Syngress knows what passing the exam means to you and to your career. And we know that you are often financing your own training and certification; therefore, you need a system that is comprehensive, affordable, and effective.

Boasting one-of-a-kind integration of text, DVD-quality instructor-led training, and Web-based exam simulation, the Syngress Study Guide & DVD Training System guarantees 100% coverage of exam objectives.

The Syngress Study Guide & DVD Training System includes:

- **Study Guide with 100% coverage of exam objectives** By reading this study guide and following the corresponding objective list, you can be sure that you have studied 100% of the exam objectives.
- **Instructor-led DVD** This DVD provides almost two hours of virtual classroom instruction.
- **Web-based practice exams** Just visit us at **www.syngress.com/certification** to access a complete exam simulation.

Thank you for giving us the opportunity to serve your certification needs. And be sure to let us know if there's anything else we can do to help you get the maximum value from your investment. We're listening.

www.syngress.com/certification

SYNGRESS®

YNGRESS®

MCSA/MCSE

Exam 70-290: Managing and Maintaining a Windows Server 2003 Environment

STUDY GUIDE & DVD TRAINING SYSTEM

ɔorah Littlejohn Shinder
Thomas W. Shinder
ra E. Hunter Technical Reviewer
Schmied DVD Presenter

KEY	SERIAL NUMBER
001	PV43SLUGGY
002	Q2TQRGN7VA
003	8C38A9R7FF
004	Z6TDAVAN9Y
005	P33JEET8MS
006	3SHX6SN$RK
007	CH3W7E42AK
008	9EU6V4DER7
009	SUPACM4NFH
010	5BVF3MEV2Z

PUBLISHED BY
Syngress Publishing, Inc.
800 Hingham Street
Rockland, MA 02370

Managing and Maintaining a Windows Server 2003 Environment Study Guide & DVD Training System

Printed in the United States of America

1 2 3 4 5 6 7 8 9 0

ISBN: 1-932266-60-7

Technical Editor:Deborah Littlejohn Shinder and Thomas W. Shinder M.D
Technical Reviewer: Laura Hunter
Acquisitions Editor: Jonathan Babcock
DVD Production: Michael Donovan

Cover Designer: Patricia Lupien
Page Layout and Art by: Patricia Lupien
Copy Editors: Beth Roberts, Michelle Melani
Indexer: Rich Carlson
DVD Presenter: Will Schmied

Acknowledgments

We would like to acknowledge the following people for their kindness and support in making this book possible.

Karen Cross, Meaghan Cunningham, Kim Wylie, Harry Kirchner, Kevin Votel, Kent Anderson, Frida Yara, Jon Mayes, John Mesjak, Peg O'Donnell, Sandra Patterson, Betty Redmond, Roy Remer, Ron Shapiro, Patricia Kelly, Andrea Tetrick, Jennifer Pascal, Doug Reil, David Dahl, Janis Carpenter, and Susan Fryer of Publishers Group West for sharing their incredible marketing experience and expertise.

Duncan Enright, AnnHelen Lindeholm, David Burton, Febea Marinetti, and Rosie Moss of Elsevier Science for making certain that our vision remains worldwide in scope.

David Buckland, Wendi Wong, Daniel Loh, Marie Chieng, Lucy Chong, Leslie Lim, Audrey Gan, and Joseph Chan of Transquest Publishers for the enthusiasm with which they receive our books.

Kwon Sung June at Acorn Publishing for his support.

Jackie Gross, Gayle Voycey, Alexia Penny, Anik Robitaille, Craig Siddall, Darlene Morrow, Iolanda Miller, Jane Mackay, and Marie Skelly at Jackie Gross & Associates for all their help and enthusiasm representing our product in Canada.

Lois Fraser, Connie McMenemy, Shannon Russell, and the rest of the great folks at Jaguar Book Group for their help with distribution of Syngress books in Canada.

David Scott, Annette Scott, Geoff Ebbs, Hedley Partis, Bec Lowe, and Mark Langley of Woodslane for distributing our books throughout Australia, New Zealand, Papua New Guinea, Fiji Tonga, Solomon Islands, and the Cook Islands.

Winston Lim of Global Publishing for his help and support with distribution of Syngress books in the Philippines.

A special thanks to Deb and Tom Shinder for going the extra mile on our core four MCSE 2003 guides. Thank you both for all your work.

And to Will Schmied, thank you for being a trooper on the DVD part of this project!

Technical Editors

Debra Littlejohn Shinder (MCSE) is a technology consultant, trainer, and writer who has authored a number of books on networking, including Scene of the Cybercrime: Computer Forensics Handbook, published by Syngress Publishing (ISBN: 1-931836-65-5), and Computer Networking Essentials, published by Cisco Press. She is co-author, with her husband, Dr. Thomas Shinder, of Troubleshooting Windows 2000 TCP/IP (ISBN: 1-928994-11-3), the best-selling Configuring ISA Server 2000 (ISBN: 1-928994-29-6), and ISA Server and Beyond (ISBN: 1-931836-66-3). Deb is also a technical editor and contributor to books on subjects such as the Windows 2000 MCSE exams, the CompTIA Security+ exam, and TruSecure's ICSA certification. She edits the Brainbuzz A+ Hardware News and Sunbelt Software's WinXP News and is regularly published in TechRepublic's TechProGuild and Windowsecurity.com. Deb currently specializes in security issues and Microsoft products. She lives and works in the Dallas-Fort Worth area and can be contacted at deb@shinder.net or via the web-site at www.shinder.net.

Thomas W. Shinder M.D. (MVP, MCSE) is a computing industry veteran who has worked as a trainer, writer, and a consultant for Fortune 500 companies including FINA Oil, Lucent Technologies, and Sealand Container Corporation. Tom was a Series Editor of the Syngress/Osborne Series of Windows 2000 Certification Study Guides and is author of the best selling books Configuring ISA Server 2000: Building Firewalls with Windows 2000 (Syngress Publishing, ISBN: 1-928994-29-6) and Dr. Tom Shinder's ISA Server and Beyond (ISBN: 1-931836-66-3). Tom is the editor of the Brainbuzz.com Win2k News newsletter and is a regular contributor to TechProGuild. He is also content editor, contributor and moderator for the World's leading site on ISA Server 2000, www.isaserver.org. Microsoft recognized Tom's leadership in the ISA Server community and awarded him their Most Valued Professional (MVP) award in December of 2001.

Technical Reviewer

Laura E. Hunter (CISSP, MCSE, MCT, MCDBA, MCP, MCP+I, CCNA, A+, Network+, iNet+, CNE-4, CNE-5) is a Senior IT Specialist with the University of Pennsylvania, where she provides network planning, implementation, and troubleshooting services for various business units and schools within the University. Her specialties include Microsoft Windows NT and 2000 design and implementation, troubleshooting and security topics. As an "MCSE Early Achiever" on Windows 2000, Laura was one of the first in the country to renew her Microsoft credentials under the Windows 2000 certification structure. Laura's previous experience includes a position as the Director of Computer Services for the Salvation Army and as the LAN administrator for a medical supply firm. She also operates as an independent consultant for small businesses in the Philadelphia metropolitan area and is a regular contributor to the TechTarget family of websites.

Laura has previously contributed to the Syngress Publishing's *Configuring Symantec Antivirus, Corporate Edition* (ISBN 1-931836-81-7). She has also contributed to several other exam guides in the Syngress Windows Server 2003 MCSE/MCSA DVD Guide and Training System series as a DVD presenter, contributing author, and technical reviewer.

Laura holds a bachelor's degree from the University of Pennsylvania and is a member of the Network of Women in Computer Technology, the Information Systems Security Association, and InfraGard, a cooperative undertaking between the U.S. Government other participants dedicated to increasing the security of United States critical infrastructures.

Contributors

Chad Todd (MCSE: Security, MCSE, MCSA: Security, MCSA, MCP+I, MCT, CNE, A+, Network+, i-Net+) author of *Hack Proofing Windows 2000 Server* (Syngress, ISBN: 1-931836-49-3) co-owns a training and integration company (Training Concepts, LLC) in Columbia, SC. Chad first certified on Windows NT 4.0 and has been training on Windows operating systems ever since. His specialties include Exchange messaging and Windows security. Chad was awarded MCSE 2000 Charter Member for being one of the first two thousand Windows 2000 MCSEs and MCSA 2002 Charter Member for being one of the first five thousand MCSAs. Chad is a regular contributing author for Microsoft Certified Professional Magazine. Chad has worked for companies such as Fleet Mortgage Group, Ikon Office Solutions, and Netbank.

Chad would like to first thank his wife Sarah. Without her love and support all of the late nights required to write this book would not be possible. He would also like to thank Kirk Vigil and Jim Jones for their support and encouragement. Lastly, Chad would like to thank Olean Rabon and Theresa Johnson for being his greatest fans.

Jeffery A. Martin (MCSE, MCDBA, MCT, MCP+I, MCP, MCNE, CNE, CNA, CNI, CCNA, CCNP, CCI, CCA, CTT, A+, Network+, I-Net+, Project+, Linux+, CIW, ADPM) has been working with computers and computer networks for over 15 years. Jeffery spends most of his time managing several companies that he owns and consulting for large multinational media companies. He also enjoys working as a technical instructor and training others in the use of technology.

Feridun Kadir (MCP, MCP+I, MCSE, MCT) is a freelance IT consultant and trainer who has worked in the field of IT since 1988. He remembers selling a TRS-80 home PC with 4Kilobytes RAM (yes kilobytes!) in the early 1980s for over $1,000. His early IT experience was with UNIX systems and local area networks. In more recent years he has worked with Microsoft products. Having discovered that he liked giving presentations he became an MCT and regularly teaches Microsoft technical courses including Windows NT 4.0, Windows 2000, Windows XP, TCP/IP, SQL Server Administration and Small Business Server. Feridun also provides IT consulting services to all types of businesses. Feridun lives with his wife, Liz and son, Jake in Stansted, Essex in England.

Colin Bowern (MCSE, MCAD, MCSD, MCDBA, CCNA, CCDA, Network+) is a Senior Consultant at Microsoft Services in Toronto, Canada. Through his work with enterprise customers and partners, Colin helps information technology professionals and business leaders understand how to leverage and make better decisions about how to use technology in their business to gain competitive advantages. Clients span several industry verticals including financial services, public utilities, and government. In addition to consulting, Colin is also an active presenter, speaking regularly in the Microsoft Developer Network's web casts as well as at a variety of public events including the TechNet Tour series in Canada. Colin's involvement with the industry also includes providing technical review for Addison-Wesley's .NET development series and the Windows Server 2003 series from Microsoft Press. In addition he is also working on a M.Sc. degree from the University of Liverpool, England.

Chris Peiris (MVP) currently lectures on Distributed Component Architectures (.NET, J2EE & CORBA) at Monash University, Caulfield, Victoria, Australia. He also works as an independent consultant for .NET and EAI implementations. He is been awarded the title "Microsoft Most Valuable Professional" (MVP) for his contributions to .NET Technologies. He has been designing and developing Microsoft solutions since 1995. His expertise lies in developing scalable, high-performance solutions for financial institutions and media groups. He has written many articles, reviews and columns for various online publications including 15Seconds, Developer Exchange (www.Devx.com) and Wrox Press (www.wrox.com). He co-authored the book *C# Web Service with .NET Remoting* and *ASP.NET* by Wrox Press. It was followed by *C# for Java Programmers* by Syngress Publishing as a primary author. Chris frequently presents at professional developer conferences on Microsoft technologies.

His core skills are C++, Java, .NET, DNA, MTS, Site Server, Data Warehousing, WAP, and SQL Server. Chris has a Bachelor of Computing, Bachelor of Business (Accounting), and a Masters of Information Technology degree. He is currently undertaking a PhD on "Web Service Management Framework." He lives with his family in Civic, Canberra ACT. Chris dedicates his contributions to this book to the Tennakoon family. In his own words "to Kusum, Rohan, Fiona & Timothy, Gayathrie & Lachlan, Ranil & Ranita. This is a token of my gratitude for the friendship, inspiration, acceptance, love and tolerance you have shown me over the years. And most of all, thanks for the curry."

Michael Cross (MCSE, MCP+I, CNA, Network+) is an Internet Specialist / Computer Forensic Analyst with the Niagara Regional Police Service. He performs computer forensic examinations on computers involved in criminal investigations, and has consulted and assisted in cases dealing with computer-related/Internet crimes. In addition to designing and maintaining their Web site at www.nrps.com and Intranet, he has also provided support in the areas of programming, hardware, network administration, and other services. As part of an Information Technology team that provides support to a user base of over 800 civilian and uniform users, his theory is that when the users carry guns, you tend to be more motivated in solving their problems.

Michael also owns KnightWare (www.knightware.ca), which provides computer-related services like Web page design; and Bookworms (www.bookworms.ca), where you can purchase collectibles and other interesting items online. He has been a freelance writer for several years, and published over three dozen times in numerous books and anthologies. He currently resides in St. Catharines, Ontario Canada with his lovely wife Jennifer and his darling daughter Sara.

Eriq Oliver Neale is an Information Technology manager for a large manufacturing company headquartered in the southwest. His IT career spans 16 years and just about as many systems. He has contributed to a number of technical publications, including several MCSE exam preparation titles. His article on MIDI, still considered one of the seminal works on the topic, has been reprinted in hundreds of publications in multiple languages. Most recently, he has been focusing on electronic data privacy issues in mixed platform environments. When not working in and writing about Information Technology, Eriq spends time writing and recording music in his home studio for clients of his music publishing company. On clear nights, he can be found gazing at the moon or planets through his telescope, which he also uses for deep-space astrophotography. His PGP public key can be found at http://eriq.neale.com/EriqNeale.asc.

DVD Presenter

Will Schmied, (BSET, MCSE, CWNA, TICSA, MCSA, Security+, Network+, A+), is the president of Area 51 Partners, Inc., a provider of wired and wireless networking implementation, security and training services to businesses in the Hampton Roads, Virginia area. Will holds a Bachelor's degree in Mechanical Engineering Technology from Old Dominion University in addition to various IT industry certifications.

Will has previously authored and contributed to several other publications from Syngress Publishing, including *Building DMZs for Enterprise Networks* (ISBN: 1-931836-88-4), *Implementing and Administering Security in a Microsoft Windows 2000 Network: Exam 70-214 Study Guide and DVD Training System* (ISBN: 1-931836-84-1), *Security+ Study Guide and DVD Training System* (ISBN: 1-931836-72-8), and *Configuring and Troubleshooting Windows XP Professional* (ISBN: 1-928994-80-6).

Will currently resides in Newport News, Virginia, with his wife, Chris, and their children, Christopher, Austin, Andrea, and Hannah. You can visit Area 51 Partners at www.area51partners.com.

MCSA/MCSE 70-290 Exam Objectives Map and Table of Contents

COVERS ALL 100% CERTIFIED EXAM OBJECTIVES

All of Microsoft's published objectives for the MCSA/MCSE 70-290 Exam are covered in this book. To help you easily find the sections that directly support particular objectives, we've listed all of the exam objectives below, and mapped them to the Chapter number in which they are covered. We've also assigned numbers to each objective, which we use in the subsequent Table of Contents and again throughout the book to identify objective coverage. In some chapters, we've made the judgment that it is probably easier for the student to cover objectives in a slightly different sequence than the order of the published Microsoft objectives. By reading this study guide and following the corresponding objective list, you can be sure that you have studied 100% of Microsoft's MCSA/MCSE 70-290 Exam objectives.

Exam Objective Map

Objective Number	Objective	Chapter Number
1	**Managing and Maintaining Physical and Logical Devices.**	2, 3
1.1	Manage basic disks and dynamic disks.	2
1.2	Monitor server hardware. Tools might include Device Manager, the Hardware Troubleshooting Wizard, and appropriate Control Panel items.	3
1.3	Optimize server disk performance.	2
1.3.1	Implement a RAID solution.	2
1.3.2	Defragment volumes and partitions.	2
1.4	Install and configure server hardware devices.	3
1.4.1	Configure driver signing options.	3
1.4.2	Configure resource settings for a device.	3
1.4.3	Configure device properties and settings.	3
2	**Managing Users, Computers, and Groups.**	4, 5
2.1	Manage local, roaming, and mandatory user profiles.	4

Objective Number	Objective	Chapter Number
2.2	Create and manage computer accounts in an Active Directory environment.	4
2.3	Create and manage groups.	4
2.3.1	Identify and modify the scope of a group.	4
2.3.2	Find domain groups in which a user is a member.	4
2.3.3	Manage group membership.	4
2.3.4	Create and modify groups by using the Active Directory Users and Computers Microsoft Management Console (MMC) snap-in.	4
2.3.5	Create and modify groups by using automation.	4
2.4	Create and manage user accounts.	4
2.4.1	Create and modify user accounts by using the Active Directory Users and Computers MMC snap-in.	4
2.4.2	Create and modify user accounts by using automation.	4
2.4.3	Import user accounts.	4
2.5	Troubleshoot computer accounts.	4
2.5.1	Diagnose and resolve issues related to computer accounts by using the Active Directory Users and Computers MMC snap-in.	4
2.5.2	Reset computer accounts.	4
2.6	Troubleshoot user accounts.	4
2.6.1	Diagnose and resolve account lockouts.	4
2.6.2	Diagnose and resolve issues related to user account properties.	4
2.7	Troubleshoot user authentication issues.	5
3	**Managing and Maintaining Access to Resources.**	5, 6
3.1	Configure access to shared folders.	5
3.1.2	Manage Shared folder Permissions.	5
3.2	Troubleshoot Terminal Services.	6
3.2.1	Diagnose and resolve issues related to Terminal Services security.	6
3.2.2	Diagnose and resolve issues related to client access to Terminal Services.	6
3.3	Configure file system permissions.	5
3.3.1	Verify effective permissions when granting permissions.	5

Objective Number	Objective	Chapter Number
3.3.2	Change ownership of files and shared folders.	5
3.4	Troubleshoot access to files and shared folders.	5
4	**Managing and maintaining a Server Environment**	1, 3, 7, 8, 9
4.1	Monitor and analyze events. Tools might include Event Viewer and System monitor.	9
4.2	Manage software update infrastructure	1
4.3	Manage software site licensing.	1
4.4	Manage servers remotely.	7
4.4.1	Manage a server by using Remote Assistance.	6
4.4.2	Manage a server by using Terminal Services remote administration mode.	6
4.4.3	Manage a server by using available support tools.	7
4.5	Troubleshoot print queues.	7
4.6	Monitor system performance.	9
4.7	Monitor file and print servers. Tools might include Task Manager, Event Viewer, and System Monitor.	9
4.7.1	Monitor disk quotas.	1
4.7.2	Monitor print queues.	7
4.7.3	Monitor server hardware for bottlenecks.	3
4.8	Monitor and optimize a server environment for application performance.	9
4.8.1	Monitor memory performance objects.	9
4.8.2	Monitor network performance objects.	9
4.8.3	Monitor process performance objects.	9
4.8.4	Monitor disk performance objects.	9
4.9	Manage a Web server.	8
4.9.1	Manage Internet Information Services (IIS).	8
4.9.2	Manage security for IIS.	8
5	**Managing and Implementing Disaster Recovery.**	10
5.1	Perform system recovery for a server.	10
5.1.1	Implement Automated System Recovery (ASR).	10
5.1.2	Restore data from shadow copy volumes.	10
5.1.3	Back up files and System State data to media.	10
5.1.4	Configure security for backup operations.	10

Objective Number	Objective	Chapter Number
5.2	Manage backup procedures.	10
5.2.1	Verify the successful completion of backup jobs.	10
5.2.2	Manage backup storage media.	10
5.3	Recover from server hardware failure.	10
5.4	Restore backup data.	10
5.5	Schedule backup jobs.	10

Contents

Foreword xxxv

Chapter 1 Overview of Windows Server 2003 1

Introduction 2
History of the Windows Operating System Family 2
Out of MS-DOS: Where It All Began 3
Windows as a Graphical Shell 4
OS/2: an IBM/Microsoft Joint Venture 8
After the "Divorce": A New Technology Emerges 8
Windows 9*x* versus Windows NT-Based Operating Systems 9
The NT OS Family Tree 10
Windows NT 3.*x* 10
Windows NT 3.1 11
Windows NT 3.5 11
Windows NT 3.51 11
Windows NT 4.0 11
Windows NT 4.0 Server 12
Windows NT Server 4.0 Enterprise Edition 12
Windows NT Server 4.0 Terminal Server Edition 12
Windows 2000 12
Windows XP/Windows Server 2003 12
Windows XP Home Edition 14
Windows XP Professional 14
Windows XP Professional 64-Bit Edition 15
Windows XP Media Center Edition 15
Windows XP Tablet PC Edition 16
Windows Server Operating System Basics 16
Client-Server Networking 17
Centralized Authentication 17
Centralized Administration 17

Client-Server versus Peer-to-Peer Networking 17
The Domain Concept 18
NT Domains 19
Windows 2000/Server 2003 Domains 19
Directory Services 20
What Are Directory Services? 20
History of Directory Services 21
Directory Services Standards 21
NT Directory Services 22
Active Directory 22
What's New in Windows Server 2003? 23
Why a New Server Operating System? 23
New Features 23
New Active Directory Features 24
Improved File and Print Services 28
Revised IIS Architecture 30
Enhanced Clustering Technology 31
New Networking and Communications Features 33
Improved Security 35
Better Storage Management 38
Improved Terminal Services 39
New Media Services 41
XML Web Services 42
The Windows Server 2003 Family 44
Why Four Different Editions? 44
Members of the Family 44
Web Edition 45
Standard Edition 45
Enterprise Edition 45
Datacenter Edition 46
4.3 Manage Software Site Licensing 47
Product Activation 48
4.2 Manage Software Update Infrastructure 50
Common Installation Issues 51
Common Upgrade Issues 52

Summary of Exam Objectives 54
Exam Objectives Fast Track 55
Exam Objectives Frequently Asked Questions 58
Self Test 60
Self Test Quick Answer Key 65

1 Chapter 2 Managing Physical and Logical Disks 67

Introduction 68
Understanding Disk Terminology and Concepts 68
Microsoft Disk Terminology 71
Physical vs Logical Disks 71
Basic vs Dynamic Disks 71
Partitions vs Volumes 74
Partition Types and Logical Drives 75
Volume Types 78
Using Disk Management Tools 84
Using the Disk Management MMC 85
Using the Command-Line Utilities 86
Using diskpart.exe 87
Using fsutil.exe 90
Using rss.exe 91
1 Understanding and Managing Physical and Logical Disks 91
1.1 Manage Basic Disks 92
When to Use Basic Disks 92
Creating Partitions and Logical Drives 92
How to Assign a New Drive Letter 100
How to Format a Basic Volume 102
How to Extend a Basic Volume 106
1.1 Managing Dynamic Disks 108
Converting to Dynamic Disk Status 108
Creating and Using Dynamic Volumes 110
1.3 Optimize Server Disk Performance 128
1.3.2 Defragmenting Volumes and Partitions 128
Understanding Disk Fragmentation 128
Using the Graphical Defragmenter 131
Using defrag.exe 137
Defragmentation Best Practices 138

4.7.1 Configuring and Monitoring Disk Quotas 139
Overview of Disk Quotas 139
Enabling and Configuring Disk Quotas 140
Monitoring Disk Quotas 145
Exporting and Importing Quota Settings 147
Disk Quota Best Practices 150
Using fsutil.exe to Manage Disk Quotas 151
1.3.1 Implementing RAID Solutions 152
Understanding Windows Server 2003 RAID 152
Hardware RAID 153
RAID Best Practices 154
Understanding and Using Remote Storage 155
Understanding Remote Storage Concepts 155
What is Remote Storage? 156
Storage Levels 156
Relationship of Remote Storage and Removable Storage 157
Setting Up Remote Storage 159
Using Remote Storage 166
Remote Storage Best Practices 170
Troubleshooting Disks and Volumes 170
Troubleshooting Basic Disks 171
New Disks Are Not Showing Up in the Volume List View 171
Disk Status is Not Initialized or Unknown 172
Disk Status is Unreadable 173
Disk Status is Failed 173
Troubleshooting Dynamic Volumes 174
Disk Status is Foreign 174
Disk Status is Online (Errors) 175
Disk Status is Offline 176
Disk Status is Data Incomplete 177
Troubleshooting Fragmentation Problems 177
Computer is Operating Slowly 178
The Analysis and Defragmentation Reports Do Not Match the Display 178
Volumes Contain Unmovable Files 178
Troubleshooting Disk Quotas 178
The Quota Tab is Not There 178

Deleting a Quota Entry Gives you Another Window 179
A User Gets an "Insufficient Disk Space"
Message When Adding Files to a Volume 180
Troubleshooting Remote Storage 180
Remote Storage Will Not Install 180
Remote Storage Is Not Finding a Valid Media Type 180
Files Can No Longer Be Recalled from Remote Storage ...181
Troubleshooting RAID 181
Mirrored or RAID-5 Volume's
Status is Data Not Redundant 181
Mirrored or RAID-5 Volume's
Status is Failed Redundancy 181
Mirrored or RAID-5 Volume's Status is Stale Data 183
Summary of Exam Objectives 184
Exam Objectives Fast Track 184
Exam Objectives Frequently Asked Questions 187
Self Test 189
Self Test Quick Answer Key 196

Chapter 3 Configuring, Monitoring, and Troubleshooting Server Hardware 197

Introduction 198
Understanding Server Hardware Vulnerabilities 198
Understanding How Windows
Server 2003 Interacts with the Hardware 198
The Hardware Abstraction Layer (HAL) 199
Device Drivers 200
Plug and Play 201
1.4.1 Installing and Configuring Server Hardware Devices 203
1.4 Configuring Driver Signing Options 203
Ensuring Your Device Drivers Are Digitally Signed 206
Using the New Hardware Wizard 210
1.4.3 Using Device Manager to Configure and Manage Devices 211
General Device Properties 213
Advanced Device Properties 214
Managing the Device Driver 215
1.4.2 Configuring Resource Settings 216
Device Installation and Configuration Best Practices 217

1.2 Monitoring Server Hardware 218
Using Device Manager 218
Using Event Viewer 219
Using Control Panel Applets 219
Using Command-Line Utilities 220
Device Console Utility (devcon.exe) 220
Service Control Utility (sc.exe) 225
4.7.3 Using Performance Console 227
Hardware Monitoring Best Practices 230
Troubleshooting Hardware Devices 231
Diagnosing and Resolving Issues
Related to Hardware Settings 234
Diagnosing and Resolving Issues
Related to Drivers and Driver Upgrades 235
Last Known Good Configuration 237
Safe Mode 238
System Configuration Utility 238
Recovery Console 239
Emergency Management Services 241
Automated System Recovery 241
Repairing the Windows Server 2003 Installation 242
Hardware Troubleshooting Best Practices 242
Summary of Exam Objectives 244
Exam Objectives Fast Track 245
Exam Objectives Frequently Asked Questions 247
Self Test 249
Self Test Quick Answer Key 254

2 Chapter 4 Managing User, Group, and Computer Accounts 255

Introduction 256
2.1 Understanding Security Objects 256
Understanding the Role of User Accounts 256
Understanding the Role of Group Accounts 257
Understanding the Role of Computer Accounts 257
Understanding the Role of Active Directory 258
Using Management Tools 258

Using the Active Directory Users and Computers (ADUC) Administrative Tool 259
Using Command-Line Utilities 261
Becoming Familiar with Using Command-Line Tools 262
Using dsadd.exe 264
Using dsmod.exe 265
Using dsget.exe 267
Using dsmove.exe 268
Using dsquery.exe 269
Using gpresult.exe 270
Using whoami.exe 274
Using cmdkey.exe 275
2.4 Creating and Managing User Accounts 277
2.4.1 Using the ADUC MMC Snap-In to Create and Manage Users 277
2.6.2/2.6.1/ 2.1 Managing and Troubleshooting User Accounts Via the Properties Tabs 280
Managing User Accounts Via the Pop-Up Menu 296
Using the Command Line to Create and Manage Users 300
Using dsadd.exe user 300
Using dsmod user 303
Using dsquery user 306
Using dsget.exe 309
2.3.5/ 2.4.2 Automating User and Group Account Creation 313
2.4.3 Importing User Accounts 315
2.6 Troubleshooting User Accounts 317
2.3 Creating and Managing Group Accounts 318
2.3.1 Understanding Group Types and Scopes 319
Security and Distribution Groups 319
Local, Domain Local, Global, and Universal Groups 320
2.3.3/ 2.3.4 Using the ADUC MMC Snap-In to Create and Manage Groups 324
Managing Group Accounts Via the Properties Tabs 326
Managing Group Accounts Via the Pop-Up Menu 332
Using the Command Line to Create and Manage Groups 333
Using dsadd.exe Group 333
Using dsmod.exe group 335
Using dsquery group 337

Using dsget group 340
Group Management Tasks 343
Identifying and Modifying the Scope of a Group 343
2.3.2 Determining to which Groups a User Belongs 344
Group Membership Management Best Practices 345
Using Domain Local Groups 345
Using Global Groups 346
Using Universal Groups 346
Understanding AGUDLP 347
Using Groups in a Single Domain 348
Using Groups in a Multiple Domain Forest 349
2.2 Creating and Managing Computer Accounts 349
2.5.1 Using the ADUC MMC Snap-In to Create and Manage Computers 350
Managing Computer Accounts Via the Properties Tabs 353
2.5.2 Managing Computer Accounts Via the Pop-Up Menu 359
2.5 Using the Command Line to Create, Manage, and Troubleshoot Computers 362
Using dsadd computer 363
Using dsmod computer 364
Using dsquery computer 365
Using dsget computer 368
Creating and Managing Domain Controllers 370
Creating a New Domain Controller for an Existing Domain 370
Creating a Domain Controller for a New Forest 377
Creating a Domain Controller for a New Child Domain 381
Creating a Domain Controller for a New Domain Tree 384
Assigning Domain Controller Operations Master Roles 388
2.5 Troubleshooting Computer Accounts 395
Summary of Exam Objectives 396
Exam Objectives Fast Track 398
Exam Objectives Frequently Asked Questions 400
Self Test 402
Self Test Quick Answer Key 407

3 **Chapter 5 Managing Access to Resources 409**
Introduction 410
Understanding Access Control 410
Defining Access Control 411
Access Control Terminology 411
Access Control Process 412
3.1 Understanding and Using Access Permissions 412
3.3 Setting File-Level Permissions (NTFS Security) 413
NTFS Permissions Defined 414
Assigning NTFS Permissions 416
NTFS Special Permissions 419
Copying or Moving Files and Folders 423
3.1.2 Setting Shared-Folder Permissions 424
Shared-Folder Permissions Defined 424
Understanding the Interaction of
Share Permissions and NTFS Permissions 425
Assigning Share Permissions 426
Copying or Moving Shared Folders 428
Shared Folders in Active Directory 429
Creating an Active Directory Share 429
Setting Active Directory Object Permissions 430
3.3.1 Understanding How Permissions Are Inherited 431
Setting User Rights and Privileges 439
Understanding the Role of User Rights 439
3.4 Using Group Policy to Set User Rights 442
2.7/ 3.4 Troubleshooting Access Problems 444
Identifying Common Access Problems 445
Basic Troubleshooting Guidelines 445
Using New Command-Line Utilities 447
Using where.exe 447
Using takeown.exe 448
Using EFS Encryption 450
Understanding Disk Encryption 451
Understanding How EFS Works "Under the Hood" 452
Domain Recovery Policies 455
Encrypting Files and Folders Using the Graphical Interface ...456
Using the cipher.exe
Command to Perform Encryption Tasks 458

Applying EFS Best Practices 459
Implementing a Public Key Infrastructure 460
Understanding the Function of a PKI 460
Public Key Cryptography 461
Digital Certificates 463
Certification Authorities 464
Installing and Using the
Windows Server 2003 Certificate Services 465
Creating the Certificate Authority Hierarchy 466
Applying PKI Best Practices 470
Summary of Exam Objectives 473
Exam Objectives Fast Track 474
Exam Objectives Frequently Asked Questions 477
Self Test 479
Self Test Quick Answer Key 486

Chapter 6 Managing and Troubleshooting Terminal Services 487

Introduction 488
Understanding Windows Terminal Services 488
Terminal Services Terminology and Concepts 489
How Terminal Services Works 489
Thin Client Computing 490
Terminal Services Components 491
Remote Desktop for Administration 492
Remote Assistance 492
3.2.2 The Terminal Server Role 493
4.4.2 Manage a Server by Using
Terminal Services Remote Administration Mode 497
Using Remote Desktop for Administration 497
Configuring RDA 497
Setting Up Authentication 498
Advantages of RDA over
other Remote Administration Methods 498
3.2.1 Diagnose and Resolve Issues
Related to Terminal Services Security 499
4.4.1 Using Remote Assistance 500
How Remote Assistance Works 501
Configuring Remote Assistance for Use 501
Asking for Assistance 502

Downloading, Installing, and Configuring the
Windows Messenger Tool for Use with Remote Assistance ...504
Downloading Messenger 504
Creating an Account 505
Using an Existing Account to Log On 505
Adding Contacts 507
Completing the Connection 511
Managing Open Invitations 515
Remote Assistance Security Issues 516
Installing and Configuring the Terminal Server Role 517
Installing the Terminal Server Role 518
3.2.2 Installing Terminal Server Licensing 520
3.2.2 Using Terminal Services Client Tools 521
Installing and Using the Remote
Desktop Connection (RDC) Utility 522
Installing the Remote Desktop Connection Utility 523
Launching and Using the
Remote Desktop Connection Utility 523
Configuring the Remote Desktop Connection Utility 525
Installing and Using the Remote Desktops MMC Snap-In 529
Installing the Remote Desktops MMC Snap-In 531
Adding a New Connection 531
Configuring a Connection's Properties 533
Connecting and Disconnecting 534
3.2.2 Installing and Using the
Remote Desktop Web Connection Utility 535
Installing Internet Information Services 6 535
Installing the Remote Desktop Web Connection Utility ...536
Using the Remote Desktop Web
Connection Utility from a Client 537
Using Terminal Services Administrative Tools 540
3.2.2 Using the Terminal Services Manager 541
Using Terminal Services Manager to Connect to Servers ...541
Managing Users with the Terminal Services Manager Tool ...542
Managing Sessions with the
Terminal Services Manager Tool 543
Managing Processes with the
Terminal Services Manager Tool 546

Using the Terminal Services Configuration Tool 547
Understanding Listener Connections 547
3.2.2 Modifying the Properties of an Existing Connection 548
Terminal Services Configuration Server Settings 558
User Account Extensions 560
The Terminal Services Profile Tab 560
The Sessions Tab 561
The Environment Tab 562
The Remote Control Tab 563
3.2.2 Using Group Policies to Control Terminal Services Users 564
Using the Terminal Services Command-Line Tools 565
3.2 Troubleshooting Terminal Services 567
Not Automatically Logged On 567
"This Initial Program Cannot Be Started" 568
Clipboard Problems 568
License Problems 569
Summary of Exam Objectives 570
Exam Objectives Fast Track 571
Exam Objectives Frequently Asked Questions 574
Self Test 576
Self Test Quick Answer Key 581

Chapter 7 Using Server Management Tools 583

Introduction 584
4.4.3 Recognizing Types of Management Tools 584
Administrative Tools Menu 584
Custom MMC Snap-Ins 585
MMC Console Modes 586
Command-Line Utilities 588
Wizards 589
Windows Resource Kit 589
The Run As Command 589
4.4 Managing Your Server Remotely 589
Remote Assistance 590
Using Web Interface for Remote Administration 591
Remote Desktop for Administration 593
Administration Tools Pack (adminpak.msi) 594
Windows Management Instrumentation (WMI) 595

Using Computer Management
to Manage a Remote Computer 595
Which Tool To Use? 597
Using Emergency Management Services 598
4.7.2/ 4.5 Managing Printers and Print Queues 601
Using the Graphical Interface 601
Creating a Printer 602
Sharing a Printer 603
Adding Printer Drivers for Earlier Operating Systems 603
Setting Permissions 603
Managing Print Queues 605
Managing Printer Pools 606
Scheduling Printers 606
Setting Printing Priorities 607
Using New Command-Line Tools 607
The Printer Spooler Service 610
The Internet Printing Protocol 613
Managing and Troubleshooting Services 614
Service Configuration 614
Service Name 614
Service States 614
Service Startup Type 614
Service Logon 615
Service Recovery 615
Dependencies 616
Service Permissions 616
Using the Graphical Interface 616
Using New Command-Line Utilities 619
sc.exe 619
schtasks.exe 619
setx.exe 620
shutdown.exe 620
tasklist.exe 621
taskkill.exe 622
Using Wizards to Configure and Manage Your Server 623
Using the Configure Your
Server and Manage Your Server Wizards 624

File Server Role 625
Print Server Role 625
Application Server (IIS, ASP.NET) Role 626
Mail Server (POP3/SMTP) Role 627
Terminal Server Role 627
Remote Access/VPN Server Role 627
Domain Controller (Active Directory) 628
DNS Server Role 629
DHCP Server Role 629
Streaming Media Server Role 629
WINS Server Role 629
Summary of Exam Objectives 632
Exam Objectives Fast Track 633
Exam Objectives Frequently Asked Questions 636
Self Test 638
Self Test Quick Answer Key 644

4.9 Chapter 8 Managing Web Servers with IIS 6.0 645

Introduction 646
Installing and Configuring IIS 6.0 646
Pre-Installation Checklist 646
Internet Connection Firewall 647
Installation Methods 650
Using the Configure Your Server Wizard 650
Using the Add or Remove Programs Applet 654
Using Unattended Setup 655
Installation Best Practices 657
What's New in IIS 6.0? 657
New Security Features 657
Advanced Digest Authentication 657
Server-Gated Cryptography (SGC) 658
Selectable Cryptographic Service Provider (CSP) 659
Configurable Worker Process Identity 660
Default Lockdown Status 660
New Authorization Framework 661
New Reliability Features 661
Health Detection 662
New Request Processing Architecture: HTTP.SYS Kernel Mode Driver 662

Other New Features 663
ASP.NET and IIS Integration 663
Unicode Transformation Format-8 (UTF-8) 664
XML Metabase 664
4.9.1 Managing IIS 6.0 666
Performing Common Management Tasks 667
Site Setup 667
Common Administrative Tasks 677
4.9.2 Managing IIS Security 684
Configuring Authentication Settings 684
Troubleshooting IIS 6.0 687
Troubleshooting Content Errors 687
Static Files Return 404 Errors 687
Dynamic Content Returns a 404 Error 688
Sessions Lost Due to Worker Process Recycling 688
ASP.NET Pages are Returned as Static Files 688
Troubleshooting Connection Errors 689
503 Errors 689
Clients Cannot Connect to Server 690
401 Error – Sub Authentication Error 690
Client Requests Timing Out 691
Troubleshooting Other Errors 691
File Not Found Errors for UNIX and Linux Files 691
ISAPI Filters Are Not Automatically Visible as Properties of the Web Site 692
The Scripts and Msadc Virtual Directories Are Not Found in IIS 6.0 692
Using New IIS Command-Line Utilities 692
iisweb.vbs 692
create 693
start, stop, pause, and delete 694
query 696
iisvdir.vbs 696
create 696
delete 697
query 698
iisftp.vbs 698
create 699

start, stop, pause, and delete 700
query 700
Active Directory set and get Calls 700
iisftpdr.vbs 701
create 701
delete 702
query 703
iisback.vbs 703
Back Up IIS Configuration 704
Restore IIS Configuration 704
delete 705
list 705
iiscnfg.vbs 706
import 706
export 707
copy 708
save 708
Summary of Exam Objectives 710
Exam Objectives Fast Track 710
Exam Objectives Frequently Asked Questions 713
Self Test 714
Self Test Quick Answer Key 719

Chapter 9 Monitoring Performance and Security 721

Introduction 722
4.6 Monitoring Performance 722
4.7 Using Task Manager to Monitor Performance 722
4.1 Using the Performance Utility to Monitor Performance 725
4.7 Using the System Monitor 725
Adding Performance Counters 727
Using Performance Logs and Alerts 733
Using Command-Line Tools 738
logman.exe 738
relog.exe 740
typeperf.exe 742
4.8 Optimizing Servers for Application Performance 743
4.8.1 Monitoring Memory Objects 743
4.8.2 Monitoring Network Objects 745
4.8.3 Monitoring Process Objects 747

4.8.4 Monitoring Disk Objects 748
Auditing Security Events 749
Defining and Modifying Auditing Policies for Event Categories 751
Policies for the Local Computer 751
Policies for Domain Controllers 752
Policies for a Domain or OU 753
Enabling Auditing of Object Access 754
Auditing Settings on Objects 754
Understanding Operation-Based Auditing of Files and Folders 755
Applying and Modifying Audit Policy Settings 755
Understanding the Effect of Inheritance on File and Folder Auditing 759
Viewing the Security Log 759
Using Event Viewer 760
Event Types 760
Understanding Event Logs 761
Event Log Types 762
Managing Event Logs 764
Setting Logging Options 764
Configuring Log Size 765
Clearing Logs 766
Archiving Logs 767
Troubleshooting Event Logs 768
Using Command-Line Tools 769
eventcreate.exe 769
eventquery.vbs 770
eventtriggers.exe 771
tracerpt.exe 774
Using the Shutdown Event Tracker 775
Shutdown Events Overview 775
Configuring the Shutdown Event Tracker 776
Working with the Shutdown Event Tracker 777
Using the Registry to Manage Shutdown Event Tracker 780
Defining Custom Shutdown Reasons 781
Summary of Exam Objectives 784
Exam Objectives Fast Track 785

Exam Objectives Frequently Asked Questions 788
Self Test 790
Self Test Quick Answer Key 795

Chapter 10 Planning and Implementing Disaster Recovery 797

Introduction 798
Defining and Understanding Disaster Recovery 798
Understanding the Components of Disaster Recovery 799
Developing Business Continuity Plans 800
Developing the Disaster Recovery Plan 805
Threat Assessment and Prioritizing 806
Legal and Administrative Considerations 806
Asset Evaluation 807
Incident Response Planning 808
Using Disaster Recovery Best Practices 809
5.2 Creating a Backup Plan 812
Backup Concepts 813
5.1.3 Backup Media 814
Types of Tapes 814
Managing Media 816
Offsite Storage 817
Backing Up Data Files with the Backup Utility 817
Starting the Backup Utility 818
Using the Backup Utility in Advanced Mode 818
Advanced Backup Settings 824
Backing Up System State Data 827
5.1.4 Configuring Security for Backup Operations 829
5.2.1 Verifying Successful Completion of Backup Jobs 830
5.2.2 Managing Backup Media 831
5.4 Restoring Backed-Up Data 833
5.5 Scheduling Backup Jobs 836
Backup Rotation Schemes 844
Using the ntbackup Command-Line Utility 845
5.1 Creating a System Recovery Plan 847
Backing up System State Data 847
Primary, Nonauthoritative, and Authoritative Restores 849
5.1.1 Creating an Automated System Recovery Set 850

Installing and Using the Recovery Console 851
Using Windows Startup Options 856
Safe Mode 856
Safe Mode with Networking 856
Safe Mode with Command Prompt 857
Enable Boot Logging 857
Enable VGA Mode 857
Last Known Good Configuration 857
Directory Service Restore Mode 858
Debugging Mode 858
5.1.2 Working with Volume Shadow Copies 859
Making Shadow Copies of Shared Folders 859
Enabling Shadow Copies on the Shared Resource 860
Changing Settings for Shadow Copies 861
Defining Storage Options for Shadow Copies 862
Scheduling Shadow Copies 863
Deploying the Client Software for Shadow Copies 864
Restoring Previous Versions of a File 865
Shadow Copies Best Practices 866
5.3 Recovering from Server Hardware Failure 867
The Role of Fault-Tolerant Disks 867
RAID 1 867
RAID 5 868
The Role of Server Clustering 868
Summary of Exam Objectives 870
Exam Objectives Fast Track 870
Exam Objectives Frequently Asked Questions 872
Self Test 874
Self Test Quick Answer Key 879
Self Test Questions, Answers, and Explanations 881
Index 957

Foreword

This book's primary goal is to help you prepare to take and pass Microsoft's exam number 70-290, *Managing and Maintaining a Microsoft Windows Server 2003 Environment*. Our secondary purpose in writing this book is to provide exam candidates with knowledge and skills that go beyond the minimum requirements for passing the exam, and help to prepare them to work in the real world of Microsoft computer networking.

What is Exam 70-290?

Exam 70-290 is one of the two core requirements for the Microsoft Certified Systems Administrator (MCSA) and one of the four core requirements for the Microsoft Certified Systems Engineer (MCSE) certifications. Microsoft's stated target audience consists of IT professionals with at least six months of work experience on a medium or large company network. This means a multi-site network with at least three domain controllers, running typical network services such as file and print services, database, firewall services, proxy services, remote access services and Internet connectivity.

However, not everyone who takes Exam 70-290 will have this ideal background. Many people will take this exam after classroom instruction or self-study as an entry into the networking field. Many of those who do have job experience in IT will not have had the opportunity to work with all of the technologies covered by the exam. In this book, our goal is to provide background information that will help you to understand the concepts and procedures described even if you don't have the requisite experience, while keeping our focus on the exam objectives.

Exam 70-290 covers the basics of managing and maintaining a network environment that is built around Microsoft's Windows Server 2003. Objectives are task-oriented, and include the following:

- **Managing and Maintaining Physical and Logical Devices**: This includes managing basic and dynamic disks; monitoring server hardware; optimizing disk performance on the server; troubleshooting hardware devices; and installing and configuring hardware devices.

- **Managing Users, Computer and Groups:** This includes managing different types of user profiles; creating and managing computer accounts in the Active Directory environment; creating and managing groups and user accounts; troubleshooting computer and user accounts; and troubleshooting user authentication issues.
- **Managing and Maintaining Access to Resources:** This includes configuring access to shared folders; troubleshooting Terminal Services; configuring file system permissions; and troubleshooting access to files and shared folders.
- **Managing and Maintaining the Server Environment:** This includes monitoring and analyzing logged events; planning and managing software updates; managing software site licensing; remote management of servers, using Remote Assistance, Terminal Services, and available support tools; troubleshooting printing problems; monitoring performance; monitoring disk quotas, print queues, and server hardware; monitoring and optimizing the environment for better application performance; and managing a Web server.
- **Managing and Implementing Disaster Recovery:** This includes performing a system recovery for a server; managing backup procedures and scheduling backup jobs; restoring backed up data; and recovery from hardware failure.

Path to MCP/MCSA/MCSE

Microsoft certification is recognized throughout the IT industry as a way to demonstrate mastery of basic concepts and skills required to perform the tasks involved in implementing and maintaining Windows-based networks. The certification program is constantly evaluated and improved; the nature of information technology is changing rapidly and this means requirements and specifications for certification can also change rapidly. This book is based on the exam objectives as stated by Microsoft at the time of writing; however, Microsoft reserves the right to make changes to the objectives and to the exam itself at any time. Exam candidates should regularly visit the Certification and Training Web site at www.microsoft.com/traincert for the most updated information on each Microsoft exam.

Microsoft presently offers three basic levels of certification:

- **Microsoft Certified Professional (MCP)**: to obtain the MCP certification, you must pass one current Microsoft certification exam. For more information on exams that qualify, see www.microsoft.com/traincert/mcp/mcp/requirements.asp.
- **Microsoft Certified Systems Administrator (MCSA):** to obtain the MCSA certification, you must pass three core exams and one elective exam, for a total of four exams. For more information, see www.microsoft.com/TrainCert/mcp/mcsa/requirements.asp.

- **Microsoft Certified Systems Engineer (MCSE):** to obtain the MCSE certification on Windows Server 2003, you must pass six core exams (including four network operating system exams, one client operating system exam and one design exam) and one elective. For more information, see www.microsoft.com/traincert/mcp/mcse/windows2003.

Exam 70-290 applies toward all of the above certifications.

NOTE

Those who already hold the MCSA in Windows 2000 can upgrade their certifications to MCSA 2003 by passing one upgrade exam (70-292). Those who already hold the MCSE in Windows 2000 can upgrade their certifications to MCSE 2003 by passing two upgrade exams (70-292 and 70-296).

Microsoft also offers a number of specialty certifications for networking professionals and certifications for software developers, including the following:

- **Microsoft Certified Database Administrator (MCDBA)**
- **Microsoft Certified Solution Developer (MCSD)**
- **Microsoft Certified Application Developer (MCAD)**

Exam 70-290 does not apply to any of these specialty and developer certifications.

Prerequisites and Preparation

There are no mandatory prerequisites for taking Exam 70-290, although Microsoft recommends that you meet the target audience profile described earlier. Exam 70-290 is the logical choice for the first step in completing the requirements for MCSA 2003 or MCSE 2003.

Preparation for this exam should include the following:

- Visit the web site at www.microsoft.com/traincert/exams/70-290.asp to review the updated exam objectives.
- Work your way through this book, studying the material thoroughly and marking any items you don't understand.
- Answer all practice exam questions at the end of each chapter.
- Complete all hands-on exercises in each chapter.
- Review any topics that you don't thoroughly understand.

- Consult Microsoft online resources such as TechNet (www.microsoft.com/technet), white papers on the Microsoft Web site, and so forth, for better understanding of difficult topics.
- Participate in Microsoft's product-specific and training and certification newsgroups if you have specific questions that you still need answered.
- Take one or more practice exams, such as the one available at www.syngress.com/certification.

Exam Overview

In this book, we have tried to follow Microsoft's exam objectives as closely as possible. However, we have rearranged the order of some topics for a better flow, and included background material to help you understand the concepts and procedures that are included in the objectives. Following is a brief synopsis of the exam topics covered in each chapter:

- **Overview of Windows Server 2003:** You will learn about the history of the Windows operating systems and specifically, the family tree of the NT-based operating systems from which Windows Server 2003 evolved. We discuss basic concepts involved in Windows server-based networking, including client-server networking, domains and directory services. We discuss the new features in Windows Server 2003, such as new Active Directory features, improved file and print services, the revised IIS architecture, enhanced clustering technology, new networking and communications features, improved security, better storage management, improvements to Terminal Services, new media services and support for XML Web services. You will learn about the different members of the Windows Server 2003 family: Web Edition, Standard Edition, Enterprise Edition and Datacenter Edition, and how each is used. We also discuss changes to licensing, and issues that commonly occur during installation and upgrade.
- **Managing Physical and Logical Disks:** We begin with an explanation of disk terminology and concepts as they apply to Windows Server 2003, and then discuss the disk management tools included with the operating system. You'll learn to use both the graphical tools such as the Disk Management MMC and the command-line utilities such as diskpart, fsutil and rss. We discuss how to manage both logical and physical disks, and you learn the difference between basic and dynamic disks and how each type is managed. We also discuss how you can optimize disk performance by defragmenting (using both GUI and command-line tools), configuring and monitoring disk quotas, and implementing RAID solutions. You will learn about remote storage, and you'll learn how to troubleshoot problems with disks and volumes.

- **Configuring, Monitoring and Troubleshooting Server Hardware:** You'll learn about common server hardware vulnerabilities and how to address them, and we'll walk you through the steps of installing and configuring hardware devices. You'll learn how to configure driver signing options, resource settings and device properties and settings. You'll also learn how to use Device Manager, the Hardware Troubleshooting Wizard, Control Panel applets, and command-line utilities to monitor your server's hardware. We discuss basic hardware troubleshooting procedures, including diagnosing and resolving issues related to hardware settings and diagnosing and resolving issues related to drivers and driver upgrades.
- **Managing User, Group and Computer Accounts:** We start with an overview of security objects: users, groups and computers, and how they fit into the Windows operating system and the Active Directory environment. We talk about the management tools provided with Windows Server 2003, including the Active Directory Users and Computers (ADUC) admin tool, and the wealth of command line utilities used for managing these objects, such as dsadd, dsget, dsmove, dsquery, gpresult, whoami and cmdkey. We walk you through the process of creating and managing user accounts and show you how to automate account creation and import user accounts. Then we address how to create and manage group accounts. You'll learn to identify and modify the scope of a group, find out to which domain groups a user belongs, and manage group membership in the Active Directory domain. Finally, we discuss creating and managing computer accounts.
- **Managing Access to Resources:** We provide a broad overview of access control to help you understand the concept, and then we get more specific, discussing access permissions (including the role of authentication and file ownership), shared folder permissions, file system permissions, and Active Directory object permissions. You'll learn about inheritance of permissions, and we'll discuss user rights and privileges and how to set them, as well as troubleshooting access problems. You'll learn to use new command-line utilities provided with Windows Server 2003, such as takeown.exe and where.exe. Then we'll discuss the Encrypting File System (EFS) and how EFS encryption can be used in conjunction with permissions to provide another layer of security. We also cover how to implement a Public Key Infrastructure (PKI).
- **Managing and Troubleshooting Terminal Services:** We discuss the terminology and concepts behind Windows Terminal Services, and you'll learn how to install and configure it on your server in either Remote Administration or Application Server mode. We walk you through the steps of configuring the Terminal Server itself, managing the licensing server, installing client access licenses and installing programs to be used in application server mode. We discuss client software, and show you how to use the Terminal Services administrative tools, including both the graphical and command-line tools. You'll learn to troubleshoot Terminal Services and recognize common errors and what to do about them.

- **Using Server Management Tools:** We go through the Administrative Tools menu and discuss the use of the provided tools, show you how to build custom MMCs using the available snap-ins, and show you how to use many new command-line utilities. You'll learn to manage servers remotely in a variety of different ways: using the built in Remote Assistance feature, using the Web interface for remote administration, using Terminal Services in remote admin mode, using the Administration Tools pack (adminpak.msi) from a client computer, using Windows Management Instrumentation (WMI) and using the Computer Management console's remote management capability. We discuss Emergency Management Services, how to manage printers and print queues, and how to manage and troubleshoot services with such utilities as sc, schtasks, setx, shutdown, tasklist and taskkill.
- **Managing Web Servers with Internet Information Services (IIS):** We take a long look at IIS 6.0, and you'll learn how to install and configure it and how to use its new features. These include new security features such as advanced digest authentication, server-gated cryptography, selectable CSP, configurable worker process identity, and the new authorization framework. You'll also learn about new reliability features such as health detection, new request processing architecture and the new HTTP.SYS kernel mode driver. Other new features we cover include ASP.NET and IIS integration, Unicode Transformation Format-8 (UTF-8) support, and the XML metabase. We walk you through the process of using the Web Server Security Lockdown Wizard and discuss intrusion prevention. You'll also learn how to troubleshoot problems with your Web server, and how to use IIS's new command line utilities.
- **Monitoring Performance and Security:** You'll learn how to use Task Manager, System Monitor and command-line tools to monitor your server's performance, and we discuss ways to optimize your servers for application performance. You'll learn about monitoring specific objects, including memory, network, process and disk objects. We then discuss security auditing, and you'll learn to use the Event Viewer's security, system and application logs. We'll show you how to use command line tools such as eventcreate, eventquery, eventtriggers and tracerpt. You'll also learn to use the Shutdown Event Tracker.
- **Planning and Implementing Disaster Recovery:** We start by defining disaster recovery and discussing what is involved in creating a disaster recovery policy. This includes creating a backup plan, and you will learn about backup concepts, how to choose backup media, and how to back up your data files and system state data. We discuss how to configure security for backup operations, and you'll find out how to verify successful completion of backup jobs, how to manage backup media, how to schedule backup jobs, and how to restore backed up data. Then we discuss the use of Automated System Recovery (ASR) and how you can restore data from shadow copy volumes. Finally, we address how to recover from server hardware failure and you'll learn about fault tolerant disks and the role of server clustering.

- **Software Deployment and Update:** You will learn all about software installation, and how the Windows Installer works. We'll show you how to use Group Policy for automated software installation, and you'll learn to assign applications to computers and assign or publish applications to users. We show you how to set options for Group Policy software installation, and how to use it to upgrade applications. You'll find out how to set application priorities and remove managed applications. We show you how to use administrative templates and we discuss the use of Remote Installation Services (RIS). You'll learn about the Windows Update feature and automatic updates, and you'll also learn about software restriction policies and how to apply them.

Exam Day Experience

Taking the exam is a relatively straightforward process. Both Vue and Prometric testing centers administer the Microsoft 70-290 exam. You can register for, reschedule or cancel an exam through the Vue Web site at www.vue.com or the Prometric Web site at www.2test.com/index.jsp. You'll find listings of testing center locations on these sites. Accommodations are made for those with disabilities; contact the individual testing center for more information.

Exam price varies depending on the country in which you take the exam.

Exam Format

Exams are timed. At the end of the exam, you will find out your score and whether you passed or failed. You will not be allowed to take any notes or other written materials with you into the exam room. You will be provided with a pencil and paper, however, for making notes during the exam or doing calculations.

In addition to the traditional multiple choice questions and the select and drag, simulation and case study questions introduced in the Windows 2000 exams, Microsoft has developed a number of innovative question types for the Windows Server 2003 exams. You might see some or all of the following types of questions:

- *Hot area* questions, in which you are asked to select an element or elements in a graphic to indicate the correct answer. You click an element to select or deselect it.
- *Active screen* questions, in which you change elements in a dialog box (for example, by dragging the appropriate text element into a text box or selecting an option button or checkbox in a dialog box).
- *Drag and drop* questions, in which you arrange various elements in a target area.

You can download a demo sampler of test question types from the Microsoft Web site at www.microsoft.com/traincert/mcpexams/faq/innovations.asp.

Test Taking Tips

Different people work best using different methods. However, there are some common methods of preparation and approach to the exam that are helpful to many test-takers. In this section, we provide some tips that other exam candidates have found useful in preparing for and actually taking the exam.

- Exam preparation begins before exam day. Ensure that you know the concepts and terms well and feel confident about each of the exam objectives. Many test-takers find it helpful to make flash cards or review notes to study on the way to the testing center. A sheet listing acronyms and abbreviations can be helpful, as the number of acronyms (and the similarity of different acronyms) when studying IT topics can be overwhelming. The process of writing the material down, rather than just reading it, will help to reinforce your knowledge.
- Many test-takers find it especially helpful to take practice exams that are available on the Internet and with books such as this one. Taking the practice exams not only gets you used to the computerized exam-taking experience, but also can be used as a learning tool. The best practice tests include detailed explanations of why the correct answer is correct and why the incorrect answers are wrong.
- When preparing and studying, you should try to identify the main points of each objective section. Set aside enough time to focus on the material and lodge it into your memory. On the day of the exam, you be at the point where you don't have to learn any new facts or concepts, but need simply to review the information already learned.
- The value of hands-on experience cannot be stressed enough. Exam questions are based on test-writers' experiences in the field. Working with the products on a regular basis, whether in your job environment or in a test network that you've set up at home, will make you much more comfortable with these questions.
- Know your own learning style and use study methods that take advantage of it. If you're primarily a visual learner, reading, making diagrams, watching video files on CD, etc. may be your best study methods. If you're primarily auditory, classroom lectures, audiotapes you can play in the car as you drive, and repeating key concepts to yourself aloud may be more effective. If you're a kinesthetic learner, you'll need to actually *do* the exercises, implement the security measures on your own systems, and otherwise perform hands-on tasks to best absorb the information. Most of us can learn from all of these methods, but have a primary style that works best for us.
- Although it may seem obvious, many exam-takers ignore the physical aspects of exam preparation. You are likely to score better if you've had sufficient sleep the night before the exam, and if you are not hungry, thirsty, hot/cold or otherwise distracted

by physical discomfort. Eat prior to going to the testing center (but don't indulge in a huge meal that will leave you uncomfortable), stay away from alcohol for 24 hours prior to the test, and dress appropriately for the temperature in the testing center (if you don't know how hot/cold the testing environment tends to be, you may want to wear light clothes with a sweater or jacket that can be taken off).

- Before you go to the testing center to take the exam, be sure to allow time to arrive on time, take care of any physical needs, and step back to take a deep breath and relax. Try to arrive slightly early, but not so far in advance that you spend a lot of time worrying and getting nervous about the testing process. You may want to do a quick last minute review of notes, but don't try to "cram" everything the morning of the exam. Many test-takers find it helpful to take a short walk or do a few calisthenics shortly before the exam, as this gets oxygen flowing to the brain.
- Before beginning to answer questions, use the pencil and paper provided to you to write down terms, concepts and other items that you think you may have difficulty remembering as the exam goes on. Then you can refer back to these notes as you progress through the test. You won't have to worry about forgetting the concepts and terms you have trouble with later in the exam.
- Sometimes the information in a question will remind you of another concept or term that you might need in a later question. Use your pen and paper to make note of this in case it comes up later on the exam.
- It is often easier to discern the answer to scenario questions if you can visualize the situation. Use your pen and paper to draw a diagram of the network that is described to help you see the relationships between devices, IP addressing schemes, and so forth.
- When appropriate, review the answers you weren't sure of. However, you should only change your answer if you're sure that your original answer was incorrect. Experience has shown that more often than not, when test-takers start second-guessing their answers, they end up changing correct answers to the incorrect. Don't "read into" the question (that is, don't fill in or assume information that isn't there); this is a frequent cause of incorrect responses.
- As you go through this book, pay special attention to the Exam Warnings, as these highlight concepts that are likely to be tested. You may find it useful to go through and copy these into a notebook (remembering that writing something down reinforces your ability to remember it) and/or go through and review the Exam Warnings in each chapter just prior to taking the exam.
- Use as many little mnemonic tricks as possible to help you remember facts and concepts. For example, to remember which of the two IPSec protocols (AH and ESP) encrypts data for confidentiality, you can associate the "E" in encryption with the "E" in ESP.

Pedagogical Elements

In this book, you'll find a number of different types of sidebars and other elements designed to supplement the main text. These include the following:

- **Exam Warning** These focus on specific elements on which the reader needs to focus in order to pass the exam (for example, "Be sure you know the difference between symmetric and asymmetric encryption").
- **Test Day Tip** These are short tips that will help you in organizing and remembering information for the exam (for example, "When preparing for the exam on test day, it may be helpful to have a sheet with definitions of these abbreviations and acronyms handy for a quick last-minute review").
- **Configuring & Implementing** These are sidebars that contain background information that goes beyond what you need to know from the exam, but provide a "deep" foundation for understanding the concepts discussed in the text.
- **New & Noteworthy** These are sidebars that point out changes in Windows Server 2003 from the Windows 2000/NT family, as they will apply to readers taking the exam. These may be elements that users of Windows 2000/NT would be very familiar with that have changed significantly in Windows Server 2003, or totally new features that they would not be familiar with at all.
- **Head of the Class** These are discussions of concepts and facts as they might be presented in the classroom, regarding issues and questions that most commonly are raised by students during study of a particular topic.

The book also includes, in each chapter, hands-on exercises in planning and configuring the features discussed. It is essential that you read through and, if possible, perform the steps of these exercises to familiarize yourself with the processes they cover.

You will find a number of helpful elements at the end of each chapter. For example, each chapter contains a *Summary of Exam Objectives* that ties the topics discussed in that chapter to the published objectives. Each chapter also contains an *Exam Objectives Fast Track,* which boils all exam objectives down to manageable summaries that are perfect for last minute review. *The Exam Objectives Frequently Asked Questions* answers those questions that most often arise from readers and students regarding the topics covered in the chapter. Finally, in the *Self Test* section, you will find a set of practice questions written in a multiple-choice form that will assist you in your exam preparation These questions are designed to assess your mastery of the exam objectives and provide thorough remediation, as opposed to simulating the variety of question formats you may encounter in the actual exam. You can use the *Self Test Quick Answer Key* that follows the *Self Test* questions to quickly determine what information you need to review again. The *Self Test Appendix* at the end of the book provides detailed explanations of both the correct and incorrect answers.

Additional Resources

There are two other important exam preparation tools included with this Study Guide. One is the DVD included in the back of this book. The other is the concept review test available from our Web site.

- **Instructor-led training DVD provides you with almost two hours of virtual classroom instruction.** Sit back and watch as an author and trainer reviews all the key exam concepts from the perspective of someone taking the exam for the first time. Here, you'll cut through all of the noise to prepare you for exactly what to expect when you take the exam for the first time. You will want to watch this DVD just before you head out to the testing center!
- **Web based practice exams.** Just visit us at **www.syngress.com/certification** to access a complete Windows Server 2003 concept multiple choice review. These remediation tools are written to test you on all of the published certification objectives. The exam runs in both "live" and "practice" mode. Use "live" mode first to get an accurate gauge of your knowledge and skills, and then use practice mode to launch an extensive review of the questions that gave you trouble.

Chapter 1

MCSA/MCSE 70-290

Overview of Windows Server 2003

Exam Objectives in this Chapter:

4.3 Manage Software Site Licensing.

4.2 Manage Software Update Infrastructure.

- ☑ Summary of Exam Objectives
- ☑ Exam Objectives Fast Track
- ☑ Exam Objectives Frequently Asked Questions
- ☑ Self Test
- ☑ Self Test Quick Answer Key

Introduction

This chapter provides exam candidates with important background information that is necessary to understand what Windows Server 2003 is, what it does, and how it works. Most of this information is not directly covered on the exam, because the exam is geared toward those with experience in the IT field who have worked with Microsoft products previously. If you are new to Microsoft networking, as many candidates studying for Exam 70-290 are, read this background information carefully. If you have previous experience in Microsoft networking and/or already hold a certification in Windows NT/2000, you might be able to skip the first part of this chapter and start with the section titled *What's New in Windows Server 2003?*

We start with a discussion of the NT operating system (OS) family tree because, to fully appreciate the features and capabilities of Microsoft's new server operating system, Windows Server 2003, you need to understand its origins. Although vastly more powerful and feature-rich, Windows Server 2003 is based on the same operating system kernel—the core code—as Windows NT. Windows NT Server was Microsoft's first operating system that was built on the idea of client-server networking, and introduced the idea of domains as administrative units to which computers and users belong. Then, with the release of Windows Server 2000, Microsoft fully embraced the use of a powerful directory service called Active Directory to provide centralized object-oriented management. In this chapter, we will discuss these important concepts on which a Microsoft enterprise-level network is built.

The latest incarnation of Microsoft's server product, Windows Server 2003, brings many new features and improvements that make the network administrator's job easier. This chapter will briefly summarize what's new in Windows Server 2003, and introduce you to the four members of the Windows Server 2003 family: the Web Edition, the Standard Edition, the Enterprise Edition, and the Datacenter Edition. We'll also discuss how licensing works with Windows Server 2003, and provide a heads up on some of the issues you might encounter when installing the new OS or upgrading from Windows 2000.

History of the Windows Operating System Family

Microsoft has been in the OS market since the early 1980s. It is amazing how far they (and computers in general) have come in such a short time. Microsoft has two OS family lines, MS-DOS and Windows NT. Each line is made up of multiple families such as Windows 3.*x*, Windows 9*x*, Windows NT 3.*x*, Windows NT 4.0, Windows 2000, Windows XP, and Windows Server 2003. This book is about Windows Server 2003, which is a descendant of the NT family. This section will give you an overview of both family lines starting with MS-DOS and transitioning into Windows NT.

Out of MS-DOS: Where It All Began

In 1980, IBM approached Microsoft about developing a new OS for their personal computers. At that time, Microsoft had never created an OS before, and recommended that IBM check with Gary Kildall of Digital Research about his "Control Program for Microcomputers" (CP/M) OS. CP/M had sold over 600,000 copies and was one of the most successful OSs on the market. After trying unsuccessfully to reach an agreement with Kildall, IBM went back to Microsoft and contracted with them to write the new OS.

The OS created for IBM was based on the "Quick and Dirty Operating System" (QDOS) created by Tim Paterson. Ironically, Paterson used a CP/M manual (written by Gary Kildall) as the basis for QDOS. It took him all of six weeks to write the new OS, which he sold to Microsoft for $50,000. Microsoft tweaked QDOS a little, renamed it, and then sold it to IBM under the name Personal Computing Disk Operating System (PC-DOS). Even though PC-DOS was designed for IBM, Microsoft retained the rights to the OS. This allowed them to market the OS to vendors other than IBM under the name Microsoft Disk Operating System (MS-DOS). MS-DOS (commonly just referred to as DOS) was officially released in 1981. Figure 1.1 shows the MS-DOS family line.

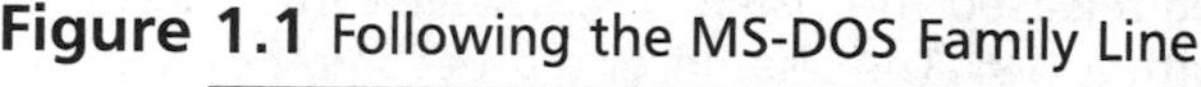
Figure 1.1 Following the MS-DOS Family Line

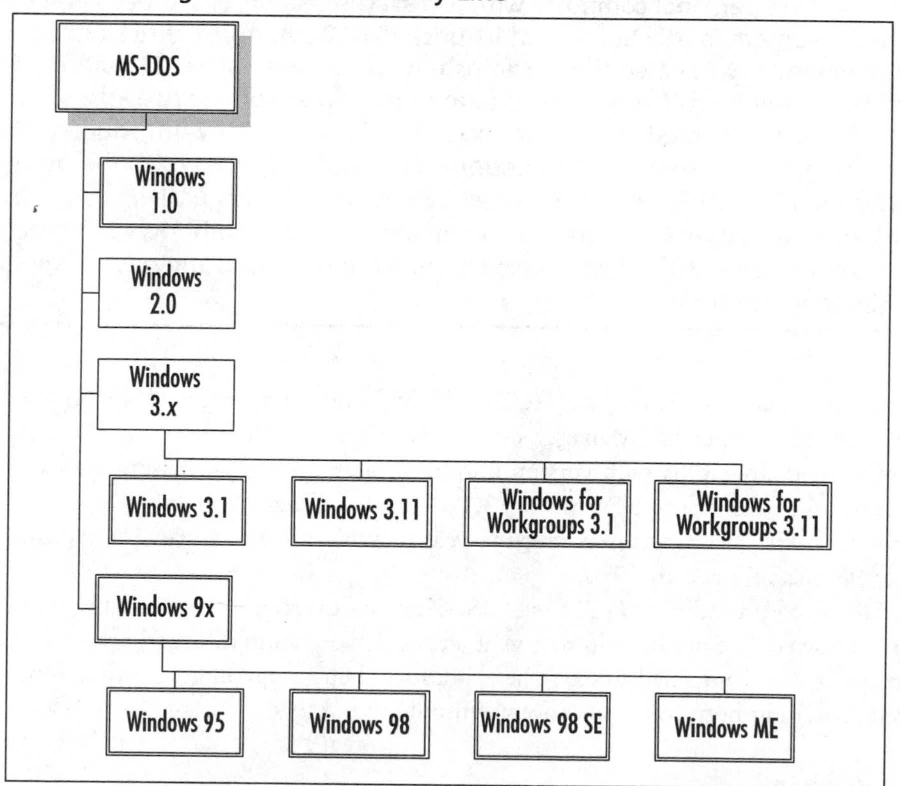

Windows as a Graphical Shell

MS-DOS was a *character-based* operating system; it used keyboards and text commands to control the OS. This worked fine for "nerds"; however, it became apparent that if Microsoft wanted more people to buy their OSs, they needed to make them easier to use. The next logical step was to give their OSs a graphical user interface, or GUI (pronounced GOO-EE), and a pointing device (for example, a mouse). A GUI makes the OS more user friendly (as illustrated by the saying that "a picture is worth a thousand words"). With a GUI, you don't have to remember a long list of text commands; instead, you can just use your mouse to point and click on menu items and icons to accomplish the same thing.

NOTE

Microsoft has created some of the most popular GUIs of all time, but they did not invent the GUI. The Xerox Corporation developed it in the 1970s. Xerox created a computer system called the Alto, which used a three-button mouse, a bitmapped display, and graphical windows. To buy an Alto in the late 1970s would have cost you over $30,000 (that is over $75,000 in today's dollars).

Even though the GUI was created in the early 1970s, it really didn't become popular until the early 1980s. Apple released the Lisa in 1983, which was considered the first personal computer with a GUI. The Lisa never did become popular with consumers, partly because of its price ($10,000). Apple struck out again in 1984 when they released the Macintosh. It had a lower price ($2,500) than the Lisa did, but it still wasn't very popular (although it was more popular than Lisa was).

Microsoft entered the GUI market in 1983 when they introduced Windows 1.0. The first two versions of Windows (1.0 and 2.0) weren't huge performers. However, in 1990 Microsoft released Windows 3.0. This GUI was a runaway hit and was immediately embraced by consumers. Since Windows 3.0, Microsoft has created over 20 different versions of Windows, and they don't appear to be slowing anytime soon.

Microsoft created Windows as a GUI for DOS. When they began work on it in 1981, the GUI was called Interface Manager, but was later renamed Windows. In the early years, Microsoft named their OSs with version numbers. These numbers incremented as new releases came out (for example, Windows 3.1 was released after Windows 3.0). Starting with Windows 95, each OS was named after the year in which it was released (for example, Windows 98 was released in 1998).

In addition to providing a GUI for DOS, Windows overcame the inability to multitask. DOS only allowed one application to run at a time. If you wanted to go back and forth between applications, you had to exit one application before opening the other. Windows supported switching between applications without having to shut them down first.

Windows 1.0

Windows 1.0 was Microsoft's first attempt at a GUI. Windows 1.0 was officially released on November 10, 1983, although it didn't appear in retail outlets until November 1985, due to a number of delays in development. Windows 1.0 was not an OS in itself; it was an extension of DOS—a graphical shell that ran on top of DOS. It used bitmap displays and added the mouse as a way to navigate the OS, giving users an alternative to having to type their commands at the command prompt.

Windows 1.0 also allowed users to switch between programs (multitask). This was a huge improvement over DOS, which required that you quit one application before opening another. Since Windows 1.0 was still based on DOS, only one application ran at a time, but users could multitask and switch between paused applications without closing them.

NOTE

Early versions of Windows used a form of multitasking called *cooperative multitasking.* This method required that application programs be written to "give up" the processor after a time so that another program could use it. When programs were not written correctly, they could "hog" the processor, denying its use to other applications. This is in contrast to the *preemptive multitasking* used by Windows 9*x* and later OSs, in which the OS—not the application—controls the scheduling of processor time.

Even with this earliest version of Windows, Microsoft had already begun the tradition of including a number of applications and utilities built into the OS: a calendar, cardfile, clock, text editor (Notepad), and rudimentary word processing and graphics programs (Windows Write and Paint).

Windows 2.0

Windows 1.0 was not a resounding sales success, but Microsoft was determined to improve on the concept. Windows 2.0 was released in April 1987. It allowed users to control screen layout and overlap windows (Windows 1.0 only supported tiled windows). Icons to represent programs were added and files that made the OS much more appealing to use and boosted its popularity over Window 1.0. Windows 2.0 supported the Video Graphics Array (VGA) display system, which allowed you to use 16 colors at 640x480. Out of the box, Windows 2.0 supported the 286 processor, but to keep up with the changing times, Microsoft released a provisional version of Windows 2.0 called Windows/386 2.03 to support the new 386 processor. The 386 version was able to run more than one MS-DOS application at a time in extended memory in addition to multitasking Windows applications. Many major applications were developed for Windows 2.0, such as Excel and Word for Windows, CorelDraw, and PageMaker.

Windows 3.0

Windows 3.0 was released on May 22, 1990, and this was when Windows began to take off in sales. Building upon the success of Windows 2.0's improved graphics, the GUI in Windows 3.0 was updated with all new icons. For backward compatibility, Windows 3.0 allowed users to run and multitask older DOS software, but the environment was completely overhauled. Windows 3.0 was able to make use of memory beyond 640K so that much more powerful applications could be developed. One of the driving forces behind the popularity of Windows 3.0 was the Windows Software Development Kit (SDK), which made it easier for developers to write applications for Windows. Prior to this version, a large portion of development time was spent creating device drivers. However, Windows 3.0 supported virtual device drivers (VxDs), which minimized hardware dependencies by adding a virtual device (another software layer) between the devices and the OS.

Windows 3.1

Windows 3.1 was released on April 6, 1992 and became the best-selling GUI in the history of computing. It added multimedia functionality, which included support for connecting to external musical instruments and MIDI devices. TrueType font support was added to provide Windows with a WYSIWYG (pronounced "wizzy wig") or "What You See Is What You Get" interface. Windows 3.1 added the ability to close applications by pressing **Ctrl+Alt+Del** and terminating hung applications from the list of running programs. Drag-and-drop functionality provided a new way to use the GUI, and support for Object Linking and Embedding (OLE) was added. OLE allowed embedding elements from different applications into one document.

Windows 3.11

Windows 3.11 was released on November 8, 1993. It did not add any feature improvements over Windows 3.1; it only corrected problems, most of which were network problems. Microsoft replaced all new retail versions of Windows 3.1 with Windows 3.11 and provided a free upgrade via their Web site to anyone who currently owned Windows 3.1 (although at that time, many Windows users did not have access to the Internet).

Windows for Workgroups 3.1

Windows for Workgroups (WFW) 3.1 was released in April 1992. It was the first Microsoft OS to provide native support for peer-to-peer networks. It supported file and printer sharing and made it easy to specify which files should be shared with other computers running DOS or Windows. WFW also included Microsoft Mail (an e-mail client) and Schedule+ (a workgroup scheduler).

Windows for Workgroups 3.11

Windows for Workgroups (WFW) 3.11 was released in February 1994 and was geared toward local area networking. This made it a hit for corporations wanting to increase productivity by sharing information. The default networking protocol was NetBEUI, which does not support routing across internetworks, but TCP/IP or IPX/SPX could be added. WFW 3.11 clients could connect to both workgroups and domains (these are explained later in this chapter), and it provided built-in support for Novell NetWare Networks. This was a strategic move, because in 1993 Novell held the majority of the market share for server OSs. WFW 3.11 also improved support for remote access services.

Windows 95

Windows 95 was released on August 24, 1995 and it changed the face of Windows forever. Windows 95 was designed with the end user in mind, with features such as Plug-and-Play to make hardware installations easier, and dial-up networking for connecting to the Internet or another network via a modem. Windows 95 was the first Microsoft OS that supported long filenames (earlier OSs required compliance with the "eight-dot-three" naming convention). Windows 95 also supported preemptive multitasking. Perhaps the most drastic change was that Windows 95 was a "real" OS; unlike it predecessors, it did not require DOS to be installed first.

Windows 95b (also called OSR2) was an improved version that was never offered for sale to the public; it was only available to Original Equipment Manufacturers (OEMs) to install on new computers that they were offering for sale. Windows 95b added support for universal serial bus (USB) devices and the FAT32 file system that allowed for larger partitions, better disk space usage, and better performance.

Windows 98

Windows 98 was released on June 25, 1998. It was the retail upgrade to Windows 95 that provided support for reading DVDs and using USB devices. Applications in Windows 98 opened and closed more quickly. Like 95b, Windows 98 included a FAT32 converter, which allowed you to use hard drives over the 2GB limit imposed by DOS. The backup program was revamped to support more backup devices (including SCSI devices) and Microsoft added the Disk Cleanup utility to help find and delete old unused files. Windows 98 also included Internet Explorer 4.0 and the Active Desktop.

Windows 98 Second Edition

Windows 98 Second Edition (SE) was released on June 25, 1998 as an incremental update to Windows 98. Windows 98 SE improved the home multimedia experience, home networking and Internet browsing. Windows 98 SE introduced Internet Connection Sharing (ICS), which allowed a Windows 98 SE machine to function as a Network Address Translation (NAT) server for other machines on the home network. In other words, you could have multiple machines connected to the Internet at the same time using only a single ISP account and a single public IP address, and all Internet traffic would go through the Windows 98 SE machine running ICS. Windows 98 SE also included NetMeeting conferencing software and Internet Explorer 5.0. Windows 98 SE was the first consumer OS capable of using the same drivers as Windows NT 4.0.

Windows ME

Windows Millennium Edition (ME) was the last OS built on the MS-DOS kernel. It was released on September 14, 2000, and added improved support for digital media through applications such as Image Acquisition, Movie Maker, and Windows Media Player. Image Acquisition was added to simplify downloading images from digital cameras. Movie Maker was included to ease editing and recording digital video media files. Media Player was used to organize and play music and video files.

To enhance reliability, Windows ME added the system restore feature, which could be used to restore any deleted system files to fix problems. Another important feature was system file protection, which prevented important OS files from being changed by applications. ME also included a new home networking wizard to ease adding peripherals and computers to a home network.

OS/2: an IBM/Microsoft Joint Venture

All of the versions of Windows (Windows 1.0—Windows ME) discussed previously are built on the MS-DOS kernel. In the mid to late 1980s, around the Windows 2.0 timeframe, Microsoft and IBM decided to work together to create a replacement for the MS-DOS kernel. This replacement was called OS/2. It supported multitasking, used up to 16MB of memory (which wasa lot at the time), and was backward compatible with DOS applications.

OS/2 1.0 was released in December 1987. It was the first OS to provide for multitasking based on hardware support. It was a text-based OS that ran on 80286 systems, but version 1.1 of OS/2 added a GUI named Presentation Manager. Version 1.20 improved the Presentation Manager and introduced the High Performance File System (HPFS), which provided many of the features later offered by Microsoft in NTFS.

Microsoft and IBM were working together on the first 32-bit OS, which was to be OS/2 2.0, when the two companies parted ways.

After the "Divorce": A New Technology Emerges

Working together on the same OS proved to be too much of a burden for both Microsoft and IBM. This was exacerbated by the success of Microsoft's Windows, to which they were devoting more and more of their time. The companies agreed to split the work. Each company would still have access to each other's source code, but IBM would create OS/2 2.0 and Microsoft would create OS/2 3.0. OS/2 2.0 was meant to be the replacement for OS/2 1.3 and Windows 3.0, whereas OS/2 3.0 would be the replacement for OS/2 2.0.

OS/2 2.0 was released in 1992, and was a 32-bit OS that ran DOS and Windows 3.1 programs (using Virtual DOS Machines, or VDMs) as well as native OS/2 applications. This version also introduced the Workplace Shell, which was an object-oriented user interface that was integrated with the OS and file system.

Microsoft made a strategic business decision at that time. They decided that instead of focusing their attention on OS/2, they should create a new 32-bit version of Windows. This new version of Windows (Windows NT) was a huge hit. Developers liked it because it used the same programming model they were used to. Unlike OS/2, which used a completely different programming model, Windows NT made it very easy to move applications from the 16-bit Windows platform to the 32-bit Windows NT platform. Consumers liked it because it used an interface similar to Windows 3.0, with which they were already familiar. After IBM caught wind of Microsoft's new product, the ties were severed between IBM and Microsoft. Each would maintain the rights for everything co-developed up to that point, but there would be no more joint development. IBM continued working on OS/2 (and went on to develop OS/2 Warp, still in use in some niche business sectors today), and Microsoft scrapped OS/2 in favor of Windows NT.

Windows 9*x* versus Windows NT-Based Operating Systems

Windows 9*x* and Windows NT support peer-to-peer and domain-based networks. Windows 9*x* supports logging on to a domain, but does not support being "joined to a domain." This means that Windows 9*x* machines cannot have a machine account on the domain and cannot be managed with domain tools such as Active Directory Users and Computers. Windows 9*x* can function as a client and/or server in a workgroup environment, but Windows NT comes in two distinct versions:

- A workstation version designed to be used primarily as a client operating system
- A server version that can operate as a standalone file/print server or as a centralized authentication server (called a domain controller in Microsoft networking terminology)

Unlike 9*x*, NT is multithreaded and can support symmetric multiprocessing (SMP), which allows you to increase the performance of an application by adding more processors (if the application was written to support multiple processors).

Windows 9*x* is based on the MS-DOS kernel and is meant to be backward compatible with older DOS and Windows 3.*x* applications. This is great for consumers who need to run older applications, but compatibility does come at a cost. Older 16-bit apps all run in the same memory address space, which means that if one 16-bit app fails, it can bring down the entire OS.

Windows NT was built with stability and security in mind. 32-bit applications run in their own separate memory spaces, and older Windows 3.*x* and DOS applications run in virtual machines. Thus, the failure of an application cannot bring down the entire OS—the reason why 9*x* machines crashed more frequently and had to be rebooted more often than NT machines did. One of the means by which NT remains more stable is by restricting applications from directly accessing the hardware. Applications must interact with the hardware through the Hardware Abstraction Layer (HAL) of the OS. As usual, there is a catch; this extra stability sacrifices compatibility. NT does not work with as many applications and drivers as 9*x* does.

The NT OS Family Tree

Windows NT was focused on business users, and was built new from the ground up to provide the stability, reliability, and security features needed in the business environment. Until Microsoft comes up with a completely new kernel, all future versions of Windows will be descendants of the NT family line. Just as with the MS-DOS family line, Microsoft started off naming Windows NT with version numbers. Starting with Windows 2000, Windows was named after the year it was released, and the letters NT were removed from the name (although the tag line "built on NT technology" remained on the splash screen). Figure 1.2 shows the structure of the NT family line.

Figure 1.2 Following the Windows NT Family Line

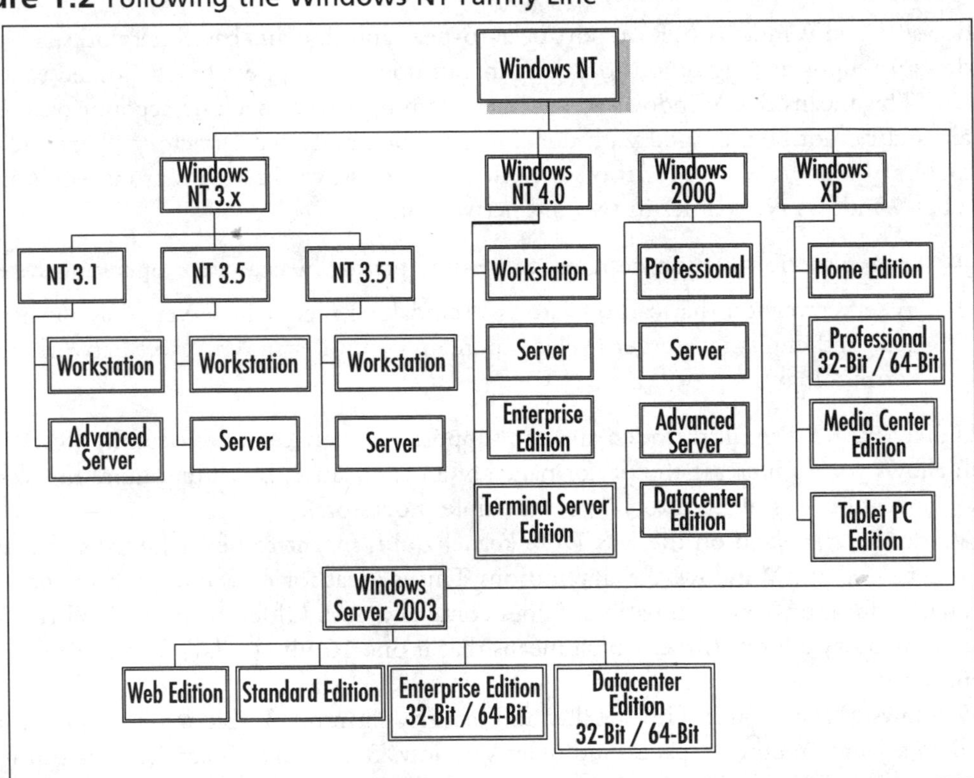

Windows NT 3.*x*

The Windows NT 3.*x* family was in production from 1993 to 1996. There were three releases within the 3.*x* family: Windows NT 3.1, Windows NT 3.5, and Windows NT 3.51. The Window NT 3.*x* GUI was similar to the Windows 3.*x* GUI, which made for an easy transition from the consumer line (Windows 3.*x*) to the business line (Windows NT 3.*x*). Each release of Windows NT 3.*x* had two versions, a desktop version called Workstation and a server version called Server in NT 3.1 or Advanced Server in NT 3.51. As we discuss the versions of NT 3.*x*, we will be referring to the server version.

Windows NT 3.1

Windows NT 3.1 was released on July 27, 1993. Even though this was the first version of NT, Microsoft chose to name it version 3.1, to build on the success of Windows 3.1. NT was created with a client/server networking model in mind. Windows NT 3.1 supported Microsoft's domain concept by functioning as a domain controller. It was also commonly used as an application server running applications such as Microsoft SQL Server (database application), Microsoft SNA Server (gateway application), and Microsoft Mail (e-mail application). Windows NT 3.1 was more scalable, fault tolerant, and secure than anything else Microsoft had produced up to that point. It provided centralized server management and centralized logons. NT 3.1 introduced NTFS, multiprocessor support, and the Win32 application programming interface (API). Win32 API was a big hit with developers because it made it easy to port over existing 16-bit apps, while making them more secure and stable.

Windows NT 3.5

Windows NT 3.5 was released in 1994. It kept the stability of Windows NT 3.1, but improved upon connectivity with other OSs. It was designed to work well in UNIX and Novell NetWare networks. To aid with server management, Microsoft added new administration tools and automatic reboot capabilities. NT 3.5 supported filenames up to 255 characters and supported high-end applications via the OpenGL graphics standard. This version also introduced new accessibility features for users with physical disabilities.

Windows NT 3.51

Windows NT 3.51 was an incremental update to Windows NT 3.5. It added a utility to assist customers with managing Client Access Licenses (CALs) for the BackOffice suite and a tool to enable over-the-network installations of Window 95. It also supported remote booting and PCMCIA (PC Card) devices.

Windows NT 4.0

The Windows NT 4.0 family was in production from 1996 to 2000. There were four releases within the 4.0 family: Windows NT 4.0 Workstation, Windows NT 4.0 Server, Windows NT 4.0 Server Enterprise Edition, and Windows NT 4.0 Terminal Server Edition. Like NT 3.*x*, the Workstation version of NT 4.0 was a desktop OS. The NT 4.0 GUI was similar to the Windows 95 GUI, just as Windows NT 3.*x* was similar to Windows 3.*x*. Once again, this made it easy to transition from the consumer line (Windows 9*x*) to the business line (Windows NT 4.0).

Windows NT 4.0 Server

Windows NT 4.0 Server shipped in 1996. This was the first version of NT to be truly 32-bit. It provided higher network throughput and made for quicker file and print services. NT 4.0 was bundled with Internet Information Server (IIS), Microsoft's Web server product, along with a suite of tools for managing and developing intranets.

Windows NT Server 4.0 Enterprise Edition

Windows NT 4.0 Enterprise Edition was released in 1997. This release was geared toward large companies that needed more than NT Server could offer. Enterprise Edition provided higher availability due to the built-in support for the Microsoft Cluster Service (MSCS) and for Windows Load Balancing (WLB). Enterprise Edition also supported more memory and more processors (up to eight) than Server, making it the most scalable Windows platform thus far. Enterprise Edition allowed applications to communicate at different times with systems on heterogeneous networks via Microsoft Message Queue Server (MSMQ).

Windows NT Server 4.0 Terminal Server Edition

Windows NT Server 4.0 Terminal Server Edition was released in 1998 and was based on technology developed by Citrix. It was a multiuser server OS that allowed multiple desktop machines to simultaneously run sessions on the Terminal Server via client software. Desktops would run the Terminal Server client software, but all processing took place on the server, thus the desktop machines could be low powered, inexpensive "thin clients." Microsoft provided client software for all Windows, UNIX, and Macintosh platforms, as well as the embedded OS in Windows-based terminal devices, thereby allowing almost any personal computer to run Windows-based applications via a Terminal Server desktop.

Windows 2000

Windows 2000 was released in February 2000, and put an end to the NT name forever. Even though it was built on the same NT kernel, it no longer bears the name. Windows 2000 shipped with four versions: Professional, Server, Advanced Server, and Datacenter Server. Professional was the replacement for NT 4.0 Workstation and was used as a desktop/client OS. Windows 2000 added many of the features on every NT 4.0 user's wish list, such as a disk defragmenter, device manager, and Plug-and-Play support. There is no separate version of Windows 2000 for Terminal Services; instead, all three server products include the ability to install Terminal Server services as part of the OS.

Windows XP/Windows Server 2003

Windows XP and Windows Server 2003 are based on the same code and are the client and server editions of the same OS, with the same relationship to one another as Windows 2000 Professional and Windows 2000 Server. In the early beta stage, both bore the code name

Whistler; however, Microsoft decided to release the desktop version before the server version was completed, and changed the names.

Windows XP is available in four 32-bit editions:

- Windows XP Home Edition
- Windows XP Professional
- Windows XP Media Center Edition
- Windows XP Tablet PC Edition

There is also a 64-bit version of XP, designed to run on the Itanium processor.

With XP, for the first time ever, Microsoft merged the consumer OS and business OS into the same family. No more 9*x* versus NT. Now everyone is using XP. Although the Home Edition and Media Center Edition are targeted toward consumers, while Professional and Tablet PC are targeted to business users, all are built on the same NT kernel.

Windows Server 2003 comes in four editions (discussed later in this chapter):

- Windows Server 2003 Web Edition
- Standard Edition
- Enterprise Edition
- Datacenter Server

Windows Server 2003 comes in both 32-bit and 64-bit versions.

Windows XP introduced a new variation to the 9*x* style GUI. The new interface is called LUNA and is also used by Windows Server 2003 (see Figure 1.3). The idea behind LUNA is to clean up your desktop and access everything that you need from the Start menu. If you don't care for LUNA, both XP and Windows Server 2003 also support the classic Windows 9x/NT 4.0 style GUI (see Figure 1.4).

Figure 1.3 Using the New LUNA Interface in Windows Server 2003

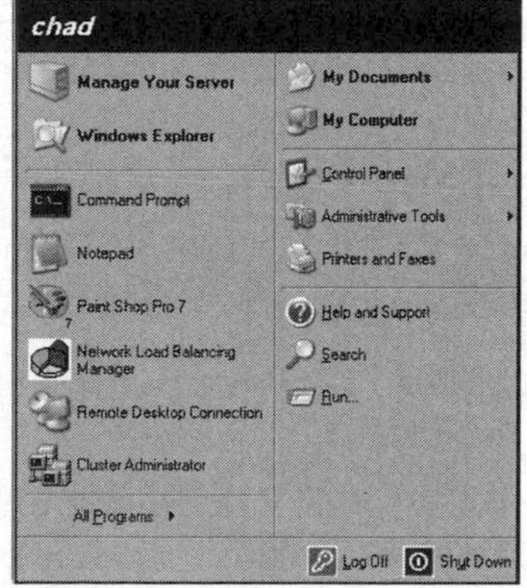

Figure 1.4 Using the Classic Start Menu in Windows Server 2003

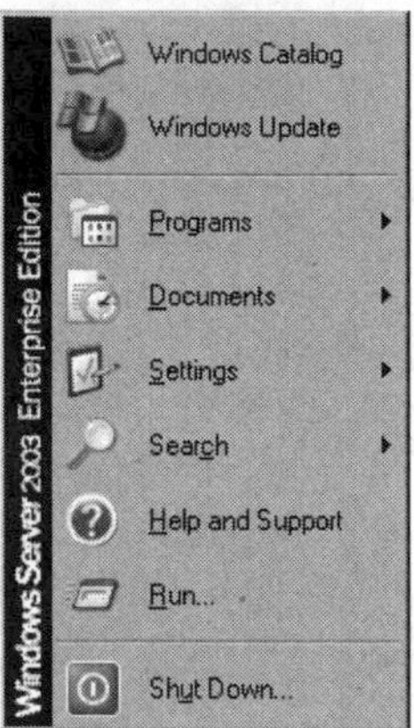

Windows XP Home Edition

Windows XP Home Edition was released in 2001. It is the first consumer OS based on the NT code, which makes it the most stable and secure Microsoft consumer OS to date. Home Edition supports the Internet Connection Firewall (ICF), which protects your computer while you are connected to the Internet. Multiple users sharing a machine is easier than ever, thanks to Fast User Switching, which allows you to switch between users' desktops without having to log off first. Home networking and multimedia capabilities have been enhanced in Home Edition. Remote Assistance is a new feature that lets you ask someone for help. The helper can then remotely control your desktop and chat with you online. Also included are features that are familiar to Windows 2000 Professional users, but were missing from the 9*x* line, such as Task Manager and System Monitor, and brand new features such as the Desktop Cleanup Wizard and taskbar grouping.

NOTE

For a full list of Windows XP Home Edition's features, see the Microsoft Home Edition Web site at *www.microsoft.com/windowsxp/home/evaluation/features.asp*.

Windows XP Professional

Windows XP Professional includes all of the features of Home Edition, and many new features geared toward business uses. Some of the new features include:

- Remote desktop, which allows XP Pro to act as a mini Terminal Server, hosting one remote session.
- Encrypting File System (EFS), which allows you to encrypt files stored on disk. EFS was included with Windows 2000 Professional, but XP Professional adds the ability to share encrypted files with other users.

- Internet Protocol Security (IPSec), which allows you to encrypt data that travels across the network to protect it from "sniffers."
- Integrated smart card support, which allows you to use smart card authentication to log on to the network, including Windows Server 2003 terminal sessions.
- Recovery console, which provides a command-line interface that administrators can use to perform repair tasks if the computer won't boot.
- The ability to join a Windows domain (domains are discussed later in the chapter). While users who have a domain account can log onto the domain from an XP Home computer, the Home computer cannot have a computer account in the domain. XP Professional computers have computer accounts, allowing the administrator to manage them centrally.

Windows XP Professional is Microsoft's current business desktop OS in use today.

Windows XP Professional 64-Bit Edition

Windows XP Professional 64-Bit Edition runs on the Itanium 2 processor and takes full advantage of its floating-point capabilities. Per Microsoft, "Windows XP 64-Bit Edition was designed to meet the demands of technical workstation users who require large amounts of memory and floating-point performance in areas such as mechanical design and analysis, 3D animation, video editing and composition, and scientific and high-performance computing applications." 64-Bit Edition supports up to 16GB of RAM and will run 32-bit applications designed for Windows XP Professional (in addition to 64-bit applications), allowing your power users to use one workstation for everything.

However, 64-bit Windows is not for everyone. The 64-bit edition of XP does not support many of the multimedia features found in 32-bit XP, such as CD recording, some of the Windows Media technologies, NetMeeting, and IEEE 1394 (FireWire) audio. It also doesn't support old subsystems and protocols such as the MS-DOS and 16-bit subsystems, IPX/SPX, AppleTalk, DLC, NetBEUI, and Services for Macintosh. System Restore is not included, and laptop features such as PC Card, IrDA, hot docking, and power management are not supported. Other features not included are Windows Messenger Service, Internet Locator Service (ILS) and SharePoint Team Services. Finally, there are a number of system administration and miscellaneous features that are not supported, including Windows Installer, Remote Assistance, Windows Product Activation (WPA), the File and Settings Transfer Wizard, and speech recognition.

Windows XP Media Center Edition

Windows XP Media Center Edition is built on Windows XP technology and comes preinstalled on Media Center PCs. Media Center Edition combines home entertainment and personal computing. It puts all of your media in one place and allows you to control it via remote control. Some of the features of Windows XP Media Center Edition include:

- Watching live TV
- Personal Video Recording (PVR)
- Electronic Program Guide (Guide)
- Playing DVDs
- Listening to music
- Watching videos
- The Media Center Remote Control

Windows XP Tablet PC Edition

Windows XP Tablet PC Edition was designed to run on tablet PCs. Tablet PCs look and function like laptops; however, you can swivel the screen around and write on them like a personal data assistant (PDA). Tablet PC Edition builds on Windows XP Professional, making it compatible with Windows XP applications, such as Office XP. Tablet PC Editions offers the following features:

- Windows Journal, which is used to take handwritten notes.
- Tablet PC Input Panel, which is used when you do not want to use your keyboard for inputting data.
- InkBall, a game that improves your skills with writing on a tablet PC.
- Sticky Notes, which are the electronic equivalent to yellow paper sticky notes.

Windows Server Operating System Basics

After discussing the timeline of the development of Windows family operating systems, we can see how Windows evolved over the years. Windows started off as a stand-alone product, with each machine independent of other machines. Next, the computer industry responded to the needs of users to share resources between machines over a network, and peer-to-peer networks were born. As networks grew larger, peer-to-peer networks started losing their appeal because of the difficulty of administration, and Microsoft moved to a client-server networking model, in which they introduced their domain concept. Eventually, as with peer-to-peer networks, companies started to outgrow their domains, and multidomain environments needed a better way for computers to interact across domains. Consequently, Microsoft introduced a new directory service called Active Directory to make it easier to locate resources within a large, complex network. Microsoft's latest server product, Windows Server 2003, still supports all of these concepts. You can use Windows Server 2003 in any network model, from peer-to-peer to Active Directory domain.

Client-Server Networking

Client-server networking is based on the idea of centralized sharing and centralized control. Think of it this way: if you had five children, you could buy each his or her own box of crayons, or you could buy one larger box that they all would share (if only it were that easy). For less than what you would pay for five individual boxes of 20 crayons, you could buy one large 100-piece box of crayons. This would allow each of the children to have more colors available and would save you some money in the process.

Client-server networking does something similar for computers. Instead of sharing resources from each other's machines, users attach to dedicated servers where all the network resources are stored. This allows you to use less powerful machines for desktops and put your money where it really matters, into your servers. As with the crayons, you are getting more for less. Users get better performance out of the higher end servers, and administrators get the benefits of centralized authentication and control. This makes for a more secure environment.

Centralized Authentication

A good rule of thumb when working with end users is to keep it simple. Most users want to log on to their PCs and work. They do not want to remember five different user account names and passwords, as is often the case when accessing resources on different workstations in a peer-to-peer network. Client-server networking makes things simple, because all shared files and printers are stored on the server. Users authenticate once to the server and they are done. They don't have to remember one password for printing and another for accessing files. One account does it all. In fact, once authenticated to the domain, they can also access resources on other workstations in the domain (to which they have permission) without needing to have local accounts on those workstations.

Centralized Administration

For an administrator, client-server networking is the only way to go. Because everything is centralized, you will find it easier to manage shared files and printers, create and manage accounts, back up and restore data, and secure the network. If you have more than 5 to 10 machines, client-server networking is much more efficient than peer-to-peer networking.

Client-Server versus Peer-to-Peer Networking

Peer-to-peer networking is networking in its simplest form. When you link two or more computers together without a centralized authentication server, you have a peer-to-peer network (also called a workgroup). Peer-to-peer networks allow file and printer sharing, but unlike client-server networking, authentication is not centralized. In a peer-to-peer network, every machine has its own local user accounts that can access files as shown in Figure 1.5. If you want to access data on four machines, then you must have an account on each of the four machines. This is fine if there are only a few machines on the network, but when there are, for example, 50 machines, you have to use 50 different accounts. This means that you have to remember the passwords for all 50 and keep them synchronized (if possible).

Figure 1.5 Using Peer-to-Peer Networking

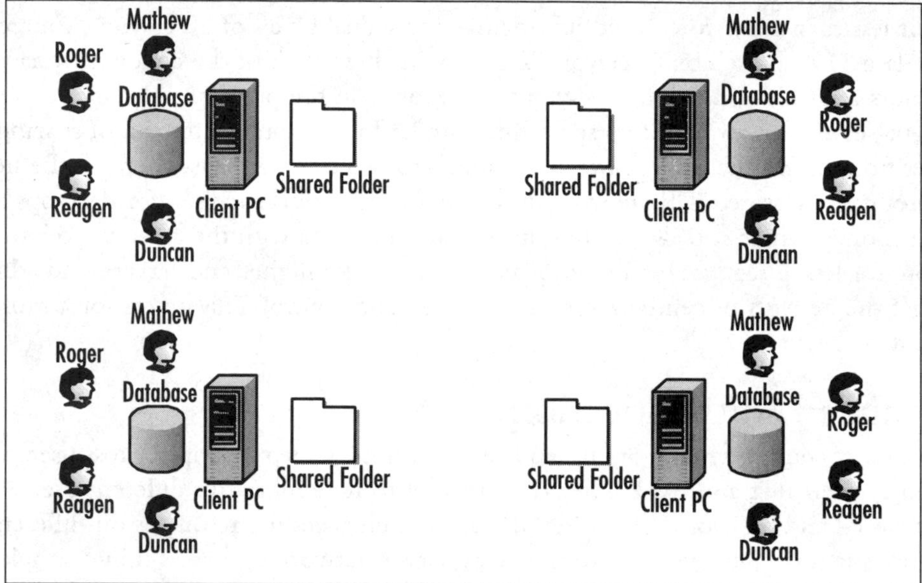

Client-server networking puts all shared objects on a centralized server, allowing everyone who has been granted permission to access them (as shown in Figure 1.6). Now, instead of having four user accounts to remember, you only have one. As discussed previously, this provides centralized administration and centralized authentication, which make it easier for administrators to manage and easier for users to understand. Microsoft used the concepts of client-server networking when they created the domain model for Windows NT.

The Domain Concept

The dictionary definition of domain is "a territory over which rule or control is exercised." In other words, a domain is a control boundary. You can control objects within a domain together, as if they were one. In Microsoft computing terminology, a domain is a logical group of computers with a common database of accounts. All of these accounts are managed and secured together in a central location (on the domain controller). Domains provide centralized authentication and centralized account management.

Figure 1.6 Using Client-Server Networking

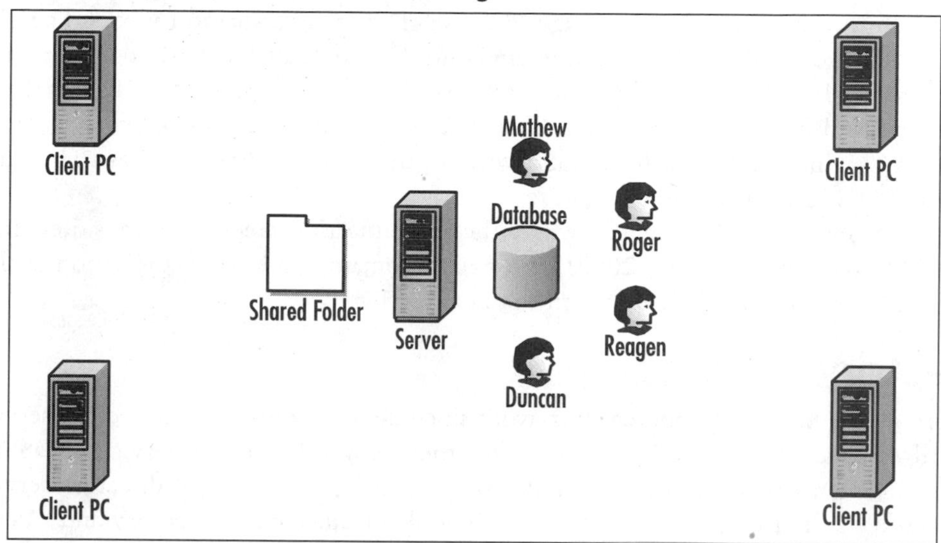

NT Domains

The idea of domains was introduced to Windows in 1993 when Windows NT 3.1 was released. Prior to the advent of Windows NT 3.1 and Windows for Workgroups, all machines were configured in a peer-to-peer network. As previously discussed, this is an inefficient way of doing things once the network grows beyond a few computers.

An NT domain consists of one or more domain controllers, member servers, workstations, users, and groups. All domain controllers share a common database called the Security Account Manager (SAM) database. Each domain controller holds its own copy of the SAM database, but there is only one writeable copy of the SAM database that is stored on the Primary Domain Controller (PDC), which is the first domian controller created in the domain. All other domain controllers are considered backup domain controllers (BDCs) and hold a read-only copy of the SAM. Whenever changes to the SAM database are made, they are made to the PDC and then replicated to the BDCs. This design is called a *single master replication model.* Member servers and workstations can be "joined to the domain," which means they have accounts in the SAM database and can be centrally managed. User and group accounts are also created within the domain, which allows centralized account management and the ability for users to use one user account to access everything they need.

Windows 2000/Server 2003 Domains

Windows 2000 and Windows Server 2003 also use the concept of domains, but with some changes. As in NT, domains provide centralized account management and centralized sign-on capabilities. The domain database is still contained on domain controllers. Workstations and servers can still be joined to the domain, and users and groups (there are more group types now) can still be created in the domain.

However, there are several differences between NT and Windows 2000/Server 2003 domains. In the latter, domains no longer use a single master replication model. There are no more PDCs and BDCs. Now, all domain controllers are equal and are just referred to as domain controllers (DCs), although there are several different *operations master roles* that can be assigned to different DCs. Windows 2000/Server 2003 domains use a *multimaster replication model*, in which all DCs can read and write to their copies of the database. This eliminates the PDC as a single point of failure.

Another important difference is where the authentication credentials are stored. Instead of the SAM database, Windows 2000/Server 2003 domains store this information in the Active Directory, which we'll discuss in the next section.

Directory Services

Directory services has been a popular buzzword since the development of directory services standards, especially since Novell implemented their Novell Directory Service (NDS) for NetWare. It seems as if everyone is talking about or using some type of directory service. OSs even have their own directory services; Novell currently has eDirectory, and Microsoft has Active Directory. One of the first network operating system directories was Banyan VINES' StreetTalk, which could be added onto Windows NT to provide a full fledged directory service.

Directory services can be used to store all types of information, including account authentication information. If you work in the computer networking field, it is likely that you will eventually implement some sort of directory service.

What Are Directory Services?

In its simplest form, a directory service is a way of storing information in a *directory* so it can easily be retrieved and used later. Directories predate electronic data; think of the telephone directory, product catalogs, and other directories published in print form. A directory service should include a set of rules to follow for naming its objects (the items entered in the directory), and a set of rules on how to store those objects. You should be able to add to and remove from a directory service as things change.

In computer networking, a directory service is a networkwide database that stores information including (but not limited to) information on people, files, printers, and applications. The directory service functions as a central point of management for the network OS in use, and assists in locating information or objects on the network. The directory can store authentication credentials, user preferences and profiles, network configuration information, and so forth. Directories differ from other databases in that they are more often read than written to. The rules that govern information format and how it is stored are located in a *schema*, which can be modified to meet the needs of your particular organization.

The basic components of a directory service include:

- A schema that defines the types of objects stored in the directory (object classes) and the attributes that can be assigned to them.

- Objects, which are representations of users, printers, applications, computers, and other entities, information about which is stored in the directory.
- Object classes, which are specific types of entities that can be stored in the directory.
- Attributes, which are the properties of an object (for example, user attributes would include the user's full name, account name, address, telephone number, and so forth.).
- A way to search the directory for information about the objects stored there.

History of Directory Services

The first directories were paper directories like the telephone book or TV guides. Some of the first electronic directories were DNS and WHOIS. Later, application directory services appeared in e-mail products such as Microsoft Exchange, Novell GroupWise, Lotus cc:Mail, and in online directory services functioning as electronic phonebooks such as Four11, Switchboard, and BigFoot.

It might be difficult to think of an electronic telephone book as a directory service, but it does match our definition. It has a set of rules for naming its objects (last name, first name) and a set of rules for storing its objects (alphabetically based on function). You can add to and remove from the telephone book as people move and their phone numbers change, and items can easily be retrieved from the phone book when needed. The most recent type of directory services to show up are network operating systems (NOS) directory services such as Novell Directory Services, Banyan VINES, and Microsoft Active Directory.

Directory Services Standards

Most directories in use today are based on the X.500 standards. The X.500 standards are recommendations published by the International Organization for Standardization (ISO) and International Telecommunications Union (ITU), that define how to organize a directory.

X.500 is not itself a directory, it is a model that vendors can use to build their own directories. Standards make compatibility between different products possible. If two separate vendors use the same model for their directories, then data sharing between the two directories should be possible. X.500 is to directories what the OSI model is to networking. X.500 defines standards for (among other things) creating a schema, defining attributes, and organizing data within the directory.

NOTE

The following two links might prove helpful for a more thorough understanding of the X.500 Standards and the OSI model:

- See www.isi.salford.ac.uk/staff/dwc/X500.htm for an explanation of the X.500 standards.
- See www.cisco.com/univercd/cc/td/doc/cisintwk/ito_doc/introint.htm for an explanation of the OSI model.

NT Directory Services

Most people think of Windows 2000 in relation to Microsoft's directory services. Some people don't even think of NT as having a directory service. However, based on our definition of a directory service (a way of storing information so it can easily be retrieved and used later), NT does have one, although it is not nearly as structured and full-featured as the Active Directory. NT's directory service (NTDS) enables users to be identified and provides access to resources throughout the network. It also allows an administrator to centrally manage the users and the network together.

NTDS was based on the domain concept and provided a means for locating objects and information within the domain. It contained users, groups, and machines; however, it was a flat database, as opposed to the hierarchical structure of more complex directories such as NDS and Active Directory.

Active Directory

Active Directory first appeared in Windows 2000 Server. Active Directory is based on the X.500 standards. It has been improved and is still in use in Windows Server 2003. Active Directory does not use the flat structure of NTDS; instead, it is hierarchical in design (sometimes referred to as a *tree structure*). This allows logical separation within the directory for organization and management.

Active Directory allows you to customize your directory into an intuitive structure for your environment. It is not a "one size fits all" directory like NT. Active Directory still uses the concepts of domains, but it changes the ways they are organized and connected. In addition to domains, Active Directory uses additional structural elements such as domain trees, forests, and organizational units (OUs) for directory organization.

NOTE

Interestingly, the NTDS name has been retained for the database file in which the Windows 2000 Active Directory database is stored, ntds.dit, which is located in the SystemRoot\NTDS directory and contains the schema, link, and data tables.

What's New in Windows Server 2003?

Windows Server 2003 improves upon previous versions of Windows in the areas of availability, reliability, security, and scalability. Windows Sever 2003 is designed to allow customers to do more with less. According to Microsoft, companies that have deployed Windows Server 2003 have been able to operate with up to 30 percent greater efficiency in the areas of application development and administrative overhead.

Why a New Server Operating System?

Microsoft has released a new server OS approximately every three years. Each time, the primary question asked by those charged with making the upgrade decision is, "Why should I switch to this version?"

Upgrading from Windows NT 3.*x* to Windows NT 4.0 got you the new Windows 9*x* style interface (among other things). Upgrading from Windows NT 4.0 to Windows 2000 got you Active Directory and Group Policy (also among other things). So, what are the significant differences in Windows Sever 2003 that should convince you to make the switch? The answer, for many, will be the strong focus on security. For others, new management and networking features might be the deciding factor. In the following sections, we will look at these more closely.

New Features

Microsoft has enhanced most of the features carried over from Windows 2000 Server and has added some brand new features for Windows Server 2003. For example:

- Active Directory has been updated to improve replication, management, and migrations.
- File and Print services have been updated to make them more dependable and quicker.
- The number of nodes supported in clustering has been increased and new tools have been added to aid in cluster management.
- Terminal Server better supports using local resources when using the Remote Desktop Protocol.
- IIS 6.0, Media Services 9.0, and XML services have been added to Windows Server 2003.
- New networking technologies and protocols are supported, including Simple Object Access Protocol (SOAP), Web Distributed Authoring and Versioning (WebDAV), IPv6, wireless networking, fiber channel, and automatic configuration for multiple networks.
- A plethora of new command-line tools have been added for easier administration.

- Software Restriction Policies allow administrators to control which applications can be run.
- All features of Windows have been updated to reflect Microsoft's security initiative.

New Active Directory Features

Windows Server 2003 enhances the management of Active Directory. There are more AD management tools now and the tools are easier than ever to use. Microsoft has made it painless to deploy Active Directory in Windows Server 2003. The migration tools have been greatly improved to make way for seamless migrations.

In the corporate world where mergers and acquisitions are common, things change all the time. It is not uncommon for a company to change its name two or three times in one year, which is a real hassle for network administrators in companies running a Windows 2000 Active Directory. Now, with Windows Server 2003, you can rename your domains. You can change the NetBIOS name, the DNS name, or both.

Another problem with mergers is the need to configure trust relationships. With Windows 2000, if two companies merge and each has a separate Active Directory, they need to either set up manual nontransitive trusts between all of their domains or collapse one forest into the other. Neither of these is an ideal choice. The trusts are easy enough to set up, but then you lose the benefits of being in a single forest. Collapsing forests can require a lot of work, depending on the environment.

Windows Server 2003 Active Directory now supports forest-level trusts. By setting the trusts at the forest roots, you enable cross-forest authentication and cross-forest authorization. Cross-forest authentication provides a single sign-on experience by allowing users in one forest to access machines in another forest via NTLM or Kerberos. Cross-forest authorization allows assigning permissions for users in one forest to resources in another forest. Permissions can be assigned to the user ID or through groups.

New & Noteworthy...

Renaming Your Domain

The Domain Rename tool allows you to rename any of your domains, as long as all domain controllers in the forest are running Windows Server 2003. It allows you to restructure domains within a tree and create new trees. However, it does not allow you to change which domain is the forest root. In addition, you cannot add and remove domains from the forest; you can only rename them and you can't reuse names.

You can get the Domain Rename tool (rendom.exe) from the server CD under the Valueadd\Msft\Mgmt\Domren folder, or you can download it from www.microsoft.com/windowsserver2003/downloads/domainrename.mspx.

Not all improvements have to do with mergers and multiple forests. In the past, it was common practice for companies with many offices spread out geographically to build their domain controllers locally and ship them to the remote offices. This was because of replication issues. When a new domain controller is created, it must pull a full copy of the Active Directory database from another domain controller. This full replication can easily oversaturate a slow network link. However, with Windows Server 2003, you can create a new domain controller and pull the Active Directory information from your backup media. The newly created domain controller now only has to replicate the changes that have occurred since the backup was made. This usually results in much less traffic than replicating the entire database.

EXAM WARNING

Active Directory now allows cross-forest authorization through forest-level transitive trusts. This allows every domain in multiple forests to share resources with each other while maintaining single sign-on capabilities. To use forest-level trusts, your forest functionality level must be set to Windows Server 2003 mode (which means you cannot have any NT or Windows 2000 domain controllers in the forest).

Transitivity means that if A trusts B and B trusts C, then A can get to C via the shared trust. It allows you to have multiple domains trust each other, while maintaining a minimal set of trusts. Windows 2000 doesn't support transitive trusts between forests; this is a new feature for Windows Server 2003.

The Active Directory Users and Computers tool (ADUC) has been improved to include a new query feature (see Figure 1.7) that allows you to write filters for the type of objects you want to view. These queries can be saved and used multiple times. For example, you might want to create a query to show you all of the users with mailboxes on a specified Exchange server. By creating a query, you can easily pull up a current list with one click of the mouse. ADUC also now supports the following:

- Multi-object selection
- Drag-and-drop capabilities
- The ability to restore permissions back to the defaults
- The ability to view the effective permissions of an object

Figure 1.7 Querying Objects in Active Directory Users and Computers

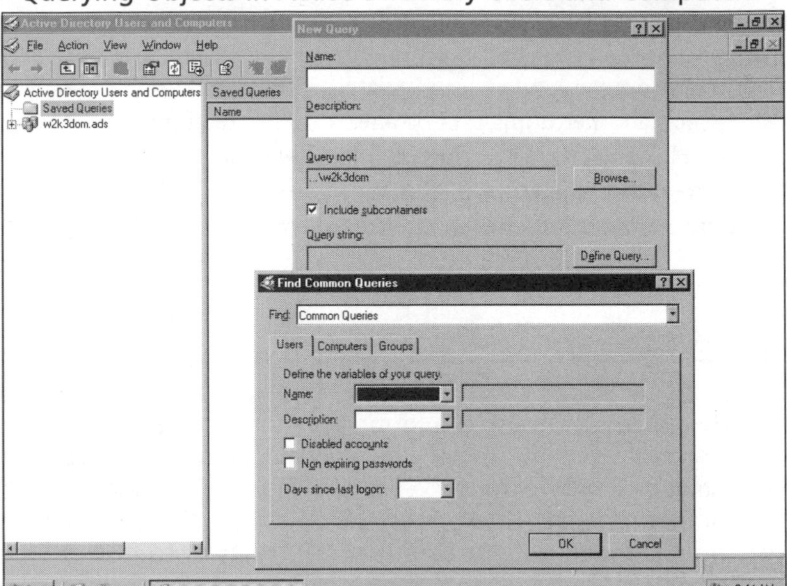

Configuring & Implementing...

Using Saved Queries in Active Directory User and Computers

The ability to create and save queries in ADUC is a convenient feature. It makes it easy to find Active Directory objects that match certain criteria. You can search for such things as:

- All printers in a certain location
- All users who use Exchange instant messaging
- All machines installed via Remote Installation Services (RIS)
- All empty groups (groups with no members)

After you create a query, it is automatically saved so you can use it again. You can even export your query to an XML file in order to export it to another machine. This makes sharing queries very easy.

Group Policy management has also been enhanced in Windows Server 2003. The Microsoft Group Policy Management Console (GPMC), shown in Figure 1.8, makes it easy to troubleshoot and manage Group Policy. It supports drag-and-drop capabilities, backing up and restoring your Group Policy objects (GPOs), and copying and importing GPOs. Where the GPMC really shines is in its reporting function. You now have a graphical, easy-to-use interface that, within a few clicks, will show you all of the settings configured in a GPO. You can also determine what a user's effective settings would be if he or she logged on to a certain machine. The only way you could do this in Windows 2000 was to actually log the user on to the machine and run gpresult (a command-line tool for viewing effective GPO settings).

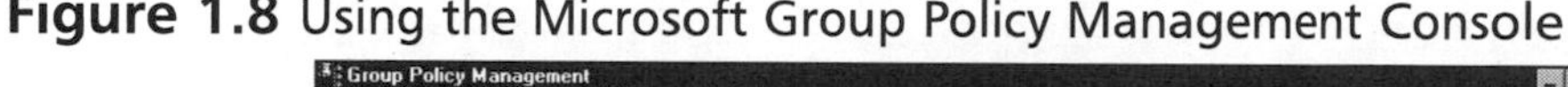

Figure 1.8 Using the Microsoft Group Policy Management Console

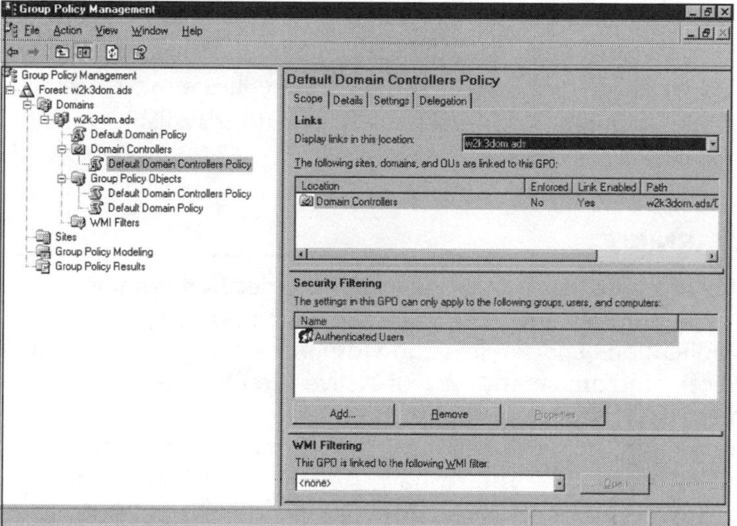

The schema can now be redefined. This allows you to make changes if you incorrectly enter something into the schema. In Windows 2000, you can deactivate schema attributes and classes, but you can not redefine them. You still need Schema Admin rights to modify the schema, but now it is more forgiving of mistakes.

The way objects are added to and replicated around the directory has been improved as well. The Inter-Site Topology Generator (ISTG) has been improved to support a larger number of sites. Group membership replication is no longer "all or nothing" as it was in Windows 2000. In Windows Server 2003, as members are added to groups, only those members are replicated to your domain controllers and global catalog (GC) servers, rather than the entire group membership list. No more worrying about the universal group replication to your GC servers.

Every domain controller caches credentials provided by GC servers. This allows users to continue to log on if the GC server goes down. It also speeds up logons for sites that do not have a local GC server. No longer is the GC server a single point of failure. In fact, you no longer are required to have one at each site.

EXAM WARNING

All domain controllers cache the credentials they receive from GC servers. This is new to Windows Server 2003 and removes the GC server as a single point of failure. Users can now log on with cached information instead of having to go through the GC server each time.

Active Directory now supports a new directory partition called the application partition. You can add data to this partition and choose which domain controllers will replicate it. This is useful if you have information you want to replicate to all domain controllers in a certain area, but you do not want to make the information available to all domain controllers in the domain.

EXAM WARNING

The application partition is only replicated to specified domain controllers. It is up to you, as the administrator, to determine which domain controllers will host a replica. Applications and services can store information in the application partition. This partition can contain any type of Active Directory object except security principles such as users, groups, computers, or services.

You might want to use the application partition to store your DNS database. This will allow you to have Active Directory Integrated (ADI) zones that replicate between different domains. In Windows 2000, there was no way to replicate ADI zones between domains.

Improved File and Print Services

Practically every organization uses file and print services, as sharing files and printers was the original reason for networking computers together. Microsoft has improved the tools used to manage your file system by making the tools run faster than before; this allows users to get their jobs done in less time and requires less downtime for your servers. The Distributed File System (DFS) and the File Replication Service (FRS) have also been enhanced for Windows Server 2003, and Microsoft has made printing faster and easier to manage.

Enhanced File System Features

Windows 2003 supports WebDAV, which was first introduced in Exchange 2000. It allows remote document sharing. Through standard file system calls, clients can access files stored in Web repositories. In other words, clients think they are making requests to their local file systems, but the requests are actually being fulfilled via Web resources.

Microsoft made it easier to manage disks in Windows Server 2003 by including a command-line interface. From the command-line, you can do tasks that were only supported from the GUI in Windows 2000, such as managing partitions and volumes, configuring RAID, and defragmenting your disks. There are also command-line tools for extending basic disk, file system tuning, and shadow copy management.

Disk fragmentation is a problem that commonly plagues file servers. This occurs when data is constantly written to and removed from a drive. Fragmented drives do not perform as well as defragmented drives. Although Windows 2000 (unlike NT) included a disk defragmentation tool, it was notoriously slow. To address this, Microsoft beefed up the defragmenter tool in Windows Server 2003 so that it is much faster than before. In addition, the new tool is not limited to only specific cluster sizes that it can defrag, and it can perform an online defragmentation of the Master Fat Table.

The venerable CHKDSK (pronounced "check disk") tool, which is used to find errors on Windows volumes, has been revamped as well. Microsoft studies show that Windows Server 2003 runs CHKDSK 20 to 35 percent faster than Windows 2000. However, since Windows Server 2003 (like Window 2000) uses NTFS—which is less prone to errors than FAT file systems—you shouldn't have to run CHKDSK often.

TEST DAY TIP

As you are learning about the enhancements made to the tools in Windows Server 2003, don't worry about remembering how much faster they are. Focus instead on learning how the tools work. For example, you will not need to know that CHKDSK is 30 percent faster than in Windows 2000, but you might be expected to know how to use CHKDSK. We discuss using CHKDSK in Chapter 2, "Managing Physical and Logical Disks."

Both the DFS and the FRS have been improved. DFS allows you to create a single logical tree view for multiple servers, so that all directories appear to be on the same server. However, they are actually on separate servers. DFS works hand in hand with Active Directory to determine site locations for clients requesting data, thereby allowing clients to be directed to a server closest to them in physical proximity. FRS is used to replicate DFS file share data. FRS now allows administrators to configure its replication topology and compress replication traffic.

One of the best file system improvements in Windows Server 2003 (in our opinion) is shadow copies. After you enable shadow copies on the server and install the shadow copy client software on the desktop computer, end users can right-click on a file and view previous versions that were backed up via shadow copies. They can then keep the current version of the file or roll back to an early version. This will remove the burden (to some extent) of simple file restores from your IT staff and allow the users to handle it themselves.

Improved Printing Features

Even though we are constantly moving toward a paperless society, printing is still an important requirement for most companies. One of the more common reasons for small companies to put in a network is for the purpose of sharing printers (a shared Internet connection and e-mail are two other reasons). Microsoft has taken many steps to improve the printing experience in Windows Server 2003. Users who print long documents should notice a performance boost over Windows 2000, because Windows Server 2003 does a better job of file spooling. In other words, print jobs should get to the printer faster.

Microsoft has also made printing easier to manage than ever before. Windows Server 2003 has command-line utilities for managing printer configuration, including print queues, print jobs, and driver management. System Monitor even has counters for managing print performance.

Installing printers is a snap in Windows Server 2003 because of Plug-and-Play (PnP) functionality. This allows you to physically connect the printer to the machine and have Windows set it up for you automatically (as long as the printer itself supports PnP). Windows Server 2003 supports over 3800 new print drivers.

Revised IIS Architecture

Internet Information Services (IIS) is Microsoft's Web server product. IIS 6.0 is included with all versions of Windows Server 2003. With this new version, Microsoft has made great leaps in the area of IIS reliability, availability, management, and security.

IIS 6.0 was designed so a problem with one application won't cause the server or other applications running on the server to crash. It provides health monitoring and disables Web sites and applications that fail too frequently within a defined period of time. IIS 6.0 can stop and restart Web sites and applications based on customized criteria (such as disk, CPU, or memory utilization). IIS 6.0 allows changing the configuration of your Web server without having to restart it. It is the most scalable version of IIS to date, supporting more Web sites on a single server than IIS 5.0. The actual IIS services stop and start much faster than before, helping to decrease Web site downtime.

Management of your Web server is easier in Windows Server 2003, thanks to command-line scripting. The metabase is now stored in a plain-text XML configuration file. This improves backing up, restoring, recovering, troubleshooting, and directly editing the metabase. IIS 6.0 supports ASP .NET, .NET Framework, and a wide variety of languages. Since the .NET Framework doesn't depend on a specific language, almost any programming language will do.

One common complaint about Windows 2000 was that IIS installed by default; thereby creating an instant vulnerability on servers that were never intended to be Web servers. Microsoft recommends that you only install IIS when needed and lock it down so it only offers the services that your organization requires. In Windows Server 2003, IIS is not installed by default and is locked down by default when you do install it. This means that it will only deliver static content, unless you specifically configure it for dynamic content. IIS 6.0 requires an administrator to add necessary dynamic extensions to the Web services extensions list. Until they are added to this list, IIS will not support them; this will stop attackers from calling unsecured dynamic pages.

EXAM WARNING

Microsoft has changed their approach to IIS in Windows Server 2003. No longer is IIS installed by default. When you do install IIS, it runs the IIS Lockdown tool automatically and secures your Web server. Basically, your Web server is set to only offer the services you select. It discards all other requests.

Enhanced Clustering Technology

A cluster is a group of servers that work together like one computer. Clusters can be used for performance reasons (to balance the load across two or more computers) or for fault tolerance reasons (to provide failover if one computer fails).

Microsoft added clustering support to its OS line in 1997 with Windows NT 4.0 Enterprise Edition. At that time, clustering was not commonly used. Only the really big IT shops could afford to put in clustered solutions because of the cost of the extra servers. Now that hardware has dropped in price, more and more customers are choosing to cluster their mission-critical systems. As Storage Area Networking (SAN) technology becomes more widespread, clusters are becoming fairly easy to set up. Like Windows 2000, Windows Server 2003 supports two types of clustering: Microsoft Cluster Service (MSCS) and Network Load Balancing (NLB).

Microsoft Cluster Service

MSCS uses two or more physically connected servers, called *nodes,* that communicate with each other constantly. If a node detects that another node is offline, it will take over the services provided by the offline node. However, this happens behind the scenes, and end users are unaware of the process (other than experiencing a small initial delay).

MSCS is traditionally used with mail servers, database servers, and file and print servers. MSCS is supported in Windows Server 2003 Enterprise Edition and Windows Server 2003 Datacenter Edition. Some of the new features of Windows Server 2003 clustering include:

- The support of more nodes in a cluster. Enterprise Edition and Datacenter Edition both support eight nodes.
- Clustering now integrates with Active Directory and creates a computer account for the virtual cluster name.
- Clustered applications can now use Kerberos authentication.

EXAM WARNING

Microsoft has increased the numbers of nodes supported in clustering. Both Enterprise Edition and Datacenter Edition now support eight nodes. Windows 2000 Advanced Server supports two node clusters, and Windows 2000 Datacenter Edition supports four node clusters. Be sure not to confuse these on the test.

Network Load Balancing

NLB is available in all versions of Windows Server 2003. Unlike MSCS, where only one server offers the services at a time, NLB nodes all offer services at the same time. The NLB cluster is accessed via a virtual name (a name that represents the group of servers as an entity), and whichever server is least busy answers the request (there is a little more to it, but this is good enough for now).

If one server goes offline, there is no transferring of services because all servers offer the services already. When a server goes offline, it is removed from the rotation of servicing requests until it comes back online. NLB is generally used with Web servers, application servers, terminal servers, and streaming media servers. NLB Manager is a new tool in Windows Server 2003 (see Figure 1.9) that provides a central point for managing and configuring NLB clusters.

Figure 1.9 Using the Network Load Balancing Manager

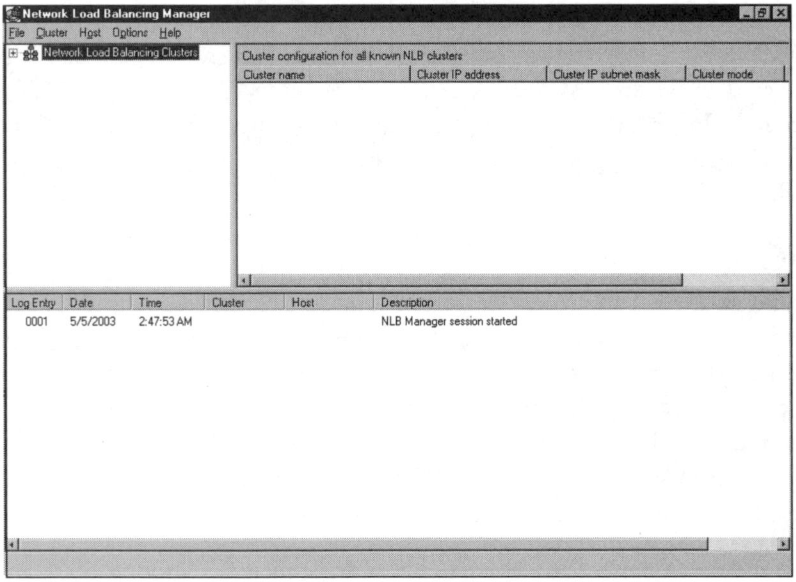

There are many new features for NLB in Windows Server 2003. NLB now supports multiple network interface cards (NICs), allowing a single server to host multiple NLB clusters. You can use virtual clusters to set up different port rules for each cluster IP address, so that each IP address represents a different resource (Web page, application, and so forth). The Internet Group Management Protocol (IGMP) is now supported when NLB is configured in multicast mode. Using IGMP limits cluster traffic on the switch to the ports that have NLB server connected to them. This helps prevent switch flooding. (Switch flooding occurs when every server in an NLB cluster sees every packet addressed to the cluster.) NLB now supports IPSec traffic.

TEST DAY TIP

Do not confuse the Microsoft Clustering Service (MSCS) with Network Load Balancing (NLB). MSCS machines actually share hardware (storage), whereas machines using NLB do not. When using MSCS, only one machine at a time is actually functioning as the server and responding to requests. It owns the resources being offered. If that machine fails, then those resources failover to another machine in the MSCS cluster. With NLB, all machines offer the resources at the same time. The NLB service routes the request to the next available machine in the NLB cluster. MSCS is implemented for fault tolerance, whereas NLB is implemented to increase performance.

New Networking and Communications Features

Windows Server 2003 adds a number of new networking technologies that enable it to grow with the needs of your business. For example:

- It supports IPv6, which was created to overcome the limited number of addresses in IPv4 (previous versions of NT use IPv4). Windows Server 2003 supports IPv4/IPv6 coexistence through technologies such as Intra-site Automatic Tunnel Addressing Protocol (ISATAP) and 6to4. Internet and remote access functionality have been enhanced in Windows Server 2003.
- Point-to-Point Protocol over Ethernet (PPPoE) allows making broadband connections to an Internet Service Provider (ISP) without having to load any software.
- Windows can now use IPSec over NAT.
- Remote Authentication Dial-In User Service (RADIUS) has been improved to provide better control over network access and easier troubleshooting of authentication problems.
- Microsoft's implementation of RADIUS, Internet Authentication Service (IAS), can send its logs to a Microsoft SQL Server and it now supports 802.1X authentication and cross-forest authentication.

New & Noteworthy...

Using L2TP over NAT

In Windows 2000, IPSec was not supported through a NAT server. This was a serious drawback for some companies, as it meant they could not VPN through the NAT server using IPSec or the Layer Two Tunneling Protocol (L2TP), which uses IPSec for encryption. This restriction has been removed in Windows Server 2003. Both IPSec connections and L2TP connections using IPSec are supported over NAT when you have a Windows Server 2003 VPN server. This is done using a technology called NAT traversal, or NAT-T. On the client end, the Microsoft L2TP/IPSec VPN client supports NAT-T. It can be downloaded at www.microsoft.com/windows2000/server/evaluation/news/bulletins/l2tpclient.asp and can be installed on Windows 98, ME, and NT 4.0 Workstation.

The Internet Connection Firewall (ICF) functions as a personal software-based firewall and provides protection for computers connected to the Internet or unsecured networks. ICF (see Figure 1.10) protects LAN,VPN, dial-up, and PPPoE connections by making it easier to secure your server against attacks.With ICF, only the services that you need to offer are exposed. For example, you can use ICF to filter the network connection of your DNS server so that only DNS requests are passed through.

Figure 1.10 Using the Internet Connection Firewall

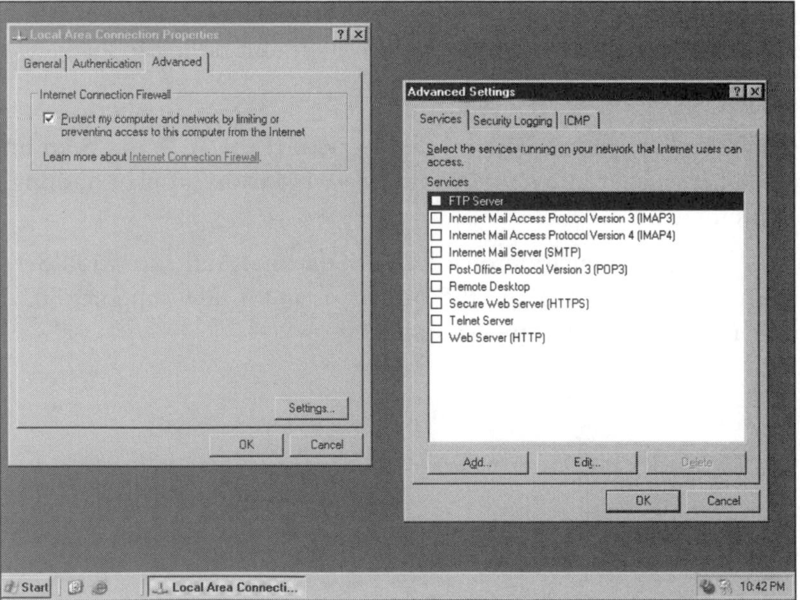

ICF is included with the 32-bit versions of the Standard and Enterprise Editions of Windows Server 2003. It is not included with the Web and Datacenter Editions, or with any of the 64-bit versions.

Improved Security

You might have noticed in the previous sections that Microsoft is paying more attention to customers' concerns about security. Many of the new features discussed thus far relate in one way or another to security. One of the key components of Windows Server 2003 security is the Common Language Runtime (CLR) software engine. It reduces the number of security vulnerabilities due to programming mistakes, and makes sure that applications have appropriate permissions to run and that they can run without any errors.

NOTE

For more information about CLR, see the article *About the Common Language Runtime (CLR)* on the .NET framework community Web site at www.gotdotnet.com/team/clr/about_clr.aspx.

EFS encrypts files that are stored on NTFS-formatted partitions so that they can only be decrypted by the person who encrypted the file, those with whom he or she shares the file, or a designated recovery agent. The sharing of encrypted files, as shown in Exercise 1.01, is new to Windows XP/Server 2003. In Windows 2000, this was not possible because only the person who encrypted the file had the correct keys to decrypt it. Now, the person who encrypts the file can choose to give other people the ability to decrypt the file as well, and the file encryption key (FEK) is protected by the public key of each additional person who is given authorization. Encrypted files appear just like normal files in Windows Explorer. However, only authorized users can access them. Anyone else will be denied access. EFS now supports encrypting offline files and storing encrypted files in Web folders.

EXERCISE 1.01

CONFIGURING MULTIPLE USERS TO SHARE EFS ENCRYPTED FILES

One of the new features of Windows Server 2003 (and Windows XP) is the ability for multiple users to share encrypted data. In Windows 2000, only the user who encrypted the data or a designated recovery agent could decrypt the data. This exercise walks you through the steps of encrypting your data and then sharing it with someone else.

To encrypt your data with EFS:

1. Right-click on the file or folder you want to encrypt. Note that Microsoft recommends encrypting at the folder level for ease of management.
2. From the **General** tab, click **Advanced**.
3. Check the box next to **Encrypt contents to secure data**.
4. Click **OK**.

NOTE

Another way to encrypt a file or folder is to use the cipher tool at the command-line.

Now, to share your encrypted data with other users, follow these steps:

1. Right-click on the file or folder you want to share.
2. From the **General** tab, click **Advanced**.
3. Click **Details**.
4. Click **Add**.
5. Click **Find User**.
6. Select the user from list.
7. Click **OK** to save your changes.

Microsoft provides a single sign-on environment for users via Credential Manager (see Figure 1.11). Credential Manager provides a secure place for users to store their passwords and X.509 certificates. When a resource is accessed, the correct credentials will be pulled from Credential Manager without prompting the user for action. In large complex environments in which you can have three or four user accounts, this is a great benefit. No longer do you have to key in your domain, username, and password each time; you set it up once and then Credential Manager does all of the work.

Figure 1.11 Using Credential Manager to Provide a Single Sign-On Environment

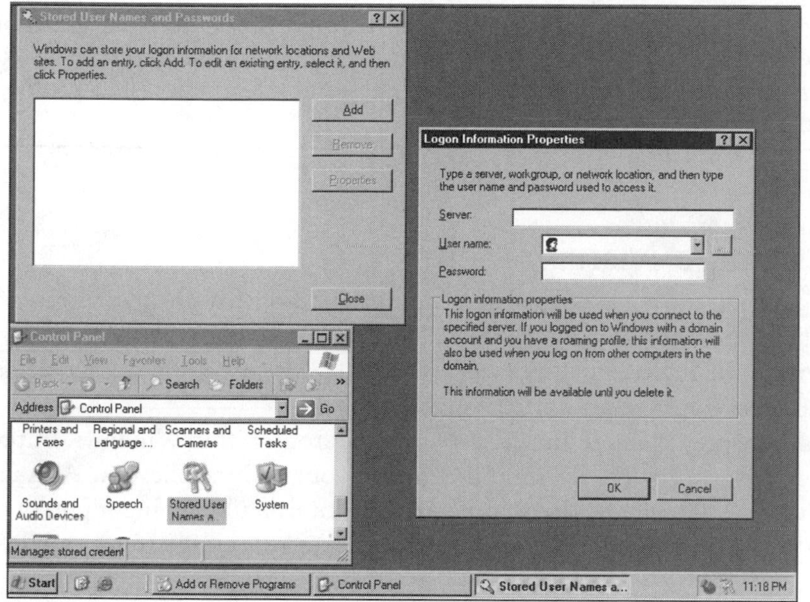

You can now control which software can run on a machine via software restriction policies. These policies can be applied at the domain, site, OU, or locally. You define a default security level that either allows or disallows software to run via the Group Policy Object Editor Snap-in. Among other things, software restriction policies can be used to prevent viruses and other harmful programs from running on your PC, and can also be used to limit end users to only running the programs needed for their job.

Windows Server 2003 supports the IEEE 802.1X protocols. This standard allows authorization and authentication of users connecting to Ethernet and wireless local area networks (WLANs). Windows Server 2003 supports authentication via Extensible Authentication Protocol (EAP) methods, such as smart cards.

Autoenrollment and autorenewal of certificates makes it easier to quickly deploy smart cards. Certificate Services now supports incremental (a.k.a. delta) Certificate Revocation Lists (CRLs), which means that the server can just push down the changes to the client and not have to push the entire CRL every time.

A couple of other new security features of Windows Server 2003 are Passport Integration and Cross-Forest Trusts. Passport is integrated with Active Directory and supports mapping Active Directory user accounts to Passport accounts. Users can use Passport for a single sign-on to all of the supported systems. In Windows 2000, trusts are set up between domains only. This means that if you have two forests, each with three domains, then you must set up trusts between all six domains. With Cross-Forest Trusts, you can set up a trust between the forests, and all domains can access each other.

NOTE

Passport is a service provided by Microsoft that lets you access a variety of services and Web sites that are Passport-enabled, using your e-mail address as your account name. The account also stores personal information in a profile, and encrypts this information to protect it.

Better Storage Management

In an effort to keep up with the changing times, Microsoft has greatly increased the level of built-in SAN support in Windows Server 2003. The Virtual Disk Service (VDS) provides a unified interface for multivendor storage devices. VDS discovers the storage devices in your network and gives you a single place to manage them.

You can now create and mount a SAN volume from within Windows. In previous versions of Windows, you had to do this from within your SAN application. Also included in Windows Server 2003, via the driver development kit, is multipathing input/output (MPIO). MPIO allows up to 32 different paths to external storage (for example, SAN).

Head of the Class...

Understanding Storage Area Networks

A SAN is a high-speed dedicated network of storage devices. SANs contain a bank of hard drives, optical drives, or other storage devices that can be divided and shared. SANs waste less storage space because you can share the disks between all of your servers. SANs provide high bandwidth with zero latency, and they eliminate I/O bottlenecks from networks.

SANs have their own private optical fiber or fibre channel network that connects them to the servers. All backing up and restoring takes place over this private fiber network, rather than going over your production Ethernet network. This saves traffic over your Ethernet network, and tremendously speeds up your backups. Ethernet networks typically run at 10 to100MB per second., whereas fiber networks run at 1 to 2GB per second.

Microsoft has put a lot of work into the backup features of Windows Server 2003. The Volume Shadow Copy Services allows you to create a snapshot (an exact copy) of volumes on your SAN. Clients can then perform shadow copy restores on their own. In other words, clients can look at a list of shadow copies performed on their data and choose to restore their own data from a given snapshot. NTBackup also uses shadow copies to make sure that all open files are backed up.

Improved Terminal Services

Terminal Server allows client workstations to function as terminal emulators. Terminal Services client software is installed on the local workstation, allowing it to connect to the terminal server and receive its own desktop session. Multiple clients can run sessions simultaneously. All processing takes place on the server. The client machine is only responsible for managing the keystrokes and mouse clicks, which are passed over the network to the Terminal Server via the Remote Desktop Protocol (RDP).

NOTE

Although RDP is the native protocol for Microsoft Terminal Server and is used with clients running the Windows 2000 Terminal Services client or the XP/2003 Remote Desktop Connection (RDC) client, the Windows Server 2003 terminal server can also be configured to accept connections from Citrix clients using the ICA protocol.

The first version of Terminal Server was a separate server OS called Windows NT Server 4.0 Terminal Server Edition. When Microsoft released Windows 2000, they included Terminal Server in the standard OS. It was a feature that could be added or removed as needed. Windows 2003 also includes Terminal Server with the OS (all editions except the Web Edition), but it has changed a little since Windows 2000.

In Windows 2000, there are two modes in which Terminal Server can run: Remote Administration mode and Application Server mode. Neither one of these is installed by default. Terminal Services in Remote Administration mode only allows two simultaneous connections, but it doesn't require any Terminal Server License. Only members of the Administrators group can connect to a terminal session. Terminal Services in Application Server mode allows unlimited connections, and sessions are not limited to administrators, but you are required to have a license for each connection and a licensing server to manage all of the connections.

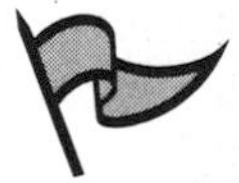

NOTE

Clients connecting to a Windows 2000 terminal server from a Windows 2000 Professional computer are not required to purchase a license, as Windows 2000 Pro includes a Terminal Services CAL. However, you still must set up a licensing server.

In Windows Server 2003, Remote Administration mode has been renamed to Remote Desktop for Administration and it is installed by default. This works like the Remote Desktop feature in Windows XP. As in Windows 2000, you are still limited to two simultaneous remote desktops at a time. However, there is one improvement: you can now take over the local console session. Terminal Services in Application Server mode is now simply called Terminal Server.

The Windows Server 2003 Terminal Server and Remote Desktop for Administration support more local client devices than in Windows 2000. Now the local client file system, audio output, printers, serial ports, smart cards, and clipboard are supported (see Figure 1.12), making it easier for clients to use their local resources while connected to the terminal server. RDP 5.1 is a much more robust client than RDP 5.0 (Windows 2000). It supports display configurations up to 24-bit color at up to 1600x1200 resolution. It also allows customizing the client experience based on available bandwidth. In other words, unnecessary features can be turned off to optimize performance when connecting over a slow link.

Figure 1.12 Configuring the Remote Desktop Connection

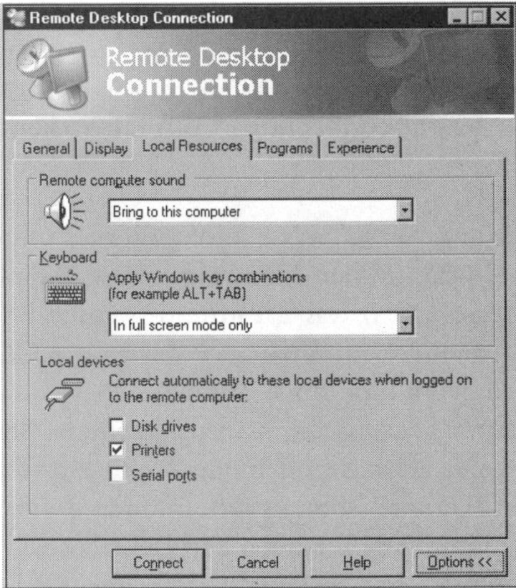

Configuring & Implementing...

Using the Remote Desktop Connection.

Terminal Server is one of the most used features of Windows 2000. It allows users to connect from their local machines and run desktop sessions off of the server. The local workstation at this point is functioning as a "thin client" because all processing is taking place on the server. One common complaint about Terminal Server in Windows 2000 is a lack of support for local resources.

This has been improved in Windows Server 2003. You can now share information easily between your local disk and the server. You no longer must map a drive back to your local workstation. You can print to locally attached printers and use locally attached serial devices. You can redirect the sound from the terminal server to come out of your local speakers. All of these things make using Terminal Server an even more transparent process to the end user.

New Media Services

Microsoft has redesigned Media Services. The version of Media Services in Windows Server 2003 is version 9.0. It is managed via the Windows Media Services Microsoft Management Console (MMC) as shown in Figure 1.13. Media Services provides audio and video content to clients via the Web (Internet or intranet). According to Microsoft, Media Services has been improved in four areas:

- Fast streaming
- Dynamic content
- Extensibility
- Industrial strength

Figure 1.13 Getting Started with Windows Media Services

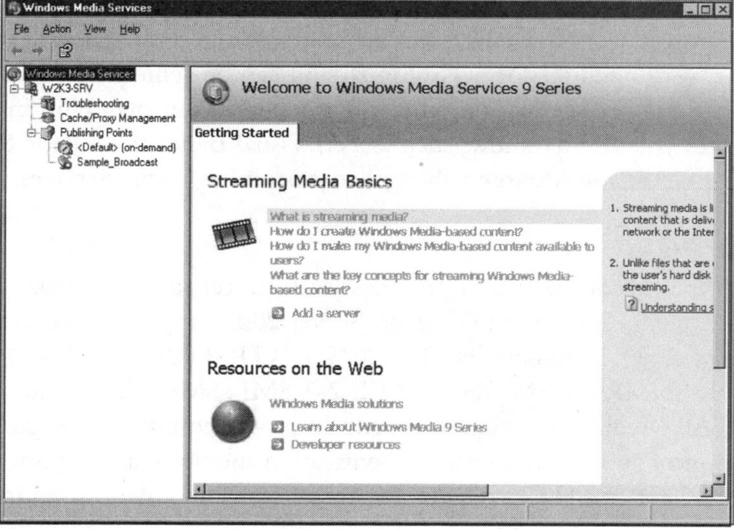

Fast Streaming

Media Services supports fast streaming to ensure the highest quality streaming experience possible even over unreliable networks (for example, wireless networks). Streaming refers to sending video and/or audio in compressed form over the network and playing the data as it arrives. There are four parts that make up fast streaming:

- **Fast start** Supplies instant-on playback without a buffering delay.
- **Fast cache** Supplies always-on playback by streaming to cache as quickly as the network will support and by playing back the stream to the client from cache.

- **Fast recovery** Sends redundant packets to wireless clients to ensure that no data is lost due to connectivity problems.
- **Fast reconnect** Supplies undisturbed playback by restoring connections if the client is disconnected during a broadcast.

Dynamic Content

Media Services supports advertisements and server-side playlists. Advertising support is very flexible, in that ads can be placed anywhere and used as often as wanted in the playlist. You can even use data gathering tools such as cookies to personalize your ads, and all ad data can be logged for further analysis. Server-side playlists are great for clients that don't support client-side playlists. Server-side playlists can contain live data or preexisting content. They allow you to customize the way your content is presented to clients and to make changes quickly and easily without any delay in service.

Extensibility

Microsoft has exposed over 60 Media Services interfaces and their properties, making Media Services a very open platform. Customization can be achieved by using the Microsoft supplied plug-ins or by using the SDK to create your own plug-ins. You can use scripting languages you already know (such as Perl, Visual Basic, Visual Basic Scripting Edition, C, Visual C++, and Microsoft JScript) to customize Media Services.

Industrial Strength

Microsoft boasts that Media Services is the most scalable, reliable, and secure solution on the market today. Media Services in Windows Server 2003 supports twice as many users per server as Windows 2000. It supports HTTP 1.0/1.1, RTP, RPSP, HTML v3.2, FEC, IPv4/6, IGMPv3, SNMP, WEBM/WMI, SMIL 2.0, SML, SML-DOM, and COM/DCOM. All Media Services plug-ins run in protected memory to guarantee reliability. Many common authorization and authentication methods are supported, such as digital rights management and HTTP Digest. Microsoft provides a Web-based interface, an MMC snap-in interface, and command-line support for administering your media servers.

XML Web Services

XML Web Services are building-block applications that connect together via the Internet. These services provide reusable components that call functions from other applications. It doesn't matter how these applications were built, the types of devices used, or the OS on the devices used, because XML is an industry standard. XML Web Services are made available in Windows Server 2003 because of the .NET framework. XML Web Services help provide effective business-to-business (b2b) and business-to-consumer (b2c) solutions.

New & Noteworthy...

What Is XML?

XML (the Extensible Markup Language) is the latest cross-platform standard for sharing formatted data on the Internet, intranets, and elsewhere. XML is a markup language, rather than a programming language. Markup languages generally use symbols or character sequences inserted into text documents to indicate the formatting, or how the document should look when displayed (for example, in a Web browser) or printed. These markup symbols are also called tags.

The most well-known markup language is HTML, the HyperText Markup Language in which most Web documents are constructed. HTML is an SGML-based language. SGML, the Standard Generalized Markup Language, is a standard for how markup languages are specified. SGML is not itself a document markup language, but a basis for standardization of markup languages. It is known as a *metalanguage* for this reason.

XML is also modeled on SGML, and is also metalanguage. XML gives users a standardized way of describing data. XML differs from HTML in that the latter's tags merely describe how the data is to be displayed. For example, the tag <b> indicates that the characters following it should be in bold type. XML tags can describe the actual contents of the data. For example, the tag <zipcode> indicates that the characters following it constitute a postal zip code. This data can then be processed by applications as a zip code. Many XML conventions will be familiar to those who have worked with HTML. For example, a slash mark (/) is used to turn the tag "off." That is, the zip code 75336 would be designated in XML as <zipcode> 75336 </zipcode>. XML and HTML can be (and are) used together in the same document. XML is called "extensible" because its markup symbols are unlimited; you can create your own tags to describe document content.

XML is important because, like HTML, it allows users to exchange data across platforms. It is not OS or network-architecture dependent. Unlike HTML, it allows applications to process the data intelligently. For example, if you search HTML documents for the word "Rob," you might get returns for pages pertaining to a man named Rob and pages instructing you on how to rob banks. With XML, "Rob" can be identified as a particular type of content using the <first-name> tag, and your search will be narrowed.

The Microsoft .NET server products are built on XML, so understanding its function is important to Windows 2000 enterprise-level administrators who will be integrating these products into their networks.

The Windows Server 2003 Family

The Windows Server 2003 family is built on the Windows 2000 Server technology. It takes the best of Windows 2000 and improves upon it. Windows Server 2003 is easier to manage and deploy than any previous versions of Windows. Windows Server 2003 is the most reliable and most secure Microsoft OS to date. It comes in four different editions, and in both 32-bit and 64-bit versions.

Why Four Different Editions?

All organizations are different. Most organizations would fall into one of three categories: small, medium, and large. The networking needs of organizations in each of these categories are different.

Typically, small organizations are concerned with performance versus cost. They want good performance, but it can't cost a fortune. Large companies want the best performance possible. They aren't as concerned with cost, as long as the product performs as expected. Medium-sized companies fall somewhere in the middle. They sometimes need a little more out of an OS than what a small company will settle for, but they don't need the high-end equipment and features used by very large companies.

Microsoft has tried to create a different edition of Windows for each type of organization, so that all companies can use Windows Server 2003 without overpaying or sacrificing performance. Companies should buy the minimum version of Windows that provides all of the needed features.

Members of the Family

As noted, there are four editions of Windows Server 2003: Web Edition, Standard Edition, Enterprise Edition, and Datacenter Edition. Each edition has its own benefits:

- Web Edition is the least expensive and least functional version. However, if your server is only used for hosting Web pages, then it is a perfect choice.
- Standard Edition is the next step up from Web Edition. Most of the features in Windows Server 2003 are supported in Standard Edition.
- If you need features not provided by Standard Edition or hardware not supported on Standard Edition, then Enterprise Edition would be the next logical choice. Almost every feature in Windows Server 2003 is supported in Enterprise Edition.
- If you need to use Windows System Resource Manager or you need super powerful hardware, then Datacenter Edition is your only choice.

Be sure to pick the version that most closely matches your needs. There are huge differences in price as your work your way up the chain. There is no reason to pay for more than what you need.

Web Edition

Prior to the release of Windows Server 2003, if you wanted to have a Windows server function only as a Web server, you would have to buy a copy of Windows 2000 Server and use IIS. This was a waste of money and functionality, because most of the features of Server would never be used. Now there is a version of Windows designed to function exclusively as a Web server, Windows Server 2003 Web Edition. This will save companies a great deal of money and possibly give Microsoft a larger share of the Web server market. There is a difference in price (list price) of around $700 to $800 between Web Edition and Standard Edition Server.

Web Edition is meant to host Web pages, Web applications, and XML services. It supports IIS 6.0, ASP.NET, and the .NET Framework. Web Edition supports up to two processors and 2GB of RAM. Client access licenses (discussed later in the chapter) are not required when connecting to Web Edition. However, you are only allowed 10 inbound simultaneous SMB connections, to be used for content publishing (this limit does not apply to Web connections). Web Edition allows you to install third-party Web server software such as Apache, Web availability management software such as Microsoft Application Center, and database engine software such as Microsoft SQL Server 2000 Desktop Engine (MSDE).

Web Edition does *not* support the following functions:

- Internet Authentication Services (IAS)
- Microsoft Metadirectory Services
- Domain controller functionality
- Universal Description, Discovery, and Integration Services (UDDI)
- Remote Installation Services

Standard Edition

Windows Server 2003 Standard Edition is the replacement for Windows 2000 Server. It is meant for small to medium-sized businesses and contains most of the features discussed thus far in the book. It is not limited in functionality like Web Edition and it supports up to four CPUs and 4GB of RAM. Standard Edition is a great choice for file and print servers, Web servers, and application servers that don't need to be clustered. It can also function as a domain controller. Microsoft expects Standard Edition to be the most widely used version of Windows Server 2003.

Enterprise Edition

Windows Server 2003 Enterprise Edition is the replacement for Windows 2000 Advanced Server. Enterprise Edition is meant for any sized business, but includes features most often desired by enterprise-level organizations. It provides high performance and reliability. All of the features supported in Standard Edition are supported in Enterprise Edition, as well as support for clustering up to eight nodes. It supports more powerful hardware than Standard Edition, and can use up to eight processors and up to 32GB of memory. There is a 64-bit version of Enterprise Edition for Intel Itanium machines. The 64-bit version supports up to eight processors and up to 64GB of RAM. Enterprise Edition is good for companies that need features or hardware not supported in Standard Edition.

Datacenter Edition

Datacenter Edition is Microsoft's high-end OS. It is meant for companies that need the most reliable and scalable platform available. You cannot buy the Datacenter Edition software and install it yourself; only approved equipment vendors can buy it and they must install it onto approved hardware. Datacenter Edition contains all of the features found in both Standard Edition and Enterprise Edition; in addition, it adds the Windows System Resource Manager to aid in system management. Datacenter Edition supports up to 32 processors and 64GB of memory in the 32-bit version. The 64-bit version supports up to 64 processors and 512GB of memory. If performance and reliability are at the top of your list (and cost is near the bottom), then Datacenter Edition is an excellent choice.

Exam Warning

You need to know the maximum hardware supported in each version of Windows Server 2003:

- Web Edition supports two processors and 2GB of RAM.
- Standard Edition supports four processors and 4GB of RAM.
- Enterprise Edition supports eight processors and 32GB of RAM.
- Datacenter 32-Bit Edition supports 32 processors and 64GB of RAM.
- Datacenter 64-Bit edition supports 64 processors and 512GB of RAM.

Test Day Tip

It is sometimes difficult to determine when to use each version of Windows Server 2003. You might be asked to identify which edition is the most appropriate in a given situation or scenario. Remember that Web Edition is for Web services only. Enterprise Edition is the starting point for clusters, while Datacenter Edition is used for high-end clusters. Unless you require Enterprise Edition or Datacenter Edition because you need the specific services offered (for example, clustering) or hardware supported (for example, 16 processors needed), you should use Standard Edition.

Manage Software Site Licensing

Microsoft based the Windows Server 2003 licensing structure on Windows 2000's structure. However, they have changed some things. This section is not the "end all be all" when it comes to Microsoft licensing. This section is meant to serve as a guide on the basics of Windows Server 2003 licensing. To order licenses, contact your Microsoft Software Advisor. In the United States, call (800) 426-9400, or visit the Microsoft Licensing Program Reseller Web page (http://shop.microsoft.com/helpdesk/mvlref.asp). In Canada, call the Microsoft Resource Centre at (877) 568-2495. Outside of the United States and Canada, please review the Worldwide Microsoft Licensing Web site (www.microsoft.com/worldwide).

There are a few rules that you need to know about Microsoft's licensing schemes:

- You have to purchase a product license for every copy of the OS you are going to install.
- Every network connection that is authenticated requires a Windows CAL. Anonymous connections do not require a CAL (for example, anonymous access to a Web page). Windows CALs are not required for Windows Server 2003 Web Edition, as it is meant to serve Web content only.
- Every Terminal Server session made by a user or device requires a Terminal Server Client Access License (TS CAL). TS CALs are not required for Windows Server 2003 Web Edition, as it is meant to serve Web content only.

Exam Warning

CALs are required every time a machine connects to a Windows Server 2003 machine. The only exception to this is an unauthenticated request (such as Web request), which does not require a CAL. TS CALs are required for every user running a Terminal Server session.

The product license allows you to install the OS onto a machine. The CAL allows devices or users to connect to that machine. Microsoft's reasoning behind this is that everyone pays the same price for the base OS, but companies with more connections pay more than companies with fewer connections. This allows them to price according to usage.

There are two licensing modes supported in Windows Server 2003:

- **Per Server mode** Requires a Windows CAL for each connection. These are assigned to each server and cannot be shared between servers. You are allowed one connection for each CAL assigned to the server. Once the maximum number has been reached, no more connections are allowed.

- **Per Device or Per User mode (formerly called "Per Seat" mode)** Requires that each device or user have its own Windows CAL. These allow the device or user to connect to an unlimited number of servers. With Per Device or Per User mode, the server will not limit the number of connections made as it does in Per Server mode.

Generally, Per Server mode will be most cost effective if you have only one or two servers, and clients that don't always connect at the same time. Per Device or Per User mode will be most cost effective if you have many servers to which your clients need to connect.

Microsoft has two types of CALs, User CALs and Device CALs. User CALs are purchased for every user that makes a connection to a Windows Server 2003 server. Device CALs are purchased for every machine that makes a connection to a Windows Server 2003 server. Microsoft recommends that you use either User CALs or Device CALs, but not both at the same time. User CALs are best when you have more machines than users and your users log on to multiple machines to access the servers. Device CALs are better when you have more employees than machines and your users share machines. User CALs and Device CALs are available for both Windows and Terminal Server. Device CALs and User CALs cost the same.

Windows 2000 supported the System Equivalency license for Terminal Server. The System Equivalency license stated that if your client was running the same OS version as the Terminal Server, then you did not have to buy a TS CAL (thus, a Windows 2000 Professional machine connecting to a Windows 2000 Terminal Server did not need a TS CAL). Windows 2003 no longer supports System Equivalency licenses. However, Microsoft does have a Terminal Server licensing transition plan. You can receive a free TS CAL for every copy of Windows XP that you own at the time of the Windows Server 2003 launch (April 24, 2003). Check out the Microsoft licensing page for more information (www.microsoft.com/licensing).

New to Windows Server 2003 is the External Connector (EC) license. ECs enable external users to access your server without requiring that you buy CALs for them. External users are people who are not employed by your company. Terminal Server also has an EC license called the Terminal Server External Connector (TS-EC). The EC license is replacing the Internet Connector and TS Internet Connector licenses.

Product Activation

Starting with Windows XP, Microsoft requires OSs to be authorized before a specified number of days pass, after which you won't be able to log on to the OS. Failure to activate only prevents logging on. Services and remote administration are not affected. Windows Server 2003 allows a 30-day grace period for product activation (for retail and OEM products). Companies that use volume licensing do not have to activate their software.

Windows includes an activation wizard, as shown in Figure 1.14. Exercise 1.02 walks you through the process of activating your software. You can activate over the Internet or by phone. One important thing to remember about product activation is that the activation process keeps track of the hardware in your machine. If the hardware changes dramatically, you will have to reactivate your software within three days in order to continue logging on to the server. Microsoft does this to prevent people from purchasing one copy of the OS, activating it, making an image of it, and deploying that image to many more machines.

NOTE

Product activation is part of Microsoft's anti-piracy campaign to ensure that software is actually purchased. It stops people from sharing their CD and CD key with other users. Even if they do share their info, the OS will only work for 30 days. After that time, users can no longer log onto the server. It must be activated to restore logon functionality. Microsoft keeps track of the keys used and verifies that they are only used by the person(s) who own them.

EXERCISE 1.02

ACTIVATING WINDOWS SERVER 2003

Unless you are using Volume Licensing for Windows Server 2003, you will at some point have to activate a server. You can activate over the Internet or via the phone. Use the following steps to activate over the Internet. These steps are based on using the new LUNA interface of Windows Server 2003. If you are using the classic Start menu, the first steps will differ.

1. Click on the **Start menu**.
2. Go to **All Programs**.
3. Click on **Activate Windows**. This will open the Activate Windows screen as shown in Figure 1.14.
4. Select **Yes, let's activate Windows over the Internet now**.
5. Click **Next**.
6. The next screen asks if you want to go ahead and register your copy of Windows. Choose Yes if you want to register, or choose No if you do not want to register. Registration is not a requirement for activation, so for this example, select **No, I don't want to register now; let's just activate Windows**.

7. The wizard will now say **You have successfully activated your copy of Windows**. Click **OK** to close the activation wizard.

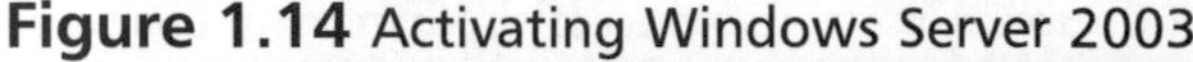

Figure 1.14 Activating Windows Server 2003

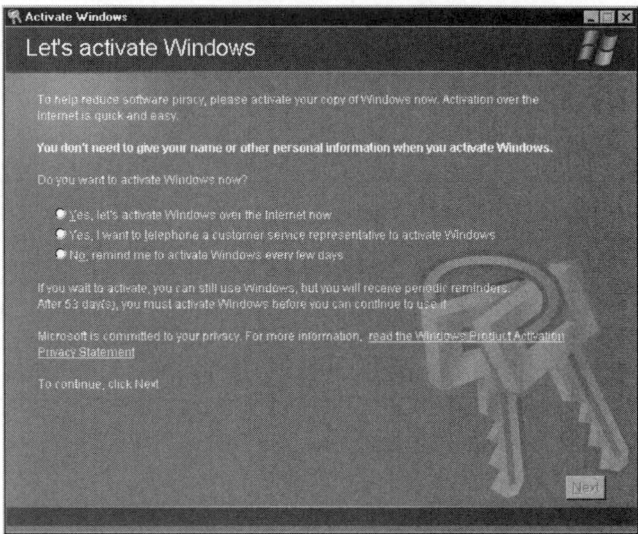

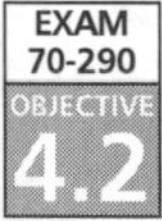

Manage Software Update Infrastructure

Unless your company is buying its first Windows server, you are going to have to decide between upgrading and performing a clean install. Each method has advantages and disadvantages:

- Upgrading preserves many of your existing settings, such as users and groups, permissions and rights, and applications.
- Performing a clean installation can improve the performance of your hard drive, as it will be reformatted during installation. This also gives you a chance to change the partition and volume sizes used on your drives. Clean installs ensure that you don't carry over any existing problems that you might have with your current OS. Some administrators (the authors of this book included) prefer clean installs because they have seen many problems related to OS upgrades in the past. There is something comforting about starting from scratch.

Common Installation Issues

The biggest problems with installing a new OS are hardware and software incompatibilities. It is important to adhere to the recommended hardware specifications for Windows Server 2003. At a minimum, you need the following hardware configuration:

- 133MHz processor
- 128MB of RAM
- 1.5GB hard drive

Remember that these are the bare minimums on which Windows Server 2003 will run. Obviously, on such old hardware, performance will suffer. Microsoft recommends at least a 550MHz processor and 256MB of RAM. The more RAM the better.

You should always verify hardware compatibility before you start your installation. There is a system compatibility check you can run from the Windows Server 2003 CD that will check out your hardware for you automatically. The System Compatibility wizard is demonstrated in Exercise 1.03. Even if all of your hardware is supported, you should always update your machine's BIOS to the most recent version.

EXERCISE 1.03

CHECKING SYSTEM COMPATIBILITY

You can check your hardware for compatibility two ways. You can look up all of the parts on Microsoft's site, or you can use the Compatibility wizard from the installation CD. The wizard is obviously the easier of the two. Follow these steps to use the Compatibility Wizard:

1. Put in the Windows Server 2003 CD.
2. Double-click on **My Computer**.
3. Double click on the **CD-ROM**. This will bring up the autorun screen shown in Figure 1.15.
4. Click on the **Check system compatibility** link.
5. Click on the **Check my system automatically** link. This will start the Compatibility Wizard.
6. You will now be prompted to get updated setup files. This is not necessary to check out your hardware. Click the radio button for **No, skip this step and continue installing Windows**.

7. Click **Next**. Windows will now check out your system. Once it is finished, it will display any issues that might interfere with installing Windows. You can click **Details** to read more about the issues, or click **Save As** to save the report to another location.
8. When finished viewing or saving the report, click **Finished** to end the wizard.

Figure 1.15 Verifying Hardware Compatibility for Windows Server

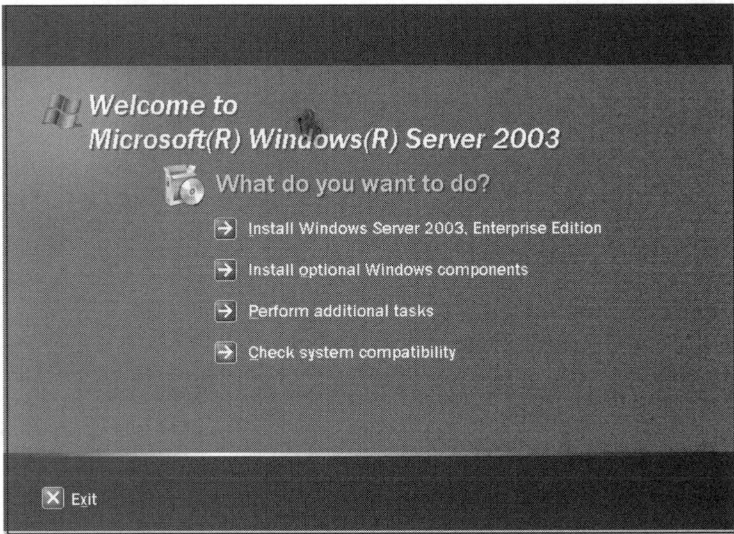

Common Upgrade Issues

As stated earlier, you should always verify hardware compatibility and BIOS versions. You should always back up your existing system before you start your upgrade. If you have applications on your server, you should read the release notes on application compatibility. These are found in the Docs folder on the setup CD (relnotes.htm).

When upgrading servers from NT 4.0 to Windows Server 2003, you must have Service Pack 5 or higher installed. You can perform upgrades from all server versions of NT 4.0 (Server, Enterprise Edition, and Terminal Server Edition). Upgrading Windows 2000 machines to Windows Server 2003 doesn't require any service packs to be installed first. Windows 2000 Server can be upgraded to Windows Server 2003 Standard Edition or Enterprise Edition. However, Windows 2000 Advanced Server can only be upgraded to Windows Server 2003 Enterprise Edition, and Windows 2000 Datacenter Server can only be upgraded to Windows Server 2003 Datacenter Edition. You must have at least 2GB of free hard drive space for all upgrades.

Test Day Tip

Generally, before you begin your test you are allowed to write information down on your scratch paper. You might want to write down the upgrade paths to Windows Server 2003 so you can refer to them later. Sometimes, writing things down before you start helps you get the facts down while you are still thinking straight, and the time you spend doing this before starting the test doesn't count against your time allotted for the test.

When upgrading Windows NT 4.0 domains to Windows Server 2003 domains, you must first make sure that DNS is installed and properly configured. You don't have to use a Microsoft DNS server, but your implementation of DNS must support service (SRV) records. Optionally, you might want it to support dynamic updates as well. If DNS does not support dynamic updates, you will have to manually create all of the needed SRV records. Before starting the upgrade, you should take one of your BDCs offline. This will allow you to roll back to your existing NT 4.0 environment if you should have problems with the upgrade. Always start your upgrades with the PDC, followed by the BDCs. After upgrading the PDC, you should set your forest functional level to Windows Server 2003 interim mode.

When upgrading Windows 2000 domains, you must first prepare the forest and the domain for Windows Server 2003 by using the ADPrep tool. You can prepare the forest by running adprep.exe /forestprep on the Schema Master, and you can prepare the domain by running adprep.exe /domainprep on the Infrastructure Master. ADPrep can only be run from the command line; there isn't an equivalent graphical tool. Unlike when you upgrade from NT 4.0 domains, you do not have to upgrade the PDC (technically the PDC Emulator) first. You can install a new Window Server 2003 domain controller into an existing Windows 2000 domain. When upgrading your domain controllers, you need to budget a little growing room for the Active Directory database. The database file (ntds.dit) might grow by up to 10 percent.

Test Day Tip

ADPrep is a new requirement for Windows Server 2003. Think of it this way: NT 4.0 did not have Active Directory, so there is nothing to prepare. When you install your first Windows Server 2003 domain controller, you are creating the Active Directory for the first time.

However, Windows 2000 already has an Active Directory, but it doesn't know anything about Windows Server 2003. You must prepare its Active Directory so it can work with Windows Server 2003. You must prepare the domain (/domainprep) and the forest (/forestprep) before you install your first Windows Server 2003 domain controller.

Summary of Exam Objectives

Windows Server 2003 is Microsoft's latest server OS. It uses Windows 2000 as its foundation, and then it gets better from there. Windows Server 2003 uses the concepts of client-server networking, domain-based administration, and Active Directory Services.

There are four different editions of Windows Server 2003: Web Edition, Standard Edition, Enterprise Edition, and Datacenter Edition. Web Edition functions as a Web server only. Standard Edition supports all features except clustering. Enterprise Edition and Datacenter Edition support all features, including clustering. Use Datacenter Edition instead of Enterprise Edition if you need more than eight processors or more than 32GB of RAM.

Most of the features in Windows Server 2003 that carried over from Windows 2000 have been updated. Some new features have also been added. Most of the improvements have to do with increasing network performance, improving security, or adding functionality for Windows Server 2003.

Active Directory speeds up domain controller installation times over slow connections by supporting the replication of new domain controllers from tape backup. Company mergers no longer mean starting over with a new AD; you can now rename and restructure domains in Windows Server 2003. Microsoft added the Group Policy Management Console to ease the burden of managing group policy. The GPMC allows you to back up and restore your group policy objects.

Windows Server 2003 enhances file security and maintenance. The Encrypting File System (EFS) supports multiple users sharing the same encrypted files. Now, departments can encrypt their shared data with built-in Microsoft tools. In the past, this would have required a third-party encryption program. If you ever need to run a repair against your disk, you should be able to do it in about 70 percent of the time expected in Windows 2000. The CHKDSK tool has been revamped to make it run faster.

No longer is IIS an instant security hole on your server. In all editions other than Web Edition, IIS is not even installed by default. IIS is more stable than ever before. It has been designed to keep applications from crashing each other. If one application fails, it should restart itself without interfering with other running applications. New command-line tools make administering IIS through scripts much easier.

Clustering support has been increased to eight nodes per single cluster. Clusters are now integrated into Active Directory, which means they support Kerberos authentication. No longer must you support down-level authentication methods just because you have a cluster. Network Load Balancing has been enhanced as well. It now supports multiple load-balanced NICs on a single server, and it will pass IPSec traffic.

Microsoft has put many convenience features into Windows Server 2003. Credential Manager provides a secure single sign-on environment for Windows users. You can extend your single sign-on experience even further by integrating your Microsoft Passport account with your Active Directory account. Shadow copies provide a method of versioning the files on your file server. A snapshot is taken of all the files, and users can roll back their files to the ones contained in any available snapshot. Users can log on to a Terminal Server and still access most of their local resources. The Remote Desktop client supports the local client file system, audio output, printers, serial ports, smart cards, and a shared clipboard.

Windows Server 2003 can be used to upgrade an existing machine or build a new one from scratch. Either way, you need to verify that your hardware is compatible by running the system compatibility check on the Server CD. If you aren't concerned with losing the existing settings on your machine, a clean installation is the preferred method. This way, you can ensure that you aren't bringing over any problems from the old OS. If you need to preserve users, groups, rights, or applications, an upgrade is your only choice. Be sure to back up your data before you start your upgrade. If you are upgrading Windows NT 4.0, you must have at least Service Pack 5 installed. When upgrading 4.0 domains, remember to take an existing BDC offline before you start and upgrade the PDC first. If upgrading a Windows 2000 domain, you must first run ADPrep to prepare the forest and the domain for Windows 2003.

Microsoft did their homework for Windows Server 2003. They listened to users' concerns about Windows 2000 problems, and they fixed them. They eased administration by updating all of the administrative tools and providing command-line scriptable tools for most services. They made the upgrade process easier and updated most of the features of Windows Server 2000.

Exam Objectives Fast Track

History of the Windows Operating System Family

- ☑ Microsoft's first OS was MS-DOS. It was text based and did not have a GUI. It was made for IBM to use on their new line of personal computers.
- ☑ Microsoft's first version of NT was Windows NT 3.1. It was numbered 3.1 to build on the popularity of Window 3.1. Even though the interface and the name were similar, the underlying technology was different. Windows 3.1 was based on the MS-DOS kernel and was not an OS in itself, but a shell that ran on top of DOS. Windows NT 3.1 was built on a new NT kernel.
- ☑ Windows Server 2003 is the latest release of Windows. It builds on the success of Windows 2000, but has been improved to make it more reliable, stable, scalable, and secure.

Windows Server Operating System Basics

- ☑ Client-server networking is preferred to peer-to-peer networking in all but the smallest networks, because it provides centralized authentication and centralized administration.
- ☑ Domains provide centralized authentication and centralized account management. All domain controllers in the same domain share a common database. As changes are made to the database, all domain controllers replicate their changes to each other.
- ☑ Windows 2000 and Windows Server 2003 use Active Directory, which provides a hierarchical way to manage your accounts. Active Directory makes it easier to secure and delegate permissions within your domain.

What's New in Windows Server 2003?

- ☑ Windows Server 2003 was designed with security in mind. Most of the features carried over from Windows 2000 have been updated to make them more secure.
- ☑ Active Directory has been enhanced to improve replication, migration, and management. In addition to adding new Active Directory tools, Microsoft also enhanced the existing tools to make them easier to use and increased their functionality.
- ☑ Windows has been improved in the area of Storage Area Networks (SANs). You can add a SAN attached drive from within Windows. Windows Server 2003 also provides a unified interface for managing your SANs.

The Windows Server 2003 Family

- ☑ There are four versions of Windows Server 2003: Web Edition, Standard Edition, Enterprise Edition, and Datacenter Edition.
- ☑ Web Edition is used as a Web server only. It supports up to two processors and 2GB of RAM.
- ☑ Standard Edition is typically used as a domain controller, file and print server, or application server. It supports up to four processors and 4GB of RAM.

- ☑ Enterprise Edition can fulfill all the same roles as Standard Edition, but it also supports clustering. Use Enterprise Edition when you need more scalability and reliability than what is offered in Standard Edition. Enterprise Edition supports up to eight processors and 32GB of RAM.
- ☑ Datacenter Edition supports all of the features included with Standard Edition and Enterprise Edition. However, it supports much more powerful hardware. It supports up to 32 processors and 64GB of RAM. Use Datacenter Edition when you need the most machine power possible.

Licensing Issues

- ☑ You must purchase a server product license for every machine on which you install Windows Server 2003.
- ☑ In order to connect over the network to the server, you must have a Client Access License (CAL). You don't need CALs if you are making an anonymous connection to a Web page.
- ☑ Terminal Server sessions require a Terminal Server Client Access License (TS CAL).
- ☑ Unless you are using a Volume Licensing version of Windows Server 2003, you must activate each installation. If you do not activate your installation, you will not be able to log on after the grace period has expired.

Installation and Upgrade Issues

- ☑ You should verify that your hardware is compatible with Windows 2003 before you start your installation. To do this, you can run the system compatibility check from the Server CD.
- ☑ Windows NT 4.0 machines must be upgraded to at least Service Pack 5 before they can be upgraded to Windows Server 2003.
- ☑ When upgrading a Windows 2000 domain to Windows Server 2003, you must update the forest first by running adprep /forestprep, and then update the domain by running adprep /domainprep.

Exam Objectives Frequently Asked Questions

The following Frequently Asked Questions, answered by the authors of this book, are designed to both measure your understanding of the Exam Objectives presented in this chapter, and to assist you with real-life implementation of these concepts. You will also gain access to thousands of other FAQs at ITFAQnet.com.

Q: What is the difference between joining my PC to an Active Directory domain and putting it into a workgroup with the same name?

A: If you do not join your PC to the domain, you will not have a machine account in AD. You will not be able to manage your PC from the domain. For example, group policy machine settings will not apply to your machine. Additionally, you will not be able to log on with user accounts from the domain. Domain user accounts can only log on to machines that are joined to the domain or joined to trusted domains.

Q: What does it mean when you say that NT was a flat directory service?

A: Think of a directory service as a file cabinet. Windows NT is like a file cabinet with only one drawer and no folders. As you add files to the drawer, it will become increasingly difficult to manage. This is a flat file structure because you can only put the files in one place. There is no way to organize them (as you could do if there were folders). Active Directory is like a file cabinet with three drawers, with each drawer having folders inside it. Now you can organize your data as you file it away. This makes it easier to manage and easier to locate the files later. This is called a hierarchical structure.

Q: How do I determine how many domain controllers I need in my organization?

A: There are no "set in stone" rules on how many you need. You should always have at least two for fault tolerance. It is recommended that you have at least one per physical location so users don't have to authenticate over wide area network (WAN) links. Microsoft provides a tool called the Active Directory Sizer (ADSizer). It serves as a good starting point for determining the number of domain controllers required. You can download ADSizer from http://download.microsoft.com/download/win2000platform/ASsizer/1.0/NT5/EN-US/setup.exe.

Q: What is the difference between running CHKDSK and defragmenting my drive?

A: CHKDSK fixes problems with disks by scanning for errors. Defragmenting fixes performance issues by reorganizing the raw data on your hard drive so that it can be accessed faster.

Q: How can I protect my server against being hacked?

A: Most hacks take place because of vulnerabilities in a service offered by your server. You can use the Internet Connection Firewall (ICF) to ensure that your server is only allowing connections to the services you want to offer. You can then concentrate on securing that service.

Q: What type of software do I need to connect my Windows Server 2003 machine to a broadband DSL connection?

A: You do not need any additional software to use broadband. Windows Server 2003 allows direct connections to broadband via the built-in PPPoE support.

Q: When should I use Enterprise Edition instead of Standard Edition?

A: Most of the time, Standard Edition will suffice. If you need to support more than four processors or more than 4GB of RAM, you need to go with Enterprise Edition. Moreover, if you need to cluster your machines, you will need Enterprise Edition because Standard Edition does not support clustering.

Q: Why is Web Edition limited to 10 incoming SMB connections at a time?

A: SMB is used to copy files between machines over the network. Web Edition is limited in the number of such connections to make sure you are using it as a Web server only and not as a file server.

Q: I can't seem to find a price for Datacenter Edition. How much does it cost?

A: You cannot buy Datacenter off of the shelf as with the other versions. Datacenter can only be purchased through Microsoft approved vendors. You buy Datacenter as a package that includes all of the needed hardware. Datacenter must be installed by an approved vendor.

Q: Why do I have to pay for the OS and then pay again to connect to my server over the network?

A: Microsoft has chosen to separate the licensing into two parts. This allows them to keep the prices down for the OS. If they didn't charge for connections (CALs), they would compensate by charging more for the OS. This way, customers who use less pay less.

Q: How do I decide if I should use Per User or Per Device licensing?

A: You should always choose the licensing structure that costs less, but still meets your needs. As a general rule, if you have roaming users and you have more users than machines, Per User is better. If you have users who share machines and you have more machines than users, Per Device is better.

Q: How do companies that host Web pages determine how many CALs to purchase?

A: Unauthenticated (anonymous) connections to a Web site do not require CALs.

Self Test

A Quick Answer Key follows the Self Test questions. For complete questions, answers, and explanations to the Self Test questions in this chapter as well as the other chapters in this book, see the Self Test Appendix.

What's New in Windows Server 2003?

1. Your company has decided to put in a Windows-based Network Address Translation (NAT) server. Your boss wants to use Windows 2000 if possible because you already own a license for it. You have been tasked with determining if Window 2000 will suffice, or if you need to go with Windows Server 2003. Which of the following required protocols will help you determine which version of Windows to use?

   A. ICMP

   B. PPTP

   C. L2TP

   D. HTTP

2. You work for an online retail company. You have been tasked with creating a Web server farm to support your company's new e-commerce initiative. All of your Web servers are running IIS 6.0 on Windows Server 2003 Enterprise Edition. You want to spread the traffic across all of your Web servers, while providing the best possible performance. Which of the following features should you use to build your Web farm?

   A. Network Load Balancing

   B. Microsoft Clustering Service

   C. DNS Round Robin

   D. Windows Media Services

3. Your company wants to put in two new e-mail servers. E-mail is mission critical for your company, so you want to configure your e-mail servers in the most fault tolerant manner possible. Which of the following features should you use for your e-mail servers?

A. Network Load Balancing

B. Microsoft Clustering Service

C. DNS Round Robin

D. Windows Media Services

4. You have been hired to restructure a company's forest. They have merged with another company and changed their name. You have upgraded all of your domain controllers to Windows Server 2003. You plan to use the Domain Rename tool (rendom.exe) from the server CD. Which of the following cannot be accomplished with this tool?

   A. Rename your domains

   B. Remove domains

   C. Create new trees

   D. Rename your domain

5. Your company has decided to migrate from Windows 2000 to Windows Server 2003. You have migrated all of your printers and file shares from a Windows 2000 server to a Windows Server 2003 server. Everything seems to be working fine after the migration, except that you cannot get to the printers Web page on the print server. This is how you administered your printers before and you would like to continue doing it this way. What could be the cause of your problem?

   A. The printers Web page is not included in Windows Server 2003.

   B. IIS is not included in Windows Server 2003.

   C. IIS is not installed by default.

   D. Your desktop doesn't have Internet Explorer 6.0.

6. You use a Windows Server 2003 machine as one of your file servers. Users are complaining that they cannot get to any shares on the file server. You can telnet to the server from a client's workstation. You log on to the server and verify that the shares exist and that the users have rights. However, whenever you try to map a drive to the server, it displays the message "network path not found." What could be the cause of the problem?

   A. The Microsoft client has been removed from the server.

   B. You do not have administrative rights on the machine.

   C. ICF is enabled on the server.

   D. The file server was promoted to a domain controller.

The Windows Server 2003 Family

7. Your company has decided to get rid of all their fax machines. Now, instead of each department having its own fax machine, everyone will share the same fax server. This fax server will allow you to send and receive faxes from within Outlook. Faxing is an important aspect to company business, so you have been tasked with making the Exchange e-mail servers as fault tolerant as possible. You decide to put in a two-node Windows Server 2003 cluster. Each node will have four processors and 2GB of RAM. Which version of Windows Server 2003 should you use?

   A. Web Edition

   B. Standard Edition

   C. Enterprise Edition

   D. Enterprise 64-Bit Edition

   E. Datacenter Edition

   F. Datacenter 64-Bit Edition

8. You work for a statistical analysis company. You are currently using Windows 2000 Server on a 1.4 GHz XEON machine. You need to upgrade to an Intel Itanium machine to support a new application. You want to use eight processors and 40GB of RAM. Which version of Windows Server 2003 should you use?

   A. Web Edition

   B. Standard Edition

   C. Enterprise Edition

   D. Enterprise 64-Bit Edition

   E. Datacenter Edition

   F. Datacenter 64-Bit Edition

Licensing Issues

9. Your company is open 24 hours a day, seven days a week. Everyone works eight-hour shifts and there are three shifts. All three shifts share the same computers. Over the next six months, you will be rolling out Windows Server 2003 and Windows XP. Your company has 1,500 workstations, 4,500 users, and 50 servers. Which licensing model should you use?

A. Per User licensing

B. Per Device licensing

C. Per Server licensing

D. External Connector licensing

10. You have been hired as a consultant to assist a company in migrating from Novell NetWare 5.0 and Windows 95 to Windows Server 2003 and Windows 2000 Professional. There will be 1,200 workstations and 10 servers. There are 600 users, and every user has two machines. Which licensing model should you use?

    A. Per User licensing

    B. Per Device licensing

    C. Per Server licensing

    D. External Connector licensing

11. Your company has partnered with another company to develop a new application. Your partner requires access to one of your company's terminal servers in order to work on the project. There will be about 1,500 users from the other company who will need to connect. Which of the following licensing models should you use?

    A. Terminal Server Per User CALs

    B. Terminal Server Per Device CALs

    C. Terminal Server External Connector

    D. Per Server CALs

Installation and Upgrade Issues

12. You have three Windows 2000 servers that need to be upgraded to Windows Server 2003. Two of your servers are running Windows 2000 Advanced Server, and one is running Windows 2000 Server. All three servers need to be running Windows Server 2003 Standard Edition. Which of the following steps should you perform? (Choose two answers.)

    A. Upgrade the servers running Windows 2000 Advanced Server to Windows Server 2003 Standard Edition.

    B. Upgrade the server running Windows 2000 Server to Windows Server 2003 Standard Edition.

    C. Perform a fresh install of Windows Server 2003 on the machines running Windows 2000 Advanced Server.

    D. Perform a fresh install of Windows Server 2003 on the machine running Windows 2000 Server.

13. You are creating a new Windows Server 2003 domain. You have installed DNS on a machine running Windows 2000 Server. You have created the correct zone and configured your soon-to-be domain controller to use the new DNS server for DNS queries. However, when you run dcpromo to create a new domain controller, you get an error message stating that a properly configured DNS server cannot be found. What should you do to get this working?

    A. You need to use a Windows Server 2003 DNS.

    B. You need to update your Windows 2000 DNS server to at least Service Pack 2.

    C. You need to enable zone transfers on your DNS server.

    D. You need to enable dynamic updates on your DNS server.

14. You have decided to upgrade your company's Windows NT 4.0 domain to a Windows Server 2003 domain. You install Service Pack 6a on all your NT 4.0 machines and you verify that all of the hardware is compatible with Windows Server 2003. You install and properly configure DNS on a Windows Server 2000 member server. What should you do next?

    A. Upgrade the PDC to Windows Server 2003.

    B. Upgrade one of your BDCs to Windows Server 2003.

    C. Upgrade your DNS server to Windows Server 2003.

    D. Install Service Pack 3 on your DNS server.

15. You have a user who is not getting the correct settings when he logs on to his PC. You are running a Windows Server 2003 domain and the user is using a Windows XP desktop. You want to see which policies are being applied to the user when he logs on to his PC. Which tool should you use?

    A. Group Policy Object Editor Snap-in

    B. Computer Management

    C. Active Directory Users and Computers

    D. Group Policy Management Console

Self Test Quick Answer Key

For complete questions, answers, and explanations to the Self Test questions in this chapter as well as the other chapters in this book, see the Self Test Appendix.

1. **C**
2. **A**
3. **B**
4. **B**
5. **C**
6. **C**
7. **C**
8. **D**
9. **B**
10. **A**
11. **C**
12. **B, C**
13. **D**
14. **A**
15. **D**

Chapter 2

MCSA/MCSE 70-290

Managing Physical and Logical Disks

Exam Objectives in this Chapter:

1.1 Manage basic disks and dynamic disks.

1.3 Optimize server disk performance.

1.3.2 Defragment volumes and partitions.

4.7.1 Monitor disk quotas.

1.3.1 Implement a RAID solution.

☑ Summary of Exam Objectives

☑ Exam Objectives Fast Track

☑ Exam Objectives Frequently Asked Questions

☑ Self Test

☑ Self Test Quick Answer Key

Introduction

Disk management is an important aspect of optimizing and maintaining any PC, and Windows Server 2003 includes a variety of tools that the administrator can use to format, partition, organize, and optimize disks. In this chapter, we take a look at how the operating system enables you to interface with the physical and logical disks in your machine, and how you can optimize disk performance to increase the overall performance of your server.

Like Windows 2000, Windows Server 2003 supports two disk types: basic and dynamic. Upgrading your disks to dynamic status enables you to take advantage of the operating system's software RAID support, so that you can create fault-tolerant volumes. A regular schedule of defragmentation is another way you can enhance disk performance, and in this chapter, we will show you how to use both the graphical interface and command-line tools to defragment your disks and perform other disk management tasks. You will also learn to configure disk quotas for better management of disk space on the file server, and we show you how to use the Remote Storage feature to manage volumes. Finally, we will discuss basic troubleshooting techniques for tracking down problems with disks and volumes.

Understanding Disk Terminology and Concepts

Computers use hard disks for storing information, but hard disks are not the only place where information is stored. Computers can store information more quickly in cache memory and random access memory (RAM), but this information is lost when we turn off our computers. Because this memory is much more expensive per megabyte than hard disk space, our total storage capacity in memory is limited. We can also store information on portable media such as floppy disks, zip disks, CD-R, CD-RW, tape, or DVD for transferring files or archiving data, but we are limited by the speed at which we can write the information to the media. Hard disks provide a good balance between fast access and lots of storage space.

A hard disk works similarly to an old-fashioned record player. Inside the hard disk casing, there are stacks of round magnetic disks that look somewhat like records. These stacks of disks are called cylinders (see Figure 2.1). Each individual disk has tracks (see Figure 2.2) on it like the grooves on a record. Each track is broken down into sectors (see Figure 2.3) and the sectors are organized into clusters (see Figure 2.4). As the disks spin around, a head (like the stylus on a record player) reads and writes data electromagnetically to the disk, one cluster at a time. Different operating systems format their disks differently, but the way the disk is physically accessed is the same for all operating systems.

Figure 2.1 Understanding Cylinders

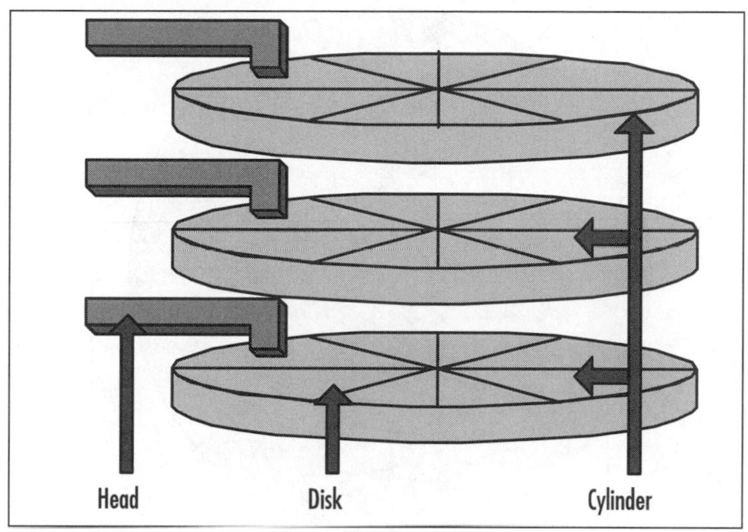

Figure 2.2 Understanding Tracks

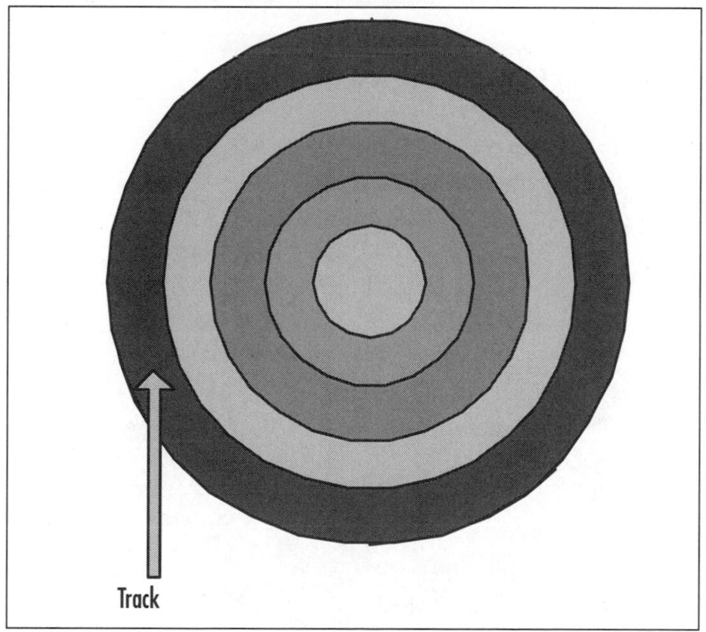

Figure 2.3 Understanding Sectors

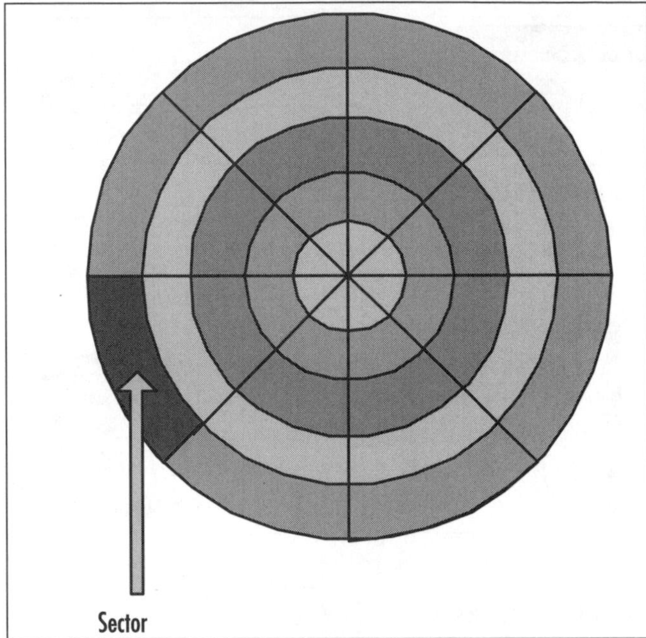

Figure 2.4 Understanding Clusters

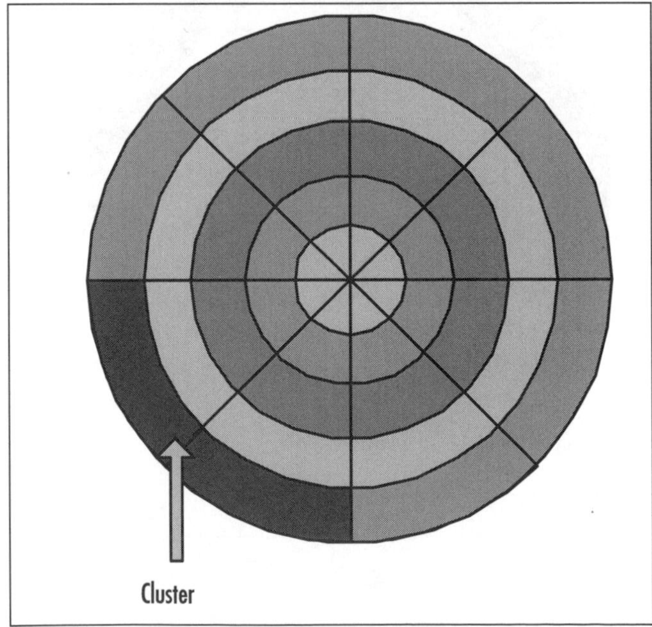

Microsoft Disk Terminology

It is important for you to know the correct terminology relating to the various disk components in Windows Server 2003. There are two primary components to understand: *physical disks* and *logical disks*. Physical disks can be either basic or dynamic. Logically, they can be separated into either partitions or volumes. This section explains when and how each of these is used.

Physical vs Logical Disks

You must be able to distinguish between a physical disk and a logical disk. *Physical* refers to the actual, tangible hard disk itself. A physical disk is a piece of hardware, which can be organized into logical disks. A physical disk by itself is of no use to Windows. It is not until you format the physical disk and create a logical disk that it becomes a resource that is accessible from within Windows.

Logical disks enable you to customize your physical disks to best fit your needs. Depending on the disk type used (basic or dynamic), logical disks consist of either partitions or volumes. These are units made up of all or part of one or more disks. Partitions are divisions of a single disk. Volumes can span multiple physical disks. Conversely, a single physical disk can contain multiple logical disks. The following scenarios illustrate a couple of real-world examples:

- You have three physical disks installed in your server, each of which contains 30GB of disk space. However, you don't want to use them as three separate disks. In other words, you do not want the operating system to "see" these disks as a C drive, a D: drive, and an E: drive. Instead, you want to access all the space contained in the three disks as if it belonged to one 90GB physical disk. To accomplish this, you can create a spanned volume (covered later in this chapter) and combine all three physical disks into one logical disk. You can now access all the storage via one drive letter (for example, D:).
- Maybe you have the opposite scenario. You have one large 100GB physical disk, but you don't want one large C: drive. You can create two or more partitions or logical drives to divide up the space. You can assign a separate drive letter for each logical disk and access the single physical disk as if it were multiple smaller physical disks.

Basic vs Dynamic Disks

Windows Server 2003 supports two types of physical disk configurations:

- Basic disks
- Dynamic disks

By default, disks are initially configured as basic. Basic disks use the same disk structure used in Windows NT 4.0 and previous operating systems all the way back to MS-DOS. That is, they are divided into primary and extended partitions, and logical drives can be created within extended partitions.

Dynamic disks use a new disk structure that was introduced in Windows 2000. The basic unit of a dynamic disk is the volume (rather than the partition). Dynamic disks support features that you don't get with basic disks and give you much more flexibility in structuring your storage space. With dynamic disks, you can extend simple volumes (make them bigger without reformatting and losing data) to any empty space on any dynamic disk, create spanned volumes across multiple physical disks and create fault tolerant (RAID 1 and 5) volumes.

A single computer can contain both basic and dynamic disks. Each physical disk installed in the computer is separately identified as either basic or dynamic. Basic disks and dynamic disks both support the same file systems (FAT16, FAT32, and NTFS).

Basic disks can be upgraded to dynamic status at any time without losing data. Later in the chapter, you will learn how to upgrade your disks. You do not even have to reboot after upgrading to dynamic unless you are upgrading the system disk or the disk being upgraded is currently in use. As mentioned, basic disks are made up of partitions and logical drives. Basic disks do not support creating volume sets or fault-tolerant volumes. MS-DOS and all versions of Windows can use basic disks.

NOTE

If you are dual booting Windows Server 2003 with a down-level operating system, such as NT, 9*x*, or MS-DOS, do not convert a disk to dynamic status if you want to be able to access its data when you are booted into the other OS. We do *not* recommend dual-boot configurations on production servers for security reasons, but it is common to dual boot a machine that is used for testing or training purposes.

Although dynamic disks (unlike basic disks) support creating volumes that span multiple disks and creating fault-tolerant volumes, dynamic disks are not always the best solution. The following are some limitations of using dynamic disks:

- Dynamic disks are currently not supported on laptop computers.
- Removable media and disks attached via FireWire (IEEE 1394), Universal Serial Bus (USB), or shared SCSI buses cannot be converted to dynamic.
- You can install Windows Server 2003 only onto a dynamic volume that was converted from a basic boot or system partition. You cannot install onto a dynamic volume that was created from free space. This is because there must be an entry in the partition table for the setup program to recognize the volume, and such an entry does not exist on a newly created dynamic volume.

- Even though Windows 2000, XP Professional, and Server 2003 all use dynamic disks, you cannot convert a basic disk that holds multiple instances of these operating systems to dynamic. The operating systems installed on the disk will not start if you do this.
- Dynamic disks are not supported by Windows Cluster Service. If you need the features of dynamic disks on a clustered shared disk, you can use a third-party program called Veritas Volume Manager 4.0 to accomplish this.

Booting Your Disk

Two disk sectors are vital to starting your computer, the master boot record (MBR) and the boot sector. The MBR is created when a disk is initially partitioned. The boot sector is created when a partition (or volume) is formatted.

The MBR is located in the first sector on the physical hard disk. It contains the master boot code, the partition table, and the disk signature for the physical disk. The master boot code is responsible for booting the machine. The partition table identifies the type and location of partitions on the physical disk. The disk signature identifies the physical disk to the operating system.

The MBR performs the following operations when a disk boots:

1. It scans the partition table (or disk configuration database) for an active partition.
2. It finds the starting sector for the active partition.
3. It loads a copy of the boot sector of the active partition into memory.
4. It passes control to the boot sector.

There is a boot sector for each partition on your physical disk. The boot sector (like the MBR) contains code that is required to boot. Among other things, it also contains information required by the file system to access the partition or volume. The boot sectors loads NTLDR (the Windows startup file) into memory and gives it control of the boot process.

Unlike basic disks, dynamic disks do not use a partition table to store their configuration information. Instead, they use a private database that is stored at the end of the disk, called the Logical Disk Manager (LDM) database. This database is exactly 1MB in size and is replicated to all the dynamic disks within a machine. This addresses the problem of the partition table as a single point of failure. The LDM database includes such information as volume types, offsets, memberships, and drive letters for each volume on the disk. The LDM replicates and synchronizes the databases across the disks, so that all dynamic disks on the system are aware of one another. There is a unique DiskID in the LDM header of each dynamic disk that enables LDM to identify each disk and distinguish it from the others.

NOTE

There can be problems when you have Storage Attached Network (SAN) drives and local disks that are all converted to dynamic status. If the SAN goes offline due to power outage, the databases may become mismatched and cause problems getting some of the disks back online. Microsoft recommends that, if you have a SAN, you make its disks dynamic and the local disks basic, or vice versa, but not make both dynamic.

New & Noteworthy...

Upgrading Disk Sets from Windows NT 4.0

Windows NT 4.0 enabled you to create spanned, striped, and fault-tolerant partitions on basic disks, which served the same purpose as the spanned, striped, and fault-tolerant volumes that now can be created only on dynamic disks. Dynamic disks were introduced with Windows 2000, and in order to create spanned, striped, and fault-tolerant volumes, you had to create them on a dynamic disk. However, Windows 2000 supported any volume sets, mirror sets, stripe sets, and stripe sets with parity that had been created in Windows NT 4.0. Thus, if your 4.0 machine was upgraded to 2000, you could still have these sets on a basic disk.

This is not the case in Windows Server 2003. If you have old NT-based volume sets, mirror sets, or stripe sets on a basic disk when you upgrade to Windows Server 2003 from Windows NT or 2000, these sets must be removed before upgrading to Windows Server 2003. For mirror sets, you need only to break the mirror before upgrading. For volume sets, stripe sets, and stripe sets with parity, you must follow these steps:

1. Back up the data.
2. Delete the set.
3. Upgrade the OS to Windows Server 2003.
4. Convert the disk to dynamic.
5. Recreate the set.
6. Restore the data.

Partitions vs Volumes

Both partitions and volumes enable us to divide one physical disk into sections so that each section appears as a separate disk. Each section is individually formatted (different sections can be formatted in different file systems) and can have its own drive letter. Basic disks contain partitions. Partitions cannot be configured to span disks and therefore cannot provide any fault tolerance. Dynamic disks contain volumes. Volumes can span disks and can provide fault tolerance.

Head of the Class...

Understanding Disk Fault Tolerance

Fault tolerance refers to the capability of a computer or network to continue to function when some component fails. Disk fault tolerance refers to methods of storing data on the disk in such as way as to create redundancy of the data, so that it can be retrieved or recreated if a disk fails. Fault tolerance is not a substitute for backing up your data, but should be used in conjunction with a regular backup schedule that includes offsite storage. Generally, a fault tolerance solution will enable you to get up and running again more quickly than if you have to restore from backup, but backups are another line of defense in case the entire computer fails or is destroyed by fire, flood, etc.

There are several different ways to achieve disk fault tolerance. The most common implementation is known as *RAID,* or Redundant Array of Independent (or Inexpensive) Disks. Multiple disks can be configured in a number of different ways to create a fault-tolerant array. Data can simply be mirrored from one disk to another, or parity information can be stored that will enable the regeneration of lost data.

RAID can be implemented either as a hardware or software solution. There are many different "levels" of RAID: 0, 1, 2, 3, 4, 5, 6, 7, 10, 0+1, and 53 are the most common. Some of these can be implemented only via the hardware. For more information about the different levels of RAID, see the RAID.edu Web site at www.acnc.com/04_01_00.html.

Windows Server 2003 has built-in support for three levels of software-implemented RAID:

- level 0 (disk striping, no parity)
- level 1 (disk mirroring)
- level 5 (striping with parity)

The biggest advantage of hardware RAID is performance; disk access is faster because you don't have the operating system overhead (the RAID disks appear as one to the operating system). The big advantage of software RAID is cost; you don't have to buy extra expensive RAID controllers or other additional hardware to use it.

We discuss the different RAID levels in more detail later in this chapter.

Partition Types and Logical Drives

There are two types of partitions:

- Primary paritions
- Extended partitions

Primary partitions are assigned drive letters and formatted as a whole; they cannot be subdivided. Extended partitions simply group free space so that it can be subdivided into logical drives, which can be individually formatted and used for storage.

Primary Partitions

After a primary partition is formatted and assigned a drive letter, it appears as a separate disk to the OS. Depending on the disk-partitioning method used, basic disks can have between four and 128 primary partitions. When using the 32-bit editions of Windows Server 2003, basic disks use the Master Boot Record (MBR) for partitioning and can have up to four primary partitions. The 64-bit editions of Windows Server 2003 can use the GUID partition table (GPT) for partitioning. The GPT utilizes primary and backup partitions for redundancy and allows for up to 128 partitions.

New and Noteworthy...

64-Bit Windows

The 64-bit editions of Windows Server 2003 can be run only on Itanium-based (either Itanium or Itanium-2) computers. Itanium is Intel's processor that supports 64-bit memory addressing. x86 computers can only run the 32-bit editions. When you install Windows Server 2003 on an Itanium-based computer, the OS must be installed on a GPT disk, but you can select either GPT- or MBR-style partitioning for other disks that are installed in the computer.

The GPT disk on which the OS is installed must have an Extensible Firmware Interface (EFI) system partition. EFI was developed by Intel as a replacement for the BIOS that is familiar to x86 computer users. It contains the platform-related information, hardware-configuration data, etc., and serves as the interface between the operating system and the platform firmware. EFI creates a standard pre-boot environment for booting an operating system, designed to solve the problems caused by lack of standardization among BIOSs created by different vendors.

While the BIOS is a program, the EFI is more like a limited operating system in its own right. It uses an area of the hard disk (a special partition) instead of being limited to flash memory or EEROM. For more information about EFI, see www.pcquest.com/content/handson/103040306.asp.

The primary partition that is marked as *active* functions as the system partition for Windows operating systems.

Head of the Class...

System and Boot Partitions

Windows NT-based operating systems (NT/2000/Server 2003) use the following terminology to describe partitions:

- **System Partition** The one on which the boot files (NTLDR, boot.ini, NTDETECT.COM) are located.
- **Boot Partition** The one on which the *systemroot* folder (which contains the operating system files) is located. This is the partition to which you select to install the OS during setup.

The system partition must be a primary active partition. The active partition is the one to which the computer looks to start the boot process. Only primary partitions can be made active. This is usually, but not always, designated as the C: partition.

The boot partition can be the same as the system partition. This occurs generally if you install the OS to the C: partition. The boot partition can also be any other (inactive) primary partition, or it can be a logical drive within an extended partition. It is generally considered best to put the operating system files on a separate partition from the boot files. Then, if something happens to one of these vital partitions, you may be able to restore just the boot files or just the system files, rather than having to restore both.

Extended Partitions

Extended partitions can be created only on an MBR-partitioned disk. Extended partitions enable you to have more than four drives on a basic disk. You can only have one extended partition per basic disk, but it can be divided into multiple logical drives. You do not format the extended partition itself. Creating an extended partition simply pools free space that can then be divided into logical drives. In other words, until you create a logical drive for your extended partition, you cannot access the space on that partition.

NOTE

You can extend primary partitions or logical drives to add space to them, if they are formatted in NTFS. You can extend basic partitions only to free space contiguous to it on the same disk. Unlike dynamic volumes, basic partitions cannot be extended across multiple physical disks.

Logical Drives

Logical drives are created when you divide up the space contained within an extended partition. Logical drives are formatted and assigned a drive letter just like primary partitions. An extended partition can contain an unlimited number of logical drives. The Windows system partition cannot be stored on a logical drive.

NOTE

Although you can create an unlimited number of partitions, there are only 26 drive letters available. A: and B: are traditionally reserved for floppy disk drives, but can be used for other drives if you have no floppy drives or only one floppy drive. If you create more than 26 partitions or volumes, you will need to use *volume mount points* instead of drive letters to access the additional ones.

Volume Types

Dynamic disks are made up of volumes. A single dynamic disk can hold up to 2,000 volumes, but Microsoft recommends that you limit the volumes per disk to 32. As with partitions, you can have multiple volumes per disk, but unlike partitions, volumes can span multiple disks. Some volume types are designed to increase performance and some types are designed to provide fault tolerance. Windows Server 2003 supports the following five volume types:

- Simple
- Spanned
- Striped
- Mirrored
- RAID-5

NOTE

Volumes can be assigned a descriptive label to make it easier to identify the purpose of each. For example, you could label the E: drive on which the operating system is installed "W2003OS" to identify it as the drive holding the OS files. You might label other drives "DATA" and "PROGRAMS" to identify their purposes.

Simple Volumes

Simple volumes are made up of free space on a single dynamic disk. They function much like primary partitions on a basic disk. If you have only one physical disk, all the volumes you create on it will be simple volumes.

Simple volumes are not fault tolerant. However, you can mirror them (discussed below) to make them fault tolerant, in which case they become *mirrored volumes*. Simple volumes can be extended on a single disk as long as the disk is not the boot or system disk. Extending a simple volume involves taking free space on a disk and adding it to the existing volume. You can also extend a simple volume across multiple disks, but then it becomes a *spanned volume*. Note that you can't combine these operations (that is, you can't mirror a spanned volume).

Simple volumes provide almost 100 percent utilization of disk space. In other words, if you purchase two 100GB disks and format them as simple volumes, you have a total of 200GB total storage, minus the 1MB per disk overhead for the LDM database. You are able to use more of the purchased disks' space than is true with other types of volumes.

EXAM WARNING

All partitions on basic disks become simple volumes when you upgrade to dynamic.

Spanned Volumes

Spanned volumes support two to 32 disks. Each disk can be a different size (as shown in Figure 2.5). Creating a spanned volume is like extending a simple volume except that it spans multiple disks (hence the name, spanned volume). In fact, if you extend a simple volume across multiple disks, it becomes a spanned volume. Spanned volumes are not fault tolerant and cannot be mirrored. Spanned volumes do not provide any performance improvements over simple volumes. They are used merely to increase the amount of space that can be accessed as a single unit. Like simple volumes, spanned volumes provide 100 percent drive utilization (minus the 1MB used for the LDM database). As data is written to the spanned volume, it is first written to the first disk in the set. When the first disk is full, the data is then written to the second disk, and so on.

EXAM WARNING

Spanned volumes do not provide fault tolerance or increased performance. They are used to create a single volume out of multiple physical disks of the same or different sizes, without wasting disk space.

Figure 2.5 Understanding Spanning Volumes

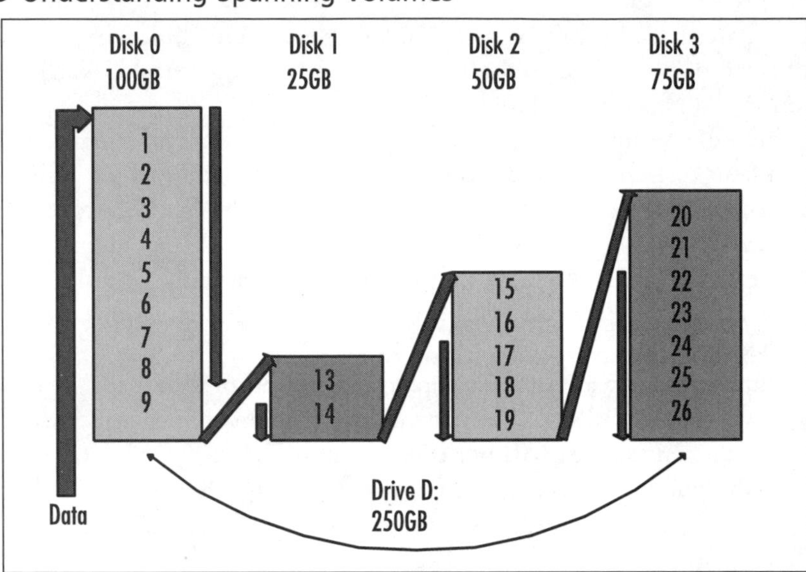

You can extend a spanned volume to make it larger (if it is formatted with NTFS). This consists of adding unallocated space to the volume, like extending a simple volume, except that the unallocated space does not have to be contiguous and can be on any dynamic disk attached to the computer. No data is lost; the new space is formatted without any impact on the existing data.

NOTE

You cannot delete any part of a spanned volume without deleting all of it. If one of the disks on which a spanned volume resides should fail, you will lose the data on the entire volume.

Striped Volumes

Striped volumes are made up of two to 32 disks. Each disk should be the same size to efficiently use all space. It is possible to use different-sized disks, but the stripe size on every disk will be limited to the amount of free space on the smallest disk, so there will be space wasted on the larger disk(s). In other words, if you created a striped volume with one 5GB drive and two 10GB drives, you would only be able to use 5GB of each drive because that is the maximum amount that is available on all disks. This would create a 15GB striped volume, wasting 10GB of disk space (5GB on each of the 10GB disks). If you use equal-sized disks, striped volumes provide 100 percent drive utilization (minus 1MB overhead for the LDM database).

Striped volumes cannot be mirrored or extended and they are not fault tolerant. However, striped volumes do provide a performance advantage. Striping increases read and write access to the volume, because all the disks are working at the same time. In fact, striped volumes offer the best performance of all Windows Server 2003 volume types. This is because of the way data is stored (as shown in Figure 2.6). Data is written evenly across all disks in 64KB chunks.

Exam Warning

Do not confuse striped volumes with RAID-5 volumes (formerly known as *stripe sets with parity*). Striped volumes (without parity) do not provide fault tolerance. Their purpose is to increase the speed of read and write access to a volume.

Figure 2.6 Understanding Striped Volumes

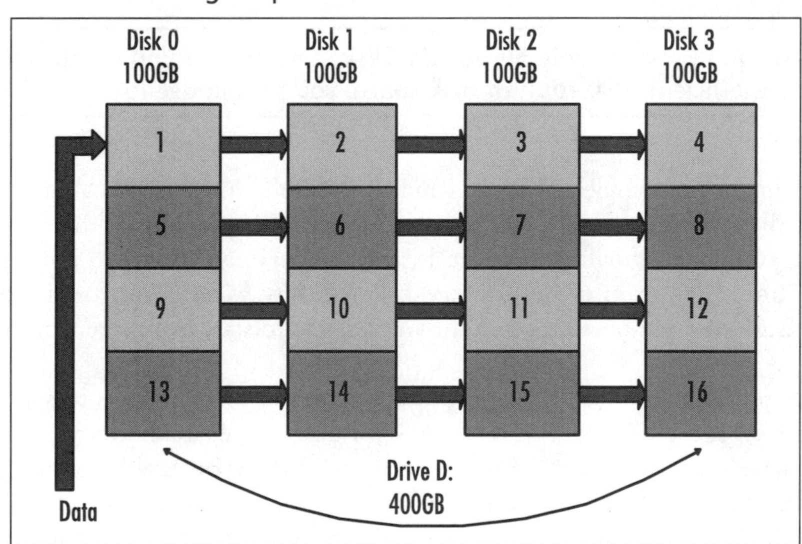

Mirrored Volumes

Mirrored volumes require exactly two disks and these two disks should be identical. Not only should they be the same size, but Microsoft recommends that both disks be the same model, from the same vendor. Mirrored volumes provide fault tolerance by making a duplicate copy of everything that is written to the volume (see Figure 2.7), with one copy on each physical disk. If one disk in the mirrored volume fails, the other disk will take its place. However, when this happens, you no longer have fault tolerance. You need to break the mirror so you can then create a new, mirrored volume with another disk, to restore fault tolerance.

Mirrored volumes cannot be extended, and they provide only 50 percent disk utilization. In other words, every 1 GB of storage space that you buy gets you 500MB of actual storage. The benefit of a mirror is that you have an exact duplicate of everything. With a mirror, you can lose one disk and still have all your data intact. Only if you lost both disks at the same time would you lose your data. Because all the data is there on the duplicate disk, you can get back up and running after a failure much faster than with a RAID-5 volume, where the data must be regenerated from the parity information following a failure before it can be accessed. Mirroring can have a negative impact on system performance, because of the overhead of writing to two disks at the same time.

An even more fault-tolerant form of disk mirroring is called *disk duplexing*. Disk duplexing is the same as disk mirroring, except that each disk in the mirror is connected to a different disk controller. This eliminates the disk controller as a single point of failure. Duplexed disks appear to the operating system the same as mirrored disks; if you have duplexed disks, they will be shown as mirrored disks in the Disk Management console.

Exam Warning

Disk mirroring provides only 50 percent disk utilization. If you need fault tolerance with more efficient utilization of disk space, you should use RAID-5.

You can mirror any simple volume, including the boot and system volumes. Microsoft recommends that you use separate controllers (duplexing) if you mirror the system or boot volumes. The controllers should be identical (same model and vendor) to prevent problems with starting from the mirror if the primary disk fails. Always test a mirrored system or boot volume to ensure that the operating system will be able to start from a remaining mirror in case of failure.

There are several conditions that must be met in order for Windows to start from a remaining mirror. If the disks in a mirror are SCSI disks on separate controllers, both controllers must have translation enabled or disabled (one cannot be enabled while the other is disabled). If the disks are SCSI disks on the same controller and there are additional disks on the controller, the controller's BIOS has to support the capability to choose which device to boot from. If the disks are IDE disks, you must ensure that the remaining disk after a failure has its jumpers set to the "master" position.

Figure 2.7 Understanding Mirrored Volumes

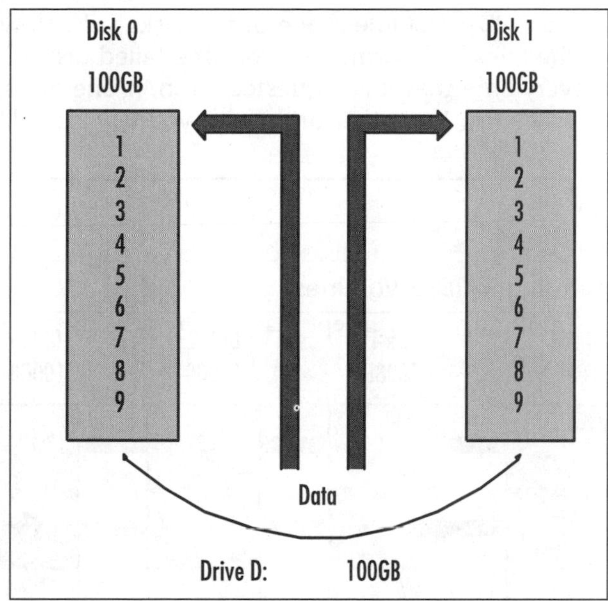

RAID-5 Volumes

RAID-5 volumes consist of three to 32 disks. RAID-5 volumes provide increased performance for read operations, as well as fault tolerance. The performance boost is due to the way RAID-5 volumes stripe data across all the disks and the fault tolerance is provided by parity information. As with a striped volume, data is written evenly across all disks in 64KB chunks (see Figure 2.8). Unlike with disk striping, the available space (the stripe) on one disk is used for parity information. To increase performance, the parity information is split across all the disks in the volume, written in stripes like the data. Write performance is lower, because the parity must be calculated during the write operation. If most operations are read-oriented (for instance, users accessing files on a file server), RAID-5 provides significant performance advantages. Windows Server 2003's RAID-5 volumes cannot be extended or mirrored, and the boot and system partitions cannot be part of a RAID-5 volume.

Disk utilization depends on how many disks are part of the RAID array. The equivalent of one disk is used for writing the parity information. If you have three disks, one-third of the total disk space is used for parity information, so you are able to utilize two-thirds of the space you purchase for data. If you have 10 disks in the array, only one-tenth of the total space is used for parity. Thus, the more disks you have in the set, the more efficient disk usage becomes.

Exam Warning

You can still access a RAID-5 volume if one of the disks fails. However, read access will be slowed as the missing information from the failed disk will have to be created from parity every time that it is requested. Also, if one drive has failed, you no longer have fault tolerance. If another drive fails, you will lose all the data on the RAID-5 volume.

Figure 2.8 Understanding RAID-5 Volumes

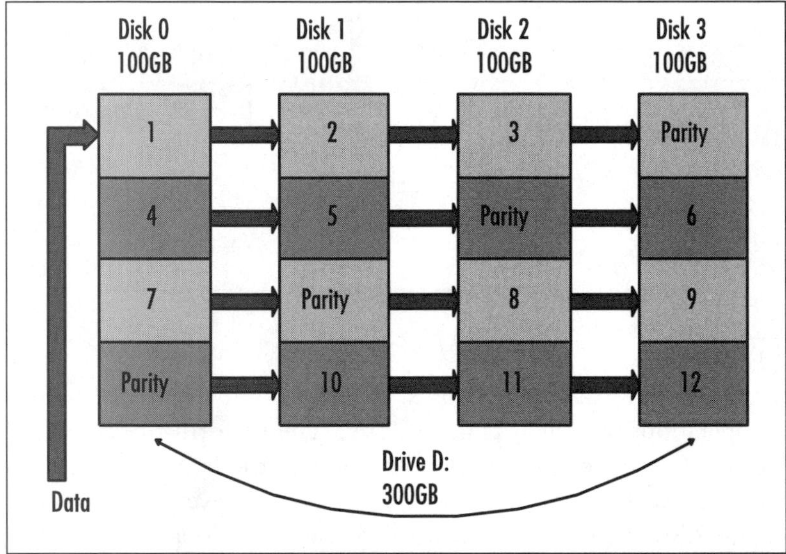

Using Disk Management Tools

Microsoft provides a variety of disk management tools in Windows Server 2003. These include command-line utilities such as diskpart.exe, fsutil.exe, and rss.exe. These tools support scripting, which enables you to automate many of your disk management responsibilities. You can also manage your disks through the graphical interface via the disk management MMC. This section will teach you to manage disks both from the GUI and from the command prompt.

Using the Disk Management MMC

You can access the disk management MMC, shown in Figure 2.9, in a couple of different ways:

- You can get there via Computer Management, by clicking **Start | Programs | Administrative Tools | Computer Management**.
- You can right-click the **My Computer** icon on the desktop or in the **Start** menu and select **Manage** from the context menu.
- You can create a custom MMC console to use the Disk Management snap-in.

Head of the Class...

Creating the Custom MMC

All MMCs share a common structure. The console pane on the left contains the console "tree," a hierarchical structure with a node for each snap-in. The details pane on the right displays items contained in the node that is highlighted in the left pane. As you navigate through the console pane by clicking the different snap-ins (for example, Removable Storage, Disk Defragmenter, Disk Management, and so forth), the details pane changes to show the specifics of that snap-in.

To create a custom MMC, follow these steps:

1. Click **Start | Run** and type **mmc**.
2. In the new empty MMC, click **File | Add/remove** snap-in.
3. On the **Standalone** tab, click the **Add** button.
4. Select **Disk Management** from the list of available snap-ins, and then click **Add**.
5. On the **Select computer** page, select **This computer to manage the disks on the local machine**, or select **The following computer** and type or browse to the name of the computer whose disks you want to manage.
6. Click **Finish**, and then click **Close** on the Add Standalone page and **OK** on the Add/Remove snap-ins page.

Now you can use the new MMC to manage disks.

Figure 2.9 shows the default view for the Disk Management MMC. Notice that the details pane is divided into two sections, a top section and a bottom section. There are three different views that you can use for either section:

- Disk list
- Volume list
- Graphical view

By default, the top section displays the volume list view and the bottom section displays the graphical view. You can change the view by clicking the **View** menu bar, choosing **Top** or **Bottom**, and selecting the view that you want.

In Figure 2.9, the top section is using the default volume list view. This view uses text in a table to show how your volumes and partitions are configured. The bottom section is using the graphical view. As the name implies, it provides a graphical representation of how your disks are configured. The third view (not shown by default) is the disk list view. It uses text to show you how your disks are configured. It looks similar to the volume list view, except it displays information on a per-disk basis instead of volume and partition information.

Most administrators find the default combination volume list and graphical view to be most efficient. Notice that there is a legend on the bottom of the MMC, as shown in Figure 2.10. The color codes enable you to look at each disk and easily determine what type of volume(s) or partition(s) it contains. You can use the **View** menu bar to change the colors assigned to each disk region.

Figure 2.9 Using Disk Management from within Computer Management

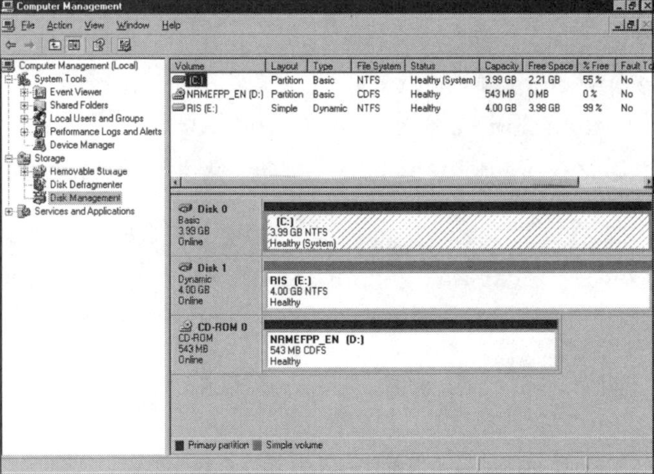

Using the Command-Line Utilities

Microsoft has increased the number of functions that administrators can perform from the command prompt in Windows Server 2003. This gives you more flexibility in accomplishing administrative tasks. Windows Server 2003 includes the following command-line tools for performing disk-related tasks:

Figure 2.10 Using the Legend in the Disk Management MMC

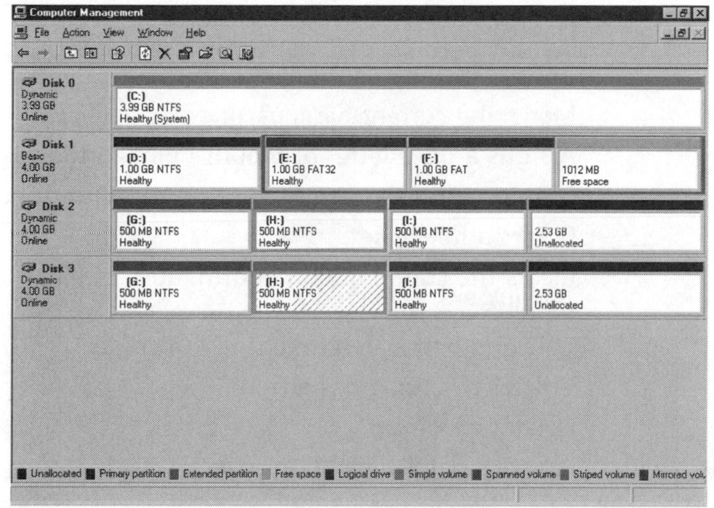

- **diskpart.exe:** For managing disks
- **fsutil.exe:** For managing the file system
- **rss.exe:** For managing remote storage

In the following sections, we will discuss each of these utilities in detail.

Using diskpart.exe

diskpart.exe enables you to manage disks, partitions, or volumes from the command prompt. You can type the commands directly at the command prompt via interactive mode or you can configure diskpart.exe to use a script for its input.

diskpart.exe scripting is beneficial if you are automating the deployment of Windows Server 2003 by using unattended setup files. Microsoft recommends that you put all your diskpart.exe commands into a single script to avoid conflicts between multiple scripts. If you must use separate scripts, you must allow at least 15 seconds after each script finishes before the next one starts to execute. Put the command *timeout /t 15* at the beginning of each script to force a 15-second delay.

The syntax for using diskpart.exe with scripts is:

```
diskpart [/s <script>]
```

If you want to use diskpart.exe in interactive mode, type **diskpart.exe** at the command prompt. This will take you to the **DISKPART>** prompt, shown in Figure 2.11. Whenever you see **DISKPART>**, you are in interactive mode and diskpart.exe is awaiting your input. Typing **help** in interactive mode will display all the utility's available commands, as shown in Table 2.1.

Table 2.1 Using Diskpart.exe Commands

Command	Description
ADD	Adds a mirror to a simple volume.
ACTIVE	Marks the current basic partition as active.
ASSIGN	Assigns a drive letter or mount point to the selected volume.
AUTOMOUNT	Enables and disables automatic mounting of basic volumes.
BREAK	Breaks a mirror set.
CLEAN	Clears the configuration information, or all information, off the disk.
CONVERT	Converts between different disk formats.
CREATE	Creates a volume or partition.
DELETE	Deletes an object.
DETAIL	Provides details about an object.
EXIT	Exits diskpart.exe.
EXTEND	Extends a volume.
GPT	Assigns attributes to the selected GPT partition.
HELP	Prints a list of commands.
IMPORT	Imports a disk group.
INACTIVE	Marks the current basic partition as inactive.
LIST	Prints out a list of objects.
ONLINE	Brings a disk online that is currently marked as offline.
REM	Does nothing. Used to comment scripts.
REMOVE	Removes a drive letter or mount point assignment.
REPAIR	Repairs a RAID array.
RESCAN	Rescans the computer looking for disks and volumes.
RETAIN	Places a retained partition under a simple volume.
SELECT	Moves the focus to an object.

Figure 2.11 Using diskpart.exe in Interactive Mode

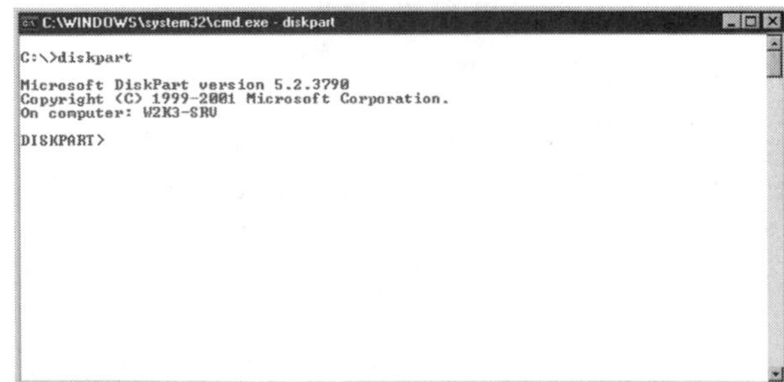

Before you can use any of these commands, you must list all disk objects and then choose one on which diskpart.exe will carry out the command(s). After you place the focus on a particular object, all commands entered will target that object until you change the focus to a different object. Exercise 2.01 shows you how to use diskpart.exe to place the focus on an object.

Exercise 2.01

Selecting a Disk for diskpart.exe

The steps below walk you through the process of focusing diskpart.exe on a disk. Figure 2.12 shows these commands as entered in the command console.

1. Use the appropriate list command from the table to list the disk, volumes, or partitions on your system. For this exercise we are going to list the disks. Type **list disk** and press **Enter**. The output is shown in Figure 2.12.
2. Now that you know which disks are available, select one for the focus of your commands. For this exercise, we select the first disk (disk 0). Type **select disk 0** and press **Enter**.
3. You can now type **list disk** again and press **Enter** to verify that the correct disk was selected. The disk on which diskpart.exe is focused has an asterisk (*) to the left of it.

Figure 2.12 Focusing Diskpart.exe on Disk 0

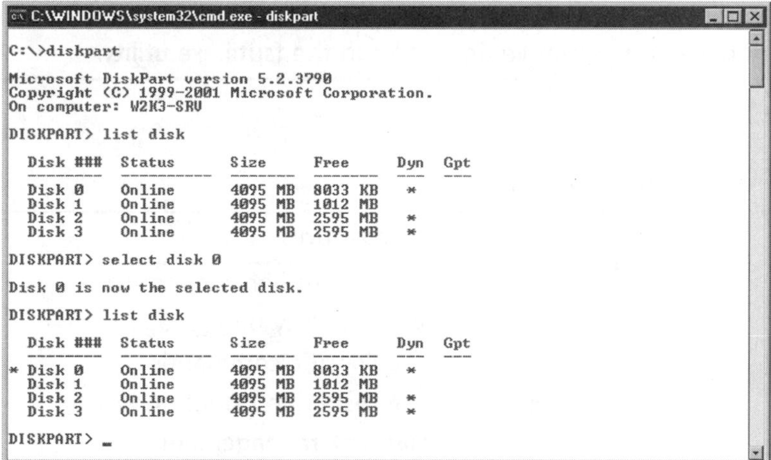

Now you can use the desired command to perform an operation on the selected disk. For example, to change a basic disk to dynamic, you use the **convert** command with the following syntax:

```
DISKPART> convert dynamic
```

NOTE

Some diskpart.exe commands change the focus automatically. If you create a new volume or partition, the focus shifts to the newly created object.

Using fsutil.exe

You can use fsutil.exe to manage FAT and NTFS file systems from the command prompt. Some of the actions you can perform with this utility include the following:

- Managing sparse files
- Managing reparse points
- Mounting and dismounting volumes
- Viewing the amount of free space on a volume

fsutil.exe supports the commands shown in Table 2.2.

NOTE

You must have administrative rights to run the fsutil.exe utility.

Table 2.2 Using fsutil.exe Commands

Command	Description
behavior	File system behavior control
dirty	Volume dirty bit management
file	File-specific commands
fsinfo	File system information
hardlink	Hardlink management
objectid	Object ID management
quota	Quota management
reparsepoint	Reparse point management

Continued

Table 2.2 Using fsutil.exe Commands

Command	Description
sparse	Sparse file control
usn	USN management
volume	Volume management

You can perform many different management tasks with this utility that do not have a GUI counterpart. For example, you can enable or disable settings for generating 8.3 file names, set the amount of disk space to be reserved for the Master File Table Zone, set a file's valid data length, and create hard links (directory entries for files).

Experimenting with fsutil.exe can create serious file system problems or even make your system unbootable, so Microsoft recommends that only advanced users run this utility.

Using rss.exe

rss.exe manages Remote Storage from the command prompt. You can use Remote Storage to extend your server's disk space by moving data off your hard disks and onto magnetic tapes or magneto-optical (MO) disks, with file data cached locally for quick access. We discuss Remote Storage in much more detail in the section titled *Understanding and Using Remote Storage.*

The rss.exe utility enables you to run scripts that enable applications to directly access Remote Storage. You can use rss.exe only after you have set up Remote Storage using the Remote Storage MMC (covered later in this chapter). The basic syntax for rss.exe is as follows:

```
RSS [ADMIN | VOLUME | MEDIA | FILE] [SET | SHOW | JOB | MANAGE | UNMANAGE
    | DELETE | SYNCHRONIZE | RECREATEMASTER | RECALL] <args> <switches>
```

NOTE

All of the rss.exe syntax has purposely not been listed here, due to its length. You can view the full list of syntax by typing **rss.exe /?** at the command prompt.

Understanding and Managing Physical and Logical Disks

We have discussed the differences between physical and logical disks, so you know that physical disks are the actual hardware devices that connect to our servers, while logical disks are units into which we divide physical disks. Physical disks can be structured as basic or dynamic disks. For the exam, you must know when to use basic versus dynamic disks and how to convert one to the other. When using basic disks, you need to be proficient at creating and using partitions and logical drives. When using dynamic disks, you need to be proficient at creating and using volumes.

Manage Basic Disks

It is important to understand the circumstances that make it desirable to use basic disks. You should not upgrade your disks to dynamic status without knowing all the consequences of that action. If you choose to stick with basic disks, you need to know how to create and delete partitions and logical drives. Basic disks can be managed via the Disk Management MMC or the diskpart.exe utility, and you can use scripts to automate many management tasks as discussed previously.

In the following sections, we discuss the most important aspects of managing basic disks, including:

- When to use basic disks instead of dynamic disks
- How to create partitions and logical drives
- How to assign a new drive letter
- How to format a basic volume
- How to extend a basic volume

When to Use Basic Disks

Basic disks are the default for Windows Server 2003. You should always use basic disks if you are going to dual-boot your machine with another operating system. MS-DOS, Windows 9*x*, Windows NT 4.0, and Windows XP Home Edition do not support dynamic disks. Windows 2000, Windows XP Professional, and Windows Server 2003 support dynamic disks, but not when dual booting.

Use basic disk if you will be moving your disks between machines. You have to go into Disk Management and import dynamic disk every time you move them from one PC to another. With basic disks, you just install them and Windows automatically sees them. Laptop hard disks must be configured as basic disks as most removable storage media.

Creating Partitions and Logical Drives

When you install Windows Server 2003, setup will prompt you to create a primary partition to use as the boot partition for Windows. If you want to create more partitions afterwards, you will need to use the disk management MMC. This section will walk you through creating a primary partition (Exercise 2.02), creating an extended partition (Exercise 2.03), and creating a logical drive (Exercise 2.04).

Exercise 2.02

Creating a Primary Partition

1. Right-click the unallocated space on the disk on which you want to create a primary partition.
2. Click **New partition** on the pop-up menu. This will start the **New Partition Wizard**, as shown in Figure 2.13.
3. Click **Next** to continue.

Figure 2.13 Creating a Primary Partition Using the New Partition Wizard

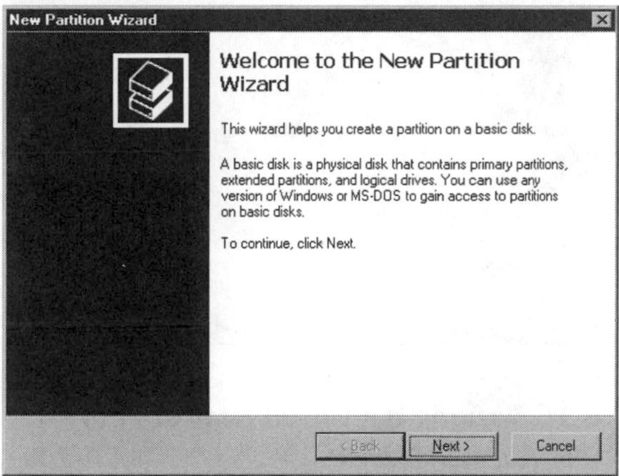

4. On the **Select Partition Type** window (Figure 2.14), select **Primary partition**.

Figure 2.14 Selecting to Create a Primary Partition

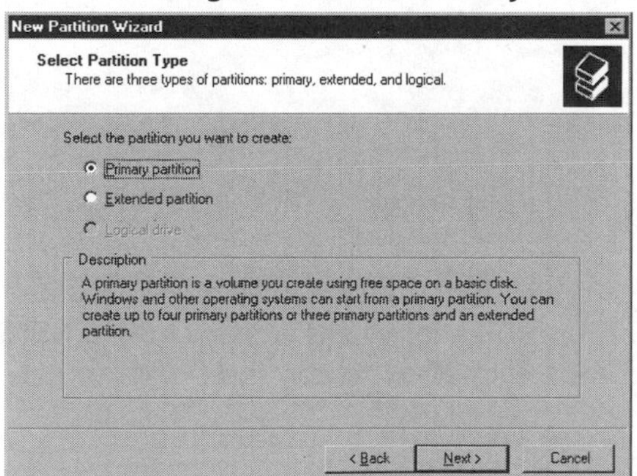

5. Click **Next** to continue. You will now be prompted to specify the partition size as shown in Figure 2.15.
6. Specify the **Partition size in MB** and click **Next** to continue.
7. Now you need to identify your new partition. Select a drive letter or choose to mount the new volume to an NTFS folder. For this exercise we are assigning our partition the drive letter **F**, as shown in Figure 2.16.
8. Click **Next** to continue.

Figure 2.15 Specifying the Partition Size

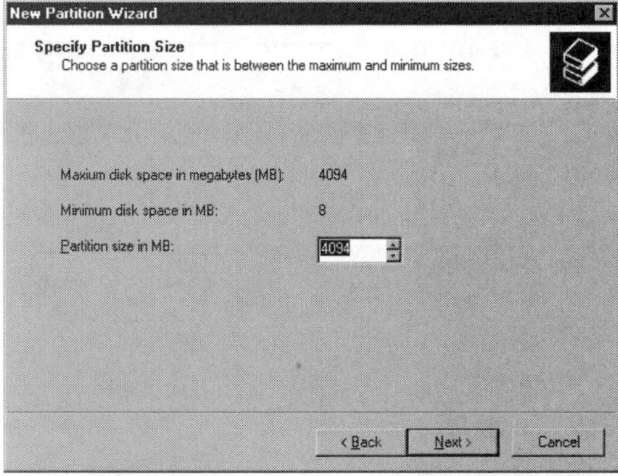

Figure 2.16 Assigning a Drive Letter or Path

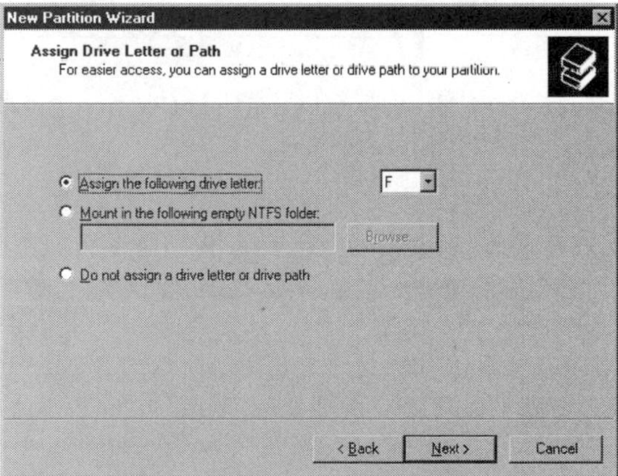

9. You must now format your new partition. You can format partitions as FAT, FAT32, or NTFS. For this exercise, choose **NTFS**, as shown in Figure 2.17, and then click **Next** to continue.

10. You will now see the **Completing the New Partition Wizard** window, as shown in Figure 2.18. Read over the summary to verify that you made the correct selections and click **Finish** to complete the process.

Figure 2.17 Formatting the Partition

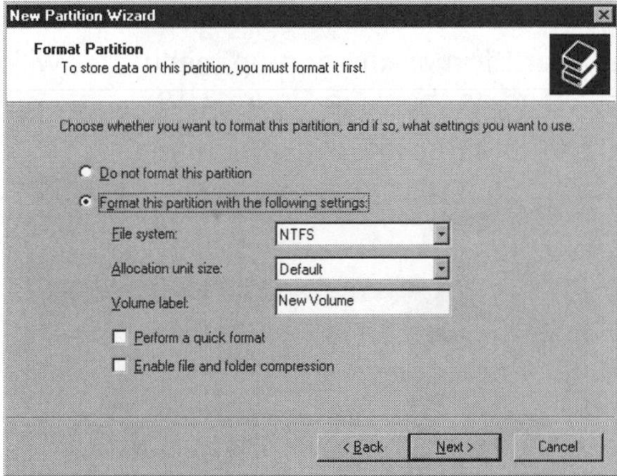

Figure 2.18 Completing the New Partition Wizard

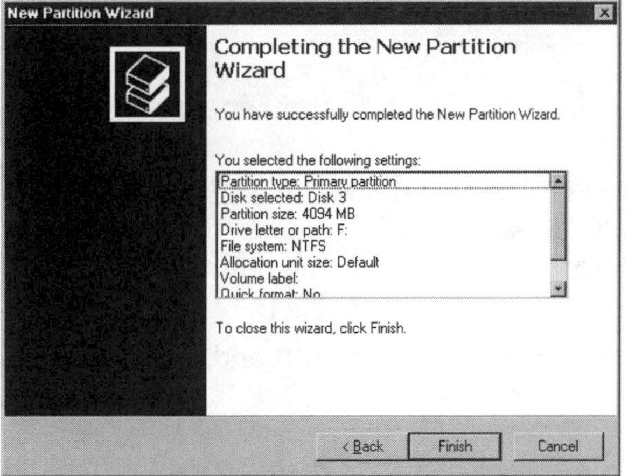

Exercise 2.03

Creating an Extended Partition

1. Right-click the unallocated space on the disk on which you want to create an extended partition.
2. Click **New partition** on the pop-up menu. This will start the New Partition Wizard as shown in Figure 2.19.
3. Click **Next** to continue.

Figure 2.19 Creating an Extended Partition with the New Partition Wizard

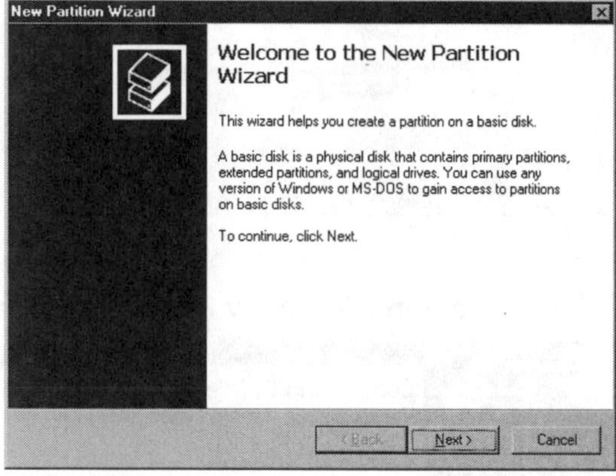

4. On the **Select Partition Type** window (Figure 2.20), select **Extended partition**.
5. Click **Next** to continue. You will now be prompted to specify the partition size as shown in Figure 2.21.
6. Specify the **Partition size in MB** and click **Finish** to create the extended partition.

Figure 2.20 Selecting to Create an Extended Partition

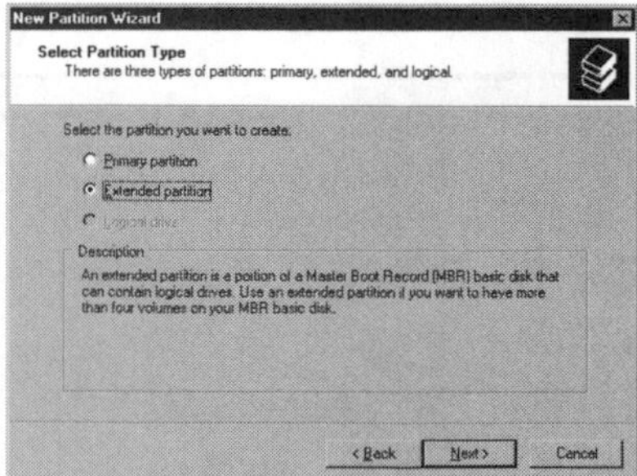

Figure 2.21 Specifying the Partition Size

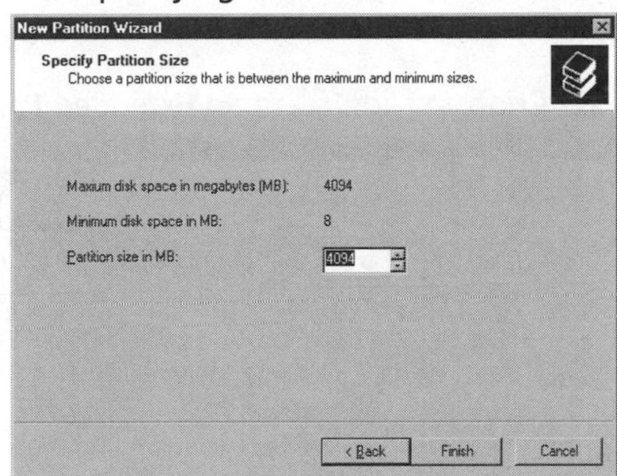

EXERCISE 2.04

CREATING A LOGICAL DRIVE

1. Right-click the Extended partition on the disk on which you want to create a logical drive.
2. Click **New Logical Drive** on the pop-up menu. This will start the New Partition Wizard, as shown in Figure 2.22.
3. Click **Next** to continue.

Figure 2.22 Using the New Partition Wizard to Create a Logical Partition

4. On the **Select Partition Type** window (Figure 2.23), select **Logical drive**.

Figure 2.23 Choosing to Create an Extended Partition

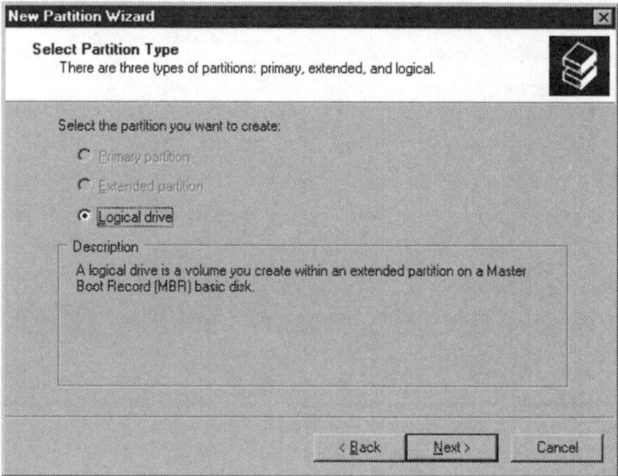

5. Click **Next** to continue. You will now be prompted to specify the partition size as shown in Figure 2.24.
6. Specify the **Partition size in MB** and click **Next** to continue.

Figure 2.24 Specifying a Partition Size

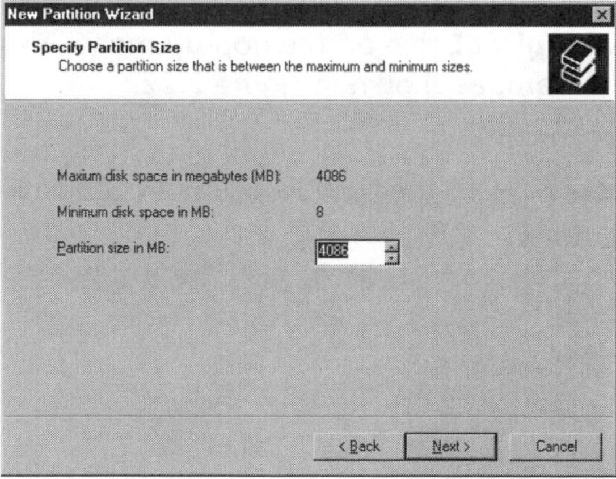

7. Now you need to identify your new partition. Select a drive letter or choose to mount the new volume to an NTFS folder. For this exercise we are assigning our partition the drive letter **G**, as shown in Figure 2.25.
8. Click **Next** to continue.

Figure 2.25 Assigning a Drive Letter or Path

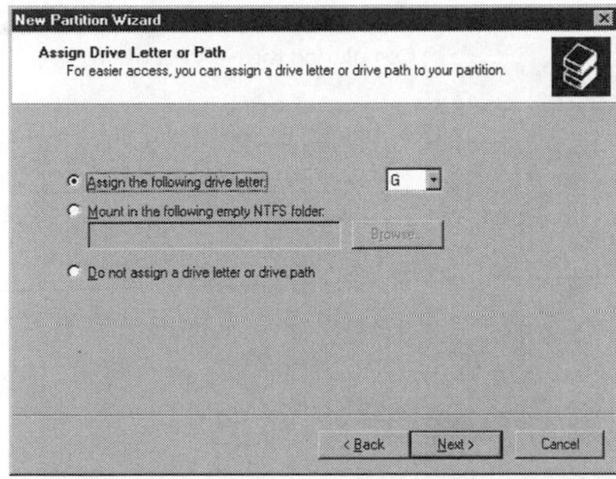

9. You must now format your new partition. You can format partitions as FAT, FAT32, or NTFS. For this exercise, choose **NTFS**, as shown in Figure 2.26, and then click **Next** to continue.

Figure 2.26 Formatting the New Partition

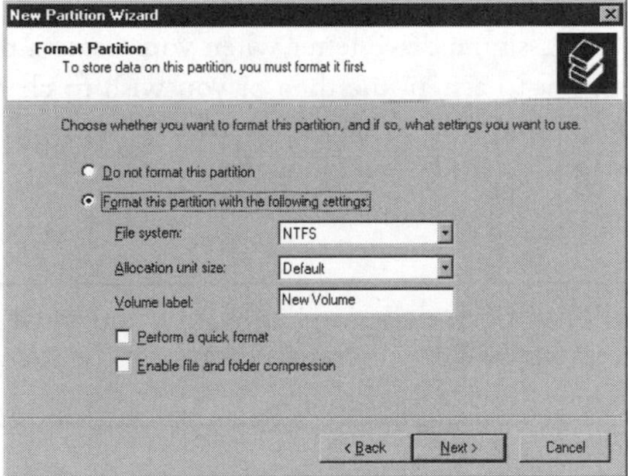

10. You will now see the **Completing the New Partition Wizard** window, as shown in Figure 2.27. Read over the summary to verify that you made the correct selections and click **Finish** to complete the process.

Figure 2.27 Completing the New Partition Wizard

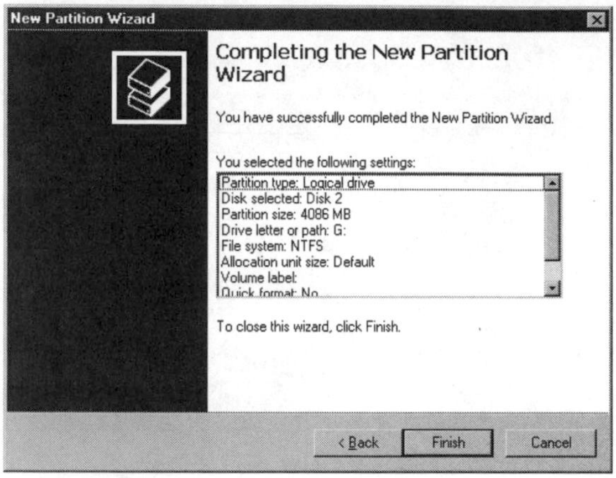

How to Assign a New Drive Letter

You are given the option to assign a drive letter when you create a primary partition or a logical drive. If you chose not to assign one then or you wish to change the letter, you can use Disk Management or diskpart.exe to assign a new drive letter. Exercise 2.05 walks you through using Disk Management to assign a new drive letter.

NOTE

Unless your account has been delegated authority, you must be a member of the Backup Operators group or Administrators group on the local computer to assign a drive letter.

EXERCISE 2.05

ASSIGNING A DRIVE LETTER

In this exercise we assign a drive letter to the first partition on Disk 1. This partition is a primary partition and is formatted with NTFS. Look at Figure 2.28 and you can see this partition is missing a drive letter. Here are the steps to assign it one:

1. Open **Computer Management** by right-clicking **My Computer** and choosing **Manage**.

2. Expand **Storage** and click **Disk Management**. This will give you the window shown in Figure 2.28.
3. Right-click the partition you want to assign a drive letter.
4. Select **Change Drive Letter and Paths** from the pop-up menu as shown in Figure 2.28. You will now see the window displayed in Figure 2.29.

Figure 2.28 Changing Drive Letter and Paths

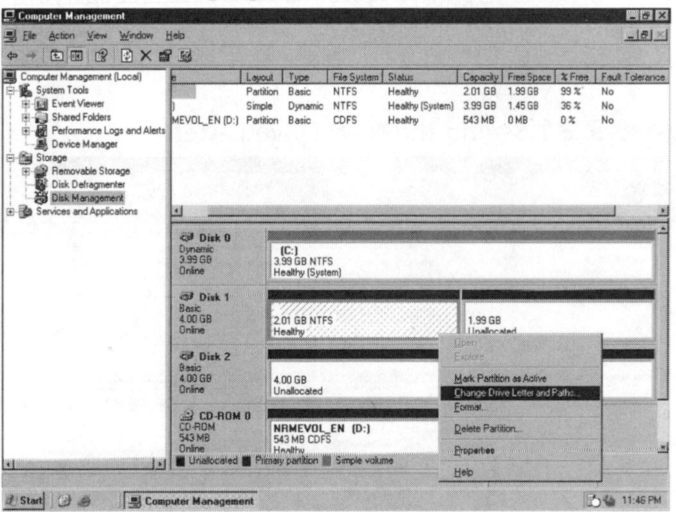

Figure 2.29 Adding a Drive Letter

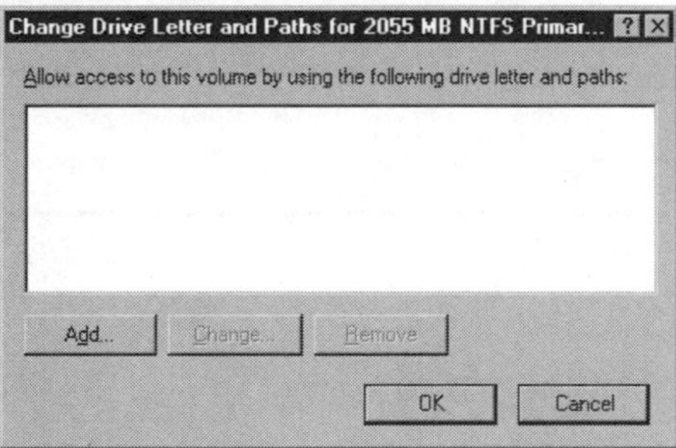

5. Click the **Add** button to add a drive letter. This will give you the window shown in Figure 2.30.
6. Use the drop-down arrow to select the drive letter you want to assign. For this exercise we are going to use **E**.

Figure 2.30 Selecting the Letter to Assign

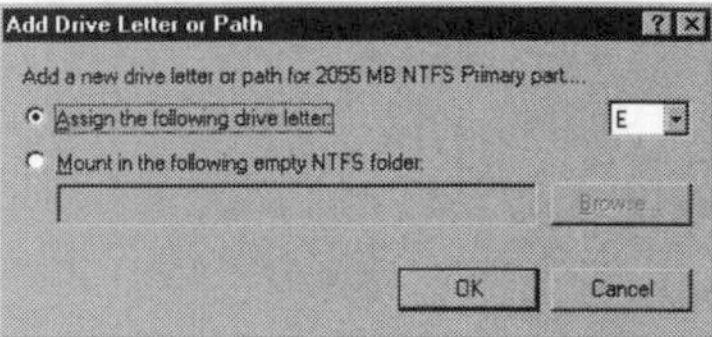

7. After you select the drive letter, click **OK** to accept your choice. This will apply your changes. Figure 2.31 shows that our partition now has the drive letter E.

Figure 2.31 Seeing the New Drive Letter

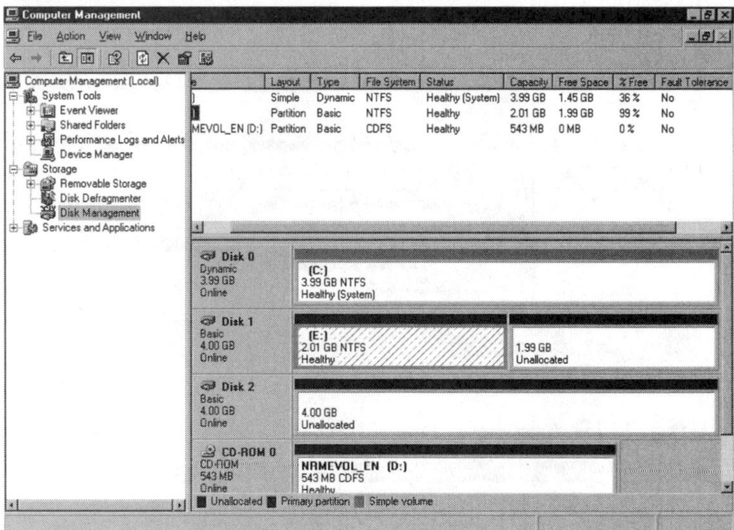

How to Format a Basic Volume

Like assigning a drive letter, you are given the option to format a drive when you create a primary partition or a logical drive. If you do not format the volume during creation, you can use Disk Management or format.exe to format the volume afterwards. Exercise 2.06 walks you through using Disk Management to format a basic volume.

NOTE

Unless your account has been delegated authority, you must be a member of the Backup Operators group or Administrators group on the local computer to format a volume. Remember, when you format a volume all data is lost.

EXERCISE 2.06

FORMATTING A VOLUME

In this exercise, we format the first primary partition on Disk 2. Look at Figure 2.32 and you can see that this partition, unlike the C: and E: drives, has not been formatted. Here are the steps to format it with NTFS:

1. Open **Computer Management** by right-clicking **My Computer** and choosing **Manage**.
2. Expand **Storage** and click **Disk Management**. This will give you the window shown in Figure 2.32.
3. Right-click the partition you want to format.
4. Select **Format** from the pop-up menu, as shown in Figure 2.32. You will now see the window displayed in Figure 2.33.

Figure 2.32 Formatting a Volume

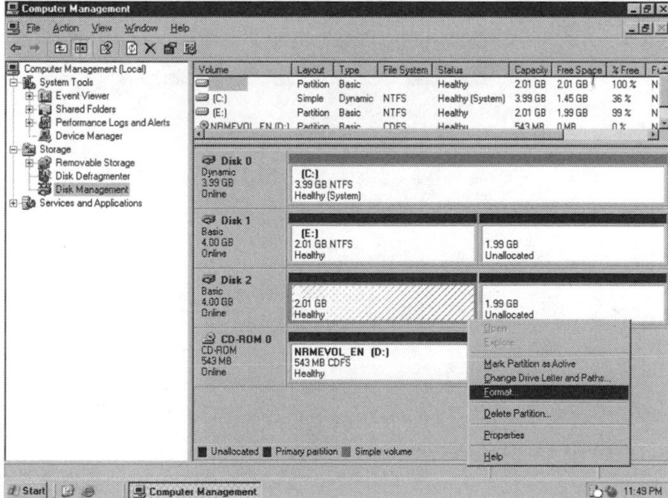

Figure 2.33 Choosing a Volume Label, File System, and Cluster Size

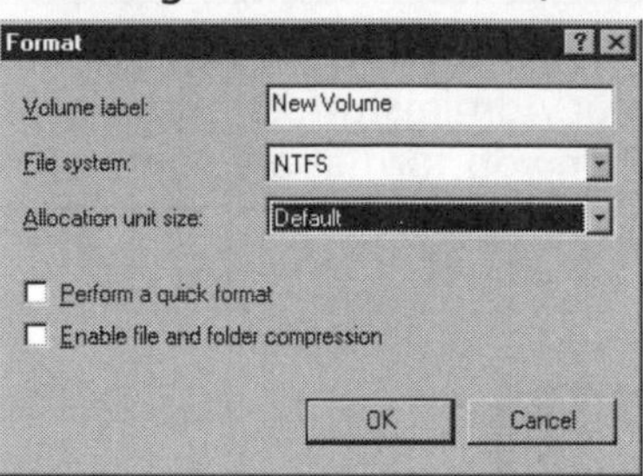

5. Enter the **Volume label** for the volume. For this exercise we are using **New Volume**.
6. Select the **File system** to use. In this exercise we are using **NTFS**.
7. Select the **Allocation unit size** (file system cluster). For this exercise we are using **Default**, which is 4 KB.
8. Optionally, you can choose to perform a quick format and to enable file and folder compression. After you make your choices, click **OK** to continue. You will now be warned that you are going to lose all data, as shown in Figure 2.34.
9. Click **OK** to start the format process. Figure 2.35 shows the volume being formatted and Figure 2.36 shows the volume after the format has completed.

Figure 2.34 Acknowledging Formatting Warning

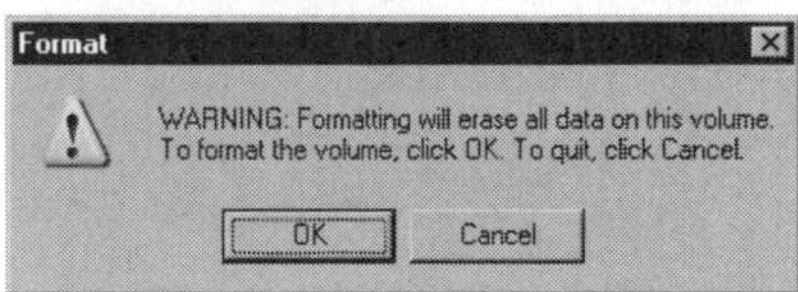

Figure 2.35 Watching the Drive Format

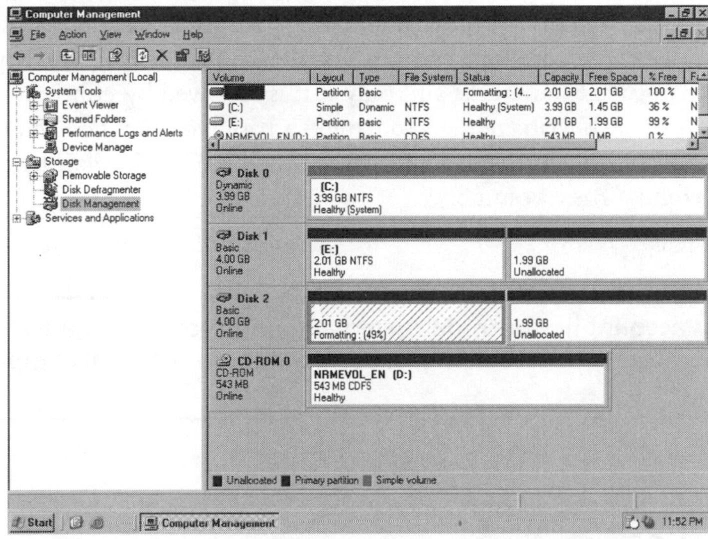

Figure 2.36 Seeing the Formatted Drive

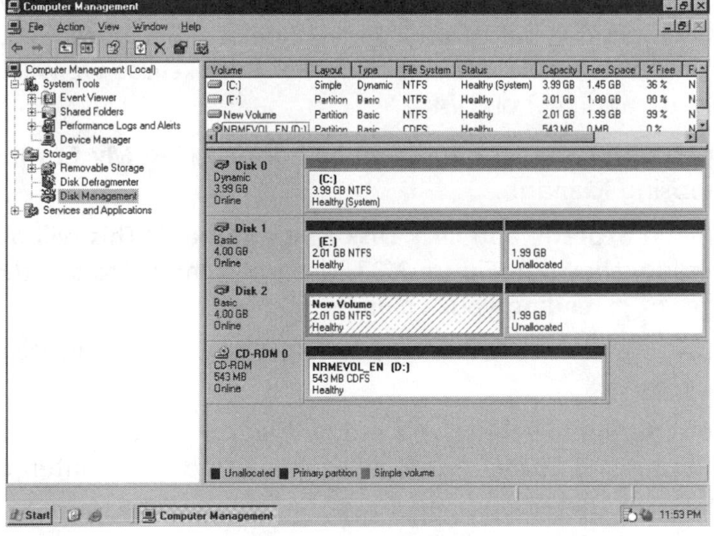

How to Extend a Basic Volume

Extending a basic volume enables you to add more space to an existing volume without losing data. This is a new feature that was not available in Windows 2000. You can extend a basic volume only onto the same disk and only if it is followed by contiguous unallocated space. You cannot use Disk Management to extend a basic volume. The only way to do it is to use diskpart.exe from the command prompt. Exercise 2.07 walks you through using diskpart.exe to extend a basic volume.

NOTE

Unless your account has been delegated authority, you must be a member of the Backup Operators group or Administrators group on the local computer to extend a basic volume.

EXERCISE 2.07

EXTENDING A BASIC VOLUME

Even though you cannot use Disk Management to extend a basic volume, let's open it anyway so that we can see our volume as it gets extended. We will use diskpart.exe to actually do the extending. For this exercise we will be extending the primary partition (F:) on Disk 2.

1. Open Computer Management by right-clicking **My Computer** and choosing **Manage**.
2. Expand **Storage** and click **Disk Management**. This will give you the window shown in Figure 2.37. Use this window to see the before and after of extending your volume.
3. Open the command prompt by selecting **Start | Run,** typing **CMD** and clicking **OK**.
4. From within the command prompt, launch diskpart by typing **diskpart** and pressing **Enter**. This will put you into diskpart interactive mode, as shown in Figure 2.38.
5. Type **list volume** and press **Enter** to display all the available volumes on your system.
6. Focus diskpart onto the volume you wish to extend by typing **select volume 3**. For this exercise we choose to extended volume 3.
7. To extend the volume, type **extend size=1024**. For this exercise we extended the volume by 1MB. To exit disk part, type **exit** when finished or just close the command prompt. Figure 2.39 shows the volume after it has been extended.

Figure 2.37 Extending a Basic Volume

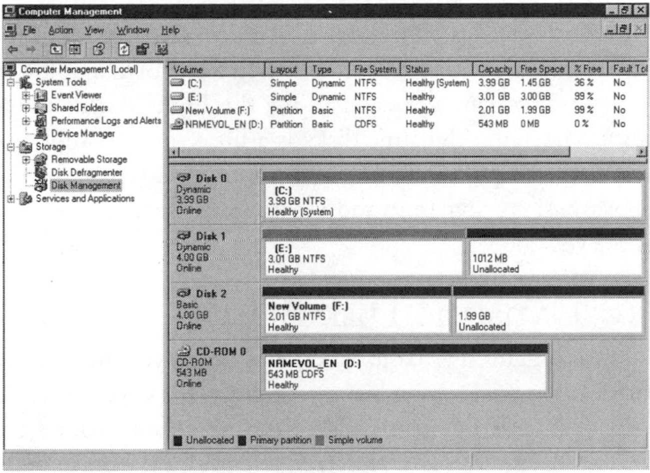

Figure 2.38 Using diskpart.exe

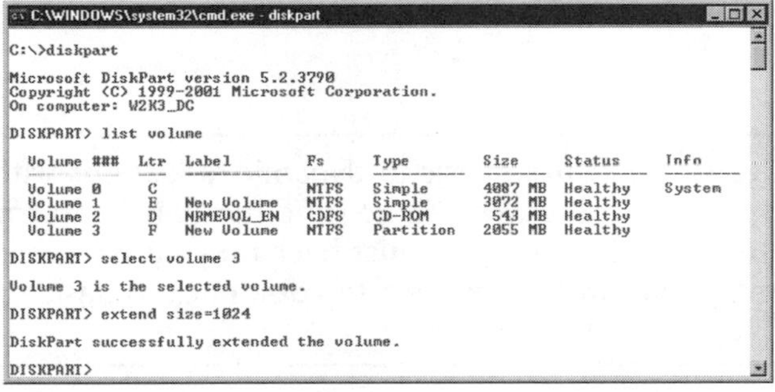

Figure 2.39 Seeing the Extended Volume

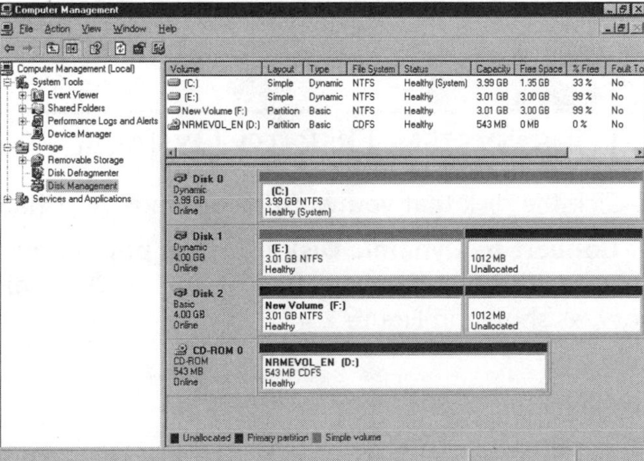

Managing Dynamic Disks

Dynamic disks are the required disk structure in Windows Server 2003 if you want to create fault-tolerant volumes or increase read and write performance by spanning disks. Dynamic disks, like basic disks, can be managed via the Disk Management MMC or with the diskpart.exe utility. Managing dynamic disks is a little more complicated than managing basic disks, as you have more options from which to choose. This section discusses converting your disks from basic to dynamic and creating the various types of volumes supported in Windows Server 2003.

Converting to Dynamic Disk Status

By default, all disks are configured as basic disks. It is up to you to convert them to dynamic if you choose to do so. Remember to carefully assess your situation and determine whether you need the features of dynamic disks (and make sure your system is one of those that cannot use dynamic disks, such as a clustered shared disk) before performing the conversion. If you convert a disk that is currently being accessed (such as the boot or system disks) then you must reboot in order to convert. Otherwise, you can convert without rebooting. Converting to dynamic does not erase any data.

WARNING

Although you can convert from basic to dynamic disk status without losing data, you cannot go back the other way. There is no mechanism to convert volumes from dynamic to basic. Instead, you must back up your data, and then delete the dynamic volumes. You can then convert the disk back to basic using the disk management MMC or the **diskpart** utility.

Exercise 2.08 walks you through the process of converting your system disk from basic to dynamic.

EXERCISE 2.08

CONVERTING YOUR SYSTEM DISK TO DYNAMIC

1. Right-click the disk that you want to upgrade to dynamic.
2. Select **Convert to Dynamic Disk** from the pop-up menu, as shown in Figure 2.40. This will give you the **Convert to Dynamic Disk** selection window, as shown in Figure 2.41.

Figure 2.40 Converting to Dynamic Disk

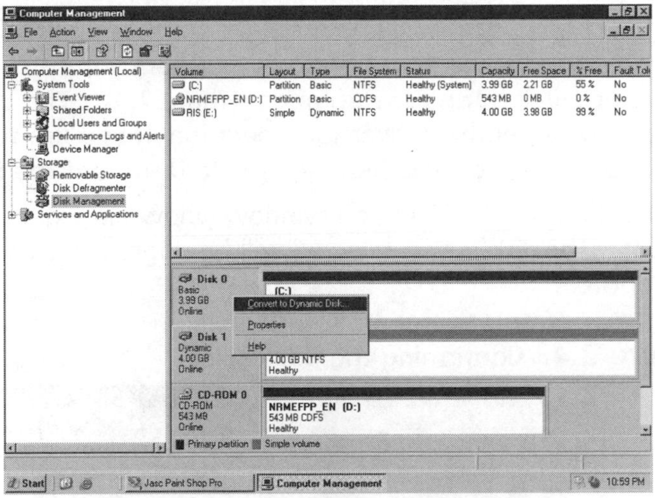

Figure 2.41 Selecting the Disk to Convert

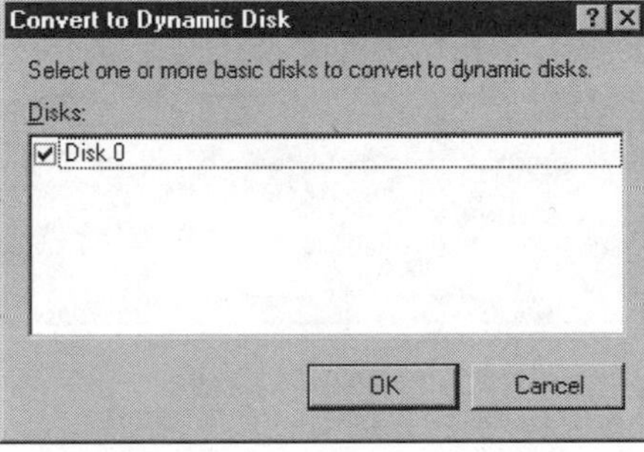

3. The disk you want to upgrade should be checked by default. If not, check its check box and click **OK** to continue.
4. You are next shown a summary screen (Figure 2.42) that indicates which disk(s) will be converted. Click **Convert** to continue.

Figure 2.42 Reviewing Disks to be Converted

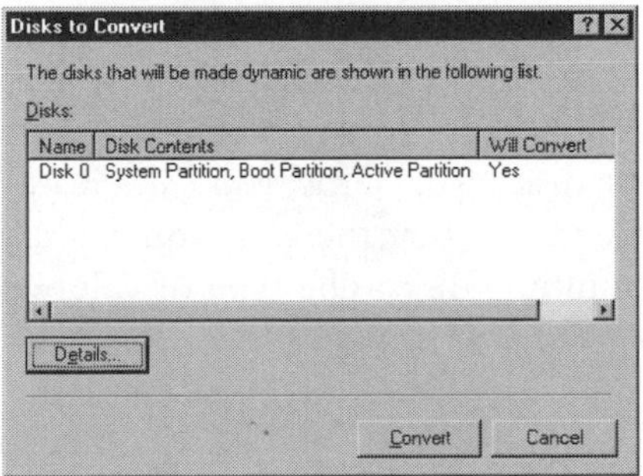

5. Windows will warn you that you are about to convert to dynamic. Click **Yes** on the warning screen (shown in Figure 2.43) to continue.
6. You are next warned that file systems currently in use on the disk will be dismounted during the upgrade (Figure 2.44). This is your last chance to cancel the conversion operation. If you are sure that you want to convert to dynamic, click **Yes** to dismount the file system.
7. Click **OK** on the confirmation window (shown in Figure 2.45) to reboot your PC. The disk(s) you selected will be upgraded when the computer is rebooted.

Figure 2.43 Confirming the Conversion

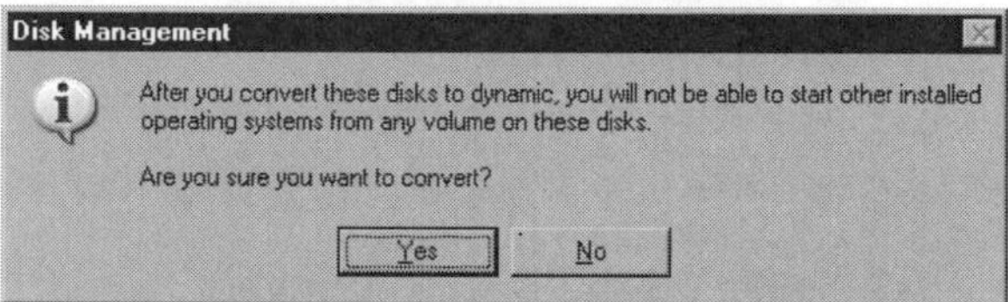

Figure 2.44 Dismounting Disk to be Converted

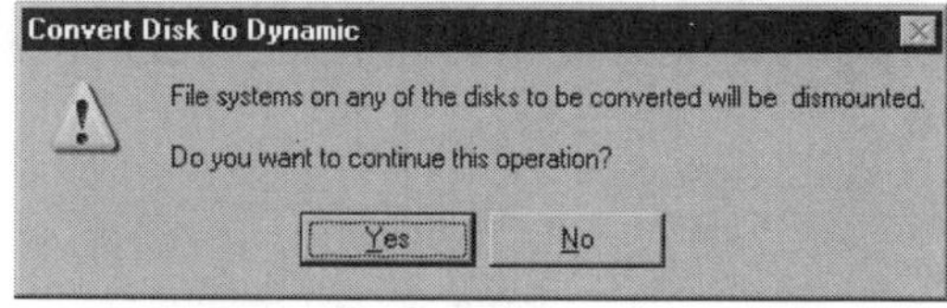

Figure 2.45 Completing the Conversion

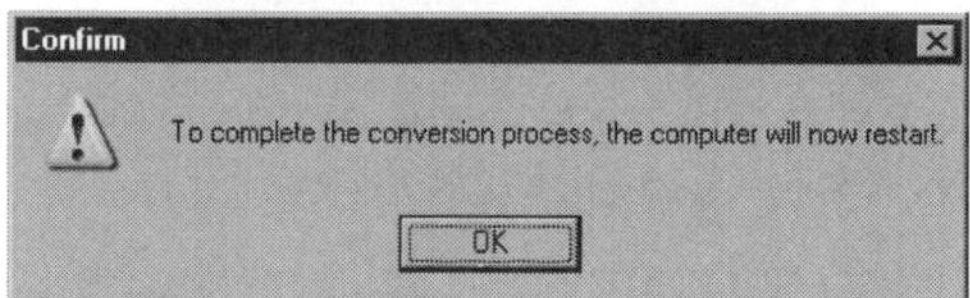

Creating and Using Dynamic Volumes

After you have converted your disk to dynamic, you can create volumes. Creating volumes is similar to creating partitions, except that there are some additional steps because, unlike partitions, volumes can span multiple disks. The type of volume you create depends on a variety of factors, such as the following:

- How many disks do you have in your machine?
- Do you want fault tolerance?
- Do you want to increase read or write performance?
- What is being stored (or will be stored) on the volume (e.g., database, system partition, print spooler, etc.)?

Creating and Using Simple Volumes

Simple volumes are the default volume type on a dynamic disk. Exercise 2.09 walks you through the process of creating a simple volume. Use simple volumes in the following situations:

- You only have one disk in a machine.
- You are not concerned with fault tolerance.
- You want the ability to dynamically extend the space used on a volume.

NOTE

When you format a dynamic volume using the Disk Management console, NTFS is the only file system choice that is available. However, if you want to format a dynamic volume in FAT or FAT32, you can do so by using the **Format** command at the command-line.

EXERCISE 2.09

CREATING A SIMPLE VOLUME

1. Right-click the unallocated space on the disk on which you want to create a simple volume.
2. Click **New Volume** on the context menu. This will start the **New Volume Wizard,** shown in Figure 2.46.
3. Click **Next** to continue.

Figure 2.46 Creating Simple Volumes

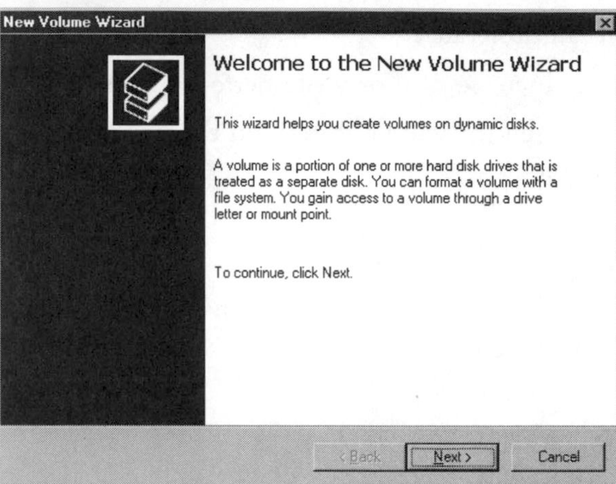

4. On the **Select Volume Type** window (Figure 2.47), select **Simple**.
5. Click **Next** to continue.

Figure 2.47 Selecting Volume Type

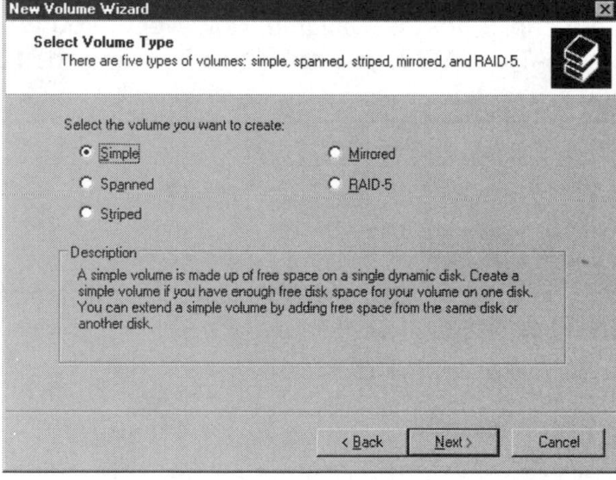

6. You will next be prompted to select the disk to use for the simple volume, as shown in Figure 2.48. The correct disk should already be selected. If not, select it.
7. Select the amount of space to be used for the simple volume and click **Next** to continue.

Figure 2.48 Selecting Disks to be Used in a Simple Volume

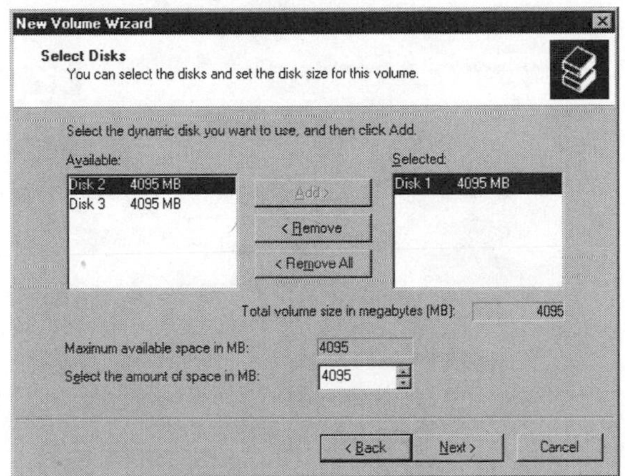

8. Next you need to identify your new volume. Select a drive letter or choose to mount the new volume to an NTFS folder. For this exercise, we assign the new volume the drive letter **D**, as shown in Figure 2.49.

Figure 2.49 Assigning a Drive Letter or Path

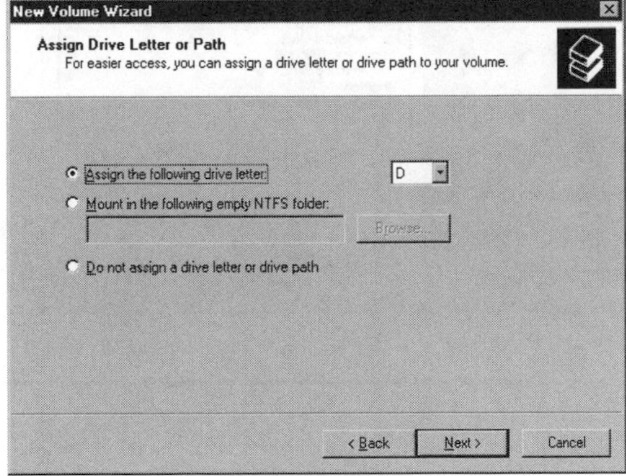

9. Next, you can format your new volume. You can format the volume as FAT, FAT32, or NTFS, or you can choose not to format the volume now. For this example, choose **NTFS,** as shown in Figure 2.50, and click **Next** to continue.
10. You will now see the **Completing the New Volume Wizard** window, as shown in Figure 2.51. Read over the summary to verify that you made the correct selections and click **Finish** to complete the process.

Figure 2.50 Formatting Your New Volume

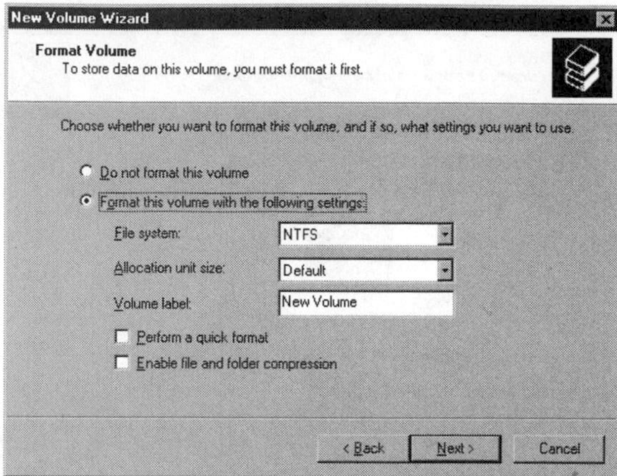

Figure 2.51 Finishing the New Volume Wizard

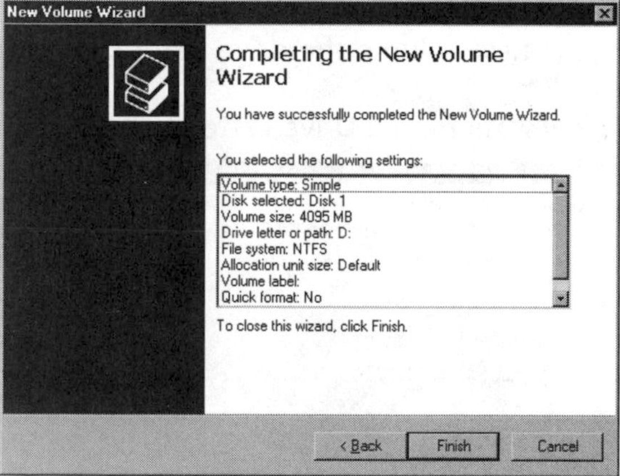

Creating and Using Spanned Volumes

Spanned volumes enable you to group different disks of the same or different sizes and access them as if they were one disk. However, only one disk in the volume is written to at a time. Spanned volumes can be created using two to 32 disks. Spanned volumes provide 100 percent drive utilization (minus the 1MB per disk overhead for the LDM partition).

Exercise 2.10 walks you through the process of creating a spanned volume. Use spanned volumes in the following situations:

- You want to access multiple disks as a single volume and you are not concerned about fault tolerance or increased read/write performance.
- Your disks are different sizes and you want to achieve 100 percent drive utilization with a single volume.
- You have a simple volume that is almost full and you need to expand it across multiple disks.

Exercise 2.10

Creating a Spanned Volume

1. Right-click the unallocated space on the disk on which you want to create a spanned volume.
2. Click **New Volume** on the context menu. This will start the **New Volume Wizard**, as shown in Figure 2.52.
3. Click **Next** to continue.

Figure 2.52 Creating a Spanned Volume

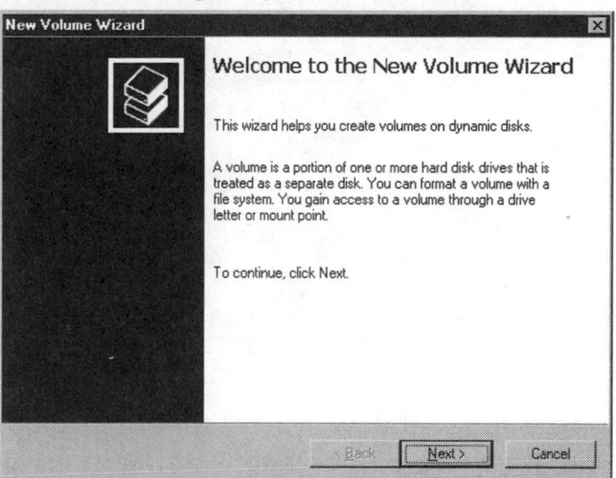

4. In the **Select Volume Type** window (Figure 2.53), select **Spanned**.
5. Click **Next** to continue.

Figure 2.53 Selecting the Volume Type to be Created

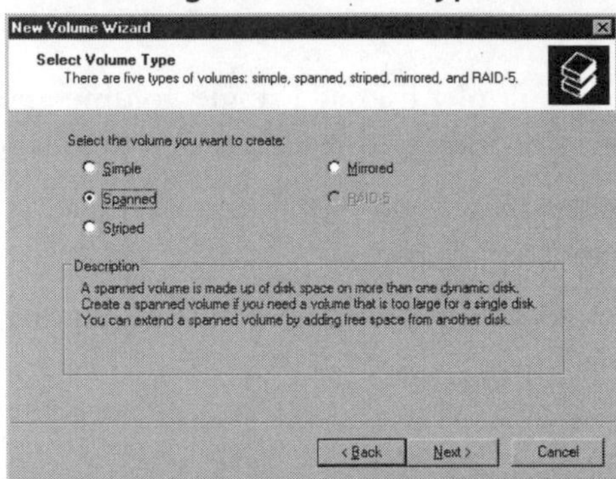

6. You will next be prompted to select the disks to use for the spanned volume, as shown in Figure 2.54. Select the disks you want to use.
7. Select the amount of space to be used for the spanned volume and click **Next** to continue.

Figure 2.54 Selecting Disks to be Used in Spanned Volume

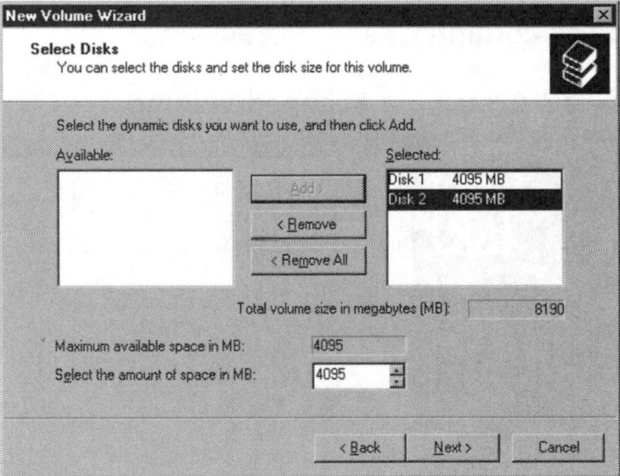

8. Next you need to identify your new spanned volume. Select a drive letter or choose to mount the new volume to an NTFS folder. For this exercise, we assign the new volume the drive letter **D**, as shown in Figure 2.55.

Figure 2.55 Assigning a Drive Letter or Path

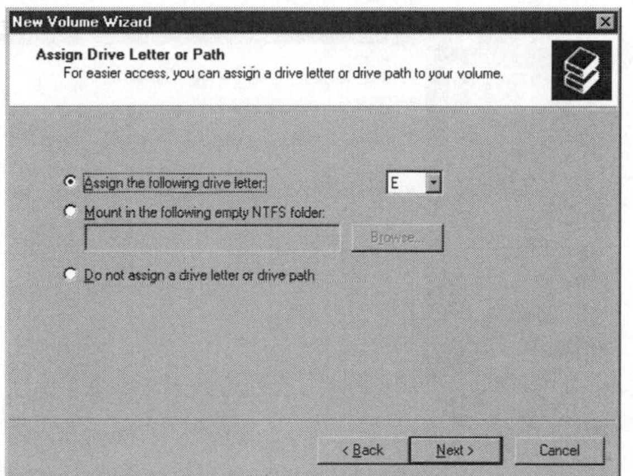

9. Next you can format your new spanned volume. You can format the volume as FAT, FAT32, or NTFS, or you can choose not to format the volume at this time. For this example, choose **NTFS,** as shown in Figure 2.56, and then click **Next** to continue.
10. You will next see the **Completing the New Volume Wizard** window, as shown in Figure 2.57. Read over the summary to verify that you made the correct selections and click **Finish** to complete the process.

Figure 2.56 Formatting the New Spanned Volume

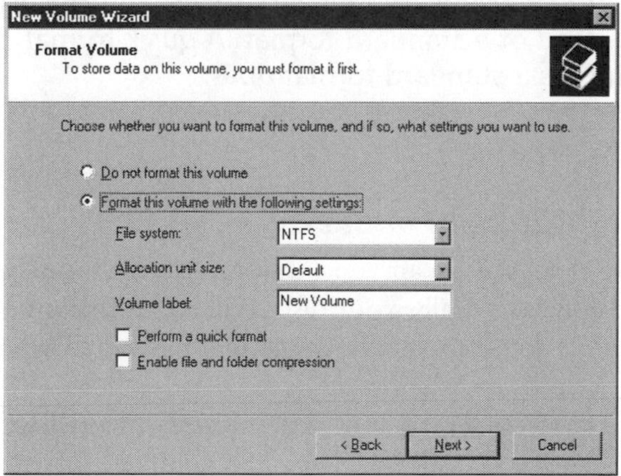

Figure 2.57 Completing the New Volume Wizard

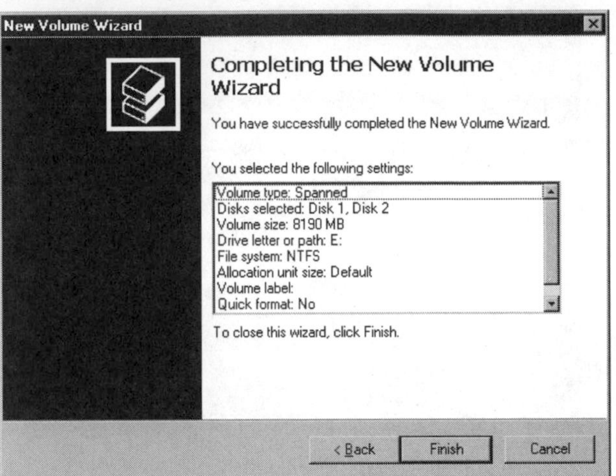

NOTE

When formatting any of the volumes created with the New Volume Wizard, you can also select the allocation unit size, give the new volume a label to more easily identify it, and/or select to enable file and folder compression (NTFS volumes only, with cluster size of 4KB or less) to save disk space. You can also choose to perform a quick format instead of a standard format. A quick format does not check the disk for bad sectors as a standard format does.

Creating and Using Striped Volumes

Striped volumes require that you use an equal amount of unallocated space on each of the disks that is part of the volume. Ideally, your disks will all be the same size and all space on each will be unallocated. If not, some of the space will be wasted when you create the volume.

Striped volumes increase both read and write performance when accessing the volume by utilizing all the disks at one time. Unlike spanned volumes, striped volumes cannot be extended. Striped volumes can be created using two to 32 disks.

Exercise 2.11 walks you through the process of creating a striped volume. Use striped volumes in the following situations:

- The primary disk operation will be reading information from a large database such as SQL or Exchange.
- The volume will be used to spool large print jobs.
- You are not concerned with fault tolerance.
- You plan to collect external data on the disk at very fast transfer rates.

Exercise 2.11

Creating a Striped Volume

1. Right-click the unallocated space on the disk on which you want to create a striped volume.
2. Click **New Volume** on the context menu. This will start the **New Volume Wizard**, as shown in Figure 2.58.
3. Click **Next** to continue.

Figure 2.58 Creating a Striped Volume

4. On the **Select Volume Type** window (Figure 2.59), select **Striped**.
5. Click **Next** to continue.

Figure 2.59 Selecting the Volume Type to be Created

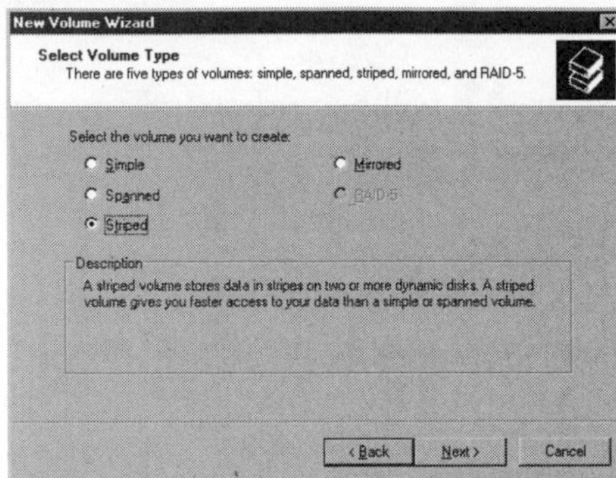

6. You will next be prompted to select the disk to use for the striped volume, as shown in Figure 2.60. Select the disks you want to use.
7. Select the amount of space to be used for the striped volume and click **Next** to continue.

Figure 2.60 Selecting Disks to be Used in the Striped Volume

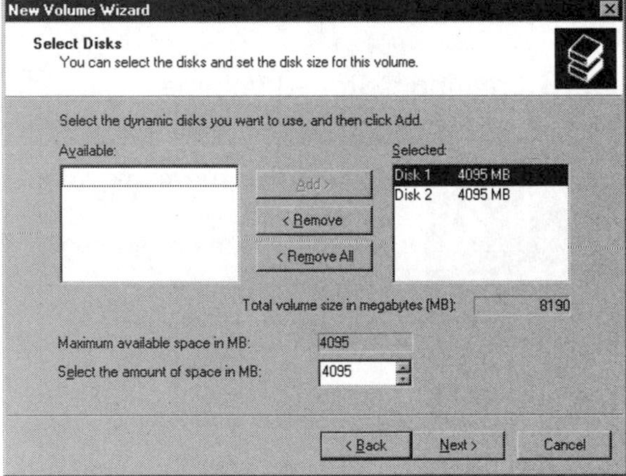

8. Next you need to identify your new striped volume. Select a drive letter or choose to mount the new volume to an NTFS folder. For this exercise, we assign the new volume the drive letter **E**, as shown in Figure 2.61.

Figure 2.61 Assigning a Drive Letter or Path

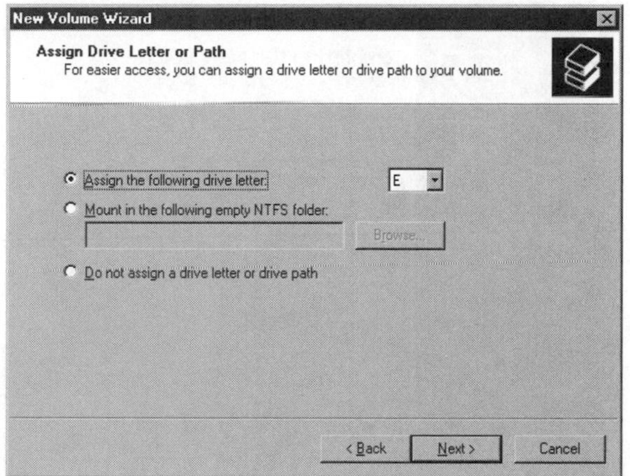

9. Next, you can format your new striped volume. You can format a striped volume as FAT, FAT32, or NTFS, or you can choose not to format the volume at this time. For this example, choose **NTFS**, as shown in Figure 2.62, and click **Next** to continue.
10. You will next see the **Completing the New Volume Wizard** window, as shown in Figure 2.63. Read the summary to verify that you made the correct selections and click **Finish** to complete the process.

Figure 2.62 Formatting the New Striped Volume

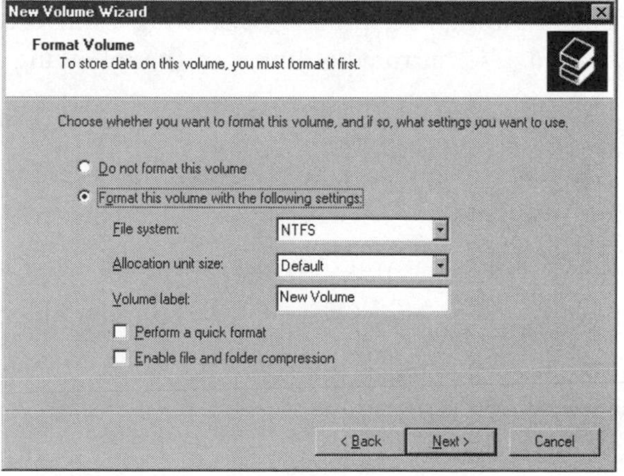

Figure 2.63 Ending the New Volume Wizard

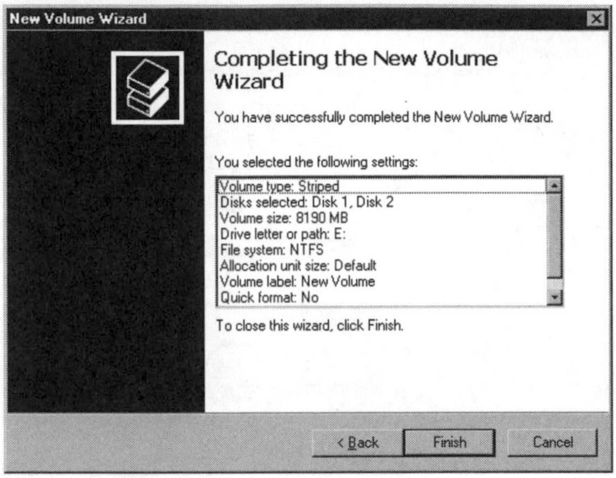

Creating and Using Mirrored Volumes

Mirrored volumes require exactly two disks and both disks must be the same size. When you write information to the mirror, it is written twice – once to each disk. This provides complete redundancy for your data. Should one disk fail, you can use the mirrored copy. Mirrored volumes provide only 50 percent disk utilization (the least cost efficient of all volume types). However, they provide excellent fault tolerance.

Exercise 2.12 walks you through the process of creating a mirrored volume. Mirrored volumes cannot be extended. Use mirrored volumes in the following situations:

- You want to provide fault tolerance for the boot and/or system partition.
- You want an easy way to roll back failed operating system upgrades (break the mirror before the upgrade).
- You need fault tolerance, but you only have two disks.
- You want to be able to get the system up and running quickly after a disk failure.

EXERCISE 2.12

CREATING A MIRRORED VOLUME

1. Right-click the simple volume you wish to mirror, as shown in Figure 2.64.
2. Choose **Add Mirror** from the context menu.

Figure 2.64 Creating a Mirrored Volume

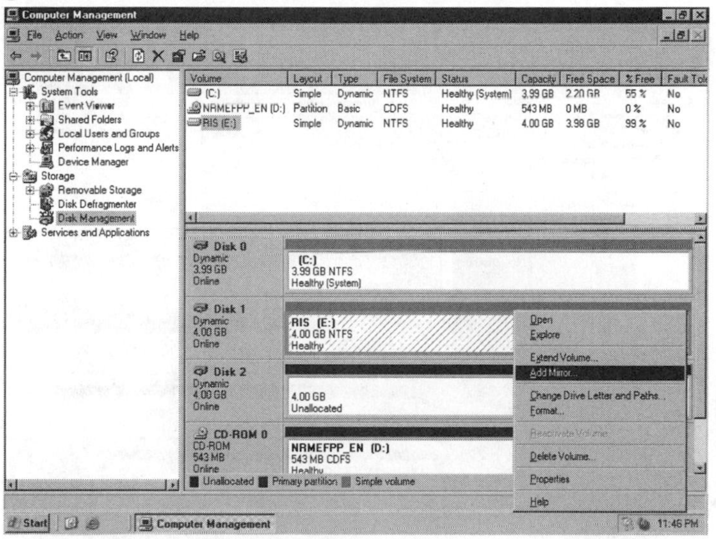

3. You are next prompted, as shown in Figure 2.65, to select a location to hold a mirror of the selected drive. Select the disk on which you want to create the mirror copy.

Figure 2.65 Selecting a Location for the Mirror

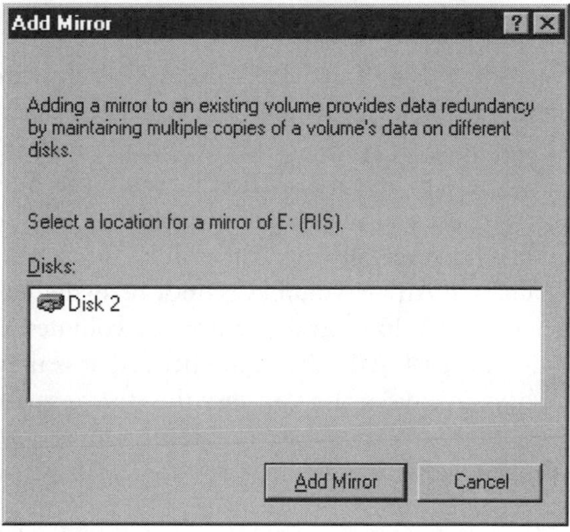

4. Click **Add Mirror** to continue. You will see your mirror being created, as shown in Figure 2.66.

Figure 2.66 Synchronizing a Mirrored Volume

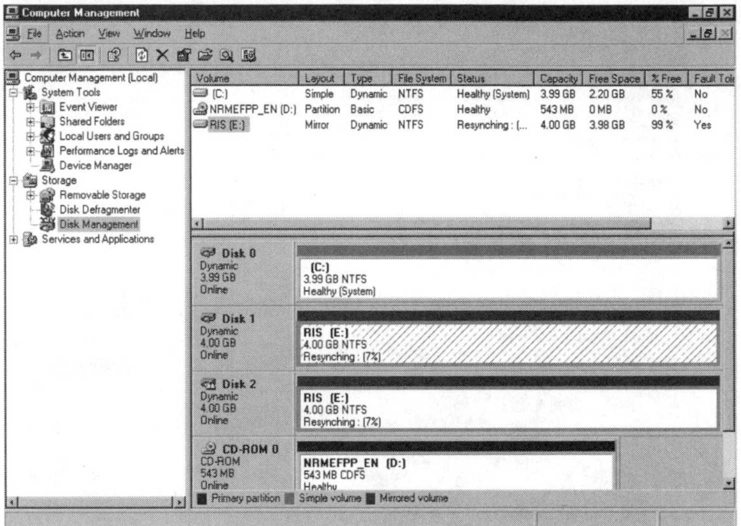

After the mirror is created, both volumes that make up the two parts of the mirror will appear in the **Disk Management** console with the same drive letter.

Creating and Using RAID-5 Volumes

RAID-5 volumes can be created using three to 32 disks. They provide fault tolerance by calculating parity information, which can be used to recreate the data on the other disks, and writing it to a block on one disk as part of the striping operation. Data is striped across all the disks in the volume, while parity information is written to one disk in each stripe. The parity information can be used to regenerate the missing data should one disk fail. If you lose more than one disk, however, all your data will be lost.

As with mirrored volumes, RAID-5 volumes cannot be extended. However, RAID-5 volumes offer more efficient disk utilization than mirrored volumes. You lose the storage space equivalent to one disk in the RAID-5 volume because it is used for parity information. For example, if you have five disks and you lose the storage space of one disk, you operate at 80 percent disk utilization. If you increase the number of disks in your RAID-5 volume, you will get even better disk utilization. For example, if you use 10 disks instead of five, you will operate at 90 percent utilization instead of 80 percent utilization. On the other hand, it takes longer to get your system back up and running after a disk failure with RAID-5, as opposed to mirrors, because you must go through the process of regenerating the data from parity.

Exercise 2.13 walks you through the process of creating a RAID-5 volume. Use RAID-5 volumes in the following situations:

- You need the boosted read performance of a striped volume, but you must have fault tolerance.
- You want fault tolerance with the most efficient level of disk utilization possible.
- You need fault tolerance, but you have too many disks to use a mirror.

EXERCISE 2.13

CREATING A RAID-5 VOLUME

1. Right-click the unallocated space on the disk on which you want to create a RAID-5 volume.
2. Click **New Volume** on the context menu. This will start the **New Volume Wizard**, as shown in Figure 2.67.

Figure 2.67 Using the New Volume Wizard to Create a RAID-5 Volume

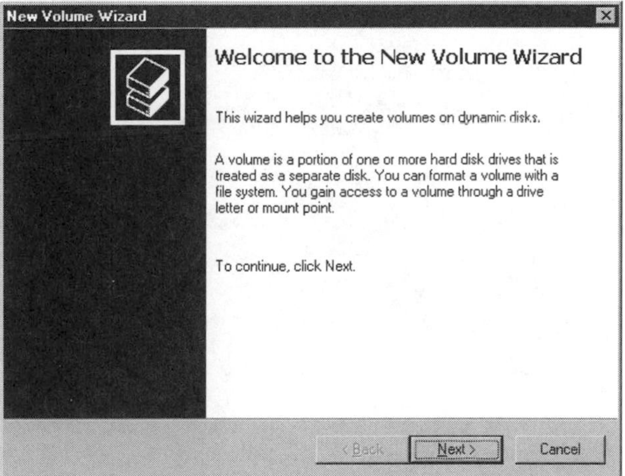

3. Click **Next** to continue.
4. In the **Select Volume Type window** (Figure 2.68), select **RAID-5**.
5. Click **Next** to continue.
6. You will next be prompted to select the disks to use for the RAID-5 volume, as shown in Figure 2.69. Select the disks you want to use.
7. Select the amount of space to be used for the striped volume and click **Next** to continue.
8. Next you need to identify your new RAID-5 volume. Select a drive letter or choose to mount the new volume to an NTFS folder. For this exercise, we assign the new volume the drive letter **D**, as shown in Figure 2.70.

Figure 2.68 Selecting to Create a RAID-5 Volume

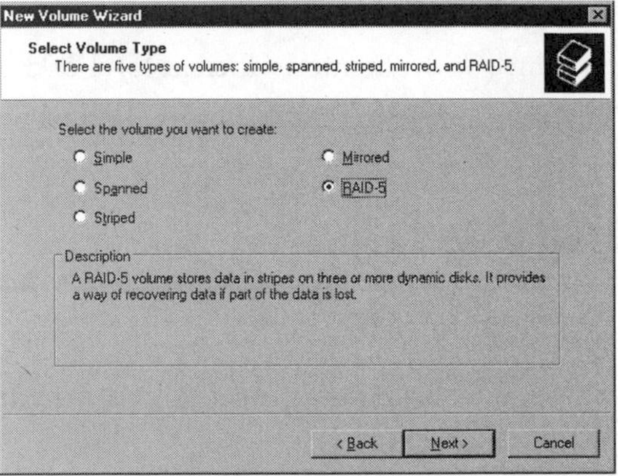

Figure 2.69 Adding Disks to the RAID-5 Volume

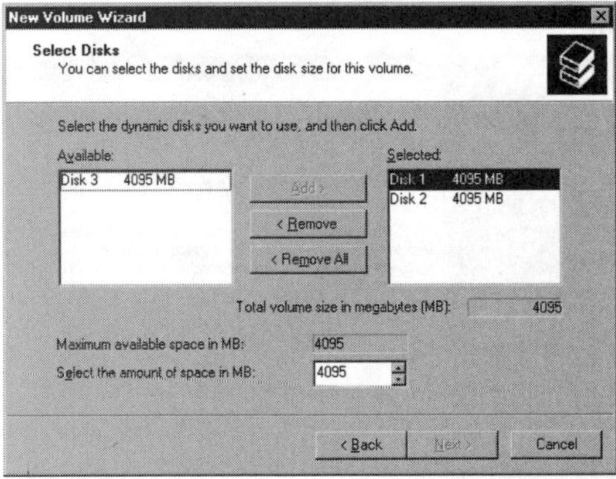

Figure 2.70 Assigning a Drive Letter or Path

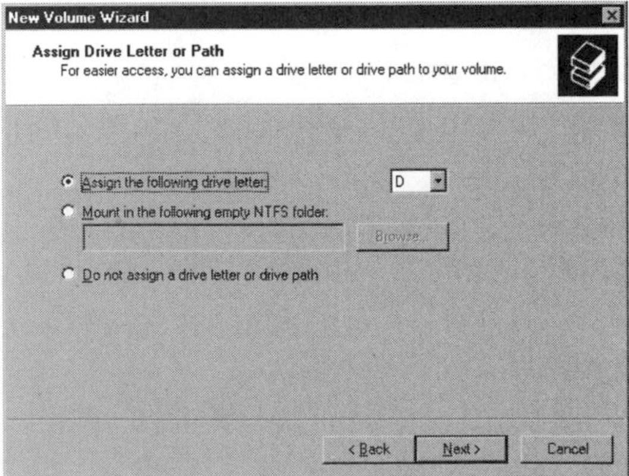

9. Next, you can format your new RAID-5 volume. You can format a RAID-5 volume as FAT, FAT32, or NTFS, or you can choose not to format the volume at this time. For this example, choose **NTFS**, as shown in Figure 2.71, and click **Next** to continue.
10. You will next see the **Completing the New Volume Wizard** window, as shown in Figure 2.72. Read the summary to verify that you made the correct selections and click **Finish** to complete the process.

Figure 2.71 Formatting the RAID-5 Volume

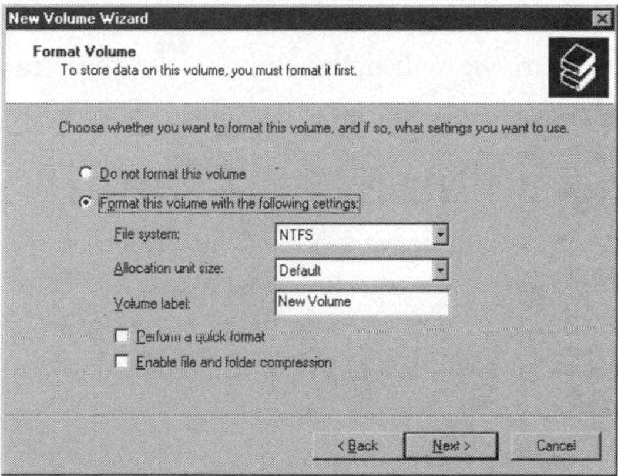

Figure 2.72 Finishing the New Volume Wizard

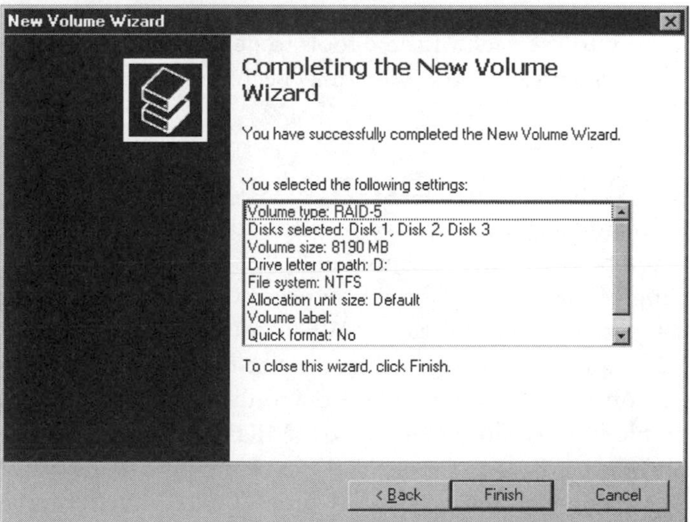

Optimize Server Disk Performance

Optimizing disk performance is an important part of managing a server. Consider the disk-oriented tasks that take place on a typical day on the typical server. Users save data to their home directories. They send e-mail back and forth (which is saved in a database on the server). They print documents. They access shared files. All of these tasks require good disk performance.

Two issues you will always run into when managing disks are disk fragmentation and insufficient disk space. Fragmentation problems are not as obvious as disk space problems; when you run out of disk space, you usually find out immediately. However, you may not notice that a disk is fragmented unless you take the time to check or you notice that performance has degraded. With Windows Server 2003, Microsoft provides ways to manage both of these concerns. The disk defragmentation utilities can ensure that your disk is performing at its peak and the disk quotas feature can ensure that you do not run out of disk space. In the following sections, we will discuss how to use these tools to keep your disks at optimum performance levels.

Defragmenting Volumes and Partitions

Defragmenting the disks on all your servers (especially file servers) can ensure optimal performance and enable you to get more use out of your disks. It is not something that you should do every day, but you definitely need to make it part of your server maintenance routine. Microsoft provides two tools for performing defragmentation. Both tools work with basic and dynamic disks that are formatted with the FAT, FAT32, or NTFS file systems. These tools are:

- Disk Defragmenter (graphical utility)
- defrag.exe (command-line tool)

You will learn how to use each of these tools to defragment your disks. First, however, in the next section we discuss how and why disks become fragmented and the effects of fragmentation.

Understanding Disk Fragmentation

To understand disk fragmentation, you have to first understand how data is written to a disk. This was covered briefly in the Understanding Disk Terminology and Concepts section at the beginning of the chapter. The smallest measurable unit on a hard disk is a sector. Sectors are joined together to make a cluster. When you save a file, Windows breaks the file into small pieces. Each piece is no bigger than the size of one cluster.

For example, if you were to save a 128KB file to disk (see Figure 2.73), Windows would separate the file into 32 clusters (based on a 4KB cluster size). Unfortunately, not all files fill up an entire cluster. If you save a 21KB file to the disk, Windows separates it into six clusters (based on a 4KB cluster size). Every time Windows writes something to disk it uses an entire cluster. You cannot have parts of two different files in the same cluster. In the case of the 21KB file, this means you have wasted 3KB of space (see Figure 2.74). This happens because Windows must use six clusters to save the file, and six 4KB clusters total 24KB of hard disk space. You really only needed 21KB to save the file, but the cluster size resulted in some space going unused. Remember that clusters are the smallest units that can be written to a disk. Even if you do not have enough data to fill an entire cluster, Windows still uses an entire cluster when it writes to disk.

NOTE

Cluster size was a source of much wasted disk space with the FAT16 file system. With FAT16, cluster sizes increase as partition size increases, so that with a 2GB partition, cluster size is 64KB. That made for a lot of wasted space that could add up to a significant portion of the disk. FAT32 helped to alleviate that problem, with cluster sizes of only 4KB for partitions from 512MB to 8GB, 8KB clusters for partitions from 8 to 16GB, and 16KB clusters for partitions up to 32GB. NTFS improves on that further, with 4KB clusters for partitions up to 2TB. For more information about cluster size in Windows file systems, see www.microsoft.com/technet/treeview/default.asp?url=/TechNet/prodtechnol/winxppro/reskit/prkc_fil_lxty.asp.

Figure 2.73 Writing Data to Your Hard Disk

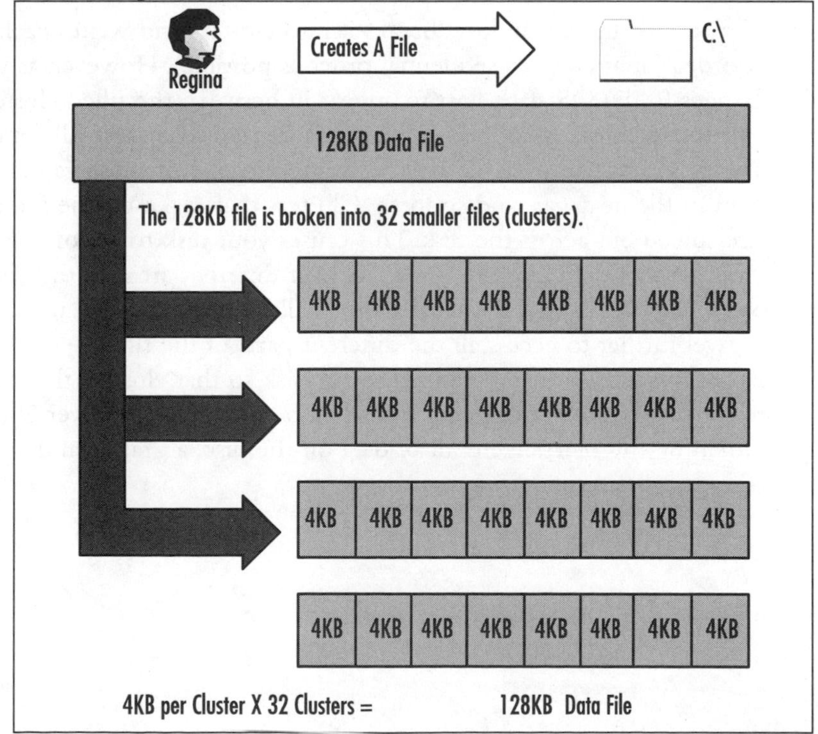

Figure 2.74 Wasting Space by Not Filling an Entire Cluster

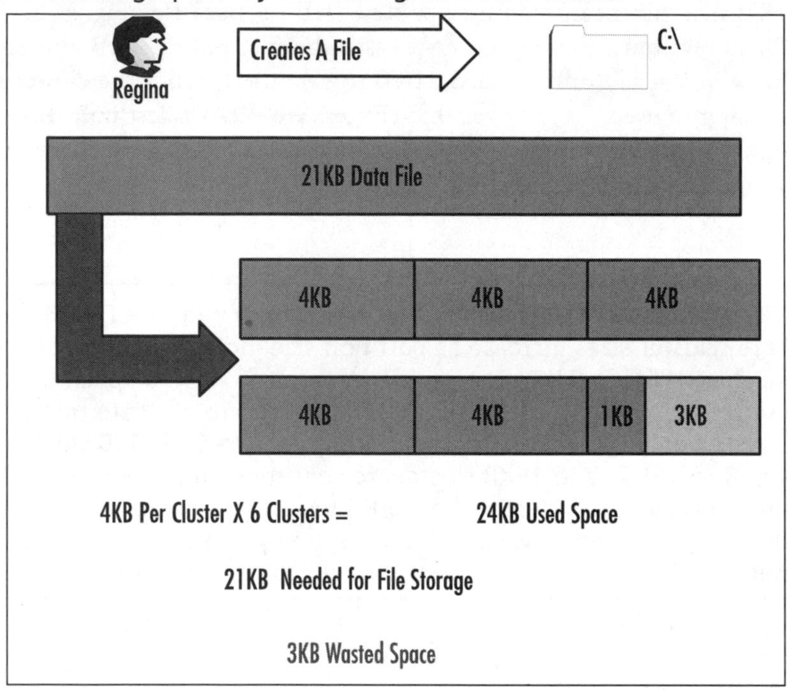

As data is saved to disk, then, Windows breaks it into clusters and writes each cluster to disk in sequential order (or as close to sequential order as possible). However, as you delete files and make changes to the OS, gaps start to appear in between the filled clusters, representing empty space on the disk. As Windows writes more files to disk, it fills in these gaps (see Figure 2.75). This means part of a file will be written in one of these gaps, then the rest of it will be written in the next gap, and so forth. Clusters that make up the file are not contiguous, but are spread out across the disk. This causes your disk to become *fragmented*. Whenever you have parts of the same file spread all over different areas of the disk, disk access will be slower and overall system performance will be degraded because the disk's read head has to travel further to access all the different parts of the file.

Defragmentation is the process of reorganizing your disk so that clusters that make up each file are stored together, instead of being spread all over. Windows Server 2003 provides two tools for performing this rearrangement of data on the disk, a graphical defragmenter and a command-prompt defragmenter.

Figure 2.75 Understanding Why Disks Get Defragmented

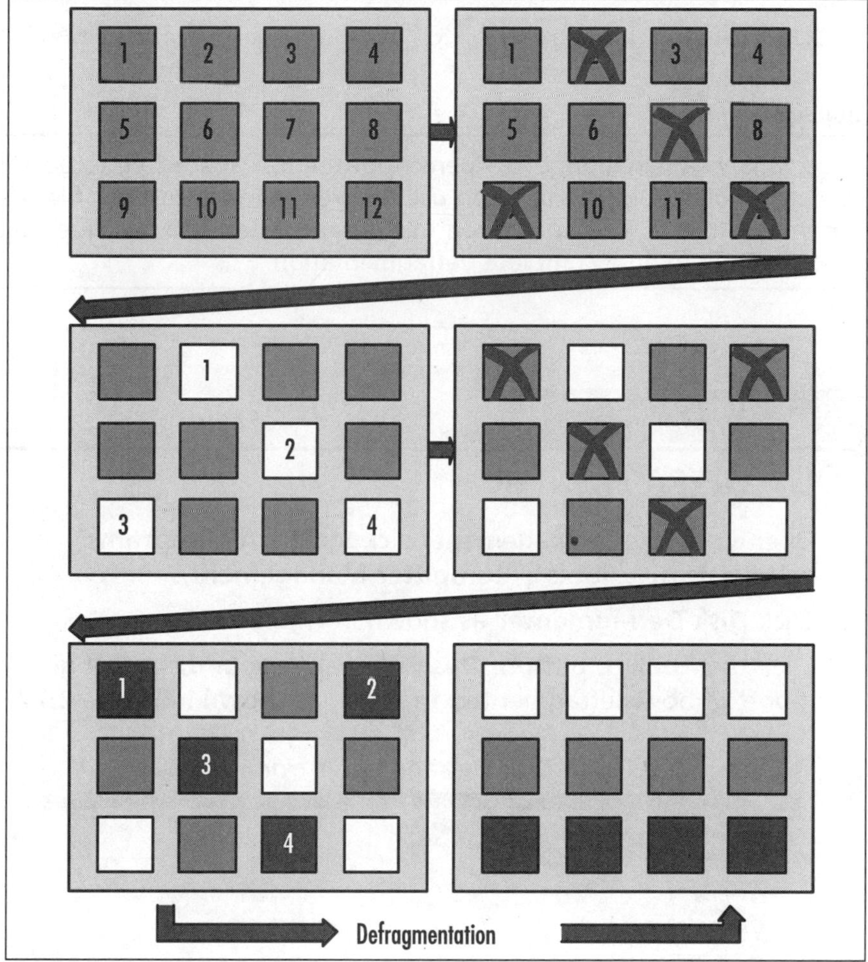

Using the Graphical Defragmenter

You can access the graphical defragmenter in several different ways:

- Click **Start | All Programs | Accessories | System Tools | Disk Defragmenter**.
- Right-click **My Computer**, select **Manage**, and click **Disk Defragmenter** in the left console pane.
- Click **Start | All Programs | Administrative Tools | Computer Management** and click the **Disk Defragmenter** in the left console pane.

For our examples, we will access the Disk Defragmenter via Computer Management. Note that anyone can open the Disk Defragmenter tool, but only an administrator, or someone with an account that has been delegated the authority, can analyze or defragment a volume.

Exercise 2.14 walks you through the process of using Disk Defragmenter.

WARNING

You need to have a minimum of 15 percent of the disk space free to be able to defragment a volume, so the tool can use the free space to sort the file fragments as it rearranges them. You can still run the defragmenter with less free space, but it will not be able to do a complete defragmentation.

EXERCISE 2.14

USING DISK DEFRAGMENTER

1. Open Computer Management (click **Start | All Programs | Administrative Tools | Computer Management**).
2. Click **Disk Defragmenter** as shown in Figure 2.76.
3. Click the **Analyze** button. This will analyze your disks and give you a report of how defragmented they are, as shown in Figure 2.77.

Figure 2.76 Using Disk Defragmenter from the GUI

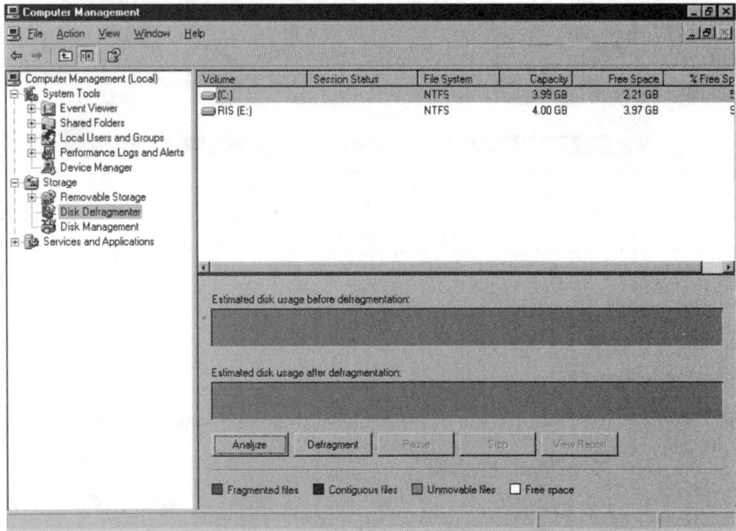

Figure 2.77 Analyzing Your Hard Disk for Defragmentation

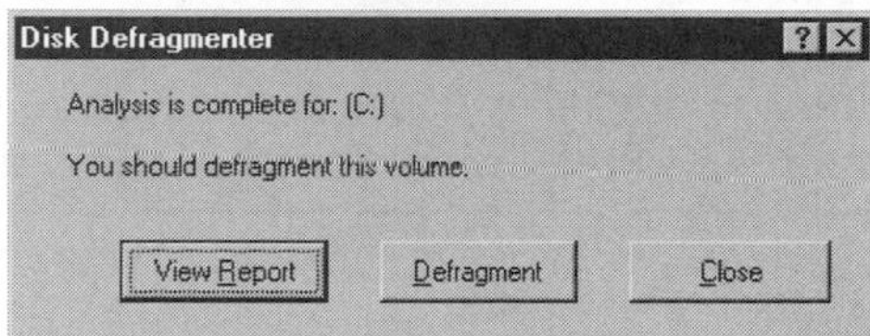

4. Click the **View Report** button to see the status of your disk. This will give you a report similar to the one shown in Figure 2.78.

Figure 2.78 Viewing the Analysis Report

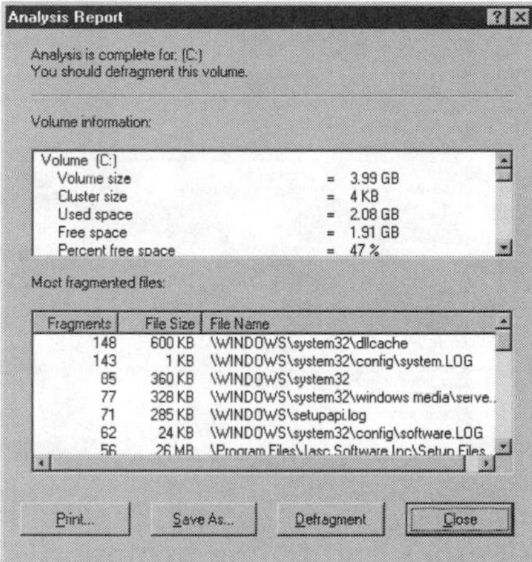

5. At this point, you can click **Close** if you do not want to defragment your disk. If you do want to defragment, click the **Defragment** button to start the process.

NOTE

You cannot defragment volumes on a remote system, only local volumes. You cannot run the Defragmenter while backing up the volume (the Disk Defragmenter will stop and refuse to run). Unlike with some tools, you cannot have more than one instance of Disk Defragmenter open at a time.

6. You will next see the screen shown in Figure 2.79. You can pause or stop the defragmentation process by clicking **Pause** or **Stop** on the **Action** menu. When the defragmentation process is complete, you will be given the option to view a defragmentation report, as shown in Figure 2.80. Click **View Report**.

NOTE

It can take quite some time to defragment a disk that is very large and very fragmented. The amount of time it takes depends on the size of the volume, the amount of fragmentation and the overall speed of the disk.

Figure 2.79 Defragmenting Your Hard Disk

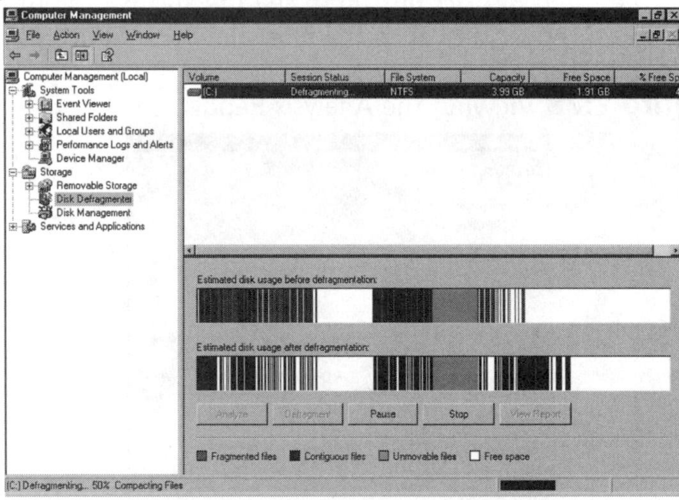

Figure 2.80 Completing Defragmentation

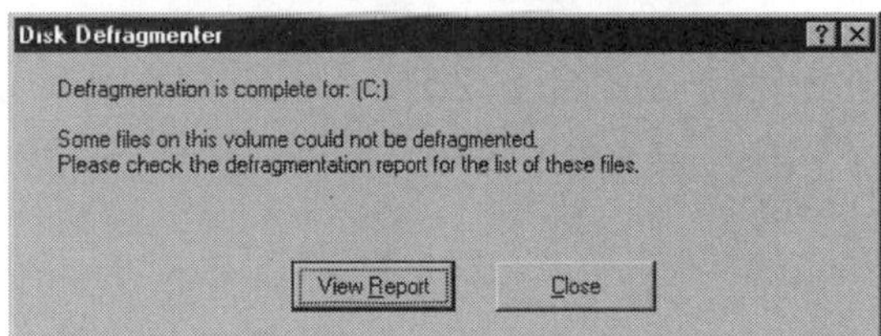

7. Compare the defragmentation report in Figure 2.81 with the analysis report in Figure 2.78. You should see a decrease in file fragmentation. You can print or save your report for later viewing. When finished, click **Close**.

Figure 2.81 Viewing the Defragmentation Report

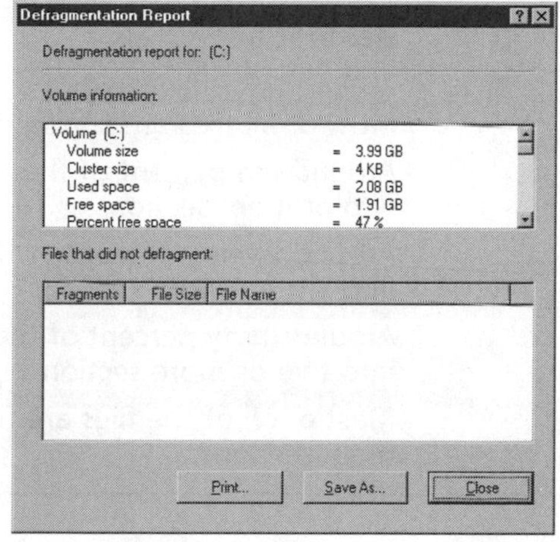

Viewing the Analysis Report

You don't have to really understand the analysis report in order to defragment your disks. The software is smart enough to let you know whether or not you need to defrag. However, a lot of good information can be found in the analysis report. This includes the following:

- **Fragmented files and folders** Displays the paths and names of the most fragmented files on the volume.
- **Volume size**
- **Amount of free space available**
- **Average number of fragments per file** You can use the average number of fragments per file to gauge how fragmented the volume is. Table 2.3 explains the possible averages.

NOTE

Microsoft recommends that you analyze disks on a weekly or monthly basis, depending on the usual rate of fragmentation. However, if you delete or add a large number of files, you should run an analysis afterward, as this can cause the volume to become fragmented. It's also a good idea to analyze the disk after you install new software or upgrade the operating system.

Table 2.3 Describing the Average Number of Fragments per File

Average Number of Fragments per File	Description
1.00	Most or all files are contiguous.
1.10	Around ten percent of the files are fragmented into two or more sections.
1.20	Around twenty percent of the files are fragmented into two or more sections.
1.30	Around thirty percent of the files are fragmented into two or more sections.
2.00	Most or all of the files are fragmented into two or more sections.

Understanding the Disk Defragmenter Interface

The Disk Defragmenter provides you with analysis reports and defragmentation reports to alert you to the fragmentation status of your disks. However, the graphical interface of the defragmenter tool also provides much of the same information if you know what to look for. The screenshot in Figure 2.82 was taken immediately after running the defragmentation utility as described in Exercise 2.15. Let's analyze the display to determine the information that is available.

Notice that Disk Defragmenter runs in a standard MMC, which gives it a familiar feel, with the console tree in the left pane and the details pane on the right. On the right side, the pane is split into a top and a bottom section. The top section shows the volumes and partitions on the machine. The bottom section shows a graphical view of the fragmentation status of the selected volume. There are two bars in the bottom pane, which indicate the following:

- Estimated disk usage before defragmentation
- Estimated disk usage after defragmentation

By examining these bars, you can see the status of the disk before the defragmentation and the changes that have occurred afterward. These bars are obviously too small to list every cluster on the disk, but they do provide an accurate representation of how fragmented the volume is.

Table 2.4 explains the color codes used in these two bars. After running Disk Defragmenter, the goal is to see most of the red in the top bar replaced with blue.

Table 2.4 Understanding the Estimated Disk Usage Bars in Disk Defragmenter

Color	Description
Red	Most of the clusters are fragmented files.
Blue	Most of the clusters are contiguous files.
Green	Most of the clusters are files that cannot be moved from their current location. This could include paging files, or files used by the file system.
White	Most of the clusters are free space.

Figure 2.82 Viewing Your Disk After Defragmentation

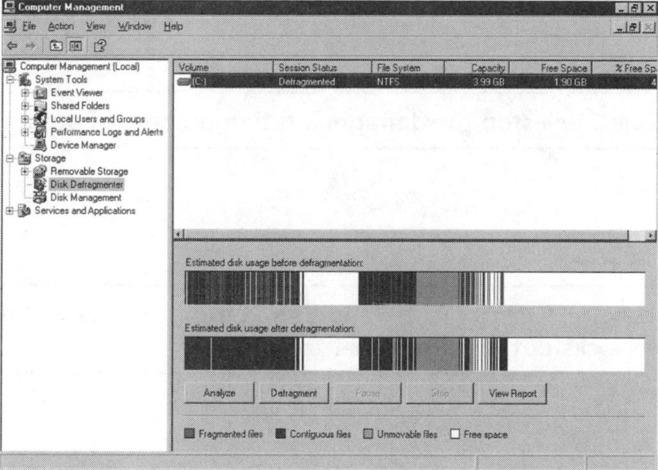

Using defrag.exe

If you are comfortable with the Disk Defragmenter tool but prefer a character-based utility, you will feel right at home with defrag.exe. It is the command prompt equivalent of Disk Defragmenter. defrag.exe does everything that Disk Defragmenter does and in addition, it supports scripting. You can use defrag.exe in a script to schedule analysis and defragmentation of your servers. Scripting is the primary reason to use defrag.exe instead of Disk Defragmenter. Table 2.5 explains the parameters for defrag.exe. defrag.exe uses the following syntax:

```
defrag <volume> [-a] [-f] [-v] [-?]
  volume  drive letter or mount point (d: or d:\vol\mountpoint)
```

Table 2.5 Understanding defrag.exe Parameters

Parameters	Description
Volume	The drive letter or mount point to be defragmented.
A	Analyzes the volume and displays an analysis summary indicating whether you should defragment the volume.
F	Forces defragmentation of the volume when low on free space.
V	Displays the complete analysis and defragmentation reports (not just a summary). When used with the /**a** switch, it displays only the analysis report. When used alone, it displays both the analysis and defragmentation reports.
?	Displays help.

Exam Warning

Pressing **CTRL+C** will stop the defragmentation process of defrag.exe.

Exam Warning

You cannot run Disk Defragmenter and defrag.exe at the same time. Whichever you open first locks out the other one.

Defragmentation Best Practices

As discussed, defragmenting your disks is a good thing. It speeds up access to your files and can make more free space available. However, for best results, here is a summary of the guidelines to follow when defragmenting your servers:

- Make sure that you have at least 15 percent of your volume's total space free. Disk Defragmenter needs to have an area to sort fragments while it is rearranging your volume. If you can't meet this requirement due to low disk space, you will only get a partial defragmentation.
- Always try to schedule your defragmentations during non-production hours. You don't want your users accessing files while the volume is being defragmented. This can cause two problems: users' performance will suffer because of the resources being consumed by Disk Defragmenter and your defragmentation will take longer.
- Always analyze before you defragment to make sure that you actually need to. You should analyze any time a large number of files are added to your server or after installing software on your server. Both of these actions tend to cause high levels of fragmentation.

EXAM WARNING

If the file system has marked your volume as "dirty," it cannot be defragmented. Use fsutil.exe (discussed earlier) to query the volume to determine if it is dirty. If it is dirty, run **chkdsk.exe** on it first to enable you to defragment it (using chkdsk is covered later in this chapter).

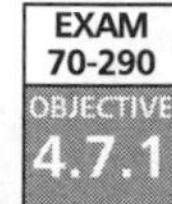

Configuring and Monitoring Disk Quotas

The capability to set disk quotas is a feature that was on the "wish list" of Windows NT administrators for a long time. Users tend to find a way of consuming every bit (and byte) of space that you offer them. Third-party products provided for setting quotas with NT, and built-in support for disk quotas was first introduced in Windows 2000. Disk quota support has been carried over to Windows XP and Windows Server 2003. In the following sections, we discuss how to enable, configure, and monitor disk quotas.

Overview of Disk Quotas

Disk quotas enable you to track and limit disk space usage on NTFS volumes. You can use disk quotas for two purposes:

- To audit how much space your users are using (enabling quotas without limiting disk space).
- To limit your users to a set amount of space (enabling quotas and setting limits on disk space).

Users are warned when they approach the specified limit. The administrator can set the level at which the warning occurs. After the limit is reached, a user can no longer save data to the volume without first deleting some files to create new space. You can also set the system to log an event to the event log when a user reaches either the warning level or the disk space limit.

Disk quota amounts are calculated based on file ownership. The size of the file is charged against its owner's limit. The only time this poses a problem is when users share single files. For example, if you have the correct permissions, you can write to a file that someone else owns and it would count against the other user's limit.

Disk quotas are set at the volume level only. You cannot create different quotas for individual folders within a volume. If you need to set different quotas for the same users on different folders, you can put those folders on separate volumes or purchase third-party software that allows for more granular setting of quotas. Likewise, you cannot set quotas at the physical disk level. If a disk has three volumes on it, each volume is managed separately. You must have administrative rights to assign quotas.

NOTE

Quotas can be set on both local and shared network volumes. You can also set quotas on volumes that are on shared removable media. However, you cannot set quotas on a volume unless it is formatted with NTFS.

Use disk quotas in the following situations:

- You have limited shared storage available on public servers and need to ensure that the disks don't become full.
- You want to keep a log of how much disk space is being consumed by each user.

EXAM WARNING

Compressed files are counted against the quota limit based on their uncompressed size. For example, if you have a 100MB file that is compressed to 85MB, 100MB is counted toward your limit. This means a user cannot compress files to "get around" or extend the quota limit.

Enabling and Configuring Disk Quotas

You can enable disk quotas by accessing the **Properties** sheet for a volume and using the **Quota** tab. If you do not see a Quota tab on the Properties sheet, either you do not have administrative rights on the machine or the volume is formatted with FAT or FAT32. Remember that disk quotas can only be configured on NTFS volumes.

Exercise 2.15 walks you through the process of enabling disk quotas and configuring limits for users, but before we walk through the steps, we will discuss the details of the Quota tab (Figure 2.83). You need to be familiar with all the options on this tab for the exam.

The first thing you see on the Quota tab is the "stop light." It indicates the status of disk quotas on the volume:

- When the light is red, disk quotas are disabled.
- When the light is yellow, the system is rebuilding disk quota information.
- When the light is green, disk quotas are enabled and active.

When you select the check box next to **Enable quota management**, the light goes from red to yellow to green. However, the light may appear to go straight to green. This just means that the quota information was built very quickly and didn't register on the light.

After you enable disk quotas, you must configure how they will be used. By default, users are not denied disk space or warned about the amount of disk space they are using. This is the proper setting if you are only using disk quotas to track how much space each user is using, but if you want to limit the amount of space available to users, you must further configure the quotas feature. This is where the **Deny disk space to users exceeding quota limit** check box comes into play. When you check this checkbox, Windows will deny additional disk space to anyone who exceeds his or her limit.

You can either set limits for users individually by using the **Quota Entries** button or you can configure a default limit that will apply to everyone. You can also import quota settings from another volume. This is useful if you want to set the quotas identically on a number of different volumes.

NOTE

You can set individual quota settings based on user accounts, but you cannot set quotas based on group accounts. Also note that you cannot set a limit on disk usage for members of the built-in administrators group. You can, however, specify a warning level.

There are two settings to configure for each user (or for all users as the default): a limit level and a warning level:

- Next to **Limit disk space to**, there are two boxes. The first box is a text field into which you can type a number. The second box is a drop-down box that contains a disk measurement unit (KB, MB, GB, TB, PB, EB). By entering a number in the first box and choosing a measurement from the second box, you can restrict each user to a disk space limit ranging from 1KB to 6 EB. The default limit is 1KB.
- Directly under the limits boxes are identical **Set warning level to** boxes. Quota warnings are configured in the same ways as quota limits. You should set the warning level to a smaller number than the disk limit so that users will know they are approaching their limits before reaching them.

Table 2.6 explains the different disk measurement options available for setting limits and warnings.

Table 2.6 Understanding Disk Measurements

Measurement	Description
KB	KB stands for kilobyte. One kilobyte equals one thousand bytes (1,024 bytes in decimal).
MB	MB stands for megabyte. One megabyte equals one million bytes (1,048,576 bytes in decimal).
GB	GB stands for gigabit. One gigabit equals one billion bytes (1,073,741,824 bytes in decimal).

Continued

Table 2.6 Understanding Disk Measurements

Measurement	Description
TB	TB stands for terabyte. One terabyte equals one thousand billion bytes (1,099,511,627,776 bytes in decimal—that is a thousand gigabytes).
PB	PB stands for petabyte. One petabyte equals one thousand terabytes (1,125,899,906,842,624 bytes in decimal).
EB	EB stands for exabyte. One exabyte equals one quintillion bytes (a billion gigabytes—1,152,921,504,606,846,976 bytes in decimal).

Finally, you can configure the logging options. Under **Select the quota logging options for this volume** you have two options:

- Log event when a user exceeds their quota limit
- Log event when a user exceeds their warning level

Both options are disabled by default and either or both can be enabled by checking the corresponding check box(es). Both settings log events to the System log of the Event Viewer. Logging options are set only on a per-volume basis; there is no setting for logging on an individual user's Quota Settings page.

Note

The limit and warning levels you set on the volume's Quota properties sheet will apply to each new user unless/until you set an individual quota setting for that user in the **Quota Entries** console.

Now that you have a good understanding of the Quota tab, go through the steps of setting it up and configuring quotas for a user by completing Exercise 2.15.

Exam Warning

If you convert a volume from FAT or FAT32 to NTFS, ownership of all files in place at the time of the upgrade are automatically assigned to the administrator. This means that users can continue to write to those files without having them count towards their own quota limits.

EXERCISE 2.15

ENABLING DISK QUOTAS AND SETTING QUOTA LIMITS

1. In Windows Explorer or My Computer, right-click the volume on which you want to set quotas and select **Properties** from the context menu. In this exercise, we enable quotas on the C: drive. Note that to manage quotas on a remote computer, you'll need to first map a network drive for the remote volume on which you want to set or manage quotas.
2. Click the **Quota** tab, as shown in Figure 2.83.
3. Check the check box next to **Enable quota management** to enable disk quotas for the C: drive.
4. Check the check box next to **Deny disk space to users exceeding quota limit** to enforce limits.
5. Click the **Quota Entries** button to open the **Quota Entries** console, as shown in Figure 2.84.

Figure 2.83 Enabling Disk Quotas

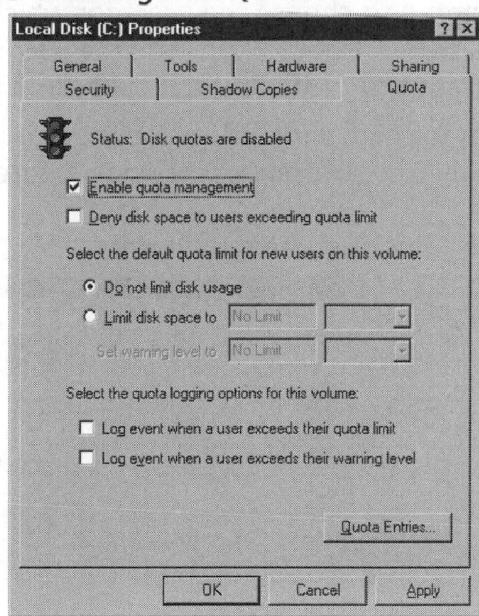

Figure 2.84 Viewing Quota Entries

Quota Entries for Local Disk (C:)

Quota Edit View Help

Status	Name	Logon Name	Amount Used	Quota Limit	Warning Level	Percent Used
OK	TC	W2K3-SRV\TC	0 bytes	100 KB	50 KB	0
OK	Family	W2K3-SRV\Family	0 bytes	150 KB	125 KB	0
OK	Paul	W2K3-SRV\Paul	0 bytes	1 MB	512 KB	0
OK	Margie	W2K3-SRV\Margie	0 bytes	5 MB	3 MB	0
OK	Salas	W2K3-SRV\Salas	0 bytes	6 MB	3 MB	0
OK	Don	W2K3-SRV\Don	0 bytes	50 MB	40 MB	0
OK	Marilyn	W2K3-SRV\Marilyn	0 bytes	50 MB	40 MB	0
OK	Malina	W2K3-SRV\Malina	0 bytes	55 MB	50 MB	0
OK	Gary	W2K3-SRV\Gary	0 bytes	150 MB	140 MB	0
OK	Holli	W2K3-SRV\Holli	0 bytes	150 MB	140 MB	0
OK	Landry	W2K3-SRV\Landry	0 bytes	155 MB	150 MB	0
OK	Kirk	W2K3-SRV\Kirk	0 bytes	200 MB	185 MB	0
OK	Vigil	W2K3-SRV\Vigil	0 bytes	210 MB	200 MB	0
OK	Mike	W2K3-SRV\Mike	0 bytes	240 MB	225 MB	0
OK	Harlene	W2K3-SRV\Harlene	0 bytes	250 MB	225 MB	0
OK	Bagley	W2K3-SRV\Bagley	0 bytes	260 MB	245 MB	0
OK	Tal	W2K3-SRV\Tal	0 bytes	500 MB	450 MB	0
OK	Mary	W2K3-SRV\Mary	0 bytes	525 MB	500 MB	0
OK	Lassiter	W2K3-SRV\Lassiter	0 bytes	600 MB	585 MB	0
OK	Chad	W2K3-SRV\Chad	0 bytes	4 EB	3 EB	0
OK	Sarah	W2K3-SRV\Sarah	2.82 MB	5 EB	4 EB	0
OK	Todd	W2K3-SRV\Todd	0 bytes	6 EB	5 EB	0
OK		NT AUTHORITY\NETWORK SERVICE	261 KB	No Limit	No Limit	N/A
OK		BUILTIN\Administrators	2.33 GB	No Limit	No Limit	N/A
OK		NT AUTHORITY\LOCAL SERVICE	218 KB	No Limit	No Limit	N/A

25 total item(s), 1 selected.

6. Click the **Quota** menu bar.
7. Select **New Quota Entry** from the menu.
8. You are prompted to choose the users for which you want to add quotas, as shown in Figure 2.85. Type the user's name in the box and click **Check Name** to verify that the user exists in the account database.
9. If the name is verified, click **OK** to continue. You next have to customize the quota entry for the user, as shown in Figure 2.86.

Figure 2.85 Choosing Users to Restrict

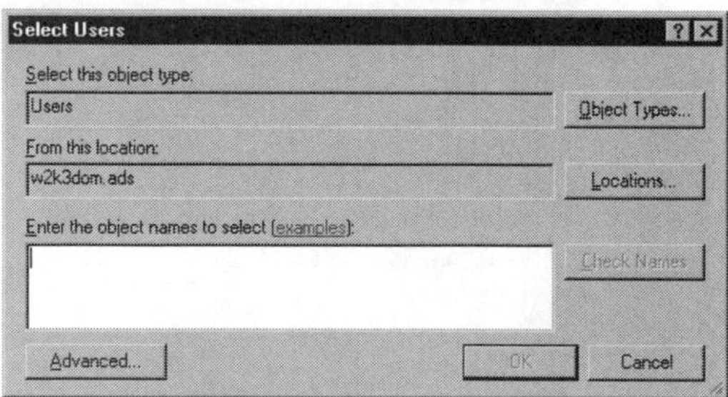

Figure 2.86 Configuring Limits and Warnings

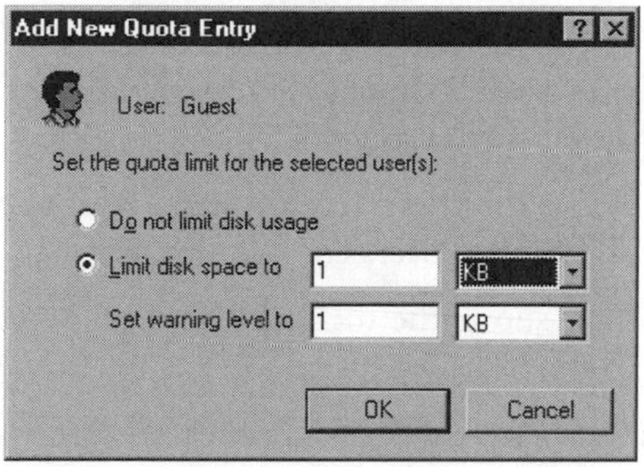

10. Select **Limit disk space to** and enter the amount of space you wish to allow the user to use on the volume. Select a unit of measurement.
11. Set the warning level for your user in the same way.
12. Click **OK** to save the settings and add the user to the Quota Entries list.

Monitoring Disk Quotas

Now that you know how to enable disk quotas, we will discuss how to analyze the quota settings and monitor disk usage. Disk quota settings are accessed and disk usage is monitored via the Quota Entries console, as previously shown in Figure 2.84.

EXAM WARNING

For the exam, you need to be able to look at this screen and analyze the disk quota entries that are shown.

The Quota Entries console displays seven items in regard to each user. You can sort by the columns by clicking the corresponding section of the column title bar or by using the View menu (**View | Arrange Items | by...**). For example, if you want to sort by the amount of disk spaced used, click on the **Amount Used** bar. This will arrange the user accounts in order of least to greatest space used. Clicking the same column header again will rearrange the accounts in the opposite order (greatest to least).

- **Status** This indicates how well the user is complying with the quota limit. There are three possible settings: **OK**, **Warning**, or **Above Limit**. A status of **OK** indicates that the user hasn't reached the warning or limit level yet. **Warning** indicates that the user has reached the warning level, but not the limit level. **Above**

Limit indicates that the user has passed both the warning and limit levels. Sorting by status makes it easy to find all users that have exceeded their limits.

- **Name** This is the user's full name as it appears in Local Users and Groups or Active Directory Users and Computers.
- **Logon Name** This is the user's account name as it appears in Local Users and Groups or Active Directory Users and Computers.
- **Amount Used** This shows the total amount of disk space currently being used by the user.
- **Quota Limit** This shows the level at which the user will no longer be allowed to save data to this volume.
- **Warning Level** This shows the level at which the user will be warned when saving data to this volume.
- **Percent Used** This displays the percentage of allocated space that has been used by the user. Sorting by Percent Used is a good way to discover which users may run out of space soon.

NOTE

When you have created a quota entry for an individual user, you won't be able to delete the entry unless that user no longer owns any files on the volume. You can move the files to a different volume or you, as administrator, can take ownership of the files to enable you to delete the user's quota entry. If you try to delete an entry when the user still owns files on the volume, you will be shown a list of those files and given the option to 1) permanently delete them, 2) take ownership of them, or 3) move them to a specified location on another volume.

Head of the Class...

Seeing SIDs in Quota Entries

When you open the Quota Entries console for the first time, you might see long numbers (see Figure 2.87) instead of logon names for some or all users. This is because quota entry information is based on a user's security identifier (SID), rather than on the username. When Quota Entries is opened for the first time, the system must resolve all the SIDs to logon names. You'll see a message to that effect ("Retrieving Name") in the Name column. After this occurs for the first time, the system caches the information into each user's profile so it won't have to be retrieved every time the console is opened. However, this caching can pose a problem if you rename a user account, because the old name might continue to show in quota entries. To rectify this, press **F5** on the keyboard or click **View | Refresh**. This will cause Quota Entries to re-associate all the SIDs with their current names.

Continued

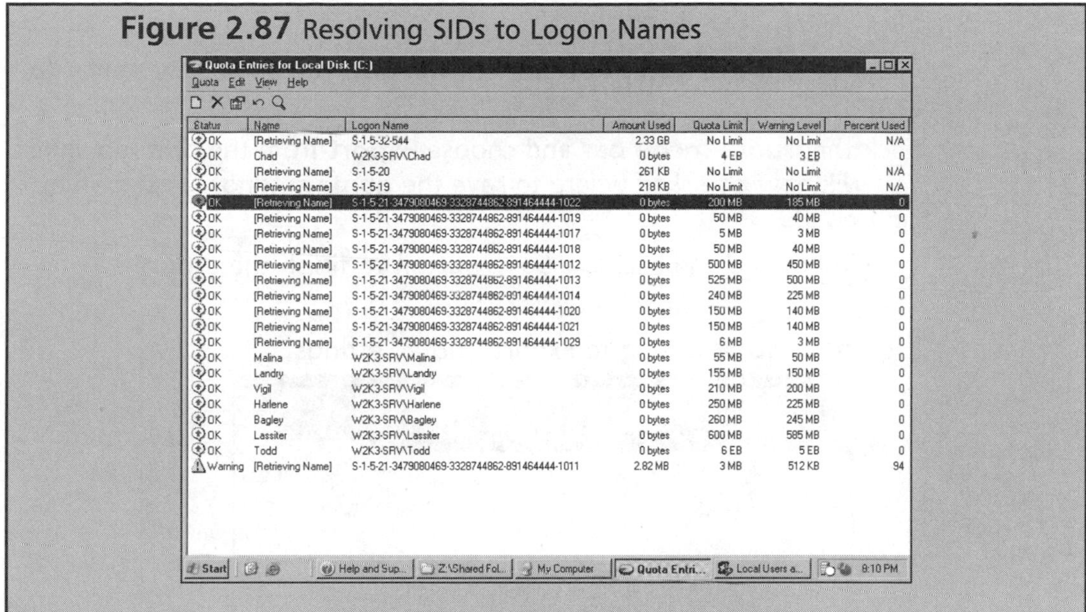

Figure 2.87 Resolving SIDs to Logon Names

Exporting and Importing Quota Settings

If you have multiple volumes that contain users' data then you will probably want to apply the same quota settings to all volumes. Also, if you migrate your users' data from one volume to another, then you need an easy way to reapply all the disk quotas.

There are a few different ways to copy disk quotas from one volume to another. If you open the Quota Entries window (as shown in Figure 2.88) for both volumes, you can drag and drop quota limits between the two windows. You can also export all quota settings to a file and import them to another volume. Exercise 2.16 walks you through exporting quota settings, and Exercise 2.17 walks you through importing quota settings.

NOTE

Unless your user account has been delegated the appropriate authority, you must be a member of the Administrators group on the local computer to export and import disk quotas.

EXERCISE 2.16

EXPORTING QUOTA SETTINGS

1. Open My Computer.
2. Right-click the volume you want to manage and choose **Properties** from the pop-up menu.

3. Click the **Quota** tab.
4. Click the **Quota Entries** button. This will give you a window similar to Figure 2.88.
5. Click the **Quota menu bar** and choose **Export** from the drop-down list. You will now be asked where to save the quota settings, as shown in Figure 2.89.
6. Type in a name and click the **Save** button to finish the export.

Figure 2.88 Choosing to Export Quota Settings

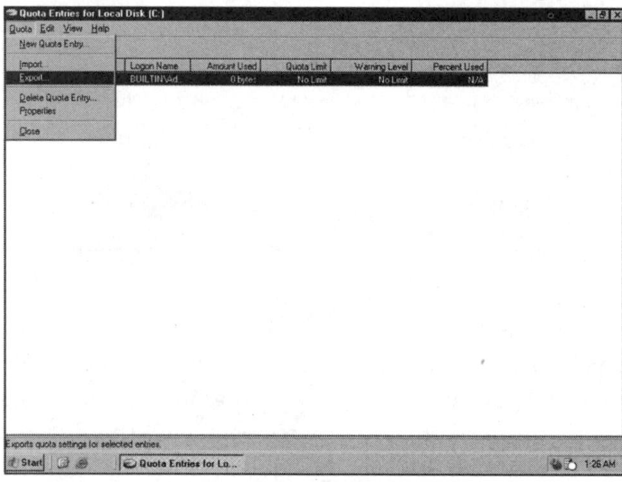

Figure 2.89 Exporting Quota Settings

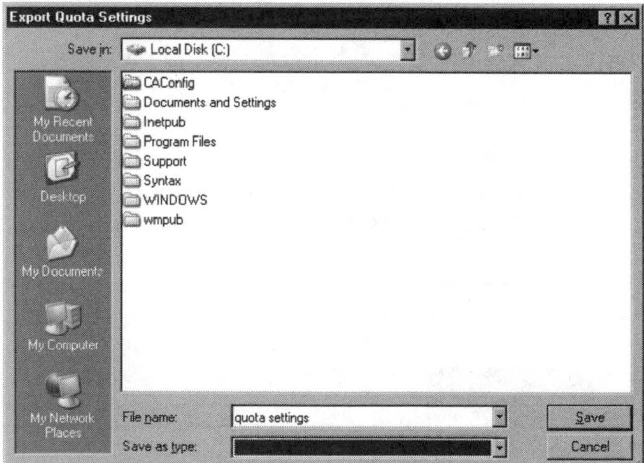

EXERCISE 2.17

IMPORTING QUOTA SETTINGS

The steps for importing quota settings are very similar to the steps for exporting quota settings.

1. Open **My Computer**.
2. Right-click the volume you want to manage and choose **Properties** from the pop-up menu.
3. Click the **Quota** tab.
4. Click the **Quota Entries** button. This will give you a window similar to Figure 2.90.

Figure 2.90 Choosing to Import Disk Quotas

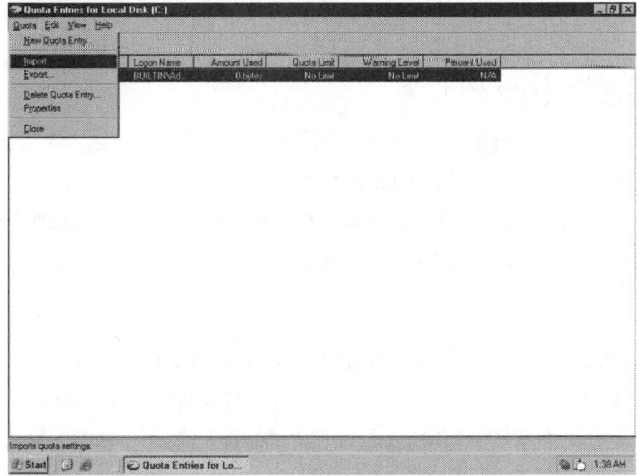

5. Click the **Quota menu bar** and choose **Import** from the drop-down list. You will now be asked which quota settings file to import, as shown in Figure 2.91.
6. Navigate to the quota settings file and click **Open** to import the settings.

Figure 2.91 Importing Disk Quotas

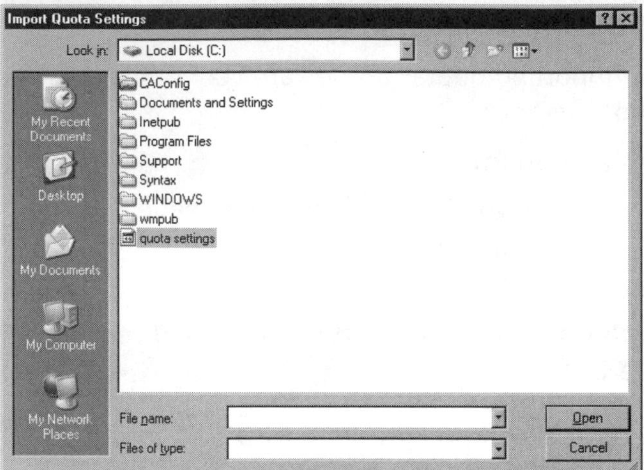

Disk Quota Best Practices

Disk quotas are a powerful feature that gives Windows Server 2003 administrators flexible control over disk usage. However, using them incorrectly can be disastrous. Don't let this keep you from using disk quotas — just learn to use them intelligently. Here are few guidelines that will ensure that enabling disk quotas makes your job as an administrator easier, not more difficult:

- Set default limits so that all users are restricted in the amount of space they can use by default. Always make your default settings as restrictive as possible, while still providing users with enough space to do their work. It is easier to give users more space if needed than to take space away. Remember that this is only a default setting. It is not a mandatory setting for all your users; it only applies to those user accounts that do not have specific individual settings configured.
- Use reasonable quota limits. Don't just take the amount of space available and divide it equally among your users. Sit down and calculate a fair limit based on user needs. Not everyone needs the same amount of disk space. Power users may need more than standard users. Those who work with and save large graphic or video files need more space than those who work primarily with plain text files.
- Be realistic in setting the quotas and stick to them unless or until there is a real need to change them. If you set the default limit at 50MB when you know most users are using 200MB, you are setting yourself up for trouble. Try not to get into

the habit of setting quotas excessively low and then increasing them when users complain. It is better to give users the right amount of space up front, and be less flexible about increasing the amount. If users know they can easily get their allocations increased by complaining, they will be less motivated to properly manage their files.

- Delete quota entries for users who no longer need to store files on the volume. Delete or move their files to another volume to free space for those who need to store data on the volume.
- When calculating the amount of disk space available for allocating quotas, remember to take into account NTFS overhead. Files can contain up to 64KB of metadata (information about the file) that is not counted against a user's quota, but does take up space on the disk.

EXAM WARNING

Each user must have at least 2MB of disk space to log on and load his or her profile. Make sure the default limit is always set to 2MB or higher.

Using fsutil.exe to Manage Disk Quotas

If you prefer using a command-line tool instead of the graphical interface, you can perform many of the tasks involved in managing disk quotas with the command-line utility fsutil.exe. Use the command *fsutil quota* with one of the following parameters to perform quota-related tasks:

- **fsutil quota disable <volumepathname>** To disable quotas on the volume.
- **fsutil quota enforce <volumepathname >** To enable quota enforcement on the volume.
- **fsutil quota modify <volumepathname>** To create a new quota or change an existing one.
- **fsutil quota query <volumepathname>** To list existing quota entries.
- **fsutil quota track <volumepathname>** To track disk usage on the volume.
- **fsutil quota violations** To display detected quota violations.

The *fsutil* commands can be used in a script to automate quota tasks (for example, to set a specified quota limit each time you add a new user).

Implementing RAID Solutions

There are several options for setting up a RAID environment. You can use either software-based RAID or hardware-based RAID. Software-based RAID is more cost effective because you don't have to purchase anything extra, but it works only in certain situations and performance is not as good. You cannot easily change from one RAID type to another. If you want to change you must do the following:

1. Back up your data.
2. Erase your existing RAID configuration.
3. Create a new RAID configuration.
4. Restore your data from backup.

For the exam, you will need to be able to determine which RAID solution is best for a given environment. This section covers the differences between hardware and software RAID and when it is best to use one instead of the other.

Understanding Windows Server 2003 RAID

Windows Server 2003 RAID is software-based RAID. With software-based RAID, all the physical disks are presented to the operating system as they are and the operating system manages them in a RAID configuration. The benefit is that software-based RAID is built into the operating system. The drawback is that the operating system incurs the entire overhead for maintaining the RAID volume. Additionally, there are limitations that apply to software-based RAID that do not apply to hardware-based RAID. You do not have as many RAID options with software-based RAID. Windows Server 2003 supports only three levels of RAID: RAID 0, RAID 1, and RAID 5. In the next sections, we discuss each in more detail.

RAID Level 0

RAID level 0 utilizes disk striping. A RAID level 0 volume in Windows Server 2003 is called a striped volume. This version of RAID does not provide any fault tolerance. It is sometimes said that RAID 0 is really "AID" rather than "RAID" because there is no redundancy of data provided. It does, however, provide the best performance of any single RAID level, and that is its purpose. Level 0 can be implemented as either a software or hardware solution and is supported by all controllers.

Because the operating system must be loaded before the striped volume is initialized and made available, a level 0 array cannot be used for the boot or system partitions. RAID level 0 should be used when you are trying to get maximum performance from your drives. Level 0 is best for data that is not mission-critical or that is backed up regularly. It is good for audio/video streaming, gaming and other applications where performance is important. Windows Server 2003's RAID level 0 works with a minimum of two disks up to a maximum of 32 disks.

RAID Level 1

RAID level 1 utilizes disk mirroring. A RAID level 1 volume in Windows Server 2003 is called a mirrored volume, and consists of two identical disks. An exact duplicate of the data is written to each disk. This version of RAID does provide fault tolerance and is the only one of Windows Server 2003's software-based RAID levels that can be used for the boot and system partitions. Level 1 is the simplest RAID implementation and can be implemented as either a software or hardware RAID solution.

RAID level 1 should be used when you want to provide fault tolerance for the boot and/or system partitions or if you need fault tolerance and have only two disks available. Level 1 is the most expensive form of Windows Server 2003 RAID because only 50 percent of the disk space that must be purchased is used for data.

RAID Level 5

RAID level 5 utilizes disk striping with parity. A RAID level 5 volume in Windows Server 2003 is called a RAID-5 volume. As with disk striping, a RAID-5 volume cannot be used for the boot or system partition because the operating system must be loaded first to initialize the volume and make it available. The parity information is distributed across multiple disks and the parity for a given block of data is always on a different disk from the disks on which the data itself is stored. This provides the fault tolerance and enables the data to be regenerated if a single disk in the array fails.

RAID-5 volumes require a minimum of three disks and work with up to 32 disks. You should use RAID level 5 when you need fault tolerance with better performance and drive utilization than RAID level 1 can provide. RAID 5 is one of the most popular RAID implementations. However, software RAID 5 is considerably slower than its hardware counterpart, because of the overhead involved in calculating the parity information. It is better for read-intensive applications as opposed to write-intensive ones.

Hardware RAID

As the name implies, hardware-based RAID uses special hardware to create RAID volumes. A RAID controller is added to your server. The controller handles the overhead of managing the RAID volumes, and this improves performance by removing the processing burden from the operating system. This also removes many of the restrictions imposed by software-based RAID.

Because the RAID controller presents the RAID volume to the OS as one disk, you can use hardware-based RAID 0 and RAID 5 volumes for the boot and system partitions. Hardware-based RAID provides you with many more RAID levels to choose from, including the following:

- **RAID 2** Splits data at the bit level and spreads it across two types of disks: data disks and redundancy disks, with redundant bits calculated with Hamming codes (a type of Error Correcting Code or ECC). Not often used due to cost and complexity. Requires a special RAID controller card.

- **RAID 3** Splits data at the byte level and stripes it across several disks, with one disk as a dedicated parity disk. Requires a RAID hardware controller; good for editing very large files.
- **RAID 4** Stripes data across multiple disks in blocks (instead of bits or bytes) and uses a dedicated parity disk. Requires a RAID hardware controller; used for the same applications as RAID 3 and 5.
- **RAID 6** Stripes data across multiple disks in blocks like RAID 4 and 5, but creates duplicate sets of parity for each data stripe. More fault tolerant than RAID 5 because it can recover the data if two disks in the array fail, but performance is not as good in write operations. Requires a special hardware controller; used for data that is especially critical and requires the extra fault tolerance.
- **RAID 7** Proprietary RAID implementation of Storage Computer Corporation. Uses multi-level cache and a special processor to manage the array. Requires special proprietary hardware; provides very high performance.
- **Nested RAID levels** Arrays that use a combination of the single levels. For example, RAID level 0+1 and 1+0 (also called 01 and 10) use "mirrored stripes" and "striped mirrors" respectively. Level 0+1 creates a stripe set and then creates a mirror of it, so you have two identical stripe sets. Level 1+0 stripes data across mirror sets. This enables you to have the performance advantages of level 0 along with the fault tolerance of level 1. Other nested RAID levels include 5+3 (also called 53), 3+0 (30), 0+5 (05), 5+0 (50), 1+5 (15) and 5+1 (51).

The only real drawback to hardware-based RAID is the price. Server-grade RAID controllers typically cost $750 and up. This can add up quickly when you have a large number of servers.

RAID Best Practices

After you have made the decision to use a RAID volume, you need to determine which solution best fits your needs. Will it be hardware RAID or software RAID? Disk striping or disk mirroring? How should you set it up? There are no hard, fast rules, only recommendations, but the following provide some general guidelines to follow when setting up your RAID volumes:

- Using Hardware RAID
  - Use hardware RAID whenever possible because it offers the best performance.
  - Try to use identical hardware for all your servers. This makes it easier to recover if you have a disaster.

    - Always keep spare disks on hand. When you lose one drive (with most RAID levels), you no longer have any fault tolerance. You need to be able to replace failed hardware as quickly as possible. (This also applies to software RAID.)
    - Keep RAID controllers updated with the current firmware revision.
    - Always back up your data before updating the firmware on RAID controllers.
- Using Software RAID
    - Use mirrored volumes for the boot and system partitions.
    - Use RAID-5 volumes for database disks (e.g., Exchange and SQL servers).
    - Use striped volumes on database servers' disks that contain transaction logs (for example, Exchange and SQL servers).
    - Use striped volumes for disks that are used for printer spooling.

TEST DAY TIP

When Microsoft refers to RAID on the test, always assume they are talking about software-based RAID unless they specifically refer to hardware-based RAID.

Understanding and Using Remote Storage

There are two ways to store files, on disks or on backup media. The benefit of disks is that you can get to the data rather quickly. The drawback is that disks cost more than backup media. On the flip side, although backup media is less expensive than disks, it doesn't lend itself as well to the purposes of end users because the data is not immediately available to them; they have to request to get their data restored from backup. This slows down the process for both users and administrators. Remote Storage is Microsoft's solution to this dilemma.

Understanding Remote Storage Concepts

Remote Storage gives you the best of both worlds. It provides fast access to data stored on disks and archival capabilities for data that isn't frequently used, and best of all, it handles switching between the two. It automates the archival process and makes accessing archived data easy for the end user.

Consider your personal data. How much of it do you use on a daily basis? Could you back up the files you only use occasionally to tape? Most people would say, "I see the benefit in backing up my files to tape to save space on the server. I just do not want to have to go through the restoration process if I need a file. I would prefer to leave everything on disk to eliminate the hassle factor."

With Remote Storage, that hassle factor is eliminated because the server backs up seldom-used files for you automatically, and then automatically restores them when you attempt to access them.

What is Remote Storage?

Remote Storage provides a means of extending the disk space on your servers without having to buy more hard disks. Instead, you use a tape or a magneto-optical (MO) disk library to archive less-frequently used files. It costs significantly less per megabyte to buy a library full of tapes compared to equivalent storage space on hard disks.

After it is set up, Remote Storage runs on autopilot. You tell Remote Storage which volume(s) to manage and you specify how much free space you want to remain available on your managed volume. When the amount of free space drops below that level, Remote Storage kicks in and moves enough files to the media library to bring the disk back within your predefined parameters. A *managed volume* refers to a disk volume in Windows whose files are monitored and managed by Remote Storage.

One big advantage of Remote Storage is that all the files on the server look the same to the end user. When a user needs to open a file, he simply double-clicks it. If the file has not yet been moved to tape, it is opened immediately. If the file has been moved to tape, Remote Storage retrieves it from storage and puts a copy on the local disk (this is called a cached copy). Users might notice a delay while this takes place, but they do not have to take any extra steps to retrieve the file. After the file is cached, it will be automatically opened for the user.

EXAM WARNING

Remote Storage is not the same thing as a backup. Backups should still be part of your daily routine. You should regularly back up the server's local volumes as well as the Removable Storage database and the Remote Storage database.

Storage Levels

Remote storage has two defined storage levels. The levels exist in a hierarchical structure:

- Local storage is the top level. It contains the NTFS disks of the computer that is running Remote Storage.
- Remote storage is the bottom level. This is the library that is connected to the server running Remote Storage.

Remote Storage keeps as much information as possible in the top level for faster access. Only when this level is reaching its storage limit is the data moved to the bottom level.

Head of the Class...

Understanding Libraries

Libraries hold the data used by Remote Storage. There are two main types of libraries, jukeboxes and stand-alone.

Jukebox libraries hold multiple disks or tapes and automatically switch to the correct one as needed. There are all sizes of jukeboxes ranging from a few disks or tapes to thousands of disks or tapes. The benefit of jukeboxes is that you do not have to manually load the correct media. The jukebox does it for you.

Stand-alone libraries hold one disk or tape at a time. You must manually add the media required by Remote Storage. If your data is spread across three tapes then you must manually load all three tapes one at a time into the library. The benefit of stand-alone libraries is the price. Stand-alones are a lot cheaper than jukeboxes. The drawback is that they require manual interaction when storing data on multiple disks or tapes.

If most of your data will fit on a single disk or tape, then stand-alone libraries are a good choice. If you are using multiple disks or tapes, a jukebox is a better option.

TEST DAY TIP

The terminology for Remote Storage can be confusing. Remote Storage (in uppercase) refers to a feature of Windows Server 2003 that integrates backup library storage with local file storage. Do not confuse this with remote storage (in lowercase), which refers to the bottom storage level for Remote Storage. When reading exam questions, pay attention to the context in which "remote storage" is used.

Relationship of Remote Storage and Removable Storage

Removable Storage is a feature of Windows Server 2003 that enables multiple programs to share the same storage media. It organizes all your available media into separate *media pools*. Microsoft defines a media pool as a logical collection of removable media that shares the same management policies. Applications use media pools to control access to specific media within the library. Removable Storage requires that all data-management programs run on the computer connected to the library.

In other words, Removable Storage provides a standard way for applications to access a media library. By having all applications access the library through Remote Storage, Microsoft has provided a level of compatibility between applications, including Remote Storage. Remote Storage uses Removable Storage to access the media stored in the library.

Media Pools

Media pools contain either media or other media pools. Using the capability to nest media pools inside each other enables you to create a hierarchical media pool structure for Removable Storage. You can group media pools together and manage them as a single unit. Media pools can span multiple libraries. There are two main types of media pools: system media pools and application media pools.

System media pools hold media not currently being used by an application. Removable Storage creates one of each of the following system media pools (as shown in Figure 2.92) for each media type in your system:

- **Free media pools** These pools hold media not currently in use by applications. This media is readily available for use.
- **Unrecognized media pools** Blank media and media not recognized by Removable Storage go into the unrecognized media pool and are unusable until they are moved into a free media pool.
- **Import media pools** These pools are recognized by Removable Storage, but they have not been used by Remote Storage before. After they have been catalogued they can be used.

Application media pools contain media created and controlled by applications. For example, Backup and Remote Storage use application media pools for storage. Application media pools dictate which media can be accessed by any given application. An application can use more multiple media pools, and more than one application can use a single media pool.

Figure 2.92 Understanding How Media Pools Work Together

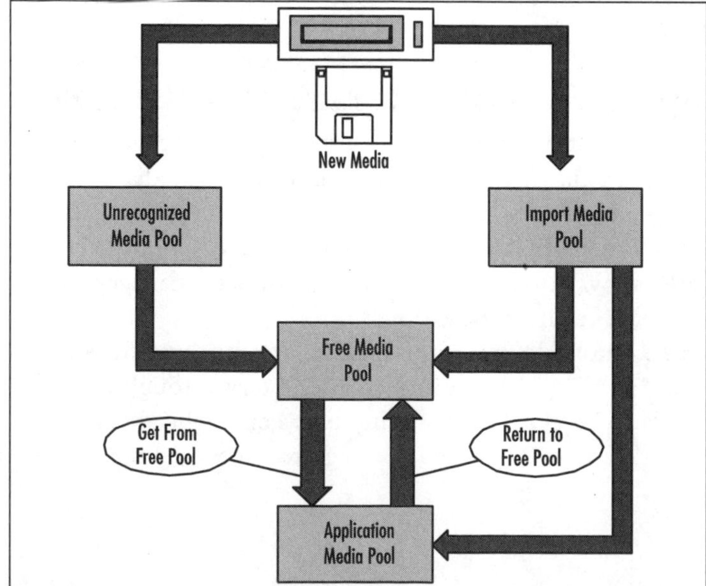

Test Day Tip

When selecting answers on the exam, be sure not to confuse Removable Storage with Remote Storage.

Note

Microsoft states that "Remote Storage supports all SCSI class 4mm, 8mm, DLT, and magneto-optical devices that are supported by Removable Storage. Using Remote Storage with Exabyte 8200 tape libraries is not recommended. Remote Storage does not support QIC tape libraries or rewritable compact disc and DVD formats."

Setting Up Remote Storage

Remote Storage is not installed by default. You add it via thc **Add or Remove Programs** applet in Control Panel. Before starting the installation, you must verify that enough tapes or disks have been moved to a free media pool in Removable Storage to hold all the files you wish to move to Remote Storage and that the local disks being managed are running Windows 2000's or Windows Server 2003's versions of NTFS (NTFS version 5). If you want compression and indexing on local disks, enable these before starting setup. You must be logged on with administrative rights to install Remote Storage. You cannot install Remote Storage into a clustered environment. Remote Storage will not fail over. Also, Remote Storage will not work with shared cluster disks but it will work with local disks that are not shared.

Exercise 2.18 walks you through the process of installing Remote Storage and Exercise 2.19 walks you through the steps involved in configuring Remote Storage after it is installed.

Note

Remote Storage is not a new feature for Windows Server 2003. Both Windows 2000 Server and Advanced Server included the Remote Storage feature. However, Windows Server 2003 Standard Edition does not support Remote Storage. Thus, if you are planning to upgrade a machine running Windows 2000 Server to Windows Server 2003 and you want to continue running Remote Storage, then you must upgrade it to Enterprise Edition rather than Standard Edition.

Exercise 2.18

Installing Remote Storage

1. Open Control Panel by clicking **Start | Control Panel**. This will display a screen similar to that shown in Figure 2.93.
2. Double-click **Add or Remove Programs**. This will display the screen shown in Figure 2.94.

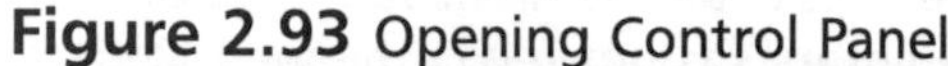

Figure 2.93 Opening Control Panel

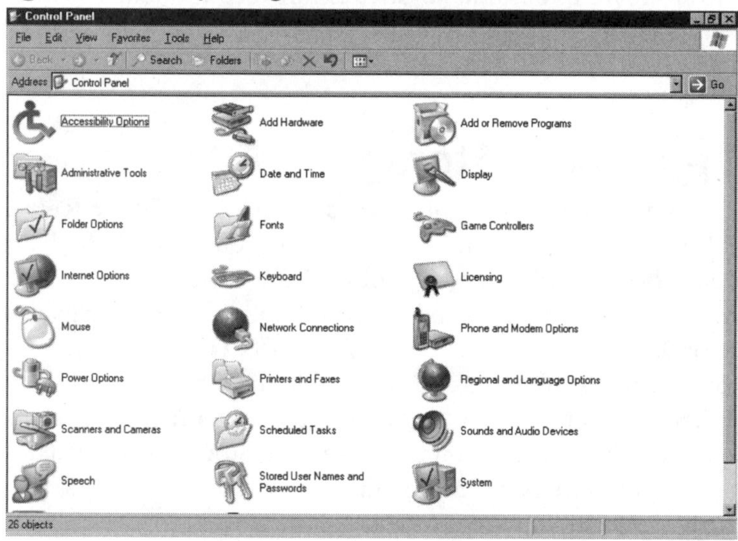

Figure 2.94 Using Add or Remove Programs

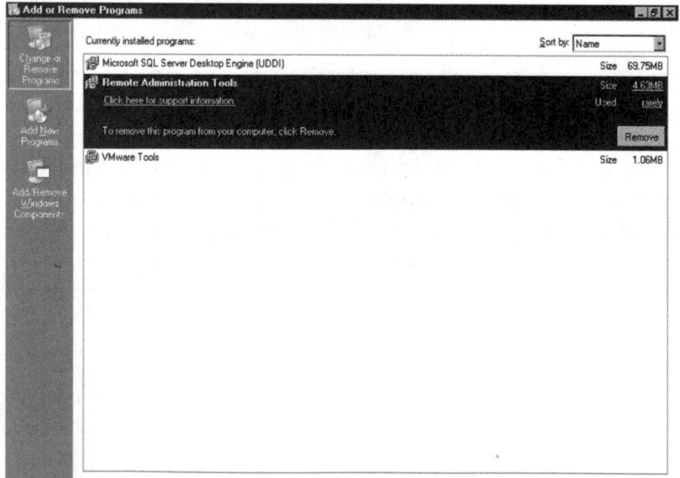

3. From the **Add or Remove Programs** window, click **Add/Remove Windows Components**. You should see a "Please wait…" message, as shown in Figure 2.95.
4. You will next be presented with the **Windows Components Wizard,** as shown in Figure 2.96.

Figure 2.95 Waiting on Windows Setup

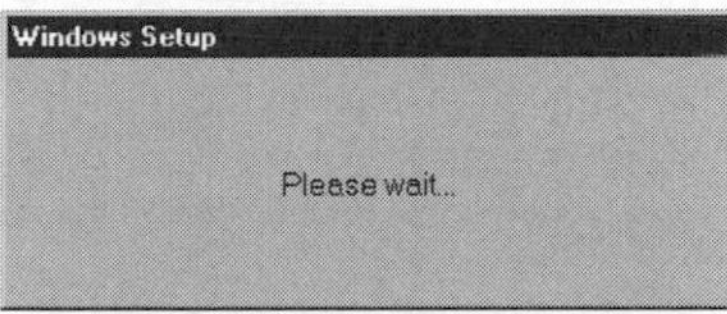

Figure 2.96 Adding Windows Components

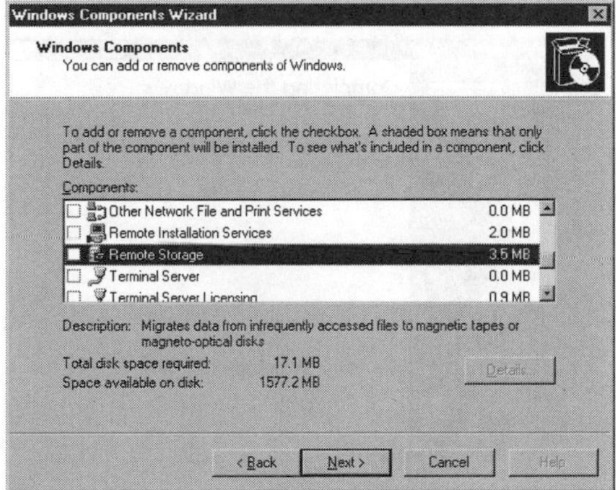

5. Scroll down and click the check box next to **Remote Storage**.
6. Click **Next** to continue.
7. Windows will now configure the newly installed components, as shown in Figure 2.97.
8. Next you will see the **Completing the Windows Components Wizard**, as shown in Figure 2.98. Click **Finish** to close the wizard.

Figure 2.97 Waiting While Windows Configures Components

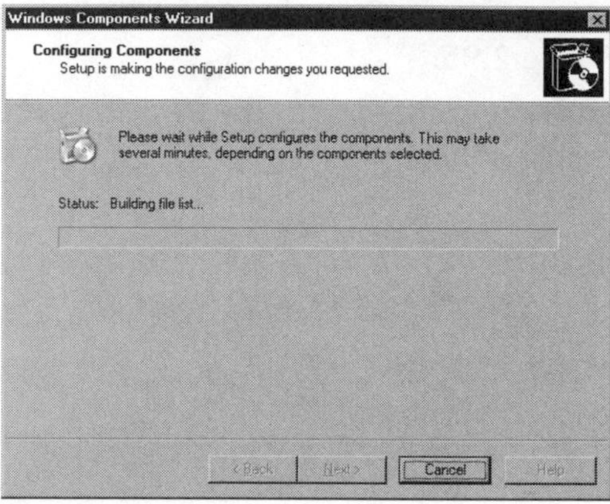

Figure 2.98 Completing the Components Wizard

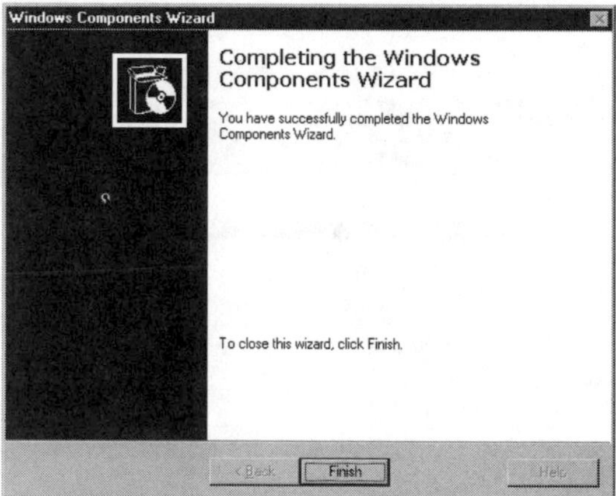

Exercise 2.19

Configuring Remote Storage

1. Open the Remote Storage MMC by clicking **Start | All Programs | Administrative Tools | Remote Storage**.
2. Because this is the first time you have opened the Remote Storage MMC, the Remote Storage Setup Wizard will automatically start, as shown in Figure 2.99. Click **Next** to continue.

Figure 2.99 Running the Remote Storage Setup Wizard

Remote Storage Setup Wizard

Welcome to the Remote Storage Setup Wizard

This wizard helps you set up Remote Storage to manage space on volumes local to this computer.

Remote Storage copies the data in infrequently used files from your managed volumes to remote storage media, such as an automated tape library.

Remote Storage frees up space used by the data in these files on the managed volumes as more free space is needed.

To continue, click Next.

< Back | Next > | Cancel

3. You will next be asked which volumes you want Remote Storage to manage, as shown in Figure 2.100. For this exercise, we select the **C** drive. Select the disk(s) that you want to manage and click **Next** to continue.

Figure 2.100 Selecting the Volumes to be Managed

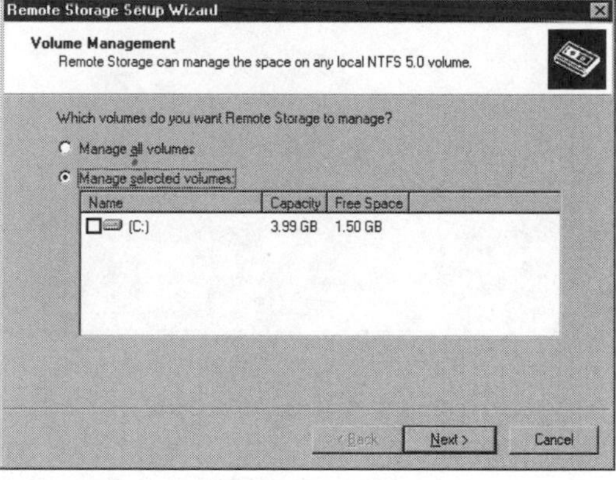

4. Set the criteria for managing free space on the volume with the **Volume Settings** dialog box shown in Figure 2.101. Click **Next** to continue.

5. Next you will be asked to choose which media type to use, as shown in Figure 2.102. For this exercise, select **Removable media** and click **Next** to continue.

Figure 2.101 Managing Free Space on Your Volumes

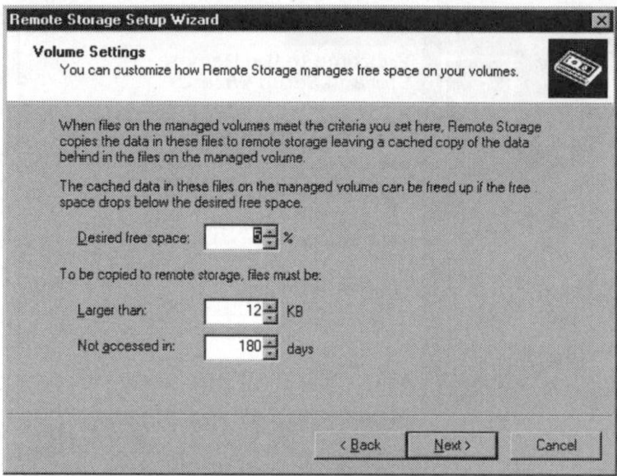

Figure 2.102 Selecting a Media Type

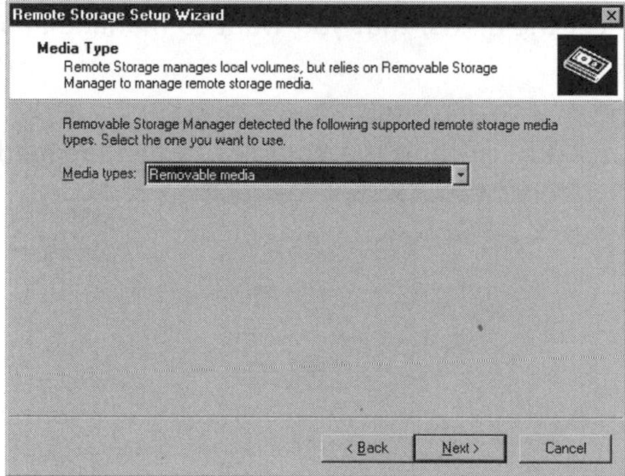

6. The last item to configure is the schedule for copying files, as shown in Figure 2.103. To accept the defaults, click **Next** and skip to step 9. To customize the schedule, click the **Change Schedule** button. This will display the **Schedule** window shown in Figure 2.104.
7. Set the schedule to copy files at a time that is least busy in your environment and click **OK**.
8. You will be returned to the screen shown in Figure 2.103. Click **Next** to continue.
9. On the **Completing the Remote Storage Setup Wizard** screen (Figure 2.105), review the settings to make sure they are correct, and then click **Finish** to complete the configuration of Remote Storage.

Figure 2.103 Verifying the Schedule for Copying Files

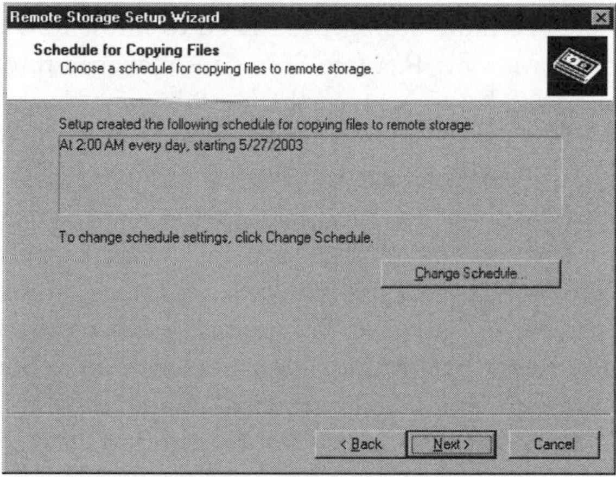

Figure 2.104 Customizing the Schedule for Copying Files

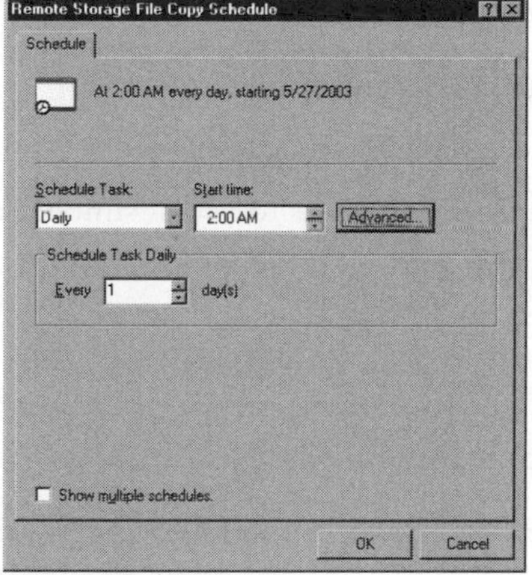

Figure 2.105 Completing the Remote Storage Setup Wizard

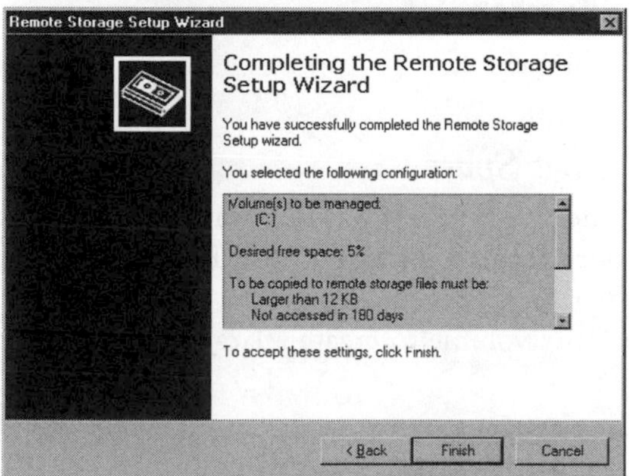

Using Remote Storage

Now that you have installed Remote Storage, you need to know how to administer it. Like Microsoft's other administrative tools, Remote Storage is managed through an MMC snap-in. The Remote Storage MMC has two panes: the console pane on the left is used to navigate the various components of Remote Storage and the details pane on the right displays specifics of whichever component is selected in the left console pane.

The Remote Storage MMC (see Figure 2.106) that is accessed from the **Administrative Tools** menu also contains the snap-ins for Removable Storage and Event Viewer. However, Remote Storage itself has only two containers to manage: the Managed Volumes container and the Media container. We previously discussed storage levels within Remote Storage. We said the top level was for local storage and the bottom level was for remote storage. The Managed Volumes container is the top level of storage and is used for managing local storage. The Media container is the bottom level and is used for managing remote storage.

The Managed Volumes container is used to perform the following tasks:

- Set the desired free space.
- Specify file-selection criteria and rules.
- Change the file-copy schedule.
- Set the maximum number of drives to access simultaneously.
- Set the runaway recall limit.
- Validate files.
- Discontinue volume management.
- Modify files on managed volumes.

The Media container is used to perform the following tasks:

- Create media copies.
- Synchronize media copies.
- Recreate the media master.

Setting the Desired Free Space

You can configure how much free space you want available on your managed volume. If the volume falls below your specified threshold, then Remote Storage deletes cached files until the volume is back within acceptable limits. You can also tell Remote Storage to delete all cached files from the volume to create a large amount of available free space.

Figure 2.106 Using the Remote Storage MMC

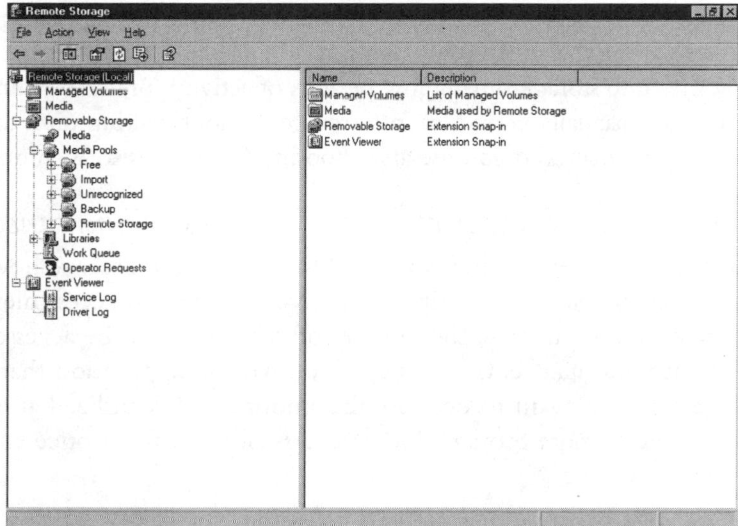

Specifying File-Selection Criteria and Rules

You tell Remote Storage which files to manage on your volume.You set criteria that must be met in order for the file to be copied to remote storage. After the criteria have been met, the files are copied. Minimum files size and elapsed time since last use are the common criteria used by Remote Storage.

In addition to using criteria to control which files get copied to Remote Storage, you can also create rules. There are two types of rules, inclusion and exclusion. Inclusion rules control which files are copied to Remote Storage and exclusion rules control which files are not copied to Remote Storage. Rules are processed in order and the first rule that matches is applied. Change the order of your rules to set their priority.

Remote Storage has a predefined list of rules available for use.You cannot modify these rules or change their order.You can create your own rules and order them however you see fit. By default, all system, hidden, encrypted, extended attribute, and sparse files are excluded from the file rule list as these files cannot be copied to remote storage.

Both types of rules are built on the same options:

- A specified folder, including subfolders
- A specified folder, excluding subfolders
- File name extension
- File name

Changing the File-Copy Schedule

The file copy schedule tells Remote Storage when to copy files from the managed volume to the library. This is set during the initial setup, but it can be changed after the fact. You should always try to copy files into storage during low periods of activity (preferably during non-business hours). You can manually copy files into storage without waiting until the scheduled time by right-clicking the managed volume and choosing Copy Files to Remote Storage.

Setting the Maximum Number of Drives to Access Simultaneously

If you have a multiple-drive device, then you need to tell Remote Storage how many drives to utilize at once. If you have multiple users trying at once to access files on different media, then you may want to increase the number of drives that can be accessed simultaneously to increase your performance. Conversely, if you have an application that accesses Removable Storage, you may want to decrease the amount of disk utilized at once by Remote Storage so that Remote Storage doesn't access all the disks at once and prevent your application from working.

NOTE

Remember, Removable Storage can be used by many different applications. For example, both Backup and Remote Storage can use Removable Storage at the same time. Limiting the number of drives used simultaneously within Remote Storage can help prevent Remote Storage conflicts.

Setting the Runaway Recall Limit

The Runaway call limit defines the number of file recalls a user can make on a file within a single session. It stops Remote Storage from copying the same file from the library to the managed volume over and over. If a user recalls a file within 10 seconds of the original file recall, the runaway recall count is increased by one. After the runaway recall limit is reached, the file is still accessible, it just will be accessed from storage and not cached on the managed volume.

Validating Files

Validation is the process of verifying that the data in Remote Storage points to the correct file on the managed volume. Validation can determine if a file has been moved between volumes. You can manually perform file validation by right-clicking the managed volume, selecting **All Tasks**, and choosing **Validate Files**. Two hours after a backup program restores a file, Remote Storage automatically forces a file validation.

Discontinuing Volume Management

You can easily tell Remote Storage to stop managing a volume by right-clicking a managed volume and choosing **Remove**. If you do so, you have to decide if you want to leave the files on the library or if you want to copy them back to the original volume. If you leave the files in Remote Storage, it will recall them as normal. However, no new files created on the volume will be copied to Remote Storage.

Modifying Files on Managed Volumes

There are special considerations to be aware of when deleting files on managed volumes and moving files between managed volumes. If files on a managed volume are deleted, you must restore the file from backup. Do not think that because the file is stored in the library that it can be restored from there. When you delete a file from the managed volume it is also deleted from the library. If you move or copy files between managed volumes, the files are recalled. If you want to move files back and forth without causing a recall, then you must back up and restore the data to the new location and then run a volume validation.

Creating and Synchronizing Media Copies

You can create copies of your media to provide fault tolerance. These copies are called *media copy sets* and they provide redundancy for your data. If there is a problem with the master media set, the media copy set will be used. In order for Remote Storage to create media copy sets, there must be two or more drives in the library. When using media copy sets, you must make sure that the master set and the copies are in sync. To synchronize the media copies, right-click **Media** and select **Synchronize Copies Now**.

Recreating the Media Master

The *media master* is the tape that holds all the files required for Remote Storage. If the media master were to fail, you could create another one from a media copy set. However, you may lose any data that was created since the last time you synchronized the media copy set with the media master. Recreate the media master only if you get errors when recalling files. Follow the steps below to recreate the media master:

1. Select **Media**.
2. Right-click the media you would like to recreate.
3. Select **Properties**.
4. Click the **Recovery** tab.
5. Click **Recreate Master**.

EXAM WARNING

If you have more data than will fit on one tape, you must have multiple media masters. A group of media masters is referred to as a *master set*.

Remote Storage Best Practices

Microsoft provides some guidelines for you to follow when using Remote Storage. You should try to adhere to these best practices whenever possible:

- Make multiple copies of your remote storage tapes and always keep a copy offsite.
- Always configure Remote Storage through the GUI before using rss.exe to manage it.
- Do not create File Replication service (FRS) replicas on a Remote Storage volume.
- Regularly validate your managed volumes.
- Stop managing all volumes before you uninstall Remote Storage.
- Do not manage full volumes.
- Do not format a managed volume.
- Schedule your tasks to run during periods of low activity.
- Do not change the drive letter of a managed volume.
- Run a system state backup as an administrator to back up the Remote Storage database files.
- Do not install Remote Storage on shared cluster disks.

Troubleshooting Disks and Volumes

Thus far in this chapter, we have focused on how to enable and configure various disk-related features of Windows Server 2003. However, a large part of any administrator's job is dealing with problems and knowing what to do when things go wrong. In this section, we address some of the most common disk-related troubleshooting scenarios. The Microsoft exams focus heavily on troubleshooting skills, so you will be expected to know how to troubleshoot disks and volumes when you take the test.

Troubleshooting Basic Disks

Many basic disk-troubleshooting scenarios involve a disk not being recognized by the operating system (and thus not showing up in the Disk Management console) or showing up in a problematic state. Remember the basic rules of troubleshooting any computer/network problem: begin at the physical level. This means you should always check the hardware first to make sure that it is functional.

In the following sections, we will cover these common situations:

- New disks don't show up in the volume list view.
- Disk status is not initialized.
- Disk status is unknown.
- Disk status is unreadable.
- Disk status is failed.

New Disks Are Not Showing Up in the Volume List View

New disks that fail to show up in the volume list view are a common concern. This is usually because there are no designators (drive letters) associated with the disk.

NOTE

By design, if you're using Windows Server 2003 Enterprise or Datacenter edition, drive letters will not be assigned by default when a new disk is installed, and the disk will not be mounted until you do it manually. This is to make it easier to use the disks in a Storage Area Network (SAN) environment.

If the disk is not mounted, you will need to use the *diskpart* and *mountvol* commands or use the Disk Management console to mount the volume and assign drive letters. The *mountvol* command enables you to mount a volume without a drive letter. This is useful if you have run out of drive letters.

You have to manually assign drive letters to each volume or partition on the disk before you can format them and use them for storage. Notice in Figure 2.107 that there are three disks shown online in the graphical view (bottom pane), but they do not have drive letters associated with them. Until they do, they will not show up in the volume list view (top pane).

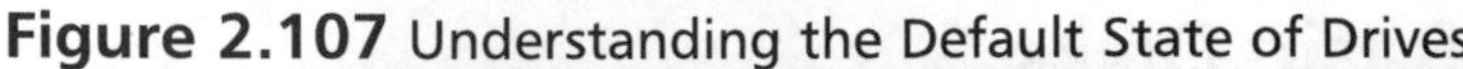

Figure 2.107 Understanding the Default State of Drives

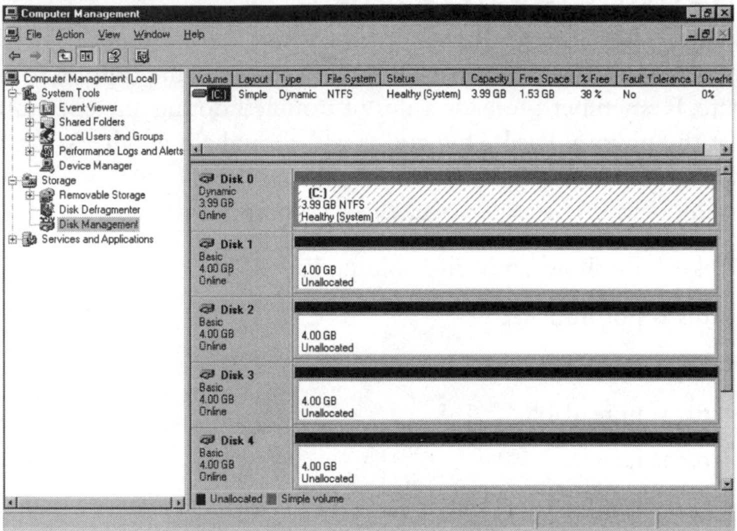

Disk Status is Not Initialized or Unknown

If your disks are showing up as unknown and not initialized, as shown in Figure 2.108, this is generally because no signature has been written to the disk by which Windows can identify it. You need to write a signature to a new disk when you install it, before you can use it. When Windows writes a signature to the disk, it also creates the master boot record (MBR) or GUID partition table. When you add a new disk and start Disk Management, the system automatically starts a wizard that prompts you to write a signature to the new disk. If you cancel the wizard, however, the disk will not have a signature and will be left in an uninitialized state.

To initialize a disk after the wizard has been cancelled, follow these steps:

1. Right-click the disk that needs to be initialized in the bottom graphical pane of the Disk Management console, and then select **Initialize Disk** from the context menu.
2. You will be prompted to select one or more disks to initialize. Ensure that the check box(es) of the appropriate disk(s) is checked and click **OK.**
3. The disk status in the graphical view will change from **Unknown** to **Basic**.

After the disk is initialized, you can create partitions.

Figure 2.108 Troubleshooting Disks That Do Not Have a Signature

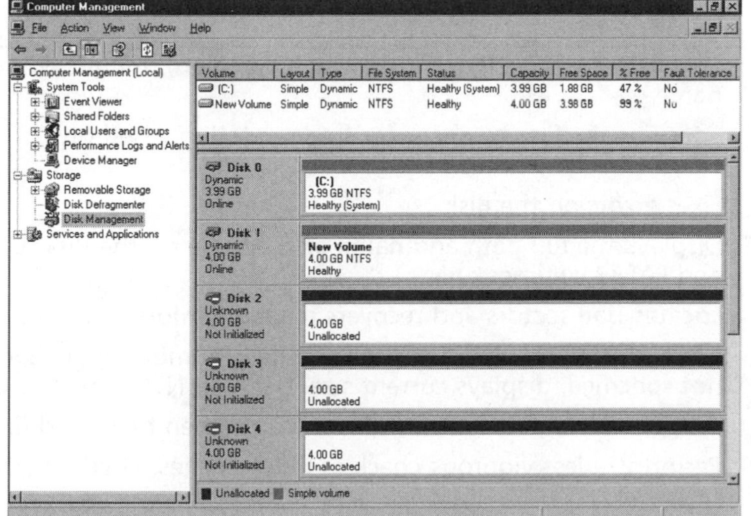

Disk Status is Unreadable

An unreadable disk indicates that you may have a hardware failure or corruption of the disk's copy of the disk configuration database. Unfortunately, there is generally no way to fix failed hardware other than to replace it. Sometimes you will get the "unreadable" message if the disks are still spinning up while you are viewing the Disk Management console. If this is the case, rescanning the computer for disks usually solves the problem. To rescan, click **Action | Rescan Disks**. If rescanning doesn't solve the problem, try rebooting the machine.

Disk Status is Failed

A failed disk indicates that the file system is corrupt, the disk is damaged, or for some other reason the volume could not start. Remember another rule of troubleshooting: always try the easy solutions first. Make sure that the disk has power and is plugged into the server. If your hardware is faulty, you will have to replace it and restore your data from backup. One of the most common causes of disk problems is a loose or bad IDE or SCSI cable. Try tightening or swapping out cables if you suspect this is the problem.

If the hardware is not faulty, we move on to troubleshooting the software. One possibility is that the file system is corrupt. If you can still access the volume, run chkdsk.exe (pronounce "check disk") against it. chkdsk.exe may not be able to recover any lost data, but it can usually bring the file system back to a consistent state. chkdsk.exe uses the following syntax.

```
CHKDSK [volume[[path]filename]]] [/F] [/V] [/R] [/X] [/I] [/C]
    [/L[:size]]
```

Table 2.7 explains chkdsk.exe parameters.

Table 2.7 Understanding Chkdsk.exe Parameters

Parameter	Desription
volume	Specifies the drive letter (followed by a colon), mount point, or volume name.
filename	Specifies the files to check for fragmentation. Used on FAT and FAT32 volumes only.
/F	Fixes errors on the disk.
/V	Displays the full path and name of every file on the disk. Used on FAT and FAT32 volumes only.
/R	Locates bad sectors and recovers readable information (implies /F).
/L:size	Changes the log file size to the specified number of kilobytes. If size is not specified, displays current size. Used on NTFS volumes only.
/X	All opened handles to the volume would then be invalid (implies /F).
/I	Performs a less vigorous check of index entries. Used on NTFS volumes only.
/C	Skips checking of cycles within the folder structure. Used on NTFS volumes only.

Troubleshooting Dynamic Volumes

Dynamic disks can have the same problems as basic disk (discussed above). When troubleshooting dynamic disks, you should always run through the scenarios given for basic disks as well. In addition to these problems that are common to both disk types, dynamic disks can have additional problems that do not apply to basic disks. In the following section, we will discuss troubleshooting scenarios that are unique to dynamic disks:

- Disk status is foreign.
- Disk status is online (errors).
- Disk status is offline or missing.
- Disk status is data incomplete.
- Disk status is Stale Data.
- Disk status is Failed or Failed Redundancy.

Disk Status is Foreign

A disk status of **Foreign** as shown in Figure 2.109 occurs when you move a dynamic disk from one machine to another. This happens because Windows stores all dynamic disk configurations in a private database in the last 1MB of disk space. This database is associated with the machine in which the disk is installed and is replicated to all the dynamic disks installed in that machine. If you connect the disk to a different machine, the second machine will detect that the database doesn't match anything in its database and the disk will be marked as foreign.

To make the new computer recognize the dynamic disk, you must import it. To do so, right-click the foreign disk and select **Import Foreign Disks** from the content menu. This will make the volume visible and incorporate it into the new machine's dynamic disks database.

NOTE

If all the dynamic disks in a system fail, the configuration database will be lost. In this case, a disk that was initialized on the system might still be marked as foreign.

Figure 2.109 Importing a Foreign Disk

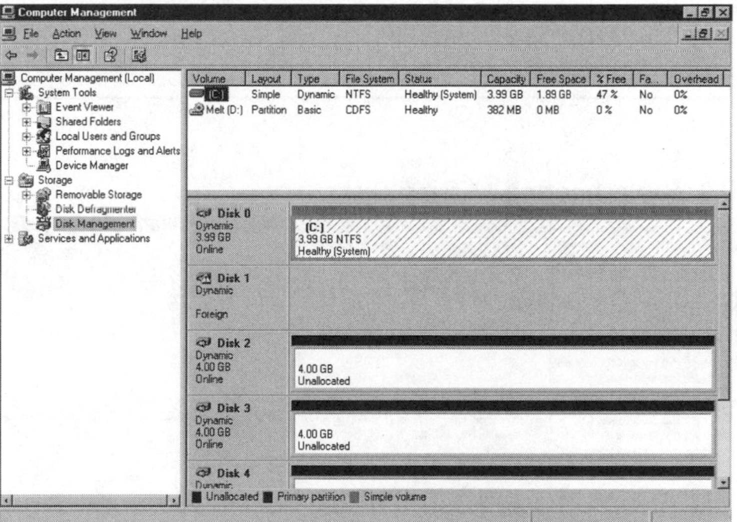

Disk Status is Online (Errors)

A disk status of Online (Errors) indicates that the disk is working, but is having problems. I/O errors are being detected somewhere on the disk. If this problem persists, you should replace the hardware. If the problem is temporary, you might be able to reactivate your volume to bring it back online. To do so, right-click the volume and choose **Reactivate Disk** from the content menu. If the reactivation works, the disk will be marked as **Online**.

You can also use the *diskpart* command with the *online* parameter to reactivate a disk (remember to first select the disk so that it is the focus).

Disk Status is Offline

A disk status of Offline, where the disk name field indicates Missing (as shown in Figure 2.110) usually means that the disk is no longer physically connected to the server. Check to make sure that the disk is powered on and correctly connected to the server. After fixing a physical connectivity problem, right-click the volume and choose **Reactivate Disk**. This will bring the disk back online and make it usable by Windows again.

If this does not fix the problem, it is possible that your disk is corrupt beyond repair. If so, you must remove it from the server. Right-click the volume(s) contained on the disk and choose **Remove Volume** from the context menu. After all volumes have been removed, right-click the disk and choose **Remove Disk**. At this point, all data is lost and the disk has been removed from your system. Do not do this unless you are sure that the disk is irreparably damaged.

NOTE

If the disk you need to remove is part of a mirrored volume, remove the mirror instead of the entire volume. This will preserve the data on the other member of the mirror.

Figure 2.110 Troubleshooting Missing Disks

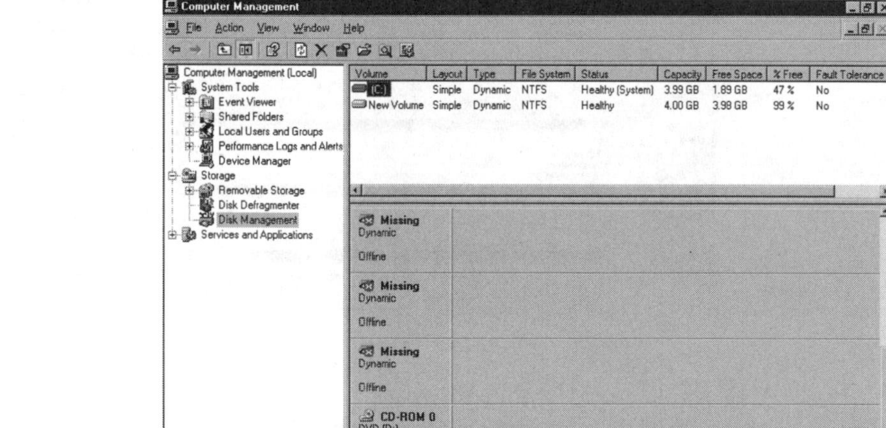

If the disk status shows Offline, but the disk name still shows as Disk 0, Disk 1, etc. (instead of "Missing"), you should be able to simply right-click and select **Reactivate** to bring the disk back online. Volumes should be returned to Healthy status after the disk comes back online.

Disk Status is Data Incomplete

As discussed earlier, when you move dynamic volumes between servers they are marked as foreign. You must import them in order for Windows to use them. If you have a volume that spans multiple disks (e.g., a spanned volume, striped volume, or RAID 5 volume) and you only import some of the disks, you will see the error message **Data Incomplete** as shown in Figure 2.111. If this happens, cancel the import process until you can move all the disks in the volume at the same time. When all the disks have been physically installed in the new machine, import them together and Windows will recognize them as being part of the same volume.

Figure 2.111 Importing Part of a Spanned Volume

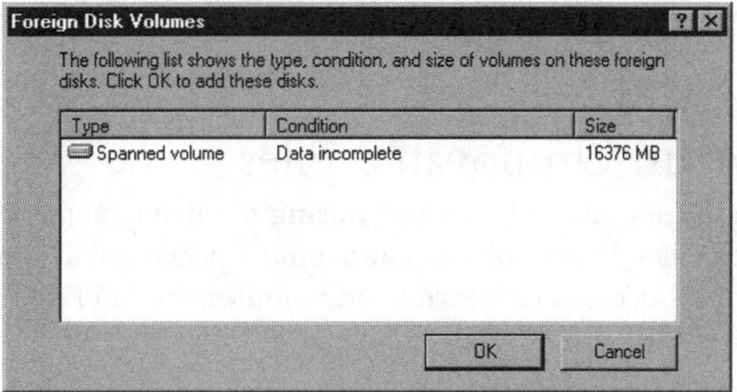

NOTE

If you don't need to use the multi-disk volume in the new computer and you only want to move one or some of the disks, you can import the disk and then delete the volume and create a new volume.

Troubleshooting Fragmentation Problems

Disk fragmentation is inevitable if you ever delete files, install programs, or otherwise use the computer for normal tasks. To optimize disk performance, you should defragment your disks as often as needed. This section covers some of the common problems that you might encounter related to disk fragmentation and the defragmentation process, including the following:

- Computer is operating slowly.
- The Analysis and Defragmentation reports do not match the display.
- Volumes contain unmovable files.

Computer is Operating Slowly

This is a common complaint from computer users. Programs seem to drag and everything goes very slowly. This is often a sign of a highly fragmented disk and commonly occurs when applications are installed or removed or many new files are created. The solution is simple: use defrag.exe or Disk Defragmenter to defragment your disks.

The Analysis and Defragmentation Reports Do Not Match the Display

The graphical display is designed to provide a quick look at the level of fragmentation of the volumes on your hard disk. The graphical representation is too small in scale to give a 100 percent accurate representation. The reports created by the defragmentation tools are much more detailed and are very accurate. When there are discrepancies between the display and reports, the information in the reports should be considered more reliable.

Volumes Contain Unmovable Files

This is normal. Certain files cannot be moved during the defragmentation process. The pagefile is one of these files. Every volume containing a pagefile will appear as having files that cannot be moved. Also, on NTFS-formatted volumes, the NTFS Change journal and the NTFS log file cannot be moved.

Troubleshooting Disk Quotas

Disk quotas are a great feature. However, they can lead to trouble if they are improperly configured or not managed properly. This section covers some of the more common issues that appear when using disk quotas. Issues such as the following:

- The Quota tab is not there.
- Deleting a Quota entry gives you another window.
- A user gets an "Insufficient Disk Space" message when adding files to a volume.

The Quota Tab is Not There

Disk quotas are set via the quotas tab on the properties of a volume. If the tab does not appear (Figure 2.112), then one of three things is the cause. Either you do not have administrative rights on the machine, the volume is formatted as FAT or FAT32 and not as NTFS, or the volume is not shared from the volume's root directory.

Figure 2.112 Missing the Quota Tab

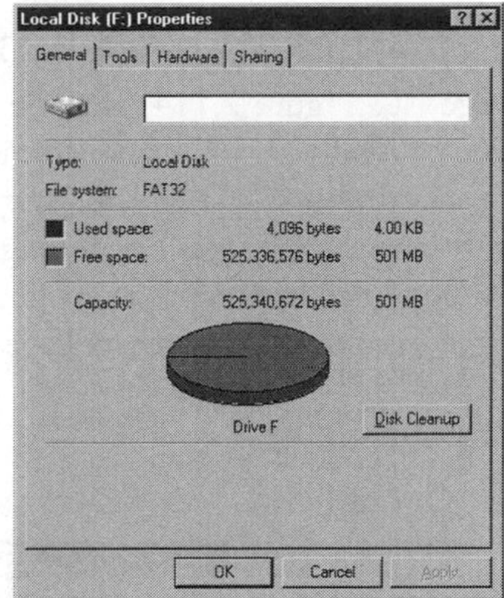

Deleting a Quota Entry Gives you Another Window

Whenever you try to delete a quota entry for a user that still retains ownership of files, you are presented with the Disk Quota window shown in Figure 2.113. This is because you cannot delete a quota entry if the user still owns files. This keeps you from having files on your server that are not being managed by disk quotas because the owner is no longer around. You have three choices:

- Permanently delete all the files.
- Take ownership of the files.
- Move the files to another volume.

After doing so, you will be able to delete the quota entry for your user.

Figure 2.113 Cleaning Up Disk Quotas

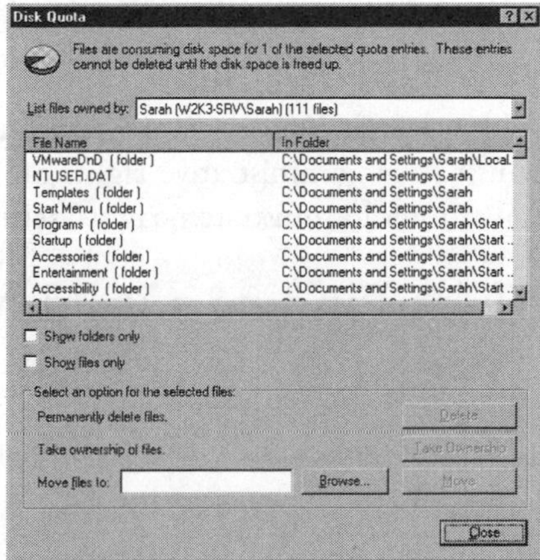

A User Gets an "Insufficient Disk Space" Message When Adding Files to a Volume

The insufficient disk space message (see Figure 2.114) is to be expected for any of your users that are over their quota limit. Usually this is a good thing because it means that disk quotas are working. The only way around it is to increase your users' quota limit or to stop denying users who exceed their disk space. If this is happening unexpectedly, verify that your users' limits are set correctly. A common error is to forget to change the quota measurement from KB to MB. You may think that your users have 150MB of available space when they only have 150KB of space.

Figure 2.114 Exceeding Your Quota Limit

Troubleshooting Remote Storage

Remember when you are troubleshooting Remote Storage that you are writing data to backup media. This is going to be slower than writing to disks. This is not to say that your performance should be terrible. Just be realistic with your expectations. Here are some common Remote Storage troubleshooting issues:

- Remote Storage will not install.
- Remote Storage is not finding a valid media type.
- Files can no longer be recalled from Remote Storage.

Remote Storage Will Not Install

Remote Storage is not installed by default. You must add it through **Control Panel | Add or Remove Programs**. You must have administrative rights on the machine on which you are installing Remote Storage. Without administrative rights, setup will not continue.

Remote Storage Is Not Finding a Valid Media Type

During initial setup, Remote Storage searches for an available media type. If Remote Storage is not finding one on your machine, you either have not waited long enough for Remote Storage to finish searching or you do not have a compatible library.

NOTE

Per Microsoft, "Remote Storage supports all SCSI class 4mm, 8mm, DLT, and magneto-optical devices that are supported by Removable Storage. Using Remote Storage with Exabyte 8200 tape libraries is not recommended. Remote Storage does not support QIC tape libraries or rewritable compact disc and DVD formats."

Files Can No Longer Be Recalled from Remote Storage

Remote Storage has a runaway recall limit to deny recalling files from storage more than a specified number of times in a row. It is possible that you have an application that is making too many recalls. Once this threshold is crossed, future recalls are denied. If the recalls are legitimate, you can increase the threshold for the runaway recall limit. If they are not valid, then you need to terminate the application making the request.

Troubleshooting RAID

When troubleshooting RAID volumes, you must first troubleshoot the disk itself, so always start with the basic disk and dynamic disk checklist. However, there are times when the problem is with the RAID volume itself and not the underlying disk. This section covers the following:

- Mirrored or RAID-5 volume's status is Data Not Redundant.
- Mirrored or RAID-5 volume's status is Failed Redundancy.
- Mirrored or RAID-5 volume's status is Stale Data.

Mirrored or RAID-5 Volume's Status is Data Not Redundant

A Data Not Redundant status indicates that your volume is not intact. This is due to moving disks from one machine to another without moving all the disks in the volume. Wait to import your disk until you have all the disks in the volume physically connected to the server. Then when you import them, Windows will see them as a complete volume and retain their configuration.

Mirrored or RAID-5 Volume's Status is Failed Redundancy

Failed Redundancy, as shown in Figures 2.115 and 2.116, occurs when one of the disks in a fault-tolerant volume fails. Your volume will continue to work, but it is no longer fault tolerant. If another disk fails, you will lose all your data on that volume. You should repair the failed disk as quickly as possible.

Your mirrored volume will need to be recreated after replacing the disk. Right-click the defective disk and select **Remove Mirror**. Then right-click the working disk and select **Add Mirror**, selecting the new disk as the mirror. To repair the RAID-5 volume, put in the disk and right-click the volume and choose **Repair RAID-5 Volume**.

Figure 2.115 Recovering a Failed Mirrored Volume

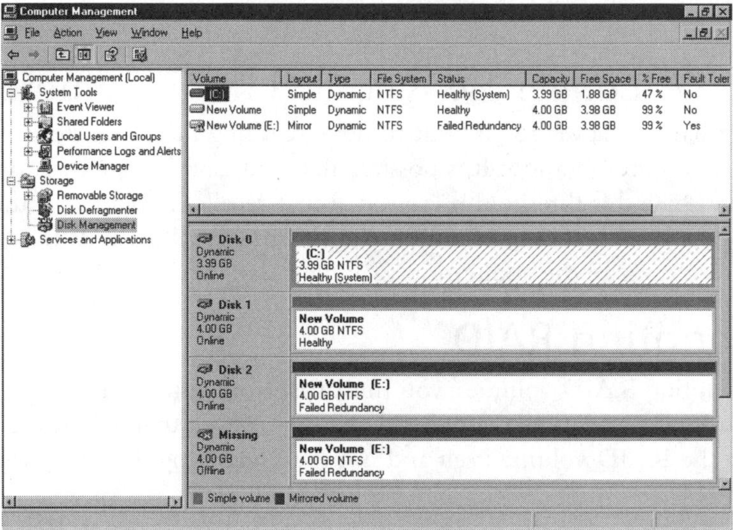

Figure 2.116 Recovering a Failed RAID-5 Volume

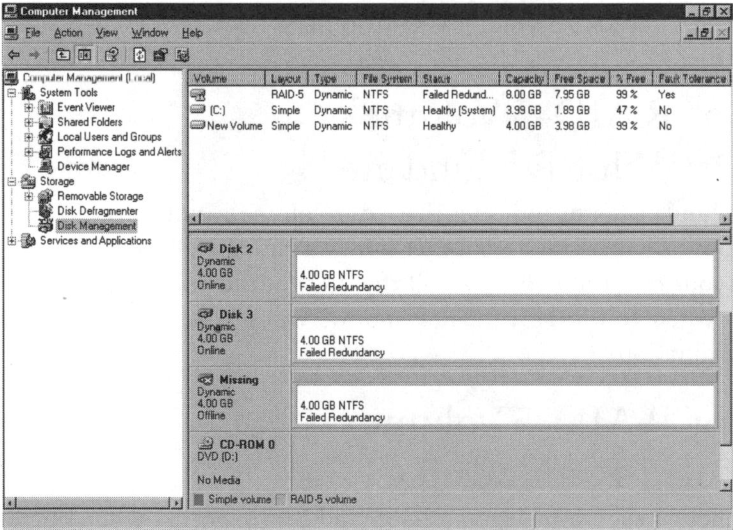

Mirrored or RAID-5 Volume's Status is Stale Data

Stale data occurs when a volume's fault-tolerant information is not completely up to date. This happens in a mirrored volume if something has been written to the primary disk, but for whatever reason it hasn't made it to the mirror disk yet. This occurs in a RAID-5 volume when the parity information isn't up to date.

If you try to move a volume while it contains stale information, you will get a status of **Stale Data** when you try to import the disk. Move the disk back to the machine it was originally in and rescan the machine for the new disk. After all the disks are discovered, wait until they say Online and Healthy before you try to move them again.

Summary of Exam Objectives

Disk management is vital to maintaining a stable server environment. Disk management encompasses different areas.

First you must determine the type of disk structure you are going to use. Windows Server 2003 supports basic and dynamic disks. Basic disks are backwards compatible with older operating systems, but they do not offer as much flexibility as dynamic disks. Dynamic disks provide better reliability due to the way they are structured and due to their support of fault-tolerant volumes.

Your partitioning method is going to depend on your disk structure. Basic disks use primary and extended partitions. Dynamic disks use simple, spanned, striped, and RAID-5 volumes. Primary partitions are the only option for booting to basic disks. Simple volumes and mirrored volumes are the only options for booting to dynamic disks. All other partition and volume types are used for storage disks only. Use Disk Management or diskpart.exe to manage your disk, partitions, and volumes.

Creating partitions and volumes is half the battle. Using your disks efficiently is the other half. You must take precautions to avoid disk fragmentation. Fragmented disks do not perform at their peak. Use Disk Defragmenter or defrag.exe on a regular basis to keep your drives defragmented and performing well. You need to also keep a close eye on disk space utilization. Running out of disk space will bring your server to a screeching halt. Use Disk Quotas on NTFS volumes to limit disk space usage or to at least track disk space usage.

Sometimes you just do not have enough disk space. Use Remote Storage to archive your least frequently used files to backup tape or disk media. When files are needed from backup, Remote Storage copies them to hard disks making them available for your users. Other than a small delay when accessing archived files, Remote Storage provides a transparent archival solution.

By using the disk features of Windows Server 2003 and the built-in disk management tools, you can ensure that your servers' disks are being used to the best of their ability.

Exam Objectives Fast Track

Disk Terminology and Concepts

☑ Basic disks are the default disk type in Windows Server 2003.

☑ Basic disks consist of primary partitions, extended partitions, and logical drives.

☑ Primary partitions are required for booting Windows. Logical drives cannot be used for booting.

☑ Dynamic disks are the preferred disk type in Windows Server 2003.

☑ Dynamic disks consist of volumes such as simple, spanned, striped, mirrored, and RAID-5.

- ☑ Simple volumes are the default volume type on dynamic disks. All partitions become simple volumes when upgraded to dynamic.
- ☑ Only mirrored and RAID-5 volumes provide fault tolerance.

Using Disk Management Tools

- ☑ The Disk Management Microsoft Management Console (MMC) provides a graphical way to manage your disks, partitions, logical drives, and volumes.
- ☑ diskpart.exe manages disks, partitions, logical drives, and volumes from the command prompt.
- ☑ fsutil.exe manages FAT and NTFS file systems from the command prompt.
- ☑ rss.exe manages Remote Storage from the command prompt.

Understanding and Managing Physical and Logical Disks

- ☑ Use basic disks whenever you are dual booting Windows Server 2003 with another operating system.
- ☑ You must have at least 1MB of unallocated space to upgrade a disk from basic to dynamic.
- ☑ You do not lose data when you convert from basic to dynamic, but you do lose all data when you convert back to basic from dynamic.
- ☑ Use the disk management MMC to create partitions, logical drives, and volumes.
- ☑ Mirrored volumes work with two disks and provide fault tolerance by writing duplicate copies of the data to both disks.
- ☑ Mirrored volumes provide 50 percent disk utilization.
- ☑ Spanned volumes work with two to 32 disks. They enable you to group different-sized disks into a single volume. They do not provide fault tolerance.
- ☑ Striped volumes offer the best performance of all volume types, but they do not provide fault tolerance. They work with two to 32 disks.
- ☑ RAID-5 volumes offer the improved performance of striping with fault tolerance. They do not perform as well as striped volumes, but they do out perform mirrored volumes. RAID-5 volumes work with three to 32 disks.

Optimizing Disk Performance

- ☑ Disk fragmentation slows disk performance.
- ☑ We can defragment our disk by using the Disk Defragmenter or defrag.exe.

- ☑ Disk Defragmenter and defrag.exe cannot be used at the same time.
- ☑ Disk quotas enable us to limit how much space a user can use on a volume.
- ☑ Disk quotas work only with volumes formatted with the NTFS file system.
- ☑ Disk quotas are based on the uncompressed size of a file.
- ☑ Disk quotas are tracked based on file ownership.

Understanding and Using Remote Storage

- ☑ Remote Storage is not installed by default.
- ☑ You must be an administrator to install Remote Storage.
- ☑ Local disks to be managed by Remote Storage must be formatted with NTFS version 5.
- ☑ You can use rss.exe to manage Remote Storage after it is installed and configured.

Troubleshooting Disks and Volumes

- ☑ Always check the hardware first. If it is faulty, replace it before you continue troubleshooting.
- ☑ Most basic disk problems are due to faulty hardware or a corrupt disk.
- ☑ Dynamic disks can suffer from the same problems as basic disks, but they also have volume problems.
- ☑ Whenever importing a foreign disk into a machine, make sure that you have all the disks that form a single volume. Without all the disks, you are going to have errors and possibly lose data.
- ☑ When a disk fails in a fault-tolerant volume, you need to replace it as quickly as possible and repair the volume to restore fault tolerance.
- ☑ Page files and NTFS journal and log files are unmovable during the defragmentation process.
- ☑ The reports are more accurate than the graphical view for determining disk utilization before and after a defragmentation.
- ☑ You cannot delete a quota limit for a user that still retains ownership to files. You must first take ownership of the files, delete the files, or move the files to another volume.

Exam Objectives Frequently Asked Questions

The following Frequently Asked Questions, answered by the authors of this book, are designed to both measure your understanding of the Exam Objectives presented in this chapter, and to assist you with real-life implementation of these concepts. You will also gain access to thousands of other FAQs at ITFAQnet.com.

Q: Why do I have to reboot my machine when I upgrade my system drive to dynamic?

A: Any time you try to upgrade a disk that has files that are currently in use, you will have to reboot. During the upgrade process the file system must be dismounted. This cannot occur if files are in use.

Q: Why isn't dynamic disk supported on my portable USB hard disk?

A: Dynamic disk contain a hidden database that holds (among other things) the disk partitioning information. This database is tied to whatever machine created the dynamic disk. If your portable hard disk were configured as dynamic, it would only work with Windows 2000 and Windows Server 2003 machines. Also, you would have to recreate the hidden database every time you moved it between machines.

Q: Why don't laptops support dynamic disks?

A: One of the main reasons for switching to dynamic disks is to be able to have volumes that span disks. Since laptops only have one disk, dynamic disks are not needed.

Q: Why do I have to wait 15 seconds between running diskpart.exe scripts?

A: You must give diskpart.exe a chance to finalize the changes currently in process before you instruct it to make more changes. Otherwise, changes may start to conflict with each other and your scripts will fail.

Q: Why would I want to use diskpart.exe when I can click my way through the disk management MMC?

A: The disk management MMC is definitely more intuitive for day-to-day disk management. However, it will not let you script activities. This is the true power of diskpart.exe. You can write scripts to automate disk management. For example, you may want to create a D: drive on all freshly built servers. You could make building a server completely automated by using an unattended file for the installation and a diskpart.exe script for creating the D: drive.

Q: How can I have my server search for new disks without rebooting?

A: From within the disk management MMC, right-click **Disk Management** and choose **Rescan Disks**.

Q: How can I switch from one volume type to another without losing data?

A: You can switch from a simple volume to a spanned volume. When you extend a simple volume to span multiple disks, it automatically becomes a spanned volume. You can also switch from a mirrored volume to a simple volume by breaking the mirror. To switch any other volumes, you would have to delete the volume and restore the data from backup.

Q: Is there a limit to the number of volumes that I can create on a single disk?

A: Windows Server 2003 supports up to 2,000 volumes per disk, but Microsoft recommends limiting yourself to 32 volumes per disk.

Q: How would you access 2,000 volumes? Aren't you limited to 24 drive letters?

A: Yes. You are limited to 24 drive letters as A: and B: are reserved for the floppy drives. However, you can get around this limit by mounting a volume to an NTFS folder. For example you could have a "data" folder on your C: drive that actually pointed to another volume. It would appear as if you were writing information to the C: drive, but it would actually be written to the mounted volume.

Q: Why can't I use defrag.exe and Disk Defragmenter at the same time?

A: They are both trying to do the same thing. Think of how defragmentation works. The defragmenter shuffles files around on disk to make them in contiguous clusters. Imagine how unorganized this would be if two programs tried to do it at the same time.

Q: Why don't I see a disk Quota tab when I go to the Properties of my volume?

A: Either you don't have administrative rights or your volume is not formatted with NTFS.

Q: How often should I defragment my servers?

A: This depends on your environment. You should do a weekly analysis to see if your volumes need to be defragmented. If you determine that weekly is too often, then drop your analysis back to monthly. Defragment only when the tools suggest that you do so.

Q: I just installed Remote Storage. Why can't I use rss.exe?

A: Rss.exe is used to manage Remote Storage. It cannot be used to set it up. If you just installed Remote Storage, then you must go into the Remote Storage MMC and set it up before rss.exe will work.

Q: Why do I get an error message when I try to install Remote Storage from Add or Remove Programs?

A: You are not logged on as an administrator. If you do not have administrative rights on the local machine, you cannot install Remote Storage.

Q: Remote Storage setup never finds my backup media. What could be the problem?

A: Make sure you are giving setup enough time to finish searching for media and verify that you are using a compatible media. Remote Storage supports all SCSI class 4mm, 8mm, DLT, and magneto-optical devices that are supported by Removable Storage, but it does not support QIC tape libraries, rewritable compact disc, or DVD formats.

Q: Why don't basic disks show up as foreign when you move them between machines like dynamic disks?

A: Dynamic disks store their configuration in a hidden database. This database is associated with the machine that created the dynamic disk. When you move it, the machines can see the disk is from somewhere else and they mark the disk as foreign. Basic disks store their configuration in the MBR and boot sector of the disk. This is tied to the disk and not to the machine. Machines see basic disks as new disks, but they cannot tell if they are from another machine so they do not mark them as foreign.

Self Test

A Quick Answer Key follows the Self Test questions. For complete questions, answers, and explanations to the Self Test questions in this chapter as well as the other chapters in this book, see the Self Test Appendix.

Understanding Disk Terminology and Concepts

1. Your domain controller currently has one 36GB dynamic disk. You want to add another disk and configure both disks into a mirror to provide fault tolerance for your domain controller. You shut down your sever and add the disk. After starting Windows, you go into the disk management MMC and verify that the disk is there. It shows up as unallocated space. You right-click on the C: drive, but Add Mirror is grayed out. You cannot select it. What could be the cause of your problem?

A. You need to format the drive with the FAT32 file system first.

B. You need to format the drive with the NTFS file system first.

C. You need to upgrade the new disk to dynamic.

D. You need to revert the C drive back to basic.

2. Your server currently has one drive that is used for the boot and system partition. You want to add a RAID-5 volume to use for storing user data. You shut down the server and add two new drives. After starting the machine back up, you go into the disk management MMC and convert both disks to dynamic. You then right-click on one of the drives and select new volume. However, the RAID-5 option is greyed out. What can you do to enable the creation of a RAID-5 volume?

A. Format both disks as NTFS.

B. Format one disk as NTFS.

C. Add another disk to the server.

D. Revert both disks back to basic.

Using Disk Management Tools

3. You add two new SCSI drives to your test server. You decide that you want to use diskpart.exe to create a new volume on each drive. Every time you type a command you get a message back saying that no disk is selected. What is the cause of your problem?

A. You need to set diskpart.exe to focus on a disk.

B. You need to go into the disk management MMC and enable the ability to use diskpart.exe.

C. You are having hardware problems with your new disks.

D. Diskpart.exe does not work with SCSI disks.

4. You have three servers that you manage offsite. You use a remote console command prompt to manage them. This enables you to open a command prompt on your local machine and have the commands sent to the remote servers. You want to mange disk quotas on the server using remote consoles. Which tool should you use?

A. diskpart.exe

B. rss.exe

C. fsutil.exe

D. quoata.exe

Understanding and Managing Physical and Logical Disks

5. Users have been complaining that printing is slow. Your print server is currently using basic disk. All spooling takes place on a primary partition. You want to create a dynamic volume to see if it increases your performance. Which of the following volume types should you create?

   A. Simple

   B. Spanned

   C. Striped

   D. Mirrored

   E. RAID-5

6. You have an old server that is no longer in production. You want to make it into an MP3 server to hold all your music. It has four drives in it. Two of the drives are 20GB in size and the other two are 5GB in size. You want to structure the disks to give the maximum storage space possible so you can store all your MP3s on one share. You are not concerned with data loss because you still have all the CDs. Which of the following volume types should you create?

   A. Simple

   B. Spanned

   C. Striped

   D. Mirrored

   E. RAID-5

7. You just bought a new server to use as a streaming media server. You want to configure it to get the best performance possible. The server has two identical 50GB drives. Which of the following volume types should you create?

   A. Simple

   B. Spanned

   C. Striped

   D. Mirrored

   E. RAID-5

Optimizing Disk Performance

8. You use Disk Defragmenter to run an analysis at lunch to determine if you need to defragment your servers. The report states that your disk is extremely fragmented and suggests that you run a defragmentation. You don't want to do it during the day due to performance reasons. You come in after hours to run your defragmentation, but you get the error message shown in Figure 2.117 every time you open Disk Defragmenter. What could be the cause of your problem?

Figure 2.117 Running Disk Defragmenter

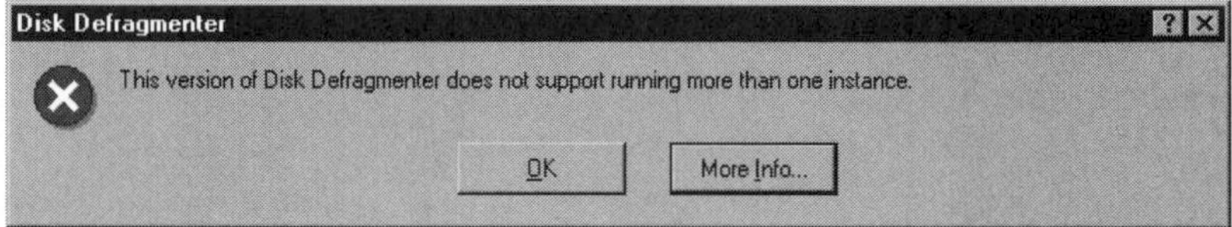

A. You are not logged in with administrative rights.

B. You installed this version of Disk Defragmenter on another machine and now you need another license.

C. You have defrag.exe running in the background.

D. You server has two disks in it. Disk Defragmenter only supports machines with one disk.

9. One of your coworkers complains that he cannot set quota limits on the file server. You check and find out that he is not in the local administrators group. You add him to the group and tell him to log off the server and back on again. When he logs on, the Quota tab is still missing. What could be the cause of the problem?

A. The volume is formatted as FAT32.

B. The volume is formatted as NTFS.

C. He is not a member of the quota admins group.

D. He is over his quota limit.

10. You have a machine with two disks. Both disks are formatted as FAT32. When you defragment both disks, they report having unmovable files. You would like to be able to completely defragment the second disk. What should you do?

A. Convert the second disk to NTFS.

B. Remove the page file from the second disk.

C. Use Disk Defragmenter to defragment the second disk instead of defrag.exe.

D. Use defrag.exe to defragment the second disk instead of Disk Defragmenter.

Understanding and Using Remote Storage

11. You have a server running Remote Storage on Windows 2000 Server. You need to upgrade the server to Windows Server 2003. You want it to continue to run Remote Storage after the upgrade. Which version of Windows Server 2003 should you upgrade to?

    A. Web Edition

    B. Standard Edition

    C. Enterprise Edition

    D. Datacenter Edition

12. You have a Windows Server 2003 machine running Remote Storage. You go into the Remote Storage MMC and try to add another local disk to be managed, but Remote Storage cannot find the disk. What could be the cause of the problem?

    A. The disk is a SCSI disk.

    B. The disk is an IDE disk.

    C. The disk is formatted with FAT32.

    D. The disk is attached to a Storage Area Network.

Troubleshooting Disks and Volumes

13. Your company has recently merged with another company named Novig. As part of the merger you are responsible for migrating all of Novig's e-mail to your Exchange servers. You do not want to migrate the mail across the WAN link, because it would be very slow. You send someone to pick up Novig's Exchange server and bring it to you so you can do the migration locally. However, when you turn on the server it has problems starting Exchange. You look in Disk Management (Figure 2.118) and see that some disks are labeled as missing. How can you fix this problem?

Figure 2.118 Troubleshooting Missing Disk

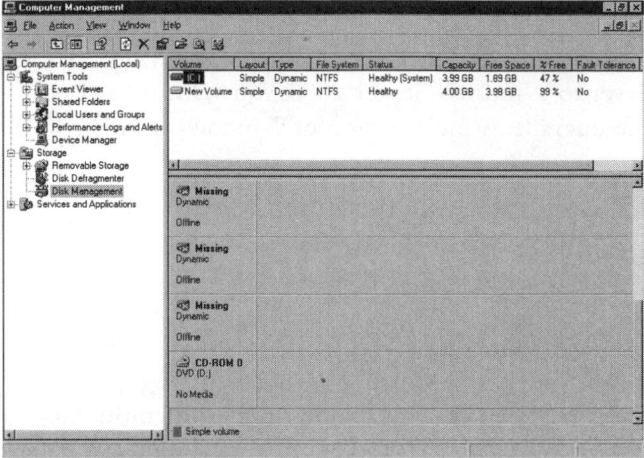

A. Format the drive as NTFS.

B. Verify that the disks are connected correctly.

C. Import the disks.

D. Assign the disks drive letters.

14. You come in to work Monday morning to find that your file server crashed over the weekend and no one can access his or her files. All user data is stored on a single disk. To get things up and running quickly you have a spare machine that you are going to rename to match the name of the crashed file server. You put the data disk from the crashed file server into the new file server, but the disk does not appear in My Computer. When you look in Disk Management (Figure 2.119), you see the disk is labeled as foreign. How do you overcome this?

Figure 2.119 Troubleshooting Foreign Disk

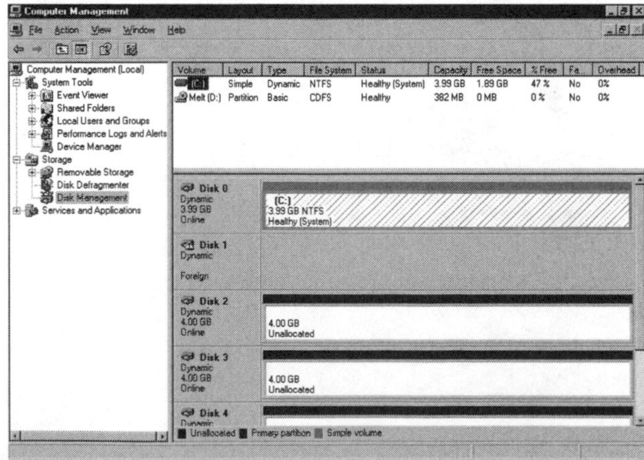

A. Format the drive as NTFS.

B. Verify that the disk is connected correctly.

C. Import the disk.

D. Assign the disk a drive letter.

15. You add four new disks to your server to use for storage. However, when you go into My Computer, the disks do not appear. You guess that the OS just isn't seeing the disks, so you reboot your server. Still they do not appear in My Computer. You open Disk Management and the disks are there as shown in Figure 2.120. Which of the following must you do to get these disks to show up in My Computer? (Choose all that apply.)

Figure 2.120 Installing New Disks

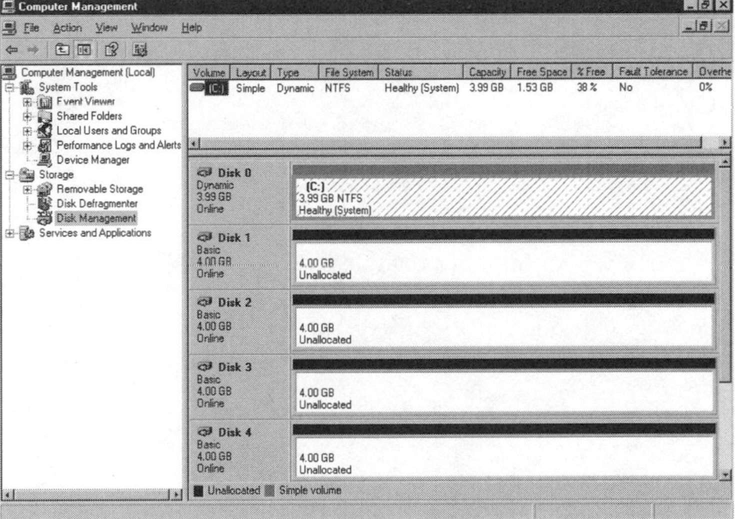

A. Format the drive as NTFS.

B. Verify that the disks are connected correctly.

C. Import the disks.

D. Assign the disks a drive letter.

Self Test Quick Answer Key

For complete questions, answers, and explanations to the Self Test questions in this chapter as well as the other chapters in this book, see the Self Test Appendix.

1. **C**
2. **C**
3. **A**
4. **C**
5. **C**
6. **B**
7. **C**
8. **C**
9. **A**
10. **B**
11. **C**
12. **C**
13. **B**
14. **C**
15. **A, D**

Chapter 3

MCSA/MCSE 70-290

Configuring, Monitoring, and Troubleshooting Server Hardware

Exam Objectives in this Chapter:

1.4 Install and configure server hardware devices.

1.4.1 Configure driver signing options.

1.4.3 Configure device properties and settings.

1.4.2 Configure resource settings for a device.

1.2 Monitor server hardware. Tools might include Device Manager, the Hardware Troubleshooting Wizard, and appropriate Control Panel items.

4.7.3 Monitor server hardware for bottlenecks.

- ☑ Summary of Exam Objectives
- ☑ Exam Objectives Fast Track
- ☑ Exam Objectives Frequently Asked Questions
- ☑ Self Test
- ☑ Self Test Quick Answer Key

Introduction

Your server hardware is the foundation on which Windows Server 2003 runs. Thus, the hardware configuration and its compatibility and interaction with the operating system play an important role in how well your Windows network operates. Even though Plug-and-Play makes working with hardware easier, it is important for the network administrator to understand how the hardware components are installed and configured, and how to manually assign resource settings (such as IRQs) and modify device properties and settings when necessary.

Device drivers are the software programs that act as liaison between the hardware and the operating system. *Driver signing* is a mechanism for ensuring that the driver files have been tested and have not been modified since they were tested, to prevent problems that can be caused by bad drivers. In this chapter, you will learn about driver signing and how to configure driver-signing options.

Inevitably, problems with hardware crop up from time to time. When those problems occur on a mission-critical server, it is essential that you be able to recognize and fix them as quickly as possible. Monitoring for problems helps you to "head them off at the pass." We will show you how to use Device Manager, the Hardware Troubleshooting Wizard, Control Panel applets, and included command-line utilities to monitor your server hardware, and we will provide some basic troubleshooting guidelines with specifics on how to diagnose and resolve issues related to hardware settings, drivers, and driver updates.

Understanding Server Hardware Vulnerabilities

Server hardware is a collection of devices. The operating system is the primary consumer of the services provided by the devices that you attach to your server environment running Windows Server 2003. Microsoft has developed a standardized framework for device vendors to develop the software necessary to leverage these devices. With the large number of possible combinations of devices, it is important to ensure that not only are the correct drivers installed, but that they are also configured correctly. Understanding how drivers interact with the operating system will go a long way to helping you understand and troubleshoot issues resulting from driver errors, failure, or misconfiguration. In this first section we cover the core principles that you should know and understand when it comes to installing, configuring, monitoring, and troubleshooting server hardware.

Understanding How Windows Server 2003 Interacts with the Hardware

The Windows Server 2003 operating system is built on a robust and mature foundation. From a high level, not much has changed in the past few releases of Windows NT/2000/XP/ Server 2003. From an infrastructure perspective, knowing how components of the operating system interact with each other and with the hardware will go a long way to helping you diagnose and resolve issues that may arise.

The operating system architecture is split up into two regions known as user-mode and kernel-mode (see Figure 3.1). The two modes function as follows:

- User mode is the mode in which most of the applications that you are familiar with (e.g., Microsoft Office) function. It protects the applications from performing illegal operations that could cause overall system instability. When these applications need to interact with the hardware, for example, draw items on the screen, they do so through drivers in kernel mode.
- Processes that run in kernel mode operate without the protection mechanisms associated with user mode. This gives these processes direct access to the underlying hardware using the hardware abstraction layer (HAL). The device drivers you install to enable Windows Server 2003 to utilize the devices you attach operate at this level. These drivers include, but are not limited to, video drivers, storage drivers, and network interface card drivers.

The whole concept of having these separate layers helps ensure system stability and enables users to mix and match hardware and devices while still enabling applications to work across the myriad of configurations.

Figure 3.1 High-Level Architecture of Windows Server 2003

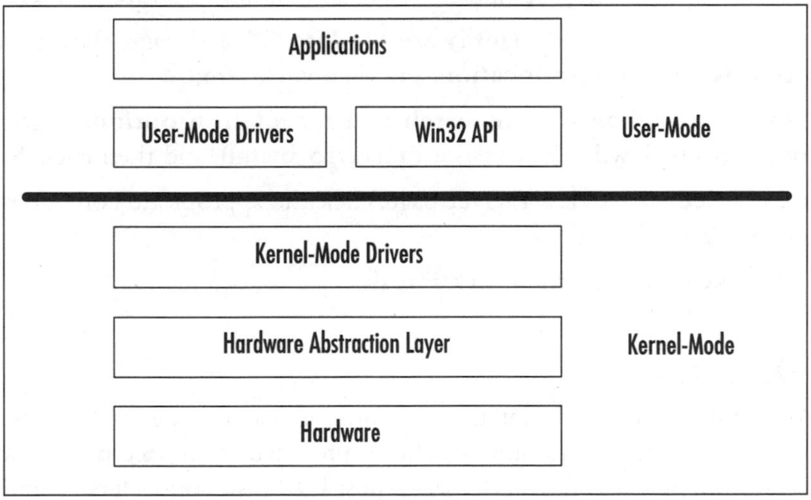

The Hardware Abstraction Layer (HAL)

The Hardware Abstraction Layer (HAL) provides a generic interface for kernel-mode drivers and processes to interact with the underlying hardware. This is a modular component that can be interchanged depending on your hardware configuration. When you deploy Windows Server 2003, it is important to ensure that you use the proper hardware abstraction layer. There are several types of HALs that ship with Windows Server 2003:

- Standard PC
- MPS Uniprocessor PC
- MPS Multiprocessor PC
- Advanced Configuration and Power Interface (ACPI) PC
- ACPI Uniprocessor PC
- ACPI Multiprocessor PC

Windows Server 2003 detects the appropriate HAL automatically during the setup process. It does this through a combination of detection of the number of processors and the presence of certain features offered by the system (e.g., Advanced Configuration and Power Interface) using information obtained from the BIOS, as well as referencing a list of known "bad BIOS" in the TXTSETUP.SIF file on the Windows CD.

After you deploy a machine with Windows Server 2003, it is likely that you will need to change the HAL only if you go from a single-processor machine to a multi-processor machine. If you do need to change the hardware abstraction layer, you can do so through Device Manager by performing the following steps:

1. Expand the **Computer** section in **Device Manager**.
2. Right-click the existing computer model and choose **Update Driver**.
3. On the **Welcome to the Hardware Update Wizard** page, choose **Install from a list or specific location**, and then click **Next**.
4. On the **Please choose your search and installation options** page, click **Don't search. I will choose the driver to install**, and then click **Next**.
5. On the **Select a Device Driver** page, click the appropriate computer type from the **Models** list.
6. Click **Next** twice, and then click **Finish**.

Device Drivers

With the HAL providing a generic interface or communications mechanisms to the core system components, device-specific functionality is provided via device drivers. While some device drivers are supplied with Windows (e.g., most IDE disk controllers), manufacturers often provide more specific device drivers that are optimized with the specific model of the device in mind and offer access to model-specific functionality.

New & Noteworthy...

Sound Drivers Disabled by Default

In the spirit of stabilizing the platform and removing unnecessary components, you will notice that sound drivers are not enabled by default in Windows Server 2003. This is a first step towards a division between client- and server-oriented operating systems. In future releases, expect other client-focused functionality to be disabled by default to allow for the server platforms to focus on what they are meant for: being a server.

If necessary, you can re-enable audio devices by performing the following steps:

1. Expand the **Sound, video and game controllers** section in **Device Manager**.
2. Verify that your sound device is listed in the section. If your device is listed and appears to be working, continue to the next step. Otherwise, do the following:
   - If you see a generic device placeholder device name, install an updated driver from the device vendor or from Windows Update.
   - If no related devices are listed, use the Add New Hardware Wizard to install the device driver (described in the "Using the New Hardware Wizard" section).
3. From the **Services** console, locate the **Windows Audio** service.
4. Right-click the service entry and select **Properties**.
5. Change the **Startup type** to **Automatic** and click the **Start** button. Click **OK** to close the **Properties** dialog box.

If you are using Windows Server 2003 as a Terminal Services machine, you are still able to re-direct sound. For more information, refer to Microsoft Support Knowledge Base article 818465 HOW TO: Use Group Policy to Permit Users to Redirect and Play Audio in a Remote Desktop Session to Terminal Services in Windows Server 2003 at http://support.microsoft.com/?id=818465.

Plug and Play

When you install a device into a system via an expansion slot or peripheral interface (e.g., serial, parallel, USB, 1394 FireWire port), it might detect the device automatically and try to install the appropriate device driver. These devices are known as Plug-and-Play (PNP) devices. The PNP specifications were developed by Intel Corporation to ensure the device installation experience is one that is possibly automatic, or if not, at least intelligent enough to ensure the appropriate driver is installed.

When a device is installed in the computer, Windows Server 2003 retrieves its PNP identification number from the hardware device via the device firmware or the system BIOS.

With this identification number, it searches all the .INF files in the device driver search path as defined in the registry, in the HKLM\Software\Microsoft\Windows\CurrentVersion key's DevicePath value. After collecting all the matches, it then ranks the matches and assigns a value from the following categories:

- 0x0000 – 0x0FFF: Exact match of the device's hardware identification number matched a hardware identification number listed in one of the .INF files.
- 0x1000 – 0x1FFF: Compatible match of the device's hardware identification number matched a compatible hardware identification number listed in one of the .INF files.
- 0x2000 – 0x2FFF: Compatible match of one of the device's compatible hardware identification numbers matched a hardware identification number listed in one of the .INF files.
- 0x3000 – 0x3FFF: Compatible match of one of the device's compatible hardware identification numbers matched a compatible hardware identification number listed in one of the .INF files.
- 0x8000 – 0x8FFF: The hardware identification match is made with an unsigned driver.
- 0x9000 – 0x9FFF: The compatible hardware identification match is made with an unsigned driver.
- 0xFFFF: All other non-matches.

As you can see, preferential treatment is given to signed drivers (for more information on signed drivers, see the section later in this chapter). If no full or partial match is found, the hardware is identified as an unknown device. You may see it listed in Device Manager with a generic name.

NOTE

With each new generation of the Windows operating system, the PNP capabilities and setup processes are streamlined. With the release of Windows Server 2003, there are no device driver installation sections during the graphical setup process. During text-mode setup, you have the option to add mass storage device drivers to the detection process. For more information, refer to the Microsoft Support Knowledge Base article 220845 Adding Third-Party or Updated Driver during Windows Setup at http://support.microsoft.com/?id=220845

If the device driver is a match, it will automatically install upon detection of the device if both of the following conditions are met:

- Digitally signed (see the "Driver Signing Options" section later in the chapter for more information).
- The driver is already pre-installed on the server.

If the device driver installation process requires user interaction or is not digitally signed, the user who is logged on when the device is plugged in will require the following rights (otherwise it will be deferred until someone with the appropriate rights can perform the operation):

- "Load and unload device drivers" privilege (the local Administrators group has this privilege by default).
- Permissions to copy files to the SYSTEM32\DRIVERS directory.
- Permissions to write settings to the registry.

Installing and Configuring Server Hardware Devices

As noted previously, when you install a device that complies with the PNP specifications, it automatically attempts to install and configure the device driver for that device. For non-PNP devices, you need to manually install the device. As part of the installation process, Windows automatically allocates the appropriate resources required for the device. This section outlines some of the ways you can control the installation process, including digitally signed driver options, manual driver installations, and configuring options associated with the drivers.

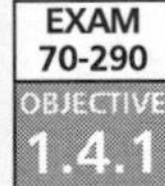

Configuring Driver Signing Options

Devices drivers play a critical role in the operation of your system, but they are also one of the major components to run in the kernel where it is not protected to the level that applications are from impacting the system stability. With the large number of devices available on the market, it is impossible to test every single combination of hardware devices and their device driver revisions.

Microsoft has put in place a program to advance the stability of systems and provide a better overall user experience through the Windows Hardware Compatibility Test (HCT) process. Hardware and software vendors work with a third-party testing firm contracted by Microsoft to ensure that rigorous functional test processes are followed. The resulting device drivers that pass the tests are signed with the Windows Hardware Quality Labs digital signature. These drivers are known as *WHQL digitally signed drivers* (or WHQL-signed drivers).

New to Windows Server 2003 is the concept of vendor-supplied Authenticode digital signatures for drivers. During the device driver installation process, there is a check for both a WHQL and a vendor-supplied Authenticode digital signature.

As the administrator, you can control how Windows Server 2003 responds to the presence of WHQL and vendor-supplied Authenticode digital signatures. This is done via the **Driver Signing Options** dialog box, which is available under the **System Properties Hardware** tab in the Control Panel, as shown in Figure 3.2.

Figure 3.2 System Properties Control Panel – Hardware Tab

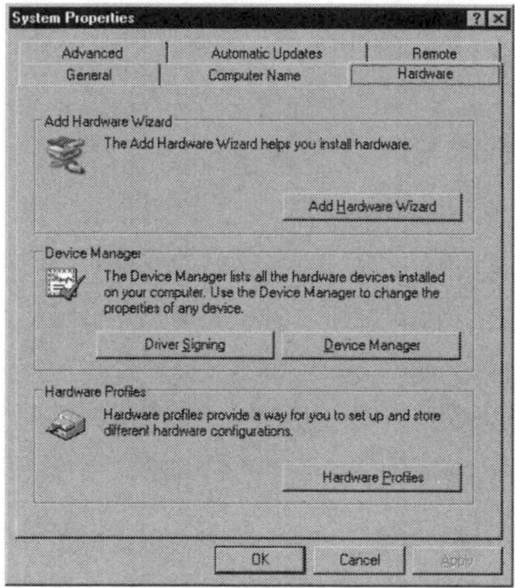

The Driver Signing Options dialog box, shown in Figure 3.3, gives you the capability to set three different levels of compliance:

- Ignore
- Warn
- Block

Figure 3.3 Driver Signing Options Dialog Box

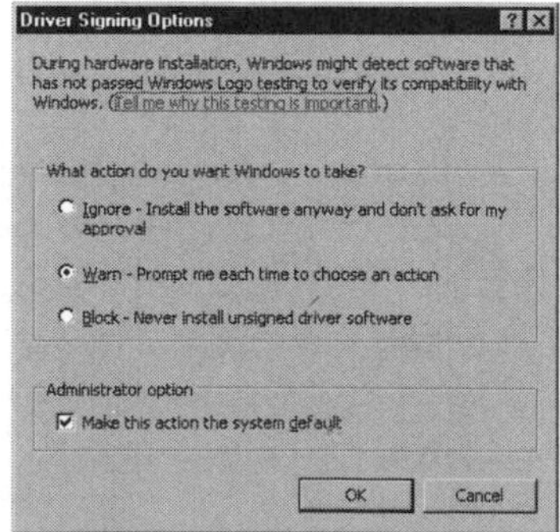

By default, it is set to **Warn** and in most environments should never be set to **Ignore**, because that can allow for unstable device drivers to enter the environment.

Depending on the validity or presence of the digital signatures and how the Driver Signing Options are configured, the installation process might respond in different ways. These can include the following:

- If the WHQL digital signature is valid, the installation process installs the driver without issue.
- If the WHQL digital signature is not valid, the installation process completes as per the option selected in the Driver Signing Options dialog box.
- If there is no WHQL digital signature and there is no valid vendor-supplied Authenticode digital signature, the installation process is completed as per the option selected in the Driver Signing Options dialog box.
- If there is no WHQL digital signature but there is a valid vendor-supplied Authenticode digital signature, the installation process checks to see if the vendor-supplied Authenticode digital signature exists in the Trusted Publishers Certificate Store. If it is and the Driver Signing Options dialog box is set to Warn, then it informs the user who published the driver that is signed with a valid Authenticode digital signature, but that it has not been certified by the Windows Hardware Quality Labs. The dialog box then gives the user the option of canceling the installation. The rest of the options operate as expected.
- If there is no WHQL digital signature but there is a valid vendor-supplied Authenticode digital signature and it is listed in the Trusted Publish Certificate Store, the driver installs silently as if it had a WHQL digital signature.

The *trusted publisher certificate store* contains all the trusted publisher certificates for that particular machine. You can install vendor-supplier Authenticode certificates to the store using one of the following methods:

- Drivers installed through the interactive user interface with a vendor-supplied Authenticode digital signature will have the certificate added to the trusted publisher certificates store automatically.
- Vendor-supplied Authenticode certificates can be deployed to machines on the network, leveraging Active Directory's Group Policy functionality.
- Vendor-supplied Authenticode certificates can be included during the unattended installation process by adding an entry in the **Unattended** section called **TrustedPublisherCertificates**. This entry specifies the path to locate the appropriate certificate store on the hard drive.

```
[Unattended]
TrustedPublisherCertificates = mycerts
```

This tells Windows Server 2003 to look in the **mycerts** directory on the root of the system drive for Trusted Publisher Certificates.

NOTE

If you are not sure about whether or not a product has been properly certified before purchasing it, check out Microsoft's Hardware Compatibility List online at www.microsoft.com/whdc/hcl.

After you have installed a device driver, you can check who signed it through **Device Manager** in the device **Properties** dialog box's **Driver** tab (see the *"Using Device Manager to Configure and Manage Devices"* section later in this chapter).

Ensuring Your Device Drivers Are Digitally Signed

Ongoing changes to the server environment bring the risk of critical system files being replaced. One of the advantages of using digitally signed device drivers is that there are several tools to help ensure that they remain intact on a continuous and on-demand basis. These tools include the following:

- Windows File Protection
- System File Checker
- File Signature Verification tool

Windows File Protection (WFP)

Windows File Protection (WFP) helps protect critical system files from being replaced or corrupted by other processes. Protecting these files helps the system remains reliable and available. WFP works by monitoring for change notifications from protected directories (e.g., %SystemRoot%\SYSTEM32). Because this process runs within the core operating system, it cannot be circumvented. If the file is changed, the following will happen:

1. WFP checks the digital signature of the changed file against the version stored in the cache (by default, %SystemRoot%\SYSTEM32\DLLCACHE) or in the digitally signed component's information file (also known as the catalog file).
2. If the file is different, it attempts to locate the correct version of the file in the following places:
    - The cache folder (by default, %SystemRoot%\SYSTEM32\DLLCACHE)
    - The original installation path (if different from the Windows Server 2003 installation media)
    - The Windows Server 2003 installation media

If WTP cannot locate it using the above locations and the person who is logged on has the appropriate rights, it prompts for the Windows CD or original installation media. Otherwise, it prompts the next time someone with the appropriate rights logs on.

3. After it locates the file, it silently replaces the file.
4. WFP creates an entry in the System event log noting the file that was replaced and the version it was replaced with.

When you do need to update a protected system file, the following processes are the only supported mechanisms:

- Windows Service Pack installations using Update.exe
- Hotfixes installed using Hotfix.exe or Update.exe
- Operating system upgrades
- Windows Update
- WHQL digitally signed driver installations.

WFP caches verified versions of these files in the cache folder. By default, this folder is located in %SystemRoot%\SYSTEM32\DLLCACHE; however, it can be modified by adding the **SFCDllCacheDir** registry value as a REG_EXPAND_SZ type in the HKLM\Software\Microsoft\Windows NT\CurrentVersion\Winlogon registry key. This cache continues to grow until it reaches any defined quota. By default, this quota is not set to a specific value (0xFFFFFFFF). You can define a quota by modifying the **SFCQuota** registry value in the HKLM\Software\Microsoft\Windows NT\CurrentVersion\Winlogon registry key.

NOTE

Windows File Protection (WFP) will stop populating the cache folder when disk space is less than 600MB plus the maximum size of the page file on the system volume.

EXERCISE 3.01

VERIFYING THAT WINDOWS FILE PROTECTION IS RUNNING

1. Open the **SYSTEM32** folder using **Windows Explorer**.
2. Find **calc.exe** in the list, right-click the entry, and then select **Delete**.

3. Wait a few moments and Windows File Protection will replace the file. After the file has been replaced, you will notice a new entry in your System event log similar to the one shown in Figure 3.4.

Figure 3.4 Windows File Protection Event Log Entry

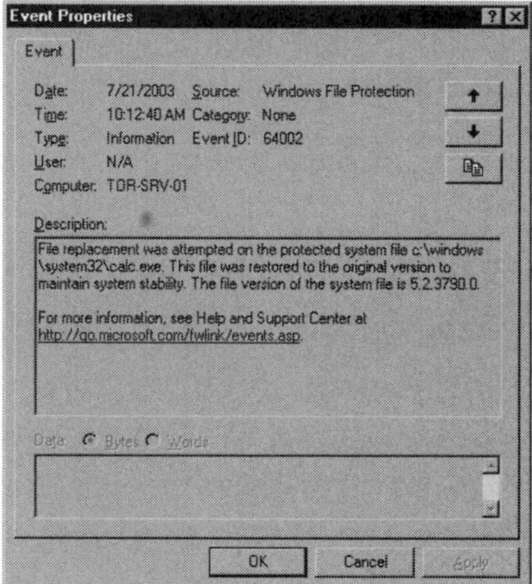

System File Checker

With Windows File Protection running on an ongoing basis, you might still want to check the critical system files on an on-demand basis. The System File Checker (sfc.exe) is a command-line tool that can be used for initiating on-demand and boot-time scans, as well as managing the contents of the Windows File Protection cache folder. To run System File Checker, you must be logged on with a user account that is a member of the Administrators group.

The System File Checker (sfc.exe) has several command-line options:

- */Scannow* Initiates an immediate scan of the protected files.
- */Scanonce* Schedules a one-time scan of the protected files the next time the computer is restarted. This option is equivalent to setting the SfcScan registry value to 2 in the HKLM\Software\Microsoft\Windows NT\CurrentVersion\Winlogon registry key.
- */Scanboot* Configures the system to scan the protected files every time the computer is restarted. This option is equivalent to setting the SfcScan registry value to 1 in the HKLM\Software\Microsoft\Windows NT\CurrentVersion\Winlogon registry key.

- *∕Revert* Resets the system to not scan for protected files during boot time. This is equivalent to the */Enable* command-line option under Windows 2000. This option is equivalent to setting the SfcScan registry value to 0 in the *HKLM\Software\Microsoft\Windows NT\CurrentVersion\Winlogon* registry key.
- */Purgecache* Purges the contents of the cache folder and initiate a scan immediately.
- */Cachesize=x* Sets the maximum size of the cache folder in megabytes (MB). For this command to take effect, you need to restart the computer and run the */PurgeCache* command to adjust the size of the cache folder. This option is equivalent to setting the SfcQuota registry value in the HKLM\Software\Microsoft\Windows NT\CurrentVersion\Winlogon registry key.

File Signature Verification Tool

sigverif.exe is a wizard-driven tool , which scans the system for the presence of unsigned drivers and critical system files. It also creates a report that lists all the files scanned along with relevant version and digital signature information. The report is stored in your Windows directory and is called sigverif.txt.

If you want to run the process without user interaction, use the */DEFSCAN* command-line option: **sigverif.exe /defscan**.

EXERCISE 3.02

SCANNING FOR UNSIGNED DRIVERS

1. From the **Start** menu, select **Run**.
2. In the **Run** dialog box, type **sigverif.exe** and click **OK**.
3. In the **File Signature Verification** dialog box, click **Advanced**.
4. In the **Advanced File Signature Verification Settings** dialog box, select the **Look for other files that are not digitally signed** option.
5. In the **Look in this folder** text box, type the full path to **SYSTEM32\DRIVERS** (e.g., C:\WINDOWS\SYSTEM32\DRIVERS).
6. Select the logging option and ensure that the **Save the file signature verification results to a log file** check box is checked, and then click **OK**.
7. In the **File Signature Verification** dialog box, click **Start**.
8. After the scanning process is complete, it displays a list of unsigned drivers. A report is also created called sigverif.txt and stored by default in the Windows directory.

9. When you are done, click **Close** to close the report and then click **Close** to exit the tool.

Using the New Hardware Wizard

The New Hardware Wizard is used to install device drivers for non-PNP devices. You can also use the wizard to install drivers for any PNP device for which you did not have the suitable device driver at the time it was connected to the system. The latter scenario is actually handled by the Hardware Update Wizard, which is invoked from within the New Hardware Wizard.

You need the following rights to use the New Hardware Wizard (by default, members of the local Administrators group hold these privileges):

- "Load and unload device drivers" privilege (the local Administrators group has this privilege by default)
- Permissions to copy files to the SYSTEM32\DRIVERS directory
- Permissions to write settings to the registry

You can access the **New Hardware Wizard** via the Control Panel's **Add Hardware** option, and from the **Hardware** tab of the **System** applet in Control Panel.

Exercise 3.03

Installing a Non-PNP Driver

1. From the **Start** menu, select **Control Panel**.
2. Select the **Add Hardware** option from the list.
3. On the **Welcome to the Add New Hardware Wizard** page, click **Next**.
4. When asked **Is the hardware connected?**, select **Yes, I already have connected the hardware** and click **Next**.
5. From the **Installed hardware list**, select **Add a new hardware device** and click **Next**.
6. On the next page, select **Install the hardware that I manually select from a list (Advanced)** and click **Next**.
7. Under the **Common hardware types** list, select **Network Adapters** and click **Next**.

8. From the list of network adapters, choose **Microsoft Loopback Adapter**. Notice that it is digitally signed as indicated by the icon to the left of it. Click **Next** twice, and then click **Finish**.

Using Device Manager to Configure and Manage Devices

After you have installed the device driver for your hardware, you might need to perform additional configurations, or make changes to the current configuration during maintenance or troubleshooting. **Device Manager** provides a graphical mechanism for managing devices, drivers, settings, and troubleshooting issues with devices. You can access **Device Manager** through one of three methods. The first is via the System control panel:

1. From the **Start** menu, select **Control Panel**, and then select **System** from the list. Or, from the **Start** menu or on the Desktop, right-click **My Computer** and select **Properties** from the context menu.
2. Select the **System** option from the list.
3. In the **System Properties** dialog box, select the **Hardware** tab.
4. On the **Hardware** tab, click **Device Manager**.

The second method is via the **Computer Management** console:

1. From the **Start** menu or the desktop icon, right-click **My Computer** and select **Manage**.
2. Select **Device Manager** from the left-hand pane of the **Computer Management** console.

The third method is via the command prompt or **Run** option on the **Start** menu. To do this, you simply go to the command prompt or **Run** option on the **Start** menu and type **devmgmt.msc** and press **Enter**.

After you open the **Device Manager,** you can view devices in four different ways. As shown in Figure 3.5, **Device Manager** defaults to the **Devices by type** view, which categorizes devices by the generic type (e.g., Display adapters, Network adapters, etc.).

In the **Devices by connection** view, shown in Figure 3.6, a hierarchy is built based on how the device is connected to the computer (e.g., your network adapter might be plugged into the PCI bus, which is connected to the computer system).

In the **Resources by type** view, shown in Figure 3.7, the four main types of resources—direct memory access (DMA) channels, input/output ports (I/O ports), interrupt request (IRQ), and memory addresses—are shown along with which device is using which resource.

Figure 3.5 Device Manager, Devices by Type

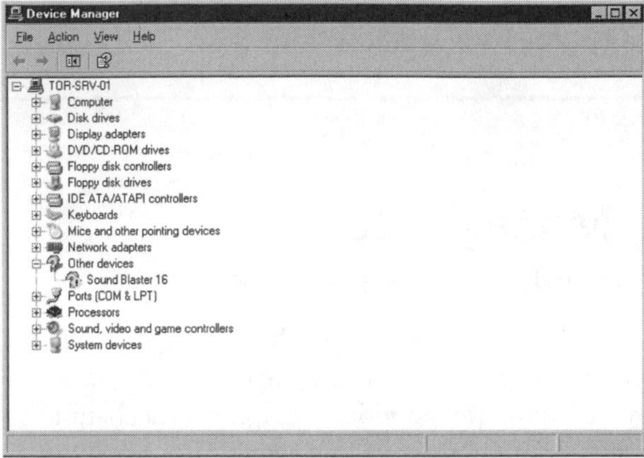

Figure 3.6 Device Manager, Devices by Connection

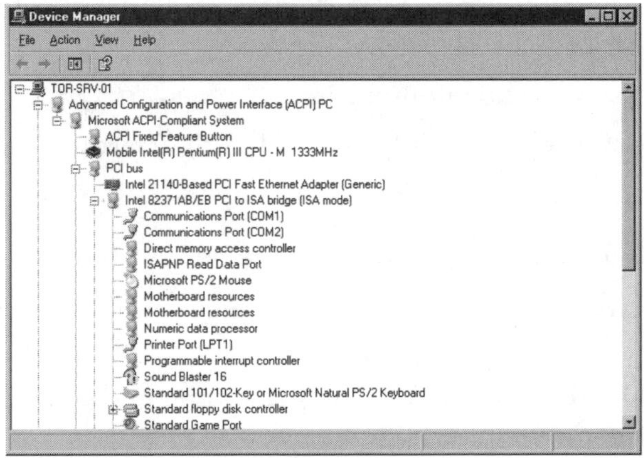

Figure 3.7 Device Manager, Resources By Type

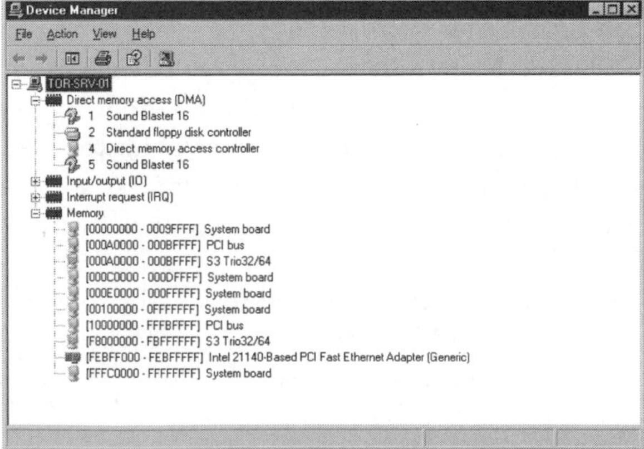

The **Resources by connection** view, shown in Figure 3.8, is similar to the **Resource by type** view, but instead of displaying the resource user directly under the type, it builds a hierarchy similar to the **Devices by connection** view. Devices that are using subsets of resources of other devices are shown as part of a hierarchy (e.g., an IDE disk controller uses a subset of the IO ports used by the PCI bus).

Figure 3.8 Device Manager, Resources by Type

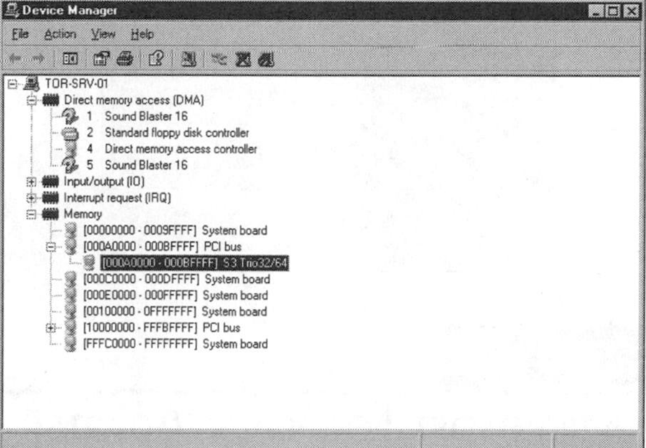

Some devices are not shown in **Device Manager** by default. These include some non-PNP devices, "phantom devices" (ones that have been removed but the drivers are still waiting for them—USB devices often fall under this class), and system devices. To view these devices, choose **Show hidden devices** from the **View** menu.

Before looking at how to manage device properties, there are two more items to note. From **Device Manager**, you can initiate a scan for new PNP devices by choosing the **Scan for Hardware Changes** option from the **Action** menu. You can also print a list of devices on the system along with summary information by choosing the **Print** option from the **Action** menu.

To view the properties of a device, right-click the entry in **Device Manager** and choose the **Properties** option from the context menu.

General Device Properties

When you first open the **Properties** dialog box for a device, you are placed into the **General** tab, as shown in Figure 3.9. In this area you can get basic information about device properties and the current status, the option to enable/disable the device, and the option to troubleshoot any device issues (we will cover this particular function later in this chapter).

Figure 3.9 Device Properties, General Tab

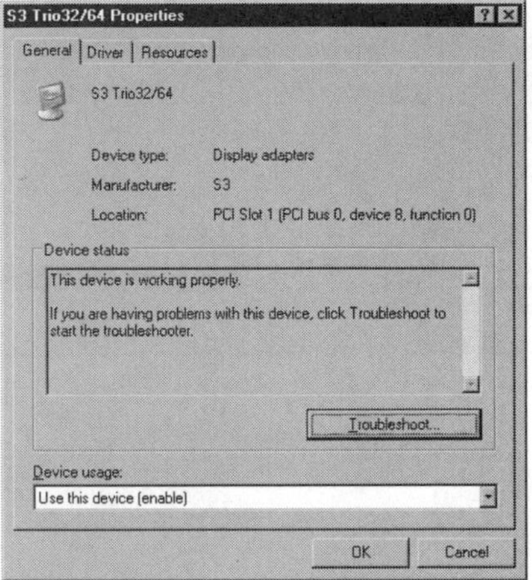

EXERCISE 3.04

DISABLING THE MICROSOFT LOOPBACK ADAPTER

1. Open **Device Manager** using one of the methods described earlier in the chapter.
2. Locate the **Microsoft Loopback Adapter** in the list and right-click it.
3. Select **Properties**.
4. In the **Microsoft Loopback Adapter Properties** dialog box, choose **Do not use this device (disable)** from the **Device usage** list.
5. Click **OK**. (Alternatively, you can select **Disable**. When asked **Do you really want to disable it?**, click **Yes.)**

Advanced Device Properties

Some devices have advanced properties that can be set to help tune their functionality for your particular usage or to assist in troubleshooting the device. These properties vary from device driver to device driver. If the device has no advanced properties exposed, there will be no **Advanced** tab in the device **Properties** dialog box, as shown in Figure 3.10.

Before changing the settings in the **Advanced** tab, refer to the device documentation to ensure that it will not cause any malfunction or instability within your system.

Figure 3.10 Device Properties, Advanced Tab

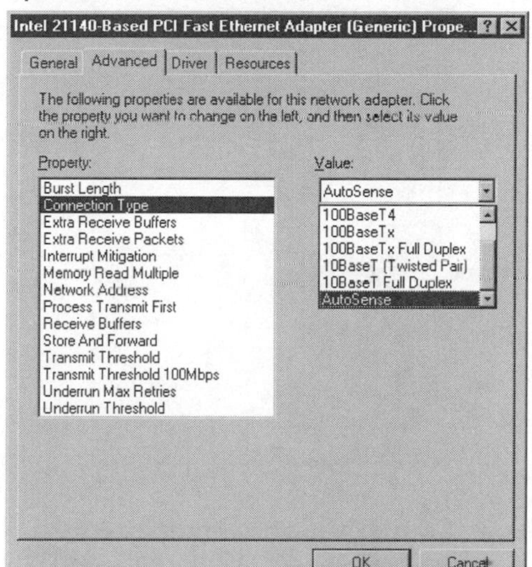

Managing the Device Driver

The **Driver** tab of the device **Properties** dialog box, shown in Figure 3.11, manages the specific version of the driver that is being used to control the device. On this tab you will find information about who wrote the driver and when, the version, and whether or not it is digitally signed.

Figure 3.11 Device Properties, Driver Tab

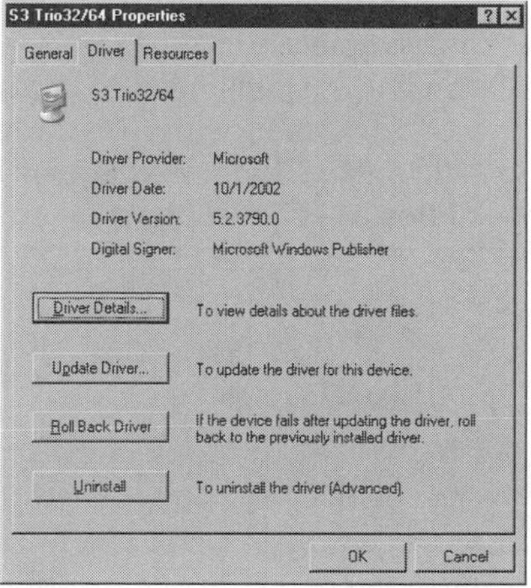

By clicking the **Driver Details** button, you can see a list of files associated with the driver currently installed as shown in Figure 3.12.

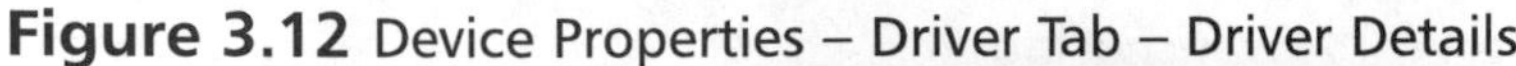

Figure 3.12 Device Properties – Driver Tab – Driver Details

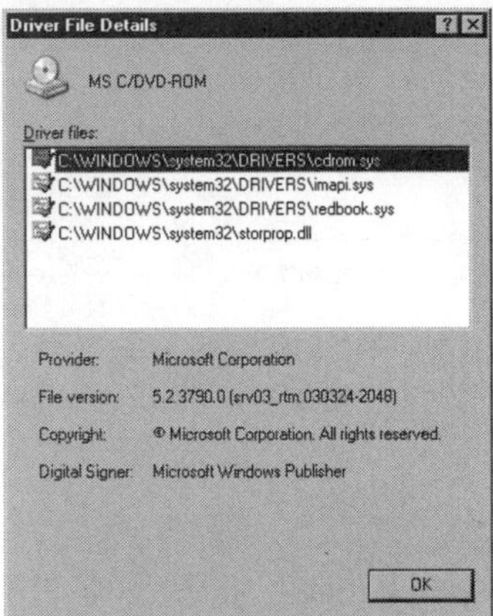

If you have a new version of the driver, you can update it by clicking the **Update Driver** button and following the **Hardware Update Wizard**. If there are problems associated with the driver you just updated, you can roll back to the previous version by clicking the **Roll Back Driver** button. Finally, if you need to uninstall the driver, you can do so with the **Uninstall** button.

NOTE

When updating drivers with WHQL-signed versions, in rare cases, you might experience other drivers being affected because the setup process overwrites files with the same name. It does not compare versions, file dates, or other driver details. If you have such a conflict, it is recommended that you contact the device vendor(s) to let them know. There is no simple way to rename the file and guarantee that it will still function. The device vendor(s) will need to provide a package without the conflicting filenames. For more information on this issue, refer to the Microsoft Support Knowledge Base article **815364 Signed Driver Install Overwrites Newer Versions of Shared Driver Files** at http://support.microsoft.com/?id=815364.

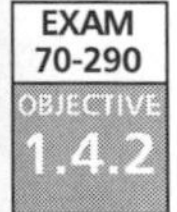

Configuring Resource Settings

Devices either exclusively or cooperatively share resources such as DMA, interrupt request (IRQ), input/output (I/O) port, and memory address resources. From time to time you might experience a conflict, or need to change which part of that resource the device uses to function. You can make these changes and check the status of any conflicts through the **Resources** tab in the device **Properties** dialog box, as shown in Figure 3.13.

Figure 3.13 Device Properties – Resources Tab

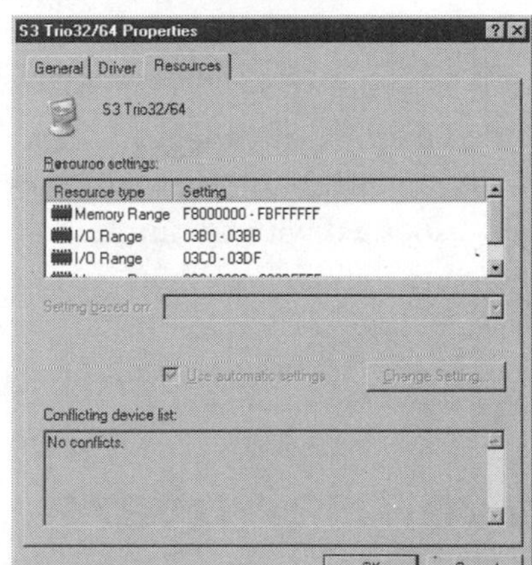

Most systems today allocate the resources appropriately for you. If you need to configure resources manually and the system bus supports it (e.g., for ISA-based devices), you can uncheck **Use automatic settings** and change the settings using the **Change Setting** button. The device might also have some pre-built resource configuration profiles that you can select through the **Settings based on** drop-down list.

Changing resource settings can disable your hardware or cause your system to malfunction, so make sure to consult your device documentation before making changes. In the case of devices that require exclusive use of resources, ensure there are no conflicts listed in the **Conflicting device list** text box.

Device Installation and Configuration Best Practices

When installing and managing devices in your system, there are a few best practices that you should consider following:

- **Always use signed drivers.** When working in a server environment, it is highly recommended that you make it a policy to use only those drivers that have been digitally signed with a Windows Hardware Quality Labs X.509 digital certificate. When you obtain the drivers from your hardware vendor, look for the *Designed for Microsoft Windows Server 2003* logo on the packaging, on the vendor's Web site, or on the device itself. If you are unable to obtain WHQL-signed drivers, at a minimum ensure that they are digitally signed by the vendor or obtained from a trusted source. Drivers operate in unprotected areas of the operating system and can cause severe system instability or expose security vulnerabilities if they are written improperly.

- **Check for device resource conflicts and issues.** After installing a new device, ensure that there are no resource conflicts by checking the **Resource** tab. Also check the **General** tab to ensure the device is working properly.
- **Manage drivers with minimum privileges.** With the advent of Windows Server 2003, there is a new emphasis to ensure that not only is the technology secure, but the processes associated with administering a system are done in a secure fashion. This section noted the minimum rights required to manage the average device driver. Consider delegating privileges to the person(s) responsible for managing server hardware instead of giving them full local Administrator access.

Monitoring Server Hardware

After you have installed and configured your device, you should monitor it on a regular basis to ensure that it is functioning as expected. Monitoring can help you be pro-active about device issues, including device failures, drivers or capacity issues, before users experience the problems first-hand. In this section we take a look at the essential tools used for monitoring the overall health of the devices, including capacity planning.

Using Device Manager

Earlier in the chapter we discussed **Device Manager** as a tool that can be used to manage device properties. In order to be able to manage the properties, **Device Manager** presents a list of devices installed in the system. Choose **Show hidden devices** from the **View** menu. These include some non-PNP devices, "phantom devices" (ones that have been removed but the drivers are still waiting for them—USB devices often fall under this class), and system devices. To view these devices, choose **Show hidden devices** from the **View** menu.

For devices that are disabled or have issues, you will see them automatically called out by having their sections expanded in the default view and an icon with an 'X' (disabled) or exclamation point (error) in the icon. If the device has an issue or is disabled without cause, you should investigate it by opening the device **Properties** dialog box by right-clicking the device entry and selecting **Properties** from the context menu to get access to the **Device status** section of the device **Properties**, as shown in Figure 3.14.

The **Device status** text box gives you basic information on why that device is having an issue.

Figure 3.14 Device Properties, General Tab (Device Status Error Shown)

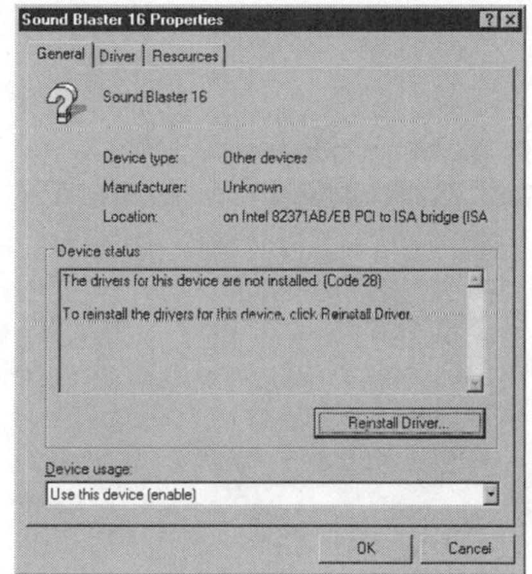

Using Event Viewer

Found under the **Administrative Tools** | **Event Viewer** is one of the essential tools for monitoring system health. It records information, warning, and error events raised by various components of the system, including device drivers and the device management services. As you navigate **Event Viewer**, you might see events that are generated by various devices. Figure 3.15 shows an example of an information message generated by the TCP/IP driver.

Figure 3.15 Event Properties

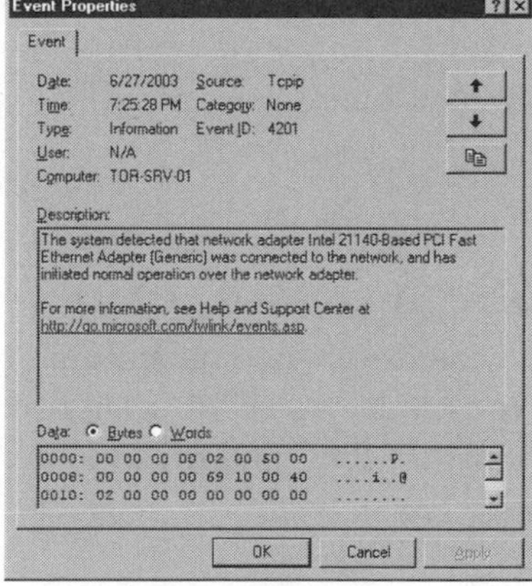

Using Control Panel Applets

Certain Control Panel applets expose hardware status information as you work with the functional properties that involve those devices. When it comes to actually managing the hardware side, these applets often bring you back to **Device Manager**'s **Properties** dialog boxes to do actual management. Applets that involve this sort of functionality include **Network Connections, Mouse** (shown in Figure 3.16), **Keyboard, Sounds and Audio Devices,** and more.

Figure 3.16 Mouse Control Panel – Hardware Tab

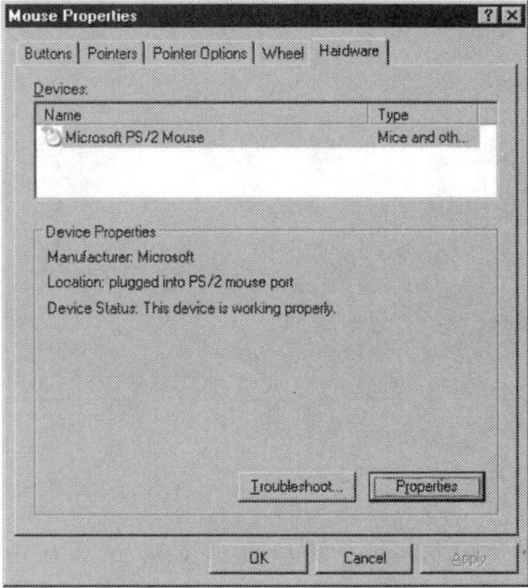

Using Command-Line Utilities

One of the management objectives that the Windows Server team had when developing Windows Server 2003 was to make all administrative functionality in the graphical interface accessible via the command-line. There are two notable command-line utilities that ship with Windows Server 2003:

- Device Console Utility (devcon.exe)
- Service Control Utility (sc.exe)

Device Console Utility (devcon.exe)

The Device Console Utility (devcon.exe) is a command-line utility that can be used as an alternative to Device Manager. It provides a level of detail that is not available in Device Manager. This tool is installed as part of the Windows Support Tools.

NOTE

The Windows Support Tools can assist you in managing systems and troubleshooting problems. They are not installed by default with Windows Server 2003. To install them, you need to run the installation process separately by executing **SUPTOOLS.MSI** from the **SUPPORT\TOOLS** folder on the Windows Server 2003 installation media.

There are four modes of operations in the Device Console Utility:

- Display the following properties of devices and their drivers on local and remote computers:
  - Hardware identification numbers, compatible hardware identification numbers, device instance identification strings
  - Categories in which devices are grouped, also known as device setup classes
  - Devices in a particular device setup class
  - Components of a driver package (e.g., driver files, installation files, etc.)
  - Hardware resources (e.g., direct memory access (DMA) channels, input/output ports (I/O ports), interrupt request (IRQ), and memory addresses)
  - Current device status
  - Device driver and service dependencies (also known as the driver stack)
- Search for devices (whether or not they have drivers installed) on local and remote computers by hardware identification numbers, device instance identification strings, or device setup class.
- Change the status or configuration of devices on the local computer, including the following:
  - Enable or disable the device.
  - Install or remove device drivers.
  - Update existing device drivers (both interactive and non-interactive installations).
  - Initiate a rescan for Plug and Play devices.
  - Add, delete, and reorder the hardware IDs of devices.
  - Change the device driver and service dependencies for a device setup class.
- Restart devices or the system on the local computer.

The high-level command-line operations are discussed in the following section.

Display-Related Commands

Table 3.1 displays information about display-related commands.

Table 3.1 Display-Related Commands

Command	Description
Classes	Lists all the known device setup classes, including the ones not in use.
DriverFiles	Displays the full path and filename of the installed device installation information files (.INF files) and the associated device driver files.
DriverNodes	Lists all the compatible driver packages for a particular device along with the version and ranking of the package. (For more information on the ranking, see the earlier Plug and Play section.)
HwIDs	Displays the hardware identification numbers, compatible hardware identification numbers, device instance identification strings.
ListClass	Lists all devices in the specified device setup classes.
Resources	Lists the system resources (e.g., DMA channels, I/O ports, IRQ, and memory addresses) allocation to a specified device.
Stack	Displays the device driver and service dependencies (also known as the driver stack) for a specified device, including the unique identifier and the name of the device setup class for each device.
Status	Displays the current status (running, stopped, or disabled) of device drivers on the computer.

The following is an example of using Device Console Utility to list all the IDE devices within the system:

```
C:\> devcon driverfiles *IDE*


IDE\DISKIC25N040ATCS05-0------------------------------------------
CS40A61A\5&D235F77&0&0.0.0
    Name: IC25N040ATCS05-0
    Driver installed from c:\windows\inf\disk.inf [disk--install]. 1
    file(s) used by driver:
        C:\WINDOWS\System32\DRIVERS\disk.sys
PCIIDE\IDECHANNEL\4&6401B72&0&0
    Name: Primary IDE Channel
    Driver installed from c:\windows\inf\mshdc.inf [atapi--Inst--primary].
    2 file(s) used by driver:
        C:\WINDOWS\System32\DRIVERS\atapi.sys
        C:\WINDOWS\System32\storprop.dll
PCIIDE\IDECHANNEL\4&6401B72&0&1
    Name: Secondary IDE Channel
    Driver installed from c:\windows\inf\mshdc.inf [atapi--Inst--secondary].
        2 file(s) used by driver:
        C:\WINDOWS\System32\DRIVERS\atapi.sys
```

```
        C:\WINDOWS\System32\storprop.dll
3 matching device(s) found.
```

Search-Related Commands

The operations shown in Table 3.2 search for information about devices on the computer.

Table 3.2 Search-Related Commands

Command	Description
Find	Locates and displays all the devices attached to the computer that match the specified search pattern.
FindAll	Locates and displays all the devices attached to the computer along with devices that have been detached or moved (known as non-present or phantom devices) that match the specified search pattern.

The following is an example of using Device Console Utility to find all devices from the media device class:

```
C:\> devcon find @root\media*

ROOT\MEDIA\MS_MMACM                                 : Audio Codecs
ROOT\MEDIA\MS_MMDRV                                 : Legacy Audio Drivers
ROOT\MEDIA\MS_MMMCI                                 : Media Control Devices
ROOT\MEDIA\MS_MMVCD                                 : Legacy Video Capture
    Devices
ROOT\MEDIA\MS_MMVID                                 : Video Codecs
5 matching device(s) found.
```

Change-Related Commands

Table 3.3 shows operations that manipulate the device or change its configuration.

Table 3.3 Change-Related Commands

Command	Description
Enable	Enables a specified device driver on the system.
Disable	Disables a specified device driver on the system.
Update	Replaces a specified device driver on the system with one specified by the updated driver's INF file.
UpdateNI	Replaces a specified device driver on the system with one specified by the updated driver's INF file without any user interaction.
Install	Installs a new device driver on the system.

Continued

Table 3.3 Change-Related Commands

Command	Description
Remove	Removes a specified device driver from the system.
Rescan	Initiates the Plug and Play service to scan the system for new devices.
SetHwID	Adds, deletes, or modifies the order of hardware identification numbers.
ClassFilter	Adds, displays, deletes, or modifies the order of filter drivers.

The following is an example of using Device Console Utility to disable and then re-enable all USB devices attached to the system:

```
C:\> devcon disable USB*

USB\ROOT_HUB\4&1F4031C5&0                                  : Disabled
USB\ROOT_HUB\4&31F9E26A&0                                  : Disabled
USB\ROOT_HUB20\4&7D3C0D5&0                                 : Disabled
3 device(s) disabled.

C:\> devcon enable USB*

USB\ROOT_HUB\4&1F4031C5&0                                  : Enabled
USB\ROOT_HUB\4&31F9E26A&0                                  : Enabled
USB\ROOT_HUB20\4&7D3C0D5&0                                 : Enabled
3 device(s) enabled.
```

Restart-Related Commands

Table 3.4 shows operations that restart the device or reboot the system.

Table 3.4 Restart-Related Commands

Command	Description
Restart	Stop and restart a specified device.
Reboot	Restart the system.

The following is an example of using Device Console Utility to restart the Microsoft Loopback Adapter:

```
C:\> devcon restart *MSLOOP*

ROOT\NET\0000                                   : Restarted
1 device(s) restarted.
```

For additional information, refer to the Device Console Utility reference in the Windows Support Tools help.

Service Control Utility (sc.exe)

The Service Control utility is used to communicate with both services and with device drivers. The functionality provided is only a subset of the Device Console utility focused on device drivers themselves; however, unlike the Device Control Utility, the Service Control Utility is installed with Windows Server 2003.

Display-Related Commands

Table 3.5 lists operations that display information about devices.

Table 3.5 Display-Related Commands

Command	Description
Enumdepend	Displays the dependencies of a specified service or device driver.
Getdisplayname	Displays the associated display name of a specified service or device driver.
Getkeyname	Displays the associated key name of a specified service or device driver display name.
Qc	Displays configuration information for a specified service or device driver.
Qdescription	Displays the associated description of a specified service or device driver.
Qfailure	Displays the actions that the Service Control Manager will execute if the specified service or device driver fails.
Query	Displays the current state information of all or specified service or device driver.
Queryex	Displays the current extended state information of all or specified service or device driver.
Querylock	Displays the current lock status of the Service Control Manager database.
Sdshow	Displays the security descriptor using SDDL for a service or device driver.

The following is an example of using the Service Control Utility to retrieve the status of all active network interface drivers:

```
C:\> sc queryex type= driver group= NDIS


SERVICE_NAME: E100B

DISPLAY_NAME: Intel(R) PRO Adapter Driver
```

```
        TYPE               : 1  KERNEL_DRIVER
        STATE              : 4  RUNNING
                                (STOPPABLE,NOT_PAUSABLE,IGNORES_SHUTDOWN)
        WIN32_EXIT_CODE    : 0  (0x0)
        SERVICE_EXIT_CODE  : 0  (0x0)
        CHECKPOINT         : 0x0
        WAIT_HINT          : 0x0
        PID                : 0
        FLAGS              :

SERVICE_NAME: Ndisuio
DISPLAY_NAME: NDIS Usermode I/O Protocol
        TYPE               : 1  KERNEL_DRIVER
        STATE              : 4  RUNNING
                                (STOPPABLE,NOT_PAUSABLE,IGNORES_SHUTDOWN)
        WIN32_EXIT_CODE    : 0  (0x0)
        SERVICE_EXIT_CODE  : 0  (0x0)
        CHECKPOINT         : 0x0
        WAIT_HINT          : 0x0
        PID                : 0
        FLAGS              :
```

Change-Related Commands

The following operations shown in Table 3.6 change the state of the machine, service control manager, or the service/device driver.

Table 3.6 Change-Related Commands

Command	Description
Boot	Specifies whether or not the last boot should be saved as the last known good configuration.
Config	Modifies the basic configuration information for a specified service.
Continue	Resumes a paused service.
Control	Sends a control code to the service.
Create	Creates a service entry in the Service Control Manager's database.
Delete	Removes a service entry in the Service Control Manager's database.
Description	Sets the description for a specified service or device driver.

Continued

Table 3.6 Change-Related Commands

Command	Description
Failure	Specifies what action to take upon failure of the service.
Interrogate	Sends an interrogate control code to the service.
Lock	Locks the Service Control Manager's database.
Pause	Pauses a service.
Sdset	Sets the security descriptor using SDDL for a service or device driver.
Start	Starts a specified service or device driver.
Stop	Stops a specified service or device driver.

Using Performance Console

Monitoring the key metrics of system performance is an important part of ensuring that you are maintaining a healthy system. Performance data is extremely useful for understanding when a system has surpassed certain thresholds, spotting trends in system usage, and helping to evaluate performance tuning of your system.

The **Performance** console hosts **System Monitor** and **Performance Logs and Alerts**. **System Monitor**, shown in Figure 3.17, delivers a real-time graphical view of what is happening in the system in various forms (graph, histogram, and report). Reports can be exported in HTML format as well. **System Monitor** is often used in production environments for viewing data logged with **Performance Logs and Alerts**.

Figure 3.17 Performance Console – System Monitor

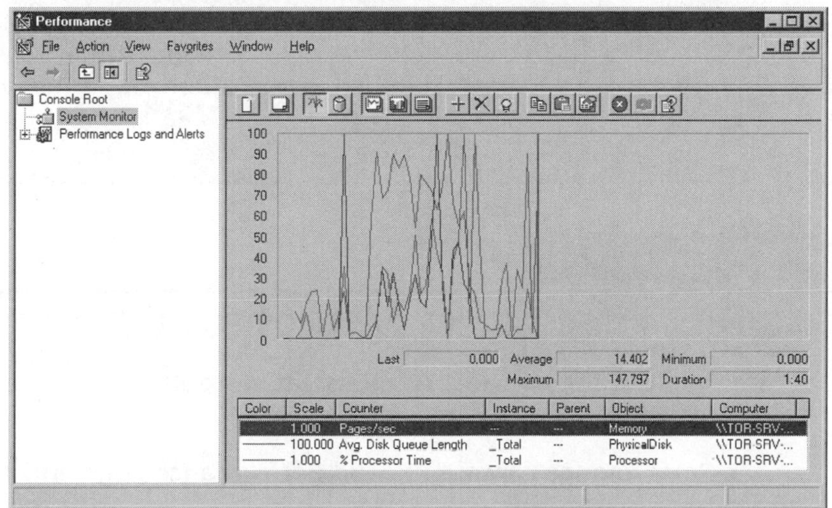

Performance Logs and Alerts, shown in Figure 3.18, is a low-overhead collection tool used to capture specified metrics for later analysis. It runs as a background service in Windows Server 2003, continuously collecting data. **Performance Logs and Alerts** also allows for collection to occur under alternative credentials as well as a variety of log formats, including comma- and tab-separated value files as well as an SQL Server database.

Figure 3.18 Performance Console – Performance Logs and Alerts – Counter Logs

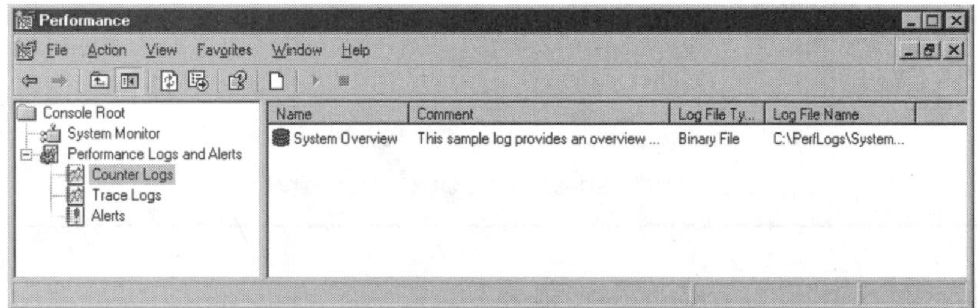

New & Noteworthy...

System Monitor and Performance Logs and Alerts Security

As part of the *Security by Design* initiative, the Windows Server product group made some fundamental changes to security around the performance monitoring tools in Windows Server 2003. If you are not a member (explicitly or through inheritance) of the local Administrators, you cannot access the performance monitoring tools or data unless you are a member of one of the following groups:

- **Performance Monitor Users** Monitor performance counters locally or from a remote computer.
- **Performance Log Users** Manage performance counters, logs, and alerts locally or from a remote computer.

If you are coming from Windows 2000 you will notice that the ability to configure logging using Performance Logs and Alerts under alternative credentials is a new feature.

Exercise 3.05

Capturing Disk Performance Metrics for Later Analysis

1. From the **Start** menu, select **Administrative tools**.
2. Select the **Performance** option from the list.
3. In the **Performance** console, expand **Performance Logs and Alerts** in the left pane.

4. Right-click **Counter Logs** and select **New Log Settings** from the context menu.
5. In the **New Log Settings** window, give the log settings a name and click **OK.**
6. In the **Properties** dialog box, click **Add Counters**.
7. In the **Add Counters** dialog box, select **PhysicalDisk** from the **Performance object** list.
8. Select **Current Disk Queue Length** from the **Counters** list, as shown in Figure 3.19.

Figure 3.19 Selecting Current Disk Queue Length

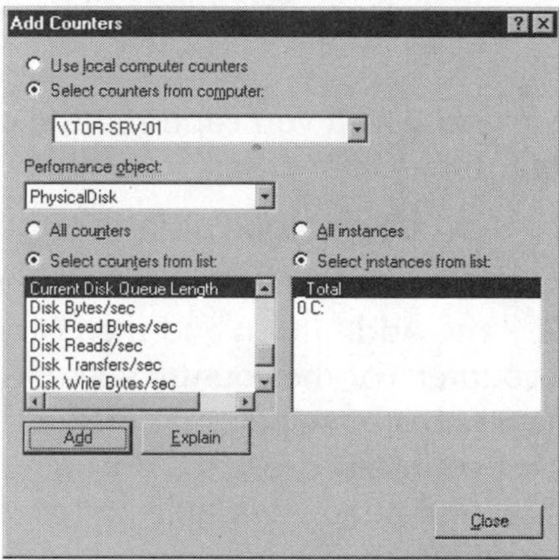

9. Select the **All instances** option, click **Add**, and then click **Close**, which results in a dialog box that looks similar to Figure 3.20.

Figure 3.20 Performance Logs and Alerts

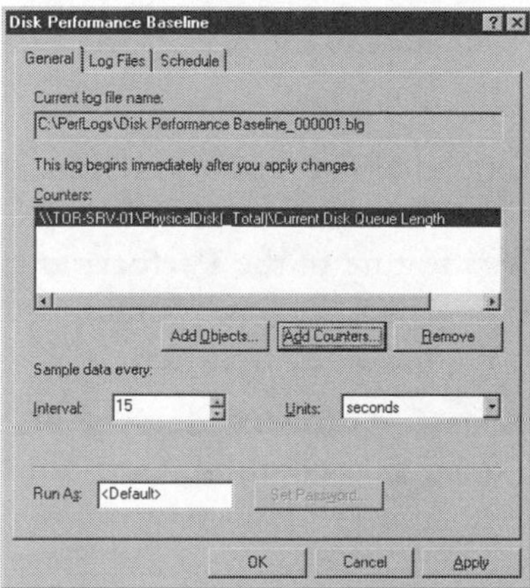

10. You are prompted with a question to create the log file; click **Yes**. **Performance Logs and Alerts** starts capturing data automatically. You need to create some activity on the disk to capture some data that can be viewed. Run something like Disk Defragmenter on your system to generate disk activity.
11. After you have generated some disk activity for a period of time, right-click the log entry in the right pane of the **Counter Logs** section of **Performance Logs and Alerts** and select **Stop** from the context menu.
12. Now it's time to view the data. Start by selecting **System Monitor** from the left pane.
13. Click the **View Log Data** button on the toolbar in the right pane.
14. In the **Data Source** section of the dialog box, select **Log files** and click the **Add** button.
15. Locate the log file to which you captured the performance data, select it, and click **Open**; then click **OK**.
16. Click the **Add** button on the toolbar in the right pane.
17. In the **Add Counters** dialog box, the one counter you added should be highlighted. Click the **Add** button and then click **Close**. This draws a graph for that counter. For the counter you added above, the suggested threshold is the number of spindles on the hard disk plus 2. As you add and explore other counters, check the documentation from your device vendor as well as information available on Microsoft's TechNet site (www.microsoft.com/technet) and other third-party sources.

Hardware Monitoring Best Practices

When monitoring devices on your system, there are a few best practices that you should consider following:

- **Create and maintain a performance baseline.** Consider capturing a baseline of key performance metrics on your system during an "average" timeframe using the **Performance Logs** feature of the **Performance** console. When it comes to troubleshooting issues or doing capacity planning, this data will go a long way toward helping you make informed decisions.
- **Monitor the event logs for unusual device-related messages and performance counters to ensure acceptable thresholds have not been exceeded.** Management tools such as Microsoft Operations Manager (MOM) assist you in automatically identifying new and unusual messages in the event logs

as well as watching performance counters for items that violate set thresholds. These tools do this by accessing the system through the Simple Network Management Protocol (SNMP) or by querying Windows Management Instrumentation (WMI). Some devices expose additional proprietary counters and details, so be sure to investigate that with your device documentation.

- **Leverage device vendor's tools where appropriate.** Some devices come with management software to enable access to more advanced monitoring. When you add a new device to your system, test the software to see if it provides any additional value. If it does not, keep your system as simple as possible and uninstall it. If you do plan to use the tool, you should ensure that the management tool also carries the *Designed for Microsoft Windows Server 2003* logo software certification when installing it in a server environment.

Troubleshooting Hardware Devices

When it comes to troubleshooting hardware devices, there are two scenarios that you will encounter. Either a device will not work or will cause the system to become unstable immediately after installation, or a device fails at a later date. Troubleshooting the first scenario can be somewhat easier because you know what has changed in the system recently. If you are troubleshooting device failure at a later date, it can often be more difficult unless you have maintained good change management documentation that records the operations that have been performed on the system.

The basic process of troubleshooting any issue is as follows:

1. Collect relevant data on the problem. This includes error messages, event log entries, and performance metrics.
2. Using past experience and research, analyze the symptoms.
3. Establish a set of potential causes that can lead to possible workarounds and/or resolutions.
4. Execute the most likely workaround and/or resolution to recover the system in a timely manner.
5. Document the problem, symptoms, and resolutions for future reference.

Windows Server 2003 provides a comprehensive set of tools to assist you in troubleshooting resource allocation issues as well as device-driver-related issues. In addition to the tools that ship with Windows Server 2003, new tools and resources are being made available online over time. Some of the notable online resources available through http://support.microsoft.com include the following:

- Windows Server 2003 Support Center
- Knowledge Base Search

- Windows Server 2003 Events and Errors Search
- Windows Server 2003 Support WebCasts
- Windows Server 2003 Newsgroups

New & Noteworthy...

Help & Support Troubleshooting Tools

Through extensive usability research, the Windows Server product group decided to move away from the **Hardware Troubleshooting Wizard** in favor of a more detailed and context-specific troubleshooting tool. Windows Server 2003 leverages a series of Troubleshooters, which first appeared in Windows XP, that walk you through a problem. This includes asking for details on the symptoms, suggesting resolutions and linking to more information on the problem. Currently, there are 17 built-in troubleshooters that cover a variety of areas, including the following:

- System setup
- Startup/Shutdown
- Display (shown in Figure 3.21)
- Home networking
- Hardware
- Multimedia and games
- Digital Video Discs (DVDs)
- Input Devices
- Drives and Network Adapters
- USB
- Sound
- Modem
- Internet Connection Sharing
- Internet Explorer
- Outlook Express (Messaging)
- File and Print Sharing
- Printing

Continued

Figure 3.21 Help and Support Center – Display Troubleshooter Step 3

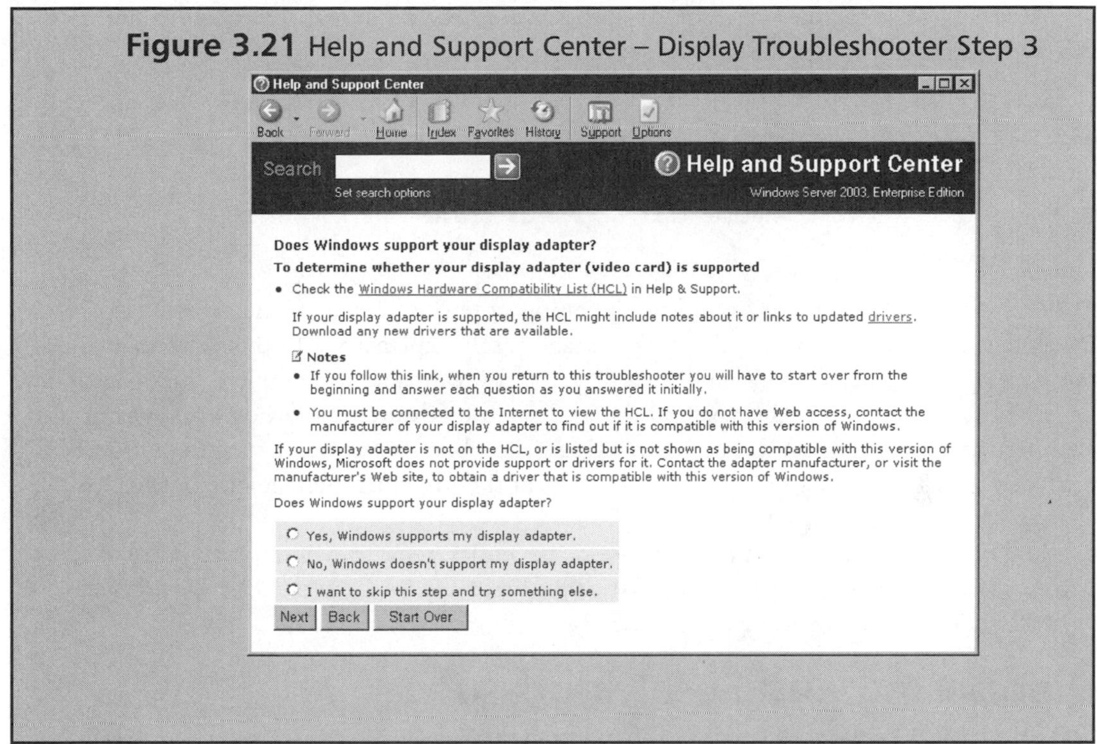

The first stop for device status is to use **Device Manager**. As mentioned earlier the chapter, **Device Manager** can give you a high-level indication of whether or not the device is having issues through the icon in the **Device Manager** console, as well as through the **Device status** text box in the device **Properties** dialog box, as shown in Figure 3.22.

Figure 3.22 Device Properties – General Tab (Drivers Not Installed)

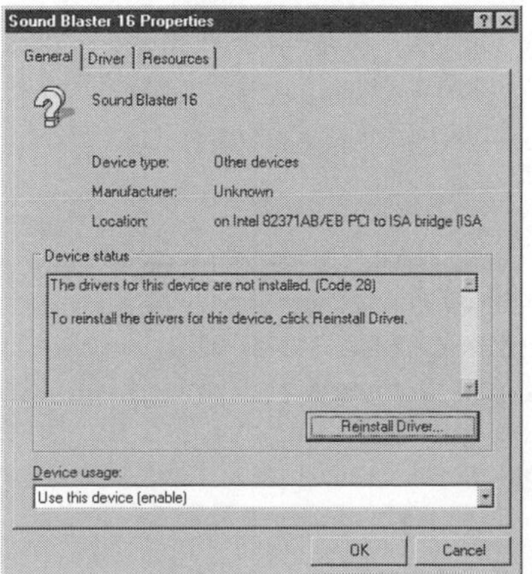

A variety of status messages could appear in the **Device status** text box. An example of a message you might see is as follows:

```
This device is either not present, not working properly, or does not
have all the drivers installed. (Code 13)

To have Windows detect whether this device is present or not, click
Detect Hardware.
```

Unlike previous generations of the operating system where error messages might be somewhat cryptic, you can see that this message is self-explanatory. In this particular case the system attempted to load the device driver and was unable to complete the operation because the device driver did not find the associated hardware. The dialog box dynamically changes the button on the device **Properties** dialog box to a context-specific button that mirrors the recommended solution. In the case of the previous message, the button would change to **Detect Hardware**.

For more information on other device status codes, refer to Microsoft Support Knowledge Base article 125174, Explanation of Error Codes Generated by Device Manager at http://support.microsoft.com/?id=125174.

Diagnosing and Resolving Issues Related to Hardware Settings

If your device is not functioning because of resource conflicts, you can use either Device Manager or System Information to identify the conflicts by the particular type of resource.

In **Device Manager**, you can view the properties of any of the devices. Under the **Resources** tab is a text box named **Conflicting device list**. This text box shows all the devices that are using conflicting resources. If your BIOS and/or device supports changing these values, you can also change the settings until you find a combination of DMA, IRQ, I/O port, and memory address resources that does not cause a conflict.

Another way to view conflicts within the system is through the **System Information** tool. This provides a summary view of all device resource conflicts throughout the system, as shown in Figure 3.23. To access this tool, at the command prompt or **Run** option on the **Start** menu, type **msinfo32.exe** and press **Enter**.

NOTE

The USB class of devices has a specific resource to note: power. If you are using non-powered hubs there might be issues with power allocation across the devices attached to a USB hub. You can view the power allocation for USB hubs in **Device Manager** by locating the hub (you might need to choose **Show Hidden Devices**), opening the device **Properties** dialog box, and selecting the **Power** tab.

Figure 3.23 System Information – Conflicts/Sharing Option

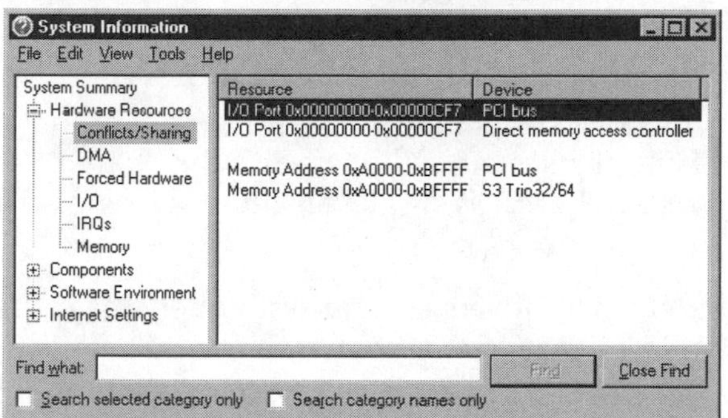

Diagnosing and Resolving Issues Related to Drivers and Driver Upgrades

When drivers cause problems within a system, you might experience two levels of severity. The first is the device simply not being enabled on system startup or installation. A more severe level will result in the system not starting up due to a bug check (also known as a blue screen or STOP error).

If the problem is caused during a driver upgrade, you can leverage the capability to roll back a driver. To roll back a driver from a previous version, open the device **Properties** dialog box in **Device Manager** and select the **Driver** tab. In that tab is a button called **Rollback** that you can select to roll back the driver to the previous version.

If the problem is caused during installation, you might have an incorrect driver or no driver installed. You can view the status of the driver with **Device Manager** and/or check for any startup messages with **Event Viewer.** Beyond being unable to start, the messages are usually specific to the device driver, so we recommend that you check with your device vendor's support services for assistance when troubleshooting these types of issues.

NOTE

Not only is a complete memory dump large and increases system recovery time, it also might expose some sensitive data because it dumps the entire contents of system memory to disk. It is recommended that you use a small or kernel memory dump unless instructed by your device vendor or Microsoft's support organization.

Head of the Class...

Reading and Understanding Bug Checks (Also Known as Blue Screens or STOP Errors)

Bug checks occur when the system encounters a condition that compromises safe operations. As a result, the system is halted and the "blue screen" with the bug check information or STOP error is displayed. These types of errors can occur for several reasons:

- Software defects in drivers or core system services cause an invalid instruction to be sent to the processor.
- Defective hardware causes unhandled messages to be sent to the operating system.
- Core system services have been terminated (e.g., Local Security Authority or Client/Server Runtime Subsystem).

Bug checks provide diagnostic information such as STOP codes and driver names that can help lead to problem resolution. Because of the volatile state of the system, this information cannot always be recorded when the event occurs. It is important that you record the information associated with the bug check and driver information sections. Many of the bug check messages have relevant information that you should read and understand if they apply to your situation. Finally, if you have enabled memory dumps, wait until the dump is complete before restarting the computer (if you do not have automatic restart enabled). Your device vendor and/or Microsoft use the memory dumps to help understand the state of the system at the time that the bug check occurred. You can change the memory dump settings through the **Startup and Recovery** button in the **System Properties' Advanced** tab, as shown in Figure 3.24.

Figure 3.24 Startup and Recovery Properties

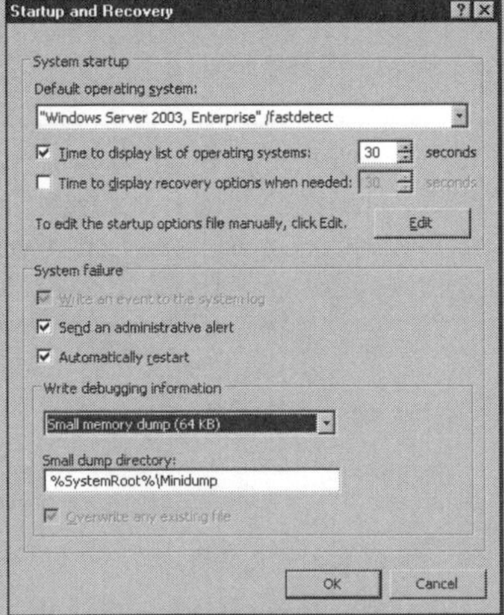

Continued

While the STOP messages might not always indicate the root cause of the problem, in combination with other sources of data, it can help direct a trained support technician to track down the root cause of the problem.

There are two sources of bug check information that you can use as a reference:

- **Windows XP Professional Resource Kit: Appendix C – Common Stop Messages** at www.microsoft.com/technet/prodtechnol/winxppro/reskit/prmd_stp_tnvo.asp.
- **MSDN Library – Device Development Kit: Bug Check Codes** at http://msdn.microsoft.com/library/en-us/ddtools/hh/ddtools/bcintro_3dkj.asp.

If you cannot get Windows fully started, chances are you are encountering either hardware failure, an improperly configured driver, or a bad driver. In these cases, Windows Server 2003 has several facilities to help you troubleshoot these startup issues:

- Last Known Good Configuration
- Safe Mode
- System Configuration Utility
- Recovery Console
- Emergency Management Services
- Automated System Recovery
- Installation Repair

In the following sections, we look at each of these in detail.

Last Known Good Configuration

If the system is unable to start up correctly after you have installed a new device or made a configuration change, this option should be the first tool you use. It will restore the HKEY_LOCAL_MACHINE\System\CurrentControlSet registry key to a copy of the one that was used during the last successful system startup. Note that this tool does not solve any issues with corrupt or missing driver files. To access this tool, perform the following steps:

1. Press **F8** during startup when you see the *Please select the operating system to start* message. (Note: to see this you need to have a timeout value of greater than 0 set in the **System** Control Panel applet, under the **Advanced** tab, in the **Startup/Recovery** options.)
2. In the **Windows Advanced Option Menu** (as shown in Figure 3.25), select **Last Known Good Configuration** and press **Enter**.

Figure 3.25 Windows Advanced Options Menu

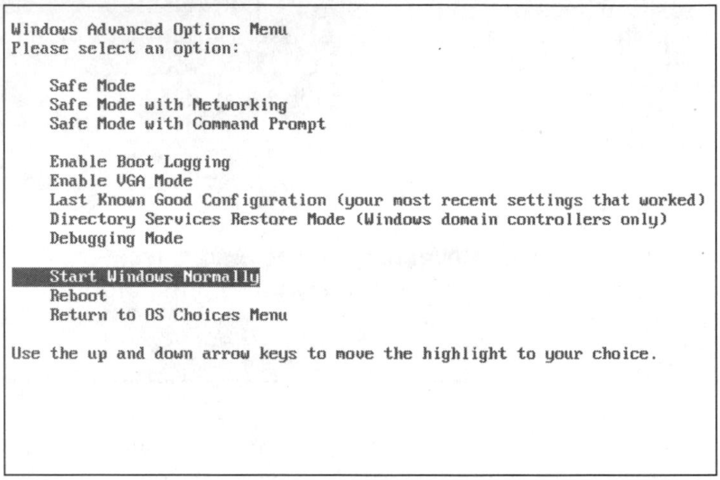

```
Windows Advanced Options Menu
Please select an option:

    Safe Mode
    Safe Mode with Networking
    Safe Mode with Command Prompt

    Enable Boot Logging
    Enable VGA Mode
    Last Known Good Configuration (your most recent settings that worked)
    Directory Services Restore Mode (Windows domain controllers only)
    Debugging Mode

    Start Windows Normally
    Reboot
    Return to OS Choices Menu

Use the up and down arrow keys to move the highlight to your choice.
```

After you are able to recover, you can then use **Event Viewer**, **Device Manager**, and/or **System Information** to identify any problematic devices.

Safe Mode

Starting your system in Safe Mode causes Windows Server 2003 to load the minimum set of drivers and services that the operating system needs to function. This option can be used to help identify and resolve problems created by corrupt or incorrect drivers, a corrupt registry, or system services that might prevent the system from starting. After you have started in Safe mode, you can disable or remove devices and services that might be preventing the system from starting, using **Device Manager** and/or the **Registry Editor**. To access this tool, perform the following steps:

1. Pres **F8** during startup when you see the *Please select the operating system to start* message.
2. In the **Windows Advanced Option Menu**, select **Safe Mode** and press **Enter**.

After you are able to recover, you can use **Event Viewer**, **Device Manager**, and/or **System Information** to identify any problematic devices. If the problem occurred late enough in the startup process, it might have also been captured as part of the Safe Mode log file, **ntbtlog.txt**, which is located in the System Root directory (by default, the WINDOWS folder). The log file contains a list of devices and services that were loaded along with whether or not each was successful.

System Configuration Utility

The **System Configuration Utility** helps you diagnose services that are related to startup and that can cause issues. It is geared more towards system services as opposed to device drivers, but can be useful because some devices include services as well as more traditional device drivers. To access this tool, at the command prompt or **Run** option on the **Start** menu, type **msconfig.exe** and press **Enter**.

After you open the tool, you will notice a variety of options that can be used to configure the startup process, as shown in Figure 3.26. After you make the necessary changes, restart Windows Server 2003 for the settings to take effect.

Figure 3.26 System Configuration Utility – General Tab

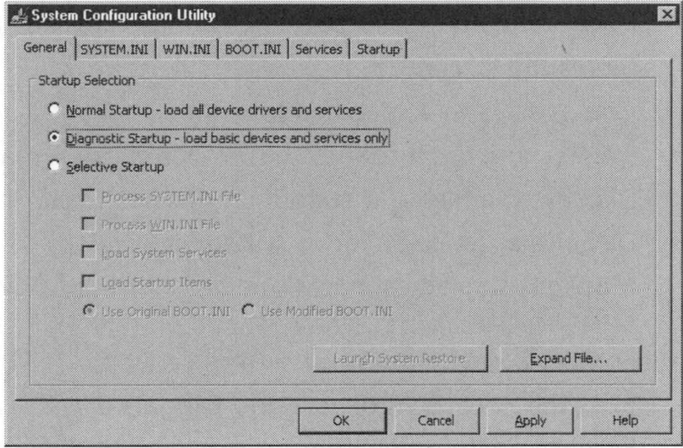

Recovery Console

When you start the **Recovery Console**, it looks very much like being in a command-prompt environment. The **Recovery Console** is used when Last Known Good Configuration and Safe Mode tools are not successful. It is recommended that you use this tool only if you are an advanced user and comfortable with a command-line interface to navigate and manipulate files. With the Recovery Console you can perform the following tasks:

- Enable or disable device drivers or system services.
- Copy files from the installation media for the operating system.
- Create a new boot sector and new master boot record (MBR).

To access this tool:

1. Insert the Windows Server 2003 CD into the CD/DVD-ROM drive.
2. When prompted, press a key to enter setup.
3. At the **Welcome to Setup** screen, press **R** to start the **Recovery Console**.

The Recovery Console gives you access to a command prompt-like environment with access to the following commands shown in Table 3.7.

Table 3.7 Commands Available from the Recovery Console

Command	Description
Attrib	Modifies the attributes of a file or directory.
Batch	Executes the commands in a specified file.
Bootcfg	Displays and modifies the boot configuration.
Chdir (CD)	Changes the current directory or displays the name of the current directory.
Chkdsk	Checks the disk for logical errors and display a status report.
Cls	Clears the screen
Copy	Copies a file to a specified location.
Delete (DEL)	Deletes one or more files that match a given mask.
Dir	Displays the files and subdirectories in the current directory.
Disable	Disables a device driver or system service.
Diskpart	Manages the logical partitions on your hard drive (similar to FDISK).
Enable	Enables a device driver or system service.
Exit	Exits the Recovery Console and triggers a system reboot.
Expand	Extracts a file from a compressed cabinet file.
Fixboot	Writes a new partition boot sector.
Fixmbr	Repairs the master boot record of the partition boot sector.
Format	Formats a logical partition.
Help	Displays a list of commands you can use inside the Recovery Console.
Listsvc	Lists the device drivers and services on the system along with their startup state (Auto, Boot, Disabled, Manual, or System).
Logon	Switches the Windows Server 2003 installation you are logged onto with the Recovery Console.
Map	Displays a list of drive letter mappings
Mkdir (MD)	Creates a new directory.
More (TYPE)	Displays the contents of a file. If you use *More*, it will pause after every screen full of content.
Rename (REN)	Renames a specified file.
Rmdir (RD)	Removes a specified directory.
Set	Sets an environment variable. If used without parameters, it displays a list of all environment variables currently set.
Systemroot	Sets the current directory to the Windows system root.

Head of the Class

Installing the Recovery Console

Instead of scrambling to locate your Windows CD when you need to access the Recovery Console, you can install it ahead of time on the server. The process is easy:

1. Insert your Windows Server 2003 CD into the CD/DVD-ROM drive.
2. At the command prompt or **Run** option on the **Start** menu, type **<driveletter>:\i386\winnt32.exe /cmdcons** (*<driveletter>* is the letter of your CD/DVD-ROM drive) and press **Enter**.
3. A setup dialog appears to confirm whether or not you want to install the **Recovery Console.** Click **Yes**. The setup process installs the Recovery Console. The next time you restart the computer, the **Recovery Console** will be available in the **Windows Advanced Option** Menu.

Emergency Management Services

Emergency Management Services (EMS) was introduced in Windows Server 2003 to facilitate out-of-band management of servers when they are not running correctly. EMS works over a range of out-of-band communications media including serial connections and terminal concentrators/emulators. The features of EMS are available during startup when the operating system is loading. Through EMS you can, for example, diagnose items as serious as a bug check or troubleshoot in situations where resource utilization is extremely heavy.

EMS works in conjunction with hardware-based out-of-band management services as well as providong management during all phases of startup. If you do not have the proper hardware available, you can gain access to the console as soon as the operating system or setup process loads.

For more information, refer to the Windows Server 2003 product documentation or the Windows Server 2003 Resource Kit sections on EMS.

Automated System Recovery

If you are using the Automated System Recovery (ASR) feature in Windows Server 2003, you can perform an ASR restore for system state data and services, which includes configuration information for devices. To access this tool, perform the following steps:

1. Insert the Windows Server 2003 CD into the CD/DVD-ROM drive.
2. When prompted, press **F2** to start **Automated System Recovery**.

For more information, refer to the Windows Server 2003 product documentation and/or the Windows Server 2003 Resource Kit sections on ASR.

Repairing the Windows Server 2003 Installation

The Windows Server 2003 setup process includes the option to repair the installation. The repair process has three main tasks:

- **Inspect the Startup Environment** Checks the boot.ini file to ensure that all the contents are correct.
- **Inspect the Boot Sector** Checks to see if the active system partition's boot sector is valid. If not, it reinstalls the boot loader functionality.
- **Recopy Windows system files** The selected installation of Windows Server 2003 has its core files re-copied to the partition.

To access this tool, perform the following steps:

1. Insert the Windows Server 2003 CD into the CD/DVD-ROM drive.
2. When prompted, press a key to enter **Setup**.
3. At the **Welcome to Setup** screen, press **Enter**.
4. When prompted to accept the licensing agreement, press **F8**.
5. If Setup is able to successfully find your installation, select the appropriate installation and press **R** to initiate repair. If it is unable to locate your installation, you will need to recover by using a backup or a new installation of Windows Server 2003.

Hardware Troubleshooting Best Practices

When troubleshooting devices in your system, there are a few best practices that you should consider following:

- **Record error messages and symptoms in detail.** It is especially useful when researching to have exact error messages to use with search facilities. The details also help if you need to contact your support organization, a device vendor's support services, or Microsoft's Product Support Services.
- **Keep accurate change logs.** Keeping a history of what has changed in the system, software or hardware, helps you understand where potential conflicts might arise based on previous experience or research into problem symptoms.
- **Leverage device vendor's and third-party tools where appropriate.** Some devices come with management software to enable access to more advanced troubleshooting. When you get a new device, test the software to see if it provides any additional value. If it does not, keep your system as simple as possible and uninstall it. If you do plan to use the tool, ensure that the management tool also carries the *Designed for Microsoft Windows Server 2003* logo software certification when installing it in a server environment.

- **Ensure drivers are signed and critical system files are intact.** Use tools such as the System File Checker and File Signature Verification tool to help locate and repair corrupt drivers or identify unsigned drivers. Unsigned drivers can be the source of system instability because they have not undergone the level of testing prescribed by the Windows Hardware Quality Labs team.

Summary of Exam Objectives

Components of the server need to be installed and configured for users to be able to leverage their services. When choosing devices for your server, it is important to find ones that have drivers that are compatible; if possible, use devices that have the *Designed for Windows Server 2003* logo certification and WHQL-signed drivers. Device drivers often operate at the kernel mode of the operating system, which is an unprotected area of the operating system designed to give the device drivers rapid access to the peripherals that they control using the Hardware Abstraction Layer (HAL). Windows Server 2003 enables you to set policy to enforce whether or not drivers should be WHQL signed before they are installed on the system. Plug and Play drivers automatically configure their resource settings, whereas non-PNP drivers require a little more manual work to get them installed in the system.

After you install the device driver through Plug and Play or the **New Hardware Wizard**, you can manage its configuration using **Device Manager**. Through this management console you can see the status of the device and configure various options for the particular device.

Monitoring devices on a regular basis is important to maintaining a healthy system. Windows Server 2003 provides several tools to help you monitor and investigate device issues. These tools include Device Manager, Event Viewer, Performance console, Device Console Utility (devcon), and various Control Panel applets. With Event Viewer you should watch for unusual warnings or errors produced by device drivers. Using the tools in the Performance console, you can establish a performance baseline to help you understand when devices are unable to keep up with the utilization of the system. In mid- to large-sized environments, consider the use of enterprise management tools such as Microsoft Operations Manager (MOM) to monitor devices across multiple systems.

Troubleshooting device issues is much like troubleshooting any other system issue. You need to collect the symptoms, research the issue using the symptoms to come up with some potential causes, and rule out the causes until you get to a set of workarounds or resolutions to the problem that meet your needs. When it comes to troubleshooting device issues, resource conflicts can be detected using **Device Manager** or the **System Information** tool. Device driver issues can cause more severe problems with the system, including not being able to start the system. Windows Server 2003 has several tools to help you recover from serious driver-related issues, including Last Known Good Configuration, Safe Mode, System Configuration Utility, Recovery Console, Emergency Management Services, Automated System Recovery and Installation Repair. The first is the least potentially destructive to the system, while the last is the most destructive to the existing system configuration.

Exam Objectives Fast Track

Understanding Server Hardware Vulnerabilities

☑ Device drivers usually operate in kernel mode and access peripherals through the Hardware Abstraction Layer, whereas applications operate in user mode.

☑ Windows Server 2003 supports Plug and Play and non-PNP device drivers. Most new devices ship with PNP drivers. Sound drivers are disabled by default.

Installing and Configuring Server Hardware Devices

☑ To install device drivers, you need to be a member of the local Administrators group or have equivalent rights.

☑ When installing devices, you can set policy as to whether or not to allow WHQL-signed drivers. The policy options include **Block, Warn**, and **Ignore**. By default, Windows Server 2003 is set to **Warn**.

☑ Several operating system tools help you maintain integrity and detect unsigned drivers: Windows File Protection, System File Check, and File Signature Verification.

☑ Non-PNP drivers are installed using the **New Hardware Wizard**.

☑ **Device Manager** is used to configure driver resources and settings as well as monitor device status. From a driver perspective, you can see the files associated with the driver, uninstall, upgrade, and roll back to the previously installed version.

☑ **Device Manager** enables you to view the system from a device or resource-centric view. Each view is further divided into a hierarchy based on type or connectivity.

Monitoring Server Hardware

☑ Use **Device Manager** and **Event Viewer** as the primary tools for monitoring. Other tools include **Performance** console, **Device Console Utility** (devcon), and various Control Panel applets.

☑ Watch for abnormal warnings or errors in the event log from device drivers, because this is usually the first sign of trouble.

- ☑ Use **Performance Logs and Alerts** to establish a baseline of key performance metrics on your system. You can store the data in textor binary files or in an SQL Server database.
- ☑ **System Monitor** can be used to view real-time metric data in a graphical fashion, or logged data resulting from **Performance Logs and Alerts**.
- ☑ **Performance** Console tools are secured to prevent anyone who is not part of the local Administrators group from accessing them. You can add users to the Performance Monitor Users group to enables them to monitor counters or the Performance Log Users group to enable them to manager counters, logs, and alerts.

Troubleshooting Hardware Devices

- ☑ Collect the symptoms, research the issue using the symptoms to come up with some potential causes, and rule out the causes until you get to a set of workarounds or resolutions to the problem that meet your needs.
- ☑ Resource conflicts can be detected using Device Manager or the System Information tool.
- ☑ Last Known Good Configuration restores the HKLM\System\CurrentControlSet registry key from a copy of the one that was last used to successfully boot the system.
- ☑ Safe Mode starts the system with the minimum number of services and drivers to operate.
- ☑ System Configuration Utility enables you to configure settings related to startup. It is more service-centric than device-centric.
- ☑ Recovery Console gives you access to a command prompt-like environment where you can replace files, enable/disable drivers and services, and work with partitions.
- ☑ Emergency Management Services is an out-of-band management tool that enables you to control the system remotely from when the operating system starts to load.
- ☑ Automated System Recovery leverages the backup of the system state data and your backup media to restore critical system configuration information.
- ☑ Installation Repair is a potentially destructive re-installation of the core operating system files that might overwrite any third-party drivers.

Exam Objectives Frequently Asked Questions

The following Frequently Asked Questions, answered by the authors of this book, are designed to both measure your understanding of the Exam Objectives presented in this chapter, and to assist you with real-life implementation of these concepts. You will also gain access to thousands of other FAQs at ITFAQnet.com.

Q: What's the difference between the kernel mode and user mode?

A: Components that run in kernel mode do not benefit from the same level of protection against software defects (e.g., illegal function calls, accessing areas of memory that are not allocated to that process). To facilitate this protection, user mode components (such as the typical Windows application) do not interface with the hardware directly. Instead, they use an abstracted interface using the Windows (Win32) APIs and user-mode drivers, which interact with kernel-mode counterparts.

Q: I'm trying to play some audio files on Windows Server 2003 and Windows Media Player is telling me that I do not have a sound device available. I know there is a sound card; how do I get it working?

A: Windows Server 2003 does not install sound device drivers by default. You should contact your device vendor for Windows Server 2003-compatible drivers and install them.

Q: I plugged in my new device and I can't see the functionality in my applications. What should I do?

A: Check to see that the driver was installed and the device is working correctly. Refer to the device documentation to ensure that the device supports Plug and Play. If not, install the device driver manually with the New Hardware Wizard.

Q: I'm installing Windows Server 2003 Enterprise Edition (64-bit) on my Itanium-based computer. Can I use my 32-bit drivers?

A: It is recommended that you obtain 64-bit drivers from your device vendor. This will ensure the driver can take full advantage of the 64-bit platform.

Q: I've recently installed a multiprocessor main board in my system and Windows Server 2003 uses only the first processor. How can I take advantage of the additional processors?

A: You might need to upgrade the Hardware Abstraction Layer to a multiprocessor version. You can do this by locating the computer in the **Computers** section of **Device Manager** and running the process to update the driver.

Q: Plug and Play detects several compatible devices. Which one should I use?

A: Some devices are listed with multiple compatible drivers because they are based on a generic chipset. You should choose the one that the system recommends (usually the first one highlighted) or the one that is closest in name of make/model to the device that you are installing. If you are still unsure, you should contact your device vendor for guidance on the proper driver to install.

Q: When installing Windows Server 2003, Setup is unable to locate my mass storage device to install the operating system on. What should I do?

A: During text-mode Setup, you will be prompted to press **F6** to include additional mass storage devices in the setup process. Make sure to have a copy of your mass storage device drivers on hand for Setup to use.

Q: My device is not operating as efficiently as it was six months ago. How can I tell what is wrong?

A: If you need immediate insight, use **System Monitor** to view the counters associated with the device functionality to see if the system is experiencing a higher than normal volume of usage. Consider monitoring it over a period of time using **Performance Logs and Alerts** to ensure that you have some data to compare the current performance level with a period of time that you considered the system to be operating in a healthy state.

Q: How do I know if my system is healthy?

A: Develop a regular routine of monitoring Event Manager for any device-related error messages. You can also use Device Manager to look for devices that have been disabled or are experiencing issues.

Q: Can I use drivers from Windows 2000 or earlier with Windows Server 2003?

A: Although the driver specifications are somewhat similar between Windows 2000, Windows XP, and Windows Server 2003, it is recommended that you obtain drivers that were designed for Windows Server 2003. With the changes in the kernel, support for 64-bit processors, and security model changes, an older driver might not run properly in Windows Server 2003.

Q: A particular device on my system is not functioning. What should I do?

A: The first step is to check with Device Manager and Event Viewer to see if there are any messages relating to that device. If everything appears to be working, consult your device documentation and vendor for troubleshooting steps focused on the device itself.

Q: I recently installed a device and now Windows Server 2003 will not start. I am getting bug checks (blue screens or STOP errors) when I try to start the server. What should I do?

A: Faulty or incorrectly configured device drivers can be the source of the bug checks that you are experiencing. Windows Server 2003 has several tools to help you recover from serious driver-related issues, including Last Known Good Configuration, Safe Mode, System Configuration Utility, Recovery Console, Emergency Management Services, Automated System Recovery, and Installation Repair. The first step is to record the information, examine the root cause of the error using the resources noted we've discussed in the chapter, and then leverage one of the tools mentioned to recover the system back to an operational state.

Self Test

A Quick Answer Key follows the Self Test questions. For complete questions, answers, and explanations to the Self Test questions in this chapter as well as the other chapters in this book, see the Self Test Appendix.

Understanding Server Hardware Vulnerabilities

1. You are attempting to play an audio file using Windows Media Player on a server running Windows Server 2003. Windows Media Player tells you that the sound device is not working. What could be the cause of the problem?

   A. Your audio file is the incorrect format.

   B. The speakers attached to the system are not turned on.

   C. Sound devices are not enabled by default.

   D. You need to upgrade the version of Windows Media Player

2. What two conditions must exist for a device driver to be installed when someone who is a member of the local Users group attached a new device to a system?

   A. The drivers must be digitally signed by WHQL and require no user interaction.

   B. The drivers must be digitally signed by the vendor and require no user interaction.

   C. The drivers must reside anywhere on the hard disk.

   D. The drivers must be located in the device driver search path.

Installing and Configuring Server Hardware Devices

3. You have recently installed a new device into the system. You cannot locate an entry for the device in Device Manager, nor have you been prompted to install device drivers at any point. What should you do?

   A. Use **Windows Update** to locate and install an updated version of the device driver.

   B. Copy the device drivers to a directory in the device driver search path.

   C. Use the **Add New Hardware Wizard** to install the device drivers.

   D. Change the **Driver Signing Policy** options from **Ignore** to **Warn**.

4. A server in your company has recently been upgraded to Windows Server 2003. One of the technicians installs a new device using an older Windows NT 4.0 driver he found on the hard drive from prior to the installation. Now when the system boots you experience a bug check (also known as the blue screen or STOP error). You have disabled the driver using the Recovery Console. What should you do?

   A. Reconfigure the device resource settings to use another I/O port.

   B. Contact the vendor for a Windows Server 2003-compatible driver.

   C. Install the device into a different peripheral interface connection.

   D. Replace the device with a new one.

5. Your company has recently set a policy that all servers will use WHQL-signed drivers. You need to enforce this policy on the server. Which Driver Signing options setting should you use?

   A. Ignore

   B. Warn

   C. Block

   D. Use the setup default

Monitoring Server Hardware

6. You have recently installed a new non-PNP device using the Add New Hardware Wizard. You need to configure some resource settings in the device driver but you are unable to find it in Device Manager. You verify that the device is attached and working. You need to complete this task with the least administrative effort. How can you gain access to the device properties?

A. Restart the system with the **Recovery Console**.

B. Restart the system in **Safe Mode**.

C. Select **Resources by Type** in **Device Manager**.

D. Select **Show Hidden Devices** in **Device Manager**.

7. Your server is reporting that the AFD Networking Support Environment driver is unable to start because of dependencies failing to start. You need to find the status of these dependencies. What should you do?

   A. Use the **Service Control** utility to enumerate dependencies of the driver.

   B. Locate the device driver entry in the HKLM\System\CurrentControlSet\Services registry hive and inspect the Enum key.

   C. Launch the **System Information** utility and export a report of the system drivers.

   D. Restart the system and enable **Boot Logging**.

8. You have been asked to make sure that the critical system files are intact on a server. What tool would you use?

   A. File Signature Verification tool

   B. System File Checker tool

   C. Device Console utility

   D. System Configuration utility

9. You have installed a new device into the system, however the drivers that you were given with the device are not being accepted by the system as compatible. How can you determine if you have the correct device drivers?

   A. Check the **Event Viewer** for the hardware identification number and cross-reference that with the device driver's INF file.

   B. Use the **System File Checker** to initiate an on-demand scan of the critical system files.

   C. Use the **Device Console** utility to list the hardware identification number and cross-reference that with the device driver's INF file.

   D. Use the **Recovery Console** to install the device driver.

10. Your company has recently merged with another company. You have been put in charge of assessing the servers from the other company to see if they meet your company policies. You need to check to see if there are any unsigned drivers running on the system. You need to complete this task with the least administrative effort. What should you do?

A. Launch the **File Signature Verification** tool on the servers to generate reports.

B. Look in the event log message detail for entries from the **Service Control Manager** on startup.

C. Check the contents of the Trusted Publishers certificate store and create a list of its contents to compare against the servers in your original environment.

D. Compare the contents of the SYSTEM32\DRIVERS directory with the ones on the original environment.

Troubleshooting Hardware Devices

11. You have recently installed an additional network card into your server for users on a new network segment to access the resources. One of the support analysts calls you several weeks later to tell you that users on that network segment cannot access the server. You use Remote Desktop to access the console from one of the other segments. Opening the command prompt you run ipconfig to see that the device is not listed. What should you do?

    A. Configure the network interface to use static instead of dynamic IP addressing.

    B. Enable the network interface card using **Device Manager**.

    C. Replace the network cable attached to the network interface card.

    D. Plug the network cable into another switch/hub port.

12. You have recently made some changes to the resources on one of the devices in your system. Since those changes, you have restarted the server and it now locks up before it is able to get to the logon prompt. What should you do?

    A. Disable support for Plug and Play operating systems in the BIOS.

    B. Boot the system with the **Recovery Console** and create a new **Master Boot Record (MBR)**.

    C. On startup in the **Windows Advanced Option Menu**, select the **Last Known Good Configuration**.

    D. On startup in the **Windows Advanced Option Menu**, select **Debugging Mode**.

13. You have connected a new device to the system. You go to use the device and find that you cannot access it. In Device Manager you see an entry for the device with the following Device status message: "This device is either not present, not working properly, or does not have all the drivers installed. (Code 13)" What should you do?

A. Copy the driver to the SYSTEM32 directory and restart the computer.

B. Use the **Add New Hardware Wizard** to install the driver.

C. Launch **Device Manager** and enable the device.

D. Change the resource settings on the driver to point to a different memory address.

14. You have acquired a new device for your system. After installing the new device drivers and restarting the computer several times, you are still unable to access the device. You look to the Device status in Device Manager to find the following message: "Windows is in the process of setting up this device. (Code 26)". What should you do to resolve this error?

A. Unplug and re-plug in the device.

B. Restart the computer once more.

C. Launch the **File Signature Verification** and initiate a scan for unsigned drivers.

D. Launch **Device Manager** to remove the driver, and then run the **Add New Hardware Wizard**.

15. When you start your server you notice that the keyboard stops working when you reach graphical mode. You connect to the server using Remote Desktop and open Device Manager to find that the keyboard device entry has a yellow exclamation mark beside it. Under Device status you see the following message: "The device is not working properly because Windows cannot load the drivers required for this device (Code 31)." You need to get the keyboard at the console working. What should you do?

A. On startup in the **Windows Advanced Option Menu**, select **Debugging Mode**.

B. Replace the keyboard.

C. Launch **Device Manager**, locate the device entry and disable and then re-enable the device.

D. Launch **Device Manager**, locate the device entry and uninstall and re-install the keyboard driver.

Self Test Quick Answer Key

For complete questions, answers, and explanations to the Self Test questions in this chapter as well as the other chapters in this book, see the Self Test Appendix.

1. **C**
2. **A, D**
3. **C**
4. **B**
5. **C**
6. **D**
7. **A**
8. **B**
9. **C**
10. **A**
11. **B**
12. **C**
13. **B**
14. **D**
15. **D**

Chapter 4

MCSA/MCSE 70-290

Managing User, Group, and Computer Accounts

Exam Objectives in this Chapter:

- 2.1 Manage local, roaming, and mandatory user profiles.
- 2.4 Create and manage user accounts.
- 2.4.1 Create and modify user accounts by using the Active Directory Users and Computers MMC snap-in.
- 2.6.2 Diagnose and resolve issues related to user account properties.
- 2.6.1 Diagnose and resolve account lockouts.
- 2.3.5 Create and modify groups by using automation.
- 2.4.2 Create and modify user accounts by using automation.
- 2.4.3 Import user accounts.
- 2.6 Troubleshoot user accounts.
- 2.3 Create and manage groups.
- 2.3.1 Identify and modify the scope of a group.
- 2.3.3 Manage group membership.
- 2.3.4 Create and modify groups by using the Active Directory Users and Computers Microsoft Management Console (MMC) snap-in.
- 2.3.2 Find domain groups in which a user is a member.
- 2.2 Create and manage computer accounts in an Active Directory environment.
- 2.5.1 Diagnose and resolve issues related to computer accounts by using the Active Directory Users and Computers MMC snap-in.
- 2.5.2 Reset computer accounts.
- 2.5 Troubleshoot computer accounts.

Introduction

In a Windows Server 2003 Active Directory domain, security object—users, groups, and computers—are represented as account objects that exist within the directory hierarchy and can be created, modified, moved, and removed. Managing these security objects is an important part of the network administrator's job. Luckily, Microsoft has included many administrative tools, both graphical and command-line, with which you can manipulate and manage these accounts.

In this chapter, you will learn about how Windows Server 2003 treats users, groups, and computers in the Active Directory environment, and we will walk you through the process of using the common management tools, including Active Directory Users and Computers (ADUC) and other useful utilities. We will show you how to create and modify user, group, and computer accounts with ADUC, and you'll learn to automate account creation and import user accounts.

Groups are special objects that contain users, and security groups are used to simplify management of multiple user accounts by enabling you to apply permissions, user rights, and so forth to an entire group of users in a single operation instead of having to apply them to individual user accounts. You'll learn to identify and modify the scope of a group, manage group memberships, and find out to which domain groups a user belongs.

Understanding Security Objects

A security object is an object in Active Directory that can be assigned permissions to other objects. When security objects are created, they are given a security identifier (SID). This number identifies the objects to Windows. Objects have friendly names to make it easier for us to remember them. Humans use names to reference accounts, but Windows uses SIDs. This section will focus on user, group, and machine security objects.

Understanding the Role of User Accounts

User Accounts represent people and are used by people to log on to a Windows machine. Windows NT, Windows 2000, Windows XP, and Windows Server 2003 require mandatory logon. By default, unless you press **CTL+ALT+DEL** and log on to the machine you cannot interact with the desktop. User accounts are also used as service accounts for applications. This enables programs to utilize the permissions assigned to its service account.

User accounts are used for the following:

- **Authentication** This is the process of proving your identity. User accounts and passwords are used to authenticate users to a domain.
- **Authorization** This is the process of being granted permissions to a resource. Authorization is different from authentication.
- **Auditing** By requiring all your users to use a unique user account, you can easily audit access to resources.

Active Directory contains three user accounts by default. These accounts are created when you create the domain (creating domains is discussed at the end of this chapter). The default user accounts are as follows:

- **Administrator** This account has full control over Active Directory. It is a member of the Administrators, Domain Admins, Enterprise Admins, Group Policy Creator Owners, and Schema Admins groups. By default the administrator account is enabled. It can be disabled, but not deleted. It is a good idea to rename the Administrator account for security purposes.
- **Guest** This account is meant to be a shared account by people who do not have an account in the domain. The Guest account is disabled by default. Most companies leave it disabled and do not use it. It is a member of the built-in Guests group and the Domain Guests global group.
- **HelpAssistant** This account is used to make a Remote Assistance Connection. It has limited access to the computer. It is created and deleted dynamically when Remote Assistance requests are pending and in progress.

NOTE

Remote Assistance is a new feature of Windows Server 2003 (and Windows XP). It enables remotely assisting with computer problems. A remote user can view and control the screen of the machine having problems. Remote Assistance also has a chat window for communicating while working on the computer.

Understanding the Role of Group Accounts

Without groups, you would have to manually assign all permissions to individual user accounts. Groups enable you to organize your users. You can group user accounts and assign permissions to everyone in the group at once. Any permissions assigned to a group are automatically granted to members of that group. Groups can also be used for e-mail distribution. By putting users into a group and assigning an e-mail address to that group, you can e-mail everyone in the group at once.

Understanding the Role of Computer Accounts

Just like user accounts represent people, computer accounts represent machines. Computer accounts provide authentication and auditing for machines. Computer accounts are created for all computers that run Windows NT, Windows 2000, Windows XP, and Windows Server 2003 if the computer is joined to a domain. Computers running Windows 3.*x*, Windows 9*x*, or Windows ME do not have computer accounts and can't be members of a domain, although a user who has an account in the domain can use it to log on to the domain.

Understanding the Role of Active Directory

Active Directory (AD) first appeared in Windows 2000. If you are going to support Windows Server 2003, you will eventually have to understand AD. Microsoft has multiple certification tests devoted to AD alone. This book is not meant to prepare you for those tests, because its focus is on preparing you for the Server test. However, there is a lot of overlap between the tests. Microsoft expects you to be familiar with AD and you should expect to see it in one way or another of all your tests.

Active Directory is the directory service for Windows Server 2003 (and Windows 2000). A directory service in its simplest form is a way of storing information in a directory so it can easily be retrieved and used later. Active Directory functions as a central repository for information such as user accounts, groups, and machine accounts. AD provides centralized authentication and centralized administration. AD contains many components, including the following:

- Domains
- Forest
- Trees

Figure 4.1 illustrates the layout of AD. It starts off with the tc.org domain. For this example, assume that tc.org was the first domain created. This makes it the *forest root* domain. Underneath tc.org are two *sub-domains* (also called *child domains*). These three domains (tc.org, columbia.tc.org, and charleston.tc.org) form the tc.org *tree*. The training.ads has two subdomains (microsoft.training.ads and win2003.microsoft.training.ads) and forms another tree. Lastly, the consulting.net domain is a third tree. Notice that a domain does not need subdomains in order to be considered a tree. All these domains make up the tc.org *forest*.

You need to remember a few things here. A forest is always named after the first domain created in the forest (tc.org). A tree is always named after the first domain created in a given tree (tc.org, training.ads, and consulting.net). Child domains always share the naming scheme of their parent (training.ads, microsoft.training.ads and win2003.microsoft.training.ads).

Using Management Tools

In Windows Server 2003, Microsoft gives us multiple ways to accomplish the same thing. We can use the graphical user interface or GUI (pronounced Goo-E) or we can use command-line utilities. Each has its own advantages and disadvantages. Typically, the GUI is easier to use. You do not have to worry about syntax. You just click your way around and get everything done. The command prompt is usually better when you need to make changes in bulk. It can be more complex than the GUI, but it supports scripting, which opens up a whole realm of possibilities.

Figure 4.1 Understanding the Structure of Active Directory

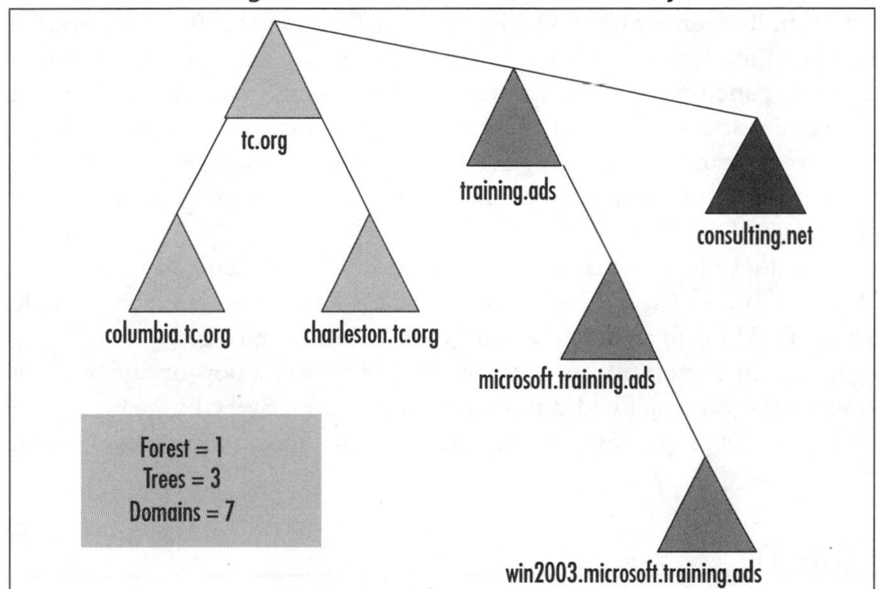

Using the Active Directory Users and Computers (ADUC) Administrative Tool

The tool most commonly used to manage user, group, and computer accounts is Active Directory Users and Computers (ADUC). ADUC is found in the Administrative Tools folder (**Start** | **Programs** | **Administrative Tools** | **Active Directory Users and Computers**). In this chapter we will cover the details of using ADUC to create and manage users, groups, and computers. First, familiarize yourself with the layout of ADUC as shown in Figure 4.2.

Figure 4.2 Getting Familiar with Active Directory Users and Computers

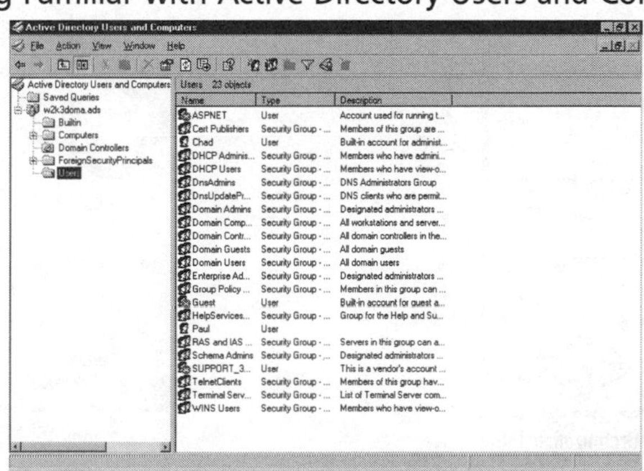

Like all of Microsoft's administrative tools in Windows Server 2003 (and Windows 2000), ADUC is built from a Microsoft Management Console (MMC). This gives all the tools a similar look and feel. The MMC is broken into two panes: the console pane on the left and the details pane on the right. The console pane is used for navigating through the domain and organizational unit (OU) structure. When you select an object in the console pane, its members appear in the details pane. For example, in Figure 4.2, the Users container is selected and all its members are listed on the right. Figure 4.3 shows the most common objects in ADUC.

ADUC has a query feature that is new to Windows Server 2003. You can use the saved queries folder to create and save XML queries that can later be reused. For example, you may want to query AD daily for members of the Domain Admins group.

Right-clicking an object (OU, user, group, etc.) gives you a pop-up menu. A lot of your administration can be accomplished directly from this menu. Everything else is accomplished by going to the properties of an object. We discuss this in more detail throughout the chapter.

TEST DAY TIP

Your machine may not have ADUC installed. By default, it is installed on all domain controllers. ADUC is installed as part of the adminpak. Run adminpak.msi from the I386 directory on the Windows Server 2003 server.

Figure 4.3 Recognizing Objects in Active Directory

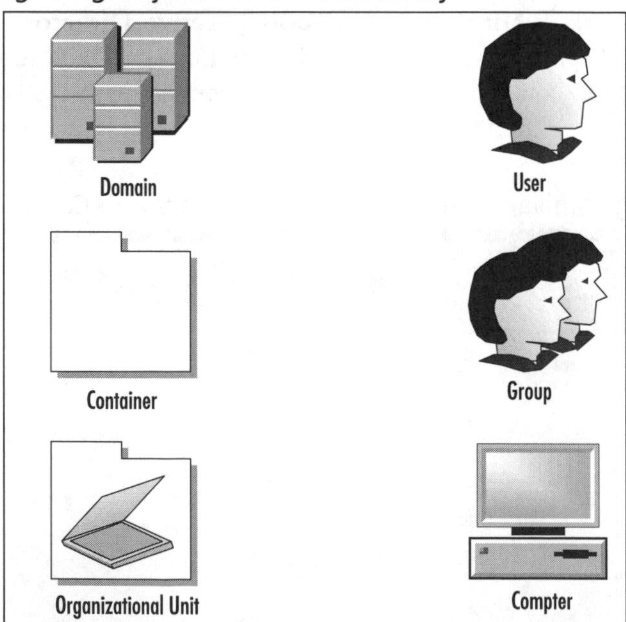

NOTE

Organizational unit containers and default containers serve the same purpose. They organize objects within a domain. Default containers appear as folders in ADUC. OU containers appear as folders, but they have the picture of a gray book on them as shown in Figure 4.3. The difference between OU containers and default containers is that you can assign group policy to an OU container, but not to a default container. People commonly refer to the default containers as OUs, but technically there is a difference between the two.

Using Command-Line Utilities

Sometimes you need the capability to script changes to Active Directory. This is where command-line utilities come in handy. Microsoft has increased the number of things that can be done from the command line. Some of the command-line tools are so easy to use you may find yourself using them regularly and not even going into ADUC. This chapter covers the following command-line tools:

- dsadd.exe
- dsget.exe
- dsmove.exe
- dsquery.exe
- gpresult.exe
- whoami.exe
- cmdkey.exe

All these tools are described in the following sections. The basic commands and syntax for each tool is listed. Some tools are covered more in the chapter later and are not given as much detail right now. Some tools contain a table of all the supported options for the given tool. These tables are here for reference; you do not need to memorize them for the test. Reading switches and help files from the command prompt can sometimes be confusing, so we have summarized that information into tables to make it easier to understand. Each tool is followed with examples. The purpose of the examples is to make sense of the syntax and to give you some easy-to-understand commands that you can use right away.

NOTE

The syntax for all these commands is available by typing the particular command followed by a question mark. For example, to see the syntax for modifying group membership, type **dsmod.exe group /?**. Additional steps and syntax for each command is listed throughout the chapter under the *Using the Command Line to Create and Manage Users, Using the Command Line to Create and Manage Groups*, and *Using the Command Line to Create and Manage Machine* sections.

Becoming Familiar with Using Command-Line Tools

Before we dive into the various commands, we'll cover command-line syntax in general. If you are a pro at using command-line tools, you may want to skip ahead to the next section (*Using dsadd.exe*), because you may find this section fairly basic. For the rest of you, we hope this will make using command-line tools a joy instead of a burden.

Using command-line tools can be difficult at times. The sticking point for most people isn't figuring out which tool to use. The problem is making sense of the syntax for the tool. Syntax refers to the structure of the command and the ordering and relationship of the structural elements. You can view the available syntax for a tool by typing the tool name followed by **/?**. For this section, we are going to analyze the **NET USE** command. You use this command to map drives to network resources. After you are familiar with reading the syntax for this tool, you are ready to tackle all other tools because they all use the same format. To view the syntax for the **NET USE** command, type the following:

```
NET USE /?
```

After typing this command and pressing **Enter** (always press **Enter** at the end of your command), you are given the syntax for the **NET USE** command. (There is more syntax than this, but this is where we are going to focus):

```
NET USE [devicename | *] [\\computername\sharename[\volume] [password
    | *]]
        [/USER:[domainname\]username]
        [/USER:[dotted domain name\]username]
        [/USER:[username@dotted domain name]
```

At first glance, this can seem intimidating. The syntax is spread across multiple lines. However, **all the commands are used on a single line** at the command prompt (your line may wrap around, but it is still one continuous command). When you are reading help, remember that the commands wrap around because they won't all fit on one line, but this does **not** mean that you enter the commands in multiple parts.

Look at each component of the **net use** syntax, starting with the following:

```
NET USE [devicename | *] [\\computername\sharename[\volume] [password
    | *]]
```

NET USE is the command and all the other words are the options for the command. Brackets **[ ]** are used to separate the options. Everything in one set of brackets goes together. The first set of brackets **[devicename | *]** tells us to pick a device name (a drive letter such as x:) or to key in an * (asterisk). If you key in an *, **NET USE** will pick the next available drive letter.

The second set of brackets **[\\computername\sharename[\volume] [password | *]]** actually contains brackets within brackets. This tells you that this section is made up of two smaller sections, but both smaller sections should be used together.

The first section within the second set of brackets **\\computername\sharename[\volume]** tells you to put in the network path to the share you want to map to. You can either map to a share by using **\\computername\sharename** or you can map to a folder within the share by using the optional **[\volume]** option. The second section within the second set of brackets **[password | *]** tells you to key in your password or key in an * to have *NET USE* prompt you for your password. Now that you know how this works, look at some examples:

The following example maps a *G:* drive to a share named *data* on a machine called *server03*:

```
NET USE G: \\server03\data
```

If you wanted to do the same thing but have *NET USE* pick a drive letter for you, you could key in an * instead of G:

```
NET USE * : \\server03\data
```

To take it a step further, you could use the [\volume] option and have *NET USE* map you to a folder inside the share:

```
NET USE * : \\server03\data\excel
```

So far you haven't used the password option. If you leave this option blank, net use will use the password of the user you are currently logged on as. To tell *NET USE* to use the password *syngress*, you the following command.

```
NET USE * : \\server03\data\excel syngress
```

The problem with keying in the password is that the password is exposed for someone to see. If we use the * options, *NET USE* prompts you for your password and it will not display it on the screen as you key it in:

```
NET USE * : \\server03\data\excel *
```

Now that you have an idea of how all the options fit together, look at the third set of brackets. This section specifies the username to be used when mapping a drive. It comes in three varieties:

[/USER:[domainname\]username]

[/USER:[dotted domain name\]username]

[/USER:[username@dotted domain name]

The first one [/USER:[domainname\]username] tells you to specify the username in the format of domain name followed by the username. This format uses the one-word NetBIOS-compatible domain name. The second one tells you to specify the username in the format of fully qualified domain name followed by the username. This is the hierarchical Active Directory domain name. The third one tells you to specify the username by using the user principal name (UPN). This format uses the @ sign between the user account name and the domain name, like an Internet e-mail address.

Add this to what you learned earlier and finish up by putting all the pieces together. The following example uses *NET USE* to map a drive using the next available drive letter to a folder named *excel* within a share named *data* on a server named *server03*. Use the password *syngress* for the user account *ctodd* in the *childdom.w2k3doma.ads* domain.

First, use the domainname\username format:

```
NET USE * : \\server03\data\excel syngress /user:childom\ctodd
```

Now, try the same thing with the fully qualified domain name format:

```
NET USE * : \\server03\data\excel syngress /user:childom.
    w2k3doma.ads\ctodd
```

Lastly, try it with the user principal name:

```
NET USE * : \\server03\data\excel syngress /user:ctodd@childom.
    w2k3dom.ads
```

TEST DAY TIP

Do not get discouraged if you cannot remember all the syntax for all the tools in this chapter. What you need to focus on is what each tool is capable of doing and becoming familiar with reading and understanding the syntax.

Using dsadd.exe

As the name implies, dsadd.exe adds objects to Active Directory. dsadd.exe can add computer, contact, group, organization unit, or user objects. dsadd.exe supports the following commands:

- **dsadd computer** Adds a computer to the directory.
- **dsadd contact** Adds a contact to the directory.

- **dsadd group** Adds a group to the directory.
- **dsadd ou** Adds an organizational unit to the directory.
- **dsadd user** Adds a user to the directory.
- **dsadd quota** Adds a quota specification to a directory partition.

Examples

To add a contact, use the following syntax:

```
dsadd contact <ContactDN> [-fn <FirstName>] [-mi <Initial>]
        [-ln <LastName>] [-display <DisplayName>] [-desc <Description>]
        [-office <Office>] [-tel <Phone#>] [-email <Email>]
        [-hometel <HomePhone#>] [-pager <Pager#>] [-mobile <CellPhone#>]
        [-fax <Fax#>] [-iptel <IPPhone#>] [-title <Title>]
        [-dept <Department>] [-company <Company>]
        [{-s <Server> | -d <Domain>}] [-u <UserName>]
        [-p {<Password> | *}] [-q] [{-uc | -uco | -uci}]
```

Here is an example that adds a contact for Chad Todd. The company is set for Training Concepts, LLC and the e-mail address set to chad@trainingconcepts.org.

```
dsadd contact "CN=Chad Todd,OU=contacts,DC=trainingconcepts,DC=org" -
    fn Chad
-ln Todd -company "Training Concepts, LLC" -email chad@trainingconcepts.
    org
```

To add an OU, use the following syntax:

```
dsadd ou <OrganizationalUnitDN> [-desc <Description>]
        [{-s <Server> | -d <Domain>}] [-u <UserName>]
        [-p {<Password> | *}] [-q] [{-uc | -uco | -uci}]
```

Here is an example that adds an OU called Trainers in the trainingconcepts.org domain with the description "This OU contains all trainer user accounts."

```
dsadd ou "OU=Trainers,DC=trainingconcepts,DC=org" -fn -desc "This OU
    contains all trainer user accounts."
```

Using dsmod.exe

dsmod.exe modifies attributes of objects in Active Directory. dsmod.exe can modify computers, contacts, groups, servers, organization units, users, quotas, and partitions. dsmod.exe supports the following commands:

- **dsmod computer** Modifies attributes of one or more computers in the directory.
- **ddsmod contact** Modifies attributes of one or more contacts in the directory.
- **dsmod group** Modifies attributes of one or more groups in the directory.
- **dsmod server** Modifies attributes of one or more servers in the directory.
- **dsmod ou** Modifies attributes of one or more OUs in the directory.
- **dsmod user** Modifies attributes of one or more users in the directory.
- **dsmod quota** Modifies attributes of one or more quotas in the directory.
- **dsmod partition** Modifies attributes of one or more partitions in the directory.

Examples

To modify a contact, use the following syntax:

```
dsmod contact ContactDN [-fn FirstName] [-mi Initial] [-ln LastName] [-
    display DisplayName] [-desc Description] [-office Office] [-tel
        PhoneNumber] [-email Email] [-hometel HomePhoneNumber] [-pager
            PagerNumber] [-mobile CellPhoneNumber] [-fax FaxNumber] [-iptel
                IPPhoneNumber] [-title Title] [-dept Department] [-company
                    Company] [{-s Server | -d Domain}] [-u UserName] [-p
                        {Password | *}] [-c] [-q]
```

Here is an example that modifies the description and e-mail address for the contact for Chad Todd. The description is set to Microsoft Trainer and the e-mail address set to ctodd@trainingconcepts.org.

```
dsmod contact "CN=Chad Todd,OU=Contacts,DC=trainingconcepts,DC=org" -desc
    "Microsoft Trainer" -email ctodd@trainingconcepts.org
```

To modify an OU, use the following syntax:

```
dsmod ou OrganizationalUnitDN [-desc Description] [{-s Server | -d
    Domain}] [-u UserName] [-p {Password | *}] [-c] [-q] [{-uc | -uco | -
        uci}]
```

Here is an example that changes the description of the trainers OU.

```
dsmod ou "OU=Trainers,DC=trainingconcepts,DC=org" -fn -desc "This OU
    contains all trainer user accounts."
```

Using dsget.exe

dsget.exe is used to see the properties of objects in Active Directory. It shows selected attributes of computers, contacts, groups, organizational units, servers, or users. You input objects into dsget.exe and it outputs a list of properties for those objects. dsget.exe supports the following commands:

- **dsget computer** Displays properties of computers in the directory.
- **dsget contact** Displays properties of contacts in the directory.
- **dsget subnet** Displays properties of subnets in the directory.
- **dsget group** Displays properties of groups in the directory.
- **dsget ou** Displays properties of OUs in the directory.
- **dsget server** Displays properties of servers in the directory.
- **dsget site** Displays properties of sites in the directory.
- **dsget user** Displays properties of users in the directory.
- **dsget quota** Displays properties of quotas in the directory.
- **dsget partition** Displays properties of partitions in the directory.

Examples

To get information about a contact, use the following syntax:

```
dsget contact ContactDN ... [-dn] [-fn] [-mi] [-ln] [-display] [-desc] [-
   office] [-tel] [-email] [-hometel] [-pager] [-mobile] [-fax] [-iptel]
      [-title] [-dept] [-company] [{-s Server | -d Domain}] [-u UserName]
         [-p {Password | *}] [-c] [-q] [-l] [{-uc | -uco | -uci}]
```

Here is an example that gets the e-mail address for the Chad Todd contact:

```
dsget contact "CN=Chad Todd,OU=Contacts,DC=trainingconcepts,DC=org" -email
```

To get information about an OU, use the following syntax:

```
dsget ou OrganizationalUnitDN ... [-dn] [-desc] [{-s Server | -d Domain}]
    [-u UserName] [-p {Password | *}] [-c] [-q] [-l] [{-uc | -uco |
       -uci}]
```

Here is an example that gets the description for the trainers OU:

```
dsadd ou "OU=Trainers,DC=trainingconcepts,DC=org" -desc
```

Using dsmove.exe

The name dsmove.exe implies that it moves objects within the directory service. This is, however, only part of what it does. dsmove.exe moves a single object to a new location in the same domain. However, it will also rename a single object without moving it. dsmove.exe uses the following syntax. (Table 4.1 explains all the syntax in detail.)

```
dsmove <ObjectDN>

            [-newparent <ParentDN>]
            [-newname <NewName>]
            [{-s <Server> | -d <Domain>}]
            [-u <UserName>]
            [-p {<Password> | *}]
            [-q]
            [{-uc | -uco | -uci}]
```

NOTE

Every Active Directory object has a relative distinguished name (RDN) and a distinguished name (DN). The RDN identifies an object within its parent container. The DN identifies the object within the entire directory. The DN consists of the RDN and its entire parent container objects.

For example, the RDN for the Chad user account in the Authors organizational unit in the trainingconcepts.org domain is CN=chad. The DN for the same object is CN=chad, OU=authors, DC=trainingconcepts, DC=org. As you read through this chapter, remember that DN is the distinguished name of an object.

Table 4.1 Understanding dsmove.exe

Value	Description
<ObjectDN>	Distinguished name (DN) of object to move or rename.
-newparent <ParentDN>	DN of the new parent location where the object should be moved.
-newname <NewName>	New relative distinguished name (RDN) value that the object should be renamed to.
{-s <Server> | -d <Domain>}	-s <Server> connects to the domain controller (DC) with name <Server>. -d <Domain> connects to a DC in domain <Domain>. Default: a DC in the logon domain.

Continued

Table 4.1 Understanding dsmove.exe

Value	Description
-u <UserName>	Connect as <UserName>. Default: the logged-on user. Username can be: username, domain\username, or user principal name (UPN).
-p <Password>	Password for the user <UserName>. If * is used, then the command prompts for a password.
-q	Quiet mode: suppress all output to standard output.
{-uc | -uco | -uci}	-uc Specifies that input from or output to pipe is formatted in Unicode. -uco Specifies that output to pipe or file is formatted in Unicode. -uci Specifies that input from pipe or file is formatted in Unicode.

Examples

The following examples move the Chad Todd user from one OU to another and rename the Sarah Smith user account.

To move the user object Chad Todd from the Training OU to the Consulting OU, type the following command:

```
dsmove "cn=Chad Todd,ou=training,dc=trainingconcepts,dc=org" -newparent
    ou=consulting,dc=trainingconcepts,dc=org
```

To rename the Sarah Smith user object to Sarah Todd, type the following command:

```
dsmove "cn=Sarah Smith Doe,ou=sales,dc=trainingconcepts,dc=org" -newname
    "Sarah Todd"
```

Using dsquery.exe

dsquery.exe enables you to query Active Directory for objects that match a specified criterion. This is useful if you need to search all of AD for objects that have similar characteristics. For example, you may want to search for all disabled user accounts or for all groups that do not have a description. dsquery.exe supports the following command:

- **dsquery computer** Finds computers in the directory.
- **dsquery contact** Finds contacts in the directory.
- **dsquery subnet** Finds subnets in the directory.
- **dsquery group** Finds groups in the directory.
- **dsquery ou** Finds organizational units in the directory.

- **dsquery site** Finds sites in the directory.
- **dsquery server** Finds domain controllers in the directory.
- **dsquery user** Finds users in the directory.
- **dsquery quota** Finds quota specifications in the directory.
- **dsquery partition** Finds partitions in the directory.
- **dsquery *** Finds any object in the directory by using a generic LDAP query.

Examples

You can pipe results from dsquery.exe into dsget.exe. In other words, you can use dsquery.exe to find objects in Active Directory and have dsget.exe show their properties.

To find all users with names starting with "Chad" and display their office numbers, type the following command:

```
dsquery user -name Chad* | dsget user -office
```

To find all servers that have been inactive for the past six weeks, type the following command:

```
dsquery computer -inactive 6
```

To find all users in the organizational unit "ou=training,dc=trainingconcepts,dc=org", type the following command:

```
dsquery user ou=training,dc=trainingconcepts,dc=org
```

Using gpresult.exe

gpresult.exe displays the Resultant Set of Policy (RSoP) information for a target user and computer. RSoP is a tool that can show the effective policy applied to a user or computer or what the policy would be, for planning purposes. This tool is very helpful for troubleshooting Group Policy, because it shows you all the policy applied and the effective policy. gpresult.exe uses the following syntax (Table 4.2 explains the syntax in detail):

```
GPRESULT [/S system [/U username [/P [password]]]] [/SCOPE scope]
        [/USER targetusername] [/V | /Z]
```

Table 4.2 Understanding gpresult.exe

Value	Description
/S System	Specifies the remote system to connect to.
/U [domain\]user	Specifies the user context under which the command should execute.

Continued

Table 4.2 Understanding gpresult.exe

Value	Description
/P [password]	Specifies the password for the given user context. Prompts for input if omitted.
/SCOPE scope	Specifies whether the user or the computer settings needs to be displayed. Valid values: "USER," "COMPUTER."
/USER [domain\]user	Specifies the username for which the RSOP data is to be displayed.
/V	Specifies that verbose information should be displayed. Verbose information provides additional detailed settings that have been applied with a precedence of 1.
/Z	Specifies that the super-verbose information should be displayed. Super-verbose information provides additional detailed settings that have been applied with a precedence of 1 and higher. This enables you to see if a setting was set in multiple places. See the Group Policy online help topic for more information.
/?	Displays this help message.

Examples

To show the RSoP data for the current logged-on user, type **gpresult** without any parameters, as shown in the following example:

```
GPRESULT
```

This gives you input similar to the following (Titles have been bolded to make them stand out):

```
Microsoft (R) Windows (R) Operating System Group Policy Result tool v2.0
Copyright (C) Microsoft Corp. 1981-2001


Created On 6/28/2003 at 1:18:01 AM



RSOP data for W2K3DOMA\chad on W2K3_DC : Logging Mode
-------------------------------------------------------


OS Type:                    Microsoft(R) Windows(R) Server 2003,
    Enterprise Edition
OS Configuration:          Primary Domain Controller
OS Version:                 5.2.3790
Terminal Server Mode:      Application Server
```

```
Site Name:                     Default-First-Site-Name
Roaming Profile:               c:\profiles\Chad
Local Profile:                 C:\Documents and Settings\Administrator
Connected over a slow link?: No


COMPUTER SETTINGS
------------------
    CN=W2K3_DC,OU=Domain Controllers,DC=w2k3doma,DC=ads
    Last time Group Policy was applied: 6/28/2003 at 1:13:28 AM
    Group Policy was applied from:      w2k3_dc.w2k3doma.ads
    Group Policy slow link threshold:   500 kbps
    Domain Name:                         W2K3DOMA
    Domain Type:                         Windows 2000

    Applied Group Policy Objects
    -----------------------------
        Default Domain Controllers Policy
        Default Domain Policy
        Local Group Policy

    The following GPOs were not applied because they were filtered out
    -------------------------------------------------------------------
        GPO Demo
            Filtering:  Not Applied (Empty)

    The computer is a part of the following security groups
    -------------------------------------------------------
        BUILTIN\Administrators
        Everyone
        BUILTIN\Pre-Windows 2000 Compatible Access
        BUILTIN\Users
        Windows Authorization Access Group
        NT AUTHORITY\NETWORK
        NT AUTHORITY\Authenticated Users
        This Organization
        W2K3_DC$
        Domain Controllers
        NT AUTHORITY\ENTERPRISE DOMAIN CONTROLLERS
```

```
USER SETTINGS
--------------
    CN=Chad,CN=Users,DC=w2k3doma,DC=ads
    Last time Group Policy was applied: 6/28/2003 at 12:38:02 AM
    Group Policy was applied from:      w2k3_dc.w2k3doma.ads
    Group Policy slow link threshold:   500 kbps
    Domain Name:                         W2K3DOMA
    Domain Type:                         Windows 2000

    Applied Group Policy Objects
    -----------------------------
        Default Domain Policy

    The following GPOs were not applied because they were filtered out
    -------------------------------------------------------------------
        GPO Demo
            Filtering:  Not Applied (Empty)

        Local Group Policy
            Filtering:  Not Applied (Empty)

    The user is a part of the following security groups
    ---------------------------------------------------
        Domain Users
        Everyone
        BUILTIN\Administrators
        BUILTIN\Users
        BUILTIN\Pre-Windows 2000 Compatible Access
        NT AUTHORITY\INTERACTIVE
        NT AUTHORITY\Authenticated Users
        This Organization
        LOCAL
        Enterprise Admins
        Group Policy Creator Owners
        Domain Admins
        Schema Admins
```

You can target gpresults.exe toward a certain user or machine, as shown in the following examples:

```
gpresult /user chad
```

```
gpresult /s chadlaptop
```

Using whoami.exe

whoami.exe displays usernames and group membership information about the currently logged-on user. It can display the security identifier (SID) and all privileges assigned to that SID. This tool is great if you need to quickly see which groups a user belongs to.

NOTE

Privileges enable certain tasks to be accomplished on the local machine and in Active Directory. Examples of AD privileges include **act as part of the operating system, add workstations to a domain,** and **back up files and directories**.

whoami.exe has three variations of syntax, as shown in the following examples (Table 4.3 explains all the syntax in detail):

- Syntax 1

  ```
  WHOAMI [/UPN | /FQDN | /LOGONID]
  ```

- Syntax 2

  ```
  WHOAMI { [/USER] [/GROUPS] [/PRIV] } [/FO format] [/NH]
  ```

- Syntax 3

  ```
  WHOAMI /ALL [/FO format] [/NH]
  ```

Table 4.3 Understanding whoami.exe

Value	Description
/UPN	Displays the username in User Principal Name (UPN) format.
/FQDN	Displays the username in Fully Qualified Distinguished Name (FQDN) format.
/USER	Displays information on the current user along with the security identifier (SID).
/GROUPS	Displays group membership for current user, type of account, security identifiers (SID), and attributes.

Continued

Table 4.3 Understanding whoami.exe

Value	Description
/PRIV	Displays security privileges of the current user.
/LOGONID	Displays the logon ID of the current user.
/ALL	Displays the current username, groups belonged to along with the security identifiers (SID), and privileges for the current user access token.
/FO format	Specifies the output format to be displayed. Valid values are TABLE, LIST, CSV. Column headings are not displayed with CSV format. Default format is TABLE.
/NH	Specifies that the column header should not be displayed in the output. This is valid only for TABLE and CSV formats.
/?	Displays this help message.

Examples

To display the user principal name of the currently logged-on user, type the following command:

```
whoami /upn
```

To display the fully qualified name of the currently logged-on user, type the following command:

```
whoami /fqdn
```

To display the SID of the currently logged-on user, type the following command:

```
whoami /loginid
```

To display the group membership for the currently logged-on user, type the following command:

```
whoami /groups
```

To display the username, group membership, SID, and privileges for the currently logged-on user, type the following command:

```
whoami /all
```

Using cmdkey.exe

cmdkey.exe enables you to manage Stored Usernames and Passwords from the command prompt. It displays, creates, and deletes stored usernames and passwords. cmdkey.exe uses the following syntax. (Table 4.4 displays the syntax for cmdkey.exe in detail.)

```
CMDKEY [{/add | /generic}:targetname {/smartcard | /user:username
    {/pass{:password}}} | /delete{:targetname | /ras} | /list
        {:targetname}]
```

Table 4.4 Understanding cmdkey.exe Syntax

Value	Description
/add:	Adds a username and password to the list.
/generic	Adds generic credentials to the list.
TargetName	The computer or domain name that this entry will be associated with.
/smartcard	Retrieves the credential from a smart card.
/user: username	Specifies the user or account name to store with this entry. If UserName is not supplied, it will be requested.
/pass: password	Specifies the password to store with this entry. If Password is not supplied, it will be requested.
/delete: targetname	Deletes a username and password from the list. If TargetName is specified, that entry will be deleted.
/ras	If /ras is specified, the stored remote access entry will be deleted.
/list: targetname	Displays the list of stored usernames and credentials. If TargetName is not specified, all stored usernames and credentials will be listed.
/?	Displays help at the command prompt.

Examples

To list available credentials for the currently logged-on user, type the following command:

```
cmdkey /list
```

To list available credentials for the user named ctodd, type the following command:

```
cmdkey /list:ctodd
```

To display a list of stored credentials with usernames, type the following command:

```
cmdkey /list
```

To use *cmdkey* to add a username and password for user ctodd to access the computer win2k3srv with the password syngress, type the following command:

```
cmdkey /add:win2k3srv /user:ctodd /pass:syngress
```

To delete existing credentials for the user ctodd, type the following command:

```
cmdkey /delete:ctodd
```

Creating and Managing User Accounts

User accounts are required to log on to a Windows network. Active Directory only gives us two built-in user accounts (administrator and guest) to log on with by default. All other accounts must be manually created. You can create user accounts through the GUI with Active Directory Users and Computers (ADUC). You can create them from the command prompt by using tools such as dsadd.exe, csvde.exe, and ldiffde.exe.

Using the ADUC MMC Snap-In to Create and Manage Users

This section discusses using ADUC to create and manage users. Exercise 4.01 covers creating users. It is important to know how to create users. However, for the test you also need to know how to manage users. This section walks you through all the tabs of an Active Directory user account with screenshots and explanations.

Exercise 4.01

Using Active Directory Users and Computers to Create Users

1. Open Active Directory Users and Computers (**Start | Programs | Administrative Tools | Active Directory Users and Computers**).
2. Right-click the **domain** or **OU** where you want to create a user, as shown in Figure 4.4.
3. Click **New** from the pop-up menu.
4. Click **User** from the pop-up menu. The **New Object – User** screen appears, as shown in Figure 4.5.
5. Fill in the new user's information. For this example, you are creating a user named Sarah Todd with the username stodd. At a minimum, you must fill in the **Full name** and the **User logon name**. However, if you fill in the **First name** and **Last name** fields, ADUC automatically transfers that information to the **Full name** field. Typing the **User logon name** automatically fills in the **User logon name (pre-Windows 2000)** field as well. When you have filled in all necessary information, click **Next** to continue. This will bring you to the password window shown in Figure 4.6.
6. The only requirement here is to **enter a password** for the new user account. By default the user account will be set to force the user to change his or her password at the next logon. You can undo this by clearing the corresponding check box. Optionally, you can set the user's password to never expire or you can make it so the user cannot change

Figure 4.4 Creating a New User

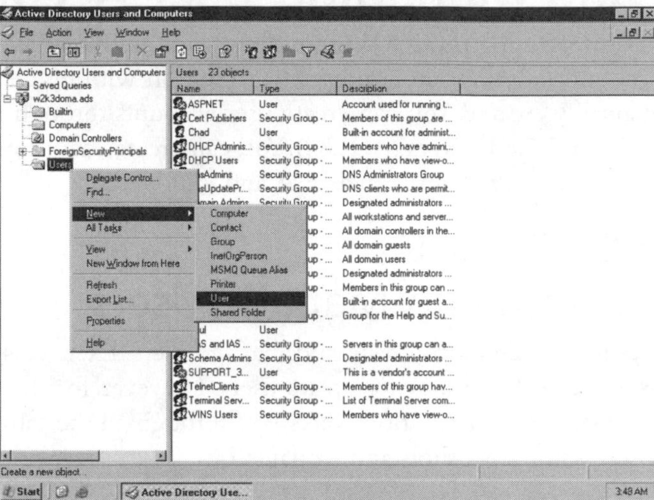

Figure 4.5 Naming the New User

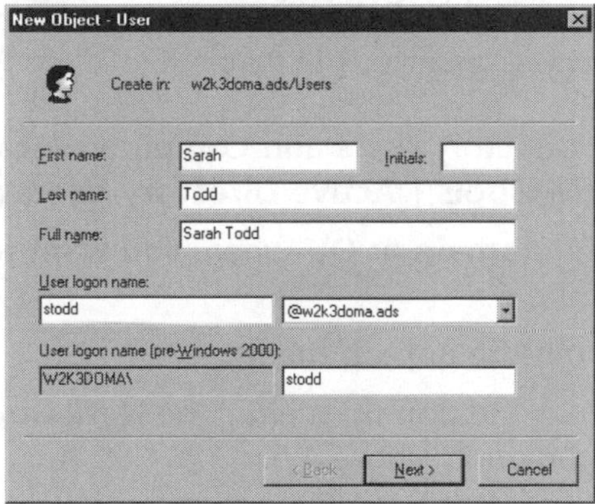

Figure 4.6 Setting the Password

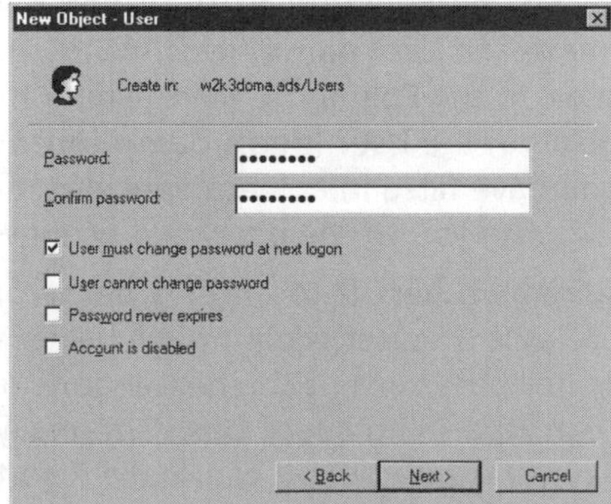

the password. If the account is not going to be used for some time, you may want to disable it now so as to avoid it being used until needed. After you have entered a password and made your selections, click **Next** to continue.

7. The summary screen appears, as shown in Figure 4.7. Verify that the settings are correct and click **Finish** to create the user. Figure 4.8 shows us that our new user account for Sarah Todd was created.

Figure 4.7 Verifying Settings

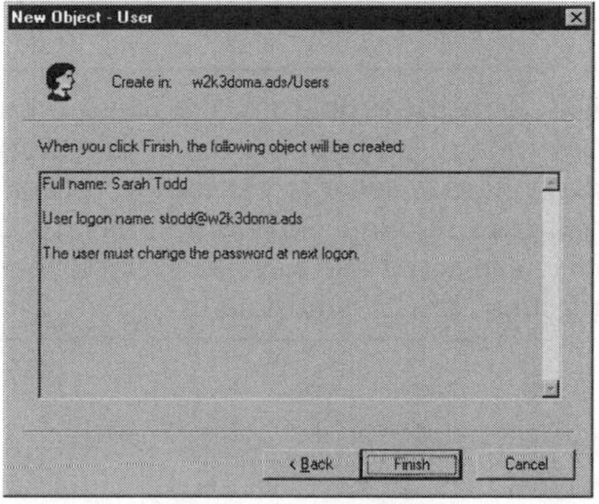

Figure 4.8 Viewing the New User Account in the Users Container

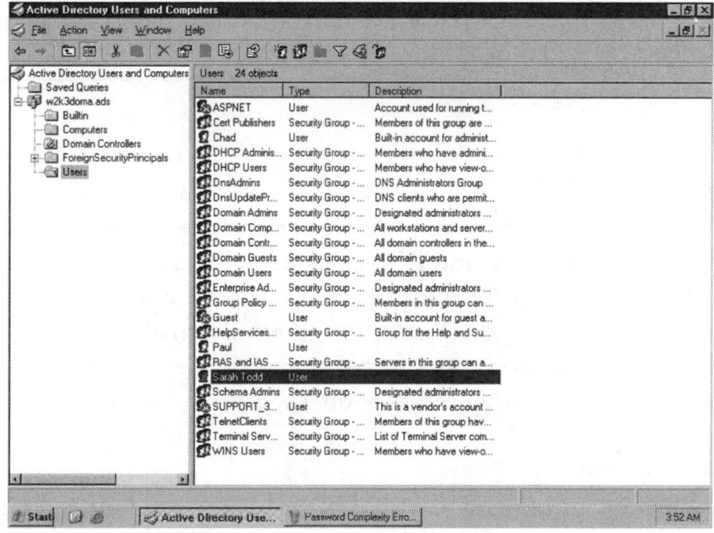

Managing and Troubleshooting User Accounts Via the Properties Tabs

As you have seen, creating user accounts is fairly simple. Managing user accounts after creation is a little more difficult. There are a lot more options for managing user accounts than for creating them. For the Server test you need to be familiar with the properties of user accounts, including what each tab is used for. This section provides screenshots with explanations for each of these tabs. To access a user's properties sheet, right-click the **user account name** in the right pane of ADUC and select **Properties**.

EXAM WARNING

You need to be familiar with the properties of a user account for the test. This test uses exhibits to test your knowledge of the Active Directory Users and Computers interface. For example, you may see a screenshot of a user's properties and have to select the tab that manages Terminal Server idle timeouts or you may see a screenshot with the correct tab selected and have to click on the option that is needed for that particular question. KNOW your tabs!

NOTE

Throughout this chapter we will be looking at the various tabs for users, groups, and machines. To see all of the tabs discussed, you must enable the advanced view within ADUC. To do this, click the **View** button on the menu bar (Figure 4.8) and select **Advanced** from the drop-down menu.

Using the General Tab

The **General** tab, as shown in Figure 4.9, contains descriptive information about the user account. The First name, Last name, and Display name fields are carried over from when you created the user. The other fields must be filled in after account creation. Some companies use the description field as a placeholder for other information so they can search on it later. For example, if you enter everyone's birthday into the description field, then you can use that field to find everyone with a birthday on a specified day.

Using the Address Tab

The **Address** tab, as shown in Figure 4.10, is self-explanatory. It contains the user's address, including the following:

- Street Name
- P.O. Box

- City
- State
- Zip Code
- Country

Figure 4.9 Understanding a User's General Tab.

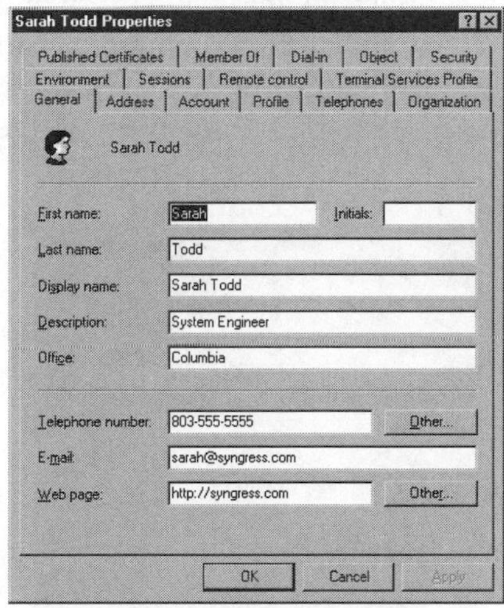

Figure 4.10 Understanding a User's Address Tab

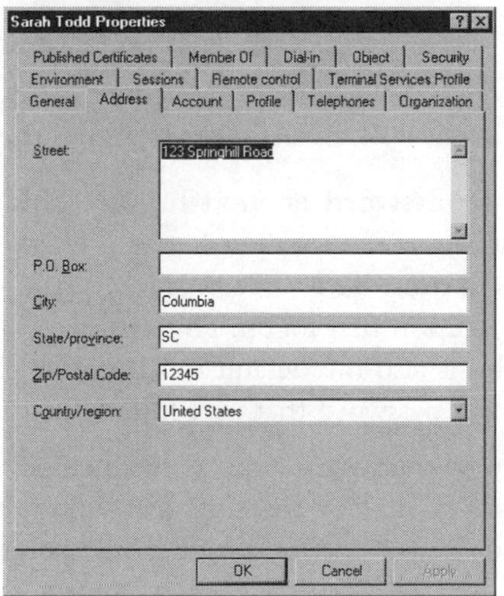

Using the Account Tab

The **Account** tab, as shown in Figure 4.11, is where most of the action takes place. This is where you change a user's logon name, the user principal name (UPN), or a user's UPN suffix. User accounts are unlocked from the account tab. Whenever a user logs on with an incorrect password a preconfigured number of times, their account is locked. This makes it unusable until an administrator unlocks it. You also set the account to expire after a set date. This is a good feature if you have contract or temporary employees working for you. If you know they are on a six-month contract, go ahead and set their accounts to expire in six months. Some companies set all temporary employee user accounts to expire monthly as a security precaution. If the temporary user leaves the company without notifying the IT department, the account can only be used (or abused) for 30 days.

Figure 4.11 Understanding a User's Account Tab

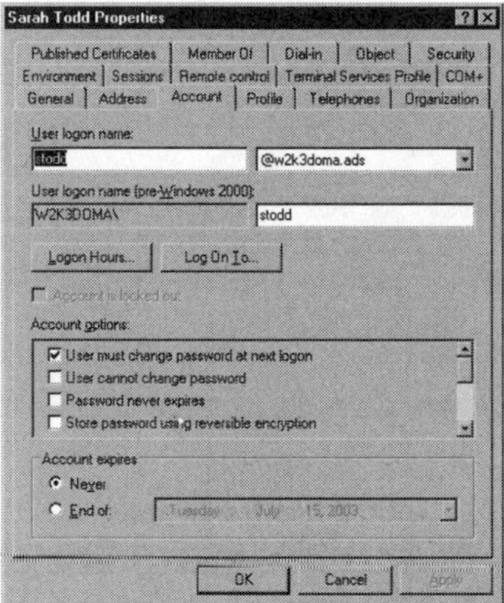

The **Account options** section of the **Account** tab has the following options:

- **User must change password at next logon** This forces a user to change his or her password the next time the user logs on. This is used when someone forgets the password and must have it reset. It resets it to something easy, and the user has to change it upon first logon. This ensures that only the user knows his or her password. This is also the default when you initially create the account, so the user can set a new password that isn't known to the administrator.
- **User cannot change password** This prevents users from changing their passwords. This is a good choice for accounts that will be running services (a.k.a. service accounts) or for shared accounts such as classroom or kiosk accounts.
- **Password never expires** When this is checked, the user's password will not expire. This option overrides the account policy configured for the domain (in the default domain policy GPO). Use this option sparingly. If a hacker stumbles

across an account with the password set to not expire, he has unlimited use of that account until someone decides to change the password. This is a good option to use for service accounts, because you don't want the quarterly password change to affect the services on your machines.

- **Store passwords using reversible encryption** This option is required when using Digest Authentication in Internet Information Services (IIS), when logging on to a Windows domain from an Apple computer, and when using Challenge-Handshake Authentication Protocol (CHAP) authentication through a remote access server. This setting instructs Active Directory to store a plain text copy of the password. Unless explicitly required, you should leave this check box cleared.
- **Account is disabled** Disabling an account does not change any permissions assigned to or settings configured for the user account. It just disables logging on with the account. This is a good thing to do for accounts that are seldom logged on with, such as test or never as template accounts. It is also a good idea to disable accounts for people that are going on extended leave from the company. If you know they will not need access to their accounts, then disable them. Disable accounts rather than deleting them any time a user leaves but there is a possibility the user might return and need to resume using the account. If you delete the account, you'll have to recreate it completely (and it won't have the same SID). If you just disable it, you can easily enable it again when it is needed.
- **Smart card is required for interactive logon** This option disables logging on without a smart card. The user's password is randomly changed and set to never expire. Active Directory manages the password for the account. This is good for security, but it can be a problem if a user forgets his or her smart card or needs to log on to a machine that does not have a smart card reader.

NOTE

Smart cards provide a secure method of logging on to a Windows Server 2003 domain. Smart cards are physical cards that contain a certificate. This certificate identifies a user to Windows. Using smart cards is more secure than standard logons, because users must have possession of their card to logon. Smart cards are protected with a pin code in case of accidental loss or theft. In addition to logging on to a domain, smart cards are used for client authentication to applications and for securing e-mail.

A drawback of smart cards is that if users leave their cards at home, they cannot logon. Also, every machine that users need to log on to must have a smart card reader attached. This can become expensive in a large environment.

- **Account is trusted for delegation** This tab should be left unchecked most of the time. Selecting it could weaken your network security. Setting an account to be trusted for delegation enables a service running as this account to impersonate a client to get access to resources on another machine running the same service.

NOTE

Delegation enables services to impersonate a user account or a computer account to access network resources. This can be used in N-tier programs where users authenticate to a middle-tier service and the middle-tier service authenticates to a back-end data server on behalf of the user.

For example, a user accesses a Web page that runs a program. The server running the program is trusted for delegation. That program accesses multiple SQL databases on various servers. After the user authenticates to the Web server, the server can access all the SQL servers as the user.

- **Account is sensitive and cannot be delegated** Enables control over a user account, such as for a guest or temporary account. You can use this option if the account cannot be assigned for delegation by another account.
- **Use DES encryption types for this account** Provides support for the Data Encryption Standard (DES) such as MPPE Standard (40-bit), MPPE Standard (56-bit), MPPE Strong (128-bit), IPSec DES (40-bit), IPSec 56-bit DES, and IPSec 168-bit Triple DES (3DES).
- **Do not require Kerberos preauthentication** Enables using this account with different implementations of the Kerberos protocol, such as a UNIX Kerberos realm.

The **Account** tab enables you to configure Logon Hour restrictions (Figure 4.12) and Machine Log-On restrictions (Figure 4.13).

Use the **Logon Hours** button to restrict the times that a user can log on to the domain. There are no restrictions by default. A user can log on anytime on any day of the week. To change the times, select the hours that you want to manage by clicking and dragging the mouse over the correct sections and clicking either the **Logon Permitted** button or the **Logon Denied** button. You may want to restrict what times users can log on because of security reasons. If they should be working only from 9 AM to 5 PM, why enable their accounts to be used on weekends?

The **Log On To** button enables you to restrict a user account to logging on to specified machines. By default, a user account can log on to any machine in its domain or a trusted domain. To use this restriction, you must have the NetBIOS protocol enabled. Restrictions are based on the NetBIOS name of the machine and without NetBIOS it will not work. This works great for accounts used in a classroom or lab.

Figure 4.12 Setting Logon Hours

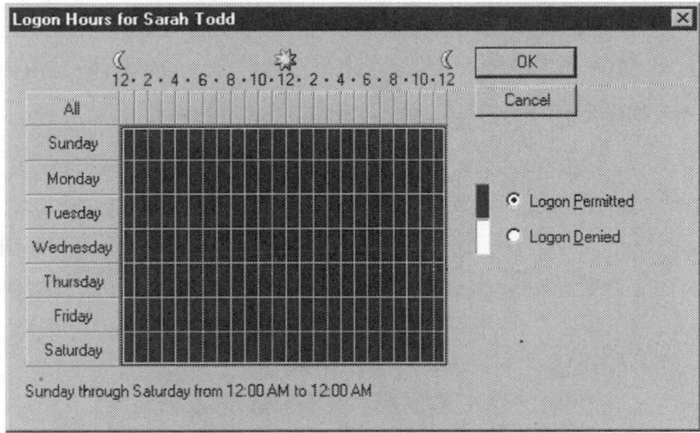

Figure 4.13 Setting Workstation Restrictions

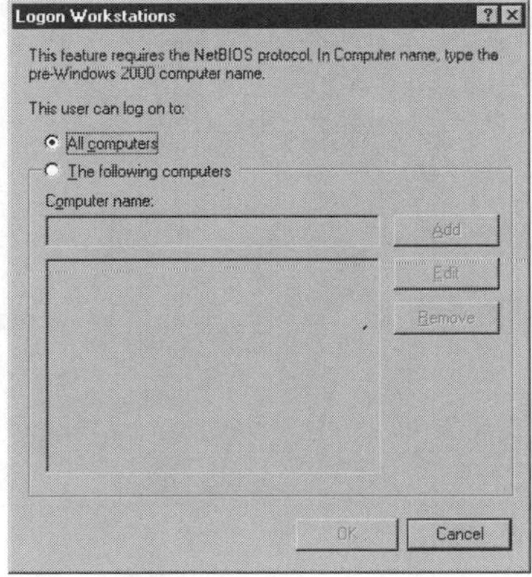

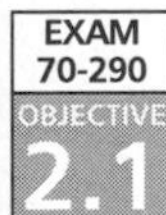

Using the Profile Tab

The user's **Profile** tab, as shown in Figure 4.14, enables you to configure the user to use a roaming profile and specify the profile's path. Roaming profiles are stored on a share, and enable a user to log on to any machine and using the same profile (this includes the desktop, Start menu, and application data). To use a roaming profile, configure the Profile path field to point to a share via a universal naming convention (UNC) such as \\server\users\%username%. The logon script field tells the user account which logon script to run. You enter the name of the logon script (e.g., ntlogon.bat) and make sure that the script is stored in the Netlogon share on your domain controllers.

The **Home Folder** section has two choices:

- **Local Path** This points to a local folder on the user's machine. If this is left blank (which is the default setting), the local user profile folder (%system-drive%\Documents and Settings\%username%) is used.
- **Connect** This tells the user account to connect to a network location for its home folder. This option requires picking a drive letter to use and entering in the UNC of the share used for the home folder. This method will automatically map the corresponding drive letter to the user's home folder.

Figure 4.14 Understanding a User's Profile Tab

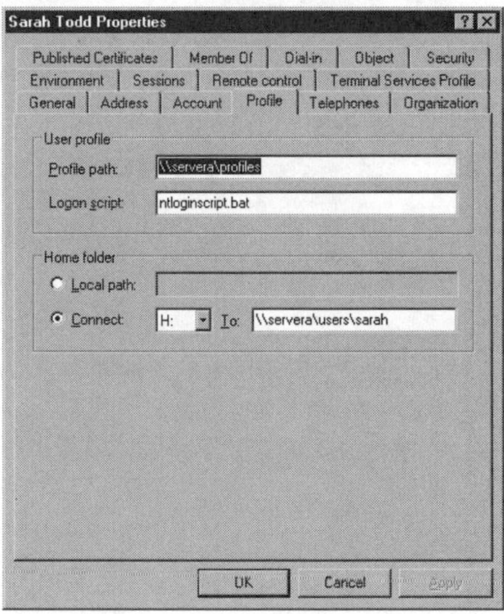

Using the Telephones Tab

The **Telephones** tab, shown in Figure 4.15, contains the phone numbers for the specified user. It also holds notes about the user account in the **Notes** field. You can enter phone numbers for the following:

- Home
- Pager
- Mobile
- Fax
- IP Phone

If a user has multiple phone numbers in a particular category (for example, two mobile numbers), you can enter them using the **Other** button.

Figure 4.15 Understanding a User's Telephone Tab

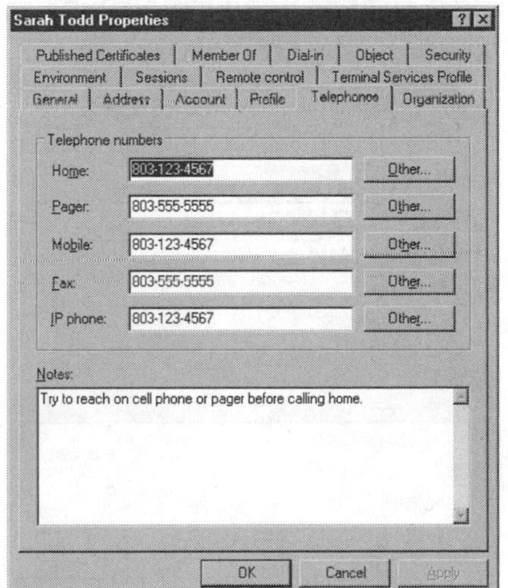

Using the Organization Tab

The **Organization** tab, shown in Figure 4.16, contains organizational chart type information. This information is useful if you want to find everyone who works in a particular department, or if you want to find everyone that reports to a certain manager. You do not fill in the **Direct reports** field. It is automatically filled in with the names of user accounts that have this account listed as their manager. In other words, when you fill in the **Manager** tab for a user account, that account is automatically listed as a direct report on the properties of the manager's account. Thus, if you enter bobsmith in the Manager field on Sarah Todd's account properties (by clicking the **Change** button and entering the name), when you open the **Organization** tab on the properties sheet for the bobsmith account, you see Sarah Todd's account name under **Direct reports**.

Using the Environment Tab

The **Environment** tab, shown in Figure 4.17, configures the Terminal Services startup environment. You can configure a user's properties so that a specified program is launched every time the user logs onto a Terminal Server. To do so, check the box next to **Start the following program at logon** and enter the program filename and the working directory for the file. The **Environment** tab also enables you to configure how clients' local devices are handled when they log onto Terminal Services. You can enable the following options:

- **Connect client drives at logon** Automatically reconnects to mapped client drives. This option works only with ICA (Citrix) clients.
- **Connect client printers at logon** Automatically reconnects to all of a client's mapped printers.

Figure 4.16 Understanding a User's Organization Tab

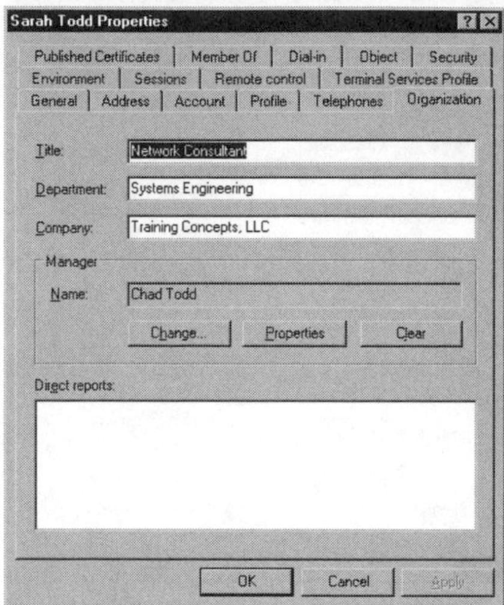

- **Default to main client printer** Automatically prints to the client's default printer.

Figure 4.17 Understanding a User's Environment Tab

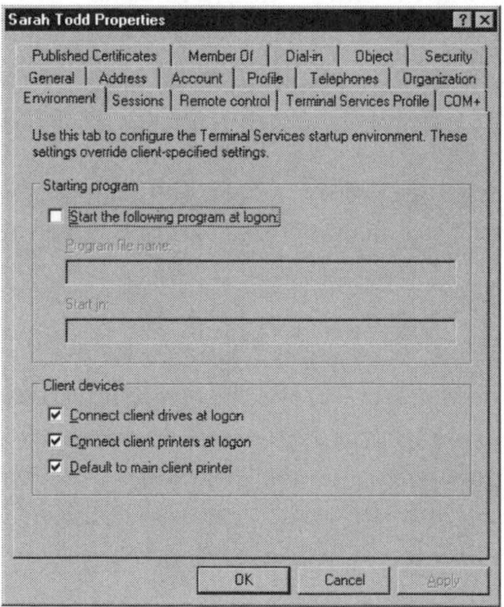

Using the Sessions Tab

The **Sessions** tab, shown in Figure 4.18, controls Terminal Services timeout and reconnection settings. It configures the timeouts for the following:

- **Disconnected sessions** These are sessions that are closed by mistake. This can be due to loss of network connectivity while connected, or by accidentally clicking the **Close** button when using the Remote Desktop Connection client. It is a good idea to enable this one to prevent wasted system resources. If your users disconnect from their Terminal Session but never log off, resources are wasted on the Terminal Server. Be careful about setting this too low, because you want to give your users time to reconnect if they accidentally lose their connections.
- **Active session limits** This controls the maximum amount of time that a user can stay connected.
- **Idle session limits** This controls the maximum amount of time that a session can remain idle without any keyboard or mouse activity.

The possible timeouts for each of these limits are as follows:

- Never (no limit)
- 1 minute
- 5 minutes
- 10 minutes
- 15 minutes
- 30 minutes
- 1 hour
- 2 hours
- 3 hours
- 1 day
- 2 days

The **Sessions** tab also controls what happens when a client's Terminal Services session is broken or the limit is reached. The session can either be disconnected or ended. If it is ended, all programs are closed and any unsaved data is lost. If it is set to disconnect, all programs continue to run, and open files are preserved until the user logs back on. However, the session remains available only until the user reaches one of the session limits (if they are defined), at which time the session is ended and all unsaved data is lost. This tab also enables you to decide from what location(s) a client is enabled to reconnect to a disconnected session. The default is to enable the client to reconnect from any client machine. This is good when the reason the user was disconnected was due to hardware failure on the local machine. You can also require that the user reconnect from the same system that initiated the connection. This is more secure, but can lead to problems if the original machine that connected is no longer available.

Figure 4.18 Understanding a User's Sessions Tab

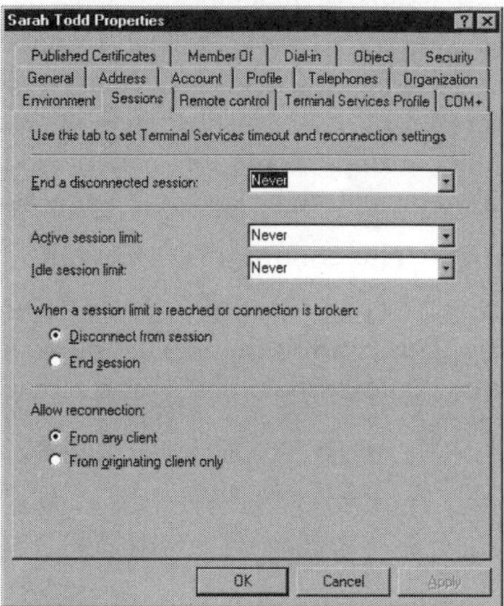

Using the Remote Control Tab

The **Remote control** tab, shown in Figure 4.19, controls the level of remote control enabled when a user is connected via Terminal Services. The default is to enable taking remote control and interacting with a session after the user has been granted permission. You have the following remote control options:

- **Enable remote control** This enables this user account to remotely control another user's Terminal Services session.
- **Require user's permission** This prompts the user for permission before remote control is granted. If the user declines, remote control is denied for that session.
- **View the user's session** This specifies that after the user takes control of another session, that user can only see what the remote user is doing. The first user cannot actually move the mouse or use the keyboard to input to the remote machine. This is good for troubleshooting purposes, because it enables an administrator to watch the steps that a user is taking.
- **Interact with the session.** This specifies that once the user takes control of another session, he or she can interact with the remote desktop. This includes the capability to move the mouse and use the keyboard to input to the remote machine.

Figure 4.19 Understanding a User's Remote Control Tab

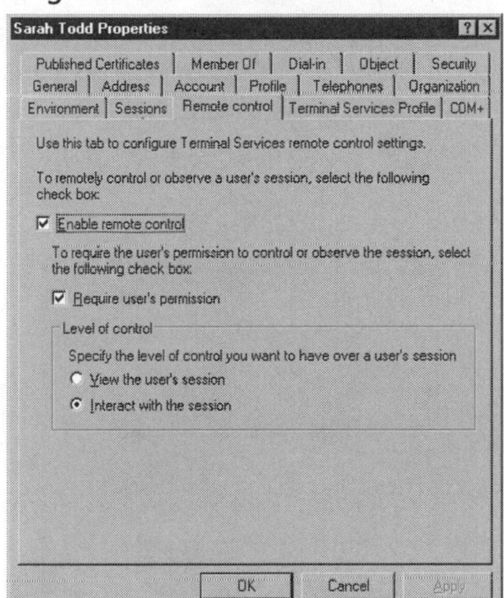

Using the Terminal Services Profile Tab

The **Terminal Services Profile** tab, shown in Figure 4.20, enables or disables the ability for a user to log on via Terminal Services. You control this by checking or clearing the **Allow logon to terminal server** check box (checked by default). All other settings on this tab are the same as the settings on the **Profile** tab previously discussed.

Figure 4.20 Understanding a User's Terminal Services Profile Tab

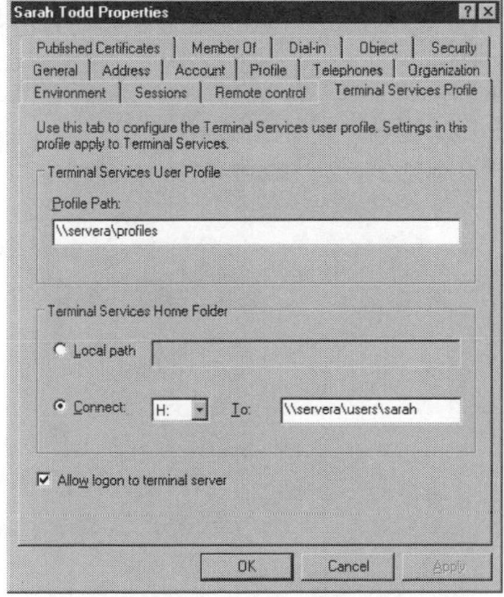

Using the COM+ Tab

The **COM+** tab, shown in Figure 4.21, lists the COM+ partition sets that can be assigned to this user. COM+ partition sets enable tailoring access of a certain set of domain users to a set of applications. Security is applied to the users in each set. After grouping your COM+ partitions into a COM+ partition set, you use this tab to assign a user to a particular set.

Figure 4.21 Understanding a User's COM+ Tab

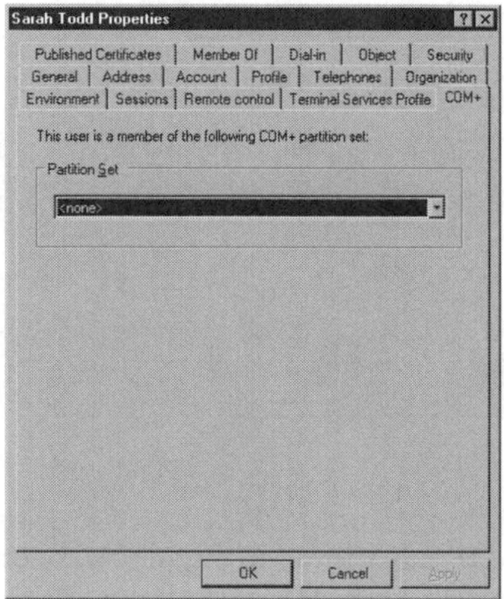

Using the Published Certificates Tab

The **Published Certificates** tab, shown in Figure 4.22, manages X.509 certificates for the selected user account. You can use this tab to view the details of the user's certificates. You can also use it to add, remove, and copy certificates. Certificates can be added from the certificate store or from a file.

Figure 4.22 Understanding a User's Published Certificates Tab

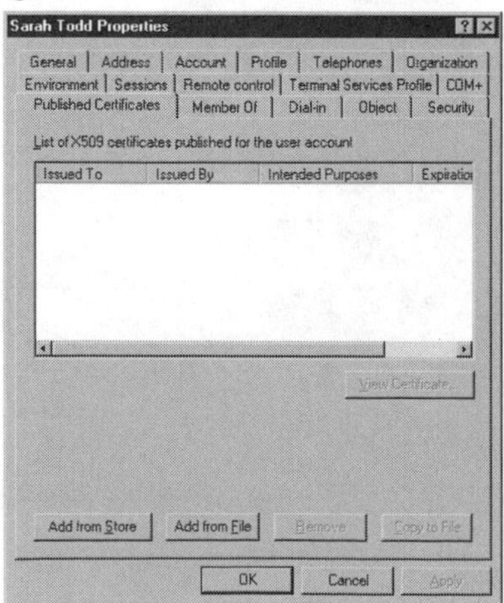

Using the Member Of Tab

The **Member Of** tab, shown in Figure 4.23, manages the groups of which the selected user is a member. By using the **Add** and **Remove** buttons, you can add and remove this user from groups. If you are using Apple clients or POSIX-compliant applications, you can use this tab to set the primary group as required. If a user account is a member of only one group, that group is automatically configured as the primary group as shown in Figure 4.23. If a user account is a member of multiple groups, click the group you want to make primary and click the **Set Primary Group** button.

Figure 4.23 Understanding a User's Member Of Tab

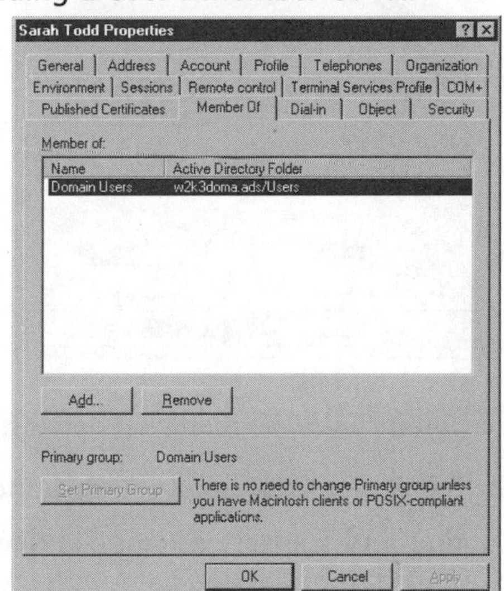

Using the Dial-In Tab

The **Dial-in** tab, shown in Figure 4.24, controls dial-in and VPN options for the selected user account. This tab contains two main sections, Remote Access Permissions and Callback Options. Remote Access Permissions determine if a user is allowed to connect to the Routing and Remote Access Service (RRAS) server for dial-in or VPN capabilities. The Callback Options controls how the phone call is managed when using a dial-in solution.

The Remote Access Permission section includes the following options:

- **Allow Access** If remote access conditions are met, setting the user account to enable access will permit connecting to the RRAS server.
- **Deny Access** Setting the user account to deny access will forbid connecting to the RRAS server.
- **Control Access through Remote Access Policy** If remote access conditions are met and there is a matching policy that enables access, setting the user account

to Control Access through Remote Access Policy will enable connecting to the RAS server. If there is not a matching policy that enables access, connecting to the RRAS server is denied.

Figure 4.24 Understanding a User's Dial-In Tab

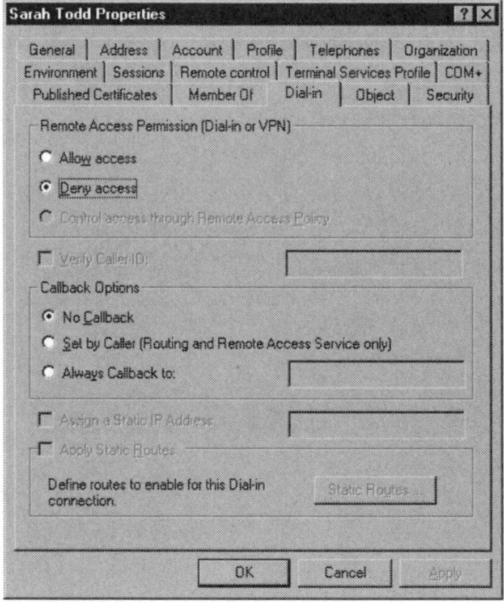

The Callback Options section includes the following options:

- **No Callback** The RRAS server does not call back the user dialing in.
- **Set by Caller (Routing and Remote Access Service only)** The RRAS server prompts the dial-in user for a phone number. It then disconnects the user and calls the user back at the number specified. This is a good option if you want the company to pay the long-distance charges when employees use a dial-in solution.
- **Always Callback to** When the user dials in to the RRAS server, the call disconnects after the user enters his or her credentials and automatically calls back at the number specified here. This is good for security purposes because it enables you to control the location of your dial-in users, and makes it less likely that someone who finds out a user's account name and password can use it to make an unauthorized connection, because the unauthorized user probably would not be calling from the legitimate user's location.

In addition to the Remote Access Permissions and the Callback Options, the **Dial-in** tab has the following options:

- **Verify Caller-ID** If the number the user is calling from does not match the number specified here, the connection to the RRAS server is dropped. This is different from **Always Callback to**, because it only verifies the phone number and it doesn't call the user back. This can be used if you want the caller to bear the long-distance charges.

- **Assign a Static IP Address** This enables you to assign static IP addresses to your RRAS clients.
- **Apply Static Routes** This enables you to apply static routes to your RRAS clients. This is useful if you want to use routing rules to limit the machines that your clients can get to once they are connected.

Using the Object Tab

There is nothing to configure on the user's **Object** tab, shown in Figure 4.25. This tab shows you the location of the object in Active Directory (the Canonical name). It shows you the type of object you are looking at (Object class). It shows you when the object was created and when it was last modified. For replication purposes, the **Object** tab also lists the current and original Update Sequence Numbers (USNs).

Active Directory uses USNs to determine what directory changes need to be replicated between domain controllers (DCs). A local counter on each domain controller assigns USNs. Using local counters ensures that the counters are accurate. However, USNs on one DC are not used by other DCs; each DC must use its own USNs.

Figure 4.25 Understanding a User's Object Tab

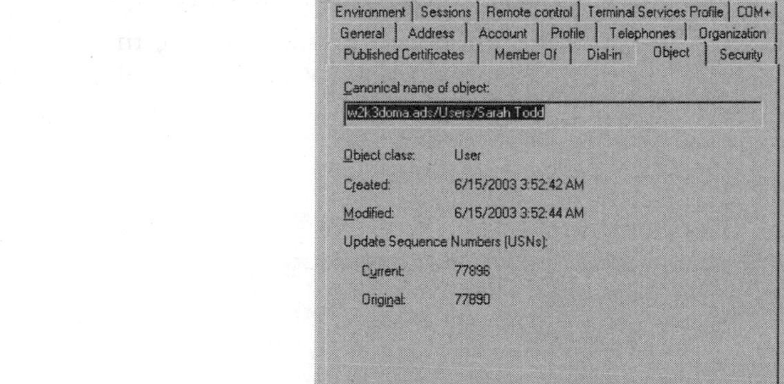

Using the Security Tab

The **Security** tab, shown in Figure 4.26, controls the Active Directory permissions for the selected user account. The top portion of this tab shows you what groups or users have been assigned permissions. After you select a group or user in the top portion, the bottom portion shows the permissions assigned to the selected group or user. You can add and remove groups and users by using the respective **Add** and **Remove** buttons. The **Advanced** tab configures special (and more granular) permissions and advanced settings such as inheritance, auditing, and ownership.

Figure 4.26 Understanding a User's Security Tab

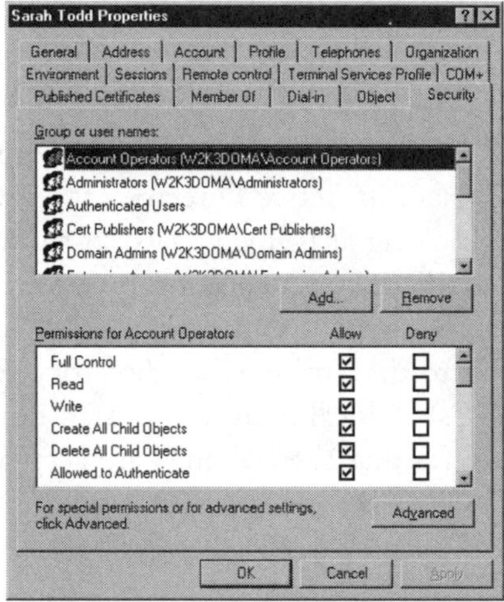

Managing User Accounts Via the Pop-Up Menu

We just saw in detail how to use ADUC to manage user accounts by going to the properties of the user and working through each tab. Some items can be managed quickly via the pop-up menu when you right-click a **user account name** in the right details pane, as shown in Figure 4.27.

Figure 4.27 Administering User Accounts

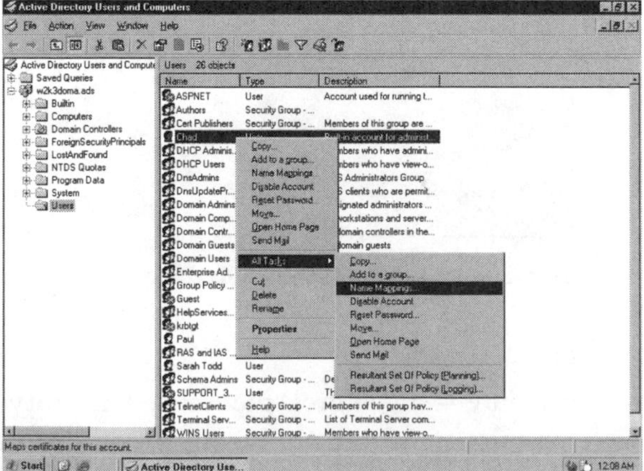

You can perform the following tasks by right-clicking on a user:

- **Copy** Copy certain properties of the user account to be used when creating a new user.
- **Add to a group** Add user to a group or groups.
- **Name Mappings** Configure X.509 certificate and Kerberos mappings.
- **Disable Account** Disable the user account.
- **Reset Password** Reset the user's password.
- **Move** Move the user to another location within the domain.
- **Open Home Page** Open the user's home page as listed on the user's General tab.
- **Send Mail** Send mail to a user's e-mail address if the user has one configured.
- **Resultant Set Of Policy (Planning)** Create *what if* scenarios to see what would happen if you configured group policy a certain way.
- **Resultant Set Of Policy (Logging)** Review existing policy settings that have been applied to computers and users.

Copying a User

It is common practice to create template user accounts for each department or for each position/job description. The template is configured according to the requirements of the specified department. When you need to create a new user account, right-click the template user account and select **Copy**. This gives you the **Copy Object – User** window shown in Figure 4.28. When copying a user account, the following attributes are copied:

- Password settings
- Description
- Groups
- Profile
- Dial-in information

These are attributes that are common to all users in the particular department or position. When copying a user account, the following attributes are *not* copied:

- Password
- Full Name
- Username

These are attributes that are unique to each user and must be configured for each individual account.

Figure 4.28 Copying a User Account in ADUC

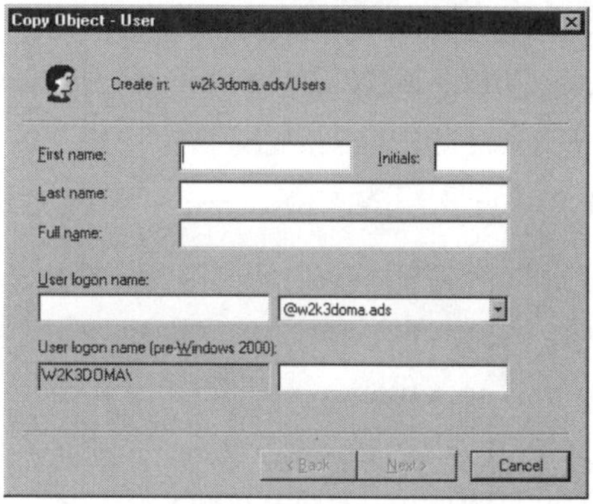

Adding a User to a Group

Right-clicking a user account and choosing **Add to a group** gives you the window shown in Figure 4.29. This window enables you to add the selected user account to a group. Type the name of the group and click the **Check Names** button to verify that the group exists. If the group exists and you spelled it right, it will be underlined. Click **OK** to add the user to the selected group.

Figure 4.29 Changing Group Membership

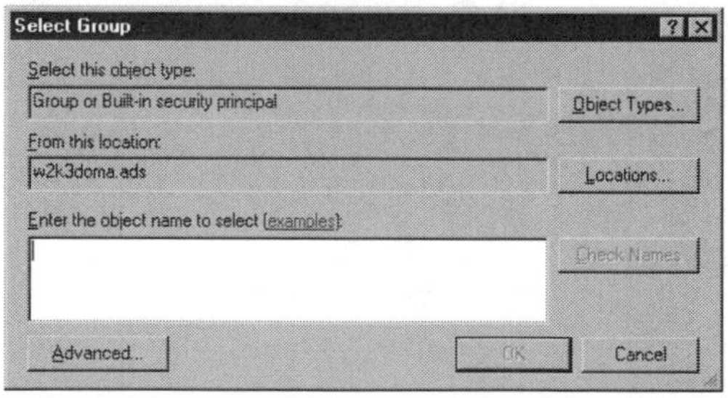

Managing Security Identity Mappings

You can map an Active Directory user account to a Kerberos Name to be used in a trusted non-Windows Kerberos realm. Active Directory also supports mapping user accounts to X.509 Certificates as shown in Figure 4.30. You have three options when mapping X.509 certificates:

- Map the certificate to one account. This is known as a one-to-one mapping.
- Map any certificate with the same subject to the user account, regardless of the issuer of the certificate. This is known as a many-to-one mapping.

- Map any certificate with the same issuer to the user account, regardless of the subject of the certificate. This is known as a many-to-one mapping.

By mapping user accounts to certificates, certificates can be used in place of user accounts. For example, certificates can enable or deny access to a Web site. Depending on the certificates mapped, users are automatically granted access to the Web site without having to provide additional authentication information.

Figure 4.30 Mapping User Accounts

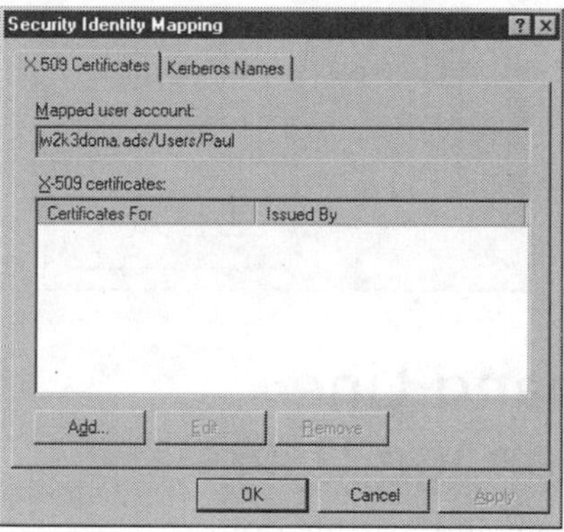

Resetting a User's Password

A common mistake with NT 4.0 administrators transitioning to Windows 2000 or Windows Server 2003 is going to the Properties page of a user account to reset the password. This is not an option in Windows 2000. The only way to reset the password in the GUI is to right-click on the user account and select **Reset Password**. Doing so will display the window shown in Figure 4.31. Type the user's new password twice and click **OK** to change it. You can also force the user to change the password the next time he or she logs on by checking the corresponding check box.

Figure 4.31 Resetting Passwords

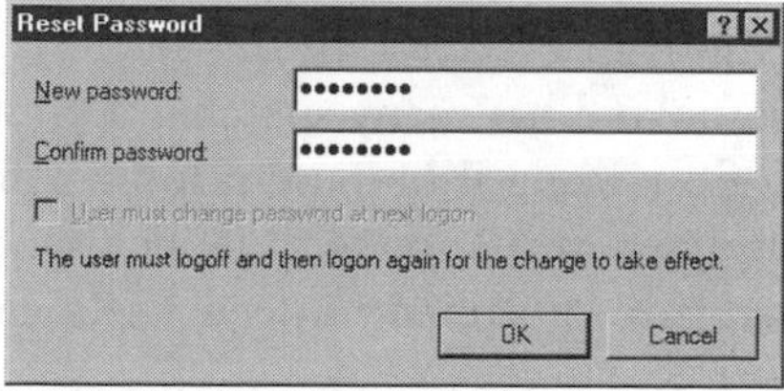

Moving a User Account

There are two ways to move user accounts in ADUC. The simplest way is to click and hold on the user object that you want to move and drag the account into the correct OU. The problem with this method is that you can easily drop the user into the wrong OU. Another way to do it (shown in Figure 4.32) is to right-click the user object and choose **Move**. Select the OU that you want to move the user to and click **OK** to move the user.

Figure 4.32 Moving Users

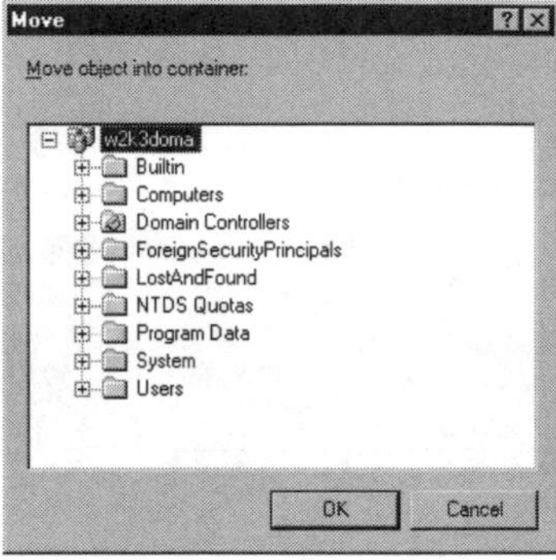

Using the Command Line to Create and Manage Users

Use the following tools to create and manage users:

- dsadd.exe
- dsmod.exe
- dsget.exe
- dsquery.exe

Using dsadd.exe User

Adding users from the GUI is fine when you have to add a few users. However, when you have to add a lot of users at the same time, the command line is more efficient. Using dsadd.exe enables you to quickly add multiple users. dsadd.exe has a lot of features. These are overviewed in the beginning of this chapter. In this section we are going to look at the syntax for **dsadd user**. This command has many switches. Do not let the complexity of options for this tool deter you from using it because it looks difficult. It is a very powerful tool that can be of great use and save you a lot of time. The syntax and options for dsadd.exe user are as follows, and are explained in detail in Table 4.5.

```
dsadd user <UserDN> [-samid <SAMName>] [-upn <UPN>] [-fn <FirstName>]
        [-mi <Initial>] [-ln <LastName>] [-display <DisplayName>]
        [-empid <EmployeeID>] [-pwd {<Password> | *}] [-desc
            <Description>]
```

```
[-memberof <Group ...>] [-office <Office>] [-tel <Phone#>]
[-email <Email>] [-hometel <HomePhone#>] [-pager <Pager#>]
[-mobile <CellPhone#>] [-fax <Fax#>] [-iptel <IPPhone#>]
[-webpg <WebPage>] [-title <Title>] [-dept <Department>]
[-company <Company>] [-mgr <Manager>] [-hmdir <HomeDir>]
[-hmdrv <DriveLtr:>] [-profile <ProfilePath>] [-loscr
    <ScriptPath>]
[-mustchpwd {yes | no}] [-canchpwd {yes | no}]
[-reversiblepwd {yes | no}] [-pwdneverexpires {yes | no}]
[-acctexpires <NumDays>] [-disabled {yes | no}]
[{-s <Server> | -d <Domain>}] [-u <UserName>]
[-p {<Password> | *}] [-q] [{-uc | -uco | -uci}]
```

Table 4.5 Understanding dsadd.exe user Syntax

Value	Description
<UserDN>	Required. Distinguished name (DN) of user to add.
-samid <SAMName>	Set the SAM account name of user to <SAMName>. If not specified, *dsadd* attempts to create SAM account name using up to the first 20 characters from the common name (CN) value of <UserDN>.
-upn <UPN>	Set the upn value to <UPN>.
-fn <FirstName>	Set user first name to <FirstName>.
-mi <Initial>	Set user middle initial to <Initial>.
-ln <LastName>	Set user last name to <LastName>.
-display <DisplayName>	Set user display name to <DisplayName>.
-empid <EmployeeID>	Set user employee ID to <EmployeeID>.
-pwd {<Password> | *}	Set user password to <Password>. If *, then you are prompted for a password.
-desc <Description>	Set user description to <Description>.
-memberof <Group ...> <Group ...>.	Make user a member of one or more groups
-office <Office>	Set user office location to <Office>.
-tel <Phone#>	Set user telephone# to <Phone#>.
-email <Email>	Set user e-mail address to <Email>.
-hometel <HomePhone#>	Set user home phone# to <HomePhone#>.
-pager <Pager#>	Set user pager# to <Pager#>.
-mobile <CellPhone#>	Set user mobile# to <CellPhone#>.

Continued

Table 4.5 Understanding dsadd.exe user Syntax

Value	Description
-fax <Fax#>	Set user fax# to <Fax#>.
-iptel <IPPhone#>	Set user IP phone# to <IPPhone#>.
-webpg <WebPage>	Set user Web page URL to <WebPage>.
-title <Title>	Set user title to <Title>.
-dept <Department>	Set user department to <Department>.
-company <Company>	Set user company info to <Company>.
-mgr <Manager>	Set user's manager to <Manager> (format is DN).
-hmdir <HomeDir>	Set user home directory to <HomeDir>. If this is UNC path, a drive letter that will be mapped to must also be specified through -hmdrv.
-hmdrv <DriveLtr:>	Set user home drive letter to <DriveLtr:>.
-profile <ProfilePath>	Set user's profile path to <ProfilePath>.
-loscr <ScriptPath>	Set user's logon script path to <ScriptPath>.
-mustchpwd {yes | no}	User must change password at next logon or not. Default: no.
-canchpwd {yes | no}	User can change password or not. This should be "yes" if the -mustchpwd is "yes". Default: yes.
-reversiblepwd {yes | no}	Store user password using reversible encryption or not. Default: no.
-pwdneverexpires {yes | no}	User password never expires or it does expire. Default: no.
-acctexpires <NumDays>	Set user account to expire in <NumDays> days from today. A value of 0 implies account expires at the end of today; a positive value implies the account expires in the future; a negative value implies the account already expired and sets an expiration date in the past; the string value "never" implies that the account never expires.
-disabled {yes | no}	User account is disabled or not. Default: no.
{-s <Server> | -d <Domain>}	-s <Server> connects to the domain controller (DC) with name <Server>.-d <Domain> connects to a DC in domain <Domain>. Default: a DC in the logon domain.
-u <UserName>	Connect as <UserName>. Default: the logged in user. Username can be: username, domain\user-name, or user principal name (UPN).
-p {<Password> | *}	Password for the user <UserName>. If * is entered, you are prompted for a password.
-q	Quiet mode: suppress all output to standard output.

Continued

Table 4.5 Understanding dsadd.exe user Syntax

Value	Description
{-uc | -uco | -uci}	-uc specifies that input from or output to pipe is formatted in Unicode. -uco specifies that output to pipe or file is formatted in Unicode. -uci specifies that input from pipe or file is formatted in Unicode.

Adding Users

Use the *dsadd* command to create a user account. Use the following syntax:

```
dsadd user UserDN [-UPN UPN] [-samid SAMName] -pwd {Password|*}
```

All the switches are covered in Table 4.5, but they're summarized here. *UserDN* is the distinguished name of the user you want to add. *UPN* specifies the user's user principal name (UPN). *Pwd* specifies the user account's password. If set to * you are prompted to enter the password.

The following example uses the *dsadd* command to create a new user, Chad Todd, in the Trainers OU:

```
dsadd user "CN=Chad Todd,CN=Users,DC=trainingconcepts,DC=org" -UPN
    chad@trainingconcepts.org -samid chadtodd -pwd *
```

Using dsmod user

dsmod user modifies the attributes of users in Active Directory. dsmod.exe uses the following syntax. All syntax is explained in detail in Table 4.6.

```
dsmod user <UserDN ...> [-upn <UPN>] [-fn <FirstName>]
            [-mi <Initial>] [-ln <LastName>] [-display <DisplayName>]
            [-empid <EmployeeID>] [-pwd {<Password> | *}]
            [-desc <Description>] [-office <Office>] [-tel <Phone#>]
            [-email <Email>] [-hometel <HomePhone#>] [-pager <Pager#>]
            [-mobile <CellPhone#>] [-fax <Fax#>] [-iptel <IPPhone#>]
            [-webpg <WebPage>] [-title <Title>] [-dept <Department>]
            [-company <Company>] [-mgr <Manager>] [-hmdir <HomeDir>]
            [-hmdrv <DriveLtr>:] [-profile <ProfilePath>]
            [-loscr <ScriptPath>] [-mustchpwd {yes | no}]
            [-canchpwd {yes | no}] [-reversiblepwd {yes | no}]
            [-pwdneverexpires {yes | no}]
            [-acctexpires <NumDays>] [-disabled {yes | no}]
            [{-s <Server> | -d <Domain>}] [-u <UserName>]
            [-p {<Password> | *}] [-c] [-q] [{-uc | -uco | -uci}]
```

Table 4.6 Understanding dsmod.exe user Syntax

Value	Description
<UserDN>	Required. Distinguished names (DNs) of one or more users to modify.
-upn <UPN>	Sets the UPN value to <UPN>.
-fn <FirstName>	Sets user first name to <FirstName>.
-mi <Initial>	Sets user middle initial to <Initial>.
-ln <LastName>	Sets user last name to <LastName>.
-display <DisplayName>	Sets user display name to <DisplayName>.
-empid <EmployeeID>	Sets user employee ID to <EmployeeID>.
-pwd {<Password> | *}	Resets user password to<Password>. If *, then you are prompted for a password.
-desc <Description>	Sets user description to <Description>.
-office <Office>	Sets user office location to <Office>.
-tel <Phone#>	Sets user telephone# to <Phone#>.
-email <Email>	Sets user e-mail address to <Email>.
-hometel <HomePhone#>	Sets user home phone# to <HomePhone#>.
-pager <Pager#>	Sets user pager# to <Pager#>.
-mobile <CellPhone#>	Sets user mobile# to <CellPhone#>.
-fax <Fax#>	Sets user fax# to <Fax#>.
-iptel <IPPhone#>	Sets user IP phone# to <IPPhone#>.
-webpg <WebPage>	Sets user Web page URL to <WebPage>.
-title <Title>	Sets user title to <Title>.
-dept <Department>	Sets user department to <Department>.
-company <Company>	Sets user company info to <Company>.
-mgr <Manager>	Sets user's manager to <Manager>.
-hmdir <HomeDir>	Sets user home directory to <HomeDir>. If this is UNC path, then a drive letter to be mapped to this path must also be specified through -hmdrv.
-hmdrv <DriveLtr>:	Sets user home drive letter to <DriveLtr>:
-profile <ProfilePath>	Sets user's profile path to <ProfilePath>.
-loscr <ScriptPath>	Sets user's logon script path to <ScriptPath>.
-mustchpwd {yes | no}	Sets whether the user must change his password (yes) or not (no) at his next logon.
-canchpwd {yes | no}	Sets whether the user can change his password (yes) or not (no). This setting should be "yes" if the -mustchpwd setting is "yes."

Continued

Table 4.6 Understanding dsmod.exe user Syntax

Value	Description
-reversiblepwd {yes | no}	Sets whether the user password should be stored using reversible encryption (yes) or not (no).
-pwdneverexpires {yes | no}	Sets whether the user's password never expires (yes) or does expire (no).
-acctexpires <NumDays>	Sets user account to expire in <NumDays> days from today. A value of 0 sets expiration at the end of today. A positive value sets expiration in the future. A negative value sets expiration in the past. A string value of "never" sets the account to never expire.
-disabled {yes | no}	Sets whether the user account is disabled (yes) or not (no).
{-s <Server> | -d <Domain>}	-s <Server> connects to the domain controller (DC) with name <Server>. -d <Domain> connects to a DC in domain <Domain>. Default: a DC in the logon domain.
-u <UserName>	Connect as <UserName>. Default: the logged-on user. Username can be: username, domain\username, or user principal name (UPN).
-p <Password>	Password for the user <UserName>. If *, then prompt for password.
-c	Continuous operation mode. Reports errors but continues with next object in argument list when multiple target objects are specified. Without this option, the command exits on the first error.
-q	Quiet mode: suppresses all output to standard output.
{-uc | -uco | -uci}	-uc Specifies that input from or output to pipe is formatted in Unicode. -uco Specifies that output to pipe or file is formatted in Unicode. -uci Specifies that input from pipe or file is formatted in Unicode.

Resetting a User's Password

Use the *dsmod* command to reset a user's password. Use the following syntax:

```
dsmod user UserDN -pwd NewPassword -mustchpwd {yes|no}.
```

All this syntax and the switches are covered in Table 4.7, but they're summarized here. UserDN is the distinguished name of the user account whose password you want to reset. The *–mustchpwd* option indicates whether or not the user will be forced to change his or her password upon the next logon attempt. The following example uses the *dsmod* command to reset the password of user Chad Todd:

```
dsmod user "CN=Chad Todd,CN=Users,DC=trainingconcepts,DC=org" -pwd * -
    mustchpwd yes
```

Enabling a User

Use the *dsmod* command to enable a user account: Use the following syntax:

```
dsmod user UserDN -disabled {yes|no}.
```

The following example uses the *dsmod* command to enable the user account of Chad Todd:

```
dsmod user "CN=Chad Todd,CN=Users,DC=trainingconcepts,DC=org" -disabled no
```

Disabling a User

Use the *dsmod* command to disable a user account: Use the following syntax:

```
dsmod user UserDN -disabled {yes|no}.
```

The following example uses the *dsmod* command to disable the user account of Chad Todd:

```
dsmod user "CN=Chad Todd,CN=Users,DC=trainingconcepts,DC=org" -disabled
    yes
```

Using dsquery user

dsquer user searches Active Directory for users that match specified credentials.You can use *dsquery* to find users and then send a list of those users to another command. For example, you could use *dsquery* to query AD for all disabled users and have those results imported into *dsmod* to enable all the users. *dsquery* uses the following syntax. (Table 4.7 explains all the switches in detail.)

```
dsquery user [{<StartNode> | forestroot | domainroot}]
           [-o {dn | rdn | upn | samid}]
           [-scope {subtree | onelevel | base}]
           [-name <Name>] [-desc <Description>] [-upn <UPN>]
           [-samid <SAMName>] [-inactive <NumWeeks>] [-stalepwd <NumDays>]
           [-disabled] [{-s <Server> | -d <Domain>}] [-u <UserName>]
           [-p {<Password> | *}] [-q] [-r] [-gc] [-limit <NumObjects>]
           [{-uc | -uco | -uci}]
```

Table 4.7 Understanding dsquery Syntax

Value	Description
{<StartNode> | forestroot | domainroot}	The node where the search starts.
-o {dn | rdn | upn | samid}	Specifies the output format. Default: DN.

Continued

Table 4.7 Understanding dsquery Syntax

Value	Description
-scope {subtree | onelevel | base}	Specifies the scope of the search. Default: subtree.
-name <Name>	Finds users whose name matches the filter given by <Name> e.g. "jon*" or "*ith" or "j*th."
-desc <Description>	Finds users whose description matches the filter given by <Description> e.g. "jon*" or "*ith" or "j*th."
-upn <UPN>	Finds users whose UPN matches the filter given by <UPN>.
-samid <SAMName>	Finds users whose SAM account name matches the filter given by <SAMName>.
-inactive <NumWeeks>	Finds users that have been inactive (not logged on) for at least <NumWeeks> number of weeks.
-stalepwd <NumDays>	Finds users that have not changed their password for at least <NumDays> number of days.
-disabled	Finds users whose accounts are disabled.
{-s <Server> | -d <Domain>}	-s <Server> connects to the domain controller(DC) with name <Server>. -d <Domain> connects to a DC in domain <Domain>. Default: a DC in the logon domain.
-u <UserName>	Connects as <UserName>. Default: the logged-on user. Username can be: username, domain\username or user principal name (UPN).
-p <Password>	Password for the user <UserName>. If * is specified, you are prompted for a password.
-q	Quiet mode: suppresses all output to standard output.
-r	Recurses or follows referrals during search. Default: do not chase referrals during search.
-gc	Searches in the Active Directory global catalog.

Continued

Table 4.7 Understanding dsquery Syntax

Value	Description
-limit <NumObjects>	Specifies the number of objects matching the given criteria to be returned where <NumObjects> is the number of objects to be returned. If the value of <NumObjects> is 0, all matching objects are returned. If this parameter is not specified by default, the first 100 results are displayed.
{-uc | -uco | -uci}	-uc specifies that input from or output to pipe is formatted in Unicode.-uco specifies that output to pipe or file is formatted in Unicode. -uci specifies that input from pipe or file is formatted in Unicode.

Finding All Users

If you do not specify user credentials or a domain, *dsquery* uses the credentials of the currently logged-on user and the current logon domain. To view all the users in the default domain, use the following syntax:

```
dsquery user
```

This will display all the users in the current domain. The following is sample output from the *dsquery user* command.

```
"CN=Chad,CN=Users,DC=trainingconcepts,DC=org"
"CN=Guest,CN=Users,DC=trainingconcepts,DC=org"
"CN=SUPPORT_388945a0,CN=Users,DC=trainingconcepts,DC=org"
"CN=ASPNET,CN=Users,DC=trainingconcepts,DC=org"
"CN=krbtgt,CN=Users,DC=trainingconcepts,DC=org"
"CN=Paul,CN=Users,DC=trainingconcepts,DC=org"
"CN=Sarah Todd,CN=Users,DC=trainingconcepts,DC=org"
```

Finding Disabled Users

To use *dsquery* to find all disabled users, use the following syntax:

```
dsquery user -disabled
```

Finding Users by Description

To find all users that match a certain description, use the following syntax:

```
dsquery user -desc <Description>
```

The following examples list all the user accounts with the description *Sales Managers*. Because the description contains spaces, we must put it in quotes.

```
dsquery user -desc "Sales Manager"
```

Finding Users by Password Change Date

To search for users based on the last time they changed their passwords, use the following syntax:

```
dsquery user -stalepwd <NumDays>
```

The following example lists all the user accounts that haven't changed their password in 60 days:

```
dsquery user -stalepwd 60
```

Finding Users by Last Logon Date

This command lists users based on how many weeks they have been inactive (in other words, based on the number of weeks since they last logged on). To search for users based on the last time they logged on, use the following syntax.

```
dsquery user -inactive <NumWeeks>
```

The following example lists all users that have not logged on for six weeks:

```
dsquery user -inactive 6
```

Using dsget.exe

dsget displays properties of users in Active Directory. There are two variations of the *dsget user* command. The first one shows the properties of multiple users. The second one shows the group memberships of a user. *dsquery user* uses the following syntax. All switches are explained in detail in Table 4.8.

```
dsget user <UserDN ...> [-dn] [-samid] [-sid] [-upn] [-fn] [-mi]
             [-ln] [-display] [-empid] [-desc] [-office] [-tel] [-email]
             [-hometel] [-pager] [-mobile] [-fax] [-iptel] [-webpg]
             [-title] [-dept] [-company] [-mgr] [-hmdir] [-hmdrv]
             [-profile] [-loscr] [-mustchpwd] [-canchpwd]
             [-pwdneverexpires] [-disabled] [-acctexpires]
             [-reversiblepwd] [-part <PartitionDN> [-qlimit] [-qused]]
             [{-s <Server> | -d <Domain>}] [-u <UserName>]
             [-p {<Password> | *}] [-c] [-q] [-l] [{-uc | -uco | -uci}]
```

```
dsget user <UserDN> [-memberof [-expand]]
            [{-s <Server> | -d <Domain>}] [-u <UserName>]
            [-p {<Password> | *}] [-c] [-q] [-l]
            [{-uc | -uco | -uci}]
```

Table 4.8 Understanding dsquery syntax

Value	Description
<UserDN>	Required/stdin. DNs of one or more users to view. If the target objects are omitted, they are taken from standard input (stdin) to support piping of output from another command to input of this command.
-dn	Shows the DN of the user.
-samid	Shows the SAM account name of the user.
-sid	Shows the user Security ID.
-upn	Shows the user principal name of the user.
-fn	Shows the first name of the user.
-mi	Shows the middle initial of the user.
-ln	Shows the last name of the user.
-display	Shows the display name of the user.
-empid	Shows the user employee ID.
-desc	Shows the description of the user.
-office	Shows the office location of the user.
-tel	Shows the telephone number of the user.
-email	Shows the e-mail address of the user.
-hometel	Shows the home telephone number of the user.
-pager	Shows the pager number of the user.
-mobile	Shows the mobile phone number of the user.
-fax	Shows the fax number of the user.
-iptel	Shows the user IP phone number.
-webpg	Shows the user Web page URL.
-title	Shows the title of the user.
-dept	Shows the department of the user.
-company	Shows the company info of the user.
-mgr	Shows the user's manager.
-hmdir	Shows the user home directory. Displays the drive letter to which the home directory of the user is mapped (if the home directory path is a UNC path).

Continued

Table 4.8 Understanding dsquery syntax

Value	Description
-hmdrv	Shows the user's home drive letter (if home directory is a UNC path).
-profile	Shows the user's profile path.
-loscr	Shows the user's logon script path.
-mustchpwd	Shows if the user must change his/her password at the time of next logon. Displays: yes or no.
-canchpwd	Shows if the user can change his/her password. Displays: yes or no.
-pwdneverexpires	Shows if the user password never expires. Displays: yes or no.
-disabled	Shows if the user account is disabled for logon or not. Displays: yes or no.
-acctexpires	Shows when the user account expires. Display values: a date when the account expires or the string "never" if the account never expires.
-reversiblepwd	Shows if the user password is allowed to be stored using reversible encryption (yes or no).
<UserDN>	Required. DN of group to view.
-memberof	Displays the groups of which the user is a member.
-expand	Displays a recursively expanded list of groups of which the user is a member.
{-s <Server> | -d <Domain>}	-s <Server> connects to the domain controller (DC) with name <Server>. -d <Domain> connects to a DC in domain <Domain>. Default: a DC in the logon domain.
-u <UserName>	Connect as <UserName>. Default: the logged-on user. Username can be: username, domain\username, or user principal name (UPN).
-p {<Password> | *}	Password for the user<UserName>. If *, then prompt for password.
-c	Continuous operation mode: reports errors but continues with next object in argument list when multiple target objects are specified. Without this option, command exits on first error.
-q	Quiet mode: suppresses all output to standard output.
-L	Displays the entries in the search result set in a list format. Default: table format.
{-uc | -uco | -uci}	Specifies that input from or output to pipe is formatted in Unicode.
-part <PartitionDN>	Connects to the directory partition with the distinguished name of <PartitionDN>.

Continued

Table 4.8 Understanding dsquery syntax

Value	Description
-qlimit	Displays the effective quota of the user within the specified directory partition.
-qused	Displays how much of the quota the user has used within the specified directory partition.

Getting a User's Description

To get a user's description, use the following syntax:

```
dsget user <userDN> -desc
```

The following example gets the description for the Chad Todd user account in the trainingconcepts.org domain:

```
dsget user "CN=Chad Todd,CN=Users,DC=trainingconcepts,DC=org" -desc
```

Getting a User's E-Mail Address

To get a user's e-mail address, use the following syntax:

```
dsget user <userDN> -email
```

The following example gets the e-mail address for the Chad Todd user account:

```
dsget user "CN=Chad Todd,CN=Users,DC=trainingconcepts,DC=org" -email
```

Determining If a User Must Change His or Her Password

To determine if a user must change his or her password upon next logon, use the following syntax:

```
dsget user <userDN> -mustchpwd
```

The following example determines if the user Chad Todd must reset his password upon next logon:

```
dsget user "CN=Chad Todd,CN=Users,DC=trainingconcepts,DC=org" -mustchpwd
```

Getting a User's Group Membership

To determine a user's group membership, use the following syntax:

```
dsget user <userDN> -memberof
```

The following example gets the group membership for the Chad Todd user account in the trainingconcepts.org domain:

```
dsget user "CN=Chad Todd,CN=Users,DC=trainingconcepts,DC=org" -memberof
```

Following is a sample output from using the *dsget.exe user <userDN> -memberof* command:

```
"CN=Group Policy Creator Owners,CN=Users,DC=trainingconcepts,DC=org"
"CN=Domain Admins,CN=Users,DC=trainingconcepts,DC=org"
"CN=Enterprise Admins,CN=Users,DC=trainingconcepts,DC=org"
"CN=Schema Admins,CN=Users,DC=trainingconcepts,DC=org"
"CN=Administrators,CN=Builtin,DC=trainingconcepts,DC=org"
"CN=Domain Users,CN=Users,DC=trainingconcepts,DC=org"
```

Automating User and Group Account Creation

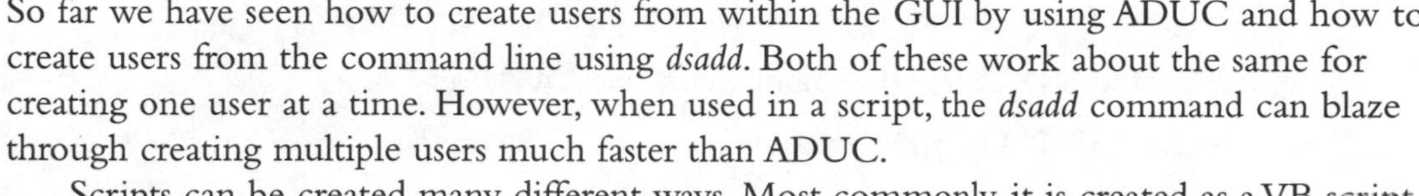

EXAM 70-290 OBJECTIVE 2.4.2

So far we have seen how to create users from within the GUI by using ADUC and how to create users from the command line using *dsadd*. Both of these work about the same for creating one user at a time. However, when used in a script, the *dsadd* command can blaze through creating multiple users much faster than ADUC.

Scripts can be created many different ways. Most commonly, it is created as a VB script or as a batch file. In this section you learn how to use the *for* command to automate the process of creating user accounts, and how to create a batch file to automate the process. The *for* command uses the following syntax, which is explained in detail in Table 4.9:

```
for %variable IN (set) DO command [command-parameters]
```

Table 4.9 Understanding the for Command

Value	Description
%variable	Specifies a single-letter replaceable parameter.
(set)	Specifies a set of one or more files. Wildcards may be used.
command	Specifies the command to carry out for each file.
command-parameters	Specifies parameters or switches for the specified command.
/?	Shows the help for the *For* command. There are many more options available that are not listed here due to length.

Simply put, the *for* command enables you to instruct a command such as *dsadd* to run multiple times, while using different input each time. The *For* command uses variables and plain text files to accomplish this. The variable is named using a percent sign followed by a single letter (e.g., %f) and is case sensitive.

To parse a line of text, the *for* command breaks the line into tokens. A token is a portion of an input line delimited by delimiter spaces such as commas or spaces. The tokens are then assigned to the variable and parsed line by line.

The following example uses the command to automate the process of creating users from the command-line.

```
for /f %I in (c:\test\users.txt) do dsadd user %I -pwd password
```

Table 4.9 explains the syntax in detail, but we'll discuss it here anyway. *For* is the command. The */f* instructs the *for* command to use file token parsing (explained previously). The *%I* is a variable. *In (c:\users.txt)* instructs the *%I* variable to use the data stored in the **users.txt** file. *Do dsadd user %I –pwd password* instructs the *for* command to do this command (*dsadd user –pwd password*), but to replace the variable *%I* with the information stored in the variable file. The *For* command reads the users.txt file line by line and it processes each line in turn.

Now that you understand what the previous command means, we'll discuss what it actually does. First, look at the users.txt file.

CN=User1,CN=Users,DC=trainingconcepts,DC=org

CN=User2,CN=Users,DC=trainingconcepts,DC=org

CN=User3,CN=Users,DC=trainingconcepts,DC=org

CN=User4,CN=Users,DC=trainingconcepts,DC=org

CN=User5,CN=Users,DC=trainingconcepts,DC=org

Each line represents the distinguished name of an object we want to create. This example assumes that you want to create your users in the default Users container in the trainingconcepts.org domain. The *For* command looks in c:\users.txt file and runs the command *dsadd user %I –pwd password* for each line; replacing the *%I* variable with the fully qualified name of the user we want to create. This command creates the user account and assigns it the password of "password."

You can script this by saving it to a batch file. However, you need to change the *%I* variable to use double percent signs %%I. Look at the output from placing the line *for /f %%I in (c:\test\users.txt) do dsadd user %%I -pwd password* into a batch file and running the batch file.

NOTE

When using the *For* command in a script file you must use a double percent sign (%%) before the variable. If you are typing the command directly into the command prompt, use only one percent sign (%).

NOTE

To create a batch file, open a blank Notepad document and type the commands you want to run. Save the file as *somename.bat* (where *somename* is the name of your file). You can now run the batch file by double-clicking it. This saves you the trouble of having to manually enter everything into the command prompt. You can key it into the batch file once and use that one file over and over.

```
C:\for /F %I in (c:\users.txt) do dsadd user %I -pwd password

C:\>dsadd user CN=User1,CN=Users,DC=trainingconcepts,DC=org -pwd password
dsadd succeeded:CN=User1,CN=Users,DC=trainingconcepts,DC=org

C:\>dsadd user CN=User2,CN=Users,DC=trainingconcepts,DC=org -pwd password
dsadd succeeded:CN=User2,CN=Users,DC=trainingconcepts,DC=org

C:\>dsadd user CN=User3,CN=Users,DC=trainingconcepts,DC=org -pwd password
dsadd succeeded:CN=User3,CN=Users,DC=trainingconcepts,DC=org

C:\>dsadd user CN=User4,CN=Users,DC=trainingconcepts,DC=org -pwd password
dsadd succeeded:CN=User4,CN=Users,DC=trainingconcepts,DC=org

C:\>dsadd user CN=User5,CN=Users,DC=trainingconcepts,DC=org -pwd password
dsadd succeeded:CN=User5,CN=Users,DC=trainingconcepts,DC=org
```

Notice that by running your simple batch file, you created five users automatically. As you can see, this makes creating users a snap. You can create 1000 users with the same amount of effort as creating one user. The only real work is setting up the batch file the first time and populating your input text file (e.g., users.txt).

The real beauty of the *for* command is that it works with any command-line tool. For example, you could automate the process of creating machine and group accounts by simply changing your batch file to use *dsadd computer* and *dsadd group* instead of *dsadd user*. Also, you need to populate your input file with the correct names of your machines and groups.

Importing User Accounts

Realizing that administrators may have the need to import and export data into and out of Active Directory and other Lightweight Directory Access Protocol (LDAP) directory services, Microsoft has provided two utilities to accomplish just that task.

- **csvde (CSV Directory Exchange)** *csvde* uses files formatted in the Microsoft comma-separated value (CSV) format. The advantage of the CSV format, is that it is supported by many other applications, such as Microsoft Excel and Microsoft Access, thus enabling you to manipulate data in these applications before importing it. The downside to using *csvde* is that it only enables the addition of new objects—*ldifde* enables the modification of existing objects.
- **ldifde (LDAP Data Interchange Format Directory Exchange)** *ldifde* can be used to extend the Active Directory schema, export data from Active Directory into other LDAP applications and services, and populate the Active Directory database with LDAP data from other directory services. LDIF is an Internet standard file format for performing batch import and export operations that conform to LDAP standards.

csvde and *ldifde* use the same syntax as follows and explained in Table 4.10.

```
csvde(or ldifde) [-i] [-f FileName] [-s ServerName] [-c String1 String2]
    [-v] [-j Path] [-t PortNumber] [-d BaseDN] [-r LDAPFilter] [-p Scope]
        [-l LDAPAttributeList] [-o LDAPAttributeList] [-g] [-m] [-n] [-k]
            [-a UserDistinguishedName Password] [-b UserName Domain
                Password]
```

Table 4.10 Understanding csvde.exe and ldifde.exe Syntax

Value	Description
-i	Specifies import mode. If not specified, the default mode is export.
-f FileName	Identifies the import or export filename.
-s ServerName	Specifies the domain controller to perform the import or export operation.
-c String1 String2	Replaces all occurrences of String1 with String2. This is generally used when importing data from one domain to another and the distinguished name of the export domain (String1) needs to be replaced with that of the import domain (String2).
-v	Sets verbose mode.
-j Path	Sets the log file location. The default is the current path.
-t PortNumber	Specifies an LDAP port number. The default LDAP port is 389. The global catalog port is 3268.
-d BaseDN	Sets the distinguished name of the search base for data export.
-r LDAPFilter	Creates an LDAP search filter for data export.
-p Scope	Sets the search scope. Search scope options are Base, OneLevel, or SubTree.
-l LDAPAttributeList	Sets the list of attributes to return in the results of an export query. If this parameter is omitted, all attributes are returned.
-o LDAPAttributeList	Sets the list of attributes to omit from the results of an export query. This is typically used when exporting objects from Active Directory and then importing them into another LDAP-compliant directory. If attributes are not supported by another directory, you can omit the attributes from the result set using this option.
-g	Omits paged searches.
-m	Omits attributes that only apply to Active Directory objects such as the ObjectGUID, objectSID, pwdLastSet and samAccountType attributes.

Continued

Table 4.10 Understanding csvde.exe and ldifde.exe Syntax

Value	Description
-n	Omits export of binary values.
-k	Ignores errors during the import operation and continues processing. The following is a complete list of ignored errors: "Object already exists," "Constraint violation," and "Attribute or value already exists."
-a UserDistinguishedName Password	Sets the command to run using the supplied UserDistinguishedName and Password. By default, the command runs using the credentials of the user currently logged on to the network.
-b UserName Domain Password	Sets the command to run as Username Domain Password. By default, the command runs using the credentials of the user currently logged on to the network.
-?	Displays the command menu.

The following is an example of what a CSV file might look like for the addition of five users into Active Directory.

```
dn,cn,givenName,sn,description,objectClass,SAMAccountname,user
    PrincipalName
"CN=Chad Todd,CN=Users,DC=trainingconcepts,DC=org","Chad Todd",Chad,Todd,
    "Owner",user,ctodd,chad@trainingconcepts.org
"CN=Paul Salas,CN=Users,DC=trainingconcepts,DC=org","Paul Salas",
    Paul,Salas,"Owner",user,paul,paul@trainingconcepts.org
"CN=Mike Bagley,CN=Users,DC=trainingconcepts,DC=org","Mike Bagley",
    Mike,Bagley,"Sales Manager",user,mike,mike@trainingconcepts.org
"CN=Gary Landry,CN=Users,DC=trainingconcepts,DC=org","Gary Landry",
    Gary,Landry,"Trainer",user,gary,gary@trainingconcepts.org
"CN=Tal Lassiter,CN=Users,DC=trainingconcepts,DC=org","Tal Lassiter",
    Tal,Lassiter,"Sales Manger",user,tal,tal@trainingconcepts.org
```

Troubleshooting User Accounts

Let's look at how some of these techniques are used in real world troubleshooting. The most common problems with user accounts are due to group membership, password problems, or account lockouts. Group membership problems manifest themselves by users not being able to access resources that are assigned through group membership. This can easily be verified and corrected via Active Directory Users and Computers or from the command line using the dsget.exe and dsmod.exe commands. Password problems are usually due to users forgetting their password and needing it reset. This can be accomplished via Active Directory Users and Computers or via the dsmod.exe command. Lastly, users often lockout their accounts because they enter in their password incorrectly. This is usually due to them forgetting their password because they just changed it recently, in which case you would need to unlock their account and reset their password. Sometimes they just can't type or CAPS LOCK is on and they enter in their password incorrectly too many times and lock their account. User accounts can be unlocked by using Active Directory Users and Computers or by using the dsmod.exe command.

Creating and Managing Group Accounts

Before you can effectively start working with groups in Windows Server 2003, you need to first understand what groups are and why they are used. A group is a collection of user and/or computer accounts, contacts, and even other groups that are managed as a single object. The users and computers that belong to the group are known as group members. In Windows, as with most operating systems, groups are used to simplify the administrative process of assigning permissions and rights to a large number of user and computer accounts at the same time, resulting in these groups' members having inherited (or implicit) permissions from the group. This is contrary to the older and more labor-intensive practice of applying permissions and rights directly to users, which are then known as explicit permissions.

A set of default groups is created during the installation of Windows Server 2003 on a computer and are known as local groups. Computers that are part of an Active Directory domain environment also have a set of default groups, but these are objects that reside within the Active Directory database structure. You can create additional groups as required for both workstation and domain-based computers. For the purposes of this discussion, assume that you are working in an Active Directory environment when creating and management of groups.

When using groups in Active Directory, you are provided with three major benefits:

- Security groups enable you to simplify and reduce administrative requirements by assigning permissions and rights for a shared resource (think printer or file share) to the group rather than to each individual user that requires access. In this way, all users (and groups) that are members of the group will receive the configured permissions and rights through inheritance. This is much more efficient and accurate than explicitly assigning these permissions and rights to users on an individual basis. In addition, this provides you with the capability to move users in and out of groups as their jobs and task requirements dictate.
- Security groups enable you to quickly and efficiently delegate administrative responsibilities for performing specific tasks in Active Directory. As an example, you might have a group of six help desk workers to whom you wish to assign the capability to reset user passwords. By placing these six users in a group and then delegating this capability to the group, you can easily enable these users to perform this specific task that might otherwise be above their standard permissions. Again, using groups in this way enables you to move users in and out of the group as required.
- Security and distribution groups enable you to quickly create e-mail distribution groups by assigning an e-mail address to the group itself. All members of the group that are mailbox enabled will receive an e-mail when it is sent to the group's e-mail

address. This is an added capability of security groups and the only usage for distribution groups—which will be discussed later in the "Group Type" section.

When you talk about groups, you need to understand two basic group characteristics: type and scope. These topics are discussed in the next sections.

Understanding Group Types and Scopes

Group type refers to one of two types:

- distribution
- security

Group type identifies the purpose of the group. Group scope refers to one of four scopes:

- local
- domain local
- global
- universal

Group scope refers to how the group is used.

Security and Distribution Groups

Two types of groups can be created in Windows Server 2003:

- **Distribution groups** Use distribution groups for distributing messages to group members. Use distribution groups with e-mail applications, such as Microsoft Exchange, to send an e-mail to all members of the group in a rapid and efficient fashion by sending it to the group e-mail address. All members of the distribution group that are mailbox enabled will receive the e-mail message. Distribution groups are not security enabled, and therefore cannot be used to assign permissions to Windows resources.
- **Security groups** Use security groups for the distribution of e-mail as described for distribution groups, but also use them to assign permissions to Windows resources. You can also use security groups to assign user rights to group members. User rights include actions such as *Backup files and directories* or *Restore files and directories*, both of which are assigned to the Backup Operators group by default. You can delegate rights to groups to enable the members of the group to perform a specific administrative function that is not normally allowed by their standard user rights. You can also assign permissions to security groups to enable them to access network resources, such as printers and file shares.

NOTE

Permissions, which should not be confused with user rights, determine which users can access specified resources and what they can do (read, write, execute, etc.) to that resource. By assigning these permissions to a group instead of individual users, you can ensure that all members of the group have the required permissions.

Local, Domain Local, Global, and Universal Groups

Unlike group types, which are fairly simple to understand, group scopes can be frustrating to those new to working with Windows Server 2003 and Active Directory. The scope of the group identifies the extent to which the group is applied throughout the domain tree or forest. There are four group scopes:

- **Local groups** Local groups can contain user accounts from the local machine, user accounts from the domain the local machine is joined to, or user accounts from any trusted domains of the domain the machine is joined to. Only local groups can manage permissions for local resources (local to a single machine).
- **Domain local groups** Domain local groups can include other groups and user/computer accounts from Windows Server 2003, Windows 2000 Server, and Windows NT domains. Permissions for only the domain in which the group is defined can be assigned to domain local groups.
- **Global groups** Global groups can include other groups and user/computer accounts from only the domain in which the group is defined. Permissions for any domain in the forest can be assigned to global groups.
- **Universal groups** Universal groups can include other groups and user/computer accounts from any domain in the domain tree or forest. Permissions for any domain in the domain tree or forest can be assigned to universal groups. Universal groups are only available if your domain functional level is set to Windows 2000 native mode.

New & Noteworthy...

Domain and Forest Functionality

Domain and forest functionality is a new feature introduced in Windows Server 2003. By having differing levels of domain and forest functionality available within your Active Directory implementation, you have different features available to your network.

As an example, if all of your network's domain controllers are Windows Server 2003 and the domain functional level is set to **Windows Server 2003**, all domain features become available. You can make use of the new capability to rename a domain controller only if the domain functional mode is set to

Continued

Windows Server 2003. If your entire Active Directory forest is set at the Windows Server 2003 functional level, you also gain the new capability to rename entire domains—something that administrators have been requesting for many years. Three domain functional levels are available:

- **Windows 2000 mixed** The default domain functional level; allows for Windows NT 4.0 backup domain controllers (BDCs), Windows 2000 Server domain controllers, and Windows Server 2003 domain controllers.
- **Windows 2000 native** The minimum domain functional level at which universal groups become available, along with several other Active Directory features; allows for Windows 2000 Server and Windows Server 2003 domain controllers.
- **Windows Server 2003** The highest domain functional level, providing the most features and functionality; allows for only Windows Server 2003 domain controllers.

Be forewarned, however, once you have raised the domain functional level, domain controllers running earlier operating systems cannot be used in that domain. As an example, should you decide to raise domain functional level to **Windows Server 2003**, Windows 2000 Server domain controllers cannot be added to that domain.

Configuring & Implementing...

Nesting Groups

You've seen how groups can have other groups as members. This concept is known as *group nesting*. Groups can be nested to help consolidate large numbers of user and computer accounts to reduce replication traffic. The type of nesting you can perform is determined by the domain functional level of the domain.

If the domain functional level is set to Windows 2000 native or Windows Server 2003, groups can have the following members:

- **Domain local groups** Other domain local groups in the same domain, global groups from any domain, universal groups from any domain, user accounts from any domain, and computer accounts from any domain.
- **Global groups** Other global groups in the same domain, user accounts in the same domain, and computer accounts in the same domain.
- **Universal groups** Other universal groups from any domain, global groups from any domain, user accounts from any domain, and computer accounts from any domain.

Continued

If the domain functional level is set to Windows 2000 mixed, distribution groups can have the same membership as detailed for Windows 2000 native or Windows Server 2003 functional-level security groups.

If the domain functional level is set to Windows 2000 mixed, security groups can have the following members:

- **Domain local groups** Other global groups from any domain, user accounts from any domain, and computer accounts from any domain.
- **Global groups** User accounts in the same domain and computer accounts in the same domain.

Group nesting is pictured in Figure 4.33. As you can see, nesting makes it easier to change permissions around. For example, if a user moves from a Tier 2 position in Desktop Support to the Windows server team, removing the user from and adding the user to a single group automatically grants membership to the necessary groups. However, nesting groups too deeply can make it difficult to troubleshoot problems, because you have to work your way through the entire group hierarchy to find the problem.

Figure 4.33 Utilizing Group Nesting

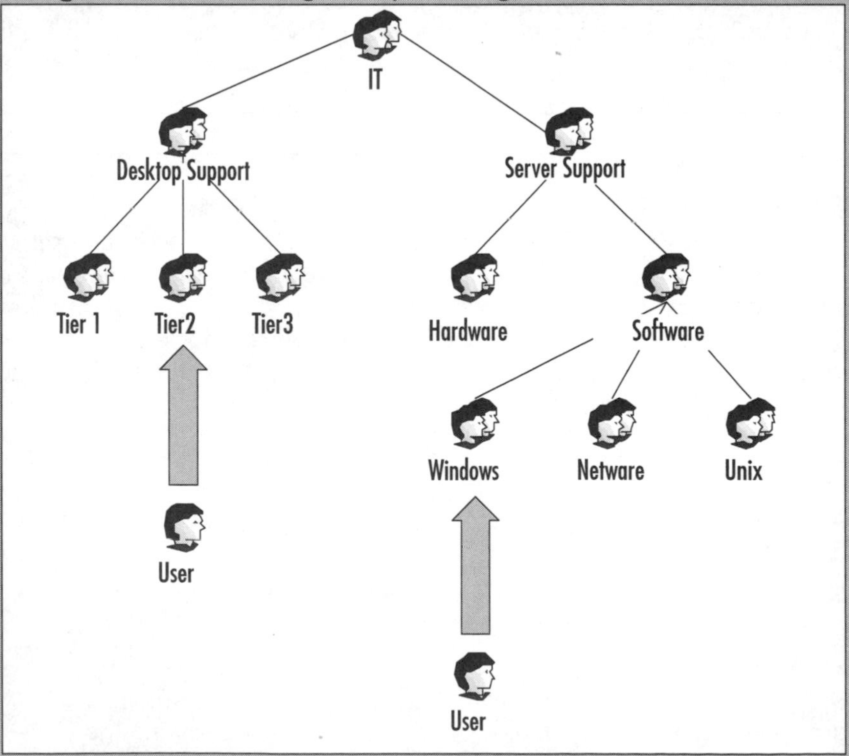

Table 4.11 outlines the behavior and usage of the scopes of domain groups as the domain functional level changes.

Table 4.11 Group Scope Behavior versus Domain Functional Level

Domain Status	Behavior	Universal Group	Global Group	Domain Local Group
Windows Server 2003 or Windows 2000 native	Group membership	Members can include user accounts, computer accounts, and other universal groups from any domain.	Members can include user accounts, computer accounts, and other global groups from the same domain.	Members can include user accounts, computer accounts, global groups, and universal groups from the same domain.
Windows 2000 mixed	Group membership	Universal groups cannot be created.	Members can include user and computer accounts from the same domain.	Members can include user accounts, computer accounts, and global groups from any domain.
Windows Server 2003 or Windows 2000 native	Group nesting	Can be added to other groups.	Can be added to other groups.	Can be added to other domain local groups.
Windows Server 2003 or Windows 2000 native	Group permissions	Can be assigned permissions in any domain.	Can be assigned permissions in any domain.	Can be assigned permissions only in the same domain.
Windows Server 2003 or Windows 2000 native	Group scope changes	Can be changed to global groups as long as no group members are other universal groups. Can be converted to domain local groups with no restrictions.	Can be changed to universal groups as long as the group is not a member of any other global group.	Can be changed to universal groups as long as no group members are other domain local groups.
Windows 2000 mixed	Group scope changes	Not allowed.	Not allowed.	Not allowed.

Using the ADUC MMC Snap-In to Create and Manage Groups

This section discusses using ADUC to create and manage groups. Exercise 4.02 covers creating groups. It is important to know how to create groups. However, for the test, you also need to know how to manage groups. This section walks you through all the tabs of an Active Directory group account with screenshots and explanations.

Exercise 4.02

Using ADUC to Create Groups

1. Open **Active Directory Users and Computers** (**Start | Programs | Administrative Tools | Active Directory Users and Computers**).
2. Right-click the **domain** or **OU** where you want to create a group, as shown in Figure 4.34.
3. Click **New** from the pop-up menu.
4. Click **Group** from the pop-up menu. This gives you the window shown in Figure 4.35.

Figure 4.34 Creating a New Group

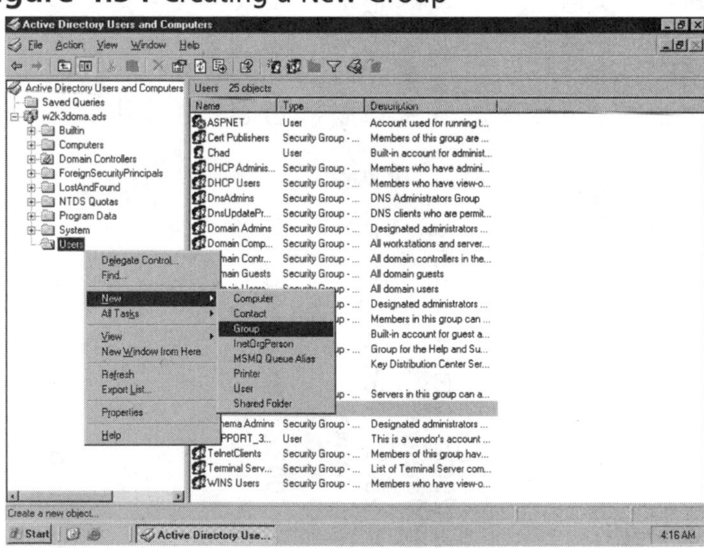

5. Fill in the **Group name.** This automatically fills in the pre-Windows 2000 group name.
6. Choose the **Group scope** by clicking the appropriate radio button.

Figure 4.35 Naming the Group

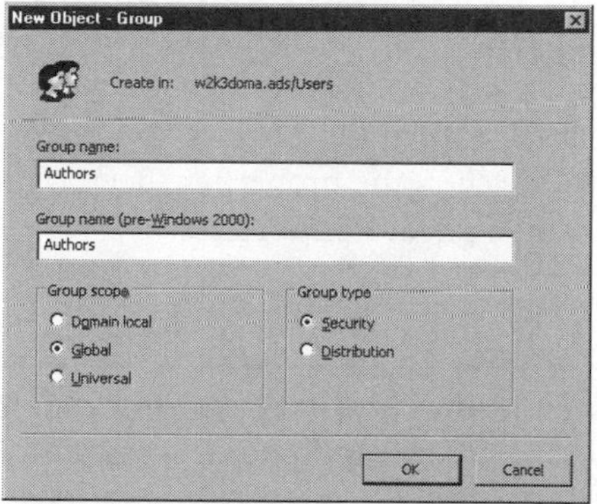

7. Choose the **Group type** by clicking the appropriate radio button.
8. Click **OK** to create the group. Figure 4.36 shows your newly created group (Authors).

NOTE

By default, when you create a new group the scope is global and the type is security.

Figure 4.36 Seeing the New Group

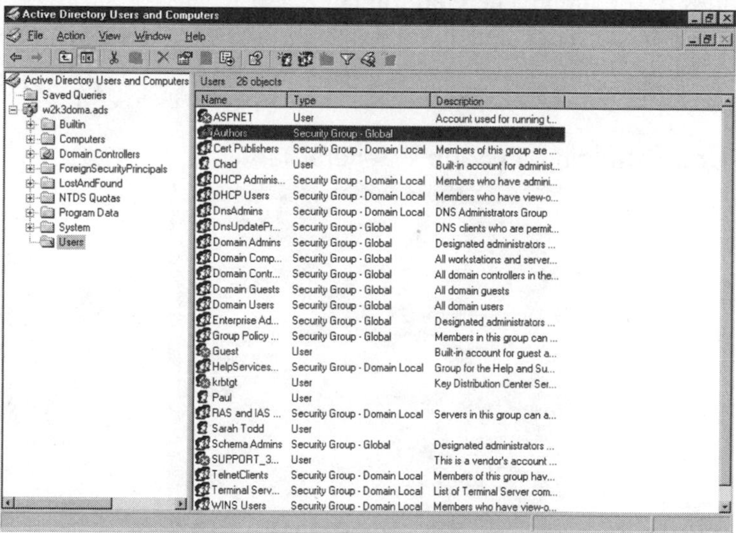

Managing Group Accounts Via the Properties Tabs

Managing groups in ADUC is easier than managing users, because there are not as many tabs to configure. For the Server test you need to be familiar with the properties of group accounts, including what each tab is used for. This section provides screenshots with explanations for each of these tabs. To access the properties sheet, right-click the group name in the right pane of ADUC and then select **Properties**.

EXAM WARNING

You need to be familiar with the properties of group accounts for the test. This test uses exhibits to test your knowledge of the ADUC interface. For example, you might see a screenshot of a group's properties and have to select the tab that manages the group's scope, or you might see a screenshot to click the option that is needed for that particular question.

Using the General Tab

The **General** tab of a group's properties is shown in Figure 4.37. Use this tab to change the group's name and description. Always give your groups a descriptive name and fill in the description. Use the **Notes** field to key in additional information about the group, such as the group's point of contact, who created the group, why the group was created, etc. If the group is mail-enabled for Exchange 2000, the **E-mail** field is automatically populated with the primary e-mail address of the group. The **General** tab is also where you change a group's scope (domain local, global, or universal) and a group's type (security or distribution).

Figure 4.37 Understanding a Group's General Tab

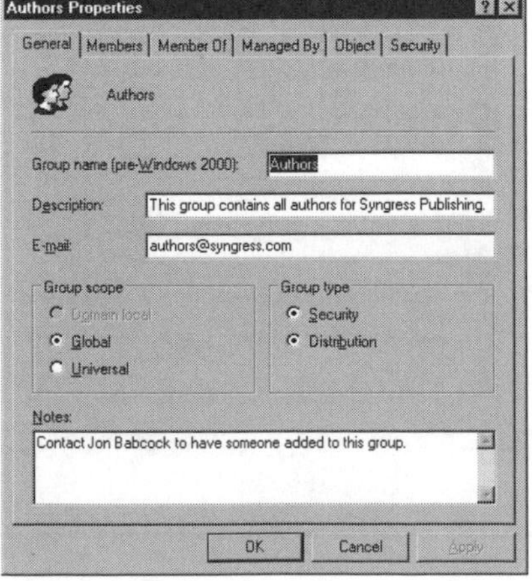

Using the Member's Tab

A group's **Members** tab is shown in Figure 4.38. This lists all the members of the group. It shows the members' names and locations in Active Directory. Click **Add** to add members to the group. This gives you the window shown in Figure 4.39. Type the **name of the account** (user or group) you want to make a member of the group and click **Check Names** to verify that the user or group exists and that the name is spelled correctly. Click **OK** to add the account to the group.

Figure 4.38 Understanding a Group's Members Tab

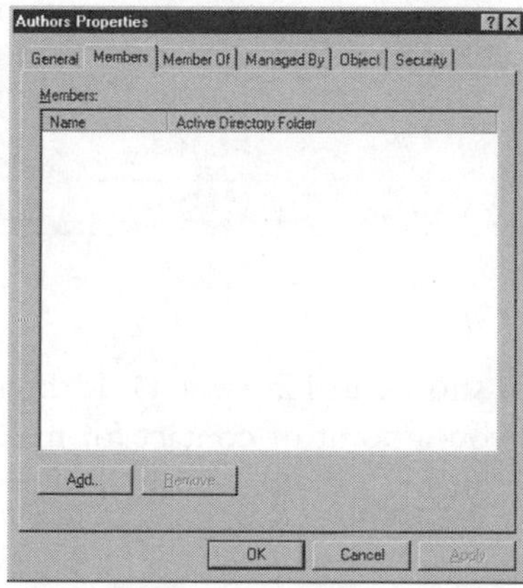

Figure 4.39 Adding Members to a Group

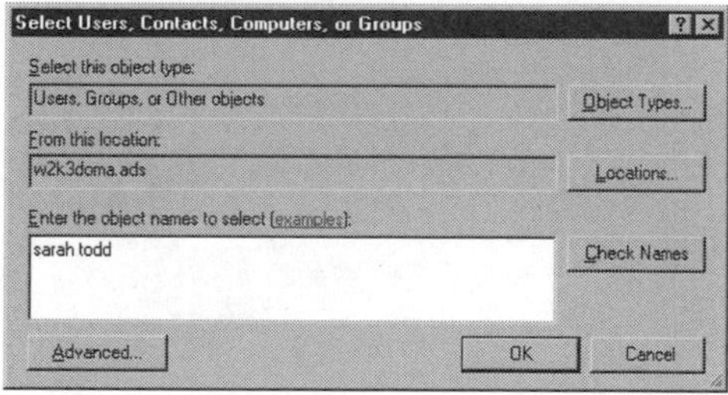

Using the Member Of Tab

Figure 4.40 shows the **Member Of** tab. This tab looks like and is managed the same as the **Members** tab. It shows the name and Active Directory location of other groups that this group is a member of. Click **Add** to add this group to other groups. The **Member Of** tab only shows groups from the local domain, or groups that are stored on the Global Catalog server.

Figure 4.40 Understanding a Group's Member Of Tab

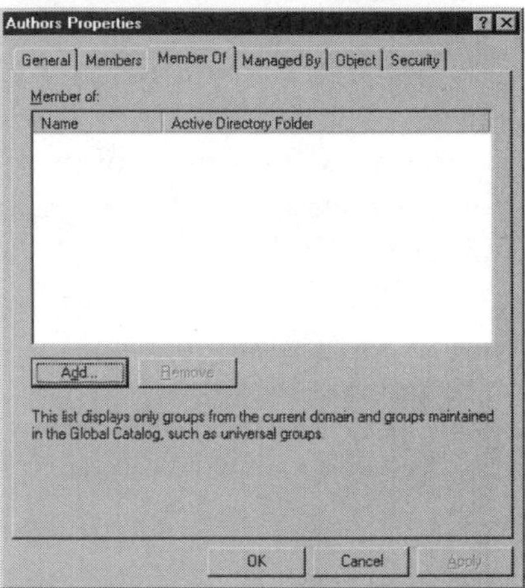

Using the Managed By Tab

The group's **Managed by** tab is shown in Figure 4.41. It shows who is responsible for managing the group. This gives you a point of contact for making changes to the group. This tab shows the following about the manager of the group:

- Name
- Office Location
- Street Address
- City
- State
- Country
- Telephone Number
- Fax Number

You do not have to enter all this information manually. After you enter the username, all the other information is populated from the user's **Telephones** and **Address** tabs. Clicking the **Properties** box enables you to customize the user's information. The **Clear** button removes the user as the group manager. You can optionally give the user the ability to update the membership of this group by selecting the check box next to **Manager can update membership list**.

Using the Object Tab

There is nothing to configure on the group's **Object** tab, shown in Figure 4.42. This tab shows the location of the object in Active Directory (the Canonical name). It shows the type of object you are looking at (Object class). It shows you when the object was created and when it was last modified. For replication purposes, the **Object** tab also lists the current and original USNs.

Figure 4.41 Understanding a Group's Managed By Tab

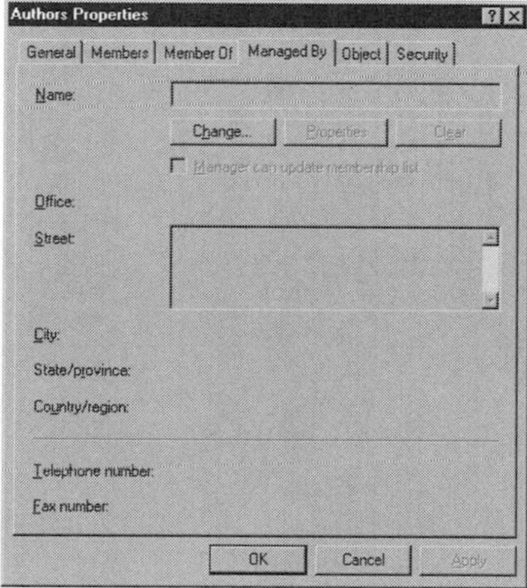

Figure 4.42 Understanding a Group's Object Tab

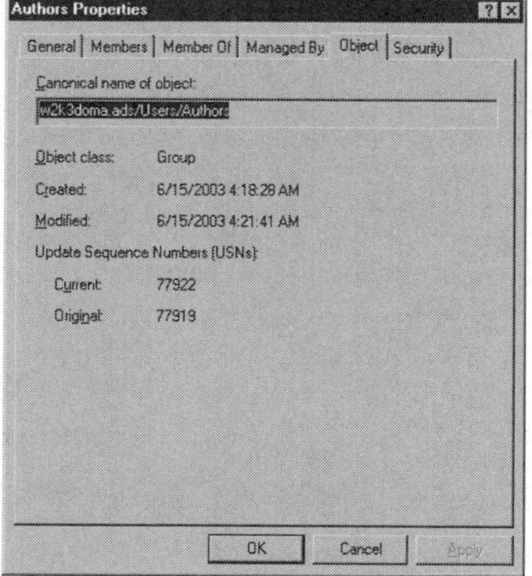

Using the Security Tab

The group's **Security** tab is shown in Figure 4.43. Use this tab to add and remove permissions to this group for other accounts (users and groups). Use the **Add** button to add the accounts, and then use the check boxes at the bottom to select the permissions for the newly added accounts. Read is the default permission assigned when you add an account to the security tab of a group. The **Advanced** button enables you to manage permissions to the group on a more granular level. This is also where you manage auditing, ownership, as well as view effective permissions.

Figure 4.43 Understanding a Group's Security Tab

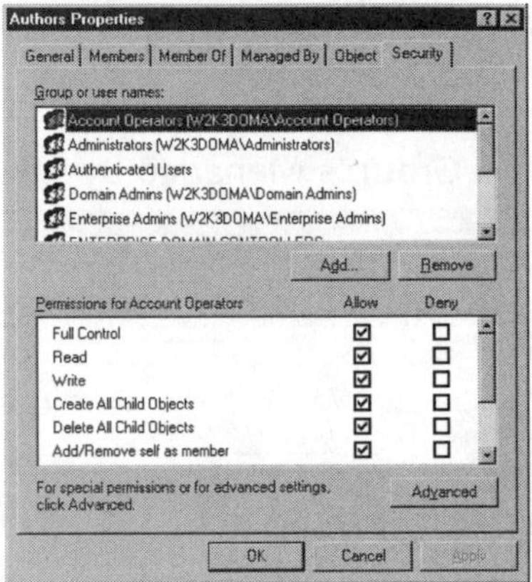

There are four tabs to manage for the advanced security settings of a group:

- Permissions
- Auditing
- Owner
- Effective Permissions

The first tab is the advanced **Permissions** tab, as shown in Figure 4.44. This tab can restore the default permissions to the group, and enable or disable inheritance for the group. The **Add**, **Remove**, and **Edit** buttons manage the permissions for the group. This is different from the permissions shown in Figure 4.43. Figure 4.43 shows permission roles. Each role is automatically assigned a number of permissions from the advanced tab. For example, the Full Control role is assigned all the permissions on the Advanced tab. If you need more granular control than what is provided by the permission roles shown in Figure 4.43, use the advanced **Permissions** tab.

Figure 4.44 Understanding the Advanced Permissions Tab

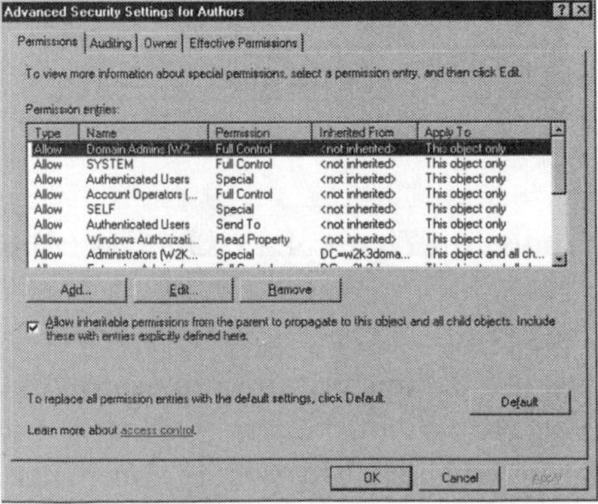

The **Auditing** tab is shown in Figure 4.45. This tab is self-explanatory: it manages what is audited for the particular group. The **Add**, **Remove**, and **Edit** buttons manage auditing.

Figure 4.45 Understanding the Auditing Tab

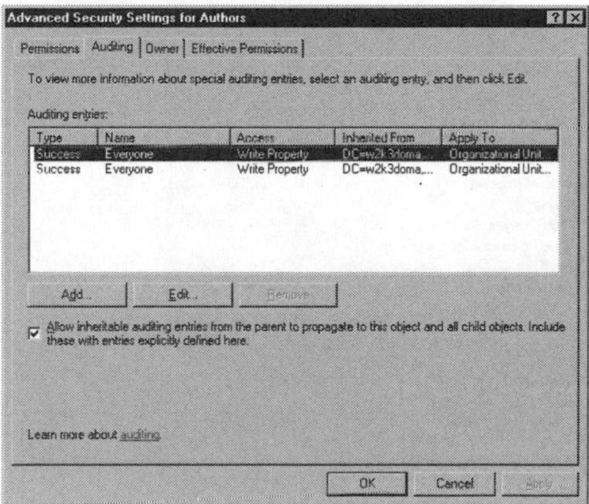

The **Owner** tab is shown in Figure 4.46. This tab shows who owns the group. The owner of a group has Full Control of the group. Typically, the owner is the person who created the group. As an administrator, you can take ownership of a group by using the **Other Users or Groups** button. By giving yourself ownership of the group, you are effectively giving yourself full control of the group.

Figure 4.46 Understanding the Owner Tab

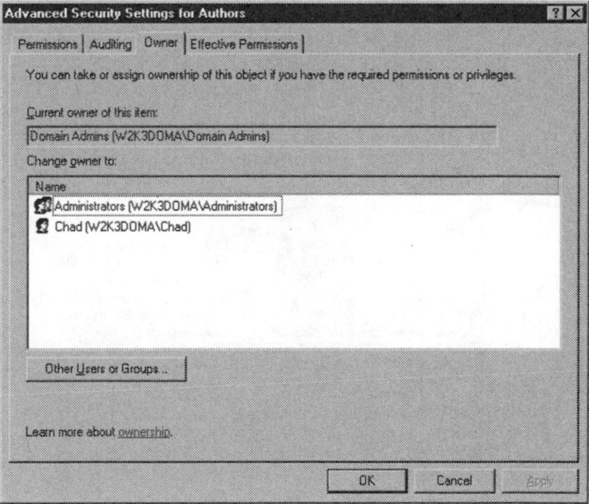

The **Effective Permissions** tab, shown in Figure 4.47, is new for Windows Server 2003. It provides a way to calculate a user's or group's effective permissions to a group. Use the **Select** button to choose the user or group that you want to investigate. Select the user and click **OK**. This shows you all the rights granted to the selected user or group for the group you are managing.

Figure 4.47 Understanding the Effective Permissions Tab

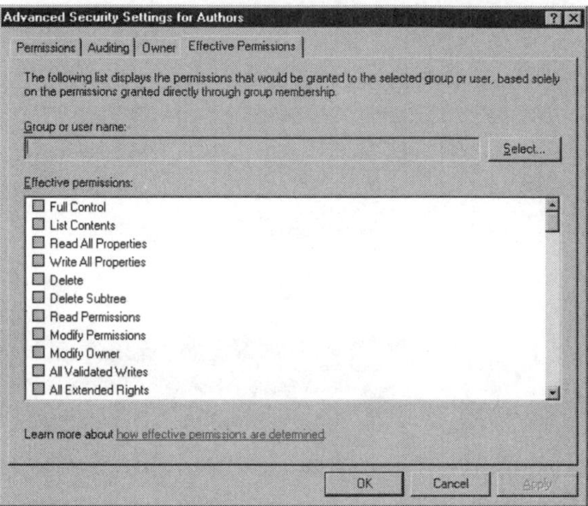

Managing Group Accounts Via the Pop-Up Menu

Like users, groups can be managed by right-clicking on the object, as shown in Figure 4.48, and selecting the desired command from the pop-up menu. However, group management offers fewer options in the context menu than user management. You can move a group to another location, as shown in Figure 4.49, or you can send the group an e-mail (if the group is mail enabled).

Figure 4.48 Using the Pop-Up Menu

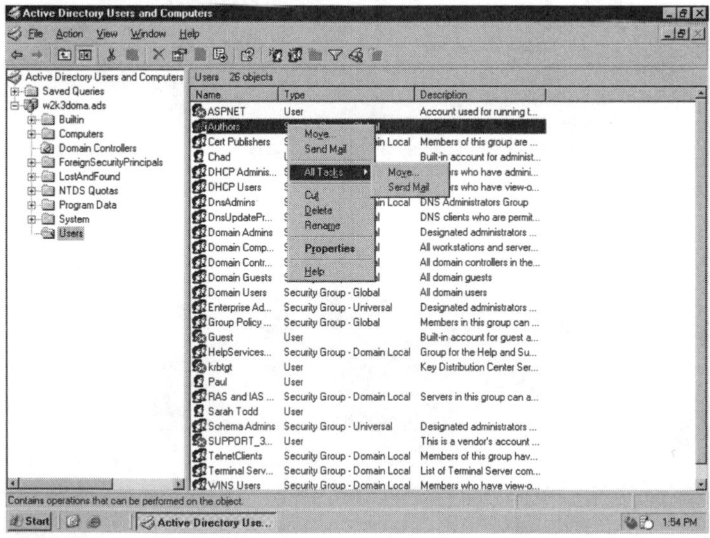

Figure 4.49 Moving Groups in Active Directory

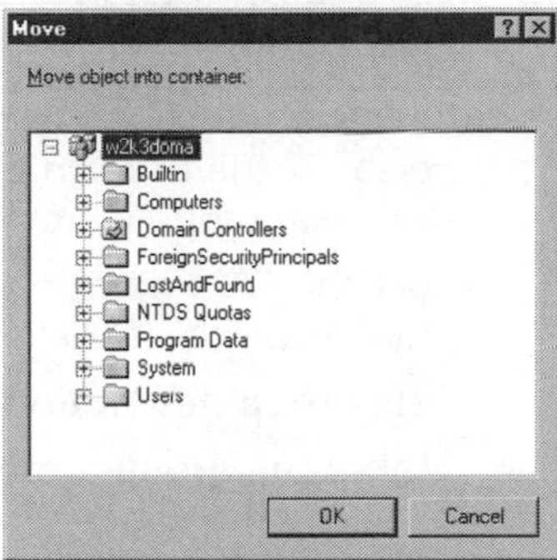

Using the Command Line to Create and Manage Groups

Use the following tools to create and manage groups:

- dsadd.exe
- dsmod.exe
- dsget.exe
- dsquery.exe

Using dsadd.exe Group

dsadd.exe enables you to quickly add multiple groups. In this section, you learn the syntax for *dsadd group*. Like the other *dsadd* commands, there is a lot of syntax for this command. The syntax for *dsadd group* is as follows, and available switches are explained in detail in Table 4.12.

```
dsadd group <GroupDN> [-secgrp {yes | no}] [-scope {l | g | u}]
[-samid <SAMName>] [-desc <Description>] [-memberof <Group ...>]
[-members <Member ...>] [{-s <Server> | -d <Domain>}] [-u  UserName>][-p
{<Password> | *}] [-q] [{-uc | -uco | -uci}]
```

Table 4.12 Understanding dsadd.exe Group

Value	Description
<GroupDN>	Required. DN of group to add.
-secgrp {yes | no}	Sets this group as a security group (yes) or not (no). Default: yes.

Continued

Table 4.12 Understanding dsadd.exe Group

Value	Description
-scope {l | g | u}	Sets the scope of this group: local, global, or universal. If the domain is still in mixed-mode, the universal scope is not supported. Default: global.
-samid <SAMName>	Sets the SAM account name of group to <SAMName> (for example, operators).
-desc <Description>	Sets group description to <Description>.
-memberof <Group>	Makes the group a member of one or more groups given by the space-separated list of DNs <Group ...>.
-members <Member>	Adds one or more members to this group. Members are set by space-separated list of DNs <Member ...>.
{-s <Server> | -d <Domain>}	-s <Server> connects to the domain controller (DC) with name <Server>. -d <Domain> connects to a DC in domain <Domain>. Default: a DC in the log-on domain.
-u <UserName>	Connects as <UserName>. Default: the logged-on user. Username can be: username, domain\username, or user principal name (UPN).
-p {<Password> | *}	Password for the user <UserName>. If * is entered, you are prompted for a password.
-q	Quiet mode: suppresses all output to standard output.
{-uc | -uco | -uci}	-uc specifies that input from or output to pipe is formatted in Unicode. -uco specifies that output to pipe or file is formatted in Unicode. -uci specifies that input from pipe or file is formatted in Unicode.

Creating Groups

Use *dsadd group* to create a new universal group with the following syntax:

```
dsadd group <GroupDN> [-secgrp {yes | no}] [-scope {l | g | u}]
        [-samid <SAMName>] [-desc <Description>]
```

The following example creates a universal group named Microsoft Trainers in the trainingconcepts.org domain:

```
dsadd group "CN=Microsoft Trainers,DC=trainingconcepts,DC=org"
     -secgrp yes -scope u -samid MicrosoftTrainers -desc "This group
         contains all of the Microsoft Trainers for Training Concepts"
```

Using dsmod.exe group

dsmod group modifies the attributes of groups in Active Directory. *dsmod group* uses the following syntax. All syntax and switches are explained in Table 4.13.

```
dsmod group <GroupDN ...> [-samid <SAMName>]
[-desc <Description>] [-secgrp {yes | no}] [-scope {l | g | u}]
[{-addmbr | -rmmbr | -chmbr} <Member ...>]
[{-s <Server> | -d <Domain>}] [-u <UserName>]
[-p {<Password> | *}] [-c] [-q] [{-uc | -uco | -uci}]
```

Table 4.13 Understanding dsmod group Syntax

<table>
<tr><th>Value</th><th>Description</th></tr>
<tr><td><GroupDN></td><td>Required. DNs of one or more groups to modify. If target objects are omitted, they will be taken from standard input (stdin) to support piping of output from another command to the input of this command. If <GroupDN ...> and <Member ...> are used together, only one parameter can be taken from standard input, requiring that at least one parameter be specified on the command line.</td></tr>
<tr><td>-samid <SAMName></td><td>Sets the SAM account name of group to <SAMName>.</td></tr>
<tr><td>-desc <Description></td><td>Sets group description to <Description>.</td></tr>
<tr><td>-secgrp {yes | no}</td><td>Sets the group type to security (yes) or non-security (no).</td></tr>
<tr><td>-scope {l | g | u}</td><td>Sets the scope of group to local (l), global (g), or universal (u).</td></tr>
<tr><td>{-addmbr | -rmmbr | -chmbr}</td><td>-addmbr adds members to the group.
-rmmbr removes members from the group.
-chmbr changes (replaces) the complete list of members in the group.</td></tr>
<tr><td><Member></td><td>Space-separated list of members to add to, delete from, or replace in the group. If target objects are omitted, they will be taken from standard input (stdin) to support piping of output from another command to the input of this command. The list of members must follow the -addmbr, -rmmbr, and -chmbr parameters. If <GroupDN ...> and <Member ...> are used together, only one parameter can be taken from standard input, requiring that at least one parameter be specified on the command line.</td></tr>
</table>

Continued

Table 4.13 Understanding dsmod group Syntax

Value	Description
{-s <Server> | -d <Domain>}	-s <Server> connects to the domain controller (DC) with name <Server>. -d <Domain> connects to a DC in domain <Domain>. Default: a DC in the logon domain.
-u <UserName>	connects as <UserName>. Default: the logged-on user. Username can be: username, domain\username, or user principal name (UPN).
-p <Password>	Password for the user <UserName>. If *, then prompt for password.
-c	Continuous operation mode. Reports errors but continues with next object in argument list when multiple target objects are specified. Without this option, the command exits on first error.
-q	Quiet mode: suppresses all output to standard output.
{-uc | -uco | -uci}	-uc specifies that input from or output to pipe is formatted in Unicode. -uco specifies that output to pipe or file is formatted in Unicode. -uci specifies that input from pipe or file is formatted in Unicode.

Adding Members to Groups

Use *dsmod group* to add user accounts to groups with the following syntax:

```
dsmod group GroupDN -addmbr UserDN
```

The following example uses the *dsmod* command to add three user accounts to the Microsoft Trainers group:

```
dsmod.exe group "CN=Microsoft Trainers,DC=trainingconcepts,DC=org"
    -addmbr "CN=Chad Todd,CN=Users,DC=trainingconcepts,DC=org"
dsmod.exe group "CN=Microsoft Trainers,DC=trainingconcepts,DC=org"
    -addmbr "CN=Gary Landry,CN=Users,DC=trainingconcepts,DC=org"
dsmod.exe group "CN=Microsoft Trainers,DC=trainingconcepts,DC=org"
    -addmbr "CN=Paul Salas,CN=Users,DC=trainingconcepts,DC=org"
```

Removing Members from Groups

Use *dsmod group* to remove members from a group with the following syntax:

```
dsmod group GroupDN -rmmbr UserDN
```

The following example removes the user Paul Salas from the Microsoft Trainers group:

```
dsmod group "CN=Microsoft Trainers,DC=trainingconcepts,DC=org" -rmmbr
    "CN=Paul Salas,CN=Users,DC=trainingconcepts,DC=org"
```

Converting Group Type

Use *dsmod group* to convert a group's type with the following syntax:

```
dsmod group GroupDN [-secgrp {yes | no}]
```

The following examples convert the Microsoft Trainers group into a distribution group and then back into a security group:

```
dsmod group "CN=Microsoft Trainers,DC=trainingconcepts,DC=org"
    -secgrp no

dsmod group "CN=Microsoft Trainers,DC=trainingconcepts,DC=org"
    -secgrp yes
```

Using dsquery group

dsquery group searches Active Directory for groups that match specified credentials. You can use *dsquery group* to find groups and then send a list of those to another command. For example, you could use *dsquery group* to query AD for all groups without any members and have those results imported into *dsmod* to delete all the empty groups. *Dsquery.exe group* uses the following syntax. Table 4.14 explains all the syntax and available switches in detail.

```
dsquery group [{<StartNode> | forestroot | domainroot}]
[-o {dn | rdn | samid}] [-scope {subtree | onelevel | base}]
[-name <Name>] [-desc <Description>] [-samid <SAMName>]
[{-s <Server> | -d <Domain>}] [-u <UserName>]
[-p {<Password> | *}] [-q] [-r] [-gc]
[-limit <NumObjects>] [{-uc | -uco | -uci}]
```

Table 4.14 Understanding dsquery group Syntax

Value	Description
{<StartNode> | forestroot | domainroot}	The node where the search starts: forest root, domain root, or a node whose DN is <StartNode>. Can be "forestroot," "domainroot," or an object DN. If "forestroot" is specified, the search is done via the global catalog. Default: domainroot.
-o {dn | rdn | samid}	Specifies the output format. Default: DN.
-scope {subtree | onelevel | base}	Specifies the scope of the search: subtree rooted at start node (subtree); immediate children of start node only (onelevel); the base object represented by start node (base). Note that subtree and domain scope are essentially the same for any start node unless the start node represents a domain root. If forestroot is specified as <StartNode>, subtree is the only valid scope. Default: subtree.
-name <Name>	Finds groups whose name matches the value given by <Name>; e.g., "jon*" or "*ith" or "j*th."
-desc <Description>	Finds groups whose description matches the value given by <Description>; e.g., "jon*" or "*ith" or "j*th."
-samid <SAMName>	Finds groups whose SAM account name matches the value given by <SAMName>.
{-s <Server> | -d <Domain>}	-s <Server> connects to the domain controller(DC) with name <Server>. -d <Domain> connects to a DC in domain <Domain>. Default: a DC in the log-on domain.
-u <UserName>	Connects as <UserName>. Default: the logged-on user. Username can be: username, domain\username, or user principal name (UPN).
-p <Password>	Password for the user <UserName>. If * is specified, you are prompted for a password.
-q	Quiet mode: suppresses all output to standard output.
-r	Recurses or follows referrals during search. Default: do not chase referrals during search.
-gc	Searches in the Active Directory global catalog.

Continued

Table 4.14 Understanding dsquery group Syntax

Value	Description
-limit <NumObjects>	Specifies the number of objects matching the given criteria to be returned, where <NumObjects> is the number of objects to be returned. If the value of <NumObjects> is 0, all matching objects are returned. If this parameter is not specified, by default the first 100 results are displayed.
{-uc | -uco | -uci}	-uc specifies that input from or output to pipe is formatted in Unicode. -uco specifies that output to pipe or file is formatted in Unicode. -uci specifies that input from pipe or file is formatted in Unicode.

Finding Groups Based on Description

To use *dsquery group* to query Active Directory for groups with a specified description, use the following syntax:

```
dsquery group -desc <Description>
```

The following example queries Active Directory for all groups with the description "Microsoft Trainers."

```
dsquery group -desc "Microsoft Trainers"
```

You can use wildcards in the name as well. The following example queries Active Directory for all groups with trainers in the description.

```
dsquery group -desc *trainers*
```

Finding Groups Based on Name

To use *dsquery group* to query Active Directory for groups that match a specified name, use the following syntax:

```
dsquery group -name <Name>
```

The following example queries Active Directory for the authors group.

```
dsquery group -name authors
```

You can use wildcards in the name as well. The following example queries Active Directory for any group beginning with the letter "a".

```
dsquery group -name a*
```

The following sample output is from querying the trainingconcepts.org domain for all groups that start with the letter "a" (previous example):

```
"CN=Administrators,CN=Builtin,DC=w2k3doma,DC=ads"
"CN=Account Operators,CN=Builtin,DC=w2k3doma,DC=ads"
"CN=Authors,CN=Users,DC=w2k3doma,DC=ads"
```

Finding Groups on the Global Catalog Server

By default, when you use *dsquery.exe group* to search for groups, only the domain partition of your domain is searched. Use the *–gc* option to search the global catalog server. The following example shows the previous examples modified to search the global catalog server.

```
dsquery group -desc "Microsoft Trainers" -gc
dsquery group -desc *trainers* -gc
dsquery group -name authors -gc
dsquery group -name a* -gc
```

Using dsget group

dsget group displays the properties of groups in Active Directory. There are two variations of this command. The first one displays the properties of multiple groups. The second one displays the group membership information of a single group. *dsget group* uses the following syntax. Table 4.15 explains all the syntax and switches for *dsget group* in detail.

```
dsget group <GroupDN ...> [-dn] [-samid] [-sid] [-desc] [-secgrp]
[-scope] [{-s <Server> | -d <Domain>}] [-u <UserName>]
[-p {<Password> | *}] [-c] [-q] [-l] [{-uc | -uco | -uci}]
[-part <PartitionDN> [-qlimit] [-qused]]

dsget group <GroupDN> [{-memberof | -members} [-expand]]
[{-s <Server> | -d <Domain>}] [-u <UserName>]
[-p {<Password> | *}] [-c] [-q] [-l] [{-uc | -uco | -uci}]
```

Table 4.15 Understanding dsget group Syntax

Value	Description
<GroupDN>	Required. DNs of one or more groups to view. If the target objects are omitted, they will be taken from standard input (stdin) to support piping of the output from another command to input of this command.
-dn	Displays the group DN.
-samid	Displays the group SAM account name.
-sid	Displays the group Security ID.
-desc	Displays the group description.

Continued

Table 4.15 Understanding dsget group Syntax

Value	Description
-secgrp	Displays if the group is a security group or not.
-scope	Displays the scope of the group—Local, Global, or Universal.
<GroupDN>	Required. DN of group to view.
{-memberof | -members}	Displays the groups of which the group is a member (-memberof), or displays the members of the group (-members).
-expand	For -memberof, displays the recursively expanded list of groups of which the group is a member. This option takes the immediate group membership list of the group and then recursively expands each group in this list to determine its group memberships and arrive at a complete set of the groups. For -members, displays the recursively expanded list of members of the group. This option takes the immediate list of members of the group and then recursively expands each group in this list to determine its group memberships and arrive at a complete set of its members.
{-s <Server> | -d <Domain>}	-s <Server> connects to the domain controller (DC) with name <Server>. -d <Domain> connects to a DC in domain <Domain>. Default: a DC in the log-on domain.
-u <UserName>	Connects as <UserName>. Default: the logged-on user. Username can be: username, domain\username, or user principal name (UPN).
-p {<Password> | *}	Password for the user <UserName>. If *, then prompt for password.
-c	Continuous operation mode: reports errors but continues with next object in argument list when multiple target objects are specified. Without this option, command exits on first error.
-q	Quiet mode: suppresses all output to standard output.
-L	Displays the entries in the search result set in a list format. Default: table format.
{-uc | -uco | -uci}	Specifies that input from or output to pipe is formatted in Unicode. -uco specifies that output to pipe or file is formatted in Unicode. -uci specifies that input from pipe or file is formatted in Unicode.
-part <PartitionDN>	Connects to the directory partition with the distinguished name of <PartitionDN>.

Continued

Table 4.15 Understanding dsget group Syntax

Value	Description
-qlimit	Displays the effective quota of the group within the specified directory partition.
-qused	Displays how much of its quota the group has used within the specified directory partition.

Determining a Group's Scope

To use *dsget group* to determine a group's scope, use the following syntax:

```
dsget group <GroupDN> -scope
```

The following example queries Active Directory for the scope (domain local, global, or universal) of the authors group.

```
dsget group authors -scope
```

Determining a Group's Type

To use *dsget group* to determine a group's type, use the following syntax:

```
dsget group <GroupDN> -secgrp
```

The following example queries Active Directory to determine whether the authors group is a security or distribution group.

```
dsget group authors -secgrp
```

Determining a Group's Members

To use *dsget group* to determine a group's members, use the following syntax:

```
dsget group <GroupDN> -members
```

The following example queries Active Directory for the members of the authors group.

```
dsget group authors -members
```

Determining a Group's Membership

To use *dsget group* to determine a group's membership, use the following syntax:

```
dsget group <GroupDN> -memberof
```

The following example queries Active Directory for the groups the authors group is a member of.

```
dsget group authors -memberof
```

Group Management Tasks

So far we have discussed the different types and scopes of groups. You have seen how to create these groups from the GUI and from the command line. Now look at some common group management tasks, such as changing group scope and determining group membership.

Identifying and Modifying the Scope of a Group

A group's scope determines its purpose and where it can be used. There are three group scopes available (if domain functionality is Windows 2000 native or later).

- Domain Local
- Global
- Universal

When to use each group scope was discussed earlier in this chapter. For this section, we focus on determining a group's current scope and changing the group scope. Both of these tasks can be accomplished via the GUI or from the command line.

Group scope can be found and modified by using ADUC. Figure 4.50 shows how to use ADUC to view a group's scope. To modify the group's scope, click the option button next to the scope type you want to convert the group to and click the **Apply** button. Groups' scope can be converted as explained in the following list:

- Universal groups can be converted to domain local groups or global groups.
- Domain local groups can be converted to universal groups.
- Global groups can be converted to universal groups.
- Global groups cannot be converted to domain local groups and vice versa.

Figure 4.50 Viewing Group Scope

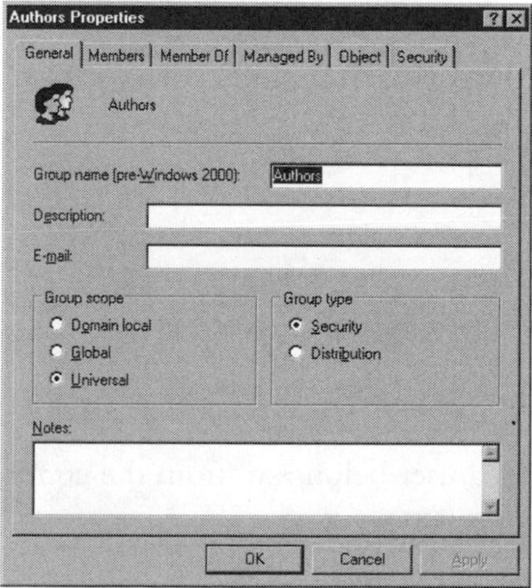

Group scope can be found and modified from the command line by using *dsget* and *dsmod*.

Use *dsget group* with the following syntax to determine a group's scope:

```
dsget group <GroupDN> -scope
```

The following example shows the group scope for the authors group in the trainingconcepts.org domain:

```
dsget group "CN=authors,CN=users,DC=trainingconcepts,DC=org" -scope
```

Use *dsmod group* with the following syntax to convert a group's scope:

```
dsmod group GroupDN [-scope {l | g | u}]
```

The following example converts a group into a global group and then into a universal group:

```
dsmod group "CN=Microsoft Trainers,DC=trainingconcepts,DC=org" -scope g
dsmod group "CN=Microsoft Trainers,DC=trainingconcepts,DC=org" -scope u
```

Determining to which Groups a User Belongs

Determining group membership can be accomplished through the GUI by using ADUC or from the command line by using *dsget.exe*. There are two ways to find this information in ADUC:

- From the properties of a user account (as shown in Figure 4.51)
- From the properties of a group account (as shown in Figure 4.52)

Figure 4.51 Finding Group Membership Via a User's Properties

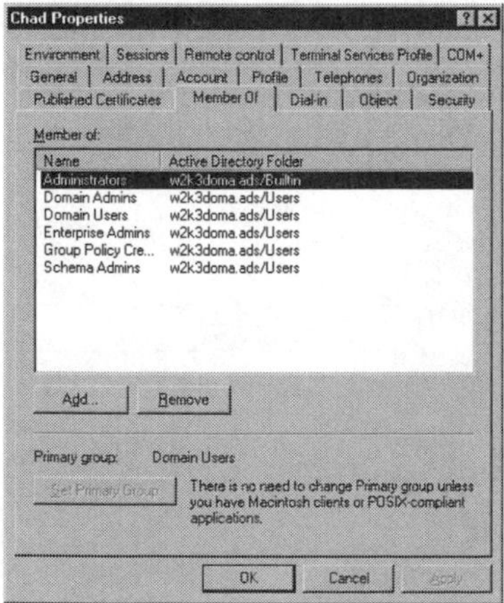

To determine what groups a user belongs to from the command line, use the *dsget user* command with the following syntax:

```
dsget user UserDN -memberof
```

Figure 4.52 Finding Group Membership Via Group Properties

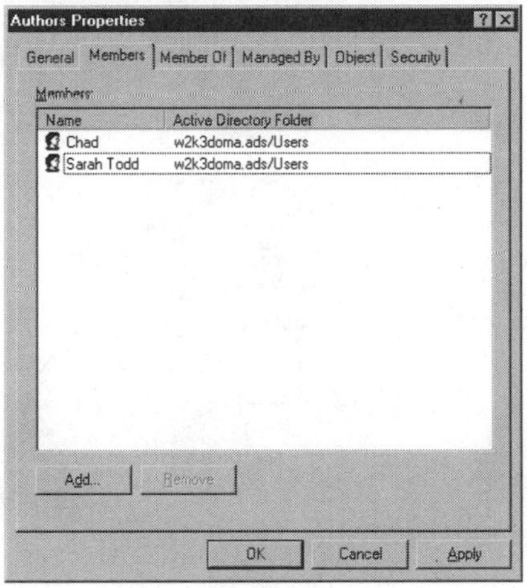

The following example determines the group membership of user Chad Todd:

```
dsget user "CN=Chad Todd,CN=Users,DC=trainingconcepts,DC=org" -memberof
```

To determine all members of a group from the command line, use the *dsget group* command with the following syntax:

```
dsget group GroupDN -members
```

The following example shows the group membership for the Trainers group in the trainingconcepts.org domain:

```
dsget group "CN=Trainers,CN=Users,DC=trainingconcepts,DC=org" -members
```

Group Membership Management Best Practices

The next few sections explain when to use each group scope and show you how all the groups fit together using the AGUDLP method. AGUDLP is an acronym to make it easier to remember when to use each group. Following the AGUDLP guideline is not a requirement, but it is a best practice recommended by Microsoft.

Using Domain Local Groups

Domain local groups manage access to resources within a domain. Figure 4.53 gives a graphical example of how domain local groups are used in an enterprise. Shares are created and permissions to those shares are assigned to domain local groups. Notice that this happens in each domain. This is the DLP portion of AGUDLP (AGUDLP is discussed in full in the subsection titled "Understanding AGUDLP"). Domain Local (DL) groups are assigned permissions (P).

Figure 4.53 Assigning Permissions Through Groups

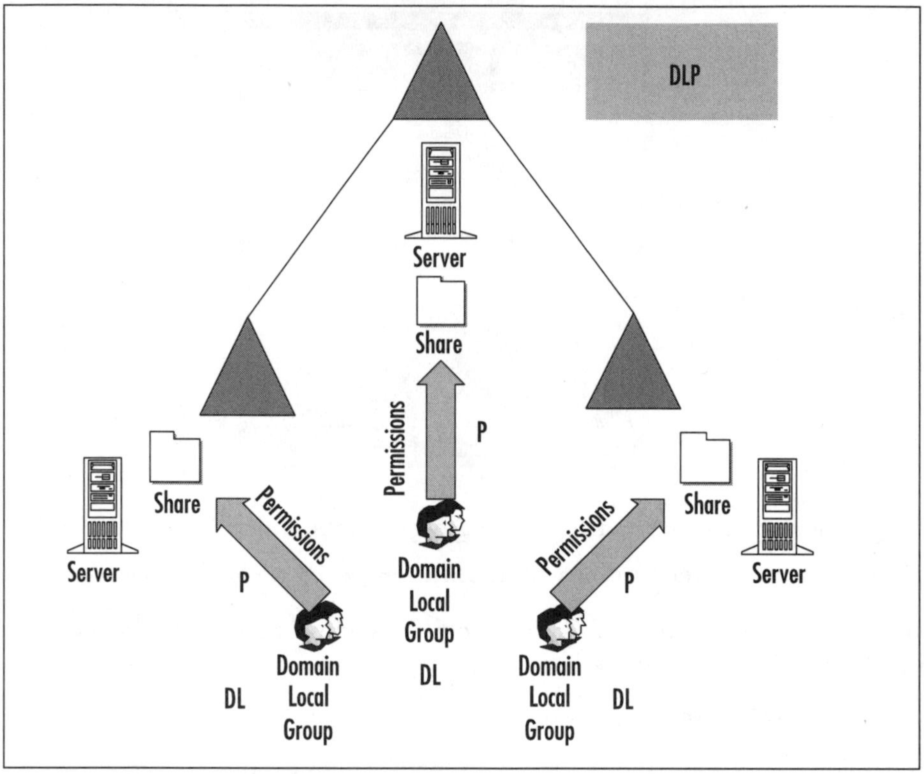

Using Global Groups

Global groups should be used to manage objects that are likely to require frequent maintenance and management operations, such as user accounts and computer accounts. Global groups are not replicated beyond the boundaries of their own domains, thus changes can be made to global group members without creating large amounts of replication traffic to the Global Catalog servers. (This is in direct contrast to universal groups, as is discussed shortly.) Permissions and user rights that are assigned to global groups are only valid in the domain in which they are assigned. You should use global groups (or universal groups) when you are applying permissions on domain objects that are replicated to the Global Catalog.

Using Universal Groups

Universal groups are best used to consolidate global groups into one location. Since user accounts are added to the global groups, membership changes in the global groups do not have an effect on the universal group. Consider the example shown in Figure 4.54 where you have three domains. User accounts are added to their respective global groups. The three global groups are added to one universal group. The universal group can be used anywhere within the enterprise and changes that might be made to the global groups do not cause replication to occur for the universal group – this provides a bandwidth (and cost) savings. This is the AGU portion of AGUDLP. User Accounts (A) go into Global groups (G) and Global Groups go into Universal groups (U).

NOTE

Membership in universal groups should not change often, because changes to universal groups are replicated to every Global Catalog server in the forest, a potentially bandwidth-intensive operation.

Figure 4.54 Organizing Users Into Groups

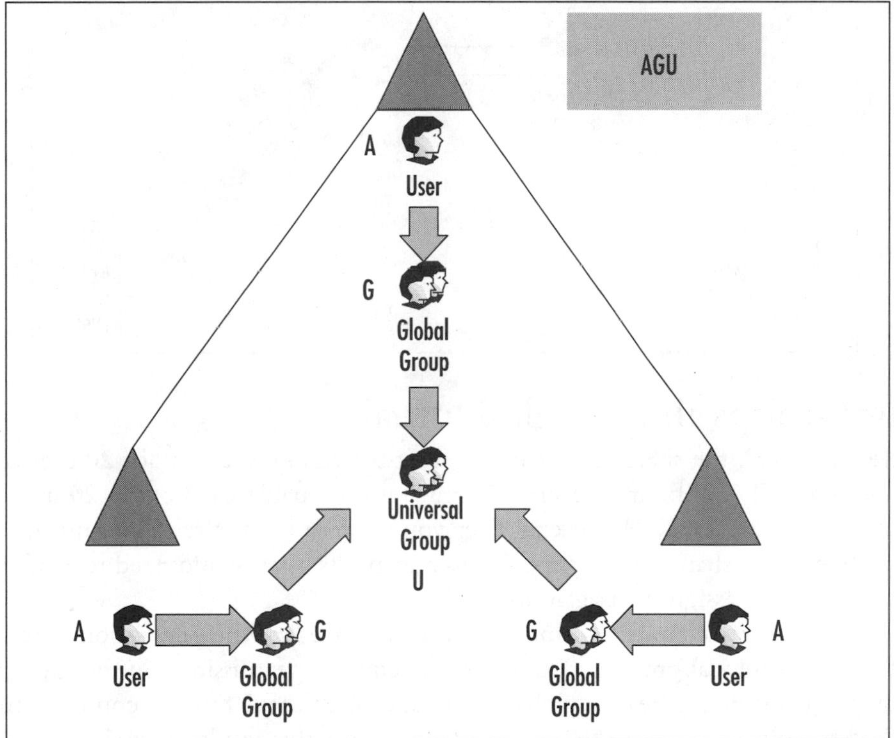

Understanding AGUDLP

As mentioned previously, AGUDLP is an acronym to help you remember how the different group scopes fit together. Figure 4.55 shows how this is used in an enterprise. User Accounts (A) go into Global groups (G) within their domains. Global groups get organized into forest-wide Universal groups (U). Universal groups get placed into Domain Local groups (DL), which have been assigned permissions (P) resources. Look at the following real-world examples.

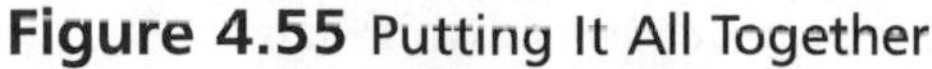

Figure 4.55 Putting It All Together

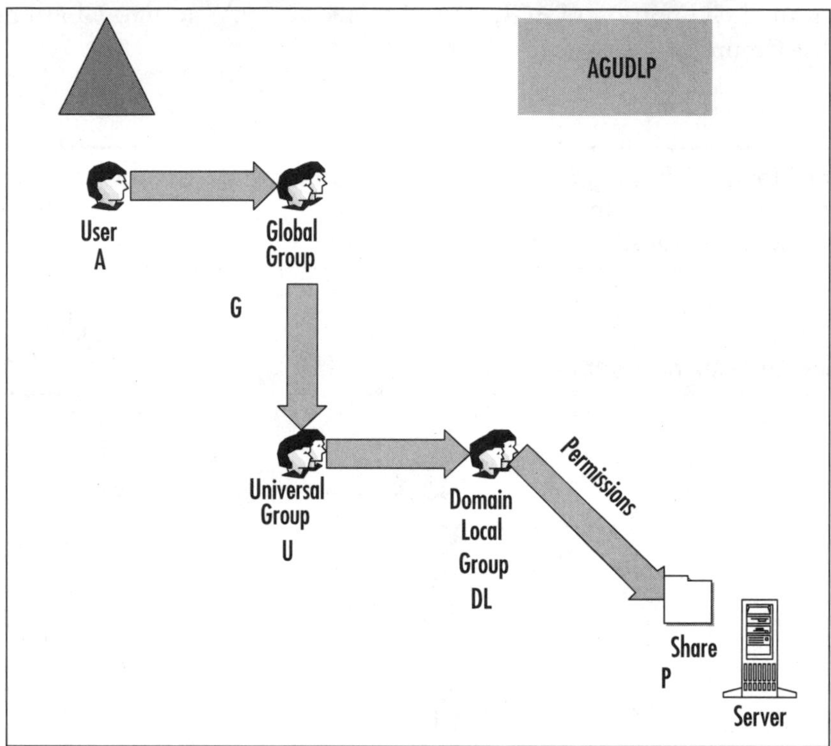

Using Groups in a Single Domain

You have a network file share to which you want to configure access for 20 user accounts. You could manually configure the share permissions to enable each of the 20 user accounts to have the required access. However, if later you need to configure the permissions on a second network file share for the same 20 user accounts, you would need to perform the manual permissions assignment again for all 20 users.

The easier, more accurate, and more secure way to assign the permissions you need is to create a domain local group and assign it the required permissions on the files shares. After this has been done, create a global group and place the 20 user accounts in the global group. Add the global group to the domain local group; this results in all 20 users inheriting the domain local group's assigned permissions, which therefore enables them to gain access to the two file shares.

This might seem like a lot of extra work at first, but it saves you a lot of work in the long run. You simply create two groups (domain local and global), configure the required permissions for the domain local group, add the users to the global group, and then add the global group to the domain local group. This is much faster and more accurate than attempting to manually configure permissions for 20 users on two different file shares. Now imagine how this example could be scaled out to include dozens, perhaps hundreds, of shared objects in a network.

Using Groups in a Multiple Domain Forest

Use the same example for a multiple domain forest. You have the same network file share. You want to give 20 users from each domain access to this share. You create a domain local group and assign it the correct permissions to the network share. You create a global group in each domain to hold the users that need permissions. You then add all those global groups to a single universal group. Next, you add the universal group to the domain local group.

Creating and Managing Computer Accounts

Computer accounts serve the same basic function as user accounts: they are used to determine the rights and permissions that a computer will have in the domain. Although computer accounts can be created for any Windows computer on your network running Windows NT or later, only Windows 2000 or later computers will be able to fully participate in Active Directory and receive security and management configuration from Active Directory. Windows 9*x* and Windows NT computers require the use of System Policies to configure security and management options. Computers running Windows 3.x, Windows 9*x*, Windows ME, and Windows XP Home Edition do not have computer accounts and thus are not domain members.

NOTE

You can learn more about System Policies at www.microsoft.com/technet/prodtechnol/windowsserver2003/proddocs/server/tattooing.asp.

Computer accounts can be created in one of three ways:

- Manually via the Active Directory Users and Computers console
- From the command line
- Automatically by joining a Windows 2000, Windows XP, or Windows Server 2003 computer to the domain

Each of these methods is examined in more detail in the following sections.

EXAM WARNING

By default, Authenticated Users are assigned the *Add workstations to a domain* user right and can create up to 10 computer accounts in the domain. This right can be removed or the number of allowed account creations can be changed from 10 to some other number. This is done by editing the Group Policy Object (**Computer Configuration | Windows Settings | Security Settings | Local Policies | User Rights Assignment**).

Using the ADUC MMC Snap-In to Create and Manage Computers

This section discusses using ADUC to create and manage computers. Exercise 4.03 covers creating computers. It is important to know how to create computer accounts. However, for the test you also need to know how to manage computer accounts. This section walks you through all the tabs of an Active Directory computer account with screenshots and explanations.

EXERCISE 4.03

USING ADUC TO CREATE COMPUTERS

1. Open **Active Directory Users and Computers** (**Start | Programs | Administrative Tools | Active Directory Users and Computers**).
2. Right-click the **domain** or **OU** where you want to create a computer account, as shown in Figure 4.56.

Figure 4.56 Creating a New Computer Account

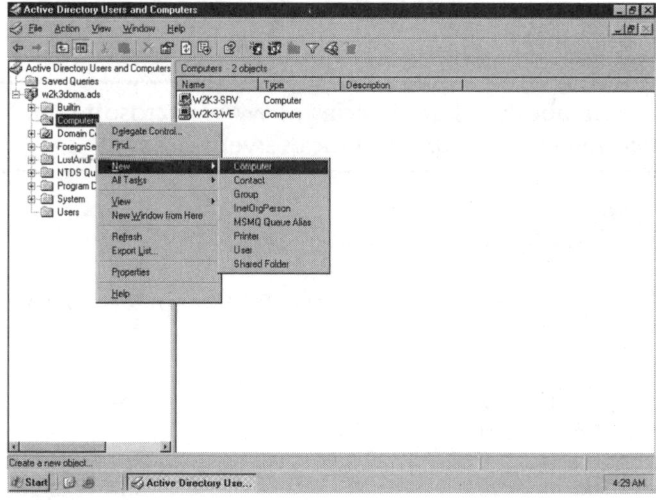

3. Click **New** from the pop-up menu.
4. Click **Computer** from the pop-up menu. This gives you the window shown in Figure 4.57.
5. Type the **name** for the computer account in the **Computer name** field. This automatically fills in the pre-Windows 2000 computer name.

Figure 4.57 Naming the New Computer Account

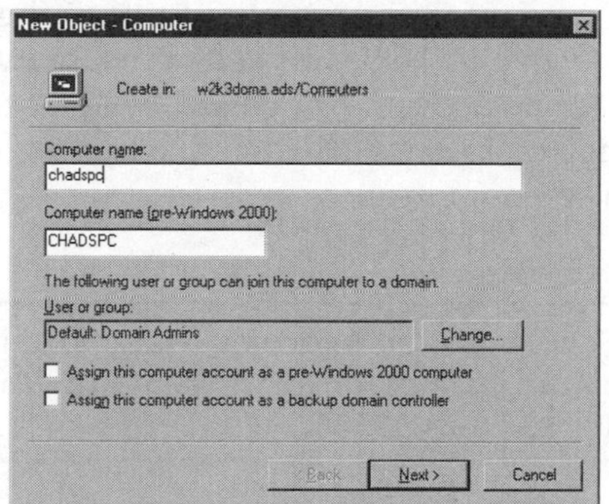

6. Select the **user** or **group** that can join the PC to the domain. By default, the built-in Domain Admins group has these rights. This option enables you to create computer accounts in advance and enables users without administrative rights to join the machines to the domain.
7. If the computer account is for a machine running a Windows NT operating system, select the check box next to **Assign this computer account to a pre-Windows 2000 computer**.
8. If the computer account is for a Windows NT backup domain controller (BDC), select the check box next to **Assign this computer an account as a backup domain controller**.
9. Click **Next** to continue. This gives you the window shown in Figure 4.58.

Figure 4.58 Managing a Computer Account

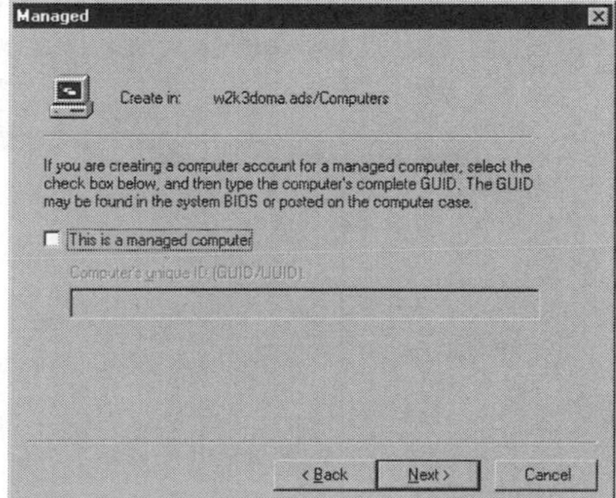

10. If this will be a managed computer, select the check box next to **This is a managed computer** and type the GUID of the object in the Computer's unique ID field. This setting is used when you are pre-staging a machine account to be used by Remote Installation Services (RIS). Pre-staging prevents RIS from deploying an operating system to unknown client computers.

Note

Remote Installation Services is used to deploy unattended installations to machines over the network. You can learn more about RIS at http://support.microsoft.com/default.aspx?scid=kb;en-us;325862.

11. Click **Next** to continue. This gives you the summary window shown in Figure 4.59. Click **Finish** to create the object. Figure 4.60 shows the newly created machine account.

Figure 4.59 Verifying Settings

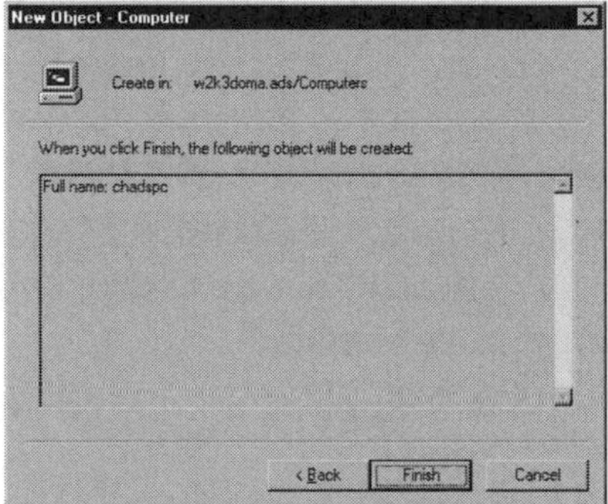

Figure 4.60 Seeing the New Computer Account

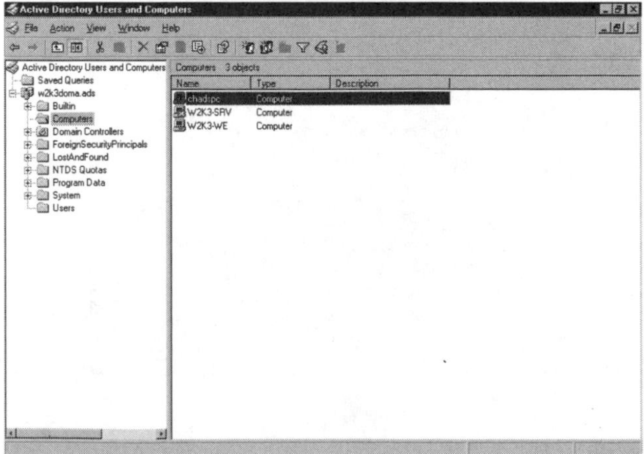

Managing Computer Accounts Via the Properties Tabs

For the Server test, you need to be familiar with the properties of machine accounts, including what each tab is used for. This section provides screenshots with explanations for each of these tabs.

EXAM WARNING

You need to be familiar with the properties of computer accounts for the test. This test uses exhibits to test your knowledge of the ADUC interface. For example, you may see a screenshot of a computer's properties and have to select the tab that manages the computer's group membership or you may see a screenshot with the correct tab selected and have to click the option that is needed for that particular question.

Using the General Tab

A computer's **General** tab, shown in Figure 4.61, displays the computer's NetBIOS (pre-Windows 2000) name and its fully qualified DNS (host) name. It also shows the computer's role. There are two possible roles:

- Workstation or server
- Domain controller

The **General** tab is also where you set the description for the server. It is a good idea to explain the server's purpose in the **Description** field. This makes it easier to remember what all of your servers do as your enterprise gets larger. For workstations, it is a good idea to list the owner of the workstation here. This makes it easy to find a particular user's workstation when browsing through a list of workstations.

Figure 4.61 Understanding a Computer's General Tab

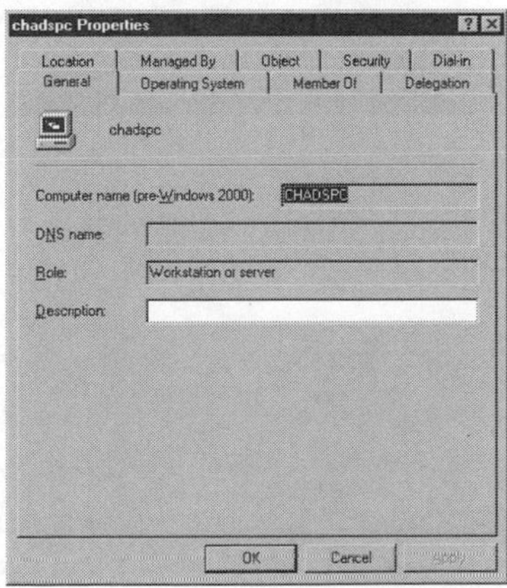

Using the Operating System Tab

The **Operating System** tab, shown in Figure 4.62, lists the operating system name and version. It also lists the current service pack installed.

Figure 4.62 Understanding a Computer's Operating System Tab

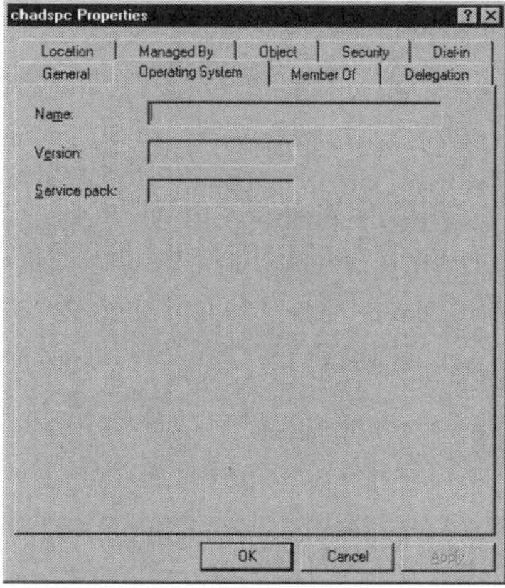

Using the Member Of Tab

The **Member Of** tab, shown in Figure 4.63, shows the name and location in Active Directory for all the groups this machine is a member of. Use the **Add** and **Remove** buttons to modify which groups this machine belongs to. If you are using POSIX-compliant applications or Macintosh clients, use the **Set Primary Group** button to set one of the groups as the primary group.

Figure 4.63 Understanding a Computer's Member Of Tab

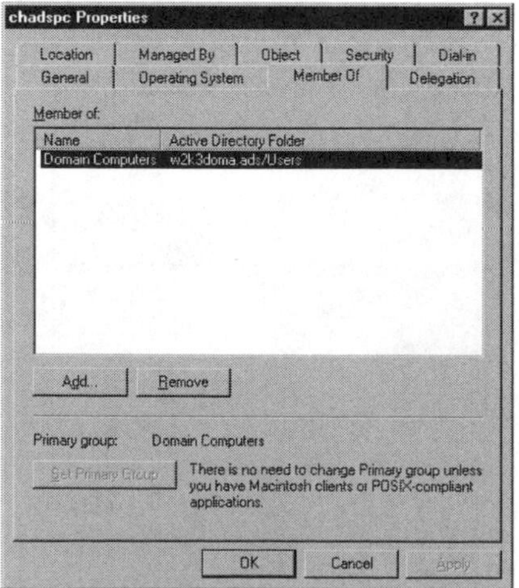

Using the Delegation Tab

The **Delegation** tab, shown in Figure 4.64, enables you to use the computer for delegation. There are three choices for delegation:

- **Do not trust this computer for delegation** This is the default for Windows Server 2003 machines.
- **Trust this computer for delegation to any service (Kerberos only)** This option makes all services under the Local System account trusted for delegation. In other words, any installed service has the capability to access any network resource by impersonating a user.
- **Trust this computer for delegation to specified services only** This feature was not available in previous versions of Windows. It enables an administrator to choose the services that are delegated by selecting a specific service or computer account. This is commonly referred to as *constrained delegation*.

Figure 4.64 Understanding a Computer's Delegation Tab

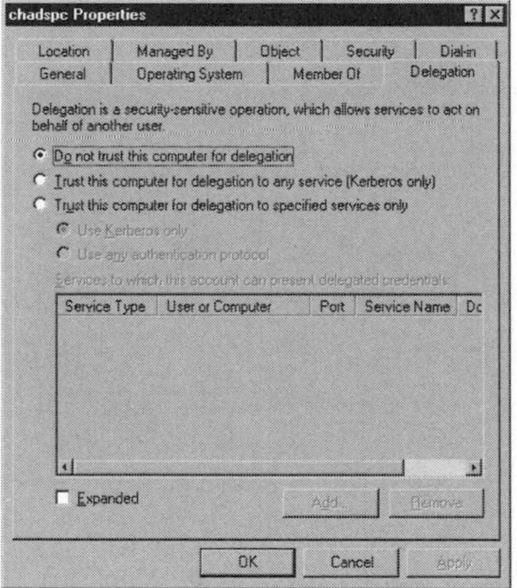

Using the Location Tab

Use the **Location** tab, shown in Figure 4.65, to configure the computer's location. This refers to the physical location of the computer. A typical location is in the format *Building Name/Floor Number/Room Number*.

Using the Managed By Tab

The computer's **Managed By** tab, shown in Figure 4.66, shows who is responsible for managing the computer. This tab shows the following about the manager of the machine:

- Name
- Office Location
- Street Address
- City
- State
- Country
- Telephone Number
- Fax Number

Figure 4.65 Understanding a Computer's Location Tab

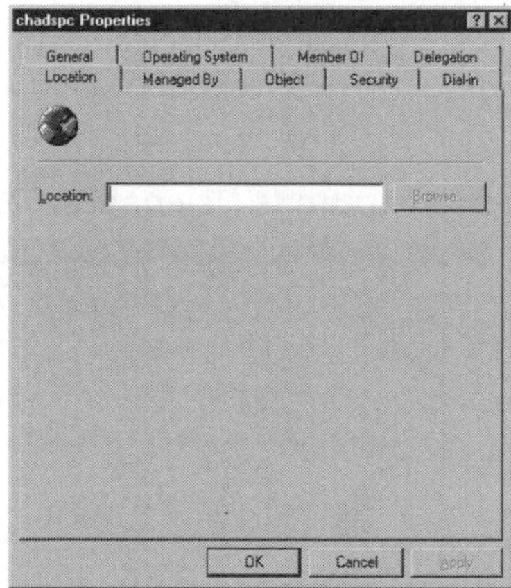

You do not have to enter all this information manually. After you enter the username, all the other information is populated from the user's telephones and address tabs. Clicking the **Properties** box enables you to customize the user's information. The **Clear** button removes the user as the computer manager.

Figure 4.66 Understanding a Computer's Managed By Tab

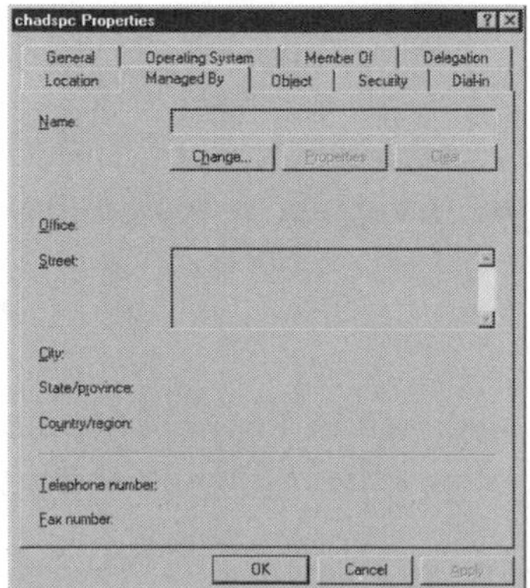

Using the Object Tab

There is nothing to configure on the user's **Object** tab, shown in Figure 4.67. This tab shows you the location of the object in Active Directory (the Canonical name). It shows you the type of object you are looking at (Object class). It shows you when the object was created and when it was last modified. For replication purposes, the **Object** tab also lists the current and original USNs.

Figure 4.67 Understanding a Computer's Object Tab

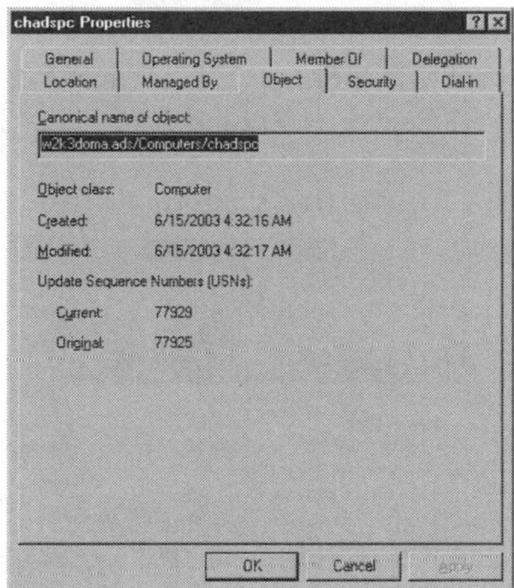

Using the Security Tab

The **Security** tab, shown in Figure 4.68, enables you to add and remove permissions to this computer for other accounts (users and groups). Use the **Add** button to add the accounts and then use the check boxes at the bottom to select the permissions for the newly added accounts. Read is the default permission assigned when you add an account to the security tab of a computer. The **Advanced** tab enables you to manage permissions to the computer on a more granular level. This is also where you manage auditing, manage ownership, and view effective permissions.

Using the Dial-In Tab

The **Dial-in** tab, shown in Figure 4.69, controls dial-in and VPN options for the selected computer account. You will recognize this as very similar to the **Dial-in** tab on a user's account properties. This tab contains two main sections: Remote Access Permissions and Callback Options. Remote Access Permissions determine whether a computer is enabled to connect to the Routing and Remote Access Server (RRAS) for dial-in or VPN capabilities. The **Callback Options** section controls how the phone call is managed when using a dial-in solution.

Remote Access Permissions include the following:

- **Allow Access** If remote access conditions are met, setting the computer account to enable access permits connecting to the RRAS server.
- **Deny Access** Setting the computer account to deny access forbids connecting to the RRAS server.
- **Control Access through Remote Access Policy** If remote access conditions are met and there is a matching policy that enables access, setting the computer account to **Control Access through Remote Access Policy** enables connecting to the RAS server. If there is not a matching policy that enables access, connecting to the RRAS server is denied.

Figure 4.68 Understanding a Computer's Security Tab

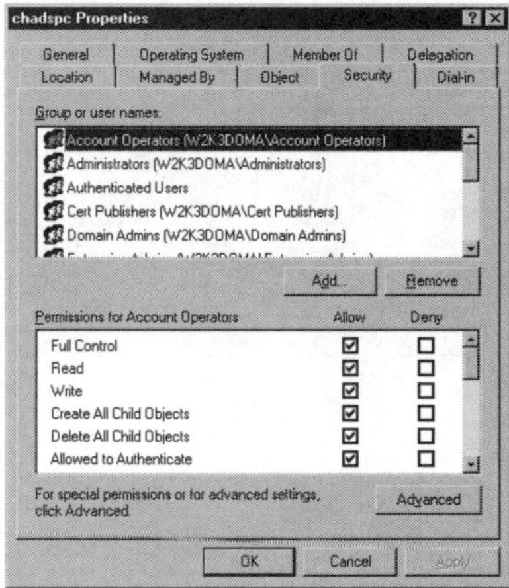

Callback Options include the following:

- **No Callback** The RRAS server does not call back the computer dialing in.
- **Set by Caller (Routing and Remote Access Service only)** The RRAS server prompts the dial-in user for a phone number. It then disconnects the user and calls back the number specified. This is a good option if you want the company to front the long-distance charges of using a dial-in solution.
- **Always Callback to** When the computer dials in to the RRAS server, it is disconnected and automatically called back at the number specified here. This is good for security purposes, because it enables you to control the location of your dial-in computers and makes it less likely that an unauthorized user who finds out a legitimate user's account name and password will be able to access the server or network.

In addition to the Remote Access Permissions and the Callback Options, the **Dial-in** tab has the following options:

- **Verify Caller-ID** If the number the computer is calling from does not match the number specified here, the connection to the RRAS server is dropped. This is different from **Always Callback to** because it only verifies the phone number; it doesn't call the user back. This is useful if you want the caller to bear the long-distance charges.
- **Assign a Static IP Address** This enables you to assign static IP addresses to your RRAS clients.
- **Apply Static Routes** This enables you to apply static routes to your RRAS clients. This is useful if you want to use routing rules to limit the machines that your clients can get to after they are connected.

Figure 4.69 Understanding a Computer's Dial-In Tab

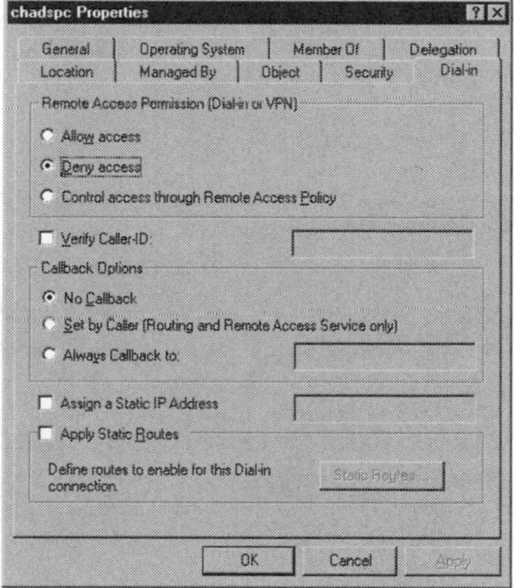

Managing Computer Accounts Via the Pop-Up Menu

Right-clicking a computer object, as shown in Figure 4.70, enables you to perform the following:

- Configure name mappings.
- Reset the computer account.
- Move the computer account.
- Delete the computer account.
- View the properties of the computer account.

Figure 4.71 shows how to configure security identity mappings for a machine account. Like with user accounts, you can map computer accounts to a Kerberos Name to be used in a trusted non-Windows Kerberos realm and to X.509 Certificates. You have three options when mapping X.509 certificates:

- Map the certificate to one account. This is known as a one-to-one mapping.
- Map any certificate with the same subject to the machine account, regardless of the issuer of the certificate. This is known as a many-to-one mapping.
- Map any certificate with the same issuer to the machine account, regardless of the subject of the certificate. This is known as a many-to-one mapping.

Figure 4.70 Using the Right-Click Pop-UP Menu

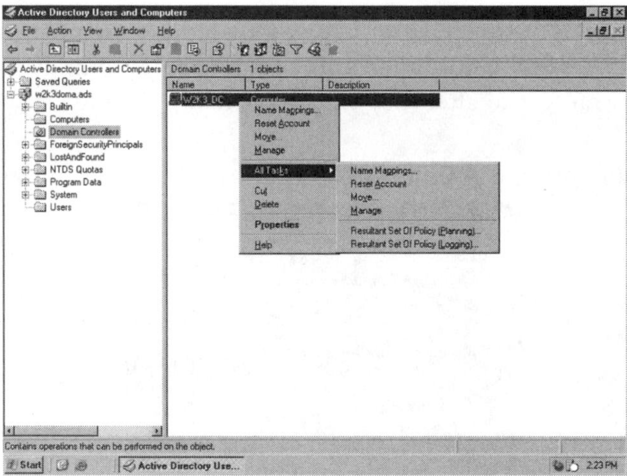

Figure 4.71 Mapping Computer Accounts to Certificates

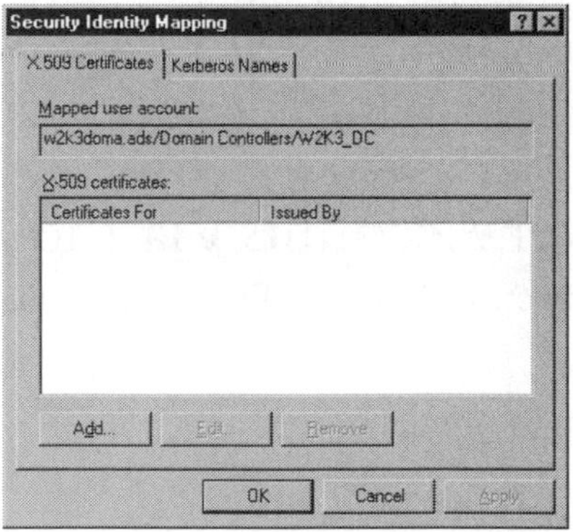

Figures 4.72 and 4.73 show how to reset computer accounts. The dialog box in Figure 4.72 asks you if you are sure that you want to reset the computer account. Clicking **No** cancels the reset. Clicking **Yes** resets the account and gives you the confirmation window shown in Figure 4.73.

Figure 4.72 Resetting Computer Accounts

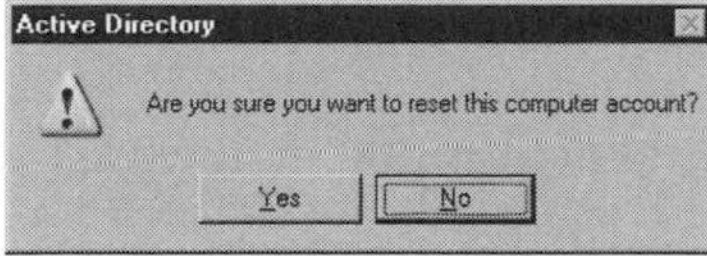

Figure 4.73 Acknowledging Reset Computer Accounts

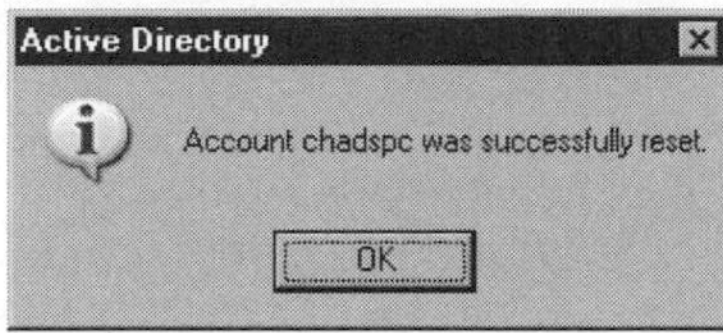

TEST DAY TIP

When you join a computer to a domain, a computername$ account is created and a password is shared between the computer and the domain. Computers use this password to authenticate with each other. This password is changed every 30 days by default. Each computer keeps a machine account password history. The history contains the current and previous passwords. When two computers try to authenticate with each other and a change to the current password is not yet received, the previous passwords are used. If the sequence of password changes exceeds two changes, you might receive an error because the two computers might not be able to communicate.

You can move computer objects by right-clicking the object and choosing **Move** from the pop-up menu, as shown in Figure 4.74. Clicking **Cancel** aborts the move. Clicking **OK** moves the computer account to the selected domain, organizational unit (OU), or container.

Figure 4.74 Moving Computer Objects

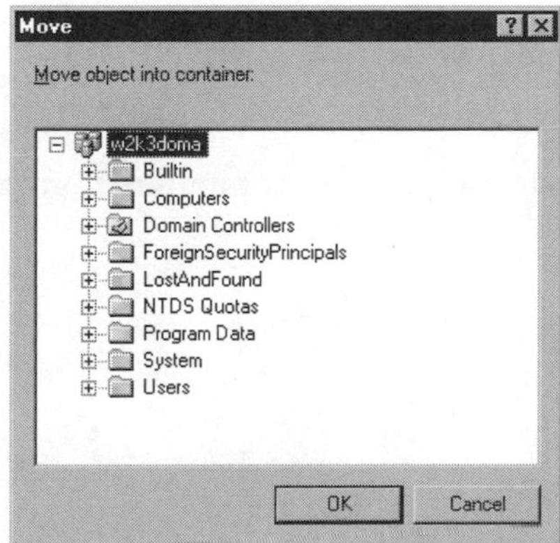

Right-clicking a computer object and clicking **Manage** opens Computer Management and connect it to the selected computer, as shown in Figure 4.75. Using Computer Management is discussed throughout this book in almost every chapter. The Computer Management MMC enables you to perform the following tasks:

- View the event logs.
- Managed shared folders.
- Use System Monitor.
- Use Device Manager.
- Manage Removable Storage.
- Defragment Disks.
- Manage Disks.
- Manage installed services and applications.

Figure 4.75 Using Computer Management

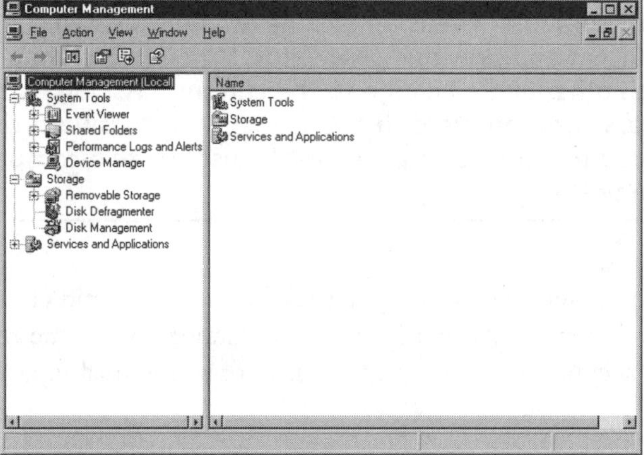

Using the Command Line to Create, Manage, and Troubleshoot Computers

Use the following tools to create and manage computers from the command line:

- dsadd.exe
- dsmod.exe
- dsquery.exe
- dsget.exe

Using dsadd computer

dsadd computer creates computer accounts in Active Directory. *dsadd computer* uses the following syntax. Table 4.16 explains all the syntax and switches for *dsadd computer* in dctail.

```
Syntax:  dsadd computer <ComputerDN> [-samid <SAMName>] [-desc
    <Description>]
         [-loc <Location>] [-memberof <Group ...>]
         [{-s <Server> | -d <Domain>}] [-u <UserName>]
         [-p {<Password> | *}] [-q] [{-uc | -uco | -uci}]
```

Table 4.16 Understanding dsadd computer Syntax

Value	Description
<ComputerDN>	Required. Specifies the DN of the computer you want to add. If the target object is omitted, it will be taken from standard input (stdin).
-samid <SAMName>	Sets the computer SAM account name to <SAMName>. If this parameter is not specified, a SAM account name is derived from the value of the common name (CN) attribute used in <ComputerDN>.
-desc <Description>	Sets the computer description to <Description>.
-loc <Location	Sets the computer location to <Location>.
memberof <Group	Makes the computer a member of one or more groups given by the space-separated list of DNs <Group ...>.
{-s <Server> | -d <Domain>}	-s <Server> connects to the domain controller (DC) with name <Server>. -d <Domain> connects to a DC in domain <Domain>. Default: a DC in the log-on domain.
-u <UserName>	Connect as <UserName>. Default: the logged-on user. Username can be: username, domain\username, or user principal name (UPN).
-p {<Password> | *}	Password for the user <UserName>. If * is entered, you are prompted for a password.
-q	Quiet mode: suppress all output to standard output.
{-uc | -uco | -uci}	-uc specifies that input from or output to pipe is formatted in Unicode. -uco specifies that output to pipe or file is formatted in Unicode. -uci specifies that input from pipe or file is formatted in Unicode.

Adding Computer Accounts

To add computer accounts to Active Directory, use the following syntax:

```
dsadd computer <ComputerDN>
```

The following command adds a computer account named chadspc:

```
dsadd computer <ComputerDN>
```

Using dsmod computer

Dsmod computer modifies attributes for computer objects in Active Directory. *dsmod computer* uses the following syntax. Table 4.17 explains all the *dsmod.exe computer* syntax in detail.

```
dsmod computer <ComputerDN ...> [-desc <Description>]
[-loc <Location>] [-disabled {yes | no}] [-reset]
[{-s <Server> | -d <Domain>}] [-u <UserName>]
[-p {<Password> | *}] [-c] [-q] [{-uc | -uco | -uci}]
```

Table 4.17 Understanding Dsmod.exe Computer Syntax

Value	Description
<ComputerDN>	Required. DNs of one or more computers to modify. If target objects are omitted, they will be taken from standard input (stdin) to support piping of output from another command to input of this command.
-desc <Description>	Sets computer description to <Description>.
-loc <Location>	Sets the location of the computer object to <Location>.
-disabled {yes | no}	Sets whether the computer account is disabled (yes) or not (no).
-reset	Resets computer account.
{-s <Server> | -d <Domain>}	-s <Server> connects to the domain controller (DC) with name <Server>. -d <Domain> connects to a DC in domain <Domain>. Default: a DC in the logon domain.
-u <UserName>	Connect as <UserName>. Default: the logged-on user. Username can be: username, domain\username, or user principal name (UPN).
-p <Password>	Password for the user <UserName>. If *, then prompt for password.
-c	Continuous operation mode. Reports errors but continues with next object in argument list when multiple target objects are specified. Without this option, the command exits on first error.

Continued

Table 4.17 Understanding Dsmod computer Syntax

Value	Description
-q	Quiet mode: suppresses all output to standard output.
{-uc | -uco | -uci}	-uc specifies that input from or output to pipe is formatted in Unicode. -uco specifies that output to pipe or file is formatted in Unicode. -uci specifies that input from pipe or file is formatted in Unicode.

Setting a Computer's Description

To set a computer's description, use the following syntax:

```
dsmod computer <ComputerDN> -desc <Description>
```

The following example sets the description for the chadspc computer account to Chad's Laptop.

```
dsmod computer chadspc -desc "Chad's Laptop"
```

Resetting a Computer's Password

To reset a computer's password, use the following syntax:

```
dsmod computer <ComputerDN> -reset
```

The following example resets the password for the chadspc computer account:

```
dsmod computer chadspc -reset
```

Disabling a Computer Account

To disable a computer's account, use the following syntax:

```
dsmod <ComputerDN> computer -disabled yes
```

The following example disables the chadspc computer account:

```
dsmod computer chadspc -disabled yes
```

Using dsquery computer

dsquery computer searches Active Directory for computers that match specified credentials. You can use *dsquery computer* to find groups and then send a list of those computers to another command. For example, you can use *dsquery computer* to query AD for all disabled computer accounts and have those results imported into *dsmod* to change the computers' description to disabled. *dsquery computer* uses the following syntax. Table 4.18 explains all the syntax in detail.

```
dsquery computer [{<StartNode> | forestroot | domainroot}]
[-o {dn | rdn | samid}] [-scope {subtree | onelevel | base}]
[-name <Name>] [-desc <Description>] [-samid <SAMName>]
[-inactive <NumWeeks>] [-stalepwd <NumDays>] [-disabled]
[{-s <Server> | -d <Domain>}] [-u <UserName>]
[-p {<Password> | *}] [-q] [-r] [-gc]
[-limit <NumObjects>] [{-uc | -uco | -uci}]
```

Table 4.18 Understanding the dsquery computer Syntax

Value	Description
{<StartNode> | forestroot | domainroot}	The node where the search starts: forest root, domain root, or a node whose DN is <StartNode>. Can be "forestroot," "domainroot," or an object DN. If "forest-root" is specified, the search is done via the global catalog. Default: domainroot.
-o {dn | rdn | samid}	Specifies the output format. Default: DN.
-scope {subtree | onelevel | base}	Specifies the scope of the search: subtree rooted at start node (subtree); immediate children of start node only (onelevel); the base object represented by start node (base). Note that subtree and domain scope are essentially the same for any start node unless the start node represents a domain root. If forestroot is specified as <StartNode>, subtree is the only valid scope. Default: subtree.
-name <Name>	Finds computers whose names match the value given by <Name>; e.g., "jon*" or "*ith" or "j*th."
-desc <Description>	Finds computers whose descriptions match the value given by <Description>; e.g., "jon*" or "*ith" or "j*th."
-samid <SAMName>	Finds computers whose SAM account names match the filter given by <SAMName>.
-inactive <NumWeeks>	Finds computers that have been inactive (stale) for at least <NumWeeks> number of weeks.
-stalepwd <NumDays>	Finds computers that have not changed their password for at least <NumDays> number of days.
-disabled	Finds computers with disabled accounts.
{-s <Server> | -d <Domain>}	-s <Server> connects to the domain controller(DC) with name <Server>. -d <Domain> connects to a DC in domain <Domain>. Default: a DC in the log-on domain.
-u <UserName>	Connect as <UserName>. Default: the logged-on user. Username can be: username, domain\username, or user principal name (UPN).

Continued

Table 4.18 Understanding the dsquery computer Syntax

Value	Description
-p <Password>	Password for the user <UserName>. If *, then prompt for password.
-q	Quiet mode: suppresses all output to standard output.
-r	Recurses or follows referrals during search. Default: do not chase referrals during search.
-gc	Searches in the Active Directory global catalog.
-limit <NumObjects>	Specifies the number of objects matching the given criteria to be returned, where <NumObjects> is the number of objects to be returned. If the value of <NumObjects> is 0, all matching objects are returned. If this parameter is not specified, by default the first 100 results are displayed.
{-uc | -uco | -uci}	-uc specifies that input from or output to pipe is formatted in Unicode. -uco specifies that output to pipe or file is formatted in Unicode. -uci specifies that input from pipe or file is formatted in Unicode.

Finding Computers Based on Their Descriptions

To use *dsquery computer* to query Active Directory for computers with a specified description, use the following syntax:

```
dsquery computer -desc <Description>
```

The following example queries Active Directory for all computers with the description "Human Resources."

```
dsquery computer -desc "Human Resources"
```

Finding Computers Based on Their Inactivity

To find computers based on inactivity, use the following syntax:

```
dsquery computer -inactive <NumWeeks>
```

The following example queries Active Directory for all computers that have been inactive for 10 weeks:

```
dsquery computer -inactive 10
```

Finding All Disabled Computer Accounts

To find all disabled computers, use the following syntax:

```
dsquery computer -disabled
```

Using dsget computer

dsget computer displays the properties of computers in Active Directory. There are two variations of this command. The first one displays properties of multiple computers. The second one displays the group membership information of a single computer. *Dsget.exe computer* uses the following syntax. Table 4.19 explains all the *dsget computer* syntax in detail.

```
dsget computer <ComputerDN ...> [-dn] [-samid] [-sid] [-desc]
[-loc] [-disabled] [{-s <Server> | -d <Domain>}] [-u <UserName>]
[-p {<Password> | *}] [-c] [-q] [-l] [{-uc | -uco | -uci}]
[-part <PartitionDN> [-qlimit] [-qused]]

dsget computer <ComputerDN> [-memberof [-expand]]
[{-s <Server> | -d <Domain>}] [-u <UserName>]
[-p {<Password> | *}] [-c] [-q] [-l] [{-uc | -uco | -uci}]
```

Table 4.19 Understanding dsget computer Syntax

Value	Description
<ComputerDN>	Required. DNs of one or more computers to view. If the target objects are omitted, they will be taken from standard input (stdin) to support piping of output from another command to input of this command.
-dn	Displays the computer DN.
-samid	Displays the computer SAM account name.
-sid	Displays the computer Security ID (SID).
-desc	Displays the computer description.
-loc	Displays the computer location.
-disabled	Displays if the computer account is disabled (yes) or not (no).
-memberof	Displays the groups of which the computer is a member.
-expand	Displays the recursively expanded list of groups of which the computer is a member. This option takes the immediate group membership list of the computer and then recursively expands each group in this list to determine its group memberships and arrive at a complete set of the groups.

Continued

Table 4.19 Understanding dsget computer Syntax

Value	Description
{-s <Server> | -d <Domain>}	-s <Server> connects to the domain controller (DC) with name <Server>. -d <Domain> connects to a DC in domain <Domain>. Default: a DC in the log-on domain.
-u <UserName>	Connects as <UserName>. Default: the logged-on user. Username can be: username, domain\username, or user principal name (UPN).
-p {<Password> | *}	Password for the user <UserName>. If *, then prompt for password.
-c	Continuous operation mode: report errors but continue with next object in argument list when multiple target objects are specified. Without this option, command exits on first error.
-q	Quiet mode: suppresses all output to standard output.
-l	Displays the entries in the search result set in a list format. Default: table format.
{-uc | -uco | -uci}	-uc specifies that input from or output to pipe is formatted in Unicode. -uco specifies that output to pipe or file is formatted in Unicode. -uci specifies that input from pipe or file is formatted in Unicode.
-part <PartitionDN>	Connects to the directory partition with the distinguished name of <PartitionDN>.
-qlimit	Displays the effective quota of the computer within the specified directory partition.
-qused	Displays how much of its quota the computer has used within the specified directory partition.

Getting a Computer's Description

To use *dsget computer* to display a computer's description, use the following syntax:

```
dsget computer <ComputerDN> -desc
```

The following example displays the description for the computer account name chadspc:

```
dsget computer chadspc -desc
```

Getting a Computer's Location

To use *dsget computer* to display a computer's location, use the following syntax:

```
dsget computer <ComputerDN> -loc
```

The following example displays the description for the computer account name chadspc:

```
dsget computer chadspc -loc
```

Getting a Computer's Group Membership

To use *dsget computer* to display a computer's group membership, use the following syntax:

```
dsget computer <ComputerDN> -memberof
```

The following example displays the description for the computer account name chadspc:

```
dsget computer chadspc -memberof
```

Creating and Managing Domain Controllers

Creating domain controllers is a necessity unless you are going to keep all your computers in a workgroup. The Active Directory (AD) Installation Wizard helps you to create domain controllers. You start the AD Installation Wizard by typing **dcpromo** in the **Run** field (on the **Start** menu). Depending on the choices made during the AD Installation Wizard (Figure 4.76), you will create one of the following four types of domain controllers (DC).

- A replica DC for an existing domain
- A DC for a new forest
- A DC for a new sub-domain
- A DC for a new tree

The following four sections describe each of these scenarios in detail. All the tools you have learned about thus far can be used with DCs in each of these categories.

Creating a New Domain Controller for an Existing Domain

Creating a new controller for an existing domain (as shown in Figure 4.77) is referred to as creating a replica DC. It is called this because the new DC holds a replica (copy) of the database held on the existing DC. You should never have a production domain with only one DC. By creating a replica DC, you eliminate having a single point of failure. One DC could fail, but your domain would still be intact.

It is also a good idea to create a replica DC for each physical site within your organization. This enables users to log on locally and reduce traffic over your WAN links. Having replica DCs is also good for disaster recovery. If one site were destroyed, you could rebuild it from an offsite DC.

Figure 4.76 Understanding the Flow of DCPromo

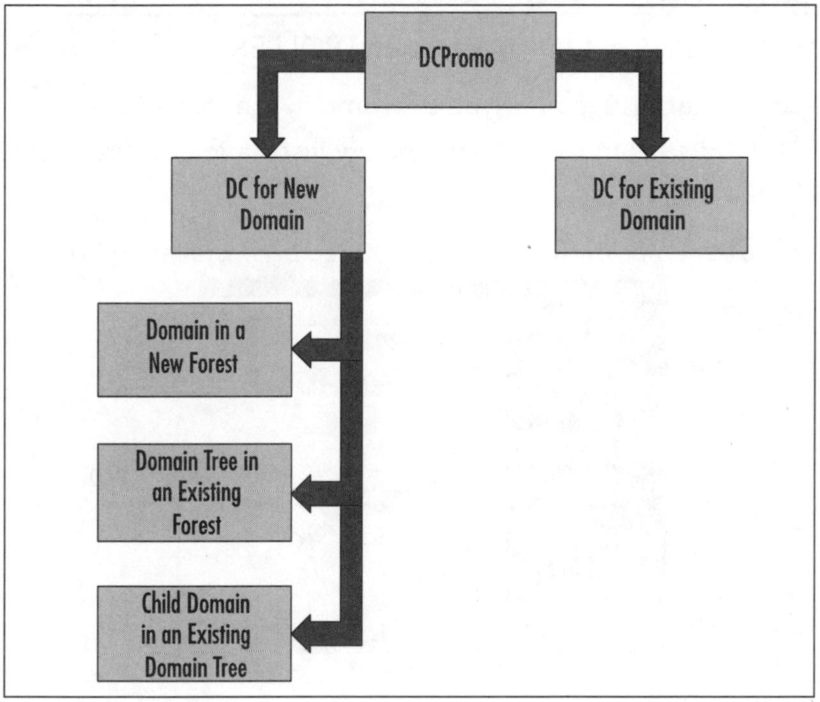

DCPromo
DC for New Domain
DC for Existing Domain
Domain in a New Forest
Domain Tree in an Existing Forest
Child Domain in an Existing Domain Tree

Exercise 4.04 walks you through creating a replica DC.

Figure 4.77 Creating a Replica DC

w2k3doma.ads
Existing Domain Controller
New Domain Controller
DCPromo

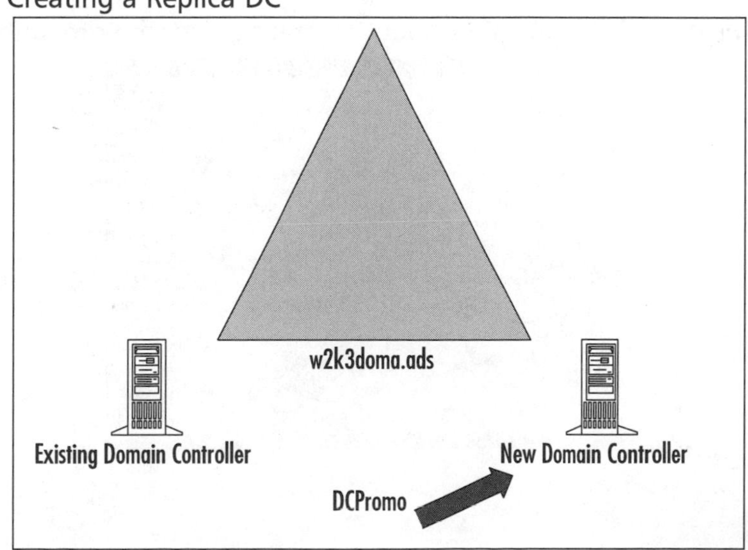

Exercise 4.04

Creating a Replica Domain Controller

1. Select **Start | Run** and type **dcpromo** in the **Open** field.
2. Click **OK** to start the Active Directory Installation Wizard, as shown in Figure 4.78.

Figure 4.78 Starting the Active Directory Installation Wizard

3. Click **Next** to continue.
4. You are warned in the dialog box shown in Figure 4.79 that Windows 95 and Windows NT 4.0 machines not running at least Service Pack 4 will not be able to logon to a domain controller running Windows Server 2003. Click **Next** to accept the warning and to continue.

Figure 4.79 Warning About Operating System Compatibility

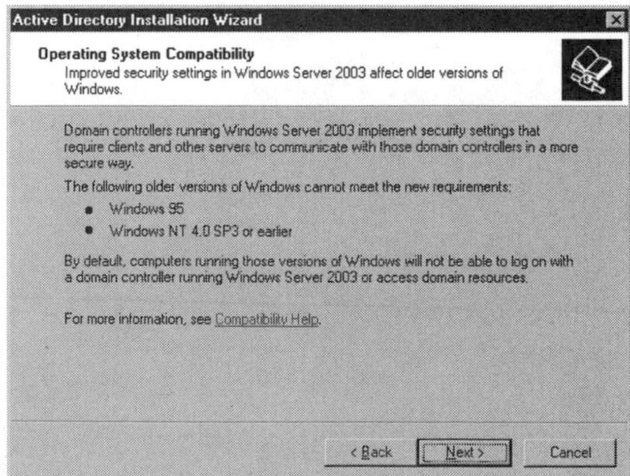

5. Select the type of domain controller to create, as shown in Figure 4.80. For this example you are creating a replica domain controller for an existing domain. Select **Additional domain controller for an existing domain** and click **Next** to continue.

Figure 4.80 Selecting Domain Controller Type

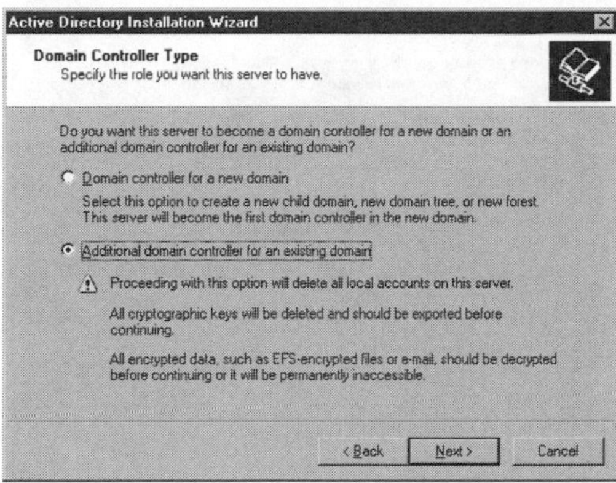

6. You are prompted (see Figure 4.81) to supply network credentials with permissions to create a replica domain controller. Enter the **User name, Password,** and **Domain,** and then click **Next** to continue.

Figure 4.81 Supplying Network Credentials

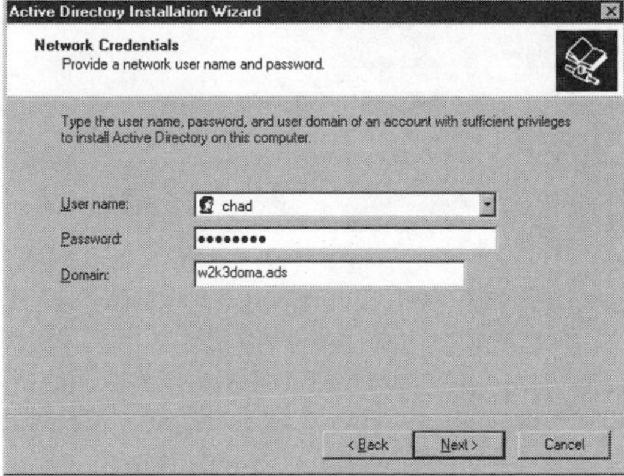

7. Tell the Active Directory Installation Wizard which domain you want to create a replica domain controller for (see Figure 4.82). Type the **fully qualified DNS domain name** and click **Next** to continue.
8. You are prompted to select a location for the Active Directory database and the Active Directory log files, as shown in Figure 4.83. Microsoft

recommends that you store the database and log files on separate physical disks. The default location for both is C:\windows\ntds. Choose a location and click **Next** to continue.

Figure 4.82 Specifying the Domain Name

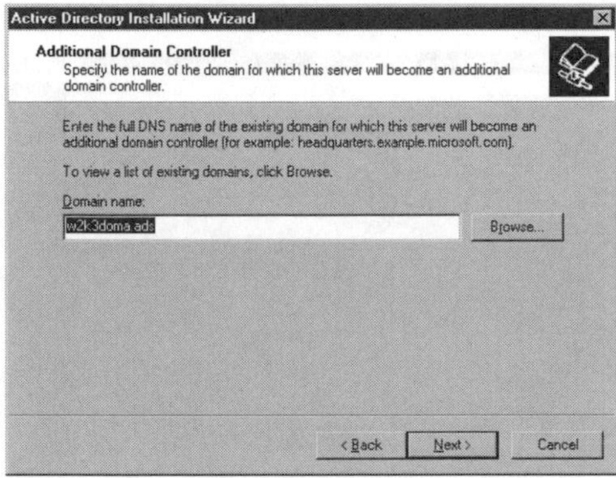

Figure 4.83 Choosing a Volume for the Database and Log Folders

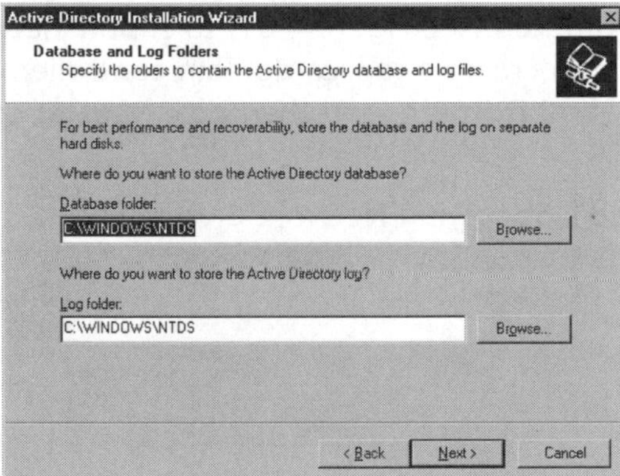

9. After choosing a location for the database and log files, choose a location for the SYSVOL folder, as shown in Figure 4.84. This volume must be formatted with the NTFS file system. The default location is C:\windows\sysvol. Select a location for SYSVOL and click **Next** to continue.
10. Figure 4.85 shows the **Directory Services Restore Mode Administrator Password** window. The password entered here is used when the domain controller must be booted into Directory Services Restore mode for Active Directory restoration and maintenance. Type the desired **Restore Mode password** and click **Next** to continue.

Figure 4.84 Selecting a Volume to Hold Sysvol

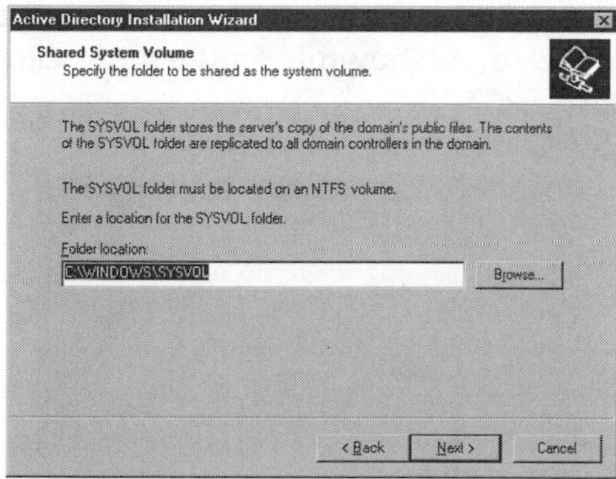

Figure 4.85 Setting a Directory Services Restore Mode Administrator Password

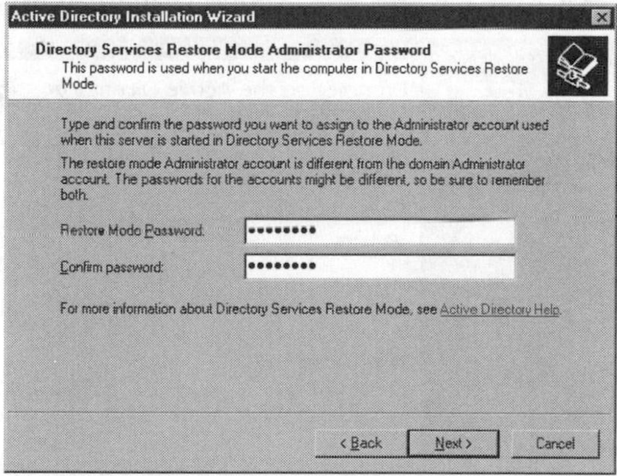

11. The Active Directory Installation Wizard displays the summary screen shown in Figure 4.86. Verify that you have made the correct selections and click **Next** to start the process of creating a replica domain controller.

Figure 4.86 Verifying Settings

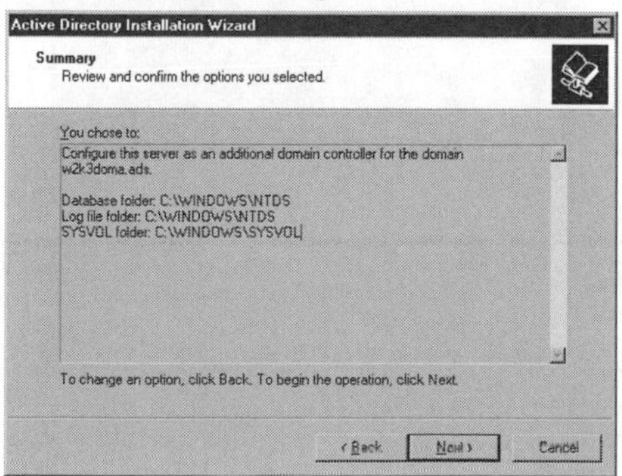

12. Figure 4.87 shows Active Directory being installed and configured. After this is complete, you are prompted to end the Active Directory Installation Wizard, as shown in Figure 4.88. Click **Finish**.

Figure 4.87 Configuring Active Directory

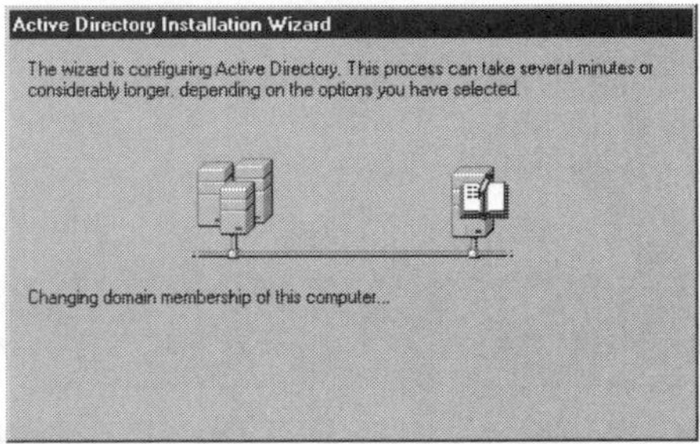

Figure 4.88 Completing the Active Directory Installation Wizard

13. You are prompted to reboot, as shown in Figure 4.89. Click **Restart Now**.

Figure 4.89 Restarting Your Computer

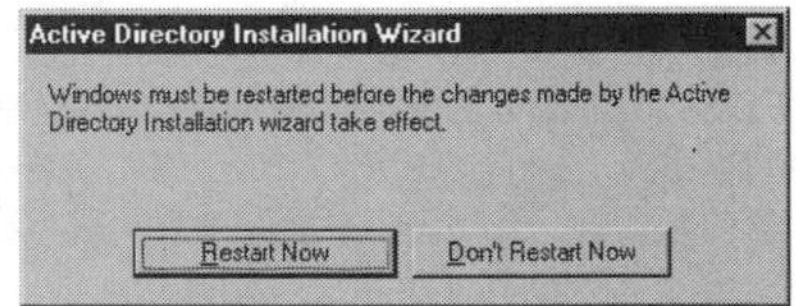

Creating a Domain Controller for a New Forest

If you have ever installed Active Directory on the first DC in a domain, you have used *dcpromo* to create a new forest, as shown in Figure 4.90. It is common for companies to have multiple forests within their organization. Usually one forest is for development or testing and the other one is for production. By creating a DC as the first DC in a new forest, you are creating a new Active Directory with a unique schema, configuration, and global catalog. Exercise 4.05 walks you through the process of creating a new forest.

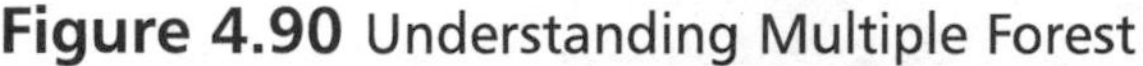

Figure 4.90 Understanding Multiple Forest

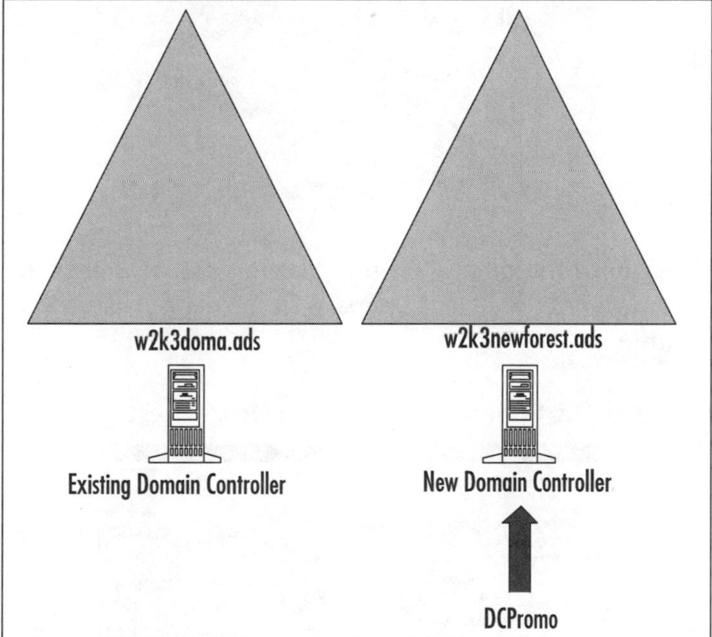

EXERCISE 4.05

CREATING A NEW FOREST

1. Select **Start | Run** and type **dcpromo** in the **Open** field.
2. Click **OK** to start the Active Directory Installation Wizard, as previously shown in Figure 4.78.
3. Click **Next** to continue.
4. You are warned (in the dialog box previously shown in Figure 4.79) that Windows 95 and Windows NT 4.0 machines not running at least Service Pack 4 will not be able to log on to a domain controller running Windows Server 2003. Click **Next** to accept the warning and continue.

5. Select the type of domain controller to create, as shown in Figure 4.91. For this example you are creating a new forest. Select **Domain controller for a new domain** and click **Next** to continue.

Figure 4.91 Selecting Domain Controller Type

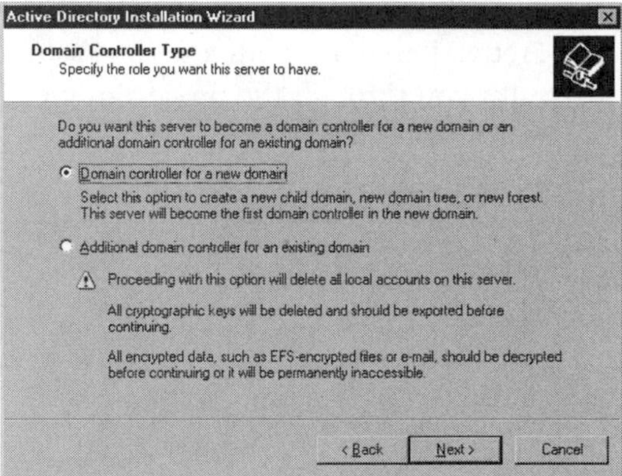

6. You are prompted, as shown in Figure 4.92, to select the type of new domain to create. Select **Domain in a new forest** and click **Next** to continue.

Figure 4.92 Choosing to Create a New Forest

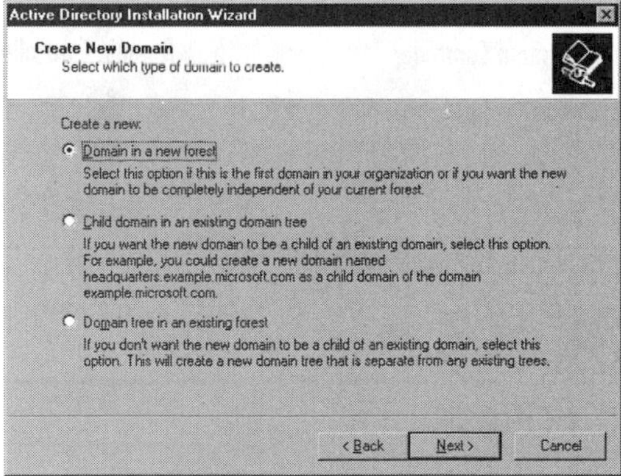

7. Tell the Active Directory Installation Wizard the name of the new domain you want to create a domain controller for, as shown in Figure 4.93. Type the **fully qualified DNS domain name** and click **Next** to continue.
8. Type the NetBIOS name of the new domain you are creating, as shown in Figure 4.94. This name is limited to 15 characters or less due to

NetBIOS restrictions. Type a compatible **NetBIOS name** and click **Next** to continue.

Figure 4.93 Specifying the New Domain Name

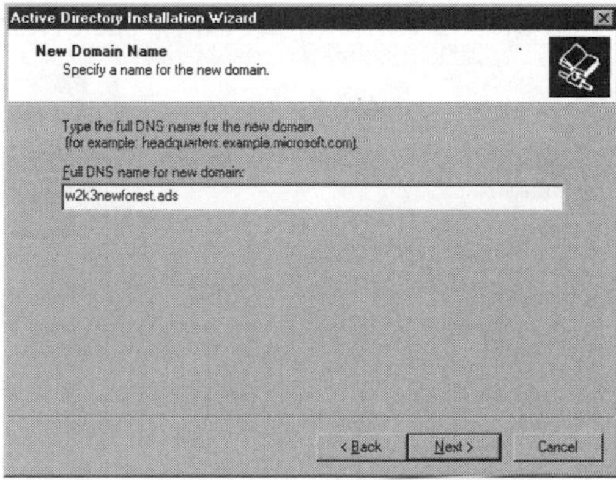

Figure 4.94 Specifying the Domain Name

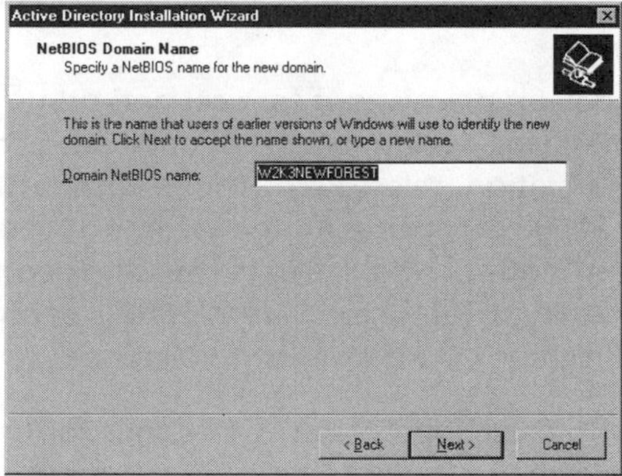

9. You are prompted to select a location for the Active Directory database and the Active Directory log files, as previously shown in Figure 4.83. Microsoft recommends that you store the database and log files on separate physical disks. The default location for both is C:\windows\ntds. Choose a location and click **Next** to continue.
10. After choosing a location for the database and log files, choose a location for the SYSVOL folder, as previously shown in Figure 4.84. This volume must be formatted with the NTFS file system. The default location is C:\windows\sysvol. Select a location for SYSVOL and click **Next** to continue.

11. The Active Directory Installation Wizard now verifies that DNS is properly configured, as shown in Figure 4.95, to support the new domain. If the test fails, you must install and configure, or have the Active Directory installation wizard install and configure, DNS for the new domain. When DNS is working properly, click **Next** to continue.

Figure 4.95 Verifying DNS Settings

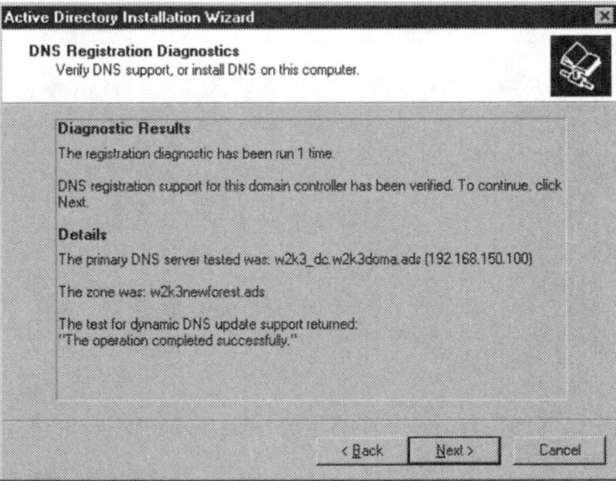

12. Select the default permissions for user and group objects, as shown in Figure 4.96. If you need to enable anonymous access for users to read domain information, select **Permissions compatible with pre-Windows 2000 server operating systems**. If you do not need to enable anonymous access, select **Permissions compatible only with Windows 2000 or Windows Server 2003 operating systems**. Choose the desired setting and click **Next** to continue.

Figure 4.96 Selecting Default Permissions for User and Group Objects

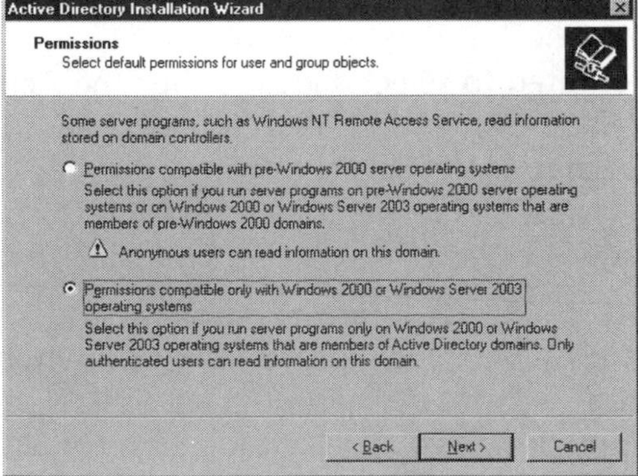

13. Figure 4.85 (previously shown) displays the **Directory Services Restore Mode Administrator Password** window. The password entered here will be used when the domain controller must be booted into Directory Services Restore mode for Active Directory restores and maintenance. Type the desired **Restore Mode password** and click **Next** to continue.
14. Figure 4.87 (previously shown) displays Active Directory being installed and configured. After this is complete you are prompted to end the Active Directory Installation Wizard (as previously shown in Figure 4.88). Click **Finish**.
15. You are prompted to reboot (as shown previously in Figure 4.89). Click **Restart Now**.

Creating a Domain Controller for a New Child Domain

Sometimes you need two domains, but you do not want a separate forest. There are a lot of benefits to having domains located in the same forest. These benefits include automatic transitive trusts between domains, a shared schema, a shared configuration, and a shared global catalog.

If you want the new domain to share its parent's namespace, as shown in Figure 4.97, you need to create the new domain as a sub-domain (child domain) of an existing domain. Exercise 4.06 walks you through creating a sub-domain.

Figure 4.97 Creating a Child Domain

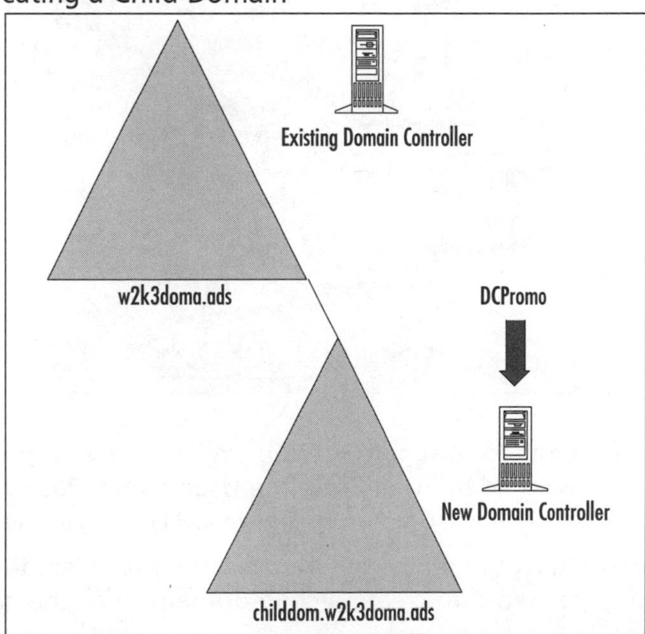

Exercise 4.06

Creating a New Child Domain

1. Select **Start | Run** and type **dcpromo** in the **Open** field.
2. Click **OK** to start the Active Directory Installation Wizard, as previously shown in Figure 4.78.
3. Click **Next** to continue.
4. You are warned (in the dialog box previously shown in Figure 4.79) that Windows 95 and Windows NT 4.0 machines not running at least Service Pack 4 will not be able to log on to a domain controller running Windows Server 2003. Click **Next** to accept the warning and continue.
5. Select the type of domain controller to create (as previously shown in Figure 4.91). For this example you are creating a new forest. Select **Domain controller for a new domain** and click **Next** to continue.
6. You are prompted, as shown in Figure 4.98, to select the type of new domain to create. Select **Child domain in an existing domain tree** and click **Next** to continue.

Figure 4.98 Choosing to Create a Child Domain in an Existing Domain Tree

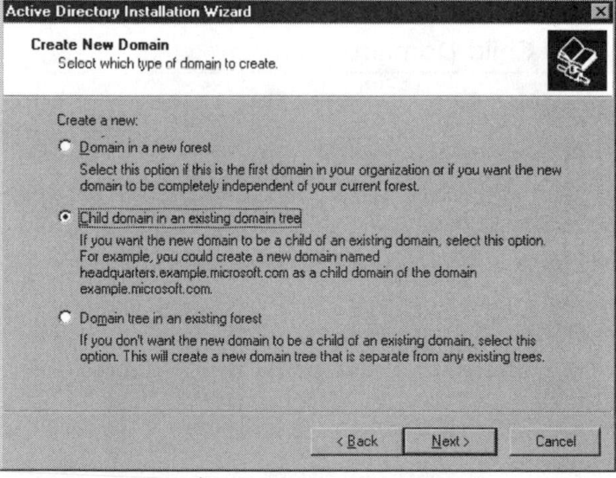

7. You are prompted to supply network credentials with permissions to create a new child domain. Enter the **User name**, **Password**, and **Domain** (as previously shown in Figure 4.81) and click **Next** to continue.
8. As shown in Figure 4.99, you are prompted to select the parent domain in which you want to create a child domain. Type the name of the

parent domain in the **Parent domain** field or click **Browse** to select it from the list of available domains.

Figure 4.99 Specifying the Domain Name

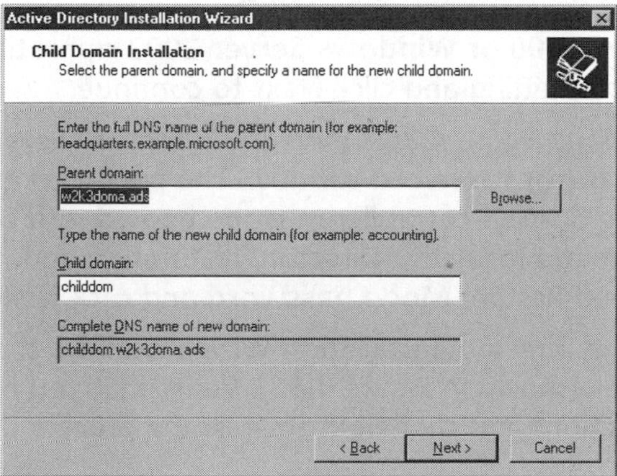

9. Type the name of the child domain in the **Child domain** field.
10. Click **Next** to continue.
11. Type the NetBIOS name of the new child domain you are creating (as previously shown in Figure 4.94). This name is limited to 15 characters or less due to NetBIOS restrictions. Type a compatible NetBIOS name and click **Next** to continue.
12. You are prompted to select a location for the Active Directory database and the Active Directory log files (as previously shown in Figure 4.83). Microsoft recommends that you store the database and log files on separate physical disks. The default location for both is c:\windows\ntds. Choose a location and click **Next** to continue.
13. After choosing a location for the database and log files, choose a location for the SYSVOL folder (as previously shown in Figure 4.84). This volume must be formatted with the NTFS file system. The default location is c:\windows\sysvol. Select a location for SYSVOL and click **Next** to continue.
14. The Active Directory Installation Wizard verifies that DNS is properly configured (as previously shown in Figure 4.95) to support the new child domain. If the test fails, you must install and configure, or have the Active Directory installation wizard install and configure, DNS for the new child domain. After DNS is working properly, click **Next** to continue.

15. Select the default permissions for user and group objects (as previously shown in Figure 4.96). If you need to enable anonymous access for users to read domain information, select **Permissions compatible with pre-Windows 2000 server operating systems**. If you do not need to enable anonymous access, select **Permissions compatible only with Windows 2000 or Windows Server 2003 operating systems**. Choose the desired setting and click **Next** to continue.
16. The previous Figure 4.85 shows the **Directory Services Restore Mode Administrator Password** window. The password entered here is used when the domain controller must be booted into Directory Services Restore mode for Active Directory restoration and maintenance. Type the desired Restore **Mode password** and click **Next** to continue.
17. The Active Directory Installation Wizard displays the summary screen (previously shown in Figure 4.86). Verify that you have made the correct selections and click **Next** to start the process of creating a child domain.
18. The previous Figure 4.87 shows Active Directory being installed and configured. After this is complete, you are prompted to end the Active Directory Installation Wizard (as previously shown in Figure 4.88). Click **Finish**.
19. You are prompted to reboot (as previously shown in Figure 4.89). Click **Restart Now**.

Creating a Domain Controller for a New Domain Tree

As mentioned previously, sometimes you need two domains, but you do not want a separate forest. If you do not want the new domain to share its parent's namespace, as shown in Figure 4.100, you need to create the new domain as a new tree (domain tree) within an existing forest. This method gives you the benefits of a single forest (automatic transitive trusts between domains, a shared schema, a shared configuration, and a shared global catalog, etc.) without having to maintain a contiguous name space for your domains. Exercise 4.07 walks you through the process of creating a new tree.

Figure 4.100 Creating a New Tree

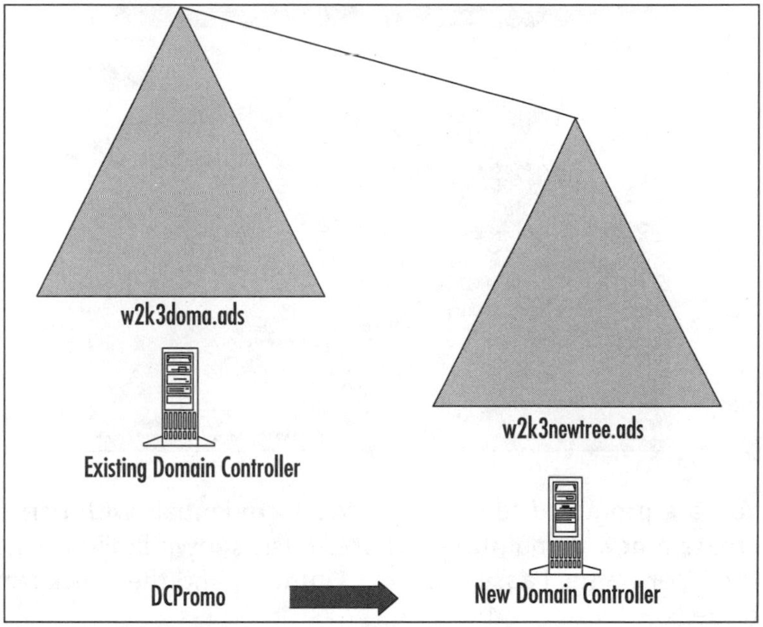

Exercise 4.07

Creating a New Tree

1. Select **Start | Run** and type **dcpromo** in the **Open** field.
2. Click **OK** to start the Active Directory Installation Wizard, as shown previously in Figure 4.78.
3. Click **Next** to continue.
4. You are warned (in the dialog box shown previously in Figure 4.79) that Windows 95 and Windows NT 4.0 machines not running at least Service Pack 4 will not be able to log on to a domain controller running Windows Server 2003. Click **Next** to accept the warning and continue.
5. Select the type of domain controller to create, as shown previously in Figure 4.91. For this example you are creating a new forest. Select **Domain controller for a new domain** and click **Next** to continue.
6. You are prompted, as shown in Figure 4.101, to select the type of new domain to create. Select **Domain tree in an existing forest** and click **Next** to continue.

Figure 4.101 Selecting to Create a New Forest

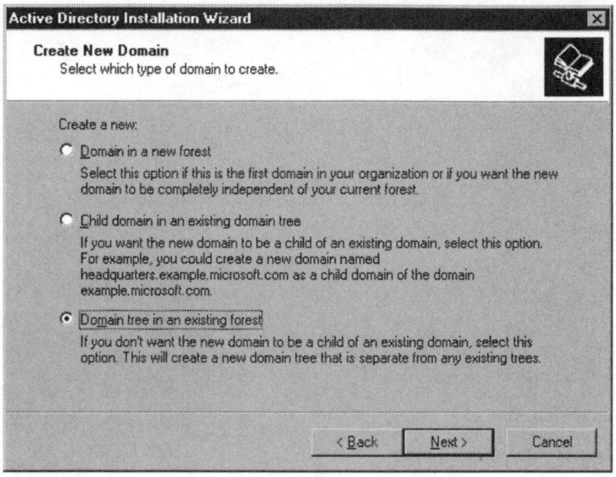

Active Directory Installation Wizard

Create New Domain
Select which type of domain to create.

Create a new:

( ) Domain in a new forest
Select this option if this is the first domain in your organization or if you want the new domain to be completely independent of your current forest.

( ) Child domain in an existing domain tree
If you want the new domain to be a child of an existing domain, select this option. For example, you could create a new domain named headquarters.example.microsoft.com as a child domain of the domain example.microsoft.com.

(•) Domain tree in an existing forest
If you don't want the new domain to be a child of an existing domain, select this option. This will create a new domain tree that is separate from any existing trees.

< Back | Next > | Cancel

7. You are prompted to supply network credentials with permissions to create a new domain tree (as previously shown in Figure 4.81). Enter the **User name**, **Password**, and **Domain**, and then click **Next** to continue.
8. Tell the Active Directory Installation Wizard the domain name for the new domain tree that you want to create (see Figure 4.102). Type **the fully qualified DNS domain name** and click **Next** to continue.

Figure 4.102 Naming a Domain Tree Name

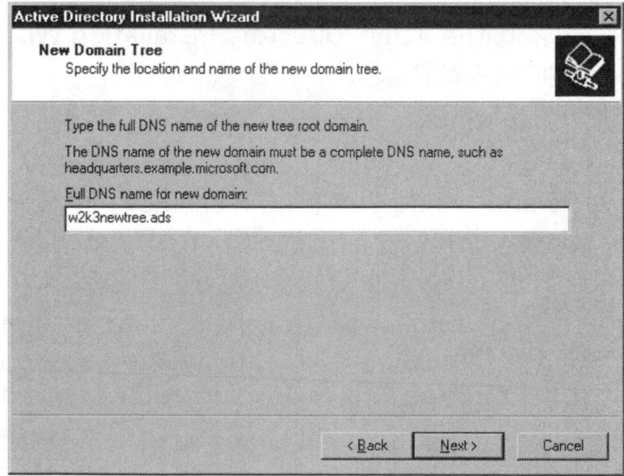

9. Type the NetBIOS name of the new domain you are creating (as shown previously in Figure 4.94). This name is limited to 15 characters or less due to NetBIOS restrictions. Type a **compatible name** and click **Next** to continue.

10. You are prompted to select **a location for the Active Directory database and the Active Directory log files** (as shown previously in Figure 4.83). Microsoft recommends that you store the database and log files on separate physical disks. The default location for both is C:\windows\ntds. Choose a location and click **Next** to continue.
11. After choosing a location for the database and log files, choose a location for the SYSVOL folder (as shown previously in Figure 4.84). This volume must be formatted with the NTFS file system. The default location is C:\windows\sysvol. Select a location for SYSVOL and click **Next** to continue.
12. The Active Directory Installation Wizard verifies that DNS is properly configured to support the new domain (as previously shown in Figure 4.95). If the test fails, you must install and configure, or have the Active Directory installation wizard install and configure, DNS for the new domain. When DNS is working properly, click **Next** to continue.
13. Select the default permissions for user and group objects (as previously shown in Figure 4.96). If you need to enable anonymous access for users to read domain information, select **Permissions compatible with pre-Windows 2000 server operating systems**. If you do not need to enable anonymous access, select **Permissions compatible only with Windows 2000 or Windows Server 2003 operating systems**. Choose the desired setting and click **Next** to continue.
14. The previous Figure 4.85 shows the Directory Services Restore Mode Administrator Password window. The password entered here is used when the domain controller must be booted into Directory Services Restore mode for Active Directory restores and maintenance. Type the desired **Restore Mode password** and click **Next** to continue.
15. The Active Directory Installation Wizard displays the summary screen previously shown in Figure 4.86. Verify that you have made the correct selections and click **Next** to start the process of creating a new domain tree.
16. The previous Figure 4.87 shows Active Directory being installed and configured. After this is complete, you are prompted to end the Active Directory Installation Wizard (as shown previously in Figure 4.88). Click **Finish**.
17. You are prompted to reboot (as shown previously in Figure 4.89). Click **Restart Now**.

Assigning Domain Controller Operations Master Roles

Active Directory uses a multimaster replication model. The benefit of a multimaster replication model is that it helps eliminate a single point of failure by enabling each domain controller to write to the database. However, a multimaster model doesn't work well for all situations.

Special roles are assigned to domain controllers to handle changes that don't work well in a multimaster replication model. These roles are called *operations master* roles. There are two operations master roles that are forest-wide and three that are domain-wide. Forest-wide roles are assigned to only one DC in the forest. Domain-wide roles are assigned to one DC in each domain in the forest.

The forest-wide roles are as follows:

- **Schema Master** Controls additions and changes to the schema.
- **Domain Naming Master** Controls the addition or removal of domains in the forest.

The domain-wide roles are as follows:

- **RID Master** Allocates relative IDs (RIDs) to each domain controller in a domain.
- **PDC Emulator** Acts as a Windows NT primary domain controller for down-level clients.
- **Infrastructure Master** Updates group-to-user references whenever the members of groups are changed or renamed.

Exercises 4.08 through 4.10 walk you through transferring operations master roles.

Exam Warning

The operations master roles are also referred to as flexible single master operations (FSMO) roles (pronounced Fiz-Moe). On the test, it is likely that you will see them referred to as operations masters or operations master roles.

Test Day Tip

When a domain controller creates users, groups, or computers, it assigns a unique security ID (SID) to each object. This SID is the method by which the domain controller identifies domain objects. The SID consists of a domain SID and a RID. The domain SID is the same for all SIDs created in the domain. The RID is unique for each SID created in the domain.

Exercise 4.08

Using Active Directory Users and Computers to Transfer Operations Master Roles

You can use ADUC to manage the RID Master, PDC Emulator, and Infrastructure Master operations master roles. This exercise walks you through the process of transferring these roles from one domain controller to another.

1. Open Active Directory Users and Computers (**Start | All Programs | Administrative Tools | Active Directory Users and Computers**). To transfer the selected role to another machine, open Active Directory Users and Computers on the machine you want transfer the role to.
2. Right-click the domain and choose **Operations Masters** from the pop-up menu, as shown in Figure 4.103.

Figure 4.103 Viewing Operations Master Roles

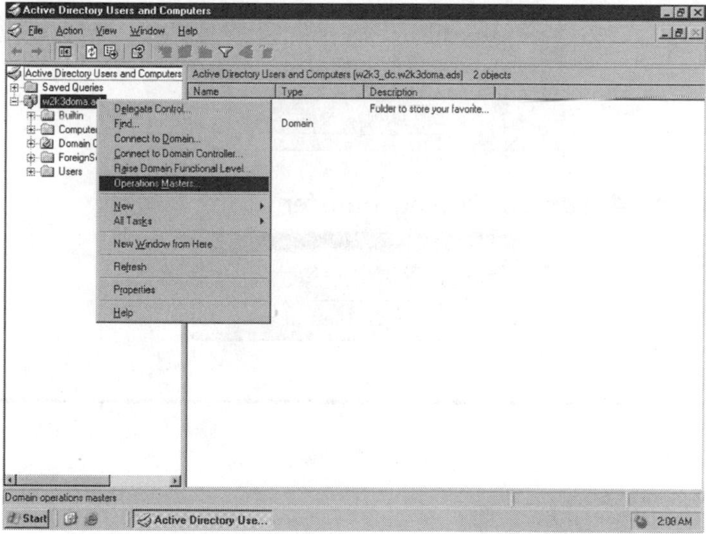

3. The **Operations Masters** window appears, as shown in Figure 4.104. Use the tabs to pick the operations master that you want to manage. Your choices are RID Master, PDC Emulator, and Infrastructure Master. Click **Change** to start the transfer process.
4. You are prompted to verify that you want to transfer the roles, as shown in Figure 4.105. Click **Yes** to transfer the selected role.
5. A confirmation window appears, as shown in Figure 4.106. Click **OK** to close the window.

Figure 4.104 Viewing the RID Master

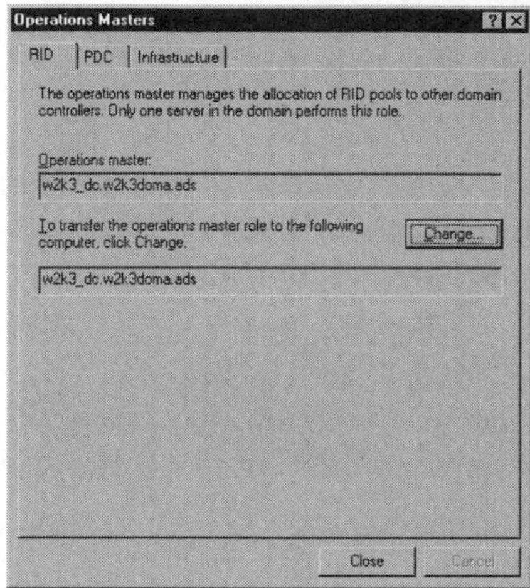

Figure 4.105 Verifying Transfer

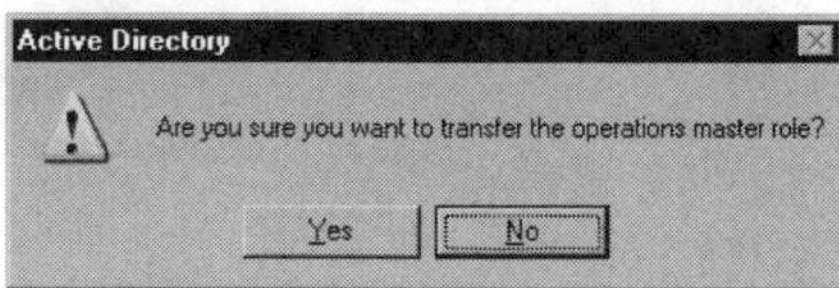

Figure 4.106 Confirming Transfer

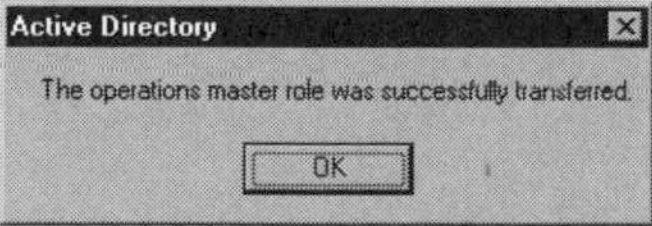

EXERCISE 4.09

USING ACTIVE DIRECTORY DOMAINS AND TRUSTS TO TRANSFER OPERATIONS MASTER ROLES

You can use Active Directory Domains and Trusts to manage the Domain Naming Master operations master role. This exercise walks you through the process of transferring this role from one domain controller to another.

1. Open Active Directory Domains and Trusts (**Start | All Programs | Administrative Tools | Active Directory Domains and Trusts**). To transfer the selected role to another machine, open Active Directory Users and Computers on the machine you want to transfer the role to.

2. Right-click the **domain** and choose **Operations Masters** from the pop-up menu, as shown in Figure 4.107.

Figure 4.107 Viewing Operations Master Roles

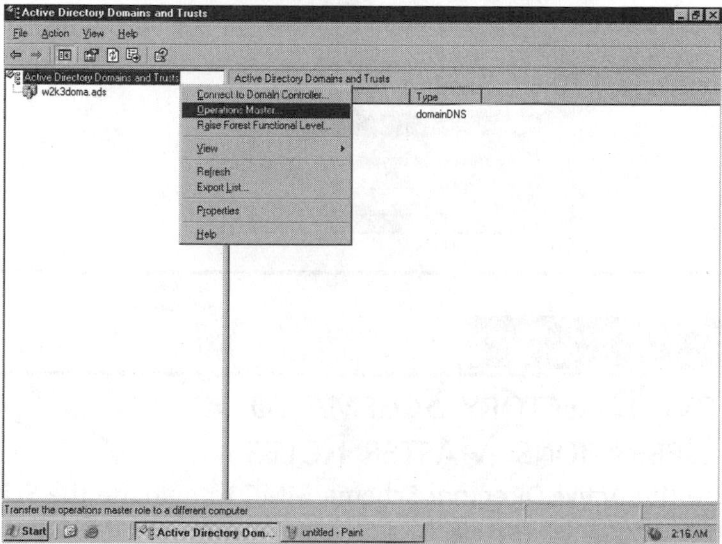

3. Next, you see the window shown in Figure 4.108. Click **Change** to start the transfer process.

Figure 4.108 Viewing the Domain Naming Master

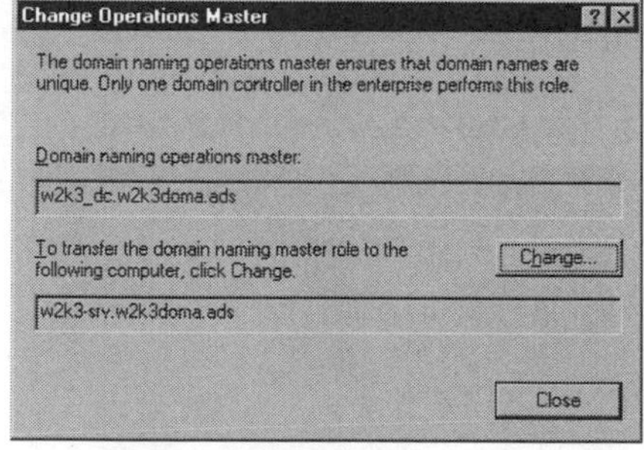

4. You are prompted to verify that you want to transfer the roles, as shown in Figure 4.109. Click **Yes** to transfer the selected role.
5. You are given the confirmation window shown in Figure 4.110. Click **OK** to close the window.

Figure 4.109 Verifying Transfer

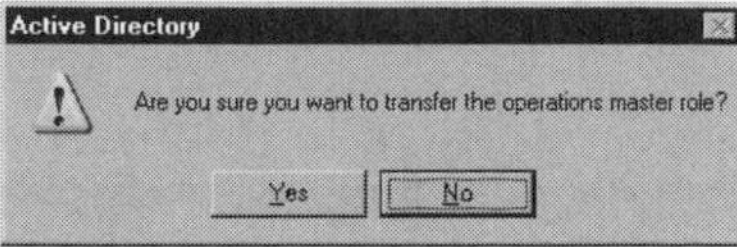

Figure 4.110 Confirming Transfer

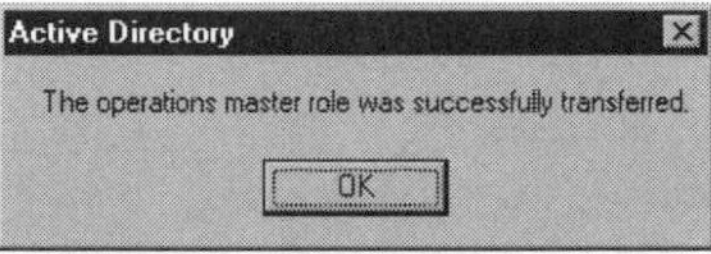

Exercise 4.10

Using Active Directory Schema to Transfer Operations Master Roles

You can use the Active Directory Schema MMC to manage the Schema Master operations master role. This exercise walks you through the process of transferring this role from one domain controller to another.

1. Transferring the Schema Master is similar to transferring the other operations master roles, except that the tool used to do so is hidden by default. To enable it you must register a dll file. Type the following in the **Run** dialog box (**Start | Run**), as shown in Figure 4.111: **regsvr32 schmmgmt.dll**.

Figure 4.111 Registering Schmmgmt.dll

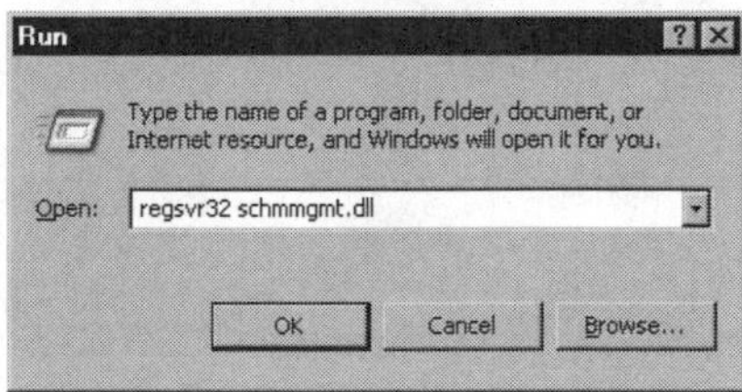

2. Click **OK** to register the DLL. A confirmation window appears, as shown in Figure 4.112.
3. Click **OK**.

Figure 4.112 Confirming DLL Registration

4. Now that you have registered the dll file, create a custom Microsoft Management Console (MMC) to transfer the Schema Master operations master role. Open a blank MMC by typing **MMC** in the **Run** dialog box and clicking **OK**. This gives you the window shown in Figure 4.113.

Figure 4.113 Adding Snap-Ins

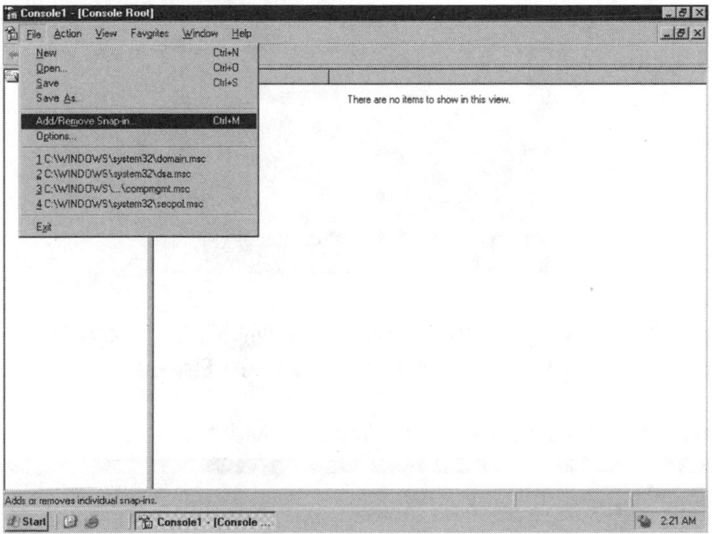

5. Select **File | Add/Remove Snap-in** from the menu bar. The screen shown in Figure 4.114 appears.

Figure 4.114 Selecting the Active Directory Schema Snap-In

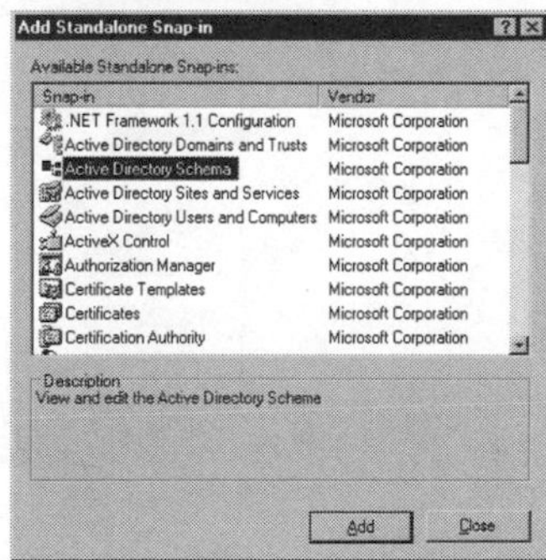

6. Select Active Directory Schema from the list of available snap-ins and click **Add** to continue.
7. Click **Close**. The window shown in Figure 4.115 appears.

Figure 4.115 Saving Snap-Ins to the MMC

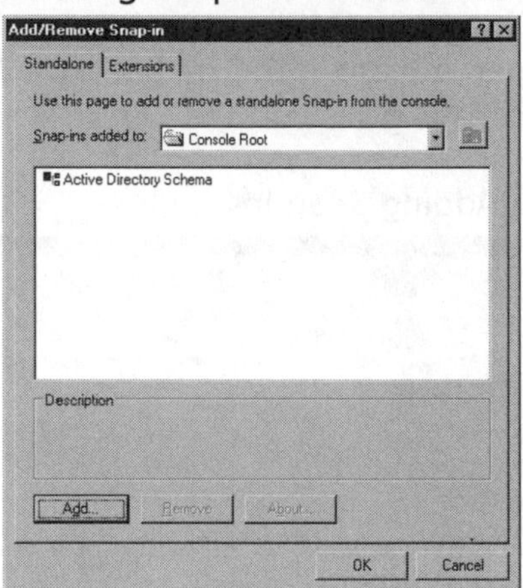

8. Click **OK**. This takes you back to the MMC, but now the Active Directory Schema snap-in is available, as shown in Figure 4.116.

Figure 4.116 Viewing the Schema Master

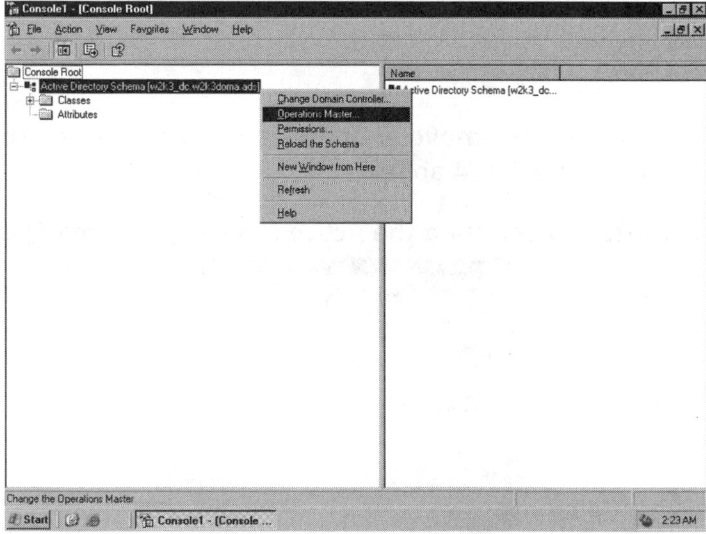

9. Right-click the **Active Directory Schema** and choose **Operations Master** from the pop-up menu. The window shown in Figure 4.117 appears.
10. Click **Change** to transfer the Schema Master role. To transfer the selected role to another machine, open ADUC on the machine to which you want transfer the role.

Figure 4.117 Transferring the Schema Master

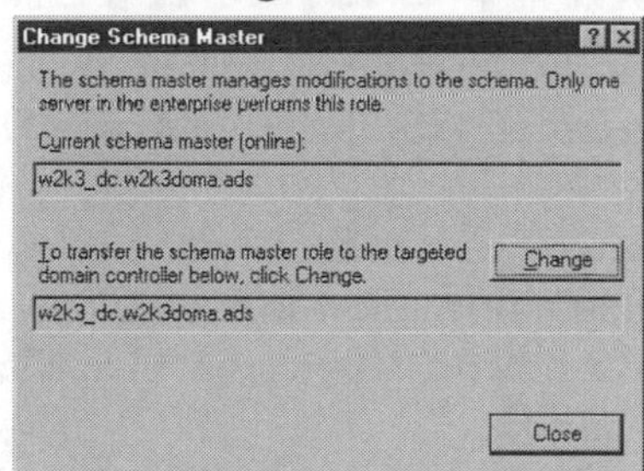

11. A verification window appears, as shown in Figure 4.118. Click **Yes** to perform the transfer.

Figure 4.118 Verifying Transfer

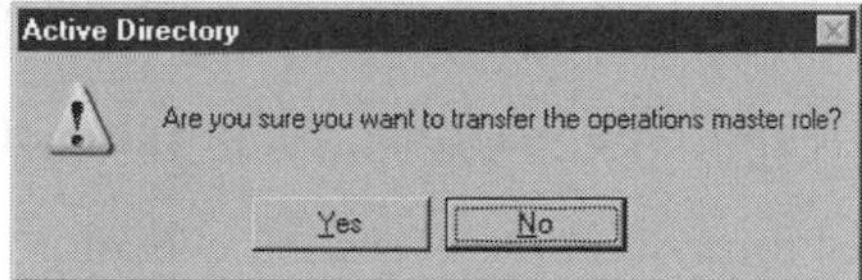

12. After the transfer is complete, a confirmation window appears, as shown in Figure 4.119. Click **OK** to close the window.

Figure 4.119 Confirming Transfer

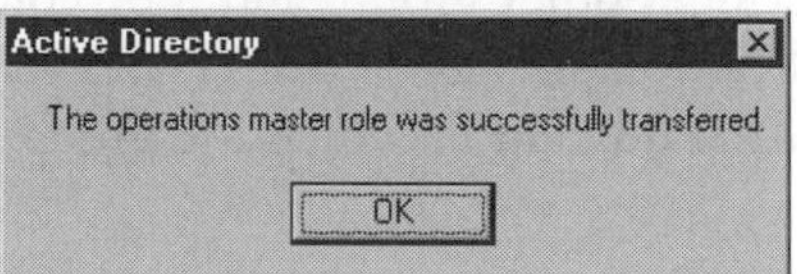

Troubleshooting Computer Accounts

Computer accounts do not typically have as many problems as user accounts. The most common problems for computer accounts occur when the computer account is not applying the correct group policy and the computer account domain password gets out of synch. Machines apply group policy based on the Organization Unit (OU), site and the domain that they are in. If your machine is not getting the correct policy because it is in the wrong OU you can use Active Directory Users and Computers to move the machine to the correct OU by right clicking the machine account and choosing Move from the pop-up menu. If the computer's password gets out of synch you can right click on it in Active Directory Users and Computers and choose Reset from the pop-up menu or use the dsmod.exe command.

Summary of Exam Objectives

This chapter talks about creating and managing security objects such as user, group, and machine accounts. Security objects refer to objects in Active Directory that can be assigned permissions to other objects.

Active Directory is the directory service for Windows Server 2003 (and Windows 2000). It provides a way of storing information so it can easily be retrieved and used later. It functions as a central repository for security objects, which allows for centralized authentication and centralized administration.

User accounts represent people and are used by people to log on to Windows machines. User accounts can also be used as application service accounts. User accounts provide authentication, authorization, and auditing.

Groups are objects that contain other objects such as users, other groups, and machines. Groups simplify management of user accounts by enabling you to apply permissions and user rights to an entire group of users at once instead of having to apply them to individual user accounts.

There are two types of groups (type identifies the purpose of the group):

- **Distribution** Used for e-mail purposes. An e-mail is sent to the group and all members get a copy.
- **Security** Used for assigning permissions to resources.

There are three scopes of groups (scope refers to how the group is used):

- **Domain Local** Includes other groups and user/computer accounts from Windows Server 2003, Windows 2000 Server, and Windows NT domains. Permissions for only the domain in which the group is defined can be assigned to domain local groups.
- **Global** Includes other groups and user/computer accounts from only the domain in which the group is defined. Permissions for any domain in the forest can be assigned to global groups.
- **Universal** Includes other groups and user/computer accounts from any domain in the domain tree or forest. Permissions for any domain in the domain tree or forest can be assigned to universal groups. Universal groups are only available if your domain functional level is set to Windows 2000 native mode.

Computer accounts serve the same purpose for machines as user accounts do for people. They determine the domain rights and permissions assigned to a machine. All Windows NT 4.0, 2000, and 2003 machines have computer accounts in the domain. Computers running Windows 3.*x*, Windows 9*x*, Windows ME, and Windows XP Home Edition do not have computer accounts and cannot be domain members.

Windows Server 2003 provides graphical tools and command-line tools for managing Active Directory objects. Most people new to managing domain accounts prefer the GUI-based tool Active Directory Users and Computers (ADUC) because it is easier to use. However, the command prompt is usually better when you need to make changes in bulk, because it supports scripting. Windows Server 2003 provides the following command-line tools.

- **dsadd.exe** Adds objects to Active Directory.
- **dsget.exe** Displays attributes for Active Directory objects.
- **dsmove.exe** Moves Active Directory objects from one location to another.
- **dsquery.exe** Queries Active Directory for objects that match the specified criteria.
- **gpresult.exe** Displays the effective policy applied to a machine or user.
- **whoami.exe** Displays information about the currently logged-on user.
- **cmdkey.exe** Manages stored username and password credentials.

Active Directory consists of (among other things) forest, trees, and domains. dcpromo.exe creates domain controllers for each of these. With dcpromo.exe you can choose to create domain controllers for an existing domain or a new domain. The new domain could be in an existing tree or forest or it could be in a new tree or forest.

Because Active Directory uses a multimaster replication model (meaning all DCs can write to the directory), Microsoft created the operations master roles to overcome the problems inherent with multimaster environments. Two of the roles are unique to the forest and three of the roles are unique to each domain.

The forest-wide roles are as follows:

- **Schema Master** Controls additions and changes to the schema.
- **Domain Naming Master** Controls the addition or removal of domains in the forest.

The domain-wide roles are as follows:

- **RID Master** Allocates relative IDs (RIDs) to each domain controller in a domain.
- **PDC Emulator** Acts as a Windows NT primary domain controller for down-level clients.
- **Infrastructure Master** Updates group-to-user references whenever the members of groups are changed or renamed.

Exam Objectives Fast Track

Understanding Security Objects

☑ User accounts are required for users to access resources in a Windows Server 2003 environment.

☑ Groups enable the assigning of permissions and rights. By assigning permissions to a group, all group members inherit the same permissions.

☑ Machine accounts provide authentication and auditing for machines used in a domain.

Using Management Tools

☑ Active Directory Users and Computers is a graphical tool used to create and manage Active Directory objects such as users, groups, and machines.

☑ *dsadd.exe* can add computers, contacts, groups, OUs, users, and quotas.

☑ *dsget.exe* shows the properties of objects in Active Directory. It works with computers, contacts, subnets, groups, OUs, servers, sites, users, quotas, and partitions.

☑ *dsmove.exe* moves objects within Active Directory.

☑ *dsquery.exe* enables you to query all Active Directory objects for a set of objects that match a specified criterion.

☑ *gpresult.exe* displays Resultant Set of Policy (RSoP). RSoP shows the effective policy for a particular user and a specified machine.

☑ *whoami.exe* displays the username and group membership information about the currently logged-on user.

☑ *cmdkey.exe* enables you to configure and manage stored usernames and passwords from the command line.

Creating and Managing User Accounts

☑ You can create user accounts from within the GUI using ADUC.

☑ You can create user accounts from the command line using the *dsadd* command.

☑ You can use *ldifde* and *csvde* files to import and export users from Active Directory.

☑ You can use dsmode to manage user account properties from the command prompt.

- ☑ You can manage a user in ADUC by going to the properties of the user or by right-clicking the user and using the pop-up menu options.

Creating and Managing Group Accounts

- ☑ You can create group accounts from within the GUI using ADUC.
- ☑ You can create group accounts from the command line using the *dsadd.exe* command.
- ☑ You can use *ldifde* and *csvde* files to import and export groups from Active Directory.
- ☑ You can use dsmod.exe to manage group properties from the command prompt.
- ☑ You can manage groups in ADUC by going to the properties of the group or by right-clicking the group and using the pop-up menu options.

Creating and Managing Computer Accounts

- ☑ You can create computer accounts from within the GUI using ADUC.
- ☑ You can create computer accounts from the command line using the *dsadd* command.
- ☑ You can use *ldifde* and *csvde* files to import and export computers from Active Directory.
- ☑ You can use dsmode.exe to manage computer account properties from the command prompt.
- ☑ You can manage computer accounts in ADUC by going to the properties of the computer account right-clicking the computer object and using the pop-up menu options.

Exam Objectives Frequently Asked Questions

The following Frequently Asked Questions, answered by the authors of this book, are designed to both measure your understanding of the Exam Objectives presented in this chapter, and to assist you with real-life implementation of these concepts. You will also gain access to thousands of other FAQs at ITFAQnet.com.

Q: If I don't have Active Directory Users and Computers (ADUC) on my machine, where can I get it?

A: ADUC is automatically installed on domain controllers. For other machines, you need to install the adminpak.msi from the Windows Server 2003 CD (under the i386 folder). You can install the administrative tools pack on client computers (such as Windows XP Pro) so that you can manage your domain remotely from the client.

Q: I understand that user accounts are needed to log on to a Windows Server 2003 environment. I also understand that computer accounts are used to enable machines to authenticate to and be audited by Active Directory. However, I don't understand what groups are used for?

A: Groups are used for assigning permissions and organizing users for e-mails. Using groups enables you to assign permissions once to a group and have all of the permissions automatically applied to all group members.

Q: Can I use a Windows Server 2003 machine if I do not have a user account?

A: No. You must have a user account to log on to a Windows Server 2003 machine. This can be a unique account for you or it can be a shared account such as the Guest account.

Q: My corporate policy mandates that everyone use the same screen saver. However, I have a user who is using a different screen saver. I think this user is not receiving the correct policy. Which tools can I use to view a user's effective group policy?

A: ADUC and gpresult.exe.

Q: Which tools can I use to create new Active Directory objects?

A: ADUC and dsadd.exe.

Q: Which tools can I use to move objects in Active Directory?

A: ADUC and dsmove.exe.

Q: I need to reset a user's password. I want to use the GUI to reset it. How do I reset a user's password with the GUI?

A: Open ADUC. Right-click the user account and choose **Reset Password**. Type the new password twice and click **OK**.

Q: If I don't want to use ADUC to reset user's passwords, what other choices do I have?

A: You can use third-party tools such as Hyena or Dameware. You can also use the built-in command-line tool *dsmod*. Here is an example of using *dsmod* to reset a user's password:

```
dsmod user "CN=Chad Todd,CN=Users,DC=trainingconcepts,DC=org" -pwd * -
    mustchpwd yes
```

Q: I have recently taken over the responsibility for setting up new users in my company. I have never worked with domains before. What options do I have for creating users?

A: You can use ADUC to create users with the GUI or dsadd to create users from the command line. To use the GUI, open ADUC. Right-click the domain or OU that you want to create the user in. Choose **New | User** from the pop-up menu. Fill in the required information in the new user wizard and click **Finish**. Here is an example of using *dsadd* to create a user account:

```
dsadd user "CN=Chad Todd,CN=Users,DC=trainingconcepts,DC=org" -UPN
    chad@trainingconcepts.org -samid chadtodd -pwd *
```

Q: Which one of the graphical Active Directory tools do I use to create groups?

A: ADUC is used to create groups. Open ADUC. Right-click the domain or OU that you want to create the group in. Choose **New | Group** from the pop-up menu. Fill in the required information in the new group wizard and click **Finish**.

Q: Can I create groups from the command line?

A: Yes. Use the *dsadd* command. Here is an example of using dsadd.exe to create a universal group:

Use *dsadd group* to create a new universal group with the following syntax:

```
dsadd group "CN=Microsoft Trainers,DC=trainingconcepts,DC=org"
    -secgrp yes -scope u -samid MicrosoftTrainers -desc "This
        group contains all of the Microsoft Trainers for Training
            Concepts"
```

Q: How do I add a user to a group with Active Directory Users and Computers?

A: There are a few different ways to add users to groups from within ADUC. One method is to go to the properties of a group (right-click and select **Properties**) and click the **Members** tab. Use the **Add** button to add the required users.

Q: How do I add a user to a group from the command line?

A: Use the *dsmod.exe* command. Here is an example of using *dsmod.exe* to add a user to a group:

```
dsmod group "CN=Microsoft Trainers,DC=trainingconcepts,DC=org" -addmbr
     "CN=Chad Todd,CN=Users,DC=trainingconcepts,DC=org"
```

Q: How do I reset the password for a computer account with the GUI?

A: Open ADUC. Right-click the computer whose password you want to reset and select **Reset Password**. Click **Yes** in the confirmation dialog box to confirm resetting the password.

Self Test

A Quick Answer Key follows the Self Test questions. For complete questions, answers, and explanations to the Self Test questions in this chapter as well as the other chapters in this book, see the Self Test Appendix.

Using Management Tools

1. You are a consultant and you work for several companies at one time. You keep your laptop in a workgroup because you are at a different company every day. You want to use Stored Usernames and Passwords to add credentials for each of the companies' domains so that you don't have to manually authenticate every time you map drives and print. Which tool would you use?

   A. dsadd.exe

   B. dsget.exe

   C. dsmod.exe

   D. gpresult.exe

   E. whoami.exe

   F. cmdkey.exe

2. You have a user who is complaining that he cannot perform certain functions when he is logged on to his workstation. You log in as yourself and it works. You log back in as the user and it does not work. You want to see what privileges are enabled for the user. Which tool should you use?

   A. dsquery.exe

   B. dsmove.exe

   C. gpresult.exe

   D. whoami.exe

   E. cmdkey.exe

3. You want to create departmental OUs for each department in your company. You need to create a list of all users who are in the quality control department so you will know which user accounts to place in the Quality Control OU. Which tool should you use?

   A. dsadd.exe

   B. dsget.exe

   C. dsmod.exe

   D. dsquery.exe

   E. dsmove.exe

4. Your company recently replaced one of its fax lines. Doing so caused the fax machine to have a new number. You need to find everyone who is listed as using the old fax number. Which tool should you use?

   A. ADUC.

   B. dsget.exe

   C. Active Directory Domains and Trusts

   D. dsmod.exe

   E. dsmove.exe

Creating and Managing User Accounts

5. You have an administrator named Jeff who cannot log on to any of the servers. You are able to log on to all the servers with no problem. Jeff can log on to his two workstations without any problems. You verify that Jeff has the correct rights to log on to the servers. You think that someone has changed the properties of Jeff's user account to play a joke on him. What could be the cause of the problem?

A. Jeff's logon hours have been changed.

B. Jeff's logon workstations have been changed.

C. Jeff's phone number has been changed.

D. Jeff's account has been disabled.

E. Jeff's account has been set to expire in two weeks.

6. You want to enable the user account for Will Carver. You decide to use the *dsmod.exe* tool. Which of the following commands will enable the Will Carver account?

   A. dsmod user "CN=Will Carver,CN=Users,DC=trainingconcepts,DC=org" -disabled no

   B. dsmod user "CN=Will Carver,CN=Users,DC=trainingconcepts,DC=org" -disabled yes

   C. dsmod user "CN=Will Carver,CN=Users,DC=trainingconcepts,DC=org" -enabled no

   D. dsmod user "CN=Will Carver,CN=Users,DC=trainingconcepts,DC=org" -enabled yes

7. You need to reset the password for Sarah Todd. You want to reset it from the command line. For security purposes, you want to be prompted to key in the password manually. Which of the following commands will reset the password?

   A. dsmod user "CN=Sarah Todd,CN=Users,DC=trainingconcepts,DC=org" –password *

   B. dsmod user "CN=Sarah Todd,CN=Users,DC=trainingconcepts,DC=org" –pwd *

   C. dsadd user "CN=Sarah Todd,CN=Users,DC=trainingconcepts,DC=org" –password *

   D. dsadd user "CN=Sarah Todd,CN=Users,DC=trainingconcepts,DC=org" –pwd *

8. Your security team has requested a report listing all disabled user accounts. You want to write a batch file for them that will give them the information at any time. Which of the following commands would you put into a batch file?

   A. dsquery user –disabled

   B. dsquery user –disabled yes

   C. dsquery user –enabled no

   D. dsquery user –locked

9. You need to change the password for all laptop users. All laptop users have the description "Laptop User." You need to change their passwords to Password01. To ease the process, you want to write a batch file to do it for you. Which commands should you put into your script file?

   A. dsquery user –desc "Laptop User" | dsmod.exe user –pwd Password01

   B. dsmod user –pwd Password01 | dsquery.exe user –desc "Laptop User"

   C. dsget user –desc "Laptop User" | dsmod.exe user –pwd Password01

   D. dsmod user –pwd Password01 | dsquery.exe user –desc "Laptop User"

Creating and Managing Group Accounts

10. You have a multiple domain forest. You want to use groups to assign permissions to shared resources in a single domain to users through the forest. You will then grant permissions to the network resources by adding users or other groups into these groups. Which group scope should you use?

    A. Domain Local

    B. Global

    C. Universal

    D. Distribution

11. You have a multiple domain forest. You want to use groups to organize your users. Users from each domain need to be in the same group. These groups will be used to assign permissions forest wide. Which group scope should you use?

    A. Domain Local

    B. Global

    C. Universal

    D. Distribution

12. You want to create three new groups to assign permissions to resources across the forest. You want these groups to be universal security groups. However, you notice that when you create a group, the option to make it a Universal group is grayed out. You can create domain local and global groups, but not universal. What could be the problem?

    A. You are not logged in as a schema administrator.

    B. You need to create the group on the global catalog server.

    C. Your domain is in Windows 2000 mixed-domain functionality.

    D. Your domain contains Windows NT 4.0 member servers.

13. You have a universal group that you need to convert to a domain local group. You want to use the *dsmod.exe* tool to make the change via the command prompt. Which of the following will convert the universal group to a domain local group?

    A. dsmod "CN=Authors,DC=trainingconcepts,DC=org" –scope g

    B. dsmod "CN=Authors,DC=trainingconcepts,DC=org" –scope u

    C. dsmod "CN=Authors,DC=trainingconcepts,DC=org" –scope dl

    D. dsmod "CN=Authors,DC=trainingconcepts,DC=org" –scope l

    E. dsmod "CN=Authors,DC=trainingconcepts,DC=org" –scope dlo

Creating and Managing Computer Accounts

14. You have a laptop that you want to join to the domain. Which of the following tools will enable you to create a machine account in Active Directory for your laptop? (Choose all that apply).

    A. dsadd.exe

    B. Active Directory Users and Computers

    C. Active Directory Domains and Trusts

    D. dsmod.exe

15. Your domain consists of a single domain controller and three member servers. You are worried that your only domain controller will fail and you will lose your domain. You want to make one of the member servers into a domain controller. Which of the following commands should you use?

    A. Active Directory Users and Computers

    B. dsadd

    C. dcpromo

    D. Active Directory Domains and Trusts

Self Test Quick Answer Key

For complete questions, answers, and explanations to the Self Test questions in this chapter as well as the other chapters in this book, see the Self Test Appendix.

1. **F**
2. **D**
3. **D**
4. **A**
5. **B**
6. **A**
7. **B**
8. **A**
9. **A**
10. **A**
11. **C**
12. **C**
13. **D**
14. **A, B**
15. **C**

Chapter 5

MCSA/MCSE 70-290

Managing Access to Resources

Exam Objectives in this Chapter:

3	Managing and maintaining access to resources.
3.1	Configure access to shared folders.
3.3	Configure file system permissions.
3.1.2	Manage Shared folder permissions.
3.3.1	Verify effective permissions when granting permissions.
2.7	Troubleshoot user authentication issues.
3.4	Troubleshoot access to files and shared folders.
3.3.2	Change ownership of files and shared folders.

- ☑ Summary of Exam Objectives
- ☑ Exam Objectives Fast Track
- ☑ Exam Objectives Frequently Asked Questions
- ☑ Self Test
- ☑ Self Test Quick Answer Key

Introduction

In today's business environment, security is a top priority, and controlling access to network resources is a major goal of any network security plan. Windows Server 2003 was designed with security in mind, and provides network administrators with the capability to implement multiple levels of security to protect sensitive data and control the capability of users to perform actions on the computer and network.

In this chapter, we will look at some of the ways you can manage access to files and folders, printers, computers, and other resources on the network. You'll learn about different types of permissions and user rights that can be configured, how permissions are inherited, and how you can use new command-line utilities such as takeown.exe and where.exe as part of your access control plan.

Although securing your data from unauthorized users is of utmost importance, ensuring that authorized users are able to access the data they need is equally important. Thus, we will discuss how to troubleshoot common access problems.

Encrypting data is not a substitute for setting permissions, but encryption can be used in conjunction with permissions to add a layer of security. Windows Server 2003 includes the Encrypting File System introduced with Windows 2000, and improvements to EFS now enable users to share encrypted files with other selected users. You will learn how to use EFS to encrypt files and folders, both through the GUI and using the cipher.exe tool.

Another tool for controlling access is an authentication scheme based on digital certificates and a public key infrastructure. We will provide an overview of how to implement a PKI using Windows Server 2003's Certificate Services.

Understanding Access Control

Just about everyone understands the concept of "access control" in non-technology terms. We have locks on our houses and cars to keep out others that we don't want to allow inside. Valuable items we want to keep secure we may store in a personal safe or in a safe deposit box.

The same concepts apply to electronic resources that apply to physical ones. The growth of the Internet over the past few years has even brought technophobes into an understanding of basic electronic access. Parents can now place restrictions on channels their children can access on television and satellite receivers. They can apply "parental controls" to limit the Web sites their children can access. They can block certain channels on their cable boxes or satellite dishes.

When you are responsible for managing a server or a network of servers, it is imperative that you understand access control and how to implement it in your environment. The remainder of this chapter will help you learn the mechanisms for securing your environment if you are new to the concept. It will also get you up to speed on the security implementations specific to Windows Server 2003 if you are already familiar with the concepts.

Defining Access Control

Access control is, quite simply, the process of determining who can access resources in an environment. In the Microsoft world, access control is comprised of physical access, logon access, file access, printer access, share access, and so on. This concept is occasionally referred to in general as security, or the lack thereof.

On a Windows 95 or Windows 98 computer, access control is determined by whether you can power on the PC and interact with the keyboard and mouse. The Windows 95 and 98 operating systems do not have any native logon or file access at the local PC. A user could set up file shares on the Windows 95/98 PC that would enable access to portions of the hard drive across the network, but anyone who sat down in front of the PC had full access to any of the data on the hard drive.

Windows NT, Windows 2000, and Windows XP have additional access controls over what was provided with previous Microsoft desktop operating systems. All require logon access before anyone can access the resources of the PC. With NTFS, file access became more limited as well. These security mechanisms available at the desktop mimic the access control that has been available with Microsoft server products for some time.

Access Control Terminology

How does the Microsoft operating system determine who has access to a resource and who does not? First, we will define some of the terms and look at the components that play a part in access control, and then we will examine how the process works in general. In later sections, we will provide specific ways to control access to the various resources of a Windows Server 2003 system.

The components involved in determining access control are listed in Table 5.1. This list is not complete, but does include those components that will be referred to throughout this chapter.

Table 5.1 Access Control Components

Component	Description
Access Control Entry (ACE)	Contains the access permissions for a single object, such as a user account or a group.
Access Control List (ACL)	Contains any number of ACEs to govern how an access request should be handled. There are two types of ACLs: DACL and SACL.
Discretionary Access Control List (DACL)	Determines which objects have access to a specific resource, such as a file, folder, or share.
System Access Control List (SACL)	Determines whether an audit activity should be performed when an object attempts to access a resource.
Security Identifier (SID)	A unique identifier associated with a specific resource, such as a user account object or a computer.

Continued

Table 5.1 Access Control Components

Component	Description
Access Token	A package comprised of the SIDs and other security information about an object that is making an access request of the system. For file/folder access, the token will provide at least the user SID, group SID, and computer SID to determine if the user has access.

Access Control Process

Opening a file on a network share seems like a pretty simple task. That's the way it should appear to the user. But a number of activities are happening in the background to determine if the user should be able to see the file, much less open it or save changes to it (Figure 5.1).

When the user double-clicks a file listed in the Explorer window, the local PC builds an access token to send off to the server hosting the file. This access token contains the user's SID from his or her network account, the group SID for each of the groups to which the account belongs, the SID of the computer the user is logged on to, along with other information. When the server receives the request and the access token, it compares information in the token to the ACLs for the object. The server examines each of the ACEs in the DACL for the requested file and compares those ACEs to each of the SIDs in the access token. If no ACEs on the file match up with any of the information in the access token, the user's request is denied. If one of the ACEs does match with one of the components in the token, access is granted, and the user sees the file open on the screen.

In addition, the server checks the access token against the SACL to determine if any audit events need to be triggered. (See Chapter 9 for more information about auditing and audit event triggers.) If no ACEs in the SACL match any items in the access token, then no audit events will occur.

Understanding and Using Access Permissions

Now that you have seen the terms and definitions, take a look at what they mean in the big picture. We will start by setting permissions on various objects and discussing how those permission settings work together or come into conflict with each other. In the following sections, we'll discuss how to use different types of permissions to provide security:

- File-level permissions (NTFS Security)
- Shared-folder permissions
- Active Directory permissions

Figure 5.1 Requesting a File

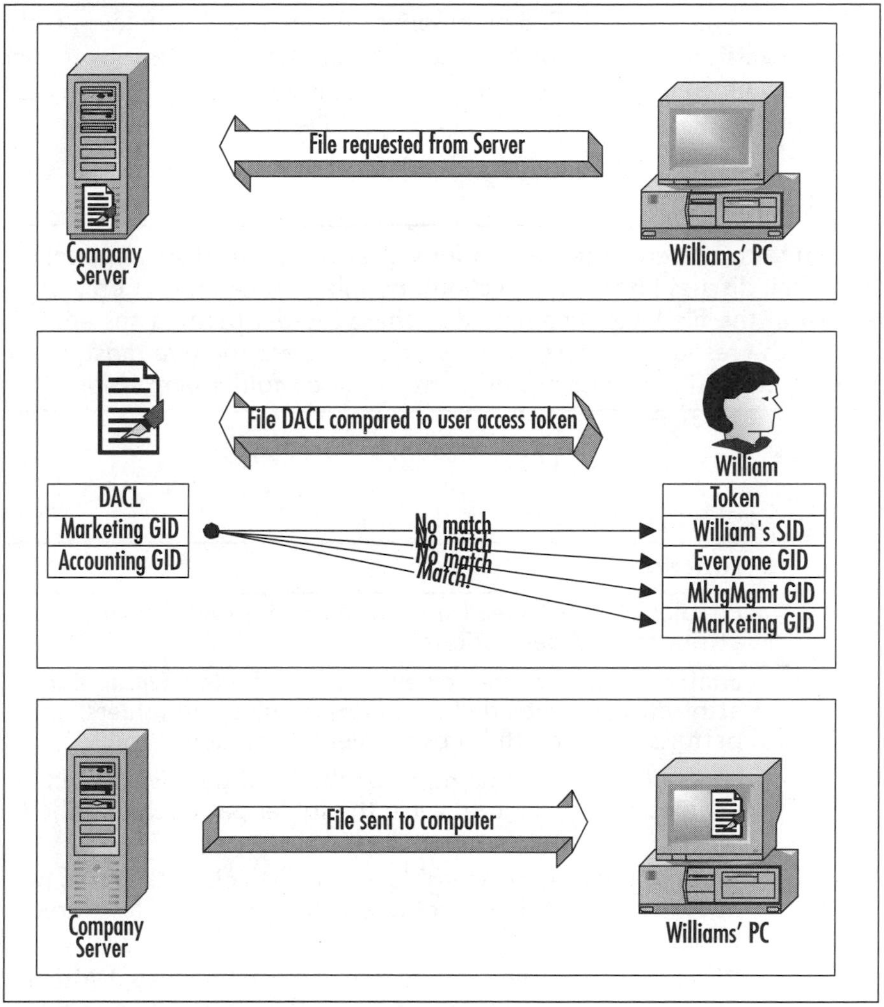

We will also discuss the inheritance of permissions. Starting with the lowest level and moving upward, we will start with file-level permissions.

EXAM 70-290 OBJECTIVE 3.3

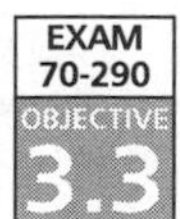

Setting File-Level Permissions (NTFS Security)

The NTFS file system used since Windows NT provides the base framework for file and folder security in Windows Server 2003. These permissions are set on the files and folders stored on the server's disk system and apply to authenticated users no matter how they access the file system (that is, whether they access it across the network or sitting at the local machine). By default, all users can read and execute files on the disk system, with the exception of certain system areas that are protected by default at installation. Applying NTFS permissions will control who has access to which areas of the disk system.

NTFS Permissions Defined

As an administrator, you can set NTFS permissions on files as well as folders. Table 5.2 describes the permissions available for NTFS folders, and Table 5.3 describes the permissions that can be applied to files. Even though the permissions are similar, there are some key differences when these permissions are applied to files and not to folders.

Exam Warning

Note that with shared-folder permissions, previously called share permissions (which we'll discuss later in this section), permissions can be set only at the folder level, not at the file level. Also note that shared-folder permissions apply only when accessing the resources across the network. These are the two most important ways in which NTFS permissions differ from shared-folder permissions.

Table 5.2 NTFS Folder Permissions

Permission	Function
Read	Enables objects to read the contents of a folder, including file attributes and permissions.
Write	Enables objects to create new files and folders within a folder, write attributes and extended attributes on files and folders, and can read permissions and attributes on files and folders.
List Folder Contents	Gives objects the same rights as the Read permission, but also enables the object to traverse the folder path beneath the folder where this permission is applied.
Read & Execute	Gives objects the same rights as the List Folder Contents permission, but also enables the object to execute program files stored in the folder.
Modify	Gives the object the same permissions as the Read, Write, List Folder Contents, and Read & Execute permissions, but also enables the object to delete files and folders within the designated folder.
Full Control	Gives objects full access to the entire contents, including the capability to take ownership of files and change permissions on files and folders.

Table 5.3 NTFS File/Folder Permissions

Permission	Function
Read	Enables objects to read the contents of a file, including file attributes and permissions.
Write	Enables objects to change the contents of or append to an existing file, as well as read the attributes and permissions on the file.
Read & Execute	Gives objects the same rights as the Read permission, but also enables the object to execute a program file.
Modify	Gives the object the same permissions as the Read, Write, and Read & Execute permissions, but also enables the object to delete the designated file.
Full Control	Gives objects full access to the file, including the capability to take ownership of the file and change permissions on the file.

When permissions are applied to a folder, those permissions apply to the files within the folder as well. For instance, if you set the Read permission on a folder, the object (user account or group) to which that permission applies is able to see the files stored in the folder and read the contents of the files within the folder. If you wanted to give a group access to write to a particular file in that folder, but not all files in the folder, you would assign the Write permission to the specific file.

Head of the Class...

When to Assign Permissions to Folders and Files

To keep file system management reasonable, your best bet is to keep permission assignments as simple as possible. Because permissions assigned to a folder apply to all the files within a folder, you should make permission assignments at the folder level most of the time. A well-planned directory structure enables you to assign folder rights at a high level in the directory structure, keeping subsequent permissions changes further down in the directory structure to a minimum.

In general, you should apply permissions to a specific file only when access to that file is significantly different from the other files in that folder. If you find that you are making file permission assignments to several files within a directory structure, it might be better to relocate those files to a different folder where the appropriate permissions can be assigned to the parent folder and not to the individual files.

Assigning NTFS Permissions

NTFS permissions for a file or folder can be assigned to any Active Directory object. Most commonly, user and group objects are assigned permissions. In general, the best way to assign and manage access to files and folders is by assigning rights to group objects, then adjusting membership of the user objects in the group object. One exception to this general principle is for user home directories. In most cases, permissions to a user home directory are assigned directly to the use object and not a group.

Assigning Folder Permissions

Assigning permissions to a folder is fairly straightforward. Right-click the folder and select **Sharing and Security** from the context menu. The folder's Properties window appears with the **Sharing** tab selected. Click the **Security** tab to view the NTFS permissions already set on the folder. Alternatively, you can right-click the folder and select **Properties** from the list, then click the **Security** tab. Or you can even select the folder, click **File** in the Explorer window, choose **Sharing and Security** from the menu, and then click the **Security** tab. No matter how you bring up the Security tab, it appears like the image in Figure 5.2. A set of permissions has been assigned to the Accounting global group, which assigns the Modify, Read & Execute, List Folder Contents, Read, and Write permissions to the group. The Administrators global group also has rights to this folder, and the Full Control permission has been assigned to that group. The CREATOR OWNER and SYSTEM groups also have permissions to this folder. Like the Administrators group, the SYSTEM group has full access to the contents of this folder by default. This scenario can be changed, and we will cover that later in this section under NTFS Special Permissions.

Figure 5.2 Setting Security Properties for a Folder

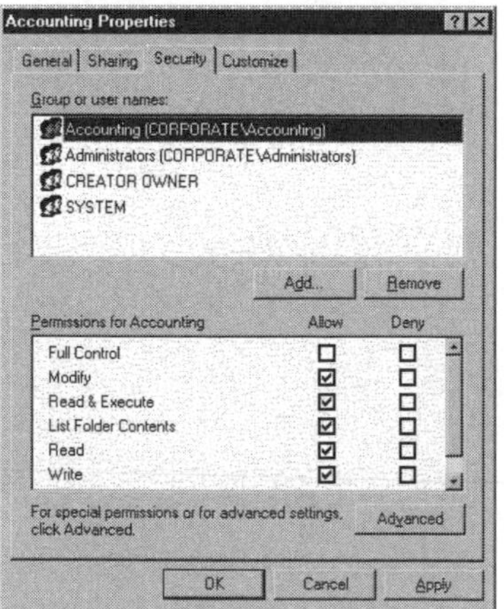

To add a user or group to the access list for the file, click the **Add** button and specify the user or group object that will be added to the access list. When the object appears in the **Group or user names** list, you can assign the desired permissions to the object. There are some shortcuts to assigning permission, fortunately. Since the Modify permission includes all the permissions of Read & Execute, List Folder Contents, Read, and Write, clicking the **Modify** check box in the **Allow** column automatically enables the other permissions. The same holds true for clicking the **Full Control** check box – all the permissions below will be enabled by default. Clicking **Read**, **Write**, or **List Folder Contents** enables only those individual permissions. Clicking **Read & Execute** enables that permission as well as **List Folder Contents** and **Read**.

After you have made the desired changes to the security permissions list, click **Apply**, then **OK**, to enable the changes on the network. The changes take effect immediately. If a user is working in a folder where he or she has Write permissions and the security settings are changed so that the user only has Read permissions in the folder, the next time the user attempts to change a file or create a new file, the action will be denied.

Assigning File Permissions

As mentioned previously, you should generally apply security permissions to folders and not to files. In the case where you do need to apply permissions to a specific file, the process differs from assigning permissions to a folder. First, you will notice that if you right-click on a file, there is no **Sharing and Security** item in the context menu. This is primarily because you cannot share a file. You can still access the security settings by opening the file's **Properties** window and selecting the **Security** tab, as shown in Figure 5.3. You will see that the List Folder Contents permission is not displayed, because it does not apply to the file. You will also notice that the CREATOR OWNER system group does not appear. Plus, the permissions selected for the Accounting group, while the same as shown in the previous figure, are grayed-out here. This indicates that the permissions are inherited from the parent folder and cannot be changed directly. We will discuss permission inheritance and how to make changes to these permissions in the "Understanding How Permissions Are Inherited" section later in the chapter.

Figure 5.3 Setting Security Permissions for a File

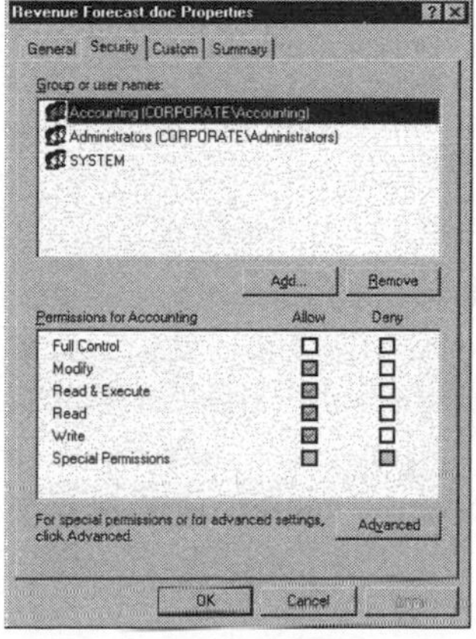

Adding a new object to the security list for the file is the same as described for a folder. Click **Add**, specify the object name, and then make the appropriate security changes. Similar shortcuts apply when enabling file permissions. Clicking **Read** or **Write** enables only those permissions. Clicking **Read & Execute** enables **Read** as well. Clicking **Modify** enables all permissions below it, as will clicking **Full Control**.

Configuration & Implementing...

Security Permissions Applied in Combination

One concept that is especially important to master in order to be able to manage permissions effectively is that the effects of security permissions are *cumulative*. If an object is a member of multiple groups (and which user objects aren't these days?) and two or more of those groups are given different permissions on a specific folder, the user object will have all the permissions assigned in each group.

Say that you have created two groups called Reviewers and Editors. In a particular folder, you assign Read permissions to the Reviewers group and Write permissions to the Editors group. Your goal is to enable the reviewers to read the files in the folder but not make changes to them. Only the editors would be able to make changes. If you accidentally add a user who is in the Reviewers group to the Editors group, when that user accesses files in the folder, the user will be able to read and make changes to the files in the folder. If this person is not supposed to be able to do this, it may take some time to track down exactly why the access restrictions are not working as expected.

A special consideration occurs when using the Deny permission to restrict access. The Deny permission overrides all other permissions explicitly assigned or applied in cumulative fashion. Suppose you give the Editors group Full Control permission on the folder, and you assign the Deny Write permission to the Reviewers group. This rights assignment will prevent members of the Reviewers group from making changes to the contents of the folder. However, if a user is a member of both the Editors and Reviewers groups, he or she will be unable to make changes to the folder because of the Deny Write permission for the Reviewers group. Even though the user should have Full Control permissions because of the rights assigned to the Editors group, the Deny Write permission on the Reviewers group will override the other settings.

Denying Permissions

Up to this point, we've been addressing file and folder security from the standpoint of enabling those permissions. There may be times that you need to specifically deny a permission to a user or group for a particular file or folder. You've already seen in previous figures that there are check boxes labeled Allow and Deny for each permission. If a Deny permission is selected, it overrides any Allow permission that may be enabled.

Suppose you have data in a share that you want to be available to everyone in the organization, but you only want members of the Accounting group to be able to edit. You assign Modify permissions to the Accounting group and Read permissions to the Everyone group. Just to make sure that no one else can make changes to the files in the share, you also add the Deny Write permission to the Everyone group. While this setup may seem to achieve the goal, it really does not. As expected, members of the Everyone group will be able to read files in the share, but they will not be able to write to any files, just like you wanted. The problem comes in when members of the Accounting group try to write to files in the share. Because the members of the Accounting group are also members of the Everyone group, the Deny Write permission assigned to the Everyone group overrides the Modify permission assigned to the Accounting group, and members of the Accounting group are not able to make changes to the files. A better way to accomplish this goal is to assign Read permissions to the Everyone group and Modify permissions to the Accounting group. Unless the Everyone group inherits Write permissions from a parent directory, only members of the Accounting group will be able to change the contents of the data in the share.

Again, a well-planned directory structure and folder security approach should minimize the need to use the Deny permission when setting access. In those cases where permissions do need to be denied, make an effort to deny the least restrictive permission necessary. For instance, if you want to restrict a group from writing to files in a specific directory, deny only the Write permission. If you deny the Modify permission, that group will not be able to do *any* of the functions covered by the Modify permission, including reading files and folders, traversing folder hierarchies, as well as writing to files.

In addition, be extremely careful when altering permissions for the Administrators and Users groups. While there are times that you may want to restrict access for the Administrators group, be *very* careful of using Deny to restrict that access. If you were to deny Full Control to the Administrators group to a folder and no other group had Full Control access to that folder, you would lose your capability to do any further management on that folder from any level. On the other hand, if you deny permissions to the Users group on any folder, you deny access to every account on the system, including administrators. In the "Understanding How Permissions Are Inherited" section later in the chapter, you will learn better ways of restricting access to certain files and folders.

NTFS Special Permissions

The basic file and folder permissions can actually be broken into smaller, more specific permissions. These are commonly referred to as Special Permissions. Table 5.4 lists the Special Permissions and their functions.

Table 5.4 NTFS Special Permissions

Special Permission	Description
Traverse Folder/Execute File	For folders, enables the object to navigate through the folder structure below the folder where the permission is applied. For files, enables the object to execute an application program stored in the folder.
List Folder/Read Data	For folders, enables the object to see the names of files and subfolders stored in the folder where the permission is applied. For folders, enables the object to view the contents of files stored in the folder.
Read Attributes	Enables the object to view the attributes of a file or folder.
Read Extended Attributes	Enables the object to view the extended attributes of a file or folder. Extended attributes are generally defined by an application and vary from program to program.
Create Files/Write Data	For folders, enables the object to create new files within the folder. For files, enables the object to change or replace the contents of an existing file.
Create Folders/Append Data	For folders, enables the object to create new subfolders within the folder. For files, enables the object to add data to the end of an existing file without other-wise altering the content of the file, including deleting the file.
Write Attributes	Enables the object to change the attributes on an existing file or subfolder within the folder.
Write Extended Attributes	Enables the object to change the extended attributes on an existing file or subfolder within the folder. Extended attributes are generally defined by an application and will vary from program to program.
Delete Subfolders and Files	Enables the object to delete a file or sub-folder, even if the Delete permission has not been granted to the object.
Delete	Enables the object to delete a file or folder. An object can still delete a file or folder without this permission set if the object has been granted the Delete Subfolders and Files permission.

Continued

Table 5.4 NTFS Special Permissions

Special Permission	Description
Read Permissions	Enables the object to view the security permissions set on files and subfolders within the folder.
Change Permissions	Enables the object to change security permissions on files and subfolders within the folder.
Take Ownership	Enables the object to change the owner of a file or folder to the object's user ownership.
Full Control	Enables the object to perform all Special Permissions.

In Figure 5.3, you saw an entry for Special Permissions in the File Permissions window that was grayed out. That entry is also present in the Folder Permissions window, but it is not displayed in the window without scrolling down. You cannot access these Special Permissions from this window, however. To modify any Special Permissions settings, you must click the **Advanced** button in the **Permissions** window.

Setting Special Permissions

Figure 5.4 shows the Advanced Security Settings window. In this sample, there are four groups that have permissions listed. These are the same four groups that were assigned permissions at the folder level in Figure 5.2. The difference is that while the Accounting, Administrators, and SYSTEM groups have been assigned their permissions at the folder level, the CREATOR OWNER group has its permissions assigned in the Advanced Security Settings window. Looking at the permissions assigned to the CREATOR OWNER group in the folder properties window seen in Figure 5.4, you can see that the only permissions identified for that group are Special Permissions, and the box is grayed out, meaning that those permissions cannot be set in that window. Like the SYSTEM group, the CREATOR OWNER group is a special system-level group that cannot have members added to or removed from it. The CREATOR OWNER group always has Full Control special permissions applied unless specifically excluded (Figure 5.5). The CREATOR OWNER group is discussed in more detail in the next section.

Ownership of Files and Folders

Whenever a file or folder is created, the user object that created the file becomes the owner of the file. No matter what other permissions the user object may have in the folder where the file was created, the user object will have full control over the file it created.

Figure 5.4 Viewing Advanced Security Settings for the Accounting Folder

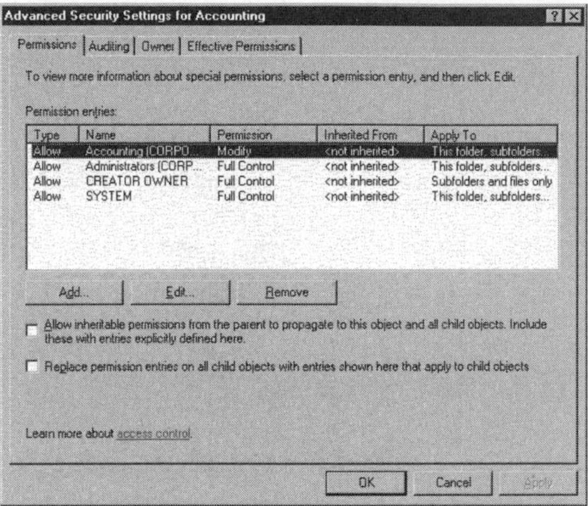

Figure 5.5 Viewing Permissions for the CREATOR OWNER Group on the

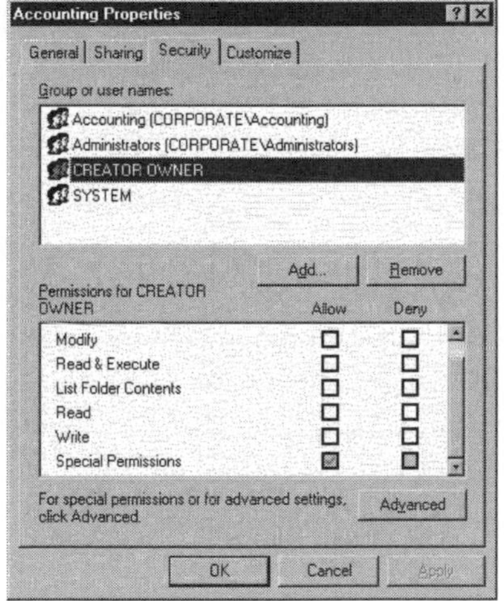

NOTE

Ownership of a file impacts more than just security access. If quotas are enabled on a disk system, file ownership helps determine how much space is used toward a user's quota.

The file owner's capability to maintain full control over a file is governed through the CREATOR OWNER group. By default, the CREATOR OWNER group has full control over certain files through special permissions. The basic rule of thumb is that if you have the capability to create a file somewhere on the volume, then you should be able to have complete control over it, which would happen if you have Full Control permissions on the file. The CREATOR OWNER group is set up for exactly that reason. When looking at the permissions on the folder in Figure 5.5, you see that the CREATOR OWNER group has no permissions explicitly defined, but the Special Permissions box under the Allow column is checked. If you open the Advanced Permissions window for the folder, you will see a listing indicating that the CREATOR OWNER group has Full Control permissions. These permissions apply only to files and folders that the user created. Just because the CREATOR OWNER group has Full Control permissions identified in a folder, everyone does not have full access to the folder. Users have full access only to files they created in the folder.

In addition, administrators in the domain have the capability to take ownership of files and folders. If an administrator takes ownership of a file, the creator of the file no longer has full control over the file. Changing ownership of the file effectively removes the user that created the file from the CREATOR OWNER group for that file, and that user's access to the file reverts to the default access he or she has based on the folder permissions.

Copying or Moving Files and Folders

NTFS permissions on files and folders that are moved or copied to other locations do not always stay the same after the move. A number of factors impact the security settings that will be placed on the file in its new location, including the following:

- Whether the file is copied or moved
- Whether the destination is an NTFS volume or not
- Whether the destination is on the same volume as the original location

Files and folders that are moved or copied to non-NTFS volumes lose all permissions. If the destination is on an NTFS volume, the security permissions the file will have after the transfer will depend on several factors. In the following sections, we'll discuss copying and moving files and folders.

Copying Files and Folders

When copying files or folders to a location on an NTFS volume, the user must have permission to create files in the destination location. When the file or folder is copied, it is created as a new object in the destination, and the user object that copied the file or folder becomes the owner of the newly created item.

Moving Files and Folders

Just as when copying files or folders, the user moving a file or folder must have permissions to create objects in the new location as well as have permission to delete objects from the original location. The file or folder created in the destination is owned by the user object that moves it, and the original file or folder is deleted from the original location. The NTFS permissions that will be assigned to the file or folder in the new location are detailed in Table 5.5.

Table 5.5 NTFS Permissions Applied to Moved Files and Folders

Destination	Permissions
Objects moved within the same NTFS volume	Objects retain their original NTFS permissions in the new location
Objects moved to a different NTFS volume	Objects inherit the permissions of the new location

Exam Warning

Be prepared to answer at least one question on the exam related to NTFS permissions on files and folders copied or moved form one location to another. This has been a favorite topic to address in Microsoft exams, because a lack of understanding of changes in permissions can lead to data access problems.

Setting Shared-Folder Permissions

Setting the NTFS file and folder permissions correctly for the entire server does no good if your users cannot get to the directory structure. Since most users do not log on at the server, the file system must be made available through shares. When a folder is shared, it becomes visible on the network. The permissions on the share also determine the level of access that a user has to the data accessed through the share. The share permissions are applied in conjunction with, not instead of, the NTFS permissions. We will discuss how this works in the section titled "Understanding the Interaction of Share Permissions and NTFS Permissions."

Shared-Folder Permissions Defined

The permissions that apply to a shared folder differ from the NTFS permissions that can be set on the same folder. There are significant differences in the way the permissions are applied to a share as compared to permissions set on a file or folder. The specific permissions that can be applied to folder shares are listed in Table 5.6. Remember that "object" in this context refers to a user or group account.

Table 5.6 Shared-Folder Permissions

Permission	Description
Read	Enables objects to see file and folder names, open files and programs, and see file and folder attributes.

Continued

Table 5.6 Shared-Folder Permissions

Permission	Description
Change	Enables objects to perform all actions associated with the Read permission, plus create new files and folders, modify file contents, delete files and folders, and modify file attributes.
Full Control	Enables objects to perform all actions associated with the Read and Change permissions, plus change permissions on files and take ownership of files.

Effective permissions on a shared folder are calculated in much the same way as with NTFS permissions. Individual permissions can be allowed or denied, and denied permissions always override allowed permissions, including inherited permissions. When a user object is assigned permissions from multiple sources, the effect is cumulative. For example, say Bob is a member of both the Accounting group and the Accounting Managers group because he is one of the accounting managers for the company. If the Accounting group is assigned Read permissions to a share, and the Accounting Managers group is assigned Change permissions to the same share, Bob's effective permissions for the share will be Change.

Understanding the Interaction of Share Permissions and NTFS Permissions

When a user accesses data through a file share, the share permissions and NTFS permissions both impact the level of access the user has to the files and folders in the share. The user access level is determined by the *more restrictive* access defined by the total cumulative permissions in either the share or NTFS security. This is easy to understand if the NTFS permissions are more limited, but many new system administrators can get confused when the share permissions are more limited. You need to remember that the permissions applied to the share impact not only your ability to access the share itself but also your ability to access the data within the share.

It is easy to get caught in the logic that says "I do not want to give users Full Control access on the share because they might delete the share or make other changes to the share." This is not the case. Giving uses Full Control on the share means that all security on the data accessed through the share is determined by the NTFS permissions. If you only assign Read permissions on the share, the user accessing data through the share will have read-only access to the entire contents, no matter what the NTFS permissions are. When setting up a file system, make sure you assign NTFS permissions to control access to the data as if the user were logging on to the machine locally. Then you can assign Full Control permissions on the share and not worry about the users having more access than you want them to have. Table 5.7 shows how share permissions and NTFS permissions combine to generate the effective permissions a user has on a folder accessed through a share.

Table 5.7 Share and NTFS Permissions in Combination

Groups	Share Permissions	NTFS Permissions	Effective Permissions
Everyone	Full Control	Read	Read
Accounting	Read	Modify	Read
Accounting Managers	Change	Full Control	Modify
IT	Full Control	Modify	Modify
Administrators	Full Control	Full Control	Full Control

EXAM WARNING

Because many access problems can arise from incorrectly configured Share and NTFS permissions, you can expect to see at least one exam question related to setting Share and NTFS permissions. When encountering one of these questions, remember that the *more restrictive* permission (of the cumulative total of each type of permission) is the one that takes precedence in determining access. Look first at the permissions defined on the share before you look at the NTFS permissions defined. If the user only has Read permissions on the share, he or she will only have read access to the contents. If the user has Full Control permissions on the share, then look to the NTFS permissions defined to determine the level of access the user has.

Assigning Share Permissions

You can set share permissions in much the same way you set NTFS permissions. Before you can set permissions on a share, however, you must first create the share.

Creating a Shared Folder

You can create a folder share from the **Properties** window of a folder. In the **Properties** window, click the **Sharing** tab. In the **Sharing** tab, you can enable and disable the share for the folder and set the permissions on the share. A typical share setup is shown in Figure 5.6. In this window, you can specify the name and comment for the share, specify whether there should be a limit to the number of users accessing the share, and set the permissions on the share. In addition, you can create multiple shares for a single folder, each one having different permissions.

Figure 5.6 Creating a Shared Folder

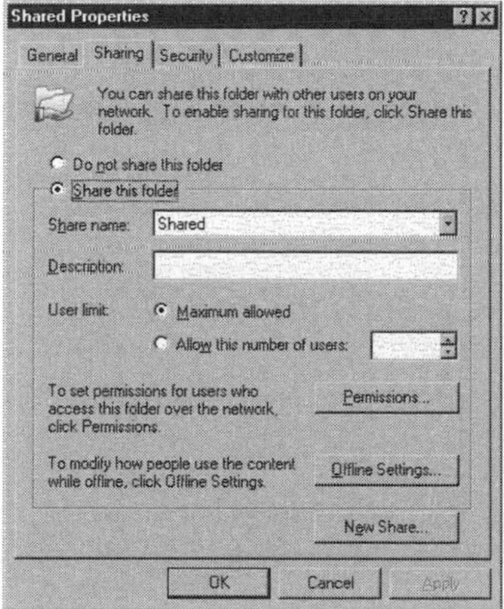

After you have created the share, it appears on the network from the server where the folder resides (a share can be created on a workstation; "server" in this sense means any computer that is sharing its resources over the network and does not refer to only computers running a server operating system). If the server is named CORPADFP1 and the share name is Shared, users with access to the share can map a drive to the share at \\CORPADFP1\Shared. This UNC name can be used to map drives in logon scripts or to access the share directly from the workstation.

NOTE

Note that while you can create share names that mirror the folder name, such as "My Documents" or "Program Files." If you have Windows 95 or Windows 98 workstations operating in your environment, your share names cannot be longer than eight characters and cannot contain any spaces. If you do have longer share names with spaces, the 95 and 98 workstations will not be able to see the share on the network.

Setting Share Permissions

After you have created the share, you can set permissions on the share. You can set permissions by clicking the **Permissions** button in the window shown in Figure 5.6. This opens the **Permissions** window for the folder as shown in Figure 5.7.

Figure 5.7 Viewing Permissions of a Shared Folder

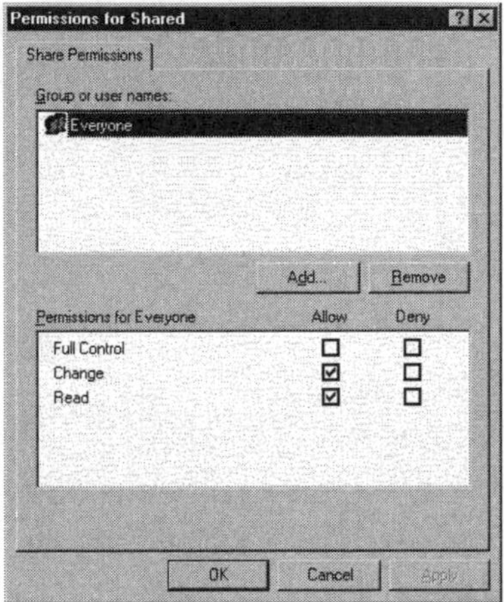

Exam Warning

By default, when you create a new share, the *Everyone* group has Read permissions assigned to it. This is different from the default response in Windows 2000 server where *Everyone* was granted Full Control by default.

As with NTFS permissions, share permissions can be set for Allow or Deny for multiple groups or users. The same rules apply for share permissions as for NTFS permissions.

- Permissions on shares are cumulative. If a user belongs to multiple groups, and two or more of those groups have permissions on a share, the user has all the permissions allowed by all the groups.
- Deny permissions override Allow permissions. If a user belongs to multiple groups, and one of those groups has Allow permissions on a share while another has Deny permissions, the user will be denied access to the share based on the Deny permission.

Note that there are no special permissions related to shares. What you see is what you get!

Copying or Moving Shared Folders

When you copy or move a shared folder to a different location, the way share permissions are affected differs from NTFS permissions.

- If you copy or move a folder to a new location, the folder in the new location will not have a share associated with it.
- If you copy a shared folder to a new location, the original folder will continue to have the original share pointing to it.
- If you move a folder, the share for the folder is deleted along with the original folder.

If you do need to move a folder share from one location to another, you have more than just share permissions to take into consideration. Changing the name of a share by changing its location can impact logon scripts that map user drives to the share. Any user that maps a drive to the share from a workstation will get errors when trying to access the drive letter if the share is removed. Relocating a share to a different file path on the same server will not necessarily cause this issue if the share for the new location has the same name as the share for the old location. If you have to relocate a share onto a different server, the share name will change because the share will be accessed from a different server name, which is part of the share's UNC path name.

Shared Folders in Active Directory

You can avoid several problems related to shares by advertising the share in Active Directory instead of from the server hosting the folder. Advertising a share in Active Directory makes it easier for users to find shares, because they do not need to know the server name where the share is located in order to look for it. The only drawback to advertising shares in Active Directory is that down-level clients will not be able to see the Active Directory shares. If this is not the case in your environment, then you should strongly consider advertising your shares in the Active Directory.

Creating an Active Directory Share

To create a share in Active Directory, you first need to create the share on the server and configure the permissions accordingly. Set up the share on the server as though your users will be accessing the share directly. When the share is set up, use the Active Directory Users and Computers tool to create the share in the directory. In Active Directory Users and Computers, select the area where you want the share to advertise, ideally at the root of the directory or in the top level of one of the OUs associated with the share. Select **Action | New | Shared Folder** to open the New Object – Shared Folder window, shown in Figure 5.8. Enter the name of the share and the network path to the share on the server. Click **OK** to create the share.

Figure 5.8 Creating the Share in the Directory

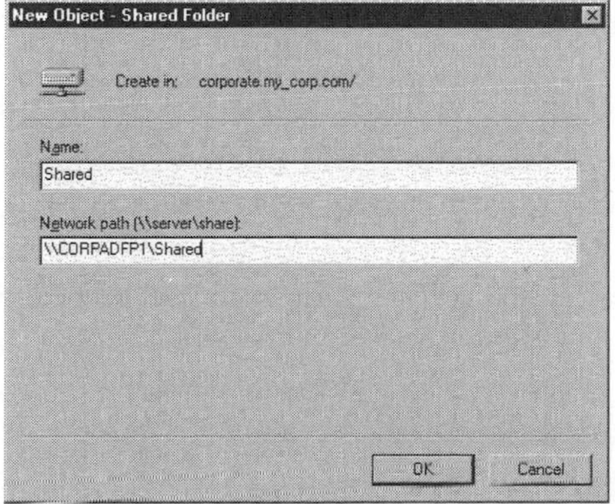

Users can now search for and find the share in the directory. One way they can do this is by opening **My Network Places** and clicking **Search Active Directory**. They can then select **Shared Folders** from the **Find** drop-down menu and click **Find** to locate the share. Figure 5.9 displays the Find Shared Folders window after a search is complete. The user can now right-click the share and map a drive to the share.

Figure 5.9 Searching for a Shared Folder in Active Directory

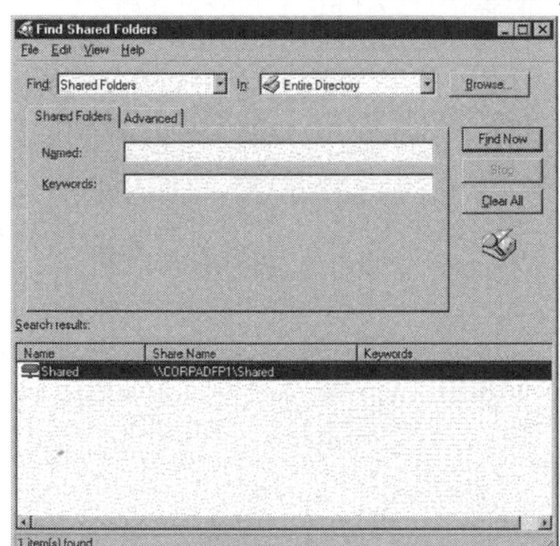

Setting Active Directory Object Permissions

You can also set permissions on the share object in the Active Directory to control access to the share object in the directory. To set permissions on the Active Directory share, open the properties of the share within Active Directory Users and Groups. Figure 5.10 shows the Permissions tab of the Shared Folder Properties window. Because you are looking at the permissions on the directory object, they will be different from those on the share itself. The permissions assigned to the directory share control access to the object in the directory, not the share that it points to. These permissions differ slightly from the permissions available on a standard share. In addition to Read, Change, and Full Control, there is also a Special Permissions option.

When a shared folder is created in Active Directory, a number of default permissions are assigned directly to the object. The Authenticated Users group is assigned Read rights to the object, the Domain Admins and SYSTEM groups are given Full Control to the object, and the Pre-Windows 2000 Compatible Access group is given no permissions.

Again, the permissions granted to objects for the directory share apply only to the directory share, not the server share. For example, the Read permission granted to the Authenticated Users group enables every user logged on to the directory to see the share. However, only users with access to the actual share are able to open it. If a user only has read access to the directory share, but Change access to the server share, and Full Control on the NTFS folder, the user will be able to map a drive to the folder using the directory share and still be able to edit and make changes to the data in the folder. The permissions on the directory share are not considered when determining access to the actual contents of the folder.

Figure 5.10 Setting Permissions on the Active Directory Shared Folder

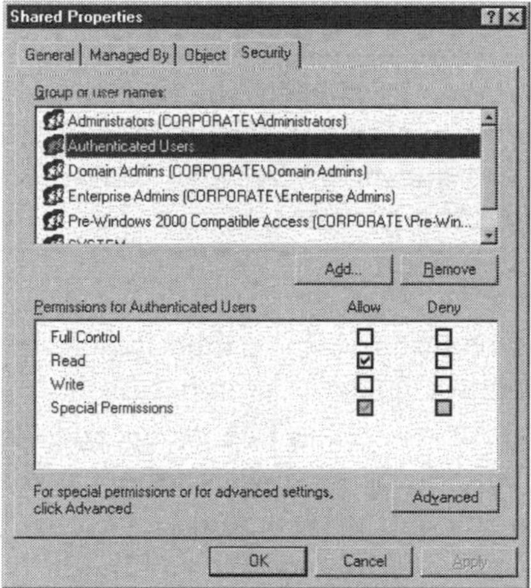

If you want to limit visibility to the directory share to certain groups, you need to grant Read permissions to the group for the directory share. Then you can go back and remove the Authenticated Users group from the ACL. Now only members of that group, and not the entire organization, are able to view the shared folder in the directory.

Understanding How Permissions Are Inherited

When setting NTFS permissions on a folder, those permissions are automatically transferred to all files and subfolders within the folder. This is by design; otherwise, you would have to set permissions on every folder on the disk to control access, and that would place a huge burden on system administrators who would have to keep up with all the changes they would have to make each time some folder setting was modified.

Say that you create a folder on your server and name it Public. You then assign Modify permissions to the Everyone group for that folder. Anyone who accesses that folder has modify rights on every file and folder beneath that folder, as far down as the directory tree goes. Now suppose that you want to restrict a certain group from accessing a certain set of files or folders beneath the Public folder. You could go in and deny rights to that group and the level where you do not want them to have access, but that could get ugly. How do you go through and set this up?

Fortunately, permission inheritance for a folder can be turned off when needed. This is an action you must handle with care, however. When you turn off inheritance for a folder, you must decide what will happen to the permissions that would otherwise flow down to that folder. You can choose to keep the permissions intact, and the operating system will automatically create new ACEs for all the groups with permissions assigned in a parent folder. Or you can choose to delete the permissions, and the operating system will remove all access to the folder except for any ACEs that you assigned directly to the folder.

TEST DAY TIP

When you take the exam, you will likely see several questions related to inheritance, and not just for file and folder permissions. Just be sure to approach the exam calmly and read the questions carefully. Make sure you fully understand the question before selecting the answer.

Why would you want to keep some of the inherited permissions intact? At the root of every volume, certain groups are assigned specific permissions. The Administrators group, the CREATOR OWNER group, the SYSTEM group, and others have default permissions applied at the root of the volume that pass down through inheritance. You really do not want to change the access for some of theses groups. For instance, if you did not enable the Administrators group's permissions to flow down, you might end up cutting off your capability to administer the file structure at that point in the directory and below.

Another group you must be mindful of is the CREATOR OWNER group. As discussed earlier, this special group determines the access that a user has to files and folders he or she has created. By default, the Full Control special permissions assigned to this group automatically apply to every folder created on the volume. If you remove this group from the inheritance list, it is possible that you could set up a situation where a user is able to create a new file in a folder and then not be able to modify it afterward. So, unless there is a really good reason, you should continue to enable the permissions for the CREATOR OWNER group to pass down to folders when you turn off automatic inheritance.

EXERCISE 5.01

SECURING AND SHARING A DATA FOLDER

Consider this scenario related to the material that has been covered thus far: You are a system administrator for a small company that has a Windows Server 2003 system set up for file and print sharing. Each department in the company has a shared directory on the server for that department's data. One of the managers of the Marketing department contacts you about setting up a secure area for the managers of the Marketing department. She wants to be able to share information such as employee reviews and budget projections with other managers in the department, but not with the entire marketing department. She asks you to create a new folder in the Marketing area called Management, and she wants the managers in her department to be able to create new files and folders in the Management folder. She also wants a new share created specifically for that folder so that all her managers can access the data quickly. She would like for the share to be called MktgMgmt, and she wants it available only to the managers in her department. In addition, she would like the share to be created in Active Directory so members of her department can locate it easily.

Before you get started with the steps required to fulfill her request, make a few assumptions. First, you already have Active Directory groups created for both the Marketing team and the Marketing managers. Second, all the departments in the company have a folder that employees can access through a share called Shared. The root of the share is actually located on the server on drive E: in a folder named Shared. OK, now you can get started!

1. Browse to the **Marketing** folder under **E:\Shared** and create a new folder called **Management**. Figure 5.11 shows how this directory structure might look.

Figure 5.11 Viewing the New Management Folder

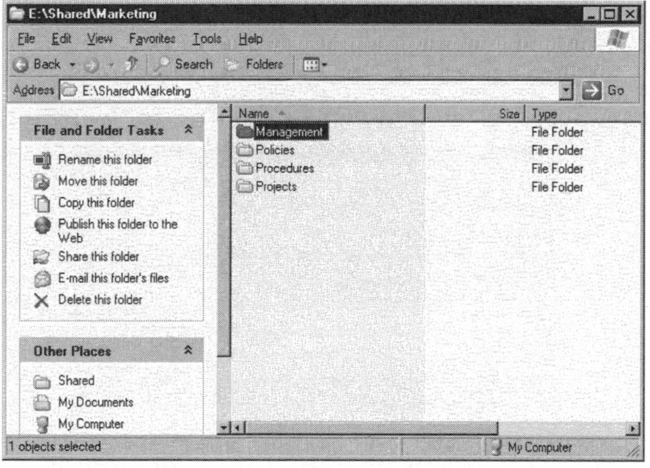

2. Right-click the folder and select **Sharing and Security**.
3. Click the **Security** tab. Figure 5.12 shows the default permissions assigned to the folder when it is created. You can see that the Marketing permissions boxes are grayed out, indicating that those permissions are inherited from the parent folder.
4. Click the **Add** button to add a new group to the permissions list.

Figure 5.12 Viewing Default Permissions on a Newly Created Folder

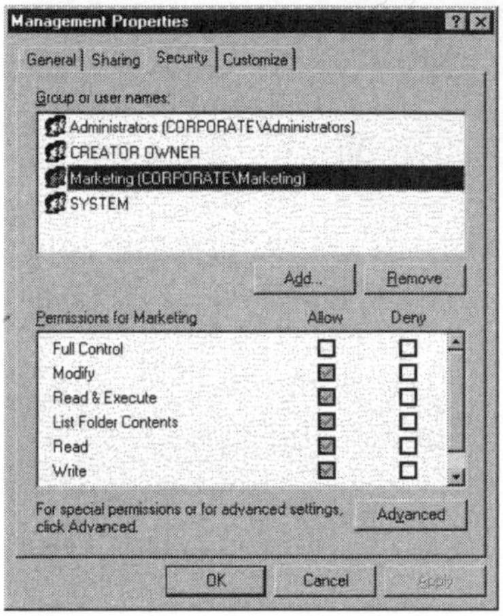

5. Type the name of the group, in this case it is **Marketing Management**, and click **Check Names**. When the group is located in Active Directory, the name is underlined in the object name window, as shown in Figure 5.13.

Figure 5.13 Selecting an Object to Add to the Permissions List

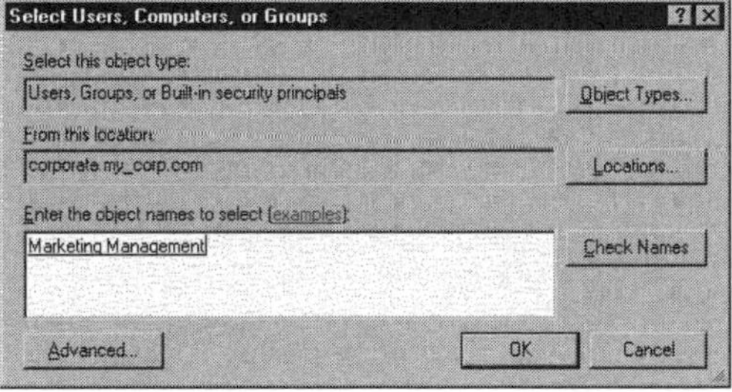

6. Click **OK**. The **Select Users, Computers, or Groups** window closes, and you can see the default permissions added to the Marketing Management group, as shown in Figure 5.14.
7. Click the **Modify** check box under the **Allow** column to add the remaining permissions for the group to the folder. Unless you want the marketing managers to be able to completely control the folder, do not click the **Full Control** check box.
8. Now that you've set up the management group to be able to access the data in the folder, you need to restrict access to the rest of the Marketing team. Click the **Advanced** button to open the Advanced Security Settings window, shown in Figure 5.15. Note that the

Administrators and the Marketing groups have a set of permissions enabled that are inherited from the parent folder. The Marketing Management group lists permissions that are not inherited from the parent folder, meaning that those permissions have been explicitly assigned to this folder.

Figure 5.14 Adding a New Group to the Folder Permissions

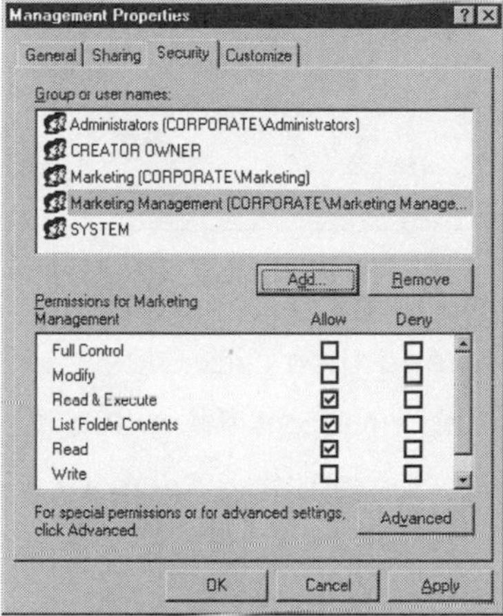

Figure 5.15 Viewing the Advanced Security Settings for the Folder

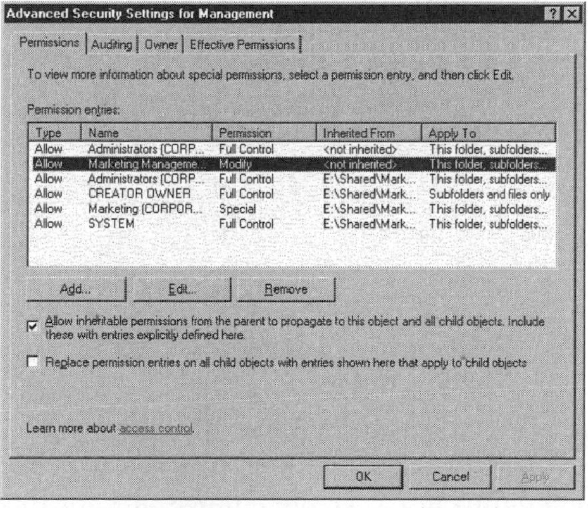

9. To remove the Marketing group's access to the folder, you need to disable the permission inheritance for the folder. Uncheck the **Allow inheritable permissions** check box. When you do, a security box, shown in Figure 5.16, pops up advising you about removing the

folder's capability to inherit permissions. If you click **Remove**, all inheritance will be removed. Since you want to maintain access for the special groups, click **Copy** instead.

Figure 5.16 Choosing to Copy or Remove Inherited Permissions

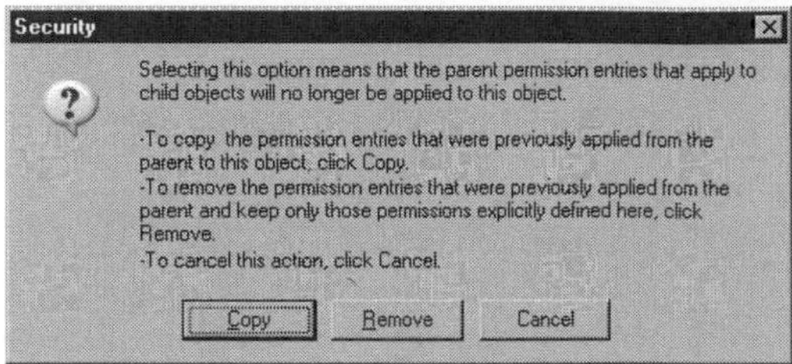

10. When the **Security** box closes, click **Apply** in the **Advanced Security Settings** window, and then click **OK**.
11. Click the **Marketing** group in the group list and click **Remove**.
12. Figure 5.17 shows the resulting **Security** window. Click **Apply** to put the new security permissions into effect.

Figure 5.17 Final Security Settings Displayed in the Folder's Properties Window

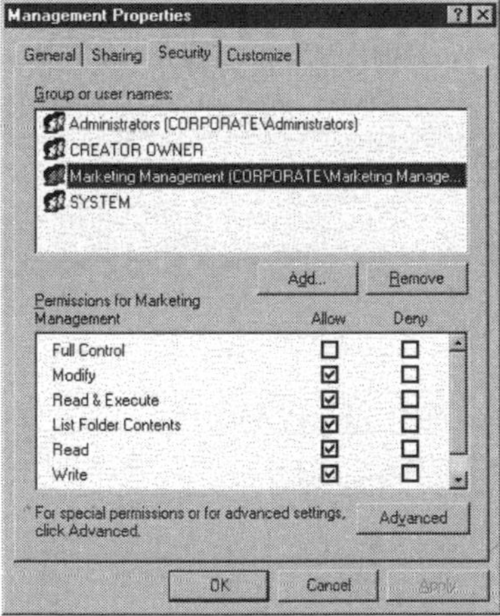

13. Click the **Sharing** tab to create a new share for this folder.
14. In the Sharing window, click the **Share this folder** radio button. Enter the requested **Share name** in the field, as shown in Figure 5.18.

Figure 5.18 Setting the Name of the New Share

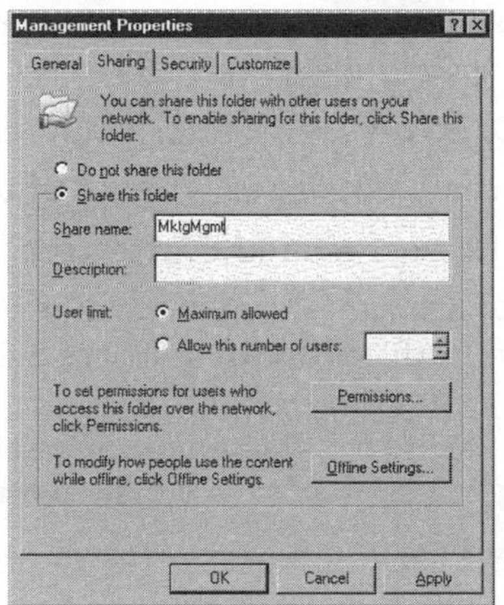

15. Click the **Permissions** button.
16. Click **Add**, enter the name of the group, and then click **Check Names**.
17. Click **OK** to close the **Select Users, Computers, or Groups** window.
18. Select **Marketing Managers** in the group list, and then click the **Full Control** check box under the **Allow** column to assign all rights to the group.
19. Select **Everyone** in the group list, and then click **Remove**. Your permissions window now looks similar to Figure 5.19.

Figure 5.19 Viewing Final Settings for Share Permissions

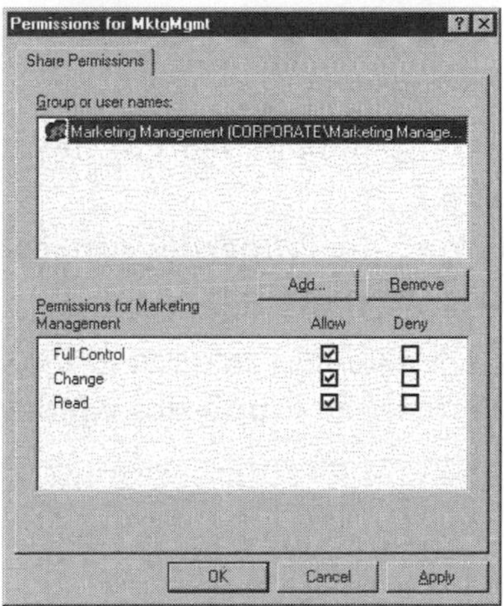

20. Click **Apply** and then click **OK** to close the **Share Permissions** window.
21. In the **Folder Permissions** window, click **Apply** and then click **OK** to close the **Permissions** dialog box.
22. Open **Active Directory Users and Computers**.
23. Select the directory root in the left pane of the window.
24. Select **Action | New | Shared Folder** from the menu.
25. Enter **MktgMgmt** for the share name and **\\CORPADFP1\MktgMgmt** for the network path, as shown in Figure 5.20.

Figure 5.20 Setting the Name of the Directory Share

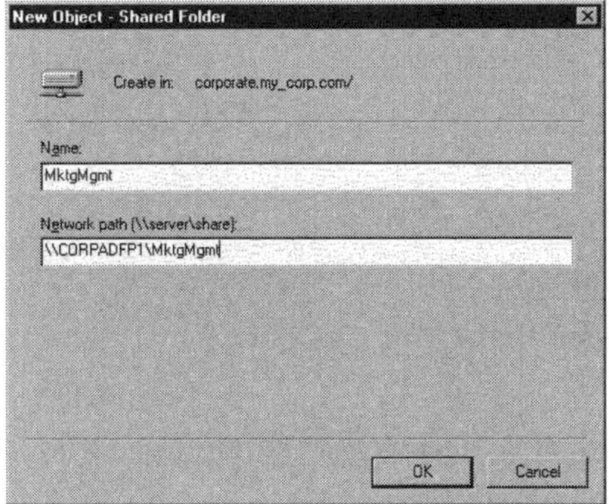

26. Click **OK**.
27. Double-click the **MktgMgmt** shared folder to open the **Properties** window.
28. Click the **Security** tab.
29. Click the **Add** button.
30. Enter the **Marketing Management** as the name of the group and click **Check Names**.
31. Click **OK** to return to the **Properties** window.
32. Select **Authenticated Users** from the group list and click **Remove**.
33. The **Properties** window now looks like Figure 5.21. Click **Apply** and then click **OK** to close the **Properties** window.

Figure 5.21 Verifying Correct Permissions on the Directory Share

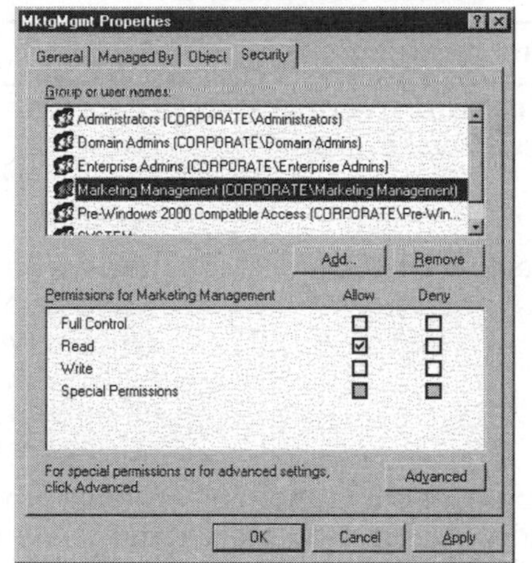

Now, the Marketing managers are able to access the Management folder through the MktgMgmt share on the network and the rest of the Marketing department cannot. In addition, the directory share is only visible to the members of the Marketing Management group and system administrators.

Setting User Rights and Privileges

Working with file, folder, and share permissions is only one way to grant or restrict access to resources on the Windows Server 2003 server. User rights give you another level of control over use of resources. This section will cover the following topics:

- Understanding the role of user rights
- Using Group Policy to set user rights

Understanding the Role of User Rights

Every object has a default set of rights governed initially by where the object is created in Active Directory. User rights are inherited from parent objects just like share and security permissions are inherited. Whereas NTFS and share permissions grant or restrict access to files and folders, user rights can affect how a user logs on to a system, how processes can affect system memory, and who can shut down a server, among other things.

There are a number of user rights that can be configured. Table 5.8 lists a few of the rights, which objects have the rights by default, and a description of the right or privilege. The items listed in the table refer to roles that can be assigned to user objects.

Table 5.8 User Rights and Default Assignments

Privilege	Default Assignments	Description
Access this computer from the network	Administrators, Authenticated Users, Everyone	Users with this right can attach to the server from across the network. This right does not affect Terminal Services.
Add workstations to domain	Authenticated Users	Users with this privilege can add workstations to the Active Directory. When a workstation is added to Active Directory, the workstation inherits the network and security settings for the Active Directory.
Allow log on locally	Account Operators, Administrators, Backup Operators, Print Operators, Server Operators	Users with this right can log on to the server console interactively.
Allow log on through Terminal Services	Administrators	Users with this right can log on to the server with the Terminal Services client.
Back up files and directories	Administrators and Backup Operators	Users with this privilege can access all files and folders on a server for the purpose of backing up the data, despite any access restrictions that have been placed on those files and folders.
Change the system time	Administrators and Server Operators	Users with this privilege can change the system time and date on the computer.
Deny access to this computer from network	None	Users with this right cannot access the server across the network. This right overrides the **Access this computer from the network** right when an object is assigned both rights.
Deny log on locally	None	Users with this right cannot log on interactively to the server. This right overrides any other rights related to local log on. If this right is assigned to the Everyone group, no one will be able to log on interactively at the server console.

Continued

Table 5.8 User Rights and Default Assignments

Privilege	Default Assignments	Description
Deny log on through Terminal Services	None	Users with this right cannot log on to the server with a Terminal Services client. This right overrides the **Allow log on through Terminal Services** right.
Force shutdown from a remote system	Administrators and Server Operators	Users with this privilege can shut down a computer or server without being at the server console.
Restore files and directories	Administrators, Backup Operators, Server Operators	Users with this privilege can restore files and directories from a backup device, including restoring the file/folder permissions and ownership of the data. This privilege bypasses any file or folder permissions that would otherwise restrict the user from accessing the data being restored.
Shut down the system	Account Operators, Administrators, Backup Operators, Server Operators, Print Operators	Users with this privilege can shut down a server from the console.
Take ownership of files or other objects	Administrators	Users with this privilege can take ownership of any object in the system with owner properties. This includes, but is not limited to, files, folders, printers, and processes.

As you can see from reading the table, these user rights govern a different type of access control than NTFS and share permissions. There is still some overlap between the two areas, specifically related to data backup and restore functions. By default, the Administrators and Backup Operators groups have the Back up files and directories and Restore files and directories privileges. This way, the data on the server can be backed up and restored even if NTFS permissions have been set to deny access to a particular directory path. So in this instance, the user privileges can override the NTFS security permissions – sort of. The backup operators still can't access (open and read) the files and folders to which they're denied access in the traditional way, but they can bypass permissions to perform specific operations (backup and restore) on them.

NOTE

To understand the difference between permissions and user rights, think of it this way: permissions control access to *specific* objects (files, folders). User rights define *tasks* that the user or group can or cannot perform on the system.

As with security permissions, denying or revoking a privilege or right supercedes the granting of the same. A user object will have only the specific privilege or right if the object belongs to a group that has been granted that right. So only members of the Administrators group will be allowed to log on to a domain controller via Terminal Services, because only that group has been granted that right. If you had a subset of accounts that belonged to the Administrators group that you wanted to prohibit from using Terminal Services to access the domain controller, you could create a new group, add the user objects to that group, then enable the Deny log on through Terminal Services right for that group. That way, only user objects that belonged to Administrators but not to this other group would be able to log on to the domain controller via Terminal Services.

Using Group Policy to Set User Rights

You have read several times in this chapter that you should apply security configurations to groups and not to users. This holds true for user rights as well. Wherever possible, user rights should be granted to a group and not an individual user object.

If you are logged on to a domain controller, the most direct way to assign user rights is through the Domain Controller Security Policy. You can find the link to this in the Administrative Tools folder, either in the Control Panel folder or in the Programs folder in the Start menu. User rights assignments are in the Local Policy group under User Rights Assignment. You can access the security editor from Windows XP workstations if you have the Windows Server 2003 Administration Tools Pack installed. Figure 5.22 shows the security policy editor (an MMC with a subset of the Group Policy Object Editor console) with the user rights listed. Next to the listing of each policy is the list of groups that have the policy assigned. If nothing is listed next to the policy name, no groups have been assigned to that policy. In some cases, such as the Create global objects policy, the policy setting is shown as Not Defined. That indicates that the policy has not been enabled and the system will take the default action related to that function if requested.

NOTE

User rights can be assigned in a domain environment by editing a GPO assigned to the domain. To access the default domain policy and set user rights on its GPO, open Active Directory Users and Computers console from the Administrative Tools menu, right-click the domain name in the left console pane, select **Properties.** Click the **Group Policy** tab, select the GPO, and then click **Edit.** This opens the Group Policy Object Editor. Under **Computer Configuration** in the left pane, expand **Windows Settings,** expand **Security Settings,** expand **Local Policies**, and select **User Rights Assignment**.

Figure 5.22 Viewing the User Rights Assignment Window in Domain Controller Security Policy Editor

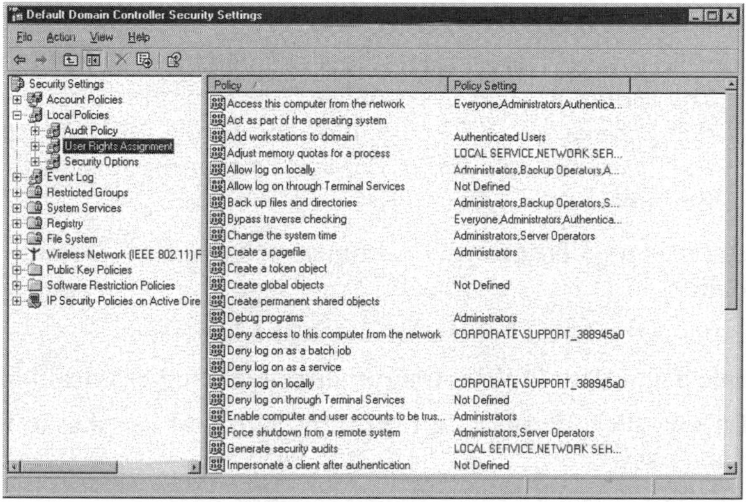

To modify the groups assigned to a particular policy, double-click the policy, and then add the desired group by clicking the **Add User or Group** button. Figure 5.23 shows what these settings might look like after the configuration was changed. After you have made the desired changes, click **Apply**, and the new policy setting will take immediate effect.

Figure 5.23 Viewing the Back Up Files and Directories Security Policy Window

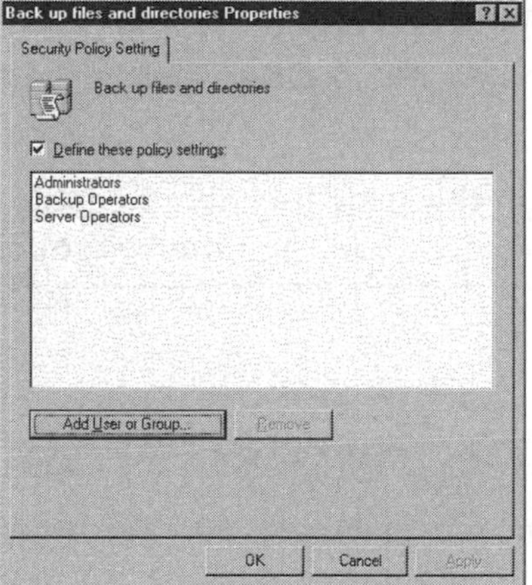

EXERCISE 5.02

ASSIGNING USER RIGHTS

In this exercise, you will go through the steps necessary to assign the capability to log on to a terminal server to an Active Directory group. You have just set up a new Windows Server 2003 computer and configured it to run as a terminal server. Now the employees in the Sales department want to be able to access the terminal server when they are on the road.

1. Open **Start | Programs | Administrative Tools | Domain Security Policy**.
2. Expand the **Local Policies** object in the left pane.
3. Select the **User Rights Assignment** object under **Local Policies**.
4. Double-click **Allow log on through Terminal Services** in the right pane.
5. Enable the **Define these policy settings** check box.
6. Click the **Add User or Group** button.
7. Click **Browse**.
8. Enter the group name (**CORPORATE\Sales** in this case) and click **Check Names**.
9. When done adding groups, click **OK**.
10. Click **OK** to return to the **Security Policy Setting** window.
11. Click **Apply** and then click **OK** to close the **Security Policy Setting** window.

You can go through the same process to enable other groups to log on through Terminal Services, or you can remove groups if needed.

Troubleshooting Access Problems

As access control tools become more powerful, they also become more complex, and the number of ways that access problems can arise increases. If you are supporting an organization that has a poorly planned or poorly implemented access structure, then a user calling to say "I can't get to my files this morning" can pose a major problem. Even if you are supporting a well-designed and maintained system, these calls can still happen and cause you a lot of extra work. This next section is devoted to giving you some pointers for common problems and resolutions. It covers the following topics:

- Identifying common access problems
- Basic troubleshooting guidelines

Identifying Common Access Problems

The most common cause of access problems is a change in permissions or rights. When a user says that the files he or she could work with yesterday are not there today, you know something has changed. What's most likely is that someone changed something and didn't check to make sure the change yielded the desired result. But knowing where to start looking for these changes can separate the successful system administrators from the unsuccessful ones. Some of the common access problems are listed here:

- **Lack of permissions** The user or group does not have permissions assigned to access the data. This could result from the user thinking that he or she already had access when none was given, or for some reason access was removed.
- **Too many permissions** This can result from resulting from an over-zealous admin not wanting to troubleshoot access problems and assigning Full Control rights in various locations until the apparent problem was resolved. Too many permissions can be more problematic than a lack of permissions.
- **Permission conflicts** Permission conflicts usually result from denying a permission incorrectly. In most cases, restricting access to a resource can be handled more cleanly by removing the permissions from the ACL of an object rather than specifying Deny permissions in an ACL.
- **Files or folders moved or copied** If data was copied or moved from one location to another, the permissions on the data in the new location may not have been set correctly.
- **NTFS and Share permissions in conflict** This is one of the most common problems a new system administrator encounters. When NTFS and share permissions are not set correctly, user access to data will not work as expected.

Basic Troubleshooting Guidelines

Whether the call comes in as "I'm getting this error when mapping a drive" or "I can't save changes to any of my files," the troubleshooting *process* is the same. Rather than promise you a guaranteed, one-size-fits-all troubleshooting process, we will outline some troubleshooting guidelines for access problems. All technicians develop their own troubleshooting mantras based on their own experiences. Here are some general "should do's" related to access problems:

- **First and foremost, listen.** Listen to the user and understand exactly what the problem is. Regardless of how good you are technically, if you cannot fully understand the problem the user is encountering, you might take your outstanding troubleshooting skills down the completely wrong path. Listening can usually distinguish between "the server is down" and "your network cable is unplugged."

- **Look at the groups to which the user object belongs.** Even though you may not know what groups the user was a member of yesterday, you can tell what group memberships he or she has right now. Look also for obvious problems with group membership. Chances are, a user who is primarily a traveling salesperson for the company should not be a member of the Backup Operators group. Likewise, the user should have some group membership defined, even if it is just Users or Everyone. A user with no group memberships likely cannot access anything on the network.
- **Look at the files and folders the user is trying to access.** Start with the actual folders and not the shares. Check the simple things first—is the folder present on the volume? Is the file in the folder? Is the file marked as read only? Then check for the NTFS permissions on the files and folders. If permissions are set on specific files, try to determine why. In general practice, NTFS permissions should only apply to folders, so see if there's an obvious reason for setting permissions on a file. Then look at the NTFS permissions on the folder. Are there appropriate ACEs in the ACL? Are the folder permissions inherited from the parent folder? Do any of the ACEs match group memberships for the user? Is the CREATOR OWNER group assigned permissions in the folder? Are there any Deny permissions that may be stomping on otherwise correctly-configured ACLs? You might need to go all the way up to the root of the volume to determine if the NTFS permissions are set correctly for the end-level folder and files. Also be on the lookout for any Deny permissions applied. If you find any Deny permissions, work out the way the Deny permission impacts access to the file or folder for all groups, then determine if that impacts the user having the access problem.
- **Examine the permissions set on the share.** Determine which share the user is accessing, remembering that a folder on disk can have multiple network shares pointing to it with different access permissions. Examine the share ACL and look for access granted to each entity. Does the user belong to a group that has permissions to the share? Are there any Deny permissions on the share that may be impacting the user's access? Does the level of access to the share match the desired level of access granted through NTFS?

Configuring & Implementing...

NTFS and Share Permissions

One of the best ways to learn how NTFS and share permissions impact user access is to set up a share and change the permissions on the share and the folder and see how access works. If you have access to a server that is not in production, you should be able to test to your heart's content. If you only have access to servers in production, be very careful when working on the system to ensure that you do not impact access to users working with the system. In a pinch, you can also use a Windows 2000 or Windows XP Professional workstation to set up and test the shares.

We highly recommend VMWare (www.vmware.com) as an essential tool for any network administrator (or networking student) who wants to be able to set up multiple-server scenarios and test configurations without having to purchase a lot of expensive hardware.

However you do your testing, start by granting a user object Full Control NTFS permissions on a folder, then share the folder and give the user Read permission on the share. Access the share as the user and see what your level of access is. Then go through and make changes to the share and NTFS permissions and see how those changes look to the user account. This will go a long way towards helping you identify NTFS and share permission conflicts when users call reporting access problems.

Using New Command-Line Utilities

Windows Server 2003 introduces a number of new command-line tools to help simplify administration of the server. Two of these new command-line tools, takeown and where, can be particularly helpful in managing access to resources on the server. You can use these commands as standalone commands or in batch files to assist in automating support of the system. The specific tools we will cover in this section are as follows:

- where.exe
- takeown.exe

Using where.exe

Administrators have been longing for a tool like where.exe ever since the inception of Windows. Similar tools have been available for UNIX and NetWare systems, and many administrators have been frustrated by the lack of such a tool—even from third-party vendors—when working in the Windows environment. Now, with Windows Server 2003, where.exe is a much-welcomed addition to the Windows command-line arsenal. where.exe is a tool designed for one purpose only—to determine the location of a file or files on a hard disk. By default, where.exe searches the current directory and the directories specified in the PATH statement to locate a particular filename or wildcard search. Using this default search pattern is helpful for determining where an application is running from if a tool does not work as expected. For example, the **cipher.exe** command-line tool that is discussed later in the chapter is different on Windows Server 2003 than on Windows 2000 Server or Professional. If you set up a batch file for your users that includes cipher.exe and it does not yield the desired results, you can use where to see which cipher.exe is being run in the batch file. To do this, open a command-prompt window and change to the directory where the cipher.exe program is being executed. Then type **where cipher.exe** at the command prompt to get a listing of all the locations where cipher.exe resides.

where.exe also enables you to use system environment variables to search for files. To have where.exe list all the files in your home directory, type **where $homedir:*.*** at the command prompt. Any environment variable can be used in this format to give *where* a location to search. Entering **where $windir:*.dll** at the command prompt lists all the .dll files in the main system directory of the computer.

Where.exe is also good for locating user documents on the server or other computers. If your server has drive E: set up for user data, you can find all Word and Excel documents on that drive by using the command **where /r e:\ *.doc *.xls**. Or if you want to do the same search on a computer named MKTG01, you can use the command **where /r \\MKTG01\C$ *.doc *.xls**. Table 5.9 lists some of the command-line parameters for the *where* tool. To get a complete listing of the parameters available, you can type **where /?** at the command prompt.

Table 5.9 Command-Line Parameters for where.exe

Parameter	Action
/R *dir*	Recursively searches starting in the directory specified by *dir* for the specified file patterns. Do not use this parameter if you specify an environment variable pattern as the search location.
/F	Displays the filenames found in double quotes.
/T	Displays the file size, file modification date and time for the filenames found.
/Q	Operates in quiet mode, only returning an error level and not displaying any output on the screen.

where.exe will also return an error-level value that can be used in a batch file. where.exe returns an error level 0 if the search is successful, error level 1 if the search failed to find any files matching the pattern, and an error level 2 if an error occurred.

Using Takeown.exe

Another command-line tool useful for managing files is takeown.exe. As you might guess, this tool enables the user to change the ownership of a file or files specified on the command line. takeown can set the new owner of a file as a specific user or as the administrators group, depending on the command-line parameters used. By default, takeown assigns the user of a file to be the user who ran the tool.

Table 5.10 lists some of the command-line parameters used with takeown. Several examples of how you might use takeown follow the table.

Table 5.10 Command-Line Parameters for takeown.exe

Parameter	Action
/F *filename*	Changes the owner of the file or files specified by *filename*. *Filename* can be a specific filename or a wildcard pattern.
/A	Changes the owner of the file or files to the Administrators group instead of the current user.
/R	Changes all files in the directory specified with the /F parameter and its subfolders.
/S *system*	Operates on the remote computer specified by *system*.
/U [*domain*\]*user*	Operates as the user specified by *user* and the optional domain specified by *domain*.
/P [password]	Uses the password specified by password to authenticate as the user specified with the */U* flag. Prompts for a password if this parameter is omitted.

To change the owner of a specific file, such as Readme.doc, enter **takeown /f readme.doc** at the command prompt. This changes the owner of the file to you, provided you have sufficient permissions to change the file owner. If you want to change the owner of the file to the Administrators group, enter **takeown /f readme.doc /a** at the command prompt. You can also use environment variables, as you can with where.exe. To change the ownership of all text files in the Windows system directory and all subdirectories to the Administrators group, enter **takeown /f %windir%*.txt /r /a**.

EXERCISE 5.03

CHANGING OWNERSHIP OF FILES

In this exercise, you will go through the process of changing ownership of files for an employee who has left the company. The manager of the Marketing department has let you know that one of her employees has left the company without notice, and she wants to have access to all the data that was in his home directory on the server. Since you cannot assign ownership of this employee's files directly to her, you will have to first take ownership of the files, grant her the take ownership permission on the files, and then show her how to use takeown.exe to make herself the owner of the files.

For this example, the Marketing manager is Patricia Chapman, and her network ID is *chapmap*. The employee who left the company is Brad Barron, whose network ID was *barronb*. His home directory is *\\CORPADFP1\Home\barronb*. All users in the company map drive H: to *\\CORPADFP1\Home*.

1. Open a command prompt.
2. Change to drive H: and change to the *barronb* directory.
3. Type **takeown /f * /r /a** and press **Enter** to change ownership of all files and folders in the current directory to the Administrators group.
4. Scroll through the responses from takeown to verify success on each ownership change.
5. Close the command window.
6. Open **My Computer** and double-click drive **H:**.
7. Right-click the **barronb** folder and select **Properties**.
8. Click the **Security** tab and click **Advanced**.
9. Click the **Add** button.
10. Enter the username (chapmap) and click **Check Names**.
11. Click **OK**.
12. Scroll to the bottom of the permissions list and click the **Take Ownership** check box under **Allow**.
13. Click **OK**
14. Click **Apply** and then click **OK**.
15. Have the Marketing manager open a command prompt on her PC.
16. Have her change to the *barronb* directory on drive H:.
17. Have her type **takeown /f * /r** and press **Enter**.
18. Have her scroll through the responses from *takeown* to verify success on each ownership change.

Now the Marketing manager is the owner on all the files belonging to the departed employee.

Using EFS Encryption

There are times when securing data through file and share access is not enough. Because administrators and backup operators can still get to data on the server, it is possible that a "rogue" net admin might be tempted to go looking through sensitive company data. With Encrypting File System (EPS) encryption, you can still keep sensitive data from prying eyes, even if they can access the files directly on the server. Topics covered in this section include the following:

- Understanding disk encryption
- Understanding how EFS works "under the hood"
- Using EFS graphical tools
- Using EFS command-line tools
- Applying EFS best practices

Understanding Disk Encryption

Encrypting files on disk is not a new technology. Those of us who were around to support WordPerfect 4.2 should remember its ability to password-protect files. When selected, the user would provide a password to WordPerfect and the program would use the password to scramble the data in the file before writing the file to disk. The program used a complex algorithm that took the data in the file and the contents of the password and processed the two together. Anyone looking at the file with a binary file reader would see nothing meaningful in the file contents. When the correct password was supplied to the WordPerfect program, the contents of the file and the password would go through a reverse algorithm and extract the meaningful data from the file and display it on the screen. Without the password, however, no one could translate the data back into human-readable form, not even the technicians at WordPerfect.

Many applications now support some form of password-protecting files to protect the contents. This protection ranges from not being able to make changes to a file without the correct password, to the WordPerfect method of not being able to use the file at all. Disk encryption does the same thing, but at a higher level. Instead of providing a password to access a specific file within a specific program, disk encryption can lock a file folder or an entire disk at the operating system level with an encryption key. Disk encryption also gives you the capability to unlock an encrypted file without the original encryption key, something WordPerfect could not do.

There is still one thing that even disk encryption cannot do – prevent users with sufficient access from deleting files from the server. All disk encryption can do for you is to make the contents of the files unreadable to prying eyes. A malicious user bent on wreaking havoc can still cause damage by deleting data, but you can at least make sure that the malcontent cannot walk out with any usable, sensitive data.

EFS is not a complete security solution for data, however. It is merely one piece of the larger data security puzzle. You will read later in this section that EFS-encrypted files are decrypted automatically under a number of different circumstances, including copying or transferring the files from one location to another. The contents of the files are unencrypted during this transport, and unless other encryption technologies are used, the data is in a readable format at that time. Other data security tools, such as SSL or IPSec, can be used to securely transfer the data between locations when you do not want to expose the data at any point along the way.

Understanding How EFS Works "Under the Hood"

Instead of using passwords that the user must remember each time he or she wants to access a file, EFS uses a system of keys based on public key technology. When a user encrypts a file on an EFS-enabled NTFS volume, several keys are created related to the file. First, if the user does not have a digital certificate suitable for EFS, one is automatically created by the system, which also generates a public key for the user based on the certificate. Next, a randomly generated key is created and used to encrypt the file. This random key, called a file encryption key (FEK), is itself encrypted using the user's public key. Each file has two FEKs created – one created using the user's public key and another with the recovery key of the recovery agent. The recovery agent can be the local system administrator or a third-party Certification Authority (CA). If more than one recovery agent is identified, a separate FEK is created for each one.

Configuring & Implementing...

Managing Keys

There is no way a user can recover encrypted data with a missing or corrupt certificate (unless a recovery agent was identified at the time the file was encrypted). Suppose you enable EFS on a local folder and your hard disk crashes. How would you regain access to the encrypted data? Even if you can restore the disk from a system backup, your encryption certificate may not return in the process. Therefore, it is important to keep a secure backup of the certificate used to encrypt data.

You can make back-up copies of your certificates through Internet Explorer. To make a backup of your certificates, you can follow these steps:

1. Open Internet Explorer.
2. Select **Tools | Internet Options**.
3. Click the **Content** tab.
4. In the **Certificates** pane, click **Certificates.**
5. If more than one certificate is listed, select each certificate individually until **Encrypting File System** is displayed in the **Certificate Intended Purposes** pane.
6. Click **Export** to start the **Certificate Export Wizard**.
7. In the first page of the wizard, click **Next**.
8. Select the **Yes, export private key** radio button and click **Next**.
9. Place a check mark in the **Enable strong protection** check box and click **Next**.
10. Type a password for the certificate and click **Next**.
11. Select a filename for the certificate and click **Next**.

Continued

12. Click **Finish** to complete the wizard.
13. Store the key file in a secure location.

You can import the certificate to your system at a later time, if needed, in the Certificates area of Internet Options. You will need to do this not only if your hard disk crashes and is recovered from backup, but also if you need to recover your certificates if you move from one computer to another.

You can also use the Certificates snap-in within MMC to manage your certificates. You can launch the Certificate Export Wizard from within the Certificates snap-in. Open the wizard by finding the certificate you want to export, right-clicking the certificate, and selecting **Export** from the **All Tasks** sub-menu.

When the user goes to access an encrypted file, the user's public key is used to decrypt the FEK associated with the user, and then the decrypted FEK is used to decrypt the file. Although the process is transparent to the user, there is some overhead associated with the encryption/decryption process, and it is possible that a user might notice some delay when reading or writing files on an encrypted volume. In the case that the file contents need to be accessed without the use of the user's public key (if the user's account were deleted from the domain before all the encrypted files were decrypted), the recovery agent can log on and decrypt the files. Alternately, the encrypted files can be transferred to a system where the recovery agent can decrypt the files. When the recovery agent accesses the file, the recovery agent's public key is used to decrypt the correct FEK and then decrypt the file. Only a recovery agent that was active at the time the file was encrypted will be able to decrypt the file. Otherwise, access to the encrypted data will fail just like it will for any other user who tries to access the data.

Configuring & Implementing...

Recovery Agents

Great caution should be used when dealing with a recovery agent and decrypting user files. Since the recovery agent's keys can decrypt any file on the network, those keys need to be kept in a secure location where no one can access them. In some cases, organizations set up the recovery agent information on a PC that is not connected to the network to ensure physical security of the keys.

If you need to use the recovery agent to decrypt user data, you should first look to transfer the data to the recovery agent's computer and perform the decryption there. This keeps the integrity of the recovery agent's keys and ensures that only the specific files sent to the recovery agent's computer are decrypted.

If you choose to have the recovery agent decrypt the files in their original location, you need to pay attention to the security surrounding the agent's keys. By doing the recovery on the network, you expose the agent's keys to potentially

Continued

unscrupulous users who may try to snag the keys and use them to access other encrypted data.

By default, the Administrator account is set up as a recovery agent in the Active Directory. Many agencies create a new account to act as the recovery agent and remove the Administrator account as a recovery agent. However, with Windows Server 2003, you are no longer required to have a recovery agent in a domain. By not requiring a default recovery agent, you can have greater assurance that an administrator will not be able to access encrypted data without prior authorization. This was actually a drawback in the Windows 2000 implementation of EFS – if an organization did not completely manage the EFS environment by removing the recovery agent's keys from the network and storing them in a difficult-to-access location, an administrator could, with those keys still on the network, go through a user's encrypted files at will.

The problem with not having a default recovery agent is what to do if something happens to the user who encrypted the files. If the user's keys become corrupt or otherwise unavailable, the files cannot be decrypted. This can be avoided by authorizing other users to share the encrypted files, which is discussed in the "Sharing Encrypted Files" sidebar later in this section.

To ensure better security, you should encourage users who want to use EFS to enable encryption at the folder level and not the file level. This way any files stored in an EFS-enabled folder are encrypted, including temporary files. Encryption settings for files are also affected when files are moved or copied to other folders. Table 5.11 details the results of taking actions on encrypted files.

Table 5.11 Encryption Settings Resulting from File Activities

Destination	Status
Encrypted file or folder moved or copied to a volume without EFS enabled (FAT32, FAT16, or Windows NT NTFS volumes)	Encryption is removed.
Encrypted file or folder copied or moved to an NTFS volume on the same computer	Encryption is maintained.
Encrypted file or folder copied or moved to another computer	File cannot be moved or copied.

In addition, no system files can be encrypted, nor can the Windows system directory be marked for encryption. EFS cannot work with compressed files, either. If compression is enabled on a folder and any data in that folder is marked for encryption, the encrypted files are uncompressed and will remain uncompressed. Enabling compression on an encrypted folder has no effect, because file encryption supercedes compression.

EFS uses the DESX algorithm for file encryption by default. DESX is a variation of the Data Encryption Standard (DES) algorithm that has been in use since 1977. DESX has improved on the original standard by adding additional computations to the encrypting algorithm, reducing the likelihood of the encryption being cracked.

Optionally, a stronger encryption algorithm can be used for EFS to provide additional file security. Triple-DES (3DES) uses longer keys (128-bit or 168-bit as opposed to the 64-bit keys used by DES) and additional computations to make cracking the encrypted contents much more difficult. 3DES use for EFS must be enabled through Group Policy. After 3DES encryption is enabled, all new encryption is completed using 3DES, although existing DESX-encrypted data can still be accessed.

Domain Recovery Policies

You can control the EFS environment for your organization through Group Policy. Domain-level Group Policy settings can enforce a recovery policy, specify recovery agents for the domain, and restrict users in the domain from using EFS altogether.

To view or configure EFS settings in the domain, follow these steps:

1. Open **Active Directory Users and Computers**.
2. Right-click the appropriate domain and select **Properties**.
3. Click the **Group Policy** tab.
4. Select the appropriate policy object from the list and click **Edit**.
5. Expand **Computer Configuration | Windows Settings | Security Settings | Public Key Policies | Encrypting File System**.

In this area of the Group Policy Editor, you will see a list of the active certificates for designated recovery agents. You can add to the list of recovery agents in two ways. First, you can select from a list of existing certificates in the directory and add the certificate to the list. To do this, right-click **Encrypting File System** and select **Add Data Recovery Agent**. This opens the **Add Recovery Agent Wizard**, which walks you through the steps of selecting an existing user with an EFS certificate in the directory to add to the list of recovery agents. Second, you can create a new certificate to add to the list. To do this, right-click **Encrypting File System** and select **Create Data Recovery Agent**. This creates a new EFS certificate for the logged-in user and makes that user a recovery agent in the domain. If you want to remove a recovery agent, right-click the recovery agent certificate and select **Delete**.

EXAM WARNING

Windows Server 2003 differs from Windows 2000 Server in the way recovery agent certificates are handled. In a Windows 2000 server environment, removing all recovery agent certificates from a Group Policy Object (GPO) disables EFS for the container to which the GPO was applied. Not so in Windows Server 2003.

Removing all recovery agent certificates in a Windows Server 2003 environment simply means that files encrypted after the recovery agent certificates have been removed will not have a recovery agent that can decrypt them if the encrypting user's key is damaged or lost.

If you want to disable EFS altogether for the domain, right-click **Encrypting File System** and select **Properties**. In the **Properties** window, uncheck the **Allow users to encrypt files using Encrypting File System** check box. Making this change prevents users using any computer in that domain from using EFS on the local system. When implementing a new Active Directory structure, it is best to disable EFS for the directory until you have had a chance to plan and implement your EFS policy for the environment. You can add and create recovery agent certificates in a GPO before enabling EFS for the environment.

Encrypting Files and Folders Using the Graphical Interface

Marking a file or folder for encryption is a simple process. Open the **Properties** window for the desired file or folder and click the **Advanced** button in the **General** tab. This opens the **Advanced Attributes** window shown in Figure 5.24. Clicking the **Encrypt contents to secure data** check box and clicking **OK** will mark the folder so that all new data in the folder is encrypted. When you apply the changes to the folder, you are asked if you want to apply the changes to the folder only or to the entire folder contents, including files and subfolders. If you select the folder only, all existing data remains intact (unencrypted) but all new data stored in the folder becomes encrypted. Additionally, if you make changes to a file that was not encrypted when the encryption settings were made, that file becomes encrypted when you save it.

Figure 5.24 Setting Encryption on a Folder

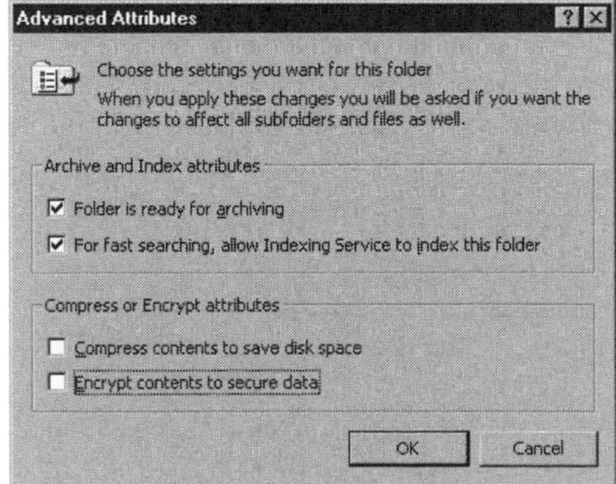

You can check on the encryption status of a file or folder from directly in Windows Explorer. When you select an encrypted file or folder in an Explorer window, the window displays **Encrypted** in the **Attributes** field, as shown in Figure 5.25. You can also set encrypted folders to display in a different text color in Explorer. By default, you will see encrypted file and folder names in green if you are logged in locally on a Windows Server 2003 computer.

Figure 5.25 Viewing Encrypted Attributes on a Folder

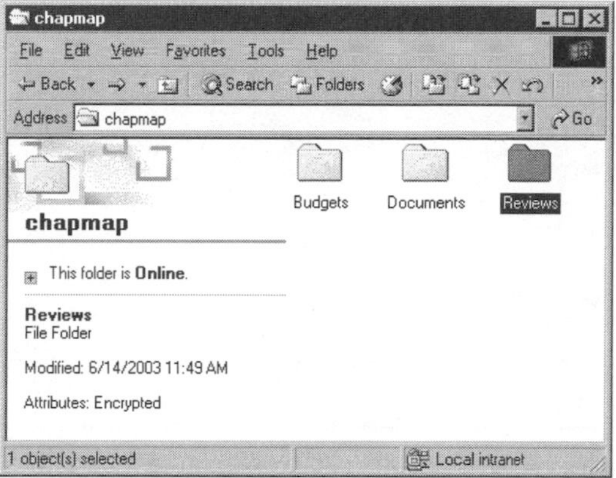

New & Noteworthy...

Sharing Encrypted Files

New with Windows Server 2003 and Windows XP is the ability to share files that have been encrypted. With the Windows 2000 version of NTFS used by Windows 2000 Professional workstations and Windows 2000 server, users could encrypt files on NTFS volumes, but only the user and the recovery agent could open the file after it was encrypted. In the new revision to NTFS used by Windows Server 2003 and Windows XP Professional, users encrypting a file can add other users to a list of those authorized to open the file.

To give other users the ability to decrypt a file, open the **Properties** for the file, and then click the **Advanced** button in the **General** tab (the same steps to set the encryption flag for the file). After a file has been encrypted, a **Details** button appears in the **Advanced Attributes** window next to the **Encryption** check box. Clicking the **Details** button opens the **Encryption Details** window, shown in Figure 5.26. The upper portion of the window displays the users who are able to access the file, while the lower portion of the window lists the recovery agents who are authorized to recover the encrypted file, if necessary. Clicking the **Add** button enables you to select other users to add to the user list. When the settings are applied to the file, the users in the user list are able to access the file, even though the contents are encrypted.

Additional users can only be added to specific files, not an entire folder.

Continued

Figure 5.26 Sharing Encrypted Files

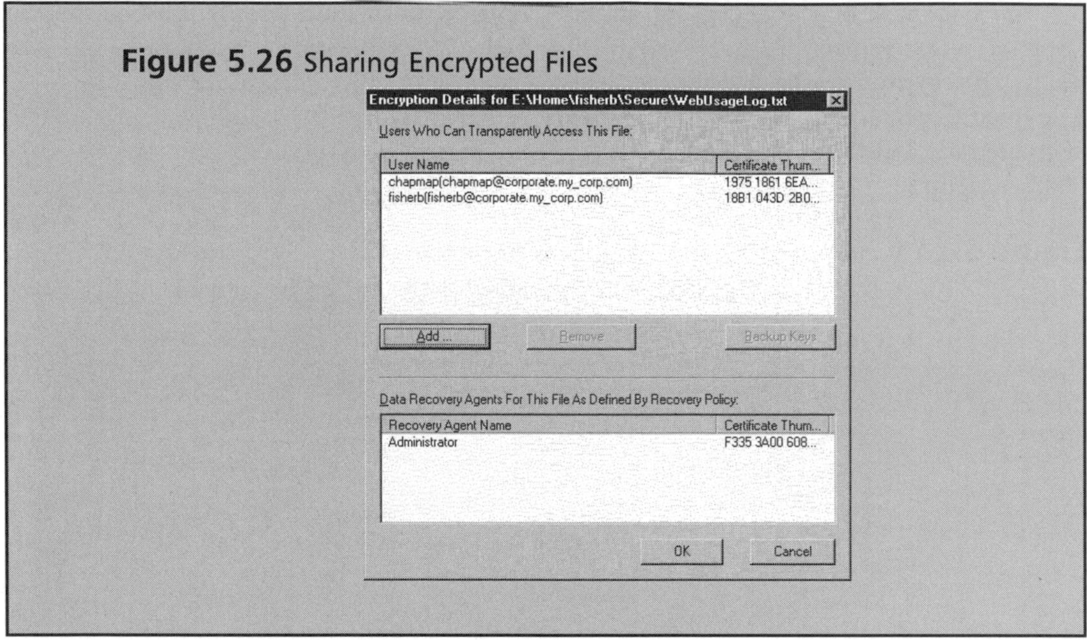

Using the Cipher.exe Command to Perform Encryption Tasks

Those who are more comfortable using command-line tools to perform administrative tasks can use the cipher.exe program to work with EFS. Using cipher.exe, you can accomplish all the functions just described, plus there are a number of additional tasks you can complete with this tool. In addition, you can use cipher.exe to automate EFS tasks if you choose.

Opening a command prompt and typing **cipher.exe** displays the current encryption state of the folder. Figure 5.27 shows the output of the cipher command in the same folder as shown previously in Figure 5.24. The output indicates that the current folder, E:\Home\chapmap\, is not set for encryption, but the Reviews folder is.

Figure 5.27 Using Cipher.exe to View Encryption Settings

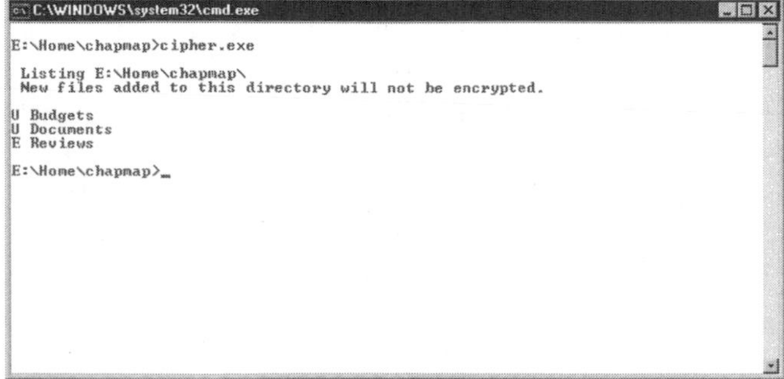

To encrypt a folder from the command line, type **cipher.exe /e** and the path to the folder to be encrypted. This marks the folder so that all files saved in the folder in the future will be encrypted. As typed, however, you will not encrypt any of the files that already exist in the folder. To encrypt the folder and all the files within the folder, type **cipher.exe /e /a** and the path to the folder. This command does not encrypt the contents of the subfolders in the directory. To do that, type **cipher.exe /e /s:*foldername***, where foldername is the name of the folder whose files and subfolders should be encrypted.

As you can see, cipher.exe is a complex tool that has a number of command-line switches to determine what functions it should perform. To see all the different command-line switches that can be used with cipher, type **cipher.exe /?** at the command prompt. Some of the common uses of cipher are listed in Table 5.12.

Table 5.12 Examples of Cipher Commands to Perform EFS Tasks

Command	Purpose
Cipher	Displays the encryption status of the current directory.
Cipher /e *name*	Encrypts the file named *name* or marks the folder *name* for future encryption.
Cipher /e /a *foldername*	Encrypts the files within the folder *foldername*, but none of the subfolders or their contents. Marks the folder *foldername* so that all new data in the folder will be encrypted.
Cipher /e /s:*foldername*	Encrypts the contents of the folder *foldername*, including all subfolders. The folder *foldername* and all the subfolders are marked so all new data will be encrypted.
Cipher /d *name*	Decrypts the file *name* or marks the folder *name* so that any new data in the folder will not be encrypted and any existing encrypted contents will be decrypted when changed.
Cipher /d /s:*foldername*	Decrypts the contents of the folder *foldername*, including all subfolders. The folder *foldername* and all its subfolders will no longer store encrypted data by default.

Cipher.exe can also be used to manage other security functions. You can back up your EFS certificate and key by typing **cipher.exe /x *filename*** at the command line. The file *filename*.pfx stores your EFS certificate information and can be copied to a secure location in case your EFS certificate becomes unusable at some point. You can also use *cipher* to remove data from unused areas on an NTFS volume. Type **cipher.exe /w:*directory*** to designate the volume that will be cleaned. You will want to close down any applications that are open when running this cleaning tool.

Applying EFS Best Practices

There are a number of different ways to make use of EFS in your environment. The following guidelines will help you manage your EFS implementation more effectively.

- Encrypt Temp folders on the system. This keeps any secure data out of the wrong hands if someone decides to go snooping through these directories.
- Set encryption on entire folders. Encrypting a single file in a folder might not maintain encryption on that file if it is deleted and recreated. Additionally, any temporary files that get written into the directory will be encrypted along with the other documents.
- Keep your recovery agent keys and certificates stored in a secure location off a file server. This prevents anyone from being able to access the key and certificate to import into their certificate store and access encrypted data.
- Create a new account or accounts to act as recovery agents. Remove the Administrator account's capability to serve as recovery agent.
- Disable EFS in the environment until you have had a chance to plan and implement your EFS policy.

Implementing a Public Key Infrastructure

Public key security is not new in the technology world, but it has not been widely used until recently. Increased concerns about access control and data security have brought more and more public key solutions into the mainstream. Microsoft is no different. With the release of Windows 2000 Server, Microsoft has included Certificate Services as a standard add-on for the OS. The service is also bundled with Windows Server 2003. You should expect to hear more about Public Key Infrastructure (PKI) in the coming years.

In this section, we will cover several areas related to Public Key Infrastructure, including the following:

- Understanding the function of a PKI
- Installing/Using Windows Server 2003 Certificate Services
- Creating the Certificate Authority Hierarchy
- Applying PKI best practices

Understanding the Function of a PKI

Digital certificates are becoming more and more common in today's computing environment. These certificates offer a way for individuals to verify the authenticity of e-mail messages, encrypt files, and so on. Several third-party organizations have been providing digital certificates or other key services for a number of years. There can be a number of drawbacks to relying solely on third-party certificate providers to generate and verify user keys. One of the most significant roadblocks is cost. While the per-user cost of issuing a valid certificate has decreased recently, it can still be cost-prohibitive for a large organization to rely solely on external resources for certificate security. Ease of management is another drawback. Again, managing certificates through an external organization can be cumbersome, confusing, and time-consuming, especially for large organizations.

With a Windows-based network infrastructure, you have the option of developing and hosting your own PKI within your organization. Microsoft provides a number of tools for creating and managing digital certificates within Active Directory. There are a number of advantages to using an internal PKI structure. First, there is no per-user cost to generate digital certificates. So these certificates can be created for every individual within the organization, no matter how large. Second, certificates can be managed internally. You can monitor use of certificates within the organization and automatically revoke certificates when a user leaves the organization or no longer has the need to use a certificate. One of the drawbacks to using a completely internal PKI is that of trust. If all your certificates are generated and managed internally, you may have difficulty getting external organizations to recognize the validity of the certificates created within your organization.

The most complete implementation of a PKI includes certificates generated internally and externally. Acquiring a certificate from a trusted third-party organization lends credence to the validity of certificates used in your organization. Generating and managing internal certificates cuts down on the costs associated with public key security. Ultimately, how you implement your PKI depends largely on the needs you have for public key security within your organization.

Public Key Cryptography

Public key cryptography is a significant improvement over secret key cryptography. In the secret key method, only one key is needed to encrypt and decrypt data, but both parties must have the secret key. Managing and keeping track of changes to secret keys is a difficult process, and whoever has a copy of the secret key, no matter how they acquired it, is able to decrypt any data encrypted with the secret key.

In public key cryptography, a pair of keys are assigned to a user. These keys are the mathematical inverse of each other. What one key does, only the other key can undo. These keys are called public and private keys. When the user creates the key pair, he or she shares the public key with others, but keeps the private key secured. If the user wants to perform public key cryptography operations on multiple computers, he or she must have access to his or her private key from each system used.

Take a look at two common operations using public key cryptography. In the first example, Byron is going to send a file to Patricia, and he wants to sign the file so that she will know that the file came from him. Figure 5.28 shows the flow of this process. Byron has a public and a private key that belong to him. Patricia also has a public and a private key that belong to her. Byron has a copy of Patricia's public key and Patricia has a copy of Byron's public key. Byron takes the original file, signs it with his private key, and sends the signed file to Patricia. When Patricia receives the file, she verifies the file using Byron's public key. The verification process tells Patricia whether or not the file came from Byron and if the contents of the file changed after the time Byron signed it. In fact, anyone who receives the file from Byron and has his public key is able to verify the file with his public key.

Figure 5.28 Signing a File

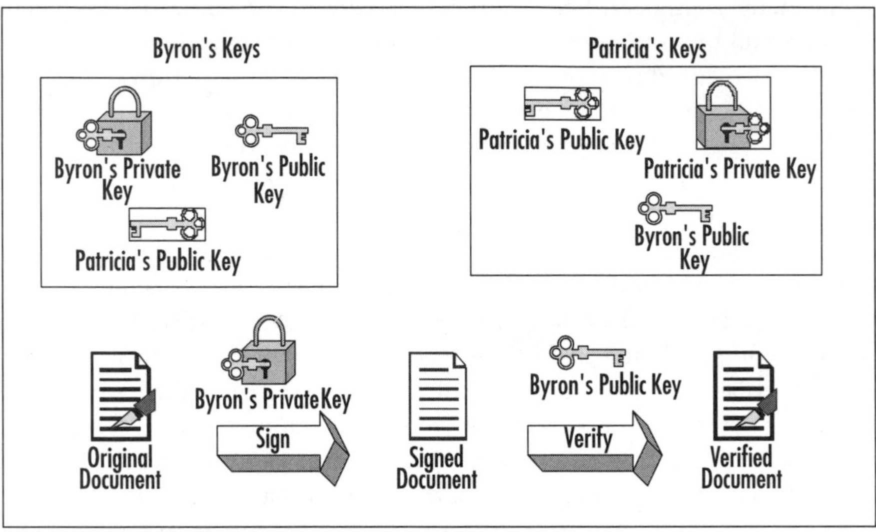

The process of signing a file actually results in two files – the original file and the digital signature for the file. The digital signature is a small file that is constructed with information from the original file and the signer's private key. The first step in signing a file is generating a "fingerprint" for the original file, usually through a hash function. This fingerprint is then combined with the signer's private key to generate the digital signature file. When Patricia receives the file and the digital signature from Byron, her computer decodes the digital signature using Byron's public key to get the fingerprint of the original file. The computer then generates another fingerprint from the file and compares it with the fingerprint decoded from the digital signature. If the fingerprints match, she knows the file did come from Byron and its contents have not been changed between the time he signed it and she verified it.

In the second example, Byron wants to send a file to Patricia so that only Patricia can read it. To do this, he can encrypt the file using a combination of their public and private keys. Figure 5.29 shows this process. Byron takes the original file and encrypts it using his private key and Patricia's public key. He then sends the encrypted file to Patricia. When Patricia receives the encrypted file, she decrypts the file using her private key and Byron's public key. In fact, only someone that has both Byron's public key and Patricia's private key is able to decrypt the file.

There are a number of other uses for public key cryptography. EFS operations are based on public key certificates. Secure Socket Layer (SSL) communications between networked systems use digital certificates to perform encrypted data transmissions. The most common use of SSL is for secure Web traffic to protect sensitive personal data, such as credit card numbers used for purchase transactions, medical information, and so on. IPSec and other communications methods can make use of public key cryptography as well. Plus, smart cards and other electronic authentication devices use this methodology to verify a person's identity in a number of places.

Figure 5.29 Encrypting a File for a Specific User

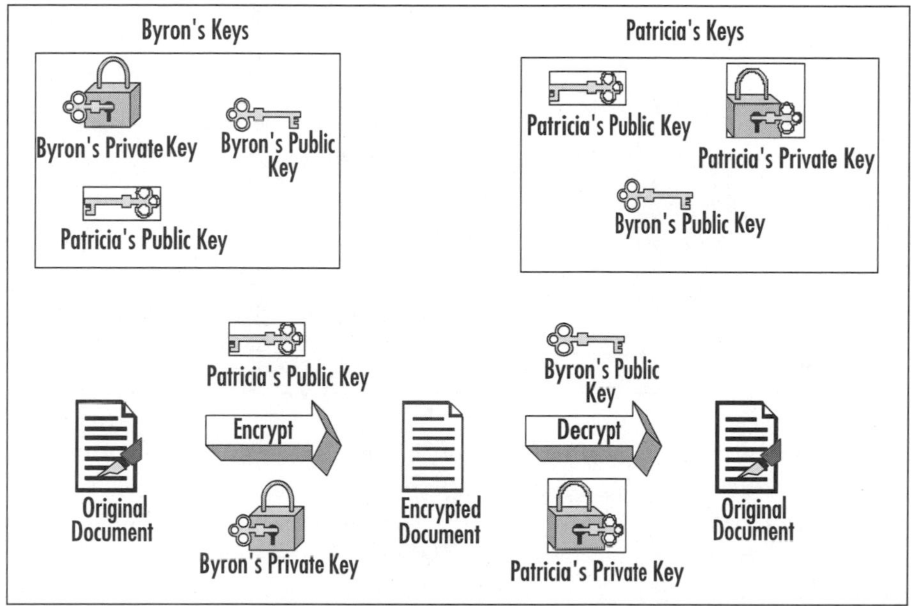

The problem with this approach, though, is this: how do you know that the public key you have from a person is a valid key and is really from that person? In other words, how do you authenticate the authentication method?

Digital Certificates

One way to validate the key holder's identity is through the use of digital certificates. Either third-party organization trusted by the recipient of a set of keys or an internal Certificate Authority validates the authenticity of the keys and the key holder and generates a unique certificate to the user. The organization that issues the certificate takes the responsibility for validating the identity of the user and authenticates the certificate of the key holder. As long as you continue to trust the integrity of the issuing entity, you can trust that any digital certificates generated by them are valid, and therefore the identity of the key holder is valid as well.

The digital certificate is a document that contains information about the individual associated with the certificate, his or her public key information, an expiration date, and a digital signature for the issuer. Many applications now internally support digital certificates as a way of identifying users or systems, and a number of different hardware devices are in development or already on the market that make use of digital certificates for identification. Figure 5.30 shows a certificate as displayed in Microsoft Windows. In this figure, you can see the numeric thumbprint of the certificate file for the user.

Figure 5.30 Viewing a Digital Certificate

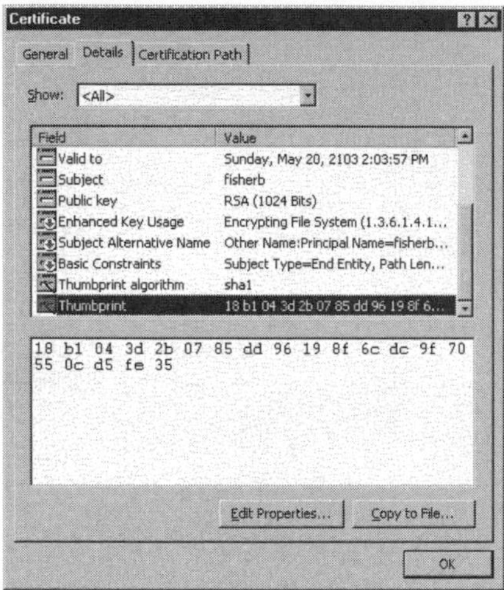

Users have two ways of requesting new certificates. One is using the Certificates MMC snap-in; the other is through Web enrollment. From within the Certificates console, users can expand the **Personal** object, right-click the **Certificates** folder, and select **Request New Certificate**. This sends a request to the CA to generate a new certificate for the user, and the newly generated certificate is stored in the user's certificate list.

Windows Server 2003 servers running Certificate Services also provide a Web interface for requesting and enrolling certificates. Users can point their browsers to http://*servername*/certsrv, where *servername* is the name of the server running Certificate Services. From the Web page, they can perform a basic certificate request, or select an advanced request where they can specify a certificate template to use, a specific cryptographic service provider, the size of the key, whether to generate a new key or use an existing one, and so on.

Certification Authorities

A provider that generates and validates digital certificates is known as a certification authority (CA). VeriSign, GlobalSign, Entrust, and other companies are third-party CAs that provide digital certificates, usually for a fee. For an enterprise organization, purchasing a digital certificate for every employee can be cost prohibitive, especially if the company is large or experiences high employee turnover. Microsoft provides tools to implement and maintain your own CAs within your organization, which enables you to generate and verify digital certificates "in house" at a significantly reduced cost. Depending on the nature of certificate use in your organization, using a completely internal CA structure may meet your needs. Or, you may choose to implement a hybrid structure that uses both internal and external CAs. Some agencies, for security reasons, may be required to rely completely on external CAs.

A root CA is the cornerstone of a PKI, no matter how large or small the organization. For small organizations, a single CA might be sufficient to handle the certificate verification process. A fully developed PKI generally has more than one CA set up in a hierarchical structure, and can include internal and external CAs in combination. Microsoft Certificate Services can function in any of the CA roles within the PKI. In the next sections, we will look at installing Certificate Services and developing the CA hierarchy in an organization.

Another important role within a PKI is managing revoked certificates. When an employee leaves a company or if a private key is compromised, the digital certificate for that employee should no longer be considered valid. CAs keep track of a certificate revocation list (CRL) and use the CRL when validating certificates upon request. When a validation request comes in for a certificate that is published on the CRL, the CA reports the certificate as revoked. Because an organization with a great degree of turnover can generate large CRLs, they can be time-consuming to distribute updates. A *delta CRL* can be used to minimize the update time. A delta CRL contains a list of changes to the last fully published CRL, and when a CA receives a delta CRL, it will combine the CRL it has on file with the delta CRL to generate an effective CRL, which will be used until a full CRL update is received.

In addition, if you implement an internal PKI, you can also specify specific CRL distribution points (CDPs) in the PKI structure. The CDP is the location that a client uses to check to see if a certificate is on the CRL. A CDP can be placed into a certificate as well, so that any client attempting to validate that certificate uses the CDP identified in the certificate instead of its default CDP.

Installing and Using the Windows Server 2003 Certificate Services

A Windows Server 2003 computer can function as a CA if you install and configure Certificate Services. The Certificate Services component can be installed either during the base setup or from Add/Remove Programs in the Control Panels folder. If you choose to install Certificate Services when first installing the server, select it from the list of optional components that can be selected during setup. Although the tools are installed with the rest of the server software, you will not be able to completely finish the installation until after you reboot and log on to the server. At that point, you will be prompted to complete the installation of Certificate Services.

If you choose to install Certificate Services on a server already running Windows Server 2003, open the **Control Panel** folder and then open **Add/Remove Programs**. The detailed instructions for installing Certificate Services using this method are provided in Exercise 5.04 at the end of this section.

When installing Certificate Services, you will be prompted to specify the CA role. There are four options for this, as explained in Table 5.13.

Table 5.13 Certificate Authority Roles for Certificate Services

CA Role	Description
Enterprise root CA	This CA is a top-level CA in the hierarchy and is the role you must select for the first CA installed in the enterprise. This role requires Active Directory. Generally, this role does not provide user and computer certificates directly, but does provide resources to other CAs in the organization. In other words, it issues the certificates to the subordinate CAs. This is the most trusted CA and should be carefully secured.
Enterprise subordinate CA	This CA requires Active Directory and receives its certificate from another CA in the organization. This CA provides certificates to users and computers and can provide certificates to other CAs.
Stand-alone root CA	This CA is a top-level CA in the hierarchy but does not require Active Directory. It is the first CA role you must install if you choose not to install an enterprise CA. It will make use of Active Directory, if available, but can be removed from the network and placed in a secure area when creating a secure offline root CA. It can issue certificates to subordinate CAs or function as the single CA in a small organization.
Stand-alone subordinate CA	This CA does not require Active Directory but can participate if Active Directory is available. This role receives its certificate from another CA and can provide certificates to users, computers, and other CAs.

Creating the Certificate Authority Hierarchy

The first step in creating the CA hierarchy is installing the root CA, the highest point of trust in the organization. If the root CA is the only CA in the hierarchy, it will issue certificates to all objects in the PKI. If the structure is larger, the root CA can issue certificates to other CA servers alone, or it can be used to serve users and computers as well (although the latter scenario is not recommended). The root CA generates a self-signed certificate that will be used to authenticate all other CAs and certificates in the organization.

NOTE

Security of the root CA is very important. Because the root CA ultimately verifies the validity of every certificate issued within the PKI, any root CA that is compromised could lead to the compromise of every CA in the PKI.

The CA structure is set up in a hierarchy for several reasons, including but not limited to the following:

- **Management of certificates** The root CA can dictate organizational settings to lower-level CAs, such as whether subordinate CAs can authenticate new CAs within the organization. Lower-level CAs can have specific settings for generating certificates to their coverage area, reducing the complexity of the policies set at the root CA.
- **Security of the root CA** Configuring the root CA so that it only certifies and controls policy for subordinate CAs means that the root CA can be set up in a more secure location. If the root CA does not have to manage object certificates, it can be set in a location where only the subordinate CAs can access it.

When installing the root CA with Certificate Services, you must decide if the server is to be a stand-alone server or an enterprise server. An enterprise server requires an Active Directory schema to interface with and can make use of certificate templates, which simplify the creation of certificates. Enterprise CAs can generate certificates automatically, and only enterprise CAs can issue certificates for use with smart card logons. A stand-alone CA does not require Active Directory and does not use certificate templates. When a certificate request comes to a stand-alone CA, the certificate request is held in a storage area until a CA administrator approves the request. Because a stand-alone CA does not require Active Directory, the CA can be taken off the network for additional security. Table 5.14 summarizes the differences between an enterprise CA and a stand-alone CA.

Table 5.14 Differences Between an Enterprise CA and a Stand-Alone CA

Function	Enterprise CA	Stand-Alone CA
Authenticate certificate requests in Active Directory	X	
Publish certificates in Active Directory	X	
Verify certificate requests in Active Directory	X	
Remove from network for additional security		X
Automatically issue certificate requests	X	
Approve certificate requests manually		X
Build certificates from templates	X	

Subordinate CAs are all CAs that do not function as a root CA. They must receive their certificates from the root CA or another subordinate CA that is above them in the hierarchical structure of the PKI, and they generate certificates for user and computers as well as for other CAs that are below them in the hierarchy. In general, CAs reporting directly to the root CA are called intermediate CAs (also referred to as policy CAs). Intermediate CAs can be used to help break down certificate policy by geographic, political, or other factors. CAs below the intermediate CAs are often referred to as issuing CAs. These CAs usually just provide certificates to users and computers and not other CAs. Figure 5.31 diagrams a typical PKI using several levels of CAs to generate and validate certificates for the organization.

Figure 5.31 Diagramming a Potential PKI Structure

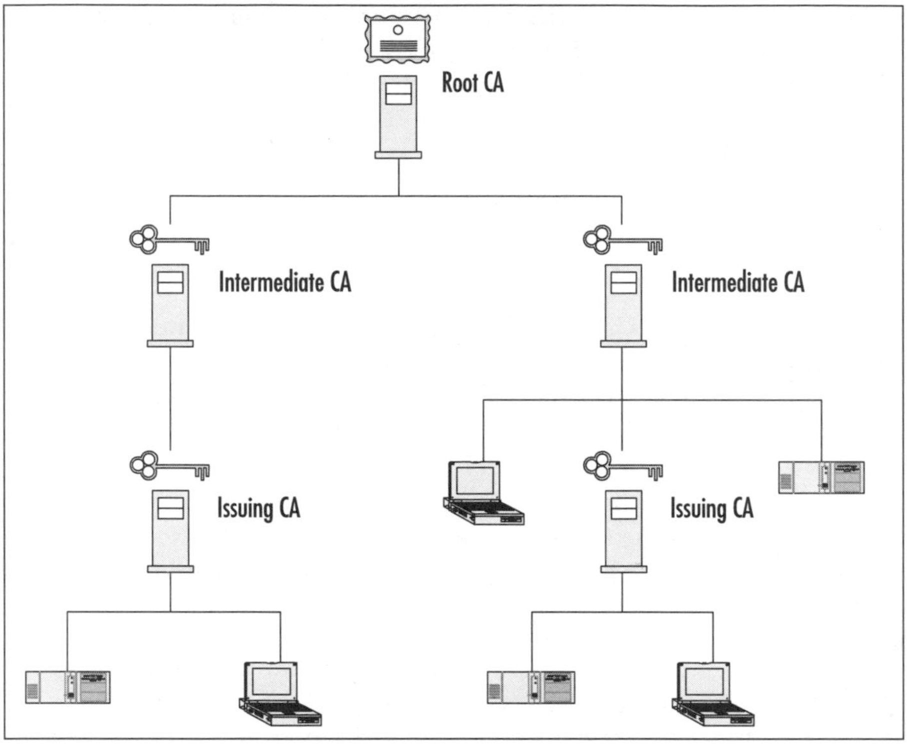

Root CA

Intermediate CA

Intermediate CA

Issuing CA

Issuing CA

New & Noteworthy...

New Features of Windows Server 2003 PKI

The following items have been added to or enhanced in Certificate Services for Windows Server 2003.

- **Editable certificate templates** Although a number of certificate templates were provided in Windows 2000 Certificate Services, they could not be modified. With the new Certificate Template MMC snap-in, certificate administrators can perform the following functions:
  - Create new templates by duplicating and renaming existing templates
  - Modify settings within the certificate template
  - Enable users and computers to auto-enroll certificates based on the template
  - Configure access control on certificates to filter the capability for users and computers to enroll or auto-enroll certificates based on the template

Continued

The new certificate templates are in a new format (version 2) from the templates provided with Windows 2000. Windows 2000-based systems can use only the original (version 1) templates. Windows XP and Server 2003 systems can use both version 1 and 2 templates. Version 1 templates are treated as read-only in XP and Server 2003, but if those templates are copied, the copy is saved in the version 2 format and can be edited.

- **Certificate auto-enrollment and auto-renewal** Windows 2000 allowed for auto-enrollment of computer certificates and EFS certificates. Not until Windows Server 2003 were users able to auto-enroll certificates. Clients using Windows XP or Windows Server 2003 systems can auto-enroll a number of certificate types based on certificate templates. In addition, if a certificate is generated based on a certificate template, certificate administrators can now specify that a valid certificate can be automatically renewed upon expiration.
- **Role-based administration** Windows Server 2003 enables Certificate Services to be managed based on a number of roles established in the PKI. Role-based administration is not enabled by default when Certificate Services are installed. The roles defined include CA Administrator, Certificate Manager, Backup Operator, Auditor, and Enrollee.
- **Key archival and recovery** Windows Server 2003 Certificate Services can automatically archive keys associates with certificates generated by the CA. If keys become lost or damaged, they can be recovered with a key recovery agent certificate.
- **Event auditing** Activities that occur on a CA can now be logged by the CA. This can be helpful for tracking activities on the CA.
- **Qualified subordination** With qualified subordination, you can specify how a subordinate CA will manage CA activities. You can limit the namespaces for which a CA can issue certificates, the functions for which a certificate generated by a qualified subordinate CA can be used, the policies that will apply to the certificate created by the CA, and the ways in which a certificate can be used in external PKI hierarchies.
- **Command-line tool enhancements** There are new ways to use the *certutil.exe* command-line tool. Using the *–dspublish* parameter with *certutil.exe* enables you to publish a certificate or CRL to Active Directory.

Applying PKI Best Practices

Consider the following items when implementing a PKI in your organization:

- Determine early on if you are going to include third-party CAs as part of your PKI. If you are going to use third-party CAs, decide if you will use them for validation of certificates or generation of certificates as well. Be aware that using third-party CAs can be expensive and time-consuming.
- Keep the root CA on the network as secure as possible. The root CA is ultimately responsible for all certificate validation and trust in the PKI, and if the root CA is compromised, the entire PKI can be compromised as well.
- Use Microsoft's guidelines related to the performance of a Certificate Services server to determine how many CA servers you will need to install in your organization. This information, along with geographic and political restrictions, will help you plan for the count and locations of the CA servers.

Exercise 5.04

Installing and Configuring Certificate Services

In this exercise, you will install and configure Certificate Services on an existing Windows Server 2003 computer. This exercise assumes the server is up and functioning and has not had Certificate Services installed previously.

1. Open the **Add/Remove Programs** control panel from **Start | Settings | Control Panel**.
2. Click **Add/Remove Windows Components.** This brings up the Windows Components Wizard.
3. Click the **Certificate Services** check box in the Wizard, as seen in Figure 5.32.

Figure 5.32 Selecting the Certificate Services Install

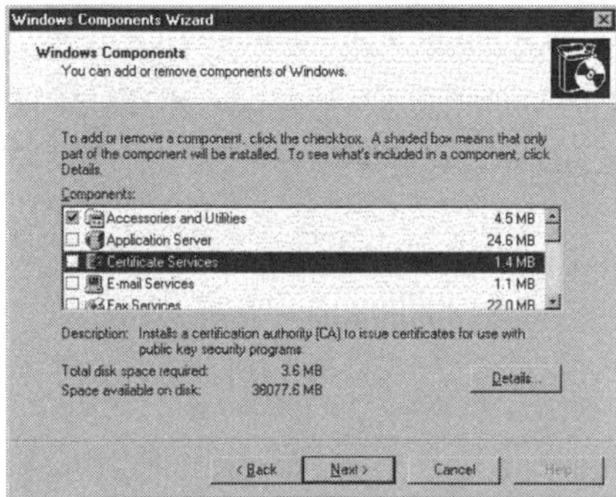

4. When you click the **Certificate Services** check box, the warning window shown in Figure 5.33 appears. Click **Yes** to continue.

Figure 5.33 Viewing the Certificate Services Warning

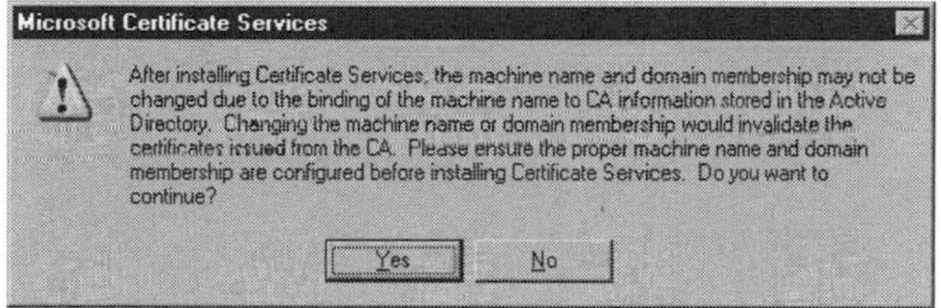

5. Click **Next**.
6. Select from one of the four CA roles. If this is the first CA being installed, select **Enterprise root CA** as shown in Figure 5.34, or **Stand-alone root CA**. Click **Next**.

Figure 5.34 Selecting the CA Role for Security Services

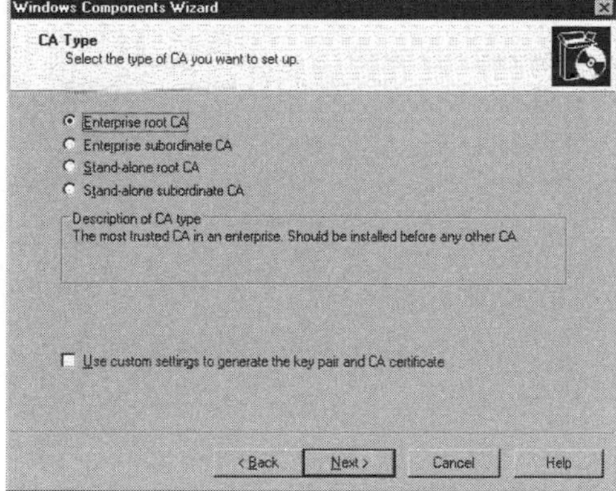

7. Complete the **Common Name for the CA** field in the window shown in Figure 5.35. The other items in the window can be customized or left at their default settings.
8. Click **Next**.
9. Setup takes a moment to configure files and settings.
10. Enter the desired location for the certificate database and certificate log, shown in Figure 5.36. You can change the locations of these items as needed. Click **Next**.

Figure 5.35 Specifying the CA Common Name

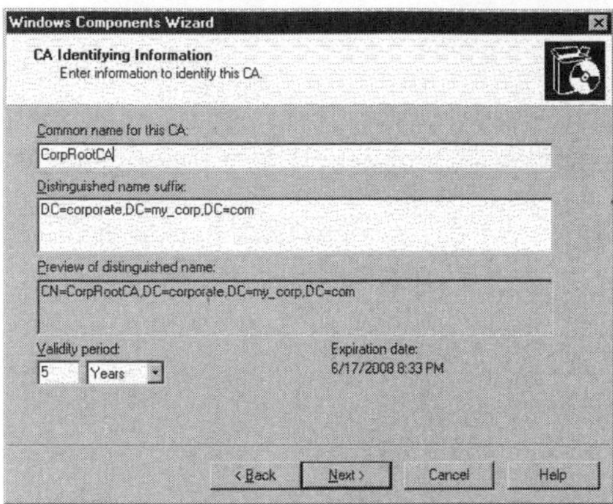

Figure 5.36 Specifying the Location for the Database and Log Files

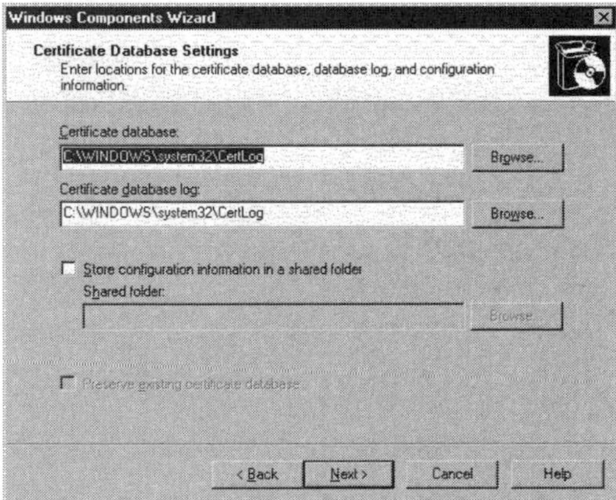

11. Provide the location of the Windows Server 2003 setup files (usually the installation CD).
12. Setup copies the files and completes the installation wizard. Click **Finish** to close the installation.

Summary of Exam Objectives

Access control is more than just a set of tools. A fully developed data security plan combines aspects from a number of different tool sets and concepts. True access control comes into play after a user logs on to the network. When the user logs on, an access token is created that contains information about the user: the user's Security ID (SID), the SID for all groups the user belongs to, and the SID from the workstation the user logged on from. When the user attempts to access resources on the network, information from the access token is used to determine if the user has the necessary permissions to access the resource.

Each resource on the network has an Access Control List (ACL) that lists the network objects that have been given permission to access the resource and what permissions have been applied. Each ACL is made of any number of Access Control Entries (ACEs) that list the specific object that has been granted permission and the type of permission granted. When access to a resource is requested, the server compares the access token to the ACL. If there is no match, the object presenting the access token is denied access to the resource. If there is a match, the object presenting the access token is granted access based on the permissions listed.

The most commonly accessed resources on the network are files and folders. Access to files and folders is governed at the volume level by NTFS permissions. An object can be granted Read, Write, List Folder Contents, Read & Execute, Modify, or Full Control permissions on a file or folder. An object can also be denied a specific permission. If an object matches multiple ACEs in a resource's ACL, all the permissions granted apply to the object, unless one of the permissions is a Deny permission. A Deny permission overrides any permissions allowed to the object.

Because most users do not log on to the file server console to access files and folders on a server volume, the data stored on the volume is made available through network shares. Users must be granted permissions to access network shares to reach the data on the server volume. Shares have their own permission set—Read, Change, and Full Control. Deny permissions can be set on a share as well. When accessing data through a share, the user object's access is determined by the more restrictive permissions on either the share or the volume. If a user object has Read permissions on a share and Full Control permissions on the volume, the object will only have Read access to the data. Folder shares can also be advertised in Active Directory to make locating a file share on the network a little easier.

Two new command-line tools can make administration of files and folders easier. The *takeown* tool enables a user with sufficient permission to become the owner of a file on the system. The *where.exe* tool can help users find files on the system more easily.

In addition to NTFS and share permissions, you can assign user objects different user rights, usually at the group level. These user rights can determine a separate level of access to the data on a server than what has been assigned through NTFS and share permissions. Any object assigned the Backup files and folders right has read access to every file on the volume, regardless of the NTFS permissions. Otherwise, the object would not be able to successfully back up the data on the server. User rights can also determine how a user logs on to a system. Most user objects are not given the user right allowing them to log on at the server console, but users may be given rights to log on to a server through terminal services. This access is granted through user rights.

Since administrators and other users with specific user roles can access all files on a volume, some users might choose to encrypt their data on the volume using Encrypting File System (EFS). When a file is encrypted, only the user that created or modified the file can access the contents, unless he or she selects to share the encrypted data specified others. The capability to share EFS-encrypted data with others is an important new feature in Windows Server 2003 and XP. The file can still be backed up and restored for disaster recovery purposes, but the contents of the data are meaningless to anyone who does not have the correct encryption key to decrypt the file. You can use the *cipher* command-line tool to automate certain encryption functions and can make it easier for some users or administrators to manage EFS. A data recovery agent designated for the network can decrypt user files when access to the file is unsuccessful through standard interfaces. This is because a file is encrypted with a public key belonging to the user who wrote the file and a key belonging to the recovery agent. Care must be taken to protect encryption keys to prevent unwanted access to encrypted data.

A tool that can be used to protect and secure public keys is Certificate Services. Part of a larger PKI, Certificate Services provides digital certificate creation and validation to users and resources on a network. A PKI is usually made up of several Certificate Authorities, resources that generate and validate digital certificates. Certificate Services can be installed and run on a Windows Server 2003 computer to enable the server to function as one of several different types of CAs in the environment. Each PKI must have at least one root CA that controls the trust for the entire organization, but there can be any number of subordinate CAs distributed through the network. Certificate Services servers acting as CAs must run either in enterprise mode or stand-alone mode. Enterprise-mode CAs require Active Directory and can automatically generate certificates based on security templates. Stand-alone CAs do not require Active Directory, must generate certificates manually, and do not use templates.

Because access control issues play a major part in the job of a network administrator in today's security-conscious business world, the material in this chapter is designed not only to help you pass Exam 70-290, but also to assist you on the job in better securing various aspects of your network.

Exam Objectives Fast Track

Understanding Access Control

☑ Access control is the last line of defense for the security of your data, following physical security and account security.

☑ Access Control Lists (ACLs) contain a number of Access Control Entries (ACEs), each of which maps a permission to a specific user or group.

- ☑ Access tokens are created at logon for each user and contain the Security IDs (SIDs) for the user account, group membership, and computer.

Understanding and Using Access Permissions

- ☑ Both NTFS and share permissions are cumulative. If a user belongs to more than one group, and two or more of these groups are assigned permissions on a file or folder, the user's effective permissions (NTFS or share) on the file or folder is the sum of all the groups' permissions.
- ☑ Deny permissions override Allow permission, regardless of which group has the Allow permission assigned.
- ☑ When determining the effective permissions on a file or folder access through a share, the more restrictive permissions (that is, the cumulative effective NTFS permissions or the cumulative effective share permissions) are the ones applied.
- ☑ NTFS permissions are inherited by the files and folders beneath the folder where the permissions are applied (child objects beneath the parent object).
- ☑ Files or folders that are copied to other volumes inherit their permissions from the new parent folder.

Setting User Rights and Privileges

- ☑ User rights can override NTFS permissions in certain cases (a user with the Backup files and directories right is able to read all files on the volume, regardless of the NTFS permissions assigned, but only for the purpose of backing up and restoring data).
- ☑ Assign user rights to groups whenever possible. Assigning user rights to individual user accounts is difficult to manage.
- ☑ User rights are set using Group Policy.

Troubleshooting Access Problems

- ☑ Listen to the user to get a full understanding of the problem he or she is having.
- ☑ Examine ACLs for permissions conflicts.
- ☑ Look for conflicting rights between folder shares and NTFS permissions.
- ☑ Check a user account's group membership for possible conflicts.

Using New Command-Line Utilities

- ☑ *where.exe* is used to find files in the current directory or in the path by default.
- ☑ You can give *where* several file patterns to search for in a single command-line statement.
- ☑ *takeown* can be used to change the owner of files and folders to the user who is running the tool or to the Administrators group.
- ☑ A user must have Take Ownership permission on a file in order to change the file ownership using *takeown*.

Using EFS Encryption

- ☑ Only the creator, recovery agent, and specific users to whom the creator has granted permission can read encrypted files. Other users trying to access the files get "access denied" errors.
- ☑ Entire folders should be marked for encryption rather than single files. This offers greater protection for the data.
- ☑ Temporary directories on a system should be encrypted to prevent temporary copies of sensitive documents from being accessed by unauthorized users.

Implementing a Public Key Infrastructure

- ☑ A Windows Server 2003 computer running Certificate Services can be used as a Certificate Authority (CA) within an organization, with or without including external CAs.
- ☑ CAs set up using Microsoft Certificate Services must be either enterprise CAs or stand-alone CAs.
- ☑ Enterprise CAs use Active Directory and can automatically generate certificates using templates.
- ☑ Stand-alone CAs do not require Active Directory (but will use the information in it if available) and must manually generate certificates without using templates.

Exam Objectives Frequently Asked Questions

The following Frequently Asked Questions, answered by the authors of this book, are designed to both measure your understanding of the Exam Objectives presented in this chapter, and to assist you with real-life implementation of these concepts. You will also gain access to thousands of other FAQs at ITFAQnet.com.

Q: What is the difference between ACLs, DACLs, and SACLs?

A: ACLs (Access Control Lists) are lists associated with an object that determine which users or groups have what type of access to the object. ACLs usually refer to the concept of control lists in general, but the term is often used synonymously with DACLs. DACLs (Discrete Access Control Lists) are the permissions placed on objects that specifically allow or deny certain rights to the object. When you grant a group Read permissions on a share, you have added an entry to the share's DACL. SACLs (System Access Control Lists) are lists associated with an object that trigger an audit even when a member of an entity listed in the SACL accesses the object.

Q: What are the main elements of access control?

A: The first is physical security, which limits who or what can access the object. The most secure server in the world is one that is not attached to a network, has no keyboard or mouse, and is locked in a vault that no one can get into. It may be secure, but it's not very useful. Another is logon security, which requires a unique username and password combination to gain access to the resource either at the console or via network connection. Logon security is only as secure as the username and password combination. Most systems can set restrictions on user IDs and passwords to help keep them from being easily guessed or hacked by a malevolent entity. A balance must be struck between making user IDs and passwords secure and making them easy for the user to use on a daily basis. Another element is file and folder security, which limits access to files and folders on the network storage volume to certain groups of users. Even with good physical and logon security, data could end up in the wrong hands if good file and folder security is not in place.

Q: What is an access token?

A: An access token is like a passport for your network. A unique token is created every time you log on to the network and contains information about you culled from the user ID you used to access the network, the computer used to connect to the network, the group memberships your username has, and other information. Each time you attempt to access a resource on the network, the network examines your access token to determine if you should be able to access the resource.

Q: What are some of the common mistakes made when setting file and folder access?

A: Probably the biggest mistake made by inexperienced system administrators related to file and folder access is giving too much access to too many people. Often, system administrators simply grant greater access to files and folders than is needed to get around an access problem a user is having. The experienced system administrator looks for the root cause of the access problem and identifies the solution, whereas someone with less experience might just add greater and greater access until the access problem "goes away." Other common mistakes are granting Deny permissions on an object when removing a user or group from the ACL would accomplish the desired access change, turning off permission inheritance on a folder, and not setting the appropriate ACLs on the folder to make sure the appropriate system resources continue to have access to the folder.

Q: Why should I set up a share in Active Directory when all it does is point me to the server and share name directly?

A: For clients using an Active Directory aware system, such as PCs running Windows XP and Windows 2000, placing a share in Active Directory makes it easier to find the shared resource on a larger network.

Q: I know that Windows servers and Windows XP and 2000 PCs have default shares on the root on the hard drives that are hidden. Can I create a folder share that is hidden on the network but accessible by those who have been given permissions to it?

A: Yes. To make a share hidden on the network, simply put a $ at the end of the share name. For instance, to make the share named **MktgMgmt** a hidden share, name the share **MktgMgmt$** and it will not appear in the share list for the server (the network browse list displayed in **My Network Places** or via the ***net view*** command). Users have to know the name of the share to be able to access it.

Q: Are there any limits on how long I can make a share name?

A: A file share can have a name that looks just like a filename on a Windows PC (that is, up to 256 characters). However, Windows 95 and Windows 98 PCs that are accessing shares on the network can only see shares with names that are no longer than eight characters and have no spaces. If you are working in an environment that has a number of Windows 95 and Windows 98 PCs, be careful how you name the file shares on your servers.

Q: Why would I want to use the *takeown* command-line command instead of going through the folder properties to change ownership of files and folders?

A: The *takeown* tool is useful for automating support tasks. Because it is a command-line tool, it can be included in batch files and other command scripts. In addition, some administrators and users find it quicker and easier to work with the command line, rather than the GUI.

Q: If I encrypt files in a folder on the network, will I be able to access those files from another computer on the network?

A: Yes, as long as you are logged on with the account that you used to encrypt the files.

Q: If I copy an encrypted file onto a floppy diskette and give it to someone, will that person be able to read the file?

A: Yes. File encryption is only supported on NTFS volumes on Windows 2000 and newer systems. If you copy files to a non-NTFS file system, such as a floppy diskette, the file is saved in unencrypted format.

Self Test

A Quick Answer Key follows the Self Test questions. For complete questions, answers, and explanations to the Self Test questions in this chapter as well as the other chapters in this book, see the Self Test Appendix.

Understanding Access Control

1. A user attempts to open a file on the network. The user is not listed explicitly in the SACL for the file or its containing folder, nor are any of the groups to which the user belongs. What happens when the user attempts to open the file?

   A. The user is denied access to the file.

   B. The user is granted access to the file and an audit is triggered upon access.

   C. The user is granted access to the file and no audit is triggered.

   D. The user is granted read-only access to the file.

2. A user who just transferred to the Marketing department calls you and complains that he cannot access the files in the Marketing share on the network from his Windows 2000 computer. You look at his account and find that he was not added to the Marketing group when he transferred to the department. You add him to the Marketing group and tell him he should be able to access the folder. He calls back five minutes later complaining that he still cannot access the folder. What is the most likely cause of the problem?

A. The share name is too long.

B. He has not logged off and logged back on since you added him to the group.

C. He has not been given permissions to the files on the network, only to the share.

D. The user needs to wait 15 minutes before accessing the share so the security changes can replicate across the Active Directory network.

Understanding and Using Access Permissions

3. The employees in Marketing access their shared data through a share named **Marketing**, which gives them access to read, write, create, and delete files in the folder. They have created a new folder in the shared folder named **Public**. They have asked you to create a new share to this public folder so they can make the contents of the folder available to the entire company, yet restrict access so only marketing employees can modify any of the files in this new share. How will you set up the permissions for the Domain Users group on this folder?

   A. Set the share permissions and the NTFS permissions on the folder to **Read** for the Domain Users group.

   B. Set the share permissions on the folder to **Read** for the Domain Users group and set the NTFS permissions to **Full Control** for the Domain Users group.

   C. Set both the share permissions and the NTFS permissions on the folder to **Full Control** for the Domain Users group.

   D. Set the share permissions to **Full Control** and set the NTFS permissions to Allow **Read** and to Deny **Write** and **Modify**.

4. You have set up a folder share that your IT technicians can access to install application updates or service packs on end user workstations. You want to create a new subfolder that contains updates and service packs that have not been fully tested yet, and you do not want all your technicians to be able to access this folder. You decide to create a new group for members of your staff whom you want to have access to this new folder. How will you set up NTFS permissions on this new folder so that only members of this new group will be able to access the files?

   A. Assign the desired permissions on the new folder for the new group. Delete the entry for the existing group on the new folder.

   B. Assign the desired permissions on the new folder for the new group. Turn off permission inheritance for the new folder and delete the permissions from the parent folder.

C. Assign the desired permissions on the new folder for the new group. Turn off permission inheritance for the new folder and copy the permissions from the parent folder. Delete the entry for the group or groups that should not access the new folder.

D. Assign the desired permissions on the new folder for the new group. Deny all permissions on the new folder for the old groups that had access.

5. You have two data volumes on your server, drives E: and F:. On E:, there is a folder named **Marketing** that has been shared to the employees of the Marketing department. The Marketing group has **Full Control** permission on the **Marketing** share, and they have **Modify** NTFS permissions on the folder. Drive space is running low on E:, so you want to move the **Marketing** folder to drive F:. The Marketing group currently has **Read** NTFS permissions on the root of F:. After you move the folder contents, what permission changes will you need to make on the folder so the Marketing employees still have access?

   A. You will not need to make any changes to the permissions on the folder or the share.

   B. You will not need to make any changes to the permission on the folder, but you will need to create a new share and give **Full Control** permissions on the share to the group.

   C. You will need to change the NTFS permissions on the folder to **Full Control** and change the share permissions from **Read** to **Full Control**.

   D. You will need to change the NTFS permissions on the folder to **Modify**, and you will need to create a new share and give **Full Control** permissions on the share to the group.

6. Your company's Benefits department is currently under the Human Resources department. The Benefits group has **Modify** permissions on their shared folder, which is located on the server in **E:\Shared\HR\Benefits**. The HR group has **Modify** permissions on the HR folder **E:\Shared\HR**. Your company goes through a reorganization, and Benefits no longer reports to HR. You are asked to move the Benefits data folder from **E:\Shared\HR\Benefits** to **E:\Shared\Benefits**. You remove the employees in the Benefits department from the HR group. None of the other HR employees are members of the Benefits group. What NTFS permissions will you need to change so that Benefits still has access to the folder, but HR does not?

   A. No NTFS permission changes are needed.

   B. Give the Benefits group **Modify** rights on the folder after it is moved.

   C. Remove the HR group from the ACL on the Benefits folder.

   D. Add the HR group to the ACL for the Benefits folder and **Deny** all access to the folder.

Setting User Rights and Privileges

7. You take over administration of a server after the previous administrator left the company. You notice that several users who are not server administrators have been logging on to the server at the console. You modify user rights in Group Policy to prevent these users from logging on to the server locally. After you make the changes, you can no longer log on to the server from the console, nor can any of the other administrators. What did you likely do?

   A. Removed your account from the Administrator group.

   B. Added the Everyone group to the **Deny access to this computer from the network user** right.

   C. Added the Everyone group to the **Deny logon locally** user right.

   D. Set the **Deny** permission in the **Log on locally** user right

Troubleshooting Access Problems

8. The Marketing department has created a folder in their shared directory called **Marketing Management**. They ask you to create a new share pointing to this folder and to give the share the same name as the folder. One user in the department is not able to access the share from his computer. When he logs on at another computer, he is able to see and access the share. What is the likely cause of this problem?

   A. The user's computer has a local policy enabled that prevents him from seeing the share.

   B. The user is not logging on to the network and therefore cannot see the share.

   C. The user does not have access to the share.

   D. The user is running Windows 98 on his primary workstation and the other computers in the department are running Windows 2000 or later on their PCs.

Using New Command-Line Utilities

9. A user is attempting to use the *cipher.exe* command-line tool to make changes to the encryption settings on a folder but keeps getting errors related to incorrect parameters. When the user asks you about the errors, you suspect that he might be using an older version of *cipher* that does not support the command-line parameter he is trying to use. How would you find this older version of *cipher* for the user?

A. Have the user open a command prompt on his PC and type **where cipher** at the command prompt.

B. Have the user do a file search for **cipher.*** on his local C: drive.

C. Search all network shares for **cipher.***

D. Have the user open a command prompt on his PC and type **cipher /where** at the command prompt.

10. An employee, Barbara Russell, whose username is russellb, has left the company and you want to reassign ownership of her files. You open a command prompt and change to the directory where her home folder resides. Which command would you type to change the ownership of her files and folders to the administrator's group?

A. **takeown /u russellb**

B. **takeown /a russellb**

C. **takeown /f /r /a russellb***

D. **takeown /f /r ***

Using EFS Encryption

11. A user asks you about enabling encryption on a folder he is using on the server. Because he is trying to reduce the amount of disk space used, he has been compressing the data on the folder for several weeks. How can he change the settings on the folder so he can encrypt the contents of his compressed files?

A. Instruct the user to run the *cipher* command on the folder using the **/e** parameter.

B. Instruct the user to uncompress the files in the folder, enable encryption on the folder, and then compress the files again.

C. Instruct the user to open the **Properties** window for the folder, click the **Advanced** button, and then click the check box to enable encryption on the folder.

D. Advise the user that encrypted files cannot be compressed.

12. A department wants to set up encryption on a shared folder so that only the members of the department can view the contents of the folder. How would you set up this encryption?

A. Open the folder's **Properties** window, click **Advanced**, and enable encryption on the folder.

B. You cannot set up shared encryption on a folder.

C. Open a command prompt and run **cipher.exe /d** on the folder.

D. Have each user open the folder properties and enable encryption for him or herself on the folder.

13. A user calls because he just e-mailed a file from his work account to his home account to edit at home. He just realized that the file was encrypted. What will he need to do to be able to work with the file at home?

A. He will not be able to work with the file at home.

B. He will need to decrypt the file before e-mailing it to himself.

C. He will be able to work with the file at home so long as his PC is running Windows 2000 or later.

D. He will be able to work with the file at home, even if his home computer is a Macintosh.

14. You have an encrypted file that you want to share with another user, William. The file is stored on your local Windows 2000 computer. You create a share on your computer, and give William share and NTFS permissions to the folder where the file is located. How will you prepare the file with EFS so that only the recipient can access the contents of the file?

A. Open a command prompt and encrypt the file using **cipher /e /u username filename**.

B. Open a command prompt and encrypt the file using **cipher /e /x:outputfile filename**.

C. Open the **Properties** window of the file, click **Advanced**, select the **Encrypt this file** check box, click **Details**, and then add William to the list of users who can decrypt the file.

D. You cannot do this with EFS.

Implementing a Public Key Infrastructure

15. You've been asked to implement a PKI in your organization using Microsoft Certificate Services on Windows Server 2003 servers. Your department is expecting a large volume of certificate and verification requests for your two office locations in Dallas and Denver. Your department head wants to ensure that there is no delay in generating new certificates when requested. How would you choose to implement a PKI to meet these requests?

A. A stand-alone root CA located either in Dallas or Denver, plus at least one intermediate CA in each of the Dallas and Denver offices.

B. An enterprise root CA located either in Dallas or Denver, plus at least one intermediate CA in each of the Dallas and Denver offices.

C. A stand-alone root CA and an intermediate CA in each of the Dallas and Denver offices.

D. An enterprise root CA and an intermediate CA in each of the Dallas and Denver offices.

Self Test Quick Answer Key

For complete questions, answers, and explanations to the Self Test questions in this chapter as well as the other chapters in this book, see the Self Test Appendix.

1. **C**
2. **B**
3. **A**
4. **C**
5. **D**
6. **A**
7. **C**
8. **D**
9. **A**
10. **C**
11. **D**
12. **B**
13. **D**
14. **D**
15. **B**

Chapter 6

MCSA/MCSE 70-290

Managing and Troubleshooting Terminal Services

Exam Objectives in this Chapter:

4.4.2 Manage a server by Using Terminal Services remote administration mode.

3.2.1 Diagnose and resolve issues related to Terminal Services security.

4.4.1 Manage a server by using Remote Assistance.

3.2 Troubleshoot Terminal Services.

3.2.2 Diagnose and resolve issues related to client access to Terminal Services.

- ☑ Summary of Exam Objectives
- ☑ Exam Objectives Fast Track
- ☑ Exam Objectives Frequently Asked Questions
- ☑ Self Test
- ☑ Self Test Quick Answer Key

Introduction

Windows Server 2003, like Windows 2000, includes the Terminal Services component that enables you to connect from remote computers using a Terminal Services client (such as the Remote Desktop Connection [RDC] utility built into Windows XP and Windows Server 2003). A Windows Server 2003 terminal server can function in one of several ways. Using a client such as the RDC utility, administrators can perform management tasks on the server from any location on the network. When the terminal server role is installed, it turns the server into an application server, which enables multiple users to connect to the terminal server from "thin clients" or other computers running the client software. These clients can then run applications on a Windows Server 2003 desktop even if they are using older, less powerful operating systems or client hardware.

In this chapter, we will provide an overview of the benefits of using Windows Server 2003 Terminal Services and how to select the Terminal Services functionality that best fits your needs. We will discuss installation and configuration of the terminal server role, the Terminal Services client software, and licensing issues. You'll learn how to use the Terminal Services administrative tools, including the Terminal Services Manager and Terminal Services Configuration console tools. In addition, we'll discuss the Remote Desktop MMC snap-in, using group policies to control Terminal Services users and clients, Terminal Services extensions to the properties of user accounts and the Terminal Services command-line tools. Finally, we look at how to troubleshoot problems with Terminal Services.

Understanding Windows Terminal Services

The Microsoft Terminal Services feature has evolved and undergone major changes since Microsoft first licensed the technology from Citrix. In the beginning, using Terminal Services required purchasing a separate operating system (Windows NT 4.0 Terminal Server Edition). In Windows 2000, it was included with the Server products, but it was a component that required separate installation. In Windows Server 2003, the core service is installed with the operating system. This is to enable administration of the server from remote clients right out of the box, with very little additional configuration being necessary, and serves the same purpose as Terminal Services running in remote administration mode in Windows 2000. This Remote Administration capability is expected to be the subject of many of the exam questions that relate to Terminal Services. Although each exam-taker will encounter different questions, the key is to remember that this exam is focused on administration of Windows Server 2003 servers, and the capability to perform administrative activities without actually having to visit the server is a key feature of the operating system.

Despite its many enhancements and new features in the area of remote administration, Terminal Services still maintains its traditional capability of serving as an application server to which multiple remote clients can connect and run sessions simultaneously. In Windows 2000, this was called Application Server mode; now it is referred to as the terminal server role. When the Terminal Server role is installed, users can connect and use applications that are installed on the server as if they were sitting at its keyboard. By default, when users connect, they will see a Windows Server 2003 desktop from the server displayed on their local systems and be able to interact with it. Most importantly, all of their session settings and application information will be kept separate from other users. This application-sharing and multi-user capability exists only when the terminal server role is installed; it does not exist with the Terminal Services remote administration feature that is available right out of the box.

NOTE

In Windows 2000, by default only members of the administrators group could use Terminal Services in remote administration mode. In Windows Server 2003, administrators can use remote administration by default, but you can also add other users to the list of authorized remote users who can connect via Remote Desktop.

Terminal Services Terminology and Concepts

As noted, back in the days of Windows NT 4.0, Microsoft sold a separate server product called Terminal Server Edition. In Windows 2000, the Terminal Services feature was integrated into all Microsoft server operating systems. With Windows Server 2003, Microsoft has again included it with their server product line. All versions of Microsoft Windows Server 2003 come with it, except Windows Server 2003 Web Server Edition (the Web Server Edition includes the core terminal service and the Remote Desktops console and can be remotely administered, but it cannot function as a full fledged terminal server for application sharing).

When used for remote administration, Microsoft enables two clients to connect simultaneously with no additional license purchases being required. You do not have to install Terminal Services Licensing.

How Terminal Services Works

When a client connects to Terminal Services, the server creates an isolated session for its use. This session is, in many ways, a virtual Windows Server 2003 computer running within the Windows Server 2003 operating system. In fact, if you look at the processes running on the server, you will see several instances of key operating system processes, such as the client/server subsystem. This is because each session has its own set of these key components initialized in memory.

It is important to realize that when you are working within a Terminal Services session, you are actually working on the server. You are considered and treated as if you were a local user sitting at a keyboard connected to the server itself. When you are running applications and doing work, none of the processing is taking place on the client machine at which you're sitting. The client software sends mouse movements and keyboard strokes to your session on the server. In response, the server updates the image of the desktop or application that is running on the server and sends it to the client. Thus, only these input signals and images travel across the network. Best of all, this typically takes less than 20Kbps of bandwidth per session. This means that many clients can connect, using very little bandwidth on the underlying network, which makes Terminal Services an ideal solution in wide area networks (WANs), where overall bandwidth is limited.

Thin Client Computing

Low bandwidth use is one of the keys to the concept of thin client computing. Another is the minimal use of resources on the client. Because all the processing is occurring on the server, very few resources are used on a client system that is connected to a Terminal Services session. Thin clients can be typical, low-powered desktop PCs (for example, 80486 computers) running any Windows operating system or other devices such as personal digital assistants (PDAs) running the Windows CE or Pocket PC operating systems.

NOTE

You don't have to be running any form of Windows to connect to the Windows Terminal Server. The Remote Desktop Connection (RDC) client software is also available from Microsoft for Macintosh OS X, and Terminal Services clients for MS-DOS and Linux are available from third-party vendors such as Terminal-Services.net (www.terminal-services.net).

The term "thin client" can also refer to special computer systems that contain a processor, memory, video card, and network card, but no hard drive. These systems, called Windows-based Terminals (WBTs) store a Windows-based operating system in memory (called an *embedded* OS). When booted, they enable the user to launch a Terminal Services client and establish a session to a terminal server. Because they do not require the latest hardware, these units are relatively inexpensive when compared with typical desktop systems.

Through the use of Terminal Services, users are able to enjoy much of the same functionality they would on a normal Windows XP/Server 2003-based desktop system, without the purchase of hardware that is capable of running Windows XP/Server 2003.

New & Noteworthy...

Web-Based Administration and Remote Console Connection Support

An outstanding new feature in the Windows server product line is the capability to perform Remote Administration from any MSIE 5.0 or later browser without a locally installed client. This means that you can be away from your desk, at virtually any client system that is capable of running MSIE, and connect to and remotely administer a server using Terminal Services. This feature has been on the wish list of many administrators for a long time and is a very welcomed addition to the product.

Another fantastic new feature is the capability to connect to the console session. Countless administrators have been forced to rely on third-party products (such as PC Anywhere) to connect to, view, and interact with the console sessions on their servers, because so many server-based applications on the market are capable of delivering their messages only to the server's primary console session. With Windows Server 2003, you can finally connect to the console and see these important messages. More importantly, you can save the money you've been spending to license all those third-party connection utilities.

Note that only a single console session can run at a time, and the console screen on the server itself is locked when the remote session is established. In addition, to run a direct console session remotely, you'll need to run a Terminal Services client that uses version 5.1 or later of the Remote Desktop Protocol (RDP). This would include the RDP client built into Windows XP. Although you can connect to the terminal server with the older RDP client that came with Windows 2000 server, you cannot use it to run a console session.

Terminal Services Components

The Terminal Services service in Windows Server 2003 supports a number of components. These include the following:

- Remote Desktop for Administration Formerly called Remote Administration mode in Windows 2000
- Remote Assistance (RA) A feature introduced in Windows XP
- The terminal server role Formerly called Application Server mode in Windows 2000

As we've mentioned, the exam objectives focus on your ability to use Terminal Services components to remotely administer a Windows Server 2003 server. Consequently, you can expect an emphasis on client and server applications relating to the Remote Desktop for Administration and RA features. However, it's important to understand that Terminal Services does not end there. Many organizations use Terminal Services to deploy multi-user application servers. In this chapter, we also thoroughly cover how to implement and manage the terminal server role, because it is a key component that is supported by the Terminal Services service, and no discussion of Terminal Services can be complete without it.

Remote Desktop for Administration

Remote Desktop for Administration is the key component of Terminal Services that enables remote server administration. It is installed by default, but is disabled; it must be manually enabled and configured by an administrator before you can connect to it. This component enables a maximum of two concurrent connections for the purposes of remotely administering the server. By default, when a Terminal Services client connects to this component, a new session is created and a copy of the Windows Server 2003 desktop is displayed in a window on the client machine.

It's important to note that this copy of the desktop is not the actual server desktop that the user would see if he or she were sitting down at the server's keyboard. That session is called the console. This is an important distinction, because often the operating system or an installed application will send a popup message to the server console. An administrator connecting to the server using Terminal Services will not see the console by default, and thus will not see the popup messages. You also will not see any applications that might be running on the console session – unless you use the RDP 5.1 or later client to run a remote console session.

In Windows 2000, there was no way to view the console session remotely. However, one of the new Terminal Services client utilities (discussed in more detail later in the chapter) includes this capability. This is a dramatic improvement that ensures administrators will be able to more fully take advantage of Terminal Services for remote administration. Because this feature was missing from earlier versions, many companies had no choice but to use third-party software to connect to the console sessions on their Windows servers.

Remote Assistance

Remote Assistance (RA) depends on and uses the Terminal Services service. However, the way you connect to it is substantially different from the methods used to establish a session with Remote Desktop for Administration or a client session connecting to the multi-user terminal server. RA enables a user at one computer (whom we'll call the Novice) to ask for help from a user at another computer (whom we'll call the Expert or the assistant), on the LAN or across the Internet. This request can be made through Windows Messenger, e-mail, or through a transferred file. The Expert can also offer remote assistance without receiving an explicit request from the Novice (if Group Policy settings are configured to enable offering of remote assistance and the Expert user is listed as an assistant in the Offer Remote Assistance policy, or is a local administrator), but the Novice must grant permission; the Expert can never take over the Novice's computer without the Novice's agreement. This differs from Remote Desktop, in that administrators and users on the Remote

Desktop Users list can start a remote session without getting permission from the person who is using the computer locally.

When an Expert receives a request from a Novice, he or she can initiate a connection to the Novice's computer. When connected, the Expert is able to view the actual desktop and applications that are being used by the Novice on his or her computer. In addition, a special application is launched on the Novice's computer that enables him or her to chat with the Expert and control the session, either via text messages or audio (as long as both computers are equipped with full-duplex sound cards, speakers, and microphones). If the Novice desires, the Expert can be allowed to control the Novice's desktop and applications, including taking control of the Novice's cursor. In addition, files can be transferred easily between the two through the RA interface.

RA requires that both computers be running Windows XP or Server 2003. Because security is always a concern in the business environment, RA invitations can require that the assistant provide a password, to prevent an imposter from connecting to the computer while pretending to be the assistant. You can also specify the amount of time for which an RA invitation will remain valid. Users also have the option to turn off the RA feature entirely.

NOTE

Both Remote Desktop and Remote Assistance are also included in the Windows XP Professional operating system (only Remote Assistance is included in Windows XP Home Edition). However, whereas a Windows Server 2003 computer can have two Remote Desktop for Administration sessions running simultaneously, only one Remote Desktop session at a time can connect to an XP Professional system. In addition, when you connect via Remote Desktop to an XP Professional computer, you will see all the applications that are running on the desktop of that XP computer, just as if you were sitting at that local machine. If Word is open on the local desktop, it will be open in your RDC session. Conversely, when you connect to a Windows Server 2003 via the Remote Desktop, you will not see applications that are open on the local (console) session. When a remote session is connected to an XP computer, the local session is locked and can't be accessed until the remote session is terminated. With Windows Server 2003, an administrator sitting at the console can continue to do tasks while the remote administrator runs a session.

The Terminal Server Role

Despite the fact that the exam objectives focus on using Terminal Services for remote administration, the original purpose of the service was to enable Windows servers to be used in a thin client environment without expensive third-party software such as Citrix MetaFrame. The development of Microsoft's Terminal Services involved the creation of several components that worked together, including a special presentation layer protocol called the Remote Desktop Protocol (RDP) and a core architectural component known as Multi-Win.

The Multi-Win Component

The Multi-Win component sits at a very low level in the operating system and enables more than one user to be logged in locally. The Multi-Win technology was originally created by Citrix for WinFrame and licensed to Microsoft for Windows NT 4.0 Terminal Server Edition. It is a core component of Terminal Services and is used in Remote Desktop for Administration, RA, and the terminal server role. Prior to its development, only the user that actually logged on at a server's keyboard (the local console session) was considered a local user. The creation of Multi-Win enabled remote users to log on and use the server as if they were local users. In other words, they could use the Terminal Services computer in a way similar to a person who was actually sitting down at its console session. The Multi-Win component not only allows for multiple local users, but it also keeps each of their system and application settings separate, even when many are logged on at the same time.

This new capability enables remote users to actually launch and use applications on the remote system. This is very different from simply installing applications to a network share for a local client computer. With a network share, the client simply goes out to the network share, transfers the application files to the computer's memory, and launches the program using the client's local processor and memory resources (by double-clicking the icon to launch the application).

A Terminal Services session is altogether different. When you establish a terminal server session, by default you see a copy of the desktop from the server to which you have connected. When using Remote Desktop for Administration or the terminal server role, by default each terminal user works in his or her own virtual Windows Server 2003 computer that has been created for that user by the Terminal Services service on the Windows Server 2003 server. When you double-click an icon within this session and launch an application, it launches in your session on the server. It uses the server's processor, the server's memory, and accesses the server's hard disk. Only images of the screen transfer to the local computer; the application files never leave the server.

NOTE

You can run the terminal session in a window on the client computer's desktop, or you can run it full screen. Either way, all the other applications on your local machine are still fully functional, and you can switch back and forth between the terminal session and other programs you're running locally. You can even copy and paste data from an application on the local computer to an application in the terminal session, although you can't cut and paste files and folders or drag and drop between the two.

The Remote Desktop Protocol (RDP)

The second important Terminal Services component, the Remote Desktop Protocol (RDP), handles the transfer of the screen information from the server to your client. It also ensures that your cursor movements and keystrokes make it from the client back to your session on the server. RDP was based on a set of International Telecommunications Union (ITU) T.120 protocol family. The early version of RDP (v4.0) used in NT 4.0 Terminal Server Edition did not perform well over low bandwidth connections (such as WAN connections). Windows 2000 Terminal Services included RDP v5.0, which increased performance. Windows XP and Server 2003 use RDP 5.1.

RDP communicates on port 3389; it uses encryption to protect the information that is sent between the terminal server and the client computer.

NOTE

Vulnerabilities have been discovered in the Windows 2000 and XP RDP clients, and security patches have been released to address this problem. See www.winguides.com/security/display.php/287/ for more information.

RDP is the native protocol for Microsoft Terminal Services. However, clients using the Citrix Independent Computing Architecture (ICA) protocol can also connect to Windows terminal servers. Some advantages of ICA include the fact that it supports 16-bit client software for MS-DOS and Windows 3.*x*, as well as Java and UNIX clients (Microsoft has licensed RDP to other vendors, and RDP clients for non-Microsoft operating systems, such as rdesktop for UNIX, are available from third parties). The ICA client also works over IPX, SPX, NetBEUI, and Asynchronous connections, whereas RDP works only with TCP. Many of the features that once required the ICA client, such as audio redirection and local printer support, are now available with the latest versions of RDP.

Head of the Class...

Where It All Began

A company called Citrix Systems, Inc. created the original components of Terminal Services. Headed by a former IBM executive, Citrix became the only company ever to license the Windows NT source code from Microsoft for resale as a separate product. Their popular product derived from Windows NT 3.51 was known as WinFrame. Prior to the release of a Windows NT 4.0-related version, Citrix and Microsoft struck a deal in which Microsoft licensed the Multi-Win component.

This component lies at the heart of Terminal Services and enables multiple users to log on locally, as if they were sitting down at the actual server itself. It creates individual sessions for each user and keeps all of their session and application settings separate. The protocol Citrix created to access Terminal Services was not licensed by Microsoft. It enables a wide range of Terminal Services clients not sup-

Continued

ported by Microsoft's RDP protocol. It also enables a wider range of application delivery and load balancing methods than does RDP. Citrix calls their protocol the Independent Computing Architecture (ICA) protocol. They currently sell this protocol in their popular MetaFrame product line.

Comparing Remote Desktop for Administration and the Terminal Server Role

The same basic process occurs, whether you are using Terminal Services for remote administration or with the terminal server role installed. The primary difference between Remote Desktop for Administration and the Terminal Server role is the number of simultaneous connections that are allowed and the extent to which settings from multiple users are accommodated and kept separate. As we mentioned in the section titled *Remote Desktop for Administration*, RDA enables only two simultaneous remote connections. With the Terminal Server role installed, you are enabled a number of connections equal to the number of Terminal Server licenses you have purchased. Unlike the two connections allowed for remote administration, connections to a Windows Server 2003 server with the Terminal Server role installed are not free. Clients will be allowed to log on to the Terminal Server without licenses for 120 days (evaluation period) after the first logon.

Remote Desktop for Administration does not have extra software installed to keep all (or rather, both) of the remote users' application settings separate. It still maintains some separation, but is not designed to have additional applications, such as Microsoft Office, installed and used by multiple users. Installation of an application using Remote Desktop for Administration installs the software for single-user use, just as an ordinary client system would. This means that if a user alters the settings in the software, the new settings are saved by the application generally, not for the user individually. The next user who launches the application may see the settings of the previous user, rather than his or her previously configured options. Of course, some application settings are based on a user's profile, even in a single-user environment, and in that case different settings can be available to different users based on the profile that is logged on.

With the Terminal Server role installed, applications are installed in special way that enables Terminal Services to make sure all settings are always kept and tracked separately. However, keeping up with all this information requires system resources. Thus, while it is likely you will never notice the overhead involved with the Remote Desktop for Administration component, a tremendous amount of resources are used up by the Terminal Server role to keep track of multiple user sessions and maintain all of their settings separately. Because of the overhead associated with the terminal server role, it is recommended that you do not install it on a domain controller or other resource-intensive application server, such as an SQL server or e-mail server. Unlike Remote Desktop for Administration and RA, an administrator must explicitly install the Terminal Server role.

It is important to know the differences between these two Terminal Services components, because they are used for very different purposes. In the following sections, we will examine in detail how to configure and use the Windows Server 2003 Terminal Services in each of these ways.

Manage a Server by Using Terminal Services Remote Administration Mode

Most of what is new in Windows 2003 Terminal Services relates to remote administration. Microsoft has really listened to customer feedback and created some major improvements in this area of the operating system. The test objectives focus on two major Terminal Services components, Remote Desktop for Administration and RA. Although a predecessor to Remote Desktop for Administration (Terminal Services in remote administration mode) existed in Windows 2000, it has received many changes in the current release. RA is a new component for Microsoft's server operating systems. It was initially released with Windows XP.

Using Remote Desktop for Administration

As we've mentioned, no installation is necessary for the Remote Desktop for Administration component of Terminal Services. It is installed with the operating system by default. However, for security purposes it is not enabled by default. After it is enabled, members of the administrators group can connect and use it by default. Non-administrators must be specifically granted access. Let's take a look at how to enable and configure this critical component.

Configuring RDA

To configure Remote Desktop for Administration, select **Start | Control Panel | System** and click the **Remote** tab. To enable the feature, simply check the box next to **Allow users to connect remotely to this computer** located in the **Remote Desktop** section of the tab, as shown in Figure 6.1.

Figure 6.1 The System Properties Window

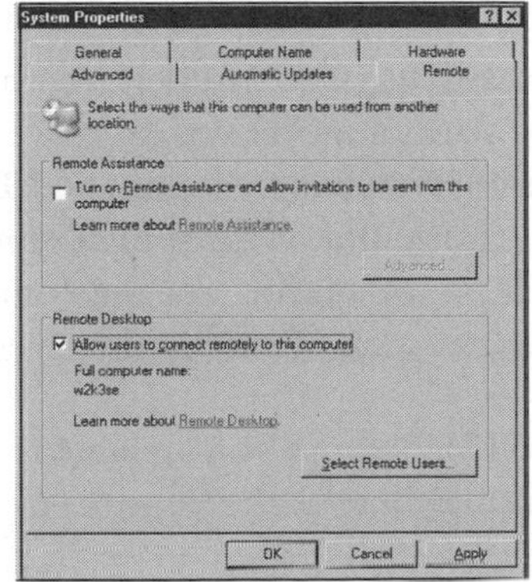

Setting Up Authentication

When RDA is enabled, any user accounts that are members of the Administrators built-in group on the server will be allowed to establish a remote session. However, other accounts must be explicitly approved for access. There are two different ways this can be accomplished. The first is to simply add any accounts that require access to the Remote Desktop Users group on the server. To grant a user access using this method, perform the following steps:

1. Open **Computer Management** and expand the **Systems Tools**, **Local Users and Groups**, and **Groups** nodes in the console tree on the left side of the utility.
2. Right-click the **Remote Desktop Users** group.
3. Select **Add to Group** from the context menu, and then click the **Add** button.
4. Type (or search for and select) the account name of the user to whom you wish to grant access.
5. Click the **OK** button.

The second, simpler way to access the Remote Desktop Users group and grant access is to use an option provided in the **Remote** tab in the **System** properties located in **Control Panel**. To use this method, perform the following steps:

1. In the Remote Desktop section of the **Remote** tab, click the **Select Remote Users** button.
2. In the **Remote Desktop Users** dialog box that appears, click the **Add** button.
3. Type (or search for and select) the account name of the user requiring access. (See Chapter 4, *Managing User, Group, and Computer Accounts,* if you need additional information on group management and how to add users to groups in Windows Server 2003).
4. Click the **OK** button.

Advantages of RDA over other Remote Administration Methods

Windows Server 2003 includes many ways to remotely administer your servers. You can install server administration tools (including Active Directory Users and Computers, Active Directory Sites and Services, Active Directory Domains and Trusts, and many others) on a client computer. You can use the Computer Management console on one computer on the network to connect to and manage another. You can use command-line tools to connect to and manage computers across the network. What are the advantages of using Remote Desktop for Administration?

Many administrators prefer RDA because you are able to see and use the entire server desktop, exactly as if you were sitting there at the console. You can do things such as promote or demote a domain controller or defrag the server's disk, install applications, run a backup job, or even upgrade the operating system. You can change configurations, such as Control Panel settings, that are difficult or impossible to configure by other remote methods. You can control the server from a computer on which you would not want to install the administrative tools. With the Remote Desktop Web Connection, you don't even have to have RDC or the Terminal Services client installed on the computer from which you initiate a terminal session; only MSIE v5.0 or later is required. Because of the efficiency of the latest version of RDP, performance over the LAN is almost as fast as if you were physically sitting at the server.

Diagnose and Resolve Issues Related to Terminal Services Security

When enabled, Remote Desktop for Administration opens port 3389 and listens for connection requests. This port is a significant target and is often sought during port scans. Most open ports link to applications that must be attacked in complex ways to permit administrator level access to a computer. This service is designed to actually provide it, which makes it a prime target for attackers. There are several best practices that you should follow to maximize the security of this component.

Remember, with the exception of administrators, users must be authorized to connect using Remote Desktop for Administration. This is accomplished by adding a user's account to the Remote Desktop Users group using one of the methods previously mentioned. If a user does not require this access, his or her account should never be a member of this group. You should control membership in this group through Group Policy or review it manually on a regular basis.

It is important to enforce strong security precautions on all accounts that are enabled to connect using Remote Desktop for Administration. Strong passwords and the use of account lock out are essential to make it difficult for an attacker to successfully use a brute force attack to gain system access. Administrators should be required to log on using a standard user account and perform administrative duties in the session using the **Run as** feature. This will ensure maximum security of the administrator credentials, minimal damage to the Windows Server 2003 computer if the session is hijacked, and make it more difficult to accidentally install trojans and other malicious code.

All users should be required to use the most recent client available for their platform. This will ensure that the latest security features are available to them. It should be standard policy to check frequently for software updates to both client and server components, because these may contain critical security fixes. In addition, users should be discouraged from storing their logon credentials in the properties of the client. This enables anyone with physical access to the user's machine to establish a session. It also stores sensitive information such as the user's username and domain in a clear text file with an RDP extension in the user's My Documents folder.

Finally, denial of service (DoS) is a significant possibility when using Remote Desktop for Administration because it enables only two sessions to exist on the server. Both active and disconnected sessions count. So, if your company has three administrators and two of them leave disconnected sessions, the third will not be able to connect using Terminal Services until one of the existing sessions has been terminated. The solution to this may appear to be setting the time out settings so that sessions are reset shortly after they enter the disconnected state. However, this can cause serious problems.

An administrator may establish a session, begin an installation process and then disconnect to enable the installation to finish unmonitored. The previous settings would terminate the session, including the installation routine it was running, with potentially disastrous effects for the server. Special circumstances like these must be taken into account when configuring your policies. Because session timeout settings can be set at the user property level, Microsoft recommends the use of a special shared administrative account for circumstances like this. The strategy applies a timeout for disconnected sessions that are started by every user account except the shared account, which has no timeout settings applied. In this way, there should always be one connection available to a server, even though the second allowed connection is being consumed by a session involving the shared administrative account.

Using Remote Assistance

As with Remote Desktop for Administration, the Remote Assistance (RA) components of Windows Server 2003 install with the operating system. And, just as Remote Desktop for Administration needs to be enabled and configured before you can use the feature, the same is true for RA.

Two major components comprise the default installation: the Terminal Services service and the Remote Desktop Help Session Manager service. In addition to installing these two components, Microsoft also creates a special user account for connections involving RA, called HelpAssistant_*XXXXXX*. On your system, the X's will be replaced with a unique alphanumeric code and the account name will appear as something similar to this: HelpAssistant_e4bb43. This account will be disabled until you enable RA. As we've mentioned, although RA is based on and uses Terminal Services, it works very differently from Remote Desktop for Administration or the terminal server role. Let's take a closer look at how RA works.

Test Day Tip

Be sure that you are familiar with Remote Assistance (RA). As a new component in the Windows server family, and one that relates directly to test objectives, it is likely to be featured in one or more exam questions.

How Remote Assistance Works

Remote Assistance (RA) enables a user at one computer, the Novice, to request help from a user at another computer, the Expert. The underlying technologies are Windows Terminal Services and the RDP protocol. Although these are the same technologies that were originally developed for thin client computing, and that are used for RDA and terminal server, RA is *not* a thin client solution; in fact, both computers must be running Windows XP or Windows Server 2003. Another difference between RA and traditional Terminal Services is that, typically, the session is initiated when the Novice sends an invitation to the Expert, soliciting his or her assistance. The Novice must typically be present at the machine that needs assistance, to allow the Expert to access his or her system after the Expert receives and accepts the invitation. With Remote Desktop for Administration or the terminal server role, a user can connect from a wide range of client systems without permission, provided the user has a valid username and password.

Using RA, the Expert actually views and (if allowed) interacts with the same desktop and applications that the Novice is using, at the same time. This is very different from the other forms of Terminal Services, in which a connection is established to a unique session on the Terminal Services computer. During an RA session, both the Novice sitting at the keyboard and the remote assistant (Expert) can control the computer at the same time.

However, with any form of Terminal Services, the RDP protocol is still used so that only screen updates are sent to the client (which in this case is the Expert) while keystrokes and mouse movements are sent back to the server (which in this case is the Novice). So, the net result continues to be remote administration and control involving very little use of bandwidth.

Configuring Remote Assistance for Use

RA is relatively easy to configure; you use the same tab that is used to configure Remote Desktop for Administration. To enable RA, go to **Control Panel** and select the **Remote** tab in the **System** properties. Select the check box next to **Turn on Remote Assistance and allow invitations to be sent from this computer**, located in the **Remote Assistance** section of the tab (as shown in Figure 6.1).

Invitations do not stay valid indefinitely. They have an expiration time of one hour by default, but the Novice can alter the expiration time of the invitations he or she sends, from 0 minutes to 99 days. The acceptance and opening of a session in response to an invitation does not cause it to expire; it is good until it reaches the specified expiration time. In other words, if you save an invitation to a file with an expiration time of 30 days, that invitation can be used to establish RA connections as many times as desired within that 30-day timeframe. To modify the default expiration time, perform the following steps:

1. Click **Start | Control Panel | System**.
2. Click the **Remote** tab.
3. Click the **Advanced** button.

4. Choose the desired number (0 to 99) and interval (minutes, hours, or days) under the **Invitations** section in the **Remote Assistance Settings** dialog box, as shown in Figure 6.2.

Figure 6.2 The Remote Assistance Settings Dialog Box

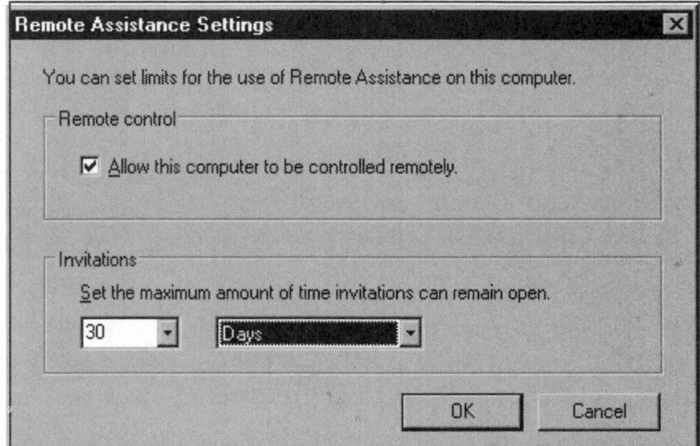

In addition to modifying the expiration time, the **Remote Assistance Settings** dialog box can be used to enable (or not enable) the Expert to control the Novice's desktop and applications during an RA session. When the **Allow this computer to be controlled remotely** box is checked, the Expert will be allowed to send mouse and keyboard input to the Novice's system and interact directly with his or her desktop and applications. When it is unchecked, the Expert will be able to see the Novice's desktop and any actions the Novice performs, but cannot control the cursor or send keyboard commands. This is the same dialog box shown in Figure 6.2.

NOTE

It is important to be aware that, when you enable Remote Assistance (RA), the **Allow this computer to be controlled remotely** checkbox is enabled by default.

Asking for Assistance

A Novice can use a variety of methods to request help by sending an invitation using RA:

- The request can be sent using Windows Messenger.
- The request can be sent via e-mail.
- The request can be saved to a file.

To create an invitation, open **Help and Support** from the Windows **Start** menu. On the right side of the **Help and Support Center** utility, click **Remote Assistance** under the Support heading. In the next screen, click the **Invite someone to help you** link. You will then be able to select the method that you want to use in asking for assistance, as shown in Figure 6.3.

Figure 6.3 The "Pick how you want to contact your assistant" Screen in Remote Assistance

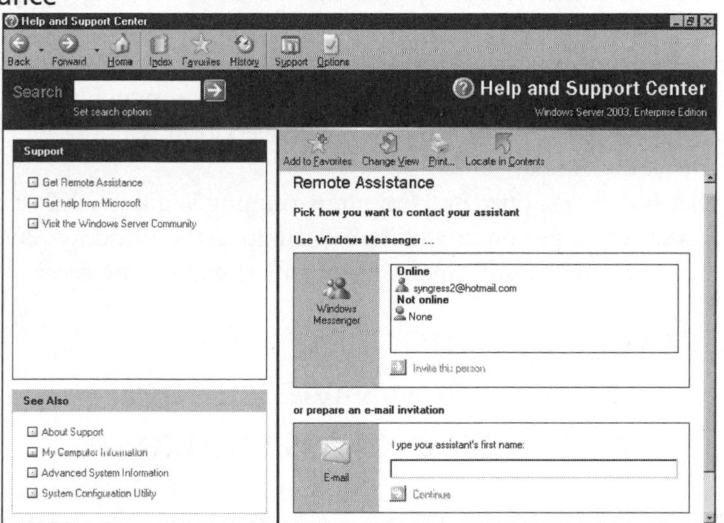

Exam Warning

Although a Remote Assistance (RA) session can be solicited using an invitation sent in a file or via e-mail, Microsoft emphasizes sending an invitation using Windows Messaging. You should make sure you are very familiar with all of the details of this method of solicitation.

Using Windows Messenger to Request Help

Windows Messenger is a chat program available at no cost from Microsoft (and installed in Windows XP by default) that is similar to ICQ and AOL Instant Messenger. (MSN Messenger is a separate but related application; both use the .NET Messenger Service.) When you use Windows Messenger for RA, the invitation travels through a messaging server infrastructure that can include the Internet, or can work with Microsoft Exchange Server within the LAN. Expert and Novice "tickets" (data packets) that contain connection information are exchanged through this infrastructure. However, after these have been exchanged, the actual RDP connection attempt and subsequent session take place directly between the Novice and Expert computers.

Windows Server 2003 does not install Windows Messenger by default. If you have not installed it prior to arriving at the Remote Connection screen, you will only see a link notifying you that it is not installed and prompting you to download and install it. If Messenger is installed, the user from whom you wish to solicit help must be on the network and logged on to his or her Windows Messenger client. If this is the case, you can click the name of the contact from whom you want to solicit assistance, followed by the **Invite this person** link. The person you invited can then accept the invitation. A Remote Assistance dialog box will display on your screen until the person accepts, or until you click the **Cancel** button in the dialog box.

You can also request assistance from within the Windows Messenger application, by double-clicking a contact to establish a conversation with him or her and then selecting the **Ask for Remote Assistance** link on the right side of the conversation window. This will add a notification to your conversation window, with a link on which you can click to cancel the request. You will also be notified in the conversation window when the person receives and accepts your request.

Remember that RA works only on computers running Windows XP and Server 2003. If your invitation is sent to a person at a computer running the Windows 2000 or earlier operating system, or a non-Microsoft operating system, it will not be received.

Downloading, Installing, and Configuring the Windows Messenger Tool for Use with Remote Assistance

If you do not have Windows Messenger installed, you can begin the process from the **Help and Support Center** by clicking on the **Download Windows Messenger** link, after beginning the process of asking for RA. This will open an Internet Explorer window with a Web page that displays the Windows XP version of Windows Messenger for download. At the time of this writing, there is no Windows Server 2003 version of Windows Messenger available; however, the Windows XP version works just fine.

Downloading Messenger

To download the Messenger application, follow these steps:

1. On the Web page, click the **Download Now** button.
2. On the next page that opens, click an identical button.
3. When the **Save As** dialog box opens, click the **Open** button.
4. After the download has completed, click **Yes** in the **Security Warning** dialog box that appears.
5. In the **Messenger 4.7** (or current version) dialog box, click **Yes** to accept the license agreement and begin the installation.
6. When installation has completed, the application will launch and ask you to sign in. If you have a username and password provided by your administrator, or a valid Microsoft .NET Passport account (such as a Hotmail e-mail account), click the **Click here to sign in** link in the Windows Messenger window. If you are unsure about which account you should use, contact your administrator.

The **Click here to sign in** link will open up the **.NET Passport Wizard.** This wizard is used to associate a .NET Passport account with your Windows user account.

Creating an Account

Follow these steps if you want to create a new Hotmail account:

1. Read the initial screen and then click **Next.** The next screen in the wizard enables you to choose between using an existing e-mail account or creating a new Hotmail account.
2. To create a new Hotmail e-mail account, select the radio button next to **No. I would like to open an MSN Hotmail e-mail account** and click the **Next** button.
3. The following screen alerts you to the fact that when you click the **Next** button, an Internet Explorer window will open with the Get a .NET Passport Web page displayed. This page will enable you to simultaneously register for a Hotmail e-mail account and a .NET Passport account. When you have completed the registration form, click the **I Agree** button.
4. On the following page, click the **Continue** button. The browser window will close, and you will be taken to the **Associate your .NET Passport with your Windows user account?** page in the wizard. Choose to clear or leave selected the **Associate my Passport with my Windows user account** and click the **Next** button, and then finish the wizard.

Using an Existing Account to Log On

Follow these steps if you already have an account with which you want to log on:

1. To use an existing account (including the Hotmail account you just created), select the radio button next to **Yes** on the **Do you have an email address?** page of the **.NET Passport Wizard**.
2. The next page in the wizard will ask if you have already registered the address with .NET Passport. If the e-mail address you plan to use is not already registered, select the radio button next to **No. I want to register my email address with Passport now** and click the **Next** button.
3. The following screen alerts you that clicking **Next** will open Internet Explorer and guide you through the registration process. Click the **Next** button after you have read the information it contains. When you complete the registration form, click the **I Agree** button.

4. On the following page, click the **Continue** button. The browser window will close, and you will be taken to the **Associate your .NET Passport with your Windows user account?** page in the wizard. Choose to clear or leave selected the **Associate my Passport with my Windows user account** and click the **Next** button, and then finish the wizard.

NOTE

All Hotmail addresses are automatically considered registered with .NET Passport, so if you plan to use a Hotmail e-mail address, you do not need to complete this registration process.

5. If you have a registered address, select the radio button next to **Yes. I want to sign in with my Passport.** on the **Have you already registered your email address with .NET Passport?** wizard page and click the **Next** button to continue.

   The next page in the wizard asks for the username and password associated with your .NET Passport account. Type your full e-mail address in the E-mail Address field, followed by your password in the Password field. The **Associate my Passport with my Windows user account.** check box on this screen is selected by default. If you leave this checked, you will not be prompted to log on to .NET Passport-enabled applications (such as Windows Messenger) and some .NET Passport-enabled Web sites when you visit them. Instead, you will automatically be logged on with the credentials associated with your user account.

   All three of the previous options contain this check box. Leaving it selected may not be ideal if you have several different .NET Passport accounts that you use for different purposes. Likewise, your company may have created a .NET Passport logon for employees to use in accessing partner Web sites, such as the Microsoft partner site, and you may have a personal .NET Passport account that you use for everything else. Finally, it is possible that the account you are logged on to is an account that the company has created for someone filling a role, such as the regional server administrator, rather than an account assigned specifically to you. In cases such as these, you will likely not be serving in this role forever. If you associate your personal .NET Passport account with this user account, the administrator who takes your place at the company will continue to use your personal .NET Passport account each time he or she logs in with the user account associated with that role at the company.

6. After you have made your selections on the **Sign in with your .NET Passport** page of the wizard, click the **Next** button.

7. The final screen in the wizard is a review screen that enables you to examine the selections you have made, go back and make changes, or finish up. Click the

Finish button to accept your selections and close the wizard. After the wizard closes, the Windows Messenger application will log on, using the .NET Passport account you provided.

Adding Contacts

At this point, you are still not finished with the configuration of Windows Messenger. If you don't add someone to contact, you won't be able to solicit help using Windows Messenger and RA.

Follow these steps to add a contact:

1. In the Windows Messenger window, click the **Add a Contact** link. This will bring up another wizard.
2. On the first page, you can opt to search for a contact or type one in. If you need to search for a contact, select the radio button next to **Search for a contact** and click the **Next** button. On the next screen, you can conduct a search based on the contact's **First Name**, **Last Name**, **Country/Region**, **City**, or **State**. You can also select to conduct the search in the **Hotmail Member Directory** or the **Address Book on this computer**. When you have entered your search criteria and selected the search location, click the **Next** button. *Note that this button will not activate until Windows Messenger feels that you have given it enough information to conduct the search.*
3. The next screen displays the search results. Click the name of the contact you wish to add and click the **Next** button. In most cases, privacy restrictions will prevent your selection from being added because the individual does not want his or her e-mail address to be made publicly available. In this case, the wizard will offer to send the person an e-mail, which you can customize. The e-mail message will tell your selected contact how to download Windows Messenger and will ask him or her to add you to as a contact after doing so. If too many users match your search criteria, you will be asked to click the **Back** button and further refine your search. This will also happen if no records are found that match your search criteria.
4. It is usually best to simply contact the person or people from whom you expect to request assistance, and ask for their .NET Passport account names. When you have a name, on the first page of the wizard, select the radio button next to **By e-mail address or sign-in name** and click the **Next** button.
5. On the next screen, enter the person's e-mail address in the text box provided and click the **Next** button. The following screen lets you know that the person has been added to your contact list, and gives you the option to send the person an e-mail, letting him or her know how to download and install the software. Click the **Next** or **Finish** button on this screen.

6. If you clicked the Next button, you will see a final screen, telling you to click **Next** to add another contact or **Finish** to close the wizard. Click the **Finish** button to close the wizard. Believe it or not, you've finally finished installing and configuring Windows Messenger on the system in a way that will enable you to use it to send RA invitations!

Responding to a Request for Help Using Windows Messenger

If the Expert to whom an invitation is sent has the Windows Messaging application running, a request from a Novice for assistance will be displayed in a Conversation window on the Expert's system. The Expert can click the **Accept** link in the window (or use the key combination **Alt + T**) to initiate the connection, or click the **Decline** link (or use the key combination **Alt + D**) to reject it. If it is neither accepted nor declined before the invitation expires, the Expert will be unable to establish a connection in response to that invitation.

Using E-Mail to Request Help

To use e-mail to send an RA invitation, you must first have a default mail client configured on the Windows Server 2003 computer. This mail client can be Microsoft Outlook Express, which is installed with Windows, Outlook (installed as a separate application or with Microsoft Office), or a third-party mail application. To create an RA invitation using e-mail, follow these steps:

1. Open the **Help and Support** utility from the Window's Start menu.
2. On the right side of the **Help and Support Center** screen, click **Remote Assistance** under the **Support** heading.
3. On the next screen that is displayed, click the **Invite someone to help you** link.
4. On the next screen, under the **or prepare an e-mail invitation section**, type the first name of the person you want to use as an Expert in the **Type your assistant's first name**: text box and click the **Continue** link.
5. The next screen contains two sections. The first is entitled **Set the invitation to expire** and contains a drop-down box for specifying a number between 0 and 99 and an interval drop-down box with selections for minutes, hours, or days. This means the possible time period during which the invitation is valid ranges from 0 minutes to 99 days.
6. The second section of this screen is entitled **Require the recipient to use a password** and is enabled by a check box. The check box is selected and this section is enabled by default. The intent is that, should the invitation accidentally fall into the wrong hands, a password would still be required to use it. Obviously, you should not include the password in the e-mailed invitation. Instead, you should communicate it to the person in some other manner (for example, by telephone).

The password is entered twice, once in the **Type password:** text box and again in the **Confirm password:** text box.

7. After the password had been entered into each box, the **Create Email Invitation** button at the bottom of the screen activates and can be clicked.
8. The final screen is entitled **Was the e-mail invitation successfully sent?** When you clicked the **Create Email Invitation** button on the previous screen, your default e-mail program should have launched, with an e-mail created and ready to be sent to the person whose assistance you are requesting. This final screen alerts you to this and gives you the option to recreate the mail message in case you accidentally closed the window when it popped open. At the bottom of the screen are links to manage your outstanding invitation requests and create additional invitations. After you send the e-mail, you've finished the process of asking for remote assistance using the e-mail method.

Responding to a Request for Help From an E-Mail Request

When e-mail has been used to send you an invitation for remote assistance, a short e-mail message entitled "YOU HAVE RECEIVED A REMOTE ASSISTANCE INVITATION" will show up in your inbox. The message will contain a link to click, which will look something like this: https://www.microsoft.com/remoteassistance/ s.asp#1AjK8A2TD,4H8SQYYfvIpQF5prHYajrReyrAd2j6oHb4Qe/Eo1Ahs=,zb2.0RJ81UIfxb4Xfkp8thzdy8A=Z.

When you click the link, your browser will open to a page on Microsoft's Web site. The entire process of the two computers finding each other using this method takes place through Microsoft's Web site. In addition, e-mail-based remote assistance depends on a downloaded control.

When you visit the site, a **Security Warning** dialog box will appear and you will be prompted to specify whether you wish to install the **Remote Assistance Server Control**. If you select **Yes**, the control will download and the page will load. If you are not accessing the page from a Windows XP or Server 2003 computer, a message will display, informing you that you must be running one of these operating systems to complete the connection. If you are accessing the Web page from a Windows XP or Server 2003 computer, you will see a button entitled **Start Remote Assistance** in the middle of the Web page. When you click this button, a small Remote Assistance dialog box appears, prompting you to enter the password associated with the invitation (if one was used). After you have typed in the password, click the **Yes** button to begin the connection.

Using a Saved File to Request Help

The third and final way of requesting assistance is to use a saved file. Obviously, if you use this method, you need to somehow transfer the file containing the invitation to the Expert. This can be done in one of several ways:

- You can e-mail the file.
- You can save the file to a share on the network.
- You can create a link to the file on a Web page.
- You can save the file on a floppy diskette and hand it to the person.

To create an RA invitation using a saved file, open the **Help and Support** utility from the Windows **Start** menu. On the right side of the **Help and Support Center** screen, click **Remote Assistance** under the Support heading. In the next screen that is displayed, click the **Invite someone to help you** link.

At the bottom of the next screen, click the **Save invitation as a file (Advanced)** link. This leads to a screen that contains two parts. The first is entitled **Enter your name** and it contains a text box into which you type your name. When you send someone a request using Windows Messenger or e-mail, the recipient can easily see who sent the request. This is not true with a file-based request, so this dialog box is used to embed that information into the request and make it readily available to the Expert.

The second portion of this screen is entitled **Set the invitation to expire** and contains a drop-down box that enables you to specify a number between 0 and 99, and an interval drop-down box with selections for minutes, hours, or days. The possible range for the duration of a valid invitation is from 0 minutes to 99 days.

After you fill in the requested information, click the **Continue** button at the bottom of the screen. The following page contains a section entitled **Require the recipient to use a password**, which can be enabled by checking a check box. By default, the check box is selected and this requirement is enabled. Again, the intent is that if the invitation accidentally falls into the wrong hands, at least a password will be required to use it. The password must be entered twice, once in the **Type password:** text box and again in the **Confirm password:** text box.

After the password has been entered into each box, the **Save Invitation** button at the bottom of the screen activates and can be clicked. This displays a **Save As** dialog box that enables you to specify a name and location for the file. The file will be saved with an *.msrcincident* extension. After it is saved, the final screen is displayed. It confirms the file name and where it was saved. At the bottom of the screen, there are links to manage your outstanding invitation requests and create additional invitations.

Exercise 6.01

Creating a Saved File for Requesting Help

1. Open the **Help and Support** utility from the Windows **Start** menu.
2. On the right side of the Help and Support Center screen, click **Remote Assistance** under the Support heading.

3. On the next screen that is displayed, click the **Invite someone to help you** link.
4. At the bottom of the next screen, click the **Save invitation as a file (Advanced)** link.
5. In the **Enter your name** text box, type your name
6. In the **Set the invitation to expire** drop-down boxes, specify when the invitation should expire and then click the **Continue** button.
7. Type the password you would like to use in the **Type password:** and **Confirm password:** text boxes. If you do not wish to use a password, clear the check box next to **Require the recipient to use a password**.
8. Click the **Save Invitation** button at the bottom of the screen.
9. In the **Save As** dialog box, specify a name and location for the file.
10. Review the information on the final screen and close the Help and Support utility.

Responding to a Request for Help that was made using a Saved File

Responding to a remote assistance request that has been saved to a file is a simple matter of double-clicking the file. When you do this, a small Remote Assistance dialog box appears, asking you to enter the password associated with the invitation (if one was specified). After you type in the password, click the **Yes** button to initiate the connection. In the following section, we show you how to complete the connection process for each of the methods described, and demonstrate what you can do when the connection has been established.

Completing the Connection

After the Expert user accepts a request for assistance, a small **Remote Assistance** dialog box pops up on the Expert's computer with a message indicating that a connection is being attempted. When the connection is established, the full **Remote Assistance** application opens, displaying a status message that says it is waiting for an answer from the Novice computer. When the connection is accepted by the Novice user, the status of the **Remote Assistance** application changes to **connected**.

During this time, the Novice's system displays a small **Remote Assistance** dialog box that asks the user if he or she wants to allow the Expert to view the computer's screen and chat with him or her. If the Novice clicks the **No** button, the connection is rejected. If the Novice clicks the **Yes** button, the connection is established. If too much time passes after the Expert attempts to establish the connection and before the Novice accepts it, a dialog box opens to inform the Novice that the invitation was accepted but has expired. This dialog box also states that a new invitation needs to be generated and offered. A dialog box is also displayed on the Expert's computer, indicating that the remote connection could not be established.

When a connection is successfully established, a **Remote Assistance** application opens on the Novice's system.

Using the Completed Connection as the Expert

The Remote Assistance application on the Expert's computer consists of a tool bar across the top, a chat option on the left side and a replica of the Novice's remote desktop on the right. This is shown in Figure 6.4.

Figure 6.4 The Remote Assistance Utility on the Expert's Computer

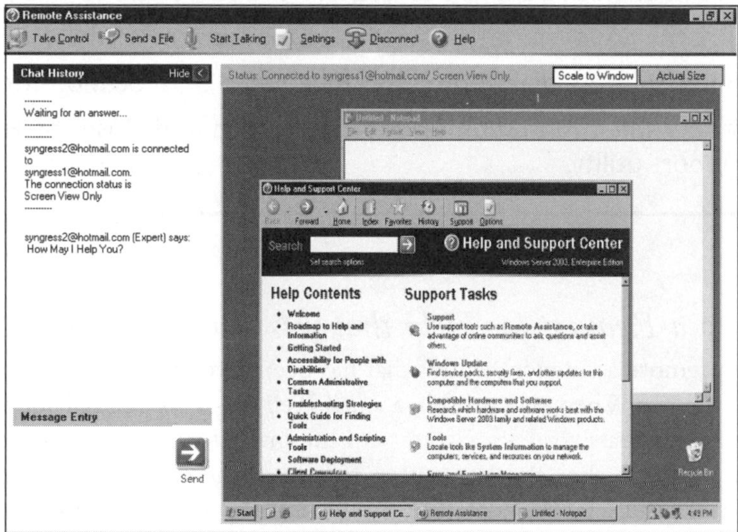

The buttons on the tool bar across the top include the following:

- **Take Control** Initiates a request to enable the Expert to remotely control the cursor and keyboard input on the Novice's computer. When this button is clicked, a dialog box pops up on the Novice's computer, asking the Novice to allow or reject control by the Expert. Remote control is only possible if the **Allow this computer to be controlled remotely** box is checked on the **Remote** tab of the **System** properties in **Control Panel**. If remote control is accepted by the Novice, a dialog box appears in the **Remote Assistance** application on the Expert's computer over the display of the Novice's desktop, stating that remote control has been accepted. Either party can end the remote control at any time by using the **ESC** key. After remote control is established, the Remote Control button changes to read **Release Control** and can be clicked to end the remote control of the session without ending the RA session itself. Both the Novice and Expert can control the cursor and keyboard input for the Novice's system, so it is recommended that only one party be using the pointing device or typing at any given time. The Expert can use Remote control by clicking on the Novice desktop that is displayed in his or her **Remote Assistance** application.

- **Send a File** Enables you to transmit a file from the Expert's to the Novice's computer.
- **Start Talking** Establishes an audio connection between the Novice's and Expert's computers for voice and/or video communication. When this button is clicked, the **Audio and Video Tuning Wizard** opens. The wizard enables you to specify and test your microphone, audio card, and other related settings.
- **Settings** Opens the **Remote Assistance Settings** dialog box and enables adjustment of audio quality in accordance with the capacity of the underlying network. **The Audio and Video Tuning Wizard**, mentioned in the previous bullet point, can also be opened from this dialog box.
- **Disconnect** Terminates the connection between the Novice's and Expert's computers and ends the RA session.
- **Help** Displays the About Remote Assistance help screen.

The left side of the Remote Assistance application on the Expert's computer contains a chat window. This enables the Novice and Expert to exchange text messages. In addition to chat communication, this portion of the application also contains status messages (such as the names of users who are part of the connection, whether remote control is enabled, how to stop remote control, etc.

The right side of the **Remote Assistance** application on the Expert's computer displays the desktop of the Novice's system. When the connection is initially established, the desktop appears in View Only mode. This enables the Expert to view the desktop of the Novice, but the Expert cannot interact with it. The Expert can still exchange text messages or voice communications with the Novice in this mode, and can exchange files. If the Expert and Novice agree to switch from View Only to Remote Control, the Expert can then interact with the remote desktop and applications on the Novice's system. To do this, the Expert uses his or her pointing device and keyboard to select and input data into the desktop that is displayed on the right side of the **Remote Assistance** application.

Using the Completed Connection as the Novice

The Remote Assistance application on the Novice's computer consists of a chat window on the left side and a series of option buttons along the right, shown in Figure 6.5.

Figure 6.5 The Remote Assistance Utility on the Novice's Computer

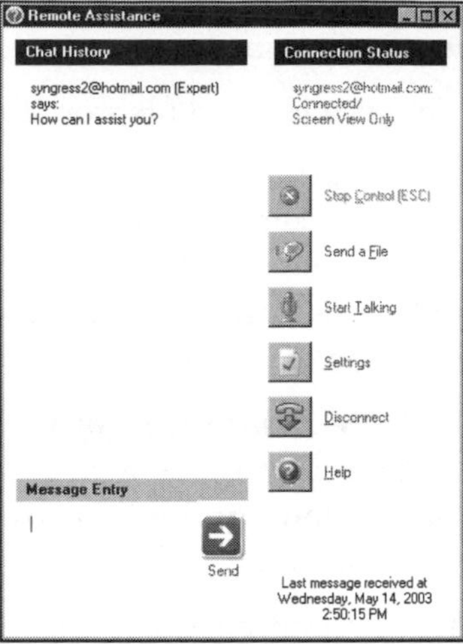

This application enables the Novice to send messages to and receive messages from the Expert. It also contains the following buttons:

- **Stop Control** Terminates the ability of the Expert to control the cursor and keyboard input on the Novice's computer.
- **Send a File** Enables transmitting a file from the Novice's to the Expert's computer.
- **Start Talking** Establishes an audio connection between the Novice and Expert computers for voice and/or video communication. When clicked, the **Audio and Video Tuning Wizard** opens. The wizard enables you to specify and test your microphone, speaker, and related settings.
- **Settings** Opens a dialog box that enables the adjustment of audio quality in accordance with the capacity of the underlying network. The **Audio and Video Tuning Wizard** can also be opened from this dialog box.
- **Disconnect** Terminates the connection between the Novice's and Expert's computers and ends the RA session.
- **Help** Brings up the **About Remote Assistance** help screen.

The left side of the Remote Assistance application on the Novice's computer contains a chat window. This enables the Novice and Expert to exchange text messages. In addition to chat communication, the left side of the application also displays status messages such as the names of users who are part of the connection, whether remote control is enabled, how to stop remote control, and so forth.

Managing Open Invitations

Sometimes you might want to know the names of users with whom you have active RA invitations open. You might want to cancel an invitation because you've solved the problem or because you want someone else to help you. Help and Support Center provides a number of options for managing open invitations.

To manage your active invitations, follow these steps:

1. Open the **Help and Support** utility from the Windows **Start** menu.
2. On the right side of the Help and Support Center screen, click **Remote Assistance** under the Support heading.
3. On the following screen, click the **View Invitation Status (*X*)** link. The (X) will be replaced on your screen by the number of invitations you have outstanding.
4. The next screen will show you a list of the invitations that are outstanding. The list consists of three columns: Sent To, Expiration Time, and Status. The Sent To column contains the name of the person to whom you sent the Windows Message or e-mail. If you saved the request to a file, this column will display the word "Saved." The Expiration Time column will show the date and time that the invitation will expire. The Status column will show whether the invitation's status is Open or Expired. Now you can view or modify any of these invitations.

Each invitation will have a radio button next to it, as shown in Figure 6.6. You can click a radio button to select one of the invitations, and then choose an action to perform using the buttons under the list box. The buttons include:

- **Details** Enables you to view to whom the invitation was sent, when it was sent, when it expires, its current status, and whether it is password protected.
- **Expire** Enables you to cause an invitation to expire immediately, regardless of the expiration time that was set when the invitation was originally created.
- **Resend** Can be used only with expired invitations. When selected, this option displays a screen that walks you through the creation process for the invitation all over again. Remember that the request was originally saved to a file or sent via e-mail. Because of this, the screens and options presented are identical to those outlined earlier in the chapter.
- **Delete** Enables you to permanently delete the invitation. If the invitation's status is Open when you select to delete it, a dialog box will pop up, informing you that the invitation will not be usable for connection. If the invitation's status is Expired, it is simply deleted and no pop-up box appears.

Figure 6.6 The "View or change your invitation settings" Screen in Remote Assistance

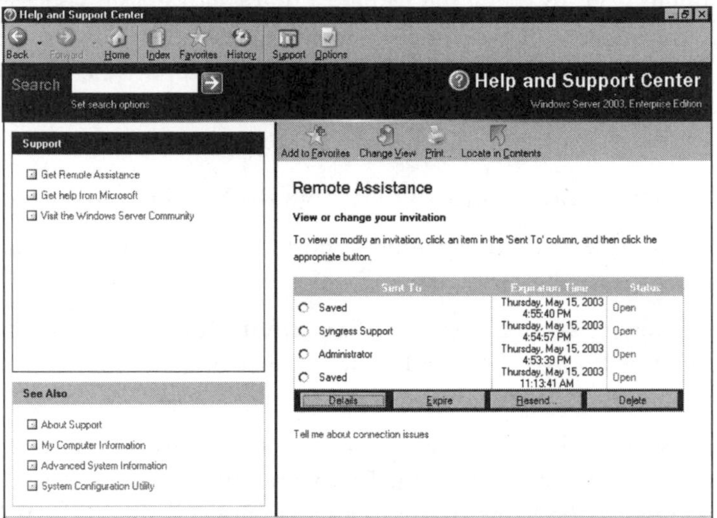

Remote Assistance Security Issues

RA is a valuable tool, but it also contains serious security risks that must be planned for and managed. RA makes it easy for any user to ask virtually anyone using a Windows XP or Server 2003 computer to connect to his or her desktop. This person can be inside or a friend that is outside of your company. Although an outside person may be qualified to assist the user, in doing so they will likely receive full control of a client in your network.

This, of course, is unacceptable, because they could place malicious software on the system while in control of it, view sensitive company information that normally isn't allowed outside of the organization, etc. The best way to prevent this is to use your company's firewalls to prevent connection to RA from outside the company's network. RA uses the same port that all Terminal Services components do, 3389. Simply blocking this port on your external firewalls prevents this type of unauthorized access.

Several other key security concerns should be addressed in your company's remote assistance policies. E-mail and file-based invitations enable you to specify passwords. An invitation without password protection can be used by anyone that receives it by accident or intercepts it illegitimately. Because of this, always mandate the use of these passwords.

Your company may also want to protect traffic that contains RA requests. E-mail is normally sent in unencrypted form on the network. This means that the URL that is sent in the e-mail invitation is available for easy interception while it is in transit on the network. Likewise, a simple XML format is used for the invitation file. A simple pattern match could be used when monitoring the network to detect and automatically save this information to an unauthorized system while it is being sent across the network. If the e-mail or file invitations do not have passwords, they can be used immediately when they are captured in this way. Even if a password is specified, there is no limit to the number of times requests like these can be used for connection. A brute force attack could be used to attempt to break the password and successfully establish a session. For this reason, it is important that your remote assistance policy also specify a short expiration time for the invitation. Once expired, no connections are possible with it. A shorter time reduces the chances of success using a brute force attack. And, if no password is specified, at least the open window for misuse of the invitation is shorter.

You should also educate your users on when it is appropriate to accept RA requests. As mentioned previously, a request saved to a file is stored in a standard XML file. These can easily be modified to perform malicious actions when run by a user on a local system. The e-mail request contains a URL to click and can also be altered. In this case it may take the user to a page that performs malicious actions on their local system, or requires the download and installation of an unauthorized ActiveX control that is designed to appear legitimate to the user. Even an unsolicited request received through Windows messaging has security worries.

The best option is to maintain a tight policy that asks users to reject RA invitations in all but a few instances. What is acceptable will relate specifically to your company. Some organizations allow acceptance only from immediate co-workers and known help desk staff. Others are more liberal and allow invitations to be accepted from any verifiable employee within the company. The most important rule is to not allow connections from outside of the organization. Again, this can be further prevented by the use of firewall rules.

Installing and Configuring the Terminal Server Role

Unlike the remote administration components in Windows 2003, the terminal server role requires separate installation by an administrator. In addition, it requires the terminal server licensing component to be added to a Windows Server 2003 server on the network. If the license server component is not added, or if it is added but valid client licenses are not installed on it, no remote connections to the terminal server will be allowed starting 120 days after the first client connects. Let's take a look at how to install the terminal server role and terminal server licensing component.

TEST DAY TIP

Although not mentioned specifically in Microsoft's exam outline, be sure you are familiar with the basics of the terminal server role and its requirements. This is a critical component of Terminal Services, and it can be used for remote administration in addition to application serving.

Installing the Terminal Server Role

The terminal server role can be installed from the **Manage Your Server** utility, which is opened from the Windows **Start | Administrative Tools** menu. Open the utility and follow these steps:

1. Click the **Add or remove a role** link. This will display the **Configure Your Server Wizard** with its first page displayed.
2. Read the recommendations and click the **Next** button.
3. A **Configure Your Server Wizard** dialog box will pop up, informing you that the underlying network settings are being detected. When detection is complete, you will see the **Configuration Options** screen in the wizard.
4. Select the radio button next to **Custom configuration** and click the **Next** button.
5. On the **Server Role** screen, click **Terminal Server** to highlight the role in the list (it should say **No** under the **Configured** column if the terminal server role has not already been installed). Click the **Next** button.
6. The **Summary of Selections** screen should read **Install Terminal Server**. Ensure that it does, and then click **Next**.
7. At this point, another **Configure Your Server** pop-up dialog box will appear to inform you that the server will reboot automatically as part of the installation process. Click the **OK** button in this dialog box.
8. The wizard will switch to the **Applying Selections** screen, launch the **Windows Component Wizard**, finish the installation based on your selections, and reboot.
9. When the reboot has completed, log on as an administrator. When your logon is completed, the **Configure Your Server Wizard** will appear to let you know that your server is now a Terminal Server. Click the **Finish** button.
10. The **Manage Your Server** utility will reappear in the background. A help window also opens when you log on with the Terminal Server help topic displayed.

In the following exercise, you will practice installing the Terminal Server role on your Windows Server 2003 computer.

New & Noteworthy...

The Old Modes Are Gone!

In Windows NT 4.0, Terminal Server Edition, Terminal Services was only installed in application mode. With Windows 2000, the Terminal Services service was added to all versions of the server products and Terminal Server Edition as a stand-alone product disappeared. In Windows 2000, Terminal Services was installed as a separate component in one of two modes: Application Server or Remote Administration. With Windows Server 2003, a whole new evolution occurs.

Remote Administration mode is now called Remote Desktop for Administration. It is installed by default with Windows 2003, but must be activated manually by an administrator. A new component that first appeared in Windows XP, RA also installs by default and requires manual activation.

Microsoft now refers to the Application Server mode as the Terminal Server role or Terminal Server component. It requires separate installation and configuration. As with Windows 2000, the Windows Server 2003 version of Terminal Services requires the Terminal Services License component to be installed to support the Terminal Server role.

Exercise 6.02

Installing the Terminal Server Role

1. Log on to your Windows Server 2003 server as an administrator.
2. If it does not open automatically, open the **Manage Your Server** utility from the Windows **Start | Administrative Tools** menu.
3. Click the **Add or remove a role** link.
4. Read the initial page in the **Configure Your Server Wizard** and click the **Next** button.
5. In the **Configuration Options** page in the wizard, select the radio button next to **Custom Configuration** and click the **Next** button.
6. On the Server Role page, select **Terminal server** in the list, followed by the **Next** button.
7. Click the **Next** button on the Summary of Selections page.
8. Click the **OK** button in the dialog box that pops up to alert you that the installation process will require a reboot to complete.
9. When the reboot has completed, log on as an administrator.
10. Click the **Finish** button in the **Configure Your Server Wizard**.
11. Close the **Manage Your Server** utility.

Installing Terminal Server Licensing

After you have installed the Terminal Server role on one of your servers, it's time to install Terminal Server licensing. If you fail to do so, all Terminal Server connections will be rejected starting 120 days after the first client logs on. Microsoft recommends that you install Terminal Server licensing on a server that does not host the terminal server role. So, it will take at least two Windows Server 2003 servers to properly implement a terminal server environment.

The terminal server licensing component is not available from the Configure Your Server Wizard and must be added using **Add or Remove Programs** from Control Panel in the Windows Start menu. To install it, follow these steps:

1. In the **Add or Remove Programs** utility, click the **Add/Remove Windows Components** button on the left side of the screen. A Windows Setup pop-up dialog box will briefly appear, followed by the **Windows Components Wizard**.
2. In the Components list, scroll down to select the check box next to **Terminal Server Licensing** and click the **Next** button.
3. On the Terminal Server Licensing Setup page of the wizard, select the way you will use this license server on your network.

NOTE

Click the radio button next to **Your entire enterprise** if you currently have or will be installing Terminal Servers across multiple Windows 2000 and/or 2003 domains in your forest. Click the radio button next to **Your domain or workgroup** if you will be installing your Terminal Servers only into a single domain, you wish to have a separate license server for each of the domains in your enterprise, you do not have a domain, or you have Windows NT Server 4.0, Terminal Server Edition computers on your network that will need to use the license server. When installed in this mode, a Terminal Server can access the license server only if it is a member of the domain in which the license server is installed, unless a workgroup is being used.

4. You can also specify where you would like to place the license database. The default location, **C:\WINDOWS\System32\LServer** is displayed in the **Install license server database at this location** text box. When you have made your selections, click the **Next** button.
5. The wizard will switch to the **Configuring Components** screen and will begin the installation. Unlike the terminal server role installation, the license component requires the Windows 2003 installation CD-ROM. If it is not in the CD-ROM drive, you will be prompted for it.
6. The final screen in the wizard is entitled **Completing the Windows Component Wizard**. Review the information it contains and click the **Finish** button.

7. When the wizard disappears, if you do not wish to add additional components, close the **Add or Remove Programs** utility.

It is important to note that you can also install the terminal server role and most other Windows components from the **Add or Remove Programs** utility in **Control Panel**.

After you have installed the licensing component, you must complete the licensing process by adding client licenses. Refer to Microsoft's Web site for additional details on how to complete this process. While it is also covered in Windows Server 2003's help materials, this can be a complex process and it is best to ensure that you have the latest information and fixes from Microsoft.

Configuring & Implementing...

Activation Required

Simply installing the terminal server role and Terminal Services License Server component is not enough to use your Terminal Server as an application server. After it is installed, the license server must be activated and at least one client license key pack must be installed on it. Client license key packs enable the license server to issue licenses to terminal server clients. Clients cannot connect to the Terminal Server (after the 120-day evaluation period expires) without a license (however, you can still use Remote Desktop for Administration as described earlier in this chapter, with no license required).

Both the license server activation and client license key pack installation processes occur through the Microsoft Clearinghouse. The Microsoft Clearinghouse is a database hosted by Microsoft that contains information about all activated terminal servers and license key packs issued. When a client initially connects to a server running the terminal server role, if the evaluation period is over, the terminal server contacts the license server and obtains a valid license for the client.

Using Terminal Services Client Tools

There are three primary tools you can use to connect from a client system to Terminal Services. These tools include:

- The Remote Desktop Connection (RDC) utility
- The Remote Desktops MMC snap-in
- The Remote Desktop Web Connection utility

Each is designed to fill a very specific role, and it is important for you to be familiar with the capabilities and uses of each. In the following sections, we examine how to install and use these utilities.

TEST DAY TIP

Be sure to familiarize yourself with the properties available for configuration in each of the client tools prior to taking the exam.

Installing and Using the Remote Desktop Connection (RDC) Utility

The Remote Desktop Connection (RDC) utility (formerly the Terminal Services Client Connection Manager) is the standard client for connecting to Terminal Services, via RDA on a server or Terminal Services on a Terminal Server. It can be used for Remote Administration or full Terminal Server client use. It enables a user to connect to a single server running Terminal Services using the RDP protocol over TCP/IP. The utility is installed with the operating system in Windows XP and Server 2003. It is accessed via the **Start | Programs | Accessories | Communications** menu in those operating systems. If you use the client often, you might want to create a shortcut to it on your desktop.

The RDC utility can also be installed and used on a number of older Windows operating systems, including Windows 2000, NT, ME, 98, and 95.

The older Terminal Services Client Connection Manager can still be used to connect to a terminal server from a Windows 3.11 computer with the 32-bit TCP/IP stack installed. There is also a 16-bit version of the Windows 2000 Terminal Service client for Windows for Workgroups 3.11 and a Macintosh client. If you need to connect MS-DOS, Linux, or other client operating systems, you will need third-party RDP or ICA client software. The Remote Desktop Connection utility is backward compatible and capable of communicating with Terminal Services in Windows XP, Windows 2000, and Windows NT 4.0, Terminal Server Edition. Let's take a look at how to install, configure, and use this critical utility.

EXAM WARNING

The Remote Desktop Connection utility is the primary end user client connection tool for Terminal Services. Don't forget that it comes preinstalled on Windows XP and Server 2003 and does not need to be installed separately.

Installing the Remote Desktop Connection Utility

If you want to use the Remote Desktop Connection utility on systems older than Windows XP, you'll need to install it first. This means you'll need the installation files. You can get them from the Microsoft Web site, or if you have installed Windows Server 2003, you can share the client setup folder located at %SystemRoot%\system32\clients\tsclient. After you share this folder, computers on the network can connect to the share and run the Setup.exe utility in the Win32 folder. If you want to deploy the client using Group Policy, Microsoft also includes an MSI installation file, Msrdpcli.msi, in this directory.

Perform the following steps to install the RDC client:

1. When you double-click the **Setup.exe** file, the installation wizard will launch. Read the initial welcome screen, and then click the **Next** button.
2. Review the license agreement, and then click the radio button next to **I accept the terms of the license agreement**, followed by the **Next** button.
3. On the Customer Information screen, enter your name for licensing purposes in the **User Name** text box, and your company for licensing purposes in the **Organization** text box.
4. In the Install this application for section, select the radio button next to **Anyone who uses this computer (all users)** if you want the utility to be available on the Windows Start menu for every user that logs on to the system. Select the radio button next to **Only for me (-)** if you want the utility to appear only in your Windows Start menu. When you've finished making your selection, click the **Next** button.
5. On the next screen, click the **Install** button to proceed with the installation or the **Back** button to review your choices. The application will remove any previously installed similar applications, and then complete its own installation.
6. Click the **Finish** button to close the wizard.

Launching and Using the Remote Desktop Connection Utility

After the application is installed, open the Windows **Start** menu and click **Remote Desktop Connection** in the **Programs | Accessories | Communications** menu. This will open the utility, with most of its configuration options hidden. To proceed with the connection at this point, simply type the name or IP address of the Terminal Server, Windows Server 2003 computer, or Windows XP Professional computer to which you want to connect in the **Computer** drop-down box, or select it from the drop-down list if you have previously established a session to it. By default, the name or IP address of the last computer to which you connected will be displayed. Finally, click on the **Connect** button.

A Remote Desktop window will open. If the user name and password with which you are logged on to your current system are valid for connection to Terminal Services on the server, you will be automatically logged on and a session will appear. If not, you will be prompted to enter a valid user name and password. When you are connected, the remote desktop will appear in a window on your system by default. You can move your cursor over it, click, and use any item in the remote desktop just as you would if you were using your local system. You can also copy and paste between the remote and local computers, using the standard methods of doing this.

Connecting is a simple process; however, terminating your session requires a bit more explanation. There are two methods that you can use to end your session:

- Logging off
- Disconnecting

To log off, simply click the Windows **Start** menu on the remote desktop, and then click the **Log Off** button. When you do this, it will completely log you out of the remote system in much the same way as if you logged out on your local system. Registry entries are properly written, programs are elegantly closed, etc. The session is completely removed from the Terminal Services computer, freeing up any system resources that were being used by your session. Make sure that you select **Log Off,** rather than **Shut Down**. If you select **Shut Down**, and you are logged onto the remote session with rights that enable your account to shut down the server, it will power down or reboot the server. This will affect everyone who is currently using the server.

The second method of terminating your session is to use the process known as disconnection. When you disconnect from Terminal Services, your session remains on the server and is not removed. It continues to consume resources, although the video stream coming to your local computer and input stream going from your local computer to the Terminal Services system are terminated. When you launch the RDC utility again and connect to the same computer running Terminal Services, your session will still be there, exactly as you left it, and you can take up where you left off. This can be helpful in cases where you are running an application that requires lengthy processing. You do not have to remain connected for the application to run and you can check back in later and obtain the result.

In general, it is best to properly log off and free up the resources being used by a session you no longer need. As we'll see a bit later, an administrator can cause a disconnected session to be reset if you don't return to it for a specified period of time. If you've left unsaved documents or other files open in your session, resetting will cause you to lose all work. Thus, it is usually safest to save your work and disconnect. You can disconnect from your session by clicking the close button (the X) in the top right corner of the Remote Desktop window.

You can also log off or disconnect using the Windows Security dialog box. This can be accessed by opening the Windows **Start** menu and selecting **Windows Security**, or by using the **CTRL + ALT + END** key combination from within the session (this has the same effect as **CTRL+ALT+DEL** on the local machine). Once in the dialog, you can log off by clicking the **Log Off** button, or by selecting **Log Off** from the drop-down box that appears if you click the **Shut Down** button. This same drop-down box also contains the option to **Disconnect**.

Configuring the Remote Desktop Connection Utility

In the previous section, we simply launched the Remote Desktop Connection utility and established a connection. When you initially launch the utility, most of its configuration information is hidden. To display it before you use it to establish a connection, click the **Options** button. This will reveal a series of tabs and many additional settings that have be configured. Let's take a look at each in the following sections.

The General Tab

The General tab contains the **Computer** drop-down box, which contains names and IP addresses of computers to which you have previously connected, along with an option to browse the network for computers not listed. It also contains **User name**, **Password**, and **Domain** text boxes. Remember, by default the credentials with which you are logged on locally are used to establish your remote session. If you always want to ensure that a specific set of credentials is used to log on to Terminal Services, you can type the account information into these text boxes.

You might be using an earlier Windows operating system that does not require you to log on. These boxes can be used in this instance if you want to avoid being prompted for a user name and password when you connect with the utility.

NOTE

In general, it is a poor security practice to leave the user name and password information saved in the utility. If you choose to do this, keep in mind that anyone with access to your computer can use the utility to establish a Terminal Services session while you are away.

This tab also enables you to save your connection settings. You might have several different systems to which you connect using Terminal Services. If so, it is helpful to not have to configure the utility each time you open it. When you click the **Save As** button, a **Save As** dialog box opens, asking you where you'd like to save the file that contains your configuration information. You can save the file with an RDP extension and can double-click it later to establish a terminal session. You can also use the **Open** button on this tab to specify that the settings from a previously saved RDP file be loaded into the utility.

The Display Tab

The Display tab controls how the remote desktop appears on your client computer. The top portion of the screen contains a slider that controls the size of the remote desktop that will be displayed on your screen. The slider has four possible positions: 640x480, 800x600, 1024x768, and Full Screen. The default is 800x600.

The next portion of this tab controls the color depth (in bits) of the remote desktop when it is displayed on your local computer. The drop-down list box contains the following options: 256 colors, High Color (15-bit), High Color (16-bit), and True Color (24-bit). Higher color depths require more resources. Note that the settings on the server itself may override your selection.

Finally, the bottom of the tab contains a check box entitled **Display the connection bar when in full screen mode**. When selected, this setting places a small bar, shown in Figure 6.7, at the top of a full screen remote desktop, which makes it easier to size, minimize or maximize (to full screen), or close the Remote Desktop window.

Figure 6.7 The Full Screen Connection Bar

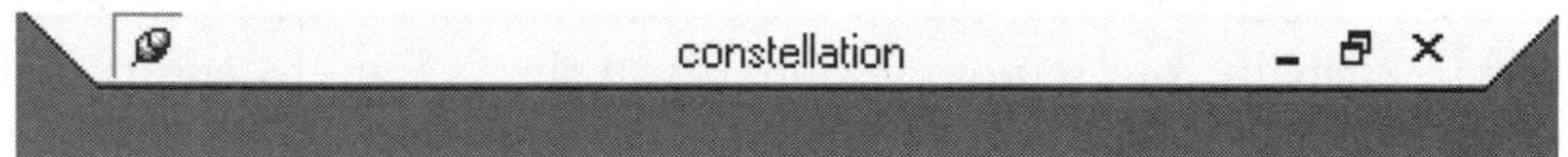

The Local Resources Tab

The Local Resources tab enables you to control whether or not client resources are accessible in your remote session. Remember that when you are working in a session, you are actually working on the remote computer. This means that when you open Windows Explorer, the disk drives you see are the ones that are physically located on the Terminal Services computer, not the ones installed on your local computer. Selections on the Local Resources tab can be used to make your local drives, client-attached printers, and similar client-side resources available for use within your remote desktop session.

The first setting on the tab deals with whether audio will be used in the session. The default setting, **Bring to this Computer**, enables you to transfer any sounds played in the session from the Terminal Services computer to the client. Audio transfer can be bandwidth intensive in a thin client environment, so Microsoft also gives you the opportunity to not transfer this audio. The **Leave at Remote Computer** setting plays the audio in the session on the Terminal Services computer but does not transfer the audio to the client. The **Do not play** setting prevents audio in the session altogether.

NOTE

The capability to transfer audio is one of the important differences between the RDC client and the older Windows 2000 Terminal Services client.

The next setting on the Local Resources tab relates to whether keyboard shortcut combinations are used by the local operating system or the Remote Desktop window. There are three possible settings for keyboard shortcut combinations:

- **In full screen mode only** In this mode (which is the default), when you use a shortcut combination, the system applies it to the local operating system, unless there is a full screen Remote Desktop window open.
- **On the local computer** This setting applies all shortcut combinations to the local operating system.
- **On the remote computer** This setting applies all shortcut combinations to the Remote Desktop window.

It is important to note that you cannot redirect the **CTRL + ALT + DEL** keyboard combination. This combination works only on the local operating system. An equivalent that can be used in the Remote Desktop window (mentioned earlier in the chapter) is **CTRL + ALT + END**.

The final section of the tab contains a series of check boxes that can be selected to determine which devices from the client system are automatically made available to the user within the remote desktop session. By default, the following are selected: Disk drives, Printers, and Smart cards (if installed). An additional one, Serial ports, is not selected by default. When Disk drives, Serial ports, or Smart cards are selected, you may see a Remote Desktop Connection Security Warning box pop up when you begin the connection process. This happens because opening up devices that enable input or may relate to the underlying security of your local machine can be risky. You should consider carefully whether these settings are actually needed, and configure the utility appropriately.

The Programs Tab

By default, when you connect to a Terminal Services session, you will receive a Windows 2003 desktop. The selections on this tab enable you to receive only a specified application instead. If Terminal Services is being used to provide only a single application for each user, this setting can increase security by ensuring that users do not receive a full desktop upon connection. This will prevent them from performing tasks on the server other than running the specified application. If the check box next to **Start the following program on connection** is selected, only that application will be available in the session.

NOTE

Because the Programs tab on the RDC utility can be configured by the user at the client computer, this is not the best way to control what the user can do on the terminal server. Administrators can use Group Policy to configure Terminal Server connection settings and user policies for better security.

Selecting the box enables the **Program path and file name** text box. If the path to the application is already contained in one of the Windows path variables on the Terminal Services computer, you can just type the name of the application's executable file in this box. If not, you must include the full path and file name of the executable. The check box also enables the **Start in the following folder** text box. If the application requires the specification of a working directory, enter it here. This is often the same directory in which the application itself is installed.

After the connection is made with a specified program starting, the traditional methods of ending your session (discussed earlier) will not always be possible. Most programs have an Exit command on a menu, embedded in a button or contained in a link. When you have specified an initial program, the Exit command is the equivalent of logging out. To disconnect, simply close the Remote Desktop Connection utility.

NOTE

If you are connecting to the console session, the settings on this tab are ignored because a new session is not being created for you when you connect.

The Experience Tab

The Experience tab enables you to customize several performance features that control the overall feel of your session. All of these settings except **Bitmap Caching** can generate substantial amounts of additional bandwidth and should be used sparingly in low bandwidth environments. The check boxes on this page include the following:

- **Desktop background** Enables the background image of the desktop (wallpaper) in the remote session to be transferred to and displayed on the client.
- **Show contents of window while dragging** Rapidly refreshes a window so that its contents are visible as the user moves it around the screen in his or her Remote Desktop window.
- **Menu and window animation** Enables some sophisticated effects, such as the Windows Start menu fading in and out, to be displayed in the Remote Desktop window on the client computer.
- **Themes** Enables any themes used in the remote session to be enabled and transferred to the Remote Desktop window on the client.
- **Bitmap Caching** Enables bitmaps to be stored locally on the client system and called up from cache, rather than being transmitted multiple times across the network. Examples of bitmaps include desktop icons and icons on application toolbars. This setting improves performance, but not all thin client systems have a hard drive or other storage mechanism in which to store the bitmaps.

At the top of this tabbed page, there is a dropdown box that contains several predefined combinations of these settings that Microsoft has optimized for different levels of available bandwidth. Table 6.1 shows which bandwidth level corresponds to which settings:

Table 6.1 Preconfigured Bandwidth Settings

Connection Speed Selection	Desktop Background	Show Contents of Window while Dragging	Menu and Window Animation	Themes	Bitmap Caching
Modem (28.8Kbps)					X
Modem (56Kbps) – default				X	X
Broadband (12 Kbps – 1.5Mbps)		X	X	X	X
LAN (10Mbps or higher)	X	X	X	X	X
Custom				X	X

The Experience tab also contains a check box entitled **Reconnect if connection is dropped,** which is selected by default. The versions of Terminal Services included with Windows Server 2003 and Windows XP SP1 or later include the Automatic Reconnection feature. If dropped packets, network service interruptions, or other network errors cause your Terminal Services connection to disconnect, this feature will automatically attempt to reconnect to your session without requiring you to reenter your logon credentials. By default, there will be a maximum of twenty reconnection attempts, which occur at five-second intervals. Generally, a notification message will pop up, informing you that the connection has been lost and counting down the remaining connection attempts.

Installing and Using the Remote Desktops MMC Snap-In

The Remote Desktops (RD) MMC snap-in is another utility that can be used to establish Terminal Services connections to Windows 2003 servers and terminal servers. The RD MMC snap-in can safely be considered the primary Terminal Services client connection tool for administrators. It contains two outstanding features that are not found in the Remote Desktop Connection (RDC) utility:

- **The RD MMC can be used to connect to multiple Windows 2003 servers using Terminal Services.** An administrator can configure and save the MMC with connection information for multiple servers. These connections can be used to establish and switch between sessions. As an example, you could configure the snap-in with connections for each of your servers and have a single tool that enables remote administration of them. With the RDC utility, you must open a new instance of the utility for each server to which you want to connect simultaneously. With the RD MMC, you can quickly click between multiple, running terminal sessions, as shown in Figure 6.8.

Figure 6.8 The Remote Desktops MMC Snap-In

- **The Remote Desktops MMC enables a remote connection to the console session.** Inability to connect to the console session has prevented many administrators from being able to use Terminal Services in the past for remote administration. In Windows 2000, this was not possible and as a result many administrators continued to use other remote administration utilities such as PC Anywhere and VNC. There are a number of server-based applications that send notification pop-up windows only to the console session on a server. Their messages cannot be redirected to another system, the Event Viewer, etc. If one or more of these applications is running on a server, the administrator needs to be able to view the actual console session to see these messages. With the Remote Desktop Connection utility and previous versions of Terminal Services and its clients, when an administrator connects to Terminal Services, a new session is established. There is simply no way for the Administrator to connect to the existing console session and see these messages.

Exam Warning

Remember, the Remote Desktops MMC snap-in is designed to enable administrators to connect to multiple terminal servers, as well as the console session. The Remote Desktops MMC snap-in is *not* available on Windows XP Professional computers, only on Windows Server 2003. However, you can use it on your Windows XP computer to manage your servers, by installing the Admin Pack (adminpak.msi, located in the i386 folder on the Windows Server 2003 installation CD).

Installing the Remote Desktops MMC Snap-In

To prepare the Remote Desktops MMC snap-in for use, you begin by opening a blank MMC console. Click **Start | Run** and type **MMC** in the **Open** dialog box.

In the MMC window that appears, click **File | Add/Remove Snap-in**. In the Add/Remove Snap-in dialog box, click the **Add** button. Select **Remote Desktops** from the **Available Standalone Snap-ins** list in the Add Standalone Snap-in dialog box and click the **Add** button followed by the **Close** button. In the Add/Remove Snap-in dialog box, click the **OK** button. Remote Desktops should now be visible in the tree view on the left side of the window under Console Root. By default, no connections are configured, so if you click the Remote Desktops node at this point, nothing will appear to happen.

Adding a New Connection

Now that you've created the new MMC, it's time to learn how to configure it to connect to Terminal Services on your servers. Begin by right-clicking the **Remote Desktops** node in the tree view on the left side of the utility. From the context menu that appears select **Add new connection**. This will open the Add New Connection window, as shown in Figure 6.9.

Figure 6.9 The Add New Connection Dialog Box in the Remote Desktops MMC Snap-In

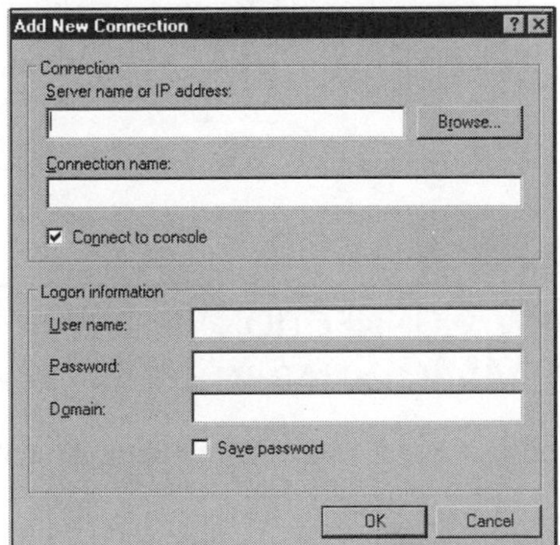

The top portion of the window contains the connection information. In the **Server name or IP address** text box, enter the fully qualified domain name (FQDN), NetBIOS name, or IP address of the server to which you wish to connect. If you use an FQDN or NetBIOS name, you must make sure that you have the necessary name resolution services running and properly configured on your network.

Next, enter a name to identify the connection in the **Connection Name** text box, or accept the default (which will be the same as the server name or IP address you entered in the previous field). This name will be used only to identify the connection within the utility.

Finally, leave the **Connect to console** check box selected if you want to connect to the server's console as mentioned earlier. Because this snap-in is intended for remote administration, this is the default setting. If you deselect the check box, Terminal Services will create a new session for you to use when you connect. If you leave it checked, you will be able to view and interact with the console session. Note that after you are authenticated, if someone else is connected to and using the console session (either locally or remotely) when you attempt your connection, you will be notified. The notification message will include the user name, whether the user is connected locally or remotely and the session state. It is important to realize that only one user can be connected to and using the console session at any time. This means that if someone is using the console, whether remotely or locally, your new connection will force him or her out.

The lower half of the Add New Connection window enables you to store logon information to be used with the session. For security reasons, it is recommended that you *not* store user names and passwords in utilities such as this one. However, if you wish to do so, enter your log-on name in the **User name** text box, followed by your password in the **Password** text box. Finally, in the **Domain** text box, type the name of your domain and select the **Save Password** check box if you wish to have your password information saved. When you are finished entering the information in the Add New Connection window, click the **OK** button to save the connection. The connection should now appear under the Remote Desktops node in the tree view on the left of the MMC window.

In the following exercise, you will practice creating a Remote Desktops MMC and configuring a new connection.

Exercise 6.03

Configuring a New Connection in the Remote Desktops MMC Snap-in

1. From the Windows **Start** menu, click **Run**, and type **MMC** in the **Open** dialog box.
2. In the MMC window that appears, click **File | Add/Remove Snap-in**.
3. In the Add/Remove Snap-in dialog box, click the **Add** button.

4. Select **Remote Desktops** from the **Available Standalone Snap-ins** list in the Add Standalone Snap-in dialog box and click the **Add** button; then click the **Close** button.
5. In the Add/Remove Snap-in dialog box, click the **OK** button.
6. Right-click the **Remote Desktops** node in the tree view in the left console pane.
7. Select **Add new connection** from the context menu.
8. In the **Server name or IP address** text box, enter the fully qualified domain name (FQDN), NetBIOS name, or IP address of the server to which you wish to connect.
9. Next type an identifying name for the connection in the **Connection Name** text box, or accept the default.
10. Leave the **Connect to console** check box selected if you want to connect to the server's console. Deselect the check box if you want Terminal Services to create a new session for you to use.
11. To store your user credentials in the connection, enter your log-on name in the **User name** text box, enter your password in the Password text box, and enter the name of the domain in the **Domain** text box.
12. Select the **Save Password** check box if you want the entered password saved.
13. Click the **OK** button to save the connection.

Configuring a Connection's Properties

You can configure several properties for saved connections. Right-click the node in the left pane of the MMC that represents the connection you want to modify, and select **Properties** from the context menu. The Properties window will appear, with the General tab displayed. This tab is essentially the same as the Add New Connection window and contains the same fields for configuration. You can change any of the settings you made when you created the connection.

Click the **Screen Options** tab to bring it to the foreground. This tab enables you to choose the size of the remote desktop window that will appear in the snap-in. The desktop will appear in the currently blank space on the right side of the MMC window. You can select the size of desktop that appears there. The default is for the desktop to fill all the available space in the right pane of the MMC window. This default setting is called **Expand to fill MMC Result Pane** in the **Properties** window. You can change this by selecting the radio button next to one of the other choices on the tab. The second choice is entitled

Choose desktop size. When selected, it enables a drop-down box containing two standard resolutions: 640x480 and 800x600. The final option on the tab is **Enter custom desktop size.** When selected, it enables two text boxes: **Width** and **Height**. If the other available options do not provide you with the desired desktop size, you can manually enter the size you want into these text boxes.

NOTE

It should be noted that the desktop size will be set at connection and will not change. If you start with the MMC not maximized, connect to the remote server and then maximize the MMC window, the desktop will not fill the right side of the utility. If you change the properties to choose a specific desktop size or custom size while the session is running, you won't see any change. You can right-click the connection name, select **Disconnect**, then right-click again and select **Connect** to see the size change.

Click the **Other** tab at the top of the Window to view the final set of options. You will see some settings that are familiar from your experience with the RDC utility: the capability to start a program and/or redirect local drives.

By default, you will receive a Windows Server 2003 desktop when you connect to a terminal session. The first selection on this tab enables you to receive only a specified application instead. If the check box next to **Start the following program on connection:** is selected, only that application will be available in the session. Selecting the box enables the **Program path and file name** text box. If the path to the application is already contained in one of the Windows path variables, you can type the filename of the application's executable file in this box. If not, you must include the full path and filename of the executable. The check box also enables the **Working directory** text box. If the application requires the specification of a working directory, enter it here. This is often the same directory into which the application itself is installed.

At the bottom of this tab is another check box, entitled **Redirect local drives when logged on to the remote computer**. If this check box is selected, the drives on the client will be visible from within the session. This provides you with access to those local drives from Windows Explorer, as well as Open and Save As dialog boxes within applications. If it is not necessary to allow clients access to their local drives, you should leave this option disabled for security purposes. Note that there is no option to redirect local printers, serial ports, and smart cards as with the RDC utility.

Connecting and Disconnecting

When you have your connection added and configured, connecting is a snap. To connect, simply right-click the node that represents your saved connection in the tree view in the left MMC pane and select **Connect** from the context menu. If you did not save your log-on information in the properties of the connection, the information you provided was incorrect, or you want to log on with a different account, you will be required to enter a user name and password when the session appears in the right pane of the snap-in.

Disconnecting is just as simple. Right-click the node that represents your saved connection in the tree view in the left MMC pane, and then select **Disconnect** from the context menu. You can also use some of the other methods for logging off and disconnecting that we mentioned earlier in the chapter.

EXAM WARNING

Only the Remote Desktop MMC snap-in and the *mstsc /console* command can be used to connect to the console session of a Terminal Services computer. However, an administrator actually sitting at the server and using the console session can request help by using the Remote Assistance functionality in Terminal Services. It is important to note that for security reasons, a console session cannot be viewed using Remote Control.

Installing and Using the Remote Desktop Web Connection Utility

The Remote Desktop Web Connection utility is designed to access a Terminal Services session through Microsoft Internet Explorer (MSIE) over TCP/IP. It consists of an ActiveX component that is downloaded to the client browser and sample Web pages that the client uses IE to connect to. It replaces Windows 2000's Terminal Services Advanced Client (TSAC).

This utility depends on Internet Information Services 6 (IIS6), which is not installed by default. Thus, to use the Remote Desktop Web Connection utility, you must begin by installing IIS6.

Installing Internet Information Services 6

IIS6 can be installed from the **Manage Your Server** utility, which is opened from the Windows **Start** | **Programs** | **Administrative Tools** menu. To do so, follow these steps:

1. Click the **Add or remove a role** link. This will bring up the **Configure Your Server Wizard** with its first page displayed. Read the recommendations it contains and click the **Next** button.
2. A **Configure Your Server Wizard** dialog box will pop up and inform you that the underlying network settings are being detected. When this completes, you will see the **Configuration Options** screen in the wizard. Select the radio button next to **Custom configuration** and click the **Next** button. (Note that you may not see this page, in which case you will be taken directly to the next screen.)

3. On the **Server Role** screen, click **Application server (IIS, ASP.NET)** to highlight the role in the list, and then click the **Next** button.
4. On the **Application Server Options** page, select the **FrontPage Server Extensions** and/or **Enable ASP.NET** check boxes if you want to use either of these options on your IIS Web server. Click the **Next** button.
5. Click the **Next** button on the **Summary of Selections** screen.
6. The wizard will switch to the **Applying Selections** screen, launch the **Windows Component Wizard**, and prompt you to insert the Windows 2003 CD-ROM if you have not done so already, or you can enter the location of the i386 folder on a network share. IIS6 is a major component, and it can take several minutes for the installation to complete.
7. When the installation finishes, the **Configure Your Server Wizard** will appear to let you know that your server is now an application server. Click the **Finish** button. The **Manage Your Server** utility will reappear in the background and can be closed.

Installing the Remote Desktop Web Connection Utility

The Remote Desktop Web Connection utility does not install automatically with IIS6. It is not available for installation from the Configure Your Server Wizard, but must be added using **Add or Remove Programs** from **Control Panel** in the Windows **Start** menu. To install it, follow these steps:

1. In the **Add or Remove Programs** utility, click the **Add/Remove Windows Components** button on the left side of the screen. A **Windows Setup** pop-up dialog box will briefly appear, followed by the **Windows Components Wizard**.
2. In the **Components** list, scroll down to select the check box next to **Application Server** and click the **Details** button.
3. In the **Application Server** dialog box that appears, select **Internet Information Services (IIS)** and click the **Details** button.
4. In the **Internet Information Services (IIS)** dialog box, select **World Wide Web Service** and click on the **Details** button.
5. In the **World Wide Web service** dialog box, select the check box next to **Remote Desktop Web Connection**, as shown in Figure 6.10, and click the **OK** button. Also click the **OK** buttons on the **Internet Information Services (IIS) and Application Server** dialog boxes.

Figure 6.10 Installing the Remote Desktop Web Connection Utility

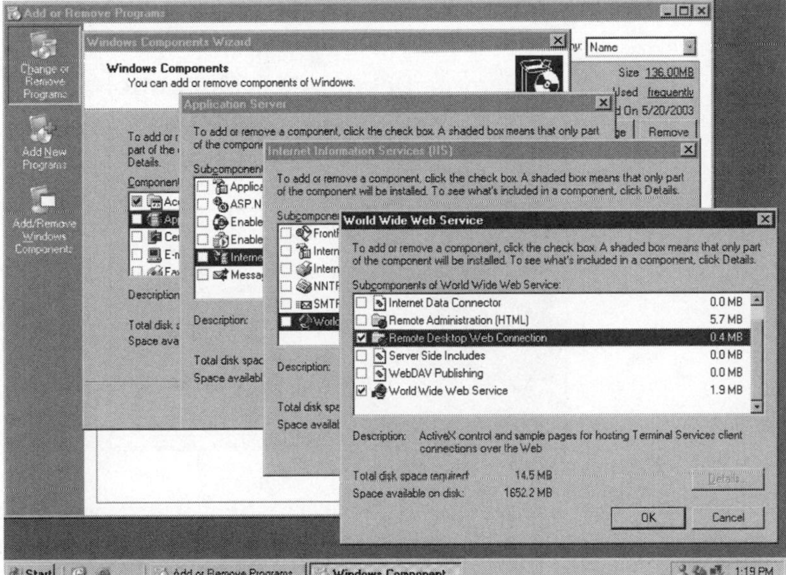

6. This will return you to the main screen of the **Windows Components Wizard**, where you should click the **Next** button. You should still have the Windows Server 2003 CD-ROM in the drive if you are installing from the CD. If you are installing from a network share, you will need to enter its path or browse to it again.
7. The wizard will switch to the **Configuring Components** screen and begin the installation. The final screen in the wizard is entitled **Completing the Windows Component Wizard**. Review the information it contains and click the **Finish** button to close the wizard.
8. A small Windows Setup pop-up box may appear briefly. When the wizard disappears, if you do not wish to add more components, close the **Add or Remove Programs** utility.

Using the Remote Desktop Web Connection Utility from a Client

To use the Remote Desktop Web Connection utility, open a version of Internet Explorer 5 or later on a client computer on the network, and connect to the following URL: http://*SERVER NAME OR IP address*/tsweb. When you do so, the default.htm Web page for the utility will appear. It will automatically detect whether you have the Remote Desktop ActiveX Control installed. If you do not, a **Security Warning** dialog box will appear, asking if you'd like to install it. Click the **Yes** button, as shown in Figure 6.11, to proceed with the installation. The control will then download and install on your system, and the default Web page will appear when installation is complete.

Figure 6.11 Installing the Remote Desktop ActiveX Control

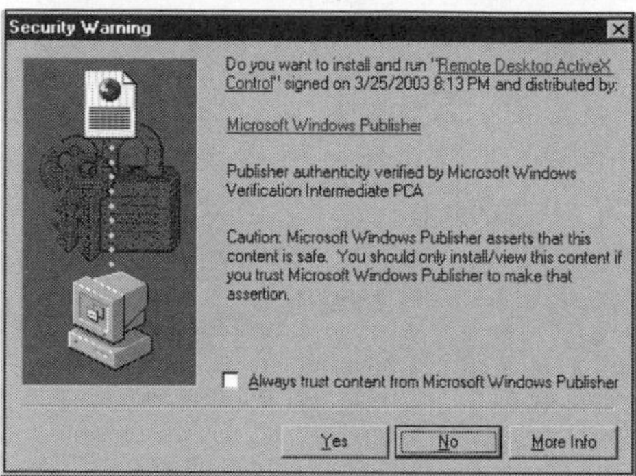

The default Web page contains two options. The **Server** text box is used to enter the name or IP address of the server to which you want to connect. The **Size** drop-down box contains a number of different screen resolutions that can be specified for the connection. The default is Full Screen, but other available options include: 640x480, 800x600, 1024x768, 1280x1224, and 1600x1200. There is also a check box entitled **Send logon information for this connection**. When selected, it adds two text boxes to the screen:

- **User name** can be used to specify the account with which you want to connect
- **Domain** can be used to specify the domain in which the account is located.

If you do not select this check box, you will be prompted for log-on information when you attempt to connect. After you have made your selections, click the **Connect** button, shown in Figure 6.12.

Figure 6.12 The Remote Desktop Web Connection Log-On Page

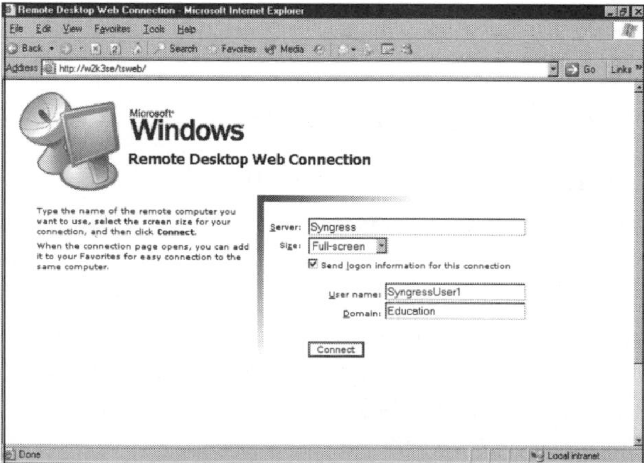

If you select any size setting less than Full Screen, the session will appear in the Web page itself, as shown in Figure 6.13.

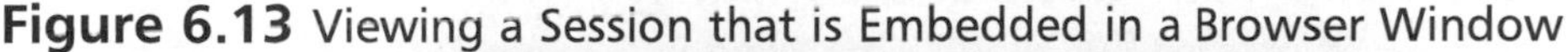

Figure 6.13 Viewing a Session that is Embedded in a Browser Window

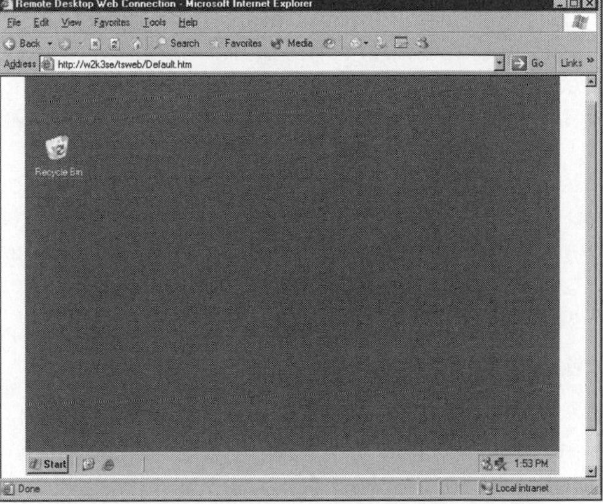

When you scroll through the Web page, the Terminal Services session will move with it. When you log off using the method described earlier in the chapter, the desktop disappears and the Web page displays the connection information and text boxes again. If you select Full Screen, a separate connection window is launched. The Web page changes to display a large blank box with text at the bottom of the page that indicates you are connected. The Remote Desktop can be minimized, sized, disconnected from, and logged off, in all the ways mentioned earlier in the chapter.

Regardless of how you connect, a full session is established, which enables you to interact with a complete Windows Server 2003 desktop and all applications, as with the other clients. An important advantage of the Web client is that it does not require any client software to be installed. The ActiveX control that downloads to the browser upon connection to the default Web page is the only client software needed. In other words, if you are away from the computer you normally use for administration, this client can be used to administer one of your servers in an emergency from anywhere in the world. All that is needed on the client system is IE 5 or later.

Configuring & Implementing...

Configuring IE for Use with the Remote Desktop Web Connection Utility

Internet Explorer 6 is installed by default on a Windows Server 2003 server. During the installation, a special security configuration is applied to it that places significant restrictions on its use. The Internet Explorer Enhanced Security Configuration feature can significantly affect the way in which Web sites are displayed in the browser. Among other things, it prevents the download and installation of ActiveX components.

Because the Remote Desktop Web Connection utility relies on an ActiveX control, by default you cannot use the browser on a Windows Server 2003 server to establish a Terminal Services session. You can configure the Enhanced Security Configuration so it will not apply to administrators. This can be accomplished by performing the following steps:

1. Open **Add or Remove Programs** from Control Panel.
2. Click the **Add/Remove Windows Components** button on the left side of the window.
3. In the **Windows Component Wizard** dialog box, scroll down and select **Internet Explorer Enhanced Security Configuration**.
4. Click on the **Details** button.
5. In the **Internet Explorer Enhanced Security Configuration** window, clear the check box next to **For administrator groups** and click the **OK** button. It may take a few moments for the configuration changes to be made.
6. Click the **Next** button, followed by the **Finish** button on the final page of the wizard.
7. Close the **Add or Remove Programs** dialog box.

Using Terminal Services Administrative Tools

Microsoft provides several utilities to administer different aspects of Terminal Services. The two primary tools are as follows:

- Terminal Services Manager, which is used to administer sessions
- Terminal Services Configuration, which is use to create and manage the properties of listener connections

In addition to these tools, Microsoft also provides extensions to the properties of user accounts, which enable them to receive individual Terminal Services settings. Virtually all of the settings available at the user properties level, as well as in the properties of a connection in the Terminal Services Configuration utility, can also be configured within Group Policy. Finally, there are a number of command-line utilities that can be used for administrative scripting of Terminal Services. In the following sections, we take a detailed look at these tools.

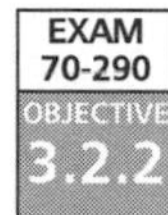

Using the Terminal Services Manager

Terminal Services Manager is the primary utility for managing existing Terminal Services sessions. It can, in many ways, be regarded as the primary administration tool for Terminal Services. You can use it to administer a single server or multiple servers that are spread across your enterprise. This centralized administrative power means that one administrator can be responsible for managing all of a company's Terminal Services computers. Let's take a look at the configuration options available.

Using Terminal Services Manager to Connect to Servers

The **Terminal Services Manager** is opened from the **Start | Programs | Administrative Tools** menu. The left pane contains a tree view that shows servers and sessions. The primary top-level nodes in the tool are as follows:

- This Computer
- Favorite Servers
- All Listed Servers

If the tool is used on a Terminal Services computer, or from within a session, **This Computer** appears in the tree to represent the local computer. You can right-click the name of any Terminal Services computer in the tree and select **Add to Favorites** from the menu that appears. Doing so will add the server under the **Favorite Servers** node in the tree. Finally, **All Listed Servers** shows aggregate information from all the Terminal Services computers to which the utility is connected.

NOTE

Some features of the Terminal Services Manager are disabled when you run the tool from the console session. The **Remote Control** and **Connect** features work only when the tool is run from a Terminal Services client session.

The **Action** menu can be used to connect to additional Terminal Services computers by selecting the **Connect to Computer** option (You can also do this by right-clicking **All Listed Servers** and selecting **Connect to Computer** in the context menu.) New Terminal Services systems that are added will appear in the tree view on the left side of the screen.

You can disconnect from any server listed in the tree view by right-clicking its name and selecting **Disconnect**. When you are connected to a server, the utility tracks statistics, such as which users are connected, the number of disconnected sessions per server, and much more. This all consumes bandwidth, so if you have added a number of servers to the utility, it may be best not to leave them all connected to prevent excessive use of network resources by the utility. Microsoft recommends that you connect to only one terminal server at a time with the TS Manager. By default, the servers to which you connect are not remembered if you close and reopen the TS Manager. To have them remembered, click **Options** in the **Tools** menu and select the check box next to **Remember server connections**.

Managing Users with the Terminal Services Manager Tool

When you select any of the server nodes or the **All Listed Servers** node in the tree view in the left pane of TS Manager, a series of tabs appears in the **Results** pane on the right side of the screen, labeled as follows:

- Users
- Sessions
- Processes

The **Users** tab can be used to view information about and manage the users who are consuming terminal server resources. It shows both currently connected users and users who have disconnected sessions still running on the server. By default, the following information is displayed about each user:

- The name of the user
- Whether the session is active or disconnected
- If the session is active, the session identifier
- If the session is disconnected, how long it has been idle
- If the session is active, the date and time the user logged on

Right-clicking a user's name brings up a number of different options, including the following:

- **Connect** Can be used to establish a connection to a disconnected user session.
- **Disconnect** Can be used to disconnect a user from his or her session. Note that this option is grayed out for console sessions; you cannot disconnect a console session.
- **Send Message** Can be used to send a message to a user in the form of a pop-up box on the user's session screen. The user's session must be in the active or

connected state (includes the console session), and you must have Message permission to send messages. Permissions for connections can be managed on a per-computer or per-connection basis.

- **Remote Control** Can be used to remotely view or direct input to a user's session (if you have Full Control permission). Your session has to be able to support the video resolution that is being used by the session you want to control. Note that you cannot remotely control the console session, and you cannot remotely control another session from the console.
- **Reset** Can be used to immediately terminate the session. This is similar to turning off a computer without properly shutting it down. All unsaved work is lost, and user and application Registry changes may not be properly saved. You need Full Control permission to reset another user's session.
- **Status** Brings up a dialog box displaying a wide range of network traffic statistics for the session. This includes the number of incoming and outgoing bytes, frames, bytes per frame, frame errors, timeout errors, and compression ratio. You can refresh the information or reset the counters within this status box. You can view the status information for your own sessions, but must have the proper permissions (Full Control, User Access, or the Query Information permission) to view statistics for another user's session. You cannot view status information for console sessions.
- **Log Off** Used to remotely log off a user and terminate the user's session. Like the Reset option, this does not save any work opened by the user. However, it does properly end the session and is not as harsh as resetting it. When it is necessary for you to terminate a user's session, this is the best option for doing so. It is always nice if you can use the Send Message command to notify the user to save any modified documents and other work, because you will be ending his or her session soon.

The Users tab is shown in Figure 6.14.

Managing Sessions with the Terminal Services Manager Tool

When you select any of the server nodes or the **All Listed Servers** node in the tree view in the left pane of the Terminal Services Manager, a series of tabs appear in the results pane on the right side of the screen. The Sessions tab is used to view information about, and manage, the sessions that are consuming terminal server resources. The tab shows currently connected sessions, disconnected sessions, listener sessions, and the console session.

Figure 6.14 The Users Tab in Terminal Services Manager

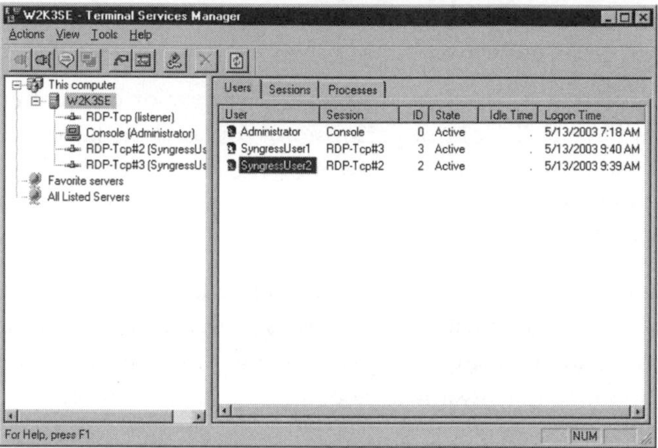

Note

Listener sessions create new sessions for client requests by listening for and accepting new RDP connections. Clients connect through a stack of drivers that's called the RDP listener stack. After the client connects, the connection is transferred to a new RDP stack, and the listener stack goes back to listening for more new client requests.

By default, the following information is displayed about each session:

- The name of the session
- The user name that is associated with the session
- The ID number of the session (the console session is always 0)
- The session state (whether the session is active, disconnected, or listening)
- The type of session (RDP, ICA, or Console)
- The name of the client associated with the session (Computer name)
- If the session is disconnected, how long it has been idle
- If the session is active, the date and time the user logged on
- A comment field, usually used for denoting the system console

Right-clicking on a session brings up a number of different options, which are the same as those discussed in regard to the Users tab, except that there is no **Log off** option. The options include the following:

- **Connect** Used to establish a connection to a disconnected user session.
- **Disconnect** Used to disconnect a user from his or her session. This will be grayed out for console and listener sessions.
- **Send Message** Used to send a message to a user in the form of a pop-up box on the session screen, as shown in Figure 6.15. (Messages can also be sent using the **msg** command).

Figure 6.15 Sending a Message to a User in a Session

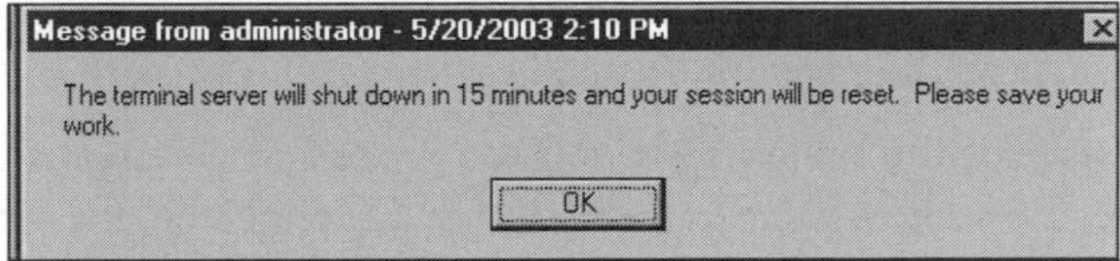

- **Remote Control** Used to remotely view or direct input to a user's session (requires Full Control permission).
- **Reset** Used to immediately terminate a user's session. This is similar to turning off a computer without properly shutting it down. All unsaved work is lost, and any user and application Registry changes may not be properly saved. It is always nice if you can use the Send Message command to notify the user to save any modified documents and other work, because you will be ending his or her session soon.
- **Status** Brings up a dialog box displaying a wide range of network traffic statistics for the session, as previously described.

The Sessions tab is shown in Figure 6.16.

Figure 6.16 The Sessions Tab in Terminal Services Manager

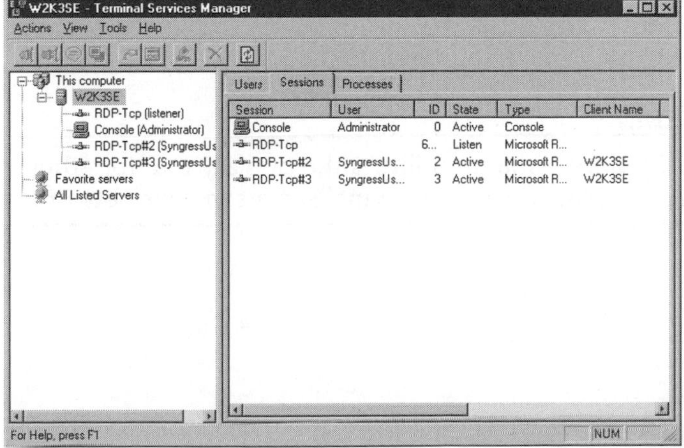

Managing Processes with the Terminal Services Manager Tool

The Processes tab is the third and final tab that is available when you select any of the server nodes or the **All Listed Servers** node in the tree view in the left pane of the Terminal Services Manager. The Processes tab can be used to terminate individual processes that are running on the server, including those running inside sessions. This tab displays the following information by default:

- The user name associated with the process (for many processes, this will be the System, local, or network service).
- The state of the session in which the process is running. If the session state is active, the session name appears. If it is disconnected, the word Disconnected appears.
- The session ID number associated with the process.
- The processor identifier (PID) of the process on the Terminal Services computer.
- The Image, or filename, associated with the process. This identifies the executable program that created this process.

NOTE

Any of these columns can be used to sort the information on the screen. Simply click the column to sort by it. Sorting by session ID number can be especially helpful as it groups all of the sessions for a particular session together in the display.

To terminate a process, simply right-click it and select **End Process** from the context menu. Then click the **OK** button in the Terminal Services Manager pop-up box that asks you to verify the termination. The process will be terminated and removed from the list. Figure 6.17 shows the Processes tab.

EXAM WARNING

The Terminal Services Manager utility is the primary tool for administering user sessions that are established to the terminal servers in your network.

Figure 6.17 The Processes Tab in Terminal Services Manager

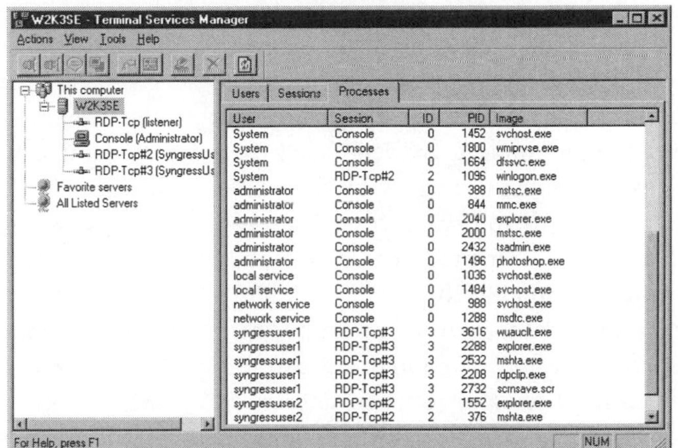

Using the Terminal Services Configuration Tool

A listener connection (also called the RDP-Tcp connection) must be configured and exist on the server for clients to successfully establish Terminal Services sessions to that server. Administrators use the Terminal Services Configuration tool to create new listener connections and configure the ones that currently exist. This tool can also be used to configure connections for ICA (Citrix) clients using IPX, SPX, Asynchronous, or NetBIOS as well as TCP. Finally, the Configuration tool is also used to configure some server policy settings.

Microsoft recommends that you use Group Policy to configure Terminal Services connection settings, if possible. However, the Configuration tool enables you to specify settings separately for multiple connections on the same computer—something that you can't do with Group Policy. You can also use the Configuration tool for terminal servers that run pre-Windows Server 2003 operating systems.

NOTE

Computer and user-level Group Policies (if set) take precedence over local configurations that are set using the Terminal Services Configuration tool.

Understanding Listener Connections

Listener connections can be configured for RDP only over TCP/IP, and only one listener can be configured for each network interface card (NIC) in the Terminal Services computer. By default, the RDP-Tcp listener is created that is bound to all of the NICs in the server. If the server has more than one NIC, an administrator can configure the default listener connection to only be associated with one NIC, and create new listener connections for each of the other NICs in the Terminal Services computer. You must be a member of the Administrators group, or be delegated the authority, in order to create new listener connections.

Creating new listener connections might be desirable if each NIC is attached to a separate segment, and only certain users should be enabled to access the Terminal Services computer from each segment. Permissions can be granted within the listener connection that specify who can and cannot connect. By default, all users are configured to connect using Terminal Servers. If you disable this in a user's properties, he or she will not be able to access any Terminal Services. If you want to enable a user to connect, but only from one segment that is attached to the terminal server, you can use the permissions associated with a listener connection to accomplish this.

In truth, it's pretty unusual for people to create their own listener connections, so the following section focuses on how to configure existing ones. All of the settings that relate to configuring listener connections also relate to settings you provide when you create one. You should also note that the term "listener connection" is an older term that is not used in Windows Servers 2003. The Windows Servers 2003 documentation refers to it as an RDP-TCP connection. We're using it here because there is no distinction made in the Windows Server 2003 Help files between a connection as configured in the Terminal Services Configuration tool, and a connection made from a client to Terminal Services running on a server. While we'll be using the term *listener connection* to help you keep them straight, the exam may not be so kind.

Modifying the Properties of an Existing Connection

To modify an existing listener connection, open the **Terminal Services Configuration** tool from the **Administrative Tools** folder in the **Start | Programs** menu, and follow these steps:

1. In the tree view on the left pane of the Configuration tool, click the **Connections** node.
2. Existing listener connections should appear in the **Results** pane on the right side of the screen.
3. The default listener connection that is created during installation is entitled RDP-Tcp. Right-click this (or any other listener connection you may have) and click **Properties**. This will open a multi-tabbed dialog box with which you can configure the settings for this connection. We will discuss each tab in detail in the following sections.

NOTE

Note that the listener connection can be **Enabled** or **Disabled** from the **All Tasks** item on the context menu when you right-click the connection name. If you disable a listener connection, no one will be able to connect to Terminal Services on the NIC for which it is configured until you re-enable it.

The most important thing to remember is that *every property you set affects all users who connect through the listener connection*. Many of the property settings for a listener connection can also be set at the client and user account property levels. By default, the listener connections are almost always set to default to the client– or user-level setting. This is to give you greater granularity of control. If you change these settings to be applied at the listener connection level, the client and user account-level settings will be ignored.

Now let's look at each of the tabs in the RDP-Tcp Properties dialog box. Keep in mind that you must be an administrator, or be delegated the proper authority, to change the settings we discuss in the following sections.

The General tab

This tab identifies the connection type (RDP-Tcp) and RDP version number. There is a Comment text box in which you can store information for administrative purposes.

More importantly, this tab enables you to specify the level of encryption that will be required for connection to Terminal Services. The default encryption setting is Client Compatible. This setting attempts to use the maximum level of encryption allowed on the client. If you have multiple clients that use different encryption levels, this is the preferred setting. The other possible settings are:

- Low (56-bit)
- High (128-bit)
- FIPS Compliant

All encryption levels use RC4 encryption. If you select **High**, any client that does not support 128-bit encryption will be unable to connect. The same will be true if you select Low and the client cannot support 56-bit encryption.

FIPS stands for Federal Information Processing Standard and should be used where required for work with the government. If the **System cryptography: Use FIPS compliant algorithms for encryption, hashing and signing** Group Policy has been enabled, you will not be able to change the encryption level using the Configuration tool. Remember that Group Policy settings take precedence over settings made with the Configuration tool.

NOTE

The encryption levels set by the Configuration tool apply to data that is sent from the client to the server. Data sent the other way (server to client) is not encrypted.

The bottom of the tab contains a check box entitled **Use standard Windows authentication**. It is not checked by default and under normal circumstances, selection of this check box is not required. However, if you have installed a third-party authentication provider, but you want to use Windows authentication for Terminal Services connections instead of the third-party provider, check this box.

The General tab is shown in Figure 6.18.

Figure 6.18 The General Tab in the RDP-Tcp Connection's Properties

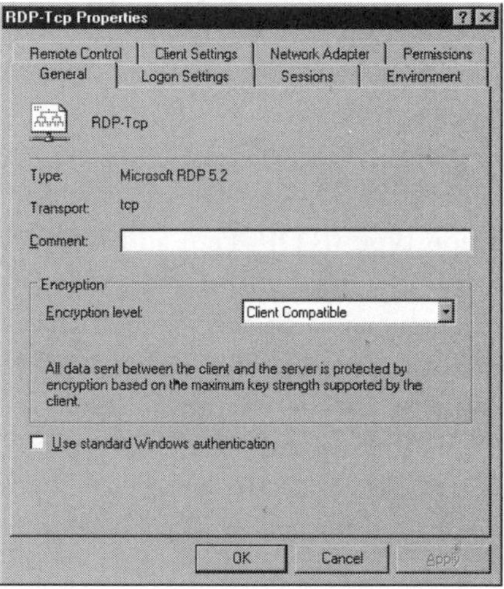

The Logon Settings tab

All Terminal Services clients are capable of providing log-on information to the Terminal Services computer. Typically, this includes a user name, password, and domain. The default setting on this tab, **Use client-provided logon information**, ensures that the credentials passed from the client are accepted at the server. If no credentials are passed, or incorrect credentials are passed, the user will be prompted for valid log-on information.

The other major option on this page is entitled **Always use the following logon information**. When selected, it enables the **User name**, **Domain**, **Password**, and **Confirm password** text boxes. Information entered in these fields will be used for logon. This will enable users to log on to the server automatically, without providing credentials.

It is important to remember that settings done at the listener connection level affect everyone who connects using the NIC or NICs to which it is bound. As a result, if this option is enabled, *everyone attempting to establish a session through this listener connection will be logged on with the same credentials*. This will make it virtually impossible to audit "who did what" later. If the credentials typed into these text boxes are incorrect, the users will still be prompted for valid log-on information. It is usually best for automatic log-on credentials to be set at the client level.

The last setting on this page is entitled Always prompt for password. If it is selected, the password in the Password and Confirm password fields will be ignored and the user will be prompted to supply a valid password. The Logon Settings tab is displayed in Figure 6.19.

Figure 6.19 The Logon Settings Tab in the RDP-Tcp Connection's Properties

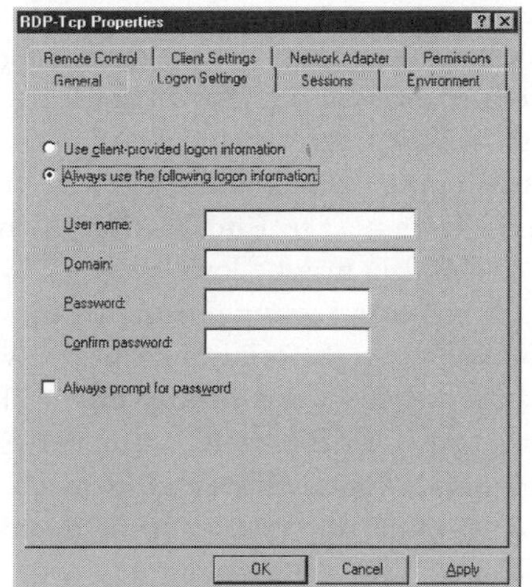

The Sessions tab

The Sessions tab enables you to control how long a user may remain actively connected to a session and how long a disconnected session should be allowed to remain on the Terminal Services computer. Even though they are not active, disconnected sessions can use substantial resources on the Terminal Services computer because applications are still running on them. Depending on your environment, it may be advisable to terminate them after a specific period of time.

By default, most of the settings on this page are configured to use the user account property settings and several settings are grayed out. This can be overridden by selecting the check box next to **Override user settings**. When user settings are overridden, several settings are no longer grayed out; these include:

- **End a disconnected session** Used to specify the amount of time a disconnected session can remain running on the Terminal Services computer.
- **Active session limit** Used to specify the amount of time an actively used session can remain connected and in use.
- **Idle session limit** Used to specify the amount of time an idle session can remain connected to the Terminal Services computer.

Each of these settings has a drop-down box that follows it. The drop-down box contains a range from Never (the default) to 2 days. If you select Never, sessions will be allowed to continue indefinitely. If the setting you prefer is not listed in the box, you can type it in and it will be added. For instance, if you type in **5 days,** a new entry (5 days) will appear in the box and be selected. Just be certain to follow the correct format when typing it in, as shown in the other entries (<number> <minutes/hours/days>).

The next configuration item on the screen is **When a session limit is reached or connection is broken**. This setting contains two possible options and relates to the **Active session limit** and **Idle session limit** settings. When one of these limits is reached, you can choose to have the user disconnected from the session, but leave the session running until the **End disconnected session** limit is reached by choosing the radio button next to the **Disconnect user from session** option. Or, you can chose to simply have the session terminated by selecting the radio button next to **End session**. If you do this, applications that are running will be shut down and data may be lost.

The final setting on this tab is **Allow reconnection**. You can use it to specify whether a user can reconnect to a session only from the original client that was used to establish it (**From previous client**) or from any client (**From any client**). This setting can be used only with ICA (Citrix) clients. If you do not have ICA clients, this option will be grayed out.

Remember that all of these time limits apply to all users who log on to the terminal server using this connection. Also remember that all of these settings can also be made using Group Policy (Microsoft's recommended method).

The Sessions tab is shown in Figure 6.20.

Figure 6.20 The Sessions Tab in the RDP-Tcp Connection's Properties

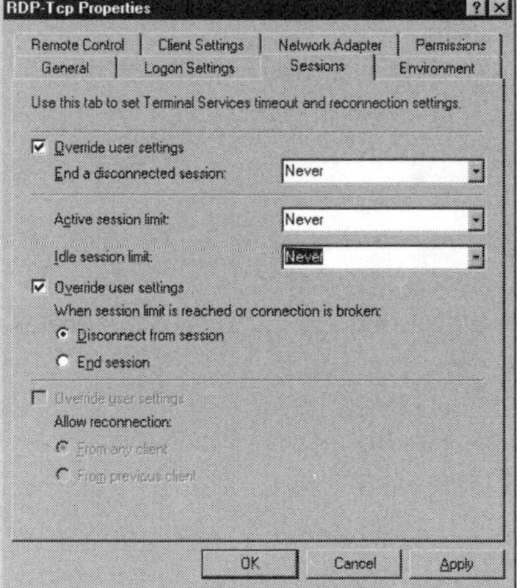

The Environment Tab

The Environment tab can be used to specify that upon connection, the user should see only a running application, instead of receiving the default desktop. It can also be used to provide a custom shell or run a batch script, which in turn calls the desktop. By default, the setting is configured to be inherited from the client or user account properties. If you override the client and user settings at the listener connection level, two previously grayed out text boxes become activated:

- **Program path and file name** is used to enter the full path to the program, including the name of the executable file.
- **Start in** This text box is where you can enter a working directory for the application if it requires one. This is often the same folder that contains the executable.

NOTE

Not all client settings are applied if a terminal session is made to a console session. If you connect to a Windows XP computer via Remote Desktop, you can only connect to the console session, and the default desktop will appear even if you've specified an application to start when you connect.

The Environment tab is shown in Figure 6.21.

Figure 6.21 The Environment Tab in the RDP-Tcp Connection's Properties

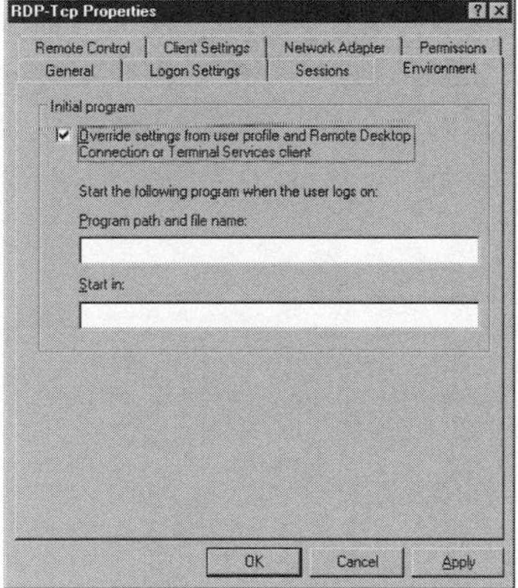

The Remote Control Tab

As mentioned in the Terminal Services Manager section of the chapter, remote control is a feature that enables an administrator to connect to, view, and interact with a user's session. It is ideal for remote troubleshooting or educating a user on the proper way to do something without leaving your desk.

The default setting on this tab is **Use remote control with user default settings**, which accepts the remote control configuration settings stored in the properties of a user's account. The second option on this tab, **Do not allow remote control,** blocks any use of remote control and should be used in secure environments where this might be necessary. Finally, you can select the third option to both enable remote control and customize its settings at the listener connection level, instead of at the user property level. This setting is entitled **Use remote control with the following settings** and when chosen it activates a number of options. As with all listener-level configurations, these settings will apply to all users who connect to the terminal server using this connection.

You can choose to enable remote control of a session with or without the user's permission by selecting or deselecting the check box next to **Require user's permission**. If this box is checked, a message will be displayed on the client, requesting permission to view or control the session.

You can specify the level of control you have over the sessions by selecting the radio button next to the appropriate option. The first option, **View the session,** enables you to see the user's desktop but does not enable you to provide any input to it. The second option, **Interact with the session,** enables you to view the desktop and provide cursor and keyboard input.

Any changes you make to the Remote Control settings won't apply to sessions that are already connected when you make the changes.

The Remote Control tab is shown in Figure 6.22.

Figure 6.22 The Remote Control Tab in the RDP-Tcp Connection's Properties

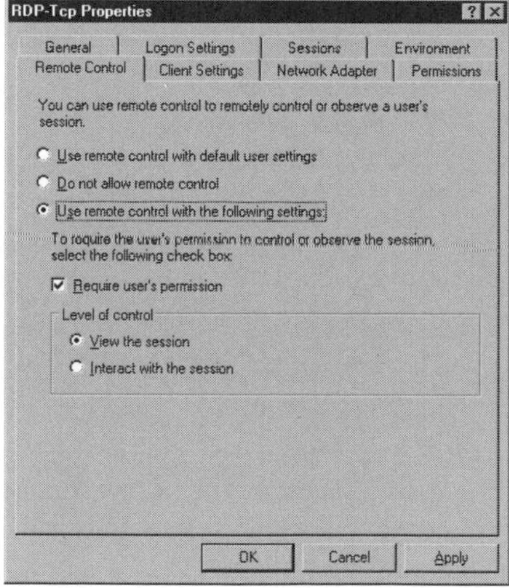

The Client Settings Tab

Remember that when you connect to a Terminal Services session, you are really working on the server. The desktop that is displayed on your local system reflects what is happening on the server. When you open Windows Explorer, the local drives displayed are actually the server's disk drives. The **Client Settings** tab contains a number of settings that can be used to make your local client resources (disk drives, printers, bar code scanner, etc.) also available from within your session.

As with many of the settings on these tabs, some of the configuration items default to settings at the user account property level. To override these settings at the listener connection level (that is, for all users using this connection), clear the check box next to **Use connection settings from user settings**. The settings include the following:

- **Connect client drives at logon** Makes your mapped local client's drives accessible from within Windows Explorer, Save As, and Open windows in the session. Note that this option is available for clients running any edition of Windows Server 2003; it is not supported for other clients.
- **Connect client printers at logon** Makes the mapped printers installed in your local client's Printers folder accessible within the session.
- **Default to main client printer** Makes the default printer in the session the same as the default printer that is specified on the client computer. If you don't select this option, the default printer for the session will be the server's default printer.

It is important to realize that these settings can cause substantial additional bandwidth to be used. When you access client drives from within your session, the data must transfer from the client system to the Terminal Services computer. Likewise, when you print to a client-attached printer from within a session, the print job must transfer from the Terminal Services computer to your local client. In most cases, these transfers occur outside the RDP protocol and can consume substantial additional bandwidth.

The next section on this tab contains the **Limit Maximum Color Depth** drop-down box. This can be used to specify the maximum color bit depth settings that will be available for connecting clients and overrides the settings in the client software. Even if a client asks to use a higher setting in a session, and is capable of doing so, it will not be allowed. The higher the bit depth settings, the more bandwidth consumed. The available settings are: 8-, 15-, 16-, and 24-bit.

The final section on the tab is entitled **Disable the following**, and contains settings that enable you to prevent certain types of communication from occurring between the client and server or being made available within the session. The options include the following:

- **Drive mapping** Blocks connection to and use of client drives from within a session. You might be asking yourself how this differs from the previous similar setting. If **Connect client drives at logon** is not selected, the drives will not be added to the session upon connection, but this does not prevent them from being manually added later. Disabling them here prevents this. Drive mapping is enabled by default.
- **Windows printer mapping** Blocks connection to and use of client printers from within Windows. If you want to block all use of client printers, you should also be sure to disable **LPT port mapping** and **COM port mapping**. The **Windows printer mapping** setting will not prevent someone from connecting

to the client printer manually at the command prompt using LPT port mapping or COM port mapping. Printer mapping is enabled by default.

- **LPT port mapping** Blocks connection to and use of devices connected to the LPT ports on the local client computer and makes these ports unavailable in the port list of the Add Printer Wizard. LPT port mapping is enabled by default.
- **COM port mapping** Blocks connection to and use of devices (including printers) connected to the COM ports on the local client computer and makes COM ports unavailable in the port list of the Add Printer Wizard. COM port mapping is enabled by default.
- **Clipboard mapping** Prevents clipboard synchronization between the remote session and the local client operating system. Although clipboard mapping can be very convenient, it can be very bandwidth intensive and may be too resource intensive for a thin client environment. When enabled, it essentially results in a shared clipboard between the session running on the Terminal Services system and the local operating system, which can be used for copying and pasting data between applications on the local machine and applications on the terminal server. When data is copied to one of the clipboards, it is transferred across the network to the other machine (note that you do not have full clipboard functionality between the local computer and terminal server; you can only copy and paste data, not files and folders).
- **Audio mapping** Prevents the transmission of audio information from the Terminal Services computer to the local client's audio subsystem. Audio mapping is disabled (the box is checked) by default.

The Client Settings tab is displayed in Figure 6.23.

Figure 6.23 The Client Settings Tab in the RDP-Tcp Connection's Properties

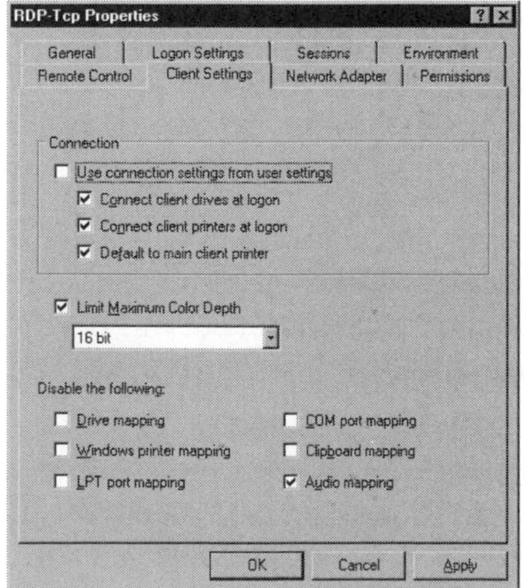

The Network Adapter Tab

As mentioned previously, only one listener connection can be associated with each NIC in the Terminal Services computer. However, by default one listener connection is associated with all NICs in the system. On this tab, you can specify with which NIC the listener connection is associated.

The top of the tab has a **Network Adapter** drop-down box, which contains an entry for each NIC as well as an entry for **All network adapters configured for this protocol**. Remember that by default, there is only one set of protocols enabled, RDP over TCP/IP. The lower portion of the tab enables you to specify the maximum number of sessions that can connect to this listener connection at any given time. If you have not installed the terminal server role, the maximum number in this box is 2 (which is the limit for Remote Desktop for Administration). If the terminal server role is installed, you can select **Unlimited connections** or set a number in the **Maximum connections** box to prevent overloading the terminal server.

The Network Adapter tab is shown in Figure 6.24.

Figure 6.24 The Network Adapter Tab in the RDP-Tcp Connection's Properties

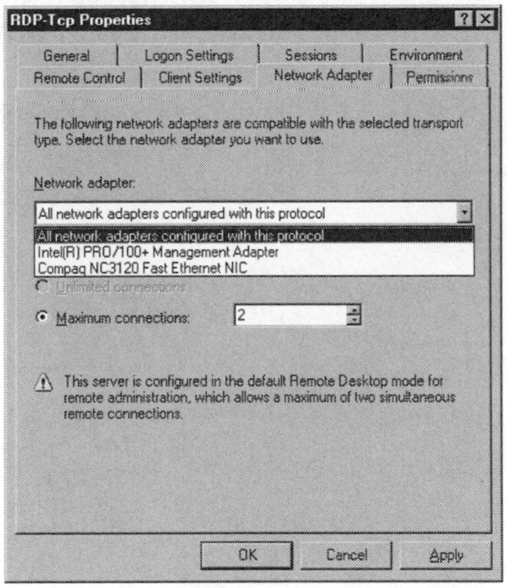

The Permissions Tab

As we mentioned earlier, you can set access permissions on each listener connection. This is accomplished using settings contained in the Permissions tab. The tab contains a standard Windows access control list, but the permissions available differ from those found elsewhere and are shown in Table 6.2.

It's important to note that by clicking the **Advanced** button, you can set specialized permissions and enable auditing for Terminal Services connections.

Table 6.2 Standard Permissions

Standard Permission	What the Permission Allows
Full Control	Lets you query to find out information about a session.
	Lets you change connection parameters.
	Lets you terminate a session using Reset.
	Lets you take control of another user's session.
	Lets you log on to a session that is running on the server.
	Lets you log off another user from an existing session.
	Lets you send a message to another user within an existing session.
	Lets you connect to an existing session.
	Lets you disconnect another user's session.
	Lets you use virtual channels to provide access to client devices from a program on the server.
Service	Lets the service query to find out information about a session.
	Lets the service send a message to another session.
User Access	Lets you log on to a session that is running on the server.
	Lets you query to find out information about a session.
	Lets you send messages to another user within an existing session.
	Lets you connect to an existing session.
Guest Access	Lets you log on to a session that is running on the server.

Terminal Services Configuration Server Settings

The **Server Settings** node in Terminal Services Configuration controls a number of server-wide settings that affect all sessions running on the server. In an Active Directory environment, these settings can also be configured using Group Policy. If configured in both Group Policy and within Terminal Services Configuration, the Group Policy settings will take precedence.

To configure these settings, click the **Server Settings** node in the tree view in the left pane of the Terminal Services Configuration tool. The configuration options, described below, will appear in the Results pane on the right side of the screen. To configure one of the options, right-click it and select **Properties** from the context menu. If the option is a simple Yes/No setting, the context menu will contain whichever selection is the opposite of the current configuration setting and can be changed from this menu.

- **Delete temporary folders on exit** Deletes a session's temporary folder when the user logs off. This setting is configured to **Yes** by default.
- **Use temporary folders per session** Creates a separate temporary folder for each new user session created on the server. This typically does not need to remain on the server after the session has been terminated. This setting is configured to **Yes** by default.
- **Licensing** Allows for the administrator to configure the server as a terminal server or Remote Desktop for Administration computer. This setting is configured to Remote Desktop for Administration if the terminal server role has not been installed. If it has, this setting reflects the licensing choice made when you installed the terminal server role (per Device or per User) and can be changed here.
- **Active Desktop** Enables the use of Active Desktop technologies in Terminal Services sessions. These desktops can use considerably more bandwidth than traditional desktops. This setting is configured to be enabled by default.
- **Permission Compatibility** Full security is the only choice available for Remote Desktop for Administration. A second mode, Relaxed Security, is added when the terminal server role is installed on the server, which loosens security to accommodate older Windows computers and legacy applications. This is configured as Full Security by default.
- **Restrict each user to one session** Can be used to ensure that users do not establish more than one session to a Terminal Services system. Savvy users may be able to work around this setting by specifying a different program to start upon connection for each different session.

NOTE

The **Relaxed Security** setting under **Permission Compatibility** is sometimes required if you want to use older, legacy programs. However, it should not be selected unless absolutely necessary because it provides full access to Registry and file system locations for all users and can result in security breaches.

User Account Extensions

Windows Server 2003 user accounts contain four property tabs that are designed for the control of the Terminal Services session at the user level. The tabs are entitled Terminal Services Profile, Sessions, Environment, and Remote Control. The same tabs exist in domain and local user accounts. The same tabs are present whether the Terminal Services computer is configured for Remote Desktop for Administration or the terminal server role. You can use these dialog boxes to control Terminal Services settings on a per-user basis. The settings you make here will apply only to that user account.

To access these tabs, right-click the user account you wish to configure in either the **Active Directory Users and Computers**, **Computer Management**, or **Local Users and Groups** MMC snap-in. From the context menu, select **Properties** and click the appropriate tab.

The Terminal Services Profile Tab

The bottom of the **Terminal Services Profile** tab contains perhaps the most important check box contained on any of the Terminal Services property tabs, **Allow logon to terminal server**. This check box is selected by default on all user accounts and enables any user to log on and use either Remote Desktop for Administration (if his or her account is added to the Remote Desktop Users list) or the terminal server. If you want to prevent a single user from accessing Terminal Services, simply clear this check box in the user's account properties.

The top section of this tab enables you to specify a separate profile and home directory for use when the user is logged on to a Terminal Services session. By default, these are blank. That means that the effective settings come from the Profile tab in the user's properties. The Profile tab was originally intended to be used to specify the profile and home directory locations when the user is logged on locally. Many companies leave the Terminal Services Profile tab blank, allowing the settings on the user's Profile tab to be the effective settings whether the user is logged on locally or with Terminal Services. Because the user's profile contains that user's desktop settings, sometimes a user can get confused when logging on to a session and finding a different desktop than when logged on locally. Likewise, if the user saves files to the home directory all day long and then is connected to a different home directory when using Terminal Services, this can be confusing.

Figure 6.25 shows the Terminal Services Profile tab on a user's account properties.

Figure 6.25 The Terminal Services Profile Tab in a User's Properties

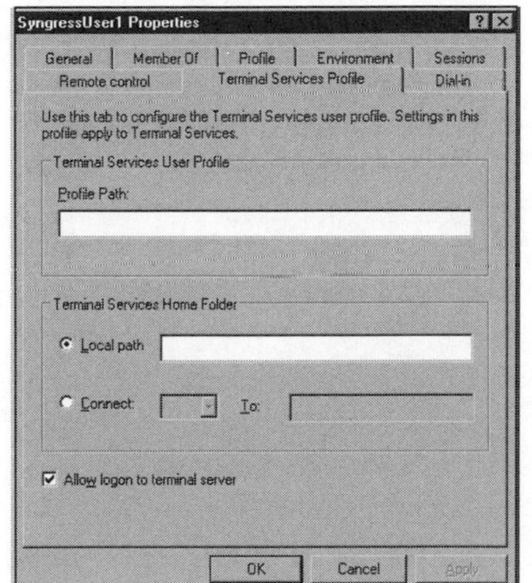

The Sessions Tab

The **Sessions** tab in the user's properties contains many of the same settings that we saw while we were examining the Terminal Services Configuration tool. At that level, they applied to all users connecting over a specified connection to the server. Here they apply to only one user. Thus, if the **Override user settings** check box is selected on any of the settings at the connection level, those that are set here at the user level are ignored. Likewise, if the defaults are left in place at the connection level, the configurations in the user's properties are the effective settings.

The settings on this tab include the following:

- **End a disconnected session** (select a duration from Never to 2 days)
- **Active session limit** (select a duration from Never to 2 days)
- **Idle session limit** (select a duration from Never to 2 days)
- **When a session limit is reached or broken**:
  - Disconnect from session
  - End session
- **Allow reconnection**:
  - From any client
  - From originating client only

Again, the settings on this tab affect only the user whose properties are being modified. However, they perform the exact same actions as described in the Terminal Services Configuration section. This tab is displayed in Figure 6.26.

Figure 6.26 The Sessions Tab in a User's Properties

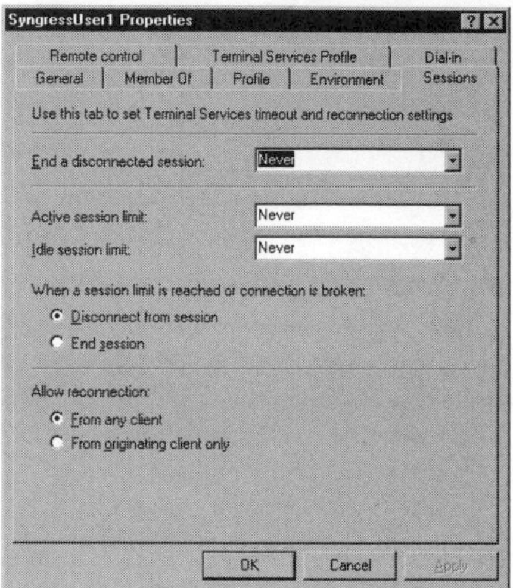

The Environment Tab

As with the **Sessions** tab, the settings on the **Environment** tab in the user's properties are identical to several settings we've already seen in the Terminal Services Configuration tool. As with the **Sessions** tab, when overridden at the connection level or by Group Policy, the settings on this tab are ignored. However, by default they are the effective settings. The top section of the tab contains the **Start the following program at logon** check box, which is not selected by default. When selected, the **Program file name** and **Start in** text boxes are enabled. The **Program file name** text box corresponds to the **Program path and file name** text box on the **Environment** tab in the Terminal Services Configuration tool. Likewise, the **Start in** text box is identical to the box of the same name on that tab in Terminal Services Configuration. Refer to the Terminal Services Configuration section of this chapter for more information about how to use these.

The lower section of the **Environment** tab in the user's properties also contains settings identical to several we've already discussed in the section on the Client Settings tab in the Terminal Services Configuration tool. These include the following:

- Connect client drives at logon
- Connect client printers at logon
- Default to main client printer

Again, by default the user's settings are effective unless overridden with the Terminal Services Configuration tool or by Group Policy. The **Environment** tab is shown in Figure 6.27.

Figure 6.27 The Environment Tab

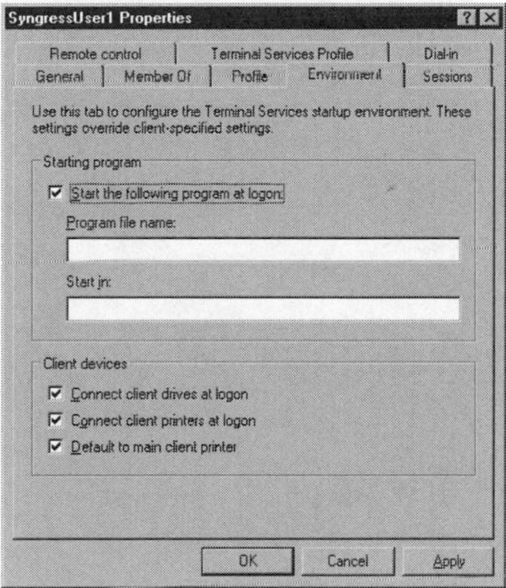

The Remote Control Tab

As with the previous two tabs, the settings on the **Remote Control** tab also mirror those in the Terminal Services Configuration tool and were described in that section of this chapter. As with the other settings, the default is for the settings at the user property level to be effective. As we saw earlier, these settings can be overridden at the connection level using Terminal Services Configuration if desired, or by Group Policy. The following settings are available at the user property level:

- **Enable remote control**
- **Require user's permission**
- **Level of control:**
  - View the user's session
  - Interact with the session

For more detailed information on each of these settings, refer to the Terminal Services Configuration section of the chapter. The **Remote Control** tab is shown in Figure 6.28.

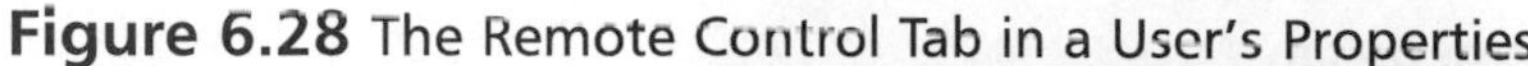

Figure 6.28 The Remote Control Tab in a User's Properties

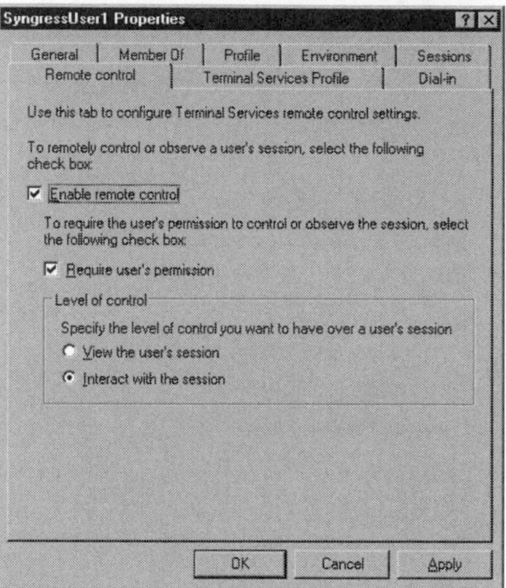

Using Group Policies to Control Terminal Services Users

There are over 900 group policy settings in Windows Server 2003, of which approximately 50 relate specifically to Terminal Services components. There are separate settings that can be applied at the computer and user levels, as well as separate settings for Terminal Services and RA. Virtually all of the actions performed by these settings have already been described, because similar settings exist on many of the tabs and property sheets we've already discussed.

Exam Warning

When the same setting is configured in both Group Policy and one of the Terminal Services utilities or clients, the setting specified in Group Policy will used.

Terminal services settings can be found in the following locations within the **Group Policy Object Editor**:

- **Computer Configuration | Administrative Templates | Windows Components | Terminal Services**
- **Computer Configuration | Administrative Templates | System | Remote Assistance**
- **User Configuration | Administrative Templates | Windows Components | Terminal Services**

Some of the key Group Policy settings that have not already been covered elsewhere in this chapter include the following:

- **Deny log off of an administrator logged in to the console session**, which can be used to prevent the automatic logoff of the administrator currently using the Terminal Services computer's console session by another administrator attempting to connect to it. Remember that by default, only one administrator can be logged on and viewing the console session at a time. When an administrator attempts to connect, by default any currently connected administrator is logged off and all unsaved work is lost. It is also important to note that the console session is the only one that cannot be used with Remote Control, in either View Only or Interaction mode.
- **Remove Windows Security item from Start menu**, which can be used to control how a user may terminate his or her session. The Windows Security dialog is the dialog box that comes up on a local system when you use the key combination **CTRL + ALT + DEL**. Because this key combination is never redirected to a remote session, Microsoft puts a link to it on the Start menu in a session. The Windows Security dialog box contains buttons for locking the remote desktop, logging off, shutting down (if you have the appropriate permissions and this is not grayed out, it will shut down the Terminal Services computer not the local computer), changing your password, and accessing Task Manager on the Terminal Services computer. It may be appropriate in your environment to remove this link for security or log-off control purposes. However, even if this link is not present, the key combination **CTRL + ALT + END** can be used to bring up the Windows Security dialog box within the terminal session.
- **Remove Disconnect option from Shut Down dialog**, which enables you to remove the disconnect option from the Shut Down Windows dialog box. This dialog box appears when you select Shut Down from the Windows Start menu or Windows Security dialog box. It is important to note that removing this option from the Shut Down dialog does not prevent someone from disconnecting. The user can still click the **X** button in the top righthand corner of the Remote Desktop window to disconnect.

There are many more Group Policy templates that can be used to control Terminal Services. For some settings, Group Policy is the only way to configure a particular setting. For example, you can specify whether to allow time zone redirection, prevent license upgrade, or enable users to offer remote assistance.

Using the Terminal Services Command-Line Tools

In addition to the graphical tools and clients described earlier, Windows Server 2003 also provides a number of command-line utilities for both administrators and end users to manage connections. The primary benefit of these command-line tools is that they can be used in scripts to automate Terminal Services tasks. The basic set of commands, as listed in the Windows Server 2003 Help files, is described in Table 6.3.

Table 6.3 Terminal Services Command-Line Tools

Command	Description
change logon	Temporarily disables logons to a terminal server
change port	Used to change COM port mappings for MS-DOS program compatibility
change user	Changes the .ini file mapping for the current user
Cprofile	Removes user-specific file associations from a user profile
Flattemp	Enables or disables flat temporary directories
Logoff	Logs off a user from a session and deletes the session from the server
Msg	Sends a message to a user or group of users
Mstsc	Displays the Remote Desktop Connection to establish a connection with a terminal server
query process	Displays information about processes running on a terminal server
query session	Displays information about sessions on a terminal server
query termserver	Displays a list of all terminal servers on the network
query user	Displays information about user sessions on a terminal server
Register	Registers applications to execute in a global context on the system
reset session	Resets a session to known initial values
Shadow	Monitors another user's session
Tscon	Connects to another existing terminal server session
Tsdiscon	Disconnects a client from a terminal server session
Tskill	Ends a process
Tsprof	Copies user configuration and changes profile path
Tsshutdn	Shuts down a terminal server

Test Day Tip

Be sure to familiarize yourself with the Terminal Services command-line utilities, as you never know when they will pop up on the exam in conjunction with a related graphical utility.

In Exercise 6.04 you will practice using the Terminal Services Manager utility to reset a session.

EXERCISE 6.04

USING TERMINAL SERVICES MANAGER TO RESET A SESSION

1. Open Terminal Services Manager from **Administrative Tools** in the Windows **Start | Programs** menu.
2. If necessary, expand the **This Computer** node.
3. If necessary, expand the node that corresponds to the name of your Windows Server 2003 server.
4. Right-click the session you wish to terminate.
5. In the context menu that appears, select **Reset**.
6. Close Terminal Services Manager.

Troubleshooting Terminal Services

Troubleshooting Terminal Services components is never an easy task. The complexity of Terminal Services often makes for strange occurrences, which are difficult to track down. Nonetheless, some of the exam objectives published by Microsoft relate to troubleshooting Terminal Services, so this is an important section with which you should become familiar.

The most important keys to understanding how to troubleshoot Terminal Services come from all the background knowledge presented in this chapter. Knowing how it all works is essential to answering the troubleshooting questions correctly. In this section, we will provide an overview of common problems and solutions that are drawn from Microsoft's support materials, have not been previously covered in earlier parts of the chapter, and relate to the exam objectives.

Not Automatically Logged On

A common problem occurs when you want to be able to automatically log on to the server, but you're still prompted for your user credentials when you connect to the terminal server. There are a number of possible causes and solutions.

If you are using a Windows NT 4.0 Terminal Services client, be aware that these clients are not always able to detect and pass on the underlying system logon credentials to the Windows Server 2003 terminal server even if your system logon credentials are the same as those for the terminal server. In the NT 4.0 Client Connection Manager, configure **Automatic logon** on the **General** tab in the **Properties** box for the connection. Enter the appropriate logon credentials in the **User name**, **Password** and **Domain** text boxes.

If you are using a Windows 2000 TS client or the RDC client, it is possible that you entered the incorrect credentials on the **General** tab. If you mistyped the user name or password, the terminal server will not be able to verify your credentials and will prompt you for the correct ones. The solution is to edit the **User name**, **Password**, and/or **Domain** text box(es) on the **General** tab of the client utility.

Another possibility is that your client settings are configured correctly, but Group Policy is configured to require users to enter at least part of the credentials (the password). Group Policy settings override client settings. The only way to correct this is to remove the Group Policy setting that is enforcing this restriction.

"This Initial Program Cannot Be Started"

Occasionally a client may receive a message stating, "This initial program cannot be started." At the client level, a user can specify that program be launched when they connect to a server instead of receiving a desktop. Likewise, an administrator can specify this at the connection level for all users that connect to a specific listener connection. Finally, this can also be set in Group Policy.

The error may be caused by something as simple as an input error. You should first check to ensure that the path and executable names specified are correct. If you have entered them incorrectly, they will be pointing to a file that does not exist. This will make it impossible for Windows Server 2003 to launch the application.

Another possibility is that the correct permissions are not set on the executable file. If Windows cannot access the file, it will not be able to launch the program for you. You should verify that the appropriate read and execute permissions are applied to both the file and the working directory (if specified). If neither of these two possible solutions resolves the issue, the application may have become corrupt. Try to launch the application from the server console. If it will not open, you may need to uninstall and reinstall the application.

Clipboard Problems

Ordinarily, when you copy text to the clipboard in a session, it is synchronized with the local clipboard on the client. Because the text is available on each clipboard, it should be available to paste into local applications as well as applications running remotely in a session. You should note that it works the same way when you copy text to the clipboard locally. It is synchronized with the clipboard running in your Terminal Services session and can be used in either local or remote applications.

Microsoft states that there are instances in which text that is copied to the clipboard in a remote session is unable to be pasted into an application on the local client. Currently, there is no fix available for this problem. First, try to reinstall the client application you are using. If it is still malfunctioning, try to uninstall the client application and reinstall it.

License Problems

For remote administration, licenses come built in to the Windows Server 2003. The Terminal Server role, however, requires the installation and proper configuration of the terminal server licensing component. Because of this, license problems typically relate only to the terminal server role. If you receive messages similar to those below, you have license component problems.

- The remote session was disconnected because there are no terminal server client access licenses available for this computer. Please contact the server administrator.
- The remote session was disconnected because there are no Terminal Server License Servers available to provide a license. Please contact the server administrator.

Error messages such as these can indicate several different types of issues. First, verify that the license server is online and able to communicate on the network. It's also important to verify name resolution during this step. Next, ensure that the license server component has been activated properly. Check event logs on the license server and look for more subtle problems than simple connectivity checks will not spot.

Verify that the license server has a sufficient number of valid client licenses for your network, and that the licenses are valid. The Terminal Server draws licenses from the license server so you should also ensure that these two servers can communicate with each other. Finally, don't forget to check the clients. It is possible that the clients never received a valid license. By default, clients often receive temporary licenses that expire after 90 days and prevent further connections. If they did receive full licenses, the licenses may have become corrupt and need to be replaced or overwritten.

TEST DAY TIP

When faced with a troubleshooting question on the exam, focus on whether or not it is a connectivity issue. Underlying connection problems are often the root cause when you have problems in a Terminal Services environment.

Summary of Exam Objectives

Terminal services is a Windows component that enables users and administrators to connect using the RDP protocol (or ICA, with Citrix client software) and obtain a desktop from a remote server. The connection transmits cursor and keyboard input from the client to the server and transfers the image of the desktop with any running applications back to the client. All applications that are run from within a session execute on the server. Unlike previous versions, Windows Server 2003's Terminal Services component is installed by default with the operating system for remote administration use (but must be enabled). The full terminal server role (formerly the Application Server mode) is still installed separately.

Terminal services contains two components for remote administration. The first, Remote Desktop for Administration, enables up to two administrators to simultaneously connect remotely to the server. Each receives his or her own session with a separate desktop. Using this mode, an administrator can also connect to the console session of the server. This option was not available in Windows 2000 and it enables the administrator to view the server's main desktop, just as if sitting at its keyboard. The second mode, Remote Assistance (RA), enables a user, called the Novice, to request assistance from someone more knowledgeable, called the Expert. An invitation is sent from the Novice to the Expert, which enables the Expert to connect to and view the actual desktop of the Novice's computer. Only one RA session can exist on a computer at any given time. The Novice can also allow the Expert to have cursor and keyboard input within the Novice's session. Both the Remote Desktop for Administration and Remote Access components must be enabled manually on the server.

The terminal server role must be installed and configured after installation of the operating system. If the Terminal Services License component is not installed and configured correctly, terminal server connections will no longer be allowed 120 days after the first client connects (expiration of the evaluation period). The terminal server role can be installed from either the **Manage Your Server** utility or via **Add or Remove Programs** in Control Panel. The terminal server licensing component can only be installed from **Add or Remove Programs**.

Three basic client tools can be used to establish a Terminal Services connection. The Remote Desktop Connection utility is the primary tool designed for end users. It enables connection to a single terminal server per instance of the utility and has a wide range of configuration options. The Remote Desktops MMC snap-in enables connections to multiple Terminal Services computers within the same interface and also enables you to connect to the console session. It is primarily designed for administrators. The Remote Desktop Web Connection utility is an IIS component that is installed from Add or Remove Programs in Control Panel. IIS 6.0 must be installed on the terminal server to enable Web connections. It uses a client side ActiveX control as the client. When used in full screen mode, it launches a session window independent of the browser window. The Web client requires MSIE 5.0 or later, with security settings configured to enable ActiveX controls to be downloaded and installed.

Terminal Services Manager is the primary graphical tool for managing users who are connected to a server. It can be used to manage multiple servers simultaneously through a single interface. As an administrator, you can use this utility to monitor, connect to, disconnect from, log off, remotely control, and reset sessions. The Terminal Services Configuration utility can be used to configure new listener connections (RDP-Tcp connections), or modify the properties of existing ones, and control settings on a per-connection basis (applying to all users who connect to the terminal server via the connection). User account extensions are installed by default and add several tabs related to Terminal Services to the user account properties interface. These tabs enable you to control a wide range of Terminal Services settings on an individual per-user basis.

You can also use Group Policy to manage Terminal Services settings. Most settings that can be configured at the client, user account, or connection property level have a corresponding Group Policy setting. When settings conflict between these various levels, the Group Policy settings always take precedence. There are some settings that can only be configured using Group Policy.

In addition to these graphical utilities, Microsoft makes a wide range of command-line utilities for Terminal Services available. These are primarily designed for use in creating administrative scripts to automate tasks.

Finally, it is especially important to have a good understanding of the Terminal Services architecture. This makes it easier to troubleshoot problems that occur. Simple connection issues between a terminal server and the license server can cause severe problems. Because Terminal Services environments are much more complex than standard client-server environments, they often exhibit strange problems that require hours of research. The reasons for this are easy to understand when you consider that you have multiple users essentially using the same computer at the same time.

Exam Objectives Fast Track

Understanding Windows Terminal Services

☑ Terminal services uses technology originally developed for the thin client environment to send cursor movements and keystrokes to the server and receive updated screen shots in return.

☑ In Windows Server 2003, Terminal Services installs as part of the operating system for remote administrative purposes (RDA).

☑ There are three major components of terminals services: Remote Desktop for Administration, Remote Assistance, and the terminal server role.

Using Terminal Services Components for Remote Administration

- ☑ Remote Desktop for Administration enables up to two administrators to remotely connect to the server simultaneously, each in his or her own session, to perform administrative tasks.
- ☑ Remote Assistance enables a user, called the Novice, to request help from someone more knowledgeable, called the Expert. The Expert is able to view and interact with the Novice's desktop remotely (if permission is granted by the Novice).
- ☑ Though installed with the operating system, both Remote Desktop for Administration and Remote Assistance must be enabled manually after installation before they can be used.

Installing and Configuring the Terminal Server Role

- ☑ For a Windows Server 2003 computer to function properly as an application server, both the terminal server role and terminal server licensing component must be installed.
- ☑ The terminal server role can be installed from either the Manage Your Server utility or the Add or Remove Programs applet (or utility) in the Control Panel.
- ☑ The terminal server licensing component can only be installed via Add or Remove Programs in the Control Panel.
- ☑ If the terminal server licensing component is not installed or proper licenses are not configured on it, terminal server connections will be rejected when the evaluation period expires (starting 120 days after the first client connection occurs).

Using Terminal Services Client Tools

- ☑ The Remote Desktop Connection utility is the primary Terminal Services client for end users. It comes with Windows Server 2003 and Windows XP, and can be installed on Windows *9x*, NT, and 2000 computers.
- ☑ The Remote Desktop MMC snap-in is designed for administrators. It enables connections to multiple servers within a single interface, as well as console session connections.
- ☑ The console session is the server's primary desktop, the one you would see if you were actually sitting at its physical keyboard.

- ☑ Only one administrator can be logged on to the console session at any given time. If another administrator attempts to log on, the current administrator will be logged off unless Group Policy prevents this.
- ☑ The Remote Desktop Web Connection utility can be used from client machines that do not have one of the other Terminal Services clients installed. It requires and is a subcomponent of IIS6. When a user connects, an ActiveX control is downloaded to his or her system to serve as the local Terminal Services client. This utility is supported only by MSIE 5.0 and later.

Using Terminal Services Administrative Tools

- ☑ Terminal Services Manager is the primary session management tool. It enables an administrator to monitor, connect to, disconnect from, log off, remotely control, and reset sessions.
- ☑ The Terminal Services Configuration utility is used to create listener (RDP-Tcp) connections on the server and configure server settings that apply to all users who use a particular connection. There can only be one listener connection bound to each network card.
- ☑ Connections can be used to control a wide range of user settings, from encryption levels to how long the user can remain connected.
- ☑ Settings at the connection level, when enabled, override settings at the user and client property levels.
- ☑ Terminal Services user account extensions are installed and enabled by default. They add additional tabs to the user account properties and enable administrators to control a wide range of settings on an individual basis. Most user level settings can be overridden at the connection level.
- ☑ Group Policy can be used to control many of the same settings that can be configured at the connection, user, and client levels. When settings conflict between Group Policy and one of these other levels, the Group Policy settings take precedence.
- ☑ Windows Server 2003 Terminal Services contains a wide range of command-line tools that can be used in scripts. Console connections can be created with the *mstsc /console* command.

Troubleshooting Terminal Services

- ☑ Licensing error messages can occur because the Terminal Server cannot contact the license server or because the client's license has become corrupt.

- ☑ If clipboard mapping fails between the client and server, the client may have become corrupted and should be removed and reinstalled. However, you don't have full clipboard functionality between the local computer and the terminal session. You can cut and paste data, but not files and folders.
- ☑ Using a password-protected screen saver can cause the screen to go blank when you minimize the Remote Connection window.

Exam Objectives Frequently Asked Questions

The following Frequently Asked Questions, answered by the authors of this book, are designed to both measure your understanding of the Exam Objectives presented in this chapter, and to assist you with real-life implementation of these concepts. You will also gain access to thousands of other FAQs at ITFAQnet.com.

Q: What is the difference between Remote Desktop for Administration and the terminal server role?

A: Both are designed to enable remote Terminal Services connections. However, the terminal server role contains additional multi-user code that keeps user session and application settings separate. This enables many users to connect using Terminal Services without having problems with the applications they are using. By default, Terminal Services enables only two connections for remote administration. When the terminal server role is installed, an unlimited number of users can connect simultaneously.

Q: How can I connect to, view, and interact with the console session using Terminal Services?

A: The Remote Desktop MMC snap-in is designed for administrator use. It enables connection to multiple Terminal Services computers, in addition to defaulting to console session access. You can also connect to the console from the command line by typing **mstsc /console**.

Q: Is Remote Assistance a part of Terminal Services or a separate component?

A: Like Remote Desktop for Administration, Remote Assistance exists in both Windows XP and Server 2003 (Remote Desktop is included only in XP Pro, not XP Home, but Remote Assistance comes with both editions of XP). It is an additional service that uses the Terminal Services service to provide its core capabilities.

Q: There seem to be a number of different utilities that can be used to connect to Terminal Services and establish a session. Which one is the primary client tool for end users?

A: The Remote Desktop Connection utility is the primary end user connection tool. It comes pre-installed with Windows XP and Server 2003 and can be installed on Windows *9x*, NT, and 2000 computers. It can be used to save connection settings to a file so that reconfiguration is not necessary when connecting to different servers. It also has a wide range of options that allow for optimization over almost any bandwidth. It includes several improvements over the Windows 2000 Terminal Services client, including the capability to redirect audio from the server to the client.

Q: I've enabled Remote Desktop connections. Why are administrators the only ones who can log on?

A: By default, only administrators can establish remote administration sessions. This makes sense when you think about it, because they are most likely to be the ones that will be connecting to the server remotely to do the work. However, if you need to enable others to connect, you can add them to the Remote Desktop Users group. This differs from Windows 2000 Terminal Services in remote administration mode, where there was no way to enable non-administrative users to connect.

Q: Yesterday I was able to connect to our terminal server with no problems, but this morning no one can log on. We keep getting a license message. What's going on?

A: It sounds as if you may have hit the 120-day limit. In a nutshell, you have 120 days from your first terminal server client connection to install and configure the terminal server licensing component. Microsoft provides this evaluation period so you can try the terminal server role and decide whether you want to use it before having to purchase TS CALs. After this time, you won't be able to establish a session unless you install the License Server component and install at least one client license.

Q: What is the best utility to use for managing existing client connections?

A: Terminal Services Manager is designed for just this purpose. It enables you to monitor, connect to, disconnect from, log off, remotely control, and reset sessions. Using it, you can manage all your servers from one interface.

Q: Can Group Policy be used to manage Terminal Services?

A: In Windows Server 2003, there are approximately 50 dedicated Terminal Services settings in Group Policy. Using them, you can manage just about everything you can possibly imagine. These Group Policy settings override conflicting settings in other utilities, allowing for centralized management consistency.

Self Test

A Quick Answer Key follows the Self Test questions. For complete questions, answers, and explanations to the Self Test questions in this chapter as well as the other chapters in this book, see the Self Test Appendix.

Understanding Windows Terminal Services

1. One of your co-workers asks how to install Terminal Services on his newly installed Windows Server 2003 server so he can perform administrative tasks on the server. Which of the following is the correct advice to give him?

   A. Add the terminal server role from the Manage Your Server utility.

   B. Add the terminal server role from the Add or Remove Programs utility.

   C. The terminal server role is installed by default.

   D. Do nothing.

2. A co-worker asks you what type of system can be used as a thin client to a Windows Server 2003 terminal server. Which of the following answers would you give her? (Choose all that apply.)

   A. A PDA running Windows CE

   B. A PDA running Windows Pocket PC

   C. A desktop computer running Macintosh OS X

   D. A desktop computer running Windows 95

3. Try as you might, you can't seem to get your co-workers to grasp the concept of Terminal Services. Then it occurs to you that you could explain what happens on the client and server during a terminal session. To explain what the server does, which of the following do you tell them? (Choose all that apply.)

   A. You tell them that the server initiates the final connection with the client.

   B. You tell them that when a user connects to the server, it begins a session just for that user.

   C. You tell them that when they are connected to Terminal Services, everything that they see in their Remote Desktop window is actually occurring on the server.

   D You tell them it no longer requires any client software.

Using Terminal Services Components for Remote Administration

4. You are attempting to describe the remote assistance process to a co-worker. The co-worker asks what the correct terms are for the person requesting assistance and the person providing assistance so that he can look them up in Windows Help. Which of the following do you reply with? (Select two.)

   A. Administrator

   B. Novice

   C. Expert

   D. End user

5. No matter how hard you try, you just can't seem to figure out how to access your e-mail using the new application that was installed over the weekend in your office. You decide to use the Remote Assistance feature to ask an administrator to walk you through the process. Which of the following are valid methods that you can use to request assistance? (Choose all that apply.)

   A. E-mail an administrator.

   B. Use ICQ to contact an administrator.

   C. Use Windows messaging to contact an administrator.

   D. Save the request to a file and transfer it to an administrator.

Installing and Configuring the Terminal Server Role

6. Several months ago, you installed the terminal server role on one of the servers at your company. This morning, clients are having difficulty connecting to Terminal Services but are still able to use file and print services on the server. The error message says it is a licensing issue but you are sure that you properly licensed your Windows Server 2003 server, as well as all your client systems. What might be causing this? (Choose all that apply.)

   A. The temporary evaluation period has expired.

   B. You failed to properly configure Terminal Services client licenses on the license server.

   C. The server was installed with a temporary license code, which has expired.

   D. You did not properly install a license server.

7. Another administrator in a different region of the country is installing the terminal server role. Knowing that you recently did this, the administrator asks for your advice. You mention to him that he must also be sure to install the Terminal Server licensing component. What will you tell him about installing this component?

   A. That the license server role must be installed from the Manage Your Server utility.

   B. That terminal server license must be selected and installed from Add or Remove Programs.

   C. That License Server is automatically installed with Terminal Services.

   D. That Terminal Services License server must be purchased separately.

Using Terminal Services Client Tools

8. Your company's network consists of Windows 2000, XP, and Server 2003 client systems. You've been asked to ensure that the Remote Desktop Connection utility is installed on all clients. Which of the following might be a component of your plan to accomplish this? (Choose all that apply.)

   A. Share the WINDOWS\system32\clients\tsclient directory to enable installation over the network.

   B. Report that the utility cannot be installed on Windows 2000.

   C. Send an e-mail providing the download source to the latest client on the Microsoft Web site.

   D. Report that the utility installs with the Windows XP and Server 2003 operating systems.

9. The person in the workspace next to yours seems to have no problem using the Remote Desktop Web Connection utility. However, despite your best efforts, you can't seem to connect. What might be wrong? (Choose all that apply.)

   A. IIS is not installed on the server properly.

   B. You Web browser is blocking the installation of ActiveX controls.

   C. You have not enabled JavaScript in your Web browser.

   D. You are not using the correct version of Internet Explorer.

10. You have installed Internet Information Services on your Windows Server 2003 server. In addition, you have verified that the Terminal Services service is running. Despite this, you cannot connect to the Remote Desktop Web Connection utility using your Web browser. Which of the following have you most likely failed to do?

A. You have failed to install the terminal server role.

B. You have failed to add an Application Server role to the server.

C. You have failed to configure and start the Web service, which is stopped by default after installation for security reasons.

D. You have failed to install the Remote Desktop Web Connection component.

11. A user recently sent you a file that contained a saved remote assistance request. Which of the following is true of such a request? (Choose all that apply.)

A. The user can determine when it expires.

B. The user can expire it at any time.

C. A password cannot be used to protect the invitation.

D. The invitation can be used as many times as desired until the expiration time has passed.

Using Terminal Services Administrative Tools

12. One of your co-workers has been reading up on Terminal Services and asks if she can run a few questions by you to see if she understands the concepts. Which of the following statements will you tell her are accurate? (Choose all that apply.)

A. Many Terminal Services settings have a corresponding setting in Group Policy.

B. In Group Policy, Terminal Services settings can be found under both the User and Computer Configuration nodes.

C. When different Terminal Services settings are specified at the user properties, connection properties, and Group Policy levels, the connection properties are the effective settings.

D. Group Policy can be used to prevent an administrator from being forcibly logged off from a console session when another administrator is attempting to connect.

13. Which of the following command-line tools can be used to return user-specific information? (Choose all that apply.)

A. query user

B. query termserver

C. query process

D. query session

Troubleshooting Terminal Services

14. Your network uses Windows NT clients running the Terminal Services Client Connection Manager utility. The user working next to you notices that when you connect to a terminal server, you are automatically logged on, while she is always prompted for a password. She asks if you can help to configure her system to automatically log on as well. Which of the following will you recommend?

    A. Configure **Automatic logon** on the **General** tab in the **Properties** of the connection, and enter the appropriate log-on credentials in the **User name**, **Password**, and **Domain** text boxes.

    B. Log on to her Windows 2000 client using your user name and password.

    C. Configure **Always use the following logon information** on the Logon Settings tab in the connection properties of the Terminal Services Configuration utility.

    D. Configure the **User name**, **Domain**, **Password**, and **Confirm password** text boxes on the Logon Settings tab for the connection in the Terminal Services Configuration utility.

15. You have just finished setting up a special terminal server that is designed to serve a single application to users. For security purposes, you decide not to enable them to connect to a full desktop. In the Terminal Services Configuration utility, you have configured the only connection to enable an initial program to be launched immediately when users connect. However, when you test the system by attempting to connect to it, you receive messages informing you that the initial program could not be started. Which of the following should you check in an effort to fix the problem? (Choose all that apply.)

    A. You should make sure that you have spelled the path and executable correctly in the Terminal Services Configuration utility.

    B. You should verify the path to the application.

    C. You should verify that you have the appropriate permissions to the application.

    D. You should verify the name of the executable for the application.

Self Test Quick Answer Key

For complete questions, answers, and explanations to the Self Test questions in this chapter as well as the other chapters in this book, see the Self Test Appendix.

1. **D**
2. **A, B, C, D**
3. **B, C**
4. **B, C**
5. **A, C, D**
6. **A, B, D**
7. **B**
8. **A, C, D**
9. **B, D**
10. **D**
11. **A, B, D**
12. **A, B, D**
13. **A, C, D**
14. **A**
15. **A, B, C, D**

Chapter 7

MCSA/MCSE 70-290

Using Server Management Tools

Exam Objectives in this Chapter:

4.4.3 Manage a server by using available support tools.

4.4 Manage servers remotely.

4.5 Troubleshoot print queues.

4.7.2 Monitor print queues.

☑ Summary of Exam Objectives

☑ Exam Objectives Fast Track

☑ Exam Objectives Frequently Asked Questions

☑ Self Test

☑ Self Test Quick Answer Key

Introduction

The network administrator's daily tasks can be made easier (or more difficult) by the number and quality of administrative tools available to perform those tasks. In Windows Server 2003, Microsoft has provided administrators with a wealth of graphical and command-line utilities for carrying out their job duties. The Administrative Tools menu is the place to start; it's there you'll find predefined management consoles for configuring and managing most of Server 2003's services and components, including Active Directory tools, distributed file system (DFS), DNS, Security policies, Licensing, Routing and Remote Access, Terminal Services, Media Services, and more.

But that's only the beginning. Administrators can create customized Microsoft Management Consoles as well, just as with Windows 2000. This makes it easier to perform tasks yourself and easier to delegate them to others, because you can create consoles for specific purposes and enable only limited user access to them for specified users or groups.

For those who prefer the power and flexibility of the command line, many of these same administrative tasks can be performed there, as well as other tasks that have no GUI interface. Windows Server 2003 includes a huge number of command-line utilities, including dozens of new ones that were not included in Windows 2000 Server.

Many of the more complex configuration tasks performed by administrators can be done via Wizards that walk you through the steps. This makes it easier to set up services and server components for those who are unfamiliar with the process.

In this chapter, we introduce you to many of the graphical management consoles and command-line administrative utilities that are included in Windows Server 2003, and show you how to use them to manage your server and your network.

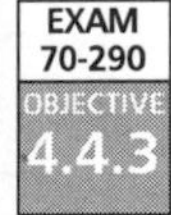

Recognizing Types of Management Tools

So many administrative tools are available in so many different places, that it can be daunting for a new administrator of a Windows computer to know where to look. Of course, in the fullness of time experience brings familiarity—but even experienced administrators occasionally discover a tool that they haven't seen before. In this section we will review where most of the common administrative tools are located.

Administrative Tools Menu

The Administrative Tools menu is where many important tools are located. Click **Start | Programs | Administrative Tools** to see what is available. You can change what appears in this folder by editing the **All Users** profile in the **Documents and Settings** folder as shown in Figure 7.1.

Figure 7.1 Location of the Administrative Tools Folder

Another way to access the same folder is by clicking **Start | Settings | Control Panel**, and then double-clicking the **Administrative Tools** icon.

Note that the items in the Administrative Tools menu folder are shortcuts, rather than the programs or console files themselves. Many of the actual management console files (.MSC files) are located in the **<systemroot>\system32** folder. You can find the location of the .MSC file by right-clicking the shortcut in the right pane as shown in the figure, selecting **Properties**, and then checking the **Target** field on the **Shortcut** menu.

NOTE

If you want specific tools to be available in the menu only when the Administrator account (or another specific account) is logged on, you can move the shortcuts for those tools from the **All Users | Start Menu | Programs | Administrative Tools** folder to the same folder under that user's profile (for example, **Administrator | Start Menu | Programs | Administrative Tools**).

Custom MMC Snap-Ins

The Microsoft Management Console (normally referred to as an MMC) is the framework for nearly all Windows graphical administrative tools. It provides a blank sheet to which you can add your favorite administration tools. The idea is that all administrative tools have a common look and feel and that the management tool for an administrative task, such as adding users and groups, is written as a snap-in for an MMC. The administrator can then choose which snap-ins to have in a console or use one of the many pre-configured ones found in the **Administrative Tools** folder. Some of the MMC snap-ins can be used to manage remote computers as well as the local computer (assuming you have the appropriate rights). Many vendors of third-party management tools provide snap-ins for their products, that you can add to your MMC consoles.

Note that some of the tools in the **Administrative Tools** folder, such as **Licensing**, are stand-alone programs that don't work with an MMC. When you look at the properties of those shortcuts, you'll find that the target files are executables (.EXE) instead of MMCs (.MSC).

After you've created an MMC, it can be saved as a stand-alone file and even e-mailed to another administrator to use. Possession of an MMC file does not in itself give a user any additional rights. So if you e-mail an MMC file with the Disk Management snap-in to a non-administrative user, for example, that user won't be able to complete any disk management tasks even though he or she can see the snap-in.

MMC Console Modes

MMC consoles can be configured to prevent anyone from changing them. A console can be saved in one of four modes, each of which has varying restrictions. Table 7.1 shows the four modes and the functionality of each.

Table 7.1 MMC Console Modes

Console Mode	Functionality
Author mode	Full access to the MMC and ability to change all aspects.
User mode – full access	Full access to the windowing commands but can't add or remove snap-ins.
User mode – limited access, multiple window	Access only to the areas of the console as it was when saved. Can create new windows but not close existing windows.
User mode – limited access, single windows	Access to the console as it was when saved. Can't open new windows.

Exam Warning

Make sure that you are familiar with creating custom MMC consoles to manage local and remote servers. Practice creating your own consoles and adding snap-ins to manage the local computer and remote servers.

Exercise 7.01

Create a Custom MMC

In this exercise, you create a custom MMC that includes snap-ins for a couple of common tasks for the local and a remote computer.

1. To create a new console, click **Start** | **Run** and type **mmc** in the dialog box.
2. Select **Add/Remove Snap-in** from the **File** pull-down menu.
3. In the **Add/Remove Snap-in** dialog-box, click the **Add** button.
4. In the **Add Standalone Snap-in** dialog box, scroll through the list and click **Event Viewer**, and then click the **Add** button.
5. In the **Select Computer** dialog box, click **Finish**.
6. Click **Close** in the **Add Standalone Snap-in** dialog box, and then click **OK** in the **Add/Remove Snap-in** dialog box.
7. Repeat steps 2 through 6, but for step 5 select **Another Computer** and enter the name of or browse to another computer on your network.
8. Repeat steps 2 through 6, but for step 4 select **Services** and in step 5 select **Local Computer**.
9. In the left-hand pane, click the **plus signs (+)** next to the two Event Viewer folders to expand them.
10. Click **Application** under the **Event Viewer (Local)** folder.
11. You should now have a console similar to the one shown in Figure 7.2.

Figure 7.2 Viewing the Application Log for the Local Computer

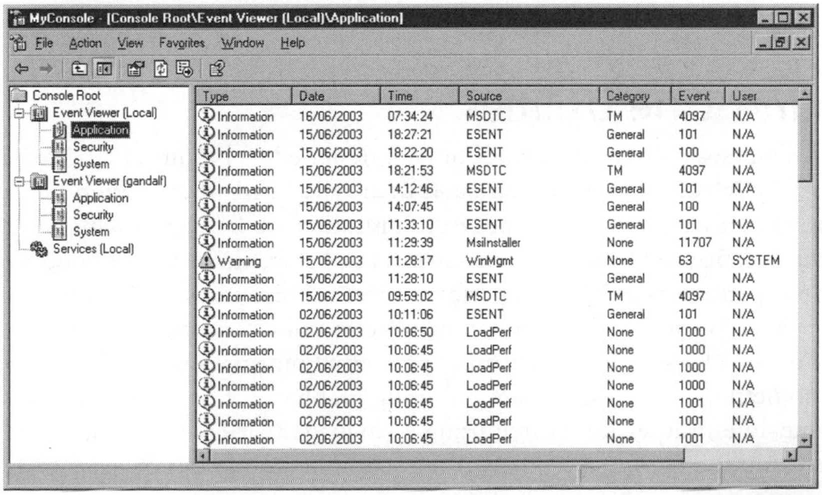

MyConsole - [Console Root\Event Viewer (Local)\Application]

File Action View Favorites Window Help

Console Root
- Event Viewer (Local)
  - Application
  - Security
  - System
- Event Viewer (gandalf)
  - Application
  - Security
  - System
- Services (Local)

Type	Date	Time	Source	Category	Event	User
Information	16/06/2003	07:34:24	MSDTC	TM	4097	N/A
Information	15/06/2003	18:27:21	ESENT	General	101	N/A
Information	15/06/2003	18:22:20	ESENT	General	100	N/A
Information	15/06/2003	18:21:53	MSDTC	TM	4097	N/A
Information	15/06/2003	14:12:46	ESENT	General	101	N/A
Information	15/06/2003	14:07:45	ESENT	General	100	N/A
Information	15/06/2003	11:33:10	ESENT	General	101	N/A
Information	15/06/2003	11:29:39	MsiInstaller	None	11707	N/A
Warning	15/06/2003	11:28:17	WinMgmt	None	63	SYSTEM
Information	15/06/2003	11:28:10	ESENT	General	100	N/A
Information	15/06/2003	09:59:02	MSDTC	TM	4097	N/A
Information	02/06/2003	10:11:06	ESENT	General	101	N/A
Information	02/06/2003	10:06:50	LoadPerf	None	1000	N/A
Information	02/06/2003	10:06:45	LoadPerf	None	1000	N/A
Information	02/06/2003	10:06:45	LoadPerf	None	1000	N/A
Information	02/06/2003	10:06:45	LoadPerf	None	1000	N/A
Information	02/06/2003	10:06:45	LoadPerf	None	1001	N/A
Information	02/06/2003	10:06:45	LoadPerf	None	1001	N/A
Information	02/06/2003	10:06:45	LoadPerf	None	1001	N/A

12. To save this console for future use, select **Save** from the **File** pull-down menu. Type **MyConsole** in the **File name** box and click **Save**.
13. The console is saved and can be started again via **Start | Programs | Administrative Tools | MyConsole.msc**.
14. We will now look at opening multiple windows. Highlight **Event Viewer (Local)**, and then right-click and select **New Window from Here**. You now have two windows open, which can be managed using the **Window** pull-down option.
15. Click **Window** and explore the various options for how the two windows are laid out.
16. Switch to the **Event Viewer (Local)** window and close this window by typing **Ctrl + F4**. You should now have only one window called **Console Root**.
17. Click **File** and select **Options**.
18. In the **Options** dialog box that appears, click the pull-down menu for the **Console mode** box and select **User mode – limited access, single window**, and then click **OK**.
19. Click **File** and select **Save**.
20. Click **File** and select **Exit**.
21. Re-open the console by selecting **Start | Programs | Administrative Tools | MyConsole.msc**.
22. Note that the **Window** pull-down option is no longer present, that you cannot add new snap-ins via the **File** pull-down menu, and that you cannot close any of the snap-ins that are in the MMC.

Command-Line Utilities

As the name suggests, command-line utilities are designed to be run in a command window (start by selecting **Start | Run**, and then type **cmd** in the **Open** box and press **Enter**) or as part of batch files or scripts. Administrators are forever looking for ways to simplify administration, and using command-lines in batch files is a very good way of handling routine, repetitive tasks. You can perform some administrative tasks using only a graphical interface, some using only a command-line utility, and others can be done using either. Later in the chapter we will examine printer administration, which is a good example of something that can be managed using graphical or command-line tools.

Command-line utilities are written using a language that has to be run using a scripting host such as Windows cscript and others run as compiled programs or executables.

Command-line utilities are harder to find because they are not in any of the Start menus (although you can add them). A good place to look for information is in **Windows Help and Support**. Search for **Command-line Reference** and you get an alphabetical list of Windows command-line tools.

Wizards

Wizards guide you through potentially complex tasks by taking you through a series of dialog boxes where you answer questions or make choices; they are essentially wrappers around the underlying graphical or command-line based tool. Each version of Windows increases the number of wizards in an attempt to make administration easier for the inexperienced administrator. However, in some cases it can be quicker for the experienced administrator to perform a task directly using the appropriate administrative tools rather than using a wizard.

Many wizards can be accessed through the Manage Your Server tool and the Configure Your Server Wizard in Administrative Tools.

Windows Resource Kit

The Windows Resource Kit, available for download from Microsoft's Web site, provides even more tools for administrators to use to manage Windows servers in a large network. If you are responsible for many servers, you should download this kit and spend some time reviewing its contents.

The Run As command

It is good practice for administrators not to log on using an account that has administrative rights. This prevents accidental changes to the file server, allowing potential attackers and viruses administrative rights to the console. As an administrator, you should log on using an ordinary user account and when you need to perform an administrative task you can use the **Run as** option to choose an administrator account. **Run as** is available by right-clicking an item in the start menu.

The **Run as** option won't appear in the right context menu for every Start menu item, just for executables, management consoles, and other programs that can be run.

You can also use the *runas* command in a command prompt for command-line utilities. Start a command prompt and then type **runas /user:administrator cmd.** This will start a new command prompt with administrator privileges.

Managing Your Server Remotely

How often have you had to walk to the other end of a building to perform a server task, or—even worse—had to drive or fly to another office? One of the main aims for any administrator is to be able to manage all the servers without leaving his or her desk! Windows Server 2003 provides you with a variety of methods to remotely manage your servers depending on your scenario.

Remote Assistance

Remote Assistance is designed for users to request help on their PCs (which must be running Windows XP or later) from another user. The user requesting help sends an invitation to assist, using Windows Messenger or e-mail via the **Help and Support Center**. The request includes an attachment (which contains details of how to connect to the user's PC) that the recipient double-clicks to start a Remote Assistance session with the requesting user's PC. Once connected, the helper can view the desktop of the requesting user and chat online with him. The helper can also, with the user's permission, take control of his desktop.

The request can optionally include an "expiry" (expiration) date, after which the Remote Assistance request is no longer valid. This is used to reduce the risk of unauthorized access to the user's computer. The user requesting help can also require the helper to use a password to connect to his computer. The user must communicate this password to the helper.

The user can review his invitations in the **Help and Support Center**. Figure 7.3 shows a summary of invitations that have been sent out.

Although the usual method is for the user requesting help to initiate the Remote Assistance session, it is also possible within a domain for a helper to offer assistance. An administrator can set group policy to prevent users from requesting Remote Assistance, or to restrict whether users will be able to enable a helper to remotely control their computers or only view them.

Both users need to be connected to the Internet in order to use Remote Assistance. If firewalls are in use, port 3398 must be open. You can disable Remote Assistance completely to prevent any Remote Assistance invitations being sent.

To configure Remote Assistance, right-click **My Computer** and select **Properties**, and then click the **Remote** tab.

Figure 7.3 Summary of Remote Assistance Invitations

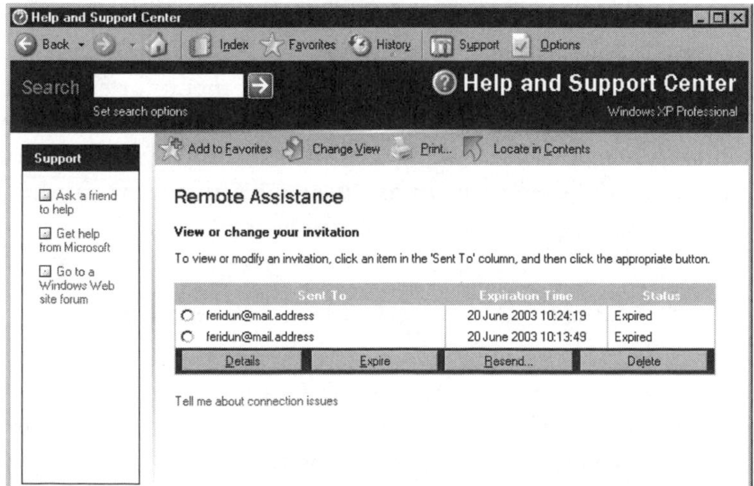

Using Web Interface for Remote Administration

If you need to manage your servers from home or perhaps from another office, one option is to use a standard Web browser to administer your servers using the remote administration component of Windows Server 2003. You must configure your server first, but after you have done this you can simply point the browser to your server's IP address and you can administer it from anywhere in the world. To access the server over the Internet, the following conditions must be met:

- The Remote Administration (HTML) component must be installed on the server. It is not installed by default (with the exception of Windows Server 2003 Web Edition).
- Port 8098 on the server must be accessible through your Internet connection.
- Your server must have a valid external IP address.

If you want to access your servers only over your company network, an external IP address is not necessary, but you must still be able to communicate with port 8098 on the server. Microsoft recommends that the browser you use for remote administration be Internet Explorer version 6.0 or later.

NOTE

Remote administration over the Web is not available for servers that are domain controllers.

To access your server over the Web, browse to **https://servername:8098**. You must use a secure connection. The **:8098** in the URL directs the browser to connect to port 8098 on the server instead of the default port 80. You can change your server to work on a different port in Internet Information Services (IIS) Manager. After you've connected to the server, you'll see the Welcome page as shown in Figure 7.4.

Through this Web site, you can carry out the more common administration tasks such as configuring Web sites, managing network settings, and administering local user accounts.

Figure 7.4 Welcome Page for Server Web Administration

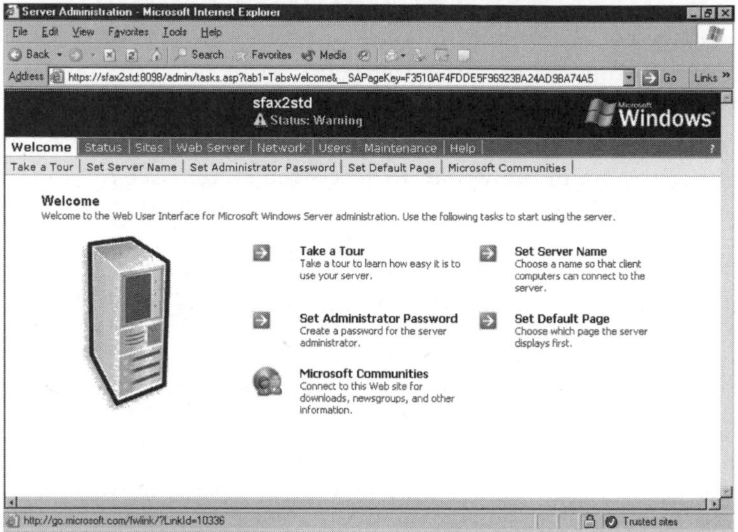

Exercise 7.02

Install Remote Administration (HTML) and Create a Local Group

In this exercise, you will install Remote Administration (HTML) on your server, and then use it to create a local group on the server:

1. Open the **Windows Components Wizard** by clicking **Start | Settings | Control Panel**. Double-click the **Add or Remove Programs** icon, and then click the **Add/Remove Windows Components** icon.
2. In the **Windows Components Wizard**, highlight **Application Server**, and then click **Details**. In the **Application Server** window, highlight **Internet Information Services (IIS)** and then click **Details**.
3. In the **Internet Information Services (IIS)** window, highlight **World Wide Web Service** and then click **Details**.
4. In the **World Wide Web Service** window, click the **Remote Administration (HTML)** check box to select it.
5. Close all the windows until you get back to the **Windows Components Wizard**, and then click **Next** to start installation. You might need your Windows Server 2003 installation CD at this point.
6. When installation has finished, click **Finish** to close the wizard.

7. Open a Web browser on any computer (or even on the server) that has connectivity to your server and type **https://servername:8098**, where *servername* is the name of your server.
8. On the welcome page, click **Users** on the blue bar.
9. On the **Users** page click **Local Groups**. The **Local Groups on Server** page appears, showing a list of groups already defined on the server and a list of tasks on the right-hand side.
10. On the **Local Groups on Server** page, click the **New** button underneath **Tasks**.
11. On the **Create New Group** page, type **DemoGroup** in the **Group name** box and **Demo Group** in the **Description** box, and then click the **OK** button at the bottom of the page. The **Local Groups on Server** page appears as shown in Figure 7.5.

Figure 7.5 Viewing Local Groups Using the Web Interface for Remote Administration

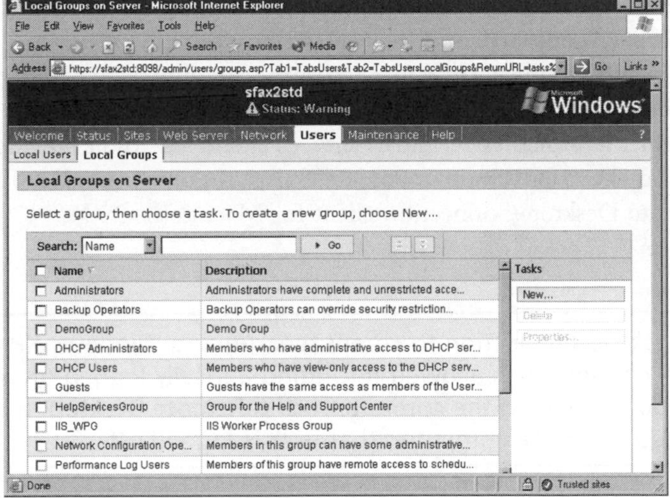

Remote Desktop for Administration

The Remote Desktop (RD) for Administration facility enables users to connect to a Windows Server 2003 or a Windows 2000 Server computer desktop from any computer that has the Remote Desktop client software. In Windows 2000, this facility was called Terminal Services Administration mode. Remote Desktop for Administration is effectively

Terminal Server installed in a special mode that enables up to two remote users and one local user (at the console) to connect to a server for administration purposes and does not require any additional licensing. Terminal Server can also be used in application mode to enable many users to connect to your server using Remote Desktop from their computers and run applications in a "thin client" computing model. Application mode requires Terminal Server licensing to be set up.

Before you can use Remote Desktop, you must enable it in System properties. Select **Start | Settings | Control Panel** and double-click the **System** icon. In the **System Properties** dialog box, click the **Remote** tab and then ensure that **Allow users to connect remotely to this computer** box is checked. The **Select Remote Users** button enables you to choose which users can connect to the computer remotely. Administrators can always connect by default.

To connect to a server using Remote Desktop on a Windows XP system, select **Start | Programs | Accessories | Communications | Remote Desktop Connection**. In the Remote Desktop Connection dialog box, type the name or IP address of the server you want to manage and then press **Connect**. The normal logon screen appears and you can log on to the server and manage it exactly as if you were at the server. Note that you are not remotely controlling the server desktop; you are working in your own session. That is, a user sitting at the server console cannot see the actions you are performing (as he or she could if you were using a third-party remote-control program such as pcAnywhere).

You can connect to the server from any client computer running the Remote Desktop Connection client or the Windows Terminal Services client. Microsoft provides an Remote Desktop Connection client for Windows 95, 98/98SE, ME, NT 4.0 and 2000. You can also download an Remote Desktop Connection client for Macintosh OS X.

NOTE

A Remote Desktop Connection to computers running Windows XP is also possible, but only one connection is allowed (including a locally logged on user). This means that when you connect to the computer using Remote Desktop, if someone is already logged on at the computer, that user is logged off.

The Remote Desktop snap-in is a very useful tool for adding Remote Desktop functionality to an MMC. With this tool, you can connect to the server's console session.

Refer to Chapter 6 for more details on configuring and using Terminal Services.

Administration Tools Pack (adminpak.msi)

The Windows Server 2003 Administration Tools Pack is used on client computers running Windows XP Professional to provide management tools for Windows Server 2003 computers. The client computers must have Windows XP Service Pack 1 applied.

You can install the Administration Tools from the adminpak.msi file, which you can find on the Windows Server 2003 CD or in the system32 folder of a computer running Windows Server 2003. Double-click the **adminpak.msi** file to install the tools.

After the tools are installed, you'll have all the administrative tools that we looked at earlier in this section available on your Windows XP computer and you'll be able to perform server and network administrative tasks from the XP client. In particular, this includes tools for server-based services such as DNS, DHCP, and Active Directory.

EXAM WARNING

The Windows Server 2003 Administration Tools Pack can be installed only on computers running Windows XP or later. However, they can be used to manage servers running Windows 2000 Server as well as Windows Server 2003.

Windows Management Instrumentation (WMI)

Windows Management Instrumentation (WMI) provides an object-based method for accessing management information in a network. It is based on the Web-Based Enterprise Management (WBEM) standard specified by the Distributed Management Task Force (DTMF) organization and is designed to enable the management of a wide range of network devices. WMI is Microsoft's implementation of WBEM for Windows operating systems.

WMI is used with programs or scripts to retrieve management information or change configurations of Windows computers, but using WMI is not trivial and requires programming skills. WMI can be used at the command-line by typing **WMIC**, but you need knowledge of the WMI database of objects. For more information on this topic, refer to Microsoft's WMI Software Development Kit.

Some enterprise Microsoft tools, such as Systems Management Server (SMS) and Health Monitor in the Back Office products use WMI to manage computers.

For more information on WMI, have a look at Microsoft's Web site at www.microsoft.com/windows2003/techinfo/howitworks/management/wmiscripts.asp.

Using Computer Management to Manage a Remote Computer

Computer Management is available on client and server computers to perform management tasks, and is actually a pre-configured MMC console. To start Computer Management, select **Start | Settings | Control Panel**, double-click **Administrative Tools**, and then double-click **Computer Management**. Alternatively, right-click the **My Computer** icon and select **Manage**.

You can also use computer management to connect to another computer (providing you have the appropriate rights). Select **Connect to another computer** from the **Action** pull-down menu, and then enter the name of the remote computer in the **Another computer** box or browse for it by clicking the **Browse** button.

Figure 7.6 shows Computer Management on a server with the Disk Management snap-in expanded. On a server computer, Computer Management has additional snap-ins for server-based services, so you won't see exactly the same snap-ins in Computer Management on a computer running Windows 2000 Professional or Windows XP Professional.

Figure 7.6 Computer Management MMC

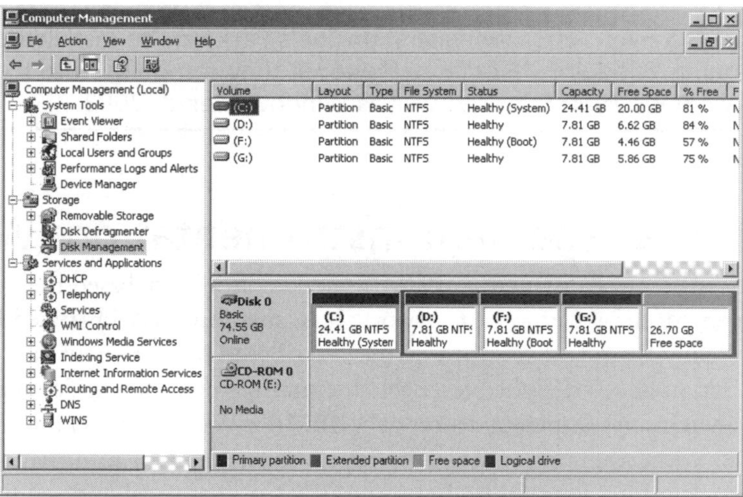

Computer Management has three nodes that group the management tasks, as shown in Table 7.2. Expanding each node reveals the snap-ins. System Tools contains snap-ins for local management tasks, the Storage node contains snap-ins for tasks related to local disks and storage devices (such as tape drives), and the Services and Applications node contains snap-ins for other server-based applications. The contents of this node vary depending on whether the computer is running a client or server operating system, as well as the server components that have been installed. Table 7.2 shows only some of the possible snap-ins under Services and Applications.

Table 7.2 Management Snap-Ins in Computer Management

Computer Management Node	Management Snap-In	Use
System Tools	Event Viewer	Display event logs
	Shared Folders	View shared folders, open files, and active sessions
	Local Users and Groups	Manage local user and group accounts

Continued

Table 7.2 Management Snap-Ins in Computer Management

Computer Management Node	Management Snap-In	Use
	Performance Logs and Alerts	Configure performance data logs
	Device Manager	Manage computer hardware
Storage	Removable Storage	Manage devices with removable media
	Disk Defragmenter	Defragment local disks
	Disk Management	Configure disk partitions and volumes
Services and Applications	DHCP *(if installed)*	Configure the DHCP service for allocating IP addresses
	Services	Manage services
	WMI Control	Configure Windows Management Instrumentation
	Indexing Service	Configure the Indexing Service to provide fast searches
	Routing and Remote Access *(if installed)*	Manage routing and remote access
	DNS (if installed)	Configure the DNS service

Which Tool To Use?

In this section we've seen a variety of tools for remotely managing servers. How do you decide which one to use in a given situation? It really depends on what you are trying to do. In cases where you can accomplish the same thing with different tools, you might have your favorite tools for administering a server.

- Remote Assistance is really a tool for end users and you are unlikely to use it for remote server management. You should, however, be aware that Remote Assistance invitations can be sent from a Windows Server 2003 computer, and you should know how to turn off Remote Assistance.

- The Remote Desktop tool is useful when you need to have full control of a single server. Because you are effectively *at* the server, you can administer any function. With the Remote Desktop snap-in, or using **RD** from the command-line, you can even connect to the server console session remotely.
- The Web Interface for Remote Administration is useful in situations where you need to carry out basic tasks when you are away from the corporate network, but still have access to the Internet. It is limited, however, as to which administrative tasks you can carry out.
- The administration tools pack and Computer Management in conjunction with custom MMCs are likely to be among the tools you use the most, especially if you have to administer a large number of servers. You can put together customized MMCs that contain the snap-ins for tools that you use the most often and for the servers that you have to regularly manage.

TEST DAY TIP

Make sure that you have a good understanding of the different types of tools and when each type is useful. Remember that some management features are not enabled by default.

Using Emergency Management Services

Emergency Management Services (EMS) is a new feature in Windows Server 2003 that enables you to remotely manage a server when normal network connectivity has failed. Under normal conditions, you use the tools described in this and other chapters to manage your server either by being physically present at the server or over the network. However, what happens if the network crashes or the server doesn't boot properly?

Provided the server has the appropriate hardware and firmware, you can remotely manage it without the presence of a local keyboard, mouse, or display. This is called out-of-band or "headless" operation. A key aim of out-of-band management is to get a server that is not working properly back to a normal operating state.

A number of situations might require you to resort to out-of-band management:

- The server has stopped responding to normal network management commands.
- The network card in the server has failed.
- The server hasn't booted properly.
- The server has been shut down and you need to bring it up again.

The extent to which you can use out-of-band management depends on the hardware of your server. On a server with Windows Server 2003, a serial port and EMS enabled, at the very least you can connect a VT100-type terminal or a computer with a terminal emulator to the serial port and perform certain tasks using the Special Administration Console (SAC). However, the server must be up and running to be able to manage it in this way.

If you need to be able to manage the server remotely when it has crashed or even been switched off, you need special hardware and firmware on the motherboard that provide features such as firmware console redirection. This means that you can monitor the server via the serial port right from the moment it starts up, and even check out BIOS settings.

EMS is not enabled by default, but can be enabled during an installation, an upgrade, or after setup has been completed.

New & Noteworthy...

Managing Several Windows Server 2003 Computers with EMS

EMS provides a useful service for managing your servers in an emergency situation. But what if you have a large number of computers running Windows Server 2003 in a computer room? What's the best way of hooking to EMS on all of them without having an array of terminals? A tidy way of providing access is to use a *terminal concentrator* (sometimes called a terminal server, not to be confused with Terminal Services).

A terminal concentrator has several serial ports (sixteen is a common number) and a network connection. You use a program like Telnet to connect to the terminal concentrator over the network, and then choose a particular port on the concentrator to connect to the device attached to that port. Connect each of the serial ports on the servers to the serial ports on the terminal concentrator and you can then connect to EMS over the network. Of course, if the terminal concentrator fails, then you won't be able to connect to any of the servers.

Exercise 7.03

Connect to Emergency Management Services

This exercise requires two computers (one with Windows Server 2003 and the other with any operating system and a terminal emulator) and a special serial cable (the cable must have two female ends and include a cross-over, sometimes called a null-modem cable). Alternatively, you can use a single computer and a terminal that connects to the serial port of the server computer.

In this exercise, you will enable EMS on the server computer and then connect to it from the second computer running the terminal emulator.

1. Connect the serial cable between the two computers using COM1: on both computers.
2. On the server computer, open a command window and run the command **Bootcfg /ems on /id 1 /port COM1**. This enables EMS on serial port COM1. The **/id** option specifies the operating system in the boot.ini list on which EMS is to be enabled. If you have more than one operating system on your computer, be sure to adjust the value of **/id** accordingly.
3. On the second computer, start Hyperterminal or any other terminal emulator and connect to COM1: using a baud rate of 9,600. You won't see anything in the terminal window yet.
4. Reboot the server computer. Watch the terminal window as the server computer restarts. You should see the normal startup messages, including the operating system loader where you can choose which operating system to boot. At this stage, you can interact with the boot process through the terminal window.
5. When the computer has finished booting, the **SAC** prompt appears as shown in Figure 7.7.

Figure 7.7 The Special Administration Console

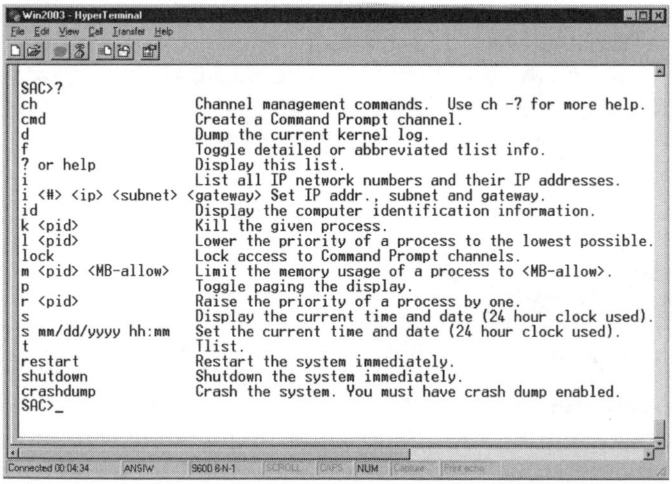
Win2003 - HyperTerminal
File Edit View Call Transfer Help
SAC>?
ch Channel management commands. Use ch -? for more help.
cmd Create a Command Prompt channel.
d Dump the current kernel log.
f Toggle detailed or abbreviated tlist info.
? or help Display this list.
i List all IP network numbers and their IP addresses.
i <#> <ip> <subnet> <gateway> Set IP addr., subnet and gateway.
id Display the computer identification information.
k <pid> Kill the given process.
l <pid> Lower the priority of a process to the lowest possible.
lock Lock access to Command Prompt channels.
m <pid> <MB-allow> Limit the memory usage of a process to <MB-allow>.
p Toggle paging the display.
r <pid> Raise the priority of a process by one.
s Display the current time and date (24 hour clock used).
s mm/dd/yyyy hh:mm Set the current time and date (24 hour clock used).
t Tlist.
restart Restart the system immediately.
shutdown Shutdown the system immediately.
crashdump Crash the system. You must have crash dump enabled.
SAC>_
Connected 00:04:34 ANSIW 9600 8-N-1 SCROLL CAPS NUM Capture Print echo

6. Enter **cmd** to start a command-prompt channel.

7. To switch to the command-prompt channel type **ch si 1** and press the spacebar to view the channel.
8. Enter your logon name, domain, and password. Use the name of the computer for the domain if your computer is not part of a domain.
9. After you have successfully authenticated, you get the normal command prompt where you can navigate the directory tree and run commands. Note: Don't attempt to run any Windows-based programs; they won't work.

Managing Printers and Print Queues

Managing printing, which involves many tasks, is a routine part of almost every administrator's job. In this section we will examine the tools that you can use to manage your printers.

EXAM 70-290 OBJECTIVE 4.7.2

Windows Server 2003 offers a variety of methods for managing printers; these include the Control Panel, the Manage Your Server tool, and command-line tools.

Printer management tasks include the following:

- Creating a printer
- Sharing a printer
- Adding printer drivers for earlier operating systems
- Setting permissions
- Managing print queues
- Creating printer pools
- Scheduling printers
- Setting printing priorities

You can carry out all these tasks using graphical or command-line tools. First, we'll cover how to carry out these tasks using the graphical interface.

Using the Graphical Interface

The Graphical Interface for managing printers and print queues includes a number of tools:

- Control Panel | Printers and Faxes folder
- Add Printer Wizard
- Add Printer Driver Wizard
- Manage Your Server

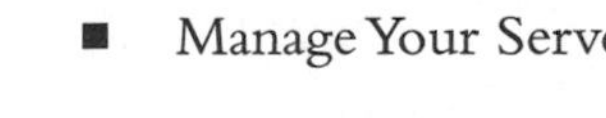

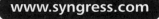

The **Printers and Faxes** folder is where printers defined on the computer are stored. Configuring the properties of printers in this folder carries out nearly all printer tasks.

The **Manage Your Server** tool enables you to configure various server roles, including the print server role, by using the **Configure Your Server** Wizard. We cover roles later in this chapter.

Here, we'll examine the key printer management tasks using the graphical interfaces.

Creating a Printer

Use the **Add Printer Wizard** to create a printer by selecting **Start | Settings | Printers and Faxes** and clicking the **Add Printer** icon.

The wizard asks you a series of questions about which port to use, the driver to use, what name to give the printer, whether it should be shared, optional location and comment information, and whether to print a test page.

The port to choose depends on how the printer is physically connected to the computer. It might be connected to a serial port, parallel port, or USB port. If the printer is connected directly to the network, you need to use a TCP/IP port and specify the IP address of the printer. Usually, if you connect a printer to a USB port, Windows uses Plug and Play to automatically install the printer for you.

Printer drivers are used to convert a print job to the specific commands that a print device understands. Print devices vary in the command languages that they use; for example, most HP printers use PCL. It is therefore very important that you select the correct driver for your printer. Often a new printer comes with an installation CD or disk that contains the driver.

After you've created a printer, it appears in the **Printers and Faxes** folder and you can double-click the printer to change its properties.

Configuring & Implementing...

Managing Printers Connected Directly to the Network

If you have printers that connect directly to the network rather than to a port on a computer, you have a choice as to how to manage printing. The first method is to create a local printer queue on every computer that needs access, specifying a TCP/IP port (with the appropriate IP address). This means that each computer prints directly to the network printer independently of the other computers.

The second method is to create a local printer queue on one computer, usually a file and print server, and then to share the printer queue. On every other computer, create a network printer queue that points to the share on the print server.

The first method is more efficient in network bandwidth because print jobs are sent directly to the printer and not via a print server. However, it is more complicated to set up because each client computer has to be configured and there is no centralized queue management. The second method is simpler and provides greater control, and is the recommended approach for most networks.

Sharing a Printer

If you do not share a printer, only the computer on which you create the printer can use it. Sharing a printer makes it available over the network to other computers.

To share a printer: highlight it, right-click, and then click **Sharing**. In the **Properties** dialog box, select **Share this printer** and choose a share name. This is the name by which the printer will be known over the network.

You need to consider the operating system that the computers using the printer share will be running. When you share a printer on a Windows Server 2003 computer, the installed driver is also suitable for Windows XP and Windows 2000 clients. When a computer running Windows 2000 or Windows XP connects to the share, it automatically downloads the driver. If you have client computers running Windows NT 4.0, or Windows 95/98 or Windows Millennium Edition (ME), install additional drivers.

Adding Printer Drivers for Earlier Operating Systems

To make a shared printer available to users of computers with earlier operating systems, install the appropriate driver on the server computer. To do this, select the **Sharing** tab for the printer and click the **Additional Drivers** button to load the drivers for earlier operating systems. The benefit of doing this is that when a computer running, for example, Windows 98 connects to the shared printer, it downloads the appropriate driver automatically rather than asking the user for the location of the printer driver.

TEST DAY TIP

Microsoft exams place a lot of emphasis on networks that have a mixture of operating systems. Be sure that you are familiar with installing additional drivers for earlier operating systems on the print server.

Setting Permissions

Printer permissions control who can print to a printer and whether a user can manage the printer. There are three permissions for printers (refer to Table 7.3), and these can be applied to users and groups. As with file and folder permissions, printer permissions are cumulative; if a user has permissions to a printer and is also a member of a group that has permissions, the user will have the cumulative effect of the user and group permissions. The exception to this is that if any of the printer permissions have been denied, the user can never have that permission regardless of any groups that he belongs to. Figure 7.8 shows the default permissions on a Windows Server 2003 computer.

Figure 7.8 Default Printer Permissions

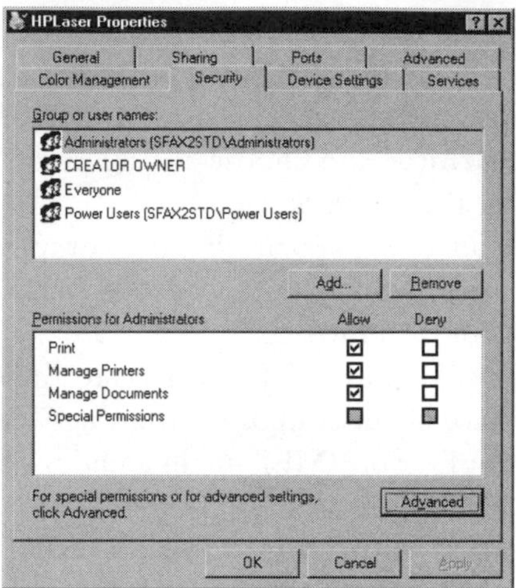

The **Special Permissions** permission enables you to fine-tune security by specifying who is allowed to read what the permissions are, who can change the permissions. and who can take ownership. The person that a printer is considered its owner, and that person can always change permissions on the printer. To make someone else the owner of a printer, give that user the **Take Ownership** permission and then have the other user exercise the **Take Ownership** option. The user will then own the printer and can change permissions.

Table 7.3 Printer Permissions

Permission	Use
Print	Users can print and delete their own jobs.
Manage Documents	Users can pause, resume, restart, delete, and change the print order of documents submitted by other users. However, this permission does not by itself enable a user to print to the printer.
Manage Printers	Users have complete control over the printer and can change any of its characteristics.

Test Day Tip

Make sure you know how to restrict access to a printer. As well as specifying who can print, you need to remove the default permission of **Print** for the Everyone group. This permission is added by default whenever you create a printer and must therefore be removed if access is to be restricted.

Head of the Class...

Local and Network Printers

Students in network administration classes often ask whether to choose a local or network printer when creating printers, especially when adding printers that are connected directly to a hub or switch rather than a computer via a parallel or USB cable. The way to decide is to realize that, in Windows terminology, a printer is a logical device that interfaces with the physical device that does the printing. You could also think of this as a printer queue.

Bearing this in mind, decide which server will manage the printing for the new print device. Add the print device as a local printer on this server and then share the printer. On any other computer that needs to use the new print device, add the print device as a network printer and specify the share name for the printer.

In Windows 2000, the **Add Printer Wizard** did not make this very clear, but in Windows Server 2003 and Windows XP the wizard includes a reminder to use the "local printer" option when you first create a queue for a network print device (refer to Figure 7.9).

Figure 7.9 The Windows Server 2003 Add Printer Wizard

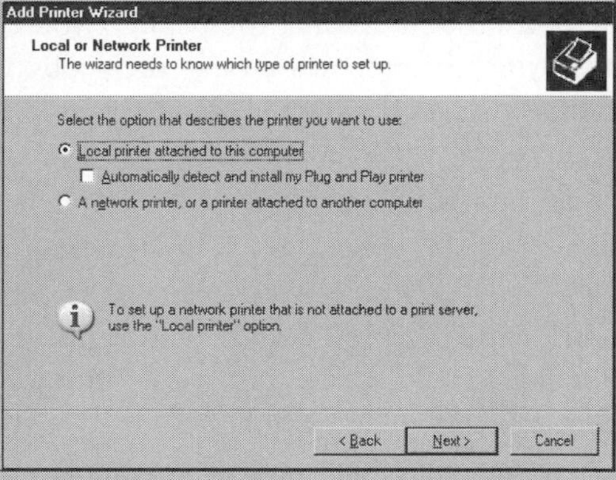

Managing Print Queues

You will often need to see what jobs are waiting to print and perhaps to delete some. You accomplish this via the print queue for a printer. To look at the queue, double-click the printer of interest. In the dialog box that appears, you will see a list of jobs waiting to be printed. You can delete or cancel a job by highlighting it and then pressing **Delete**, or by highlighting it and then right-clicking and selecting **Cancel**.

To cancel all jobs in a queue, highlight the printer, right-click, and select **Cancel All Documents**. If you have the dialog box for the printer queue open, you can also select **Cancel All Documents** from the **Printer** pull-down menu.

Pausing a print job prevents it from printing but won't delete it from the queue. You might do this if someone has submitted a very large print job and you want to hold it back until all the other jobs have printed. To pause a print job, highlight the job, right-click, and then select **Pause**. To release the job for printing, highlight the job, right-click, and then select **Resume**.

You can also pause the entire queue, perhaps because the printer has failed or jammed and you want to stop a flood of error messages. To pause a printer, highlight it, right-click, and then select **Pause Printing**. To restart printing, highlight the printer, right-click, and then select **Resume Printing**.

Managing Printer Pools

Imagine your printer has become very busy and long queues develop. In this situation, rather than replacing the printer with a much more powerful one, you could purchase another identical printer (perhaps saving money). Connect the printer, and instead of creating a new printer queue on the server, modify the properties of the existing queue. On the **Ports** tab, select **Enable Printer Pooling** and choose the new port that you used to connect the printer (this could be a TCP/IP port).

Whenever a user prints to this queue, the print job is sent to the first printer that is not busy, thus pooling the jobs. You must ensure that the printers you connect are identical, because users cannot control which printer will service their jobs. Differences in capabilities between the printers might mean that a job fails to print properly. You should also locate the printers physically close to each other, because users will not know which printer has printed their job.

Scheduling Printers

Along with controlling which users can use a printer, you can also control when they print by using scheduling. By setting a schedule, users can still submit jobs at any time, but the jobs will only be printed during the scheduled hours.

Consider a scenario where some users print large reports to a printer that is shared by other users. With a single printer queue, printing the large report holds up printing for everyone else. To resolve this, create a second printer queue that points to the same port as the first queue, change the availability time to out-of-office hours and advise users to use the second printer for the large reports and the first queue for shorter jobs.

To set a schedule for a printer, highlight it, right-click and select **Properties**, and then select the **Advanced** tab. The default is for a printer to be available at all times. Figure 7.10 shows an example of a printer with restricted availability.

Figure 7.10 Example of Restricted Printing Hours

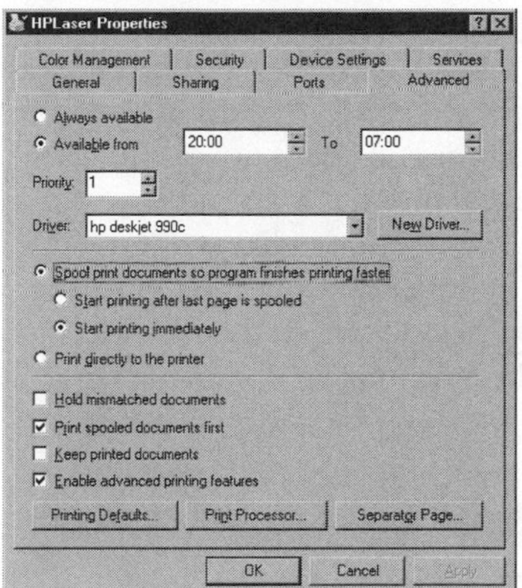

Setting Printing Priorities

You can use priorities to control the order in which print jobs are processed. Normally, jobs are printed in the order in which they are received. All printers and print jobs have a priority setting that can be changed. The default priority is 1 but can range from 1 to 99, with 99 being the highest. When a print job arrives, its priority setting is the same as the priority of the printer. Once in the queue, the priority setting can be changed by anyone with the **Manage Documents** permission. Typically, the priority of a print job will be increased to make it print next despite its position in the queue. Note that by changing the default priority of the printer to 50, for example, it is possible to reduce the priority of a job.

You can also use priorities to give certain users preferential access to a printer. For example, you have a group of managers whose print jobs need to be dealt with before other users'. To achieve this, create two print queues pointing to the same printer. Let's say they are called A4 and A4Mgrs. Remove the **Print** permission for the Everyone group from A4Mgrs and add the **Print** permission to the Managers group. This means that only the managers can use this queue. The final step is to increase the priority on the A4Mgrs print queue so that the managers' print jobs get serviced first.

Using New Command-Line Tools

Windows Server 2003 introduces a number of command-line-based scripts to manage printers. If you have large numbers of printers on your network with many servers, using these new command-line scripts in batch files can save you a lot of time compared with using the graphical interface.

The scripts are written in Visual Basic and have to be run in a command window using *cscript*, as in this example: **cscript prncnfg.vbs**.

It isn't necessary to include the .vbs extension. But using *cscript* is necessary because the default scripting host is *wscript* (which is for graphical windows-based scripts) and the printer management scripts have been written for the command line. You can change the default scripting host to *cscript* by using the command **cscript //h:cscript**.

If you change the default scripting host, you can run the command-line tools without having to type *cscript* each time (however, you will then have to type *wscript* before any windows-based scripts you run). You might also like to set the option that suppresses the *cscript* logo. This prevents a couple of extra lines appearing in the output. Figure 7.11 shows the output of the *prnjobs* script with and without the logo and using the *cscript* command to suppress the appearance of the logo lines.

Figure 7.11 Using the //nologo Option with *cscript*

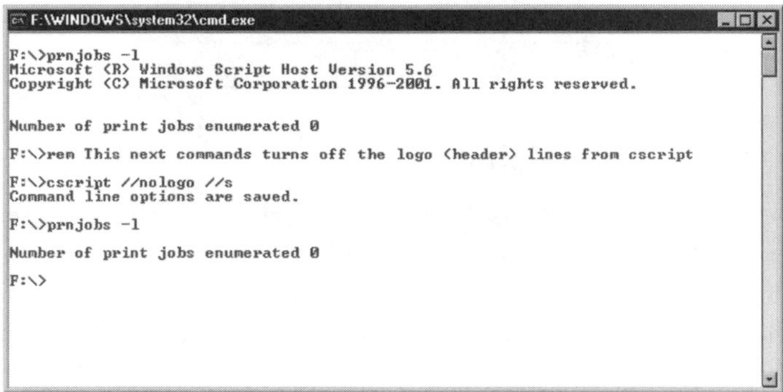

Most of the scripts can also be used to manage printers on a remote computer by using the *–s computername* option. If you want to use a script to connect to a remote computer, you might also need to use the *–u username* and *–w password* options to connect as a user who has administrative privileges on the remote computer.

Each script has many options, so use Windows Help or run the script with the */?* option to display additional help on each option.

Note that with all these scripts you must leave a space between the option and the argument. For example, you should enter **prnport –l –s computername** instead of **prnport –l –scomputerrname**.

The following list describes each of the new scripts:

- **prncnfg.vbs** Use *prncnfg* to display or change configuration information about a printer or rename a printer on a local or remote computer.
- **prndrvr.vbs** Use *prndrvr* to delete, add, or list the printer drivers installed on a local or remote computer.
- **prnjobs.vbs** Use *prnjobs* to manage print jobs. You can pause, resume, or cancel (delete) individual print jobs or list all the jobs in a print queue on a local or remote computer. Note that *prnjobs* is used to manage individual print jobs, not the whole queue. To manage a queue, use *prnqctl*.

- **prnmngr.vbs** Use *prnmngr* to add and delete printers, list printers, and to display or change the default printer. Some of the options for *prnmngr* work only on the local computer.
- **prnport.vbs** Use *prnport* to manage TCP/IP ports. You can display or change configuration information, create, delete, or list TCP/IP ports on a local or remote computer.
- **prnqctl.vbs** Use *prnqctl* to manage a printer queue. You can pause or resume printing of jobs in the queue, cancel all print jobs in the queue, or print a test page.

Table 7.4 shows the main options for each script. Note that you will need to include additional options over and above what is shown in Table 7.4 to specify the particular printer, driver, port, and so on that is to be affected. Table 7.5 shows the command to use for each of the common printer management tasks.

Table 7.4 Options for Printer Management Scripts

Script and Options	Use
prncnfg -g	Display configuration information for a printer.
prncnfg -t	Configure a printer.
prncnfg -x	Rename a printer.
prndrvr -l	List installed printer drivers.
prndrvr -a	Install a printer driver.
prndrvr -d	Delete a printer driver.
prnjobs -l	List print jobs.
prnjobs -z	Pause a print job.
prnjobs -m	Resume a print job.
prnjobs -x	Cancel a print job.
prnmngr -a	Add a printer.
prnmngr -d	Delete a printer.
prnmngr -l	List all the printers on a computer.
prnport -l	List TCP/IP ports.
prnport -g	Display configuration information for a TCP/IP port.
prnport -t	Change configuration information for a TCP/IP port.
prnport -a	Create a TCP/IP port.
prnport -d	Delete a TCP/IP port.
prnqctl -z	Pause the queue.
prnqctl -m	Resume printing of the queue.
prnqctl -x	Cancel all print jobs in the queue.
prnqctl -e	Print a test page.

Test Day Tip

Don't feel that you have to learn and memorize every single option for every single command. What you should do is learn what the commands can do and practice using them.

Table 7.5 Example of Commands for Printer Management Tasks

Task	Example of Command To Use
Create a printer	prnmngr –a –p printername –m drivername –r portname
Share a printer	prncnfg –t –p printername –h sharename +shared
Add a printer driver	prndrvr -a -m drivername -v versionnumber –e environment
Set permissions	Not available
Manage print queues	prnjobs or prnqctl
Create printer pools	Not available
Schedule printers	prncnfg –t –p printername –st starttime –ut endtime
Set printer priorities	prncnfg –i prioritynumber

The Printer Spooler Service

All printing is managed by the spooler service. If this service is not running, users cannot print. The spooler has a number of configuration options. To change these, open the **Printers and Faxes** folder and select **Server Properties** from the **File** pull-down menu. This opens the **Print Server Properties** dialog box containing four tabs: **Forms**, **Ports**, **Drivers**, and **Advanced**, which are used as follows:

- Use the **Forms** tab to define custom paper sizes.
- Use the **Ports** tab to define new ports (especially TCP/IP ports) and to configure properties of existing ports.
- Use the **Drivers** tab to add new drivers or configure existing drivers.
- Use the **Advanced** tab to modify the behavior of the spooler service.

In particular, note the **Spool Folder** under the **Advanced** tab. This location is where print jobs are stored until they are printed. On larger networks with many printers, the spool folder can get quite large.

Exam Warning

You need to know that the location of the spool folder can be changed. A common problem with printing in larger networks is that the spool folder gets so large that it fills up all available space on the disk drive. To get around this, move the spool folder to a different disk partition that has plenty of free space. Open the **Print Server Properties** dialog box, select the **Advanced** tab and type in a new location for the spool folder.

Exercise 7.04

Install and Configure a Printer for Shared Use

In this exercise, you will add an HP Laserjet 2200 printer and configure it for shared use using both the graphical tools and the command-line tools.

1. To create a printer using the graphical tools, click **Start | Settings | Printers and Faxes.**
2. Double-click **Add Printer** to start the wizard. The first page of the wizard gives you information about Plug and Play printers. Click **Next** to continue.
3. On the next page, ensure that **Local printer attached to this computer** is selected and clear the **Automatically detect and install my Plug and Play printer**. Click **Next**.
4. The next page asks you which printer port to use. Select **LPT2: (Printer Port)** as shown in Figure 7.12. Click **Next**.

Figure 7.12 Selecting a Printer Port

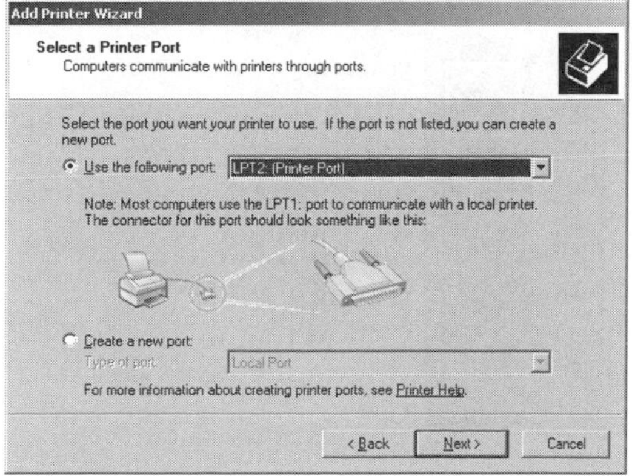

5. The **Install Printer Software** page appears, asking you to choose the driver for your printer. Choose **HP** in the **Manufacturer** list and **HP Laserjet 2200 Series PCL** in the **Printers** list. Click **Next**.
6. Enter **HPLaser** in the **Printer Name** box. Click **Next**.
7. Select **Share Name** and enter **HPLaser** in the box as shown in Figure 7.13. Click **Next**.

Figure 7.13 Sharing a Printer

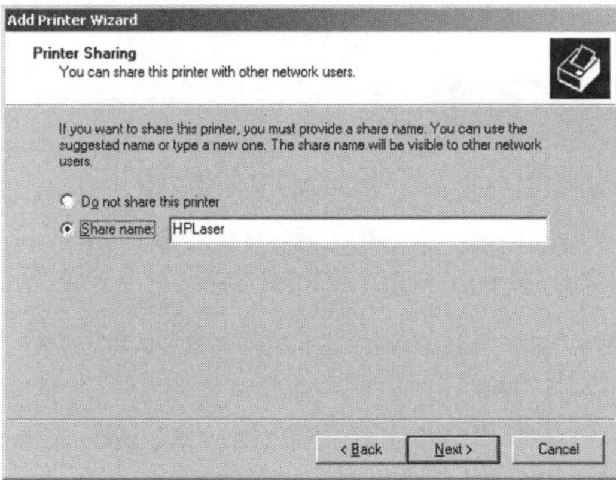

8. Enter appropriate descriptive information in the **Location** and **Comment** boxes. Click **Next**.
9. Select **No** on the **Print Test Page** page (unless you do have a printer attached). Click **Next** and review the settings that are to be used to create the printer as shown in Figure 7.14. Click **Finish** to create the printer, which should now be visible in the **Printers and Faxes** folder.

Figure 7.14 Completing the Add Printer Wizard

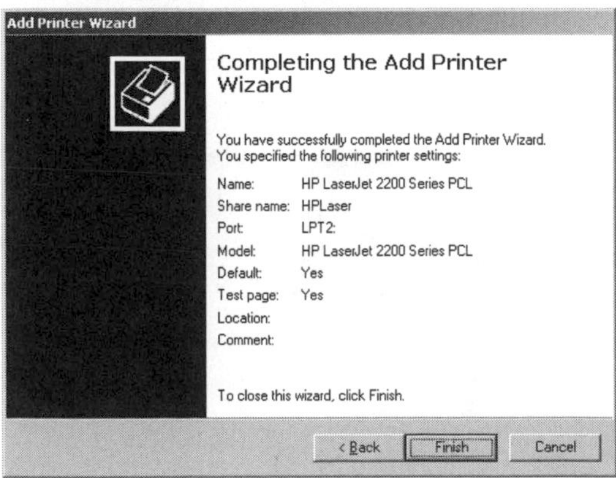

10. To create a printer using the command-line tools, click **Start | Run,** type **cmd** in the box, and then press **Enter**. This starts a command-line window.
11. Type **cscript //H:cscript //S** and press **Enter** to set the default script host to cscript.
12. Type **prnmngr –a –p HPLaserCmd –m "HP Laserjet 2200 Series PCL" –r LPT1:** and press **Enter**. This command adds a new printer called HPLaserCmd, which should appear in **Printers and Faxes**. You now need to share the printer.
13. Type **prncnfg –t –p HPLaserCmd –h HPLaserCmd +shared** and press **Enter**. This shares the printer.
14. To stop sharing the printer, type **prncnfg –t –p HPLaserCmd –shared**.

This exercise shows you how easy it is to add and share printers using the wizard but also how quick it can be to add printers (especially if there are many) using the command-line commands.

The Internet Printing Protocol

Windows Server 2003 enables users to print to printers over the Internet or an intranet. Users have to know the URL for the printer so that they can connect to it via their Web browsers. For servers running Windows 2000 Server or Windows Server 2003, the URL http://server/printers shows the printers available on the server. At this URL, users can connect to a printer, review the queue, and manage printers and jobs for which they have permissions. Figure 7.15 shows an example of viewing a queue using a Web page. Internet Printing requires Internet Information Services (IIS) to be running on the server. Internet Printing is installed by default on Windows 2000, but on Windows Server 2003 it has to be specifically installed, as does IIS (which is also not installed by default).

Figure 7.15 Viewing a Printer Queue using a Web Page

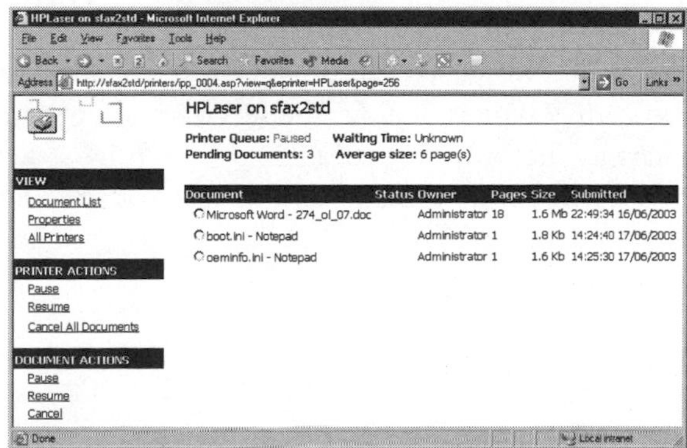

Managing and Troubleshooting Services

Services are system programs that run in the background regardless of whether anyone is logged on. Depending on the configuration of your server, eighty or so services might be running.

As an administrator, you need to check that services are running, perhaps restart them, and occasionally modify the configuration of a service.

Service Configuration

In this section, we examine the configuration and characteristics of services. Later in the chapter, we'll see how to modify the way a service works.

Service Name

Every service has a name and a display name. The display name is used in the graphical interface and the service name is used in the registry. The full configuration of a service is stored in the registry under the HKEY_LOCAL_MACHINE\System\CurrentControlSet\Services key.

Service States

A service can be in one of three states: started, stopped, or paused. The difference between stopped and paused is that in the paused state, the service continues to run but no new connections to the service are allowed. Not all services can be paused. You might see that a service is starting or stopping, but this should be only for a few seconds.

Service Startup Type

The service startup type controls when the service starts. There are three startup types:

- automatic
- manual
- disabled

If the startup type is *automatic*, the service starts when the operating system boots up. For a *manual* startup type, the service won't start automatically, but if another service needs to start it, it will be started. If the startup type is *disabled*, the service will not start automatically and another service cannot start it. The only way to start such a service is for the administrator to change the startup type to manual or automatic, and then to start the service.

Test Day Tip

The problem of services not starting is a common issue. Make sure that you fully understand the difference between the service startup types, especially manual and disabled.

Service Logon

Every service has to run in the context of an account. You can choose any user account for a service but most services run as **Local System**. This is a built-in account that is part of the operating system and has full access to everything on the local computer. The local system account does not have access to network resources unless it is on a domain controller. Using a dedicated service account from the domain works best for some network applications, such as Exchange and SQL Server. If you use a domain account for a service, you must make sure that you enter the correct password for that account. Otherwise, the service won't start.

There are also the **Local Service** and **Network Service** accounts. The local service account is a built-in account that has the same level of access as local users; this limits what a service running as local service can do. The local service account accesses network resources using no credentials; this restricts what it can access over the network. The network service account is a built-in account that is similar to the local service account in that it has the same level of access as local users but it accesses network resources using credentials of the local computer account.

Exam Warning

Passwords for domain accounts usually expire. If you use a domain account for a service, make sure that the password for that account is set not to expire. If the password for the account for your service expires, the next time you start the service (perhaps by rebooting the server), the service will fail to start because it won't be able to log on with the expired password.

Service Recovery

Windows Server 2003 enables you to specify actions to take if a service fails. The actions include the following:

- Restart the service.
- Restart the computer.
- Run a program.

You can specify different actions for the first, second, and subsequent failures. So, for example, the first action might be to take no action, on the second failure to restart the service, and on the next failure to restart the computer.

Dependencies

Some services need other services to be running before they can run—this is called a *dependency*. The operating system uses dependencies in deciding the order in which to start services. For example, the Netlogon service depends on the Workstation service. This means that if the Workstation service fails to start, the Netlogon service won't start either. Sometimes, you might see many error messages in Event Viewer that, on investigation, are caused by the failure of a single service.

Service Permissions

Permissions specify what users or groups can do regarding a service. The permissions include starting, stopping, pausing, and resuming a service, deleting a service, changing the permissions, and changing its configuration (e.g., startup type). Use Security Configuration and Analysis to configure service permissions.

Using the Graphical Interface

Most of the time, you will use the graphical interface for managing services. You can start it in a number of ways:

- Select **Start** | **Programs** | **Administrative Tools** | **Computer Management**. In the Computer Management window, expand **Services and Applications**, and then click **Services**.
- Create a custom Microsoft Management Console that contains the Services snap-in. (Refer to Exercise 7.1 earlier in this chapter.)
- Select **Start** | **Programs** | **Administrative Tools** | **Services**.

Exercise 7.05

Manage Services Using Control Panel

In this exercise, you will review the configuration of the Telnet service and see how its configuration can be changed.

1. Select **Start** | **Programs** | **Administrative Tools** | **Services**.
2. Maximize the window that appears and note the list of services in the right-hand pane. On the tabs at the bottom there is an Extended and Standard view. Ensure that the Extended view is selected. Scroll through the list of services and click **Telnet**.

3. Note the description that appears to the left. This is the same as the description under the **Description** column.
4. Note the **Startup Type** is **Disabled** and the **Log On As** is **Local Service**.
5. Double-click **Telnet**. This brings up the **Properties** dialog box. Note the four tabs: **General, Log On, Recovery**, and **Dependencies**.
6. On the **General** tab, review the **Service name** (as stored in the registry), the **Display name**, and the **Path to executable**. This provides the location of the Telnet server executable.
7. Note that the service is stopped and the startup type is disabled.
8. Click the pull-down arrow in the **Startup Type** box, select **Manual**, and then click **Apply**. The **Start** button becomes active and you can supply start parameters that will be passed to the Telnet program.
9. Click the **Start** button and note that the service status becomes **Started** and that the **Stop** and **Pause** buttons become active. Figure 7.16 shows how the **General** tab should look.

Figure 7.16 Properties for the Telnet Service

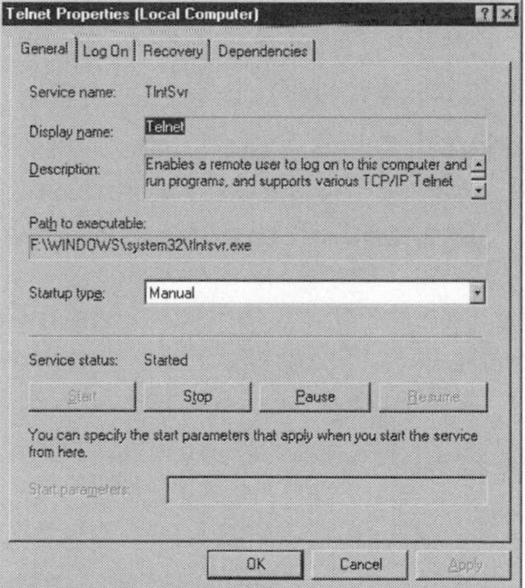

10. Click the **Log On** tab. Note the account that is being used, NT AUTHORITY\Local Service, which gives the Telnet service some access to the local computer. If you want or need to use another account, such as a domain account, click **Browse** and search for the relevant account or just type it in. Make sure that you enter the correct password for the account that you choose.

11. Click the **Recovery** tab. Note the failure boxes where you can specify what action to take when the service fails. Click the pull-down arrow to see the possible actions.
12. If you select **Run a program**, the bottom part of the dialog box is made active where you can specify the program to run.
13. If you select **Restart the Service**, the **Restart service after** box becomes enabled where you can specify how many minutes to wait before trying to restart the service following a failure.
14. If you select **Restart the Computer**, the **Restart Computer Options** box becomes enabled where you can specify how many minutes to wait before restarting the computer and whether to send a message to network computers.
15. In the **Reset fail count after** box, you can specify the number of days after which the number of times a failure has occurred should be reset to 0.
16. Click the **Dependencies** tab. In the top half of the dialog box is a list of services that Telnet requires to be running before it can start. In the bottom half is a list of services that depend on Telnet (there should be none).
17. Click **OK** to close the **Properties** dialog box.
18. Note that the description of the Telnet service now includes links for managing the state of the service, as shown in Figure 7.17.You can also use the Stop, Pause, and Start buttons on the toolbar.

Figure 7.17 Links for Managing the State of the Telnet Service

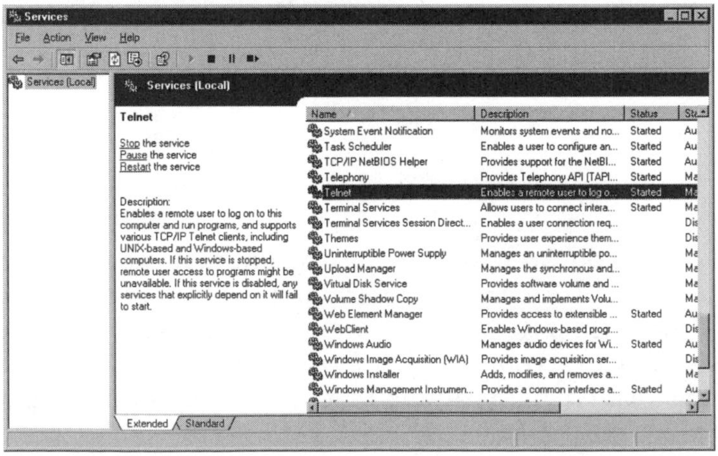

Using New Command-Line Utilities

In addition to the graphical interface, Windows Server 2003 has a number of command-line-based programs to manage and troubleshoot services and perform a few other server tasks. These are executable programs rather than scripts, so they do not need to be run with the *cscript* command. In the following sections, we examine each program.

sc.exe

The sc.exe program communicates with the Service controller and has twenty-four different options. We won't examine them all here, but you can refer to the online help for more information. In general, **sc** is used to configure services and manage their status, name, and permissions. For example, **sc stop <servicename>** is used to stop a service but *<servicename>* must be the name as stored in the registry and not the display name. Use **sc getkeyname** to determine the registry name of the service. Figure 7.18 shows how to find the registry name for the Telnet service, how to check the service's current status, and how to stop the Telnet service.

Figure 7.18 Stopping the Telnet Service Using sc

```
F:\WINDOWS\system32\cmd.exe

F:\>sc getkeyname telnet
[SC] GetServiceKeyName SUCCESS
Name = TlntSvr

F:\>sc query tlntsvr

SERVICE_NAME: tlntsvr
        TYPE               : 10  WIN32_OWN_PROCESS
        STATE              : 4  RUNNING
                                (STOPPABLE, PAUSABLE, ACCEPTS_SHUTDOWN)
        WIN32_EXIT_CODE    : 0  (0x0)
        SERVICE_EXIT_CODE  : 0  (0x0)
        CHECKPOINT         : 0x0
        WAIT_HINT          : 0x0

F:\>sc stop tlntsvr

SERVICE_NAME: tlntsvr
        TYPE               : 10  WIN32_OWN_PROCESS
        STATE              : 3  STOP_PENDING
                                (STOPPABLE, PAUSABLE, ACCEPTS_SHUTDOWN)
        WIN32_EXIT_CODE    : 0  (0x0)
        SERVICE_EXIT_CODE  : 0  (0x0)
        CHECKPOINT         : 0x0
        WAIT_HINT          : 0x0

F:\>_
```

schtasks.exe

You use schtasks.exe to set programs to run at scheduled intervals, delete or change existing scheduled tasks, and stop or run a scheduled task immediately. Table 7.6 lists the six options for *schtasks*. *schtasks* doesn't provide as much control over scheduled tasks as using the graphical interface.

NOTE

To manage scheduled tasks graphically, select **Start | Settings | Control Panel** and click the **Scheduled Tasks** folder. This opens a new window showing the scheduled tasks and an **Add Scheduled Task** icon that starts a wizard for adding new tasks.

Table 7.6 Options for the schtasks Command

Schtasks option	Use
schtasks create	Create a new scheduled task.
schtasks change	Change the properties of a scheduled task but not the actual schedule.
schtasks run	Run a scheduled task immediately.
schtasks end	Stop a scheduled task that is currently running.
schtasks delete	Delete a scheduled task.
schtasks query	List all the scheduled tasks on the local or a remote computer.

setx.exe

You use setx.exe to configure environment variables for either the user (the variables apply only to a specific user) or the system environment (variables apply to all users). You can set variables explicitly by specifying their value or using the value of a registry key or the contents of a file. *setx* is the only way to permanently (i.e., remembered between reboots) set a variable name via the command line.

NOTE

You can also set variable names graphically via **Start | Control Panel | System**. Click the **Advanced** tab and then **Environment Variables**. Create variables for the user in the top half and for the system in the bottom half of the window.

shutdown.exe

Use the shutdown.exe command to shut down or restart local or remote computers. You can also use it for shutting down several computers at once using the */i* option. With this option, a new window appears where you add the names of the computers that you want to shut down or restart. Figure 7.19 shows the dialog box for the */i* option.

Figure 7.19 The Remote Shutdown Dialog Box

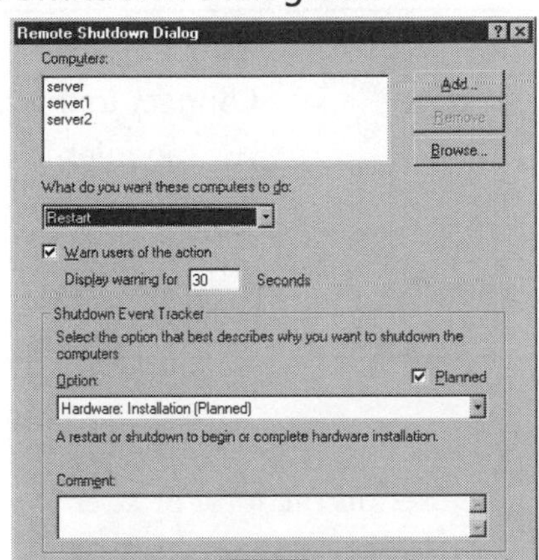

tasklist.exe

tasklist.exe shows all the tasks that are running on the local or remote computer. *tasklist* is a really useful command given its many options as shown in Table 7.7.

- The */S* option connects to a remote computer. You might also have to specify the */U* option to connect as a particular user and the */P* option to specify the password for that user.
- The */M* option lists all the DLL modules that a process has loaded. However, you can also use this option to list all the processes that have loaded a particular module by specifying **/M module name**. For example, to list all processes that have loaded the user32.dll module, use **tasklist /M user32.dll**.
- The */FI* option is particularly useful for restricting the output to list only the tasks that are of interest. This option is used with a variety of filters, which can, for example, be used to display tasks with a particular name, process number, or processes that have used more than a certain amount of CPU time. As an example, to list all processes that start with *H*, use the command **tasklist /FI "IMAGENAME eq H*"**.
- The */FO* option controls how the output is displayed. There are three formats: Table, List, or CSV.
- The */V* option adds information to the output.

Table 7.7 Some of the Options for the tasklist Command

tasklist Option	Use
/S	Connect to a remote computer (system).
/M	List modules loaded by processes.
/FI filter	Display only processes that match the filter.
/FO format	Specify how the output is displayed.
/V	Display verbose information.

taskkill.exe

Use taskkill.exe to terminate processes on the local or a remote computer. You need to use *tasklist* first to identify the process that needs to be terminated. *Taskkill* has many options and if used without care you could end up ending more processes than you expected.

- The */S* option connects to a remote computer. You might also have to specify the */U* option to connect as a particular user and the */P* option to specify the password for that user.
- The */F* option forcefully terminates a process. Without the */F* option a process might not actually terminate, particularly if it raises a dialog box asking whether changes should be saved. The */F* option overrides this but there is a risk of losing the user's work.
- Use the */FI* option with extreme care, because it can terminate all processes that match a given filter. For example **taskkill /FI "IMAGENAME eq H*"** terminates all processes that start with H.
- The */PID* option terminates a process with a specific process number.
- The */T* option terminates a process and all child processes that it started.
- The */IM* option is functionally the same as */FI* with *IMAGENAME* in that it terminates processes with a specific name or names. You can use wildcards to specify the process names.

Table 7.8 Some of the Options for the taskkill Command

taskkill Option	Use
/S	Connect to a remote computer (system).
/F	Forcefully terminate a process.
/FI filter	Terminate processes that match the filter. **Use with care!**
/PID process id	Terminate the process with this ID.

Continued

Table 7.8 Some of the Options for the taskkill Command

taskkill Option	Use
/T	Terminate a process and all its child processes.
/IM process name	Terminate all processes that match the given image name.

Try Exercise 7.06 to get used to how to use *tasklist* and *taskkill*.

Exercise 7.06

Use tasklist and taskkill

In this exercise, you will start Notepad and then use *tasklist* to identify the process ID for Notepad. You will then use *taskkill* to end the process.

1. Start Notepad and enter any text into the new document.
2. Start a command prompt by clicking **Start | Run**, typing **cmd** in the **Open** box, and then pressing **Enter**.
3. An the command prompt, type **tasklist**. You should see a list of processes running on your computer, including Notepad. Note the image name is listed as **notepad.exe**.
4. Type **tasklist /fi "IMAGENAME eq notepad.exe"**. These options tell *tasklist* to list only processes whose image name is **notepad.exe**. You should get a list with just one entry for **notepad.exe**.
5. Make a note of the process ID (PID).
6. Type **taskkill /pid <processid>** where *processid* is the number you noted in Step 5. Note the warning box that appears in the Notepad window asking if you want to save changes. Click **No**. Terminating a process in this case is the same as using **File | Exit** in Notepad.

Using Wizards to Configure and Manage Your Server

A lot of effort has been made in Windows Server 2003 to make administrative tasks easy for the administrator through the use of wizards. A key wizard is the **Configure Your Server Wizard**, which, in conjunction with the **Manage Your Server** tool, guides an administrator through the most common administrative tasks.

Using the Configure Your Server and Manage Your Server Wizards

Windows Server 2003 introduces the concept of server roles, which brings related administrative tasks together for management purposes. These roles include the following:

- File server
- Print server
- Application server
- Mail server
- Terminal server
- Remote Access/VPN server
- Domain Controller (Active Directory)
- DNS server
- DHCP server
- Streaming media server
- WINS server

We'll examine each of these roles later in this section. Figure 7.20 shows the server role page of the **Configure Your Server Wizard**. This page shows whether a role has been configured.

You must install server roles using the **Configure Your Server Wizard** before you can manage them using **Manage Your Server**. In the rest of this section we'll look at each of the roles in more detail. The **Configure Your Server Wizard** and **Manage Your Server** can be found in **Start | Programs | Administrative Tools**.

Note that the use of server roles is completely optional and there is no reason you can't perform server administrative tasks without setting up server roles.

Figures 7.22, 7.23, 7.24, and 7.25 show Manage Your Server with all the server roles added.

To remove a role, run the **Configure Your Server Wizard**. Highlight the role and follow the instructions in the wizard. Removing a role usually stops everything associated with the role. For example, if you install the file server role, share several folders and then remove the file server role, sharing will also be removed from all folders.

Figure 7.20 Server Roles

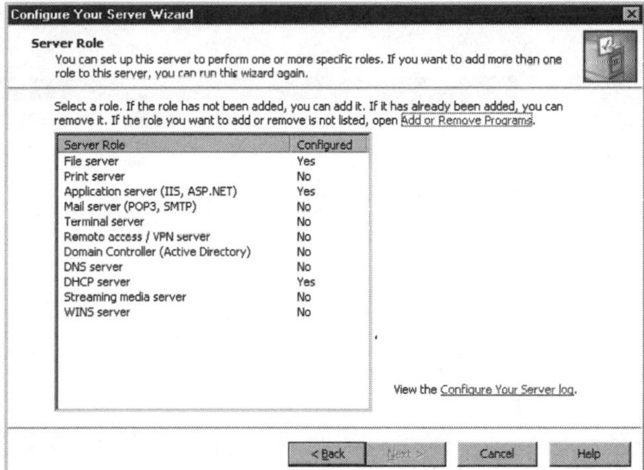

EXAM WARNING

Server roles are a new concept in Windows Server 2003. Even though you might not use the Configure Your Server wizard to implement them, make sure that you are familiar with the different roles. Practice installing and configuring them.

File Server Role

Use the file server role to configure disk quotas for users, run the indexing service to make searching for files faster, share folders using the **Share a Folder Wizard**, and install the **File Server Management** MMC. A quirk of installing the file server role is that you must complete the **Share a Folder Wizard**; otherwise, the installation of the role doesn't complete. The **File Server Management** MMC is similar to the **Computer Management** MMC, but it is more task-oriented, as Figure 7.21 shows.

After it is installed, the role shows up in **Manage Your Server** where there are links to the **File Server Management** MMC and the **Share a Folder Wizard**.

Print Server Role

Installing the print server role guides you through the **Add Printer Wizard** to create printers. It also asks whether you want to include printer drivers for operating systems earlier than Windows 2000.

After you have installed the print server role, there are links to the **Printers & Faxes** folder, the **Add a Printer Wizard** and the **Add a Printer Driver Wizard** in **Manage Your Server**.

Figure 7.21 The File Server Management MMC

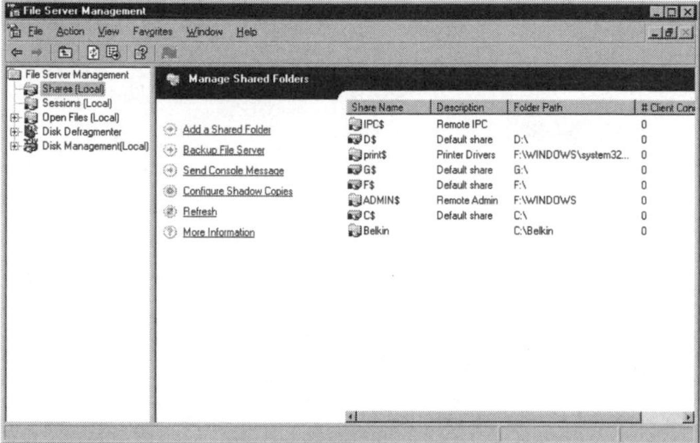

Figure 7.22 The File and Print Server Roles in Manage Your Server

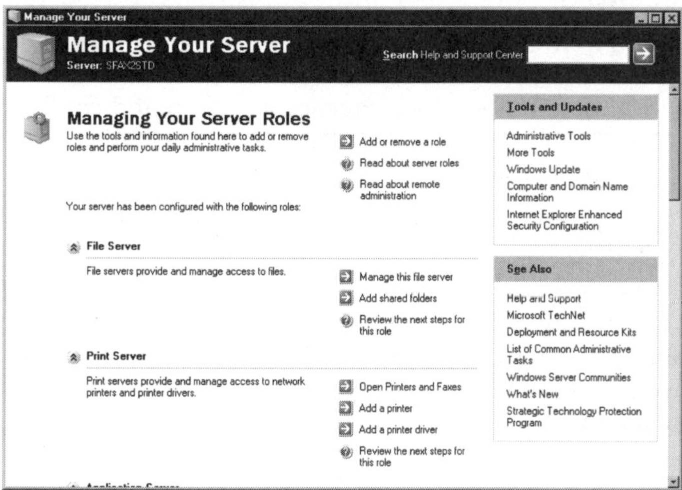

Application Server (IIS, ASP.NET) Role

Use the application server role to install Internet Information Services (Microsoft's Web server software) on the server. You can optionally install Front Page Server extensions (used by end-users to publish Web pages) and ASP.NET (Web-based programming framework) when adding this role. COM+ and DTC are installed automatically. You need access to the Windows installation files (which might be on CD or on the network) to install this role.

After it is installed, just one task in **Manage Your Server** includes a link to the **Application Server** MMC.

Mail Server (POP3/SMTP) Role

The mail server role adds the capability to receive mail using POP3 or SMTP. You specify how users are authenticated and which e-mail domain name the server is to receive mail for. Access to the Windows installation CD or installation files is required to complete installation of the role.

In **Manage Your Server**, installing the mail server role creates a link to the **POP3 Service** MMC.

NOTE

The mail server role provides only a basic mail service for collecting mail using SMTP, and mailboxes for users using the POP3 service on a single server. It effectively just moves mail around rather than providing centalized storage and management. For a more featured enterprise mail server that includes centralized storage of mail, distribution lists, and scalability, consider using a product like Microsoft Exchange.

Terminal Server Role

Installing this role configures the server as a Terminal Server. This refers to what was called an "Application mode" Terminal Server in Windows 2000, which enables multiple users to run Terminal Sessions and run multi-user applications. It is *not* necessary to install this role in order to remotely administer the server via Terminal Services (Remote Desktop for Administration).

No questions are asked during installation of the Terminal Server role, and the server is rebooted after installation completes. After the server has restarted, a dialog box appears to say that the server is now a Terminal Server and that a licensing server must be added to the network within 120 days. Access to the Windows installation files is required to complete installation of the role.

The tasks in **Manage Your Server** include the **Terminal Services Manager** for managing sessions and **Terminal Services Configuration**.

Remote Access/VPN Server Role

Adding this role runs the **Routing and Remote Access Server Setup Wizard**. This wizard enables you to choose from a number of common remote access configurations, as shown in Table 7.9.

Figure 7.23 The Application, Mail, and Terminal Server Roles in Manage Your Server

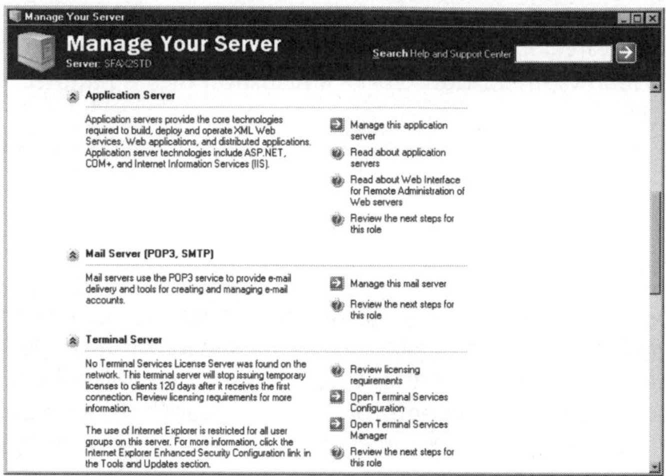

Table 7.9 Remote Access Configurations Available During the Setup Wizard

Remote Access Configuration	Use
Remote access (dial-up or VPN)	Enables remote clients to connect to the server using a dial-up connection or a VPN connection over the Internet
Network Adddress Translation (NAT)	Enables computers on the internal network to connect to the Internet using a single public IP address
VPN and NAT	Enable remote clients to connect using VPN and internal computers to connect to the Internet using a single public IP address
Secure connection between two private networks	Enables connection to a remote network (e.g. a branch office)
Custom Configuration	Enables manual configuration of Routing and Remote Access

After the role is installed, a link to the **Routing and Remote Access** MMC appears in **Manage Your Server**.

Domain Controller (Active Directory)

The domain controller role takes you through the **Active Directory Installation Wizard** to make the server a domain controller in an existing or new domain. Selecting this role has the same effect as running **dcpromo** at the command-line. During Active Directory installation, you are able to choose from four different domain controller roles.

The tasks in **Manage Your Server** for this role include links to **Active Directory Users and Computers**, **Active Directory Domains and Trusts**, and **Active Directory Sites and Services**.

DNS Server Role

Installing the DNS server role configures the server as a DNS server and runs the **Configure a DNS Server Wizard**. After installing this role there is a link to the **DNS** MMC in **Manage Your Server**.

Figure 7.24 The Remote Access, Domain Controller, and DNS Server Roles in Manage Your Server

DHCP Server Role

Adding the DHCP server role configures the server as a DHCP server, enabling it to provide IP addresses to DHCP clients. After installing this role there is a link to the **DHCP MMC** in **Manage Your Server**.

Streaming Media Server Role

Configuring the streaming media server role adds Windows Media Services to the server, enabling it to deliver audio and video presentations to client computers. After adding this role there is a link to the **Windows Media Services MMC** in **Manage Your Server**.

WINS Server Role

Installing the WINS server role installs WINS server, enabling the server to service requests for NetBIOS name to IP lookups. Just one task is added to Manage Your Server—a link to the **WINS MMC**.

Figure 7.25 The DHCP, Streaming Media, and WINS Server Roles in Manage Your Server

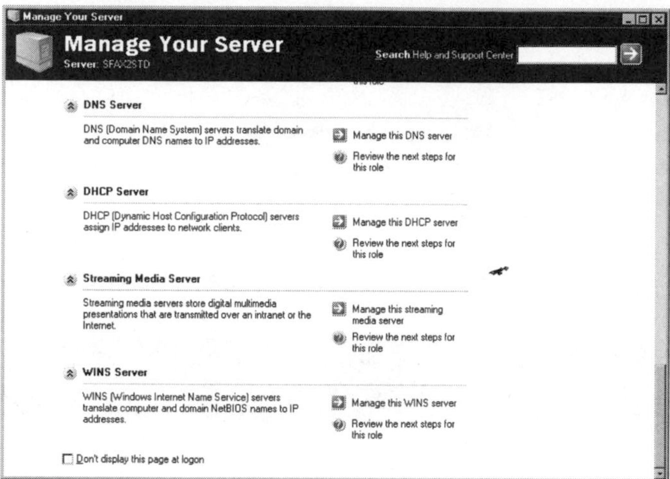

EXERCISE 7.07

INSTALL THE FILE SERVER ROLE

In this exercise, you will use Configure Your Server to add the file server role, set up disk quotas and share a folder, and then use File Management to check that the folder has been shared.

1. To start **Configure Your Server**, click **Start | Programs | Administrative Tools | Configure Your Server**.
2. In the first page of the **Configure Your Server Wizard**, click **Next** to continue.
3. Read through the next page and then click **Next** to continue.
4. On the server role page, highlight **File Server** in the list of roles and then click **Next**.
5. The **File Server Disk Quotas** page appears. Here you can choose to restrict the amount of disk space users are allowed on NTFS volumes on the server. Click **Next** to continue.
6. The **File Server Indexing Service** page appears, enabling you to choose whether to run the Indexing Service. Ensure that **No, leaving Indexing service turned off** is selected and then click **Next**.
7. Read through the **Summary of Selections** page and then click **Next**.
8. The **Share a Folder Wizard** starts. You must share a folder, otherwise the file server role will not be installed. Click **Next**.

9. On the **Folder Path** page, enter or browse to any folder that exists on your server and click **Next**.
10. On the **Name, Description and Settings** page, review the options and enter any description for the share, and then click **Next**.
11. On the **Permissions** page, ensure that **All users have read-only access** is selected and click **Next**.
12. On the **Sharing was Successful** page, click **Close**.
13. On the **This Server Is Now a File Server** page, click **Finish**.
14. The file server role has now been installed and **Manage Your Server** appears, enabling you to further configure the file server role. Click **Manage this file server**.
15. The **File Server Management** MMC appears. Highlight **Shares (Local)** in the left-hand pane and check that the folder you shared in Step 9 appears in the list of shares in the right-hand pane.
16. Highlight the share created in Step 9 and notice that additional tasks appear in the pane.

Summary of Exam Objectives

Windows Server 2003 provides a wide range of management tools. Some are graphical and others are command-line based and you should know where to find each of them. There are also many wizards to help less experienced administrators through particular tasks.

Many of the graphical tools are built using the MMC and snap-ins. You can use snap-ins to configure your own customized administrative tools. It is important to realize that most tools (graphical and command-line) work over the network so that you can manage remote servers from your computer.

When you need to manage a server remotely, you can choose from a variety of tools, including a browser (for remote administration), Remote Desktop connection (using Terminal Services), snap-ins for the MMC, and the Administration Tools Pack. Some tasks, such as adding a user, can be carried out using any of the remote administration tools, whereas others require you to use a specific tool.

End-users can use Remote Assistance to allow others access to their desktop to guide them through resolving a problem or show them how to do something.

Sometimes you won't be able to connect to a server over the network at all, or it might have crashed completely. If the server is physically distant from you, consider using Emergency Management Services. Provided that you have the appropriate hardware, you can establish access to the server even when the operating system is not running. Even with a server with no special hardware, you can still use EMS via the serial port to remotely manage the server using the Special Administration Console, but this will work only while the operating system is running.

Managing printers and printer queues is an important task that probably requires attention every day. You must ensure that printers are created and available to users as required.

Many of the routine tasks involve deleting print jobs or making them print more quickly. You need to plan and implement security requirements so that certain printers can be restricted to certain people. You might have computers with a variety of desktop operating systems, so you need to ensure that printer drivers for these operating systems are installed on the print servers.

Many new command-line scripts have been introduced for managing printers; you might be able to incorporate these into printer-management batch files if you have a large number of printers to manage. Services are system programs that always run on a computer. You need to check the state of services if a particular part of the operating system fails. A service can be stopped, started, or paused, and an administrator can change the state of a service using graphical tools or command-line tools.

All services authenticate to the computer using a logon account, which can be any local or domain account. Three special accounts give varying degrees of access to the local computer and the network: local system, local service, and network service.

Several new command-line utilities are available for managing services, scheduling tasks, setting variables, shutting down a computer, and managing processes.

Wizards play an increasing part in Windows operating systems as Microsoft endeavors to make life easier for administrators. Configure Your Server and Manage Your Server together cover almost all administrative tasks that an administrator is likely to encounter on a day-to-day basis. The key concept behind these wizards is the idea of server roles, which you add using Configure Your Server and then manage using Manage Your Server. Although these wizards can make administration simpler, their use is not mandatory.

Because server management is the crux of a network administrator's job, this chapter provides information that is not only necessary to mastering the exam objectives, but will also be invaluable as you go about your day-to-day duties.

Exam Objectives Fast Track

Recognizing Types of Management Tools

- ☑ Windows Server 2003 provides administrators with a variety of management tools including wizards, graphical administration tools, and command-line utilities.
- ☑ Most graphical administration tools can be found as pre-configured management consoles, accessible via **Start | Programs | Administrative Tools**.
- ☑ Many graphical management tools are built using the Microsoft Management Console and snap-ins.
- ☑ You can create your own customized management tools by using snap-ins provided by the operating system or third-party products.

Managing Your Server Remotely

- ☑ End-users can use Remote Assistance to invite another person to view or take control of their desktops.
- ☑ The Web Interface for Remote Administration enables you to manage a server from anywhere in the world using a Web browser. However, the range of administration tasks is limited.
- ☑ Remote Desktop for Administration enables you to connect to a Windows 2000 Server or a Windows Server 2003 desktop via Terminal Services, and act as if you were at the server. This enables you to perform any task on the server.
- ☑ You can install the Administration Tools Pack on a Windows XP computer to enable you to remotely manage servers.
- ☑ Windows Management Instrumentation (WMI) provides a programming interface for developers to design management tools.

- ☑ Computer Management (a pre-configured MMC) and other MMC snap-ins provide local and remote management capability.

Using Emergency Management Services

- ☑ Emergency Management Services (EMS) provides a means for managing a server even when network connectivity has failed.
- ☑ To manage a server even when the operating system is not running, special hardware is required.
- ☑ Emergency Management Services provides a Special Administration Console (SAC) that runs on the serial port and enables remote access via a serial cable or modem. The SAC runs when the operating system is running.
- ☑ EMS must be installed before it can be used.

Managing Printers and Print Queues

- ☑ The Printers and Faxes folder is the primary starting point for managing printers and queues using the graphical tools.
- ☑ You must share printers for users on other computers to be able to access them and you might have to install drivers for earlier operating systems on the print server.
- ☑ Access to printer queues can be restricted by using permissions and scheduling availability.
- ☑ Printer priorities are used to alter the order in which print jobs are printed.
- ☑ The Spooler service manages all printing and might have to be restarted in case of problems.
- ☑ You can use command-line tools to carry out nearly all printer management tasks; they are particularly useful when dealing with a large number of printers.

Managing and Troubleshooting Services

- ☑ Services run in the background all the time, even if no one is logged on.
- ☑ All services have a registry and display name.
- ☑ The startup type of a service controls whether the service starts automatically, manually, or not at all (disabled).
- ☑ All services must log on and can use a local or domain account.

- ☑ Some services depend on other services (dependencies) that need to be running before they can start.
- ☑ You can configure actions to take if a service fails, such as restarting the service or even the server.
- ☑ Services can be managed using a graphical interface at **Start | Programs | Administrative Tools | Services**.
- ☑ To manage services from the command line, use sc.exe.
- ☑ Use *tasklist* and *taskkill* to list running processes and to terminate processes.
- ☑ Scheduled tasks can be created and managed graphically or using *schtasks*.

Using Wizards to Configure and Manage Your Server

- ☑ Server roles are installed and removed using **Configure Your Server**.
- ☑ Server roles are managed using **Manage Your Server**.
- ☑ **Manage Your Server** is a "launch-pad" to other administrative tools, such as MMCs or wizards grouped by server roles.
- ☑ The use of server roles is optional; you can manage your server without using them.

Exam Objectives Frequently Asked Questions

The following Frequently Asked Questions, answered by the authors of this book, are designed to both measure your understanding of the Exam Objectives presented in this chapter, and to assist you with real-life implementation of these concepts. You will also gain access to thousands of other FAQs at ITFAQnet.com.

Q: What type of administrative tools does Windows Server 2003 provide?

A: You can work with graphical tools, command-line utilities, or wizards.

Q: Can I create my own administrative tool, like **Computer Management,** that only shows the tools that I use?

A: Yes. From the **Run** command, enter **mmc**. This starts a blank Microsoft Management Console where can you add your favorite administration tools.

Q: Which type of remote management tool would be most appropriate if you needed to manage your server from a customer's office?

A: The Web Interface for Remote Administration is generally best, assuming that your customer has Internet access.

Q: What management feature can users use to request help from someone else?

A: Computers running Windows XP or later include the Remote Assistance feature. This enables a user to send an invitation to another person to remotely view or take control of the user's desktop and provide assistance. Remote Assistance is enabled by default, but you can turn it off via the **Control Panel | System | Remote** tab.

Q: Can you manage Windows Server 2003 computers from your desktop computer?

A: Yes, there are several methods: Remote Desktop, Web Interface, Administration Tools Pack, and MMCs.

Q: What does Emergency Management Services provide?

A: The capability to manage a server, even when there is no network connectivity and sometimes even when the operating system has crashed (if you have the proper server hardware).

Q: What is the name of the management tool that EMS provides over the serial port?

A: SAC, the Special Administration Console. This enables you to run command-line programs in a terminal emulator.

Q: What is out-of-band management?

A: Out-of-band management refers to using a different set of tools from the standard ones; including tools that don't run over the network.

Q: I have a mixture of operating systems on my client computers. Can I make my network printer available to all of them without having to install drivers on each client computer?

A: Yes. Configure the printer on a print server, share it, and then use the **Additional drivers** option to install drivers on the server for the operating systems used on your network. The correct drivers are downloaded to the client systems when the clients first attempt to use the printer.

Q: Why would you change the priority of a print job?

A: The priority of a print job affects when it is printed in relation to other jobs in the queue. The job with the highest priority prints first after the current job has finished. Increasing the priority of a print job makes it print sooner, and decreasing it makes it print later. Priorities can be set from 1 to 99.

Q: I need to create fifteen printers on my server; what is the most efficient way to do this?

A: Write a batch file that uses the **prnmngr** command-line tool to create each printer (there will be fifteen lines) and then run the batch file. Creating and running the batch file should be quicker then adding fifteen printers using the graphical tool. You can also use the batch file again should the need arise.

Q: Is it possible to stop some users from printing to certain printers?

A: Yes; you can change the permissions on the printer to exclude the users.

Q: What are services?

A: Services are system programs that run in the background regardless of whether anyone is logged on.

Q: If a service fails do I have to reboot the computer?

A: Probably not. Normally, just restarting the service is sufficient, but occasionally the operating system gets into such a muddle that only a reboot will work.

Q: Why do services have to log on?

A: All activity on a computer has to run in the context of an account, whether it is a logged-on user or system task. The same applies to services. For convenience, most services using the Local System account, although you can choose any account you like.

Q: How do I configure a role after it has been installed?

A: Use the **Manage Your Server** tool. This contains links to the common tasks for each role and links for further reading in Help and Support.

Self Test

A Quick Answer Key follows the Self Test questions. For complete questions, answers, and explanations to the Self Test questions in this chapter as well as the other chapters in this book, see the Self Test Appendix.

Recognizing Types of Management Tools

1. You are logged on to the server using an ordinary user account (i.e., without administrator privileges). You need to add several new printers on the server and you decided to use the *prncnfg* command-line utility. How do you do this without logging off?

   A. Select **Start | Run**, and then type **runas /user:administrator cmd**. In the command window run the prncnfg command.

   B. Select **Start | Programs | Administrative Tools | Prncnfg**, and then right-click and select **Run as**.

   C. Select **Start | Settings | Command**. In the command window type **runas /user:administrator cmd** and run the prncnfg command in the new command window that appears.

   D. Select **Start | Run** and then type **cmd**. In the command window run the *prncnfg* command.

2. One of your users is having problems getting a productivity application to work correctly. You suspect that he is performing the steps involved in using the application incorrectly, but the application interface is complex and it's difficult for you to explain over the phone what he needs to do. The user is running Windows XP, and you want to connect to his PC and show him how to perform the task in question so that he can actually see you go through the steps. How would you arrange to do this?

   A. Send the user a Remote Assistance Request.

   B. Get the user to send a Remote Assistance Invitation.

   C. Connect to the user's PC using Remote Desktop.

   D. Connect to the user's PC using the Web Interface for Remote Administration.

3. You are at a branch office of your company assisting a user on her PC. While assisting the user, you receive a call that requires you to alter a DNS setting on the server back at the main office. The user has many applications open and you would prefer to not have to log her out if at all possible. What would be the best way to connect to the server?

   A. Install the Windows Administration Tool Pack on the user's PC.

   B. Connect to the server using the Web Interface for Administration.

   C. Use Computer Management on the PC and connect to the server.

   D. Connect to the server using Remote Desktop for Administration.

Managing Your Server Remotely

4. You recently installed Windows Server 2003 on some of your company's servers. You plan to manage the servers locally using the Windows Administration Tools Pack and remotely from home and other locations using the Web Interface for Remote Administration. You have checked that your network firewalls enable incoming access to the Web Interface. What else do you need to do to enable the Web Interface for Remote Administration?

   A. Install Remote Administration (HTML).

   B. Enable it in System Properties.

   C. No need to do anything; it is already installed and configured for use.

   D. Install Remote Administration (HTML) and configure the administration Web site using IIS Manager to enable administrators to connect.

5. You are at a client's site when you receive a call from your manager. He needs you to check out a problem on a server called sfax2std. You start a browser on one of the PCs on the client's network and try to connect to the Web Interface for Remote Administration for your server. However, this does not work, as shown in Figure 7.26. What is the most likely reason that the connection did not work?

Figure 7.26 Exhibit for Question 5

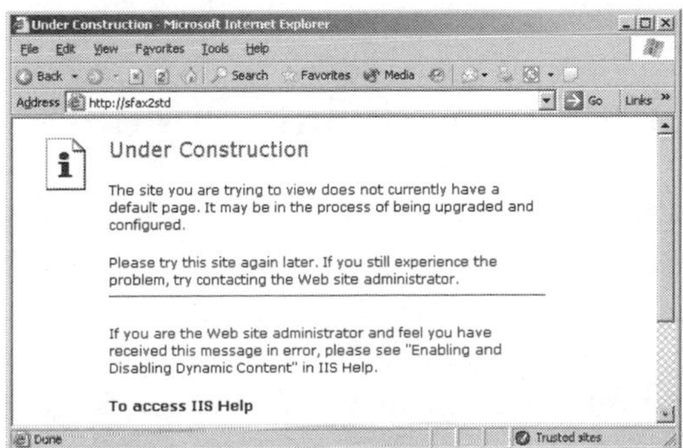

A. Remote Admin (HTML) has not been installed.

B. You don't have permissions to connect.

C. The URL is not correct.

D. IIS isn't running on the server.

Using Emergency Management Services

6. During a review of disaster recovery planning at your company, the need to manage your servers remotely when the network has failed has been raised as an issue. You decide to use the Emergency Management Services feature of Windows Server 2003. To test this, you connect a terminal to the serial port of your Windows Server 2003 computer. However, you find that you are getting no response on the terminal. What is the most likely reason for this?

   A. EMS operates only when the operating system has failed.

   B. EMS hasn't been enabled on the computer.

   C. Your computer doesn't have the special hardware required to support EMS.

   D. EMS works only over the network.

7. You have a computer that has Windows Server 2003 and Windows XP Professional installed on it. You've connected a terminal to the serial port of the computer so that you can manage it remotely using EMS. You reboot the server and see the list of available operating systems on the terminal. You select Windows XP Professional from the boot list and then find that there is no further response on the terminal. What has happened?

   A. The computer crashed while booting into Windows XP Professional.

   B. EMS was enabled on the wrong serial port in the Windows XP Professional installation.

   C. EMS wasn't enabled in the Windows XP Professional installation.

   D. Windows XP Professional doesn't support EMS.

Managing Printers and Print Queues

8. One of your users frequently submits a very large print job prompting complaints from other users whose print jobs are delayed because of the large job. The server also handles requests for other print queues. You decide to try changing the default priority of the queue that is causing the complaints. What would be the benefit of changing the priority from the default of 1 to say 50?

A. To make print jobs appear faster.

B. To make print jobs from the queue appear before those in other queues.

C. To enable you to reduce the priority of individual jobs as well as increase the priority.

D. To be able to give some users preferential access so that their jobs print more quickly.

9. A user calls you and asks you to ensure that his document is printed next. The user's print job is shown highlighted in Figure 7.27. You examine the queue and note that there is a long print job before the user's document and you agree to prioritize it. What is the best way to arrange for the user's document to be printed next?

Figure 7.27 Exhibit for Question 9

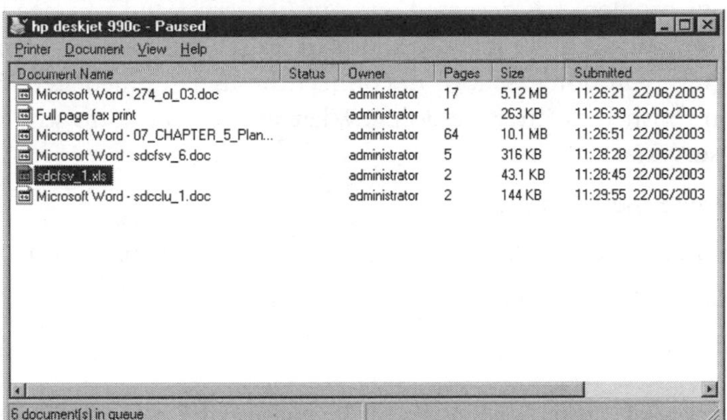

A. Delete all the jobs above the highlighted one.

B. Pause all the jobs above the highlighted one, wait for it to print, and then resume the paused jobs.

C. Drag it to the top of the queue.

D. Double-click the job and increase its priority.

10. The only laser printer on your network is now very heavily used and users often have to wait a long time for their print jobs. Management has agreed to buy another printer that is the same as the current one. The same print server will manage both printers. The original printer is connected to LPT1 and the new printer will be connected to LPT2. What is the most efficient way to deploy the new printer?

A. Create a new queue on the print server using LPT2. Modify the current printer queue to send jobs to the new printer when it is busy.

B. Modify the queue for the existing printer to enable printer pooling and configure the printer to use LPT2 as well as LPT1.

C. Create a new printer queue on the print server using LPT2. Configure the users' computers so that half use the current printer and the other half use the new printer.

D. Create a new printer queue on the print server using LPT2. Create a printer pool that contains both the new and the current printers.

Managing and Troubleshooting Services

11. A serious problem has occurred on your file server and you need to shut down the computer, but users are still connected. Because the users have important work that is in progress, you don't want to disconnect the users immediately, but instead you want them to finish what they are doing. What should you do to stop new users connecting to the server?

    A. Disable the Server service.

    B. Shutdown the server anyway; users can save their files locally.

    C. Stop the Server service.

    D. Pause the Server service.

12. Your company hosts DNS zones on several servers. Because the proper operation of the DNS servers is crucial to your network, one of your tasks is to check that the DNS service is running on all these servers and you have to perform this task on a regular basis. What is the most efficient way to do this?

    A. Write a script that uses ***sc*** with the remote computer option to check the DNS service on each server.

    B. Create a custom MMC and add the services snap-in for each server and check the state of the DNS service in each snap-in.

    C. Log on to each server using Remote Desktop and run Computer Management to check the DNS service in the services folder.

    D. Install the Administration Tools Pack and run DNS Manager, connecting to each server in turn to see if DNS is running.

13. You are installing SQL Server on a Windows Server 2003 computer. The SQL Server needs to be able to send e-mail via Exchange Server, which is installed on another Windows Server 2003 computer. What type of account should you use for the SQL Server service?

    A. Domain User

    B. Local User

    C. Local System

    D. Local Service

Using Wizards to Configure and Manage Your Server

14. A new administrator has joined your company and you have tasked him with setting up Routing and Remote Access on one of your servers. The new administrator has very little experience in managing Windows Server 2003 servers. Which tool should you advise the new administrator to use in the first instance?

    A. Manage Your Server

    B. Configure Your Server Wizard

    C. Administration Tools Pack

    D. Computer Management

15. Your company has acquired a new printer and you've been asked to set up the printer so that all the users can use it. You decide to set up the printer on your server so that you can centrally manage printing. You successfully install the printer and print a test page. However, you then find that the users cannot connect to the printer. What is the most likely reason?

    A. The File Server role isn't installed.

    B. The File & Print Server role isn't installed.

    C. The Print Server role isn't installed.

    D. You forgot to share the printer.

Self Test Quick Answer Key

For complete questions, answers, and explanations to the Self Test questions in this chapter as well as the other chapters in this book, see the Self Test Appendix.

1. **A**
2. **B**
3. **D**
4. **A**
5. **C**
6. **B**
7. **D**
8. **C**
9. **D**
10. **B**
11. **D**
12. **A**
13. **A**
14. **B**
15. **D**

Chapter 8

MCSA/MCSE 70-290

Managing Web Servers with IIS 6.0

Exam Objectives in this Chapter:

- 4.9 Manage a Web server.
- 4.9.1 Manage Internet Information Services (IIS).
- 4.9.2 Manage security for IIS.

- ☑ Summary of Exam Objectives
- ☑ Exam Objectives Fast Track
- ☑ Exam Objectives Frequently Asked Questions
- ☑ Self Test
- ☑ Self Test Quick Answer Key

Introduction

Microsoft's Internet Information Services (IIS) is one of the most popular Web servers in use on the Internet and in intranets throughout the world. Windows Server 2003 includes the latest version, IIS 6.0. There have been changes, additions and improvements to the software in the areas of core functionality and services, administration, security, and performance. IIS 6.0 has been redesigned to provide better reliability and more flexibility in configuring application environments.

A Web server is a common point of vulnerability to hackers. In the past, it has been common for servers to be running "rogue" Web services without the knowledge of administrators. Thus, for security reasons, IIS 6.0 is not installed by default on Windows Server 2003 servers (with the exception of the Web Server Edition). When you do install it, it is initially configured in a high security ("locked") mode. Because Web servers are common targets of attack due to their exposure to those outside the local network, security is a priority in this new version. Consequently, a number of important Web services features that worked automatically in previous versions that now have to be explicitly enabled before they will work. This new focus on security means administrators need to familiarize themselves with these changes to provide the Web server services needed on their networks.

In this chapter, we take you through the installation and configuration process for IIS 6.0 and introduce you to its new features, including security features, reliability features, and other new features. We'll show you how to use the Web Server Security Lockdown Wizard and how to manage security issues for your Web servers. We'll also discuss troubleshooting issues, and you'll learn to use the new IIS command-line utilities.

Installing and Configuring IIS 6.0

Before you can use IIS's services, you have to install it (unless you're using the Web Server Edition of Windows 2003 Server), so we will first concentrate on the installation process. Remember that IIS is not installed by default in any of the other Windows Server 2003 family members. This is to minimize unauthorized access to the server. You will learn about all these new security features as we progress though this chapter. First, let's learn about the prerequisites for installing IIS 6.0 on Windows Server 2003.

Pre-Installation Checklist

You should take some precautions before installing IIS. These steps will ensure that your new IIS installation will run smoothly. Here is a checklist to go through prior to the installation:

- **Domain Name Registration for an IP address for the IIS server** If it is to be an Internet Web server (as opposed to an intranet server), the IIS server will be referred by the Domain name from outside the enterprise, so you must register a domain name and obtain a public IP address for it. You'll also need to obtain DNS services for your domain, from your ISP or another public DNS server (just registering the name does not do this). You also need to assign an IP address or a unique machine name for references inside the enterprise. These details should be taken care of before you do any installations.

- **Access privileges for installation** Make sure you are logged in with an account (*Administrator* or a member of the *Administrator group* for the machine) that has the correct authentication privileges to access the machines and network components. (for example, configuring routers to channel IIS requests).

NOTE

Microsoft strongly recommends that IIS be installed on an NTFS–formatted drive. The executable files and the virtual directories should reside on NTFS volumes. NTFS will provide more secure file access than the FAT32 file system. It is recommended that you convert the file system if you are upgrading from an IIS 5.0 FAT32 system. A command-line utility called convert.exe can be used for this purpose.

Internet Connection Firewall

Windows Server 2003 comes with a very basic internal software firewall called the Internet Connection Firewall (ICF). This facility is disabled by default. If you enable it, the firewall can be configured to enable or disable protocol access through IIS. (The protocols in question that relate to IIS are HTTP, HTTPS, FTP, and SMTP). IIS 6.0 will *not* function correctly if the ICF is *enabled* and the relevant protocols are *disabled*. (For example, the IIS 6.0 Web server will not function if the HTTP and HTTPS protocols are disabled.) You basically have two options when it comes to the ICF:

1. Disable the firewall. (Warning: You are at the mercy of the corporate firewall!)
2. Enable the firewall and filter the correct protocols.

The most cost-effective method is to use the second option and maximize Windows Server 2003's built-in functionality. Follow these steps to configure the protocols:

1. Open **Start | Control Panel | Network Connections | Local Area Connection**.
2. Navigate to the **Advanced** tab and select the **Protect my computer and network by limiting or preventing access to this computer from the internet** checkbox. (See Figure 8.1.)

New & Noteworthy...

Firewall Protection for Web Servers

Microsoft recommends that you use the ICF for small- to medium-size Web project developments if you do not have a more sophisticated firewall solution (such as Internet Security and Acceleration Server) deployed. ICF is adequate to protect Internet traffic on most Web sites. However, large organizations should consider ISA or another heavy-duty firewall product. You do not need to enable the ICF if you have a corporate firewall to protect your Web servers.

It is common to place Web servers that are to be accessed from the Internet in a "DMZ" or perimeter network (also sometimes called a screened subnet). This can be done in one of several ways. You can configure a "tri-homed DMZ" in which you have a firewall server (such as ISA) with three interfaces (an internal network interface to the LAN, a public interface with a public IP address, and a DMZ interface with a public address). Alternatively, you can configure a "back-to-back DMZ," where you have two firewall servers, an external one and an internal one.

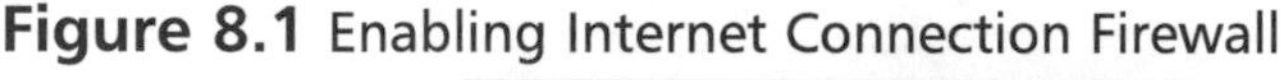
Figure 8.1 Enabling Internet Connection Firewall

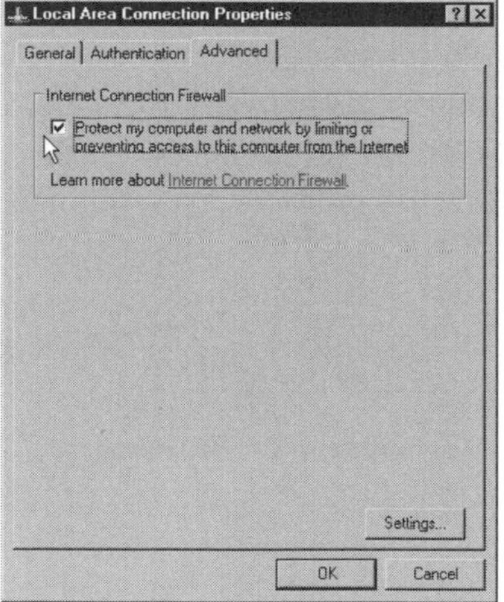

3. Click the **Settings** button and navigate to the **Services** tab. This will bring up a window to select or deselect the access protocols to your server. This is the list of protocols the IIS server will understand to process user requests. Select the correct checkbox next to the protocol name to enable requests using the particular protocol. You can disable the protocol access by clearing the checkbox. Your screen should be similar to Figure 8.2.

Figure 8.2 Available Protocol Configuration Window

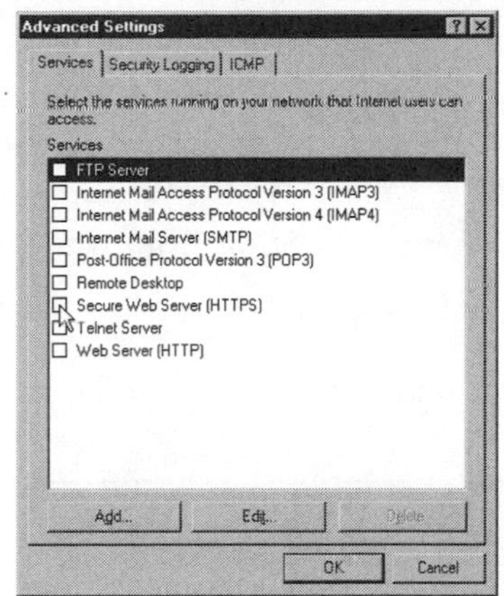

4. Select the appropriate protocols for your organization. Most organizations will enable HTTP, HTTPS, SMTP, and FTP access through the firewall. Each time you select a protocol, a small window will appear, prompting you to enter the machine name or IP address of the server that hosts the service. Figure 8.3 shows the entry to enable HTTPS access to a machine called **home-net**.

Figure 8.3 Entering Machine Name or IP Address to Configure the Firewall

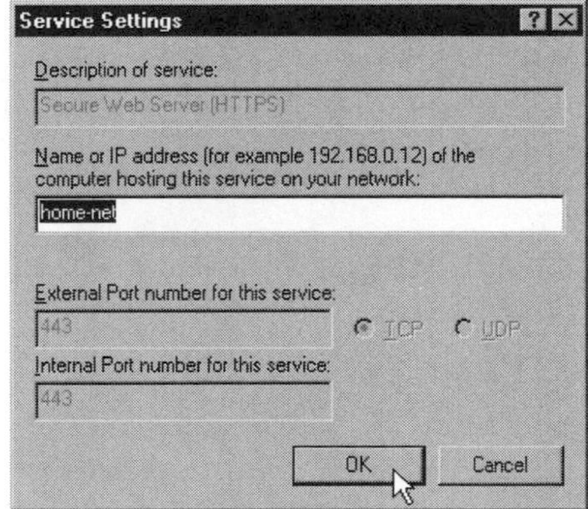

5. Click **OK** and repeat the process for all other protocols.

When you complete these steps, you have enabled the correct access to your organization through the ICF.

These are some of the prerequisites for your IIS 6.0 installation. Application of IIS security templates and operating system hardening are some of the other prerequisites. The next step is to initiate the installation process. There are several ways to install IIS in Windows Server 2003. We will discuss each of these in the next section.

Installation Methods

IIS is not installed by default in the Windows 2003 Server setup, except in the Web Server Edition. There are three different ways to install IIS. They are listed below:

- Use the Configure Your Server Wizard.
- Use the **Add or Remove** option from the **Control Panel**.
- Use the Unattended Setup.

We will investigate each option closely in the next section.

Head of the Class...

Default IIS Access options

All of the installation methods described here install IIS in "locked" mode. That means you get access only to static Web material. All the ASP.NET scripts, Server Side Includes, WEBDAV access, and Front Page Extensions will be disabled by default. If you try to access any of these facilities, you will get a 404 (Page not found) error. You must enable these features through Web Services Extensions node in IIS Manager if you want to use them.

The details regarding how to enable dynamic features will be discussed in the section titled *Common Administrative Tasks*. If you enable these features, you can disable them later to increase security. This involves using the Web Service Extensions node in the IIS Management console. Any Web service extension can be enabled or disabled individually as long as it's registered in the Web Service Extensions node, or you can prohibit all extensions from running. You can also add new extensions, and you can configure IIS so that a specific application will be able to use the Web service extensions. Please refer to the *Common Administrative Tasks – Enabling Web Service Extension* section to learn about Web service extensions.

Using the Configure Your Server Wizard

In addition to its other possible roles (domain controller, file server, DNS server, and so forth), the Windows Server 2003 can act as an application server, and the components of the application server can be configured through Configure Your Server Wizard. The Application server components are COM+, ASP.NET, and IIS.

NOTE

In this context, the term "application server" has a different meaning from the one you may have used in the past. Here, we are not talking about a server that provides a network location on which productivity applications such as Microsoft Office are installed, nor or we talking about a server that you connect to and run applications from a thin client (a terminal server functioning as an application server). Instead, the "applications" we are referring to are Web-based applications such as Web-hosting services, as well as newsgroup services, FTP services, and SMTP services.

Follow these steps to install IIS 6.0 from the **Configure Your Server** Wizard:

1. Click the **Start** | **Manage Your Server** option. You will see the **Manage Your Server** window. (Please refer to Figure 8.4.) Click the **Add or remove a role** link.

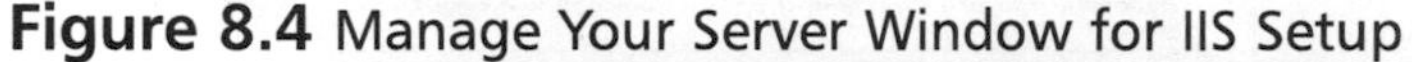

Figure 8.4 Manage Your Server Window for IIS Setup

2. The next screen is the **Preliminary Steps** window. This is a warning screen that prompts the user to confirm that all prerequisites are met for the installation. Most of these warnings relate to hardware not being configured correctly. The screen should be similar to Figure 8.5. Click **Next**.

Figure 8.5 Preliminary Steps to Install IIS 6.0

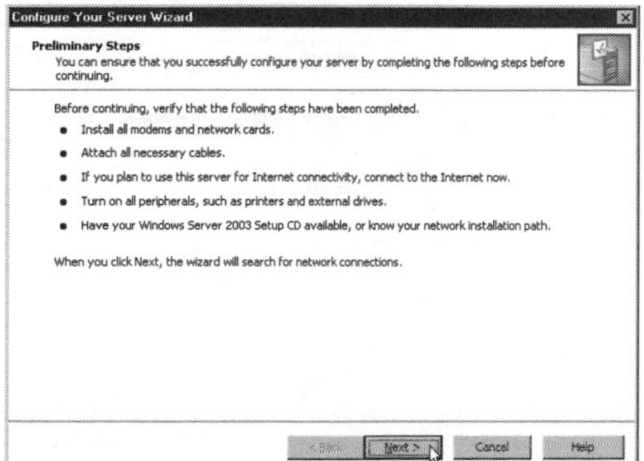

3. The next screen is the **Configuration Options** screen. This screen is presented to the user only once. You can select from two options to configure the server. The **Typical configuration for a first server** option will enable the basic server communication options. It will set up a domain controller by installing Active directory, DNS services, and DHCP services. The second option is **Custom Configuration**. This will enable you to configure your server by selecting specific options from a list. For this walk-through, we will choose the second option. The screen should be similar to Figure 8.6.

Figure 8.6 Configuration Options Screen

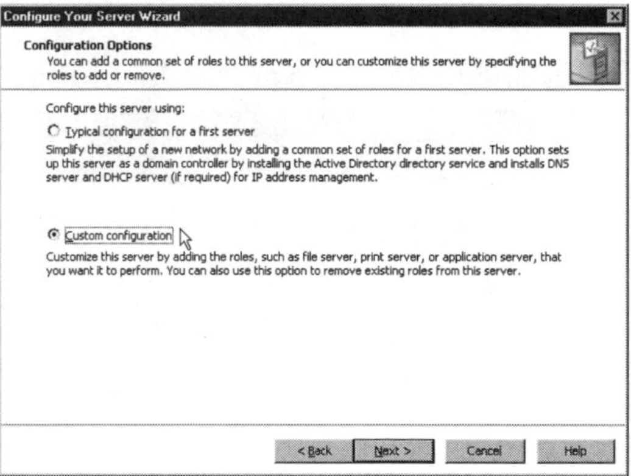

4. The next screen displays a list of server roles that you can assign to your Windows 2003 server. This screen lists all the server services that are available. We will select the **Application Server (IIS, ASP.NET)** option from the list. You can also use this screen to install Print, Terminal, DNS, DHCP services, and more. (Refer to Figure 8.7 for the complete list.) Click **Next**.

Figure 8.7 Server Role Screen

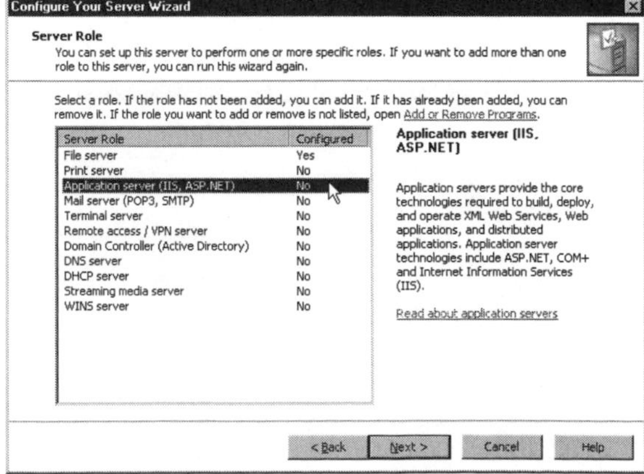

5. The next screen is the **Application Server Options** window (see Figure 8.8). This screen enables you to configure dynamic options for IIS installation. The options you can select here include **ASP.NET** and **FrontPage Extensions**. ASP.NET is a scripting framework that is used to execute IIS applications. The FrontPage extensions will enable your Web applications to be ported to another Integrated Development Environment (IDE). That is, the same Web project can be modified using Visual Studio .NET and Web Matrix. The FrontPage extensions will also enable users to develop Web content and manage the Web site remotely. Click **Next.**

Figure 8.8 Application Server Options Window

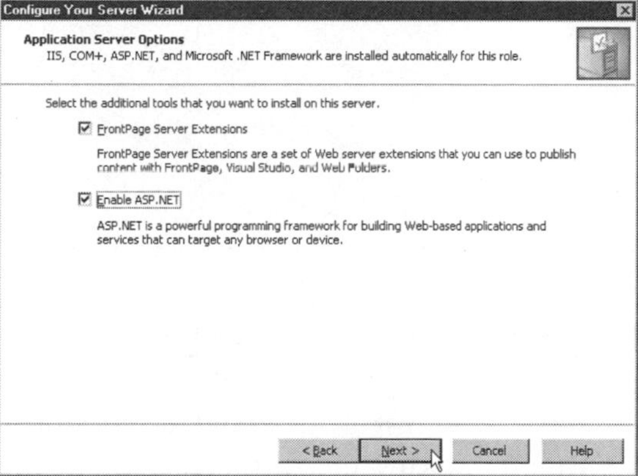

6. The next screen is a summary of the items you have selected. Review these, and use the **Back** button if you want to change anything. Note that **Enable COM+ for remote transactions** option is added by the installation process. Your screen should be similar to Figure 8.9. Click **Next**.

Figure 8.9 Summary of Selections Window

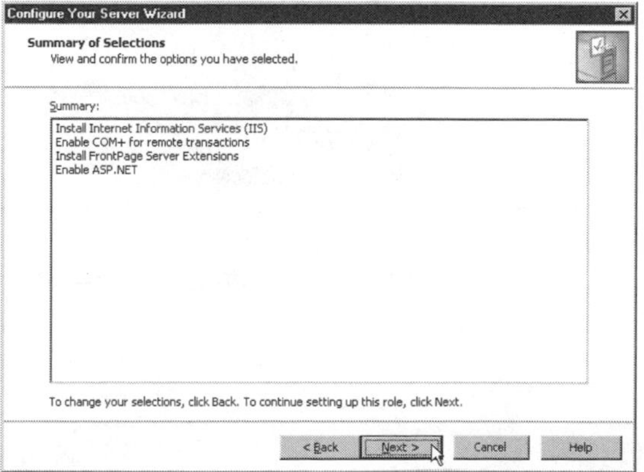

7. The installation process will commence now. You will be presented with an **Application Selections** screen and a progress bar will indicate the installation progress. The installation process will automatically bring up the **Configuration Components** window and will start to copy the correct files from the Windows Server 2003 installation CD, DVD, or network share. This window is shown in Figure 8.10. Finally, a confirmation screen will appear to complete the installation.

Figure 8.10 Configuring Components Window

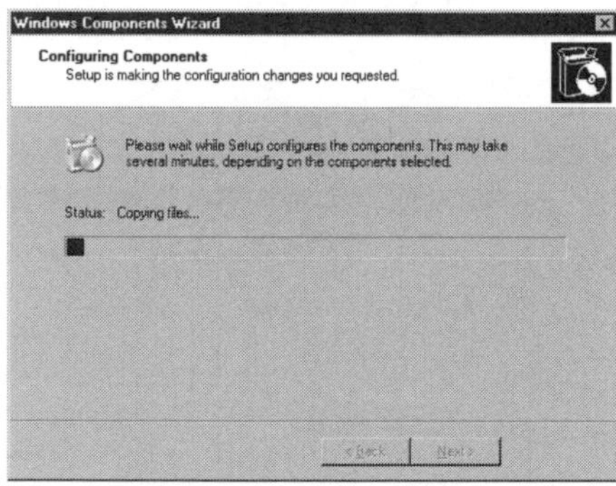

Using the Add or Remove Programs Applet

The previous section explained how to install IIS 6.0 by using the **Configure Your Server Wizard**. The second option is to install IIS through the **Add or Remove Programs** applets in **Control Panel**. To do this, follow these steps:

1. Navigate to **Start | Control Panel | Add or Remove Programs**.
2. Click the **Add/Remove Windows Components** button.
3. Select the **Application Server** option button. Refer to Figure 8.11 for an illustration of this. Next, click the **Details** button to configure the application server options.

Figure 8.11 Selecting the Application Server Option from Windows Components Window

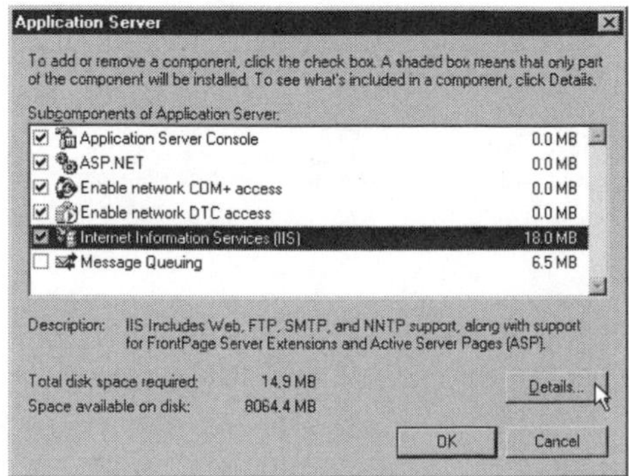

4. You will see a screen similar to Figure 8.12. This screen will enable you to select any additional IIS components you want to install. The **World Wide Web Service** is the only default selection on this screen. We recommend that you also select **Internet Information Server Manager** to enable GUI editing for IIS-related functions. Select the options you want and click the **OK** button. (You can also further configure each setting by selecting the individual item and clicking the **Details** button.) The installation will start and a screen similar to Figure 8.10 will be presented. Ensure that the Windows Server 2003 CD-ROM/DVD is available in the CD-ROM drive if you are installing from the CD-ROM. After you click **Next**, you will be presented with a confirmation screen.

Figure 8.12 Selecting Options for IIS

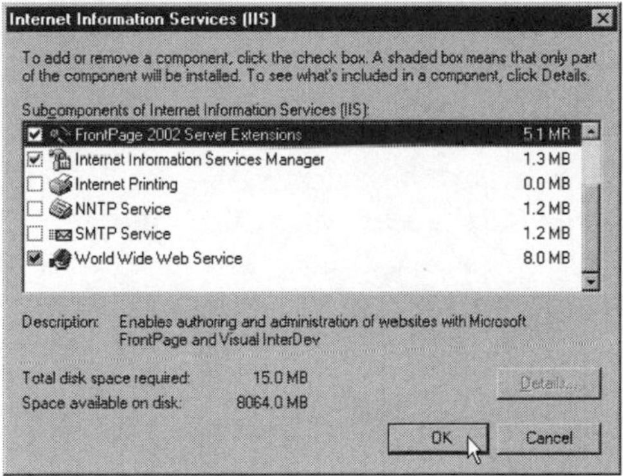

Using Unattended Setup

The third option for installing IIS is using the unattended setup feature, which is commonly used by system administrators to install IIS 6.0 on multiple computers. When you use this option, the setup program does not need any manual intervention. The configuration settings (the selections that you would make during an attended setup) are read from a text file and applied automatically by the operating system. You only need to initiate the process and IIS 6.0 will be installed according to the text file settings.

The script that provides the configuration settings is referred to as an *Answer Script* or *answer file* (because it provides answers to the installation questions that you encounter in an attended setup). After you create the answer file, you then run winnt32.exe or the sysocmgr.exe command-line utility with the answer script as the parameter. The answer file has a .INF file extension. Some of the important options that are included in the answer file are shown in Table 8.1.

Table 8.1 Answer File Parameters for IIS Unattended Setup

Component	Answer File Parameter
ASP.NET	asp.net = on/off
FTP service	iis_ftp = on/off
IIS Manager	iis_inetmgr = on/off
NNTP Service	iis_nntp = on/off
SMTP Service	iis_smtp = on/off
WWW Service	iis_www = on/off
Active Server Pages	iis_asp = on/off
WebDAV Publishing (discussed later)	iis_webdav = on/off

Head of the Class...

Difference between winnt32.exe and sysocmgr.exe

Winnt32.exe is used to install Windows Server 2003. Using winnt32.exe, system administrators can install the Windows 2003 operating system and its components (including IIS 6.0). When you use a properly configured answer file with winnt32.exe, it will install Windows Server 2003 with IIS 6.0. In some cases, you might need to install IIS 6.0 after the operating system is installed. The sysocmgr.exe utility is used to install IIS 6.0 with unattended setup after the operating system has been installed. Here are the steps to use sysocmgr.exe:

1. First we need to create the answer file. Open a text editor (e.g., Notepad or Wordpad) and type the following:

```
[DefaultInstall]
Asp.net=on
Iis_inetmgr=on
Iis_www=on
Iis_asp=on
```

2. Save the file as .INF on specified directory. (We will use *c:\temp\iisSetup.inf* for demonstration purposes.)
3. Click on **Start | Run**.
4. Type in **sysocmgr.exe /i:sysoc.inf /u:c:\temp\iisSetup.inf** and the installation will begin. The *"/i:sysoc.inf"* attribute is the Windows Server 2003 Server master initialization file for the unattended setup.

Installing IIS with unattended setup is very straightforward. You can also get the help files available for unattended setup by using the *syscomgr.exe /?* syntax.

Installation Best Practices

Now you should be familiar with all the different IIS setup processes. It is worthwhile to spend some time learning about the installation best practices. Installation best practice will ensure the optimum scalability and performance of IIS 6.0. Here are some of the important steps to ensure maximum value from IIS:

- The file system onto which you install IIS should be NTFS. If the partition is not already formatted as NTFS, upgrade the FAT32 file system to NTFS prior to installation or during the upgrade process.
- Make sure the Internet Connection Firewall (ICF) is enabled and configured properly unless you will be relying on a separate firewall product.
- Use unattended setup to install IIS on multiple machines.
- **Configure Your Server Wizard** will enable you to install multiple application server components (DNS, File server, etc.). Therefore, you can install other components parallel to the IIS 6.0 setup.

What's New in IIS 6.0?

There are many new features in IIS 6.0. Many of these features are designed to address technical and architectural issues in IIS 5.0. The new features can be divided into several broad categories. The most important categories are security and reliability. Microsoft has invested a large number of resources on its new Trustworthy Computing initiative. IIS 6.0 is one of the first products to be developed under this security-focused strategy. Performance is also enhanced by some key architectural modifications to the IIS 6.0 object model. In the following sections, we investigate these changes in detail.

New Security Features

IIS 5.0 and earlier versions were constantly patched up by HotFixes from Microsoft. IIS was once considered one of the main security holes in Windows architecture. This was a major deterrent to using IIS as a commercial Web server. IIS 6.0 comes with an impressive list of new security features designed to win back commercial users. You will learn about these new features in the next sections.

Advanced Digest Authentication

Advanced Digest authentication is an extension of *Digest security*. Digest security uses MD5 hashing to encrypt user credentials (user name, password, and user roles).

What's the purpose of MD5 hashing? *Basic authentication* sends the user name and password details over the network medium in base64-encoded format. These details can be easily "sniffed" (captured with a protocol analyzer) and decoded by an intruder, who could then use the credentials for nefarious purposes. The MD5 hash enhances security by applying more sophisticated, more difficult-to-crack cipher algorithms to deter these intruders. An MD5 hash is made up of binary data consisting of the user name, password, and realm. The *realm* is the name of the domain that authenticates the user. All of this means Digest security is more secure than Basic authentication. (These security features are explained in more detail in the *Managing IIS Security* section.)

EXAM WARNING

An MD5 hash is embedded in an HTTP 1.1 header. This is only supported by HTTP 1.1-enabled browsers. Digest or Advanced Digest authentication mechanisms cannot be enabled if the target browsers do not support HTTP 1.1. Internet Explorer 5.0 and later versions support HTTP 1.1, as well as recent versions of Netscape, Opera, Mozilla and other popular browsers.

Advanced Digest authentication takes the Digest authentication model a bit further by storing the user credentials on a domain controller as an MD5 hash. The Active Directory database on the domain controller is used to store the user credentials. Thus, intruders would need to get access to the Active Directory in order to steal the credentials. This adds another layer of security to protect access to Windows Server 2003 Web sites, and you do not need to modify the application code to accommodate this security feature.

TEST DAY TIP

Both Digest and Advanced Digest Authentication work only on Web Distributed Authoring and Versioning (WebDAV) enabled directories. WebDAV is a file sharing protocol that is commonly used in Windows Internet-related applications. WebDAV was referred to as Web Folders before. It is a *secure* file transfer protocol over intranets and the Internet. You can download, upload, and manage files on remote computers across the Internet and intranets using WebDAV. WebDAV is similar to File Transfer Protocol (FTP). WebDAV always uses password security and data encryption on file transfers. (FTP does not support these tasks.)

Server-Gated Cryptography (SGC)

Communication between and IIS Web server and the Web client is done using Hypertext Transfer Protocol (HTTP). These HTTP network transmissions can be easily compromised due to their text-based massaging formats. Therefore, we need to encrypt these HTTP calls between the client and the server. Secure Sockets Layer (SSL) and Transport Layer Security (TLS) are the most common encryption mechanisms used on Web sites. SSL/ TLS will enable a secure communication by encrypting the communication channel with a cipher algorithm. TLS is the later version of the SSL protocol. (It is more secure than SSL.)

IIS 5.0 and earlier versions included SSL/TLS for secure communication between the Web client and the server. Server-Gated Cryptography (SGC) is an extension of SSL/TLS. It uses a strong 128-bit encryption mechanism to encode the data. SGC does not require an application to run on client's machine. It has been available since IIS 4.0. SGC needs a valid certificate at the client Web browser, which can encode and decode. A special SGC certificate is needed to enable SGC support built into IIS 6.0. We can obtain a certificate by contacting a certificate authority. This certificate can be added to IIS as any other certificate. (Please refer to the *Configure Authentication Settings* section.) IIS 6.0 supports both 40-bit and 128-bit encryption sessions. This means your old 40-bit SGC certificates are still valid in IIS 6.0. SGC is commonly used for financial sector applications (banking and financial institutions) to protect data.

NOTE

If you try to open an existing 40-bit SGC certificate, you may get a "*The certificate has failed to verify for all of its intended purposes*" warning. These certificates are targeted to Windows 2000 servers. Thus, you can have a valid certificate and can be misled by this warning. Windows 2000 supports only 40-bit encryptions and Windows 2003 supports both 40-bit and 128-bit encryptions.

Selectable Cryptographic Service Provider (CSP)

SSL/TLS offer a secure environment in which to exchange data. The downside is performance. SSL/TLS are very CPU intensive. IIS 6.0 comes with a new feature called **Selectable Cryptographic Service Provider (CSP)** that enables the user to select from an optimized list of cryptography providers. A cryptographic provider will provide you with an interface to encrypt communication between the server and the client. CSP is not specific to IIS and can be used to handle cryptography and certificate management. Microsoft implements two default security providers. Those are Microsoft DH SChannel

Cryptographic provider and Microsoft RSA SChannel Cryptographic provider. The Microsoft implementations are optimized to IIS 6.0 for faster communications. The private keys for these two Microsoft implementations are stored in the registry. The Microsoft Cryptographic API (Crypto API) for every provider contains identical interface for all providers. This will enable developers to switch between providers without modifying the code. Each provider will create a public and a private key to enable data communication. The private key is stored on hardware devices (such as PCI cards, smart cards, and so forth) or in the Registry. The other CSP keys can also be stored in the registry. It makes more sense to store private keys as registry settings for computer access to the server. The private key will be stored on smart cards and other portable devices if we have a mobile distribution environment. (This is similar to *Plug and Play* support for devices on Windows 2000 and Windows Server 2003 environments.) The CSP can be configured using the **Welcome to the Web Server Certificate Wizard**. (Click on **Properties** of a Web site and select the **Directory Security** tab. Then click the **Server Certificate** button.)

Configurable Worker Process Identity

One of the most serious problems with previous IIS versions was the instability of the World Wide Web (WWW) Publishing Service. The failure of this service could result in the shutdown of the machine. IIS 6.0 runs each Web site in an isolated process environment. This isolated process environment is called a *worker process*. Therefore, a Web site malfunction could be limited to its process environment. (Hence, not lead to a Web server shutdown.) IIS 5.0 did not implement a worker process model. IIS 6.0 can also run IIS 5.0 isolated environment. The IIS system administrator can choose between worker process model or IIS 5.0 isolation model by selecting the correct option from **Services** tab by right-clicking **Web Sites**. You can click the **Run WWW service in IIS 5.0 isolation mode** option box to run IIS in IIS 5.0 isolation mode. IIS will run on worker process model if you do not check the box. IIS can run only at one mode at a time. Therefore we will not be able to run worker process model Web sites and IIS 5.0 isolation mode Web sites simultaneously.

The worker process can be run with a lower level of permission than the system account. The worker process will shut down the application if the IIS server is targeted with malicious code. IIS 6.0 (which is by default run by the local system account) is not affected since the worker process can be configured to run under a less-privileged account.

Default Lockdown Status

The default installation of IIS 6.0 will result in a *light-weight* Web server. The only default feature available will be the access to static content. This is to deter any malicious access by the intruders. This *restricted* functionality is referred as *Default Lockdown* status. This feature will force the system administrators to manually enable and disable the features that are necessary for the applications. They can do this through the Web Services Extensions node of the IIS Manager. (Please refer to the *Managing IIS 6.0* and *Web Service Extensions* sections.)

New Authorization Framework

Authorization refers to the concept of confirming a user's access for a given resource. (Authentication refers to obtaining access to the resource. When a user is authenticated we need to make sure that he or she is authorized to perform any tasks on the resource. This is the basis of authorization.) There are two types of ASP.NET authorization options available for IIS 6.0:

- **File Authorization** *FileAuthorizationModule* class is responsible for file authorization on Windows Server 2003 systems. The module is activated by enabling **Windows Authentication** on a Web site. This module does access control list (ACL) checking on the authorization access on an ASP.NET file for a given user. (It could be either an .ASMX file for ASP.NET application or an .ASMX file for a Web service.) The file is available for the user if the ACL confirms the user access to the file.
- **URL Authorization** *URLAuthorizationModule* class is responsible for URL authorization on Windows Server 2003. This mechanism uses the URL namespace to store user details and access roles. The URL authorization is available to use at any time. The authorization information is stored in a text file on a directory. The text file will have *<authorization>* tag to allow or deny access to the directory. (This will apply to the subdirectories if not specified.) Here is a sample authorization file:

```
<authorization>
    <allow users="Chris"/>
    <allow roles="Admins"/>
    <deny users="kirby"/>
    <deny users="?"/>
</authorization>
```

This file will enable *Chris* to access its content. It will also enable anyone with *Admins* user roles. The user *Kirby* is denied access. Any one else will not be able to gain access to this directory (indicated by the *?* wild card).

New Reliability Features

Microsoft has done a great job of re-designing IIS to be more reliable and robust. Perhaps the most significant modification is the emphasis on the *Worker Process Model*. This concept was initially embedded into IIS 4.0 as *Running an application in a separate memory space*.

IIS separates all user code from its WWW service. The user application (different Web sites) functions as a separate Internet Server Application Programming Interface (ISAPI) application. The separate ISAPI workspace is referred as a worker process. IIS 5.0 ran each Web site within its own **inetinfo.exe** memory space. (inetinfo.exe is the application that implements IIS 5.0.) The IIS 6.0 worker process Web sites do not run within the inetinfo.exe (WWW services) memory space. Because the worker process runs in an isolated environment from the WWW service, an error in the Web site application code (or malicious attack) will not cause the Web server to shut down. The worker process can also be configured to run on a specified CPU. The worker process model can store application-specific data on its own memory space. IIS 5.0 stored all the application data within the inetinfo.exe memory space. Therefore, we can assign a Web site to run on specific CPU. This mechanism will enable us to dedicate more resources to popular Web sites.

Head of the Class...

Is This the Same as IIS 5.0 Isolation Mode?

IIS 6.0 runs worker process model by default. You can also configure IIS 6.0 to run in *IIS 5.0 isolation mode*. The worker process model is more flexible than the IIS 5.0 isolation model. The worker process can isolate individual sites. This will minimize the risk of a malicious attack on the WWW service. IIS 5.0 isolation mode still runs *within* the inetinfo.exe memory space, so an error in the application can bring down the whole server. IIS 5.0 used ASP as the default scripting mechanism. IIS 6.0 uses ASP.NET. IIS 6.0 can run ASP and all the code should run smoothly in an upgrade from IIS 5.0 to IIS 6.0. If the ASP code is not compatible you may need to revert to IIS 5.0 isolation mode.

Health Detection

Health detection simplifies IIS Web site management. Health detection is performed by IIS over all its worker processes. This adds another level of reliability to the Web applications. The inetinfo.exe process (IIS) will check the availability of each worker process (different Web sites) periodically. IIS manager can configure this time limit. (It is 240 seconds by default.) Therefore IIS will maintain a *heartbeat* between its worker processes. (Heartbeat is similar to the *ping* facility. The IIS server will try to communicate with worker processes to make sure that they are alive.)

New Request Processing Architecture: HTTP.SYS Kernel Mode Driver

In Windows Server 2003, the HTTP stack is implemented as a kernel mode device driver called HTTP.sys. All incoming HTTP traffic goes through this kernel process. This kernel process is independent of application process. IIS 6.0 is an application process and external to HTTP.sys (Application processes run in *user mode* and the operating system functions are run in *kernel mode*) the IIS that runs in *user mode*. HTTP.sys is responsible for the following: connection management (managing the database connections from the ASP.NET pages to data bases), caching, (reading from a static cache as opposed to recompiling the ASP.NET page), bandwidth throttling (limiting the size of the Web requests to a Web site), and text-based logging. (Writing IIS information into a text log file.)

In IIS 5.0, the HTTP request was processed by the IIS inetinfo.exe. HTTP.sys in IIS 6.0 relieves IIS of this responsibility. In doing so, it enhances IIS performance in the following ways:

- HTTP.sys enables caching (referred as *flexible caching*) at kernel level so that static data can be cached for faster response time (independent of the user-mode caching). This will be faster than user-mode caching. We need to be careful with flexible caching. Because HTTP.sys is separate from IIS we may still cache old data after an IIS restart.
- HTTP.sys introduces a mapping concept called *application pool*. Application pooling enables Web sites to run together in one or more processes, as long as they share the same pool designation. Web sites that are assigned different application pools never run in the same process. A central Web site (credit card verification Web site) can be accessed by all the other miscellaneous sites (shopping cart e-commerce sites) by using this method. By using the correct application pool information HTTP.sys can route the HTTP traffic to the correct Web site.
- HTTP.sys increases the number of Web sites you can host using the application pool concept. This architecture also increases performance and more controlled access to valuable IIS resources.

Other New Features

Lets' concentrate on some of the other new features in IIS 6.0. All of these changes are designed to improve IIS scalability. Some of these changes are a byproduct of the Microsoft .NET strategy.

ASP.NET and IIS Integration

IIS is a Web server, and one of its functions is to accept HTTP requests. We need to have scripting language that can communicate with IIS in order to do this. Earlier versions of IIS (2.0 through 5.0) used a scripting language called Active Server Pages (ASP). IIS 6.0 uses ASP.NET scripting languages for the same purpose. There are some significant changes to the ASP.NET architecture (compared to the older ASP). Some of those advantages include the following:

- ASP.NET is based on MS .NET framework. ASP.NET can be coded in multiple languages (C#, VB.NET, Jscript.NET, etc.).
- You can have multiple language code in the same ASP.NET page. In other words, you can have a VB.NET function in a C# ASP.NET page.

- ASP code is interpreted (the code is complied *line by line*, not as the complete source file at once), while ASP.NET code is compiled. (The complete source file is complied once, not line-by-line compilation.) This makes for a *significant performance increase* in IIS 6.0.
- ASP.NET allows you three levels of caching. You can cache complete pages. The second option is to cache selected parts of the pages. (Referred to as *fragment caching.*) The third option is to use *Caching API.* Developers can use this to exert extensive control over caching behavior, and thus increase performance.

Unicode Transformation Format-8 (UTF-8)

The earlier version of IIS log file was only in English. This was a major issue for multilingual Web sites. Multilingual support is enabled by supporting UCS Transformation Format (UTF) 8 characters codes. Computer applications do not understand human-readable characters. They only understand binary code. There are conversion tables available to convert a key value to a human readable character (those tables are referred as *Local Character Sets* or *Unicode formats*). The tables were language specific. Therefore, we could not read an English log file entry in Japanese. UTF-8 format rectifies these problems. We can instruct HTTP.sys to log details in specific language format. FTP site login does not support UTF-8 login. Therefore, we can maintain multiple log files in multiple languages. UTF-8 support is available for URLs and filenames in IIS 6.0. Active Server Pages (ASP) will also have the UTF-8 support. The Unicode code is converted into UTF-8 in this instance.

XML Metabase

The information store that contains IIS configuration settings is referred as the *metabase*. The metabase is a hierarchical database in which all the information needed to configure IIS is stored.

The metabase data was in binary format in earlier IIS versions. It was difficult to edit the entries, or even to read them, since the information was in binary. The IIS 6.0 metabase, on the other hand, is in *XML format*. These Extensible Markup Language files are plain text. You can use a general text editor to change the XML entries, and these changes can even be performed when ISS 6.0 is running. Editing the XML metabase while IIS is running is referred to as *edit while running*. You do not need to restart IIS to reflect the changes. (Unless you make overwrite the schema file with a new version.)

This design change has also significantly increased the performance of IIS 6.0. It has reduced the start-up and shutdown time of ISS considerably. (All the IIS settings were in the inetinfo.exe and system registry. This resulted in multiple reads from the registry and accessing system resources as start-up time. We also needed to clear all memory references at the shutdown time. We do not need to do these functions in IIS 6.0 due to the XML metabase.)

The metabase consists of the following two XML files:

- **Metabase.xml** An XML document that contains IIS configuration values for the server (for example, Web site details, virtual directory details). It can be edited while IIS is running (*edit-while-running*), which is a new feature to IIS 6.0.
- **MBSchema.xml** An XML document in which the metabase XML schema is stored, which acts as a *validation tool* to enter correct metabase values in metabase.xml.

The metabase files are located in the Systemroot\System32\Inetsrv directory. You need administrator permission to view the contents of the metabase entries. The schema changes are enabled by using Active Directory Service Interface (ADSI). Editing a metabase.xml file is a tedious task. A simple approach is to use the IIS Manager interface to make the changes. However, this could save some effort for the expert users. It is possible to have simultaneous changes to the metabase.xml. (The schema is changed by ADSI while the administrator is making some changes to the metabase.xml file.) We can prevent this by using access control lists (ACLs) on the metabase files. This will prevent the XML file changes when the schema changes are made. The metabase history feature stores a history of the metabase.xml file changes. This is valuable for IIS to execute new metabase changes.

Configuring & Implementing...

Backup/Restore Metabase

The metabase entries can be backed up by using the **Backup/ Restore Configuration** option of the **All Tasks** menu item. Perform the following steps:

1. Click **Start | Programs | Administrative Tools | Internet Information Services (IIS) Manager**.
2. Right-click the server name in the left console pane.
3. Select **All Tasks** from the context menu.
4. Select **Backup/Restore Configuration**.
5. Click the **Create Backup** button.
6. Type a name for the configuration backup.
7. Select whether to encrypt the backup with a password by checking or unchecking the **Encrypt backup using password** checkbox. If you check the box, type and confirm the password.
8. Your new backup will appear in the list of backups. Restoring IIS from a backup is done through the same interface. (When you select an existing backup from the list, the **Restore** button will be enabled on the interface.) Select the backup and click the **Restore** button if you wish to restore the backup.

When backing up the metabase, you can encrypt it with a password to protect it. If the computer running IIS fails, the metabase can be restored from backup

Continued

on a new installation of Windows Server 2003 or even on a different computer (if you use secure backup). It is also possible to restore the metabase with a previous version of the metabase files that are saved in the history folder. However, you can't restore a backup from an earlier version of IIS, and if you restore from the history files, you can't restore to a different IIS installation or different computer.

IIS automatically makes regular backups of the metabase, in addition to manual backups made by the administrator. History files are also created automatically, as long as the history feature is enabled (by default, it is). You can use IIS Manager to restore history files, as well as restoring from backup.

Thus far, you have learned about the installation process and the new features in IIS 6.0. In the following sections, we will practice using the interface to perform common IIS management tasks. You will learn how to create, manage, stop, start, and delete IIS components (Web, FTP, NNTP, and SMTP servers).

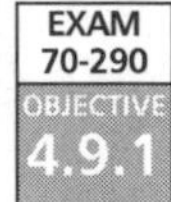

Managing IIS 6.0

The primary tool for managing IIS 6.0 is an MMC called IIS Manager. Most of the management of IIS functions can be done using the IIS Manager. Figure 8.13 displays the IIS Manager in action. In the left pane, there is a node for each instance of IIS that is installed. Folders/subnodes underneath each node (identified by the server name) contain the FTP, Application Pool, Web site, Web Service Extensions, NNTP, and SMTP server information. For example, Figure 8.13 displays all the IIS nodes for a computer called *Home-net*. Let's investigate some of the common functions of the IIS manager.

Figure 8.13 IIS Manager Console Application

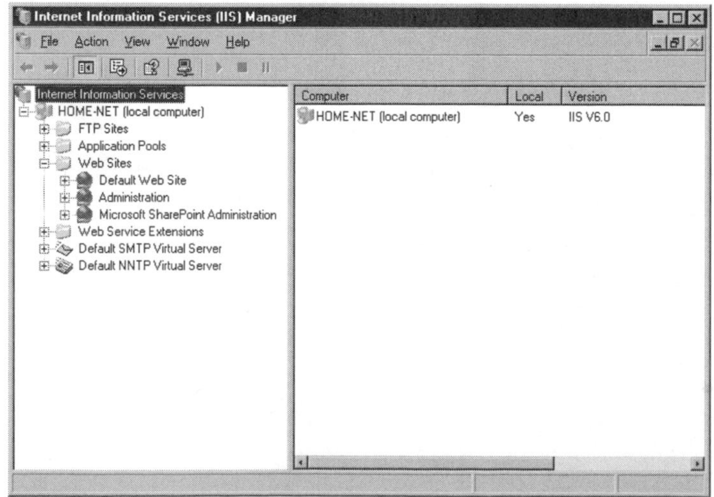

Performing Common Management Tasks

First of all, let's get familiar with the IIS Manager console. How can we start the IIS Manager? We can load the IIS Manager in the following ways.

1. Go to **Start | Administrative Tools | Internet Information Services (IIS) Manager**.
2. Go to **My Computer | Manage.** Select and expand **IIS Manager** node.

IIS Manager is the primary interface to handle all Internet-related functions. We can set up Web sites, FTP sites, SMTP servers, and NNTP servers using this console. We can also stop and restart IIS servers from this interface. Some other IIS Manager functions are to stop and restart Web, FTP, NNTP, and SMTP servers. Different IIS server instances also can be managed from one IIS Manager console. For example, we have a Web server farm with A, B, C, and D machines. We can manage all these four servers from machine A's IIS Manager Console. We will investigate setting up Web, FTP, NNTP, and SMTP sites in the next section.

Site Setup

We can set up Web and FTP sites using IIS Manager. We can also configure SMTP and NNTP virtual servers using IIS Manager. The WWW, FTP, NNTP, and SMTP servers can be installed manually or using scripts (unattended setup). Please follow these steps to install the components manually:

1. Navigate to **Start | Control Panel | Add Remove Programs**.
2. Click the **Add Remove Windows Component** button.
3. Select the **Application Server** option from the Windows Components window, and then click **Details**.
4. Select **IIS** and click **Details** in the **Application Server** window.
5. Select the options you want to install (Web, NNTP, FTP, and SMTP).
6. Click **OK** and the installation process will begin.
7. You will be presented with a confirmation screen at the end of the installation process.

Let's look closely on how to create and maintain Web, FTP, NNTP, and SMTP sites. All these subjects will be discussed as a subsection from now on.

Setting up a Web Site

All Web sites can be created and managed in IIS Manager. This is a wizard-driven exercise. Therefore, it is a simple task to create a Web site from scratch. Let's learn the process to create a Web site using IIS Manager.

1. Start **IIS Manager** (refer to the previous section on *Site Setup*).

2. Navigate to **Web Sites** node and right-click it.
3. Select **New** then **Web Site**. You should get a screen similar to Figure 8.14. (You can also create a Web site from XML file settings. This option is commonly used to create Web sites from a backup configuration. In most case you will be using the wizard to create a new Web site.)

Figure 8.14 Creating a New Web Site in IIS Manager

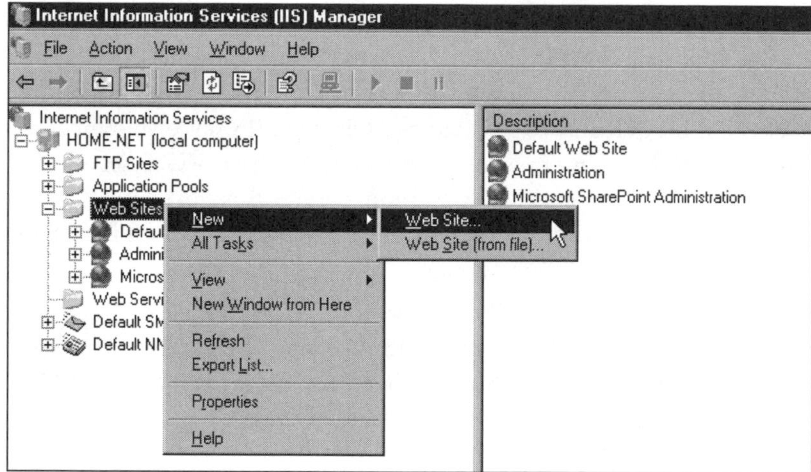

4. You will be greeted with the Welcome to the **Web Site Creation Wizard**. Click **Next** on this screen.
5. In the **Web Site Description** window enter the Web site name. We will create a Web site called **TestWebSite**. Then click **Next**. Your screen should be similar to Figure 8.15

Figure 8.15 Entering the Web Site Name

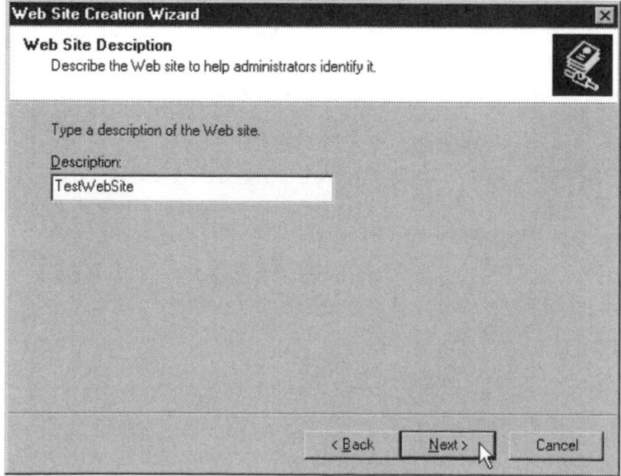

6. The next screen will be the **IP Address and Port Settings** window. Let's assume my Web site domain name is www.mytestwebsite.com and it runs on port 80. Put these details under the **Host Header** (please refer to *Hosting Multiple Web Sites* in the next section for further details) and **TCP Port this Web site should** use text boxes. Let's assume that we don't assign a specific IP address for this Web site. Therefore, leave the **Enter the IP address to use for this web site** combo box with the **(All Unassigned)** property. (This is the default value.) We will not be able to refer to the Web site by its IP address if we do not assign an IP address. This could be handy for intranet development. We rely on Host Headers to find the site by selecting (All Unassigned) option. We also don't need to assign port 80 as the default port. If any port is assigned other than port 80, then we need to change the URL to reflect that. (For example, if we run www.mytestwebsite.com on port 100, we will use www.mytestwebsitecom:100 as the URL.) After all the values are entered, please click **Next**. The screen should be similar to Figure 8.16.

Figure 8.16 Entering IP Address and Port Settings for a Web Site

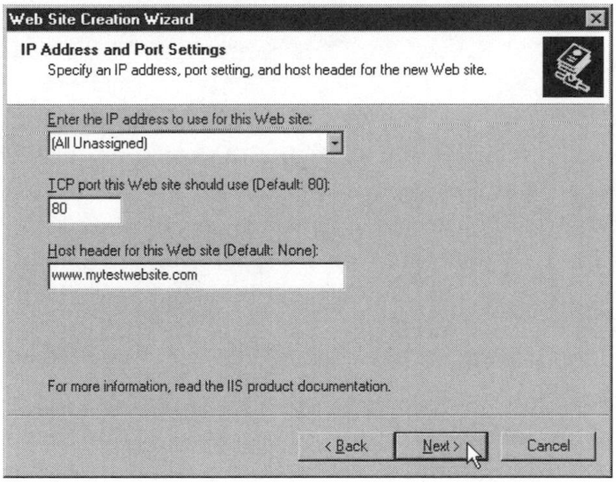

7. The next window is the **Web Site Home Directory** window (Figure 8.17). The *home directory* is where the physical files of a Web site reside. All the content and executable files are stored here.

8. Enter the path to find the ASP.NET files that associate with the Web site. In this example, the files are found at C:\inetpub\wwwroot\testWebSite directory. Therefore, when a user enters www.mytestwebsite.com, it will point to this directory. Microsoft strongly recommends that the home directory volume is an NTFS drive. Please click the **Browse** button and navigate to that folder. The **Allow anonymous access to this web site** flag is checked by default. Allowing anonymous access will enable the users to navigate the site without authenticating

themselves. This is not recommended for sites with sensitive business information. Please refer to the *Configuring Authentication Settings* section for further details. Click **Next** to navigate to the next window.

Figure 8.17 Entering the Home Directory for a Web Site

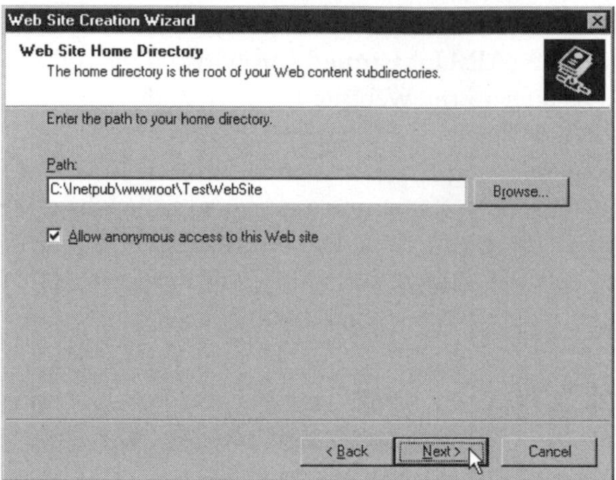

9. The next window is the **Web Site Access Permissions** screen. This is a very important screen. We can configure the access to our Web site using this screen. The **Read** and **Run scripts** options are selected by default. The **Execute** option refers to granting execute permission for Dynamic Link Libraries (such as ISAPI DLLs or CGI applications) in IIS space. Most of the business logic and interfaces to third-party business models will be stored as ISAPI DLLs or CGI Applications. Therefore we may need to enable **Execute** access to communicate with these entities. The **Write** option will enable the user of the Web site to upload/write data into the Web site's source directories (in this case, c:\inetpub\wwwroot\testWebSite directory). Finally, the **Browse** option will enable *directory browsing* on the Web site. This option will produce a complete directory information list (files and their attributes – size, last modified time stamp, etc.) when a user navigates to the directory. Therefore, we can get a complete file list using a Web browser interface. This is not widely recommended. (Since it exposes all the files and interfaces to Web site users. It will be a large security breach if Anonymous access is also enabled.) We have selected the default options and the screen should be similar to Figure 8.18. Finally, click **Next** to finish the creation of the Web site. You will get a window confirming your creation of the Web site.

Figure 8.18 Entering Access Permissions for a Web Site

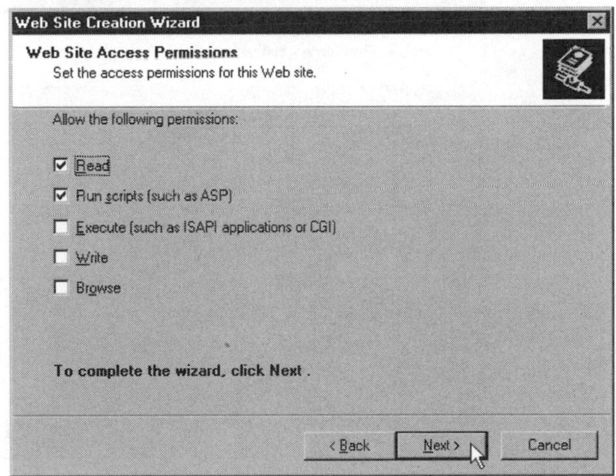

Setting up an FTP Server

The FTP site setup is similar to Web site setup. Most of the setup has the same information as the Web site setup. An FTP site will enable the user to share data with others. The users can upload data or download data from our FTP site. Let's learn how to create an FTP site using IIS Manager.

1. Open **IIS Manager**.
2. Click the **FTP sites**, right-click and select **New**.
3. Select **FTP Site** from the context menu. (You can also read the FTP site settings from an XML configuration file.)
4. Click **Next** from the **Welcome to the FTP site Creation Wizard**.
5. Enter the FTP site name in the **FTP Site Description** window. We will name our FTP site "TestFTPSite" and click **Next**.
6. Let's enter the IP address and the port number for the Web site in the **IP Address and Port Settings** window. The default port number for an FTP site is 21. You can use a different port number than 21. (Most corporate firewalls will open port 80 for Web and 21 for FTP access. If you change the FTP port to another number, we need to reconfigure the firewall to let the traffic into the enterprise.) The next step is to select the correct IP address from the combo box. We will use the default **(All Unassigned)** for our demonstration. You can also assign a dedicated IP address for the FTP site. The user will use this IP address to access the FTP site. The site will use the IP address of the IIS machine if we leave the **(All Unassigned)** option selected. The screen should be similar to Figure 8.19. Click **Next** to navigate to the next window.

Figure 8.19 Entering IP Address and Port Numbers for an FTP Site

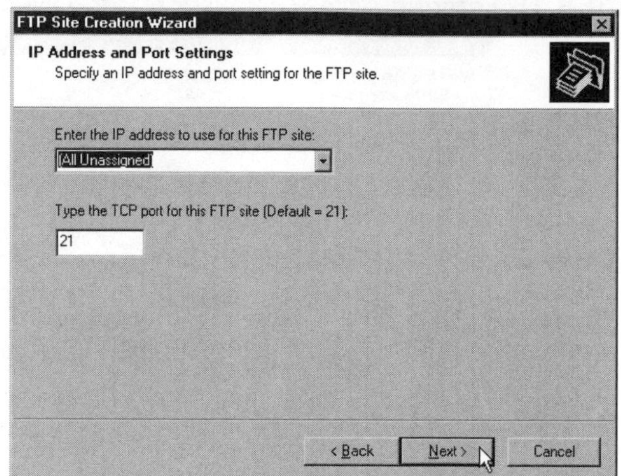

7. The next window is the **FTP User Isolation** window. This window will enable you to configure the security settings for the FTP site. The user access for an FTP server can be managed in several ways. The default setting is that every user has access to other user directories. This will not be a problem in many cases since a company FTP site will distribute generic information regardless of the user (e.g., enable Beta product download to the test users). The user will have access to *all files* if the user is authenticated. In some cases this model may not work. We may need to give different users to access different information. We need to *isolate* users to different directories in this case. FTP user isolation prevents users from accessing the FTP home directory of another user on this FTP site. We can select **Isolate users** to accommodate this scenario. This option uses NTFS directory authentication to perform this task. We can also go a step further by asking Active Directory to authenticate the user and assign an FTP home directory for the user. This can be configured using the **Isolate the users using Active Directory** option. We can also use iisftp.vbs script to perform these functions at a command line with the */isolation* switch. This will be discussed later in the chapter. We will stick with the default and click the **Next** button. (Figure 8.20 shows the isolation options.)
8. The next window will enable you to enter a physical directory path where the FTP site is located. We will put C:\Inetpub\ftproot\TestFTPSite as the physical directory for our FTP site. This directory will be exposed to the public access. Therefore, make sure the data in this directory is not sensitive to the organization. Click **Next.**

Figure 8.20 FTP Site User Isolation Options

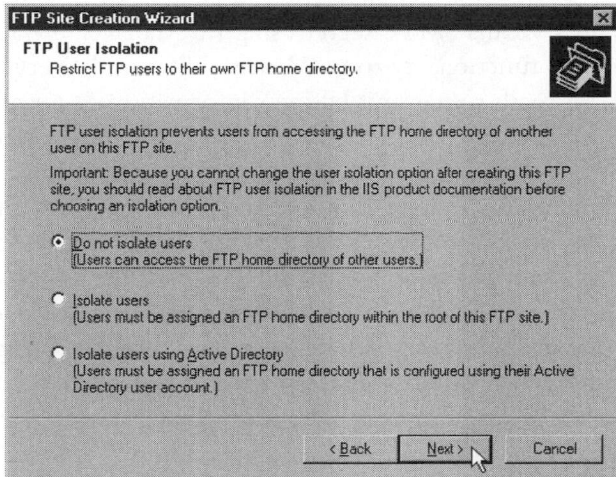

9. The Next window is the **FTP Site Access Permission** window. The default is just read access to users. You can also enable the **Write** access if the users need to upload files to the server. This option can be helpful in some cases (for example, your sales team needs to upload sales data to the FTP server for weekly accounting purposes). This option will enable users to upload malicious content to the server. Therefore, it is not recommend to enable **Write** access unless necessary. The screen should be similar to Figure 8.21. Click **Next** and the FTP site creation process will be completed.

Figure 8.21 FTP Site Access Permissions Window

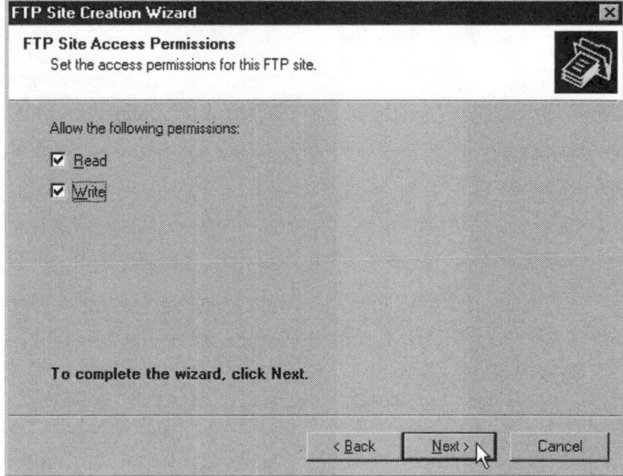

Setting up an SMTP Server

We can also set up a virtual SMTP server using IIS Manager. SMTP servers help IIS to deliver simple e-mail functionality to its Web sites. E-mail delivery is a common task for Web sites. We use e-mails to transmit business information or for administration purposes (e.g., e-mail error message to the system administrators) from our IIS components. Therefore, Microsoft included the SMTP server to be installed with IIS 6.0. SMTP server fully supports Simple Mail Transfer Protocol and is compatible with SMTP clients. SMTP servers use TLS encryption to protect the e-mail information. The SMTP server will communicate with the Domain Name System (DNS) to validate the recipient's e-mail address. The sent e-mails are transferred to the drop directory. The SMTP server will transmit all the messages in the drop directory. Therefore, other non-IIS 6.0 applications can also send e-mail by putting the application messages in the drop directory. The delivered e-mail will be picked up from a pickup directory. Let's learn the process to set up an SMTP server.

1. Start IIS Manager.
2. Navigate to the correct computer and select **Default SMTP Server**.
3. Right-click and select **New**. Then select **Virtual Server**.
4. Enter the SMTP site name in the **New SMTP Virtual Server Wizard** window. We will use **TestSMTPServer** for our demonstration. Click **Next**. You should have a screen similar to Figure 8.22

Figure 8.22 Entering the Name of the SMTP Virtual Server

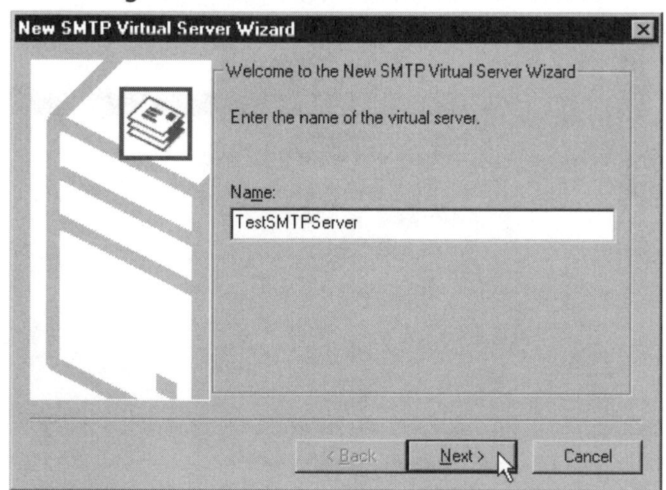

5. Select the correct IP address settings from the **Select IP Address** window. We will select 127.0.0.1. Click **Next**.

Configuring & Implementing...

Entering IP Address Details SMTP Server

The IIS installation creates default SMTP and NNTP virtual servers, which are bound to the **(All Unassigned)** IP address. Therefore, if you try to select the default for **IP Address and Port Settings** screen (that is, **All Unassigned** option) the operation will fail. Please use the 127.0.0.1 IP address if you want to refer to the local machine. You can also use any other valid IP address available. You can run multiple SMTP servers on a single IP address by using multiple port numbers. You can add these extra port numbers by navigating to the **Properties | General** tab, clicking the **Advanced** button, and entering IP and port number settings. You can also run multiple SMTP virtual servers on a single IIS 6.0 node. The best practice is to use multiple IP addresses for each virtual server. (For example, run a single SMTP server for intranet use and dedicate another SMTP virtual server to Internet use.)

6. Select a home directory for the virtual server by using the **Browse** button of the Select a Home Directory screen. We will refer to C:\Inetpub\mailroot\Mailbox for our home directory. Non-IIS 6.0 applications can also use the SMTP server to send e-mail. Therefore, it is a good practice to have general access to the home directory. (It shouldn't have any restricted NTFS permissions on it. It shouldn't be an OS drive if it will be performing generic mail access from other applications.) Click **Next.**
7. Enter the domain name of the SMTP server at the **Default Domain** window and click **Finish.** You will get a message to confirm the creation of the server.

Setting up an NNTP Server

The Network News Transfer Protocol (NNTP) server helps the IIS 6.0 server to facilitate discussion group functionalities. The IIS setup creates an NNTP server by default. Let's try to create a new NNTP server.

1. Load IIS Manager.
2. Navigate to the correct computer and select **Default NNTP Server**.
3. Right-click and select **New.** Then select **Virtual Server**.
4. Enter the NNTP site name in the **New NNTP Virtual Server Wizard.** We will use **TestNNTPServer** for our demonstration. Click **Next.** The screen should be very similar to the initial SMTP screen.

5. Select the correct IP address settings from the **Select IP Address** window. We will select 127.0.0.1. You also need to provide a different port number for each NNTP server. The default port number associated with NNTP servers is 119. You can also use another port number. We will use 1001 for this demonstration. You can also have multiple NNTP servers. The best practice is to use different IP addresses for each NNTP site. If a lot of IP addresses are not available, then we can use multiple port numbers on a single IP address. Click **Next**. The screen should be similar to Figure 8.23.

Figure 8.23 Entering IP Address and Port Numbers for the NNTP Server

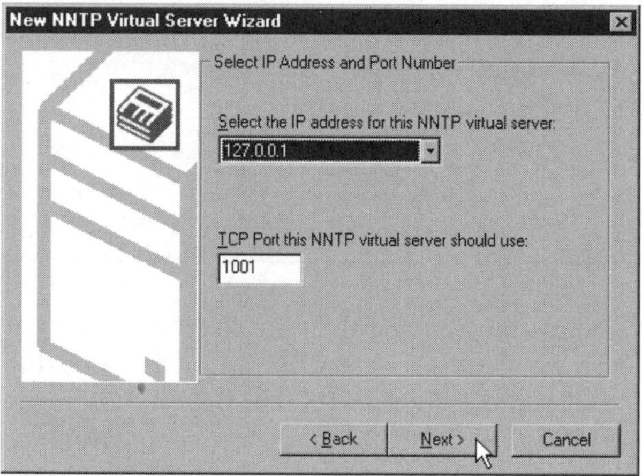

6. The next screen will allow you to to select a home directory for the NNTP virtual server. We will select C:\Inetpub\nntpfile\root as our home directory. Click **Next.**

7. The next window is **Select Storage Medium**. This option will enable us to choose between **File System** and **Remote Share**. This is where the news messages are stored. The **File System** option will enable the user to store the news content on the local machine. The **Remote Share** option will enable it to be stored remotely. We need to know the machine name and user details (i.e., user name and password details) in order to store news content remotely. We will select the default **File System** option. The screen should be similar to Figure 8.24. Click **Next**.

Figure 8.24 Selecting a File System for the NNTP Server

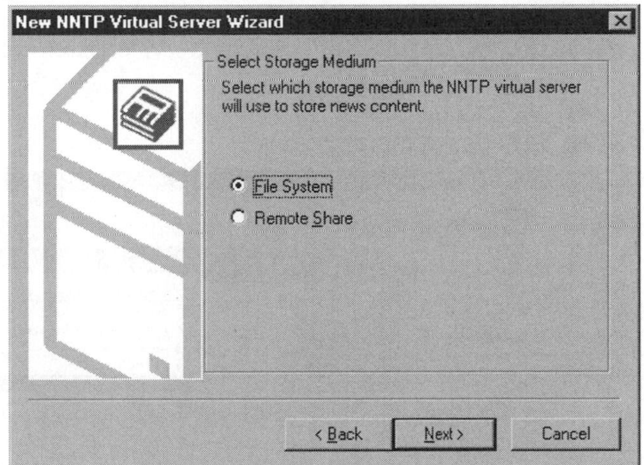

8. The next screen will enable you to define the physical directory in which the messages are going to be stored. Click the **Browse** button and navigate to the directory. We will use C:\Inetpub\nntpfile\drop as our file system location. Click **Finish** to create the NNTP virtual server. You will get a message to confirm the creation of the server.

Common Administrative Tasks

We have learned to install Web, FTP, NNTP, and SMTP servers. Now we are in a stage to practice our knowledge and dive further into the IIS 6.0 world. Let's concentrate on learning some common administrative tasks.

Enabling Web Service Extensions

Web Service Extensions is a new feature in IIS 6.0. This utility will give a Control Panel-like functionality on your IIS components. We will be able to allow, prohibit, or change IIS properties using this tool. This will also enable you to add new IIS extensions (ISAPI applications and third-party IIS tools) to the IIS 6.0 server. You can also enable or disable **All Web Service Extensions** by using this management console. Here is a list of components the Web service extensions can enable or disable.

- ASP.NET executions
- ASP executions
- CGI and ISAPI Applications
- Front Page Server Extensions 2000 and 2002
- WebDAV support for IIS directories

We can get to the Web Service Extensions by using **Start** | **Administrative Tools** | **IIS Manager** and clicking on **Web Server Extensions** node on a selected server name. Figure 8.25 is similar to a default view of the Web Service Extensions window.

Figure 8.25 Web Service Extensions View

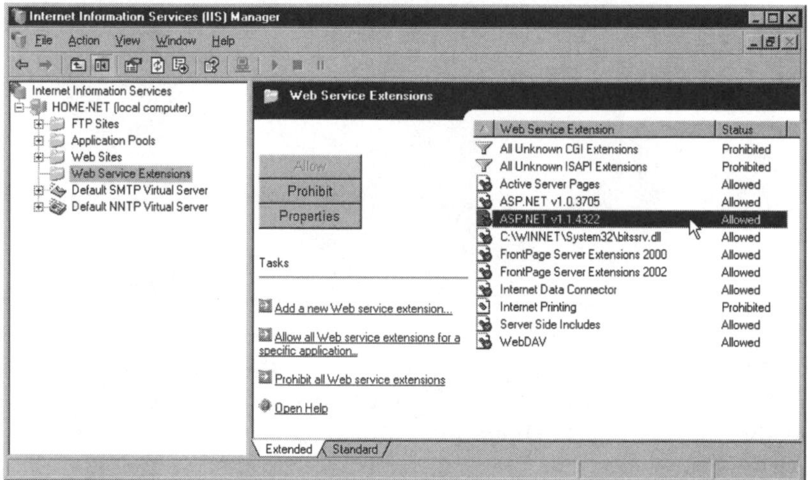

Creating and Working with Virtual Directories

Creating virtual directories is a simple task in IIS 6.0. A virtual directory is a *reference* to an existing directory by a Web or FTP site. We can get access to the subdirectories from a root Web or FTP directory. Sometimes we need to go beyond the root directoryto access information to process a Web request. We use virtual directories to remedy these scenarios. (For example, we can store all the images files in a large shopping catalogue in one directory. Then we can point multiple Web servers to access this images directory as a virtual directory. It will be low maintenance to modify one images directory.) The Web or FTP site will be able to refer to this directory as it exists within its directory structure (even if it physically exists outside of its directory structure). One of the limitations here will be Web site deployment to a new server. Because the virtual directory is not a physical subdirectory (under the home FTP or Web directory) we simply cannot copy and paste the files to the new server. We also need to configure the virtual directories manually. Here is the process to create a virtual directory for a Web site. (The FTP server virtual directory creation process is very similar to this.)

1. Open IIS Manager.
2. Select the server and right-click on the Web site. This will be the Default Web Site for our demonstration purposes.
3. Select **New** | **Virtual Directory**. The screen should be similar to Figure 8.26.

Figure 8.26 Creating a Virtual Directory for a Web Site

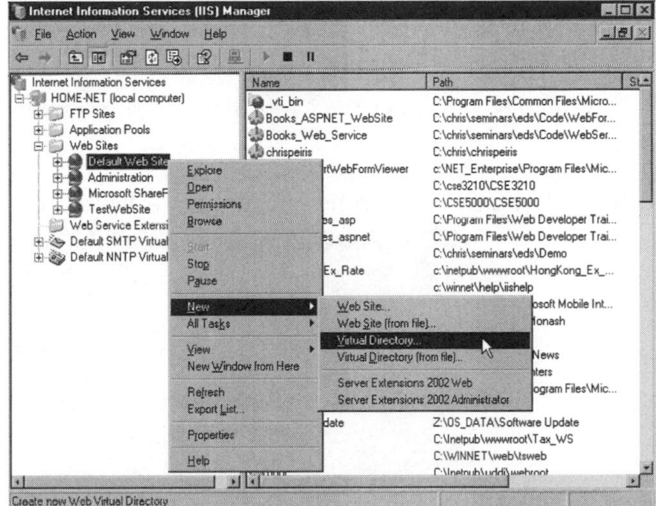

4. The **Virtual Directory Creation Wizard** will appear. Click **Next**.
5. Type the virtual directory name in the Virtual Directory Alias window and click **Next**. We will enter **TestVirtualDir** for our demonstration.
6. In the Web Site Content Directory choose the physical directory the virtual directory is point to. We will choose C:\test to point our TestVirtualDir. Therefore from the IIS point of view, every time we refer to **TestVirtualDir** it will point to C:\test. Click **Next**
7. Select the access permissions from the Virtual Directory Access Permissions window. The default is Read and Run Scripts. The options are very similar to Web site creation options. (Please refer to the *Web Site Creation* section.) Click **Next** to finish the creation process. You will be greeted with a confirmation screen. A virtual directory accessed in the same way as a subdirectory under the root directory. The external user will not know that he or she is communicating to a virtual directory (as apposed to a subdirectory under the root Web directory).

Hosting Multiple Web Sites

Hosting multiple Web sites can be done in three ways. The most common is to assign an IP address to every new Web site. This used to be the most common practice. The obvious limitation is the number of IP addresses available for the organization. This will not be a major issue for internal access within the enterprise. (Behind a corporate firewall. The enterprise will have its own private addressing range. We can use the private IP address for these Web sites.) This practice is also an expensive one to manage. The following is the IIS 6.0 process to assign an IP address for a particular site:

1. Open IIS Manager.
2. Select the server and right-click on the Web site. This will be the Default Web Site for our demonstration purposes.
3. Click **Properties** and select the **Web Site** tab. Your screen should be similar to Figure 8.27.

Figure 8.27 Assigning an IP Address for a Web Site

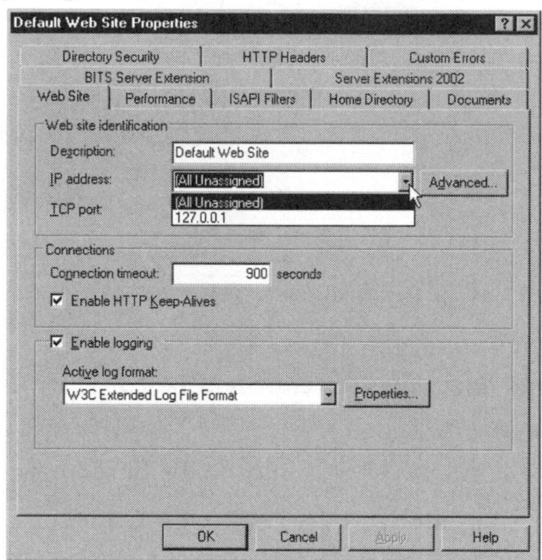

4. Click the **IP address combo box** and select or type the IP address your Web site should refer to. Click the **OK** button at the bottom. We will select **(All Unassigned)** for this example.

   The second option is to use the same IP address and use a different port number. A different port number will be assigned to each Web site. (For example, Web site A will run on port 1001 and Web site B will run on port 1002.) This will require you to change the URL of the Web site. (For example, Web site A could be accessed as www.siteA.com:1001 and site B can be accessed as www.siteB.com:1002.) This would be a great mechanism to handle internal or intranet access behind a corporate firewall.

   The last option is to assign unique host headers on a single IP address. The host headers are unique DNS names that identify different Web sites. IIS will channel all the requests for a single IP address and filter them using the *header information*. The filter process will forward them to the correct Web site according to the header name. This is a good mechanism to implement small to medium Web sites on a single machine. We need dedicated IP addresses for large Web sites. (For example, 150 Web sites running on a single IP address using host headers will affect performance and it is not scalable.) Here is the process to create a header for a site. Follow the steps from 1 to 4 from the last exercise. Then click the **Advanced** button. You will get the following window (Figure 8.28).

Figure 8.28 Entering Header Information for a Web Site

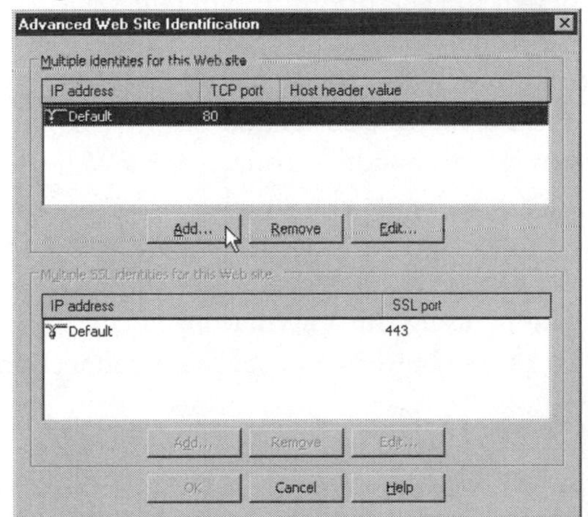

5. Click the **Add** button and you will see Figure 8.29. Choose the IP Address of the Web site and enter the port number. Then enter the header information (DNS entry) in the **Host Header value** text box and click **OK**. (We have entered a new header called **www.myDefaultSite.com** for our Default Web Site.)

Figure 8.29 Entering a New Header for Default Web Site

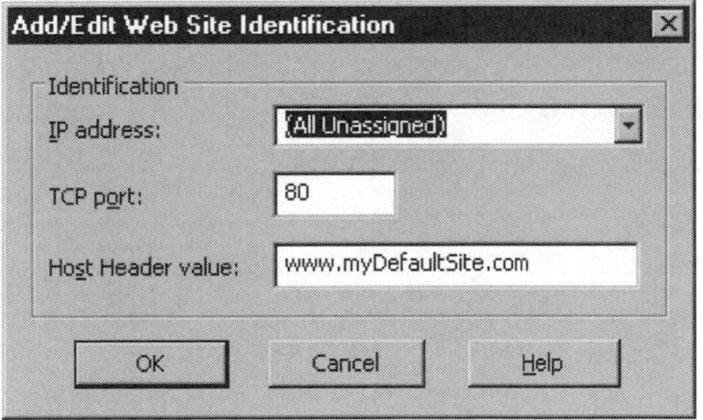

If you refer to the *Site Setup – Setting up a Web Site* section, you'll see that we already have a sample Web site called TestWebSite. It has the header www.mytestwebsite.com. Now, if we investigate closely, we have two Web sites (the **Default web site** and **TestWebSite)** running on *port 80 of the same IP address.*

Please note that the mixed case in the host header file will not matter from IIS 6.0 point of view. It is not case sensitive. The host header implementation will be an issue for SSL implementations. SSL certificates are issued for a Web site and they are tied to an IP address or machine name. The issue here is that all the Web sites use one IP address. Therefore, SSL-supported sites should have their dedicated IP address for the Web site.

Assigning Resources to Applications

Resources can be assigned to applications in different ways. The most common way is to use the **Properties** tab to control caching, performance, and process options. You can also use the bandwidth throttling option to restrict resources for a given Web site. (This option can be found under the **Performance** section on the **Properties** tab.) Bandwidth throttling will limit the network bandwidth resources for a Web site. The maximum bandwidth value is 1024 KB per second. This is also the default value. You can enable bandwidth throttling by selecting the **Limit the network bandwidth to this Web site** check box and specifying the maximum kilobytes per second value. You can also limit the number of connections to the Web site by using this **Performance** tab. Select the **Unlimited** or **Connection limit to** option buttons and specify a connection value.

Working with ASP.NET

ASP.NET is the advanced version of Active Server Pages. IIS 6.0 will enable you to run both ASP and ASP.NET applications. The ASP.NET scripts are built on the .NET model and the ASP scripts follow the old Windows Component Object Model (COM). The ASP.NET model is scalable and performs better than the ASP model. We can use ASP scripting inside ASP.NET scripts. ASP.NET applications can be built on any .NET compatible language (C#, VB.NET, Jscript.NET, etc.). We can enable ASP.NET support from the Web Service Extension Interface. Here are the steps:

1. Navigate to **Start | Administrative Tools | IIS Manager**.
2. Click the **Web Server Extensions** node on a selected server name. Figure 8.25 is similar to a default view of the Web Service Extensions window.
3. Select the **ASP.NET** option from the Web Service Extension window. You can click the **Allow** or **Prohibit** button to enable or disable ASP.NET access.

Backing up and Restoring the Metabase

The metabase stores the IIS configuration setting as XML entries. The metabase has two components. Those are the metabase.xml and the metabase schema file. It is a good practice to back up the metabase regularly. The metabase backup will back up both the metabase.xml and metabase schema files (an .md*VersionNumber* file for the metabase and an .sc*VersionNumber* file for the schema file). The metabase can be safely restored (from a backup) if we lose all the IIS settings. This utility will back up only IIS entries. It does not back up the Web site content. Therefore, you need to restore the Web site content separately. Here are the steps to create and restore backups:

1. Open IIS Manager.
2. Select the server and right-click and select **All Task | Backup/Restore Configuration**.
3. You will get the Configuration Backup/Restore window (see Figure 8.30).

4. Select the **Create Backup** button to create a backup. (It will take the next version number by default.) Otherwise select a backup and click the **Restore** button to restore the IIS settings.

Figure 8.30 Backup and Restore Metabase

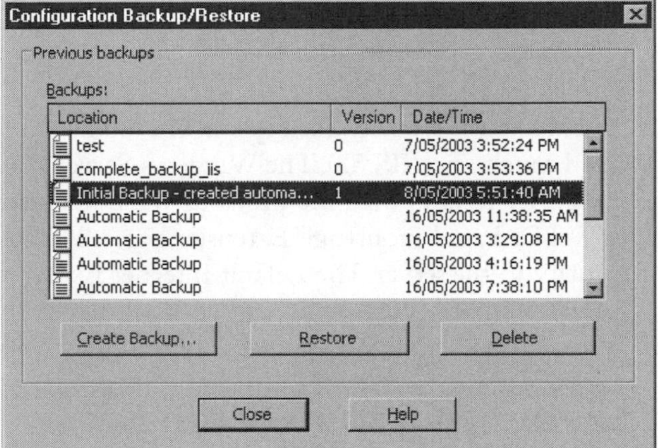

Enabling Health Detection

Health detection enables IIS to monitor its worker process functionality. We can enable pinging and configure rapid application fail over (discussed in *503 Errors* under *Troubleshooting* section later in the chapter). You can also set the startup and shutdown time for a worker process using the option.

Exercise 8.01

Enable Health Detection

You can enable health detection by following this process. This process only works if you're running in worker process isolation mode.

1. Start IIS Manager (**Start | Administrative Tools | IIS Manager**).
2. Select **Application Pools**.
3. Navigate to the correct Web site
4. Right-click on the site and click **Properties**.
5. Select the **Health** tab and enter your settings. You can configure the ping interval using the Enable Pinging group box. This interval describes the timeframe to contact a worker process to make sure it is functioning correctly. The default setting is 240 seconds. The Enable

Rapid fail-over group box functionality will be explained in the *503 Error* section. You can also configure the worker process startup time (if the worker process restarts) and shutdown time (if the worker process gets into a deadlock position) using this screen.

Managing IIS Security

We are going to investigate the security concepts in IIS 6.0 in this section. The core concepts haven't changed much since IIS 5.0. The Windows Server 2003 default installation does extend more security features than the previous Windows server versions. Internet access, ASP scripts, WebDAV, and FrontPage Extensions are all disabled by default. This adds another level of security to the server. The default Internet Explorer access is restricted to High Security Zone and no Web sites are permitted until they are added to the Trusted **Zone** links. Let's learn how to configure the security settings for a Web site in IIS 6.0.

Configuring Authentication Settings

The authentications setting are configured at the Web site level. There are several ways to protect your Web site from intruders. The security settings for a Web site can be viewed by right-clicking on a Web site in **IIS Manager** and selecting **Properties**. The settings can be found the **Directory Security** tab. Figure 8.31 displays the configurable options of security settings.

Figure 8.31 Directory Security Tab for a Web Site

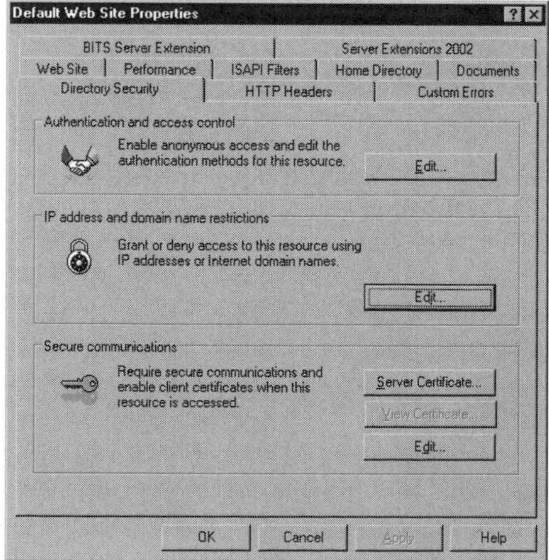

The first option is to restrict users by forcing them to authenticate to the IIS server. This can be achieved by clicking the **Edit** button of the **Authentication and Access Control** group box. Figure 8.32 describes the options available for authenticating in IIS 6.0.

Figure 8.32 Authentication Options Available in IIS 6.0

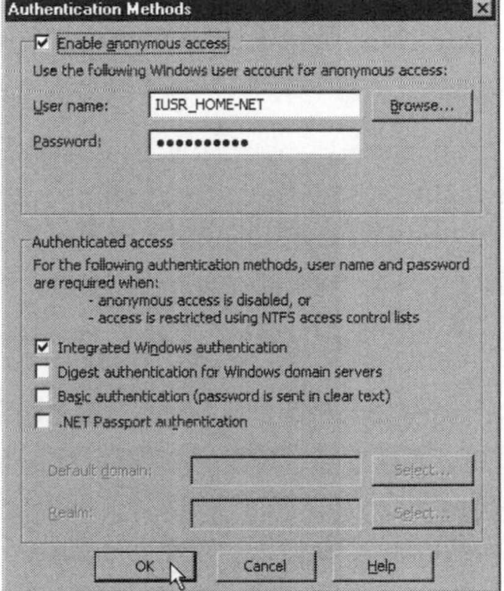

- **Enable anonymous access** This will enable the users to access the site without explicitly logging on. IIS will impersonate the IUSR_*MachineName* account to execute scripts in this instance. A safer option is to disable the anonymous access and force the user to authenticate using one of the following methods.
- **Integrated Windows authentication** This was formerly known as Windows NT Challenge/Response or NTLM. It is a secure form of authentication that hashes the user name and the password before any network transmission. It uses Kerberos version 5 for authentication if the client browser supports Kerberos. Otherwise, it will use NTLM authentication to protect user name and password data.
- **Digest authentication for Windows domain servers** This option will use Digest authentication. Please refer to *New IIS Features* section to learn about Digest security.
- **Basic authentication** This option uses cleartext username and password for authentication. This is not secure and not recommended. This could be useful in a less secure environment (e.g., a development environment behind a firewall). You can alternatively use SSL encryption to encrypt the cleartext username and password details.
- **.NET Passport Authentication** This option uses .NET passports to authenticate Web users. This is a new feature in IIS 6.0. .NET Passport is a single sign-on

mechanism. The incoming HTTP requests must have the passport credentials (user name and password) inside the query string or as a cookie value. (A hacker might compromise the cookie and expose the user to malicious attacks. Therefore, Microsoft recommends to run **.NET Passport Authentication** over SSL.) You can enable this option by clicking the **.NET Passport Authentication** check box. You will be asked to select the **Domain** the IIS server belongs to and the **Realm** to configure the .NET passport credentials. These details need to be available to the client for future requests to the Web server.

The second option is to restrict users on an IP address level. We can list all the permitted IP addresses using this method. The users are denied access if they are not accessing from this permitted list. This can be achieved by clicking the **Edit** button under IP Address and Domain Name Restrictions group box on the Web site's Properties window (Figure 8.31). You will be presented with Figure 8.33.

Figure 8.33 Assigning IP Address Restrictions on a Web Site

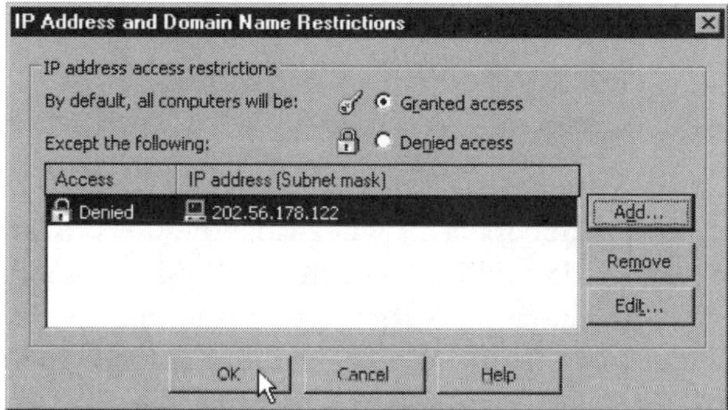

In this demonstration, we enable all computers to have access to our Web site by default. We can also restrict access to users by including their IP address in a list. You do this by clicking the **Add** button and entering the IP address. The above example will let any user access the Web site unless their IP address is 202.56.178.122.

The third option is to enable SSL and attach security certificates to the Web site. You do this by using the buttons on the **Secure Communications** group box (Figure 8.31). The **Server Certificate** button will initiate a wizard to configure a certificate for the Web site. The **Edit** button will enable you to view any existing certificate entries. The Certificate will have information on the version, serial number, signature algorithm (e.g., sha1RSA), Issuer, Valid From, Valid To, Subject, and Public Key Information. The certificate has keys that are used to authenticate the server and the client for SSL encryption. The Web server will create a Session or Encryption key according to the security certificate. This key is used to encrypt all the communication with the server and the client. The strength of the encryption is measured by the length of the encryption key (this is in bits). The encryption strength can be either 40-bits or 128-bits. The choice of the strength of the encryption depends on the sensitivity of the data. (High importance will require 128-bits—as apposed to 40.)

Troubleshooting IIS 6.0

Let's concentrate our attention on some of the troubleshooting associated with IIS 6.0. We can divide this troubleshooting section into three subsections: content errors, connection errors, and miscellaneous errors. First we look at content errors.

Troubleshooting Content Errors

Content errors are caused by ASP or ASP.NET application code. We need application code or scripts to perform business intelligence task to manipulate data. These errors are associated with these scripts. We will try to get familiar with these errors. Here are some of the common ones.

Static Files Return 404 Errors

This is the most common IIS error. This could be due to two main reasons. The user may type in an incorrect URL, or the file extension is invalid. IIS is configured to only accept requests from files that have a valid extension. (For example, IIS will understand the .ASPX extension, but it will not understand ".abc" file extension.)

Test Day Tip

We can enable IIS 6.0 to accept all requests for any file extension. We can configure this by adding **"*,application/octet-stream"** value to the MIME types list in IIS 6.0.

IIS checks for the file extension as soon as it gets a request. All the valid file extensions are available as Multipurpose Internet Mail Extensions (MIME) formats in IIS. MIME types will instruct the Web server how to process the incoming requests. (For example, if it receives .ASPX file, the Web server knows to instruct ASP.NET to process the request.) The MIME type does not have any effect on the returned data to the client. (The returned data will be in HTML for most HTTP requests.) IIS will start to process the file if the incoming file extension is present in the MIME list for IIS 6.0.

Exam Warning

If you change the MIME settings, you need to restart the World Wide Web (WWW) Publishing service. IIS 6.0 worker process needs to be recycled to detect the new MIME types. Therefore, a restart of the WWW service is necessary.

Dynamic Content Returns a 404 Error

The IIS 6.0 default installation does not activate ASP.NET and CGI applications. These have to be manually enabled using Web Service Extensions module (discussedpreviously). If the ASP.NET or CGI applications are not enabled, you will get a 404 error on dynamic content.

Sessions Lost Due to Worker Process Recycling

Sessions were very popular in ASP scripts. (A *session* could be described as a data storage mechanism for a single user on a Web site. We use sessions to manipulate HTTP cookies to store information about the user activities. This information is referred as Session data.) These ASP sessions were alive till we restarted the IIS server. IIS 6.0 works on a worker process model. Therefore, when the worker process stops, we lose all the session information. The default installation will configure IIS to recycle worker process every 120 minutes. (Session data can grow to a large amount in a high-scale Web farm. This could have an adverse affect on the performance and the memory management of the Web servers. Therefore, IIS 6.0 will *empty* the session information by recycling the worker process every 120 minutes by default.) We can either disable worker process recycling or extend the time span to correct this potential problem.

Exercise 8.02

Configure Worker Proces Recycling

1. Open the IIS Manager.
2. Select **Application Pools** and right-click the correct application pool for your Web site.
3. Select **Properties**.
4. Select **Recycling** tab.
5. To disable worker process recycling, **clear** the **Recycle worker process (in minutes)** check box. Alternatively you can select the box and enter a higher figure to extend the time.
6. Click **OK**.

ASP.NET Pages are Returned as Static Files

ASP.NET files should be processed at the server and the HTML is returned to the browser. (In some cases this could be DHTML, depending on the complexity of the browser.) If the IIS server does not recognize an ASP.NET file (.ASPX file extension), the server will return the static text as the reply. This can happen if you reinstall IIS without re-registering ASP.NET.

Troubleshooting Connection Errors

Let's concentrate on the Connection errors now. Connection issues with IIS and ASP.NET are the primary causes of these errors.

503 Errors

503 errors are generally caused by HTTP.sys overload. It could be due to two reasons. Either the request queue length has exceeded the number of available application pool resources, or the problem is **rapid-fail protection** initiated by IIS.

Every application pool has a configurable queue length. If the request pool queue exceeds this amount, the HTTP.sys will not be able to process the requests. This will result in a 503 error been thrown at the client.

Exercise 8.03

Extend the Queue Lenght of an Application Pool

We can investigate the process to increase the queue length of the application process. The default value for the queue length is 2,000 requests. We can extend the value by following these steps:

1. Open **IIS Manager**.
2. Select **Application Pools** and right-click the correct application pool for your Web site.
3. Select **Properties**.
4. Select **Performance** tab.
5. In the **Request Queue Limit** group box, select the **Limit the kernel request queue** check box and put a value in the text box.
6. Click **OK**.

IIS initiates *rapid-fail protection* when too many application pool errors are generated for a specified time frame. The default is five errors occurring in five minutes. This scenario will trigger the IIS to restart and issue a 503 error to the client.

EXERCISE 8.04

EXTENT THE QUEUE LENGTH OF AN APPLICATION POOL

Alternatively you can increase the error count and expand the timeframe. Usually this is resulting from a memory leak in the application code. Here is the process to configure rapid-fail protection:

1. Open the **IIS Manager**.
2. Select **Application Pools** and right-click the correct application pool for your Web site.
3. Select **Properties**.
4. Select the **Health** tab.
5. In the **Enable rapid-fail protection** group box, enter the value for **Failures** and **Time Period (in minutes)**.
6. Click **OK**.

Clients Cannot Connect to Server

Windows 2003 server comes with a built in software firewall. Internet Connection Firewall is disabled by default. If you enable the firewall, you need to provide the correct settings to let your clients into the system. Please refer to the *Internet Connection Firewall* section for configuration details.

401 Error – Sub Authentication Error

Anonymous accesses to Web sites are managed by the sub-authentication component (iis-suba.dll). This DLL is not enabled by default in IIS 6.0. The reason is to avoid potential security risks due to anonymous access. We can enable the sub-authentication component by registering iissuba.dll and setting the *AnonymousPasswordSync* attribute in the Metabase to **true**. The IIS administrator will issue a warning when anonymous access is enabled.

TEST DAY TIP

Sub-authentication component for anonymous access is enabled by default in IIS 5.0 and lower. Remember, it is not enabled by default in IIS 6.0.

Client Requests Timing Out

There was less emphasis on connections timing out in IIS 5.0 and below. IIS 6.0 has gained some considerable ground on this issue. IIS 6.0 has locked down and reduced the size of many client request properties. This has resulted in better efficiency and performance. Here are some new features in IIS 6.0 that deal with timeouts:

- **Limits on response buffering** We can buffer all the process output at the server end and send the whole output to the client as a single entity (as apposed to processing some data and sending the information and starting to process the next bit of the initial request). This is referred to as *response buffering*. Limits on response buffering is 4MB. A timeout will result if the buffer exceeds the limit. This feature can be modified by using the **ASPBufferingLimit** metabase property.
- **Limits on posts** The maximum ASP post size is 204,800 bytes. (**Post** refers to a HTTP POST response to the Web server. This is usually done as an HTML form submission. Sometimes these HTML form variables can be very lengthy. The maximum size allowed as HTTP POST request is referred to as Post limit/size.) Each individual field can have up to 100k of data. If these fields are exceeded, a time out error is thrown. This property can also be modified from the **AspMaxRequestEntityAllowed** property of the metabase.
- **Header size limitation** HTTP.sys only accepts a request that has less than 16K as the request header. HTTP.sys believes that anything larger is malicious and terminates the connection. You can change this value by modifying the MaxRequestBytes registry key.

Troubleshooting Other Errors

We will investigate some miscellaneous troubleshooting errors in this section. These errors do not clearly fall into the content or connection categories.

File Not Found Errors for UNIX and Linux Files

IIS 6.0 can access and share information with UNIX and Linux systems. IIS 6.0, UNIX, and Linux all support mixed-case filenames. Unfortunately, the IIS *static file cache* stores filenames as upper case. Therefore, the first file access will be trouble-free. The subsequent access to the same file will result in a File Not Found error because IIS 6.0 will try to extract it from the static file cache. The remedy is to disable static file cache if you deal with UNIX or Linux systems.

Head of the Class...

Disable Static File Cache

To disable static file cache on a Web site or a virtual directory, edit the metabase property **MD_VR_NO_CACHE to 1.** To disable static file cache for all sites, edit the **DisableStaticFileCache=1** value in the registry. Changing these settings will affect only ASP.NET files. ASP files **will not** be affected by this change. The *static file cache* will cache all the static Web content for faster response times. Performance may decrease if this facility is disabled.

ISAPI Filters Are Not Automatically Visible as Properties of the Web Site

IIS 5.0 used to display all the ISAPI filters that were associated with a particular site. IIS 6.0 does not load an ISAPI DLL until it is actually invoked from a client request. Therefore, until an ISAPI DLL is loaded, it will not show up in the **ISAPI** tab of the **Properties** window. Please run IIS 6.0 in isolation mode if you want to get a complete list of ISAPI DLLs available for a site. (Refer to the *New Reliability Features* section to learn how to run IIS 6.0 in isolation mode.)

The Scripts and Msadc Virtual Directories Are Not Found in IIS 6.0

IIS 5.0 had executable permission on the Scripts and Msadc directories. This was one of the common security breaches of IIS 5.0. A malicious user can start to execute code in these virtual directories and take control of the IIS server. Therefore, IIS 6.0 is configured not to have these two directories in order to beef up security.

Using New IIS Command-Line Utilities

IIS Manager is the GUI interface for all IIS management functions. You can also perform these management functions by using command-line tools. All these command line tools are VBScript functions with *.VBS file extensions. You can get the complete help file information by applying the */?* Switch on each utility. Let's go through them one by one.

iisweb.vbs

The insweb.vbs utility is used to create and manage Web sites in IIS 6.0. This utility is stored at System Root\system 32 directory. iisweb.vbs comes with six main switches. The main switches are listed in Table 8.2. The first argument for iisweb.vbs is one of these main switches. The rest of the arguments are further information to perform the task. The common syntax is:

```
Iisweb [switch] [parameters to switch]
```

Table 8.2 Switches Available in Iisweb.vbs

Switch Name	Description
/create	To create a Web site
/delete	To delete an existing Web site
/start	To start a Web site
/stop	To stop a Web site
/pause	To pause a Web site
/query	To check whether the Web site/sites are functioning according to plan

The parameters to the switches change from switch to switch. Let's investigate the syntax of every switch.

create

First we will look at the /create switch. The syntax is illustrated in the following example. The parameters are discussed in Table 8.3. The required parameters to run the command successfully are *Path* and *SiteName*.

```
Syntax : iisweb[.vbs] /create Path SiteName [/b Port] [/i IPAddress] [/d
    HostHeader] [/dontstart] [/s Computer [/u [Domain\]User
        [/p Password]]]
```

Table 8.3 Available Parameters for Create Switch in iisweb.vbs

Parameter	Description
Path	This field is mandatory. This is the path to find the files for the Web site. The iisweb.vbs script will create a directory if the path does not exist. This must be the first parameter.
SiteName	The name of the Web site. This field is also mandatory.
/b Port	The port number for the Web site to channel HTTP requests. The default value is 80.
/I IPAddress	The specified IP address associated with the Web site.
/d HostHeader	The host header for the site. This is the domain name of the Web site. The default configuration is *no host headers* and the Web site is identified by the IP address and port number.

Continued

Table 8.3 Available Parameters for create Switch in iisweb.vbs

Parameter	Description
/dontstart	IIS will start the Web site as soon as it creates one. Using this command we can instruct the IIS not to start the Web site immediately.
/s Computer	You can use this command if you are creating Web sites remotely. The default value is the local computer. Use the IP address or machine name if you want to create Web sites remotely.
/u [Domain\]User	The user details when you create Web sites remotely.
/p Password	The password for the above user account.
/?	List of help commands for the iisweb.vbs script.

Now let's see this command in action. We will try to create a Web site called "TestIISCommand" using the iisweb.vbs script. Here is the process:

Create a Visual Studio Command Prompt Window. (**Start | All Programs | Visual Studio .NET | Visual Studio .NET Tools | Visual Studio .NET Command Prompt.)** Refer to Figure 8.34 for the command and the output of the command.

Figure 8.34 Creating a Web site Using iisweb.vbs

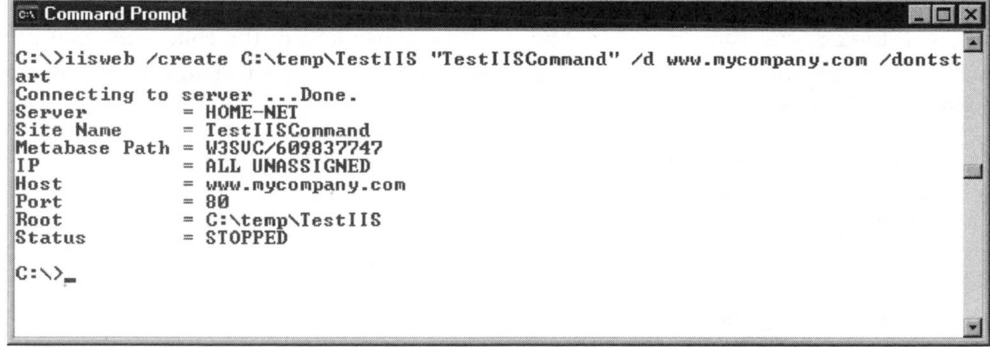

This command will create a Web site called "TestIISCommand" that refers to C:\temp\TestIIS directory. The domain name of the Web site is www.mycompany.com and we are instructing IIS not to start the Web site as soon as we create it.

start, stop, pause, and delete

We can discuss the */start, /stop, /pause,* and */delete* switches together because their parameters are the same. The general syntax is illustrated in the following example. Table 8.4 describes the common parameters for these switches.

```
Syntax : iisweb[.vbs] {/delete | /start | /stop | /pause} WebSite
    [WebSite...] [/s Computer [/u [Domain\]User [/p Password]]]
```

Table 8.4 Parameters for start, stop, pause, and delete Switches of iisweb.vbs

Parameter	Description
WebSite	The name of the site we want to start, stop, pause, or delete. Alternatively, the metabase path is also valid. Multiple values can be added to perform a common task on them.
/s Computer	You can use this command for remote access. The default value is the local computer. Use the IP address or machine name if you want to perform operations remotely.
/u [Domain\]User	The user details for the remote operation.
/p Password	The password for the above user account.
/?	List of help commands available for start, stop, pause, and delete command.

Exam Warning

In IIS 6.0 you can have multiple Web sites with the same name as long as they have different metabase entries. To delete them you need to give the exact metabase entry name (as apposed to site name).

Let's see our commands in action (refer to Figure 8.35 for reference). First we try to start the TestIISCommand Web site we created before. Then we try to stop the same Web site by using the */stop* switch. Please note that we are using the metabase entry name as apposed to the site name for this command. Then we restart the site and pause it. Finally, we delete the site using the */delete* switch.

Figure 8.35 Starting, Pausing, Stopping, and Deleting a Web Site Using iisweb.vbs

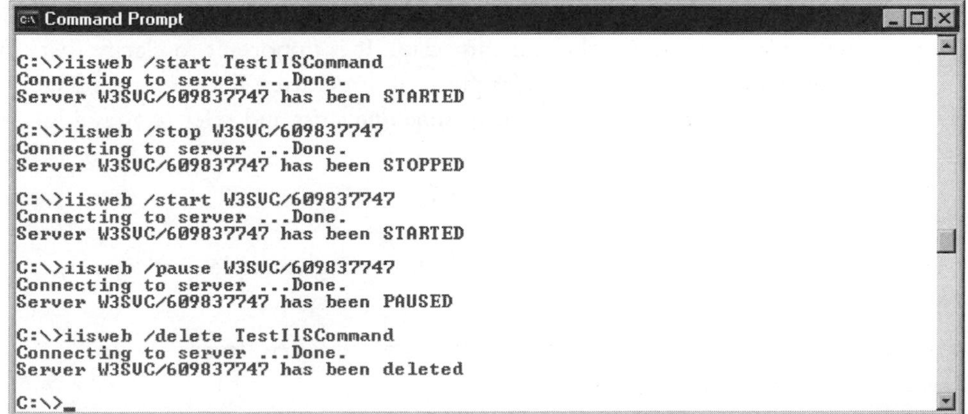

query

Use the */query* switch to display information about the active Web sites on IIS servers. *query* command without any arguments will display all Web sites under the control of IIS. Alternatively, we can give it a single site to focus on it:

```
Syntax : iisweb[.vbs] /query [WebSite [WebSite...]] [/s Computer [/u
    [Domain\]User [/p Password]]]
```

The parameter options are exactly the same as the previous Table 8.4. Here is the *query* command in action (refer to Figure 8.36).

Figure 8.36 Getting a List of Web Sites Using iisweb.vbs

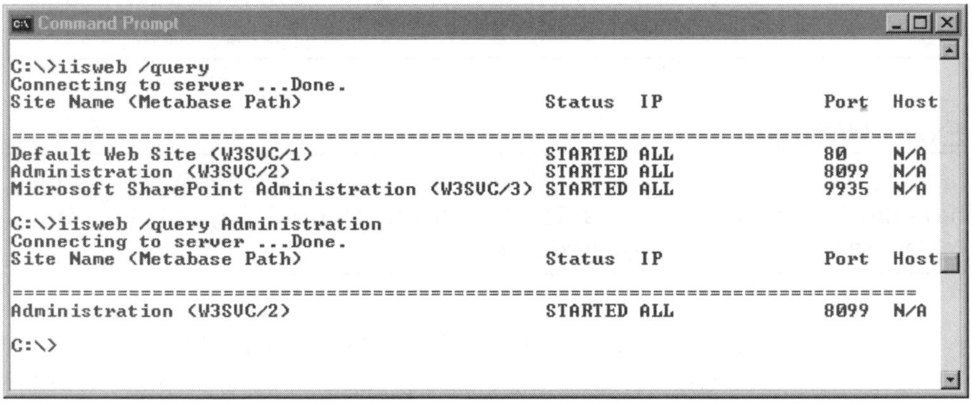

```
Command Prompt

C:\>iisweb /query
Connecting to server ...Done.
Site Name (Metabase Path)                     Status  IP          Port  Host

==============================================================================
Default Web Site (W3SVC/1)                    STARTED ALL         80    N/A
Administration (W3SVC/2)                      STARTED ALL         8099  N/A
Microsoft SharePoint Administration (W3SVC/3) STARTED ALL         9935  N/A

C:\>iisweb /query Administration
Connecting to server ...Done.
Site Name (Metabase Path)                     Status  IP          Port  Host

==============================================================================
Administration (W3SVC/2)                      STARTED ALL         8099  N/A

C:\>
```

First we use the query command to get a list of all the Web sites running on our target machine. Then we do a more specific query on a selected Web site (*Administration* web site).

iisvdir.vbs

The iisvdir.vbs command enables us to create virtual directories for a specific Web site. We can use create, delete, and query switches on this script. It is important to clarify that this command does not generate any new code or physical directories. This command will basically instruct the IIS configuration to point at *existing directories* and refer to it as a local directory of the Web site.

create

This switch will create a new virtual directory. The following example illustrates the syntax. Table 8.5 describes all the parameters available for the *create* switch.

```
iisvdir /create WebSite[/VirtualPath] Name PhysicalPath [/s Computer [/u
    [Domain\]User /p Password]]
```

Table 8.5 Parameters Available for Create Switch for iisvdir.vbs

Parameter	Description
WebSite	This field is mandatory. The name of the Web site we create the virtual directory for.
VirtualPath	Sometimes we need to create a virtual directory under an existing virtual directory. This parameter is optional. The virtual directory will be created at the root if this parameter is omitted.
Name	The name of the virtual directory. This field is mandatory.
PhysicalPath	The physical directory where the virtual directory points. This field is also required.
/s Computer	You can use this command if you are creating virtual directories remotely. The default value is the local computer. Use the IP address or machine name if you want to create the virtual directory remotely.
/u [Domain\]User	The user details when you create the virtual directory remotely.
/p Password	The password for the user account.

delete

We can delete an existing virtual directory using the */delete* switch. The following example illustrates the syntax. Table 8.6 describes the parameters available for this script.

```
Syntax : iisvdir /delete WebSite[/VirtualPath] Name [/s Computer [/u
    [Domain\]User/p Password]]
```

Table 8.6 Parameters Available for delete Switch for iisvdir.vbs

Parameter	Description
WebSite	This field is mandatory. The name of the Web site containing the virtual directory we want to delete.
VirtualPath	Sometimes we need to create a virtual directory under an existing virtual directory. This optional parameter will enable us to navigate to the correct virtual directory.
Name	The name of the virtual directory. This field is mandatory.
/s Computer	You can use this command if you are deleting virtual directories remotely. The default value is the local computer. Use the IP address or machine name if you want to delete the virtual directory remotely.
/u [Domain\]User	The user details when you delete the virtual directory remotely.
/p Password	The password for the user account.

query

The */query* switch will display all the virtual directories of a given Web site. The following example illustrates the syntax. Table 8.7 describes the parameters available for this script.

```
Syntax : iisvdir /query  WebSite[/VirtualPath][/s Computer [/u [Domain\]
    User/p  Password]]
```

Table 8.7 Parameters Available for Query Switch for iisvdir.vbs

Parameter	Description
WebSite	This field is mandatory. The name of the Web site containing the virtual directories we want to query.
VirtualPath	This field needs to be populated if you are trying to query a virtual directory inside a virtual directory.
/s Computer	For remote access. The default value is the local computer. Use the IP address or machine name if you want to query the virtual directory remotely.
/u [Domain\]User	The user details when you query the virtual directory remotely.
/p Password	The password for the user account.

iisftp.vbs

iisftp.vbs is the command-line tools to administer FTP sites on your IIS server. The functionality is very similar to iisweb.vbs. The only major difference is the association with Active Directory under iisftp.vbs. The main switches are described in Table 8.8. The common syntax is as follows:

```
Iisweb [switch] [parameters to switch]
```

Table 8.8 Switches Available for iisftp.vbs

Switch name	Description
/create	To create an FTP site
/delete	To delete an existing FTP site
/start	To start an FTP site
/stop	To stop an FTP site
/setadprop	To set Active Directory properties for a user to access FTP site
/getadprop	To get Active Directory properties for a user
/query	To check whether the FTP site/sites are functioning according to plan

The parameters to switches change from switch to switch. Let's investigate the syntax of every switch.

Create

We will investigate the */create* switch first. The following example illustrates the syntax. The required parameters to run the command successfully are *Path* and *SiteName*.

```
Syntax : iisftp /create Path SiteName [/b Port] [/i IPAddress]
    [/dontstart] [/isolation  {AD|Local} [/domain  DomainName /Admin
        [Domain\]User /AdminPwd Password]] [/s Computer [/u
            [Domain\]User/p Password]]
```

Table 8.9 describes the parameters. The required parameters to run the command successfully are *Path* and *SiteName*.

Table 8.9 Parameters Available for Create Switch for iisftp.vbs

Parameter	Description
Path	This field is mandatory. This is the path to find the files for the FTP site. This must be the first parameter.
SiteName	The name of the FTP site. This field is also mandatory.
/b Port	The port number for the FTP site to channel FTP requests. The default value is 21.
/i IPAddress	The specified IP address associated with the FTP site.
/dontstart	IIS starts the FTP site as soon as it is created. Using this command, we can instruct IIS not to start it immediately.
/isolation	iisftp.vbs accepts two isolation modes. This could be either Active Directory or local isolation mode. The default is local.
/domain	This flag is valid only when the isolation flag is set to Active Directory. This is the domain to which the Active Directory belongs.
/Admin	Only valid with Active Directory isolation mode. The Active Directory's admin account details.
/AdminPwd	Only valid with Active Directory isolation mode. The password of the admin account.
/s Computer	You can use this command if you are creating FTP sites remotely. The default value is the local computer. Use the IP address or machine name if you want to create FTP sites remotely.
/u [Domain\]User	The user details when you create FTP sites remotely.
/p Password	The password for the user account.
/?	List of help commands for the iisftp.vbs script.

The use of the *iisftp /create* is very similar to *iisweb /create*. The input parameters and the command shell output are very similar.

start, stop, pause, and delete

The */start, /stop, /pause,* and */delete* switches are also very similar to iisweb.vbs functionality. We can discuss these four switches together because their parameters are the same. Table 8.10 describes all the parameters. This is the general syntax:

```
Syntax : iisftp[.vbs] {/delete | /start | /stop | /pause} FTPSite
    [FTPSite...] [/s Computer [/u [Domain\]User [/p Password]]]
```

Table 8.10 Parameters Available for *start, stop, pause,* and *delete* Switches for iisftp.vbs

Parameter	Description
FTPSite	The name of the FTP site we want to start, stop, pause, or delete. Alternatively, the metabase path also is valid. Multiple values can be added to perform a command task on them.
/s Computer	You can use this command for remote access. The default value is the local computer. Use the IP address or machine name if you want to perform operations remotely.
/u [Domain\]User	The user details for the remote operation.
/p Password	The password for the above user account.
/?	List of help commands available for start, stop, pause, or delete command.

query

Use the */query* switch to display information about the active FTP sites on IIS servers. The *query* command without any arguments will display all FTP sites under the control of IIS 6.0. Alternatively, we can give it a single site to focus on.

```
Syntax : iisftp[.vbs] /query [FTPSite [FTPSite...]] [/s Computer [/u
    [Domain\]User [/p Password]]]
```

The parameter options are exactly same as those found in Table 8.10 for the *start, stop, pause,* and *delete* commands.

Active Directory set and get Calls

The Active Directory commands apply only when the iisftp.vbs runs on *Active Directory isolation mode*. The */isolation AD* switch must be present to enable *GetADProp* and *SetADProp* commands. Here is the syntax for both commands:

```
iisftp /GetADProp UserID [/s  Computer [/u [Domain\]User /p Password]]
iisftp /SetADProp UserID {FTPDir|FTPRoot} PropertyValue [/s Computer [/u
    [Domain\]User/p Password]]
```

GetADProp returns the property values for a specific user. *SetADProp* assigns property values for a specific Active Directory user. Table 8.11 shows the options available with these commands.

Table 8.11 Parameters Available for GetADProp and SetADProp Switches for iisftp.vbs

Parameter	Description
UserID	This is a required field. The login ID of the Active Directory user.
FTPDir | FTPRoot	This is required for SetADProp. This is a flag to indicate whether the change is at the "Directory" or the "Root" level of the FTP site.
PropertyValue	Required for *SetADProp*. Describes the home directory and relative path.
/s Computer	You can use this command for remote access. The default value is the local computer. Use the IP address or machine name if you want to perform operations remotely.
/u [Domain\]User	The user details for the remote operation.
/p Password	The password for the user account.

iisftpdr.vbs

The iisftpdr.vbs command is very similar to iisvdir.vbs. We create virtual directories for FTP sites (not Web sites) using this command. We can use *create, delete,* and *query* switches on this script.

create

The */create* switch will create a new virtual directory. The following example illustrates the syntax. Table 8.12 explains the different parameters we can use with the iisftpdr.vbs script.

```
Syntax : iisftpdr /create FTPSite[VirtualPath] Name PhysicalPath [/s
    Computer [/u [Domain\]User /p Password]]
```

Table 8.12 Parameters Available for create Switch for iisftpdr.vbs

Parameter	Description
FTPSite	This field is manatory. The name of the FTP site we create the virtual directory for.
VirtualPath	Sometimes we need to create a virtual directory under an existing virtual directory. This parameter is optional. The virtual directory will be created at the root if this parameter is omitted.
Name	The name of the virtual directory. This field is mandatory.
PhysicalPath	The physical directory where the virtual directory points.
/s Computer	You can use this command if you are creating a virtual directory remotely. The default value is the local computer. Use the IP address or machine name.
/u [Domain\]User	The user details when you create a virtual directory remotely.
/p Password	The password for the user account.

Delete

We can delete an existing virtual directory using the */delete* switch. The following example illustrates the syntax. Table 8.13 describes the parameters available for this script.

```
Syntax : iisftpdr /delete  FTPSite[VirtualPath]/Name [/s  Computer [/u
    [Domain\]User /p Password]]
```

Table 8.13 Parameters Available for delete Switch for iisftpdr.vbs

Parameter	Description
FTPSite	This field is mandatory. The name of the FTP site where we delete the virtual directory.
VirtualPath	Sometimes we need to delete a virtual directory under an existing virtual directory. This parameter is optional. The virtual directory will be deleted at the root if this parameter is omitted.
Name	The name of the virtual directory. This field is mandatory.
/s Computer	You can use this command if you are deleting a virtual directory remotely. The default value is the local computer. Use the IP address or machine name.
/u [Domain\]User	The user details when you delete a virtual directory remotely.
/p Password	The password for the user account.

query

The */query* switch will display all the virtual directories of a given FTP site. The following example illustrates the syntax. Table 8.14 describes the parameters available for this script.

```
Syntax : iisftpdr /query  FTPSite[/VirtualPath][/s Computer [/u
    [Domain\]User/p  Password]]
```

Table 8.14 Parameters Available for query Switch for iisftpdr.vbs

Parameter	Description
FTPSite	This field is mandatory. The name of the FTP site we query.
VirtualPath	This field needs to be populated if you are trying to query a virtual directory inside a virtual directory.
/s Computer	You can use this command if you are querying a virtual directory remotely. The default value is the local computer. Use the IP address or machine name.
/u [Domain\]User	The user details when you query a virtual directory remotely.
/p Password	The password for the above user account.

iisback.vbs

Use the *iisback.vbs* utility to create backups and restore IIS configurations. We can back up both the metabase and metabase XML schema data using this tool. The backup creates two files. The *.mdVersionNumber* file to back up the metabase and the *.scVersionNumber* file to back up the metabase schema.

Exam Warning

iisback.vbs only creates backups. It does not copy the IIS configuration details. Therefore, you cannot copy a backup from one machine to another and expect the IIS server to inherit the information. Please use iiscnfg.vbs if want to replicate the IIS configuration settings.

Test Day Tip

IIS 6.0 backups are encrypted with a session key. The session key is only validated when you try to restore the backup. You will be able to read and delete the backups. You will not be able to modify the encrypted session key details of the backup.

Back Up IIS Configuration

Here is the syntax for the iisback.vbs utility. Table 8.15 explains the different parameters for the utility.

```
iisback /backup [/b BackupName] [/v {Integer | HIGHEST_VERSION |
    NEXT_VERSION}] [/overwrite] [/e  EncryptingPassword] [/s Computer [/u
        [Domain\]User/p Password]]
```

Table 8.15 Parameters Available for backup Switch for iisback.vbs

Parameter	Description
/b *BackupName*	Name of the backup.
/v {*Integer*}	This value could be either the NEXT_VERSION or HIGHEST_VERSION value. The NEXT_VERSION attribute will increment the current version number by 1. The HIGHEST_VERSION value can only be used with the **/overwrite** parameter. It will create a backup of the last (highest) version number. (This will overwrite the highest version backup.) The default is NEXT_VERSION.
/overwrite	This flag will enable the iisback.vbs script to overwrite an existing backup.
/e *EncryptingPassword*	The encrypted session key password associated with the backup.
/s Computer	You can use this command if you are creating backups remotely. The default value is the local computer. Use the IP address or machine name.
/u [Domain\]User	The user details when you create a backup remotely.
/p Password	The password for the user account.

Restore IIS Configuration

Use the */restore* switch to restore settings from a given backup. The following example illustrates the syntax. Table 8.16 explains the parameters for the utility.

```
Syntax : iisback /restore /b BackupName [/v {Integer | HIGHEST_VERSION}]
    [/e EncryptionPassword] [/s Computer [/u [Domain\]User/p Password]]
```

Table 8.16 Parameters Available for restore Switch for iisback.vbs

Parameter	Description
/b *BackupName*	Name of the backup to be restored.
/v {*Integer*}	This value could be either the integer (the version number) or HIGHEST_VERSION value. The default is HIGHEST_VERSION.
/e *EncryptingPassword*	The encrypted session key password associated with the backup.
/s Computer	You can use this command if you are restoring remotely. The default value is the local computer. Use the IP address or machine name.
/u [Domain\]User	The user details when you restore backups remotely.
/p Password	The password for the user account.

delete

Use the */delete* switch to delete the backup of IIS. This will delete both the MD*VersionNumber* and SC*VersionNumber* files. The following example illustrates the syntax. Table 8.17 explains the parameters.

```
Syntax : iisback /delete [/bBackupName] [/v {Integer | HIGHEST_VERSION}]
    [/s Computer [/u [Domain\]User /p Password]]
```

Table 8.17 Parameters Available for delete Switch for iisback.vbs

Parameter	Description
/b *BackupName*	Name of the backup to be deleted.
/v {*Integer*}	This value could be either the integer (the version number) or HIGHEST_VERSION value.
/s Computer	For remote access. The default value is the local computer. Use the IP address or machine name.
/u [Domain\]User	The user details when you delete remotely.
/p Password	The password for the user account.

list

The */list* switch will display all the backups available for a given IIS server. The default is the local server. The following example illustrates the syntax and Table 8.18 displays the parameters for this utility.

```
Syntax : iisback /list [/s Computer [/u [Domain\]User/p Password]]
```

Table 8.18 Parameters Available for query Switch for iisback.vbs

Parameter	Description
/s Computer	For remote access. The default value is the local computer. Use the IP address or machine name.
/u [Domain\]User	The user details when you query remotely.
/p Password	The password for the user account.

iiscnfg.vbs

The iiscnfg.vbs script will enable you to manipulate the configuration settings for IIS 6.0. The main task is to import and export settings of the IIS metabase. You can also select a node of the IIS 6.0 and import and export settings to it. The available switches are import, export, copy, and save. Let's investigate them one by one.

Head of the Class...

Metabase Refresh with iiscnfg.vbs

Changes using iiscnfg.vbs are effective **immediately** in IIS 6.0. This is not immediately reflected in the metabase.xml file. The default refresh time for metabase.xml is five minutes. We need to use the **/save** switch to force refresh the metabase.xml if we want to update the metabase immediately.

import

The */import* switch will enable you to import configuration settings into your IIS 6.0 server. The following example illustrates the syntax. Table 8.19 describes the parameters.

```
Syntax : iiscnfg /import /f [Path\]FileName.xml /sp  SourcePath /dp
    DestinationPath[/d EncryptingPassword] [/inherited] [/children]
        [/merge][/s Computer [/u [Domain\]User [/p Password]]]
```

Table 8.19 Parameters Available for import Switch for iiscnfg.vbs

Parameter	Description
/f [*Path*\]*FileName.xml*	This required field describes the XML source file to read the data.
/sp *SourcePath*	The position of the key/node of the XML source file. This is a required field.
/dp *DestinationPath*	The destination key/node position in the metabase. This is a required field.
/d *EncryptingPassword*]	The encrypted password for the source file.
/inherited	The utility will import all the inherited data if the source key/node has inherited properties.
/children	Recursively import all subkeys of a given key/node.
/merge	We can merge different source keys into one metabase key using this parameter.
/s Computer	For remote access. The default value is the local computer. Use the IP address or machine name.
/u [Domain\]User	The user details when you import remotely.
/p Password	The password for the user account.

export

The */export* switch will help the user to export IIS configuration. The following example illustrates the syntax. The parameters are explained in Table 8.20.

```
Syntax : iiscnfg /export /f [Path\]FileName.xml /sp SourcePath [/d
    EncryptingPassword] [/inherited] [/children] [/s Computer [/u
        [Domain\]User [/p Password]]]
```

Table 8.20 Parameters Available for export Switch for iiscnfg.vbs

Parameter	Description
/f [*Path*\]*FileName.xml*	This required field describes the XML file to write the data.
/sp *SourcePath*	The position of the key/node of the metabase entries. This is a required field.
/d *EncryptingPassword*	The encrypted password for the source file.
/inherited	Instructions to import all inherited keys of the metabase entries.
/children	Recursively export all subkeys of a given key/node.
/s Computer	For remote access. The default value is the local computer. Use the IP address or machine name.

Continued

Table 8.20 Parameters Available for export Switch for iiscnfg.vbs

Parameter	Description
/u [Domain\]User	The user details when you export remotely.
/p Password	The password for the user account.

copy

The */copy* switch uses the iiscnfg.vbs script to make duplicates of the IIS configurations and copy it to the target IIS server. This will copy both the metabase.xml and metabase XML schema files. Please note these are just the IIS configuration settings. The Web site content is not replicated using this method. We need to use a content replication system for copying Web site content (for example, Microsoft Content Management Server or Site Server Replication Tools). Here is the syntax for */copy* switch. Table 8.21 explains the parameters.

```
Syntax : iiscnfg /copy /ts TargetComputer /tu TargetUser /tp
    TargetPassword [/s Computer [/u [Domain\]User [/p Password]]]
```

Table 8.21 Parameters Available for Copy Switch for iiscnfg.vbs

Parameter	Description
/ts TargetComputer	The target computer name where the configuration needs to be copied to. This required field could be the machine name or IP address.
/tu TargetUser	The user name to log on to the target machine.
/tp TargetPassword	Password for the target machine's user account.
/s Computer	For remote access. The default value is the local computer. Use the IP address or machine name.
/u [Domain\]User	The user details when you copy remotely.
/p Password	The password for the user account.

save

The */save* switch enables you to save all the changes to the metabase. All changes by iiscnfg.vbs or IIS Manager will be loaded to the memory and written to the metabase on a scheduled timeframe. This utility will force the metabase to update immediately. The following example illustrates the syntax and Table 8.22 explains the parameters.

```
Syntax : iiscnfg /save [/s Computer [/u [Domain\]User /p  Password]]
```

Table 8.22 Parameters Available for Save Switch for iiscnfg.vbs

Parameter	Description
/s Computer	For remote access. The default value is the local computer. Use the IP address or machine name.
/u [Domain\]User	The user details when you save remotely.
/p Password	The password for the user account.

Summary of Exam Objectives

This chapter explains the functionality of Internet Information Server (IIS) 6.0 in Windows Server 2003. Our objective is to get familiar with the new features and learn the main features of IIS. Internet Information Server 6.0 incorporates World Wide Web Service, FTP service, NNTP server, and SMTP server.

We investigated the new features in IIS 6.0. There are several new security features: Advance Digest Security, Server Gated Cryptography, Selectable Cryptographic Providers, and default lockdown status. The new reliability features in IIS 6.0 are Health Detection and request processing architecture using HTTP.sys. Miscellaneous new features include the XML metabase, UTF-8 support, and ASP.NET integration with IIS 6.0.

We have learned to create, start, stop, and delete all these sites and virtual servers. The management of the IIS 6.0 functions is mainly done through the IIS Manager MMC console. There are also command-line utilities available for these functions. Iisweb.vbs script is available to manage IIS 6.0 Web sites. Iisftp.vbs utility is used to manage FTP sites. Iisback.vbs can be used to make backups and restore IIS settings. Iiscnfg.vbs script is used to manipulate the IIS configuration settings.

We also learned about the different security options available in IIS 6.0. We can use Digest security, Basic Authentication, Windows Integrated Security and .NET passport security models to manage security. We can also use the new Web Service Extensions window to conveniently enable or disable ASP, ASP.NET, FrontPage extensions, and WebDAV support on an IIS server. We also spent some time learning the common troubleshooting errors of II 6.0.

Our objective was to educate you on the IIS basics and help you to avoid pitfalls with IIS 6.0. We have concentrated on a *hands-on* approach to experiment with IIS as we progress through this chapter. Please take time to read the special comments and to do the exercises. Finally, test your knowledge with the sample exam questions and get familiar with the frequently asked questions. Good Luck!

Exam Objectives Fast Track

Installing and Configuring IIS 6.0

☑ Windows Server 2003 has a built-in Internet Connection Firewall. Please configure the firewall correctly before you install IIS 6.0.

☑ IIS can be installed in three different ways. The first is by using **Configure your Server Wizard**. The second option is to use **Add/Remove Programs** from **Control Panel**. The final option is unattended setup.

☑ Systems administrators will use the unattended setup to configure multiple computers.

What's New in IIS 6.0?

- ☑ The new features can be categorized into two main sections: security and reliability.
- ☑ Advance Digest authentication, Server-gated Cryptography, Selectable Cryptography Service Provider, separate Worker Process, and Default Lockdown Wizard are the new security features.
- ☑ IIS 6.0 runs on a separate worker process model. This means that every Web site is a separate ISAPI application memory space that is detached form IIS.
- ☑ There is a Health Detection system between IIS and the separate worker processes.
- ☑ HTTP.sys is the new kernel process that accepts all incoming IIS traffic. It uses application pools to assign resources to Web sites.
- ☑ ASP.NET is the default scripting mechanism available in IIS 6.0. It will still support the old ASP applications.
- ☑ IIS configuration settings are stored in a XML metabase.

Managing IIS 6.0

- ☑ We can force the user to authenticate using Digest, Basic, Integrated Windows, and .NET Passport security.
- ☑ Anonymous access is not recommended for a Web site.
- ☑ The safest authentication is the Digest authentication option.
- ☑ We can also include IP restrictions to restrict known offenders and networks.
- ☑ Another security mechanism is to use SSL certificate to encrypt the communication between the server and the client.

Troubleshooting IIS 6.0

- ☑ Troubleshooting IIS can be categorized into two main sections: Content and Connection errors.
- ☑ A 404 error is due to a misspelled URL or an invalid file extension.
- ☑ You can also lose session data in IIS 6.0 because the worker process is recycled every two hours. (Two hours is the default configurable setting.)

- ☑ 503 errors are due to the influx of HTTP requests to HTTP.sys. This could lead to Rapid-fail protection to restart the worker process.
- ☑ The time-out parameters in IIS 6.0 are much more extensive than the IIS 5.0 settings.

Using New IIS Command-Line Utilities

- ☑ All IIS Manager functionality is available by using command-line utilities.
- ☑ **iisweb.vbs** enables you to create, start, stop, pause, and delete Web sites.
- ☑ **iisftp.vbs** enables you to create, start, stop, pause, and delete FTP sites.
- ☑ **iisvdir.vbs** enables you to create, delete, and query virtual directories for Web sites.
- ☑ **iisftpdr.vbs** enables you to create, delete, and query virtual directories for FTP sites.
- ☑ **iisback.vbs** enables you to back up, restore, delete, and list the IIS backups.
- ☑ **iiscnfg.vbs** enables you to import, export, copy, and save IIS configuration settings.
- ☑ **iiscnfg.vbs** */save* switch enables you to use the iiscnfg.vbs to make backups and copy the configuration settings to another computer.

Exam Objectives Frequently Asked Questions

The following Frequently Asked Questions, answered by the authors of this book, are designed to both measure your understanding of the Exam Objectives presented in this chapter, and to assist you with real-life implementation of these concepts. You will also gain access to thousands of other FAQs at ITFAQnet.com.

Q: How do I replicate Web content on multiple servers?

A: IIS 6.0 does not have a built-in content replication tool. Content replication is a major issue to manage large Web farms. Please use Microsoft Content Management Server (CMS) or Site Server tools for content replications.

Q: Can I remotely administer my IIS Server?

A: Yes, you can. Both IIS Manager and the command-line tools provide tools to do this. IIS Manager enables you to add remote computers as nodes to the IIS Manager console. All command-line utilities come with parameters to configure user name password support for remote computers. All command-line utilities come with */s* parameter for the remote computer name, */u* parameter for the user name to log on to the remote machine and */p* parameter for the password for the user account.

Q: Can I give different access points to different users for an FTP site?

A: Yes, you can. Using the FTP isolation utilities in IIS, we can point different FTP users to different physical FTP home directories.

Q: How can I convert a FAT system to an NTFS system?

A: There is a command-line utility called convert.exe for this purpose. The syntax is **convert *DriveLetter*: /FS:NTFS.** It is important to understand that an NTFS system cannot be converted to a FAT system using this tool.

Q: How do I obtain SSL security access information?

A: This could be achieved through the IIS Manager. Click on the Web site and select **Properties**. Then select **Directory Security** tab. Choose the **View Certificate** button under the **Secure Communications** group box. The certificate will have information on the version, serial number, signature algorithm (e.g., sha1RSA), Issuer, Valid From, Valid To, Subject, and Public Key Information.

Q: Can we have multiple SSL security certificates for a single Web site?

A: Unfortunately, no. Only one security certificate is permitted for a single Web site.

Q: Can I reuse the same server certificate for multiple Web sites?

A: Yes. You can use the same SSL security certificate in multiple Web sites. Multiple sites have to be configured separately to use the same certificate.

Q: Can I attach SSL security certificates for FTP sites?

A: Unfortunately, no. FTP sites do not support SSL without third-party add-ons.

Self Test

A Quick Answer Key follows the Self Test questions. For complete questions, answers, and epxlanations to the Self Test questions in this chapter as well as the other chapters in this book, see the **Self Test Appendix**.

Installing and Configuring IIS 6.0

1. You have been instructed to install Windows Server 2003 on a Windows 2000 machine. The current Windows 2000 Server is running under a FAT32 system. The Windows 2003 installation will permit you to upgrade or have clean installation. When you are performing the upgrade, you have an option between FAT32 and NTFS file systems. Which ones would you choose?

   A. FAT

   B. FAT32

   C. NTFS

   D. FAT64

2. You have installed the standard default installation of Windows Server 2003. You were disappointed to find out that the IIS 6.0 wasn't installed by default. You have read that you can install IIS in several ways. You pick the **Configure Your Server Wizard** option. You have discovered that the Windows server acts like an Application Server by investigating this option. What technology is not included in the Windows Server 2003 application server technologies?

   A. COM+

   B. ASP.NET

   C. ASP

   D. IIS 6.0

What's New in IIS 6.0?

3. IIS 6.0 introduces a worker process model concept. A worker process model is a separate ISAPI application (Web site) that runs in isolation. In previous IIS versions (version 5.0 and earlier) all applications ran in the same memory space as inetinfo.exe. IIS 6.0 does not enable the applications to run in the same space as inetinfo.exe. What is the IIS 6.0 concept of tracking its Web sites referred to as?

   A. Using Health Detection

   B. Using HTTP.sys

   C. Using XML metabase entries

   D. Using ASP.NET scripts that directly communicate to .NET Framework

4. ASP.NET is the new scripting mechanism available in IIS 6.0. You have read in the *Windows 2003 Magazine* about its advantages over ASP. You are experimenting with ASP.NET scripting now. What could be correct about your sample ASP.NET files?

   A. IIS understands only C# ASP.NET applications.

   B. You can have a C# function inside a Jscript.NET page.

   C. ASP.NET pages are interpreted.

   D. ASP.NET is based on Component Object Model (COM) architecture.

5. One of the new reliability features in IIS 6.0 is the introduction of HTTP.sys. HTTP.sys is the new kernel mode driver for IIS 6.0. HTTP.sys is engineered to increase the performance of IIS dramatically. You have been researching HTTP.sys functionality. Your research does not indicate one of the following options. Please select the correct one.

   A. Uses application pools to assign resources to Web sites

   B. Implements flexible caching

   C. Since HTTP.sys consumes all incoming traffic, inetinfo.exe has less to worry.

   D. Performs health detections data to IIS

Managing IIS 6.0

6. Web Services Extensions is a new feature in IIS 6.0. Using Web Services Extensions we can configure IIS 6.0 components. We can enable and disable them from the IIS Manager console. You have been experimenting on enabling and disabling these components. You couldn't notice one or more of the following items. Which item(s) fall into this category? (Choose all that apply.)

A. WebDAV

B. ASP.NET

C. File Sharing

D. ASP

7. You have read that IIS 6.0 can handle multiple Web sites on a single IP address. Your organization is running out of static IP address and this seems to be a great idea. You are investigating the steps to create multiple Web sites on the same IP address. Which of these options is the most correct one?

   A. Use single IP address with multiple Web site headers.

   B. Use single IP address with multiple HTTP 1.1 headers.

   C. Assign different port numbers to different Web sites.

   D. Use multiple Web sites with the same header.

8. There are several ways you can apply security on Web sites. You can configure all of these by the Properties tab of a Web site. Which one of the following is not a security measure to prevent intruders hacking into IIS 6.0 Web sites?

   A. Using SSL certificates

   B. Using WebDAV

   C. Using an authentication method to force the user to authenticate

   D. Applying IP restrictions on known offenders and networks

Troubleshooting IIS 6.0

9. Your Web server is running ASP.NET applications on IIS 6.0. An incorrect configuration setting has caused you to reinstall IIS 6.0 on this machine. You have used the **Control Panel | Add Remove Programs** method to uninstall and reinstall IIS 6.0. Then you tried to load up your ASP.NET pages. Unfortunately, all ASP.NET pages are displayed as text. What could be the solution to this problem?

   A. You need to reregister ASP.NET.

   B. You need to reformat the drive as NTFS and reinstall Windows Server 2003 with IIS.

   C. You need to edit the metabase XML file to recognize ASP.NET files.

   D. You need to restart IIS from IIS Manager.

10. Your company's new MP3 player is getting very popular on the Internet. You are getting close to 2,500 requests per minute to download the product. Unfortunately, your

Web server is continuously getting a 503 error for the product downloads. Your boss has asked you to look into this problem. What could be the issue?

A. There is not enough bandwidth for the users.

B. HTTP.sys cannot handle the incoming traffic.

C. The worker process is getting recycled every five minutes.

D. The FTP server needs to be run on isolation mode.

11. You are getting frequent 503 errors on your production environment. You have also noticed that a series of 503 errors will restart the IIS server automatically. IIS 6.0 recovers and starts accepting product download till we get another set of 503 error and restarts. What do you call the fail-over mechanism?

A. Self-correcting IIS

B. IIS worker process recycle

C. Backup/restore configuration

D. Rapid-fail protection

12. Your IIS 6.0 server is communicating with a UNIX server to handle sales procurement information. The first request seems to work fine. The subsequent requests from the UNIX servers results in a 404 File Not Found error from our IIS server. What could be the issue here?

A. Static file cache stores filename in uppercase.

B. Static file cache stores filename in lowercase.

C. Worker process recycles every time a UNIX request comes in.

D. UNIX communication is cookie based and IIS 6.0 needs a new cookie with every request.

13. You have installed an ISAPI application as the *Checkout* facility for your shopping cart. You bought this third-party tool to facilitate credit card transactions. This was visible under IIS 5.0 as an ISAPI application. You have installed this on the Windows Server 2003 server and looked at the ISAPI application tab. The Checkout ISAPI DLL is not visible as a live application. What could have gone wrong here?

A. You need to enter the ISAPI data into the metabase manually to recognize it.

B. You need to restart the IIS and it will show up.

C. It only comes up when a user invokes the Checkout facility.

D. The ISAPI application needs to be rewritten for IIS 6.0.

Using New IIS Command-Line Utilities

14. The iisftp.vbs command can be used to create, start, stop, pause, and list FTP sites in IIS 6.0 server. You have been experimenting with this command. What will be the outcome of a *iisftp /query* command-line invocation?

    A. An error will come up. It is not a valid command because the .VBS extension is not present.

    B. An error will come up. You haven't listed the FTP site name to query on.

    C. A list of all FTP sites will come up.

    D. The information for the "query" FTP site will come up.

15. You are creating a Web server farm to host multiple Web sites. You need to mirror the exact IIS configuration settings on every computer in the farm. This could be a tedious task if you do a manual server installation (machine by machine). Your senior architect has informed you of a command-line utility that will copy all configuration settings from one server to another. Which one is it?

    A. iisback.vbs

    B. iiscnfg.vbs

    C. iisftp.vbs

    D. iisvdir.vbs

Self Test Quick Answer Key

For complete questions, answers, and explanations to the Self Test questions in this chapter as well as the other chapters in this book, see the Self Test Appendix.

1. **C**
2. **C**
3. **A**
4. **B**
5. **D**
6. **C**
7. **A**
8. **B**
9. **A**
10. **B**
11. **D**
12. **A**
13. **C**
14. **C**
15. **B**

Chapter 9

MCSA/MCSE 70-290

Monitoring Performance and Security

Exam Objectives in this Chapter:

4.6	Monitor system performance.
4.7	Monitor file and print servers. Tools might include Task Manager, Event Viewer, and System Monitor.
4.1	Monitor and analyze events. Tools might include Event Viewer and System monitor.
4.8	Monitor and optimize a server environment for application performance.
4.8.1	Monitor memory performance objects.
4.8.2	Monitor network performance objects.
4.8.3	Monitor process performance object.
4.8.4	Monitor disk performance objects.

Introduction

Server performance is an important issue in a mission-critical business environment. Poor performance can have a huge negative impact on the ability of workers to do their jobs, and thus on productivity and the company's bottom line. Monitoring and optimizing performance of network servers is one of the administrator's most important tasks, and it is important to continually collect and analyze performance data to ensure that any problems can be taken care of before they impact end users. Security events are another important area that the administrator must stay on top of, to protect the integrity of the organization's network and data.

Windows Server 2003 provides administrators with built-in tools for monitoring performance issues and detecting security breaches (or attempted breaches). These include both simple monitoring tools such as Task Manager, powerful monitoring tools such as the System Monitor, and a set of useful command-line utilities. For auditing security events, the security log provides vital information for tracking successful and failed breaches of security.

In this chapter, we will show you how to use these tools to monitor server performance and security and provide tips for optimizing performance of common server applications.

Monitoring Performance

Performance is a key factor of a successful system implementation. Windows Server 2003 provides several tools to analyze performance. Those tools include the following:

- Task Manager
- System Monitor
- A set of command-line utilities

In the following sections, we will discuss how each of these can be used to monitor and analyze the performance of your Windows Server 2003 computer.

Using Task Manager to Monitor Performance

The Task Manager displays all the applications and processes on the Windows Server 2003 computer. It also displays some common performance measures. The Task Manager can be invoked in many ways, including the following:

- Press **Ctrl + Alt + Delete** and click the **Task Manager** button.
- Click **Start | Run** and type **taskmgr.exe**.
- Right-click an empty area of the taskbar and select **Task Manager**.

The Task Manager has five tabs in Windows Server 2003. These include: Applications, Processes, Performance, Networking, and Users. The Users tab is a new feature in Windows

Server 2003. We will investigate the Performance tab first, because our focus in this section is monitoring server performance.

The Performance tab provides graphs and statistics to illustrate the status of the system. There are eight group boxes in this tab. They are: CPU Usage, Page File Usage, CPU Usage History, Page File Usage History, Totals, Physical Memory (K), Commit Change (K), and Kernel Memory (K), as shown in Figure 9.1. In the following section, we will discuss each of these and the information that you can glean from each.

Figure 9.1 Task Manager Interface

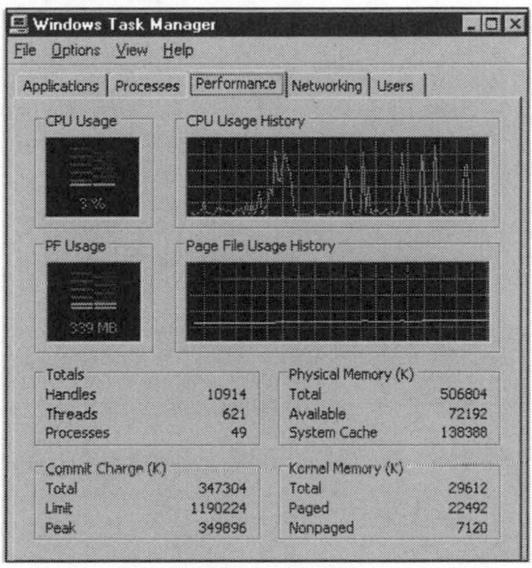

The CPU Usage group box describes the CPU usage of the system. This is displayed as a percentage of the maximum CPU utilization. This is an indication of how busy the machine is. The machine shown in Figure 9.1 has a very light CPU load (only 3 percent).

The CPU Usage History group box plots all CPU loads on a graph. Using **View | Update Speed** and choosing either the High, Normal, Low, or Paused option can modify the speed of the plotting of the graph. The CPU usage history graph is a good indicator for the behavior of the CPU utilization of the system. Our CPU has done some intensive tasks, according to Figure 9.1. The individual peaks show the fluctuating CPU usage.

The Page File Usage follows the same format. PF Usage displays the current usage in megabytes and Page File Usage History plots the figures as a graph. (We will discuss *Page Files* in more detail later in this chapter.)

The Totals group box displays the total handles (a handle is a process invocation for a particular object; or is the reference to an object in memory), threads (a thread is a single execution unit; a single thread is responsible for one unit of work in an application), and processes currently running on the system. These details can vary, depending on the application architectures.

The Physical Memory group box displays the total memory available (Random Access Memory or RAM), the amount currently available on the system, and the System Cache size. System cache holds data that was processed previously. It is faster to obtain data from cache, rather than repeating the transaction. These two items make up the Kernel Memory group box.

New & Noteworthy...

What is Paging?

A computer has a fixed amount of physical memory (RAM) installed, but there is a way to "fool" applications into thinking they have more memory available than is actually installed in the machine. This enables you to run more programs simultaneously (multitask).

This is accomplished via a *paging* mechanism that can copy the physical memory information to a *page file* on the disk. Thus, an area of hard disk space is able to emulate physical memory. The physical memory can then be used for other operating system and application functions. The amount of information in the page file is referred as *Paged Memory*. The page file is also referred to as *virtual memory*. The *NonPaged memory* is the memory that is not copied into the page file.

In early versions of Windows (and in some other operating systems), the page file is called a *swap file* because the information stored there is swapped in and out of physical memory as it is needed. The location and size of the page file can be configured via the Control Panel's **System** applet. To do so, follow these steps:

1. Click **Start | Settings | Control Panel | System**.
2. Click the **Advanced** tab and click the **Settings** button under Performance.
3. Click the second **Advanced** tab.
4. At the bottom, under **Virtual Memory** is a display that tells you the total size of the paging file. Click the **Change** button.
5. In the **Virtual Memory** dialog box, you can select the drive(s) on which you want to create paging files and set the size of the paging file for each drive. If you click **System Managed** size, the operating system grows and shrinks the paging file as needed. If you click **Custom** size, you can set an initial and maximum size for the file.
7. Click the **Set** button to apply your changes.

If you set the **Initial size** and **Maximum size** fields to the same value, the paging file is *static*; that is, it won't grow and shrink. This can improve performance because there is system overhead involved in maintaining a *dynamic* paging file that grows and shrinks.

Spreading the paging file across multiple physical disks can also improve performance, as can putting the paging file(s) on different disks than the disk on which the operating system is installed (the one on which the WINDOWS directory is located).

The Commit Charge group box is related to the Kernel Memory group box. The *virtual memory* details can be found here. (Remember, virtual memory is the maximum size of the page file.) The *Peak* item in this Commit Charge group box can exceed the physical memory value in the Physical Memory group box since page file can be utilized. The *Limit* item displays the maximum memory available.

Next, we will look at the other tabs on the Task Manager interface.

- The Application tab displays all the active applications on the system. You can right-click an application and select different options. These options include Switch to (the application receives focus on the screen) and End Task (this option ends the application).
- The Process tab lists all the processes running on the system. This has no direct relationship to the Applications tab, in that some applications have multiple processes working for them and some applications share processes. You will see several options if you right-click any of these processes. Some of the important options are End Process (as the name implies, it shuts down the process), End Process Tree (ends the process and also ends dependent processes), and Set Priority (You can assign priority on a process basis). The processes with higher priorities are executed first.
- The Networking tab displays network activity. This tab is displayed only if one or more network adapters are present. This tab provides information on the availability and the quality of network resources. A graph indicates the amount of associated traffic when you select each network resource.
- The Users tab displays all users currently connected to the computer. You can disconnect them or log them off using this tab. (You must have administrator access to perform these functions). Right-click a user's name and select the **Disconnect** or **Log off** options to perform the tasks. You can also send a message to the user by selecting the **Send Message** option in the right context menu.

Using the Performance Utility to Monitor Performance

The main utilities that monitor performance are the System Monitor and the performance logs. These tools provide a graphical user interface to analyze performance data. We will also investigate the command-line tools available in Windows Server 2003. We'll start with the System Monitor.

Using the System Monitor

The System Monitor is the primary tool for monitoring system performance. In Windows NT 4.0, it was called the Performance Monitor; in Windows 2000, Microsoft changed the name to System Monitor, within the Performance MMC.

In keeping with its old name, the System Monitor interface can be invoked by clicking **Start | Run** and typing **perfmon**, or by clicking **Start | Administrative Tools | Performance** and selecting **System Monitor**. The System Monitor runs as an ActiveX control inside the Performance Monitor console. Because the System Monitor is built as an ActiveX control, you can embed the System Monitor into a Web page or a Web form application. You can also monitor remote computer activity from your local System Monitor console. Figure 9.2 shows the System Monitor.

Figure 9.2 System Monitor

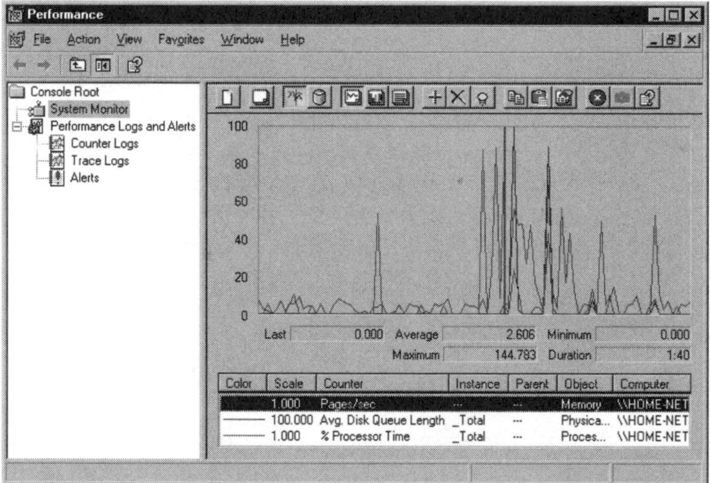

The System Monitor can be displayed in three formats. Figure 9.2 shows the System Monitor as a graph. You can also display the System Monitor as a histogram or as a text report. You can alter these views by clicking one of the three buttons in the button bar directly above the graph. (The first button is the fifth from the left of the button bar and next to the database sign.) Hover your cursor over these buttons to see the labels **View Graph**, **View Histogram**, and **View Report**.

Three performance counters are activated and monitored by default. These are displayed in Figure 9.2, and include the following:

- **Memory object** Pages/sec counter
- **Physical disk object** Average disk queue length counter
- **Processor object** % processor time counter

You can right-click any performance counter in the lower pane and select **Save As** to save the log information as an HTML file (.HTM) or a tab-delimited file (.TSV).

Adding Performance Counters

You can add performance counters by doing one of the following:

- Right-click the counter pane and select **Add counters**.
- Select the **Data** tab from the **Properties** dialog box of the System Monitor, as shown in Figure 9.3. To open the Properties dialog box, right-click within the graph area or on an item in the counter pane, and then click **Properties**, or click **CTRL + L**.
- Click the **Add** button on the button bar, which appears as a plus sign (+).
- Type **CTRL + I**.

Figure 9.3 Properties for System Monitor

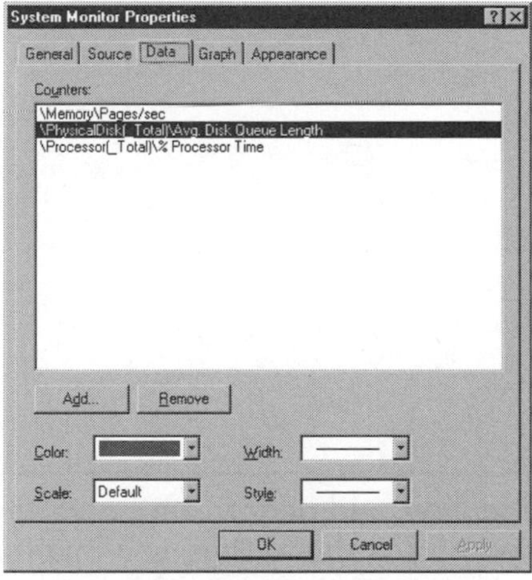

The existing counters are displayed in the **Counters** space. When you click the **Add** button or click **CTRL + I**, the **Add Counters** dialog box appears, as shown in Figure 9.4.

Figure 9.4 Add Counters Screen

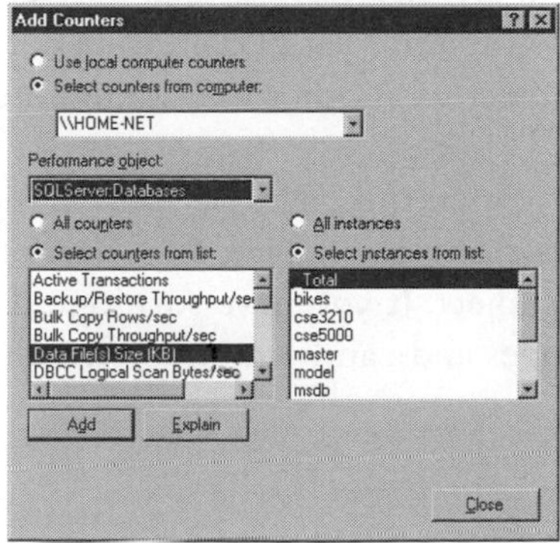

In the Add Counters dialog box, first select the machine you wish to monitor. You can monitor counters on the local computer by selecting **Use local computer counters**, or you can monitor counters on a remote machine by selecting **Select counters from computer:** and typing the UNC path to the remote system or choosing it from the drop-down box if you've monitored it from this computer previously.

Next, select the **Performance object**. A performance object is a specialized object that has performance counter information on a particular application, service, or hardware device. (For example, SQL Server has specialized performance objects that enable System Monitor to monitor their activity) There are a large number of objects from which to choose. Some of the most commonly monitored objects include the following:

- Processor
- Memory
- Logical Disk
- Physical Disk
- DNS
- DHCP Server
- Network interface
- Web service

NOTE

Some applications and services add performance objects and counters to the System Monitor when you install them. Thus, you might not see all the listed objects/counters if you don't have the related applications or services installed on the computer you're monitoring. For example, if you don't have SQL Server installed, you will not see the SQLServer:Databases object.

Finally, select the *counters* you are interested in that pertain to your selected object, or select **All counters** to track all counters that pertain to that object. (The counters are different from one performance object to another, and some objects have a large number of counters.)

Next, select the instance to which the counters apply if there is more than one instance of the object on the machine. For example, if you have dual processors installed, there are two instances for the Processor object. If you have two logical disks (C: and D:), both of these show up as separate instances and can be monitored individually, or you can select **All instances** to monitor them all.

NOTE

You can select a counter and click the **Explain** button to get help information about it. A window pops up beneath the **Add Counters** dialog box with the explanation of the counter. You can remove a counter by selecting it and clicking **Remove**.

It is important for you to be familiar with the functions of the major performance counters and their thresholds. The performance counters we''ll discuss are memory, disk, and process related. Table 9.1 discusses some of these counters and their thresholds. Some recommendations are given for thresholds values that should trigger actions on your part. There can be a myriad of reasons that the threshold is met. It is an indication that the system is not responding correctly if the counter thresholds are met, so it is important to know when this is occurring (or about to occur) and take action. System administrators should investigate the cause anytime a performance threshold is reached. You can configure the Performance utility to notify you when a threshold is met, as we will discuss later in the chapter. (All the counters are explained in the *Optimizing Servers for Applications Performance* section.)

Table 9.1 Important Performance Counters and Thresholds

Type	Object\Counter	Threshold	Action
Memory	Memory\Available Bytes	Less than 4MB	Check for memory leaks and add RAM if necessary.
Memory	Memory\Pages/sec	20	Investigate paging settings.
Paging File	Paging File\% Usage	Above 70 percent	The Paging File value should match up with the previous two values. A value exceeding 70 percent is not healthy for the system.
Disk	Physical Disk\Free Space Logical Disk\Free Space	15 percent	Clear more disk space. Increase logical or physical disk space.
Disk	Physical Disk\Disk Time Logical Disk\Disk Time	90 percent	The disk is not being read quickly enough. This could be a hardware issue. It could also be that the amount of data on the disk is too large.
Disk	Physical Disk\Disk Reads/sec, Physical Disk\ Disk Writes/sec	Depends on Manufacturer	The writing or reading from the disk is slow. You might need to upgrade the disk or disk drivers.

Continued

Table 9.1 Important Performance Counters and Thresholds

Type	Object\Counter	Threshold	Action
Processor	Processor\% Processor Time	85 percent	Find the process-intensive processes and move them to separate processors (if you have a multi-processor machine) or add more processing power (by adding another processor or by upgrading to a faster processor).
Processor	Processor\ Interrupts/sec	Processor specific; 1000 is a standard	If the counter value increases without additional processes, the cause could be hardware related.
Server	Server\Bytes Total/sec	Depends on the network	If all your servers' Bytes Total/ sec is the same and similar to the maximum network speed, you might need to increase the network bandwidth.
Server	Server\Pool Paged Peak	Physical RAM available	Should not be greater than the physical RAM value.

We have investigated the Data tab of the System Monitor. Now we'll discuss the other properties of the System Monitor.

General Tab of the System Monitor

The General tab enables you to configure the System Monitor view. Figure 9.5 displays the General tab of the System Monitor's properties. You can view the System Monitor as a graph, histogram, or a report, by selecting the option from the View group box. You can customize the System Monitor display by selecting the options from the Display elements group box. You can use the Report and histogram data group box to filter through the *amount* of data to be monitored. The *maximum* displays the maximum values of counters and *minimum* displays the minimum values. You can view the System Monitor as 3D or one dimension (the option Flat) by selecting from the Appearance drop-down box. Then you can apply a border using the Border option. The Sample automatically every *X* seconds box enables you to configure the refresh interval of the System Monitor. You can also allow duplicate counters by selecting the **Allow duplicate counter instances option** box.

Figure 9.5 General Tab of System Monitor

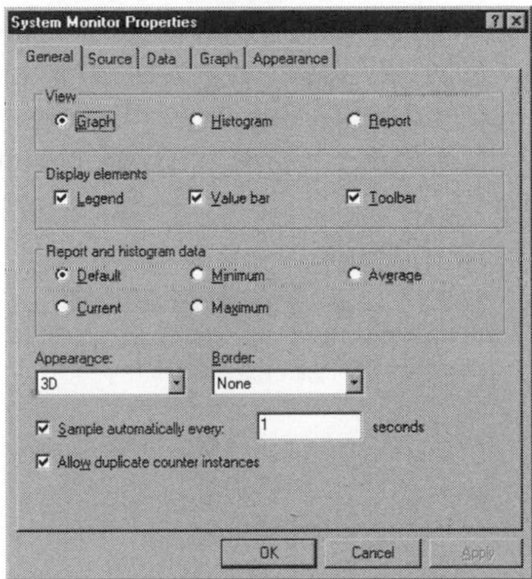

Source Tab of the System Monitor

The **Source** tab describes the data source for the System Monitor. There are three major sources. The first one is the current activity of the system. You can enable this by selecting the **Current activity** option. The second option is from a log file. You can enable this by selecting the **Log files** option. To point to the correct log files, click the **Add** button. To remove unwanted log files, click the **Remove** button. The third option is a database source. Enter the Data Source Name (DSN) and select the correct log file database by using the **Log set** options. You can also filter the data sources according to time ranges by using the **Time Range** option. Please refer to Figure 9.6 for details.

Figure 9.6 Source Tab of System Monitor

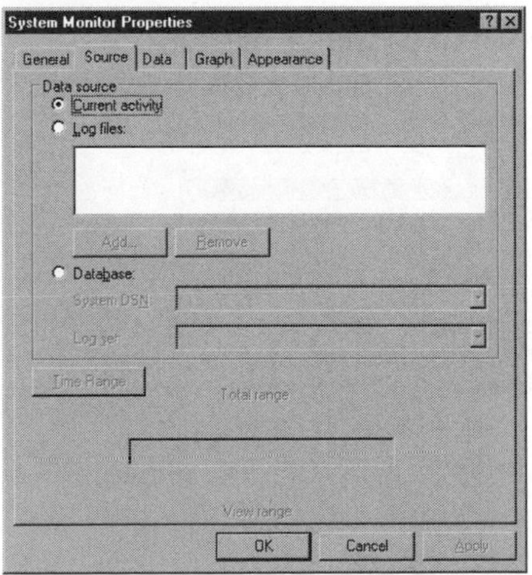

Graph Tab of the System Monitor

The Graph tab enables you to configure the display format of the System Monitor graph. You can add titles and vertical axis names for the graph using this tab. You can also display the graph as a grid using vertical and horizontal lines. Then you can configure the scale of the graph. Figure 9.7 displays the Graph tab of the System Monitor.

Figure 9.7 Graph Tab of System Monitor

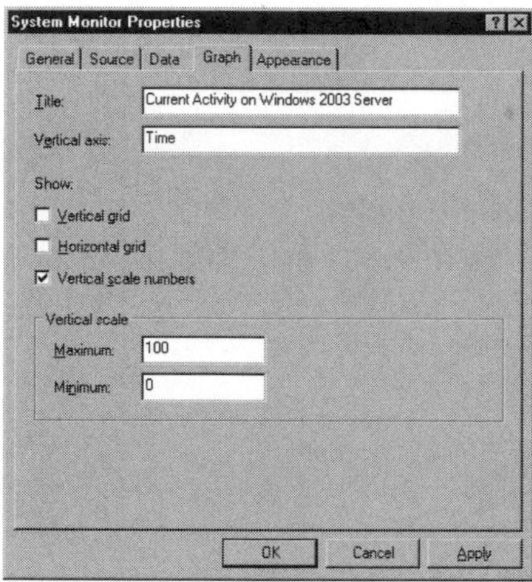

Appearance Tab of the System Monitor

The final tab is the Appearance tab. This controls the physical appearance of the System Monitor graph. You can change the background and foreground colors and font sizes using this tab. Figure 9.8 shows the Appearance tab.

Figure 9.8 Appearance Tab of System Monitor

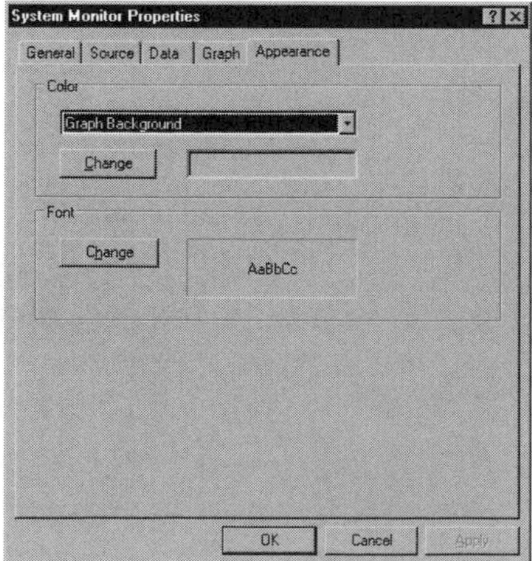

Using Performance Logs and Alerts

This section of the Performance utility enables you to configure logging of performance-related information and set up the system to alert you when thresholds are reached. We'll look closely at the **Performance Logs and Alerts** section.

In the left pane of the **Performance** MMC, expand the **Performance Logs and Alerts** node and you will see that this section has three child nodes:

- Counter Logs
- Trace Logs
- Alerts

All of these logs and alerts can be configured, started, or stopped using the Performance utility. We'll investigate the counter logs first.

Counter Logs

The counter logs store the performance counter information. You can use these logs to analyze data at a later opportunity. Now you'll learn how to create a counter log.

EXERCISE 9.01

CREATE A COUNTER LOG

1. Click **Start | Run** and type **perfmon.exe**.
2. Select **Performance logs and counters** from the Performance Monitor screen.
3. Right-click **Counter Logs** and select **New Log Settings**.
4. A text box appears to allow you to enter the counter log name. Enter **Test_Memory_Log** for demonstration purposes. A Properties screen appears for the newly created log (see Figure 9.9).
5. The log file name is automatically assigned by the system. You can configure the counters you wish to monitor by utilizing the **Counters** section. First add objects you want to monitor by using the **Add Objects** button. Then select the individual counters for each object by clicking the **Add Counters** button. (Select the memory counters to monitor memory activity for demonstration purposes.) You can also configure the frequency of the log file entries by utilizing the **Interval** and **Units** option boxes. You can configure more settings by using the **Log Files** and the **Schedule** tabs. The Log Files tab is shown in Figure 9.10.

Figure 9.9 General Tab of Counter Log

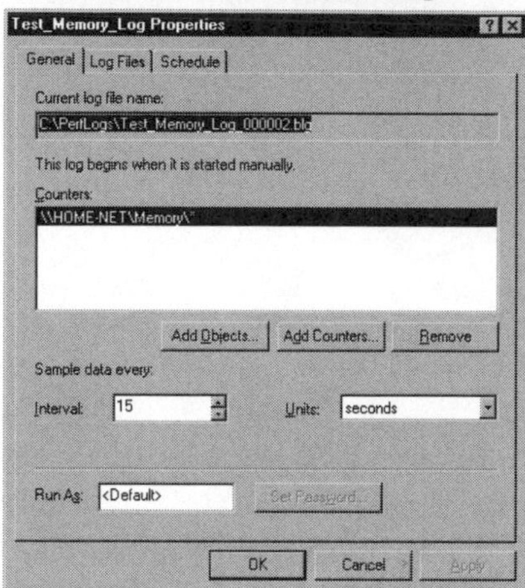

Figure 9.10 Log Files Tab of Counter Logs

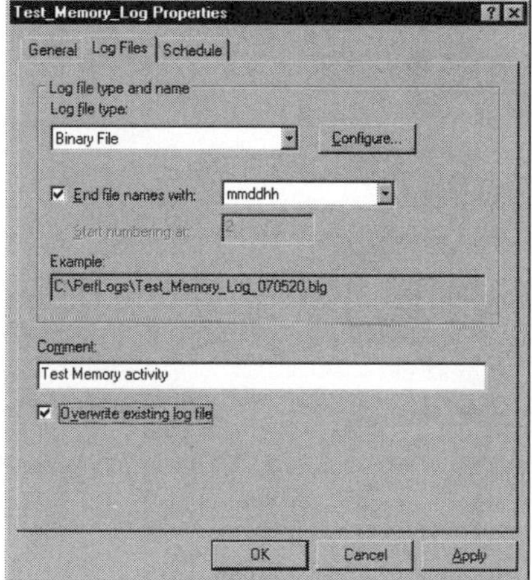

6. You can configure the log file type using the Log file type option box. Some valid types are binary format, comma-separated file format, tab-delimited format, or database. Configure these options by clicking the **Configure** button. The **End file names with** option box enables you to append a time stamp to the log file. Figure 9.10 shows the selection month–day–year format. You can put a comment about the log by using the Comment field. You can instruct the system to overwrite the existing log file by clicking the bottom option box.

Figure 9.11 Schedule Tab for Counter Logs

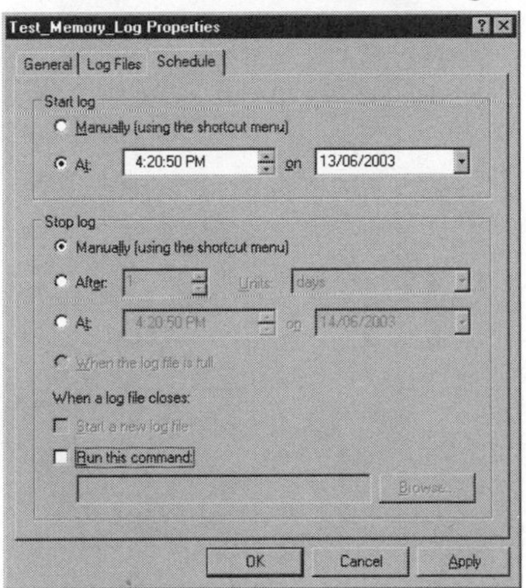

7. You can configure the start date and the end date by using the Schedule tab (Figure 9.11). You can either start the log manually or assign a time by using the controls in the **Start log** group box. The **Stop log** group box enables you to configure the end time and the subsequent operations of the termination of the log file. You can terminate the log manually, after a certain number of days, or at an exact time. Then you can use the **Start a new log file** command or **Run this command option boxes** to configure the subsequent events.
8. Click the **OK** or **Apply** button to apply the changes.

Trace Logs

The trace logs enable you to trace applications and processes. The creation of the trace logs is similar to the creation of the counter logs. You can create a trace log by right-clicking **Trace Logs** in the left pane of the Performance console and selecting **New log settings**. You are required to enter a trace name, and then a dialog box opens that enables you to select the trace sources and settings. (Please refer to Figure 9.12 for the details. You are creating a **TestTrace** file to mointor process, thread, disk, and network activity.)

Test Day Tip

You can add non-system providers by clicking the **Nonsystems providers** option box and clicking the **Add** button. (These providers are not known to the operating system.) You can also configure the system account the log file runs under by using this tab. The **<Default>** option uses the default logged-in account to enter the log entries.

Figure 9.12 General Tab for Trace Log

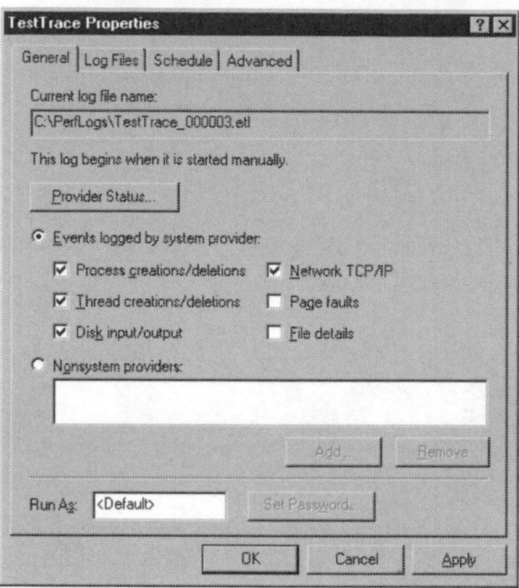

You can schedule the trace events and set log file sizes in the same way as you did with counter logs. The **Log Files** tab is similar to the **Counter Log** tab. Now we'll look at the **Advanced** tab (shown in Figure 9.13). The log entries are usually written to a memory and buffered before it is written to the log files. You can configure the memory buffer size by utilizing the **Buffer Size** option. You can also configure the number of buffers the system is using to write to trace logs. An alternative option is to write the log files directly without utilizing the memory buffer. This is achieved by enabling the **Transfer data from buffers to log file at least every** ***X*** **seconds** option.

Figure 9.13 Advanced Tab of Trace Log

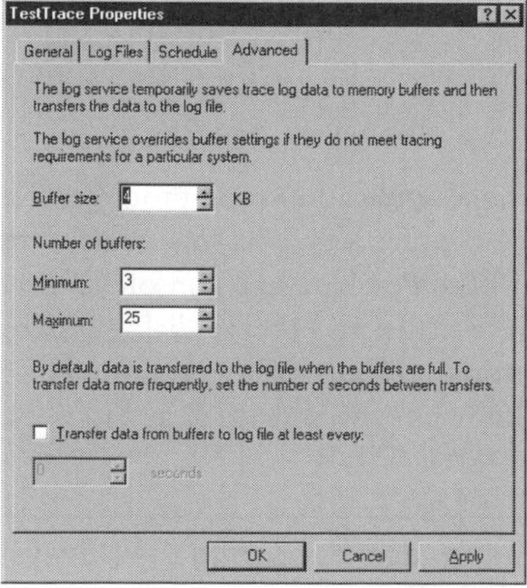

Alerts

Alerts are mechanisms that sends notifications when one of the performance thresholds is met. You can create an alert by right-clicking **Alerts** in the left console pane and selecting **New Alert Settings**. You are required to enter a name for the alert, and then you can configure the settings for it. (Enter **TestAlert** for demonstration purposes.) You can pick a performance counter from a list by clicking the **Add** button. This process is very similar to the counter logs selection process. You can specify the threshold for this counter by using the Alert when the value is option and the Limit option. You should be alarmed if the Processor(Total)\% Processor Time counter exceeds 20 percent. Figure 9.14 illustrates the condition for TestAlert alert. You can add multiple counters in a single alert. The Interval and Units options can be utilized to configure the frequency of applying the counters.

Figure 9.14 General Tab of Alerts

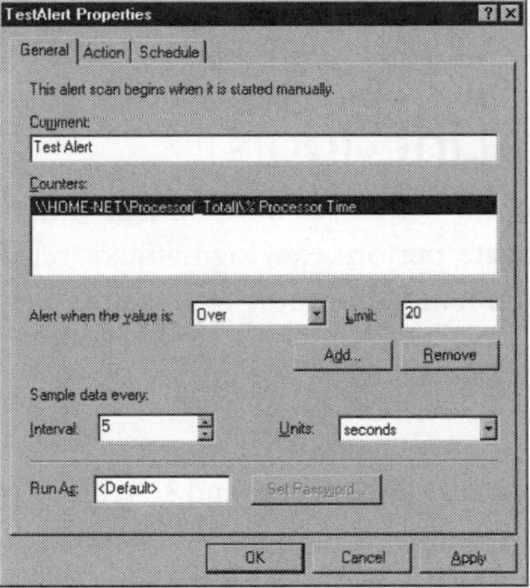

The Action tab explains the available actiopns to take when the threshold is met. Here are the options available when the counter's threshold is met:

- Create an event log entry.
- Send a messenger to a specified user account via the Messenger service.
- Start a performance data log.
- Run a specified program or script.

You can select any combination of these actions. The TestAlert example illustrates the selections to add an entry to the event log and send a message to the Administrator (refer to Figure 9.15).

Figure 9.15 Action Tab of Alerts

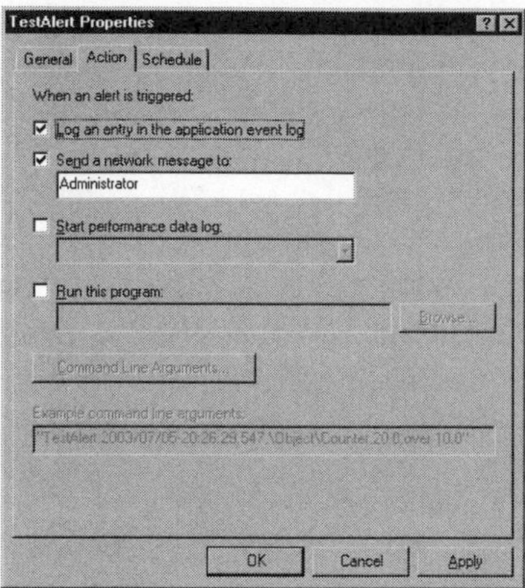

Using Command-Line Tools

Windows Server 2003 also comes with a set of command-line tools to monitor performance monitoring. We investigate perfom.exe, logman.exe, relog.exe, and typeperf.exe tools in this section. You can use command-line tools to monitor performance locally or on a remote computer.

logman.exe

The logman.exe command-line utility manages and schedules performance counters. You can also use it to manage and schedule trace logs. You can use this utility on a remote computer provided you have the proper administrator credentials. The syntax for using this command is as follows:

```
Syntax : Logman [create {counter | trace} [CollectionName]] [start
    CollectionName] [stop CollectionName] [delete CollectionName] [query
      {CollectionName | providers [ProviderName]} [update CollectionName]
```

You can create, start, stop, delete, query, and update performance counters and traces using the logman.exe commands. The parameters that make up the *CollectionName* component are explained in Table 9.2. The *CollectionName* properties can also be read from a provider. This can be configured by populating the ***providers** [ProviderName]*} details. Later in this section, we will experiment with logman.exe and provide screenshots of actual command entries.

Table 9.2 Collection Parameters for logman.exe Switches

Switch	Description
-s *ServerName*	The name of the machine on which you want to use logman.exe.
-t config	The name of the config file that contains all the logman.exe parameters.
-b *M/D/YYYY H:MM:SS* [{**AM** | **PM**}]	The begin/ start time to collect data. You can use a 24-hour format or use the AM/PM flags for a 12-hour format.
-e *M/D/YYYY H:MM:SS* [{**AM** | **PM**}]	The end time to collect data. Can be either 12- or 24-hour format.
-m [start | stop]	Manually starts or stops the trace or log. You cannot use this option with **-e**, **-b**, or **–rt** options.
-rt	Specifies the trace is in "real time" mode. The trace is not from a trace log file (which is the default).
-u *Username Password*	The account credentials to be used to execute logman.exe to run locally or remotely.
-o *[Path | DSNCounterLog]*	The output file and the path where the file is located. Alternatively, the DSN entry for the SQL database login (if you are writing the logging information into a database).
-f {bin | bincirc | csv | tsv | SQL}	Specifies the file format for counter logs or trace data. The format can be binary, circular binary, commas separated, tab separated or SQL database.
-max *Value*	Specifies the maximum size of the log. The logging will stop when the file exceeds this limit.
-c {*Path [Path..]* | **-cf** *FileName*}	Specifies the performance counter file path with *Path* and the name of the file with *FileName* attribute. This follows the *[\\Computer\Object[Parent/instance#Index] format.* Most counters do not have any indexes (e.g., \Processor(_Total)\%ProcessorTime). You can also set these counters in text files and give the file location as the **–cf** parameter. Enclosing them in quotation marks and separating them with a space can specify multiple counters. (Please refer to Figure 9.16.)
-si *[[HH]:MM:]SS*	The time interval for the performance counter in hours, minutes, and seconds. The default is 15 seconds.
/?	Help available for logman.exe.

Figure 9.16 shows the input and output of the logman command-line utility. In this example, you first create a performance counter called **test_perf_log**. You want to track the **\Processor(_Total)\%ProcessorTime** and **\Memory\Available Bytes** counters in this performance log. You start the log at 10 A.M. on 10 June 2003 and end it at 10 A.M. of 20 June 2003. You collect data on these two counters every 15 minutes. You record the log details in the *test_log* file located in the *c:\perflogs* directory.

Figure 9.16 logman.exe in Action

```
C:\>logman create counter test_perf_log -b 10/6/2003 10:00:00 -e 20/6/2003 10:00
:00 -c "\Processor\(_Total)\%Processor Time" "\Memory\Available bytes" -si 00:15
 -o "c:\perflogs\test_log"
The command completed successfully.

C:\>logman query test_perf_log

Name:            test_perf_log
Type:            Counter
Status:          Running
Start:           10/6/2003 10:00:00
Stop:            20/6/2003 10:00:00
File:            c:\perflogs\test_log_000001.blg
Run As:          <Default>

Counters:
   \Processor\(_Total)\%Processor Time
   \Memory\Available bytes

The command completed successfully.

C:\>logman stop test_perf_log
The command completed successfully.

C:\>logman delete test_perf_log
The command completed successfully.

C:\>
```

After entering the command, run a query on the performance counter using the *query* switch. Notice that the counter is already running. The system automatically starts the counter when it is created. The output of the query shows us the name, log type, status, start and stop times, file path, and account information.

Use the stop and delete switches to stop the logging process and delete the performance counter when finished.

relog.exe

You can use relog.exe to extract data from performance counter logs and convert it to tab-separated value (.TSV), Comma-Separated Value (.CSV), binary log file (.BLG), or SQL formats. This tool is commonly used to extract logs to Excel spreadsheets and to resample logs and create new ones that are based on a particular time period, sampling interval, or specified counters. It can also be used to create source data files for database manipulation tools. The following listing illustrates the syntax, and Table 9.3 explains the parameters available.

```
Syntax : relog [FileName [FileName ...]] [-a] [-c Path [Path ...]] [-cf
    FileName] [-f {bin | csv | tsv | SQL}] [-t Value] [-o {OutputFile |
        DSNCounterLog}] [-b M/D/YYYY [[HH:]MM:]SS] [-e M/D/YYYY
            [[HH:]MM:]SS] [-q]
```

Table 9.3 Parameters for relog.exe Switches

Switch	Description
FileName [FileName ...]	The name of the existing performance counter files. You can enter multiple file names.
-a	Append to the file; do not overwrite. This does not apply to SQL output. The default is to append in SQL files.

Continued

Table 9.3 Parameters for relog.exe Switches

<table>
<tr><th>Switch</th><th>Description</th></tr>
<tr><td>-b M/D/YYYY H:MM:SS [{AM | PM}]</td><td>The begin/ start time for extracting data. You can use a 24-hour or 12-hour format.</td></tr>
<tr><td>-e M/D/YYYY H:MM:SS [{AM | PM}]</td><td>The end time for extracting data. Can be either 12- or 24-hour format.</td></tr>
<tr><td>-o [Path | DSNCounterLog]</td><td>The output file and the path for it. Alternatively, the DSN entry for the SQL database login.</td></tr>
<tr><td>-f {bin | bincirc | csv | tsv | SQL}</td><td>Specifies the file format for counter logs or trace data. The format can be binary, circular binary, comma separated, tab separated, or SQL database.</td></tr>
<tr><td>-c {Path [Path..] |
-cf FileName}</td><td>Specifies the performance counter file path with Path and the name of the file with FileName attribute. This follows the [\\Computer\Object[Parent/instance#Index] format. Most counters do not have any indexes (e.g., \Processor(_Total)\ %ProcessorTime). You can also set these counters in a text file and give the file location as the –cf parameter. Enclosing them in quotation marks and separating them with a space character can specify multiple counters.</td></tr>
<tr><td>-t Value</td><td>Specifies the interval of records. This is the interval that reads X rows of performance counter data and enters the X rows to the output file.</td></tr>
<tr><td>-q</td><td>Displays the time ranges and the performance counters specified in the input files.</td></tr>
<tr><td>/?</td><td>Help available for relog.exe.</td></tr>
</table>

Figure 9.17 displays sample input and output using the relog.exe command. In this example, the utility is reading a memory performance counter log from location *c:\perflogs\test_memory_log_000001.blg.* Your commands tell the utility to write all the "Memory\Available Bytes" performance counters to a .CSV file called **test_csv_log.csv** and to read 30 records from the performance counter log at a time and insert 30 records into the .CSV file.

Figure 9.17 relog.exe in Action

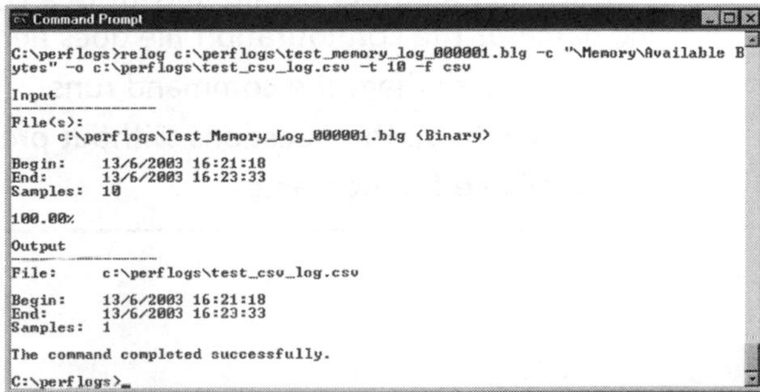

typeperf.exe

typeperf.exe is similar to relog.exe; this utility enables you to write performance log file data onto a command window or a file. This functionality distinguishes this tool from relog.exe. To stop the typeperf.exe utility, press **CTRL + C**. There are no *begin* and *end* time flags for this format. (You can, however, use the *–sc* parameter to limit the number of samples that are collected). The following listing illustrates the syntax, and the parameters are explained in Table 9.4.

```
Syntax : Typeperf [Path [Path ...]] [-cf FileName] [-f {csv | tsv | bin}]
    [-si [MM:]SS] [-o FileName] [-q [Object]] [-qx [Object]]
        [-sc Samples] [-config FileName] [-s ComputerName] [-y]
```

Table 9.4 Parameters for Typeperf.exe Switches

Switch	Description
-c {*Path [Path..]* | **-cf** *FileName*}	Specifies the performance counter file path with *Path* and the name of the file with the *FileName* attribute. You can also set these counters in text files and give the file location as the **–cf** parameter. Enclosing them in quotation marks and separating them with a space character can specify multiple counters.
-f {bin | csv | tsv }	Specifies the file format for counter logs or trace data. The format can be binary, comma separated, or tab separated.
-si *[MM:]SS*	Specifies the time between log entries. The default is one second.
-o *[Path]*	The output file and the path for it.
-q	Displays and queries all counters without instances. Include the object name if you want details about the counters for a specific object.
-qx	Displays and queries all counters with instances.
-sc	The sample count. This is how many samples you want to take. Default is to keep taking samples until you press **CTRL + C** to stop the process.
-config *FileName*	Used to read all these parameters from a configuration file. The name of the configuration file goes here.
-s *ComputerName*	The computer where the command runs.
/y	Answer yes to all the questions without prompting.
/?	Help available for logman.exe.

Figure 9.18 shows typeperf.exe in action. In this example, you want to display the *\Memory\Available Bytes* data on the screen. The data appears on the screen till **CTRL + C** is pressed. Next, the utility reads the same log data and stores it in a .CSV file called **testTypeperf.csv**. Only two samples are read and the time between samples is three seconds. The testTypeperf.csv file has two rows of data in it.

Figure 9.18 typeperf.exe in Action

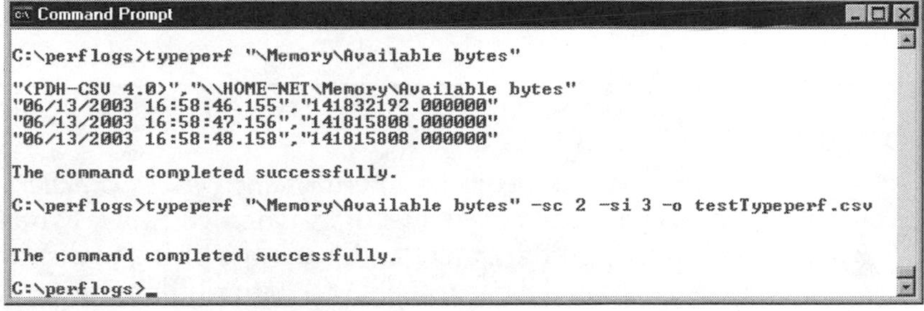

Optimizing Servers for Application Performance

In a production environment, you must optimize your servers to get the maximum throughput for your mission-critical applications. In the following sections, we will address the specifics of monitoring and optimizing memory objects, network objects, process objects, and disk objects to provide the best performance for your servers. You obtain the source data for the optimization by analyzing the performance counters related to each object. You can use the System Monitor, discussed earlier in the chapter, to monitor these counters. In each of the following sections, we will discuss which counters should be monitored and the actions you can take to address the problems you detect. Please refer to Table 9.2 to learn about the thresholds for each counter.

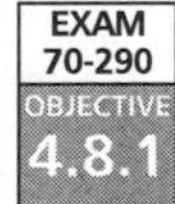

Monitoring Memory Objects

Memory issues often contribute to performance problems. You can use the System Monitor to monitor various counters related to the memory object. The most important performance counters you can monitor to detect memory problems include the following:

- **Memory:Available Bytes** This indicates the available memory capacity. We recommend that you have at least 4MB of memory available to run the server effectively. You should take immediate action if memory falls below 4MB.
- **Memory:Pages/sec** This indicates the rate at which pages are written to or read from disk, in number of pages. The recommended threshold for the **Memory:Pages/sec** counter is 20. If this counter exceeds 20, you should take action. (Alerts can be used to notify the system administrator of these events Refer to the Alerts section under *System Monitor*).

Configuring & Implementing...

Common Optimization Tips

A lack of memory is one of the most common performance issues on client workstations. You should investigate memory issues first when you have workstation performance problems. Servers, on the other hand, are more prone to disk and network problems. Here are some guidelines to help you with optimization methods:

- Make one optimization change at a time. Make the change and test the system to observe the outcome. You cannot determine the change if you make multiple changes simultaneously.
- Observe the event log closely when you are making modifications to the system. The event log displays errors when applications are unstable.
- Try to run the application locally on your system (as apposed to running it on a network server). This can give you an indication of whether a network problem is present.

The most common memory problem is a *memory leak* due to incorrect application code. Here are some recommendations to remedy memory issues:

- Investigate the minimum memory requirement for your applications to run. You can do this easily by using the Task Manager. (Read the memory values before and after the application is loaded to the memory.) Make sure the available memory exceeds this value. Add more physical RAM to the machine if it is not sufficient.
- Create multiple paging files on multiple disks. This enables faster disk access between the disks.
- Reevaluate the paging file size. It is recommended that the paging file size be 1.5 times the physical RAM installed. If the paging file/virtual memory used exceeds this limit, add extra physical memory or decrease the page file size.

- Run your most memory-intensive applications on your highest-performing computers. You can also reschedule such applications to run when the system workload is light.

Head of the Class...

Detecting a Memory Leak

The first step in detecting a memory leak is to observe the memory data by using the **Memory:Available Bytes** and **Memory:Committed Bytes** performance counters. You should suspect a memory leak when the available memory figure declines by more than 4MB. You need to isolate the applications and run them against these counters to determine which application is causing the memory leak. You might need to monitor the **Process:Private Bytes**, **Process:Working Set**, and **Process:Handle Count** counters on the suspected process to confirm the memory leak. A kernel mode application can also be leaking memory. In that case, use the **Memory:Pool Nonpaged Bytes**, **Memory:Pool Nonpaged Allocs**, **Process (Process name):Pool Nonpaged Bytes** counters. The kernel mode applications do not refer to paging mechanisms; therefore you should use non-paged counters.

Monitoring Network Objects

Monitoring network objects involves tracking the overall network traffic. You also need to track the server's process and memory data in conjunction with the network traffic. Server memory problems can be initiated by malfunctions of the network architecture.

Head of the Class...

Use Network Counter with Other Server Counters

You should monitor network counters in conjunction with **Processor:Processor Time**, **Physical Disk:% Disk Time**, and **Memory:Pages/sec**. Most network resources (network adapters and protocol software) use non-paged memory. If the computer is doing excessive paging, this might be due to the fact that networking activities are consuming the resources and the applications are being swapped to the disk. This is indicated by an increase in **Memory:page/sec** and a decrease in **Processor:Total Bytes** performance counters. Please check the Event Viewer in this case to confirm that you are running out of paged or non paged memory.

Exam Warning

The paging capabilities of a system should be approximately 1.5 times the amount of installed RAM. This is automatically set by the operating system. The system will be unstable if you exceed the 1.5 limit. (A common cause is a network issue that causes excessive swapping of applications.)

Specialized performance counters can be used to optimize network usability. The following are important network-related performance counters:

- **Network Interface\:Bytes Total/sec**, **Bytes Sent/sec**, and **Bytes Received/sec** These counters describe how the network adapters are performing against the network traffic. You should investigate any Bytes received or Sent abnormalities indicated by these counters. (The recommended threshold depends on the network adapters and network topologies).
- **Protocol_layer_object: Segments Received/sec**, **Segments Sent/sec**, **Frames Sent/sec**, and **Frames Received/sec** The *Protocol_layer* object is TCPv4, TCPv6, IPv6, and so forth. These are based on a single protocol at a time. This provides you with information on how the protocols perform against the network availability. A frame is a unit of data sent to a machine over the network. You should be concerned if the frames received or sent do not correspond to your preferred settings for the organization.
- **Server: Bytes Total/sec**, **Bytes Received/sec**, and **Bytes Sent/sec** These counters indicate how the server is using the network to receive and send data. This data is closely coupled to protocol layer and Network Interface layer data. The protocol and network activity should be high if these counters are high. You should investigate if the protocol activity and the network activity do not follow the server trends. (For example, it could be a hardware malfunction that consumes the resource of the server. Therefore network and protocol activity are slow in the face of a high server-utilization rate.)

You need to constantly monitor network traffic and make sure it does not exceed your Local Area Network (LAN) capacity. You should be using the Network Monitor tool to manage large network traffic situations. (This is not installed by default in the Windows Server 2003 installation. You might need to install it via **Add/Remove Programs** in **Control Panel** in order to use it.) Here are some recommendations to optimize your network performance:

- Unbind unwanted and infrequently used network adapters. They put an extra burden on the system that has to manage them.
- Try to place all domain users in one subnet to prevent unwanted replication traffic on the network.

- The order in which network/transport protocols are bound makes a difference if you are using multiple protocols for network communications. For example, if you have both TCP/IP and IPX/SPX installed and bound to your NIC, put the most-used protocol at the top of the protocol list. Some protocols are optimized for specific network topologies, so you should spend some time identifying the protocols you need and configuring the protocols for maximum throughput.

Monitoring Process Objects

Monitoring processor and system counters gives you a good indication of how processors are utilized in your Windows Server 2003 server. The most important performance counters to monitor in this regard include the following:

- **Processor: % Processor Time** and **Process(process): % Processor Time** These counters show *how active the processor is*. The **Process(process)** counter displays the statistics for a single process. The server is handling a lot of requests if the percentage is higher. If the counter is low, then the server is idle most of the time. It is common practice to install more processors if the counter exceeds than 80 percent. (This threshold changes depending on what the server is dedicated to do.)
- **System: Processor Queue Length** These are the requests in line to be processed. This value shouldn't be greater than one. If it is, that means that there are requests waiting in the queue to be processed. If this happens often, you should add more processors or upgrade to a faster processor to handle the extra load.
- **Processor: Interrupts/sec** This counter indicates the number of interrupts the system gets from devices (disks, network adapters, etc.). If the number of interrupts is higher, you should upgrade the device drivers or assign other processors to control these devices. (The number of interrupt thresholds can be different from processor to processor. A common benchmark is 1000 interrupts per processor. You should investigate if the interrupts are higher than 1000 per second.)
- **Server Work Queues:Queue Length** This counter indicates the queue length of the Server Work queue at a given time. The recommended threshold for this queue is four. It is an indication of processor congestion if more than four items are in the queue. You should add processing power to redirect queries or install another processor to eradicate this problem.

You can observe these counters to monitor the process objects; you can tell if the processor(s) is creating a bottleneck on the system that needs to be addressed. After memory, the processor is the most common system bottleneck.

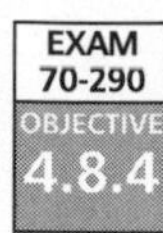

Monitoring Disk Objects

Another component that it is important to monitor to optimize your server's performance is disk activity. The hard disk is often a system bottleneck in today's fast processor, memory-packed computers. One way to increase disk performance is to spread the workload over multiple disks. You can monitor disk activity using the following performance counters.

- **PhysicalDisk: % Disk Time and % Idle Time** These two counters indicate *the percentage of time the disk was used* and *the percentage of time the disk has been idle.* If the disk usage time is high, you should consider moving some applications to other servers. The threshold for these counters is 90 percent. You should investigate if these counters exceed 90 percent.
- **PhysicalDisk: Disk Reads/sec and Disk Writes/sec** This indicates the speed of writing data on to the disk and the speed it was read from the disk, by showing the number of times the disk reads or writes per second. A long delay might indicate a disk hardware problem or a long queue of data. The thresholds for these counters change from disk manufacturer to manufacturer. (For example, an Ultra Wide SCSI disk driver can handle 50 to 70 input and output transactions per second.) You should upgrade the disk or try to eliminate the queue length if the disk threshold is met.
- **PhysicalDisk: Avg. Disk Queue Length** This indicates the length of the queue involved in writing or reading from the disk in number of requests that are waiting when the counter is measured, including requests in service. The threshold is the number of spindles plus two requests. The disk transactions are going to be slower if you exceed this queue length. Therefore, you have to assign more disk space to accommodate the extra requests.
- **LogicalDisk: % Free Space** This counter indicates the amount of free space available on the disk as a percentage of the total disk capacity. Paging problems can occur if you have little disk space to which the system can swap data out of memory, and operating system errors can occur if the partition on which the OS is installed becomes too full.

NOTE

Log the performance data onto another drive when you are testing the disk speed of a particular logical disk. Otherwise, the logging process interferes with the statistics.

- **Logical Disk sec/Transfer** This counter describes how long the disk is taking to fulfill the requests. The more time it spends on fulfilling the requests, the slower the disk controller is. It is recommended that this value be less than .3 second for most disk controllers.
- **Physical Disk Bytes/sec** This gives you the throughput of the disk activity.

Exam Warning

The following are recommendations for optimizing disk activity on the server:

- When you upgrade a disk, upgrade the disk controller and bus associated with it. It does no good to install a fast disk if the disk controller and bus don't support the faster speed.
- Try to distribute applications across multiple disks. That is, place different applications on different disks, However, you should also ensure that each individual application is not cross-referencing to multiple disks, so as to minimize disk activity.
- Use Disk Defragmenter on a regular basis (especially after deleting large amounts of data) to rearrange the data on each partition so that data belonging to a specific file is contiguous on the disk; this minimizes disk access time.

Auditing Security Events

Performance is not the only important thing to monitor in Windows Server 2003. In today's business environment, perhaps even more vital than ensuring top performance is the ability to ensure that sensitive data is kept secure. Security auditing enables you to track access to and modifications of objects, files, or folders, and to determine who has logged on (or attempted to do so) and when.

Security events are logged in the security log, accessible by administrators via the Event Viewer. An audit entry can be either a *Success* or a *Failure* event in the security log. A list of audit entries that describes the life span of an object, file, or folder is referred to as an *audit trail*. The primary types of events that you can choose to audit include the following:

- Computer logons and logoffs
- System events (when a computer shuts down or reboots, or something happens that affects system security, such as the audit log being cleared, system time is changed, or an invalid procedure call port is used to try to impersonate a client)
- User and computer account-management tasks (such as the creation of accounts or changes to account status or permissions)
- Access to files, folders, and objects

Configuring security auditing helps you to track potential security issues and provide evidence in relation to security breaches. It is best practice to create an *audit plan* before you enable auditing on your system. The audit plan details the purpose and objectives of the audit. The audit plan should contain the following:

- The type of information you want to audit
- How much time you have to review audit logs
- The resources you have for collecting and storing audit logs (disk space, memory and processor usage)
- The intended scope of the audit

You'll need to ask yourself some questions as you prepare the audit plan. Is the purpose of the audit plan to prevent security breaches from unauthorized sources? If so, enable the audit failure events on logons and collect information on it. Is the objective of the auditing to get a snapshot of the organization's activities for forensic purposes? In that case, enable both success and failure events to collect data on all applications.

It is important to remember that the audit trail information can result in a very large amount of data if both the success and failure audits are enabled. Too wide a scope for the audit can also make it difficult for you to find the information you're looking for within a huge file that records thousands of events.

Head of the Class...

Periodically Back Up Audit Information

The administrative account or administrative privileges are a prime target for hackers so there is always the possibility of intruders gaining administrator access to your system. With these privileges, an intruder can do malicious damage to your system and delete the audit events from the event log. If this happens, there will not be an audit trail to determine the cause and the damage to the system. To minimize the damage that would be caused by such an attack, duplicate the audit information periodically. You can use Microsoft Operations Manager (MOM) to copy audit events periodically and store them in a secure network drive; this provides a backup of the audit trail information.

MOM is a monitoring and management tool released by Microsoft in 2000 and used for a wide variety of enterprise-level management tasks. You can download a trial version on Microsoft's Web site at /www.microsoft.com/MOM/default.asp.

Defining and Modifying Auditing Policies for Event Categories

The audit policy has to be configured before you can log any audit information on access to files, folders, and objects. You can define audit policies for any of the following:

- Local computer
- Domain controller
- Domain
- Organization unit

The Audit account logon events and Audit logon events items are enabled for auditing by default in Windows Server 2003. By default, object access is not enabled. You can view the security audit entries under the Security section of the Event Viewer.

Policies for the Local Computer

This section covers how to define an audit policy on a local computer. The local audit policy dictates the audit procedures on the local machine. It does not dictate the audit policy for the rest of the network computers. Exercise 9.02 walks you through the steps required to enable the auditing policy on the local computer. You must have administrator access to perform any of the auditing policy changes.

EXERCISE 9.02

ENABLE AUDIT POLICY ON A LOCAL MACHINE

1. Click **Start | Programs | Administrative Tools | Local Security Policy**.
2. In the left pane of the console, expand **Local Policies,** and then click **Audit Policy**. Your screen should look similar to Figure 9.19.

Figure 9.19 Local Audit Policy Settings

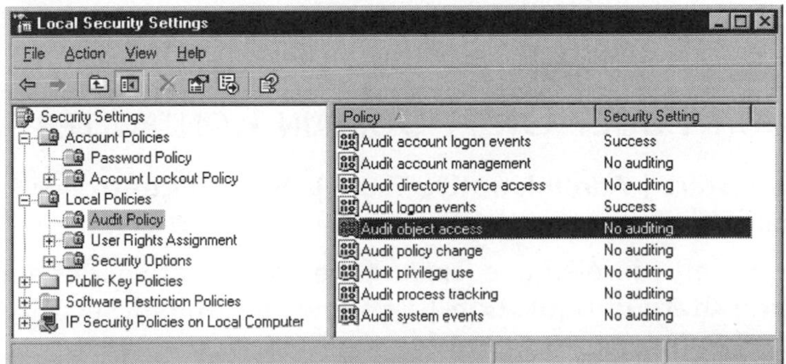

3. In the right details pane, select and double-click the option for which you want to define audit policy. For this exercise, select the **Audit object access** option. The Audit object access Properties dialog box appears (see Figure 9.20). Here you can choose to enable success and/or failure audits by checking the option box(es).

Figure 9.20 Enable Success or Failure Audit Options

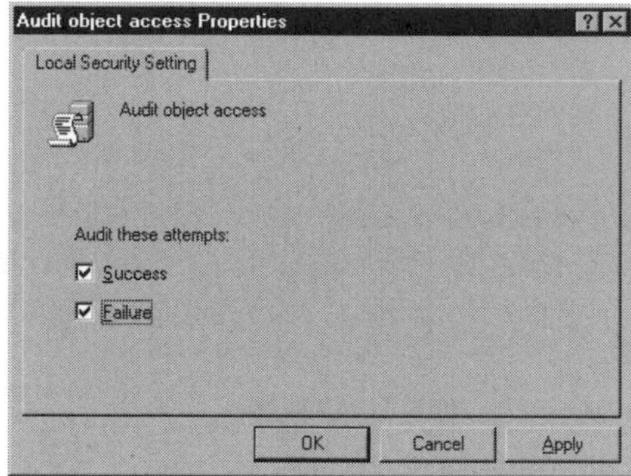

4. Click **OK** or **Apply** button. Now you can enable auditing on objects, files, and folders on the local computers. Please refer to the *Enabling Auditing of Object Access* section for further details.

Policies for Domain Controllers

The next step is to learn the steps to create an audit policy for the domain. This audit policy applies to each computer in the domain. The audit policy is defined at the domain controller machine. The individual machine does not need to specify any audit policies. (They are automatically inherited from the domain controller.) Exercise 9.03 shows the steps to enable audit policy on a domain controller. The steps are similar to the previous exercise.

Exercise 9.03

Enable Audit Policy On A Domain Controller

1. Click **Start | Administrative Tools | Domain Controller Security Policy**.
2. In the left console pane, expand the appropriate nodes and navigate to **Computer Configuration | Windows Settings | Security Settings | Local Policies | Audit Policy**.

3. Double-click the item on which you want to define the audit policy, as shown in Figure 9.20.
4. Choose to enable success and/or failure event auditing by checking the correct option box(es).
5. Click **OK** or **Apply**.

Policies for a Domain or OU

You can also define security audit policies for a domain or an organizational unit (OU). The security audit policy needs to be integrated into the Active Directory in this case. All the members of the Active Directory inherit the audit policy. The local computers settings or the domain controller does not dictate the audit policy. Exercise 9.04 shows how this is done.

EXERCISE 9.04

DEFINE AUDITING POLICY FOR DOMAIN OR OU

1. Click **Start | Administrative Tools | Active Directory Users and Computers**.
2. In the left console pane, right-click the domain or organization unit for which you want to define the audit policy.
3. Select the **Properties** tab, and then select the **Group Policy** tab.
4. Select the Group Policy object (GPO) you want to edit and click **Edit**. You can also create a new Group Policy object and click **Edit**.
5. In the left console tree of the GPO Object Editor, expand the appropriate nodes and click **Computer Configuration | Windows Settings | Security Settings | Local Policy | Audit Policy**.
6. Select the item for which you want to define the policy and double-click it.
7. Check the success and/or failure option box(es) to enable security auditing.
8. Click **OK** or **Apply**.

Enabling Auditing of Object Access

In addition to defining an audit policy as you learned to do in the exercises, you must enable auditing on each particular object for which you want to audit access. In this section, we will discuss how to enable auditing on objects, files, and folders.

Auditing Settings on Objects

Objects include Registry keys, printers, files, folders, and so forth. Every Windows object has a security information object attached to it. It is referred as the *security descriptor* of the object. The security descriptor contains *permission* and *auditing* information on the object. The security descriptor holds information about the groups and individual users that are authorized to manipulate the object, and defines what level of access each has to the object. This part of the security descriptor is referred to as Discretionary Access Control List (DACL).

EXAM WARNING

The DACL is the part of the security descriptor that grants or denies access to individuals or groups for the object. These permissions can be assigned by anyone with "change permissions" credentials. Hence, it is under the *discretion* of the owner to assign access rights.

The security descriptor also contains the auditing information for the object. This part of the descriptor is referred to as the System Access Control List (SACL). The SACL describes the auditing activity on a group basis. The SACL details the audit policy with the following features:

- The individual or group accounts that are to be audited when they access the object.
- The operation to be audited.
- The type of access to document in the security log. The available types are *success* and *failure* audits. The permission rights (which are dictated by the DACL) verifies the user access rights when you try to log *success* or *failure* audits.

You can also specify the audit permissions for objects that are in the inheritance tree using the SACL. This enables all child objects to inherit the audit policy from their parent objects. Refer to the section titled *Understanding the Effect of Inheritance on File and Folder Auditing* for more information on this.

Understanding Operation-Based Auditing of Files and Folders

Operation-based auditing is a new feature in Windows Server 2003. Operation-based auditing provides a more detailed audit trail than its Windows 2000 and XP counterparts. You could determine that a user gained access to an object in Windows 2000 or XP environments, but you could not audit the *operations* that were performed on that object. Operations are the activities, such as write or read details of an object. You can now audit these *operation details* under Windows Server 2003. You can use operation-based auditing to audit files or folders enabling you to configure logging of both the file access details and the operations on those files (e.g., read or write).

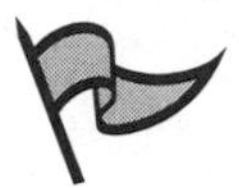

TEST DAY TIP

Operation-based audits are categorized as object audits in the security log. They are easily distinguishable by their unique event ID. The event ID is 567. These events are generated the first time the operation is invoked by the system. They only apply to files and folders, not other types of Active Directory objects.

You must first enable Audit Object Access to enable operation-based auditing. (Refer to the Defining and Auditing Policies section earlier in the chapter.)

Applying and Modifying Audit Policy Settings

In this section, you'll learn how to apply and modify the audit policy settings. We first discuss applying the audit policy on files and folders, and then we discuss how to apply the audit policy as a *Group Policy* on domain controllers.

Policy Settings for Local Files and Folders

Auditing can be enabled only for files and folders that are located on NTFS drives. Thus, the first step in auditing local files and folders on your Windows Server 2003 computer is to verify that the files and folders you want to audit are stored on an NTFS volume.

NOTE

You can use the *convert.exe* utility to convert a FAT or FAT32 partition to NTFS without losing data, but be aware that this is a one-way operation; you cannot convert back without formatting the disk and losing all the data on it. For security, reliability, and performance reasons, it is highly recommended, that all partitions on all servers in a production environment be formatted in NTFS.

Auditing can be a resource-intensive operation if you choose to audit a large number of objects. Because of this, you might need to select the files and folders you want to audit carefully, and audit only those that you really need to, in order to avoid filling your disk space and degrading performance due to the overhead of auditing.

Exercise 9.05 walks you through the process of enabling auditing on a file or a folder.

Exercise 9.05

Add An Audit Setting for Files and Folders

1. Open Windows Explorer (**Start | Accessories | Windows Explorer**).
2. Navigate to the file or folder you on which you want to enable audit policy. Select the **c:\test** directory for this exercise.
3. Click **Properties** and navigate to the **Security** tab.
4. Click the **Advanced** button and select the **Auditing** tab. Your screen should be similar to Figure 9.21. The existing audit entries on the folder are displayed. You can select the **Edit** button or the **Remove** button to modify the existing properties or remove the entry. Auditing is enabled at the user or group level. Our example shows that the built-in Administrator account has access audited on this folder. Click the **Edit** button to get the list of activities/operations for which the Administrator is audited on this folder. To add an account to be audited on this folder, click the **Add** button. (Refer to the *Understanding the Effects of Inheritance* section later in this chapter for more information about the bottom two option boxes. They are related to inheriting audit policies.)

Figure 9.21 Adding and Modifying Auditing Properties on a Folder

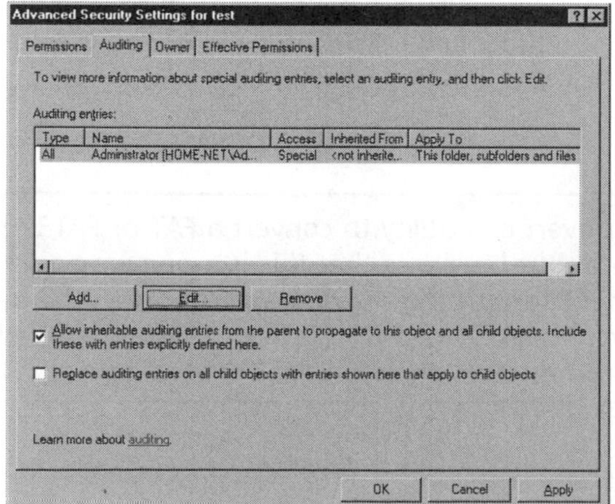

5. You are asked to select the user account or group account that is to be audited on this folder. The Select User or Group window appears, as shown in Figure 9.22. You can type the username in the text box and click the **Check Names** button to verify it. Click the **Advanced** button to extend this screen so you can query Active Directory for a specific object. You can specify whether you are only interested in the users, groups, or all accounts by clicking the **Object Types** button. Click the **Find Now** button to get a complete list of the users. (We will select the built-in Administrator account from this list for this demonstration. Use your valid user account in your case.). Click **OK** after you select the account.

Figure 9.22 Selecting a User or Group to Audit

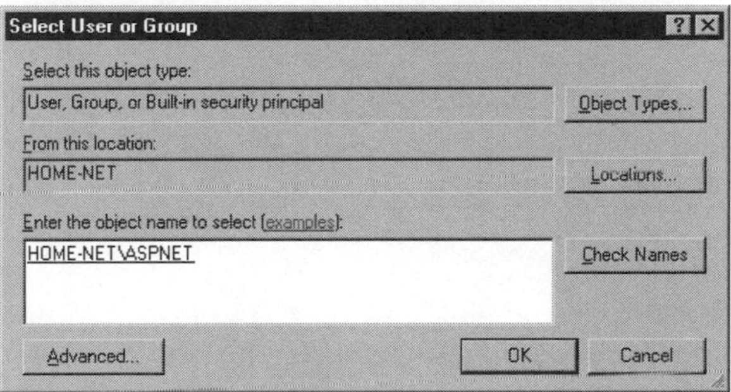

6. Next, you can select the operations you wish to audit. You can see an auditing entry for the *FolderName* window to set your audit configurations. Use the option boxes and check the success and/or failure activities you want to audit for. You can choose whether you want to apply the audit policy on the child subdirectories, file, or just test directory by selecting the correct option from the **Apply onto** list box. For this exercise, enable success and failure auditing on the test directory for child file, folder creations, and deletions. If you wish to prevent audit policy from being inherited by child directories, check the **Apply these auditing entries to objects and/or containers within this container only** check box. Click **OK** to finish applying audit policy on the test directory. See Figure 9.23.

Figure 9.23 Configuring Audit Activities

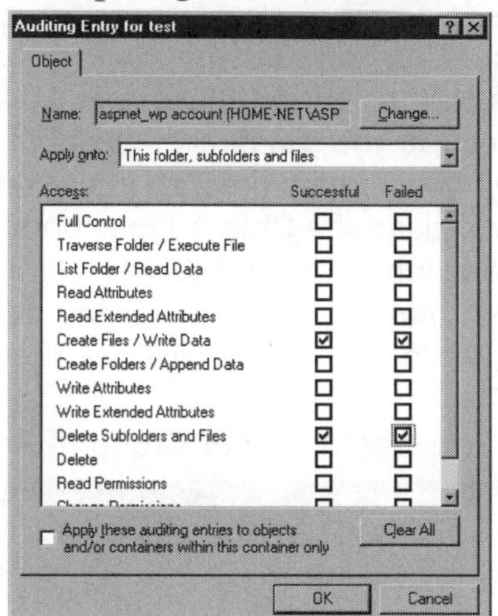

Using Group Policy

You can apply an audit policy to your active directory users and OUs by editing an applicable Group Policy object. The process is similar to enabling audit policy on files and folders. You need to modify the Group Policy on the Active Directory object (domain or OU) to do this. Exercise 9.06 walks you through the steps.

Exercise 9.06

Specify Group Policy

1. Click **Start | Run** and type **mmc** to open an empty management console.
2. Select **Add Snap in** from the **File** menu and click **Add**.
3. Select **Group Policy Object Editor** and click **Add**.
4. In the **Select Group Policy Object** dialog box, click the **Browse** button to select the correct GPO for the domain or organizational unit. The GPO opens in the Group Policy Object Editor.
5. To specify the file auditing policy, navigate to the **Computer Configuration | Windows Settings | Security Settings | File System** node in the left pane of the Group Policy Object Editor.

6. Right-click the **File System** node to add the auditing details for a file or a folder. Navigate to the file or folder on which you want to set auditing, using the browse interface, and click **Properties**. Then click **Edit Security** to enter the auditing details, as you did in steps 4 through 6 of the previous exercise.

Understanding the Effect of Inheritance on File and Folder Auditing

You can apply an audit policy on an inheritance tree. This means the child object can *inherit* the parent object's audit policies. A child object has inherited audit policy settings from a parent object if the following conditions are present:

- The option boxes in the **Access** area are not available from the **Auditing Entry for File or FolderName** window, as shown in Figure 9.23.
- The **Remove** button is grayed out from the **Advanced security settings for File or FolderName** dialog box, as shown in Figure 9.21.

It is easy to enable auditing on the child nodes. Check the **Allow inheritable auditing entries from the parent to propagate to this object and all child objects. Include these with entries explicitly defined here** checkbox as previously shown in Figure 9.21. This is enabled by default. Therefore, auditing for the child objects is enabled by default in Windows Server 2003.

You can also prevent the parent audit policy being inherited by a child node. (The inheritance does not apply in this case.) This is done by unchecking the option box **Apply these auditing entries to objects and/or containers within this container only** from the **Auditing Entry for File or FolderName** dialog box, as shown in Figure 9.23. You can change the audit policies on each child object individually by using this method. You can also make changes to the parent folder's audit policy so that the new policies propagate to the child objects. This results in the parent and child objects having the same policies.

Viewing the Security Log

You can view audit details in the security log section of the Event Viewer. (The Event Viewer is discussed in detail in the next section). The security log is displayed in Figure 9.26 in the next section. You can use it to view object, file, and folder activities on those objects for which you've configured auditing, as well as logon successes and failures and other security events.

As mentioned earlier, auditing can be expensive in terms of disk space usage and resource usage, as well as administrative time and effort. This is exacerbated if you have a large amount of traffic and/or incorrectly configured audit policies. For this reason, we recommend that you not enable Full Control Auditing for *Success* and *Failure* events on frequently accessed directories and files. Such a policy can generate a tremendously large amount of data. Carefully analyze the need before you enable auditing on files or folders and take into consideration the amount of available disk space.

The maximum size of the security log is defined in the Event Viewer and can be modified by the administrator. You can select to stop entering audits into the security log when the maximum file size limit is reached, or overwrite the oldest audit information. (Refer to the *Configure the log size* subsection in the section titled *Event Viewer*).

NOTE

Note that your system can become unstable if the Event Viewer runs out of disk space.

Using Event Viewer

The Event Viewer is used to monitor many different aspects of server activity. To access this tool, click **Start | Programs | Administrative Tools | Event Viewer.** The Event Viewer is displayed as a Microsoft Management Console (MMC) that is stored at SystemRoot\System32\eventvwr.msc. The Everyone user group has Read and Execute access to manipulate the Event Viewer. The Administrator group and the System account have Full Control. (Full Control consists of read, write, modify, and execute permissions.)

The Event Viewer displays event log data. There are at least three different event log files: the application, security, and system logs. (Each is discussed in detail later in this section.) Your Event Viewer can display additional logs, depending on applications and services you have installed on the server. For example, if the computer is configured as a DNS server, it has a DNS log in addition to the three default logs.

Event Types

There are five major event types. The *error, warning,* and *information* types occur in the application and System logs. The *Success Audit* or *Failure Audit* types occur in the Security log. Following are descriptions of each event type and its function:

- **Error** Indicates a significant problem in the system. This can have adverse effects on the application or operating system if ignored. (For example, the DHCP service not starting at reboot can lead to the lack of IP assignment for the network computers.)
- **Warning** Indicates the possibility of future errors, but conditions do not pose an immediate threat to the system (For example, *Low disk space* is a warning that can lead to various errors if ignored, but does not indicate an immediate threat.)

- **Information** Describes a successful operation of the system or an application. (For example, SQL Server logs an information event when the SQL Server starts up correctly.)
- **Success Audit** All audited security events that are completed successfully are logged in this category. (For example, a successful user logon when security auditing is enabled.)
- **Failure Audit** All audited security events that fail are logged here. (For example, you receive an authorization error if you try to log on to a shared drive to which you don't have access. This results in a failure audit entry in the security event log.)

Understanding Event Logs

In this section, we discuss the Event Viewer format and examine the way information is presented in each log. Every event log entry is comprised of several pieces of information. These components are listed in Table 9.5. All of these components can be enabled or disabled by using the **View | Add/Remove Columns** menu item.

Table 9.5 Columns Available in Event Logs

Column Name	Description
Date	The date the event occurred. This is stored in Universal Time Coordinate (UTC) format, but the date is displayed according to the user's local settings.
Time	The time the event occurred. This is also stored in UTC format and displayed according to the user's local settings.
User	The user name of the process that caused the event. This can be a *user account* name or an *impersonation* name. (Impersonation is the term used to describe when a user impersonates someone else's credentials; e.g., the IIS anonymous user logs on as IUSER_ *MachineName* account.) If the account is impersonated, *both* the impersonated account and user name are logged.
Computer	The name of the server where the event took place. This could be a remote computer name if you are accessing a remote computer's event log.
Source	The name of the application that generated the event. This could be a software program or a Windows Server 2003 component (e.g., SQL Server as a program and USB device driver as a component).
Event	Unique ID number for each event. This is supported with a brief explanation of the error (e.g., the description for Event ID (19011) is *Source (MSSQL$WEBDB) cannot be found*). You can troubleshoot the application by using these event details and the source information.

Continued

Table 9.5 Columns Available in Event Logs

Column Name	Description
Type	The type of the event. This could be any one of those event types discussed earlier: error, information, and warning in the *system* and *application* logs, or success audit or failure audit in the security log. Each type has a unique icon to represent it in the Event Viewer.
Category	This feature is primarily used in the security log. This is the category to which the event belongs according to the source of the event.

Event Log Types

The event log service is automatically started when the Windows Server 2003 systems starts. Three default log files are available in Windows Server 2003. These same logs were also available in Windows NT, 2000, and XP. The default logs are as follows:

- **Application log** This log is available for general troubleshooting as well as the application developers. It can be used to record application errors, warnings, and information events. Scripting languages (such as C#, C++, VB 6.0) include Application Programming Interface (API) calls to log entries in the application log. This log can be used to display a myriad of application errors. (e.g., The application can record a *Source file not found* error when files needed to complete a transaction are missing.)
- **Security log** Events that affect system security are included in this event log. These events include failed or successful logon attempts, creating, opening or deleting files, changing properties or permissions on user accounts and groups, etc.
- **System log** Events related to Windows system components are stored in this log file. This includes entries regarding failure of drivers and other system components during startup and shutdown.

These are the logs available for a Windows Server 2003 standalone server. The application or system event log of a Windows Server 2003 non-domain controller machine is similar to Figure 9.24. This image displays the Application event log on a machine called HOME-NET. This image clearly shows the information, warning, and error events that have occurred on this server. (For example, the first entry is an information event, followed by two warnings and two errors.) Note the different icons the Event Viewer uses for information, warning, or error events. Also note the columns that are displayed.

You can get further information about a specific event by double-clicking the event name in the list. The list view does not give any specific information about the event; it only provides you with an event ID. Double-clicking the event gives you more information. Figure 9.25 shows the Event Properties box that is displayed when you double-click the first error message in the list. You can view a detailed error message using this view. You can also use the arrow keys (*up* and *down* arrow keys) to navigate through the Event Viewer, or you can copy the event information to the clipboard by using the icon below the *down* arrow key.

Figure 9.24 Application Event Viewer

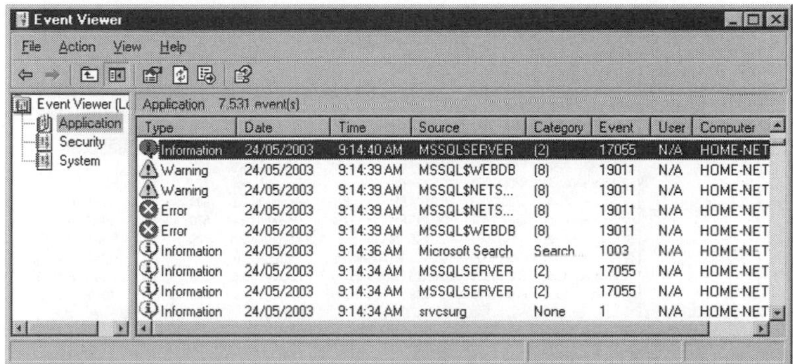

Test Day Tip

Some errors display the input and output parameters for a process. This data can be viewed via the *Data* group box at the bottom. The data can be viewed in Hexadecimal (displayed as *Bytes*) or DWORD (displayed as *Words*) format. Not all applications generate binary data. Expert programmers can use the information contained in these descriptions to troubleshoot problems.

Figure 9.25 Application Error Description

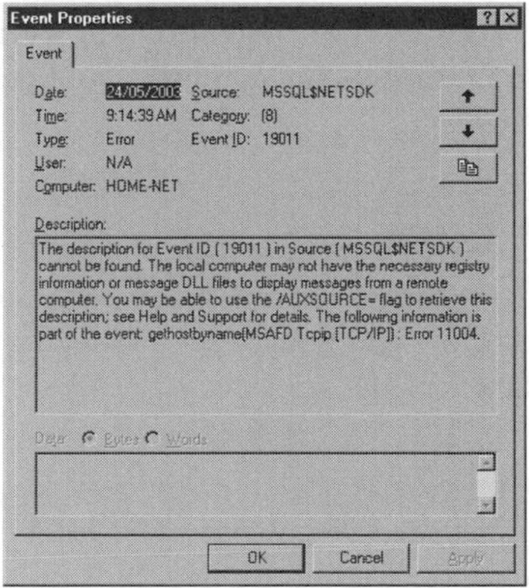

The Security Event Viewer is similar to Figure 9.26. However, there are two differences. The *type* of the Security Event Viewer is either Success Audit or Failure Audit. The other significant difference is the information in the *Category* column. The Security Event Viewer is shown in Figure 9.26.

Figure 9.26 Security Event Viewer

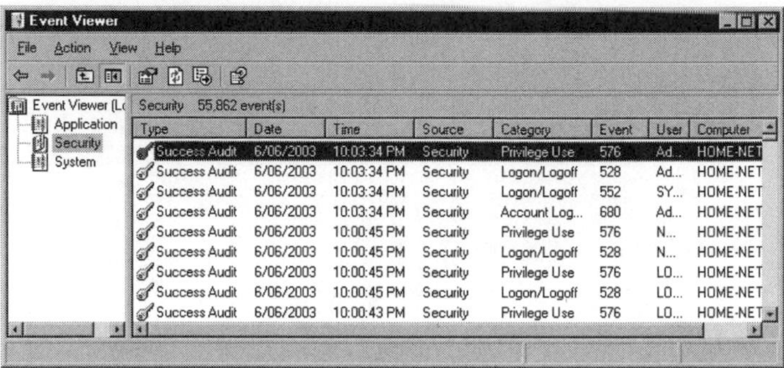

If the server is a domain controller, it displays additional event logs. Here are the additional events logs you might see on a domain controller:

- **Directory Service log** Used to log Windows Active Directory events. The Active Directory Service logs these entries in the event log. (For example, a connection error between the Active Directory global catalog and the server is recorded in this section.)
- **File Replication Service log** Contains the events logged by the File Replication Service. File replication failures and other events regarding system and shared volumes are recorded here.
- **DNS server log** Domain Name System (DNS) service log entries are include in this log file. This log appears on any computer configured as a DNS server (not just domain controllers).

Managing Event Logs

There are a number of common administrative tasks related to using the Event Viewer. In the following sections, we will show you how to set up logging options, configure the log size, clear log events, and archive log data.

Setting Logging Options

You can set logging options using the Event Viewer. This can be achieved by modifying the **Properties** options of the event log. To do this, right-click on a log file (Application, System, or Security) and select the **Properties** option. The dialog box that displays will be similar to Figure 9.27.

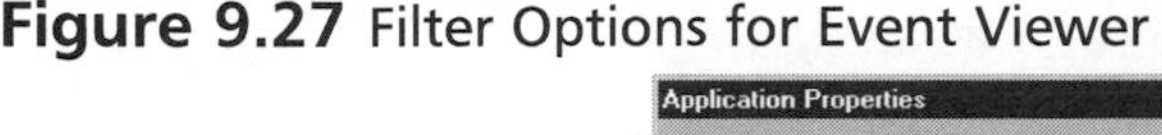

Figure 9.27 Filter Options for Event Viewer

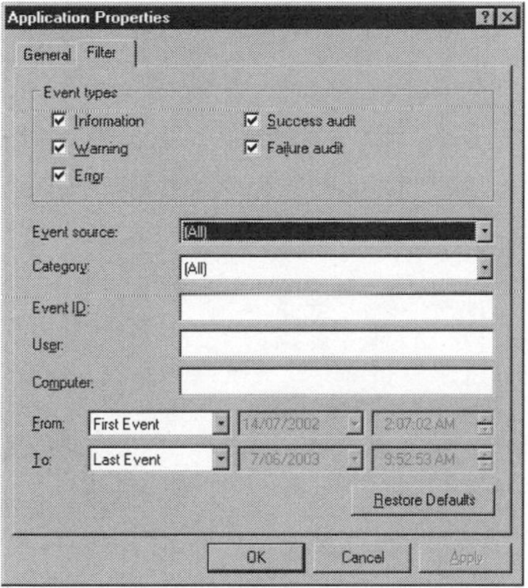

You can customize your logging options by referring to this screen. You can choose which events you want to record. You can select the option box next to Application, System, Security, Success Audit, or Failure Audit to enable or disable event logging. You can also filter the events according to the source of the events. On the **Filter** tab, you can select a single entry from the drop-down list and click the **Apply** button to filter the events. You can also filter the events by populating the Category, Event ID, User, and Computer name fields as arguments and clicking the **Apply** button. The filtering feature also supports multiple filter criteria.

Configuring Log Size

You can configure the log size of an event log by using the **General** tab of the **Properties** window. Display the **Properties** dialog box by right-clicking an event log type. Figure 9.28 displays the **Properties** of the Application log file.

Following are some of the ways you can configure the properties of log files:

- You can configure the log size by changing the properties the Log size group box.
- You can set a maximum file size limit on the log file, in kilobytes. Figure 9.28 refers to a maximum file size of 16,384KB.
- You can instruct the system to overwrite the log file when it has filled to capacity. (This is done by clicking the **Overwrite events as needed** option, which is selected by default.)
- You can instruct that the log file be purged at a specific time interval (e.g., delete all entries that are older than 7 days).

Figure 9.28 Configure Log Size

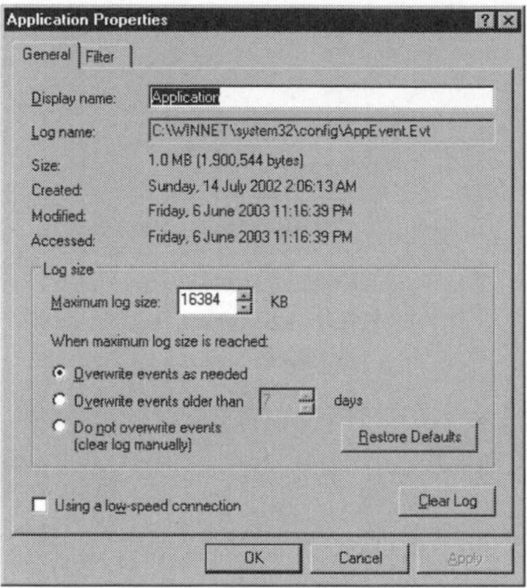

- You can specify that the log remain until it is manually deleted by a system administrator.
- You can clear the log completely by clicking the **Clear Log** button.
- You can store the event log at another computer and log information remotely. The computer might be connected using a low-speed connection (using a modem). You can configure the Event Viewer to accommodate this scenario by selecting the **Using a low-speed connection** option box. This option optimizes network resources transfer data at low speeds.

Clearing Logs

Event logs inevitably grow over time, as more and more events occur and are logged by the system. You might need to purge the event logs periodically to avoid system malfunctions, because you might run out of disk space if you continuously let the Event Viewer grow. The Event Viewer includes an option to delete all entries in a log file. You can also configure the **Properties** dialog box to clear the events, as discussed above. The steps required to clear the event log completely are shown in Exercise 9.07.

Exercise 9.07

Archive Event Logs

1. Open Event Viewer (**Start | Administrative Tools | Event Viewer**).
2. Right-click the relevant log (Application, System, or Security) and select the **Clear All Events** option.

3. A confirmation box appears to confirm that you want to delete the event data. Click **Yes**.
4. You are required to save the event log before deleting the event information. You are presented with a dialog box to enter the file name.
5. Enter the file name and save the file.
6. Click **OK**.
7. Next, to set a maximum log size, enter the maximum disk space in the **Maximum Log size X KB** text box. This is the disk space in kilobytes assigned to the log file. (Please refer to Figure 9.28.)
8. Now you can configure the events when the maximum log file is met. The options can be found directly under the maximum log file size. You can instruct the system to overwrite the log file, delete the entries after *X* number of days, or you can instruct the system not to overwrite it automatically. You have to manually delete the log entries in this case. Please refer back to Figure 9.28 for details. Select your option and click **OK**.

Archiving Logs

You can archive event logs for future reference. You can store the archives in one of several different file formats:

- Event Viewer format (.EVT)
- Comma-separated values file (.CSV)
- Text file (.TXT)

The .EVT file format is the only file type that can be loaded into the Event Viewer for direct viewing through its interface. The .TXT file can be opened with a text editor (such as Notepad) and the .CSV file can be opened with a spreadsheet program (such as Microsoft Excel).

You can save Event Viewer files locally or remotely. You have to provide the correct network share location if you wish to save events logs remotely (e.g., \\RemoteComputerName\NetworkShare). You also need to grant the correct access privileges for those who will access the files. All the events in the event logs are saved when the log is archived. However, *Sort* formats and *Filtering* options are ignored. Here are the steps required to archive files:

1. Open the Event Viewer (**Start | Administrative Tools | Event Viewer**).
2. Right-click the relevant log (Application, System, or Security) and select the **Save Log File As** option.

3. Enter the file name and select the correct file type (.EVT, .CSV or .TXT).
4. Click the **Save** button.

You can open an archived log file that was saved in .evt format in the Event Viewer by using the **Open Log File** option in the right context menu. (Alternatively, you can open it by clicking **File | Open Log File**.)

Troubleshooting Event Logs

As with any system component, sometimes problems occur when using the Event Viewer. In this section, we discuss some common troubleshooting problems related to the Event Viewer. Most of these issues turn out to be due to incorrect security privileges.

- **There is a Global Unique Identifier (GUID) or Security ID (SID) in the User field instead of the user details** This can be due to many reasons. The user ID might have been deleted for some reason (there is nothing you can do to rectify the problem in this case). It can also happen if you try to access the event log of a remote computer. The solution is to run the Event Viewer locally on the remote computer.
- **You are unable to view the security log on a remote computer, but you can view application and system logs** You must be a member of the local Administrators group to access the security log. The solution is to add your account to the Administrators group on the remote computer.
- **You can view the security log remotely, but you cannot view the application or system logs** This happens when you are a member of both the Guests and Administrators groups of the remote computer. The Guests group is denied access to the event logs, and when you belong to groups with conflicting permissions, the most restrictive permissions apply. To remedy the problem, remove your account from the Guests group from the remote computer.
- **You cannot view the details for the *Category* and *Description* fields when you access the Event Viewer remotely** This can be due to several reasons. You might not have Administrator access to obtain this information. If this is the case, add your account to the remote computer's Administrators group. Another reason can that be the Remote Registry Service on the remote computer is stopped. If so, start the Remote Registry Service on the computer to display the Description and Category fields. (You can start this service from the **Services** node under the **Services and Applications** node in the **Computer Management** console.)

Using Command-Line Tools

Windows Server 2003 includes some useful command-line tools that you can use to manipulate the events on the server. You can create, query, and trigger events by using these command-line utilities. Table 9.6 describes some common switches that are used in all the command-line utilities discussed in this section.

Table 9.6 Common Switches Available

Switch	Description
/s	You can specify the machine name or the IP address of the computer for which you wish to record events. The default is the local computer.
/u *Domain\User*	This is the user account that is used to insert the event into the event log. The default is the currently logged-in account.
/p *Password*	Password for the user account.
/?	Displays help information.

eventcreate.exe

The eventcreate.exe utility creates an event in a specified event file. The valid event files are Application and System logs. You cannot enter events in the Security log with this utility. You must have administrator access to use this utility to enter entries into the application and system logs. The Application log is the default log file for this utility. The log file in which the event is to be entered is specified by using the */l* switch. The syntax for the command is shown below. The available switches are explained in Table 9.7.

```
Syntax : eventcreate [/s Computer [/u Domain\User [/p Password]] {[/l
    {APPLICATION | SYSTEM}] | [/so SrcName]} /t {ERROR | WARNING |
        INFORMATION} /id EventID /d Description
```

Table 9.7 Switches Available for eventcreate.vbs

Switch	Description
/so *SrcName*	The source details of the event. This is a string that represents a valid application component that generated the event.
/t {*log type*}	The log type (ERROR, WARNING, or INFORMATION).
/id *EventID*	The event ID. A valid event ID is a number between 0 and 1000.
/d *Description*	The event description.
/l Logfile	Specifies the log file in which the event is to be entered (APPLICATION or SYSTEM).

Figure 9.29 shows the eventcreate.exe tool in action. We created an information event called **Create event in Application log** with the event ID 1000. The results can be seen in Figure 9.29. The source of the event is logged as **EventCreate** by default. Next, we created an event remotely on a machine called "home-net." The event description is **Creating events on a remote computer**. This is an error with event ID 1000. The results are shown in Figure 9.29.

Exam Warning

If you do not provide a user name and password for the event creation, the default credentials are passed to the remote computer. This generates a warning message so you know that it's happening.

Figure 9.29 Command-Line Example for eventcreate.vbs

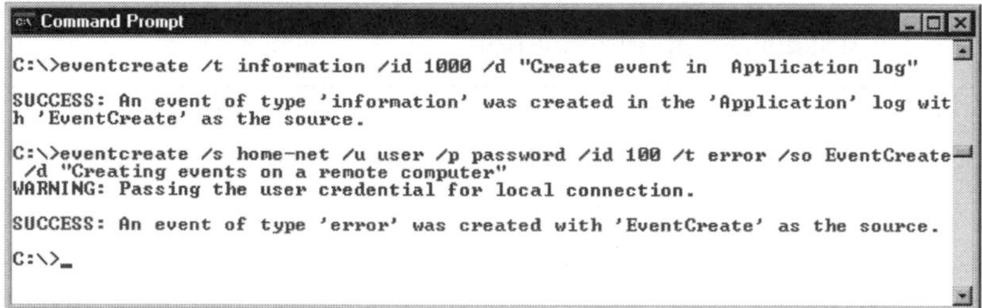

eventquery.vbs

The eventquery.vbs command-line utility is used to query log files, to list the events and properties in the files. You can query Application, System, and Security log files using this tool. The syntax is shown below and Table 9.8 describes some of the switches available for the utility.

```
Syntax : eventquery[.vbs] [/s Computer [/u Domain\User [/p Password]]]
    [/fi FilterName] [/fo {TABLE | LIST | CSV}] [/r EventRange
        [/nh] [/v] [/l [APPLICATION] [SYSTEM] [SECURITY] ["DNS server"]
            [UserDefinedLog] [DirectoryLogName] [*] ]
```

Table 9.8 Options Available for eventquery.vbs

Switch	Description
/fi *FilterName*	The filter information for the event query. The filter can be a date, type, ID, user, machine name, source, or category information. Use *eq* (equal to), *gt* (greater than), and *le* (lesser than) operators to do the validations.

Continued

Table 9.8 Options Available for eventquery.vbs

Switch	Description
/fo {*FileOutput*}	The specified format for the output file. This can be one of the TABLE (as a table), LIST (as a list), or CSV (comma-separated value file format) values.
/r *EventRange*	The range of events to list. For example, the tool displays the first 20 events if you provide "20" as the value. You get the last 20 events if you provide "-20." The value "10-20" is used to get the events between 10 and 20.
/nh	Only available in TABLE and CSV format. This suppresses the headers in the output. (*nh* stands for *no header*).
/v	Specifies to list a verbose output.
/l	The type of log file to be listed. This can be application, system, security, DNS, or any custom log files. The wild card ("*") is used to obtain all log files.

Figure 9.30 displays some examples of how to use this utility. First, we queried the Security log file, to obtain the last two events in LIST file format. Figure 9.30 displays the execution of this command. This command is followed by another command to obtain the events in the Application log. You can also apply a filter to obtain the error type entries only. The results are shown in Figure 9.30.

Figure 9.30 Examples of eventquery.vbs

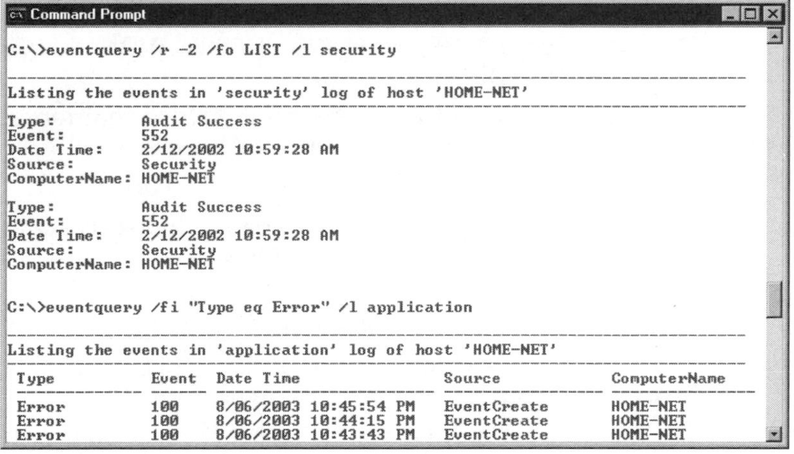

eventtriggers.exe

eventtriggers.exe is a tool used to configure and manage triggers on event logs. A trigger is a mechanism that initiates a new process or action when a threshold is met. For example, you can configure triggers on event logs to prevent the logs from filling all the available disk space and causing the server to go offline. You can create a trigger to detect a "*Low Disk Space*" event and send a message to the server's administrator, so he or she can investigate the problem before it becomes critical. (You can send the message by writing a script to interact with the mail client and creating a mail message to the Administrator.) You can use this command locally or on a remote computer.

NOTE

Configuring triggers on a system compromises speed and performance, because there is overhead involved in monitoring for the threshold events and initiating the actions specified. However, it is important to server availability.

The eventtriggers.exe command with no parameters displays all the available triggers . Three switches are available for this command: */create*, */query*, and */delete*. These switches accept the same common parameters. Table 9.9 details these parameters. Refer to the syntax of each switch and pick the corresponding parameters from the table.

Table 9.9 Options Available for eventtrigger.vbs Switches (Create, Query, and Delete)

Switch	Description
/tr *TriggerName*	The name of the trigger. This is a name you provide to identify the trigger.
/eid *ID*	The event ID. The trigger monitors the activity for this event.
/t {*logFile*}	The event type (ERROR, WARNING, INFORMATION, SUCCESSAUDIT, or FAILUREAUDIT).
/so *SrcName*	The source details of the event. This is a string that represents a valid application component that generates the event.
/d *Description*	The event description
/tk *TaskName*	Specifies the process to execute when the trigger is activated (for example, call up the disk cleanup utility when a "Low Disk Space" event is generated).
/tid *TriggerID*	The trigger ID. The unique identifier for a trigger.
/fo {*FileOutput*}	The specified format for the output file: TABLE (as a table), LIST (as a list), or CSV (comma-separated value file format).
/r *EventRange*	The range of the events to list. You get the first 20 events if you provide "20" as the value. You get the last 20 events if you provide "-20." The value "10-20" is used to get the events between 10 and 20.
/nh	Only available in TABLE and CSV format. This suppresses the headers in the output. (*nh* stands for *no header.*)

Continued

Table 9.9 Options Available for eventtrigger.vbs Switches (Create, Query, and Delete)

Switch	Description
/v	Specifies to list a verbose output.
/l	The type of log file to be listed. This could be application, system, security, DNS, or any other Event Viewer log files. The wild card "*" is used to obtain all log files.

The */create* switch creates an event rigger on a local or remote computer. The syntax for the */create* switch is shown in the following listing:

```
Syntax : eventtriggers[.exe] /create [/s Computer [/u Domain\User [/p
    Password]]] /tr TriggerName [/l [APPLICATION] [SYSTEM] [SECURITY]
        ["DNS Server"] [LOG] [DirectoryLogName] [*] ] {[/eid ID] |
            [/t {ERROR | INFORMATION | WARNING | SUCCESSAUDIT |
                FAILUREAUDIT}] | [/so Source]} [/d Description] /tk
                    TaskName
```

The */query* switch displays the triggers available on the machine. A list of all triggers can be obtained by using the eventtriggers.exe command without any parameters or switches. The syntax for the */query* switch is shown in the following listing:

```
Syntax : eventtriggers[.exe] /query [/s Computer [/u Domain\User [/p
    Password]]] [/fo {TABLE | LIST | CSV}] [/nh] [/v]
```

The */delete* switch deletes a specified trigger according to a given trigger ID. The wild card "*" is used to delete all triggers. The syntax for the */delete* switch is shown in the following listing:

```
Syntax : eventtriggers[.exe] /delete [/s Computer [/u Domain\User [/p
    Password]]] /tid {ID | *}
```

Figure 9.31 shows an experiment with the *eventtriggers.exe* tool's functionality. We created a trigger to detect low disk space on the system that corresponds to event ID 4133. (Event ID 4133 is the low disk space event for the system.) In our example, we created this trigger on a machine called "Home-net." We wanted to initiate the disk cleanup utility when this trigger was activated. Figure 9.31 illustrates the execution of this command. Enter the Administrator's password (that of the currently logged-on account with Administrator group privileges) to execute this command.

Next, we used the *eventtriggers* command with no switches or parameters to obtain a complete list of all the triggers on the server. Then we used the */query* switch to display all the triggers on the Home-net computer. (The results are the same because we are executing all commands on the Home-net computer.) Finally, we deleted all the triggers using the "*" wildcard on the server. Refer to Figure 9.31 for illustrations of the input and output described.

Figure 9.31 eventtriggers.exr Command in Action

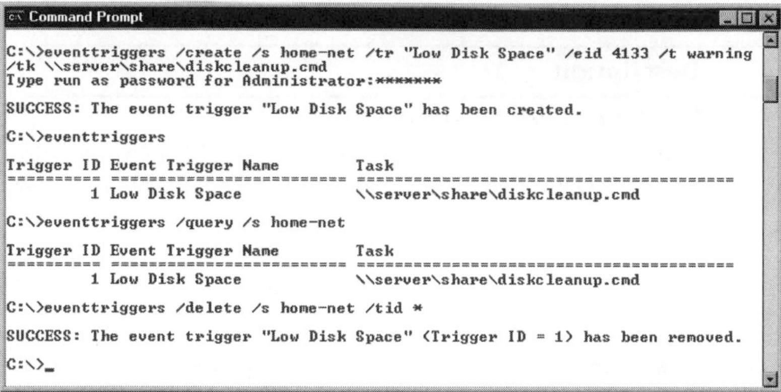

tracerpt.exe

The tracerpt.exe command-line utility generates a report for the event traces. Refer to the subsection titled *Trace Logs* in the *System Monitor* section for more information about event traces). This utility can generate several output files. A comma-separated file (.CSV) describes the report on the trace source. .csv files can be easily imported into Microsoft Excel for analysis. A summary file can also be generated by this utility. The Summary File contains the summary details for the execution of the command. You can use either a trace file or a real time source as the source for the summary. The syntax for the tracerpt.exe command is shown below. The switches and parameters are explained in Table 9.10.

```
Syntax : tracerpt [FileName [FileName ...]] [-o [FileName]] [-report
    [FileName]] [-rt SessionName [SessionName ...]] [-summary
        [FileName]] [-config [FileName] [-f {XML | TXT | HTML}] [-y]
```

Table 9.10 Options Available for tracerpt.exe

Switch	Description
FileName [FileName ...]	Specifies the source file or files to generate the report.
-o *[FileName]*	The name of the output .csv file. Dumpfile.csv is used as the default if no file name is given.
-report *[FileName]*	The name of the output report file. Workload.txt is used as the default if no name is provided.
-rt *[SessionName]*	This indicates real-time processing. Include the event trace session details.
-summary	The name of the summary file. The default is summary.txt.

Continued

Table 9.10 Options Available for tracerpt

Switch	Description
-config	You can create a configuration file to document all the parameter information. This switch is used to give the config file details.
-f	Specifies the report format. The default is TXT. You can also use HTML or XML formats.
-y	Use this option to answer "yes" to all the intermediate question while generating the report.

Using the Shutdown Event Tracker

The Shutdown Event Tracker enables system administrators to monitor the shutdowns on their servers. This is an important factor in understanding the behavior of the computer systems. You can also e-mail the shutdown information to Microsoft using this feature (e.g., to notify them of bugs encountered in beta testing).

Shutdown Events Overview

A computer can be shut down for different reasons. There are two broad categories: *expected* and *unexpected* shutdowns. An expected shutdown is one that you anticipate in response to a particular action, such as clicking **Start | Shutdown** or pressing **Ctrl + Alt + Del** and selecting **Shutdown**. The system initiates the shutdown and logs the reason for the shutdown.

An expected shutdown can be either *planned* or *unplanned*. System administrators have control over a planned shutdown (e.g., the system shutdown after an IIS upgrade process). You can also have an unplanned shutdown (e.g., one of the applications on the server can cause it to restart automatically). The *unexpected shutdowns* cause the Windows Server 2003 systems to shut down unexpectedly. This could be due to non-applications or operating system functions (e.g., due to a power failure for a server).

Shutdown events are controlled by two applications:

- Shutdown Event Tracker
- shutdown.exe

The Shutdown Event Tracker is a graphical user interface (GUI) application that monitors the shutdown. Shutdown.exe is the command-line interface used for the same purpose. It is important not to turn off the computer until a message instructs you to do so, to ensure that all applications, files, and services are closed properly. Windows Server 2003 stores valuable configuration information in memory during a shutdown and writes it to disk so it won't be lost when the computer is powered down. You can turn off the computer when the operating system displays the message "It is OK to shut down the server."

Configuring the Shutdown Event Tracker

In this section, you learn to configure the Shutdown Event Tracker. This tool is enabled by default in the Windows Server 2003 family of operating systems. You perform the configuration by using the Group Policy Object Editor to edit the local computer policy. Exercise 9.08 walks you through the steps.

Exercise 9.08

Configure Shutdown Event Tracker

1. Click **Start | Run,** type **gpedit.msc,** and then click **OK**. This activates the **Group Policy Object Editor** with the Local Computer Policy displayed.
2. Expand the nodes and navigate to **Local Computer Policy | Computer Configuration | Administrative Templates | System** and select **Display Shutdown Event Tracker**. Your screen should be similar to Figure 9.32.

Figure 9.32 Group Policy Console

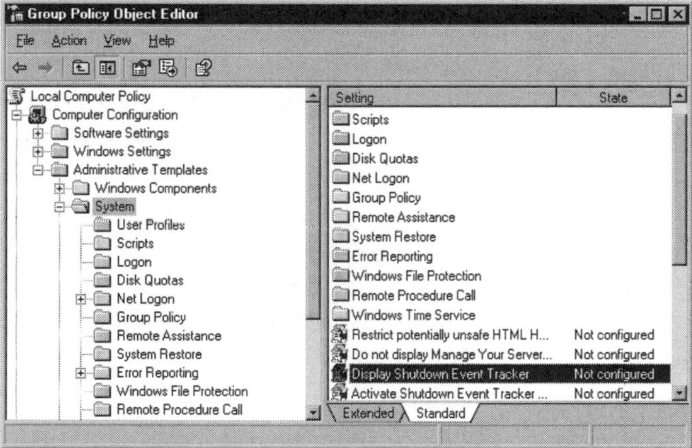

3. Double-click the **Display Shutdown Event Tracker** policy. This brings up another window with the configuration settings, as shown in Figure 9.33. You can select the **Not Configured, Enabled,** or **Disabled** options from this dialog box. A drop-down option list appears if you click **Enabled**. The available options for enabling the Shutdown Event Tracker are **Always, Server Only,** and **Workstation Only**. This determines when the Shutdown Event Tracker should be displayed. Domain administrators use the last two options to configure domain settings. The **Server Only** setting applies only to Windows Server 2003 servers,

and the **Workstation Only** setting applies only to Windows XP Professional workstations. Some comprehensive help information can be found when you click the **Explain** tab. For purposes of this exercise, select **Enabled** to enable the Shutdown Event Tracker and select **Always** from the list.

NOTE

By default, the Shutdown Event Tracker is displayed on Windows Server 2003 computers and is not displayed on Windows XP Professional computers. Shutdown Event Tracker is not available in Windows XP Home edition and previous Microsoft operating systems.

Figure 9.33 Shutdown Event Tracker Properties

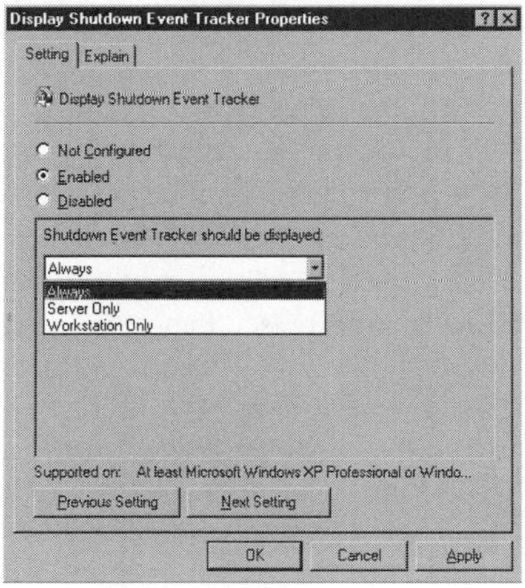

4. Click **OK**.

Working with the Shutdown Event Tracker

If the **Display Shutdown Event Tracker** policy is configured to display the Shutdown Event Tracker (this is the default on a Windows Server 2003 machine), the **Shutdown Windows** dialog box is displayed whenever the system shuts down. The dialog box is similar to Figure 9.34.

Figure 9.34 Shutdown Event Tracker Dialog Box

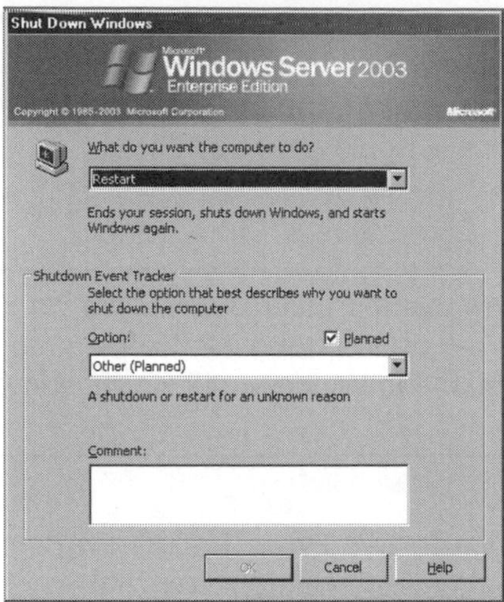

Use this screen to collect data on shutdowns. The **What do you want the computer to do** option box enables you to log off the current user, restart, or shut down. Then you can select a reason and indicate whether it is a planned or unplanned shutdown. Add a comment to complete the Shutdown Event Tracker data collection. You can also invoke the expected shutdown dialog box on a remote computer by using shutdown.exe with */i*. The **Remote Shutdown Dialog** screen appears (see Figure 9.35) when you invoke shutdown.exe with */i*.

Figure 9.35 Using Shutdown Event Tracker Remotely

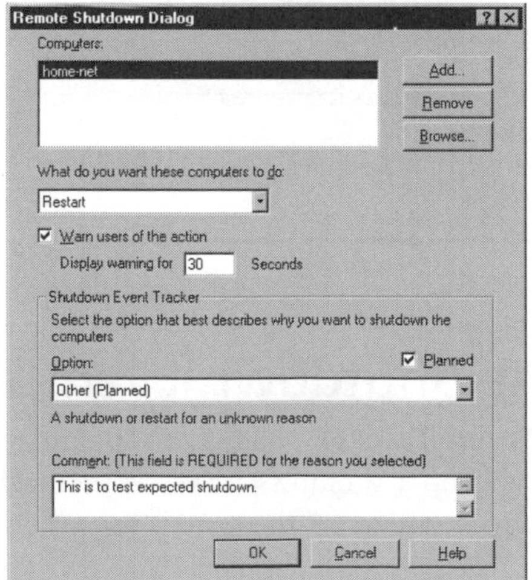

This functionality is similar to Figure 9.34. When the Shutdown Event Tracker is enabled, even expected shutdowns force the system administrator to enter the reason for the shutdown. You can view the Shutdown Event Tracker information in the **Shutdown Event** Tracker group box by selecting an option and clicking the **Planned** option box. A shutdown is unplanned if you do not select this box. You must select a reason from the **Other (Planned)** option list, as shown in Figure 9.35. You must also include a comment to support the category you selected. (Otherwise, the **OK** button is disabled.)

An unexpected shutdown does not give any warning to the system before it goes offline. This can be due to many reasons (for example, a power failure, a power connection cord being disconnected, etc.). The system forces the shutdown tracker to collect the details when an authorized user logs on again.

Test Day Tip

The *System State data* feature is a Shutdown Event Tracker option on Windows Server 2003 domain policies that can be enabled for domains or OUs by editing the GPO that applies to that domain or OU. This policy causes a system state data file to be saved when an unplanned shutdown or restart occurs. The file is located at <systemroot>\System32\LogFiles\Shutdown and can be viewed by administrators only.

Exam Warning

Shutdown Event Tracker does not record *Logoff* or *Hibernate* actions. It only logs complete shutdowns of the system.

You can use the shutdown.exe utility to enter shutdown events via the command-line. Table 9.11 explains some of the options available for the shutdown.exe command-line utility.

Note

To use the shutdown.exe utility, you must have been granted the Shut down the system user right. To annotate an unplanned shutdown, you must be an administrator.

Table 9.11 Options Available for Shutdown.exe

Switch	Description
/s *ServerName*	/*s* shuts down the computer; *Servername* indicates the name of the machine to be shut down.
/r	Restarts the computer after shutdown.
/t *nnn*	The time period for shutdown in seconds. The number of seconds can be between 0 and 600. The default is 30 seconds. This switch causes a warning to be displayed on the console.
/d [p:xx:yy]	/d lists the reason for the shutdown. p: Indicates the shutdown is planned; *XX* and *YY* identify the major and minor reason numbers. If you don't use the *p:* parameter, the system assumes the shutdown is unplanned.
/p	The power to the machine is on if this parameter is given. This has to be used with the /*d* switch.
/d[p:]xx:yy	*xx* specifies the major reason number (0 to 255). The "*yy*" describes the minor reason number (0 to 65535). This relevant number information can be found under Windows Server 2003 documentation under Shutdown Event Tracker. Please refer to http://msdn.microsoft.com/library/default.asp?url=/library/en-us/sysinfo/base/system_shutdown_reason_codes.asp for all shutdown codes.
/a	Cancels the shutdown process, during the timeout period indicated by the /*t* switch. Used with /m *computername.*
/m \\computername	Indicates the target computer.

Using the Registry to Manage Shutdown Event Tracker

You can configure the registry to enable or disable the Shutdown Event Tracker. The Windows Server 2003 default installation enables Shutdown Event Tracker by default. However, you can configure the registry settings to enable it or disable it on demand. The process is described in Exercise 9.09.

TEST DAY TIP

We prefer to use the registry to configure Shutdown Event Tracker in many cases (in comparison to the local Group Policy settings). The local Group Policy can dictate the shutdown policy for the domain. This is not feasible for a single machine configuration. Another reason is the lack of terminal server access to local Group Policy settings. You can use the Registry Editor to edit the remote computer's registry in this case.

EXERCISE 9.09

CONFIGURE REGISTRY ENTRIES FOR SHUTDOWN EVENT TRACKER

1. Open the Registry Editor. (Click **Start | Run |** and type **regedit.**)
2. Navigate to the **HKEY_LOCAL_MACHINE\Software\Microsoft\Windows\CurrentVersion\Reliability** key and select the **ShutdownReasonUI** value. This value does not exist by default; if it has not been created, create a new DWORD value and name it **ShutdownReasonUI**.
3. Double-click the **ShutdownReasonUI** key. A screen similar to Figure 9.36 appears.

Figure 9.36 Editing the Registry Key for Shutdown Event Tracker

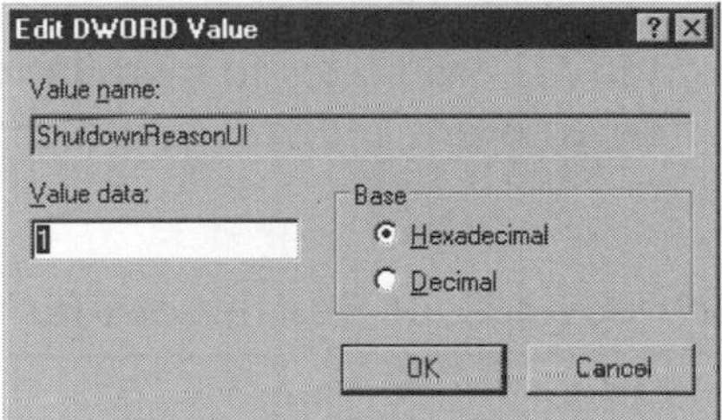

4. The value **1** in the **Value data** text box indicates that the Shutdown Event Tracker is enabled. The value **0** indicates that the Shutdown Event Tracker is disabled. Enter the appropriate data value, depending on whether you wish to enable or disable the Shutdown Event Tracker.
5. Click **OK** and close the Registry Editor. Restart the computer to apply the changes.

Defining Custom Shutdown Reasons

Predefined planned and unplanned reasons are available to choose from the list box on the Shutdown Event Tracker screen (please refer to Figure 9.34). You can also define custom shutdown reasons to use at shutdown times. This could be handy to narrow your system-specific limitations. Use the registry to define these additional reasons. The steps to add more custom reasons for the Shutdown Event Tracker are shown in Exercise 9.10.

EXERCISE 9.10

ADD CUSTOM SHUTDOWN REASONS

1. Open the Registry Editor. (Click **Start | Run** and type **regedit**.)
2. Navigate to the **HKEY_LOCAL_MACHINE\Software\Microsoft\Windows\CurrentVersion\Reliability\UserDefined** key. Create a new string value called **CSP:64:1** (for demonstration purposes). Refer to Table 9.12 for an explanation of the flags. This example indicates that a comment is required (C), the expected shutdown dialog box displays (S) and it is a planned shutdown (P). The "64:1" is a shutdown code, indicating the major and minor shutdown reasons. Refer to http://msdn.microsoft.com/library/default.asp?url=/library/en-us/sysinfo/base/system_shutdown_reason_codes.asp for a list of shutdown codes. The "64" means an **Application** and the "1" translates to **Installation** string. You can go through the shutdown event code table and choose customs settings for your system.

Table 9.12 Shutdown Code Descriptions for the Registry Settings

Flag	Description
P	Planned shutdown. Without this flag, an unplanned shutdown is assumed.
C	A comment is required.
B	An ID is required.
S	Displays the expected shutdown event dialog box.
D	Displays the unexpected shutdown dialog box. This is shown after the system restarts after an unexpected shutdown.

3. You can add more comments using the string registry value. The format for comments is *<title>/n/r<Description of the comment>*. This is the "title" of the comment that is separated by a "new line" or a "tab" character. A description of the comment follows this character. Refer to Figure 9.37 for an illustration of how this value data is entered.

Figure 9.37 Adding Comments to Your Custom Reasons

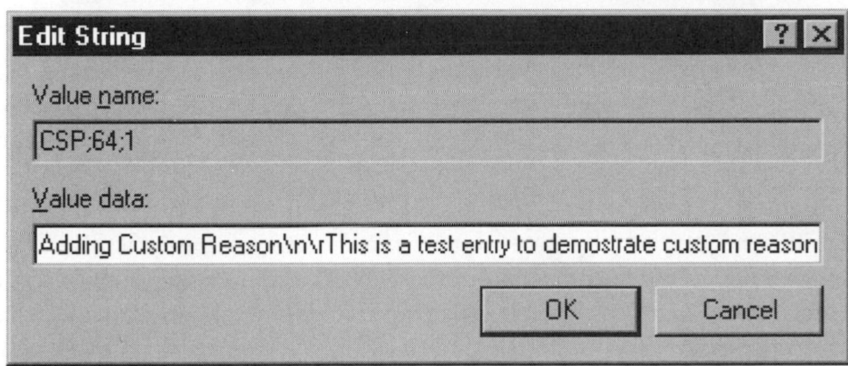

4. Click **OK** and close the Registry Editor. Restart the computer to apply the changes.

Summary of Exam Objectives

In the first section of this chapter, you learned about performance and monitoring tools. Windows Server 2003 implements a wide range of GUI and command-line tools for this purpose. The most commonly used utilities are the Task Manager and the System Monitor.

The Task Manager provides a snapshot of the applications and the processes running on the system. You can view the CPU activity and the memory utilization using graphs. You can also view, start, and stop applications using the Task Manager. Some other benefits include manipulating processes, monitoring network traffic, and monitoring user activity. The System Monitor is an ActiveX component that sits in the Performance Monitor application. The System Monitor displays graphs, histograms, or reports on different performance counters. This performance counter data can be real time, read from a log file, or from a database. This can be imported into .csv or .tsv files or databases.

Several command-line tools are included in Windows Server 2003 to help with performance and monitoring. *Perfmon.exe* is simply a command-line method of opening the Performance console that contains the System Monitor and Performance Logs and Alerts. *Logman.exe* enables you to manipulate performance counter logs or trace logs. *Relog.exe* enables you to query log files and import the data into .csv or .tsv files or database. *Typeperf.exe* enables you to read data from a log file onto the standard output (computer screen) or write to a file until **CLRT + C** is pressed.

You can use performance counters to detect bottlenecks and optimize memory, network, processor, and disk objects. There are specialized counters for each category. You can add these counters to the System Monitor to evaluate the situation. This takes measurements on the data collected by these counters and makes it easy for you to analyze the data so as to make changes that can increase productivity.

Security auditing tracks logon events, account management tasks, and creation and modifications of files, folders, and objects. You can track the behavior of your system by enabling an audit trail. An audit plan should lay out the purpose for which you are implementing auditing; for example, to track the behavior of the system or to stop intruders hacking into your systems. The purpose you define determines the scope and targets of your audit.

The Event Viewer displays *error, warning,* and *information* events on Application and System log files. The Security log displays *success audit* or *failure audit* events. The Application log details application-specific events. The Security log concentrates on events that impact the security of the system. The System log events are entered by the operating system components. You will find other logs, including Directory Service logs, File Replication Service logs, and DNS Server logs on domain controllers. In addition to the three default logs, servers might have additional logs, depending on the services and applications that are installed. A number of command-line utilities are included with Windows Server 2003 that are used to manage event logs. You can create an Application or System event using the eventcreate.exe tool. You cannot create a Security entry using this utility. You can use the eventquery.vbs script to query application, security, and system logs using filters. You can create, query, and delete triggers with the eventtriggers.exe utility. The tracerpt.exe utility is used to generate a trace report. The source for the trace report can be a trace log file or a real time resource.

Finally, we discussed the purpose and use of the Shutdown Event Tracker. This tool is enabled by default in Windows Server 2003. You can record data relating to both planned and unplanned shutdowns using this tool. You can analyze the shutdown patterns of all the Windows XP and Windows Server 2003 systems in the enterprise by evaluating this information. You also learned to create custom reasons for shutdown using Registry settings.

The objective of this chapter is to give you a thorough understanding of the performance- and security-monitoring tools and how they fit into the Windows Server 2003 architecture. You have learned the concepts and performed exercises to familiarize yourself with the interfaces. We recommend that you spend some time reviewing the *Exam Objectives Fast Track* and the *FAQ* sections to refresh your memory about the topics covered in this chapter, and then test your knowledge with the sample questions at the end.

Exam Objectives Fast Track

Monitoring Performance

☑ The Task Manager enables you to manage the applications and the processes of the system. You can monitor memory and CPU activity using graphs.

☑ The System Monitor is an ActiveX component that can be plugged into the Performance Monitor or another embedded container (Web page, Web Form).

☑ perfmon.exe starts the Performance Monitor application that contains the System Monitor ActiveX control, counter logs, trace logs, and alerts.

☑ logmon.exe enables you to manipulate performance logs or trace logs. You can create, start, stop, delete, and query logs using this utility.

☑ relog.exe extracts data from performance counter logs and converts it to TSV, CSV, binary, or SQL format.

☑ typeperf.exe enables you to write performance log file data to the screen or to a file. You must press **CTRL + C** to stop the typeperf.exe command.

Optimizing Servers for Application Performance

☑ You can optimize memory, disk, process, and network capabilities to increase performance.

☑ You can closely monitor memory activity using **Memory\Available Bytes** and **Memory\Pages/sec** counters.

☑ You can monitor network activity using **Network Interface\Bytes Total/sec**, **Bytes Sent/sec**, **Protocol_layer_object\ Segments Received/sec**, **Segments Sent/sec**, and **Frames Sent/sec** counters.

- ☑ You can monitor processor objects using **Processor\% Processor Time, System\Processor Queue Length**, and **Processor\Interrupts/sec** counters.
- ☑ You can monitor disk objects using **PhysicalDisk\% Disk Time % Idle Time, PhysicalDisk\Disk Reads/sec**, and **Disk Writes/sec** counters.

Auditing Security Events

- ☑ Security auditing enables you to track file, folder, and object creations and modifications and helps you to detect security breaches using audit trails.
- ☑ You must first define the audit policy before you enable auditing. The audit policy can be enabled on a Windows Server 2003 local computer, domain controller, domain, or an organization unit.
- ☑ You should create an audit plan before you enable auditing. The audit plan should detail the objectives behind the auditing.
- ☑ The security descriptor of an object consists of two parts: *System Access Control List (SACL)* and *Discretionary Access Control List (DACL).*
- ☑ *Operation-based auditing* is a new feature in Windows Server 2003 and is used to log both access to objects and the *operations* performed on them.
- ☑ You can also use inheritance to propagate audit policies to child objects from the parent objects.
- ☑ Security audit information can be viewed in the security log of the Event Viewer.

Using Event Viewer

- ☑ The Event Viewer displays three event logs by default: Application, System, and Security logs.
- ☑ A domain controller has additional DNS, Directory Service, and File Replication Service logs.
- ☑ An event type can be an error, warning, information, successful audit, or failure audit.
- ☑ You must be a member of the Administrator group to access the security log file on a computer.
- ☑ You can archive events as text files (.TXT), comma-separated value (.CSV) files or Event Viewer files (.EVT).

Using Command-Line Tools

- ☑ eventcreate.exe is used to create events in the log files. You can use this tool only for the application and system log files.
- ☑ The eventquery.vbs script is used to query all the event logs at the command prompt. You can also use filters on the queries.
- ☑ eventtriggers.exe helps you to create, query, and delete triggers on events.
- ☑ tracerpt.exe is used to create a report on an event trace. The source can be a trace file or a real-time trace session (configured by the *–rt* switch).

Using the Shutdown Event Tracker

- ☑ The Shutdown Event Tracker records the causes of shutdowns. It does not record logoffs or hibernations activities.
- ☑ Shutdown Event Tracker is enabled by default in Windows Server 2003 family computers.
- ☑ The Shutdown Event Tracker can be configured using the Group Policy Object Editor, which you can open to the Local Security Policy by clicking **Start | Run** and typing **gpedit.msc**.
- ☑ The Shutdown Event Tracker can be invoked on a remote system by executing **shutdown.exe /i**.
- ☑ The Shutdown Event Tracker can be enabled or disabled by editing the registry.
- ☑ You can define custom reasons for shutdowns using the registry settings.

Exam Objectives Frequently Asked Questions

The following Frequently Asked Questions, answered by the authors of this book, are designed to both measure your understanding of the Exam Objectives presented in this chapter, and to assist you with real-life implementation of these concepts. You will also gain access to thousands of other FAQs at ITFAQnet.com.

Q: Can I use the System Monitor in an ASP.NET page?

A: Yes, you can. System Monitor is an ActiveX object. Therefore, it can be plugged into multiple Microsoft interface architectures (ASP.NET, Web Form, and embedded in ASP pages).

Q: In what file formats can you store performance log details?

A: You can store performance logs in many formats, including Event Viewer format (.EVT), comma-separated value format (.CSV), or text format (.TXT).

Q: What is the purpose of the alerts in Performance Monitor?

A: The purpose of an alert is to notify the system administrator that the system is not functioning according to standard operating environment. You can configure alerts to send a network message, start a program, run a script, or log an event in the event log if a performance threshold is reached. Thresholds are limits that you specify (for example, when a disk is 90 percent full).

Q: How do you detect a memory leak?

A: Observe the **Memory\Available Bytes** and **Memory\Pages/sec** counters in the System Monitor. If the **Memory\Available Bytes** figure is less than 4MB without introducing any new applications, you are probably experiencing a memory leak from the application. The **Memory\Pages/sec** counter should be less than 20 to support this evaluation.

Q: What is virtual memory?

A: Virtual memory is space on the hard disk that is used as a "holding" area for data that is swapped in and out of physical memory. The computer writes large chunks of data to disk to process incoming requests when there is not enough room in RAM to hold all the data. The file in which these chunks of data are stored is referred to as the *Page File*. The memory that is freed by swapping it to disk is used to accommodate other processors, thus enabling you to run more applications simultaneously. Virtual memory should be approximately 1.5 times the amount of RAM installed.

Q: What is the maximum size of the page file?

A: The page file should generally be no more than 1.5 times the physical memory. (For example, if the RAM is 1GB, the maximum virtual memory is 1.5GB). However, you can set the maximum size for the page file using the **Control Panel | System | Advanced** tab as described in the text of this chapter.

Q: Where can you view security audit information?

A: You can view these details in the security log, which is accessed via the Event Viewer. Here you can see the success or failure entries relating to logon, account management, and access to files, folders, and objects.

Q: Can you duplicate the audit trail information to store it in a secure location?

A: Yes, you can. You can use Microsoft Operations Manager (MOM) to periodically store audit trail data on a secure server. This backs up the audit trial in case hackers obtain administrator privileges and delete the audit entries in the security log, or the log file data is lost for some other reason.

Q: In our organization, we store all the product information in subdirectories under a parent directory called "products." We have more than 40 products that are produced by our organization. Do we need to enable auditing on all 40 directories individually?

A: No. You can use the inheritance capabilities of the audit policies to enable auditing on the "products" directory and propagate the audit policy to the child directories.

Q: Are extra event logs available in domain controllers, in addition to the three default logs? If so, what are they?

A: Windows Server 2003 domain controllers have additional logs, including the Directory Service log, File Replication Service log, and a DNS server log (if the domain controller is a DNS server) in the Event Viewer. Other servers might have additional logs as well, depending on the applications and services installed.

Q: I was trying to access the security log of a remote computer but I could not see the log details. What could be the reason?

A: You must have Administrator access to view the security log. To remedy this problem, you must add your account to the administrators group on the remote computer.

Q: Can you save the filter options with the event log data?

A: No, Microsoft does not provide a way to do this. When you save the event log, the filter options are ignored. However, you can open the saved file and apply filters again as an alternative.

Q: Can we create security log entries with eventcreate.exe?

A: No, you cannot. You can only create Application and System log events using eventcreate.exe.

Q: Can we apply triggers to events in Windows Server 2003?

A: Yes, you can. You can configure the eventtriggers.exe command-line utility to add triggers that trigger specified actions when certain events are logged to the Event log.

Q: Can I start an application when an event activates a trigger from the event log?

A: Yes, you can utilize the */tk* parameter in the eventtriggers.exe utility to provide details about the application and configure it to start when a specific trigger is activated.

Self Test

Monitoring Performance

1. You need to query your memory trace file. The file is called "test_log" and it is stored in the root of the C: drive. You are thinking of using the *relog.exe* command-line utility to extract the data to a .csv file called "out.csv" that also resides on the root of C: drive. You are thinking of reading the log data in chunks of 10 records at a time. What will be your command-line instructions to execute this scenario?

   A. relog.exe C:\test_log.blg **–config** "\Memory\Available Bytes" **–o** C:\out.csv **–t** 10 **–f** csv

   B. relog C:\test_log.blg **–c** "\Memory\Available Bytes" **–f** C:\out.csv **–t** 10 **–o** csv

   C. relog.exe C:\test_log.blg **–a** "\Memory\Available Bytes" **–o** C:\out.csv **–t** 10 **–f** csv

   D. relog C:\test_log.blg **–c** "\Memory\Available Bytes" **–o** C:\out.csv **–t** 10 **–f** csv

2. A faulty uninstallation has caused your Microsoft Management Console (MMC) programs to give strange errors. You cannot read any performance log data from the Performance Monitor. You have read that you can input the performance counter data onto the screen using a command-line utility. That command-line utility is which of the following?

   A. logman.exe

   B. relog.exe

   C. typeperf.exe

   D. perfmon.exe

Optimizing Servers for Application Performance

3. You are investigating the slow responses of your network's file server. This file server accommodates all the business data templates that are shared by 200 internal and external employees. The machine has multiple network adapters to communicate to internal and external resources. The machine has 1GB of RAM. The page file size is 1.2GB at the moment. The page file size seems to be increasing and getting larger after a reboot. It starts at 800MB and climbs higher. What could be the cause of this issue?

   A. There is a network problem.

   B. There is a page file size problem on the server.

   C. You cannot use multiple network adapters on Windows Server 2003.

   D. File servers need at least 2GB of memory.

4. You are contemplating adding a processor to your Web server. You are trying to get performance indicators using performance counters. The **System\Processor Queue Length** is currently at three. The **Server Work Queues\Queue Length** is also at three. What is your recommendation, derived from this information?

   A. Do not add an extra processor.

   B. Add an extra processor.

   C. These counters relate to disk activity; not processor activity.

   D. Not enough information to make the decision.

5. You suspect a disk controller issue on your application drive. You can see a lot of disk activity (by observing the LED settings) and slow response times across multiple applications. You have been asked to do a performance test on the disk activity. What counter(s) would you add to the System Monitor?

   A. **Memory\Available Bytes** counter

   B. **Server\Bytes Total/sec**, **Bytes Received/sec** counters

   C. **PhysicalDisk\% Disk Time and % Idle Time** counters

   D. **System\Processor Queue Length** counter

Auditing Security Events

6. You suspect some hackers are breaking into your Web server. You have read in a tech magazine about enabling security auditing on the server. You are trying to apply security auditing and noticed some default audit properties enabled by the Windows Server 2003 installation. Which of the following security audits is enabled by default?

   A. Audit policy change

   B. Audit privilege change

   C. Audit account logon events

   D. Audit process tracking

7. You suspect some intrusions to your Windows Server 2003 file server. The hackers seem to be very diligent with their break-ins. There is no evidence to support the hacker activity. You have enabled auditing on the server. However, the hackers seem to delete the auditing details from the security log after each intrusion. You are trying to back up the audit trail periodically so you can analyze this problem further. What technology can be used for this scenario?

   A. Windows Server 2003 Event Viewer

   B. Microsoft Site Server 4.0

   C. Microsoft Application Center

   D. Microsoft Operation Manager

8. You are trying to connect to your SQL Server using the Query Analyzer to extract some product information. Your connection seems to fail with invalid user name and password errors. Your system administrator informs you that security auditing is enabled for SQL Server logons. You would like to view the logon details to validate your logon process. Where should you look for these audit details?

   A. Users section under SQL Server Enterprise Manager.

   B. Control Panel | Administrative Tools | Component Services

   C. Event Viewer

   D. Task Manager

Using Event Viewer

9. You are trying to troubleshoot an SQL Server connection error. You are looking at the SQL Server event logs remotely to track the connection failure. You can see the SQL Service errors. When you double-click the error, you get a detail view of the error. The only problem is the lack of description data in the detail view. What could be the cause of this?

   A. SQL Server does not log the error description to the event log.

   B. Remote Registry Service is stopped on SQL Server.

   C. You must have Administrators group access to view this data.

   D. The Event Viewer does not provide detailed error descriptions.

10. Your server is experiencing "Out of disk space" errors. Your investigation has concluded that purging of the logs was not configured. The option **Do not delete events** was selected. What can you do to force purging of the event logs on Windows Server 2003 machine?

    A. You cannot purge events on log files.

    B. Unselect the option **Overwrite events as needed**.

    C. Select the option **Overwrite events more than 20 days**.

    D. Click the **Clear Log** button.

11. You are trying to archive the event log to save disk space. You have a custom-made Excel spreadsheet in which you want to record all Application errors. You are a bit confused about what file format to use when you save the event log, to be able to load the data into the Excel spreadsheet. What is the most suitable format in which to save the event log?

    A. XML format (.XML file)

    B. Text file format (.TXT file)

    C. Event Viewer format (.EVT file)

    D. Comma-Separated Values format (.CSV file)

Using Command-Line Tools

12. Your servers are running out of disk space due to extensive logging information generated by Internet Information Server (IIS) traffic. This causes the Web server to crash. You need to run a disk cleanup utility when this happens. Can you use any command-line tools to help you with this issue?

A. Use eventcreate.exe

B. Use eventquery.vbs

C. Use eventtriggers.exe

D. Use eventtriggers.vbs

13. You have been having performance issues with your Web server. An external consultant has advised you to get some event trace information to analyze the issue. You ran the *tracerpt.exe* command with the source of the trace events. If you did not specify a name, which file contains the trace report?

A. DumpFile.csv

B. Summary.txt

C. Config file

D. Dumpfile.xls

Using the Shutdown Event Tracker

14. Your Web servers are getting frequent 503 errors. Rapid application failover is causing the machine to shut down. You have to frequently remove this machine form the Web farm because of this issue. As a result, this machine is subject to many logons and hibernate scenarios. Windows Server 2003 forces the shutdown tracker to collect the information each time it shut downs. The shutdown tracker logs information relating to which of the following?

A. Shutdown data only

B. Shutdown and Hibernate data

C. Shutdown, Hibernate, and Logoff data

D. Hibernate and Logoff data

15. Your machine has been upgraded from a standalone machine to a domain controller. You want to have the Shutdown Event Tracker enabled on each workstation and server of your domain. How would you go about doing this?

A. You can enable Shutdown Event Tracker only for servers. Therefore, no Windows Server 2003 workstations can enable Shutdown Event Tracker.

B. Enable Shutdown Event Tracker and select *WorkStation only* option.

C. Enable Shutdown Event Tracker and select *Domain only* option.

D. Enable Shutdown Event Tracker and select *Always* option.

Self Test Quick Answer Key

For complete questions, answers, and explanations to the Self Test questions in this chapter as well as the other chapters in this book, see the Self Test Appendix.

1. **D**
2. **C**
3. **A**
4. **B**
5. **C**
6. **C**
7. **D**
8. **C**
9. **B**
10. **C**
11. **D**
12. **C**
13. **A**
14. **A**
15. **D**

Chapter 10

MCSA/MCSE 70-290

Planning and Implementing Disaster Recovery

Exam Objectives in this Chapter:

- 5.2 Manage backup procedures.
- 5.1.3 Back up files and System State data to media.
- 5.1.4 Configure security for backup operations.
- 5.2.1 Verify the successful completion of backup jobs.
- 5.2.2 Manage backup storage media.
- 5.4 Restore backup data.
- 5.5 Schedule backup jobs.
- 5.1 Perform system recovery for a server.
- 5.1.1 Implement Automated System Recovery (ASR).
- 5.1.2 Restore data from shadow copy volumes.
- 5.3 Recover from server hardware failure.

Introduction

Regardless of how hard administrators work to protect their networks and systems from disaster, sometimes the worst occurs. Servers are subject to hardware failure due to age, overuse, or defects, data loss from hack attacks, and even natural disasters such as fire or flood that can destroy both the data and the systems themselves. Planning for disaster is an important part of every network administrator's job.

Windows Server 2003 includes tools to help you prepare for a serious system failure or attack, to ensure that your mission-critical data won't be lost and that server downtime will be minimized. A good disaster preparation plan starts with a strategy for regularly scheduled backups, and the Windows Backup utility provides you with an easy way to back up your data with the Backup and Restore Wizards. Also included is the Automated System Recovery (ASR) utility. The ASR Wizard helps you create a two-part backup of your essential system components: a floppy disk containing system settings and a backup of the local system partition on other media.

Other, more sophisticated approaches to recovering from server hardware failure are supported by Windows Server 2003 as well. Fault-tolerant disks (RAID) can be an important part of your disaster preparation plan, and if you're running the Enterprise Edition of Windows Server 2003, you also have the option of using server clustering – the ultimate in fault tolerance.

In this chapter, we will show you how to create a comprehensive disaster recovery plan for your organization's network and servers, using the backup and recovery tools included with the Windows Server 2003 operating system.

Defining and Understanding Disaster Recovery

A disaster occurs when events make continuing normal business functions impossible, and can result in some form of loss. These losses can include human life, data, equipment, money, property, or any number of other assets. Because the potential effects of a disaster can be both catastrophic and diverse, it is important to identify the types of disasters that can affect your company and implement measures to deal with them accordingly.

Disasters can result from a wide variety of sources. When people think of disasters, they generally think of storms, floods, fires, earthquakes, tornadoes, or other naturally occurring events. However, other environmental and naturally occurring threats exist. These include (but are not limited to) the following:

- Inadequate security in a building or area
- Poor air quality and temperature control in the server room
- Outdated software
- Aging equipment

Beyond these, disasters can also result from human involvement, where the deliberate or accidental actions of a person or group cause some form of damage. A hacker can gain access to sensitive information, viruses might infect a network and corrupt data, or disgruntled employees can damage equipment or sabotage data. Whatever the source, the resulting disaster has the potential to cause massive damage to a company.

Disaster recovery is the process of recognizing which threats have the potential to escalate into a disaster, and then taking steps to prevent or minimize their impact. In doing so, the most mission-critical systems of a company can be restored immediately or within a short period of time after a disaster occurs. This means that while the company might suffer some loss, it won't be crippled by it.

To understand how disaster recovery works, consider a common scenario: as network administrator, you have determined that viruses are a likely threat to your company. If one infected the network, data could be corrupted and systems could be disabled. To deal with this potential threat effectively, you can install anti-virus software to prevent viruses from infecting the network, and you can perform backups regularly. You could develop and distribute a procedure to be followed as a matter of policy if a new virus does infect the network. You might check the vendor's Web site for new anti-virus signature files and information about the virus, and restore backed-up data and system files to return them to a previous, uninfected state. In doing these tasks, you look at the cause and effect of a potential threat that is likely to affect your company, and then devise a solution to prevent and/or recover from it. That is what disaster recovery focuses on achieving.

The key to disaster recovery is being prepared. You will rarely know ahead of time exactly where and when a disaster will occur. Some disasters are more unexpected than others. Although we knew that there might be repercussions from the "Y2K bug" on a certain date, and that preparations needed to be completed by January 1, 2000, no one could have foreseen the events of September 11, 2001. In the same light, you know that your Windows software will cease to function on a particular date if you don't activate the product, but it is nearly impossible to determine when a hard disk will fail, viruses will infect systems, or when the next lightning storm will adversely affect your network. By establishing plans and procedures and having tools and technologies in place before the disaster occurs, your company will be better able to recover from a disaster and resume normal business practices quickly.

Understanding the Components of Disaster Recovery

Just as no single manual can cover every piece of hardware and software installed on a computer, no single plan or utility can adequately protect or restore a business after a disaster. Because disasters can have far-reaching effects and can affect a wide variety of systems, many components are involved in the recovery of systems and the organization as a whole. These include policies and procedures for dealing with individual systems and elements of a business. Some specific documents that should be developed as part of your overall recovery policy include the following:

- Business Continuity Plans
- Disaster Recovery Plans
- Backup Plans
- System Recovery Plans
- Hardware Recovery Plans

In the following sections, we will address each of these components individually.

Developing Business Continuity Plans

Business continuity plans are used to identify key functions of a business and pinpoint the threats that are most likely to endanger them. By identifying such threats, processes can be created to ensure that normal business operations can be restored in the event of disaster. For example, if a company sells widgets, the business continuity plan is used to restore the organization's ability to sell its product and get that product to the customer. Because business continuity plans focus on restoring the business as a whole, they consist of many different plans and procedures that address different areas of the business.

The Elements of a Business Continuity Plan

Business continuity plans begin by identifying the key functions of departments within the company. These are the elements that must exist so that people within the department can do their jobs. Because jobs within the organization vary, many of these key functions also vary. However, some elements are constant. Having facilities to perform work-related duties is a common element, so the company might plan for workers to be relocated to branch offices if the building is damaged or destroyed in a disaster. By looking at what is needed to conduct business, contingency plans can be set in place to enable those functions to resume quickly in the face of catastrophe.

One of the plans included in a business continuity plan is the disaster recovery plan. Disaster recovery plans concentrate on restoring data and technology and implementing systems that can prevent or minimize disasters. As you'll see in later sections of this chapter, there are many countermeasures that can be taken to protect systems, and numerous tools that can be used to successfully restore systems and data when problems arise. Like business continuity plans, disaster recovery plans consist of many different plans and procedures, but narrow the focus to address individual areas of Information Technology (IT).

A major portion of protecting and restoring data and other files on a server is backing them up. As you'll see later in this chapter, backups create a copy of files and folders on other media, such as tapes, magneto-optical (MO) discs, CDs, or DVDs. When a problem occurs, these files and folders can then be copied back to the server, or to another server if the original is irretrievably lost. A backup plan creates a regimen of backing up data on a regular schedule, and outlines what data is to be backed up and the procedures that need to be followed when restoring it.

Just as data can be at risk in a disaster, so can the systems themselves. Problems might arise that prevent Windows Server 2003 from starting properly, or even starting at all. In these instances, network administrators or other members of the IT staff need to intervene and follow procedures to restore the system. Such procedures are found in a system recovery plan, which we'll discus in greater detail later in this chapter.

With any of these plans, it is important that the staff members who will be involved with using them be knowledgeable and well trained in their implementation. It is important for members of an organization to know that the plans exist, and the necessary parties must have a clear understanding of how to carry out the procedures involved. If this information is not disseminated to the proper parties and employees are not properly trained, people might fumble through the steps needed to complete certain tasks, while other tasks might be missed because no one knew they were required. The time to learn how a procedure should be carried out is before it is actually needed.

The Role of Emergency Management Services

Just as procedures need to be understood, so do the tools and technologies related to a task. In Chapter 7, you learned about methods for connecting to your Windows Server 2003 computer remotely, so that you can administer it and solve problems without having to sit directly in front of the computer. Although these remote administration methods and other tools (such as Telnet) can be extremely useful in solving issues with your server, one drawback is that they require an *in-band connection*. An in-band connection is a link between two computers using standard networking technologies such as a local area network (LAN) or the Internet. The problem with these methods is that if the in-band connection is unavailable, they can't be used. Even if the network itself is functioning but the operating system on the remote computer isn't fully functional, you might not be able to use traditional remote administration methods because network drivers must be used to make the connection. The solution is to use Emergency Management Services (EMS), which uses out-of-band connections that rely on a serial port connection between the two computers. In addition, you don't need a functioning keyboard, mouse, monitor, or video card on the server you're administering with EMS. However, if you have them, you can still use the keyboard to input data to the managed computer locally and view output on a local monitor at the same time you are managing the server remotely. EMS uses redirection of character-based output to another computer (called *console redirection*) so that you can perform tasks that are necessary for disaster recovery.

NOTE

The Extensible Firmware Interface (EFI) provides console redirection. This is the firmware that takes over the functions of a traditional BIOS on Intel Itanium 64-bit computers. Some BIOSes on x86 computers also support console redirection and some do not. EMS takes over console redirection from the firmware or service processor when operating system control passes to NTLDR.

Using EMS, you can perform tasks such as the following:

- Restart or shut down a server.
- Display information about the computer on which Windows Server 2003 is running.
- View Fatal System Errors (Stop errors).
- Start and access the command prompt.
- View the text mode portion of Setup and respond to Setup prompts (graphical-mode Setup is not redirected).
- View a list of active processes, and end them as needed.
- Limit the memory used by a process and associated child processes.
- View and set the server's IP address.
- Generate Stop errors to create a memory dump file.
- Install and repair Windows Server 2003 using Remote Installation Services (RIS).
- Manage Windows using Windows Management Instrumentation (WMI).

TEST DAY TIP

New features in Microsoft products often appear in exam questions, so be prepared for topics that didn't exist in older exams. EMS is one such new feature, and (at the time of this writing) is available only for operating systems in the Windows Server 2003 family. It can be used to access servers using both in-band and out-of-band connections and provides the capability to perform numerous tasks that might be necessary to restore the server.

EMS can be enabled by using the Bootcfg tool to modify the boot.ini file. Bootcfg.exe can be run from the command prompt and can enable or disable EMS by using the */EMS* switch. The syntax for this command is as follows, while the explanation of parameters are explained in Table 10.1.

```
Bootcfg /EMS RedirectionValue [/S system] [/U domain\user] [/P password]
    [/PORT] port] [/BAUD baudrate] [/ID bootID]
```

Table 10.1 Parameters for Bootcfg /EMS

Parameter	Description
RedirectionValue	Use this parameter to enable, disable, or edit the current settings of EMS. To enable EMS, type **ON** as the *RedirectionValue*. To disable EMS, type **OFF** as the *RedirectionValue*. To edit current settings, type **EDIT** as the *RedirectionValue*.
/S system	By default, the local computer is where EMS is enabled or disabled. Use this parameter to specify the name of the remote system to connect to.
/U domain\user	Specifies the user account under which this command executes. By default the currently logged-on user is used.
/P password	Specifies the password for the user account used to execute this command.
/PORT port	Specifies the port number to use for redirection. You can use *COM1*, *COM2*, *COM3*, *COM4*, or *BIOSSET* to use *SPCR* table settings.
/BAUD baudrate	Used to specify the baud rate to use for redirection. Valid baud rates are 9600, 19200, 57600, 115200.
/ID bootID	This entry specifies the boot menu sequence number of the operating system to enable or disable EMS. If the system is a single-boot system, then **1** is used. This parameter must be used if the *RedirectionValue* is set to **ON** or **OFF**.

A number of different components in Windows Server 2003 support EMS. These include the Setup loader that installs Windows Server 2003 (win32.exe, winnt.exe, and unattended installation), Recovery Console, RIS, and Stop errors. In addition to these, two new remote-management consoles have been developed for Windows Server 2003:

- Special Administration Console (SAC)
- !Special Administration Console (!SAC)

These are both command-line tools that can be accessed through terminal software that supports VT-UTF8, VT100+, or VT100.

SAC is the primary tool used by EMS, and is available early in the boot process and throughout the running of Windows. Using SAC, you can perform a variety of tasks mentioned above. These include displaying server information, restarting or shutting down the server, viewing and ending active processes, setting the server's IP address, manually generating a Stop error to create a memory dump file, and starting command line environments that you can then access as needed.

You can use SAC to create multiple sessions. These sessions are called channels and you can switch from one channel to another. You must be a member of the Administrators group to create SAC channels and issue SAC commands. The different commands for SAC are shown in Table 10.2.

Table 10.2 SAC Commands

Command	Description
Ch	Lists all channels.
Cmd	Creates a command-line environment. This command creates Windows command-prompt channels, which require you to log on to each instance of a command prompt.
Crashdump	Manually generates a Stop error to create a memory dump file.
D	Dumps the Kernel log.
F	Toggles the output from the *T* command. This is used to control whether processes and threads or only processes are shown.
I	Displays IP information or sets the IP address, subnet mask, and gateway of a network interface device.
Id	Displays identification information on the server.
K <*PID*>	Ends a process. *PID* is used to specify the process identification number you wish to end.
L <*PID*>	Lowers the priority of a process and its child processes to the lowest level. *PID* is used to specify the process identification number you wish to lower.
Lock	Restricts access to command-prompt channels. To unlock the channel, a valid username and password is required.
M <*PID*> <*MB*-allow>	Limits the memory used by a process and its child processes. *PID* is used to specify the process identification number you wish to limit, while *MB* is the number of megabytes to limit it to.

Continued

Table 10.2 SAC Commands

Command	Description
P	Pauses the output from the *T* command.
R <*PID*>	Raises the priority of a process and its child processes to the lowest level. *PID* is used to specify the process identification number you wish to raise.
Restart	Restarts the computer.
S	Displays or sets the system date and time.
Shutdown	Shuts down the computer.
T	Lists processes that are currently running.

If SAC fails to load or function properly, then EMS automatically switches to !SAC (you cannot manually start !SAC). Because !SAC is a secondary tool, it has considerably fewer commands associated with it. It enables you to display server information and log entries, or restart the server. The commands available for !SAC are shown in Table 10.3.

Table 10.3 !SAC Commands

Command	Description
Restart	Restarts the server.
D	Displays log entries.
Id	Displays identification information about the computer.
Q	Quits !SAC. After quitting, normal out-of-band operation is resumed.

While EMS is an important tool for disaster recovery, many others are provided in Windows Server 2003. As we'll discuss later in this chapter, Windows Server 2003 provides tools for backing up data, restoring the server, and other tasks necessary to disaster recovery. In addition to these, we will also discus numerous technologies and hardware components that can protect systems and data from harm.

Developing the Disaster Recovery Plan

Each of the practices mentioned above (and covered later in the chapter) should be included as part of a disaster recovery plan. A disaster recovery plan provides procedures for recovering from a disaster after it occurs and addresses how to return normal Information Technology functions to the business. These documents recognize potential threats and provide guidance on how to deal with such events when they occur. In the following sections, we discuss some of the specific tasks and considerations that go into creating an effective disaster recovery plan.

Threat Assessment and Prioritizing

When creating a disaster recovery plan, you should try to identify all the different types of threats that might affect your company. It is important to realize that the threats faced by one company might not apply to others. For example, some disasters are more common in different geographical regions. Blizzards in Canada or major earthquakes in Mexico might be likely threats in each of these locales, but not vice-versa. To adequately deal with potential threats, it is important to look at which types of disasters are likely to occur. When you've determined the types of disasters your company could reasonably anticipate, you can then implement countermeasures to minimize the risk of those events actually happening, and develop procedures that detail what to do if one occurs.

The issues dealt with in a disaster recovery plan focus on how technologies and business functionality can be restored quickly, with the most business-critical requirements taken care of first. For example, a company that sells products on the Internet would require that the Web server be restored before most other components are addressed. After the most critical systems have been restored, then the less significant ones can be dealt with. Thus, it is important that you set priorities and document those priorities in writing as part of your plan.

Legal and Administrative Considerations

When creating the disaster recovery plan to be used by your organization, it is important to verify that the plan doesn't violate any existing policies, regulations, or laws, or put the company at risk of civil liability. Companies operating in some industries must adhere to specific rules or guidelines if they are to remain in business, and failing to meet these requirements can cause more harm than the disaster that activates the plan. For example, a hospital or physician's office in the United States that falls under the Health Insurance Portability and Accountability Act (HIPPA) regulations is required to use certain technologies or adhere to certain criteria so that patient information is kept confidential. If you restore elements of the network in a medical environment and don't adhere to these requirements, it is possible that lawsuits and/or administrative penalties can result. In some situations, a business might even be shut down for failing to abide by certain regulations or legislation.

A disaster recovery plan often incorporates or includes references to other policies, procedures or documents. Such documentation might provide information on infrastructure, procedures to be followed to fix problems, legal requirements, third-party contact numbers (such as the phone company that maintains the T-1 line to the Internet), and other important data. By including or referring to other policies, procedures, and documents, you ensure that those involved in the disaster recovery process will be able to find the information they need to solve problems quickly.

Asset Evaluation

During the development of the disaster recovery plan, you should identify and address the company assets that might be damaged or destroyed in a disaster. In any organization, there are a wide variety of assets that can be affected, including the following:

- Data
- Equipment
- Software
- Personnel
- Facilities

Omitting any element that is necessary to the recovery of the business could be detrimental and prevent normal business functions from being reestablished.

Data can be one of the most valuable assets in an organization and there should be redundant mechanisms in place to protect it. Losing a customer database or other sensitive data can have long-lasting effects and can even put a company out of business. As you will see later in this chapter, in the section titled *Creating a Backup Plan,* it is important for data stored on servers to be backed up regularly and stored in a secure, offsite location.

Dealing with damaged equipment varies in complexity, depending on availability of replacement parts or equipment and the steps required to restore necessary resources. Some companies have additional servers that are configured to be identical to the damaged ones, for use as replacements when incidents occur. Ideally, these redundant servers can be configured in server clusters with automatic failover, so that little or no downtime is experienced if the primary machine fails. Other companies are not able to afford such measures and don't have enough additional machines to replace damaged ones. In such cases, you might have to put data on other functioning servers, and then configure applications and drive mappings so the data can be accessed from the new location. Whatever the situation, you should try to anticipate possible scenarios in your disaster recovery plan, and devise contingency plans to deal with a wide variety of problems when they arise.

The cost of software can make up a considerable part of a company's operating budget. Not only do you need to buy licenses for Windows Server 2003, but also for client operating systems and applications that are installed on each computer in the organization. To deal with the potential loss of software, copies of programs and their licenses should be kept offsite so that they can be used to restore the software when systems are damaged or destroyed. Configuration information should also be documented and kept offsite, so that it can be used to quickly return each system to its previous state.

NOTE

Because hardware and software (especially proprietary software) is not always easy to install and configure, you might need to have outside parties involved. You should check your vendor agreements ahead of time, to determine whether they provide onsite service within hours or days, because waiting for outsourced workers can present a significant bottleneck in restoring the systems. You don't want to be surprised by such delays when a disaster occurs, so preparing for such possibilities is the key to readiness.

When developing the disaster recovery plan, you should identify vulnerabilities that exist in current systems. Vulnerabilities are elements that can expose a system to attack and cause more significant damage during a disaster. For example, you might find that security patches or Service Packs need to be applied to the operating system, unused accounts need to be disabled or deleted, or other steps need to be taken to address any number of other possible weaknesses. After you have identified these vulnerabilities, you need to create countermeasures to deal with them, such as regularly updating antivirus signature files, checking for new security patches, and so forth.

Because vulnerabilities often go unnoticed until a disaster occurs, following any disaster you should reevaluate and establish additional countermeasures. Rather than allowing a vulnerability to go unchecked, steps should be taken to fix existing problems as soon as they are discovered, to protect your systems. For example, if a hacker breaks into the network using a known vulnerability in the operating system, you should apply a security patch as soon as one becomes available. Meanwhile, you might take other protective steps, such as closing the applicable ports on your firewall, to keep the same thing from happening again. Otherwise, history could repeat itself and the vulnerability could be used over and over again to cause the same disaster.

Personnel are another important consideration in creating a disaster recovery plan. Certain members of the company often have distinct skill sets that can cause a major loss if that person is unavailable. If a person is injured, dies, or leaves the company, his or her knowledge and skills are also gone. Imagine a network administrator being injured in a fire and no one else fully understanding how to perform that job. This would cause a major impact to any recovery plans. Thus, it is important to provide cross training. You should have at least one secondary person with comparable skills who is capable of temporarily replacing each important employee. It is also vital that backup personnel have access to documentation on systems architecture and other elements related to recovery, as well as clear procedures to follow in performing important tasks.

Incident Response Planning

When considering the issue of personnel, you should designate members who will be part of an incident response team. This team will be responsible for dealing with disasters when they arise. Members should have a firm understanding of their roles in the disaster recovery plan, and the tasks they will need to perform to restore systems. A team leader should also be identified, so that a specific person will be responsible for coordinating efforts.

If a team already exists, its members should be included in preparing and testing the disaster recovery plan. Their insight might prove crucial to developing a plan that really works, as opposed to something that just looks good on paper. It is important for the team to perform "dry runs" of the disaster recovery plan to ensure that developed strategies work as expected, and revise any steps that are ineffective.

A disaster recovery plan approaches risks proactively, setting up controls that can be used in the event of a disaster. This requires preparation and foresight, and includes the following:

- Backing up data regularly
- Keeping needed information and tools (or copies of same) offsite
- Having the necessary physical facilities to recover normal business functions
- Having a way to replace damaged or destroyed hardware quickly and cost effectively

Failing to do any of these could result in the business being unable to recover properly from a disaster that befalls it.

Using Disaster Recovery Best Practices

As with many issues faced by network administrators, certain practices have proven successful in the field and can save valuable time when problems arise. There is no need to completely "reinvent the wheel." Instead, you can learn from the experiences of others who have survived the types of disasters to which your own company is vulnerable. By having disaster recovery components in place beforehand, you will be able to access them quickly when needed. In a disaster, every minute saved beforehand is one that won't be wasted later.

Passwords are a common security mechanism, and are often the sole method of controlling access to computers and networks. Passwords should be used on all accounts, especially administrative accounts that have the capability to modify other accounts and system settings. Passwords are also used on password-protected documents, which require that a password be entered before a person can read or modify the document. Following a disaster, these accounts and documents might be necessary to fix problems, but they won't be accessible if the people who need them don't know the required passwords.

For this reason, a list of important passwords should be stored in a location that is secure, but accessible to specific people within the organization. These lists can be stored in a sealed envelope with a responsible person's signature on it, and kept in a safe or some other place that can be locked inside a restricted area. When needed, the network administrator, manager, or other key personnel can open the envelope and use the password list. It is important that more than one person has the combination to the safe or key to the locked area, so that the list can be obtained if one or more of these people are unavailable. When it is no longer needed, the list is put in a new envelope, signed, sealed, and returned to the secure location. Following this procedure helps to ensure that anyone who isn't authorized to use the list will be unable to reuse the same envelope or duplicate the signature on a new one.

Remember that this information, or a copy of it, should be stored offsite (secured in the same way) in case the entire building is destroyed in the disaster.

NOTE

Rather than share the password to a critical account such as the built-in Administrator account, you can create secondary accounts for key persons and give those accounts administrative privileges, listing those account names and passwords on your sealed emergency document, to be revealed and used only in case of disaster.

Lists of important contact people should also be created and made accessible to members of the organization. One such list should provide contact information for members of the IT staff, so that certain employees (such as those working reception or the switchboard) can notify IT personnel of a potential problem. The list should provide information on what areas specific people are responsible for or have expertise in. That way, a programmer won't be called first about a network issue, or the network administrator won't be called about something he or she has no knowledge of. Another contact list should be created for members of the IT staff, so that they can contact vendors and contractors as needed. This list should include information for contacting companies responsible for repairing equipment, software support, phone service, ISP, and other technologies used in the business.

Procedures on how to handle specific problems should also be available to members of the IT staff, so that they can refer to them as needed. These documents can be stored in electronic format on the server, so that they can be easily accessed, but should also be printed so they can still be used if the server is unavailable. If you provide multiple methods for retrieving the same information, there is a greater chance that people will be able to access the information when needed.

As we'll discuss later in this chapter, a backup plan should be created and this should be one of the documents that is available to those who need it. Information in the backup plan should include steps on how to back up and restore data, where backed-up data is stored, and how long old backups are retained. If a server fails, or data needs to be restored for some other reason, these procedures can be used to restore the data and enable the business to resume using it.

In addition to documentation, installation CDs for all critical software should be stored in a place that's accessible to those who need it. Programs installed on the server might need to be repaired or reinstalled during a disaster, so it's important that these CDs be available when needed. IT staff should know where these CDs are located, so the functionality of necessary programs can be restored to the business.

The Windows Server 2003 installation files should also be kept in a handy location, where they can be found and used when needed. These files can be used to repair system files or (if necessary) reinstall Windows Server 2003. They can also be used to run Recovery Console and ASR.

It is a good idea to store the original Windows Server 2003 CD offsite in a secure location. You can make backup CDs to keep onsite if you don't have multiple original copies. You can also place the installation files on one or more servers, by copying the i386 folder on the installation CD to the server's hard disk and sharing the folder. If the network is functional, these files can be accessed across the network so that you don't need to bother with finding and using a CD.

Head of the Class...

Using the Recovery Console

The Recovery Console is a tool that enables you to perform administrative tasks useful in disaster recovery. Using it, you can enable, disable, and reconfigure services that could prevent Windows Server 2003 from starting; copy files to the hard drive; view and modify files; and perform other tasks. ASR enables you to back up and restore the Registry, boot files, and other System State data, as well as other data used by the operating system. Without the installation CD, the capability to restore such data might be unavailable when needed.

To avoid having to rely solely on the installation CD to run the Recovery Console, you should install it as a startup option. As you'll see later in this chapter, when the Recovery Console is installed on an x86 computer running Windows Server 2003, it appears in a list of available operating systems when the computer initially starts. You can then select **Recovery Console** from this list and run it from the computer.

Other options relating to startup and recovery can be set in Windows Server 2003, enabling you to control what happens when the system stops unexpectedly. These startup and recovery options enable you to determine whether the system should restart automatically when a fatal system error occurs, and what information is logged when problems occur. These are features of Windows Server 2003 that we'll discuss in greater detail later in this chapter.

As you saw in the previous section, EMS enables you to manage a Windows Server 2003 machine remotely, even when network connections are unavailable. This can be a vital tool when situations require you to access the computer, but you're unable to access the computer directly. To ensure that it's available when needed, servers running Windows Server 2003 should have EMS enabled prior to any problems that would require its use. EMS is enabled after installation of Windows Server 2003 through the bootcfg.exe tool or the Recovery Console, which we'll discuss later in this chapter.

EXERCISE 10.01

ENABLING EMERGENCY MANAGEMENT SERVICES

1. From the Windows Start menu, click the **Command Prompt** menu item.
2. When the Command Prompt opens, type the following:

```
BOOTCFG /EMS ON /PORT Port /ID bootID
```

   Where *Port* is the port number you wish to use, and *bootID* is the boot menu sequence number of the operating system on which you wish to enable or disable EMS. For example, if you wanted to use *COM1* as the port and it was only a single-boot system, then the command would be *BOOTCFG /EMS ON /PORT COM1 /ID 1*.
3. Type the following at the command prompt to verify that EMS has been enabled on the Windows Server 2003 server:

```
BOOTCFG /QUERY
```

4. On the output, check to see that the Boot Loader Settings show that redirect:COM1 appears, and OS Load Options show that the */redirect* switch is included.

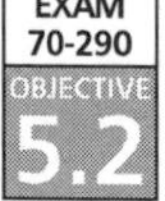

Creating a Backup Plan

A backup enables data and system files on a computer to be archived to another location on the hard disk or to other media. You can compare backups to making a photocopy of an original document, which creates a duplicate that can be stored safely in case the original is destroyed. As with a photocopy, a backup of data is a duplicate of the original data on a computer at the time the backup was taken. Unlike a photocopy, however, the quality of the backup data is equal to the quality of the original.

When problems occur, the backed-up files can be restored to the location from which the data was originally copied or to another location such as a different directory or a different machine. The capability to restore the data is just as important as performing regular backups; if the backup cannot be restored, then the backed-up data is as lost as any original data you're attempting to recover.

Backing up and restoring data is a fundamental part of any disaster recovery plan. A backup plan provides procedures that detail which data should be backed up, how this data is to be backed up, and when it is to be backed up. The plan also provides information regarding the storage of backed-up data, and how it can be restored. Such information can be used during a disaster to restore system files and other data that might have been damaged or destroyed.

As we'll discuss in the sections that follow, there are many different elements to a good backup plan. In addition to knowing how the Backup utility can be used, you need to make decisions about what data will be backed up, where it will be stored, and other issues. Such decisions need to be made far in advance of any disasters. A good backup plan should be part of every network administrator's daily routine.

Backup Concepts

Backing up data begins with deciding what information needs to be archived. Critical data, such as trade secrets that the business relies on to function, along with other important data crucial to business needs, must be backed up. Other data, such as temporary files and applications, might not need to be backed up, as they can easily be reinstalled or aren't needed in the first place. Such decisions, however, will vary from company to company and even from department to department.

In addition to data, it is important to back up the System State data, which consists of files the operating system uses. These include the boot files, system files, the Registry, COM+ Class Registration database, and other files that Windows Server 2003 (depending on the server configuration) will require you to back up as a single unit. If the server fails at any point, these files can be used to restore the system to a functioning state.

Rather than simply backing up bits and pieces of your server, it is wise to back up everything on a server at the same time. This includes all data on the server and the System State data. If the hard disk on the server fails, or the entire server is lost in a disaster, then a full backup of everything can be used to restore the server quickly.

As you'll see later in this chapter, the Backup utility provided with Windows Server 2003 enables you to create an ASR set. An ASR set is a backup of system files that can be used to restore Windows Server 2003 if a major system failure occurs. When creating an ASR set, only system files are backed up, not data.

When creating a backup, you should always have the Backup utility create log files. A backup log shows which files were backed up, and the log can be saved or printed as a reference for restoring data. If you needed to restore a particular file or folder, the log would show whether a particular backup included it in the job.

When a backup is performed, the copied data is usually kept on media other than the local hard disk. After all, if the hard disk failed, both the original data on the disk and the backup would be lost. As we'll discuss later in greater detail, other media such as tapes can be used to store backups safely. Microsoft recommends that three copies of the media be stored, with one copy kept offsite. This ensures that if one or two of the copies are destroyed in a disaster, the third can be used to restore data and the system.

To prevent backups from being stolen and used to restore data to another machine, it is important that backup devices and media be kept physically secure. Backup media should be stored in a secure location, such as a safe or locked storage device. The area in which it is stored shouldn't be easily accessible. In the same light, the devices used to create backups should also be secured. Removable devices should be stored in secure environments, while servers with backup devices installed on them should be kept secure (in locked server rooms). The physical security of devices and media should be as high as the security of data on the server.

Because backups are so important, it is important for personnel to be trained in how to perform backups and restores. Designated members of the IT staff should be knowledgeable in the steps involved in creating backups and restoring data, should know where media is stored, and should be aware of what data is to be backed up and when. If a disaster occurs, they should be able to follow the backup plan without incident.

Before a disaster occurs, however, you should test whether data can actually be restored. If a device seems to back up data properly but is actually failing to do so, you might not be aware of it until you need to restore the data. Rather than assuming everything is being backed up properly, you should test your equipment by restoring data from a previous backup job. If files and folders can be restored properly, then you will have peace of mind that such data can be restored during a disaster.

Backup Media

There are many different types of media to which backed-up data can be stored. The type you choose will determine how much data can be stored on a single media target, and the speed at which backups can be performed. In choosing the type of media you'll use, you should estimate how much data will be copied during a backup job.

The Backup utility that comes with Windows Server 2003 enables you to back up files to a tape or file. The capability to back up to a file was introduced with the version of ntbackup that came with Windows 2000. Prior to that, Windows NT's backup utility worked only with tape. Now, if you don't have a tape backup drive and wish to use the Backup utility, you can back up files to a file on the hard disk and then copy the file to a compact disk (CDR/CD-RW), digital video disk (DVD/DVD-R), or other media afterwards. While this requires an extra step in backing up data, it enables you to use the Backup utility if you don't have a tape unit or wish to store backup files on a server or in another location.

Types of Tapes

Of the different media available on which backups are stored, tapes are the most common. Tape backups use magnetic tapes to store data sequentially, which requires the tape to be cued up to the point where the data is located. This is similar to the tapes used in a micro-cassette recorder, in which you have to fast-forward or reverse the tape to find the information you want. The biggest advantage of tape backups is cost; you can store more data on tape for a lower cost than with other backup media types.

There are a number of different types of tape drives available, which support different sizes of data and enable an assorted number of tapes. Two of the most common types of tape drives are:

- Digital Audio Tape (DAT)
- Digital Linear Tape (DLT)

DAT stores data on 4mm tapes, while DLT stores it on a half-inch magnetic reel-to-reel tape, in which one reel is contained in the cartridge while the other is stored inside the DLT drive. DAT is not as fast as DLT, and doesn't provide as much storage capacity. However, it is less expensive than DLT, which makes DAT a popular method of tape backup.

DAT uses the Digital Data Storage format (DDS), which uses a process similar to that used in VCRs to store data on the DAT tape. It performs a helical scan, in which read/write heads spin diagonally across a DAT tape. Two read heads and two write heads are used. When data is written, the read heads verify that data has been written correctly to the tape. If they detect any errors, the data is rewritten. As seen in the following table, there are different formats of DDS available for tape drives.

As shown in Table 10.4, different versions of DDS provide different levels of storage capacity. In viewing this information, you can see that there are two numbers associated with the storage capacity of different formats. This is because the first number is the uncompressed amount of data that can be stored on the tape, while the second shows the compressed data that can be stored.

Table 10.4 DDS Formats for DAT Drives

Type of Format	Storage Capacity
DDS	2GB
DDS-1	2/4GB
DDS-2	4/8GB
DDS-3	12/24GB
DDS-4	20/40GB

The original DDS format enabled you to store only up to 1.3GB of data, but the next generation increased storage to 2GB of data on a 120-minute cartridge. The data on the original DDS format tapes was uncompressed, so less data could be stored on the tape than with the other methods. DDS-1 was the first format to use compression, and enables you to store up to 4GB of data on a 120-minute cartridge. DDS-2 increased compression on a 120-minute cartridge to enable up to 8GB of data. DDS-3 uses a 125-minute cartridge and enables you to store up to 24GB of compressed data. This format also introduced the use of Partial Response Maximum Likelihood (PRML), which eliminates noise so that data is transferred to the tape cleaner and with fewer errors. Finally, DDS-4 enables 40GB of compressed data to be stored on a 125-minute cartridge. Each of these formats is backward compatible. This means that if you had a DDS-3 device, you could use DDS-1 or DDS-2 cartridges.

As mentioned, DLT is faster than DDS, and provides a higher storage capacity. Using this method, you can put more data on the tape, enabling you to use this media with larger hard disks, and/or relieving you from having to change tapes quite so often. As shown in Table 10.5, there are different generations of DLT that accommodate different capacities of storage.

Table 10.5 DLT Types and Capacities

DLT Type	Capacity
DLT2000	15/30GB
DLT4000	20/40GB
DLT7000	35/70GB
DLT8000	40/80GB

Unlike DDS, each version of DLT provides data compression. DLT2000 enables you to store up to 30GB of data, DLT4000 enables up to 40GB of data, DLT7000 enables up to 70GB of data, and DLT8000 enables up to 80GB of data storage. However, if compression isn't used, then only half of these amounts can be stored on the tape.

TEST DAY TIP

While the information included here about backup tapes is useful for understanding what type of backup drive and tapes your server will need, don't expect exam questions dealing with detailed information about backup media and equipment. Instead, remember that the Backup utility is designed to store backups to file or to tape. Backups cannot be stored directly to media such as compact disks or digital video disks.

Managing Media

Backups must be effectively managed so that there is a clear understanding of what's been backed up, when, and where it is currently stored. This enables people to know which tape they should use first to restore data, and where the tape (or other media) can be found. If media isn't managed properly, then a tape could be lost, accidentally erased, or overwritten.

When a backup is made, you should write the date on the media. This enables you and others to see that the backup is a duplicate of data from a given date. As you'll see later in this section, there could be numerous backups made in an organization, so you'll want to use the most current version. This prevents users from having to reproduce more work than is needed. For example, let's say you made a backup of everything on your server on Monday and Tuesday, and the server crashed on Wednesday. If you restore the backup from Monday, any work that was performed after that time won't be included on the backup. This means that all work done by users on Tuesday will need to be redone. If the backup from Tuesday is restored, users will only need to redo work performed after that time (which would take hours rather than days).

Documenting the date also provides information on how many times a particular media type was used. Backup tapes can be used multiple times, but they don't last forever. As you might have discovered with videotapes you've used to record your favorite TV shows, reusing the same magnetic tape over and over will slowly degrade the tape. When the tape holds your backed-up data, this can result in data being lost. To avoid this, you should record how many times a medium has been used, and not use it more than the number of times recommended by the manufacturer.

It is also unwise to keep all backup media in the same location or in the same area as the computers whose data you've backed up. Because you're backing up data to protect the business from data loss, keeping backups near the backed up computer can expose the backups to the same disaster that damages or destroys the original data on that computer. In the same light, if all the backups are together in the same location, they can all be destroyed simultaneously. If a fire or flood occurs and destroys the server room, all backup tapes stored in that room could also be destroyed. To protect your data, you should store the backups in different locations, so that they'll be safe until they're needed.

Offsite Storage

Offsite storage can be achieved in a number of ways. If your company has multiple buildings, in different cities or different parts of the city, the backups from each site can be stored in one of the other buildings. Doing this makes it more likely that, if one location experiences a disaster, the original data or backups will remain safe. If this isn't possible, you can consider using a firm that provides offsite storage facilities. Some organizations store their offsite backups in a safe deposit box at a bank. The key is keeping the backups away from the physical location of the original data.

When deciding on an offsite storage facility, you should ensure that it is secure and has the environmental conditions necessary to keep the backups safe. You should ensure that the site has air conditioning and heating, as temperature changes could affect the integrity of data. It should also be protected from moisture and flooding, and have fire protection in case a disaster befalls the storage facility. The backups need to be locked up, and your organization should have policies that dictate who can pick up the data when needed. Otherwise, someone posing as a member of your organization could steal the data. Conversely, you want the data to be quickly accessible, so that you can acquire the data from the facility if you need it, without having to wait until the next time the building is open for business.

Backing Up Data Files with the Backup Utility

Windows Server 2003 provides a Backup utility that enables you to archive any files on the computer, regardless of whether the hard disk is formatted as FAT, FAT32, or NTFS. When data is backed up, it is copied to an area of your hard disk or other media that can be stored in a separate location. If a user accidentally deletes a file, data becomes corrupted, or a disaster occurs, the backup can then be used to copy this data back to the server.

NOTE

The Backup utility in Windows Server 2003 uses the *volume shadow copy* technique to create copies of your data. This means even files that are open and being used by users or the system can be backed up. We discuss volume shadow copies in more detail later in this chapter, in the section titled *Working with Volume Shadow Copies.*

Starting the Backup Utility

The Backup utility has two modes:

- Backup and Restore Wizard
- Advanced Mode

When the utility is started for the first time after you install Windows Server 2003, the Backup and Restore Wizard appears. This wizard takes you through the step-by-step process of backing up the server or restoring an existing backup from the hard disk or other media.

From the initial Welcome screen of the wizard, you can open Backup in Advanced Mode, which provides more features for those who are more comfortable with backing up and restoring data.

NOTE

The Welcome screen of the Backup utility provides a check box to configure Backup to always start in Advanced Mode. This disables the wizard.

You can open the Backup utility in one of two ways:

- Click **Start** | **Programs** | **Accessories** | **System Tools** | **Backup.**
- Click **Start** | **Run** and type **ntbackup**.

Using the Backup Utility in Advanced Mode

When you open Backup in Advanced Mode, you are presented with a Welcome to the Backup Utility Advanced Mode page. There are three buttons: one to start the Backup Wizard (Advanced), one to start the Restore Wizard (Advanced) and one to start the Automated System Recovery Wizard. We will discuss ASR later in the chapter. As you can see by Figure 10.1, the utility provides four tabs that provide the controls needed to perform various tasks, which we'll discuss here and later in this chapter.

When you switch to the **Backup** tab, the interface looks similar to that shown in Figure 10.1. If you don't want to use a wizard to control your backup, the Backup tab should be used to back up data files.

Figure 10.1 Windows 2003 Backup Utility

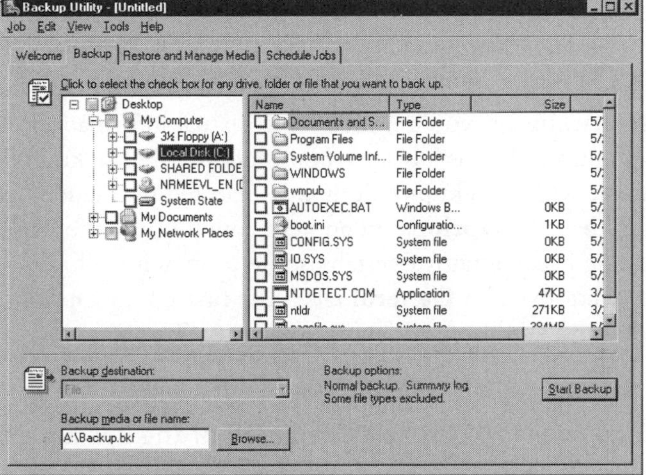

The Backup tab contains two panes that enable you to view the hierarchical listings of files and folders on the computer. The left tab enables you to navigate through the drives, and can be expanded to show the various folders on those drives. When a drive or folder is selected, the right pane is used to view the files and folders within. In both panes, check boxes appear beside the different drives, folders, and files. When these are checked or unchecked (by clicking the check box), the items are respectively selected or deselected for backup. As you can see, the Backup utility makes it easy and straightforward to choose the files, folders, or entire drives that are to be included in your backup job.

Below the two panes are other controls that are used to provide information and start the backup process. The Backup destination field provides a drop-down list of where the Backup utility is to store the data (media type). You can choose to store the backup as a file, or back up to a tape device that's installed on the machine.

NOTE

If you don't have a tape device installed, the Backup destination field is grayed out.

Below this is the Backup media or file name field, where you can specify the path and filename of the location where the backup file will be stored, or (if you are backing up data to a tape) specify the tape you wish to use. If you plan to overwrite an existing backup file, you can click the **Browse** button to find the file. Finally, when you're ready to begin the backup job, simply click the **Start Backup** button to begin the process.

NOTE

You can name the backup whatever you want and use any file extension, but Microsoft recommends that you use the .bkf extension for backup files, as this enables them to be recognized by the Backup utility.

Setting Backup Options

When looking at the Backup tab, you'll notice some textual information below the two panes dealing with Backup options. This is a brief synopsis of how the backup will be performed, and contains facts about which backup options were selected or included by default. To modify these options, click the **Options** menu item, found under the **Tools** menu.

The Options dialog box contains five tabs, some of which we'll discuss here (others we'll discuss in later sections). The **General** tab is the first tab in Options, and provides a variety of choices on how a backup of data is performed. These options are listed and explained in Table 10.6.

Table 10.6 Options Available on the General Tab of the Backup Utility

Option	Description
Compute selection information before backup and restore operations	When this option is selected, information is displayed on the number of files and bytes that are needed to perform the backup or restore job. This information is shown prior to the start of a job.
Use the catalogs on the media to speed up building restore catalogs on disk	Specifies whether to build an on-disk catalog from the on-media catalog when restoring data. This option is described in greater detail later in this chapter, when we discuss restoring data.
Verify data after the backup completes	When the data is backed up, it is compared to the original data to ensure it is the same. This option is described in greater detail later in this chapter, when we discuss verification of backups.
Back up the contents of mounted drives	Backs up the contents of a mounted drive, which is a folder on an NTFS volume that functions as a drive. If not selected, only the path information for the mounted drive is backed up.
Show alert message when I start Backup and Removable Storage is not running	Displays an alert when the Removable Storage service isn't running, and will start this service automatically.

Continued

Table 10.6 Options Available on the General Tab of the Backup Utility

Option	Description
Show alert message when I start Backup and there is recognizable media available	Displays an alert when the Removable Storage service detects that new media is available to which files can be backed up.
Show alert message when new media is inserted	Alerts you when the Removable Storage service detects that new media has been inserted into a device.
Always enable use of recognizable media without prompting	Enables the Removable Storage service to move any new media it detects to the Backup media pool, which is a collection of media used by the Backup utility.

When looking at these options, you will see that several of them deal with Removable Storage, which is a service that manages removable media (such as tapes) and storage devices on Windows Server 2003. If this service isn't running, Backup won't be able to back up files to tape. Because of its importance, if you are backing up files to tape, you should have the options relating to this service checked. As these options apply to backing up data to tape, you don't need to check these options if you are backing up data to a file.

NOTE

By default, all options are checked on the General tab except two: Verify data after the backup completes and Always allow use of recognizable media without prompting.

Understanding Backup Types

Another tab in the Options dialog box that you can use to configure backups is the Backup Type tab. As shown in the Figure 10.2, this tab provides a drop-down list that enables you to configure how backups are handled by default. The types of backups you can choose in the Windows Server 2003 Backup utility are as follows:

- Normal
- Incremental
- Differential
- Copy
- Daily

As you will see in the paragraphs that follow, different types of backups archive data in different ways. Because of this, the methods used to back up data will vary between businesses. One company might make normal backups every day, while another might use a combination of backup types. Regardless of the types used, however, it is important that data be backed up on a daily basis so that large amounts of data won't be lost in the event of a disaster.

Figure 10.2 Backup Type Tab of the Backup Utility's Options

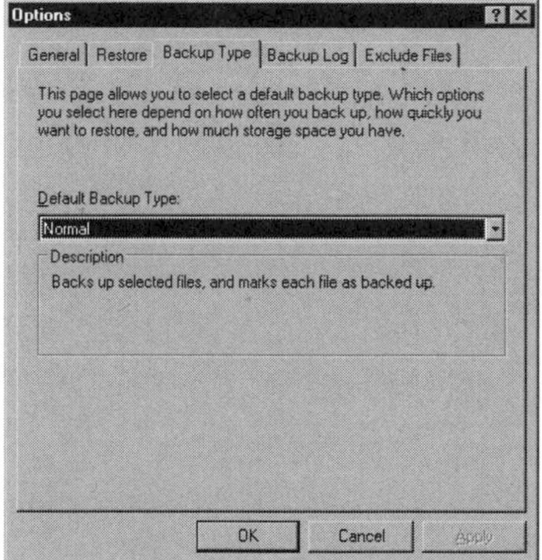

Before describing each of the backup types, it is important to understand that the type chosen will affect how the archive attribute is handled. The archive attribute is a property of a file or folder that's used to indicate whether a file has changed since the last time it was backed up. As you will see in the paragraphs that follow, depending on the backup type used, the archive attribute of a file is or is not cleared after it is backed up. When the file is modified, the archive attribute is set again to indicate it has changed and needs to be backed up again. Without the archive attribute, the Backup utility is unable to tell whether files need to be backed up or not. Here is a description of each backup type in more detail:

- Use a *normal backup* when you want to back up all the files you select in a single backup job. When you select this type of backup, the Backup utility backs up the selected files to a file or tape, ignoring whether the archive attribute is set or cleared. In other words, it doesn't matter whether the file has been backed up before; it will be backed up now. After backing up a file, it then changes the archive attribute to indicate that the file was backed up. Normal backups are commonly selected when you are performing full backups, in which all files on a volume are backed up.
- Use an *incremental backup* to back up all files that have changed since the last normal or incremental backup. When each file is backed up, the archive attribute is cleared. Because only files that have changed are backed up, this type of backup takes the

least amount of time to perform. However, it also takes the most amount of time to restore, because the last normal backup and every subsequent incremental backup must be restored to fully restore all data and make the contents of the computer as up-to-date as possible.

- Use a *differential backup* to back up all files that have changed since the last normal or incremental backup. However, when this type of backup is performed, the archive attribute isn't cleared. This means that the data on one differential backup contains the same information as the previous differential backup, plus any additional files that have changed. Since unchanged data is continually being backed up with this method, differential backups take longer to perform than incremental backups. However, when restoring backed up data, only the last normal backup and the last differential backup need to be restored. This makes the time it takes to fully restore a system faster than with a combined normal and incremental backup method.
- A *copy backup* is similar to a normal backup in that they can both be restored from a single backup job, but differ because a copy backup doesn't change the archive attribute. Because the archive attribute isn't modified, it does not affect any incremental or differential backups that are performed afterwards. This is useful if you want to make a copy of data on the computer, but don't want it to interfere with other backup operations involving normal and incremental backups.
- Use a *daily backup* to back up all selected files that have been modified on that particular day. Files that haven't been modified that day are not backed up. As with a copy backup, daily backups can be restored from a single backup and don't affect the archive attribute. Because the archive attribute is not cleared, it won't interfere with other backup operations involving normal and incremental backups.

Exam Warning

Not all backups are the same. Remember that normal and incremental backups set the archive attribute after backing up a file, but differential, copy, and daily backups do not. You can use normal, copy, and daily backups to restore files from a single backup job, whereas you can use incremental and differential backup types in conjunction with normal backups. This is because differential backups back up all files that have changed since the last normal backup (regardless of whether they were backed up by a previous differential backup), while incremental backups only back up files that have changed since the last normal or incremental backup and were not backed up previously.

Configuring Backup Logs

The **Backup Log** tab of the Backup utility is used to specify how log files dealing with the backup process should be created. There are three options on this tab:

- Detailed
- Summary
- None (turns off logging of the backup job)

When the **Summary** option is selected, only key operations in the backup process are logged. The log shows when the backup process started and ended, errors, and other events. When the **Detailed** option is selected, all information about the backup is included in the log. The log includes not only information displayed in a summary log, but also entries showing which files were backed up and their locations on the server. Although this can be handy for referencing what was backed up and when, a detailed log is also larger and uses more disk space.

Excluding Files from a Backup Job

The **Exclude Files** tab is used to identify types of files you'd like to exclude from your backup. This can be done for all users who own files on the machine, or only for the user currently logged in. On the **Exclude Files** tab, which is shown in Figure 10.3, you can click the **Add new** button to open the **Add Excluded Files** dialog box. Click a file type that's recognized by the system in the Registered file type box. File types included in the listing of the **Add Excluded Files** dialog box are ones that are tracked by Windows Server 2003 and included in the file associations of installed software on the machine.

You can also enter a custom file type by using the Custom file mask field below this listing. In this textbox, enter a period followed by the file extension to indicate types of files that shouldn't be included in your backup. If you only want to exclude file types in a certain folder, you can type the path to that folder in the Applies to path textbox that appears below the custom file mask field. When this is done, only the specified file types that are located under that path are excluded. For example, you might exclude all text files with the extension .TXT under C:\WINNT. Excluding file types makes your backup set smaller and thereby faster to restore, because unneeded data isn't included.

Advanced Backup Settings

You can set several options for a Backup job after you click the **Start Backup** button on the **Backup** tab. When you click this button, the **Backup Job Information** dialog box appears, providing information dealing with how the backup will be performed. A number of these settings can be modified for each backup job you configure.

The **Backup description** field enables you to enter information about the backup, which can be used to show when it was created and why. By default, this field contains the date and time the set was created.

Figure 10.3 Exclude Files Tab of the Backup Utility's Options

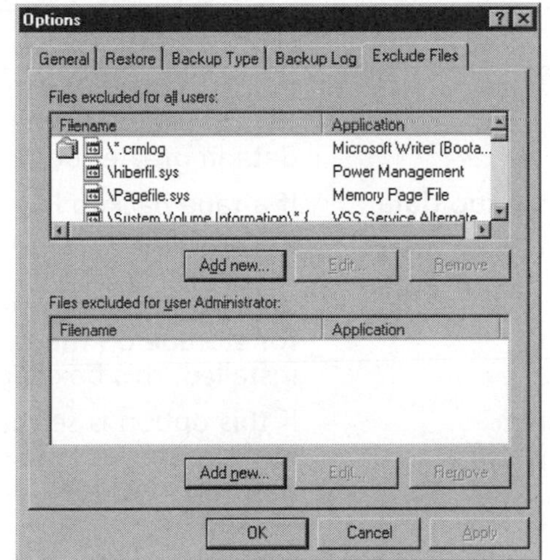

Below is a frame with two option buttons that enable you to control what happens if the media already contains a backup. If the first option is selected, the backup is appended to an existing backup set. If the second is selected, the data on the media is replaced by the new backup data. This is particularly useful if the same file is being used for multiple backup jobs. If you select the second option, a warning box appears to warn you that the data already on the backup media will be replaced.

The Backup Job Information dialog box also provides an **Advanced** button, which brings up the Advanced Backup Options dialog box when clicked. Here you can check various check boxes to control elements of the backup job, including additional data to be included and other factors. By default, none of the boxes are checked. The dialog box also provides a **Backup Type** drop-down list, which enables you to change the type of backup to be performed (Normal, Copy, Incremental, Differential, and Daily). The check boxes included on this dialog box are shown in Table 10.7.

Table 10.7 Options Available on the General Tab of the Backup Utility

Option	Description
Back up data that is in Remote Storage	If the **Back Up Data that is in Remote Storage** check box is checked, the job also backs up data that's included in Remote Storage. Remote Storage is a service that manages data that's infrequently used, and migrates it from local storage to remote storage. When the user opens the file, it is automatically recalled without the user realizing that Remote Storage was used.

Continued

Table 10.7 Options Available on the General Tab of the Backup Utility

Option	Description
Verify data after backup	Verifies that backed up data is identical to the original data. We will discuss verifying data in greater detail later in this chapter.
If possible, compress the backup data to save space	If a tape backup is performed, and the tape device supports compressed data, this option is enabled. Checking this box compresses the backed up data so that there is more room for storage on the tape. If no tape drive is installed, this box is grayed out.
Automatically backup System Protected Files with the System State	If this option is selected, system files located in the systemroot (e.g. C:\WINDOWS) and boot files included with the System State are backed up.
Disable volume shadow copy	When performing a backup, the Windows Server 2003 Backup utility by default creates a *volume shadow copy*, which is a duplicate of the volume at the time the copy process began. This enables the Backup utility to back up all selected files, including those that are currently open by users or the operating system. Because the Backup utility uses a volume shadow copy, it ensures that all selected data is backed up and any open files are not corrupted during the process. If this check box is checked, files that are open or in use are skipped when the backup is performed.

Exercise 10.02

Using The Windows Server 2003 Backup Utility

1. Start the Backup Utility by clicking **Start | All Programs | Accessories | System Tools | Backup** or by clicking **Start | Run** and typing **ntbackup**.
2. If the Backup or Restore Wizard opens, click the text link on the initial Welcome screen labeled **Advanced Mode**. This closes the wizard and opens the Backup Utility.
3. Click the tab labeled **Backup**.
4. From the **Job** menu, click **New**.

5. The left pane of the Backup tab shows a directory tree, which can be used to view the drives and folders on the computer. The right pane can be used to view files and folders within the drive or folder you've selected in the left pane. In the left pane of the Backup tab, select your C: drive. This changes the display in the right pane to shows the contents of the C: drive.
6. Scroll through the contents of your C: drive and select the files you wish to back up by clicking the check box beside each file or folder. Once checked, a file or folder is selected for backup.
7. In the **Backup Destination** drop-down menu, select whether you want to back up to a file (which is selected by default), or another medium (such as a tape device). For the purposes of this exercise, accept the default choice of backing up to a file. (Note that if you do not have a tape drive attached to your computer, this selection is grayed out and your only choice is the default.)
8. In the **Backup Media or File Name** text box, enter the path and filename for the backup file. This is where the backup file is saved. Type **C:\backup.bkf**.
9. From the **Tools** menu, click **Options**.
10. When the Options dialog appears, click the **General** tab. If the **Verify data after the backup completes** check box is not checked, click it so that a check mark appears in the box.
11. Click the **Backup Type** tab. Select **Normal** as the type of backup to perform.
12. Click the **Backup Log** tab and click the option labeled **Detailed**. This provides a detailed log of the files being backed up.
13. Click **OK** to exit the dialog box.
14. Click the **Start Backup** button.
15. When the Backup Job Information dialog appears, accept the default values and click the **Start Backup** button to begin the backup job.

Backing Up System State Data

The System State data of a computer consists of files the system specifically needs to function as configured. The files making up the System State data includes files needed to boot the computer, files to load and run the operating system, configuration information for the server, and other files that we'll discuss in greater detail later in this chapter.

Backups of the System State data can be used in a disaster to restore Windows Server 2003 if the operating system won't start or the disk must be formatted or is destroyed. System state backups are performed using the Windows Server 2003 Backup utility. As we discussed in the previous section, the **Backup** tab of this utility has panes that list the drives and directories that can be included in a backup. One of the items that appears in the list under **My Computer** is **System State**. By checking the check box beside this item, you can designate that the System State data be included in a backup.

It is important to realize that all the files that are needed to completely restore the server aren't included in the System State data. After all, the entire operating system and data on the server isn't included in the System State data, which your server needs to be restored to its previous functioning state. Microsoft recommends that when backing up the System State data, you also back up all the files on the boot and system volumes of your server. This backs up all the files used by the operating system and enables you to restore a duplicate of the server (as it was when the backup was performed).

Exam Warning

When backing up the System State data, you can only back up the System State data of the local computer. You cannot back up the System State data of a remote computer. System State data files have dependencies that require you to back them up as a unit. You cannot back up individual components of the System State data with the Backup utility.

Head of the Class...

Special Backup Situations

Some types of data require that you follow special procedures to back them up. The System State data, discussed in the text, is one such special situation.

Another special situation occurs when you want to back up files that are associated with Windows Media Services (WMS). To back up these files, you must follow the procedures that are outlined in the WMS Help files. You cannot use the normal backup procedures to back up and restore these files.

Microsoft recommends that if you want to back up database files on an SQL server, you should use the backup and restore utilities that are included with SQL Server instead of the Windows Server 2003 Backup utility.

If your Windows Server 2003 computer is running cluster services (Enterprise or Datacenter editions), you need to perform an ASR backup for each cluster node, back up the cluster disks in each node, and then back up individual applications that run on the nodes.

Configuring Security for Backup Operations

Being able to perform a backup requires that you have the proper permissions and rights. After all, if anyone could perform a backup, an unauthorized person could obtain a copy of the data stored on the computer. Note, however, that being able to back up data doesn't necessarily mean you are able to access and read it. Also note that a user who is authorized to back up data can back up and restore encrypted files without decrypting them.

The permissions and user rights needed to perform backup and restore operations in Windows Server 2003 are dependent on what is being backed up or restored, the permissions set on the files and folders, and the account being used to perform the backup and its group memberships.

To back up or restore any file or folder on the computer to which you are currently logged on as a user, you need to be a member of a group on that computer. Backup and restoration of files and folders on the local computer require you to be a member of the Administrators or Backup Operators local group. A local group is a group that's created on the computer (in contrast to a group that is created on the domain controller and used throughout the domain). A local group is assigned rights and permissions that apply only to that computer. Because the rights and permissions are limited to that machine, accounts that are a part of these groups cannot perform backup or restoration of data on other machines.

To back up or restore files and folders on any computer in a domain, you need to be a member of the Administrators or Backup Operators group on a domain controller. This also enables group members to back up or restore computers that are in a domain with which your domain has a two-way trust relationship.

NOTE

A two-way trust relationship enables authentication in one domain to be accepted in the other domain, so that you don't have to create multiple accounts for a user in each domain. This enables an Administrator or Backup Operator in one domain to back up or restore files in the other domain.

If you are not an Administrator or Backup Operator, there is still a chance that you might have the necessary permissions to perform a backup. The owner of a file or folder can generally back up his or her files. If the owner has one or more of the following permissions to a file or folder, then he or she can perform a backup:

- Read
- Read and execute
- Modify
- Full control

In addition to these rights and permissions, it is important that a user to whom you want to give the capability to back up and restore files doesn't have any disk-quota restrictions. Such restrictions make it impossible to perform backups of data.

An administrator can also *delegate the authority* to perform backups to a user without placing that user in one of the authorized groups. Delegation of control can be done through the **Delegation of Control** Wizard or via Group Policy settings.

Head of the Class...

Delegating Authority to Perform Backups via Group Policy

You can delegate the authority to perform backups by editing the Group Policy settings for a computer or Windows Server 2003 domain. To do so, open the group policy object (for a local computer, do this by clicking **Start | All Programs | Administrative Tools | Local Security Policy**).

In a domain, you do this through the Active Directory Users and Computers administrative tool. Open the console and right-click the domain name; then select **Properties**. Click the **Group Policy** tab and select the **Default Domain Policy**. In the left pane, expand the **Computer Configuration** node; then expand **Windows Settings**, and then **Security Settings**.

In either case, in the Group Policy Object Editor console, in the left pane under Security Settings, expand **Local Policies** and click **User Rights Assignment**. In the right pane, double-click **Back up files and directories**. Check the **Define these policy settings** check box if you are editing the domain policy. Click **Add User or Group**. You can select an individual user account or any group account to which you wish to delegate the authority to perform backups. The number of people who have the capability to back up and restore data varies from company to company. In some organizations, a higher level of security might be required, which limits the capability to perform backups to one person or group of Administrators. In other organizations, servers might be located in branch offices across the country. Since the Backup utility can only be used to back up and restore the System State of the local computer, and cannot be used to back up another domain controller, this might require that people in each location be authorized to perform backups and restores. The choice of how security is configured depends on the policies and needs of your organization.

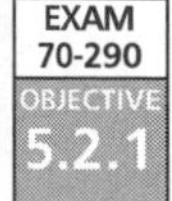

Verifying Successful Completion of Backup Jobs

Sometimes problems occur that prevent a back up from completing successfully. Errors can occur during the backup process that corrupt data or cause data not to copy properly. For example, a tape might be partially demagnetized, causing the data to be erroneously written during the backup. To ensure that backups are performed properly, you can configure the Backup utility to verify, after writing the backup copy, that the data included in a job is identical to the original files.

To verify that data was backed up properly, use the Options dialog box in the Backup Utility, by clicking **Tools | Options**. On the **General** tab, select the option **Verify data after the backup completes**. When this option is selected, the data that's been backed up is compared to the original data to ensure that they're identical.

When verifying data after a backup, you might find that some files are not the same. System files are regularly used, and can be changed while the backup is being performed. In other situations, users have files open, which they are modifying. In such situations, errors result during verification. For this reason, you should run your backups at night or during times when network activity is low. Although you can ignore a small number of such errors, a large number could indicate a problem with the media being used, or a problem with the area of the hard disk to which the backup file is being written. In such cases, you should run the backup job a second time, using a different filename or a different tape.

Managing Backup Media

The **Restore and Manage Media** tab of the Backup utility provides the capability to manage the media used for backups and restores. This tab can be used to create and delete catalogs used for restoring data. Depending on whether a tape backup device is installed on the machine, you might also be able to format and retension tapes, or mark a tape as free. Such tasks are necessary components of managing your backups.

As with disks, tapes might need to be formatted so that data can be stored on them and old data (if the tape has been previously used) can be erased. To format a tape, insert it into the tape device. In the **Restore and Manage Media** tab, select the tape as the one you want to manage. After doing this, click **Tools | Media Tools**, and then click **Format** to begin formatting the tape.

NOTE

The Media Tools selection on the **Tools** menu is grayed out if you do not have a tape device installed on the computer. This is because menu items in **Media Tools** apply only to tape backups, and not to files.

In addition to formatting tapes, which destroys any existing data on the tapes, you can also mark tapes as free. Marking tapes as free enables them to be reused for backups. Doing this indicates that the tape can be reused by the Backup utility, but won't actually destroy any data on the backup. Although marking a tape as free is useful for many organizations, this shouldn't be done if tapes need to be completely erased for legal reasons or to adhere to internal policy.

NOTE

Be aware that even formatting does not completely destroy all data on a disk; data can still be recovered with special computer forensics software. If data on magnetic media is highly sensitive and must be completely erased, the only way to ensure this is to physically destroy the media by grinding (in the case of disks), shredding (in the case of tapes), incinerating, or dissolving with acid.

To mark a tape as free, insert the tape you want to mark as free into the tape device, and then select the tape from the **Restore and Manage Media** tab. After this is done, select **Tools | Media Tools** and then click **Mark as Free**. The Backup utility then begins marking the tape.

Over time, tapes can become loose and need to be *retensioned*. If you've never experienced this with backup tapes, you might have seen it happen to music tapes used in cassette players. The tape becomes loose inside the cassette, and can cause the tape to spool out of the cassette while being played. If you've ever had a tape "eaten" by the cassette player/recorder, you can appreciate the damage this does to the tape and sometimes to the device. Retensioning the tape prevents this problem, by winding it to the end and then back to its beginning.

To retension a tape using the Backup utility, insert the tape you want to retension into the tape device. From the **Restore and Manage Media** tab, select the tape you want to retension, and then click **Tools | Retension** to begin the process.

In addition to managing tapes, the Backup utility can be used to manage *catalogs*. A catalog is a list of files and folders that have been included in a particular backup set. *On-media catalogs* are created during the backup process and stored on media to indicate which files and folders are included in the set. *On-disk catalogs* contain the same type of information, but are stored on the local hard disk. Because it is faster to read a catalog from the hard disk than from a tape, this speeds the restoration process (as we discuss in the next section).

If an on-disk catalog isn't needed anymore, it can be easily deleted from the **Restore and Manage Media** tab. On this tab, right-click the backup set that contains the catalog you wish to remove. If that backup you're dealing with was saved to a file, click **Delete Catalog** from the menu that appears. If it was stored on a tape, click **Delete From System**. In both cases, the on-disk catalog is deleted for the backup set. However, if the backup is stored on a tape, this also removes the tape from the database used by the Removable Storage service.

Just because a catalog is deleted, this doesn't mean you can't recreate it. The Backup utility has the capability to create or recreate catalogs of files and folders stored in backup sets. From the **Restore and Manage Media** tab, right-click the media containing the backup set you want to catalog and then click **Catalog** on the menu that appears. If the media is stored on a tape, you need to perform an additional step beforehand. On tapes, the catalog is stored on one of the tapes that is part of the backup set. If this tape is missing, or the catalog is corrupt or damaged in some way, click **Tools | Options**. When the Options dialog box appears, click the **General** tab and ensure that the **Use the catalogs on the media to speed up building restore catalogs on disk** check box is cleared. When you start cataloging the tape, it goes through the backup set and catalogs files and folders included in the backup to generate a catalog. If the catalog tape isn't missing and the on-media catalog is intact, ensure that the **Use the catalogs on the media to speed up building restore catalogs on disk** check box is checked. When it is checked, this creates an on-disk catalog.

Restoring Backed-Up Data

When original data is lost, deleted, or corrupted, restoring a previous backup might be the only way to get that data back. To copy the data from a backup and put it back on the computer's hard disk, you need to restore it. The Backup utility that was used to create the backup set is also used to restore it.

When the Backup utility is initially started, it opens the **Backup and Restore Wizard**, which takes you through the step-by-step process of restoring files from a backup. By clicking the **Advanced Mode** link that appears on the Welcome screen, you can switch the Backup utility to Advanced Mode. This displays the interface we've used throughout previous sections.

As noted before, the Backup utility includes four tabs, which are used for various tasks involving backups. The Welcome tab provides a button that starts the **Restore Wizard**, which is an advanced version of the Backup and Restore Wizard, and can be used to guide you through the process of restoring data. You can use the **Restore and Manage Media** tab to restore data. As shown in Figure 10.4, this tab has two panes that enable you to browse backups created with this tool. The left pane can be used to browse through a tree of different backup sets and view the drives and folders included in different backups. When a type of backup is selected in the left pane, the right pane shows the various backup sets that are available for restoration. If a backup or folders within that backup are selected in the left pane, the right pane shows its contents.

Figure 10.4 Restore and Manage Media Tab of the Backup Utility

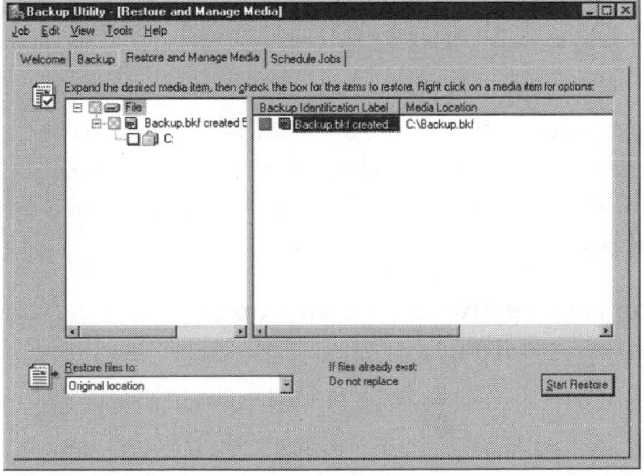

The items listed in the two console panes enable you to configure exactly what will be restored from the backup. Beside each item is a check box. By clicking a check box to check it, you select which backups, folders, and files are selected to be restored. This gives you the flexibility to restore as much or as little as you want from a backup.

The **Restore files to** drop-down list appears below these panes and designates the location to which files are restored. The following options are available:

- Original location
- Alternate location
- Single folder

If **Original location** is selected, files are restored to the same locations from which they were originally backed up. As we'll discuss later in this section, depending on how the Backup utility is configured, this might result in existing files being overwritten. If **Alternate location** is selected, files and folders are restored to a specified folder. With this option, the structure of folders and subfolders is maintained. If **Single folder** is selected, files and folders are restored to a specified folder, but the tree structure of these folders is not maintained. When either **Alternate location** or **Single folder** is selected, a textbox entitled **Alternate location** appears below this drop-down box, enabling you to specify the folder to which the backup should be restored.

When restoring from an existing backup, the Backup utility provides a number of options that can be configured. This is done through the Options dialog box that you saw earlier in this chapter. You can access the Options dialog box by clicking **Tools | Options**. Different tabs in the Options dialog box enable you to configure how the Backup utility restores data.

NOTE

If files that were backed up were originally located on an NTFS volume, you should restore them to a volume that is formatted with the same version of NTFS. Although you can restore them to a FAT/FAT32 volume or one formatted with an earlier version of NTFS, some of the features dependent on NTFS are lost if you do.

The **Restore** tab provides options on how data is restored to the computer. When files are restored, it is possible that a file might already exist on the hard disk. Given this possibility, you should decide how you want the Backup utility to deal with such instances. The **Restore** tab has several options:

- If the **Do not replace the file on my computer** option is selected, Backup won't overwrite any existing files.

- If the **Replace the file on disk only if the file is on disk is older** option is selected, older versions of files are replaced by newer ones on the backup. If a file is newer than the one in the backup set, it is skipped.
- If the **Always replace the file on my computer** option is selected, existing files on the disk are overwritten, regardless of whether they're newer or older.

As we demonstrated in the previous section, you can configure the Backup utility to create catalogs that can be used for restoring data. The **Use the catalogs on the media to speed up building restore catalogs on disk** option on the **General** tab can be used to specify whether the on-media catalog should be used to create an on-disk catalog. The on-media catalog is a list of files and folders that have been backed up as part of a single backup job. It is used during the restoration process to find the files and folders more quickly. When an on-disk catalog is used, this information can be read from the local hard disk, to speed up the restore process. When an on-disk catalog is built, the information is gathered from the on-media catalog. However, if the on-media catalog is missing or damaged, the Backup utility needs to scan the entire backup set to create this catalog, which can take a considerable amount of time depending on the size of the backup set being restored.

Head of the Class...

The Need to Perform Test Restorations

Many network administrators have followed a routine of backing up data, only to find that the backup wasn't performed properly and the data can't be restored when it's needed. This can be caused by problems with the media, the device, or the way the job was configured. A backup is only as good as its ability to be restored. If a backup can't be restored when needed, not only was it pointless to perform the backup in the first place, but time and resources were also wasted. More importantly, if a backup can't be restored, important data might be irrevocably lost. To ensure that your backups work, you should perform test restorations *before* you need them.

A test restoration involves restoring files or folders to another location and checking to determine if they were restored properly. This doesn't require restoring the entire backup, but simply a subset of it (such as several files or a folder containing files). After doing this, you can then try opening one or more of these files (such as a document or spreadsheet) to ensure that the file opens and looks as expected. If such a restoration fails, it could indicate problems such as a faulty tape device or a bad tape.

Scheduling Backup Jobs

When a backup is performed, the Backup utility uses resources on the computer to complete the job. It processes the backup, reading and writing from the hard disk as the backup set is created, using memory and processor cycles, and might use other resources (such as a tape device). This can collectively affect system performance if users are using the server at the same time. Because of this, if possible, backups should be performed when network activity is low and when few (if any) users are accessing the server.

This means network administrators generally perform backups after normal work hours, often at night and on weekends. To prevent the administrator from having to come in and manually start a backup job, the Windows Server 2003 Backup utility provides scheduling features to automatically start backups on specific days and times that you designate. This is done through the **Schedule Jobs** tab or the **Backup** tab of the Backup utility.

As shown in Figure 10.5, the **Schedule Jobs** tab provides an easy-to-use calendar interface. By selecting a date on the calendar and clicking the **Add Job** button, you invoke the Backup Wizard. The wizard guides you through the process of creating a new backup job and scheduling it for a particular date and time. This is the same wizard that can be accessed from the **Welcome** tab of the Backup utility.

Figure 10.5 Schedule Jobs Tab of the Backup Utility

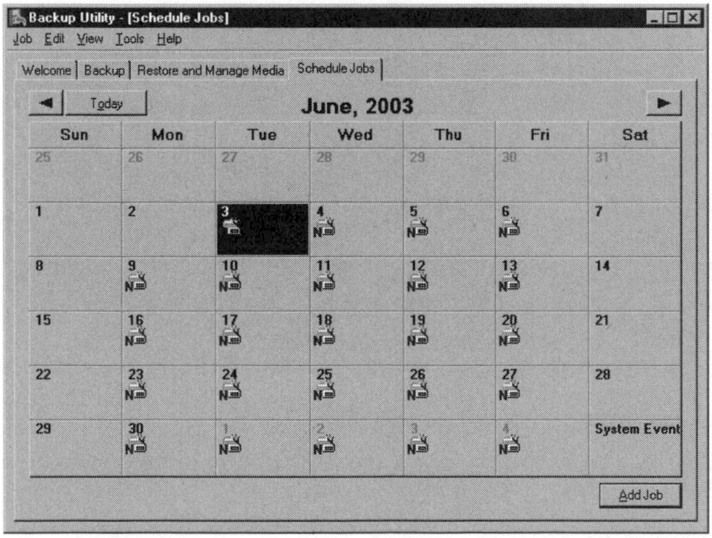

You can also schedule jobs through the **Backup** tab, which we discussed earlier in this chapter. After you select the files you want to back up and click the **Start Backup** button, the **Backup Job Description** dialog box is displayed (Figure 10.6). This dialog box has a button labeled **Schedule**, which, when clicked, displays the **Set Account Information** dialog box that enables you to enter the account information (username and password) under which you want the backup job to run.

Figure 10.6 Backup Job Information Dialog Box

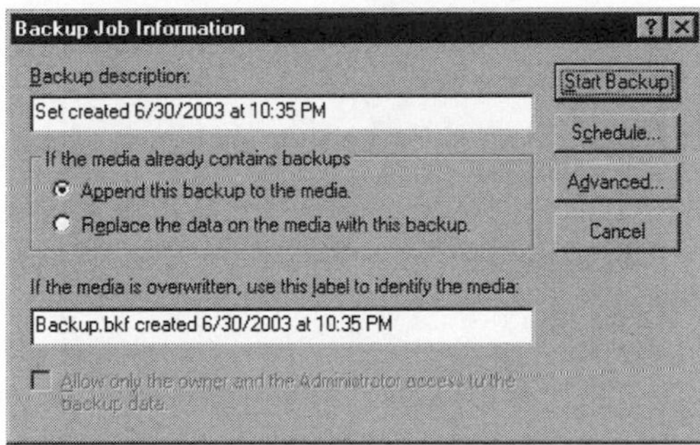

After you do this, the **Scheduled Job Options** dialog box appears. As shown in Figure 10.7, this dialog has two tabs. The **Backup Details** tab provides information on the backup, inclusive to a summary on the jobs. The **Schedule Data** tab enables you to enter the name of the backup job and configure properties.

Figure 10.7 Scheduled Job Options Dialog Box

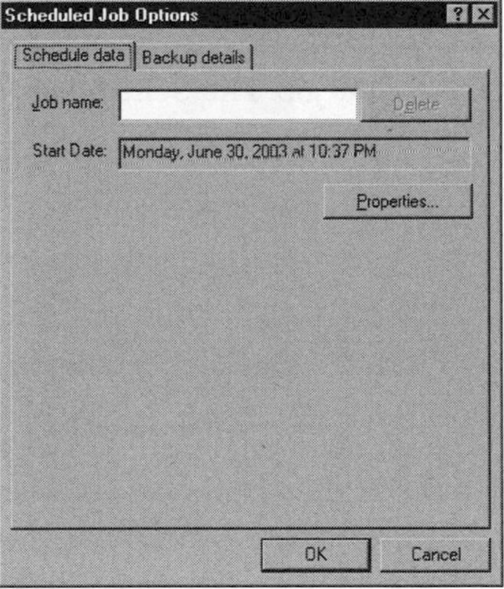

This dialog box also has a **Properties** button. When you click **Properties**, it displays the **Schedule Job** dialog box shown in Figure 10.8, where you can schedule the date, time, and other properties of the backup job. These are elements that can be changed at any time after the job has been scheduled.

Figure 10.8 Schedule Job Dialog Box

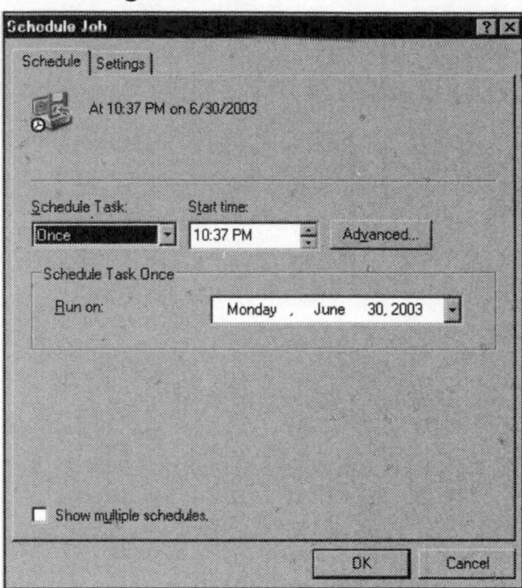

After a backup job has been created, it appears on dates of the calendar as an icon. Double-clicking an icon that appears on a date brings up the **Scheduled Job Options** dialog box, where you can reconfigure elements of the backup job. This is the same dialog box that was initially used to schedule the job. **The Scheduled Job** Options dialog box has two tabs:

- Schedule data
- Backup details

The **Schedule data** tab enables you to name the job and has a **Properties** button that displays the **Schedule Job** dialog box. The **Backup details** tab provides textual information about this job, including the backup set, device to be used, and a job summary. This information cannot be modified from this location.

The **Schedule Job** dialog box shown in Figure 10.9 is where you can set most of the configuration information used to schedule a backup job for a later time. The **Task** tab enables you to set parameters, enter comments, and set account information used to perform the backup. The Task tab appears on the **Schedule Job** dialog box after a backup job has been scheduled to run; you review the task by opening the job's properties.

When running a backup as you did in Exercise 10.2, the utility can use the username and password of the person logged onto the machine to access and back up files. When a backup is scheduled, however, there is a good chance that someone with the necessary rights and permissions to perform the backup won't be logged on. Setting account information instructs the Backup utility to use a particular username and password that has the appropriate rights to access and back up files.

Figure 10.9 Schedule Job Dialog Box

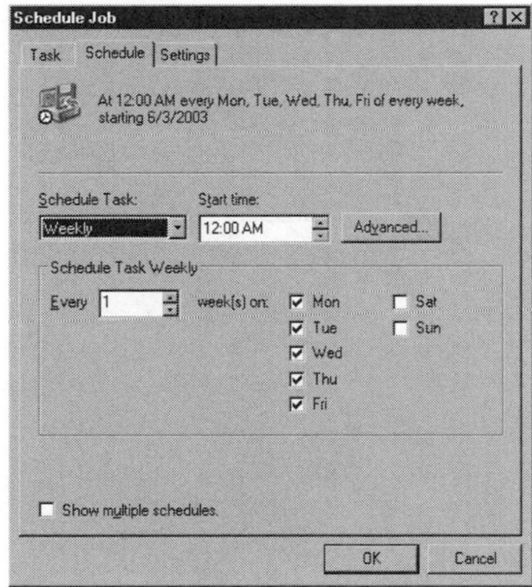

The **Schedule** tab is where you configure the time and day when the backup job runs, and how often. By setting the **Start time** field, you ensure that a backup job starts when the system's clock reaches a specified time. Because you might want certain backup jobs to run at different intervals, the **Schedule Task** drop-down list enables you to control how frequently a backup job runs. Setting the value on this drop-down list enables you to choose to run a backup job at any of the following intervals:

- Daily
- Weekly
- Monthly
- Once
- At System Startup
- At Logon
- When idle

When you choose **At System Startup** or **At Logon**, the backup job runs when Windows Server 2003 starts or when you log on to the operating system, respectively. However, when other values are selected from the **Schedule Task** drop-down list, additional fields relating to the interval you select appear. This provides the capability to control details relating to the frequency of a backup job.

When **Daily** is selected from the drop-down list, the **Schedule Task Daily** frame appears beneath these controls, as shown in Figure 10.10. Here you can designate whether the backup job runs every day, every two days, every three days, and so on. For example, if you want the backup job to run every two days, it will run every other day at the time you specify.

Figure 10.10 Schedule Task Daily

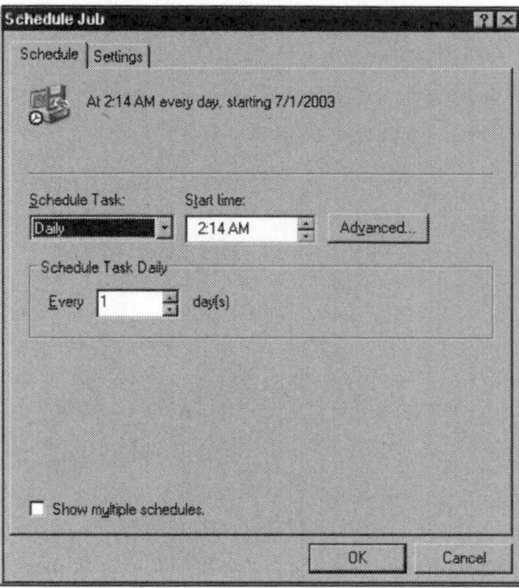

When you select **Weekly** from the **Schedule Task** drop-down list, the **Schedule Task Weekly** frame appears below the controls, as shown in Figure 10.11. You can select whether the backup runs every week, every two weeks, every three weeks, and so on. You can also use the check boxes in this frame that show different days of the week to select on which days the backup job will run. This is useful if you want to run certain backup types (such as differential or incremental) on weekdays, and larger jobs (such as normal backups) on weekends.

Figure 10.11 Schedule Task Weekly

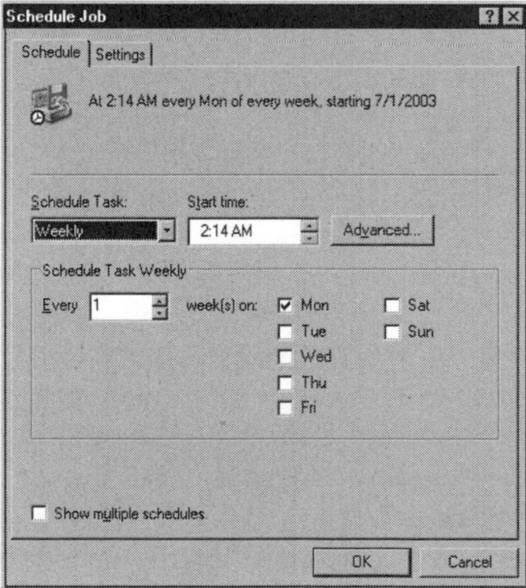

When you select **Monthly** from the **Schedule Task** drop-down list, the **Schedule Task Monthly** frame appears, as shown in Figure 10.12. This frame contains two options, which enable you to specify the day of the month that a scheduled backup will run, or if the backup should run only on occurrences of a certain weekday during the month. It also contains a **Select Months** button that displays a dialog box displaying months of the year. By checking the check boxes beside the months, you can configure the Backup Utility to run the backup job only during those months.

Figure 10.12 Schedule Task Monthly

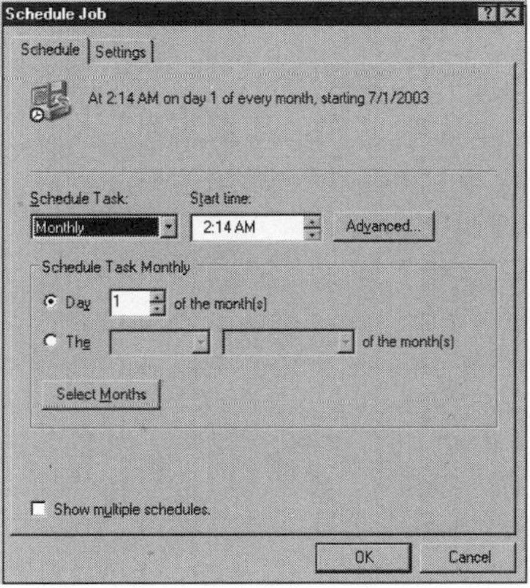

When performing monthly backups, if the first option in the **Schedule Task Monthly** frame is selected (**Day**), you can set the date on which a backup will run. The **Day** field enables you to select a number between 1 and 31 as the day of the month that a backup is run. For example, if you selected 15, then the backup would run on the fifteenth of each month. If a day between 29 and 31 is selected, the backup job will run only on months that contain those days.

If you choose the second option in the **Schedule Task Monthly** frame, you can configure backups to run on occurrences of a weekday (for example, on the first Monday of each month). When this option is selected, two drop-down lists are enabled. The first drop-down list enables you to choose whether the backup is run on the first, second, third, fourth, or last occurrence of a particular day of the week. In the second list, you select a day of the week (Monday through Sunday) on which the backup should run. For example, if you wanted the backup to run on the second Friday of every month, you would select **second** from the first list and **Friday** from the second list.

The **Schedule Task** drop-down list of the **Schedule** tab also offers the choice of running a backup one time. When Once is selected, the **Schedule Task** Once frame appears, as shown in Figure 10.13, with a field showing the current date. If you don't want to run the backup on today's date, click the arrow beside this field to display a calendar control that can be used to pick another date.

Figure 10.13 Schedule Task Once

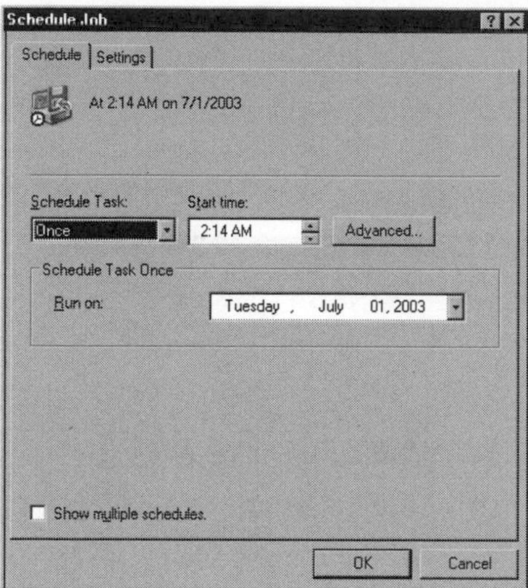

If you select **When idle** from the **Schedule Task** drop-down list, the **Schedule Task When Idle** frame appears, as shown in Figure 10.14. This enables you to set the number of minutes that the operating system should remain idle before starting the backup job. Because it is based on a time interval of minutes, the **Start time** field (which enables you to set the time to start a backup) becomes disabled. Although you can select that the system remain idle for 1 to 999 minutes, the default value is 10 minutes.

Figure 10.14 Schedule Task When Idle

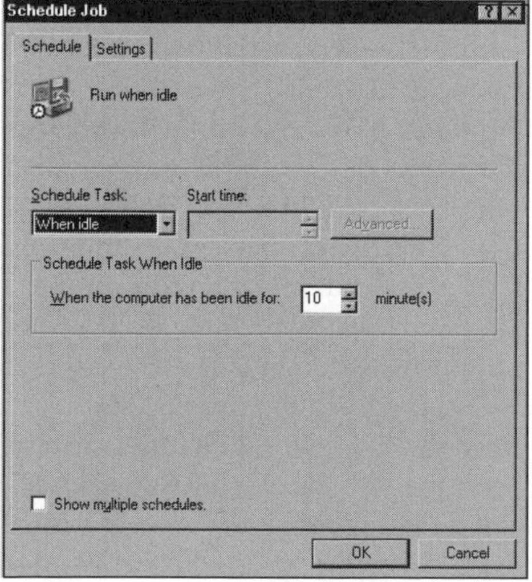

Test Day Tip

When dealing with scheduled backups, more than one backup can be created to handle a particular server's data. For example, a normal backup might be scheduled for one day of the week, while incremental or differential backups are scheduled for the rest of the week. By doing this, data is regularly backed up to other media. Don't assume that only one schedule is needed to adequately back up data.

The **Settings** tab of the **Schedule Job** dialog box, shown in Figure 10.15, provides the capability to set configuration information for scheduling a backup job. On this tab, you can control what happens to a job when it runs too long, is completed but isn't scheduled to run again, whether it should run after the system is idle, and power management options. For the settings you want to use, ensure that the check box beside each setting is checked and accept or modify the values corresponding to that setting.

Figure 10.15 Settings Tab of the Schedule Job Dialog Box

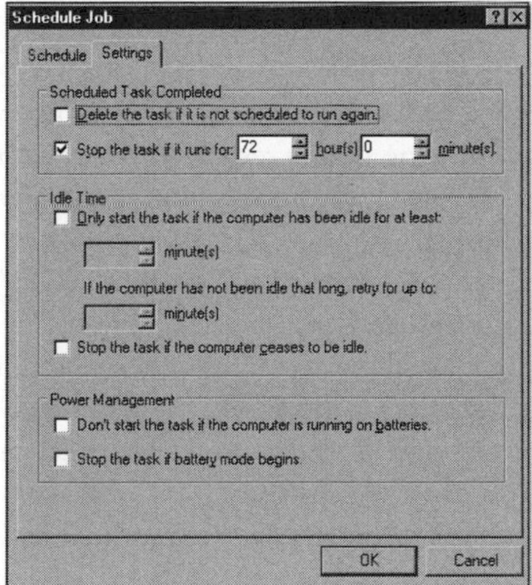

The **Scheduled Task Completed** frame on this tab determines what happens to a job once it's completed. Here you can check a box to delete the backup job if it's scheduled not to run again, and control whether the job should be stopped if it runs too long. By default, a job is configured to stop if it runs for 72 hours. However, you can set it for a different specified value of hours and minutes if you choose.

The **Idle Time** frame on this tab has several configurable settings. The first enables you to control whether the backup job will start if the computer has been idle for a specific amount of time. If the computer hasn't had any keyboard or mouse activity for the number of minutes you configure, the backup will start. If it is not idle when it first attempts to start, you can also set the number of minutes the Backup utility should continue checking to see if the computer is idle. Below this, you can also check the second check box in this frame to configure the backup job to stop if the computer is used while the backup is running.

Finally, the **Power Management** frame on this tab enables you to determine what happens with the backup job if normal power is lost. Because the Backup utility accesses the hard disk, tape devices, and other resources during a backup job, this can drain batteries faster. This could result in the server suddenly shutting down when the batteries are drained, before normal power is restored. You can set the backup job not to start if the computer is running on batteries, or to stop the job if it begins running on batteries.

NOTE

If either the **Don't start the task if the computer is running on batteries** or the **Stop the task if battery mode begins setting** is selected, the backup will *not* resume after normal power is restored.

Backup Rotation Schemes

Your goal in creating a backup schedule is to balance the number of tapes needed (cost effectiveness) with the amount of time that is required to restore the server's data completely (time effectiveness). This is most commonly done by *rotating* the type of backup made each day, week, and/or month.

A popular rotation scheme is the *Grandfather-Father-Son* (GFS) rotation, which organizes rotation into a daily, weekly, and monthly set of tapes. With a GFS backup schedule, at least one full backup is performed per week, with differential or incremental backups performed on other days of the week. At the end of the week, the daily and weekly backups are stored offsite and another set is used through the next week. To understand this better, assume the company is open from Monday to Friday. As shown in Table 10.8, a full backup of the server's volumes is performed every Monday, with differential backups performed Tuesday to Friday. On Friday, the tapes are then moved to another location, and another set of tapes is used for the following week.

Table 10.8 Sample Weekly Backup Schedule

Sun.	Mon.	Tues.	Wed.	Thurs.	Fri.	Sat.
None	Full Backup	Differential	Differential	Differential	Differential, with week's tapes moved offsite	None

Because it would be too expensive to continually use new tapes, old tapes are reused for backups. A tape set for each week in the month is rotated back into service and reused. For example, at the beginning of each month, the tape set for the first week of the previous month would be rotated back into service and used for that week's backup jobs. Because one set of tapes is used for each week of the month, this means that you have most sets of tapes kept offsite. Even if one set were corrupted, the set of tapes for the week previous could still be used to restore data.

In the Grandfather-Father-Son rotation scheme, the full backup is considered the "Father," and the daily backup is considered the "Son." The "Grandfather" segment of the GFS rotation is an additional full backup that's performed monthly and stored offsite. The Grandfather tape isn't reused, but is permanently stored offsite. Each of the Grandfather tapes can be kept for a specific amount of time (such as a year), so that data can be restored from previous backups, even after the Father and Son tapes have been rotated back into service. If someone needs data restored from several months ago, the Grandfather tape enables the network administrator to retrieve the required files.

Using the ntbackup Command-Line Utility

In addition to using the Backup utility in Windows Server 2003 that uses a graphical user interface, Windows Server 2003 also provides a command-line utility for performing backups. The command-line utility is Ntbackup, and can be started from the command prompt. This tool enables you to back up data from the computer, but doesn't provide the capability to restore files.

As with other command-line utilities, the NTBACKUP tool uses a number of parameters to control what tasks are executed and how they are performed. These parameters are shown in Table 10.9, and the syntax for using the command is as follows (note that this would all be one line):

```
ntbackup backup [systemstate] "@FileName.bks" /J {"jobname"} [/P
{"poolname"}] [/G {"GUIDName"}] [/T {"tapename"}] [/N {"medianame"}]
[/F {"filename"}] [/D {"setdescription"}] [/DS {"servername"}] [/IS
{"servername"}] [/A] [/V:{yes | no}] [/R:{yes | no}] [/L:{f | s | n}]
[/M {BackupType}] [/RS:{yes | no}] [/HC:{on | off}] [/SNAP:{on | off}]
```

Table 10.9 Ntbackup Parameters

Parameter	Description
Systemstate	Specifies that the System State is to be backed up. This option forces Ntbackup to use the normal or copy backup type.
@filename.bks	Specifies the name of the backup file. You must use the @ character before the filename you wish to use.
/J {*"jobname"*}	Specifies the name of the job to appear in the log file.

Continued

Table 10.9 Ntbackup Parameters

Parameter	Description
/P {"*poolname*"}	Specifies the media pool to use. When this parameter is used, the */A*, */G*, */F*, or */T* switches cannot be used.
/G {"*GUIDName*"}	Specifies to overwrite or append to tape. This parameter isn't to be used with the */P* switch.
/T {"*tapename*"}	Specifies to overwrite or append to this tape. This parameter isn't to be used with the */P* switch.
/N {"*medianame*"}	Specifies the name of a new tape. This parameter isn't to be used with the */A* switch.
/F {"*filename*"}	Specifies the path and filename. This parameter isn't to be used with the */P*, */G*, or */T* switch.
/D {"*setdescription*"}	Specifies the label to use for the backup set.
/DS {"*servername*"}	Specifies to back up the directory service file for Microsoft Exchange Server.
/IS {"*servername*"}	Specifies to back up the information store file for Microsoft Exchange Server.
/A	Specifies to append the backup. When this parameter is used, the */G* or */T* switch must also be used. This parameter isn't to be used with the */P* switch.
/V:{yes | no}	Specifies whether to verify the data after the backup.
/R:{yes | no}	Specifies to restrict access to the tape to members of the administrators group or the owner.
/L:{f | s | n}	Specifies the type of log file to be created. When *F* is used a full log is created; when *S* is used a summary log is created; and when *N* is used no log file is created.
/M {*BackupType*}	Specifies the backup type (*normal*, *copy*, *differential*, *incremental*, or *daily*)
/RS:{yes | no}	Specifies to back up migrated data files in Remote Storage.
/HC:{on | off}	Specifies whether to use hardware compression.

Continued

Table 10.9 NTBACKUP Parameters

Parameter	Description
/SNAP:{on | off}	Specifies whether volume shadow copy is used for the backup.

Creating a System Recovery Plan

Data is a vital component of any business, but it does the business little good if the data can't be accessed from the server. Servers provide a variety of resources, and if they are unavailable, people within the company might be unable to do any work and the business won't be able to function. System recovery plans are used to prepare for circumstances that can affect a server's capability to run properly and address how the operating system and services can be restored in the event of a disaster.

System recovery plans document procedures on how to fix many of the problems that commonly result in the operating system failing to start. The plan should include information on the types of disasters that might affect a server, and how such problems can be fixed. Procedures provide step-by-step instructions on how to restore the system, and refer to other documents and plans (such as backup plans) that are used as part of system recovery.

Because many types of disasters can affect an operating system's ability to start, Windows Server 2003 includes a variety of utilities that can be used to recover the system. These include the following:

- The capability to back up the System State data
- The creation of ASR sets using the Backup utility
- The Recovery Console
- Startup options that appear when the computer is booted

Using these tools, you can remedy many of the problems that could prevent you from starting and using Windows Server 2003. In the next sections, we will discuss each of these tools in more detail.

Backing up System State Data

The System State data is a set of files that the system uses to function; it must be backed up as a single unit. Windows Server 2003 requires these files to be backed up together, because the files included in the System State have dependencies, in which two or more files rely on one another to function. Because of this, you can't choose individual System State data files when performing a backup.

System State data files are specific to each computer running Windows Server 2003 and can't generally be swapped between servers. Since servers can have different hardware and software installed, swapping these files can result in devices, programs, and the operating system itself not functioning properly. Thus, when backing up System State data files, it is important to label the backup as belonging to a specific server so that you won't accidentally restore the wrong System State data files to a server.

NOTE

It is possible to restore the System State data to an alternate location, but if you do so, some components (the COM+ Class Registration database, the Active Directory database, and the Certificate Services database) are not restored.

As we discussed earlier in this chapter, the System State data can be backed up using the Windows Server 2003 Backup utility. The files that this utility considers to be part of the System State can vary between computers. On Windows Server 2003, it always includes the following:

- The Registry
- The COM+ Class Registration database
- System files
- Boot files

In addition to these, the Backup utility might also include other files if the server is configured for a special purpose or has certain services installed. A domain controller has the Active Directory and the SYSVOL directory included in the System State data, and a certificate server includes the Certificate Services database as part of the System State data. If the server is part of a cluster, cluster service information also is included in the System State data. If Windows Server 2003 is configured to be a Web server and has Internet Information Services (IIS) installed, the IIS Metadirectory is also included. As you can see, the role a server plays on a network and the services it has installed have a great impact on what is backed up as part of the System State data.

The System State data can be backed up by checking the **System State** check box in the hierarchical list of volumes and folders in the left pane of the **Backup** tab with the Backup utility running in Advanced mode. Alternatively, you can use the command-line interface to back up the System State data by typing **ntbackup backup systemstate** at a command prompt.

TEST DAY TIP

A number of different items can be included in a backup of System State data, and questions might appear on the exam asking which of these will be backed up for a particular server. Remember that the System State data always includes the Registry, COM+ Class Registration database, system files, and boot files. Other elements that can be included depend on the role a server plays, and that role can be

used to cue your memory. Certificate servers are the only servers that have the Certificate Services database included, just as domain controllers have elements exclusively relating to their role.

Primary, Nonauthoritative, and Authoritative Restores

There are different situations where you would restore Active Directory. In some cases, you might have only one domain controller on a network, while in other situations you might want the information on the backup to be replicated to other domain controllers on the network. Because situations will vary, Windows Server 2003 provides three different methods of restoring Active Directory:

- Primary
- Nonauthoritative (normal)
- Authoritative

Use a primary restore when you are restoring Active Directory to the only domain controller on your network or the first of multiple domain controllers being restored. This type of restore is commonly used when all of the domain controllers are no longer available (such as when a disaster has destroyed all servers or data), and you are rebuilding the network from scratch.

Use a nonauthoritative or normal restore when you are restoring Active Directory on a network with multiple domain controllers. When Active Directory is restored to the domain controller, it is generally older than the directory information stored on other DCs in the domain. To ensure all domain controllers have identical copies of Active Directory, these other domain controllers replicate updated data to the restored server.

The reason a nonauthoritative restore has its information updated from other domain controllers is because of the way updates to the directory are recorded. When the System State data changes on a domain controller that participates in replication, an update sequence number is incremented to indicate a change has occurred. Because the System State data on other domain controllers has a lower update sequence, they know that they don't have the most up-to-date data. The System State data with the higher update sequence number is then replicated to other domain controllers so they have duplicate information.

When a nonauthoritative restore is performed, the domain controller generally has older data restored to it. For example, a backup might have been performed several days ago, in which time a considerable number of changes could have been made on other domain controllers on the network. To ensure the domain controller being restored has the most recent information, information is replicated to it to bring it up-to-date.

This can be a problem in situations where you want the restored data to be used. For example, you might have made errors in modifying Active Directory objects, such as deleting a user account that is still needed. By performing the nonauthoritative restore, the deleted account is restored from the backup, but it is then deleted again when replication occurs. To enable restored data to not be affected by replication, you can use authoritative restores.

An authoritative restore is similar to a nonauthoritative restore, in that Active Directory is restored to domain controllers participating in replication. The difference is that when it is restored, it is given a higher update sequence number, so it has the highest number in the Active Directory replication system. Because of this, other domain controllers are updated through replication with the restored data.

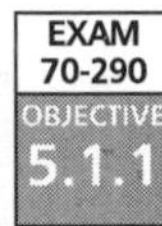

Creating an Automated System Recovery Set

An ASR set consists of files that are needed to restore Windows Server 2003 if the system cannot be started. When you create an ASR set, the following are backed up:

- System State data
- System services
- Disks that hold operating system components

In addition, a floppy disk is created that contains system settings. Because an ASR set focuses on the files needed to restore the system, data files are not included in the backup.

You should create an ASR set each time a major hardware change or a change to the operating system is made on the computer running Windows Server 2003. For example, if you install a new hard disk or network card, or apply a security patch or Service Pack, an ASR set should be created. Then if a problem occurs after upgrading the system in such ways, the ASR set can be used to restore the system to its previous state after other methods of system recovery have been attempted.

An ASR should not be used as the first step in recovering an operating system. In fact, Microsoft recommends that it be the last possible option for system recovery, to be used only after you've attempted other methods. In many cases, you'll be able to get back into the system using Safe Mode, Last Known Good Configuration (LKGC), or other options we'll discuss in later sections of this chapter.

ASR sets are easily created by using the Windows Server 2003 Backup utility, which we discussed earlier in this chapter. On the **Welcome** tab of the Backup utility, click the **Automated System Recovery Wizard** button. This starts the **Automated System Recovery Preparation Wizard**, which takes you through the steps of backing up the system files needed to recover Windows Server 2003 and create a floppy disk containing the information needed to restore the system.

You can restore an ASR set through the Windows Server 2003 setup by pressing **F2** in the text mode portion of setup. After doing this, the ASR restore starts recovery by reading configuration information that was stored on a floppy disk when the ASR set was created. This information is used to restore disk signatures, volumes, partitions, and other disk configurations. A simple installation of Windows then starts and automatically begins restoring your system from the ASR set that was created with the Automated System Recover Wizard.

Installing and Using the Recovery Console

The Recovery Console is a text-mode command interpreter that can be used without starting Windows Server 2003. It enables you to access the hard disk and use commands to troubleshoot and manage problems that prevent the operating system from starting properly. With this tool, you can do the following:

- Enable and disable services
- Format hard disks
- Repair the master boot record and boot sector
- Read and write data on FAT16, FAT32, and NTFS drives
- Perform other tasks necessary to repairing the system

The Recovery Console can be started from the installation CD for Windows Server 2003, or you can install it on an x86-based computer. When installed on the computer, you can run it from a multiple-boot menu that appears when the computer is first started. Either method starts the same program and enables you to enter different commands to repair the system.

NOTE

You cannot install the Recovery Console on an Itanium running the 64-bit version of Windows Server 2003. You can still access the Recovery Console from the CD.

To start the Recovery Console from the installation CD, run Windows Server 2003 Setup. Press **Enter** on your keyboard when the **Setup Notification** screen appears, and then press **R** on your keyboard to select the option of repairing the installation. This opens the Recovery Console and enables you to enter commands at the prompt.

To install the Recovery Console as a startup option, follow these steps:

1. Ensure that the Windows Server 2003 CD is in the CD-ROM drive.
2. Click **Start | Run**.
3. Enter the drive letter of your CD-ROM drive, then type **/I386/Winnt32.exe /cmdcons**.
4. A message box appears, asking if you'd like to install Recovery Console as a startup option and telling you that it takes approximately 7MB of disk space. Click **Yes**.
5. Windows Setup starts and the Recovery Console is installed.

Upon restarting your computer, you see a multi-boot menu that enables you to start different operating systems installed on the computer. On this menu, you also see an option labeled **Microsoft Windows Recovery Console**. Select it to highlight it and press **Enter** on your keyboard to start the Recovery Console.

When the Recovery Console starts, you must select the Windows installation you'd like to log onto, and enter the password for the Administrator account for that installation. The built-in Administrator account is the only account you can use to run the Recovery Console on Windows Server 2003.

Head of the Class...

Automatic Logon for Recovery Console

You can set the Recovery Console for automatic administrator logon, so that you won't be prompted to enter a username and password when you start it. Before doing this, be sure to consider the security implications: if someone has physical access to your server, he or she can start the Recovery Console and perform all the administrative functions that it provides. We recommend that you set automatic logon only if your server is physically secured.

To set up automatic logon, perform the following steps:

1. Log on with an administrative account.
2. Click **Start | Settings | Control Panel | Administrative Tools | Local Security Policy**.
3. Expand **Security Settings** in the left console pane. Under that, expand **Local Policies**.
4. Click **Security Options**.
5. In the right details pane, double-click **Recovery Console: Allow automatic administrative logon**.
6. On the policy properties sheet, select **Enable**.

The new policy takes effect immediately and you should not be prompted for a password when you start the Recovery Console.

You can accomplish the same thing by editing the following Registry key:

```
HKEY_LOCAL_MACHINE\SOFTWARE\Microsoft\WindowsNT\CurrentVersion\
    Setup\RecoveryConsole.
```

Create a DWORD value called **SecurityLevel** (if it does not exist) and set its value to **1**.

The Recovery Console provides a prompt where you can enter text-based commands. The commands available to you are shown in Table 10.10.

Table 10.10 Commands For Recovery Console

Command	Description
ATTRIB	Enables you to view and change attributes on a file or directory
BATCH	Executes commands in a text file
BOOTCFG	Used for boot configuration and recovery. Enables you to scan disks for Windows installations, add an installation of Windows to the boot list, set the default boot entry, list entries in the boot list, and configure other parameters related to boot configuration.
CD	Displays the name of the current directory and enables you to change to a new directory
CHDIR	Displays the name of the current directory and enables you to change to a new directory
CHKDSK	Checks the disk for errors and displays results
CLS	Clears the screen
COPY	Copies a file to another location
DEL	Deletes a file
DELETE	Deletes a file
DIR	Displays the contents of a directory
DISABLE	Disables a service
DISKPART	Used to manage partitions on a hard disk. Enables you to add and delete partitions.
ENABLE	Enables a service
EXIT	Exits the Recovery Console and restarts the computer
EXPAND	Expands a compressed file
FIXBOOT	Creates a new boot sector on the system partition
FIXMBR	Used to repair the master boot record on the boot partition
FORMAT	Formats a disk
HELP	Displays commands available to use in the Recovery Console
LISTSVC	Lists available services and drivers

Continued

Table 10.10 Commands For Recovery Console

Command	Description
LOGON	Enables you to log on to an installation of Windows
MAP	Displays a list of drive letter mappings
MD	Creates a new directory
MKDIR	Creates a new directory
MORE	Displays a text file on the screen
RD	Deletes a directory
REN	Renames a file
RENAME	Renames a file
RMDIR	Deletes a directory
SYSTEMROOT	Sets the current directory to the systemroot
TYPE	Displays a text file on the screen

Exam Warning

The Recovery Console is not a regular command prompt, so many of the commands listed in the table can only be used in the Recovery Console. Because the Recovery Console is used to recover the system when it cannot start properly, you cannot start Recovery Console after Windows Server 2003 has started. It can only be run prior to loading Windows from the multi-boot menu or from the installation CD.

Exercise 10.03

Installing And Using Remote Console

1. Insert the Windows Server 2003 installation CD into the CD-ROM of your server.
2. From the **Start** menu, click **Run**.
3. When the **Run** command box appears, type ***<cdrom>*/I386/Winnt32.exe /cmdcons**, where *<cdrom>* is the drive letter of your CD-ROM.
4. When a message box appears, asking if you would like to install the Recovery Console, click **Yes**.

5. Windows Setup starts and begins installing the Recovery Console. When this completes, another message box appears, informing you that the Recovery Console was installed. Click **OK** to exit the message box.
6. Restart the server.
7. After you restart, a menu appears, asking you which operating system you would like to start: Windows Server 2003 or the Microsoft Windows Recovery Console. Use the up and down arrow keys on your keyboard to select **Recovery Console**, and then press **Enter** on your keyboard.
8. After Recovery Console starts, a command-line interface appears on the screen, enabling you to enter commands at the prompt.
9. At the prompt, type **MAP** to view a list of drive mappings.
10. At the prompt, type **MORE C:\BOOT.INI** to view the contents of the BOOT.INI file.
11. At the prompt, type **LISTSVC** and notice as a list of available services and drivers are displayed on the screen. Press the **spacebar** on your computer to scroll through the list until you reach the end of the list and the command prompt appears again.
12. At the prompt, type **EXIT** to exit the Recovery Console.

Head of the Class...

Removing the Recovery Console

If you have installed the Recovery Console on your server and decide you want to remove it (for example, for security reasons), you can do so by deleting the files associated with it. Note that these are hidden files and folders, so you first need to ensure that the system is configured to show hidden files and folders. Do this through Windows Explorer, by clicking **Tools | Folder Options**, selecting the **View** tab, and then clicking **Show hidden files and folders** and clearing the check box for **Hide protected operating system files**.

Next, navigate to the root directory of the partition on which you installed the Recovery Console, and delete both the **Cmdcons** folder and the file named **Cmdldr**.

To remove the Recovery Console option from the boot menu, click **Start | Control Panel | System**. Under **Startup and Recovery,** click the **Advanced** tab and click **Settings.** This opens the **Startup and Recovery** dialog box. Under **System startup,** click **Edit**. This opens the **boot.ini** file in NotePad. Delete the entry that begins with **<driveletter>:\cmdcons.** Click **File | Save** to save the file.

Using Windows Startup Options

Often, problems preventing Windows Server 2003 from running properly can be resolved by using the startup options. These are different options for starting Windows that can be accessed when you boot the computer. If you install new software, devices, or other components and find Windows Server 2003 doesn't load properly afterwards, the startup options can be used to load Windows with minimal drivers, VGA display, and other minimal settings. After the operating system starts, you can then use the utilities in Windows Server 2003 to resolve issues that prevent it from starting normally.

The Windows startup options can be displayed by pressing **F8** when the computer starts. This produces a menu of different options for starting the operating system. There are eight possible methods of starting Windows from this menu:

- Safe Mode
- Safe Mode with Networking
- Safe Mode with Command Prompt
- Enable Boot Logging
- Enable VGA Mode
- Last Known Good Configuration
- Directory Service Restore Mode
- Debugging Mode

In the following sections, we will look at each of these in a little more detail.

Safe Mode

Safe Mode starts Windows Server 2003 with the minimum files and drivers needed for it to load. This includes such elements as a mouse driver (except serial mice), keyboard, monitor, and base video, mass storage device drivers, and default system services. Starting Windows 2003 in this mode does not load the drivers and files required for network connectivity, thus making the server a stand-alone machine. After Windows Server 2003 loads in Safe Mode, you can then use the tools in Windows Server 2003 to adjust settings, or uninstall software that is preventing it from loading normally.

Safe Mode with Networking

Safe Mode with Networking starts Windows Server 2003 with the same minimum files and drivers as Safe Mode, but also loads the drivers needed to make connections to the network. With network connections, you can access resources that might be needed to restore your server to a working state. For example, if you need to uninstall a device driver that was causing problems, you might need to access documentation on the device or old drivers residing on another server. Without network connectivity, such resources might be inaccessible and the problem couldn't be fixed.

Safe Mode with Command Prompt

Safe Mode with Command Prompt enables you to start Windows Server 2003 with minimum files and drivers, but does not load the Windows Server 2003 Graphical User Interface (GUI). Instead, a command prompt is displayed, enabling you to enter text-based commands. This option is particularly important when the GUI interface fails to load properly, and the only way to access the system is through a command-line interface. It is also useful when you're comfortable using text-based commands, and using such an interface restores the system faster than waiting for a GUI interface to load.

TEST DAY TIP

Although you might have questions on the exam about starting in Safe Mode to recover a system, read the question carefully to determine which option is actually being used. Safe Mode can also be started with Networking or with the command prompt, rather than the normal Windows desktop, taskbar, and Start menu.

Enable Boot Logging

When *Enable Boot Logging* is selected from the startup options, the drivers and services that are used by the system are loaded, and the results of loading them are logged to a file called ntblog.txt. The ntblog.txt file can be located in the directory containing Windows Server 2003 (the systemroot directory, named WINDOWS by default). By viewing this file after unsuccessfully attempting to start Windows Server 2003, you can determine where a problem occurred and at what point the operating system stopped loading properly.

Enable VGA Mode

Enable VGA Mode enables Windows Server 2003 to start with a basic VGA driver that provides minimal graphics support. This mode is useful when a graphics card has been installed or display settings have been changed, and consequently you can't view the Windows GUI interface or other elements of the system properly. By using Windows Server 2003 in VGA Mode, you are able to load and view Windows Server 2003's interface and then make changes to the system so the new settings or graphics driver won't be used. When you do so, you should then be able to restart Windows normally.

Last Known Good Configuration

As you've probably noticed when shutting down Windows Server 2003, the operating system takes some time to save system settings before actually shutting down the server. This information is used in case problems occur and you need to use the *Last Known Good Configuration* that's available on the startup menu. When Last Known Good Configuration is used, Windows starts using the Registry information and driver settings that were saved at the last successful logon. This option is particularly important if you incorrectly configured Windows Server 2003, because using the settings that were saved during the last successful logon will load the operating system as it was previous to these changes.

Directory Service Restore Mode

If you are having problems with a Windows Server 2003 computer acting as a domain controller, the startup options provide the *Directory Service Restore Mode*. This mode of starting Windows Server 2003 is used to restore the Active Directory database and the SYSVOL directory. Because this only applies to domain controllers, this option isn't available on servers that have not been promoted to domain controller status.

Debugging Mode

Debugging Mode is the final method of loading Windows from the startup options. Software developers use this mode, because they are the only ones who can reprogram Windows Server 2003 after finding bugs in the operating system code. When this mode is used, debugging information is sent through a serial cable to another computer as the system starts. The serial cable must be connected to COM1 port, and the baud rate must be set at 115,200 for this to work.

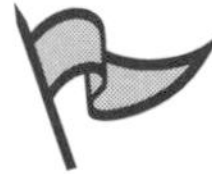

NOTE

Additional Startup options might be available if you have used Remote Installation Services to install the operating system.

Head of the Class...

Safe Mode Issues

In many cases, you can resolve issues that prevent Windows Server 2003 from starting by using Safe Mode or other startup options. You should try to solve the problem by using Safe Mode, and if this isn't successful, move on to trying to recover the system by using the Recovery Console. As a last resort, you can restore the system using the ASR set, which can be used to overwrite system files and revert the system to a previous state.

When you use Safe Mode, the local administrator account is available to use and make changes to the system. This account is enabled in Safe Mode even if you've disabled it on the server. To prevent hackers from accessing this account through Safe Mode and making changes to your system, you should ensure that the administrator account is set up to use a strong password that is difficult to guess. A strong password consists of a combination of lowercase letters (a –z), uppercase letters (A-Z), numbers (0-9), and special characters (({}[],.<> ;:'"?/|\`~!@#$%^&*()_-+=) and has a minimum length of eight characters. If a

Continued

hacker starts the server in Safe Mode, he or she still must get past the strong password that this account uses before being able to make changes to the system.

To prevent hackers from gaining access to the server and making such changes, you should have the server located in an area that is physically secure (such as a locked room with restricted access). Preventing access to the server with locks, passwords, and other security measures limits the ability for someone to use Safe Mode for less than safe purposes.

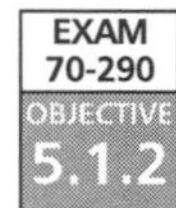

Working with Volume Shadow Copies

Volume shadow copies are used to provide copies of data at a given point in time. Users can view the contents of shared folders and see previous versions of data. This enables them to use these copies as if they were restoring a backup of data from an earlier time.

When shadow copies are made of shared folders, there are a number of benefits. If a file was deleted or corrupted in some way, you can open the previous version and copy it to the original location or another location. This also enables you to use previous versions to compare changes that have occurred between the versions.

The previous versions of files included in a shadow copy are read-only, preventing users from modifying the older version in any way. This maintains the integrity of the previous version, so it remains a duplicate of the file at the time it was initially shadow copied. If users wish to make modifications to it, the older version can be copied to another location.

NOTE

You will recall that by default, the Backup utility makes shadow copies. In this section, we are talking about additional shadow copies that can be manually configured through the Computer Management console.

Making Shadow Copies of Shared Folders

Shadow copies are created and configured by using the Computer Management tool. Using this tool, you can create multiple shadow copies for volumes and configure them individually. Configuration of shadow copies enables you to control where they are stored, the amount of disk space they take up, and schedule the frequency with which they'll be created. You can control many details in making shadow copies of shared folders on a Windows Server 2003 computer.

Creating shadow copies does have limitations, however. For example, you can't store an indefinite number of shadow copies on each volume you enable. For each volume that has shadow copies enabled, a maximum of 64 shadows copies can be created. This means you can view up to 64 previous versions of data. Once this limit is reached, the oldest shadow copy is deleted and can't be restored.

Enabling Shadow Copies on the Shared Resource

To enable shadow copies, open the **Computer Management** tool, which is available under the **Administrative Tools** folder of the **Start** menu or by right-clicking **My Computer** and selecting **Manage**. The **Computer Management** console has two panes. The left pane displays a hierarchical tree of various utilities for managing the computer. Expand the **System Tools** node and you will see a folder called **Shared Folders**. Right-click **Shared Folders**, select **All Tasks**, and click **Configure Shadow Copies**. This brings up the **Shadow Copies** dialog box, shown in Figure 10.16, which enables you to configure and manage shadow copies.

Figure 10.16 Shadow Copies Dialog Box

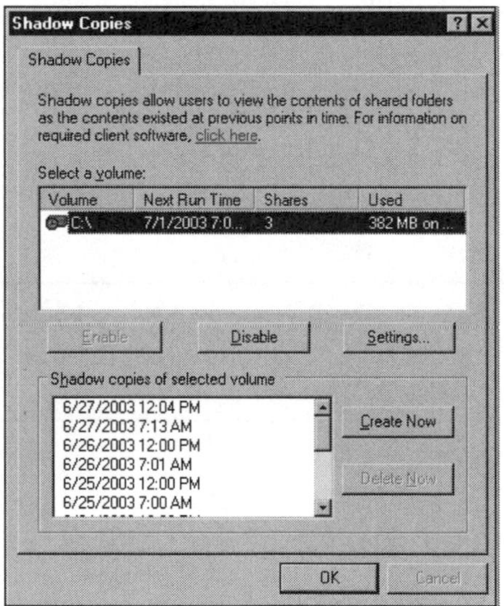

The **Shadow Copies** dialog box contains two panes. The lower pane of the **Shadow Copies** dialog box provides a listing of shadow copies that have been created, and lists the dates and times of their creation. The upper pane enables you to select a volume on the computer and click the **Enable** button below this pane to enable shadow copies on the selected volume. Note that by default, shadow copies are disabled on all volumes. To prevent a particular volume from using shadow copies, click the **Disable** button. When shadow copies are enabled, Windows configures the feature with a default schedule and settings. As you'll see later in this chapter, these settings can be modified.

NOTE

When you enable shadow copies on a volume, Windows Server 2003 presents a warning box that advises you that the default settings are not appropriate if your server has a high Input/Output (I/O) load, and that if this is the case, you should manually configure the settings to put the storage area on a volume that won't be shadow copied.

To enable shadow copies, you must be a member of the Administrators group on the local machine. If you are not a member of this group, you won't be able to make the necessary changes to the computer to enable, disable, or make modifications.

It can take some time after you click **Enable** for Windows Servers 2003 to do its work and enable the feature, so be patient. When it is done, a date and time appear in the lower pane and under **Next Run Time** in the upper pane.

Changing Settings for Shadow Copies

After shadow copies have been enabled, you can modify the configuration by using the Settings button on the **Shadow Copies** dialog box. Clicking this button displays the **Settings** dialog box. As shown in Figure 10.17, the **Settings** dialog box enables you to modify the storage area used for shadow copies and the schedule that controls how often they are created. The settings you specify apply only to the selected volume.

Figure 10.17 Settings Dialog for Configuring Shadow Copies

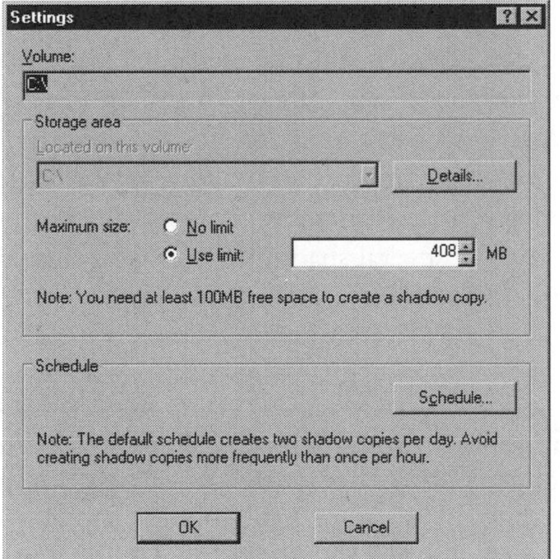

Defining Storage Options for Shadow Copies

The **Storage Area** frame of the **Settings** dialog box enables you to modify where shadow copies are stored and how much space is allocated to store them. Modifying these settings can improve system performance and enable shadow copies to be created more effectively.

The first field on this dialog box enables you to configure the volume on which shadow copies are stored. The drop-down list enables you to select different volumes on the server. However, if the computer has only one volume, then the current volume is your only choice and this drop-down list is disabled. Even if there are additional volumes, by default the storage area is on the same volume that is being shadow copied. You can click the **Details** button beside the drop-down box to view such information as available free space and total disk space.

The **Maximum Size** options below this drop-down list enable you to configure how much disk space is used for storing shadow copies. The options available to you are: **No Limit** and **Use Limit**. If you select **No Limit**, the system can use as much hard disk space as necessary to create shadow copies. If **Use Limit** is selected, you can specify the maximum number of megabytes to be used for storage.

The amount of available hard disk space is important when using shadow copies. There must be a minimum of 100MB available for the system to create shadow copies. By default, Windows Server 2003 uses 10 percent of the total disk space of the volume containing files to be shadow copied. If there is an insignificant amount of free disk space available, you should use another volume on the server for storage.

You should carefully calculate the amount of hard disk space needed for shadow copies. If a limit is set that is too small, you might prohibit the system from making an adequate number of shadow copies. If this happens, and a version of an older file is needed, it might be unavailable because Windows Server 2003 needed to delete it to make room for newer shadow copies. It is also important to remember that the number of files in a shadow copy and the frequency with which shadow copies are created affect the amount of space used. If you're creating a daily shadow copy of ten files that are approximately the same size, it takes less space than a few dozen similar files that are copied hourly. After viewing the size, number of files, and frequency of several shadow copies, you should decide whether there is enough room for the number of copies you want.

Exam Warning

Shadow copies retain only up to 64 previous versions. Once this limit is reached, the oldest shadow copy is permanently deleted. The number of previous versions is also affected by the amount of space available for shadow copies. There must be a minimum of 100MB available for the system to create shadow copies, but if this isn't enough for 64 individual copies, there will be fewer created.

Scheduling Shadow Copies

The **Schedule** button on the **Settings** dialog enables you to control when shadow copies are created. Using this tab, you can configure Windows Server 2003 to create shadow copies at any of the following intervals:

- Daily
- Weekly
- Monthly
- Once
- At System Startup
- At Logon
- When idle

You might notice that these are the same options as discussed earlier in this chapter, when we looked at how backup jobs could be scheduled using the Backup Utility. As with scheduling backups, each of these options provide the same additional configurable settings when selected. For example, if **Daily** is selected, you can control whether shadow copies are performed every day, every second day, every third day, and so on.

The **Settings** dialog box for shadow copies differs from that of the Backup utility in that you can create multiple scheduled tasks from this dialog box. By clicking the **New** button, you can create multiple scheduled tasks for creating shadow copies. By default, two shadow copies per day are made. Although a greater or lesser number can be scheduled to be created, Microsoft recommends that the frequency at which they're created shouldn't be greater than two per hour. Exceeding this recommendation limits how far back a user can access older versions of data.

EXERCISE 10.04

ENABLING AND CONFIGURING SHADOW COPIES

1. Click **Start | Programs | Administrative Tools | Computer Management**, or right-click **My Computer** and select **Manage**.
2. In the left pane of the Computer Management console, expand the **System Tools** Folder.
3. Right-click **Shared Folders**. When the menu appears, select **All Tasks**, and then click **Configure Shadow Copies**.
4. When the **Shadow Copies** dialog box appears, a list of available volumes are shown. Select the volume on which you want to enable shadow copies, and then click the **Enable** button.

5. A message box appears, asking for confirmation that you want to enable shadow copies for this volume. Click **Yes**.
6. You can now configure the storage space used for shadow copies. Click the **Settings** button.
7. When the Settings dialog box appears, click the **Use limit** option in the **Storage Area** frame and change the number of MB to **250**.
8. Click the **Schedule** button.
9. When the dialog box appears, click the **New** button to configure a new schedule.
10. Select Daily from the Schedule Task drop-down list, and then set the Start time to **11:00 PM**.
11. Under **Schedule Task Daily**, change the number of days this is to run to **Every 2 days**.
12. Click **OK** to confirm these settings and exit the dialog box.
13. Click **OK** to exit the **Shadow Copies** dialog box, and then confirm your changes.

Deploying the Client Software for Shadow Copies

To use shadow copies, client computers need special software installed. The Previous Versions Client can be installed through a Windows Installer Package that is located on your Windows Server 2003 machine in \system32\clinets\twclient\ of the systemroot directory (typically named WINDOWS). After it is installed, this tool enables users to access previous versions of files that were included in a shadow copy.

Since the Previous Versions Client is available as a Windows Installer Package, it can be deployed to client computers in a number of ways:

- You can copy the installation package to a shared folder on the server, and then notify users that it is available for those who wish to install it. Users can install it by right-clicking on the package, and then clicking **Install** on the menu that appears.
- It can also be installed by double-clicking the package. This starts a wizard that asks the user if he or she wishes to install the software. The user clicks **Next** to begin the installation.
- You can also deploy the installation package through Group Policy. Software deployment through Group Policy enables you to offer software for installation, or force it to be installed, by either publishing or assigning the software. By using Group Policy-based software deployment, you ensure that the computers or users you select will have access to the Previous Versions Client.

Restoring Previous Versions of a File

Older versions of files included in a shadow copy are retained for a limited period. As mentioned earlier, a maximum of 64 shadow copies are retained, and fewer than this if there is a limited amount of disk space available. Because these previous versions of files might be permanently removed after a time, users might wish to keep a copy of an older version for future reference. Also, if a user accidentally deletes or overwrites the current copy of a file, it must be restored. Using the Previous Versions Client, users can restore previous versions without having to bother the network administrator to restore data on their behalf.

To view previous versions of a file, access the shared folder on a volume using **My Network Places** (or **Network Neighborhood**, depending on the client operating system). After opening this folder, you can right-click a file and select **Properties** from the menu that appears. When the **Properties** dialog box opens, click the **Previous Versions** tab. This displays a listing of previous versions of the file. Select the version you want, and then click the **View** button to open a read-only version of the file.

Copying a previous version of a file is also done through the **Previous Versions** tab. After selecting the previous version you want to copy, click the **Copy** button on this tab. This opens a **Copy Items** dialog box, which enables you to specify where the older version of this file should be copied.

If you want to replace the current version of a file with an older version, you can use the **Restore** button on the **Previous Versions** tab. When this button is clicked, a warning message appears, asking if you're sure you want to roll back the current version to the previous version of the file. If you click **Yes**, the current file is overwritten with the older one.

Sometimes, when using the **Previous Versions** tab, you might find that no previous versions of files are listed, or the **Previous Versions** tab itself doesn't appear. When no previous versions are listed, it means that no changes have been made to the file. If the **Previous Versions** tab doesn't appear, it means shadow copying hasn't been enabled on that server.

Exam Warning

The Previous Versions Client must be installed or the **Previous Versions** tab does not appear in the properties of a shared file. The **Previous Versions** tab appears only when viewing files across the network. It does not appear if you view files on the local hard disk (for example, by using Windows Explorer to access a local shared folder).

EXERCISE 10.05

RESTORING FILES FROM SHADOW COPIES

1. Using Windows Explorer, go into the **<systemroot>\system32\clinets\twclient** directory on your server and open the folder relating to the type of computer that you are using (e.g., x386).
2. Double-click the Windows Installer package in this folder to start the wizard.
3. When the **Previous Versions Client Wizard** appears, click **Next**.
4. After the Previous Versions Client fully installs, use **My Network Places** to access the shared folder you shadow copied in the previous exercise.
5. Right-click a file within that folder, and then click **Properties** on the menu that appears.
6. Click the **Previous Versions** tab.
7. Select a previous version from the list on this tab, and then click the **View** button. The previous version opens in the program with which it is associated.

Shadow Copies Best Practices

While shadow copies provide a useful tool for users to view, copy, and restore older versions of files, they shouldn't be considered a substitute for regular backups. Shadow copies make copies of files stored on shared folders, but do not provide a duplicate of every file on the system that can be restored after Windows Server 2003 fails. In addition to enabling shadow copies, you should also routinely back up your system.

Shadow copies shouldn't be created on dual-boot systems. If your computer has Windows Server 2003 server and Windows NT 4.0 installed on it in a dual-boot configuration, shadow copies that persist when you restart the older operating system might be corrupted. To avoid this, enable shadow copies only on computers that exclusively run Windows Server 2003.

Scheduling when shadow copies are created should be based on the work habits of users. If multiple shadow copies are created, you don't want copies created when users haven't made any changes. For example, if no one works on the weekend, there won't be any changes to files so there is no point in creating shadow copy files during that time. As mentioned earlier, more than two shadow copies per hour shouldn't be scheduled, because a maximum of 64 shadow copies can be created on a volume. The more frequently shadow copies are made, the faster the older shadow copies are removed from the system.

If the server is heavily used, and there are a large number of disk reads and writes on the current volume, you should consider changing the volume where shadow copies are stored to a volume on a different physical disk. This enables the system to write shadow copies to a different hard disk and improve performance. However, this change needs to be made before shadow copies are created. If shadow copies are already present on the volume, you need to delete all the shadow copies on the volume before making the change.

Recovering from Server Hardware Failure

Recovering from disasters isn't limited to being able to restart the server or restore deleted files. Anyone who's ever had hard disks fail and lost important data can testify to the importance of a computer's capability to recover from hardware failure. Similarly, if a server becomes unavailable due to a major problem, network users are unable to access resources. To deal with the possibility of hardware failure, Windows Server 2003 natively supports different methods of recovery, including the use of fault-tolerant disks and server clustering.

The Role of Fault-Tolerant Disks

Fault-tolerant disks enable a computer to recover from a disaster, so that data won't be lost or corrupted. RAID (Redundant Array of Independent – or Inexpensive – Disks) provides several methods of writing data across multiple disks. If one disk in an array fails, RAID enables you to replace the damaged disk and recover the data quickly. There are many different levels of RAID available, both as hardware and as software implementations. Windows Server 2003 supports only two built-in software implementations of RAID: RAID 1 and RAID 5.

RAID 1

As discussed in Chapter 3, RAID 1 is based on disk mirroring or duplexing. Data that's written to one disk is also written to another, so that each disk has an exact copy of the data and one disk's data is a mirror image of the other's. If one of the physical disks fails, the server can continue operating by using the other disk. Because data from one disk is mirrored to another, two disks must be used to implement RAID 1.

When mirroring is used on Windows Server 2003, the first disk in the set must contain files to be mirrored. The second disk must be at least the same size as the first, because information from the first disk needs to be written to it. If it were smaller, then all the data on the first disk couldn't be copied to the second. If the second disk is larger, the extra space is wasted.

The two disks in a mirror are seen as a single volume by the operating system and share a single drive letter. If one of the mirrors in a mirrored volume fails, the mirrored volume must be broken, using the Disk Management tool. This makes the other mirror a separate volume. This gives the still-functioning volume its own drive letter and enables you to create a new, mirrored volume using the free disk space on another disk, in order to restore fault tolerance.

Additional fault tolerance can be achieved with RAID 1 by using separate disk controllers for each disk; this is called duplexing. If only mirroring is used, both disks can become unavailable if the controller on which they are installed fails. With duplexing, each disk is installed on a different controller, so that if one of the disks fails or a controller fails, the data is still available through the other disk in the pair.

Mirroring disks not only provides fault tolerance, but can also impact performance. Multiple reads and writes to the disks are performed each time new data needs to be accessed or saved. Because data is read from both mirrored volumes, this can increase performance, because two different disks are reading the data at the same time. However, when data is written to the mirrored disks, there is a decrease in performance, because both disks must have the same data written to them.

RAID 5

RAID 5 is disk striping with parity. With this level of RAID, data is striped across three or more disks, with parity information stored across multiple disks. Parity is a calculated value that's used to restore data from the other drives if one of the drives in the set fails. It determines the number of odd and even bits in a number, and this information is used to reconstruct data if a sequence of numbers is lost, which is the case if one of the disks fail.

Because RAID 5 requires parity information to be calculated, the performance of your server can decrease when data is written using this level of RAID. However, performance can increase when data is read, because the data is read from multiple disks at once. Since there can be up to 32 disks making up RAID 5 array, this can be a significant advantage. However, when a disk fails, the performance decreases because the server must reconstruct the data from parity information on the other disks.

RAID 5 also offers better disk utilization than RAID 1. When you mirror a disk, you must purchase twice the amount of disk space that you'll actually use for data. Fifty percent of the total disk space is used for redundancy. With RAID 5, the amount of space used for parity is equal to one disk in the array, so the more disks you use, the higher your percentage of disk utilization. For example, if you have 10 disks in the array, only one-tenth of the total disk space is used for redundancy and nine-tenths of the space is available for data.

The Role of Server Clustering

Just as it is important to have fault tolerance for the data stored on hard disks, it is also important to provide fault tolerance for the other resources on a server. Server clustering can be used to group individual computers running Windows Server 2003 together, so they appear to the network as a single system. If one computer fails, then others in the cluster can take over and provide services and other resources to users. Server clustering can be thought of as the ultimate fault tolerance method because the entire server is redundant.

Each computer that is part of a cluster is called a *node*. There can be up to eight nodes in a cluster, and the nodes communicate with one another by sending out messages called heartbeats. If the other computers in a cluster fail to detect the heartbeat of one of the cluster nodes, it considers this computer to be unavailable. At this point, a *failover* occurs, which means the resources of the failed computer are taken offline and another computer begins providing services in its place.

Because the cluster appears as a single system on the network, users of the network don't notice such failures. If a service is requested from one server that normally provides the service, and that server isn't available, the service is transparently provided by one of the other nodes in the cluster. This makes it appear to users of the network as if nothing is wrong with the server, and everything is functioning normally.

NOTE

In addition to making resources in the cluster highly available, another type of clustering is supported in Windows Server 2003 called Network Load Balancing (NLB). NLB enables the normal workload of a server to be divided among multiple computers. This improves performance because more than one computer is processing requests and providing services.

Server clustering is available on servers running either the Enterprise Edition or Datacenter Edition of Windows Server 2003. However, these two operating systems might be running different versions of the cluster service, which is needed to operate and manage the cluster database. Consequently, you can't mix these two operating systems in the same cluster. However, you can use Windows 2000 Servers as part of a cluster with Windows Server 2003 Enterprise or Datacenter Edition.

Summary of Exam Objectives

Disasters can occur at any time, and can result from any number of causes. To prevent disasters from causing extensive damage, you need to identify the types of disasters that can affect your business, and then implement plans and policies to deal with them effectively. Such plans include information on how to perform backups and restore data, recover from server problems, and address other issues that can make the business unable to function.

Windows Server 2003 provides a number of tools that can be used when problems arise. The Backup utility enables you to back up data, back up the System State, and create Automated System Recovery sets. By implementing these measures, you can prevent data and system files from being permanently lost during a disaster. If the system can't be started to access such tools, you can use the startup options to access the system using minimal drivers and files, or use the Recovery Console to restore the system.

Windows Server 2003 also supports methods for recovering from hardware failures on the server. RAID 1 (mirroring and duplexing) and RAID 5 (disk striping with parity) can be implemented to prevent data from being lost in the event of a disk failure. Services and other resources can also be protected from hardware failures by making them part of a server cluster.

By implementing the various measures discussed in this chapter, you will be better prepared for problems that threaten your network. Although none of these methods will keep your network completely out of harm's way, implementing them will put you in the position of being better able to restore technologies and services quickly when problems arise.

Exam Objectives Fast Track

Defining and Understanding Disaster Recovery

- ☑ A disaster recovery plan provides procedures for recovering from a disaster after it occurs and addresses how to return normal Information Technology functions to the business.
- ☑ Best practices should be followed when developing a disaster recovery plan. These include developing and implementing a backup plan, keeping installation CDs handy, using Emergency Management Services, installing the Recovery Console as a startup option, and specifying startup and recovery options.
- ☑ Disaster recovery plans should address the protection and recovery of assets within the company, including data, equipment, software, personnel, and facilities.

Creating a Backup Plan

- ☑ Backup plans help to protect data on a computer. When data is backed up, it is copied to an area of the hard disk or other media that can be stored in a separate location. If a user accidentally deletes a file, data becomes corrupted, or a disaster occurs, the backup can be used to copy this data back to the server.
- ☑ Windows Server 2003 provides a Backup utility that enables you to back up files on your server, regardless of whether the hard disks are formatted as FAT, FAT32, or NTFS. This data can be backed up to a file or tape drive and kept until it needs to be restored.
- ☑ The Backup utility provides five different types of backups that can be performed: Normal, Incremental, Differential, Copy, and Daily. The type of backup you choose determines how much data is backed up and the storage space required for the backup job.

Creating a System Recovery Plan

- ☑ System recovery plans provide procedures and information about how to restore Windows Server 2003 and other systems. You use the plans during a disaster as a guideline to restoring systems required by the business.
- ☑ The System State data is a set of files that the system uses to function and must be backed up as a single unit. It includes the Registry, COM+ Class Registration database, system files, boot files, and other files that are needed for the server's configuration and installed services.
- ☑ Recovery console is a text-mode command interpreter that enables you to access the hard disk and use commands to troubleshoot and manage problems that prevent Windows Server 2003 from starting properly.

Working with Volume Shadow Copies

- ☑ Volume shadow copies are copies of data as it is at a given point in time. Users can benefit from shared copies by being able to view, copy, or restore previous versions of data.
- ☑ The Previous Versions Client enables users to access previous versions of files across the network. When the client software is installed, users can view, copy, and restore files from the Previous Versions tab of the file's properties.
- ☑ You can schedule shadow copies just like you schedule backups. You can schedule Windows Server 2003 to make shadow copies once, at system startup, at logon, when the computer is idle, or on a daily, weekly, or monthly basis.

Recovering from Server Hardware Failure

- ☑ Fault-tolerant disks enable a computer to recover from a disaster, so that data won't be lost or corrupted. RAID (Redundant Array of Independent Disks) provides several methods of writing data across multiple disks.
- ☑ Windows Server 2003 supports RAID levels 1 and 5 as methods of creating fault-tolerant disks.
- ☑ Server clustering is used to group individual computers running Windows Server 2003 together, so they appear to the network as a single system. If one computer fails, others in the cluster can take over and provide services and other resources to users with no interruption in service.

Exam Objectives Frequently Asked Questions

The following Frequently Asked Questions, answered by the authors of this book, are designed to both measure your understanding of the Exam Objectives presented in this chapter, and to assist you with real-life implementation of these concepts. You will also gain access to thousands of other FAQs at ITFAQnet.com.

Q: I have developed a disaster recovery plan, but I'm not completely certain that the plans and procedures will be effective during a disaster. How can I be sure?

A: Perform "dry runs" of the disaster recovery plan to ensure that developed strategies work as expected, and revise any steps that are ineffective.

Q: I want users to be able to back up the files that they own. I have given them Full Control over the folders that belong to them on the server, but they still can't back up files. What is the most likely reason for this?

A: If a user isn't an Administrator or Backup Operator, he or she needs either Read, Read and Execute, Modify, or Full Control permissions over a file for which he or she has ownership. Since the users have Full Control, this isn't the problem. The problem might reside in the fact that disk quotas have been set. Disk quota restrictions prevent users from being able to perform a backup.

Q: I disabled the Administrator account on my Windows Server 2003 computer so that hackers couldn't use it to access the system, and I created a new account with administrator rights. After loading Windows Server 2003 in Safe Mode, I found that the Administrator account could still be used. I loaded Windows Server 2003 normally and found the account was once again disabled. Why is this happening?

A: You cannot prevent this account from being used in Safe Mode. Windows Server 2003 enables the Administrator account to be used in Safe Mode even if you've disabled it on the server. This enables you to use the account if other accounts are unavailable or don't have the rights necessary to make modifications to the server.

Q: I have tried modifying a previous copy of a file included in shadow copy, but find I cannot. Why is this?

A: Previous versions of files included in a shadow copy are read-only, preventing users from modifying the older version in any way. This maintains the integrity of the previous version, so it remains a duplicate of the file at the time it was initially shadow copied. To modify a copy of the file, you need to first copy it to another location.

Q: I made some configuration changes in Windows 2003, and now the server won't restart properly. What is the first thing I should try to recover from this so I can get into the system?

A: Use Last Known Good Configuration at startup. When this is used, Windows Server 2003 starts using the Registry information and driver settings that were saved at the last successful logon.

Q: I have configured a backup job to run, and now users are complaining that applications and files they're trying to retrieve from the server are slow. I need this information backed up, but want users to be able to do their jobs. What can I do?

A: Schedule the backup job to run when few people are logging on and accessing files and programs on the server. Backup enables you to configure jobs to run during non-peak hours, so that the backup process doesn't affect people.

Q: I have backed up data on domain controllers for tapes. I am concerned about leaving tapes in the same location as the domain controllers, but don't want them in an area where I can't get to them if needed.

A: Keep multiple copies of backup tapes, with one set onsite and another set offsite. By keeping a recent set onsite, you can restore data as needed using a copy that's at the same location as the servers. By keeping a set offsite, the backups are safe and won't be affected if a disaster destroys the original data on the servers.

Self Test

Defining and Understanding Disaster Recovery

1. A small company uses a single Windows Server 2003 machine to provide resources and services to users of the network. During a power failure, the drivers for the network card and graphics card for this server are corrupted. You want to connect to this server remotely so that you can repair the damage. Which of the following will you use to fix these problems?

   A. Automated System Recovery

   B. Emergency Management Services

   C. RAID

   D. Server Clusters

2. You are using the Special Administration Console to repair a Windows Server 2003 computer that has failed to start properly. When you try to use this tool, it fails to load properly. Which of the following will occur?

   A. SAC will restart, giving you limited functionality. You will only be able to display information about the computer, view log entries, and restart the server.

   B. !SAC will automatically load, giving you the capability to display information about the computer, view log entries, and restart the server.

   C. !SAC will automatically load, giving you the full functionality of the Special Administration console.

   D. !SAC will need to be manually loaded.

Creating a Backup Plan

3. Members of the organization store files on a Windows Server 2003 computer. Each department has its own folder, with subfolders inside for each employee within that department. A complaint has been made about an employee having non-work-related files on the server that are considered offensive. Upon checking the contents of that person's folder, you find it to be true. You want to back up the entire contents of this folder, without affecting the backups that are performed daily. What will you do?

   A. Perform a normal backup.

   B. Perform an incremental backup.

   C. Perform a copy backup.

   D. You cannot back up the files without affecting other backups that are performed.

4. You are developing a backup plan that will be used to routinely back up data each night. There is a considerable amount of data on the Windows Server 2003 servers on the network, so you want backups to occur as quickly as possible. Due to the mission-critical nature of much of this data, you also want data to be restored as quickly as possible following a disaster. Based on these needs, which of the following backup types will you use in your plan?

   A. Perform a normal backup each night.

   B. Perform a daily backup each night.

   C. Perform a normal backup, followed by nightly incremental backups.

   D. Perform a normal backup, followed by nightly differential backups.

5. A user has ownership of files in a shared folder located on a Windows Server 2003 computer and wants to perform a backup of her files. She is a standard user, with no special rights or group memberships. Due to the amount of free disk space and the need of users to store sizable files, there are no restrictions on how much data a user can store on the server. The user has to temporarily perform the duties of a coworker who also uses this folder for his work. After modifying documents belonging to this person over the day, she tries to back up the files but finds she cannot. She calls and complains to you about the problem, hoping you can help. What is most likely the reason for this problem? (Choose all that apply.)

   A. She doesn't have the minimum permissions necessary to back up these files.

   B. She is not an Administrator or Backup Operator.

   C. She does not have ownership of the files.

   D. Disk quota restrictions are preventing the backup.

6. You schedule a backup to run Monthly on the 30th of each month. When configuring this job, you also specify that the computer is to stop the task if it runs for 72 hours, or if the computer begins running on battery power. You also set the job to start only if the computer has been idle for at least 20 minutes and to retry for up to 60 minutes if it is not. Ten minutes before leaving at 5:00 PM on Friday, you recheck these settings. On Sunday, March 1st, you are called in to take care of a separate problem and find that the backup job didn't start. Based on this information, what is most likely the reason for this problem?

   A. You checked the settings before leaving at the end of the day.

   B. More than 72 hours has passed since the job first started.

   C. Since it is set to run every 30 days, 30 days haven't elapsed since the last backup.

   D. There aren't 30 days in this month.

7. You are using the Backup utility to back up the System State of a Windows Server 2003 computer. This server contains data files used by users of the network. It also acts as a Web server for the local intranet, and enables users to view information in HTML format on the network. Which of the following files will be included when the System State is backed up? (Choose all that apply.)

   A. IIS Metadirectory

   B. COM+ Class Registration database

   C. SYSVOL directory

   D. Certificate Services database

Creating a System Recovery Plan

8. The master boot record on the boot partition of your Windows Server 2003 computer has become damaged. When the computer tries to start, it fails before displaying the multi-boot menu that enables you to choose which operating system to start, preventing you from accessing utilities that are available after Windows Server 2003 starts. How will you fix the problem?

   A. Restore the master boot record from an Automated System Recovery set.

   B. At startup, press the F8 key to access the startup options and use the utilities that appear to fix the master boot record on the boot partition.

   C. Run the Recovery Console from the menu that appears at system startup and use the FIXMBR command to repair the master boot record on the boot partition.

   D. Run the Recovery Console from the installation CD and use the FIXMBR command to repair the master boot record on the boot partition.

9. A server on your network acts as a file server and Web server, but isn't configured as a domain controller. You have modified settings in the Registry dealing with services that load automatically in the hopes of improving system performance. After making these modifications, you try to restart Windows but find that it can't load properly. Which of the following startup options will you use to attempt to resolve this problem?

   A. Last Known Good Configuration

   B. Enable VGA Mode

   C. Directory Service Restore Mode

   D. Debugging Mode

Working with Volume Shadow Copies

10. A user attempts to view the previous versions of a file that's been shadow copied on the server. When he tries to view the previous versions, he finds that he cannot. When he views the file's properties, there is no tab for previous versions. Other users of the network are not experiencing this problem and are able to view previous versions without any issues. What is most likely the cause of this problem?

    A. Shadow copying isn't enabled

    B. There have been no modifications to the file since shadow copying was enabled.

    C. The Previous Versions Client hasn't been installed on the server.

    D. The Previous Versions Client hasn't been installed on the user's computer.

11. A user has asked for your assistance in accessing a previous version of a file and restoring it to another location on the hard disk so it can be modified. How will you assist this user?

    A. From the Previous Versions tab on the properties of the file, click **Copy** and specify the new location for the file.

    B. From the Previous Versions tab on the properties of the file, click **Restore** and specify the new location for the file.

    C. From the Previous Versions tab on the properties of the file, click **View** and specify the new location for the file when asked where the file should be copied before opening it.

    D. Right-click the file and click **Restore** from the menu that appears. When the dialog box appears, specify the new location for the file

12. A Windows Server 2003 computer has a shared folder filled with files in the local path C:\Shared. Shadow copying is enabled, and the client software is installed on the server. To confirm everything is working properly, you open Windows Explorer and attempt to view the previous version of a file by accessing it through C:\Shared. When attempting to access it, you find that there is no tab for previous versions. What is the problem?

    A. The client software cannot be installed on the server; this prevents you from viewing the previous versions.

    B. The client software has been installed prior to enabling shadow copying on the server.

    C. The Previous Versions tab is available only when clients attempt to view the properties over the network.

    D. There is nothing shared on the server, preventing shadow copying from working.

Recovering from Server Hardware Failure

13. You have decided to implement RAID to provide fault tolerance for data stored on hard disks on the server. The level of RAID you plan to implement is RAID 5. The Windows Server 2003 computer on which you plan to implement RAID has 256MB of memory, one 500MB hard disk, one 800MB hard disk, and acts as a domain controller. Can RAID 5 be installed on this machine as it is?

    A. Yes. It meets the minimum requirements for RAID 5.

    B. No. There isn't enough memory installed on the server.

    C. No. The hard disks are different sizes.

    D. No. There aren't enough hard disks installed.

14. A Windows Server 2003 computer uses RAID 5 for fault tolerance. One of the disks fails. What will happen to the data in this set?

    A. Data will be regenerated from parity information on the other disks.

    B. The mirrored volume must be broken using the Disk Management tool to make the other mirror a separate volume.

    C. RAID 5 only improves performance; it isn't fault tolerant. The data will be lost.

    D. The data will need to be reinstalled from a backup.

15. Your server is running Windows Server 2003. The machine has two disk drives installed that are 10GB and 20GB in size. You have decided to use disk duplexing for fault tolerance. Which of the following will you need to do to implement this? (Choose all that apply.)

    A. Mirror the two drives so that data from the 10GB drive is also written to the 20GB drive.

    B. Mirror the two drives so that data from the 20GB drive is also written to the 10GB drive.

    C. Install each drive on a separate disk controller.

    D. Install each drive on the same disk controller.

Self Test Quick Answer Key

For complete questions, answers, and explanations to the Self Test questions in this chapter as well as the other chapters in this book, see the Self Test Appendix.

1. **B**
2. **B**
3. **C**
4. **D**
5. **B, C**
6. **D**
7. **A, B**
8. **D**
9. **A**
10. **D**
11. **A**
12. **C**
13. **D**
14. **A**
15. **A, C**

Appendix

MCSA/MCSE 70-290

Self Test Questions, Answers, and Explanations

This appendix provides complete Self Test Questions, Answers, and Explanations for each chapter.

Chapter 1: Overview of Windows Server 2003

What's New in Windows Server 2003?

1. Your company has decided to put in a Windows-based Network Address Translation (NAT) server. Your boss wants to use Windows 2000 if possible because you already own a license for it. You have been tasked with determining if Window 2000 will suffice, or if you need to go with Windows Server 2003. Which of the following required protocols will help you determine which version of Windows to use?

   A. ICMP

   B. PPTP

   C. L2TP

   D. HTTP

   ☑ Answer **C** is correct. Windows 2000 NAT does not allow IPSec traffic. Since L2TP uses IPSec for encryption, it is not supported either. However, Windows Server 2003 does allow NAT traffic via NAT traversal.

   ☒ Answers **A**, **B**, and **D** are incorrect because all three are supported in both Windows 2000 and Windows Server 2003 implementations of NAT. ICMP is the Internet Control Message Protocol and is used when (among other things) pinging a machine to see if it is responsive. PPTP is the Point-to-Point Tunneling protocol. It is a tunneling protocol used when connecting to a virtual private network (VPN) and uses MPPE for encryption. HTTP (HyperText Transfer Protocol) is used when connecting to Web pages.

2. You work for an online retail company. You have been tasked with creating a Web server farm to support your company's new e-commerce initiative. All of your Web servers are running IIS 6.0 on Windows Server 2003 Enterprise Edition. You want to spread the traffic across all of your Web servers, while providing the best possible performance. Which of the following features should you use to build your Web farm?

   A. Network Load Balancing

   B. Microsoft Clustering Service

   C. DNS Round Robin

   D. Windows Media Services

   ☑ Answer **A** is correct. NLB is used with IP-based services such as Web Services, Terminal Services, VPNs, and Streaming Media. NLB load balances by spreading all traffic across all hosts. It also provides fault tolerance by compensating for host failure. If one of the hosts in an NLB cluster fails, its work is redistributed across the remaining hosts.

   ☒ Answer **B** is incorrect because the Clustering Service does not load balance; it only provides fault tolerance. Answer **C** is incorrect because Round Robin works by creating multiple host records in DNS for one machine. Each record points to a different IP address. As clients make requests, DNS rotates through its list of records. This isn't as preferred for load balancing because it doesn't adjust for server failure. If a server fails in Round Robin, some clients will fail to connect because DNS will still hand out the IP address of the failed server. Answer **D** is incorrect because Windows Media Services does not support load balancing.

3. Your company wants to put in two new e-mail servers. E-mail is mission critical for your company, so you want to configure your e-mail servers in the most fault tolerant manner possible. Which of the following features should you use for your e-mail servers?

   A. Network Load Balancing

   B. Microsoft Clustering Service

   C. DNS Round Robin

   D. Windows Media Services

   ☑ The Clustering Service (Answer **B**) provides fault tolerance for applications that only allow one instance at a time. Applications such as Exchange and SQL are supported in Server Clustering (MSCS), but not NLB.

   ☒ Answer **A** is incorrect because Microsoft Exchange does not support NLB. You can only have one instance of Exchange at a time, because each user's exchange account can only be on one server at a time. Answer **C** is incorrect. Round Robin is incorrect for the same reasons why NLB was incorrect. Round Robin works by creating multiple host records in DNS for one machine. Each record points to a different IP address. As clients make requests, DNS rotates through its list of records. This will not work for Exchange because only one instance of Exchange can exist at a time. Answer **D** is incorrect because Windows Media Services does not provide fault tolerance.

4. You have been hired to restructure a company's forest. They have merged with another company and changed their name. You have upgraded all of your domain controllers to Windows Server 2003. You plan to use the Domain Rename tool (rendom.exe) from the server CD. Which of the following cannot be accomplished with this tool?

   A. Rename your domains

   B. Remove domains

   C. Create new trees

   D. Rename your domain

   ☑ rendom.exe does not allow you to remove domains from your forest, therefore Answer **B** is correct.

   ☒ Answers **A**, **C**, and **D** are incorrect. Rendom.exe does allow you to (Answer **A**) rename your domains, (Answer **C**) create new trees, and (Answer **D**) rename domains.

5. Your company has decided to migrate from Windows 2000 to Windows Server 2003. You have migrated all of your printers and file shares from a Windows 2000 server to a Windows Server 2003 server. Everything seems to be working fine after the migration, except that you cannot get to the printers Web page on the print server. This is how you administered your printers before and you would like to continue doing it this way. What could be the cause of your problem?

   A. The printers Web page is not included in Windows Server 2003.

   B. IIS is not included in Windows Server 2003.

   C. IIS is not installed by default.

   D. Your desktop doesn't have Internet Explorer 6.0.

   ☑ You can only manage your printers via a Web page if IIS is running on your print server. However, IIS is not installed by default in Windows Server 2003; therefore Answer **C** is correct.

   ☒ Answer **A** is incorrect because the printers Web page is supported in Windows Server 2003 as long as IIS is installed. **B** is incorrect because IIS is included in Windows Server 2003, although not installed by default. **D** is incorrect because using the printers Web page is not dependent on Internet Explorer 6.0.

6. You use a Windows Server 2003 machine as one of your file servers. Users are complaining that they cannot get to any shares on the file server. You can telnet to the server from a client's workstation. You log on to the server and verify that the shares exist and that the users have rights. However, whenever you try to map a drive to the server, it displays the message "network path not found." What could be the cause of the problem?

   A. The Microsoft client has been removed from the server.

   B. You do not have administrative rights on the machine.

   C. ICF is enabled on the server.

   D. The file server was promoted to a domain controller.

   ☑ Answer **C** is correct. The Internet Connection Firewall (ICF) restricts traffic into your server. If you have misconfigured ICF, it could cause some traffic to be allowed (such as telnet), but not allow the traffic you want.

   ☒ Answer **A** is incorrect because removing the Microsoft client from the server would prevent the server from mapping a drive to another machine, but not the reverse. Answer **B** is incorrect because you do not need administrative rights on a machine in order to map a drive to it. Answer **D** is incorrect because promoting a server to a domain controller would not cause the server to become unavailable.

The Windows Server 2003 Family

7. Your company has decided to get rid of all their fax machines. Now, instead of each department having its own fax machine, everyone will share the same fax server. This fax server will allow you to send and receive faxes from within Outlook. Faxing is an important aspect to company business, so you have been tasked with making the Exchange e-mail servers as fault tolerant as possible. You decide to put in a two-node Windows Server 2003 cluster. Each node will have four processors and 2GB of RAM. Which version of Windows Server 2003 should you use?

   A. Web Edition

   B. Standard Edition

   C. Enterprise Edition

   D. Enterprise 64-Bit Edition

   E. Datacenter Edition

   F. Datacenter 64-Bit Edition

   ☑ Enterprise Edition is the minimum version of Windows Server 2003 that supports clustering; therefore Answer **C** is correct. It supports up to eight processors and 32GB of RAM, making it the correct choice for this scenario.

   ☒ Answers **A** and **B** are incorrect because neither Web Edition nor Standard Edition supports clustering. Answers **D** and **F** are incorrect because this scenario does not require a 64-bit operating system. Answer **E** is incorrect because there is no need to pay extra for Datacenter when Enterprise Edition meets the requirements; Datacenter is overkill for this situation.

8. You work for a statistical analysis company. You are currently using Windows 2000 Server on a 1.4 GHz XEON machine. You need to upgrade to an Intel Itanium machine to support a new application. You want to use eight processors and 40GB of RAM. Which version of Windows Server 2003 should you use?

   A. Web Edition

   B. Standard Edition

   C. Enterprise Edition

   D. Enterprise 64-Bit Edition

   E. Datacenter Edition

   F. Datacenter 64-Bit Edition

   ☑ This question requires a 64-bit operating system in order to take advantage of the Intel Itanium processor; therefore Answer **D** is correct. Enterprise 64-Bit Edition supports up to eight processors and 64GB of RAM.

☒ Answers **A**, **B**, **C**, and **E** are incorrect because they are not 64-bit operating systems, which are required to take advantage of the Itanium hardware. Answer **F** is incorrect because this question does not need any of the features provided by Datacenter 64-Bit Edition. Since all requirements are met with Enterprise 64-Bit Edition, spending more for Datacenter 64-Bit is not necessary.

Licensing Issues

9. Your company is open 24 hours a day, seven days a week. Everyone works eight-hour shifts and there are three shifts. All three shifts share the same computers. Over the next six months, you will be rolling out Windows Server 2003 and Windows XP. Your company has 1,500 workstations, 4,500 users, and 50 servers. Which licensing model should you use?

   A. Per User licensing

   B. Per Device licensing

   C. Per Server licensing

   D. External Connector licensing

   ☑ Answer **B** is correct. In this scenario, you have fewer users than machines, making Per Device licensing the most cost-effective route.

   ☒ Answers **A** and **C** are incorrect because they would require you to purchase more CALs than Per User licensing. You could use these options, but you would be paying more for no reason. Always try to buy exactly the number of licenses needed without wasting any. Answer **D** is not a valid choice for this question. The External Connector license can only be used for connections made by people who do not work for your company.

10. You have been hired as a consultant to assist a company in migrating from Novell NetWare 5.0 and Windows 95 to Windows Server 2003 and Windows 2000 Professional. There will be 1,200 workstations and 10 servers. There are 600 users, and every user has two machines. Which licensing model should you use?

    A. Per User licensing

    B. Per Device licensing

    C. Per Server licensing

    D. External Connector licensing

    ☑ Answer **A** is correct. In this scenario, you have more users than machines, making Per User licensing the best option. With Per User licensing, a CAL is purchased for each user and allows them to connect to unlimited machines.

    ☒ Answers **B** and **C** are incorrect because they would require buying more licenses than required. Per Device licensing would require buying 1200 CALs, and Per Server licensing would require buying up to 6000 CALs, compared to 600 Per User CALs. Answer **D** is not a valid choice for this question. The External Connector license can only be used for connections made by people who do not work for your company.

11. Your company has partnered with another company to develop a new application. Your partner requires access to one of your company's terminal servers in order to work on the project. There will be about 1,500 users from the other company who will need to connect. Which of the following licensing models should you use?

    A. Terminal Server Per User CALs

    B. Terminal Server Per Device CALs

    C. Terminal Server External Connector

    D. Per Server CALs

    ☑ Answer **C** is correct. TS CALs cost around $150 each. Purchasing 1,500 CALs for 1,500 users would cost around $225,000. You can purchase a Terminal Server External Connector for around $8,000. It allows unlimited users to connect, as long as they are not employees of your company.

    ☒ Answers **A** and **B** are incorrect because buying the needed licenses would cost more than a Terminal Server External Connector License. Answer **D** is incorrect because Server CALs do not license you to connect to a Terminal Server session.

Installation and Upgrade Issues

12. You have three Windows 2000 servers that need to be upgraded to Windows Server 2003. Two of your servers are running Windows 2000 Advanced Server, and one is running Windows 2000 Server. All three servers need to be running Windows Server 2003 Standard Edition. Which of the following steps should you perform? (Choose two answers.)

    A. Upgrade the servers running Windows 2000 Advanced Server to Windows Server 2003 Standard Edition.

    B. Upgrade the server running Windows 2000 Server to Windows Server 2003 Standard Edition.

    C. Perform a fresh install of Windows Server 2003 on the machines running Windows 2000 Advanced Server.

    D. Perform a fresh install of Windows Server 2003 on the machine running Windows 2000 Server.

    ☑ You can upgrade from Windows 2000 Server to Windows Server 2003 Standard Edition, but not from Windows 2000 Advanced Server to Windows Server 2003 Standard Edition; therefore Answers **B** and **C** are correct.

    ☒ Answer **A** is incorrect because you cannot upgrade from Windows 2000 Advanced Server to Windows Server 2003 Standard Edition. Answer **D** is a possible solution, but it is more work than required. Since you can upgrade directly from Windows 2000 Server to Windows Server 2003 Standard Edition, installing a fresh copy wouldn't be the best choice. By upgrading instead of installing from scratch, you can preserve your applications and system settings.

13. You are creating a new Windows Server 2003 domain. You have installed DNS on a machine running Windows 2000 Server. You have created the correct zone and configured your soon-to-be domain controller to use the new DNS server for DNS queries. However, when you run dcpromo to create a new domain controller, you get an error message stating that a properly configured DNS server cannot be found. What should you do to get this working?

    A. You need to use a Windows Server 2003 DNS.

    B. You need to update your Windows 2000 DNS server to at least Service Pack 2.

    C. You need to enable zone transfers on your DNS server.

    D. You need to enable dynamic updates on your DNS server.

    ☑ Answer **D** is correct. During dcpromo, the machine being promoted goes to its DNS server and tries to register all of its new SRV records. If dynamic updates are not enabled, the new domain controller cannot register its records and displays an error message. If you enable dynamic updates and run the wizard again, the error will go away.

    ☒ Answer **A** is incorrect because you do not have to use a DNS server running Windows Server 2003. You do not even have to use a Microsoft DNS server; any DNS server will suffice, as long as it supports SRV records. Answer **B** is incorrect because you do not need any service packs for DNS to work on Windows 2000. Answer **C** is incorrect because enabling zone transfers has no effect on registering records during dcpromo.

14. You have decided to upgrade your company's Windows NT 4.0 domain to a Windows Server 2003 domain. You install Service Pack 6a on all your NT 4.0 machines and you verify that all of the hardware is compatible with Windows Server 2003. You install and properly configure DNS on a Windows Server 2000 member server. What should you do next?

    A. Upgrade the PDC to Windows Server 2003.

    B. Upgrade one of your BDCs to Windows Server 2003.

    C. Upgrade your DNS server to Windows Server 2003.

    D. Install Service Pack 3 on your DNS server.

    ☑ After all prerequisites have been met, you can start upgrading your domain controllers. The PDC should always be the first machine upgraded when you are upgrading a Windows NT 4.0 domain; therefore Answer **A** is correct.

    ☒ Answer **B** is incorrect because you should always upgrade the PDC first. Answer **C** is incorrect because you do not have to use a Windows Server 2003 DNS server when upgrading an NT 4.0 domain. Answer **D** is incorrect because any properly configured compliant DNS server will do; it doesn't have to be running Windows 2000 or have any specific service pack level installed.

15. You have a user who is not getting the correct settings when he logs on to his PC. You are running a Windows Server 2003 domain and the user is using a Windows XP desktop. You want to see which policies are being applied to the user when he logs on to his PC. Which tool should you use?

A. Group Policy Object Editor Snap-in

B. Computer Management

C. Active Directory Users and Computers

D. Group Policy Management Console

☑ The Group Policy Management Console (Answer **D**) is a new tool in Windows Server 2003 that assists in managing group policy. It has a reporting feature that allows you to run a query to see the effective settings for a user logging on to a specified machine. It allows you to see the effective settings without having to log on the user.

☒ Answers **A**, **B**, and **C** are incorrect because these tools do not show effective group policy settings. The Group Policy Object Editor Snap-in is used to configure the settings within a specified group policy object. Computer Management is used to configure system settings on the local machine. Active Directory Users and Computers is used to manage Active Directory objects such as users, groups, and machines within the domain.

Chapter 2: Managing Physical and Logical Disks

Understanding Disk Terminology and Concepts

1. Your domain controller currently has one 36GB dynamic disk. You want to add another disk and configure both disks into a mirror to provide fault tolerance for your domain controller. You shut down your sever and add the disk. After starting Windows, you go into the disk management MMC and verify that the disk is there. It shows up as unallocated space. You right-click on the C: drive, but Add Mirror is grayed out. You cannot select it. What could be the cause of your problem?

   A. You need to format the drive with the FAT32 file system first.

   B. You need to format the drive with the NTFS file system first.

   C. You need to upgrade the new disk to dynamic.

   D. You need to revert the C drive back to basic.

   ☑ Answer **C** is correct. Mirrored volumes can be created only on dynamic disk. The default state for a disk is basic. Until you convert to dynamic, no volumes can be created.

   ☒ Answers **A** and **B** are incorrect because the file system does not have any effect on creating a mirrored volume. Answer **D** is incorrect because both disks must be dynamic to create a mirrored volume. Also, you would have to rebuild your machine if you reverted your system drive to basic, because all data would be lost.

2. Your server currently has one drive that is used for the boot and system partition. You want to add a RAID-5 volume to use for storing user data. You shut down the server and add two new drives. After starting the machine back up, you go into the disk management MMC and

convert both disks to dynamic. You then right-click on one of the drives and select new volume. However, the RAID-5 option is greyed out. What can you do to enable the creation of a RAID-5 volume?

A. Format both disks as NTFS.

B. Format one disk as NTFS.

C. Add another disk to the server.

D. Revert both disks back to basic.

☑ Answer **C** is correct. RAID-5 volumes require at least three disks. In this question you only have two available because you cannot incorporate the boot and system disk into a RAID-5 volume.

☒ Answers **A** and **B** are incorrect because the file system does not affect the ability to create RAID-5 volume. Answer **D** is incorrect because dynamic disks are required to create a RAID-5 volume.

Using Disk Management Tools

3. You add two new SCSI drives to your test server. You decide that you want to use diskpart.exe to create a new volume on each drive. Every time you type a command you get a message back saying that no disk is selected. What is the cause of your problem?

   A. You need to set diskpart.exe to focus on a disk.

   B. You need to go into the disk management MMC and enable the ability to use diskpart.exe.

   C. You are having hardware problems with your new disks.

   D. Diskpart.exe does not work with SCSI disks.

   ☑ Answer **A** is correct. Diskpart.exe must be focused on a disk for your commands to work. You can focus diskpart.exe on a certain disk by typing **select disk *X*** (where x equals the disk number) when in interactive mode.

   ☒ Answer **B** is incorrect because you do not have to enable diskpart.exe. It is built into Windows Server 2003. Answer **C** is incorrect because hardware problems would not give you this error. Answer **D** is incorrect because diskpart.exe works with any disks supported by Windows Server 2003, including SCSI disks.

4. You have three servers that you manage offsite. You use a remote console command prompt to manage them. This enables you to open a command prompt on your local machine and have the commands sent to the remote servers. You want to mange disk quotas on the server using remote consoles. Which tool should you use?

   A. diskpart.exe

   B. rss.exe

C. fsutil.exe

D. quota.exe

☑ fsutil.exe (Answer **C**) has a quota option that enables you to manage the following quota settings: Disable quota tracking and enforcement, Enable quota tracking, Enable quota enforcement, Display quota violations, Set disk quota for a user, Query disk quotas

☒ Answers **A** and **B** are incorrect because they do not support managing disk quotas. Answer **D** is incorrect because no such tool exists.

Understanding and Managing Physical and Logical Disks

5. Users have been complaining that printing is slow. Your print server is currently using basic disk. All spooling takes place on a primary partition. You want to create a dynamic volume to see if it increases your performance. Which of the following volume types should you create?

   A. Simple

   B. Spanned

   C. Striped

   D. Mirrored

   E. RAID-5

   ☑ A striped volume (Answer **C**) provides the fastest read and write access of all the dynamic volumes.

   ☒ Answer **A** is incorrect because a simple volume would not have any better performance than the primary partition you are currently using. Answer **B** is incorrect because a spanned volume writes to only one disk at a time and cannot be any faster than a simple volume or a primary partition. Answer **D** is incorrect because it is the slowest method of all. A mirror writes everything twice. Answer **E** is incorrect because a RAID-5 volume (while faster than a single disk) is slower than a striped volume because of the parity is has to write for fault tolerance. You would use a RAID-5 volume only if you wanted fault tolerance.

6. You have an old server that is no longer in production. You want to make it into an MP3 server to hold all your music. It has four drives in it. Two of the drives are 20GB in size and the other two are 5GB in size. You want to structure the disks to give the maximum storage space possible so you can store all your MP3s on one share. You are not concerned with data loss because you still have all the CDs. Which of the following volume types should you create?

   A. Simple

   B. Spanned

   C. Striped

   D. Mirrored

   E. RAID-5

☑ A spanned volume (Answer **B**) provides a 100-percent drive utilization and enables you to combine different-sized disks into one volume.

☒ Answer **A** is incorrect because you want to store everything on one share. If you used simple volumes you would have four different drives and each one would be shared out separately. Answer **C** is incorrect because a striped volume requires that all disks have the same amount of unallocated space. Because all our disks are different sizes, a striped volume would not work here. Answers **D** and **E** are incorrect because we want the maximum storage space possible, which rules out mirrored volumes and RAID-5 volumes.

7. You just bought a new server to use as a streaming media server. You want to configure it to get the best performance possible. The server has two identical 50GB drives. Which of the following volume types should you create?

   A. Simple

   B. Spanned

   C. Striped

   D. Mirrored

   E. RAID-5

☑ Striped volumes (Answer **C**) provide the best read and write performance of all volume types. This question tried to trick you into picking mirrored volume by saying there were only two disks. Remember that striped volumes work with two to 32 disks. Don't always assume mirrored volume when you see two disks.

☒ Answers **A, B, D,** and **E** are incorrect because they provide slower access than a striped volume.

Optimizing Disk Performance

8. You use Disk Defragmenter to run an analysis at lunch to determine if you need to defragment your servers. The report states that your disk is extremely fragmented and suggests that you run a defragmentation. You don't want to do it during the day due to performance reasons. You come in after hours to run your defragmentation, but you get the error message shown in Figure 2.117 every time you open Disk Defragmenter. What could be the cause of your problem?

Figure 2.117 Running Disk Defragmenter

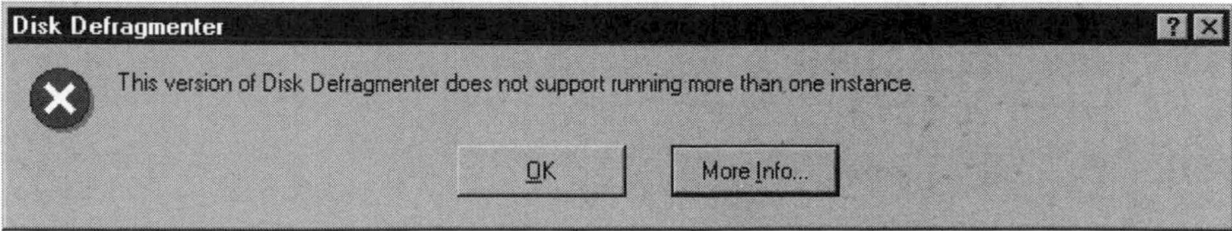

A. You are not logged in with administrative rights.

B. You installed this version of Disk Defragmenter on another machine and now you need another license.

C. You have defrag.exe running in the background.

D. You server has two disks in it. Disk Defragmenter only supports machines with one disk.

☑ Answer **C** is the cause of the problem. You cannot run defrag.exe and Disk Defragmenter at the same time.

☒ Answer **A** is incorrect because, although you do need administrative rights to defragment a machine, this is not the error that you would get. Answer **B** is incorrect because you cannot install or uninstall Disk Defragmenter. It is built into Windows Server 2003. Answer **D** is incorrect because Disk Defragmenter does work with multiple disks.

9. One of your coworkers complains that he cannot set quota limits on the file server. You check and find out that he is not in the local administrators group. You add him to the group and tell him to log off the server and back on again. When he logs on, the Quota tab is still missing. What could be the cause of the problem?

   A. The volume is formatted as FAT32.

   B. The volume is formatted as NTFS.

   C. He is not a member of the quota admins group.

   D. He is over his quota limit.

   ☑ Disk quotas are not supported on FAT 32 (or FAT) partitions; therefore Answer **A** is the cause of the problem.

   ☒ Answer **B** is incorrect because disk quotas do require NTFS. Answer **C** is incorrect because there is no such quota admins group. Answer **D** is incorrect because your coworker's personal disk quotas would not effect his ability to manage disk quotas.

10. You have a machine with two disks. Both disks are formatted as FAT32. When you defragment both disks, they report having unmovable files. You would like to be able to completely defragment the second disk. What should you do?

   A. Convert the second disk to NTFS.

   B. Remove the page file from the second disk.

   C. Use Disk Defragmenter to defragment the second disk instead of defrag.exe.

   D. Use defrag.exe to defragment the second disk instead of Disk Defragmenter.

   ☑ Answer **B** is correct. Page files cannot be moved during the defragmentation process. If you want to completely defragment the second disk, you must remove the page file.

   ☒ Answer **A** is incorrect because converting the disk to NTFS will not eliminate the problem of the disk having a page file. Actually, it will make the problem worse because the NTFS file system has system files that cannot be defragmented. Answers **C** and **D** are incorrect because neither tool will defragment a page file.

Understanding and Using Remote Storage

11. You have a server running Remote Storage on Windows 2000 Server. You need to upgrade the server to Windows Server 2003. You want it to continue to run Remote Storage after the upgrade. Which version of Windows Server 2003 should you upgrade to?

    A. Web Edition

    B. Standard Edition

    C. Enterprise Edition

    D. Datacenter Edition

    ☑ When upgrading from Windows 2000 Server to Windows Server 2003, you must upgrade to either Standard Edition or Enterprise Edition. Standard Edition does not support remote storage, but Enterprise Edition does, making Enterprise Edition (Answer **C**) the correct answer.

    ☒ Answers **A** and **D** are incorrect because they are not possible upgrade paths from Windows 2000 Server. Answer **B** is incorrect because Standard Edition does not support Remote Storage. Thus, if you are planning to upgrade a machine running Windows 2000 Server to Windows Server 2003, and you want to continue running Remote Storage, you must upgrade it to Enterprise Edition rather than Standard Edition.

12. You have a Windows Server 2003 machine running Remote Storage. You go into the Remote Storage MMC and try to add another local disk to be managed, but Remote Storage cannot find the disk. What could be the cause of the problem?

    A. The disk is a SCSI disk.

    B. The disk is an IDE disk.

    C. The disk is formatted with FAT32.

    D. The disk is attached to a Storage Area Network.

    ☑ Answer **C** is correct. Remote Storage will only manage disks that are formatted with the version of NTFS from Windows 2000 and Windows 2003.

    ☒ Answers **A**, **B**, and **D** are incorrect because Remote Storage will work with any local fixed disk as long as it is formatted with NTFS.

Troubleshooting Disks and Volumes

13. Your company has recently merged with another company named Novig. As part of the merger you are responsible for migrating all of Novig's e-mail to your Exchange servers. You do not want to migrate the mail across the WAN link, because it would be very slow. You send someone to pick up Novig's Exchange server and bring it to you so you can do the migration locally. However, when you turn on the server it has problems starting Exchange. You look in Disk Management (Figure 2.118) and see that some disks are labeled as missing. How can you fix this problem?

Figure 2.118 Troubleshooting Missing Disk

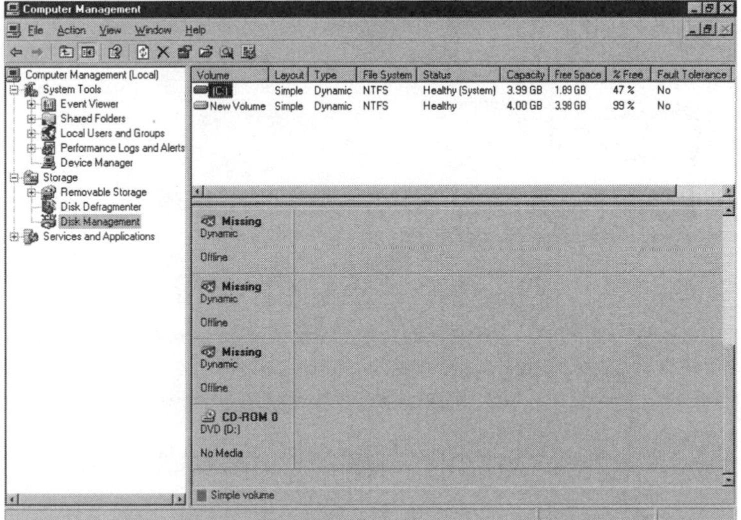

A. Format the drive as NTFS.

B. Verify that the disks are connected correctly.

C. Import the disks.

D. Assign the disks drive letters.

☑ Answer **B** is correct. Whenever you see a disk labeled as missing, it usually means that the system cannot find the disk. This is because the disk is not connected correctly or the disk has become so damaged as to be unreadable to Windows. Always check the connectivity before you assume the disk is bad.

☒ Answer **A** is incorrect because you cannot format a disk that Windows cannot see. Even if you could, you would not want to, because formatting a drive erases all its information. Answer **C** is incorrect because you should have to import a dynamic disk only if it has been moved between machines. These disks are still in the same machine, so importing is not needed. Answer **D** is incorrect because you cannot assign drive letters to disks that Windows cannot see.

14. You come in to work Monday morning to find that your file server crashed over the weekend and no one can access his or her files. All user data is stored on a single disk. To get things up and running quickly you have a spare machine that you are going to rename to match the name of the crashed file server. You put the data disk from the crashed file server into the new file server, but the disk does not appear in My Computer. When you look in Disk Management (Figure 2.119), you see the disk is labeled as foreign. How do you overcome this?

Figure 2.119 Troubleshooting Foreign Disk

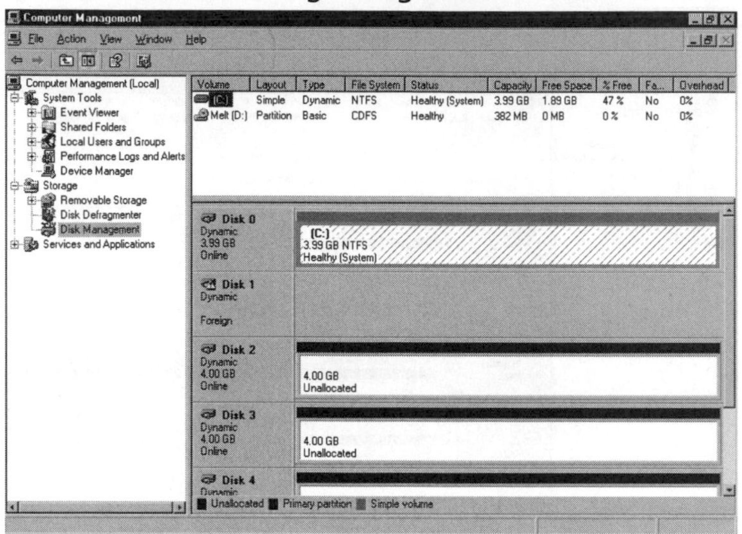

A. Format the drive as NTFS.

B. Verify that the disk is connected correctly.

C. Import the disk.

D. Assign the disk a drive letter.

☑ Answer **C** is correct. Whenever you move dynamic disks between machines, you must import the disk due to the hidden database used to store disk configuration. The server will recognize that this disk belongs to another server and will not use it until it has been imported.

☒ Answer **A** is incorrect because you cannot format a disk until Windows sees it as usable storage. Answer **B** is incorrect because a disk that is not physically connected to the server will not show up at all. Answer **D** is incorrect because you cannot assign a drive letter to a disk until Windows sees it as usable storage.

15. You add four new disks to your server to use for storage. However, when you go into My Computer, the disks do not appear. You guess that the OS just isn't seeing the disks, so you reboot your server. Still they do not appear in My Computer. You open Disk Management and the disks are there as shown in Figure 2.120. Which of the following must you do to get these disks to show up in My Computer? (Choose all that apply.)

Figure 2.120 Installing New Disks

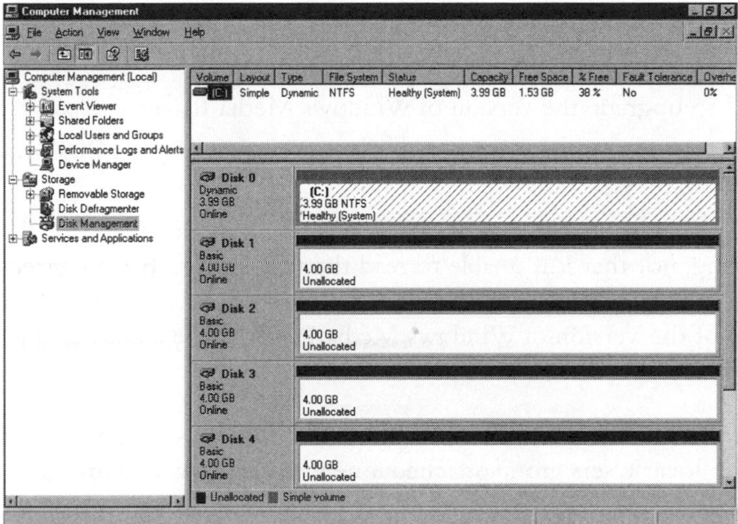

A. Format the drive as NTFS.

B. Verify that the disks are connected correctly.

C. Import the disks.

D. Assign the disks a drive letter.

☑ Answers **A** and **D** are correct. Disks are not assigned a drive letter or formatted by default in Windows. You must manually assign a drive letter and manually format the disks. Until you do both of these, the disks are not usable for storage and will not show up in My Computer.

☒ Answer **B** is incorrect because a disk that is not physically connected to the server will not show up at all. Answer **C** is incorrect because you should have to import a dynamic disk only if it has been moved between machines. These disks are new and have never been in a machine until now, so importing is not needed.

Chapter 3: Configuring, Monitoring, and Troubleshooting Server Hardware

Understanding Server Hardware Vulnerabilities

1. You are attempting to play an audio file using Windows Media Player on a server running Windows Server 2003. Windows Media Player tells you that the sound device is not working. What could be the cause of the problem?

A. Your audio file is the incorrect format.

B. The speakers attached to the system are not turned on.

C. Sound devices are not enabled by default.

D. You need to upgrade the version of Windows Media Player

☑ Sound devices are not installed by default on Windows Server 2003 systems, therefore Answer **C** is correct.

☒ Answer **A** is incorrect because Windows Media Player is saying that the sound device is not working, not that it is unable to read the file. Answer **B** is incorrect because Windows Server 2003 does not control the speakers. Answer **D** is incorrect because, regardless of the version of Windows Media Player, if the sound card is disabled it will not play audio.

2. What two conditions must exist for a device driver to be installed when someone who is a member of the local Users group attached a new device to a system?

A. The drivers must be digitally signed by WHQL and require no user interaction.

B. The drivers must be digitally signed by the vendor and require no user interaction.

C. The drivers must reside anywhere on the hard disk.

D. The drivers must be located in the device driver search path.

☑ The user is a member of the local Users group and there is no mention of administrative rights, therefore Answers **A** and **D** are correct.

☒ Answers **B** and **C** are incorrect because they will not enable a user who is not a member of the local Administrators group to install the device driver.

Installing and Configuring Server Hardware Devices

3. You have recently installed a new device into the system. You cannot locate an entry for the device in Device Manager, nor have you been prompted to install device drivers at any point. What should you do?

A. Use Windows Update to locate and install an updated version of the device driver.

B. Copy the device drivers to a directory in the device driver search path.

C. Use the Add New Hardware Wizard to install the device drivers.

D. Change the Driver Signing Policy options from Ignore to Warn.

☑ The device is a non-Plug-and-Play device that is only installed with the Add New Hardware Wizard, therefore Answer **C** is correct.

☒ Answer **A** is incorrect because Windows Update does not have the capability to install new drivers for non-PNP devices to which there is not already a driver installed. Answer **B** is incorrect because there is no process to initiate a detection of the device because it does not support PNP. Answer **D** is incorrect because the device is a non-PNP device and the driver installation has not even started to have driver-signing policy applied.

4. A server in your company has recently been upgraded to Windows Server 2003. One of the technicians installs a new device using an older Windows NT 4 driver he found on the hard drive from prior to the installation. Now when the system boots you experience a bug check (also known as the blue screen or stop error). You have disabled the driver using the Recovery Console. What should you do?

   A. Reconfigure the device resource settings to use another I/O port.

   B. Contact the vendor for a Windows Server 2003-compatible driver.

   C. Install the device into a different peripheral interface connection.

   D. Replace the device with a new one.

   ☑ The driver models have changed from Windows NT 4.0 to Windows Server 2003 and the driver is causing a bug check because it is attempting to access a function or part of memory that has been restricted in Windows Server 2003, therefore Answer **B** is correct.

   ☒ Answer **A** is incorrect because the scenario indicates that the driver used was an older Windows NT 4.0 driver that isn't compatible with Windows Server 2003. Answer **C** is incorrect because it won't matter what interface slot it is plugged into. Answer **D** is incorrect because it will not resolve the issue because the problem is the driver, not a bad device.

5. Your company has recently set a policy that all servers will use WHQL-signed drivers. You need to enforce this policy on the server. Which Driver Signing options setting should you use?

   A. Ignore

   B. Warn

   C. Block

   D. Use the setup default.

   ☑ The Block option will enforce that all drivers must be WHQL signed, therefore Answer **C** is correct.

   ☒ Answers **A** and **B** are incorrect because they will not enforce the policy. Answer **D** is incorrect because it refers to the setup default, which is Warn.

Monitoring Server Hardware

6. You have recently installed a new non-PNP device using the Add New Hardware Wizard. You need to configure some resource settings in the device driver but you are unable to find it in Device Manager. You verify that the device is attached and working. You need to complete this task with the least administrative effort. How can you gain access to the device properties?

   A. Restart the system with the Recovery Console.

   B. Restart the system in Safe Mode.

   C. Select Resources by Type in Device Manager.

   D. Select Show Hidden Devices in Device Manager.

☑ Not all non-PNP devices are listed by default in Device Manager. You need to explicitly specify to show hidden devices, therefore Answer **D** is correct.

☒ Answer **A** is incorrect because it is a lot more administrative effort and will bring down the system as a result, whereas you can access the settings using the correct answer (**D**) without having to restart the system and impact system availability. Answers **B** and **C** are incorrect because they will not give you access to the hidden devices.

7. Your server is reporting that the AFD Networking Support Environment driver is unable to start because of dependencies failing to start. You need to find the status of these dependencies. What should you do?

   A. Use the Service Control utility to enumerate dependencies of the driver.

   B. Locate the device driver entry in the HKLM\System\CurrentControlSet\Services registry hive and inspect the Enum key.

   C. Launch the System Information utility and export a report of the system drivers.

   D. Restart the system and enable Boot Logging.

   ☑ The Service Control utility's ENUMDEPEND option enables you to list the dependencies along with the status of those dependencies, therefore Answer **A** is correct.

   ☒ Answers **B**, **C**, and **D** are incorrect because they do not list dependency information.

8. You have been asked to make sure that the critical system files are intact on a server. What tool would you use?

   A. File Signature Verification tool

   B. System File Checker tool

   C. Device Console utility

   D. System Configuration utility

   ☑ The System File Checker tool will enable the user to do an on-demand scan of critical system files, therefore Answer **B** is correct.

   ☒ Answer **A** is incorrect because it will look only for unsigned drivers and not for other critical system files. Answer **C** is incorrect because it will not list the driver file versions. Answer **D** is incorrect because it will not enable the user to look at the driver files, just the overall package version.

9. You have installed a new device into the system, however the drivers that you were given with the device are not being accepted by the system as compatible. How can you determine if you have the correct device drivers?

   A. Check the Event Viewer for the hardware identification number and cross-reference that with the device driver's .INF file.

   B. Use the System File Checker to initiate an on-demand scan of the critical system files.

C. Use the Device Console utility to list the hardware identification number and cross-reference that with the device driver's INF file.

D. Use the Recovery Console to install the device driver.

☑ This will enable you to cross-reference the data that Windows Server 2003 uses to determine if the device driver is made for a particular device, therefore Answer **C** is correct.

☒ Answer **A** is incorrect because the Event Viewer will not provide the hardware identification number. Answer **B** is incorrect because it will not install device drivers. Answer **D** is incorrect because the Recovery Console will not enable you to install incorrect drivers.

10. Your company has recently merged with another company. You have been put in charge of assessing the servers from the other company to see if they meet your company policies. You need to check to see if there are any unsigned drivers running on the system. You need to complete this task with the least administrative effort. What should you do?

A. Launch the File Signature Verification tool on the servers to generate reports.

B. Look in the event log message detail for entries from the Service Control Manager on startup.

C. Check the contents of the Trusted Publishers certificate store and create a list of its contents to compare against the servers in your original environment.

D. Compare the contents of the SYSTEM32\DRIVERS directory with the ones on the original environment.

☑ The File Signature Verification tool generates the report of unsigned drivers with the least administrative effort, therefore Answer **A** is correct.

☒ Answer **B** is incorrect because the Service Control Manager event log entries do not show anything in regards to digital signatures. Answer **C** is incorrect because it won't show you if the policies are enforced for those certificates. Answer **D** is incorrect because it will not indicate if the drivers are signed.

Troubleshooting Hardware Devices

11. You have recently installed an additional network card into your server for users on a new network segment to access the resources. One of the support analysts calls you several weeks later to tell you that users on that network segment cannot access the server. You use Remote Desktop to access the console from one of the other segments. Opening the command prompt you run ipconfig to see that the device is not listed. What should you do?

A. Configure the network interface to use static instead of dynamic IP addressing.

B. Enable the network interface card using Device Manager.

C. Replace the network cable attached to the network interface card.

D. Plug the network cable into another switch/hub port.

☑ Disabled network devices do not show up in ipconfig, therefore Answer **B** is correct.

☒ Answer **A** is incorrect because it will not enable users to access the segment because the device is disabled and will not get as far as starting the TCP/IP stack. Answers **C** and **D** are incorrect because changing the cable and/or switch it is plugged into will have no effect because the device driver is disabled.

12. You have recently made some changes to the resources on one of the devices in your system. Since those changes, you have restarted the server and it now locks up before it is able to get to the log-on prompt. What should you do?

A. Disable support for Plug and Play operating systems in the BIOS.

B. Boot the system with the Recovery Console and create a new Master Boot Record (MBR).

C. On startup in the Windows Advanced Option Menu, select the Last Known Good Configuration.

D. On startup in the Windows Advanced Option Menu, select Debugging Mode.

☑ The Last Known Good Configuration option restores the components of the registry to a time in which the system was able to boot up and reach the log-on prompt, therefore Answer **C** is correct.

☒ Answer **A** is incorrect because the device resource settings are managed by the operating system, not the BIOS, so disabling support for PNP will not have any effect on the device configuration. Answer **B** is incorrect because creating a new master boot record will not have any effect on the device configuration. Answer **D** is incorrect because it will not reverse the change on the driver causing problems.

13. You have connected a new device to the system. You go to use the device and find that you cannot access it. In Device Manager you see an entry for the device with the following Device status message: "This device is either not present, not working properly, or does not have all the drivers installed. (Code 13)" What should you do?

A. Copy the driver to the SYSTEM32 directory and restart the computer.

B. Use the Add New Hardware Wizard to install the driver.

C. Launch Device Manager and enable the device.

D. Change the resource settings on the driver to point to a different memory address.

☑ **B**. The error code clearly indicates that the drivers have not been installed correctly, therefore Answer **B** is correct.

☒ Answer **A** is incorrect because it will not trigger any sort of detection process for the files copied there. Answer **C** is incorrect because the device drivers are not present to enable the device. Answer **D** is incorrect because the driver is missing and the system doesn't know how to see the device regardless of what memory address is allocated to it.

14. You have acquired a new device for your system. After installing the appropriate device drivers and restarting the computer several times, you are still unable to access the device. You look to the Device status in Device Manager to find the following message: "Windows is in the process of setting up this device. (Code 26)". What should you do to resolve this error?

   A. Unplug and re-plug in the device.

   B. Restart the computer once more.

   C. Launch the File Signature Verification and initiate a scan for unsigned drivers.

   D. Launch Device Manager to remove the driver, and then run the Add New Hardware Wizard.

   ☑ The driver's installation failed and it needs to be reinstalled from a clean state, therefore Answer **D** is correct.

   ☒ Answer **A** is incorrect because the driver installation failed and reattaching the device will leverage the existing installation. Answers **B** and **C** are incorrect because they will not fix the failed driver installation.

15. When you start your server you notice that the keyboard stops working when you reach graphical mode. You connect to the server using Remote Desktop and open Device Manager to find that the keyboard device entry has a yellow exclamation mark beside it. Under Device status you see the following message: "The device is not working properly because Windows cannot load the drivers required for this device (Code 31)." You need to get the keyboard at the console working. What should you do?

   A. On startup in the Windows Advanced Option Menu, select Debugging Mode.

   B. Replace the keyboard.

   C. Launch Device Manager, locate the device entry and disable and then re-enable the device.

   D. Launch Device Manager, locate the device entry and uninstall and re-install the keyboard driver.

   ☑ The driver needs to be uninstalled and reinstalled in order for the system to re-detect the settings associated with the driver and repair any corruption in the driver itself, therefore Answer **D** is correct.

   ☒ Answer **B** is incorrect because the drivers are the issue, not the keyboard. Answer **C** is incorrect because disabling/re-enabling the device will not solve the issue. Answer **A** is incorrect because the system in debugging mode will not result in the driver working.

Chapter 4: Managing User, Group, and Computer Accounts

Using Management Tools

1. You are a consultant and you work for several companies at one time. You keep your laptop in a workgroup because you are at a different company every day. You want to use Stored Usernames and Passwords to add credentials for each of the companies' domains so that you don't have to manually authenticate every time you map drives and print. Which tool would you use?

   A. dsadd.exe

   B. dsget.exe

   C. dsmod.exe

   D. gpresult.exe

   E. whoami.exe

   F. cmdkey.exe

   ☑ cmdkey.exe manages Stored Usernames and Passwords from the command prompt, therefore Answer **F** is correct. To add a set of credentials, type cmdkey /add:*domainname* /user:*username* /pass:*password* where *domainname* is the name of your domain, *username* is the username you want to store, and *password* is the password for the stored user account.

   ☒ Answer **A** is incorrect, because dsadd.exe adds objects to Active Directory. Answer **B** is incorrect, because dsget.exe displays information about objects in Active Directory. Answer **C** is incorrect, because dsmod.exe changes the values for objects in Active Directory. Answer **D** is incorrect, because gpresult.exe displays Resultant Set of Policy (RSoP) about users and computers. Answer **E** is incorrect, because whoami.exe displays information such as group membership, SID, and allowed privileges for the currently logged-on user.

2. You have a user who is complaining that he cannot perform certain functions when he is logged on to his workstation. You log in as yourself and it works. You log back in as the user and it does not work. You want to see what privileges are enabled for the user. Which tool should you use?

   A. dsquery.exe

   B. dsmove.exe

   C. gpresult.exe

   D. whoami.exe

   E. cmdkey.exe

☑ whoami.exe displays information such as group membership, SID, and allowed privileges for the currently logged-on user, therefore Answer **D** is correct.

☒ Answer **A** is incorrect, because dsquery.exe queries Active Directory for all objects that match the specified criteria. Answer **B** is incorrect, because dsmove.exe moves objects in Active Directory. Answer **C** is incorrect, because gpresult.exe displays Resultant Set of Policy (RSoP) about users and computers. Answer **E** is incorrect, because cmdkey.exe manages Stored Usernames and Passwords from the command prompt.

3. You want to create departmental OUs for each department in your company. You need to create a list of all users who are in the quality control department so you will know which user accounts to place in the Quality Control OU. Which tool should you use?

   A. dsadd.exe

   B. dsget.exe

   C. Dsmod.exe

   D. dsquery.exe

   E. dsmove.exe

   ☑ dsquery.exe queries Active Directory for all objects that match the specified criteria, therefore Answer **D** is correct. In this case, you would type dsquery.exe user –desc "Quality Control".

   ☒ Answer **A** is incorrect, because dsadd.exe adds objects to Active Directory. Answer **B** is incorrect, because dsget.exe displays information about objects in Active Directory. Answer **C** is incorrect, because dsmod.exe changes the values for objects in Active Directory. Answer **E** is incorrect, because dsmove.exe moves objects in Active Directory.

4. Your company recently replaced one of its fax lines. Doing so caused the fax machine to have a new number. You need to find everyone who is listed as using the old fax number. Which tool should you use?

   A. Active Directory Users and Computers

   B. dsget.exe

   C. Active Directory Domains and Trusts

   D. dsmod.exe

   E. dsmove.exe

   ☑ Active Directory Users and Computers has a query feature that enables you to search for all users that match the specified criteria, therefore Answer **A** is correct. In this case, you would create a query that searches for all users with the specified fax number. Queries are created in the **Queries** container at the top of the console pane in Active Directory Users and Computers.

☒ Answer **B** is incorrect, because dsget.exe displays information about objects in Active Directory. Answer **C** is incorrect, because Active Directory Domains and Trusts manages windows trusts and user principle name suffixes. Answer **D** is incorrect, because dsmod.exe changes the values for objects in Active Directory. Answer **E** is incorrect, because dsmove.exe moves objects in Active Directory.

Creating and Managing User Accounts

5. You have an administrator named Jeff who cannot log on to any of the servers. You are able to log on to all the servers with no problem. Jeff can log on to his two workstations without any problems. You verify that Jeff has the correct rights to log on to the servers. You think that someone has changed the properties of Jeff's user account to play a joke on him. What could be the cause of the problem?

   A. Jeff's log-on hours have been changed.

   B. Jeff's log-on workstations have been changed.

   C. Jeff's phone number has been changed.

   D. Jeff's account has been disabled.

   E. Jeff's account has been set to expire in two weeks.

   ☑ Restricting the machines Gary can log on to would cause him to get access denied messages when he tries to log on to other machines, therefore Answer **B** is correct.

   ☒ Answer **A** is incorrect, because the question states that Gary can log on to some machines. If his problem were log-on hours, then he would not be able to log on to any machines. Answer **C** is incorrect, because changing Gary's phone number would have nothing to do with logging on. Answer **D** is incorrect, because if Gary's account were disabled, he wouldn't be able to log on to any machines. Answer **E** is incorrect, because an account expiring in the future would not affect it logging on today.

6. You want to enable the user account for Will Carver. You decide to use the dsmod.exe tool. Which of the following commands will enable the Will Carver account?

   A. dsmod user "CN=Will Carver,CN=Users,DC=trainingconcepts,DC=org" -disabled no

   B. dsmod user "CN=Will Carver,CN=Users,DC=trainingconcepts,DC=org" -disabled yes

   C. dsmod user "CN=Will Carver,CN=Users,DC=trainingconcepts,DC=org" -enabled no

   D. dsmod user "CN=Will Carver,CN=Users,DC=trainingconcepts,DC=org" -enabled yes

   ☑ The correct switch for enabling a user account with dsmod.exe is *–disabled no*, therefore Answer **A** is correct.

   ☒ Answer **B** is incorrect, because using the *–disabled yes* switch disables a user account. Answers **C** and **D** are incorrect, because there is not an *–enabled switch* with dsmod.exe.

7. You need to reset the password for Sarah Todd. You want to reset it from the command line. For security purposes, you want to be prompted to key in the password manually. Which of the following commands will reset the password?

   A. dsmod user "CN=Sarah Todd,CN=Users,DC=trainingconcepts,DC=org" –password *

   B. dsmod user "CN=Sarah Todd,CN=Users,DC=trainingconcepts,DC=org" –pwd *

   C. dsadd user "CN=Sarah Todd,CN=Users,DC=trainingconcepts,DC=org" –password *

   D. Dsadd user "CN=Sarah Todd,CN=Users,DC=trainingconcepts,DC=org" –pwd *

   ☑ Answer **B** is correct. There are two parts to getting this question right. Part one is knowing that *dsmod.exe* is used to manage a user's password. Part two is knowing the correct switch to use with dsmod.exe (*-pwd*).

   ☒ Answer **A** is incorrect, because the *–password* switch is not valid. Answers **C** and **D** are incorrect, because dsadd.exe is not used to reset a user's password.

8. Your security team has requested a report listing all disabled user accounts. You want to write a batch file for them that will give them the information at any time. Which of the following commands would you put into a batch file?

   A. dsquery.exe user –disabled

   B. dsquery.exe user –disabled yes

   C. dsquery.exe user –enabled no

   D. dsquery.exe user –locked

   ☑ The correct dsquery.exe user switch for finding disabled users is *–disabled*, therefore Answer **A** is correct.

   ☒ Answers **B**, **C**, and **D** are incorrect, because they aren't valid options with the dsquery.exe command.

9. You need to change the password for all laptop users. All laptop users have the description "Laptop User." You need to change their passwords to Password01. To ease the process, you want to write a batch file to do it for you. Which commands should you put into your script file?

   A. dsquery.exe user –desc "Laptop User" | dsmod.exe user –pwd Password01

   B. dsmod.exe user –pwd Password01 | dsquery.exe user –desc "Laptop User"

   C. dsget.exe user –desc "Laptop User" | dsmod.exe user –pwd Password01

   D. dsmod.exe user –pwd Password01 | dsquery.exe user –desc "Laptop User"

   ☑ You need to use dsquery.exe to find all users that match the correct description and then import those commands into dsmod.exe to change the password, therefore Answer **A** is correct.

   ☒ Answers **B**, **C**, and **D** are incorrect, because you need to use the dsquery.exe command first to find the laptop users.

Creating and Managing Group Accounts

10. You have a multiple domain forest. You want to use groups to assign permissions to shared resources in a single domain to users through the forest. You will then grant permissions to the network resources by adding users or other groups into these groups. Which group scope should you use?

    A. Domain Local

    B. Global

    C. Universal

    D. Distribution

    ☑ Domain local groups can contain other domain local groups in the same domain, global groups from any domain, universal groups from any domain, user accounts from any domain, and computer accounts from any domain, therefore Answer **A** is correct. Domain local groups are the best choice here because they have more flexibility with their memberships than global groups or universal groups. Also, unlike with universal groups, changes to the membership of a domain local group do not force global catalog replication.

    ☒ Answer **B** is incorrect, because global groups can contain other global groups in the same domain, user accounts in the same domain, and computer accounts in the same domain. Global groups are too restrictive with their group membership to work in this scenario. Answer **C** is incorrect, because using universal groups would not give any benefits over domain local groups and would increase network replication. Answer **D** is incorrect, because Distribution is not a possible group scope. It refers to a group type. Distribution groups are used for e-mail purposes only.

11. You have a multiple domain forest. You want to use groups to organize your users. Users from each domain need to be in the same group. These groups will be used to assign permissions forest wide. Which group scope should you use?

    A. Domain Local

    B. Global

    C. Universal

    D. Distribution

    ☑ Universal groups can contain other universal groups from any domain, global groups from any domain, user accounts from any domain, and computer accounts from any domain, therefore Answer **C** is correct. Universal groups are the only groups that can contain users from any domain in the forest and be assigned permissions to any domain in the forest.

    ☒ Answer **A** is incorrect, because, although domain local groups can contain objects from any domain, they can only be assigned permissions within their own domains. Answer **B** is incorrect, because global groups can contain objects only from their own domains. Answer **D** is incorrect, because Distribution is not a possible group scope. It refers to a group type. Distribution groups are used for e-mail purposes only.

12. You want to create three new groups to assign permissions to resources across the forest. You want these groups to be universal security groups. However, you notice that when you create a group, the option to make it a Universal group is grayed out. You can create domain local and global groups, but not universal. What could be the problem?

    A. You are not logged in as a schema administrator.

    B. You need to create the group on the global catalog server.

    C. Your domain is in Windows 2000 mixed-domain functionality.

    D. Your domain contains Windows NT 4.0 member servers.

    ☑ Universal security groups cannot be created in a Windows 2000 mixed-mode domain, therefore Answer **C** is correct. To create universal security groups, your domain must be running in Windows Server 2003 native or Windows Server 2003 domain functionality.

    ☒ Answer **A** is incorrect, because you do not need to be a schema administrator to create universal groups. Answer **B** is incorrect, because, although universal groups are stored on the global catalog server, they do not have to be created there. Answer **D** is incorrect, because member servers do not affect the capability to create universal groups. If you had Windows NT 4.0 domain controllers, you would need to upgrade them to Windows 2000 or Windows Server 2003 in order to change your domain to Windows 2000 or 2003 native domain functionality.

13. You have a universal group that you need to convert to a domain local group. You want to use the dsmod.exe tool to make the change via the command prompt. Which of the following will convert the universal group to a domain local group?

    A. dsmod.exe "CN=Authors,DC=trainingconcepts,DC=org" –scope g

    B. dsmod.exe "CN=Authors,DC=trainingconcepts,DC=org" –scope u

    C. dsmod.exe "CN=Authors,DC=trainingconcepts,DC=org" –scope dl

    D. dsmod.exe "CN=Authors,DC=trainingconcepts,DC=org" –scope l

    E. dsmod.exe "CN=Authors,DC=trainingconcepts,DC=org" –scope dlo

    ☑ The *–scope l* is the correct *dsmod* option to convert a group to domain local, therefore Answer **D** is correct.

    ☒ Answers **A** and **B** are incorrect, because *–scope g* (global) and *–scope u* (universal) are not the correct options for converting to a domain local group. Answers **C** and **E** are incorrect, because *–scope dl* and *–scope dlo* are not valid options for dsmod.exe.

Creating and Managing Computer Accounts

14. You have a laptop that you want to join to the domain. Which of the following tools will enable you to create a machine account in Active Directory for your laptop? (Choose all that apply).

A. dsadd.exe.

B. Active Dirctory Users and Computers

C. Active Directory Domains and Trusts

D. dsmod.exe

☑ dsadd.exe creates Active Directory objects (such as computers) from the command line. Active Directory Users and Computers creates Active Directory objects (such as computers) from the GUI. Therefore Answers **A** and **B** are correct.

☒ Answer **C** is incorrect, because Active Directory Domains and Trusts managed trusts relationships and user principal name suffixes. Answer **D** is incorrect, because dsmod.exe modifies objects in Active Directory.

15. Your domain consists of a single domain controller and three member servers. You are worried that your only domain controller will fail and you will lose your domain. You want to make one of the member servers into a domain controller. Which of the following commands should you use?

    A. Active Directory Users and Computers

    B. dsadd.exe

    C. dcpromo.exe

    D. Active Directory Domains and Trusts

    ☑ Running dcpromo.exe from the Run window starts the Active Directory Installation Wizard that is used to create domain controllers, therefore Answer **C** is correct.

    ☒ Answer **A** is incorrect, because Active Directory Users and Computers is used to create and manage Active Directory objects such as users, groups, and computers. Answer **B** is incorrect, because dsadd.exe creates objects such as users, groups, and computers in Active Directory. Answer **D** is incorrect, because Active Directory Domains and Trusts manages domain and forest trust and user principal name suffixes.

Chapter 5: Managing Access to Resources

Understanding Access Control

1. A user attempts to open a file on the network. The user is not listed explicitly in the SACL for the file or its containing folder, nor are any of the groups to which the user belongs. What happens when the user attempts to open the file?

    A. The user is denied access to the file.

    B. The user is granted access to the file and an audit is triggered upon access.

    C. The user is granted access to the file and no audit is triggered.

    D. The user is granted read-only access to the file.

☑ Answer **C** is correct. The SACL determines if an audit event is triggered when a user accesses an object. Because neither the user nor any of the user's groups are listed in the SACL, no audit event is triggered, and the user is granted access to the file according to the DACL for the file.

☒ Answer **A** is incorrect because the SACL has no effect on whether the user can access the file, only whether an audit event is to be triggered when the user accesses the file. The user's access is determined by the DACL on the file. Answer **B** is incorrect because the absence of the user and the user's groups from the SACL does not trigger an audit event. Answer **D** is incorrect because read-only access to the file is given in the DACL, not the SACL.

2. A user who just transferred to the Marketing department calls you and complains that he cannot access the files in the Marketing share on the network from his Windows 2000 computer. You look at his account and find that he was not added to the Marketing group when he transferred to the department. You add him to the Marketing group and tell him he should be able to access the folder. He calls back five minutes later complaining that he still cannot access the folder. What is the most likely cause of the problem?

   A. The share name is too long.

   B. He has not logged off and logged back on since you added him to the group.

   C. He has not been given permissions to the files on the network, only to the share.

   D. The user needs to wait 15 minutes before accessing the share so the security changes can replicate across the Active Directory network.

   ☑ Answer **B** is correct. The user needs to log off and log back on for the new group permissions to take effect. The access token he is using does not have the Marketing group's information in it, and it will not update while he is logged in.

   ☒ Answer **A** is incorrect because his PC is running Windows 2000, which will see the nine-character share name with no problems. If he was running Windows 95 or Windows 98, this might be a problem. Answer **C** is incorrect because when you added him to the Marketing group, you gave him access to all files, folders, and shares that the Marketing group accesses. If there were access problems to the files in the share, you would have heard about it long before now. Answer **D** is incorrect because the user could wait 30 minutes and still not be able to access the share if he doesn't log off and back on. The user will gain the correct permissions at the next logon because that's when the access token is generated.

Understanding and Using Access Permissions

3. The employees in Marketing access their shared data through a share named Marketing, which gives them access to read, write, create, and delete files in the folder. They have created a new folder in the shared folder named Public. They have asked you to create a new share

to this public folder so they can make the contents of the folder available to the entire company, yet restrict access so only marketing employees can modify any of the files in this new share. How will you set up the permissions for the Domain Users group on this folder?

A. Set the share permissions and the NTFS permissions on the folder to Read for the Domain Users group.

B. Set the share permissions on the folder to Read for the Domain Users group and set the NTFS permissions to Full Control for the Domain Users group.

C. Set both the share permissions and the NTFS permissions on the folder to Full Control for the Domain Users group.

D. Set the share permissions to Full Control and set the NTFS permissions to Allow Read and to Deny Write and Modify.

☑ Answer **A** is correct. By setting both the share and NTFS permissions to Read for the Domain Users group, you ensure that everyone in the company can see the share and can read the contents of the folder. It is important to note that if members of the Marketing department access this folder through the new share, they will also be limited to read-only access to the folder. If they access the folder through their original share and not through the new share, they will still be able to make changes to the contents of the folder as expected.

☒ Answer **B** is incorrect because setting the share permissions to Read will guarantee that anyone who accesses the folder through the share will only have Read permissions on the contents of the folder. However, by setting the NTFS permissions to Full Control, if someone outside the marketing group were to access the folder by logging on directly to the server or through a different share, he or she could end up being able to make changes to the contents of the folder. Answer **C** is incorrect because setting both the share and NTFS permissions to Full Control will enable everyone in the organization to make changes to the contents of the folder and even delete items. Answer **D** is incorrect because setting Deny Write permissions on the folder will prevent anyone from making changes to the contents of the folder, including the employees of the Marketing department.

4. You have set up a folder share that your IT technicians can access to install application updates or service packs on end user workstations. You want to create a new subfolder that contains updates and service packs that have not been fully tested yet, and you do not want all your technicians to be able to access this folder. You decide to create a new group for members of your staff whom you want to have access to this new folder. How will you set up NTFS permissions on this new folder so that only members of this new group will be able to access the files?

A. Assign the desired permissions on the new folder for the new group. Delete the entry for the existing group on the new folder.

B. Assign the desired permissions on the new folder for the new group. Turn off permission inheritance for the new folder and delete the permissions from the parent folder.

C. Assign the desired permissions on the new folder for the new group. Turn off permission inheritance for the new folder and copy the permissions from the parent folder. Delete the entry for the group or groups that should not access the new folder.

D. Assign the desired permissions on the new folder for the new group. Deny all permissions on the new folder for the old groups that had access.

☑ Answer **C** is correct**.** Turning off permission inheritance for the new folder and copying the access permissions from the parent folder is the only way to ensure that all necessary permissions remain intact. Removing the entry for the group that should not have access is possible only when the permissions are assigned directly to the folder and not inherited.

☒ Answer **A** is incorrect because you cannot just delete the access entry for a group on the new folder since the permissions are inherited. You must disable inheritance before you will be able to remove the group from the list. Answer **B** is incorrect because deleting the inherited permissions might have adverse effects on the folder. If you do not copy the inherited permissions, the permissions for the Administrators, CREATOR OWNER, and other groups will not be transferred to the new folder. This can cause significant mayhem. Answer **D** is incorrect because Deny permissions supercede any other permissions assigned. If an account is in both the new group that has had permissions assigned and the old group that has had the permissions denied, that account will not be able to access the new folder. It is best to avoid denying permissions whenever possible.

5. You have two data volumes on your server, drives E: and F:. On E:, there is a folder named Marketing that has been shared to the employees of the Marketing department. The Marketing group has Full Control permission on the Marketing share, and they have Modify NTFS permissions on the folder. Drive space is running low on E:, so you want to move the Marketing folder to drive F:. The Marketing group currently has Read NTFS permissions on the root of F:. After you move the folder contents, what permission changes will you need to make on the folder so the Marketing employees still have access?

A. You will not need to make any changes to the permissions on the folder or the share.

B. You will not need to make any changes to the permission on the folder, but you will need to create a new share and give Full Control permissions on the share to the group.

C. You will need to change the NTFS permissions on the folder to Full Control and change the share permissions from Read to Full Control.

D. You will need to change the NTFS permissions on the folder to Modify, and you will need to create a new share and give Full Control permissions on the share to the group.

☑ Answer **D** is correct. When moving a shared folder from one volume to another, two things happen. First, the folder being moved inherits the permissions of the parent folder, in this case the root of F:. The Marketing group has Read permissions on the root of F:, so they will have Read permissions on the folder after it is moved. Second, the share ceases to exist when the folder is removed from E:. The share will need to be recreated to point to the new folder location, and permissions will need to be assigned to the new share.

☒ Answer **A** is incorrect because the users would only have Read access to the folder on the new volume if they could get to it, as there is no share. Answer **B** is incorrect because even though you will have to recreate the share, you will also have to change the permissions on the folder. Answer **C** is incorrect because even though you do have to change permissions on the folder, the share does not exist after the folder move for you to change the permissions on it.

6. Your company's Benefits department is currently under the Human Resources department. The Benefits group has Modify permissions on their shared folder, which is located on the server in E:\Shared\HR\Benefits. The HR group has Modify permissions on the HR folder E:\Shared\HR. Your company goes through a reorganization, and Benefits no longer reports to HR. You are asked to move the Benefits data folder from E:\Shared\HR\Benefits to E:\Shared\Benefits. You remove the employees in the Benefits department from the HR group. None of the other HR employees are members of the Benefits group. What NTFS permissions will you need to change so that Benefits still has access to the folder, but HR does not?

   A. No NTFS permission changes are needed.

   B. Give the Benefits group Modify rights on the folder after it is moved.

   C. Remove the HR group from the ACL on the Benefits folder.

   D. Add the HR group to the ACL for the Benefits folder and Deny all access to the folder.

   ☑ Answer **A** is correct. Because the folder is moved on the same volume, the NTFS permissions assigned to the folder do not change. By removing any HR employees who are not members of the Benefits department from the Benefits group, you assure that no one else in HR will have access to the folder.

   ☒ Answer **B** is incorrect because you will not need to make any permission changes to the folder after it is moved. Answer **C** is incorrect, because the HR group was not in the ACL for the Benefits folder before it was moved, so it is not in the ACL after the move. Answer **D** is incorrect because you do not need to take any action to prevent HR employees from accessing the Benefits folder, as the group is not in the ACL for the folder after it moved and folder inheritance does not move with the folder.

Setting User Rights and Privileges

7. You take over administration of a server after the previous administrator left the company. You notice that several users who are not server administrators have been logging on to the server at the console. You modify user rights in Group Policy to prevent these users from logging on to the server locally. After you make the changes, you can no longer log on to the server from the console, nor can any of the other administrators. What did you likely do?

A. Removed your account from the Administrator group.

B. Added the Everyone group to the Deny access to this computer from the network user right.

C. Added the Everyone group to the Deny logon locally user right.

D. Set the Deny permission in the Log on locally user right

☑ Answer **C** is correct. If you added Everyone to the Deny logon locally user right, this right setting will override your capability as an administrator to log on to the console. You need to remove this group assignment to be able to log on to the console again.

☒ Answer **A** is incorrect because this would likely prevent you from logging on at the console, but would have no impact on the other members of the Administrators group. Answer **B** is incorrect because setting the Deny access to this computer from the network user right does not impact the capability to log on at the server console. Answer **D** is incorrect because you cannot set a Deny permission on a user right.

Troubleshooting Access Problems

8. The Marketing department has created a folder in their shared directory called Marketing Management. They ask you to create a new share pointing to this folder and to give the share the same name as the folder. One user in the department is not able to access the share from his computer. When he logs on at another computer, he is able to see and access the share. What is the likely cause of this problem?

A. The user's computer has a local policy enabled that prevents him from seeing the share.

B. The user is not logging on to the network and therefore cannot see the share.

C. The user does not have access to the share.

D. The user is running Windows 98 on his primary workstation and the other computers in the department are running Windows 2000 or later on their PCs.

☑ Answer **D** is correct. If the user is running Windows 98 on his PC, he will not be able to see the share, because the share name is too long and has a space in it.

☒ Answer **A** is incorrect because there are no system policies that restrict a user or computer from being able to see a share if the user has the necessary permissions to access the share. Answer **B** is incorrect because it is highly unlikely that the user is logging on to the network correctly on other workstations and not his own. Answer **C** is incorrect because the user can access the share from other workstations.

Using New Command-Line Utilities

9. A user is attempting to use the cipher.exe command-line tool to make changes to the encryption settings on a folder but keeps getting errors related to incorrect parameters. When the user asks you about the errors, you suspect that he might be using an older version of cipher that does not support the command-line parameter he is trying to use. How would you find this older version of cipher for the user?

   A. Have the user open a command prompt on his PC and type where cipher at the command prompt.

   B. Have the user do a file search for cipher.* on his local C: drive.

   C. Search all network shares for cipher.*

   D. Have the user open a command prompt on his PC and type cipher /where at the command prompt.

   ☑ Answer **A** is correct. Using the where.exe tool searches the user's current directory and system path for cipher.exe.

   ☒ Answer **B** is incorrect because the search looks only on the local system for the file. If the user has a network share in his path, the older version might be out on the network and not on the local system. Answer **C** is incorrect because you might find several versions of cipher.exe in the network shares, but you will not know which one the user is calling. Answer **D** is incorrect because the cipher command does not have a /where parameter.

10. An employee, Barbara Russell, whose username is russellb, has left the company and you want to reassign ownership of her files. You open a command prompt and change to the directory where her home folder resides. Which command would you type to change the ownership of her files and folders to the administrator's group?

    A. **takeown /u russellb**

    B. **takeown /a russellb**

    C. **takeown /f /r /a russellb***

    D. **takeown /f /r ***

    ☑ Answer **C** is correct. takeown uses the /f parameter to specify which files to change, using the pattern russellb* to indicate which folder to change. The /r parameter tells *takeown* to recurse through all the folders, and the /a switch tells the tool to change the owner to the Administrator's group and not the currently logged-on user.

    ☒ Answer **A** is incorrect because the /u parameter is used to specify which account the tool should run as, not which user's files to change. Answer **B** is incorrect because takeown has been told only to act on the file or folder named russellb. Even if this were a folder name, none of the files inside russellb would be changed. Answer **D** is incorrect because all the files and folders under the current directory, the directory above the user's home directory, would be changed. Also, the /a parameter was not specified, so the files would be owned by the user running the command.

Using EFS Encryption

11. A user asks you about enabling encryption on a folder he is using on the server. Because he is trying to reduce the amount of disk space used, he has been compressing the data on the folder for several weeks. How can he change the settings on the folder so he can encrypt the contents of his compressed files?

    A. Instruct the user to run the cipher command on the folder using the /e parameter.

    B. Instruct the user to uncompress the files in the folder, enable encryption on the folder, and then compress the files again.

    C. Instruct the user to open the Properties window for the folder, click the Advanced button, and then click the check box to enable encryption on the folder.

    D. Advise the user that encrypted files cannot be compressed.

    ☑ Answer **D** is correct. Encrypted files cannot be compressed. If encryption is enabled on a folder that has been marked for compression, the contents will be uncompressed automatically when encrypted.

    ☒ Answer **A** is incorrect because while the cipher command can be used to encrypt the contents of the folder, encryption settings will still override compression settings. When the files are encrypted, they will be uncompressed automatically. Answer **B** is incorrect because the order in which encryption and compression settings are applied does not enable files to be compressed and encrypted at the same time. If you attempt to compress an encrypted file, the action will fail. Answer **C** is incorrect for the same reason – when you enable encryption on a file or folder, the contents will be uncompressed automatically when they are encrypted.

12. A department wants to set up encryption on a shared folder so that only the members of the department can view the contents of the folder. How would you set up this encryption?

    A. Open the folder's Properties window, click Advanced, and enable encryption on the folder.

    B. You cannot set up shared encryption on a folder.

    C. Open a command prompt and run cipher.exe /d on the folder.

    D. Have each user open the folder properties and enable encryption for him or herself on the folder.

    ☑ Answer B is correct. Though you can set up encryption on a folder that is shared, you can only specify shared encryption on files. If you want to enable each member of the department to access encrypted files in the folder, the owner of each file has to add each other member of the department to the encrypted users list.

    ☒ Answer **A** is incorrect because enabling encryption on the shared folder will enable encrypted files to be stored in the folder, but shared encryption settings must be applied to each file within the folder. Answer **C** is incorrect because the /d parameter on the cipher command would decrypt the folder instead of encrypting the folder. Answer **D** is incorrect because encryption is set at the folder level, not at the user level. The first person that marked the folder for encryption would enable encryption on the folder for everyone.

13. A user calls because he just e-mailed a file from his work account to his home account to edit at home. He just realized that the file was encrypted. What will he need to do to be able to work with the file at home?

    A. He will not be able to work with the file at home.

    B. He will need to decrypt the file before e-mailing it to himself.

    C. He will be able to work with the file at home so long as his PC is running Windows 2000 or later.

    D. He will be able to work with the file at home, even if his home computer is a Macintosh.

    ☑ Answer **D** is correct. When transferring an encrypted file to another system, the operating system will automatically decrypt the file and save the file in a readable format. So even if his home computer is a Macintosh, he will be able to access the contents of the file in an unencrypted format.

    ☒ Answer **A** is incorrect because the file was sent in unencrypted format through e-mail, so he will be able to use the file when he pulls it out of his e-mail. Answer **B** is incorrect because the operating system will automatically decrypt the file for him. He can choose to decrypt the file manually, but it is not necessary. Answer **C** is incorrect because he will not require any special operating system or file system to read the decrypted file.

14. You have an encrypted file that you want to share with another user, William. The file is stored on your local Windows 2000 computer. You create a share on your computer, and give William share and NTFS permissions to the folder where the file is located. How will you prepare the file with EFS so that only the recipient can access the contents of the file?

    A. Open a command prompt and encrypt the file using cipher /e /u username filename.

    B. Open a command prompt and encrypt the file using cipher /e /x:outputfile filename.

    C. Open the Properties window of the file, click Advanced, select the Encrypt this file check box, click Details, and then add William to the list of users who can decrypt the file.

    D. You cannot do this with EFS.

    ☑ Answer **D** is correct. EFS does not support this type of encryption under Windows 2000. You need to be running Windows XP on your computer or copy the file to a share on a Windows Server 2003 server where both you and William have access, set encryption on the file, and add William to the list of users who can decrypt the file.

    ☒ Answer **A** is incorrect because the /u parameter cannot be used with any other parameter but /n, and it will attempt to update all encrypted files on a volume. Answer **B** is incorrect because the /x parameter cannot be used with any other parameters and will attempt to generate a backup file of certificates and keys for an encrypted file. Answer **C** is incorrect because sharing encrypted files is not supported under Windows 2000 EFS.

Implementing a Public Key Infrastructure

15. You've been asked to implement a PKI in your organization using Microsoft Certificate Services on Windows Server 2003 servers. Your department is expecting a large volume of certificate and verification requests for your two office locations in Dallas and Denver. Your department head wants to ensure that there is no delay in generating new certificates when requested. How would you choose to implement a PKI to meet these requests?

    A. A stand-alone root CA located either in Dallas or Denver, plus at least one intermediate CA in each of the Dallas and Denver offices.

    B. An enterprise root CA located either in Dallas or Denver, plus at least one intermediate CA in each of the Dallas and Denver offices.

    C. A stand-alone root CA and an intermediate CA in each of the Dallas and Denver offices.

    D. An enterprise root CA and an intermediate CA in each of the Dallas and Denver offices.

    ☑ Answer **B** is correct. You will want to use an enterprise PKI to be able to automatically generate certificates upon request. A stand-alone PKI requires manual approval of certificate requests, and this would cause a delay in generating new certificates. The enterprise root CA can exist in either the Dallas or Denver office, whichever has the greater security. You will want to place at least an intermediate CA in each office and possibly more, depending on office size and request volume.

    ☒ Answer **A** is incorrect because a stand-alone CA will not automatically generate certificates, which puts this solution in conflict with the desired outcome. Answer **C** is incorrect because of the desire to automatically generate certificates, and having multiple root CAs implies that the two offices would be operating independently with respect to Certificate Services. Answer **D** is incorrect because you cannot have more than one enterprise root CA.

Chapter 6: Managing and Troubleshooting Terminal Services

Understanding Windows Terminal Services

1. One of your co-workers asks how to install Terminal Services on his newly installed Windows Server 2003 server so he can perform administrative tasks on the server. Which of the following is the correct advice to give him?

    A. Add the Terminal Server role from the Manage Your Server utility.

    B. Add the Terminal Server role from the Add or Remove Programs utility.

    C. The Terminal Server role is installed by default.

    D. Do nothing.

☑ Terminal Services is installed by default for remote administration purposes when you install Windows 2003; therefore Answer **D** is correct.

☒ In Windows 2000, Terminal Services was a separate component requiring installation in either Remote Administration or Application Server mode. As mentioned earlier, in Windows Server 2003, Terminal Services for Remote Administration is installed automatically with the operating system. However, Application Server mode is now called the Terminal Server role and is an additional component requiring separate installation; therefore, **C** is incorrect. Answers **A** and **B** can both be used to install the Terminal Server role, but the question specified that Terminal Services was to be used to perform administrative tasks, and did not mention a need for the Terminal Server role.

2. A co-worker asks you what type of system can be used as a thin client to a Windows Server 2003 Terminal Server. Which of the following answers would you give her? (Choose all that apply.)

   A. A PDA running Windows CE

   B. A PDA running Windows Pocket PC

   C. A desktop computer running Macintosh OS X

   D. A desktop computer running Windows 95

   ☑ **A, B, C, D.** To use a Microsoft Terminal Services client, a thin client device can be a wide range of computers, including the following: a PDA running the Windows CE or Pocket PC operating system; a full desktop computer running Windows 3.11 (with the 32-bit network stack installed), 95, 98, ME, 2000, XP, or Server 2003. It can also be a special thin client device that contains a processor, memory, video card, and network card, but no hard drive. These systems often store a Windows-based operating system in memory and when booted enable the user to launch a Terminal Services client and establish a session to a terminal server. Microsoft has also released a Terminal Services client for the Apple MAC OS X.

   ☒ All answers are correct.

3. Try as you might, you can't seem to get your co-workers to grasp the concept of Terminal Services. Then it occurs to you that you could explain what happens on the client and server during a terminal session. To explain what the server does, which of the following do you tell them? (Choose all that apply.)

   A. You tell them that the server initiates the final connection with the client.

   B. You tell them that when a user connects to the server, it begins a session just for that user.

   C. You tell them that when they are connected to Terminal Services, everything that they see in their Remote Desktop window is actually occurring on the server.

   D You tell them it no longer requires any client software.

☑ Answers **B** and **C** are correct. By default, when a client begins a session with Terminal Services, the user receives his or her own session. Terminal Services keeps the sessions and application settings of different users separate. When using a session, the user is, in effect, working on the server as a local user. The desktop is being displayed from the server, and when the user launches an application, the application executes on the server, not on the local client.

☒ Answer **A** is incorrect, because the client initiates the session with the server, not the other way around. Answer **D** is incorrect, because one of the three client utilities is still required to establish a session.

Using Terminal Services Components for Remote Administration

4. You are attempting to describe the remote assistance process to a co-worker. The co-worker asks what the correct terms are for the person requesting assistance and the person providing assistance so that he can look them up in Windows Help. Which of the following do you reply with? (Select two.)

   A. Administrator

   B. Novice

   C. Expert

   D. End user

   ☑ Answers **B** and **C** are correct. In relation to a remote assistance session, Microsoft refers to the person requesting help as the Novice and the person providing it as the Expert.

   ☒ Although valid terms in computer networking circles, Administrator (Answer **A**) and End user (Answer **D**) are not the terms Microsoft uses to officially refer to roles involved in using Remote Assistance; therefore these answers are incorrect.

5. No matter how hard you try, you just can't seem to figure out how to access your e-mail using the new application that was installed over the weekend in your office. You decide to use the Remote Assistance feature to ask an administrator to walk you through the process. Which of the following are valid methods that you can use to request assistance? (Choose all that apply.)

   A. E-mail an administrator.

   B. Use ICQ to contact an administrator.

   C. Use Windows messaging to contact an administrator.

   D. Save the request to a file and transfer it to an administrator.

☑ There are three correct answers to this question. There are three methods that a Novice can use to request help from an Expert. First, the Novice can have Remote Assistance generate an e-mail request that contains a link on which the Expert can click to begin the session (Answer **A**). Second, the Novice can initiate a remote assistance request using Windows Messaging (Answer **C**). Finally, the Novice can save the remote assistance request to a file and give it to the Expert on a floppy or transfer it to the Expert across a network (Answer **D**).

☒ Answer **B** is incorrect, because, although similar to Windows Messaging, the ICQ messaging client was not created by Microsoft and does not contain the necessary code to request a Remote Assistance session.

Installing and Configuring the Terminal Server Role

6. Several months ago, you installed the terminal server role on one of the servers at your company. This morning, clients are having difficulty connecting to Terminal Services but are still able to use file and print services on the server. The error message says it is a licensing issue but you are sure that you properly licensed your Windows Server 2003 server, as well as all your client systems. What might be causing this? (Choose all that apply.)

   A. The temporary evaluation period has expired.

   B. You failed to properly configure Terminal Services client licenses on the license server.

   C. The server was installed with a temporary license code, which has expired.

   D. You did not properly install a license server.

   ☑ Answers **A**, **B**, and **D**, could be the cause of this problem. In addition to installing the Terminal Server role, you must also install the Terminal Server licensing component and properly install Terminal Services client licenses on it. These are different from the CALs for the operating systems on your client computers. If you fail to complete any of these steps, your Terminal Services clients will be unable to connect when the evaluation period expires, which is 120 days after the first client connection occurs.

   ☒ Answer **C** is incorrect, because clients can still connect to file and print services on the Windows 2003 server hosting the Terminal Server role. It is clear that the server itself is licensed and functioning properly.

7. Another administrator in a different region of the country is installing the Terminal Server role. Knowing that you recently did this, the administrator asks for your advice. You mention to him that he must also be sure to install the Terminal Server licensing component. What will you tell him about installing this component?

   A. That the License Server role must be installed from the Manage Your Server utility.

   B. That Terminal Server license must be selected and installed from Add/Remove Programs.

   C. That License Server is automatically installed with Terminal Services.

   D. That Terminal Services License server must be purchased separately.

☑ The Terminal Server licensing component must be installed from Add/Remove Programs in Control Panel; therefore Answer **B** is correct. After it is installed, you must add valid client licenses to it so that they can be handed out for clients. If this is not done, Terminal Services clients will not be able to connect 120 days after the first client connects to the Terminal Server. Microsoft recommends installing the Terminal Server licensing component on a separate computer from the one on which you have the Terminal Server role installed.

☒ Answer **A** is incorrect, because there is no License Server role, although the computer on which the license component is installed is often called a license server. In addition, Terminal Services License component does not appear in the list of components that can be installed from Manage Your Server utility. You can, however, open the Add/Remove Programs utility from the Manage Your Server utility. Answer **C** is incorrect, because the Terminal Server license utility is not automatically installed when you install the Terminal Server role. Answer **D** is incorrect, because the Terminal Server licensing component comes with Windows Server 2003, but the individual licenses it holds must be purchased separately.

Using Terminal Services Client Tools

8. Your company's network consists of Windows 2000, XP, and Server 2003 client systems. You've been asked to ensure that the Remote Desktop Connection utility is installed on all clients. Which of the following might be a component of your plan to accomplish this? (Choose all that apply.)

   A. Share the WINDOWS\system32\clients\tsclient directory to enable installation over the network.

   B. Report that the utility cannot be installed on Windows 2000.

   C. Send an e-mail providing the download source to the latest client on the Microsoft Web site.

   D. Report that the utility installs with the Windows XP and Server 2003 operating systems.

   ☑ Answers **A**, **C**, and **D** might be part of your plan and are therefore correct. When Windows Server 2003 is installed, the Remote Desktop Connection installation files are placed in the WINDOWS\system32\clients\tsclient directory. As time goes on, however, the version that shipped with the Windows Server 2003 installation CD-ROM may not be the latest version available, so specifying a newer version on the Microsoft Web site may be a good idea. Finally, by default the Remote Desktop Connection utility is installed on Windows XP and Server 2003 computers.

   ☒ Answer **B** is incorrect, because the Remote Desktop Connection utility can be installed on Windows 2000 computers.

9. The person in the workspace next to yours seems to have no problem using the Remote Desktop Web Connection utility. However, despite your best efforts, you can't seem to connect. What might be wrong? (Choose all that apply.)

   A. IIS is not installed on the server properly.

   B. You Web browser is blocking the installation of ActiveX controls.

   C. You have not enabled JavaScript in your Web browser.

   D. You are not using the correct version of Internet Explorer.

   ☑ Answers **B** and **D** are correct. The Remote Desktop Web Connection utility depends on Internet Explorer 5.0 or later, and a downloaded and installed ActiveX control. If a non-Microsoft browser is in use on the client, or a version of Internet Explorer prior to version 5.0 is being used, the Web connection utility will not work. In addition, when the user initially connects to the Web connection page, an ActiveX client is downloaded to his or her system. If the browser security settings prevent this download, or the user accidentally rejects it when prompted, the utility will not function.

   ☒ Answer **A** is incorrect, because, since other users can access the utility, IIS 6.0 must be installed and properly configured. Answer **C** is incorrect, because the utility does not depend on JavaScript.

10. You have installed Internet Information Services on your Windows Server 2003 server. In addition, you have verified that the Terminal Services service is running. Despite this, you cannot connect to the Remote Desktop Web Connection utility using your Web browser. Which of the following have you most likely failed to do?

    A. You have failed to install the Terminal Server role.

    B. You have failed to add an Application Server role to the server.

    C. You have failed to configure and start the Web service, which is stopped by default after installation for security reasons.

    D. You have failed to install the Remote Desktop Web Connection component.

    ☑ Installing IIS does not automatically install the Remote Desktop Web Connection component; therefore Answer **D** is correct. This must be installed manually via the Add or Remove Programs applet (or utility) in Control Panel.

    ☒ Answer **A** is incorrect, because the terminal server role is not necessary to connect to Terminal Services using the Remote Desktop Web Connection utility. Answer **B** is incorrect, because IIS is an Application Server role and it is installed. Finally, Answer **C** is incorrect, because when IIS and the Remote Desktop Web Connection role are installed, the Web service is started automatically.

11. A user recently sent you a file that contained a saved remote assistance request. Which of the following is true of such a request? (Choose all that apply.)

A. The user can determine when it expires.

B. The user can expire it at any time.

C. A password cannot be used to protect the invitation.

D. The invitation can be used as many times as desired until the expiration time has passed.

☑ When a user creates an invitation, that user can specify when it will expire. Upon expiration, the invitation can no longer be used, so Answer **A** is correct. Answer **B** is also correct, because the user does not have to wait for the expiration time to expire. The user who created it can expire the invitation at any time. Finally, the invitation file can be used an unlimited number of times until it expires; therefore, Answer **D** is correct.

☒ Answer **C** is incorrect. When a user creates an invitation file, the user can set a password on it. This helps to ensure that only the authorized Expert can use the file to establish a connection to the user's system.

Using Terminal Services Administrative Tools

12. One of your co-workers has been reading up on Terminal Services and asks if she can run a few questions by you to see if she understands the concepts. Which of the following statements will you tell her are accurate? (Choose all that apply.)

A. Many Terminal Services settings have a corresponding setting in Group Policy.

B. In Group Policy, Terminal Services settings can be found under both the User and Computer Configuration nodes.

C. When different Terminal Services settings are specified at the user properties, connection properties, and Group Policy levels, the connection properties are the effective settings.

D. Group Policy can be used to prevent an administrator from being forcibly logged off from a console session when another administrator is attempting to connect.

☑ Answer **A** is correct. Many, if not most, configuration settings that can be specified in a user account's properties or at the connection level can also be specified using Group Policy settings. Within the Group Policy Object Editor, Terminal Services configuration items can be found under both the User and Computer Configuration nodes, so Answer **B** is also correct. Finally, Answer **D** is correct because the Deny log off of an administrator logged in to the console session setting enables the behavior it describes.

☒ Answer **C** is incorrect, because the Group Policy settings always override any conflicting configurations in the user account or connection properties.

13. Which of the following command-line tools can be used to return user-specific information? (Choose all that apply.)

A. query user

B. query termserver

C. query process

D. query session

☑ Answer **A** is correct because the query user command displays information regarding the user sessions on a Terminal Server. Answer **C** is also correct. The query process command shows a list of all processes running on a Terminal Server, showing which user is associated with each. Finally, the query session command shows information pertaining to all connected and disconnected sessions on a Terminal Server, again showing the user associated with each; therefore, Answer **D** is also correct.

☒ Answer **B** is incorrect, because the query termserver command shows a list of Terminal Servers in the domain or on the network.

Troubleshooting Terminal Services

14. Your network uses Windows NT clients running the Terminal Services Client Connection Manager utility. The user working next to you notices that when you connect to a Terminal Server, you are automatically logged on, while she is always prompted for a password. She asks if you can help to configure her system to automatically log on as well. Which of the following will you recommend?

A. Configure Automatic logon on the General tab in the Properties of the connection, and enter the appropriate log-on credentials in the User name, Password, and Domain text boxes.

B. Log on to her Windows 2000 client using your user name and password.

C. Configure Always use the following logon information on the Logon Settings tab in the connection properties of the Terminal Services Configuration utility.

D. Configure the User name, Domain, Password, and Confirm password text boxes on the Logon Settings tab for the connection in the Terminal Services Configuration utility.

☑ You should recommend Answer **A**. In this case, the Terminal Services Client Connection Manager cannot pass the user's system log-on credentials directly to Terminal Services running on the server. A quick fix for this is to enter them into the Client Connection Manager on the General properties tab. The only danger here is that if the user leaves the machine unattended, someone else could sit down and connect to a session without being prompted for credentials.

☒ Answer **B** is incorrect, because the problem is not with the credential being used, but with the configuration of the client utility. In addition, you should never give your log-on credentials to another user. Answers **C** and **D** are also incorrect, because the Terminal Services Configuration utility is for administrators, not users. Settings made in this tool will affect all users.

15. You have just finished setting up a special Terminal Server that is designed to serve a single application to users. For security purposes, you decide not to enable them to connect to a full desktop. In the Terminal Services Configuration utility, you have configured the only connection to enable an initial program to be launched immediately when users connect. However, when you test the system by attempting to connect to it, you receive messages informing you that the initial program could not be started. Which of the following should you check in an effort to fix the problem? (Choose all that apply.)

    A. You should make sure that you have spelled the path and executable correctly in the Terminal Services Configuration utility.

    B. You should verify the path to the application.

    C. You should verify that you have the appropriate permissions to the application.

    D. You should verify the name of the executable for the application.

    ☑ Answer **A** is correct, because you should begin by making sure that you didn't create any errors when specifying the location of the program. Answers **B** and **D** are also correct, because it's possible that the application isn't installed where you thought it was, or that the application installation didn't finish. Finally, answer **C** will also be correct if the user logging on to the session doesn't have permission to launch the application.

    ☒ All answers are correct.

Chapter 7: Using Server Management Tools

Recognizing Types of Management Tools

1. You are logged on to the server using an ordinary user account (i.e., without administrator privileges). You need to add several new printers on the server and you decided to use the prncnfg command-line utility. How do you do this without logging off?

    A. Select Start | Run, and then type runas /user:administrator cmd. In the command window run the prncnfg command.

    B. Select Start | Programs | Administrative Tools | Prncnfg, and then right-click and select Run as .

    C. Select Start | Settings | Command. In the command window type runas /user:administrator cmd and run the prncnfg command in the new command window that appears.

    D. Select Start | Run and then type cmd. In the command window run the prncnfg command.

    ☑ Answer **A** is correct. To run the prncnfg command-line utility, you need to have administrator privileges. The runas command enables you to run a command with the credentials of a different user, in this case the administrator.

☒ Answer **B** is incorrect, because prncnfg does not appear in Administrative Tools. Answer **C** is incorrect, because there is no such menu combination. Command does not appear under Start | Settings. Answer **D** is incorrect, because the command prompt is running using the un-privileged user credentials and administrator privileges are required to add a printer.

2. One of your users is having problems getting a productivity application to work correctly. You suspect that he is performing the steps involved in using the application incorrectly, but the application interface is complex and it's difficult for you to explain, over the phone, what he needs to do. The user is running Windows XP, and you want to connect to his PC and show him how to perform the task in question so that he can actually see you go through the steps. How would you arrange to do this?

   A. Send the user a Remote Assistance Request.

   B. Get the user to send a Remote Assistance Invitation.

   C. Connect to the user's PC using Remote Desktop.

   D. Connect to the user's PC using the Web Interface for Remote Administration.

   ☑ By getting the user to send you a Remote Assistance Invitation (Answer **B**), you can connect to the user's desktop and the user can follow what you are doing.

   ☒ Answer **A** is incorrect, because sending the user a Remote Assistance Request is the wrong way and it is also not called a Request. Answer **C** is incorrect, because connecting to a user's PC using Remote Desktop logs off anyone at the PC and he will not be able to see what you are doing. Answer **D** is incorrect, because Remote Administration is not available on Windows XP computers.

3. You are at a branch office of your company assisting a user on her PC. While assisting the user, you receive a call that requires you to alter a DNS setting on the server back at the main office. The user has many applications open and you would prefer to not have to log her out if at all possible. What would be the best way to connect to the server?

   A. Install the Windows Administration Tool Pack on the user's PC.

   B. Connect to the server using the Web Interface for Administration.

   C. Use Computer Management on the PC and connect to the server.

   D. Connect to the server using Remote Desktop for Administration.

   ☑ The simplest way to configure DNS on the server is to connect to the server using a Remote Desktop connection and then run the DNS Manager in the Remote Desktop session(Answer **D**). You don't even have to log the user off her PC.

   ☒ Answer **A** is incorrect, because installing the Windows Administration Tool Pack would install DNS Manager on the user's PC. But you would have to log the user off, locate the source file for the Administration Tool Pack, and run the DNS Manager as an administrator. Answer **B** is incorrect, because the Web Interface for Administration does not include a DNS management tool. Answer **C** is incorrect, because Computer Management does not include the DNS snap-in.

Managing Your Server Remotely

4. You recently installed Windows Server 2003 on some of your company's servers. You plan to manage the servers locally using the Windows Administration Tools Pack and remotely from home and other locations using the Web Interface for Remote Administration. You have checked that your network firewalls enable incoming access to the Web Interface. What else do you need to do to enable the Web Interface for Remote Administration?

   A. Install Remote Administration (HTML).

   B. Enable it in System Properties.

   C. No need to do anything; it is already installed and configured for use.

   D. Install Remote Administration (HTML) and configure the administration Web site using IIS Manager to enable administrators to connect.

   ☑ Answer **A** is correct. The Web Interface for Remote Administration uses the Remote Administration (HTML) windows component. This is not installed by default.

   ☒ Answer **B** is incorrect, because there is no setting in System Properties for the Web Interface for Remote Administration. Answer **C** is incorrect, because it is not installed by default. Answer **D** is incorrect, because configuration of the administration Web site is not necessary. Users have to authenticate when they browse to the Web site.

5. You are at a client's site when you receive a call from your manager. He needs you to check out a problem on a server called sfax2std. You start a browser on one of the PCs on the client's network and try to connect to the Web Interface for Remote Administration for your server. However, this does not work, as shown in Figure 7.26. What is the most likely reason that the connection did not work?

Figure 7.26 Exhibit for Question 5

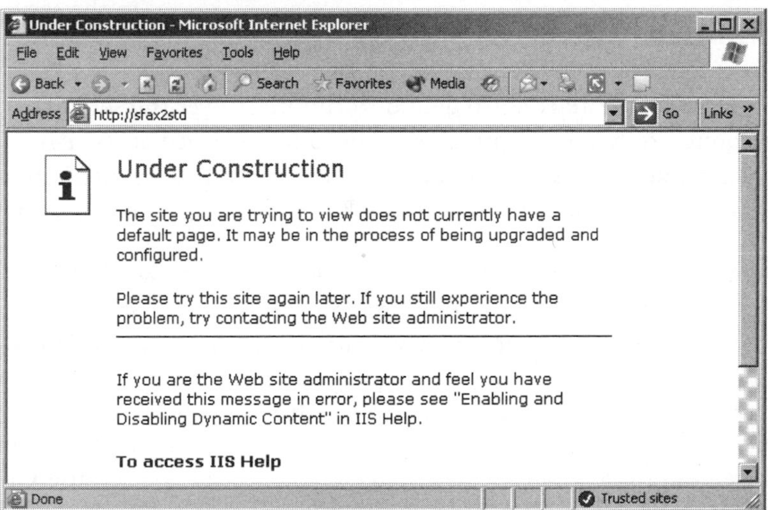

A. Remote Administration (HTML) has not been installed.

B. You don't have permissions to connect.

C. The URL is not correct.

D. IIS isn't running on the server.

☑ Answer **C** is most likely the reason the connection did not work. The URL to use is https://servername:8098. The key point is that the administration Web site is listening on port 8098.

☒ Answer **A** is incorrect, because, although it's possible that Remote Administration has not been installed, you won't know until the correct URL is tried. Answer **B** is incorrect, because authentication is carried out by the administration Web site during browsing and permission to connect is not configured separately. Answer **D** is incorrect, because if IIS were not running, a different error message would appear.

Using Emergency Management Services

6. During a review of disaster recovery planning at your company, the need to manage your servers remotely when the network has failed has been raised as an issue. You decide to use the Emergency Management Services feature of Windows Server 2003. To test this, you connect a terminal to the serial port of your Windows Server 2003 computer. However, you find that you are getting no response on the terminal. What is the most likely reason for this?

   A. EMS operates only when the operating system has failed.

   B. EMS hasn't been enabled on the computer.

   C. Your computer doesn't have the special hardware required to support EMS.

   D. EMS works only over the network.

   ☑ EMS is not enabled by default; therefore Answer **B** is correct.

   ☒ Answer **A** is incorrect, because EMS operates as soon as the boot loader is running and is therefore available while the operating system is running. Answer **C** is incorrect, because special hardware is not required to run EMS over the serial port. Special hardware is required only if the computer needs to be managed at the BIOS level. Answer **D** is incorrect, because EMS does work over serial ports. The whole point of EMS is that it provides out-of-band management even when network connectivity has failed.

7. You have a computer that has Windows Server 2003 and Windows XP Professional installed on it. You've connected a terminal to the serial port of the computer so that you can manage it remotely using EMS. You reboot the server and see the list of available operating systems on the terminal. You select Windows XP Professional from the boot list and then find that there is no further response on the terminal. What has happened?

A. The computer crashed while booting into Windows XP Professional.

B. EMS was enabled on the wrong serial port in the Windows XP Professional installation.

C. EMS wasn't enabled in the Windows XP Professional installation.

D. Windows XP Professional doesn't support EMS.

☑ Answer **D** is correct. Only Windows Server 2003 supports EMS, so as soon as Windows XP starts up there is no further communication on the serial port.

☒ Answers **A**, **B**, and **C** are all incorrect because Windows XP doesn't support EMS.

Managing Printers and Print Queues

8. One of your users frequently submits a very large print job prompting complaints from other users whose print jobs are delayed because of the large job. The server also handles requests for other print queues. You decide to try changing the default priority of the queue that is causing the complaints. What would be the benefit of changing the priority from the default of 1 to say 50?

A. To make print jobs appear faster.

B. To make print jobs from the queue appear before those in other queues.

C. To enable you to reduce the priority of individual jobs as well as increase the priority.

D. To be able to give some users preferential access so that their jobs print more quickly.

☑ Answer **C** is correct. The default priority for print jobs in a queue is 1. Although the priority can be anywhere between 1 and 99, having a default of 1 does not enable you to reduce the priority of a single print job. It might be useful to do this occasionally, if you need to hold back a large print job until the queue is empty. Setting the priority to 50 gives you the scope to reduce as well as increase priorities.

☒ Answer **A** is incorrect, because the priority has no bearing on how fast print jobs are printed. Answer **B** is incorrect, because the priority of a printer queue sets the default priority for print jobs that enter the queue and has no relevance to other queues that print to different printers. Answer **D** is incorrect, because increasing the default priority only doesn't achieve the aim of giving some users preferential access. To do this, you must configure two printer queues that point to the same printer device, change the priority on one of the queues, and then restrict access to the higher priority queue using permissions.

9. A user calls you and asks you to ensure that his document is printed next. The user's print job is shown highlighted in Figure 7.27. You examine the queue and note that there is a long print job before the user's document and you agree to prioritize it. What is the best way to arrange for the user's document to be printed next?

Figure 7.27 Exhibit for Question 9

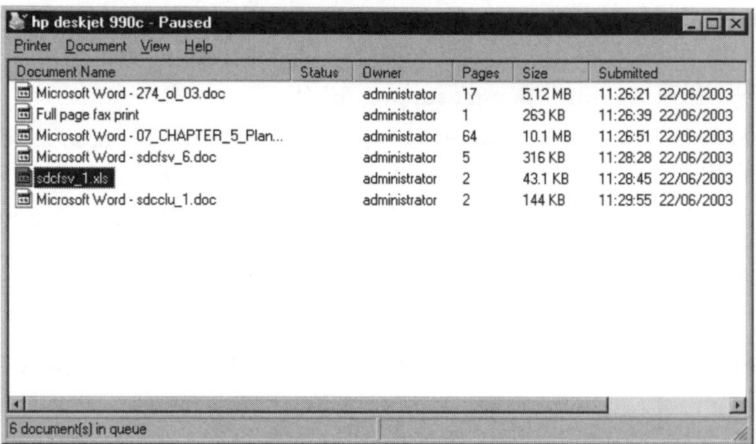

A. Delete all the jobs above the highlighted one.

B. Pause all the jobs above the highlighted one, wait for it to print, and then resume the paused jobs.

C. Drag it to the top of the queue.

D. Double-click the job and increase its priority.

☑ Answer **D** is correct. Print jobs are normally processed in the order in which they arrive. The only way to change this is to change the priority of an individual job.

☒ Answer **A** incorrect, because deleting users' jobs is not a good idea. Answer **B** is incorrect, because, although it would work, it is certainly not the best way, as it requires a lot of administrative effort. Answer **D** is incorrect, because it is not possible to drag print jobs entries.

10. The only laser printer on your network is now very heavily used and users often have to wait a long time for their print jobs. The management has agreed to buy another printer that is the same as the current one. The same print server will manage both printers. The original printer is connected to LPT1 and the new printer will be connected to LPT2. What is the most efficient way to deploy the new printer?

    A. Create a new queue on the print server using LPT2. Modify the current printer queue to send jobs to the new printer when it is busy.

    B. Modify the queue for the existing printer to enable printer pooling and configure the printer to use LPT2 as well as LPT1.

    C. Create a new printer queue on the print server using LPT2. Configure the users' computers so that half use the current printer and the other half use the new printer.

    D. Create a new printer queue on the print server using LPT2. Create a printer pool that contains both the new and the current printers.

☑ Answer **B** is the most efficient way to deploy the new printer. A printer queue sends jobs to more than one printer if printer pooling is enabled and more than one port is selected; jobs will be sent to the first free printer. Also, no changes are required on the users' computers.

☒ Answer **A** is incorrect, because a printer queue can only distribute jobs between printers by using printer pooling. It is not possible for one queue to transfer its jobs to another. Answer **C** is incorrect, because it is not the most efficient method, since it requires a change on half of the computers on the networks. Answer **D** is incorrect, because a printer pool cannot consist of separate queues, only separate ports.

Managing and Troubleshooting Services

11. A serious problem has occurred on your file server and you need to shut down the computer, but users are still connected. Because the users have important work that is in progress, you don't want to disconnect the users immediately, but instead you want them to finish what they are doing. What should you do to stop new users connecting to the server?

    A. Disable the Server service.

    B. Shutdown the server anyway; users can save their files locally.

    C. Stop the Server service.

    D. Pause the Server service.

    ☑ Answer **D** is correct. The Server service provides file server functionality. Pausing a service doesn't affect users who are connected, but no new connections are allowed.

    ☒ Answer **A** is incorrect, because, although disabling a service stops the service from starting, this has no effect until the server is rebooted. Answer **B** is incorrect, because users might well lose some of their work. Answer **C** is incorrect for the same reason as Answer **B**: stopping a service immediately disconnects all users.

12. Your company hosts DNS zones on several servers. Because the proper operation of the DNS servers is crucial to your network, one of your tasks is to check that the DNS service is running on all these servers and you have to perform this task on a regular basis. What is the most efficient way to do this?

    A. Write a script that uses ***sc*** with the remote computer option to check the DNS service on each server.

    B. Create a custom MMC and add the services snap-in for each server and check the state of the DNS service in each snap-in.

    C. Log on to each server using Remote Desktop and run Computer Management to check the DNS service in the services folder.

    D. Install the Administration Tools Pack and run DNS Manager, connecting to each server in turn to see if DNS is running.

☑ Answer **A** is the most efficient way to carry out the check. You need to write the script only once and it can then be run as required.

☒ Answers **B**, **C**, and **D** are all wrong, because, although all of them would work, they all require a lot of administrative effort, especially if the task is to be repeated. They are all incorrect because they are not the most efficient way of achieving the required task.

13. You are installing SQL Server on a Windows Server 2003 computer. The SQL Server needs to be able to send e-mail via Exchange Server, which is installed on another Windows Server 2003 computer. What type of account should you use for the SQL Server service?

    A. Domain User

    B. Local User

    C. Local System

    D. Local Service

    ☑ Only a domain user account (Answer **A**) has access to other resources on the network. Since the SQL Server service needs to be able to communicate with another server, a domain account needs to be used.

    ☒ Answers **B**, **C**, and **D** are all incorrect, because they all have access to resources on the local computer only.

Using Wizards to Configure and Manage Your Server

14. A new administrator has joined your company and you have tasked him with setting up Routing and Remote Access on one of your servers. The new administrator has very little experience in managing Windows Server 2003 servers. Which tool should you advise the new administrator to use in the first instance?

    A. Manage Your Server

    B. Configure Your Server Wizard

    C. Administration Tools Pack

    D. Computer Management

    ☑ The Configure Your Server Wizard (Answer **B**)guides inexperienced administrators through installing and configuring server roles.

    ☒ Answer **A** is incorrect, because you use Manage Your Server to configure roles after they have been installed. Answers **C** and **D** are incorrect, because they do not guide an administrator through configuring a server.

15. Your company has acquired a new printer and you've been asked to set up the printer so that all the users can use it. You decide to set up the printer on your server so that you can centrally manage printing. You successfully install the printer and print a test page. However, you then find that the users cannot connect to the printer. What is the most likely reason?

A. The File Server role isn't installed.

B. The File & Print Server role isn't installed.

C. The Print Server role isn't installed.

D. You forgot to share the printer.

☑ A printer must be shared before network users can use it; therefore Answer **D** is correct.

☒ Answers **A**, **B**, and **C** are all incorrect, because server roles are not necessary to enable shared printers. The file server role isn't relevant to printing and there isn't a File & Print Server role.

Chapter 8: Managing Web Servers with IIS 6.0

Installing and Configuring IIS 6.0

1. You have been instructed to install Windows Server 2003 on a Windows 2000 machine. The current Windows 2000 Server is running under a FAT32 system. The Windows Server 2003 installation will permit you to upgrade or have clean installation. When you are performing the upgrade, you have an option between FAT32 and NTFS file systems. Which ones would you choose?

   A. FAT

   B. FAT32

   C. NTFS

   D. FAT64

   ☑ The preferred file system is NTFS (Answer **C**). IIS 6.0 and other servers rely on NTFS security permissions to authenticate users.

   ☒ Answer **A** is incorrect. File Allocation System (FAT) is an old DOS version of a file system. This was superceded by FAT32 version. FAT32 was a 32-bit file allocation system. Therefore, answer **B** is also incorrect. The FAT64 system was a proposed 64-bit file allocation system that follows the FAT format. Answer D is incorrect because this option is not implemented yet.

2. You have installed the standard default installation of Windows Server 2003. You were disappointed to find out that the IIS 6.0 wasn't installed by default. You have read that you can install IIS in several ways. You pick the Configure Your Server Wizard option. You have discovered that the Windows server acts like an Application Server by investigating this option. What technology is not included in the Windows Server 2003 application server technologies?

   A. COM+

   B. ASP.NET

   C. ASP

   D. IIS 6.0

☑ ASP (Answer **C**) is not an application server technology.

☒ Answers **A, B,** and **D** are incorrect. COM+, ASP.NET and Internet Information Server (IIS) 6.0 are application server technologies in Windows Server 2003. These components can be configured from the Manage Your Server option from the Start menu.

What's New in IIS 6.0?

3. IIS 6.0 introduces a worker process model concept. A worker process model is a separate ISAPI application (Web site) that runs in isolation. In previous IIS versions (version 5.0 and earlier) all applications ran in the same memory space as inetinfo.exe. IIS 6.0 does not enable the applications to run in the same space as inetinfo.exe. What is the IIS 6.0 concept of tracking its Web sites referred to as?

   A. Using Health Detection

   B. Using HTTP.sys

   C. Using XML metabase entries

   D. Using ASP.NET scripts that directly communicate to .NET Framework

   ☑ Heath Detection (Answer **A**) is the technology that IIS uses to make sure they are running smoothly.

   ☒ Answer **B** is incorrect because HTTP.sys is the new kernel mode driver to accept all incoming HTTP traffic. Answer **C** is incorrect because metabase holds all the configuration settings for IIS. Answer **D** is incorrect because ASP.NET is a scripting language to perform business intelligence tasks. It does not assist IIS to synchronize its worker process.

4. ASP.NET is the new scripting mechanism available in IIS 6.0. You have read in the *Windows 2003 Magazine* about its advantages over ASP. You are experimenting with ASP.NET scripting now. What could be correct about your sample ASP.NET files?

   A. IIS understands only C# ASP.NET applications.

   B. You can have a C# function inside a Jscript.NET page.

   C. ASP.NET pages are interpreted.

   D. ASP.NET is based on Component Object Model (COM) architecture.

   ☑ Ansewr **B** is correct. ASP.NET supports multiple languages in the same page. Therefore, we can run a C# function in Jscript.NET page without any difficulty.

   ☒ Answer **A** is incorrect because ASP.NET supports multiple languages including C#. Those are VB.NET, J#.NET, Jscript.NET, and so forth. Answer **C** is incorrect because ASP.NET code is compiled. Answer **D** is incorrect because ASP.NET is based on the .NET model, not the COM model.

5. One of the new reliability features in IIS 6.0 is the introduction of HTTP.sys. HTTP.sys is the new kernel mode driver for IIS 6.0. HTTP.sys is engineered to increase the performance of IIS dramatically. You have been researching HTTP.sys functionality. Your research does not indicate one of the following options. Please select the correct one.

   A. Uses application pools to assign resources to Web sites

   B. Implements flexible caching

   C. Since HTTP.sys consumes all incoming traffic, inetinfo.exe has less to worry.

   D. Performs health detections data to IIS

   ☑ Answre **D** is correct. HTTP.sys does not deal with health detections. It is done by IIS utilizing the worker process model.

   ☒ Answer **A** is incorrect because application pool is a new concept in IIS 6.0. They are used by HTTP.sys to assign resources to Web sites. Answer **B** is incorrect because flexible caching is the mechanism of caching at kernel level using HTTP.sys. Answer **C** is incorrect because HTTP.sys specializes in incoming traffic and saving resources for the IIS process (inetinfo.exe).

Managing IIS 6.0

6. Web Services Extensions is a new feature in IIS 6.0. Using Web Services Extensions we can configure IIS 6.0 components. We can enable and disable them from the IIS Manager console. You have been experimenting on enabling and disabling these components. You couldn't notice one or more of the following items. Which item(s) fall into this category? (Choose all that apply.)

   A. WebDAV

   B. ASP.NET

   C. File Sharing

   D. ASP

   ☑ File sharing (Answer **C**) is an Application Server responsibility. It does not have any association with Web Service Extensions.

   ☒ Answer **A** is incorrect because WebDAV access can be enabled and disabled from the Web Service Extension window. Answer **B** is incorrect because ASP.NET is also under the control of the Web Service Extensions. The same goes for answer **D**.

7. You have read that IIS 6.0 can handle multiple Web sites on a single IP address. Your organization is running out of static IP address and this seems to be a great idea. You are investigating the steps to create multiple Web sites on the same IP address. Which of these options is the most correct one?

A. Use single IP address with multiple Web site headers.

B. Use single IP address with multiple HTTP 1.1 headers.

C. Assign different port numbers to different Web sites.

D. Use multiple Web sites with the same header.

☑ Answer **A** is correct. We need to use different header names on the same IP address to obtain multiple Web sites.

☒ Answer **B** is incorrect because the HTTP version does not have any relevance to having multiple Web sites on the same IP address. All the Web site communication will be done in HTTP 1.1. All Web sites run on port 80 by default. We can assign different port numbers to different Web sites. However this is not the best practice. The Web sites need to modify their URLs since they no longer run on the default port. Since **A** is a better implementation, we can discard **C**. Answer **D** is incorrect because IIS 6.0 will issue an error message if multiple sites have the same header.

8. There are several ways you can apply security on Web sites. You can configure all of these by the Properties tab of a Web site. Which one of the following is not a security measure to prevent intruders hacking into IIS 6.0 Web sites?

A. Using SSL certificates

B. Using WebDAV

C. Using an authentication method to force the user to authenticate

D. Applying IP restrictions on known offenders and networks

☑ WebDAV (Answer **B**) is a file-sharing mechanism and does not have any implications on Web site security.

☒ Answer **A** is incorrect. SSL has been used for years to encrypt communication to preserve sensitive information. Answer **C** is incorrect because, by forcing the users to authenticate, we can check their credentials and keep a log of their activity. Answer **D** is incorrect because we can restrict the user by entering IP address restrictions on a Web site.

Troubleshooting IIS 6.0

9. Your Web server is running ASP.NET applications on IIS 6.0. An incorrect configuration setting has caused you to reinstall IIS 6.0 on this machine. You have used the Control Panel | Add Remove Programs method to uninstall and reinstall IIS 6.0. Then you tried to load up your ASP.NET pages. Unfortunately, all ASP.NET pages are displayed as text. What could be the solution to this problem?

A. You need to reregister ASP.NET.

B. You need to reformat the drive as NTFS and reinstall Windows Server 2003 with IIS.

C. You need to edit the metabase XML file to recognize ASP.NET files.

D. You need to restart IIS from IIS Manager.

☑ Answer **A** is correct. You need to reregister ASP.NET when you reinstall IIS 6.0.

☒ Answer **B** is incorrect because you do not need to reformat the machine to reinstall IIS. You only need to make IIS *remember* where to find ASP.NET in this case. Answer **C** also does not make sense. You can enable ASP.NET setting using the metabase XML file, but it does not solve this particular problem. Answer **D** is incorrect because restarting IIS will not make difference.

10. Your company's new MP3 player is getting very popular on the Internet. You are getting close to 2,500 requests per minute to download the product. Unfortunately, your Web server is continuously getting a 503 error for the product downloads. Your boss has asked you to look into this problem. What could be the issue?

    A. There is not enough bandwidth for the users.

    B. HTTP.sys cannot handle the incoming traffic.

    C. The worker process is getting recycled every five minutes.

    D. The FTP server needs to be run on isolation mode.

    ☑ Answer **B** is correct. Error 503 occurs when HTTP.sys cannot handle the incoming HTTP requests. The default queue length is 2,000 requests for a minute. When you exceed this limit you start getting 503 errors.

    ☒ Answer **A** is incorrect and vague. Error 503 is a server error and bandwidth is not a major concern for this error. Answer **C** is incorrect because the worker process recycles every two hours, not every five minutes. Answer **D** is incorrect because the FTP server cannot be run in isolation mode. IIS as a whole can be run in isolation made.

11. You are getting frequent 503 errors on your production environment. You have also noticed that a series of 503 errors will restart the IIS server automatically. IIS 6.0 recovers and starts accepting product download till we get another set of 503 error and restarts. What do you call the fail-over mechanism?

    A. Self-correcting IIS

    B. IIS worker process recycle

    C. Backup/restore configuration

    D. Rapid-fail protection

    ☑ The automatic process of IIS worker process recycle is referred to as rapid-fail protection; therefore Answer **D** is correct.

    ☒ Answer **A** is incorrect. It is a made-up name to confuse the user. Answer **B** is incorrect because the IIS worker process is an architectural change to boost performance in IIS. It does not recycle after 503 errors. Answer **C** is incorrect because backup/restore configuration enables you to back up IIS configuration. It does not respond to 503 errors.

12. Your IIS 6.0 server is communicating with a UNIX server to handle sales procurement information. The first request seems to work fine. The subsequent requests from the UNIX servers results in a 404 File Not Found error from our IIS server. What could be the issue here?

    A. Static file cache stores filename in uppercase.

    B. Static file cache stores filename in lowercase.

    C. Worker process recycles every time a UNIX request comes in.

    D. UNIX communication is cookie based and IIS 6.0 needs a new cookie with every request.

    ☑ The issue is the Static file cache, which will cache all data in uppercase; therefore Answer **A** is correct. The UNIX systems are case sensitive; therefore, the UNIX requests will always conform to the correct case. But all our data is in uppercase, which will result in a File Not Found error.

    ☒ Answers **B** is incorrect because file data is cached in uppercase. Answer **C** is incorrect because the worker process does not recycle for UNIX clients. Answer **D** is incorrect because UNIX communication is not based on cookies.

13. You have installed an ISAPI application as the *Checkout* facility for your shopping cart. You bought this third-party tool to facilitate credit card transactions. This was visible under IIS 5.0 as an ISAPI application. You have installed this on the Windows Server 2003 server and looked at the ISAPI application tab. The Checkout ISAPI DLL is not visible as a live application. What could have gone wrong here?

    A. You need to enter the ISAPI data into the metabase manually to recognize it.

    B. You need to restart the IIS and it will show up.

    C. It only comes up when a user invokes the Checkout facility.

    D. The ISAPI application needs to be rewritten for IIS 6.0.

    ☑ The ISAPI application does not come up till a user invokes it; therefore Answer **C** is correct.

    ☒ Answer **A** is incorrect because the metabase does not need to be manually configured to recognize ISAPI DLL. It is automatically done when the user registers the DLL in IIS 6.0. Answer **B** is incorrect because you do not need to restart the IIS and even if you do, it will not make a difference. Answer **D** is incorrect because you do not need to rewrite any code to port it from IIS 5.0 to IIS 6.0.

Using New IIS Command-Line Utilities

14. The iisftp.vbs command can be used to create, start, stop, pause, and list FTP sites in IIS 6.0 server. You have been experimenting with this command. What will be the outcome of an iisftp/query command-line invocation?

A. An error will come up. It is not a valid command because the .VBS extension is not present.

B. An error will come up. You haven't listed the FTP site name to query on.

C. A list of all FTP sites will come up.

D. The information for the "query" FTP site will come up.

☑ The query with no arguments will produce all the active FTP sites on the IIS server; therefore Answer **C** is correct.

☒ Answer **A** is incorrect because the iisftp.vbs script will function without the .VBSextension. Answer **B** is incorrect because if no arguments are given, iisftp.vbs returns all the FTP site information. It will not result an error. Answer **D** is incorrect because query is a keyword and is not an FTP site name.

15. You are creating a Web server farm to host multiple Web sites. You need to mirror the exact IIS configuration settings on every computer in the farm. This could be a tedious task if you do a manual server installation (machine by machine). Your senior architect has informed you of a command-line utility that will copy all configuration settings from one server to another. Which one is it?

A. iisback.vbs

B. iiscnfg.vbs

C. iisftp.vbs

D. iisvdir.vbs

☑ You can use the iiscnfg.vbs (Answer **B**)with the /copy switch to replicate IIS configuration settings from one computer to another.

☒ Answer **A** is incorrect because iisback.vbs creates backups and restores them. Answer **C** is incorrect because iisftp.vbs creates and manipulates FTP site settings on IIS 6.0. Answer **D** is incorrect because iisvdir.vbs creates and manipulates Web site virtual directories.

Chapter 9: Monitoring Performance and Security

Monitoring Performance

1. You need to query your memory trace file. The file is called "test_log" and it is stored in the root of the C: drive. You are thinking of using the *relog.exe* command-line utility to extract the data to a .csv file called "out.csv" that also resides on the root of C: drive. You are thinking of reading the log data in chunks of 10 records at a time. What will be your command-line instructions to execute this scenario?

A. relog.exe C:\test_log.blg –config "\Memory\Available Bytes" –o C:\out.csv –t 10 –f csv

B. relog C:\test_log.blg –c "\Memory\Available Bytes" –f C:\out.csv –t 10 –o csv

C. relog.exe C:\test_log.blg –a "\Memory\Available Bytes" –o C:\out.csv –t 10 –f csv

D. relog C:\test_log.blg –c "\Memory\Available Bytes" –o C:\out.csv –t 10 –f csv

☑ The –c parameter is used to describe the performance counters. The –o parameter describes the output file and its path. The interval of record insertion (the chucks of data you read from the log to enter to the log file) is indicated by the –t parameter. Finally, the **–**f parameter describes the file format. Answer **D** has all the correct settings for the command.

☒ Answer **A** is incorrect, it has the –config parameter that is used to point to the configuration file to find the set of counters. Answer **B** is incorrect, because it has two incorrect settings. It switches the –o and –f parameters that describe the output file and file format, respectively. Answer **C** is incorrect, because it refers to the **–a** parameter. The counter information is given with parameter –c.

2. A faulty uninstallation has caused your Microsoft Management Console (MMC) programs to give strange errors. You cannot read any performance log data from the Performance Monitor. You have read that you can input the performance counter data onto the screen using a command-line utility. That command-line utility is which of the following?

A. logman.exe

B. relog.exe

C. typeperf.exe

D. perfmon.exe

☑ The typeperf.exe utility (Answer **C**) can query performance log files and output the data onto the screen or write it to a text file.

☒ Answer **A** is incorrect, because the logman.exe utility creates and manipulates the performance log file. It does not display the logs on the screen. Answer **B** is incorrect, because relog.exe queries log files and writes the output to text files and databases, not to the screen. Answer **D** is incorrect, because perfmon.exe brings up the Performance Monitor and does not query the log files.

Optimizing Servers for Application Performance

3. You are investigating the slow responses of your network's file server. This file server accommodates all the business data templates that are shared by 200 internal and external employees. The machine has multiple network adapters to communicate to internal and external resources. The machine has 1GB of RAM. The page file size is 1.2GB at the moment. The page file size seems to be increasing and getting larger after a reboot. It starts at 800MB and climbs higher. What could be the cause of this issue?

A. There is a network problem.

B. There is a page file size problem on the server.

C. You cannot use multiple network adapters on Windows Server 2003.

D. File servers need at least 2GB of memory.

☑ Network-related activities take up a lot of non-paged data; therefore Answer **A** is correct. This file server gets a lot of network traffic every day with 200 employees needing to obtain their business data templates on two network adapters. When the network data hogs the memory, more application data is copied to the page file. Therefore, the page file size keeps increasing. The page file size is still acceptable in this case (less than 1.5 times physical RAM.)

☒ Answer **B** is incorrect, because the page file size is less than 1.5 times the system memory. Answer **C** is incorrect, because you can use multiple network adapters in Windows Server 2003. Answer **D** is incorrect, because there is no memory standard for file servers. It depends on the organization's requirements and the software implementation.

4. You are contemplating adding a processor to your Web server. You are trying to get performance indicators using performance counters. The System\Processor Queue Length is currently at three. The Server Work Queues\Queue Length is also at three. What is your recommendation, derived from this information?

   A. Do not add an extra processor.

   B. Add an extra processor.

   C. These counters relate to disk activity; not processor activity.

   D. Not enough information to make the decision.

   ☑ Answer **B** is correct. The System\Processor Queue Length indicates the queue length or number of the requests to be processed. This should not be greater than one. If it is, it means the processor is not capable of handling all the incoming requests. Therefore, you should add another processor. The Server Work Queues\Queue Length is acceptable (the recommended threshold is four).

   ☒ Answer **A** is incorrect, because you do need to add a processor to the system. Answer **C** is incorrect, because these counters relate to processor activities. These do not reflect the disk activity of the system. Answer **D** is incorrect, because there is enough information to come to a conclusion.

5. You suspect a disk controller issue on your application drive. You can see a lot of disk activity (by observing the LED settings) and slow response times across multiple applications. You have been asked to do a performance test on the disk activity. What counter(s) would you add to the System Monitor?

   A. Memory\Available Bytes counter

   B. Server\Bytes Total/sec, Bytes Received/sec counters

   C. PhysicalDisk\%Disk Time and %Idle Time counters

   D. System\Processor Queue Length counter

☑ The disk activity is monitored by PhysicalDisk\% Disk Time and %Idle Time counters (Answer **C**). These indicate how active the disk is and how idle the disk is.

☒ Answer **A** is incorrect, because the Memory\Available Bytes counter is used to figure out memory problems. Answer **B** is incorrect, because the Server\Bytes Total/sec and Bytes Received/sec counters are used to troubleshoot network issues. Answer **D** is incorrect, because System\Processor Queue Length counter is used for processor evaluation.

Auditing Security Events

6. You suspect some hackers are breaking into your Web server. You have read in a tech magazine about enabling security auditing on the server. You are trying to apply security auditing and noticed some default audit properties enabled by the Windows Server 2003 installation. Which of the following security audits is enabled by default?

   A. Audit policy change

   B. Audit privilege change

   C. Audit account logon events

   D. Audit process tracking

   ☑ There are two security audits available by default. They are Audit account logon events and Audit logon events; therefore Answer **C** is correct.

   ☒ Answer **A** is incorrect, because audit policy change has to be manually configured to enable success and failure events. Answers **B** and **D** are incorrect for the same reasons: audit privilege change and audit process tracking are not available by default.

7. You suspect some intrusions to your Windows Server 2003 file server. The hackers seem to be very diligent with their break-ins. There is no evidence to support the hacker activity. You have enabled auditing on the server. However, the hackers seem to delete the auditing details from the security log after each intrusion. You are trying to back up the audit trail periodically so you can analyze this problem further. What technology can be used for this scenario?

   A. Windows Server 2003 Event Viewer

   B. Microsoft Site Server 4.0

   C. Microsoft Application Center

   D. Microsoft Operation Manager

   ☑ Microsoft Operation Manager (Answer **D**) enables you to duplicate the audit trail and store the backup on a secure network drive. You can analyze this data even if the hackers delete the source audit.

   ☒ Answer **A** is incorrect, because the Windows Server 2003 Event Viewer is used to view the audit information. It does not periodically back it up. (However, you can use the Save As option to save the data to disk.) Answer **B** is incorrect, because Site Server 4.0 is used to manage Web sites. It does not have any relevance to audit trails. Answer **C** is incorrect, because Application Center is used to manage Web farms and middle-tier components. It does not have any relevance to audit trails.

8. You are trying to connect to your SQL Server using the Query Analyzer to extract some product information. Your connection seems to fail with invalid user name and password errors. Your system administrator informs you that security auditing is enabled for SQL Server logons. You would like to view the logon details to validate your logon process. Where should you look for these audit details?

   A. Users section under SQL Server Enterprise Manager.

   B. Control Panel | Administrative Tools | Component Services

   C. Event Viewer

   D. Task Manager

   ☑ The security audit details are logged in the security log. The security log is viewed using the Event Viewer; therefore Answer **C** is correct. You can get to the Event Viewer by using Control Panel | Administrative Tools | Event Viewer.

   ☒ Answer **A** is incorrect, because the Users section of SQL Server lists the SQL users that have access to the databases. Answer **B** is incorrect, because a component service does not display security audit information. Answer **D** is incorrect, because the Task Manager does not display any auditing data.

Using Event Viewer

9. You are trying to troubleshoot an SQL Server connection error. You are looking at the SQL Server event logs remotely to track the connection failure. You can see the SQL Service errors. When you double-click the error, you get a detail view of the error. The only problem is the lack of description data in the detail view. What could be the cause of this?

   A. SQL Server does not log the error description to the event log.

   B. Remote Registry Service is stopped on SQL Server.

   C. You must have Administrators group access to view this data.

   D. The Event Viewer does not provide detailed error descriptions.

   ☑ The Remote Registry Service (Answer **B**) needs to be started in order to access the *Description* and the *Category* information for an event. Because the service is not started, you are not able to view the data in the Event Viewer.

   ☒ Answer **A** is incorrect, because the SQL Service populates detailed error description to the log files. Answer **C** is incorrect, because you do not need to be a member of the Administrators group to access application errors (SQL Server is an application). You do need Administrator access for security log access. Answer **D** is incorrect, because the Event Viewer provides detailed error descriptions if the remote registry service is started.

10. Your server is experiencing "Out of disk space" errors. Your investigation has concluded that purging of the logs was not configured. The option Do not delete events was selected. What can you do to force purging of the event logs on Windows Server 2003 machine?

   A. You cannot purge events on log files.

   B. Unselect the option Overwrite events as needed.

   C. Select the option Overwrite events more than 20 days.

   D. Click the Clear Log button.

   ☑ Answer **C** is correct. The purging of error logs has three options when the log exceeds the maximum log size limit. You can overwrite the file as necessary (the oldest events are overwritten). Another option is to overwrite events older than a configurable number of days. This time can be configured to 20 days.

   ☒ Answer **A** is incorrect, because the event log does have several options to purge log files. Answer B is incorrect, because you can purge the log file by selecting the Overwrite events as needed option. However, unselecting the option disables this. Answer D is incorrect, because you delete the event log data by clicking the Clear Log button.

11. You are trying to archive the event log to save disk space. You have a custom-made Excel spreadsheet in which you want to record all Application errors. You are a bit confused about what file format to use when you save the event log, to be able to load the data into the Excel spreadsheet. What is the most suitable format in which to save the event log?

   A. XML format (.XML file)

   B. Text file format (.TXT file)

   C. Event Viewer format (.EVT file)

   D. Comma-Separated Values format (.CSV file)

   ☑ The comma-separated file is the best format to load event log data into an Excel file; therefore Answer **D** is correct. You can import a .CSV file directly into Excel.

   ☒ Answer **A** is incorrect, because the Event Viewer does not enable you to save files in XML format. Answers **B** and **C** are incorrect, because, although you can save the files as text format or Event Viewer format, these options do not support the capability to import to an Excel spreadsheet.

Using Command-Line Tools

12. Your servers are running out of disk space due to extensive logging information generated by Internet Information Server (IIS) traffic. This causes the Web server to crash. You need to run a disk cleanup utility when this happens. Can you use any command-line tools to help you with this issue?

A. Use eventcreate.exe

B. Use eventquery.vbs

C. Use eventtriggers.exe

D. Use eventtriggers.vbs

☑ eventtriggers.exe (Answer **C**) is used to create triggers on a specified event that cause some action to be taken when an event trigger is activated.

☒ Answer **A** is incorrect, because eventcreate.exe creates an event on a specified log file. Answer **B** is incorrect, because eventquery queries a specified log file. Answer **D** is incorrect, because eventtrigger is an executable (.EXE) file, not a .VBS script.

13. You have been having performance issues with your Web server. An external consultant has advised you to get some event trace information to analyze the issue. You ran the *tracerpt.exe* command with the source of the trace events. If you did not specify a name, which file contains the trace report?

A. dumpfile.csv

B. summary.txt

C. config file

D. dumpfile.xls

☑ Tracerpt generates the Dumpfile.csv (Answer **A**) file as the default report file. It also generates a text file when you use the *–report* switch.

☒ Answer **B** is incorrect, because summary.txt is the summary file for the tracerpt execution. Answer **C** is incorrect, because you can use a configuration setting file to read the arguments for tracerpt. This is the config file. Answer **D** is incorrect, because tracerpt creates a .CSVfile, not an Excel file (.XLS).

Using the Shutdown Event Tracker

14. Your Web servers are getting frequent 503 errors. Rapid application failover is causing the machine to shut down. You have to frequently remove this machine form the Web farm because of this issue. As a result, this machine is subject to many logons and hibernate scenarios. Windows Server 2003 forces the shutdown tracker to collect the information each time it shut downs. The shutdown tracker logs information relating to which of the following?

A. Shutdown data only

B. Shutdown and Hibernate data

C. Shutdown, Hibernate, and Logoff data

D. Hibernate and Logoff data

☑ Answer **A** is correct. The shutdown tracker records only the shutdown information.

☒ Answer **B** is incorrect, because the Shutdown Event Tracker does not record Hibernate information. Answers **C** and **D** are incorrect, because it does not record logoff information.

15. Your machine has been upgraded from a standalone machine to a domain controller. You want to have the Shutdown Event Tracker enabled on each workstation and server of your domain. How would you go about doing this?

    A. You can enable Shutdown Event Tracker only for servers. Therefore, no Windows Server 2003 workstations can enable Shutdown Event Tracker.

    B. Enable Shutdown Event Tracker and select WorkStation only option.

    C. Enable Shutdown Event Tracker and select Domain only option.

    D. Enable Shutdown Event Tracker and select Always option.

    ☑ Answer **D** is correct. You need to enable Shutdown Event Tracker on every machine (domain controller and the workstations). Therefore, you need to enable it and select the Always option.

    ☒ Answer **A** is incorrect, because you can enable Shutdown Event Tracker on both Windows Server 2003 servers and workstations. Answer **B** is incorrect, because the Workstation only option omits the server implementing Shutdown Event Viewer. The same logic applies to answer **C**. Domain Only option does not enable Shutdown Event Tracker on workstations.

Chapter 10: Planning and Implementing Disaster Recovery

Defining and Understanding Disaster Recovery

1. A small company uses a single Windows Server 2003 machine to provide resources and services to users of the network. During a power failure, the drivers for the network card and graphics card for this server are corrupted. You want to connect to this server remotely so that you can repair the damage. Which of the following will you use to fix these problems?

    A. Automated System Recovery

    B. Emergency Management Services

    C. RAID

    D. Server Clusters

    ☑ Emergency Management Services (Answer **B**) enables you to access a Windows Server 2003 computer remotely, even if a network connection isn't available. Although other tools enable remote management, they depend on network drivers to be functioning properly or the operating system on the server to be fully functional. Emergency Management Services can use an out-of-band connection to access the server so that management tasks can be performed.

☒ Answers **A, C,** and **D** are incorrect because none of these is used to remotely connect to a server using an out-of-band connection. Answer **A** is incorrect, because Automated System Recovery is used to create backup sets that can be used to recovery the system if a major problem occurs. Answer **C** is incorrect, because RAID is a Redundant Array of Inexpensive Disks, which is used to enable data to be restored in the case of a disaster through methods like mirroring, disk duplexing, and disk striping with parity. Answer **D** is incorrect, because server clustering enables groups of individual computers running Windows Server 2003 to be grouped together, so they appear to the network as a single system. If one computer fails, then others in the cluster can take over and provide services and other resources to users.

2. You are using the Special Administration Console to repair a Windows Server 2003 computer that has failed to start properly. When you try to use this tool, it fails to load properly. Which of the following will occur?

   A. SAC will restart, giving you limited functionality. You will only be able to display information about the computer, view log entries, and restart the server.

   B. !SAC will automatically load, giving you the capability to display information about the computer, view log entries, and restart the server.

   C. !SAC will automatically load, giving you the full functionality of the Special Administration console.

   D. !SAC will need to be manually loaded.

   ☑ Answer **B** is correct. If Special Administration Console (SAC) fails to load or function properly, then Emergency Management Services switches to !SAC. Because !SAC is a secondary tool that is part of Emergency Management Services, it has considerably fewer commands associated with it. It enables you to display server information and log entries, or restart the server.

   ☒ Answer **A** is incorrect, because when SAC fails to load or function, !SAC automatically loads. **C** is incorrect, because !SAC has less functionality than SAC. Answer **D** is incorrect, because !SAC automatically loads when SAC fails to load or function.

Creating a Backup Plan

3. Members of the organization store files on a Windows Server 2003 computer. Each department has its own folder, with subfolders inside for each employee within that department. A complaint has been made about an employee having non-work-related files on the server that are considered offensive. Upon checking the contents of that person's folder, you find it to be true. You want to back up the entire contents of this folder, without affecting the backups that are performed daily. What will you do?

   A. Perform a normal backup.

   B. Perform an incremental backup.

C. Perform a copy backup.

D. You cannot back up the files without affecting other backups that are performed.

☑ Answer **C** is correct. A copy backup backs up the entire contents of the folder, without changing the archive attribute of backed-up files. Because the archive attribute isn't modified, it does not affect any incremental or differential backups that are performed. This is useful if you want to make a copy of data on the computer, but don't want it to interfere with other backup operations involving normal and incremental backups.

☒ Answer **A** is incorrect, because a normal backup changes the archive attribute of files that are backed up, which affects other backups that are performed daily. Answer **B** is incorrect, because incremental backups also affect the other backups. This answer is also incorrect because it only backs up files that have changed since the last normal or incremental backup (not the entire contents of the folder). **D** is incorrect, because a copy backup backs up the entire contents of the folder, without affecting the archive attribute of the files.

4. You are developing a backup plan that will be used to routinely back up data each night. There is a considerable amount of data on the Windows Server 2003 servers on the network, so you want backups to occur as quickly as possible. Due to the mission-critical nature of much of this data, you also want data to be restored as quickly as possible following a disaster. Based on these needs, which of the following backup types will you use in your plan?

A. Perform a normal backup each night.

B. Perform a daily backup each night.

C. Perform a normal backup, followed by nightly incremental backups.

D. Perform a normal backup, followed by nightly differential backups.

☑ Answer **D** is correct. A normal backup backs up all the selected files, while subsequent differential backups back up all data that has changed since the last normal (or incremental backup). When this type of backup is performed, the archive attribute isn't cleared, so data on one differential backup contains the same information as the previous differential backup plus any additional files that have changed. When restoring backed-up data, the last normal backup and last differential backup need to be restored.

☒ Answer **A** is incorrect, because a normal backup backs up all the files you select in a single backup job. This means that all files selected for backup are backed up, regardless of whether they've changed or not. This takes a considerable amount of time each night to back up data. Answer **B** is incorrect, because a daily backup backs up all the files you select that have been modified on that particular day. Any data before the first backup is performed won't be backed up. This means that if a disaster occurs, all of the data won't be available to be restored. Answer **C** is incorrect, because a normal backup with nightly incremental backups takes longer to restore than a differential backup. An incremental backup backs up all data that was changed since the normal or incremental backup.

Because the normal backup and every subsequent incremental backup needs to be restored in order to fully restore all data, it takes longer to restore than a combined normal and differential backup.

5. A user has ownership of files in a shared folder located on a Windows Server 2003 computer and wants to perform a backup of her files. She is a standard user, with no special rights or group memberships. Due to the amount of free disk space and the need of users to store sizable files, there are no restrictions on how much data a user can store on the server. The user has to temporarily perform the duties of a coworker who also uses this folder for his work. After modifying documents belonging to this person over the day, she tries to back up the files but finds she cannot. She calls and complains to you about the problem, hoping you can help. What is most likely the reason for this problem? (Choose all that apply.)

   A. She doesn't have the minimum permissions necessary to back up these files.

   B. She is not an Administrator or Backup Operator.

   C. She does not have ownership of the files.

   D. Disk quota restrictions are preventing the backup.

   ☑ Answers **B** and **C** are correct. If this user were an Administrator or Backup Operator, she could back up these files. However, giving her this level of security is overkill if the only reason is to enable her to back up someone else's files. While the user has the necessary permissions to the files, she must also have ownership of the file.

   ☒ Answer **A** is incorrect, because the permissions needed to back up a file that you own is Read, Read and Execute, Modify, or Full Control. Since she is able to modify the documents she's attempting to back up, she has the minimum permissions needed. Answer **D** is incorrect, because the scenario states that disk quotas are not used on the server.

6. You schedule a backup to run Monthly on the 30th of each month. When configuring this job, you also specify that the computer is to stop the task if it runs for 72 hours, or if the computer begins running on battery power. You also set the job to start only if the computer has been idle for at least 20 minutes and to retry for up to 60 minutes if it is not. Ten minutes before leaving at 5:00 PM on Friday, you recheck these settings. On Sunday, March 1st, you are called in to take care of a separate problem and find that the backup job didn't start. Based on this information, what is most likely the reason for this problem?

   A. You checked the settings before leaving at the end of the day.

   B. More than 72 hours has passed since the job first started.

   C. Since it is set to run every 30 days, 30 days haven't elapsed since the last backup.

   D. There aren't 30 days in this month.

   ☑ Answer **D** is correct. When performing monthly backups, you can set the date on which a backup will run. The Day field enables you to select a number between 1 and 31 as the day of the month when a backup will run. However, if a day between 29 and 31 is selected, the backup job will run only on months that contain those days. Since you came in to work and checked on the job on the 1st of March, this means that the previous month was February (which doesn't have 30 days in it).

☒ Answer **A** is incorrect, because when you set a task to start only if the computer has been idle for a specific number of minutes, it can recheck to see whether it is idle. In this situation, the job was configured to retry for up to 60 minutes if the computer was not idle. Answer **B** is incorrect, because it was checked on Sunday, and the job was started at the end of the day on Friday, meaning that less than 72 hours have passed. Answer **C** is incorrect, because the scenario says that the backup job was to start on the 30th of each month, not every 30 days.

7. You are using the Backup utility to back up the System State of a Windows Server 2003 computer. This server contains data files used by users of the network. It also acts as a Web server for the local intranet, and enables users to view information in HTML format on the network. Which of the following files will be included when the System State is backed up? (Choose all that apply.)

   A. IIS Metadirectory

   B. COM+ Class Registration database

   C. SYSVOL directory

   D. Certificate Services database

   ☑ Answer **A** and **B** are correct. The IIS Metadirectory, COM+ Class Registration database and Registry will be backed up. On Windows Server 2003, the System State always includes the Registry, COM+ Class Registration database, system files, and boot files. Because this server is configured to be a Web server and has Internet Information Services (IIS) installed, the IIS Metadirectory is also included.

   ☒ Answer **C** is incorrect, because Active Directory and the SYSVOL directory are included in the System State only on domain controllers. The scenario does not state that the server is a domain controller. Answer **D** is incorrect, because only certificate servers include the Certificate Services database as part of the System State. The scenario does not state that the server is a certificate server.

Creating a System Recovery Plan

8. The master boot record on the boot partition of your Windows Server 2003 computer has become damaged. When the computer tries to start, it fails before displaying the multi-boot menu that enables you to choose which operating system to start, preventing you from accessing utilities that are available after Windows Server 2003 starts. How will you fix the problem?

A. Restore the master boot record from an Automated System Recovery set.

B. At startup, press the F8 key to access the startup options and use the utilities that appear to fix the master boot record on the boot partition.

C. Run the Recovery Console from the menu that appears at system startup and use the FIXMBR command to repair the master boot record on the boot partition.

D. Run the Recovery Console from the installation CD and use the FIXMBR command to repair the master boot record on the boot partition.

☑ Answer **D** is correct. FIXMBR is a command within Recovery Console that repairs the master boot record.

☒ Answer **A** is incorrect, because an ASR set can't be used to repair damage to the master boot record. Answer **B** is incorrect, because the startup options don't provide a utility to repair damage to the master boot record. Answer **C** is incorrect, because the system is failing before the multi-boot menu appears, so you can't access Recovery Console from the menu that appears at system startup.

9. A server on your network acts as a file server and Web server, but isn't configured as a domain controller. You have modified settings in the Registry dealing with services that load automatically in the hopes of improving system performance. After making these modifications, you try to restart Windows but find that it can't load properly. Which of the following startup options will you use to attempt to resolve this problem?

A. Last Known Good Configuration

B. Enable VGA Mode

C. Directory Service Restore Mode

D. Debugging Mode

☑ Answer **A** is correct. When Last Known Good Configuration is used, Windows starts using the Registry information and driver settings saved at the last successful logon. This option is particularly important if you incorrectly configured Windows Server 2003, because using the settings that were saved during the last successful logon loads the operating system as it was before you made these changes.

☒ Answer **B** is incorrect, because Enable VGA Mode enables Windows Server 2003 to start with a basic VGA driver that provides minimal graphics support. Because the problem is that you modified configuration settings in the Registry, that has nothing to do with the display driver, so this choice doesn't apply. Answer **C** is incorrect, because Directory Service Restore Mode is used for a Windows Server 2003 computer acting as a domain controller, so that you can restore Active Directory and the SYSVOL directory. The scenario states that the server is not a domain controller. Answer **D** is incorrect, because Debugging Mode is used to send debugging information through a serial cable to another computer.

Working with Volume Shadow Copies

10. A user attempts to view the previous versions of a file that's been shadow copied on the server. When he tries to view the previous versions, he finds that he cannot. When he views the file's properties, there is no tab for previous versions. Other users of the network are not experiencing this problem and are able to view previous versions without any issues. What is most likely the cause of this problem?

    A. Shadow copying isn't enabled

    B. There have been no modifications to the file since shadow copying was enabled.

    C. The Previous Versions Client hasn't been installed on the server.

    D. The Previous Versions Client hasn't been installed on the user's computer.

    ☑ Answer **D** is correct. Until this client software is installed, the Previous Versions tab won't appear on the properties of files he views.

    ☒ Answer **A** is incorrect, because other users are able to view previous versions. Answer **B** is incorrect, because if no modifications have been made to the file since shadow copying was enabled, the user would be able to see the Previous Versions tab of the file's properties, but would not see any previous versions. Answer **C** is incorrect, because the Previous Versions Client needs to be installed on the user's machine, not on the server.

11. A user has asked for your assistance in accessing a previous version of a file and restoring it to another location on the hard disk so it can be modified. How will you assist this user?

    A. From the Previous Versions tab on the properties of the file, click Copy and specify the new location for the file.

    B. From the Previous Versions tab on the properties of the file, click Restore and specify the new location for the file.

    C. From the Previous Versions tab on the properties of the file, click View and specify the new location for the file when asked where the file should be copied before opening it.

    D. Right-click the file and click Restore from the menu that appears. When the dialog box appears, specify the new location for the file

    ☑ Answer **A** is correct. Copying a previous version of a file is done through the Previous Versions tab. After selecting the previous version you want to copy, click the Copy button on this tab. This opens a Copy Items dialog box, which enables you to specify where the older version of this file should be copied.

    ☒ Answer **B** is incorrect, because using the Restore button overwrites the current version of the file. It doesn't offer an alternate location to which it can be restored. Answer **C** is incorrect, because the View button opens the file, but doesn't offer a location to copy it to before opening it. Answer **D** is incorrect, because right-clicking the file doesn't provide a Restore menu item.

12. A Windows Server 2003 computer has a shared folder filled with files in the local path C:\Shared. Shadow copying is enabled, and the client software is installed on the server. To confirm everything is working properly, you open Windows Explorer and attempt to view the previous version of a file by accessing it through C:\Shared. When attempting to access it, you find that there is no tab for previous versions. What is the problem?

    A. The client software cannot be installed on the server; this prevents you from viewing the previous versions.

    B. The client software has been installed prior to enabling shadow copying on the server.

    C. The Previous Versions tab is available only when clients attempt to view the properties over the network.

    D. There is nothing shared on the server, preventing shadow copying from working.

    ☑ Answer **C** is correct. Attempting to view previous versions by accessing the file from the local hard disk does not work.

    ☒ Answer **A** is incorrect, because the client software can be installed on the server. Answer **B** is incorrect, because it doesn't matter if the client software is installed before shadow copying is enabled. If the client is installed first, you are able to view previous versions on other servers. When you enable shadow copying on the server on which the client is installed, you are able to view previous versions on that server over the network. Answer **D** is incorrect, because C:\Shared has been shared out, and would be used for shadow copying.

Recovering from Server Hardware Failure

13. You have decided to implement RAID to provide fault tolerance for data stored on hard disks on the server. The level of RAID you plan to implement is RAID 5. The Windows Server 2003 computer on which you plan to implement RAID has 256MB of memory, one 500MB hard disk, one 800MB hard disk, and acts as a domain controller. Can RAID 5 be installed on this machine as it is?

    A. Yes. It meets the minimum requirements for RAID 5.

    B. No. There isn't enough memory installed on the server.

    C. No. The hard disks are different sizes.

    D. No. There aren't enough hard disks installed.

    ☑ Answer **D** is correct. With RAID 5, data is striped across three or more disks, with parity information stored across multiple drives. Because there are only two disks installed, RAID 5 can't be used unless you add more disks. Because the system and boot partitions can't be part of a RAID 5 array, you need to install at least two more disks (assuming your boot and system partitions are on the same physical disk).

☒ Answer **A** is incorrect, because there aren't enough hard disks installed on the server. Answer **B** is incorrect, because there are no requirements for minimal memory to implement RAID 5. Answer **C** is incorrect, because the problem isn't that the hard disks are different sizes, but that there aren't enough hard disks installed.

14. A Windows Server 2003 computer uses RAID 5 for fault tolerance. One of the disks fails. What will happen to the data in this set?

    A. Data will be regenerated from parity information on the other disks.

    B. The mirrored volume must be broken using the Disk Management tool to make the other mirror a separate volume.

    C. RAID 5 only improves performance; it isn't fault tolerant. The data will be lost.

    D. The data will need to be reinstalled from a backup.

    ☑ Answer **A** is correct. With RAID 5, data is striped across three or more disks, with parity information stored across multiple disks. Parity is a calculated value that's used to restore data from the other disks if one of the disks in the set fails. It determines the number of odd and even bits in a number, and can use this to reconstruct data if a sequence of numbers is lost, which is the case if one of the disks fails.

    ☒ Answer **B** is incorrect, because this choice describes a mirrored volume. Answer **C** is incorrect, because RAID 5 is fault tolerant. Answer **D** is incorrect, because data can be reconstructed from the parity information on other disks.

15. Your server is running Windows Server 2003. The machine has two disk drives installed that are 10GB and 20GB in size. You have decided to use disk duplexing for fault tolerance. Which of the following will you need to do to implement this? (Choose all that apply.)

    A. Mirror the two drives so that data from the 10GB drive is also written to the 20GB drive.

    B. Mirror the two drives so that data from the 20GB drive is also written to the 10GB drive.

    C. Install each drive on a separate disk controller.

    D. Install each drive on the same disk controller.

    ☑ Answers **A** and **C** are correct. When separate controllers are used for mirrored drives, it is called duplexing. With duplexing, each disk is installed on a different controller, so that if one of the disks fails or a controller fails, the data is still available through the other disk in the pair.

    ☒ Answer **B** is incorrect, because there wouldn't be enough disk space on the second drive to mirror the first. Answer **D** is incorrect, because if both disks were on the same controller, mirroring would be implemented, not duplexing.

Index

Symbols

!SAC/SAC tool, 803–805
%% double percent sign, 314
? question mark, 262

Numerics

3DES algorithm, 455
401 errors, 690
404 errors, 687
40-bit/128-bit encryption, 659
503 errors, 689
802.1X protocols, 37

A

access control, 409–485
  how the process works, 412
  terminology of, 411
  troubleshooting, 444–447
    guidelines for, 445
  See also security; reliability
Access Control Entry (ACE), 411
Access Control Lists (ACLs), 661, 665
  types of, 411
  access tokens, 412
Account tab (ADUC tool), for user accounts, 282–285
ACE (Access Control Entry), 411
ACLs. *See* Access Control Lists
activating Windows Server 2003, 48–50
active command, 88
Active Directory (AD), 2, 16, 22, 258
  clustering integrated with, 31
  computer accounts and, 349
  domain controller role for, 628
  group accounts and, 318
  new features with Server 2003, 24–28
  RDN/DN names and, 268
  restoring, methods for, 849
  security objects and, 256
  shares and, permissions for, 429–431
  system upgrades and, 53
  user rights and, 439
  utilities for, 259–276, 303–313
Active Directory Installation wizard, 628
  creating domain controllers and, 370
Active Directory Integrated (ADI) zones, 28
Active Directory isolation mode, iisftp.vbs tool and, 700
Active Directory Users and Computers admin tool (ADUC), 259–261
  new query feature of, 25
  tabs in, displaying, 280
  using
    for computer accounts, 350–362
    for group accounts, 324–333
    for user accounts, 277–300
active partition, 77
Active Server Pages (ASP), 663
  IIS troubleshooting and, 687
  See also ASP.NET
AD. *See* Active Directory
add command, 88
Add Printer wizard, 602
Address tab (ADUC tool), for user accounts, 280
ADI zones, 28
administration, 17
Administration Tools Pack, 594
  when to use, 598
Administrative Tools menu, 584
administrative tools. *See* utilities
Administrator account, 257
administrators
  Recovery Console, automatic logon for, 852
  Run as command and, 589
  Safe Mode and, 858
adminpak.msi, 594
  when to use, 598
ADUC. *See* Active Directory Users and Computers admin tool
Advanced Digest Authentication, 657
Advanced mode (Backup utility), 818–827
AGUDLP mnemonic device, 345, 347
alerts, 733, 737
Allow logon to terminal server check box, 560
Alto computer system (Xerox Corporation), 4
answer file/Answer Script, for IIS setup, 655
Appearance tab (System Monitor), 732
Apple's Lisa computer system, 4
application log, 762
  eventcreate.exe tool for, 769
  types of events in, 760
application media pools, 158
application partition, 28
application pools, 663
  extending queue length of, 689
Application Server mode. *See* terminal server role
application server role, 626
application servers, terminology caution and, 650
ASP. *See* Active Server Pages
ASP.NET, 663
  application server role for, 626

connection errors and, 689
content errors and, 687, 688
working with, 682
See also Active Server Pages
ASR. *See* Automated System Recovery
asset evaluation, 807
assign command, 88
attributes (of objects), 21
audio devices, sound drivers for disabled by default in Server 2003, 201
audit plan, 750
audit policies, 751–759
settings for, 755–759
audit trail, 749
auditing
computer accounts and, 257
user groups and, 256
authentication, 17, 657–660
vs. authorization, 661
computer accounts and, 257
Remote Desktop for Administration and, 498
user groups and, 256
Web sites, configuring settings for in IIS, 684–686
authoritative restores, for Active Directory, 849
authorization, 661
user groups and, 256
Automated System Recovery (ASR), 241, 813, 850
automatic service startup, 614
automount command, 88

B

Backup and Restore wizard (Backup utility), 818, 833
Backup Domain Controllers (BDCs), 19
backup logs, 824
backup media, 814–817
managing, 831–833
safeguarding, 813
backup sets, managing catalogs and, 832, 835
Backup tab (Backup utility), 819
scheduling backups and, 836
Backup utility, 813, 817–845
ASR sets and, 850
backup media and, 814
exercise using, 826
backups, 800, 812–847
of audit information, 750
boot/system files and, 828
as part of business continuity plan, 800
delegating authority for, 830
excluding file types from, 824
of IIS configurations, 703–706
media for, 814–817
of metabase entries, 665
naming, 820
offsite storage of, 817
vs. Remote Storage, 156
restoring, 812, 833–835
scheduling, 835–844
frequency of, 839–844
setting options for, 820
advanced options and, 824–826
of System State data, 827
types of, 821–823
verifying successful completion of, 830
which data to back up, 813
Banyan VINES directory service, 20
basic authentication, 657
basic disks, 71–74
converting to dynamic, 108–110
managing, 92–107
tools for, 92
troubleshooting, 171–174
BDCs (Backup Domain Controllers), 19
behavior command, 90
.bkf file extension, 820
blue screens, 235–237
boot files, 77
backing up, 828
System State backups and, 848
boot partition, 77
boot sector, 73
repairing with Recovery Console, 851
Bootcfg.exe tool, using to enable EMS, 802
booting disks, 73
break command, 88
bug checks, 235–237
business continuity plans, 800–805

C

cache memory, 68
cached copies of files, 156
CALs (Client Access Licenses), 11, 47
catalogs, managing, 832, 835
CDPs (CRL distribution points), 465
Certificate Authorities (CAs), 466–472
"The certificate has failed to verify for all of its intended purposes" warning message, 659

certificate revocation lists (CRLs), 37, 465
certificate servers, System State backups and, 848
Certificate Services, 460, 463–471
  enhancements with Server 2003, 468
  installing/configuring, 465, 470–472
certificates. *See* digital certificates
certification authorities (CAs), 464
change logon command, 566
change port command, 566
change user command, 566
channels, 804
character-based operating systems, 4
chat programs, 503
child domains. *See* sub-domains
chkdsk.exe tool, 29, 173
cipher.exe tool, 458
  encrypting files and, 36
Citrix Independent Computing Architecture (ICA) protocol, 495
Citrix Systems, 495
  Multi-Win technology and, 494
  Terminal Services technology and, 488
  Windows NT Server 4.0 Terminal Server Edition and, 12
clean command, 88
Client Access Licenses (CALs), 11, 47
client computers, shadow copy software for, 864
client connection tools for Terminal Services, 521–540
client-server networking, 17
Client Settings tab (Terminal Services Configuration tool), 554–556
clipboard, troubleshooting problems with, 568
CLR (Common Language Runtime), 35
cluster services, 31–33
  nodes backups and, 828
  System State backups and, 848
clusters, 68, 70, 128–130
  editions of Server 2003 and, 46
cmdkey.exe tool, 275
COM+ Class Registration database, System State backups and, 848
COM+ tab (ADUC tool), for user accounts, 292
command-line utilities, 258, 588
  for account management
    computer accounts, 362–370
    group accounts, 333–342
    user accounts, 300–313
  for Active Directory, 261–276
  cipher.exe, 458
  for disk management, 86–91
  for event handling, 769–775
  for hardware devices/device drivers, 220–227
  for IIS 6.0, 692–709
  ntbackup, 845–847
  for performance monitoring, 738–743
  for print management, 607–610
  for server management, 447–450
  for services, 619–623
  syntax for, 262–264
  for Terminal Services, 565
comma-separated value format (CSV format), 315
Common Language Runtime (CLR), 35
compressed files
  disk quotas and, 140
  EFS encryption and, 454
computer accounts, 257, 349–395
  creating
    with ADUC tool, 350–352
    with dsadd.exe tool, 363
  group accounts and, 317
  managing, 353–395
    description of computers, 365, 369
    disabling computer accounts, 365
    finding computers, 367
    group membership of computers, displaying, 370
    location of computers, displaying, 370
    mapping computers, 359
    moving, 361
    resetting computer accounts, 360
    tools for, 258–276
  passwords for, 361
    resetting, 365
computer forensics software, 832
Computer Management MMC, 595–597
  computer accounts and, 362
  when to use, 598
Computer Management tool, creating shadow copies and, 859
Configure a DNS Server wizard, 629
Configure Your Server wizard, 602, 624–631, 650–654
configuring. *See* installing/ configuring
connection errors, troubleshooting, 689–691
console redirection, 801
console sessions, 491
    Terminal Services Manager and, 541
    vs. Terminal Services sessions, 492, 494
contacts, creating in Windows Messenger, 507
containers, 260, 261
content errors, troubleshooting, 687
Control Panel applets, using to display hardware device information, 219

Control Program for Microcomputers (CP/M), 3
convert.exe tool, 755
cooperative multitasking, 5
copy backups, 823
counter logs, 733–735
CP/M (Control Program for Microcomputers), 3
Cprofile command, 566
create command, 88
Credential Manager, 36
critical systems, restoring first, 799, 806
CRL distribution points (CDPs), 465
CRLs (certificate revocation lists), 37, 465
cross-forest authentication, 24
cross-forest authorization, 24
cross-forest trusts, 38
cryptography, 658–660
  See also Encrypting File System
cscript, 607
CSP (Selectable Cryptographic Service Provider), 659
CSV Directory Exchange tool, 315–317
.csv files, saving event logs as, 767
CSV format, 315
csvde tool, 315–317
Ctrl+Alt+Del reboot, introduced with Windows 3.1, 6
cylinders, 68, 69

D

DACLs. *See* Discretionary Access Control Lists
daily backups, 823
DAT (Digital Audio Tape), 815
data, asset evaluation and, 807
databases, striped volumes and, 119
Datacenter Edition (of Server 2003), 46
dcpromo, 370–372, 381–385
DCs. *See* domain controllers
DDS format, 815
Debugging Mode startup option, 858
Default Lockdown status, IIS and, 660
defrag.exe tool, 128, 137
Defragmenter tool, 128, 131–137
  disk optimization and, 749
defragmenting disks, 128–139
  best practices for, 138
  disk fragmentation, troubleshooting and, 178
  software analysis for, 135–137
  time required for, 134
delegation, 284
Delegation tab (ADUC tool), for computer accounts, 355
delete command, 88
demilitarized zones (DMZs), 648
dependencies, for services, 616
designators. *See* drive letters
Desktop Cleanup wizard, 14
DESX algorithm, 455
detail command, 88
devcon.exe tool, 220–225
Device Console utility, 220–225
device drivers, 198, 200
  for sound, disabled by default in Server 2003, 201
  managing, 215
  troubleshooting, 235–242
Device Manager, 233
  using to configure hardware devices, 211–217, 218
devices. *See* hardware devices
Dfs (Distributed File System), 28, 29
DH SChannel Cryptographic provider (Microsoft), 659
DHCP server role, 629
Dial-In tab (ADUC tool)
  computer accounts, 357–359
  user accounts, 293–295
differential backups, 823
Digest security, 657
Digital Audio Tape (DAT), 815
digital certificates, 452, 460–465
  managing revoked, 465
Digital Data Storage (DDS), 815
Digital Linear Tape (DLT), 815
digital media, improved support for introduced with Windows ME, 8
directories, 20
Directory Service log, 764
Directory Service Restore Mode startup option, 858
directory services, 20–22, 258
dirty command, 90
dirty volumes, defragmentation and, 139
disabled service startup, 614
disaster recovery, 797–879
  best practices for, 809–811
  components of, 799
  plans for dealing with (list), 800
  types of disasters, 798
disaster recovery plans, 800, 805–812
  as part of business continuity plan, 800
Discretionary Access Control Lists (DACLs), 411, 754

discussion groups, creating/ managing NNTP server for, 675–677
Disk Cleanup utility, introduced with Windows 98, 7
Disk Defragmenter tool. *See* Defragmenter tool
disk duplexing, 82
disk encryption. *See* encryption
disk fault tolerance, 75
disk fragmentation, 29, 128–131
  troubleshooting, 177
Disk Management MMC snap-in, 85
disk management tools, 84–91
disk quotas, 139–151
  best practices for, 150
  converted volumes and, 142
  copying, 147
  default limit for users, 151
  enabling/configuring, 140–145
  exporting/importing, 147–150
  monitoring/analyzing, 145–147
  status of, stop light indicating, 140
  troubleshooting, 178–180
  when to use, 140
disk signature, 73
  troubleshooting basic disks and, 172
diskpart.exe tool, 87–90
disks, 67–196
  basic vs. dynamic, 71–74
  booting, 73
  defragmenting, 128–139
    best practices for, 138
    software analysis for, 135–137
    time required for, 134
    tools for, 128
  monitoring, 748
    recommendations/tips for, 749
  optimizing performance of, 128–155, 748
  physical vs. logical, 71
  tools for managing, 84–91
  troubleshooting, 170–183
Display tab (RDC utility), 526
distinguished name (DN), 268
Distributed File System (Dfs), 28, 29
Distributed Management Task Force (DTMF), 595
distribution groups, 318, 319
DLT (Digital Linear Tape), 815
DMZ (demilitarized zones), 648
DN (distinguished name), 268
DNS directory service, 21
DNS server log, 764
DNS server role, 629
domain accounts, 615
domain controller role, 628
Domain Controller Security Policy, 442
domain controllers (DCs), 18–20
  Active Directory restores and, 849
  assigning operations master roles to, 388–395
  audit policies for, 752
  creating/managing, 370–387
  domain functionality and, 320
  event logs on, 764
  new features with Server 2003, 25
  System State backups and, 848
  system upgrades and, 53
domain functionality, 320–323
domain local groups, 319, 320–323
  determining/changing, 343
  using, 345
Domain name registration for IIS server, 646
Domain Naming Master Controls operations master role, 388, 390
domain rename tool, 24
domain-wide roles, 388
domains, 18–20
  Active Directory and, 258
  audit policies for, 753
  computer accounts and, 257
  configuring user access to network share and, 348
  creating new domain controller for, 370–376
  introduced with Windows NT 3.1, 19
  renaming, 24
  system upgrades and, 53
  Windows XP Pro and, 15
DOS. *See* entries at MS-DOS
double percent sign (%%), in script files, 314
downloads
  Microsoft Operations Manager, 750
  rendom.exe tool, 24
  Windows Messenger, 504
  Windows Resource Kit, 589
drag-and-drop functionality, introduced with Windows 3.1, 6
drive letters
  assigning, 100–102
  troubleshooting basic disks and, 171
driver signing, 198, 202
  configuring options for, 203–210
drives, setting number accessed simultaneously, 168
dsadd.exe tool, 264
  for computer accounts, 363
  for group accounts, 333
  for user accounts, 300–303
dsget.exe tool, 267, 309–313

for computer accounts, 368–370
for group accounts, 340–342
dsmod.exe tool, 265, 303–306
for computer accounts, 364
for group accounts, 335–337
dsmove.exe tool, 268
dsquery.exe tool, 269, 306–309
for computer accounts, 365–368
for group accounts, 337–340
DTMF (Distributed Management Task Force), 595
dual-boot configurations, 72
basic disks and, 92
dynamic content, 42
404 errors and, 688
dynamic disks, 71–74
converting from basic, 108–110
limitations of, 72
managing, 108–127
Windows 2000 and, 72, 74
dynamic volumes
creating, 110–127
troubleshooting, 174–177

E

EAP (Extensible Authentication Protocol), 37
EB (exabyte), 142
EC licenses, 48
eDirectory (Novell), 20
EFI. *See* Extensible Firmware Interface
EFS. *See* Encrypting File System
e-mail, using to request Remote Assistance, 508
embedded operating systems, 490
Emergency Management Services (EMS), 241, 598–601, 801–805
enabling as part of disaster recovery planning, 811
Server 2003 components supporting, 803
EMS. *See* Emergency Management Services
Enable Boot Logging startup option, 857
Enable VGA Mode startup option, 857
encrypted files, sharing, 457
exercise for, 35
Encrypting File System (EFS), 14, 35, 450–460
best practices for, 459
controlling environment for, 455
disabling, 456
enabled at folder level by users, 454
recovery agents and, 453
encryption
for Terminal Services, 549
See also Encrypting File System
Enterprise Edition (of Server 2003), 45
Entrust, 464
Environment tab
ADUC tool, for user accounts, 287
Terminal Services Configuration tool, 552
user accounts, 562
environment variables, setx.exe tool for, 620
errors, as event type, 760
event logs, 760–768
configuring, 764
eventtriggers.exe tool for, 771–774
purging/clearing, 766
troubleshooting, 768
event traces, tracerpt.exe tool for, 774
Event Viewer, 760–768
troubleshooting, 768
using to monitor hardware devices, 219
eventcreate.exe tool, 769
eventquery.vbs tool, 770
eventtriggers.exe tool, 771–774
.evt files, saving event logs as, 767
exabyte (EB), 142
Excel spreadsheets, extracting performance logs to, 740
exercises
audit policies, 751–753
applying, 758
Backup utility, 826
Certificate Services, installing/ configuring, 470–472
computer accounts, creating, 350–352
counter logs, creating, 733–735
Defragmenter tool, 132–135
disk performance metrics, capturing, 228–230
disk quotas
enabling/setting limits for, 143–145
exporting/importing, 147–150
disks
converting from basic to dynamic, 108–110
selecting, 89
drive letters, assigning, 100–102
driver signing, scanning for unsigned drivers, 209
EMS, 599–601, 812
encrypted files, sharing, 35
event logs, archiving, 766
files
changing ownership of, 449
audit settings for, 756–758
folders, audit settings for, 756–758
forests, creating, 377–381
group accounts, creating, 324

health detection, enabling, 683
logical drives, creating, 97–100
Microsoft Loopback Adapter, disabling, 214
MMC snap-ins, creating custom, 587
non-plug-and-play drivers, installing, 210
operations master roles, transferring, 389–395
partitions, creating, 93–97
printers, sharing, 611–613
processes, identifying/ terminating, 623
queue length of application pools, extending, 689, 690
Remote Administration (HTML) component, installing/using, 592
Remote Console, installing/ using, 854
Remote Desktops MMC snap-in, configuring connection in, 532
Remote Storage, installing/ configuring, 160–165
replica DCs, 372–376
saved file, using to request Remote Assistance, 510
Server 2003, activating, 49
server roles, installing, 630
services, managing via Control Panel, 616–618
sessions, resetting using Terminal Services Manager, 567
shadow copies, 863, 866
shared folders, 432–439
Shutdown Event Tracker, 776, 781, 782
sub-domains (child domains), creating, 382–384
system compatibility, checking, 51
terminal server role, installing, 519
trees, creating, 385–387
user accounts, creating, 277–279
user rights, assigning, 444
volumes
creating, 111–127
extending, 106
formatting, 103–105
Windows File Protection, verifying operation of, 207
worker process recycling, 688
exit command, 88
Experience tab (RDC utility), 528
extend command, 88
extended partitions, 77
creating (exercise), 96
Extensible Authentication Protocol (EAP), 37
Extensible Firmware Interface (EFI), 76, 801
Extensible Markup Language. *See* entries at XML
External Connector (EC) licenses, 48

F

failover, 869
failure audits, 754
displayed in Security Event Viewer, 763
as event type, 761
failure events, 749
fast streaming, support for, 41
Fast User Switching feature, 14
FAT file systems
clusters and, 129
FAT32, support for introduced with Windows 95b, 7
fsutil.exe tool for, 90
Quota tab and, 178
Recovery Console and, 851
fault tolerance, 74, 75
RAID volume troubleshooting and, 181–183
recovering from hardware failures and, 867
volumes and, 79–83
Federal Information Processing Standard (FIPS), 549
FEK (file encryption key), 35
file authorization, for IIS 6.0, 661
file command, 90
file encryption key (FEK), 35
file extensions, troubleshooting IIS and, 687
file-level permissions. *See* NTFS permissions
File Replication Service (FRS), 28, 29, 764
file server role, 625
file services, improvements with Server 2003, 28
file sharing, introduced with Windows for Workgroups 3.1, 6
file signature verification tool, 209
File Transfer Protocol (FTP)
FTP sites, creating/managing
with IIS Manager, 671–673
with iisftp.vbs, 698–701
ICF and, 647
vs. WebDAV protocol, 658
files
encrypted, 456–459
sharing (exercise), 35
excluding from backup jobs, 824
finding, 447
moving, NTFS permissions and, 423
operation-based auditing of, 755–759
ownership of, 421–423
changing, 448
password-protected, 451
saved file, using to request Remote Assistance, 509–511
shadow copies of, 29

restoring, 865
troubleshooting Remote Storage and, 181
UNIX/Linux, IIS troubleshooting and, 691
unmovable, defragmentation and, 178
when to assign permissions to, 415
working with under Remote Storage, 167–169
FIPS (Federal Information Processing Standard), 549
firewall software internal to Server 2003, 647–649
Flattemp command, 566
flexible caching, 663
flexible single master operations. *See* operations master roles
folders
encrypting, 456–459
moving, NTFS permissions and, 423
operation-based auditing of, 755–759
ownership of, 421–423
when to assign permissions to, 415
For command (VB script), for creating multiple user accounts, 313–315
foreign disks, 174, 177
forensics software, 832
forest functionality, 320
forest root, 258
forest-wide roles, 388
forests, 38, 258
creating domain controller for, 377–381
system upgrades and, 53
fragmentation. *See* disk fragmentation
FrontPage Server extensions, application server role for, 626
FRS. *See* File Replication Service
fsinfo command, 90
FSMO. *See* operations master roles
fsutil.exe tool, 90, 151
FTP. *See* File Transfer Protocol

G

GB (gigabit), 141
GC servers, 27
General tab
ADUC tool
computer accounts, 353
group accounts, 326
user accounts, 280
RDC utility, 525
System Monitor, 730
Terminal Services Configuration tool, 549
GFS backup rotations, 844
gigabit (GB), 141
global catalog (GC) servers, 27
global groups, 319, 320–323
determining/changing, 343
using, 346
GlobalSign, 464
GPMC (Group Policy Management Console), enhancements with Server 2003, 26
GPOs (group policy objects), 26
gpresult.exe tool, 27, 270–274
GPT (GUID partition table), 76, 172
gpt command, 88
Grandfather-Father-Son rotations, 844
Graph tab (System Monitor), 732
graphical Defragmenter. *See* Defragmenter tool
graphical user interface (GUI), 4, 258
group accounts, 257, 317–349
creating
with ADUC tool, 324
with dsadd.exe tool, 333
disk quotas and, 141
group nesting and, 321
managing, 326–342
displaying properties of, 340–342
finding groups, 337–340
tools for managing, 258–276
users, adding to, 298, 336
group members, 317
adding to/removing from group accounts, 336
determining, 342, 344
group nesting and, 321
group nesting, 321–323
group policies
server settings and, 558
Terminal Services connection settings and, 547
Terminal Services users, controlling via, 564
using to delegate authority for backups, 830
Group Policy Management Console (GPMC), enhancements with Server 2003, 26
Group Policy Object Editor, 564
Group Policy Objects (GPOs), 26
audit policies and, 758
using to set user rights, 442
group scopes, 319–323
best practices for, 345–349
changing, 343
determining, 342, 343
group types, 319–323
converting, 337
determining, 342
Guest account, 257
GUI (graphical user interface), 4, 258
GUID partition table (GPT), 76, 172

H

HAL (Hardware Abstraction Layer), 9, 199
hard disks, 68–71
  formatting with Recovery Console, 851
  writing data to, 128–131
  See also disks
hardlink command, 90
Hardware Abstraction Layer (HAL), 9, 199
Hardware Compatibility List (Microsoft), 206
hardware devices
  asset evaluation and, 807
  configuring resources settings for, 217
  device status codes, resources for further information, 234
  failures and, recovering from, 867–869
  installing/configuring, 203–218
    best practices for, 217
  managing, 197–254
  monitoring, 218–231
    best practices for, 230
  New Hardware wizard for, 210
  properties for, 213, 214
  requirements/compatibility for Server 2003, 51
  troubleshooting, 231–243
    best practices for, 242
  vulnerabilities of, 198–203
hardware recovery plans, 800, 867–869
Hardware Troubleshooting Wizard, 232
HCT (Windows Hardware Compatibility Test), 203
headless management of servers, 598
health detection, 662
  enabling, 683
heartbeats (server node messages), 662, 869
help command, 88
HelpAssistant account, 257
HelpAssistant_XXXXXX user account, 500
High Performance File System (HPFS), 8
Hotmail accounts, creating in Windows Messenger, 505
HPFS (High Performance File System), 8
.htm files, saving log information as, 726
HTML (HyperText Markup Language), 43
HTTP.sys kernel mode device driver, 662
HTTPS protocol, ICF and, 647
HyperText Markup Language (HTML), 43
Hypertext Transfer Protocol (HTTP)
ICF and, 647

I

IAS (Internet Authentication Service), 33
IBM, OS joint venture with Microsoft, 8
ICA protocol, 495
ICF (Internet Connection Firewall), 14, 34
ICS (Internet Connection Sharing), introduced with Windows 98 SE, 7
IE. *See* Internet Explorer
IGMP (Internet Group Management Protocol), 32
IIS 5.0 isolation model, 662
IIS 6.0. *See* Internet Information Services
IIS log file, multilingual support for, 664
IIS Manager, 666–686
  creating/managing Web/FTP sites with, 667–677
IIS protocol, ICF and, 647
IIS. *See* Internet Information Services
iisback.vbs tool, 703–706
iiscnfg.vbs tool, 706–709
iisftp.vbs tool, 698–701
iisftpdr.vbs tool, 701–703
iissuba.dll, troubleshooting IIS and, 690
iisvdir.vbs tool, 696–698
iisweb.vbs tool, 692–696
import command, 88
in-band connections, 801
inactive command, 88
inactive primary partitions, 77
incident response planning, 808
incremental backups, 822
inetinfo.exe, 661
.inf file extension, 655
information, as event type, 761
Infrastructure Master operations master role, 388, 389
inheritance
  file/folder auditing and, 759
  permissions and, 431–439
  user rights and, 439
"This initial program cannot be started." error message, 568
installing/configuring
  ADUC tool, 260
  Certificate Services, 465, 470–472
  disk quotas, 140–145
  hardware devices, 203–218
  IIS 6.0, 535, 646–657
    best practices for, 657
    methods for, 650
  Recovery Console, 241, 851–855
  Remote Storage, 159–165
  terminal server role, 517–521
"Insufficient Disk Space" error message, 180
Inter-Site Topology Generator (ISTG), improvements with Server 2003, 27
Internet Authentication Service (IAS), 33

Internet Connection Firewall (ICF), 14, 34, 647–649
  IIS troubleshooting and, 690
Internet Connection Sharing (ICS), introduced with Windows 98 SE, 7
Internet Explorer
  remote administration and, 491
  Remote Desktop Web Connection utility and, 535, 540
Internet Group Management Protocol (IGMP), 32
Internet Information Services (IIS)
  application server role for, 626
  improvements with Server 2003, 30
  Internet printing and, 613
  System State backups and, 848
Internet Information Services (IIS),Version 6.0, 645–719
  backing up/restoring configurations, 703–706
  configuration settings for, manipulating, 706–709
  installing/configuring, 535, 646–657
    best practices for, 657
    methods for, 650
  managing
    with command-line utilities, 692–709
    with IIS Manager, 666–686
  new features with, 657–666
  pre-installation checklist for, 646
  troubleshooting, 687–692
Internet printing, 613
Internet Protocol Security (IPSec), 15
invitations requesting Remote Assistance, 502–511
  managing open, 515
IP addresses
  authentication settings and, 686
  SMTP/NNTP servers and, 675
IPSec (Internet Protocol Security), 15
IPSec over NAT, 33
IPv6, 33
ISAPI DLLs, viewing, 692
isolated environment (IIS 5.0), 660
ISTG (Inter-Site Topology Generator), improvements with Server 2003, 27
Itanium processor
  64-bit version of Windows XP Pro and, 15
  GPTpartitioning and, 76
  Recovery Console and, 851

J

jukebox libraries, 157

K

KB (kilobyte), 141
Kerberos authentication, available with clustered applications, 31
kernel mode, 199, 662
keys, cryptography and, 452, 461–463
Kildall, Gary, 3
kilobyte (KB), 141

L

L2TP over NAT, 34
Last Known Good Configuration, 237, 857
ldifde tool, 315–317
LDM database., 73
legal considerations for disaster recovery, 806
libraries, 157
licensing, 47–50
  for terminal server role, installing/activating component for, 520
  troubleshooting problems with, 569
Linux
  IIS troubleshooting and, 691
  Terminal Services clients for, 490
Lisa computer system (Apple), 4
list command, 88
listener connections, 547–550, 557
listener sessions, 543–545
load balancing, 869
local audit policies, 751
local groups, 318, 319, 320
Local Resources tab (RDC utility), 526
local service accounts, 615
local storage (top level of Remote Storage), 156, 166
Location tab (ADUC tool), for computer accounts, 355
log file for IIS, multilingual support for, 664
log files
  backup-related, 824
  eventquery.vbs tool for, 770
Logical Disk Manager (LDM) database, 73
logical disks, 71, 91–127
  tools for managing, 84–91
logical drives, 75–78, 92
  creating (exercise), 97–100
logman.exe tool, 738–740
Logoff command, 566
logon
  automatic, troubleshooting, 567
  to Recovery Console, automatic for administrators, 852
  Run as command for, 589

Logon Hour restrictions, user accounts and, 284
logon names
  changing for users, 282
  security identifiers and, 146
Logon Settings tab (Terminal Services Configuration tool), 550
long filenames, support for introduced with Window 95, 7
Loopback Adapter (Microsoft), 214
LUNA user interface, 13

M

Machine Log-On restrictions, user accounts and, 284
Macintosh OS X, RDC client software for, 490
magneto-optical (MO) disks, 156
mail server role, 627
Manage Your Server tool, 602, 624–631
Managed By tab (ADUC tool)
  computer accounts, 355
  group accounts, 328
managed volumes, 156
  modifying files on, 169
  removing from Remote Storage, 169
  setting free space for, 166
Managed Volumes container, 166
management information, retrieving with WMI, 595
management tools. *See* utilities
manual service startup, 614
mapping user accounts, 298
master boot record (MBR), 73, 172
  repairing with Recovery Console, 851
master sets, 170
MB (megabyte), 141
MBR. *See* master boot record
MBSchema.xml, 665
MD5 hashing, 657
Media container, 166
media copies, creating/ synchronizing, 169
media master, recreating, 169
media pools, 157, 158
Media Services, improvements with Server 2003, 41
megabyte (MB), 141
Member Of tab (ADUC tool)
  computer accounts, 354
  group accounts, 327
  user accounts, 293
Members tab (ADUC tool), for group accounts, 327
memory dumps, 235
memory leaks, 744
memory objects, monitoring/optimizing, 743–745
metabase data
  backing up/restoring, 665, 682
  Web site names and, 695
metabase entries, 664–666
metabase.xml file, 665
  refresh and, 706
metalanguages, 43
Microsoft
  DH SChannel Cryptographic provider, 659
  Excel spreadsheets, extracting performance logs to, 740
  Hardware Compatibility List, 206
  Loopback Adapter, disabling, 214
  OS joint venture with IBM, 8
  security providers, 659
  Trustworthy Computing initiative by, 657
Microsoft Cluster Service (MSCS), 12, 31
Microsoft Disk Operating System. *See* MS-DOS operating system
Microsoft Management Console (MMC), 41, 585
  creating custom consoles, 85
  See also entries at MMC; Remote Desktops MMC snap-in, 529
Microsoft Message Queue Server (MSMQ), 12
Microsoft Operations Manager (MOM), 750
MIME formats, 687
mirror sets, 74
mirrored volumes, 79, 81–83
  creating, 122–124
  vs. RAID-5 volumes, 124
  recovering from hardware failures and, 867
  when to use, 122
MMC console modes, 586
MMC snap-ins, 585–588
MMC. *See* Microsoft Management Console
MO disks, 156
MOM (Microsoft Operations Manager), 750
Msadc directory, not available with IIS 6.0, 692
.msc files, 585
MSCS (Microsoft Cluster Service), 12, 31
MS-DOS operating system, 3–9
  Terminal Services for, 490
Msg command, 566
MSIE. *See* Internet Explorer
MSMQ (Microsoft Message Queue Server), 12
mstsc /console command, 535
Mstsc command, 566
Multi-Win component, 494, 495
multimaster replication model, 20, 388

Multipurpose Internet Mail Extensions (MIME), 687
multitasking, 4–8
  OS/2 and, 8

N

NAT servers, 34
  Windows 98 SE and, 7
NDS (Novell Directory Service), 20
nested RAID levels, 154
.NET Passport, 506
Network Adapter tab (Terminal Services Configuration tool), 557
Network Address Translation (NAT) servers, 34
  Windows 98 SE and, 7
network interfaces cards (NICs), 547, 557
  support for multiple, 32
Network Load Balancing (NLB), 32, 869
Network Monitor tool, 746
Network News Transfer Protocol (NNTP), 675–677
network operating systems (NOS), 21
network service accounts, 615
network share, configuring access for users, 348
networks, 17
  improvements with Server 2003, 33–35
  monitoring/optimizing, 745–747
    recommendations/tips for, 746
New Hardware wizard, 210
NICs. *See* network interface cards
NLB (Network Load Balancing), 32, 869
NLB Manager, 32
NNTP (Network News Transfer Protocol), 675–677
NNTP. *See* Network News Transfer Protocol
nodes, 31
  in server cluster, 869
non-paged memory, 745
non-system providers, 735
nonauthoritative restores, for Active Directory, 849
normal backups, 822
NOS (network operating systems), 21
Notepad, process exercise and, 623
Novell Directory Service (NDS), 20
NT directory service (NTDS), 22
NT operating system. *See* Windows NT operating system
ntbackup utility, 818, 845–847
NTBackup, shadow copies and, 38
NTDS (NT directory service), 22
NTFS file system
  disk quotas and, 139
  file/folder auditing and, 755
  fsutil.exe tool for, 90
  IIS server and, 647
  introduced with Windows NT 3.1, 11
  Recovery Console and, 851
  restoring backups and, 834
  unmovable files and, 178
NTFS permissions, 413–424
  files/folders, moving and, 423
  share permissions and, 425–429
  vs. shared-folder permissions, 414
  special, 419–423
  testing, 447

O

object classes, 21
Object Linking and Embedding (OLE), introduced with Windows 3.1, 6
Object tab (ADUC tool)
  computer accounts, 357
  group accounts, 328
  user accounts, 295
objectid command, 90
objects, 21
  enabling auditing for, 754
offsite storage of backups, 817
OLE (Object Linking and Embedding), introduced with Windows 3.1, 6
on-disk catalogs, 832, 835
on-media catalogs, 832, 835
online command, 88
Operating System tab (ADUC tool), for computer accounts, 354
operating systems (OSs), 2–22
  character-based, 4
  embedded, 490
  network, 20
  sharing printers and, 603
  See also MS-DOS operating system; Windows NT operating system; Windows operating systems
operation-based auditing, 755
operations master roles, 20, 388–395
  transferring, 389–395
Organization tab (ADUC tool), for user accounts, 287
organization units (OUs), 260
  audit policies for, 753
OS. *See* operating systems; MS-DOS operating system; Windows NT operating system; Windows operating systems

OS/2, 8
OUs (organization units), 260
  audit policies for, 753
out-of-band connections, 801
out-of-band management of servers, 598

P

page files, 178, 723–725
  optimizing memory and, 744
paged/non-paged memory, 745
Partial Response Maximum Likelihood (PRML), 815
partition table, 73
partitions, 71, 74–77
  creating, 92–97
  defragmenting, 128–139
    best practices for, 138
    software analysis for, 135–137
    time required for, 134
    tools for, 128
  diskpart.exe tool for, 87–90
  largest potential number of, 78
  vs. volumes, 74
Passport service, 38
password-protected files, 451
passwords
  for computer accounts, 361
  disaster recovery planning and, 809
  resetting
    for computer accounts, 365
    for user accounts, 299, 305
  Safe Mode and, 858
  user accounts and, 282
Paterson, Tim, 3
PB (petabyte), 142
PC-DOS (Personal Computing Disk Operating System), 3
PDAs (personal digital assistants), thin client computing and, 490
PDC (Primary Domain Controller), 19
PDC Emulator operations master role, 388, 389
peer-to-peer networking
  vs. client-server, 17
  introduced with Windows for Workgroups 3.1, 6
performance
  improvements in IIS 6.0, 646, 663, 691
  mirrored volumes and, 868
  monitoring, 722–743
    via Performance Console, 227–230
    types of objects monitored, 728
  optimizing
    for disks, 128–155, 749
    for networks, 746
    for servers, 743–749
Performance Console, 227–230
performance counters, 726–730
  adding to System Monitor, 727
  disks and, 748
  logman.exe tool for managing/ scheduling, 738–740
  memory and, 743
  networks and, 746
  processors and, 747
  relog.exe tool for extracting data from, 740
performance logs, 733–736
  typeperf.exe tool for, 742
performance logs/alerts, 227, 228
Performance Monitor, 725–732
performance objects, 728
permissions, 319, 412–439
  backups and, 829
  cumulative effects of, 418
  denying, 418
  for FTP site access, 673
  inheritance and, 431–439
  for listener connections, 548, 557
  for printers, 603
  security descriptors and, 754
  server settings and, 559
  for services, 616
  types of (list), 412
  vs. user rights, 441
  for virtual directory access, 679
  for Web site access, 670
  See also user rights
Permissions tab (Terminal Services Configuration tool), 557
Personal Computing Disk Operating System (PC-DOS), 3
personal digital assistants (PDAs), thin client computing and, 490
Personal Video Recording (PVR), 16
personnel
  backing up/restoring data and, 814
  disaster recovery and, 808–810
petabyte (PB), 142
physical disks, 71, 91–127
  tools for managing, 84–91
ping facility, 662
piracy, software activation and, 49
PKI (Public Key Infrastructure), 460–472
  best practices for, 470
Plug and Play devices (PNP devices), 201
Point-to-Point Protocol over Ethernet (PPPoE), 33
pop-up menu (ADUC tool)
  for computer accounts, 359–362

for group accounts, 332
for user accounts, 296–300
POP3, mail server role for, 627
port scans, Remote Desktop for Administration and, 499
portable storage media, 68
power management, scheduling backups and, 844
PPPoE (Point-to-Point Protocol over Ethernet), 33
preemptive multitasking, 5
Windows 95 and, 7
Presentation Manager user interface, 8
Previous Versions Client software, 864
Primary Domain Controller (PDC), 19
primary partitions, 76
as active, 77
creating, 93–95
primary restores, for Active Directory, 849
print pooling, 606
print queues, managing, 605
print server role, 625
print services, improvements with Server 2003, 29
printer drivers, adding for earlier operating systems, 603
printers, 601–613
choosing local vs. network, 605
Internet printing and, 613
print server role for, 625
sharing, 6, 603
Printers and Faxes folder, 602
spooler service and, 610
private/public keys, 452, 660
privileges, 274
PRML (Partial Response Maximum Likelihood), 815
prncnfg script, 608
prndrvr script, 608
prnjobs script, 608
prnmngr script, 609
prnport script, 609
prnqctl script, 609
processes
managing with Terminal Services Manager, 546
taskkill.exe tool for, 622
Processes tab (Terminal Services Manager), 546
processors, monitoring, 747
Profile tab (ADUC tool), for user accounts, 285
Programs tab (RDC utility), 527
programs, "This initial program cannot be started." error message, 568
Properties tabs (ADUC tool)
for computer accounts, 353–359
for group accounts, 326–332
for user accounts, 280–296
protocols, 37–40, 495, 647
FTP, 671–673, 698–701
IGMP, 32
IPSec, 15
NNTP, 675–677
PPPoE, 33
public key cryptography, 461–463
Public Key Infrastructure (PKI), 460–472
best practices for, 470
public/private keys, 452, 660
Published Certificates tab (ADUC tool), for user accounts, 292
PVR (Personal Video Recording), 16

Q

QDOS (Quick and Dirty Operating System), 3
query process command, 566
query session command, 566
query termserver command, 566
query user command, 566
querying objects, with ADUC tool, 25
question mark (?), for displaying command syntax, 262
queue length of application pools, extending, 689
Quick and Dirty Operating System (QDOS), 3
quota command, 90
Quota tab, missing, 178

R

RA. *See* Remote Assistance
RADIUS (Remote Authentication Dial-In User Service), 33
RAID 2... RAID 7, 153
RAID-5 volumes, 83
creating, 124–127
troubleshooting, 181–183
when to use, 124
RAID level 0, 152
RAID level 1, 153, 867
RAID level 5, 153, 868
RAID. *See* Redundant Array of Independent (or Inexpensive) Disks
random access memory (RAM), 68
rapid-fail protection, 689
RD MMC snap. *See* Remote Desktops MMC snap-in
RDA. *See* Remote Desktop for Administration
RDC utility. *See* Remote Desktop Connection

RDN (relative distinguished name), 268
RDP-Tcp connections, 547–550, 557
RDP-Tcp Properties dialog box, 549
RDP. *See* Remote Desktop Protocol
rebooting applications with Ctrl+Alt+Del, introduced with Windows 3.1, 6
recovery agents, 453
  specifying, 455
Recovery Console, 15, 239–241, 811
  installing/using, 851–855
recovery policies, enforcing, 455
recovery. *See* entries at disaster recovery
Redundant Array of Independent (or Inexpensive) Disks (RAID), 75
  best practices for, 154
  creating, for RAID 5 volumes, 124–127
  fault tolerance and, 867
  implementing solutions for, 152–155
  nested levels and, 154
  troubleshooting, 181–183
Register command, 566
Registry (the), System State backups and, 848
regulatory considerations for disaster recovery, 806
relative distinguished name (RDN), 268
reliability, new features with IIS 6.0, 661–663
relog.exe tool, 740
rem command, 88
remote access/VPN server role, 627
remote administration, 488
  via Internet Explorer, 491
  using Terminal Services components, 497–517
Remote Administration (HTML) component, 591–593
  when to use, 598
Remote Administration mode. *See* Remote Desktop for Administration
Remote Assistance (RA), 14, 491, 492, 590
  asking for assistance, 502–511
  completing connection for, 511–514
  configuring/using, 500–517
  how it works, 500
  responding to request for
    in Windows Messenger, 508
    via saved file, 511
    sent by e-mail, 509
  security and, 516
  when to use, 597
Remote Authentication Dial-In User Service (RADIUS), 33
Remote Console, removing from server, 855
Remote Control tab
  ADUC tool, for user accounts, 290, 563
  Terminal Services Configuration tool, 553
Remote Desktop Connection (RDC), 39, 40, 522–529
  launching/terminating sessions of, 523
Remote Desktop for Administration (RDA), 39, 492, 519, 593
  benefits of vs. other methods of remote administration, 498
  configuring/using, 497–500
  security and, 499
  vs. terminal server role, 496
  when to use, 598
Remote Desktop Protocol (RDP), 39, 40, 493, 495–497
  Remote Assistance and, 500
Remote Desktop Web Connection utility, 535–540
  configuring Internet Explorer for use with, 540
Remote Desktops, 14
Remote Desktops MMC snap-in, 529–535
  connecting to/disconnecting from, 534
remote document sharing, 28
Remote Storage, 155–170
  vs. backups, 156
  best practices for, 170
  file-selection criteria and rules for, 167
  installing/configuring, 159–165
  media master for, recreating, 169
  not supported by Windows Server 2003 Standard Edition, 159
  rss.exe tool for, 91
  troubleshooting, 180
  using, 166–170
remote storage (bottom level of Remote Storage), 156, 166
Remote Storage MMC snap-in, 166
Removable Storage, 157–159
  backup options and, 821, 825
remove command, 88
rendom.exe tool, 24
repair command, 88
reparsepoint command, 90
replica DCs, 370–376
rescan command, 88
reset session command, 566
resources
  assigning to applications, 682
  managing access to. *See* access control
resources for further information
  Common Language Runtime, 35
  device status codes, 234
  OSI model, 22

Remote Installation Services, 352
System Policies, 349
Windows Management Instrumentation, 595
X.500 standards, 22
Restore and Manage Media tab (Backup utility), 831, 833
Restore wizard, 833
restoring backups, 812, 833–835
location for, 834
Resultant Set of Policy (RSoP) data, 270–274
retain command, 88
retensioning tape backup media, 832
RID Master operations master role, 388, 390
root CA, 466–471
Routing and Remote Access Server Setup wizard, 627
RSA SChannel Cryptographic provider (Microsoft), 660
RSoP data, 270–274
rss.exe tool, 91
Run as command, 589
runaway recall limit, 168, 181

S

SAC channels, 804
!SAC commands, 805
SAC/!SAC tool, 803–805
SACLs (System Access Control Lists), 411, 754
Safe Mode, 238, 856, 858
Safe Mode with Command Prompt, 857
Safe Mode with Networking, 856
SAM (Security Account Manager), 19
SAN (Storage Area Networks), 31, 38
SAN drives, 74
sc.exe tool, 225–227, 619
Schedule Jobs tab (Backup utility), 836
Schema Master operations master role, 388, 392–395
schemas, 20
schtasks.exe tool, 619
scope. *See* group scopes
scripting, for creating user accounts, 313–315
Scripts directory, not available with IIS 6.0, 692
sectors, 68, 70
Secure Sockets Layer (SSL), 462, 658
authentication settings and, 686
security
auditing (monitoring). *See* security auditing
backups and, 829
IIS 6.0 and, 657–661
new features with Server 2003, 35–38
Remote Assistance and, 516
Remote Desktop for Administration and, 499
Safe Mode and, 858
Web servers and, 646
See also access control; reliability
Security Account Manager (SAM), 19
security auditing, 749–760
types of events audited, 749
Security by Design initiative, 228
security descriptors, 754
Security Event Viewer, 763
security groups, 318, 319
security identifiers (SIDs), 146, 411
displaying, 274
domain controllers and, 388
security objects and, 256
security log, 749, 762
displaying contents of, 759
size of, caution with, 760
security objects, 256–258
security patches, 495
security providers, 659
Security tab (ADUC tool)
computer accounts, 357
group accounts, 329–332
user accounts, 295
select command, 88
Selectable Cryptographic Service Provider (CSP), 659
Server 2003. *See* Windows Server 2003
server clustering, 868
Server-Gated Cryptography (SGC), 658
server roles, 624–630
installing (exercise), 630
Server Settings node (Terminal Services Configuration tool), 558
servers
as hardware. *See* hardware devices
backing up, 813
clustering services for, 31–33
connecting to with Terminal Services Manager, 541
disaster recovery planning for, 847–859
EMS for, 598–601
managing
command-line tools for, 447–450
via Remote Administration component, 591–593
remotely, 589–598
wizards for, 623–631
optimizing performance for, 743–749
redundant, 807
SAC/!SAC tool for, 804
server-wide settings and, 558

shutting down, 775
Service Control utility, 225–227
services
enabling/disabling using Recovery Console, 851
failing, recovery from, 615
managing/troubleshooting, 614–623
types of startup for, 614
session data, worker process recycling and, 688
Sessions tab
ADUC tool, for user accounts, 288–290
Terminal Services Configuration tool, 551
Terminal Services Manager, 543–545
user accounts, 561
sessions, creating multiple, 804
See also console sessions; terminal sessions
setx.exe tool, 620
SGC (Server-Gated Cryptography), 658
SGML (Standard Generalized Markup Language), 43
Shadow command, 566
shadow copies, 29, 38, 859–867
best practices for, 866
created by default with Backup utility, 826
maximum number of, 860, 862, 865
restoring files from, 865
scheduling, 863
share permissions
NTFS permissions and, 425–429
testing, 447
shared-folder permissions, 424–429
vs. NTFS permissions, 414
shared folders
permissions and, 424–431
shadow copies and, 859, 863–866
Shutdown Event Tracker, 775–783
enabling/disabling via the registry, 780
shutdown events, 775–783
types of, 775
shutdown.exe tool, 620, 775, 779
SIDs. *See* security identifiers
signature. *See* disk signature
signed drivers. *See* driver signing
sigverif.exe tool, 209
simple volumes, 79
creating, 111–114
when to use, 111
single master replication model, 19
Smart Cards, 37
support for in Windows XP Professional, 15
user accounts and, 283
SMTP protocol, 647
mail server role and, 627
SMTP servers, creating/managing, 674
software
asset disaster recovery and, 807, 810
computer forensics, 832
piracy and, software activation to prevent, 49
restriction policies for, 37
sound drivers, disabled by default in Server 2003, 201
Source tab (System Monitor), 731
spanned volumes, 79
creating, 114–118
when to use, 114
sparse command, 90
Special Administration Console/ !Special Administration Console, 803–805
Special Permissions, 419–423
spooler service, 610–613
SQL database files, backing up, 828
SSL. *See* Secure Sockets Layer
stale data, troubleshooting RAID volumes and, 183
stand-alone libraries, 157
Standard Edition (of Server 2003), 45
Standard Generalized Markup Language (SGML), 43
startup options for Server 2003, 856–859
displaying, 856
startup services, troubleshooting, 238
states, of services, 614
static files, IIS troubleshooting and, 687, 691
stop errors, 235–237
Storage Area Networks (SAN), 31, 38
Storage Attached Network drives (SAN drives), 74
storage media, 68
storage, improved management with Server 2003, 38
streaming media server role, 629
streaming, support for, 41
StreetTalk directory service, 20
stripe sets, 74
stripe sets with parity, 74, 81, 868
striped volumes, 80
creating, 118–122
when to use, 118
sub-authentication component, troubleshooting IIS and, 690
sub-domains, 258
creating domain controller for, 381–384
success audits, 754
displayed in Security Event Viewer, 763
as event type, 761
success events, 749

swap file. *See* page files
switch flooding, 32
syntax for command-line utilities, 262–264
sysocmgr.exe tool, 655
 vs. winnt32.exe, 656
System Access Control Lists (SACLs), 411, 754
System Configuration utility, 238
System Equivalency licenses, 48
System File Checker, 208
system files
 backing up, 828
 critical, System File Checker for, 208
 EFS encryption and, 454
 System State backups and, 848
 Windows File Protection for, 206–208
system log, 762
 eventcreate.exe tool for, 769
 types of events in, 760
system media pools, 158
System Monitor, 725–732
system monitoring, 722–743
system partition, 77
system recovery plans, 800, 847–859
system requirements/compatibility, 51
System State data, 779
 backing up, 813, 827, 847–850
 backup options and, 826
systemroot folder, 77
SystemrootSystem32Inetsrv directory, 665

T

T.120 protocol family (ITU), 495
Tablet PCs, Windows XP edition for, 16
takeown.exe tool, 448
tape backup media, 814–816
 managing, 831
tape media, 156
Task Manager, for performance monitoring, 722–725
taskkill.exe tool, 622
 exercise using, 623
tasklist.exe tool, 621
 exercise using, 623
TB (terabyte), 142
Telephone tab (ADUC tool), for user accounts, 286
terabyte (TB), 142
terminal concentrators, 599
Terminal Server, 39, 40, 594
 licensing transition plan for, 48
 terminal server role for, 627
Terminal Server External Connector (TS-EC) licenses, 48
terminal server role, 488, 493–497, 627
 installing/configuring, 517–521
 vs. Remote Desktop for Administration, 496
Terminal Services, 487–581
 administrative tools for, 540–567
 client connection tools for, 521–540
 components supported by, 491–497
 group policy settings for, 564
 how it works, 489
 improvements with Server 2003, 39
 remote administration with, 497–517
 sessions of vs. console sessions, 492, 494
 troubleshooting, 567–569
Terminal Services Advanced Client (TSAC), 535–540
Terminal Services Client Connection Manager. *See* Remote Desktop Connection (RDC) utility, 522
Terminal Services Configuration tool, 547–559
Terminal Services Manager, 541–547
 resetting sessions with (exercise), 567
Terminal Services Profile tab
 ADUC tool, for user accounts, 291
 user accounts, 560
terminal sessions, 543–545
terminating
 processes, 546
 Remote Assistance sessions, 513, 514
 Remote Desktop connections, 524
 sessions, 543
  resetting using Terminal Services Manager (exercise), 567
  Terminal Services Configuration tool for, 552
 terminal sessions, 545
thin client computing, 490
threats, 799
 assessing, 806
thresholds, alerts/actions when met, 733, 737
timing out, IIS troubleshooting and, 691
TLS (Transport Layer Security), 658
tools. *See* utilities
trace logs, 735, 774
tracerpt.exe tool, 774
tracks, 68, 69
transitive trusts, 25
Transport Layer Security (TLS), 658
trees, 258
 creating domain controller for, 384–387
triggers, 771–774
Triple-DES algorithm, 455

troubleshooting
access control problems, 444–447
guidelines for, 445
disks, 170–183
event logs, 768
Event Viewer, 768
hardware devices, 231–243
IIS 6.0, 687–692
services, 614–623
Terminal Services, 567–569
troubleshooters built into Server 2003, 232
volumes, 170–183
See also disaster recovery
trusted publisher certificates, 205
trusts, 25, 38
Trustworthy Computing initiative (Microsoft), 657
TS Client Access Licenses (TS CALs), 47
TS-EC licenses, 48
TSAC (Terminal Services Advanced Client), 535–540
Tscon command, 566
Tsdiscon command, 566
Tskill command, 566
Tsprof command, 566
Tsshutdn command, 566
.tsv files, saving log information as, 726
.txt files, saving event logs as, 767
typeperf.exe tool, 742
types. *See* group types

U

Unicode Transformation Format-8 (UTF-8), 664
universal groups, 319, 320–323
determining/changing, 343
using, 346
universal serial bus devices, support for introduced with Windows 95b, 7
UNIX, IIS troubleshooting and, 691
"unreadable disk" error message, 173
upgrading to Windows Server 2003, 52
benefits/drawbacks of, 50–53
UPN name/suffix, changing, 282
URL authorization, for IIS 6.0, 661
USB devices, support for introduced with Windows 95b, 7
user account extensions, 560–564
user accounts, 256, 277–317
creating
automating for multiple creations, 313–315
with ADUC tool, 277–279
with dsadd.exe tool, 300–303
disk quotas and, 141, 151
group accounts and, 317
importing, 315–317
managing, 280–313
adding users to groups, 298, 336
collectively, 542
copying users, 297
enabling/disabling users, 306
finding users, 306–309
individually, 560
group memberships of, 309–313, 344
mapping user accounts, 298
moving users, 299
via pop-up menu, 296–300
properties of, 309–313
resetting user passwords, 299, 305
setting properties for, 280–296
security identifiers (SIDs) and, 146
tools for managing, 258–276
user mode, 199, 662
user principal name (UPN), changing, 282
user rights, 319, 439–444
See also permissions
usernames, security identifiers and, 146
Users tab (Terminal Services Manager), 542
usn command, 90
UTF-8 format, 664
utilities
account-management, 258–276
chkdsk.exe, 173
disk quota-management, 151
disk-management, 84–91
event-handling, 769–775
for disk defragmenting, 128
for hardware devices/device drivers, 218–227
for IIS 6.0, 692–709
Network Monitor, 746
ntbackup, 845–847
performance-monitoring, 738–743
Remote Desktop Connection, 522–529
Remote Desktop Web Connection, 535–540
server-management, 583–644
shutdown.exe, 779
sysocmgr.exe, 655, 656
Terminal Services, 521–567
types of, 584–589
VMWare, 447
which to use, 597
winnt32.exe, 655, 656

V

.vbs file extension, 692
vendor-supplied Authenticode digital signatures for drivers, 204
VeriSign, 464
Veritas Volume Manager 4.0, dynamic disks and, 73
Video Graphics Array (VGA), support for introduced with Windows 2.0, 5
virtual directories, 678
  for FTP sites, 701–703
  for Web sites, 696–698
virtual memory. *See* page files
Visual Basic, printer batch files and, 607
VMWare tool, 447
volume command, 90
volume mount points, 78
volume sets, 74
volume shadow copies. *See* shadow copies
volumes, 71, 78–84
  converted, disk quotas and, 142
  creating, 110–127
  defragmenting, 128–139
    best practices for, 138
  descriptive labels for, 78
  diskpart.exe tool for, 87–90
  extending, 106
  formatting, 102–105
  vs. partitions, 74
  recommended number of per dynamic disk, 78
  troubleshooting, 170–183
  Windows 2000 and, 72
vulnerabilities, 808

W

WANs (wide area networks), Terminal Services and, 490
warnings, as event type, 760
WBEM (Web-Based Enterprise Management), 595
WBTs (Windows-based Terminals), 490
Web-Based Enterprise Management (WBEM), 595
Web browsers, managing servers remotely via, 591–593
Web Distributed Authoring and Versioning (WebDAV), 658
Web Edition (of Server 2003), 45
  IIS and, 646
Web servers, managing with IIS 6.0, 645–719
Web Service Extensions, 650
  enabling, 677
Web sites
  configuring security settings for in IIS, 684–686
  creating/managing
    with IIS Manager, 667–671
    with iisweb.vbs, 692–696
  hosting multiple, 679–681
  Microsoft licensing, 47
  names of, metabase entries and, 695
  security patches, 495
  Terminal-Services.net, 490
  for troubleshooting tools, 231
  Windows XP Home Edition, 14
WebDAV protocol, 28, 658
WFP (Windows File Protection), 206–208
WFW (Windows for Workgroups), 6
what you see is what you get (WYSIWYG), introduced with Windows 3.1, 6
where.exe tool, 447
Whistler code name, 13
whoami.exe tool, 274
WHOIS directory service, 21
WHQL digital signatures, 203, 205
  updating device drivers and, 216
wide area networks (WANs), Terminal Services and, 490
Win32 API
  introduced by Windows NT 3.1, 11
Windows 1.0, 5
Windows 2.0, 5
Windows 2000, 12
Windows 3x, 6
Windows 9x, 7
  vs. Windows NT-based operating systems, 9
Windows-based Terminals (WBTs), 490
Windows Cluster Service, dynamic disks and, 73
Windows File Protection (WFP), 206–208
Windows for Workgroups (WFW), 6
Windows Hardware Compatibility Test (HCT), 203
Windows Hardware Quality Labs digital signature, 203, 205
Windows Load Balancing (WLB), 12
Windows Management Instrumentation (WMI), 595
Windows ME, 8
Windows Media Services
  backing up files associated with, 828
  streaming media server role for, 629
Windows Messenger, 503–508
Windows Millennium Edition (ME), 8
Windows NT 3.x, 10

Windows NT 4.0, 11
Windows NT operating system, 2, 10–16
 initial creation of, 8
 version naming and, 10, 13
 vs. Windows 9x, 9
Windows operating systems, 2–16
 for servers, basics of, 16–22
Windows Resource Kit, 589
Windows Server 2003, 1–66
 activating, 48–50
 Backup utility for, 817–845
 copies of, safeguarding, 810
 different editions of, 44–46
 hardware, interactions with, 198–203
 installation repair for, 242
 installing vs. upgrading, benefits/drawbacks of, 50–53
 licensing for, 47–50
 new features with, 23–43
  ADUC tool query feature, 260
  command-line tools for print management, 607–610
  EMS, 598–601
  operation-based auditing, 755
  SAC/!SAC tool, 803
  server roles, 624
  sharing encrypted files, 457
  vendor-supplied Authenticode digital signatures for drivers, 204
 startup options for, 856–859
 system requirements and, 51
Windows XP, 12–16
Windows XP Home Edition, 14
Windows XP Media Center Edition, 15
Windows XP Professional, 14
 64-bit version of, 15
Windows XP Tablet PC Edition, 16
WinFrame (Citrix), 495
winnt32.exe tool, 655
 vs. sysocmgr.exe, 656
WINS server role, 629
wizards, 589, 623–631
WLB (Windows Load Balancing), 12
WMI (Windows Management Instrumentation), 595
worker processes, 660, 661
 configuring startup/shutdown times for, 683
 recycling for, 688
Workplace Shell user interface, 8
World Wide Web (WWW) Publishing Service, 660, 661
wscript, 608
WWW Publishing Service, 660, 661
WYSIWYG (what you see is what you get), introduced with Windows 3.1, 6

X

X.500 standards, 22
Xerox Corporation's Alto computer system, 4
XML (Extensible Markup Language), 43
XML metabase, 664–666
 See also metabase entries
XML Web Services, 42

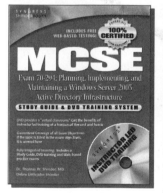